Brian Levack • Edward Muir • Meredith Veldman

The West
Encounters and Transformations
Combined Volume

Second Custom Edition for Portland Community College

Taken from:
The West: Encounters and Transformations, Fourth Edition
by Brian Levack, Edward Muir, and Meredith Veldman

Pearson Learning Solutions, 501 Boylston Street, Suite 900, Boston, MA 02116
A Pearson Education Company
www.pearsoned.com

Printed in the United States of America

8 9 10 V092 16 15

000200010271765688

TF

ISBN 10: 1-269-44478-6
ISBN 13: 978-1-269-44478-1

Dear Student,

The History faculty members at Portland Community College have selected this textbook for use in our History 101, 102, and 103 classes.

Please find packaged with each new textbook, an access code for you to have access to MyHistoryLab, an electronic resource which includes the e-text and other electronic resources, to help you succeed in your class.

*NOTE: PLEASE keep your access code for MyHistoryLab for the duration of your time attending any of these classes. You might need it for future terms, even if your current instructor does not require it!

We hope that you will find these to be valuable resources for your classes!

Sincerely,
PCC History Faculty

BRIEF CONTENTS

CONTENTS

Each chapter concludes with the following: Making Connections, Taking It Further, Chapter Review, and Time Line.

MAPS

DOCUMENTS

Note: The following documents are referenced in the margins of the text and are available at **www.myhistorylab.com**. Document titles bearing a red speaker are available with audio.

Engage your students
beyond the classroom . . .

. . . with **MyHistoryLab** and *THE WEST: Encounters and Transformations,* Fourth Edition

Would your students get more out of their introductory history course if you could engage them with history *beyond* the classroom? Would class discussion go farther if they were reading and writing more, working with primary sources, studying maps, and mastering key topics . . . *before* class meetings begin?

If your answer to these questions is yes, then it's time to consider how MyHistoryLab can help you meet these challenges. MyHistoryLab offers immersive content, tools, and experiences to engage students and help them succeed, enabling you to craft a better learning experience for them in your introductory survey course.

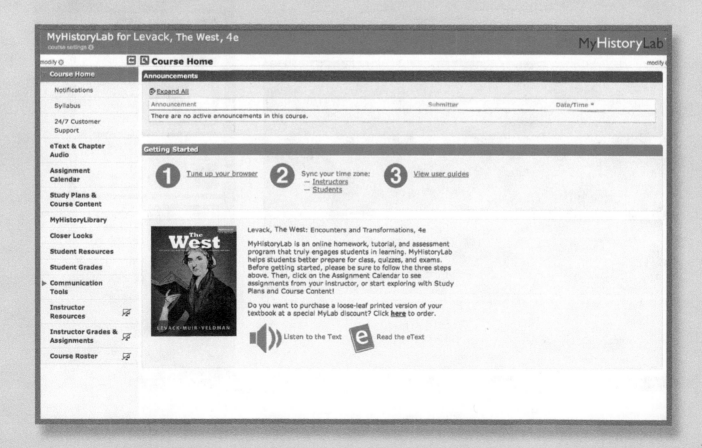

Prepare students on key topics with the MyHistoryLab Video Series

Are your introductory history students ready and eager to contend with a college textbook narrative? If not, help them get up-to-speed with the new MyHistoryLab Video Series: Key Topics in Western Civilization. Correlated to the chapters of *The West*, each video unit reviews key topics of the period, readying students to get the most from the text narrative. These engaging videos feature seasoned historians reviewing the pivotal stories of our past, in a lively format designed to demonstrate the power of historical narrative.

Drive your students into primary sources with the new MyHistoryLibrary

Now your students can read more than 200 of the most commonly assigned primary source documents, specially formatted in Pearson's powerful new eText. Students also have the option of listening to each reading in the accompanying Chapter Audio. Either way, students may access the text or the audio with various devices anytime they have access to the Internet.

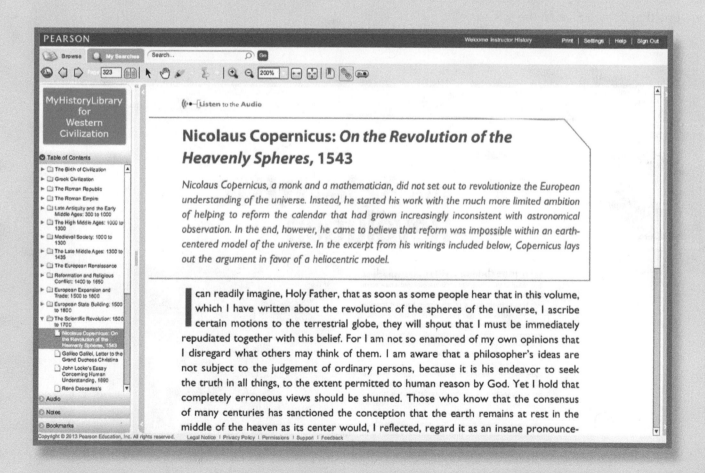

Immerse your students in a powerful eText deeply integrated with MyHistoryLab

I ntroductory survey teachers have long struggled to get students engaged in traditional textbooks. Now Pearson's MyHistoryLab offers a deeply immersive eText that transforms how students experience history. With a new pedagogically-driven design, it highlights a clear learning path through the material and offers a visually stunning learning experience in print or on a screen. With the Pearson eText, students can transition directly to MyHistoryLab resources such as primary source documents, videos, and Closer Look features. At last, history students can experience the eText they have been waiting for—one that comes alive on the screen.

Key Supplements
and Customer Support

Annotated Instructor's eText

Contained within MyHistoryLab, the *Annotated Instructor's eText* for your Pearson textbook leverages the powerful Pearson eText platform to make it easier than ever for you to access subject-specific resources for class preparation. The *AI eText* serves as the hub for all instructor resources, with chapter-by-chapter links to PowerPoint slides, content from the Instructor's Manual, and *MyHistoryLab's* ClassPrep engine, which contains a wealth of history content organized for classroom use.

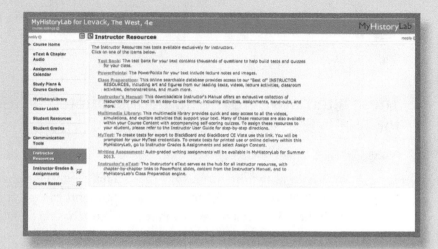

Instructor's Manual

The Instructor's Manual for *The West: Encounters and Transformations* contains learning objectives, a list of important themes discussed in the chapter, an overview of the Different Voices feature in the chapter, an annotated chapter outline with summaries of each section's content, suggestions for class activities, discussion questions, and suggestions for additional print and online resources for instructors. At the end of each chapter, MyHistoryLab Media Assignments catalog all of the MyHistoryLab resources for the chapter. The Instructor's Manual also contains a MyHistoryLab syllabus and suggestions for integrating MyHistoryLab into your course.

PowerPoint Presentations

Strong PowerPoint presentations make lectures more engaging for students. Correlated to the chapters of *The West*, each presentation includes a full lecture outline and a wealth of images, maps, and time lines from the textbook.

MyTest Test Bank

Containing a diverse set of multiple-choice, short-answer, and essay questions, the MyTest test bank supports a variety of assessment strategies. The large pool of multiple choice questions for each chapter includes factual, conceptual, and analytical questions, so that instructors may assess students on basic information as well as critical thinking.

Customer Support

Our dedicated team of local Pearson representatives will work with you not only to choose course materials but also to integrate them into your class and assess their effectiveness. Moreover, live support for MyHistoryLab users, both educators and students, is available 24/7.

Provide choices for your students through a variety of formats and price points

These alternatives to the traditional printed textbook are available for *THE WEST: Encounters and Transformations,* Fourth Edition.

 MyHistoryLab with eTextbook offers a full digital version of the print book and is readable on iOS and Android tablets. Students can get access to **MyHistoryLab** with the print book or save even more by purchasing on-line access at **www.myhistorylab.com**.

 Books a la Carte is a convenient, three-hole-punched, loose-leaf version of the traditional text at a discounted price—allowing students to carry only what they need to class. The Books a la Carte edition is also available with **MyHistoryLab** access.

 Black & White Printed Textbook, a discounted alternative, contains all the same content of the traditional text, rendered without color. To ensure full editorial integrity, some maps and illustrations in the Black & White edition have been redrawn. The Black & White edition is also available with **MyHistoryLab** access.

 CourseSmart eTextbooks offer the same content as the printed text in a convenient online format—with highlighting, online search, and printing capabilities. Learn more at **www.coursesmart.com. The CourseSmart eTextbook** is also available with **MyHistoryLab** access.

 Pearson Custom Library helps instructors build the perfect course solution. For enrollments of at least 25, create your own textbook by combining chapters from best-selling Pearson textbooks and reading selections. To begin building your custom text, visit **www.pearsoncustomlibrary.com**.

PREFACE

We wrote this textbook to answer questions about the identity of the civilization in which we live. Journalists, politicians, and scholars often refer to our civilization, its political ideologies, its economic systems, and its cultures as "Western" without fully considering what that label means and why it might be appropriate. The classification of our civilization as Western has become particularly problematic in the age of globalization. The creation of international markets, the rapid dissemination of ideas on a global scale, and the transmission of popular culture from one country to another often make it difficult to distinguish what is Western from what is not. *The West: Encounters and Transformations* offers students a history of Western civilization in which these issues of Western identity are given prominence. Our goal is neither to idealize nor to indict that civilization, but to describe its main characteristics in different historical periods.

The West: Encounters and Transformations gives careful consideration to two basic questions. The first is, how did the definition of the West change over time? In what ways did its boundaries shift and how did the distinguishing characteristics of its cultures change? The second question is, by what means did the West—and the idea of the West—develop? We argue that the West is the product of a series of cultural encounters that occurred both outside and within its geographical boundaries. We explore these encounters and the transformations they produced by detailing the political, social, religious, and cultural history of the regions that have been, at one time or another, a part of the West.

Defining the West

What is the West? How did it come into being? How has it developed throughout history? Many textbooks take for granted which regions or peoples of the globe constitute the West. They treat the history of the West as a somewhat expanded version of European history. While not disputing the centrality of Europe to any definition of the West, we contend that the West is not only a geographical realm with ever-shifting boundaries, but also a cultural realm, an area of cultural influence extending beyond the geographical and political boundaries of Europe. We so strongly believe in this notion that we have written the introductory essay "What Is the West?" to encourage students to think about their understanding of Western civilization and to guide their understanding of each chapter. Many of the features of what we call Western civilization originated in regions that are not geographically part of Europe (such as North Africa and the Middle East), while ever since the fifteenth century various social, ethnic, and political groups from non-European regions (such as North and South America, eastern Russia, Australia, New Zealand, and South Africa) have identified themselves, in one way or another, with the West. Throughout the text, we devote considerable attention to the boundaries of the West and show how borderlines between cultures have been created, especially in eastern and southeastern Europe.

Considered as a geographical and cultural realm, *the West* is a term of recent origin, and the civilization to which it refers did not become clearly defined until the eleventh century, especially during the Crusades, when western European Christians developed a distinct cultural identity. Before that time we can only talk about the powerful forces that created the West, especially the dynamic interaction of the civilizations of western Europe, the Byzantine Empire, and the Muslim world.

Over the centuries Western civilization has acquired many salient characteristics. These include two of the world's great legal systems (civil law and common law), three of the world's monotheistic religions (Judaism, Christianity, and Islam), certain political and social philosophies, forms of political organization (such as the modern bureaucratic state and democracy), methods of scientific inquiry, systems of economic organization (such as industrial capitalism), and distinctive styles of art, architecture, and music. At times one or more of these characteristics has served as a primary source of Western identity: Christianity in the Middle Ages, science and rationalism during the Enlightenment, industrialization in the nineteenth and twentieth centuries, and a defense of individual liberty and democracy in the late twentieth century. These sources of Western identity, however, have always been challenged and contested, both when they were coming into prominence and when they appeared to be most triumphant. Western culture has never been monolithic; even today references to the West imply a wide range of meanings.

Cultural Encounters

The definition of the West is closely related to the central theme of our book, which is the process of cultural encounters. Throughout *The West: Encounters and Transformations,* we examine the West as a product of a series of cultural encounters both outside the West and within it. We show that the West originated and developed through a continuous process of inclusion and exclusion resulting from a series of encounters among and within different groups. These encounters can be described in a general sense as external, internal, or ideological.

External Encounters

External encounters took place between peoples of different civilizations. Before the emergence of the West as a clearly defined entity, external encounters occurred between such diverse peoples as Greeks and Phoenicians, Macedonians and Egyptians, and Romans and Celts. After the eleventh century, external encounters between Western and non-Western peoples occurred mainly during periods of European exploration, expansion, and imperialism. In the sixteenth and seventeenth centuries, for example, a series of external encounters took place between Europeans on the one hand and Africans, Asians, and the indigenous people of the Americas on the other. Two chapters of *The West: Encounters and Transformations* (Chapters 13 and 18) and a large section of a third (Chapter 24) explore these external encounters in depth and discuss how they affected Western and non-Western civilizations alike.

Internal Encounters

Our discussion of encounters also includes similar interactions between different social groups *within* Western countries. These internal encounters often took place between dominant and subordinate groups, such as between lords and peasants, rulers and subjects, men and women, factory owners and workers, masters and slaves. Encounters between those who were educated and those who were illiterate, which recurred frequently throughout Western history, also fall into this category. Encounters just as often took place between different religious and political groups, such as between Christians and Jews, Catholics and Protestants, and royal absolutists and republicans.

Ideological Encounters

Ideological encounters involve interaction between comprehensive systems of thought, most notably religious doctrines, political philosophies, and scientific theories about the nature of the world. These ideological conflicts usually arose out of internal encounters, when various groups within Western societies subscribed to different theories of government or rival religious faiths. The encounters between Christianity and polytheism in the early Middle Ages, between liberalism and conservatism in the nineteenth century, and between fascism and communism in the twentieth century were ideological encounters. Some ideological encounters had an external dimension, such as when the forces of Islam and Christianity came into conflict during the Crusades and when the Cold War developed between Soviet communism and Western democracy in the second half of the twentieth century.

* * *

The West: Encounters and Transformations illuminates the variety of these encounters and clarifies their effects. By their very nature encounters are interactive, but they have taken different forms: They have been violent or peaceful, coercive or cooperative. Some have resulted in the imposition of Western ideas on areas outside the geographical boundaries of the West or the perpetuation of the dominant culture within Western societies. More often than not, however, encounters have resulted in a more reciprocal process of exchange in which both Western and non-Western cultures, or the values of both dominant and subordinate groups, have undergone significant transformation. Our book not only identifies these encounters, but also discusses their significance by returning periodically to the issue of Western identity.

Coverage

The West: Encounters and Transformations offers both comprehensive coverage of political, social, and cultural history and a broader coverage of the West and the world.

Comprehensive Coverage

Our goal throughout the text has been to provide comprehensive coverage of political, social, and cultural history and to include significant coverage of religious and military history as well. Political history defines the basic structure of the book, and some chapters, such as those on Hellenistic civilization, the age of confessional divisions, absolutism and state building, the French Revolution, and the coming of mass politics, include sustained political narratives. Because we understand the West to be a cultural as well as a geographical realm, we give a prominent position to cultural history. Thus, we include rich sections on Hellenistic philosophy and literature, the cultural environment of the Italian Renaissance, the creation of a new political culture at the time of the French Revolution, and the atmosphere of cultural despair and desire that prevailed in Europe after World War I. We also devote special attention to religious history, including the history of Islam as well as that of Christianity and Judaism. Unlike many other textbooks, our coverage of religion continues into the modern period. *The West: Encounters and Transformations* also provides extensive coverage of the history of women and gender. Wherever possible the history of women is integrated into the broader social, cultural, and political history of the period. But there are also separate sections on women in our chapters on classical Greece, the Renaissance, the

Reformation, the Enlightenment, the Industrial Revolution, World War I, World War II, and the postwar era.

The West and the World

Our book provides broad geographical coverage. Because the West is the product of a series of encounters, the external areas with which the West interacted are of major importance. Three chapters deal specifically with the West and the world.

- Chapter 13, "The West and the World: The Significance of Global Encounters, 1450–1650"
- Chapter 18, "The West and the World: Empire, Trade, and War, 1650–1815"
- Chapter 24, "The West and the World: Cultural Crisis and the New Imperialism, 1870–1914"

These chapters present substantial material on sub-Saharan Africa, Latin America, the Middle East, India, and East Asia. Our text is also distinctive in its coverage of eastern Europe and the Muslim world, areas that have often been considered outside the boundaries of the West. These regions were arenas within which significant cultural encounters took place. Finally, we include material on the United States and Australia, both of which have become part of the West. We recognize that most American college and university students have the opportunity to study American history as a separate subject, but treatment of the United States as a Western nation provides a different perspective from that usually given in courses on American history. For example, this book treats America's revolution as one of four Atlantic revolutions, its national unification in the nineteenth century as part of a broader western European development, its pattern of industrialization as related to that of Britain, and its central role in the Cold War as part of an ideological encounter that was global in scope.

What's New to This Edition?

This edition of *The West: Encounters and Transformations* has been revised to reflect the latest developments in historical research and has added a host of new features to assist student learning. The most significant pedagogical innovation has been the seamless integration of documents, maps, videos, illustrations, and other resources from MyHistoryLab into the textbook. A new pedagogically driven design highlights a clear learning path through the material and offers a visually stunning learning experience in print or on a screen. With the Pearson eText, students can transition directly to MyHistoryLab resources such as primary source documents, videos, and maps.

Additionally, questions have been added to the captions of all the maps. The list of Suggested Readings has been revised and updated, and many of the terms in the Glossary have been edited to improve student comprehension.

Specific changes in the contents of this edition are as follows:

- Chapter 3 expands the discussion of Corinth and adds a new illustration linking the legendary wealth of that polis to its strategic geographical position.
- Chapter 4 refines the interpretation of Alexander the Great and directs the student to a Closer Look in MyHistoryLab that analyzes the famous mosaic of Alexander at the Battle of Issus.
- Chapter 5 uses new images from the Theater of Marcellus and the Parthenon to illustrate and clarify the differences between Greek and Roman architectural style.
- Chapter 7 refers students to several new documents about early Christianity in MyHistoryLab and a selection examining the role of religion in the fall of the Roman Empire.

- Chapter 8 clarifies the causes of the growing alienation between western and eastern rite Christians. It also discusses why, on the basis of the Qur'an, Muslims might disagree about the proper attitude they should take toward Jews and Christians.

- Chapter 9 revises the discussion of the differences between the status of Germanic and Roman women, providing a much more carefully nuanced picture. It takes account of the tremendous variation among the Germanic tribes in the status of women and pays more attention to class differences among women. The discussion of monastic life notes how monks did not just copy ancient texts but made their own significant intellectual contributions. The chapter offers an enriched discussion of Viking culture and technology.

- Chapter 10 expands the discussion of the papal monarchy.

- Chapter 11 employs the latest DNA research to revise the discussion of the epidemiology of the Black Death. Rather than leaving the cause of the Black Death as an open question, the new evidence gives greater support for the thesis that the high mortality came from a form of bubonic plague. The discussions of the Mongol Empire and the Silk Road have also been enriched, as has the account of medieval guilds.

- Chapter 12 expands the discussion of Lorenzo Valla as an example of humanist critical techniques. The debt of the Italian Renaissance to Muslim science is clarified.

- Chapter 13 adds a section on Aztec religion and examines how the spread of "New World" silver altered the global economy not just in Europe but also in China.

- Chapter 14 expands both the explanation of the religious justification of violence and the ways the Jesuit missionaries contributed to a better European understanding of other cultures.

- Chapter 15 adds additional material on the limits of religious toleration during the period.

- Chapter 16 presents a more nuanced interpretation of the theory of absolutism and adds an excerpt from John Locke's *Second Treatise of Government* to illustrate the radicalism of his political thought.

- Chapter 17 expands the definition of alchemy and gives it a more prominent place in the section on the causes of the Scientific Revolution. The new illustration of dissection in 1632 is superior to the eighteenth-century image in the third edition.

- Chapter 18 adds new material on the activities of slave traders in Africa.

- Chapter 19 simplifies the Map of the Enlightenment to make the international character of the Republic of Letters clearer. References to works by Voltaire, Mary Wollstonecraft, Cesare Beccaria, and Catherine the Great reveal the diversity of the contributions that the Enlightenment made to Western culture.

- Chapter 20 includes a new illustration that highlights the militancy of the *sans-culottes* and includes new material on the Republic of Virtue. The Closer Look in MyHistoryLab on the execution of Louis XVI supplements the discussion of this event in the text and in the "Justice in History" feature.

- Chapter 21 includes new material on industrialization in Europe and an illustration of the Stockton and Darlington Railway. It also refers the student to a new map of English Railways in MyHistoryLab.

- Chapter 22 clarifies the doctrine of liberalism and includes excerpts from John Stuart Mill and David Ricardo to support the description of this new ideology. Inclusion of the Chartist People's Petition of 1838 helps explain why Britain did not experience a revolution in 1848.

- Chapter 23 includes a new map of the United Kingdom in 1910. The section titled "The Irish Identity Conflict" has been completely rewritten, incorporating new material. The section on "Russia: Revolution and Reaction" has been revised to reflect the emphasis in scholarship on nationalist upheaval within the Russian Empire and adds a discussion on the tsarist policy of Russification.

- Chapter 24 strengthens and reorganizes the section titled "The Birth of Modernism."
- Chapter 25 includes a new map on the Eastern Front that identifies the national regions of Poland, the Baltics, Ukraine, Caucasus, East Prussia, and Galicia. It adds new sub-sections titled "A War of Movement" and "Germany and the East" to reflect current research on the Eastern Front and the German occupation of Russian territories. Another new sub-section, "A Very Different Battle," deals with the influenza pandemic. The discussion of the October Revolution has also been expanded.
- Chapter 26 has been extensively reorganized to make discussions more coherent, to improve "teachability," and to take into account recent research. It adds new sub-sections titled "NEP and Nationalities" and "From Lenin to Stalin." The substantially revised section on the Irish Revolution includes new material.
- Chapter 27 includes a new section titled "The Wars Within the War" that takes into account the most recent research on the Holocaust and the Eastern Front. The section titled "The Decisive Front" has been extensively revised and includes new material.
- Chapter 28 incorporates new material in the section titled "Devastation, Death, and DPs."
- Chapter 29 adds a new sub-section, "The Turn to Terrorism," in the section on "Economic Stagnation and Political Change: The 1970s and 1980s." It also extensively revises and adds new material to the sections "Islam and the West" and "The European Union." This chapter also brings the story of Russia under Putin up-to-date.

Features and Pedagogical Aids

In writing this textbook we have endeavored to keep both the student reader and the classroom instructor in mind at all times. The text includes the following features and pedagogical aids, all of which are intended to support the themes of the book.

"What Is the West?"

The West: Encounters and Transformations begins with an essay to engage students in the task of defining the West and to introduce them to the notion of cultural encounters. "What Is the West?" guides students through the text by providing a framework for understanding how the West was shaped. Structured around the six questions of What? When? Where? Who? How? and Why?, this framework encourages students to think about their understanding of Western civilization. The essay serves as a blueprint for using this textbook.

"Encounters and Transformations"

These features, which appear in about half the chapters, illustrate the main theme of the book by identifying specific encounters and showing how they led to significant transformations in the cultures of the West. These features show, for example, how camels enabled encounters among nomadic tribes of Arabia, which led to the rapid spread of Islam; how the Mayans' interpretation of Christian symbols transformed European Christianity into a hybrid religion; how the importation of chocolate from the New World to Europe changed Western consumption patterns and the rhythms of the Atlantic economy; and how Picasso's encounter with African art contributed to the transformation of modernism. Each of these essays concludes with questions for discussion.

"Justice in History"

Found in every chapter, this feature presents a historically significant trial or episode in which different notions of justice (or injustice) were debated and resolved. The "Justice in History" features illustrate cultural encounters within communities as they try to determine the fate of individuals from all walks of life. Many famous trials dealt with conflicts over basic religious, philosophical, or political values, such as those of Socrates, Jesus, Joan of Arc, Martin Luther, Charles I, Galileo, and Adolf Eichmann. Other "Justice in History" features show how judicial institutions, such as the ordeal, the Inquisition, and revolutionary tribunals, handled adversarial situations in different societies. These essays, therefore, illustrate the way in which the basic values of the West have evolved through attempts to resolve disputes and conflict.

Each "Justice in History" feature includes two pedagogical aids. "For Discussion" helps students explore the historical significance of the episode just examined. These questions can be used in classroom discussion or as student essay topics. "Taking It Further" provides the student with a few references that can be consulted in connection with a research project.

"Different Voices"

Each chapter contains a feature consisting of two primary source documents that present different and often opposing views regarding a particular person, event, or development. An introduction to the documents provides the necessary historical context, identifies the authors of the documents, and suggests the different perspectives they take. A set of questions for discussion follows the two documents.

Questions for Discussion

This edition of *The West: Encounters and Transformations* offers many opportunities for students to address a variety of questions in each chapter.

- The main question that the chapter addresses appears after the introduction to each chapter.
- Each of the major sections of the chapter begins with the main question that the section addresses. These questions also appear at the bottom of the first page of the chapter under the "Learning Objectives" heading and are repeated in the Chapter Review at the end of the chapter.
- At the end of each chapter a set of questions under the heading "Making Connections" asks the student to think about some of the more specific issues discussed in the chapter.
- Each Encounters and Transformations, Justice in History, and Different Voices feature is followed by a set of questions under the heading "For Discussion."
- The caption for each map includes a question related to the map for which the text of the chapter provides an answer.

Maps and Illustrations

Artwork is a key component of our book. We recognize that many students often lack a strong familiarity with geography, and so we have taken great care to develop maps that help sharpen their geographic skills. Complementing the book's standard map program, we include maps focusing on areas outside the borders of Western civilization. More than 300 images of fine art and photos tell the story of Western civilization and help students visualize the past: the way people lived, the events that shaped their lives, and how they viewed the world around them.

Chronologies

Each chapter includes a varying number of chronologies in time line format that list the events relating to a particular topic discussed in the text. Chronologies present the sequence of events and can be helpful for purposes of review.

Key Terms and Glossary

We have sought to create a work that is accessible to students with little prior knowledge of the basic facts of Western history or geography. Throughout the book we have explained difficult concepts at length. For example, we present in-depth explanations of the concepts of Zoroastrianism, Neoplatonism, Renaissance humanism, the various Protestant denominations of the sixteenth century, capitalism, seventeenth-century absolutism, nineteenth-century liberalism and nationalism, fascism, and modernism. We have identified these concepts as key terms by printing them in bold in the narrative and defining them in the margins of the book. All key terms are listed in alphabetical order, together with their definitions, in the Glossary at the end of the book.

Suggested Readings

An annotated list of suggested readings for all the chapters appears at the end of the book. The items listed there are not scholarly works for the benefit of the instructor, but suggestions for students who wish to explore a topic in greater depth or to write a research paper. References to books or articles relevant to the subject of the "Justice in History" feature appear at the end of each feature under the heading "Taking It Further."

Chapter Reviews

At the end of each chapter, a Chapter Review revisits the questions that accompany each section heading and summarizes key concepts within the section that address these questions.

Time Lines

A time line at the end of each chapter lists important events discussed within the chapter.

A Note About Dates and Transliterations

In keeping with current academic practice, *The West: Encounters and Transformations* uses B.C.E. (before the common era) and C.E. (common era) to designate dates. We also follow the most current and widely accepted English transliterations of Arabic. *Qur'an,* for example, is used for *Koran; Muslim* is used for *Moslem.* Chinese words appearing in the text for the first time are written in pinyin, followed by the older Wade-Giles system in parentheses.

Acknowledgments

We are grateful to Jeff Lasser for guiding us through the long process of preparing the fourth edition and Rob DeGeorge for his help in selecting the illustrations and preparing the manuscript for publication.

We would like to thank the following reviewers for their helpful suggestions: Frank Biletz, Loyola University, Chicago; Julian Bourg, Boston College; Jace Crouch, Oakland

University; Stephanie Annette Finley-Croswhite, Old Dominion University; Nichole Gotschall, Columbia Southern University; Derrick Griffey, Gadsden State Community College; Erik Heinrichs, Bridgewater State University; Carol Herringer, Wright State University; Stephanie Lamphere, Sierra College; Alison Williams Lewin, Saint Joseph's University; Erik Lindseth, Indiana University; Michael Martin, Fort Lewis College; Lindsey McNellis, University of Central Florida; Patricia O'Neill, Central Oregon Community College; Karen Sonnelitter, Purdue University; Tamrala Swafford, Columbia Southern University; Tom Ward, Spring Hill College; Bradley Woodworth, University of New Haven; and Terry Young, Patrick Henry Community College.

We would also like to thank the following friends and colleagues for their valuable advice and suggestions: Gabor Agoston, Catherine Clinton, Catherine Evtuhov, Wojciech Falkowski, Benjamin Frommer, Andrzej Kaminski, Adam Kozuchowski, Christopher Lazarski, David Lindenfeld, Suzanne Marchand, John McNeill, John Merriman, James Miller, Daria Nalecz, Karl Roider, Steven Ross, and Mark Steinberg. Finally, we wish to thank Graham Nichols for his telecommunications assistance and expertise.

ABOUT THE AUTHORS

Brian Levack grew up in a family of teachers in the New York metropolitan area. From his father, a professor of French history, he acquired a love for studying the past, and he knew from an early age that he too would become a historian. He received his B.A. from Fordham University in 1965 and his Ph.D. from Yale in 1970. In graduate school he became fascinated by the history of the law and the interaction between law and politics, interests that he has maintained throughout his career. In 1969 he joined the history department of the University of Texas at Austin, where he is now the John Green Regents Professor in History. The winner of several teaching awards, Levack teaches a wide variety of courses on British and European history, legal history, and the history of witchcraft. For eight years he served as the chair of his department, a rewarding but challenging assignment that made it difficult for him to devote as much time as he wished to his teaching and scholarship. His books include *The Civil Lawyers in England, 1603–1641: A Political Study* (1973), *The Formation of the British State: England, Scotland and the Union, 1603–1707* (1987), *The Witch-Hunt in Early Modern Europe* (3rd edition, 2006), and *Witch-Hunting in Scotland: Law, Politics, and Religion* (2008).

His study of the development of beliefs about witchcraft in Europe over the course of many centuries gave him the idea of writing a textbook on Western civilization that would illustrate a broader set of encounters between different cultures, societies, and ideologies. While writing the book, Levack and his two sons built a house on property that he and his wife, Nancy, own in the Texas hill country. He found that the two projects presented similar challenges: It was easy to draw up the design, but far more difficult to execute it. When not teaching, writing, or doing carpentry work, Levack runs along the jogging trails of Austin and has recently discovered the pleasures of scuba diving.

Edward Muir grew up in the foothills of the Wasatch Mountains in Utah, close to the Emigration Trail along which wagon trains of Mormon pioneers and California-bound settlers made their way westward. As a child he loved to explore the broken-down wagons and abandoned household goods left at the side of the trail and from that acquired a fascination with the past. Besides the material remains of the past, he grew up with stories of his Mormon pioneer ancestors and an appreciation for how the past continued to influence the present. During the turbulent 1960s, he became interested in Renaissance Italy as a period and place that had been formative for Western civilization. His biggest challenge was finding the time to explore yet another new corner of Italy and its restaurants.

Muir received his Ph.D. from Rutgers University, where he specialized in the Italian Renaissance and did archival research in Venice and Florence, Italy. He is now the Clarence L. Ver Steeg Professor in the Arts and Sciences at Northwestern University and former chair of the history department. At Northwestern he has won several teaching awards. His books include *Civic Ritual in Renaissance Venice* (1981), *Mad Blood Stirring: Vendetta in Renaissance Italy* (1993 and 1998), *Ritual in Early Modern Europe* (1997 and 2005), and *The Culture Wars of the Late Renaissance: Skeptics, Libertines, and Opera* (2007). His books have also been published in Italian.

Some years ago Muir began to experiment with the use of historical trials in teaching and discovered that students loved them. From that experience he decided to write this textbook, which employs trials as a central feature. He lives beside Lake Michigan in Evanston, Illinois. His twin passions are skiing in the Rocky Mountains and rooting for the Chicago Cubs, who manage every summer to demonstrate that winning isn't everything.

 **Meredith Veldman** grew up in the western suburbs of Chicago, where she learned to love winter and the Cubs—which might explain her preference for all things improbable and impractical. Certainly that preference is what attracted her to the study of history, filled as it is with impractical people doing the most improbable things. Veldman majored in history at Calvin College in Grand Rapids, Michigan, and then earned a Ph.D. in modern European history, with a concentration in nineteenth- and twentieth-century Britain, from Northwestern University in 1988.

As an associate professor of history at Louisiana State University, Veldman teaches courses in nineteenth- and twentieth-century British history and twentieth-century Europe, as well as the second half of "Western Civ." In her many semesters in the Western Civ. classroom, Veldman tried a number of different textbooks but found herself increasingly dissatisfied. She wanted a text that would convey to beginning students at least some of the complexities and ambiguities of historical interpretation, introduce them to the exciting work being done in cultural history, and, most important, tell a good story. The search for this textbook led her to accept the offer Levack and Muir made to join them in writing *The West: Encounters and Transformations*.

An award-winning teacher, Veldman is also the author of *Fantasy, the Bomb, and the Greening of Britain: Romantic Protest, 1945–1980* (1994) and *Margaret Thatcher: Shaping the New Conservatism* (2014). She and her family ride out the hurricanes in Baton Rouge, Louisiana. She remains a Cubs fan and she misses snow.

What Is the West?

Many of the people who influence public opinion—politicians, teachers, clergy, journalists, and television commentators—refer to "Western values," "the West," and "Western civilization." They often use these terms as if they do not require explanation. But what do these terms mean? The West has always been an arena within which different cultures, religions, values, and philosophies have interacted; any definition of the West will inevitably arouse controversy.

The definition of the West has always been disputed. Note the difference in the following two poems, the first by Rudyard Kipling (1865–1936), an ardent promoter of European imperialism who wrote "The Ballad of East and West" at the height of the British Empire:

> OH, East is East, and West is West, and never the twain shall meet,
> Till Earth and Sky stand presently at God's great Judgment Seat. . . .

The second, "East/West Poem," is by a Chinese-American living in Hawaii, Wing Tek Lum (1946–), who expresses the confusion caused by terms that designate both cultural traits and directions around the globe:

> O
> East is East
> and
> West is West.
> but
> I never did
> understand
> why
> in Geography class
> the East was west
> and
> the West was east
> and that no
> one ever
> cared
> about the difference.

This textbook cares about the difference. It also shows that East and West have, in contrast to Kipling's view, often "met." These encounters created the idea of the East and the West and helped identify the ever shifting borders between the two.

The Shifting Borders of the West

The most basic definition of the West is of a place. Western civilization is now typically thought to comprise the regions of Europe, the Americas, Australia, and New Zealand. However, this is a contemporary definition of the West. The inclusion of these places in the West is the result of a long history of European expansion through colonization and conquest.

This textbook begins about 10,000 years ago in what is now Iraq; the final chapter returns to discuss the Iraq War, but in the meantime the Mesopotamian region is only occasionally a concern for Western history. The history of the West begins with the domestication of animals, the cultivation of the first crops, and the establishment of long-distance trading networks in the Tigris, Euphrates, and Nile River valleys. Cities, kingdoms, and empires in those valleys gave birth to the first civilizations in the West. By about 500 B.C.E., the civilizations that were the cultural ancestors of the modern West had spread from southwestern Asia and north Africa to include the entire Mediterranean basin—areas influenced by Egyptian, Hebrew, Greek, and Roman thought, art, law, and religion. The resulting Greco-Roman culture created the most enduring foundation of the West. By the first century C.E. the Roman Empire drew the map of what historians consider the heartland of the West: most of western and southern Europe, the coastlands of the Mediterranean Sea, and the Middle East.

For many centuries, these ancient foundations defined the borders of the West. During the last century, however, the West came to be less about geography than about culture, identity, and technology. When Japan, an Asian country, accepted human rights and democracy after World War II, did it become part of the West? Most Japanese might not think they have adopted "Western" values, but the thriving capitalism and stable democracy of this traditional Asian country that was never colonized by a European power complicates the idea of what is the West. Or consider the Republic of South Africa, which the white minority—people descended from European immigrants—ruled until 1994. The oppressive white regime violated human rights, rejected full legal equality for all citizens, and jailed or murdered those who questioned the government. Only when democratic elections open to blacks replaced that government did South Africa fully embrace what the rest of the West would consider Western values. To what degree was South Africa part of the West before and after these developments?

Or how about Russia? Russia long saw itself as a Christian country with cultural, economic, and political ties with the rest of Europe. The Russians have intermittently identified with their Western neighbors, especially during the reign of Peter the Great (1682–1725), but their neighbors were not always sure about the Russians. After the Mongol invasions of the thirteenth and fourteenth centuries much of Russia was isolated from the rest of the West, and during the Cold War from 1949 to 1989 Western democracies considered communist Russia an enemy. When was Russia "Western" and when not?

Thus, when we talk about where the West is, we are almost always talking about the Mediterranean basin and much of Europe (and later, the Americas). But we will also show that countries that border "the West," and even countries far from it, might be considered Western in many aspects as well.

THE TEMPLE OF HERA AT PAESTUM, ITALY Greek colonists in Italy built this temple in the sixth century B.C.E. Greek ideas and artistic styles spread throughout the ancient world, both from Greek colonists, such as those at Paestum, and from other peoples who imitated the Greeks.

WHERE IS THE WEST? The shifting borders of the West have moved many times throughout history, but they have always included the areas shown in this satellite photo. These include Europe, north Africa, and the Middle East.

Changing Identities Within the West

In addition to being a place, the West is the birthplace of Western civilization, a civilization that encompasses a cultural history—a tradition stretching back thousands of years to the ancient world. Over this long period the civilization we now identify as Western gradually took shape. The many characteristics that identify it emerged over this time: forms of governments, economic systems, and methods of scientific inquiry, as well as religions, languages, literature, and art.

Throughout the development of Western civilization, the ways in which people identified themselves changed as well. People in the ancient world had no such idea of the common identity of the West, only of being members of a tribe, citizens of a town, or subjects of an empire. But with the spread of Christianity and Islam between the first and seventh centuries, the notion of a distinct civilization in these "Western" lands subtly changed. People came to identify themselves less as subjects of a particular empire and more as members of a community of faith—whether that community comprised followers of Judaism, Christianity, or Islam. These communities of faith drew lines of inclusion and exclusion that still exist today. Starting about 1,600 years ago, Christian monarchs and clergy began to obliterate polytheism (the worship of many gods) and marginalize Jews. From 1,000 to 500 years ago, Christian authorities fought to expel Muslims from Europe. Europeans developed definitions of the West that did not include Islamic communities, even though Muslims continued to live in Europe, and Europeans traded and interacted with the Muslim world. The Islamic countries themselves erected their own barriers, seeing themselves in opposition to the Christian West, even as they continued to look back to the common cultural origins in the ancient world that they shared with Jews and Christians.

MARINER'S COMPASS The mariner's compass was a navigational device intended for use primarily at sea. The compass originated in China; once adopted by Europeans, it enabled them to embark on long ocean voyages around the world.

During the Renaissance in the fifteenth century, these ancient cultural origins became an alternative to religious affiliation for thinking about the identity of the West. From this Renaissance historical perspective Jews, Christians, and Muslims descended from the cultures of the ancient Egyptians, Hebrews, Greeks, and Romans. Despite their differences, the followers of these religions shared a history. In fact, in the late Renaissance a number of Jewish and Christian thinkers imagined the possibility of rediscovering the single universal religion that they thought must have once been practiced in the ancient world. If they could just recapture that religion, they could restore the unity they imagined had once prevailed in the West.

The definition of the West has also changed as a result of European colonialism, which began about 500 years ago. When European powers assembled large overseas empires, they introduced Western languages, religions, technologies, and cultures to many distant places in the world, making Western identity a transportable concept. In some of these colonized areas—such as North America, Argentina, Australia, and New Zealand—the European newcomers so outnumbered the indigenous people that these regions became as much a part of the West as Britain, France, and Spain. In other European colonies, especially on the Asian continent, Western cultures failed to exercise similar levels of influence.

As a result of colonialism Western culture sometimes merged with other cultures, and in the process, both were changed. Brazil, a South American country inhabited by large numbers of indigenous peoples, the descendants of African slaves, and European settlers, epitomizes the complexity of what defines the West. In Brazil, almost everyone speaks a Western language (Portuguese), practices a Western religion (Christianity), and participates in Western political and economic institutions (democracy and capitalism). Yet in Brazil all of these features of Western civilization have become part of a distinctive culture in which indigenous, African, and European elements have been blended. During Carnival, for example, Brazilians dressed in indigenous costumes dance in African rhythms to the accompaniment of music played on European instruments.

Western Values

For many people today, the most important definition of the West involves adherence to "Western" values. The values typically identified as Western include democracy, individualism, universal human rights, toleration of religious diversity, ownership of private property, equality before the law, and freedom of inquiry and expression. These values, however, have not always been part of Western civilization. In fact, they describe ideals rather than actual realities; these values are by no means universally accepted throughout the West. Thus, there is nothing inevitable about these values; Western history at various stages exhibited quite different ones. Western societies seldom prized legal or political equality until quite recently. In ancient Rome and throughout most of medieval Europe, the wealthy and the powerful enjoyed more protection under the law than did slaves or the poor. Most medieval Christians were completely convinced of the virtue of making war against Muslims and heretics and curtailing the actions of Jews. Before the end of the eighteenth century, few Westerners questioned the practice of slavery and a social hierarchy of birth that remained powerful in the West through the nineteenth century; in addition, most women were excluded from equal economic and educational opportunities until well into the twentieth century. In many places women still do not have equal opportunities. In the twentieth century, millions of Westerners followed leaders who stifled free inquiry, denied basic human rights to many of their citizens, made terror an instrument of the state, and censored authors, artists, and journalists. The Holocaust, fascism, and communism were Western phenomena.

The values that define the West have not only changed over time, they also remain fiercely contested. One of the most divisive political issues today, for example, is that of "gay marriage." Both sides in this debate frame their arguments in terms of "Western values." Supporters of the legalization of same-sex marriages highlight equality and human rights: They demand that all citizens have equal access to the basic legal protections afforded by marriage. Opponents emphasize the centrality of the tradition of monogamous heterosexual marriage to Western legal, moral, and religious codes. What this current debate shows us is that no single understanding of "Western values," or of the West itself, exists. These values have always been contended, disputed, and fought over. In other words, they have a history. This text highlights and examines that history.

Asking the Right Questions

So how can we make sense of the West as a place and an identity, the shifting borders and definitions of the West, and Western civilization in general? In short, what has Western civilization been over the course of its long history—and what is it today?

Answering these questions is the challenge this book addresses. There are no simple answers to any of these questions, but there is a method for finding answers. The method is straightforward. Always ask the *what, when, where, who, how,* and *why* questions of the text.

The *What* Question

What is Western civilization? The answer to this question will vary according to time and place. In fact, for much of the early history covered in this book, "Western civilization" did not exist. Rather, a number of distinctive civilizations emerged in the Middle East, northern Africa, and Europe, each of which contributed to what later became Western civilization. As these cultures developed and intermingled, the idea of Western civilization slowly began to form. Thus, the understanding of Western civilization will change from chapter to chapter. The most extensive change in the place of the West was through the colonial expansion of the European nations between the fifteenth and twentieth centuries. Perhaps the most significant cultural change came with acceptance of the values of scientific inquiry for solving human and philosophical problems, an approach that did not exist before the seventeenth century but became one of the distinguishing characteristics of Western civilization. During the late eighteenth and nineteenth centuries, industrialization became the engine that drove economic development in the West. During the twentieth century, industrialization in both its capitalist and communist forms dramatically gave the West a level of economic prosperity unmatched in the non-industrialized parts of the world.

The *When* Question

When did the defining characteristics of Western civilization first emerge, and for how long did they prevail? Dates frame and organize the content of each chapter, and numerous short timelines are offered. These resources make it possible to keep track of what happened when. Dates have no meaning by themselves, but the connections *between* them can be very revealing. For example, dates show that the agricultural revolution that permitted the birth of the first civilizations unfolded over a long span of about 10,000 years—which is more time than was taken by all the other events and developments covered in this textbook. Wars of religion plagued Europe for nearly 200 years before Enlightenment thinkers articulated the ideals of religious toleration. The American Civil War—the war to preserve the union, as President Abraham Lincoln termed it—took place at exactly the same time as wars were being fought for national unity in Germany and Italy. In other words, by paying attention to other contemporaneous wars for national unity, the American experience seems less peculiarly an American event.

By learning *when* things happened, one can identify the major causes and consequences of events and thus see the transformations of Western civilization. For instance, the production of a surplus of food through agriculture and the domestication

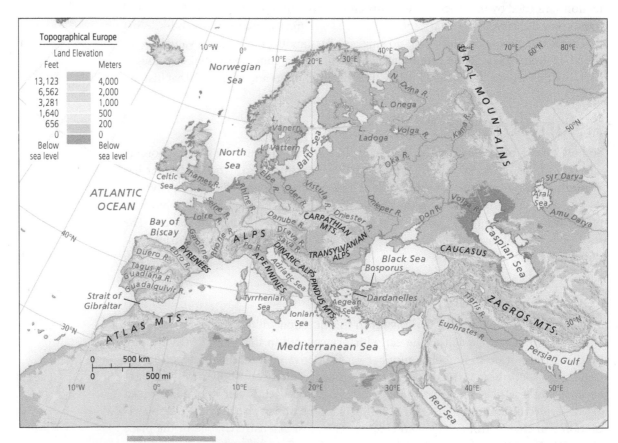

MAP **1** CORE LANDS OF THE WEST These are the principal geographical features that will appear recurrently throughout this book.

of animals were prerequisites for the emergence of civilizations. The violent collapse of religious unity after the Protestant Reformation in the sixteenth century led some Europeans to propose the separation of church and state two centuries later. And during the nineteenth century many Western countries—in response to the enormous diversity among their own peoples—became preoccupied with maintaining or establishing national unity.

The *Where* Question

Where has Western civilization been located? Geography, of course, does not change very rapidly, but the idea of where the West is does change. By tracing the shifting relationships between the West and other, more distant civilizations with which it interacted, the chapters highlight the changing "where" of the West. The key to understanding the shifting borders of the West is to study how the peoples within the West thought of themselves and how they identified others as "not Western." During the Cold War, for example, many within the West viewed Russia as an enemy rather than as part of the West. In the previous centuries, Australia and North America came to be part of the West because the European conquerors of these regions identified themselves with European cultures and traditions and against non-European values.

The *Who* Question

Who were the people responsible for making Western civilization? Some were anonymous, such as the unknown geniuses who invented the mathematical systems of ancient Mesopotamia. Others are well-known—saints such as Joan of Arc, creative thinkers such as Galileo Galilei, or generals such as Napoleon. Most were ordinary. Humble people, such as the many millions who migrated from Europe to North America or the unfortunate millions who suffered and died in the trenches of World War I, also influenced the course of events.

Perhaps most often this book encounters people who were less the shapers of their own destinies than the subjects of forces that conditioned the kinds of choices they could make, often with unanticipated results. During the eleventh century when farmers throughout Europe began to employ a new kind of plow to till their fields, they were merely trying to do their work more efficiently. They certainly did not recognize that the increase in food they produced would stimulate the enormous population growth that made possible the medieval civilization of thriving cities and magnificent cathedrals. Answering the *who* question requires an evaluation of how much individuals and groups of people were in control of events and how much events controlled them.

The *How* Question

How did Western civilization develop? This is a question about processes—about how things change or stay the same over time. This book identifies and explores these processes in several ways.

First, woven throughout the story is *the theme of encounters and transformations.* What is meant by encounters? When the Spanish *conquistadores* arrived in the Americas some 500 years ago, they came into contact with the cultures of the Caribs, the Aztecs, the Incas, and other peoples who had lived in the Americas for thousands of years. As the Spanish fought, traded with, and intermarried with the natives, each culture changed. The Spanish, for their part, borrowed from the Americas new plants for cultivation and responded to what they considered serious threats to their worldview. Many native Americans, in turn, adopted European religious practices and learned to speak European languages. At the same time, Amerindians were decimated by European diseases, illnesses to which they had never been exposed. The native Americans also witnessed the destruction of their own civilizations and governments at the hands of the colonial powers. Through centuries of interaction and mutual influence, both sides became something other than what they had been.

The European encounter with the Americas is an obvious example of what was, in fact, a continuous process of encounters with other cultures. These encounters often occurred between peoples from different civilizations, such as the struggles between Greeks and Persians in the ancient world or between Europeans and Chinese in the nineteenth century. Other encounters took place among people living in the same civilization. These include interactions between lords and peasants, men and women, Christians and Jews, Catholics and Protestants, factory owners and workers, and capitalists and communists. Western civilization developed and changed, and still does, through a series of external and internal encounters.

Second, *features in the chapters* formulate answers to the question of how Western civilization developed. For example, each chapter contains an essay titled *Justice in History*. These essays discuss a trial or some other episode involving questions of justice. Some *Justice in History* essays illustrate how Western civilization was forged in struggles over conflicting values, such as the discussion of the trial of Galileo, which examines the conflict between religious and scientific concepts of truth. Other essays show how efforts to resolve internal cultural, political, and religious tensions helped shape Western ideas about justice, such as the essay on the *auto da fé*, which illustrates how authorities attempted to enforce religious conformity.

Some chapters include another feature as well. The *Encounters and Transformations* features show how encounters between different groups of people, technologies, and ideas were not abstract historical processes, but events that brought people together in a way that transformed history. For example, when the Arabs encountered the camel as an instrument of war, they adopted it for their own purposes. As a result, they were able to conquer their neighbors very quickly and spread Islam far beyond its original home in Arabia.

The *Different Voices* feature in each chapter includes documents from the period that represent contrasting views about a particular issue important at the time. These conflicting voices demonstrate how people debated what mattered to them and in the process formulated what have become Western values. During the Franco-Algerian War of the 1950s and early 1960s, for example, French military officers debated the appropriateness of torture when interrogating Algerian prisoners alleged to be insurgents. The debate about the use of torture against terrorist suspects continues today, revealing one of the unresolved conflicts over the appropriate values of the West.

The *Why* Question

Why did things happen in the way they did in history? This is the hardest question of all, one that engenders the most debate among historians. To take one persistent example, why did Hitler initiate a plan to exterminate the Jews of Europe? Can it be explained by something that happened to him in his childhood? Was he full of self-loathing that he projected onto the Jews? Was it a way of creating an enemy so that he could better unify Germany? Did he really believe that the Jews were the cause of all of Germany's problems? Did he merely act on the deeply seated anti-Semitic tendencies of the German people? Historians still debate the answers to these questions.

Such questions raise issues about human motivation and the role of human agency in historical events. Can historians ever really know what motivated a particular individual in the past, especially when it is so notoriously difficult to understand what motivates other people in the present? Can any individual determine the course of history? The *what, when, where, who,* and *how* questions are much easier to answer; but the *why* question, of course, is the most interesting one, the one that cries out for an answer.

This book does not—and cannot—always offer definitive answers to the *why* question, but it attempts to lay out the most likely possibilities. For example, historians do not really know what disease caused the Black Death in the fourteenth century that killed about one-third of the population in a matter of months. But they can answer many questions about the consequences of that great catastrophe. Why were there so many new universities in the fourteenth and fifteenth centuries? It was because so many priests had died in the Black Death, creating a huge demand for replacements. The answers to the *why* questions are not always obvious, but they are always intriguing; finding the answers is the joy of studying history.

1 The **Beginnings** of **Civilization,** 10,000–1150 B.C.E.

In 1991 hikers toiling across a glacier in the Alps between Austria and Italy made a startling discovery: a man's body stuck in the ice. They alerted the police, who soon turned the corpse over to archaeologists. The scientists determined that the middle-aged man had frozen to death about 5,300 years ago. Ötzi the Ice Man (his name comes from the Ötztal Valley where he perished) quickly became an international celebrity. The scientists who examined Ötzi believe that he was a shepherd leading flocks of sheep and goats to mountain pastures when he died. Grains of wheat on his clothing suggested that he lived in a farming community. Copper dust in his hair hinted that Ötzi may also have been a metalworker, perhaps looking for ores during his journey. An arrowhead lodged in his back indicated a violent death, but the circumstances remain mysterious.

Ötzi's gear was state-of-the-art for his time. His possessions showed deep knowledge of the natural world. He wore leather boots insulated with dense grasses chosen for protection against the cold. The pouch around his waist contained stone tools and fire-lighting equipment. The wood selected for his bow offered strength and flexibility. In his light wooden backpack, Ötzi carried containers to hold burning embers and dried meat and seeds to eat on the trail. The arrows in his quiver featured a natural adhesive that tightly bound bone and wooden points to the shafts. The most noteworthy find among Ötzi's possessions

LEARNING OBJECTIVES

1.1 ((∙	1.2 ((∙	1.3 ((∙
What is the link between the food-producing revolution of the Neolithic era and the emergence of civilization?	What changes and continuities characterized Mesopotamian civilization between the emergence of Sumer's city-states and the rise of Hammurabi's Babylonian Empire?	What distinctive features characterized Egyptian civilization throughout its long history?

((∙ Listen to Chapter 1 on MyHistoryLab

THE THINKER OF CERNEVODA While most surviving Neolithic art focuses on the central concerns of hunting and fertility, this terracotta sculpture depicts a figure deep in thought, Just 4½ inches high, this piece was created between 5250 and 4500 B.C.E. and found at a Neolithic site in Romania.

👁 Watch the Video Series on MyHistoryLab

Learn about some key topics related to this chapter with the *MyHistoryLab Video Series: Key Topics in Western Civilization*

1.1

1.2

1.3

was his axe. Its handle was made of wood, but its head was copper, a remarkable innovation at a time when most tools were made of stone. Ötzi was ready for almost anything—except the person who shot him in the back.

Ötzi lived at a transitional moment, at the end of what archaeologists call the **Neolithic Age**, or "New Stone Age," a long period of revolutionary change lasting from about 10,000 to about 3000 B.C.E. in which many thousands of years of human interaction with nature led to food production through agriculture and the domestication of animals. This chapter begins with this most fundamental encounter of all—that between humans and the natural world.

The achievement of food production let humans develop new, settled forms of communities—and then civilization itself. The growth of civilization also depended on constant interaction among communities that lived far apart. Once people were settled in a region, they began trading for commodities that were not available in their homelands. As trade routes extended over long distances and interactions among diverse peoples proliferated, ideas and technology spread.

Neolithic Age The New Stone Age, characterized by the development of agriculture and the use of stone tools.

 Read and **View**

A Visitor from the Neolithic Age

> **This chapter focuses on two questions: How did the encounters between early human societies create the world's first civilizations? And, what was the relationship between these civilizations and what would become the "West"?**

Defining Civilization, Defining Western Civilization

1.1 What is the link between the food-producing revolution of the Neolithic era and the emergence of civilization?

Anthropologists use the term **culture** to describe all the different ways that humans collectively adjust to their environment, organize their experiences, and transmit their knowledge to future generations. Culture serves as a web of interconnected meanings that enable individuals to understand themselves and their place in the world. Archaeologists define **civilization** as an urban culture with differentiated levels of wealth, occupation, and power. One archaeologist notes that the "complete checklist of civilization" contains "cities, warfare, writing, social hierarchies, [and] advanced arts and crafts."[1] With cities, human populations achieved the critical mass necessary to develop specialized occupations and a level of economic production high enough to sustain complex religious and cultural practices—and to wage war. To record these economic, cultural, and military interactions, writing developed. Social organization grew more complex. The labor of most people supported a small group of political, military, and religious leaders. These leaders controlled not only government and warfare, but also the distribution of food and wealth. They augmented their authority by building monuments to the gods and participating in religious rituals that

culture The knowledge and adaptive behavior created by communities that helps them to mediate between themselves and the natural world through time.

civilization The term used by archaeologists to describe a society differentiated by levels of wealth and power, and in which military, religious, economic, and political control are based in cities.

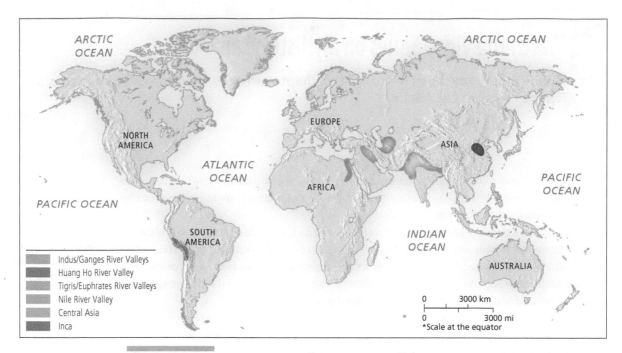

MAP **1.1** THE BEGINNINGS OF CIVILIZATION Civilizations developed independently in India, China, central Asia, and Peru, as well as in Egypt and southwest Asia. Western civilization, however, is rooted in the civilizations that first emerged in Egypt and southwest Asia. What five features make up the "complete checklist of civilization"?

linked divinity with kingship and military prowess. Thus, in early civilizations four kinds of power—military, economic, political, and religious—converged.

As **Map 1.1** shows, a number of civilizations developed independently of each other across the globe. This chapter focuses on the Mesopotamian and Egyptian civilizations because many of the characteristics of "Western civilization" originated in these areas. The history of Western civilization thus begins not in Europe, the core territory of the West today, but in what we usually call the Middle East and what ancient historians call the "Near East."* By 2500 B.C.E., when, as we will see, city-states in Mesopotamia formed a flourishing civilization and Egypt's Old Kingdom was well-developed, Europeans still lived only in scattered agricultural communities. Without the critical mass of people and possessions that accompanied city life, early Europeans did not develop the specialized religious, economic, and political classes that characterize a civilization.

Watch the Video

Ideas

Making Civilization Possible: The Food-Producing Revolution

For more than the first 175,000 years of their existence, modern humans, known as ***Homo sapiens sapiens*** ("most intelligent people"), did not produce food. Between 200,000 and 100,000 years ago, *Homo sapiens sapiens* first appeared in Africa and began to spread to other continents. Scientists refer to this stage of human history as the Paleolithic Age, or Old Stone Age, because people made tools by cracking rocks and using their sharp edges to cut and chop. These early peoples scavenged for wild food and followed migrating herds of animals. They also created beautiful works of art by carving bone and painting on cave walls. By 45,000 years ago, these humans had reached most of Earth's habitable regions.

Homo sapiens sapiens Scientific term meaning "most intelligent people"; applied to physically and intellectually modern human beings that first appeared between 200,000 and 100,000 years ago in Africa.

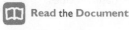

Read the Document

A Need to Remember

---

*Terms such as the "Near East," the "Middle East," and the "Far East"—China, Japan, and Korea—betray their Western European origins. For someone in India, say, or Russia or Australia, neither Mesopotamia nor Egypt is located to the "east."

The end of the last Ice Age about 15,000 years ago ushered in an era of momentous change: the food-producing revolution. As the Earth's climate became warmer, cereal grasses spread over large areas. Hunter-gatherers learned to collect these wild grains and grind them up for food. When people learned that the seeds of wild grasses could be transplanted and grown in new areas, the cultivation of plants was underway.

People also began domesticating pigs, sheep, goats, and cattle, which eventually replaced wild game as the main sources of meat. The first signs of goat domestication occurred about 8900 B.C.E. in the Zagros Mountains in southwest Asia. Pigs, which adapt well to human settlements because they eat garbage, were first domesticated around 7000 B.C.E. By around 6500 B.C.E., domestication had become widespread.

Farming and herding were hard work, but the payoff was enormous. Even simple agricultural methods could produce about 50 times more food than hunting and gathering. Thanks to the increased food supply, more newborns survived past infancy. Populations expanded, and so did human settlements. With the mastery of food production, human societies developed the mechanisms not only to feed themselves, but also to produce a surplus, which allowed for economic specialization and fostered the growth of social, political, and religious hierarchies.

The First Food-Producing Communities

The world's first food-producing communities emerged in southwest Asia. People began cultivating food in three separate areas, shown on **Map 1.2**. Archaeologists have named the first area the **Levantine Corridor** (also known as the **Fertile Crescent**)—a 25-mile-wide strip of land that runs from the Jordan River valley of modern Israel and Palestine to the Euphrates River valley in today's Iraq.* The second region was the hilly land north of Mesopotamia at the base of the Zagros Mountains. The third was Anatolia, or what is now Turkey.

Read the Document

Redefining Self: From Tribe to Village to City

Levantine Corridor Also known as the Fertile Crescent, this arc of land stretching from the Jordan River to the Euphrates River was the place where food production and settled communities first appeared in southwest Asia (the Middle East).

Fertile Crescent Also known as the Levantine Corridor, this 25-mile-wide arc of land stretching from the Jordan River to the Euphrates River was the place where food production and settled communities first appeared in southwest Asia (the Middle East).

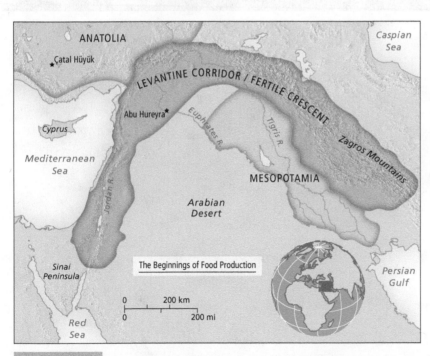

MAP **1.2** THE BEGINNINGS OF FOOD PRODUCTION This map shows early farming sites where the first known production of food occurred in ancient southwest Asia. What were the three areas in which people first began cultivating food?

---

*The term *Levant* refers to the eastern Mediterranean coastal region. "Levant" comes from the French: "the rising [sun]"—in other words, the territory to the east, where the sun rises.

The small settlement of Abu Hureyra near the center of the Levantine Corridor illustrates how agriculture developed. Humans first settled here around 9500 B.C.E. They fed themselves primarily by hunting gazelles and gathering wild cereals. But sometime between 8000 and 7700 B.C.E., they began to plant and harvest grains. Eventually they discovered that crop rotation—planting different crops in a field each year—resulted in a much higher yield. By 7000 B.C.E. Abu Hureyra had grown into a farming community, covering nearly 30 acres that sustained a population of about 400. A few generations later, the inhabitants of Abu Hureyra began herding sheep and goats to supplement their meat supply. These domesticated animals became the community's primary source of meat when the gazelle herds were depleted about 6500 B.C.E.

Families in Abu Hureyra lived in small, rectangular dwellings containing several rooms. Archaeological evidence shows that many women in the community developed arthritis in their knees, probably from crouching for hours on end to grind grains. Thus, we assume that while men hunted and harvested, women prepared food. The division of labor along gender lines indicates a growing complexity of social relations within the community.

Similar patterns of agricultural development characterized the early histories of other regions in southwest Asia. By 6000 B.C.E., for example, the Anatolian town of Çatal Hüyük (meaning "Fork Mound") consisted of 32 acres of tightly packed rectangular mud houses that the townspeople rebuilt more than a dozen times as their population expanded. About 6,000 people lived in houses built so closely together that residents could only enter their homes by walking along the rooftops and climbing down a ladder set in the smoke hole. Such a set-up, while physically uncomfortable, also strengthened Çatal Hüyük's security from outside attack. Archaeologists have

 View the Closer Look Çatal Hüyük

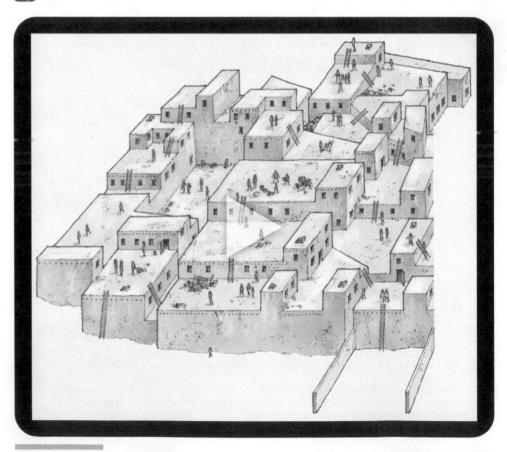

ÇATAL HÜYÜK This drawing illustrates archaeologists' reconstruction of Çatal Hüyük. In such a settlement, modern conceptions of privacy and self-determination would have been inconceivable.

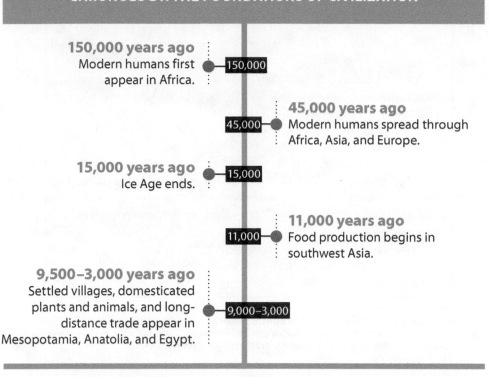

150,000 years ago
Modern humans first appear in Africa.
150,000

45,000 years ago
Modern humans spread through Africa, Asia, and Europe.
45,000

15,000 years ago
Ice Age ends.
15,000

11,000 years ago
Food production begins in southwest Asia.
11,000

9,500–3,000 years ago
Settled villages, domesticated plants and animals, and long-distance trade appear in Mesopotamia, Anatolia, and Egypt.
9,000–3,000

uncovered about 40 rooms that served as religious shrines. The paintings and engravings on the walls of these rooms focus on the two main concerns of ancient societies: fertility and death. In these scenes, vultures scavenge on human corpses while women give birth to bulls (associated with virility). These shrines also contain statues of goddesses whose exaggerated breasts and buttocks indicate the importance of fertility rites in the villagers' religious rituals.

Only a wealthy community could allow some people to work as artists or priests rather than as farmers, and Çatal Hüyük was wealthy by the standards of its era. Much of its wealth rested on trade in obsidian. This volcanic stone was the most important commodity in the Neolithic Age because it could be used to make sharp-edged tools such as arrowheads, spear points, and sickles for harvesting crops. Çatal Hüyük controlled the obsidian trade from Anatolia to the Levantine Corridor. With increasing wealth came widening social differences. While most of the burial sites at Çatal Hüyük showed little variation, a few corpses were buried with jewelry and other riches, a practice that indicates the beginning of distinctions between wealthy and poor members of the society.

The long-distance obsidian trade that underlay Çatal Hüyük's wealth also sped up the development of other food-producing communities in the Levantine Corridor, the Zagros Mountains, and Anatolia. These trade networks of the Neolithic Age laid the foundation for the commercial and cultural encounters that fostered the world's first civilization.

Transformations in Europe

In all of these developments, Europe remained far behind. The colder and wetter European climate meant heavier soils that were harder to cultivate than those in the Near East. The food-producing revolution that began in southwest Asia around 8000 B.C.E. did not spread to Europe for another thousand years, when farmers, probably from Anatolia, ventured to northern Greece and the Balkans. Settled agricultural communities had become the norm in southwest Asia by 6000 B.C.E., but not until about 2500 B.C.E. did most of Europe's hunting and gathering cultures give way to small, widely dispersed farming communities. (See **Map 1.3**.)

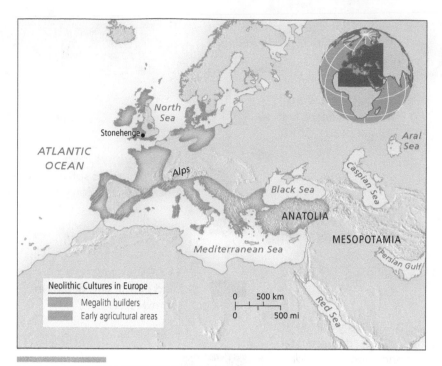

MAP **1.3** NEOLITHIC CULTURES IN EUROPE During the Neolithic period, new cultures developed as most of the peoples of Europe changed their way of life from hunting and gathering to food production. What features characterized these early European societies?

As farmers and herders spread across Europe, people adapted to different climates and terrain. A variety of cultures evolved from these differences but most shared the same basic characteristics: Early Europeans farmed a range of crops and herded domesticated animals. They lived in villages, clusters of permanent family farmsteads. Jewelry and other luxury goods left in women's graves might indicate that these village societies granted high status to women, perhaps because these communities traced ancestry through mothers.

Two important technological shifts ushered in significant economic and social change in these early European groups. The first was metallurgy, the art of using fire to shape metals. Knowledge of metallurgy spread slowly across Europe from the Balkans, where people started to mine copper about 4500 B.C.E. Jewelry made from copper and gold became coveted luxury goods. As trade in metals flourished, long-distance trading networks evolved. These networks provided the basis for the meeting and blending of different groups of peoples and different cultural assumptions and ideas.

The introduction of the plow was the second significant technological development for early Europe. The plow, invented in Mesopotamia in the late fifth or early fourth millennium B.C.E., became widely used in Europe around 2600 B.C.E. The use of plows meant that fewer people were needed to cultivate Europe's heavy soils. With more people available to clear forest lands, farming communities expanded and multiplied, as did opportunities for individual initiative and the accumulation of wealth.

As a result of these developments—and as had occurred much earlier in the Near East—the social structure within European villages became more stratified, with growing divisions between the rich and the poor. From the evidence of weaponry buried in graves, we know that the warrior emerged as a dominant figure in these early European societies. With the growing emphasis on military power, women's status may have declined.

These early Europeans constructed enduring monuments that offer tantalizing glimpses of their cultural practices and religious beliefs. Around 4000 B.C.E. Europeans began building communal tombs with huge stones called **megaliths**. Megaliths were constructed from Scandinavia to Spain and on islands in the western Mediterranean. The best-known megalith construction is Stonehenge in England. People began to

megalith A very large stone used in prehistoric European monuments between 5000 and 1500 B.C.E.

STONEHENGE This megalithic monument in southern England consists of two circles of standing stones with large blocks capping the circles. It was built without the aid of wheeled vehicles or metal tools, and the stones were dragged from many miles away.

build Stonehenge about 3000 B.C.E. as a ring of pits. The first stone circle of "blue-stones," hauled all the way from the Welsh hills, was constructed about 2300 B.C.E. Only an advanced level of engineering expertise, combined with a high degree of organization of labor, made such construction possible.

The purpose of these magnificent constructions remains controversial. Some archaeologists argue that Stonehenge was used to measure the movement of stars, the sun, and the planets. Others view it as principally a place for religious ceremonies. Recent excavations suggest a third possibility: Stonehenge may have been a complex devoted to healing ceremonies. All three theories could be correct, for ancient peoples commonly associated healing and astronomical observation with religious belief and practice.

If we recall the "complete checklist" needed for a civilization—"cities, warfare, writing, social hierarchies, [and] advanced arts and crafts"[2]—we can see that by 1600 B.C.E., Europeans had checked off all of these requirements except cities and writing—both crucial for building human civilizations. The rest of this chapter, then, will focus not on Europe, but on the dramatic developments in southwest Asia and Egypt from the sixth millennium B.C.E. on.

Mesopotamia: Kingdoms, Empires, and Conquests

1.2 What changes and continuities characterized Mesopotamian civilization between the emergence of Sumer's city-states and the rise of Hammurabi's Babylonian Empire?

Long before the early Europeans living in Britain began to build Stonehenge, the first civilization and the world's first empires emerged on the Mesopotamian floodplain. Standing at the junction of the three continents of Africa, Asia, and Europe, southwest Asia became the meeting place of peoples, technologies, and ideas.

The Sumerian Kingdoms

About 5300 B.C.E. the villages in Sumer in southern Mesopotamia began a dynamic civilization that would flourish for thousands of years. The key to Sumerian civilization was water. Without a regular water supply, villages and cities could not have survived in Sumer. The name *Mesopotamia*, an ancient Greek word, means "the land between the rivers." Nestled between the Tigris and Euphrates Rivers, Sumerian civilization developed as its peoples learned to control the rivers that both enabled and imperiled human settlement.

The Tigris and Euphrates are unpredictable water sources, prone to sudden, powerful, and destructive flooding. Sumerian villagers first built their own levees for flood protection and dug their own small channels to divert floodwaters from the two great rivers to irrigate their dry lands. Then they discovered that by combining the labor force of several villages, they could build and maintain levee systems and irrigation channels on a large scale. Villages merged into cities that became the foundation of Sumerian civilization, as centralized administrations developed to manage the dams, levees, and irrigation canals; to direct the labor needed to maintain and expand the water works; and to distribute the resources that the system produced.

By 2500 B.C.E., about 13 major city-states—perhaps as many as 35 in all—managed the Mesopotamian floodplain in an organized fashion. (See **Map 1.4**.) In Sumer's city-states, the urban center directly controlled the surrounding countryside. Uruk, "the first city in human history,"[3] covered about two square miles and had a population of approximately 50,000 people, including both city-dwellers and the peasants living in small villages in a radius of about 10 miles around the city.

Sumer's cities served as economic centers where craft specialists such as potters, toolmakers, and weavers gathered to swap information and trade goods. Long-distance

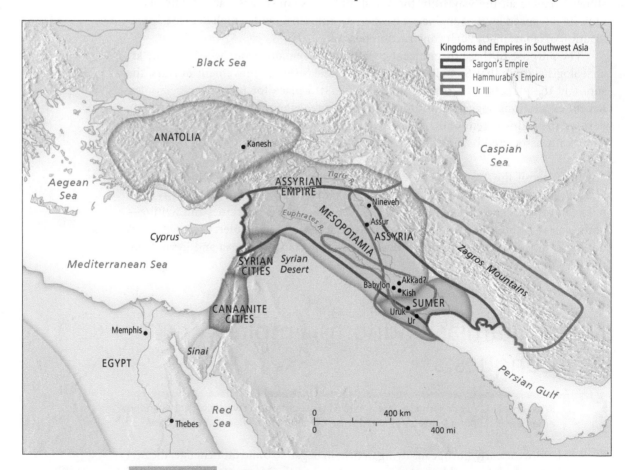

MAP **1.4** KINGDOMS AND EMPIRES IN SOUTHWEST ASIA Between 3000 and 1500 B.C.E., the Sumerian city-states, Sargon's Akkadian Empire, Hammurabi's empire in Babylon, and the Ur III dynasty emerged in southwest Asia. What features did these four different political entities share?

trade, made easier by the introduction of wheeled carts, enabled merchants to bring timber, ores, building stone, and luxury items unavailable in southern Mesopotamia from Anatolia, the Levantine Corridor, Afghanistan, and Iran.

Within each city-state, an elite group of residents regulated economic life. Uruk and the other Sumerian city-states were **redistributive economies**. In this type of economic system, the central authority (such as the king) controlled the agricultural resources and "redistributed" them to his people (in an unequal fashion!). Archaeologists excavating Uruk have found millions of bevel-rimmed bowls, all the same size and shape—and, as the archaeologist Robert Wenke notes, "surely one of the ugliest ceramic types ever made outside a kindergarten."[4] One theory is that the bowls were ration bowls—containers in which workers received their daily ration of grain. What is certain is that the bowls were mass-produced, and that only a powerful central authority could organize such mass production.

In the earliest era of Sumerian history, temple priests constituted this central authority. Sumerians believed that their city belonged to a god or goddess: The god owned all the lands and water, and the god's priests, who lived with him (or her) in the temple, administered these resources on the god's behalf. In practice, this meant that the priests collected exorbitant taxes in the forms of goods (grains, livestock, and manufactured products such as textiles) and services (laboring on city building and irrigation projects), and in return provided food rations for the workers from these collections.

As Sumer's city-states expanded, a new form of authority emerged. The ruins of monumental palaces as well as temples testify to the appearance of powerful royal households that joined the temple priesthood in managing the resources of the city-state. Historians theorize that as city-states expanded, competition for land increased. Such competition led to warfare, and during warfare, military leaders amassed power and, eventually, became kings.

The king's power rested on his military might. Yet to retain the people's loyalty and obedience, a king also needed religious legitimacy. Kingship, then, quickly became a key part of Sumerian religious traditions. Sumerians believed that "kingship descended from heaven," that the king ruled on the god's behalf. According to a Sumerian proverb, "Man is the shadow of god, but the king is god's reflection."[5] To challenge the king was to challenge the gods—never a healthy choice. The royal household and the temple priesthood thus worked together to exploit the labor of their subjects and amass power and wealth. Religious and political life were thoroughly intertwined.

Although the Sumerian city-states did not unite politically—and, in fact frequently fought each other—a number of factors created a single Sumerian culture. First, the kings maintained diplomatic relations with one another and with rulers throughout southwest Asia and Egypt, primarily to protect their trading networks. These trade networks also helped tie the Sumerian cities together and fostered a common Sumerian culture. Second, the city-states shared the same pantheon of gods. The surviving documents reveal that Sumerians in the different city-states sang the same hymns, used the same incantations to protect themselves from evil spirits, and offered their children the same proverbial nuggets of advice and warning. They did so, however, in two different languages—Sumerian, unrelated to any other known language, and Akkadian, a member of the Semitic language family that includes Hebrew and Arabic.

The Akkadian Empire of Sargon the Great

The political independence of the Sumerian city-states ended around 2340 B.C.E. when they were conquered by a warrior who took the name Sargon ("true king") and built a capital city at Agade (or Akkad), the ruins of which may rest under the modern city of Baghdad. With the reign of Sargon (ca. 2340–ca. 2305 B.C.E.), the history of Mesopotamia took a sharp turn. Sargon created the first empire in history. The term **empire** identifies a kingdom or state that controls foreign territories, either on the same

redistributive economies Type of economic system characteristic of ancient Mesopotamian societies. The central political authority controls all agricultural resources and their redistribution.

📖 **Read the Document**

Sumerian Law Code: The Code of Lipit-Ishtar

empire Large political formation consisting of different kingdoms or territories outside the boundaries of the states that control them.

continent or overseas. Except for relatively brief periods of fragmentation, imperial rule became the standard form of political statehood in southwest Asia for millennia. Because an empire, by definition, brings together different peoples, it serves as a cauldron of cultural encounters. As we will see, such encounters often transformed not only the conquered peoples, but the conquerors themselves.

Map 1.4 shows that the empire Sargon built embraced a string of territories running far west up the Euphrates River toward the Mediterranean. Sargon was probably the first ruler in history to create a standing army, one that was larger than any yet seen in the Near East. This formidable fighting force certainly helps explain how he conquered so many peoples. To meld these peoples into an empire, however, required not only military power but also innovative organizational skills. The formerly independent Sumerian city rulers became Sargon's governors, and were required to send a portion of all taxes collected to Akkad. Akkadian became the new administrative language, and a standard measurement and dating system was imposed to make record-keeping more efficient.

Raising the revenues to meet the costs of running this enormous empire was vital. Akkadian monarchs generated revenues in several ways. They, of course, taxed their people. Hence, the Mesopotamian proverb: "There are lords and there are kings, but the real person to fear is the tax collector."[6] They also leased out their vast farmlands and required conquered people to pay regular tribute. In addition, Akkadian kings depended on the revenue generated by commerce. They placed heavy taxes on raw materials imported from foreign lands. In fact, most Akkadian kings made long-distance trade the central objective of their foreign policy. They sent military expeditions as far as Anatolia and Iran to obtain timber, metals, and luxury goods. Akkadian troops protected international trade routes and managed the maritime trade in the Persian Gulf, where merchants brought goods by ship from India and southern Arabia.

Akkadian troops also waged war. Warfare during this era changed with the use of two new military technologies. The composite bow boosted the killing power of archers. Multiple layers of wood from different types of trees as well as bone and sinew added to the tensile strength of the bow and so increased the distance an arrow could fly and the speed at which it did so. The second important military innovation was an

THE SUMERIANS AT WAR This Sumerian battle wagon, a heavy four-wheeled cart pulled by donkeys, appears on the "Standard of Ur" (ca. 2500 B.C.E.). Excavated in the 1920s, the "Standard" is actually a wooden box, about 8.5 × 20 inches, with an inlaid mosaic of shells, red limestone, and lapis lazuli. One panel of the mosaic depicts a Sumerian war scene, the other a banquet; hence, archaeologists have labeled the panels "War" and "Peace."

early form of the chariot, a heavy four-wheeled cart that carried a driver and a spearman. Mounted on fixed wheels (and so incapable of swift turns) and pulled by donkeys (the faster horse did not come into use until the second millennium), the early chariot must have been a slow, clumsy instrument. Yet it proved effective in breaking up enemy infantry formations.

The cities of Mesopotamia prospered under Akkadian rule. Even so, Akkadian rulers could not hold their empire together for reasons that historians do not completely understand. One older explanation is that marauding tribes from the Zagros Mountains infiltrated the kingdom and caused tremendous damage. More recent research suggests that civil war tore apart the empire. Regardless of the cause, Akkadian kings lost control of their lands, and a period of anarchy began about 2250 B.C.E. "Who was king? Who was not king?" lamented a writer during this time of troubles. After approximately a century of chaos, the kingdom finally collapsed. Sargon, however, lived on in the memories and folk tales of the peoples of southwest Asia as the model of the mighty king.

The Ur III Dynasty and the Rise of Assyria

With the fall of Akkad, the cities of Sumer regained their independence, but they were soon—and forcibly—reunited under Ur-Nammu (r. ca. 2112–ca. 2095 B.C.E.), king of the Sumerian city of Ur, located far to the south of Akkad. Ur-Nammu established a powerful dynasty that lasted for five generations.

The Ur III dynasty (as it is called) developed an administrative bureaucracy even more elaborate than that of Sargon. Like all bureaucracies, it generated vast amounts of documents—we have more documentary sources for the Ur III era than for any other in ancient southwest Asia. Local elites, who served as the king's governors, administered the empire's 20 provinces. To assure their loyalty, they were often bound to the king by ties of marriage. As governors, these locals controlled the temple estates, maintained the canal system, and acted as the highest judge in the province. Significantly, they did not control the military. Ur III's kings set up a separate military administration and made sure that the generals assigned to each province came from somewhere else. In this way, the king could be sure that the general owed his allegiance to the royal household, not to the local elite. Ur's kings also strengthened their power by assuming the status of gods. Royal officials encouraged the people to give their children names such as "Shulgi is my god" to remind them of the king's divine authority.

Despite their sophisticated bureaucratic apparatus and their claims to divinity, the kings of Ur proved unable to stave off political fragmentation indefinitely. Rebellions increased in size and tempo. About 2000 B.C.E., semi-nomadic peoples known as Amorites began invading Mesopotamia from the steppes to the west and north. The Amorites seized fortified towns, taking food and supplies and causing widespread destruction. Their invasions destabilized the economy. Peasants fled from the fields, and with no food or revenues, inflation and famine overcame the empire. Ur collapsed, and Mesopotamia shattered again into a scattering of squabbling cities.

Assyria and Babylonia

For a long period, the political unity Sargon forged in Mesopotamia remained elusive, as states and peoples fought each other for control. This period of political fragmentation allowed for an important development: a partial "privatization" of the Mesopotamian economy, as individuals began to trade on their own behalf. Not connected in any way to the temple or the palace and, therefore, outside the redistributive economy, many of these free people grew prosperous. Merchants traveling by land and sea brought textiles, metals, and luxury items such as gold and silver jewelry and gems from lands bordering the Mediterranean and along the Persian Gulf and Red Sea.

Assyrian merchants, for example, developed an elaborate trade network linking the city-state of Assur with Anatolia. (See Map 1.4.) In Assur, they loaded up donkey caravans with tin and textiles for an arduous 50-day journey to the southern Anatolian city of Kanesh. (The surviving documentation is so detailed that we know that each donkey carried 150 pounds of tin or 30 textiles weighing about five pounds each.) Once they arrived in Kanesh, the merchants sold the donkeys, exchanged their merchandise for silver and gold, and headed back to Assur. Meanwhile, Assyrian merchants stationed in Kanesh sold the tin and textiles throughout Anatolia. The enterprise was risky—a storm, bandits, or a sick donkey could imperil it—but the profits were huge: 50 to 100 percent annually. Building on this economic prosperity, Assur (or Assyria) flourished as a powerful city-state until one of the most powerful empire-builders in the history of ancient southwest Asia reduced its power.

By 1780 B.C.E., the kingdom of Babylon had become a mighty empire under Hammurabi (r. 1792–1750 B.C.E.). Hammurabi never entirely conquered Assyria, but he dominated Mesopotamian affairs. Like Ur-Nammu and Sargon, Hammurabi developed a centralized administration to direct irrigation and building projects and to foster commerce throughout his realm. Both his law code (discussed later in this chapter) and his surviving letters to his royal agents reveal that no detail of economic life was too small for Hammurabi's notice. In one letter, for example, he ordered his agent to give "a fallow field that is of good quality and lies near the water, to Sin-imguranni, the seal-cutter."[7] Hammurabi did not, however, reverse the partial privatization of the economy that had developed during the era of political fragmentation. Babylonian society contained a prospering private sector of merchants, craftspeople, farmers, and sailors. Hammurabi liked to think of himself as a benevolent ruler, a kind of protective father. He declared, "I held the people of the lands of Sumer and Akkad safely on my lap."[8]

Nevertheless, Hammurabi and his successors imposed heavy taxes on their subjects. These financial demands provoked resentment, and when Hammurabi died, many Babylonian provinces successfully revolted. The loss of revenue weakened the Babylonian imperial government. By 1650, Hammurabi's empire had shrunk to northern Babylon, the territory Hammurabi had inherited when he first became king. Hammurabi's successors remained in control of northern Babylon for another five generations, but by 1400 B.C.E., a new people, the Kassites, ruled the kingdom.

Cultural Continuities: The Transmission of Mesopotamian Cultures

Although the rise and fall of kingdoms and empires punctuated the political history of Mesopotamia between the emergence of Sumerian civilization in 5300 B.C.E. and the collapse of Babylon in 1500 B.C.E., Mesopotamian culture exhibited remarkable continuity. Over these millennia, Sumerian religious values, architectural styles, literary forms, and other cultural concepts were absorbed, transformed, and passed on by the various peoples they encountered in both commerce and conquest.

THE MESOPOTAMIAN WORLDVIEW: RELIGION Religion—powerfully influenced by Mesopotamia's volatile climate—played a central role in the Sumerian and, hence, the wider Mesopotamian worldview. The Sumerians did not tend to think of their gods as loving or forgiving. Sumerian civilization arose on a floodplain subject to extreme and unpredictable climate conditions, with results ranging from devastating drought to torrential floods. Sumerians knew firsthand the famine and destruction that could result from sudden rainstorms, violent winds, or a flash flood They envisioned each of these natural forces as an unpredictable god who, like a human king or queen, was often unfair and had to be pleased and appeased:

> The sin I have committed I know not;
> The forbidden thing I have done I do not know.
> Some god has turned his rage against me;
> Some goddess has aimed her ire.
> I cry for help but no one takes my hand.[9]

Sumer's religion was **polytheistic**. Sumerians believed that many gods controlled their destinies. In the Sumerian pantheon, the all-powerful king Anu, the father of the gods, ruled the sky. Enlil was master of the wind and guided humans in the proper use of force. Enki governed the Earth and rivers and guided human creativity and inventions. Inanna was the goddess of love, sex, fertility, and warfare. These gods continued to dominate Mesopotamian culture long after Sumer's cities lost their political independence. After Hammurabi conquered most of Mesopotamia, Babylon's city-god Marduk joined the pantheon as a major deity.

polytheistic The belief in many gods.

Because the priests conducted the sacrifices that appeased the often-angry gods, the priesthood dominated Mesopotamian culture as did the temples in which they served and the gods to whom they sacrificed. In the center of every Sumerian city stood the temple complex, comprising temples to various gods, buildings to house the priests and priestesses, storage facilities for the sacrificial gifts, and looming over it all, the **ziggurat**. As the photograph of the ziggurat of Ur reveals, ziggurats were enormous square or rectangular temples with a striking stair-step design. Ur's ziggurat, built around 2100 B.C.E. by Ur-Nammu, had a 50-foot-high base, on which three stairways, each of 100 steps, led to the main gateways. The top of Ur's ziggurat did not survive, but in Ur-Nammu's time, a central staircase would have led upward to a temple.

ziggurat Monumental tiered or terraced temple characteristic of ancient Mesopotamia.

Ur-Nammu built Ur's ziggurat to house the chief god of the city. The Sumerians believed that one god or goddess protected each city, and that the city should serve as an earthly model of the god's divine home. Towering over the city, the deity's ziggurat reminded all the inhabitants of the omnipresent gods who controlled not only their commerce, but their very destiny.

THE MESOPOTAMIAN WORLDVIEW: SCIENCE Struggling to survive within an often hostile environment, Mesopotamians sought to understand and control their world through the practice of **divination**. To "divine"—to discern or to "read"—the future, a

divination The practice of discerning the future by looking for messages imprinted in nature.

ZIGGURAT OF UR Built of mud-brick, the Ziggurat of Ur was the focal point of religious life in the city. This vast temple was built by King Ur-Nammu of the Third Dynasty (2112–2095 B.C.E.) and restored by the British archaeologist, Sir Leonard Woolley, in the 1930s.

local wise woman or a priest looked for the messages imprinted in the natural world, such as in the entrails of a dead animal or in an unusual natural event. Once a person knew what the future was to hold, he or she could then work to change it. If the omens were bad, for example, a man could seek to appease the god by offering a sacrifice.

Divination and religious sacrifice seem to have little to do with science—and in Western culture in the twenty-first century, "religion" and "science" are often viewed as opposing or at least separate realms. Yet the Mesopotamian practice of divination helped shape a "proto-scientific" attitude toward the world. Much of divination consisted of "if . . . then . . ." equations:

> If a horse attempts to mount a cow, then there will be a decline in the land.
> If a man's chest-hair curls upward, he will become a slave.
> If the gallbladder [of the sacrificial sheep] is stripped of the hepatic duct, the army of the king will suffer thirst during a military campaign.[10]

Such statements seem silly, not scientific. Yet they rest on one of the fundamentals of modern science: close observation of the natural world. Only by observing and recording the *normal* processes of the natural world could Mesopotamians hope to recognize the omens embedded in the *abnormal*. Moreover, in the practice of divination, observation of individual events led to the formulation of a hypothesis of a general pattern—what we call **induction**, a crucial part of scientific analysis. In their effort to discern rational patterns in the natural world to improve the circumstances of their own lives, Mesopotamians were moving toward the beginnings of a scientific mentality—a crucial aspect of Western civilization.

This proto-scientific understanding is even more evident in the technological, astronomical, and mathematical legacy of ancient Mesopotamia. Sumerians devised the potter's wheel, the wagon, and the chariot. They developed detailed knowledge about the movement of the stars, planets, and the moon, especially as these movements pertained to agricultural cycles, and they made impressive innovations in mathematics. Many Sumerian tablets show multiplication tables, square and cube roots, exponents, and other practical information such as how to calculate compound interest on loans. The Sumerians divided the circle into 360 degrees and developed a counting system based on 60 in multiples of 10—a system we still use to tell time.

induction The process of reasoning that formulates general hypotheses and theories on the basis of specific observation and the accumulation of data.

THE DEVELOPMENT OF WRITING Perhaps the Sumerians' most important cultural innovation was writing. The Sumerians devised a unique script to record their language. Historians call the symbols that Sumerians pressed onto clay tablets with sharp objects **cuneiform**, or wedge-shaped, writing. The earliest known documents written in this language come from Uruk about 3200 B.C.E. Writing originated because of the demands of record-keeping. By around 4000 B.C.E., officials in Uruk were using small clay tokens of different shapes to represent and record quantities of produce and numbers of livestock. They placed these tokens in clay envelopes, and impressed marks on the outer surface of the envelopes to indicate the contents. By 3100 B.C.E., people stopped using tokens and simply impressed the shapes directly on a flat piece of clay or tablet with a pointed stick or reed.

cuneiform A kind of writing in which wedge-shaped symbols are pressed into clay tablets to indicate words and ideas. Cuneiform writing originated in ancient Sumer.

As commodities and trading became more complex, the number of symbols multiplied. Learning the hundreds of signs required intensive study. The scribes, the people who mastered these signs, became important figures in the royal and religious courts because their work enabled kings and priests to regulate the economic life of their cities. Sumerian cuneiform writing spread, and other peoples of Mesopotamia and southwest Asia began adapting it to record information in their own languages.

THE *EPIC OF GILGAMESH* Writing made a literary tradition possible. Sumerians told exciting stories about their gods and heroes. Passed on and adapted through the ages, these stories helped shape ideas about divine action and human response throughout Mesopotamian history.

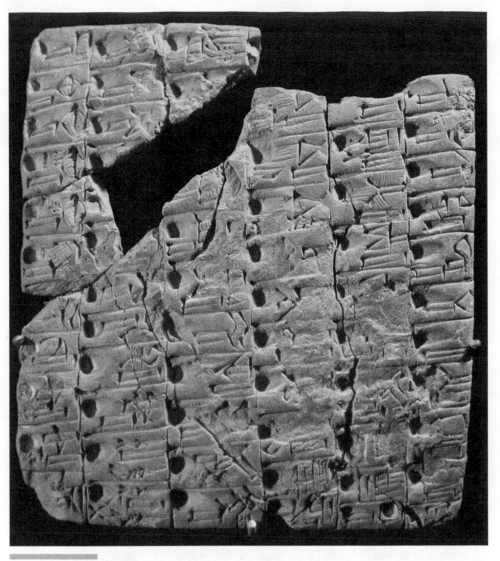

CUNEIFORM TEXTS A Sumerian scribe in the city-state of Uruk wrote in cuneiform on this stone tablet around 3200 B.C.E.

One of the most popular of these stories concerned the legendary king Gilgamesh of Uruk. Part god and part man, Gilgamesh harasses his subjects. He demands sex from the young women and burdens the young men with construction tasks. The people of Uruk beg the gods to distract this bothersome hero. The gods send the beastly Enkidu to fight Gilgamesh, but after a prolonged wrestling match that ends in a draw, the two become close friends and set off on a series of adventures. The two heroes battle monsters and even outwit the gods. Finally the gods decide that enough is enough and arrange for Enkidu's death. Mourning for his stalwart friend, Gilgamesh sets out to find the secret to living forever. In the end, immortality eludes his grasp. A mere mortal, Gilgamesh becomes a wiser king, and his subjects benefit from his new wisdom. He realizes that while he must die, his fame may live on, and so he seeks to leave behind him a magnificent city that will live forever in human memory.

The *Epic of Gilgamesh* as we know it was recorded in Akkadian, but it is clear that the stories date from long before the rise of the Akkadian Empire. Recited and read by Mesopotamian peoples for millennia, the Gilgamesh story's influence extended beyond the borders even of the empires of Sargon or Hammurabi. Its themes, plots, and characters reappear in revised form in the literatures of such diverse peoples as the ancient Hebrews (recorded in the Hebrew Bible or Old Testament) and the early Greeks. These peoples, however, reworked the stories in accordance with their own cultural

1.1

1.2

1.3

((**Read the Document**

Excerpts from the *Epic of Gilgamesh*

values. In its Sumerian form, the *Epic of Gilgamesh* demonstrates a Mesopotamian worldview: It emphasizes the capriciousness of the gods, the hostility of nature, and the unpredictability of human existence. It offers no hope of heaven, only resignation to life's unpredictability and the chance of finding some sort of reward during one's short time on Earth.

LAW AND ORDER Mesopotamian culture also made a lasting imprint on future societies through another important innovation: the code of law, preserved in written form. Archaeologists have so far uncovered three Sumerian law codes, the earliest dating to around 2350 B.C.E. The most famous lawgiver of the ancient world was the Babylonian empire-builder Hammurabi. The Law Code of Hammurabi—282 civil, commercial, and criminal laws—is the world's oldest complete surviving compendium of laws. We do not know to what extent these laws were actually implemented. Many scholars argue that the code was a kind of public relations exercise, an effort by Hammurabi both to present a social ideal and to persuade his people (and the gods) to view him as the "King of Justice." (See *Justice in History* in this chapter.)

What is clear is that Hammurabi's laws unveil the social values and everyday concerns of Babylonia's rulers. For example, many of the laws focus on the irrigation system that made Babylonian agriculture possible. One such law reads: "If a man has opened his channel for irrigation and has been negligent and allowed the water to wash away a neighbor's field, he shall pay grain equivalent to the crops of his neighbors"—or be sold as a slave.[11]

Hammurabi's law code buttressed Babylon's social hierarchy by drawing legal distinctions between classes of people. The crimes of aristocrats (called free men) were treated more leniently than were the offenses of common people, while slaves were given no rights at all. If an aristocrat killed a commoner, he or she had to pay a fine, whereas if a commoner killed an aristocrat, he or she was executed. But the code of Hammurabi also emphasized the responsibility of public officials and carefully regulated commercial transactions. If a home was robbed, and city officers failed to find the burglar, then the householder had the right to expect reimbursement for his losses from the city government. If a moneylender suddenly raised interest rates beyond those already agreed on, then he forfeited the entire loan.

Almost one-quarter of Hammurabi's statutes concern family matters. The laws' focus on questions of dowry and inheritance reflect the Mesopotamian view of marriage as first and foremost a business matter. The Sumerian word for *love* literally translates to "measure the earth"—to mark land boundaries and designate who gets

Justice in History
Gods and Kings in Mesopotamian Justice

Mesopotamian kings placed a high priority on ruling their subjects justly. Shamash, the sun god and protector of justice, named two of his children Truth and Fairness. In the preface to his law code, Hammurabi explained the relationship between his rule and divine justice:

At that time, Anu and Enlil [two of the greatest gods], for the well-being of the people, called me by name, Hammurabi, the pious, god-fearing prince, and appointed me

to make justice appear in the land [and] to destroy the evil and wicked, so that the strong might not oppress the weak, [and] to rise like Shamash over the black-headed people [the people of Mesopotamia].[12]

Mesopotamian courts handled cases involving property, inheritance, boundaries, sale, and theft. A special panel of

(continued on next page)

(continued from previous page)

royal judges and officials handled cases involving the death penalty, such as treason, murder, sorcery, theft of temple goods, or adultery. Mesopotamians kept records of trials and legal decisions on clay tablets so that others might learn from them and avoid additional lawsuits.

A lawsuit began when a person brought a dispute before a court. The court consisted of three to six judges chosen from among the town's leading men, such as merchants, scribes, and officials in the town assembly. The judges could speak with authority about the community's principles of justice.

Litigants spoke on their own behalf and presented testimony through witnesses, written documents, or statements made by leading officials. Witnesses took strict oaths to tell the truth in a temple before the statue of a god. Once the parties presented all the evidence, the judges made their decision and pronounced the verdict and punishment.

Sometimes the judges asked the defendants to clear themselves by letting the god in whose name the oath was taken make the judgment. The accused person would then undergo an ordeal or test in which he or she had to jump into a river and swim a certain distance underwater. Those who survived were considered innocent. Drowning constituted proof of guilt and a just punishment rendered by the gods.

The following account of one such ordeal comes from the city of Mari, about 1770 B.C.E. A queen was accused of casting spells on her husband. The maid forced to undergo the ordeal on her behalf drowned, and we do not know whether the queen received further punishment:

> Concerning Amat-Sakkanim . . . whom the river god overwhelmed. . . . : "We made her undertake her plunge, saying to her, 'Swear that your mistress did not perform any act of sorcery against Yarkab-Addad her lord; that she did not reveal any palace secret nor did another person open the missive of her mistress; that your mistress did not commit a transgression against her lord.' In connection with these oaths they had her take her plunge; the river god overwhelmed her, and she did not come up alive."[13]

This account illustrates the Mesopotamian belief that sometimes only the gods could make decisions about right and wrong. By contrast, the following trial excerpts come from a homicide case in which humans, not gods, made the final judgment. About 1850 B.C.E., three men murdered a temple

THE LAW CODE OF HAMMURABI Hammurabi receives the law directly from the sun god, Shamash, on this copy of the Law Code.

SOURCE: Stele of Hammurabi. Hammurabi standing before the sun-god Shamash and 262 laws. Engraved black basalt stele. 1792–1750 B.C.E., 1st Babylonian Dynasty. Louvre, Paris, France. © Giraudon/Art Resource, NY.

official named Lu-Inanna. For unknown reasons, they told the victim's wife, Nin-dada, what they had done. King Ur-Ninurta of the city of Isin sent the case to be tried in the city of Nippur, the site of an important court. When the case came to trial, nine accusers asked that the three murderers be executed. They also requested that Nin-dada be put to death because she had not reported the murder to the authorities. The accusers said:

> They who have killed a man are not worthy of life. Those three males and that woman should be killed.

In her defense, two of Nin-dada's supporters pointed out that she had not been involved in the murder and therefore should be released:

> Granted that the husband of Nin-dada, the daughter of Lu-Ninurta, has been killed, but what had the woman done that she should be killed?

The court agreed, on the grounds that Nin-dada was justified in keeping silent because her husband had not provided for her properly:

> A woman whose husband did not support her . . . why should she not remain silent about him? Is it she who killed her husband? The punishment of those who actually killed him should suffice.

In accordance with the decision of the court, the defendants were executed.

This approach to justice—using witnesses, evaluating evidence, and rendering a verdict in a court protected by the king—demonstrated the Mesopotamians' desire for fairness. This court decision became an important precedent that later judges frequently cited.

For Discussion

1. How would a city benefit by letting a panel of royal officials make judgments about life-and-death issues? How would the king benefit?

2. How do these trials demonstrate the interaction of Mesopotamian religious, social, and political beliefs?

Taking It Further

Greengus, Samuel. "Legal and Social Institutions of Ancient Near Mesopotamia," in *Civilizations of the Ancient Near East,* ed. Jack M. Sasson, Vol. 1 (Peabody, MA: Hendrickson Publishers, 2001). Describes basic principles of law and administration of justice, with a bibliography of ancient legal texts.

patriarchy A social or cultural system in which men occupy the positions of power; in a family system, a father-centered household.

what. Hammurabi's laws also highlight the **patriarchal** structure of Mesopotamian family life. In a patriarchal society, the husband/father possesses supreme authority in the family. Hence, Hammurabi's code declared that if a wife had a lover, both she and her lover would be drowned, while a husband was permitted extramarital sex. If a wife neglected her duties at home or failed to produce children, her husband had the right to divorce her. Yet Mesopotamian women, at least those in the "free" class, were not devoid of all rights. If a husband divorced his wife without sufficient cause, then he had to give her back her entire dowry. Unlike in many later societies, a married woman was an independent legal entity: She could appear in court and she could engage in commercial contracts. Some Babylonian women ran businesses, such as small shops and inns.

Many of Hammurabi's laws seem harsh: If a house caved in because of faulty workmanship and the householder died, then the builder was put to death. If a freeman hit another freeman's pregnant daughter and caused her to miscarry, he had to pay 10 silver shekels for the unborn child, but if his blow killed the daughter, then his own daughter was executed. Yet through these laws Hammurabi's Code introduced one of the fundamentals of Western jurisprudence: the idea that the punishment must suit the crime (at least in crimes involving social equals). The principle of "an eye for an eye" (rather than a life for an eye) helped shape legal thought in southwest Asia for a millennium. It later influenced the laws of the Hebrews and, thus through the Hebrew Bible (the Christian Old Testament), still molds western ideas about justice.

 Read the Document

The Code of Hammurabi

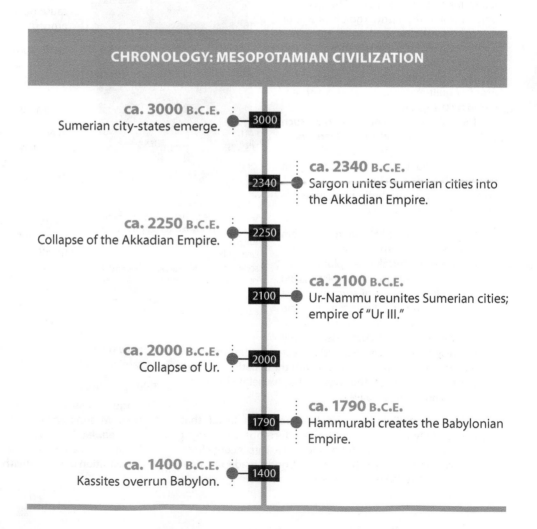

CHRONOLOGY: MESOPOTAMIAN CIVILIZATION

ca. 3000 B.C.E.
Sumerian city-states emerge.
3000

ca. 2340 B.C.E.
2340 Sargon unites Sumerian cities into the Akkadian Empire.

ca. 2250 B.C.E.
Collapse of the Akkadian Empire.
2250

ca. 2100 B.C.E.
2100 Ur-Nammu reunites Sumerian cities; empire of "Ur III."

ca. 2000 B.C.E.
Collapse of Ur.
2000

ca. 1790 B.C.E.
1790 Hammurabi creates the Babylonian Empire.

ca. 1400 B.C.E.
Kassites overrun Babylon.
1400

Egypt: The Empire of the Nile

1.3 What distinctive features characterized Egyptian civilization throughout its long history?

As the civilizations of Mesopotamia rose and fell, another civilization emerged far to the south: Egypt. A long and narrow strip of land in the northeast corner of Africa, Egypt depended for its survival on the Nile, the world's longest river, which flows north into the Mediterranean Sea from one of its points of origin in eastern Africa 4,000 miles away. The northernmost part of Egypt, where the Nile enters the Mediterranean, is a broad and fertile delta. The river flooded annually from mid-July to mid-October, leaving behind rich deposits of silt ideal for planting crops. Unlike in southwest Asia, the annual floods in Egypt came with clockwork regularity. For the Egyptians, nature was not unpredictable and random in its destruction, but a benevolent force, generous in sharing its riches.

Egypt was also fortunate in another of its physical features: It rested securely between two desert regions that effectively barricaded it from foreign conquest. Whereas Mesopotamia stood at the intersection of three continents, vulnerable to invading armies, Egyptian civilization emerged in a far more easily defended position. Egyptian history, then, is remarkable for its political stability. This stability, combined with the predictability and generosity of the Nile, may explain the confidence and optimism that marked Egyptian culture.

Historians organize the long span of ancient Egyptian history into four main periods: Predynastic and Early Dynastic (10,000–2680 B.C.E.), the Old Kingdom (ca. 2680–2200 B.C.E.), the Middle Kingdom (2040–1720 B.C.E.), and the New Kingdom (1550–1150 B.C.E.). Times of political disruption between the kingdoms are called *intermediate periods*. Despite these periods of disruption, the Egyptians maintained a remarkably stable civilization for thousands of years.

◖◖ ▢ Read the Document

An Egyptian Hymn to the Nile

Egypt's Rise to Empire

Like the peoples of Mesopotamia, the Egyptians were originally hunter-gatherers who slowly turned to growing crops and domesticating animals. Small villages, in which people could coordinate their labor most easily, appeared along the banks of the Nile between 5000 and 4000 B.C.E. By 3500 B.C.E., Egyptians could survive comfortably through agriculture and herding. Small towns multiplied along the Nile, and market centers connected by roads emerged as hubs where artisans and merchants exchanged their wares.

Toward the end of the Predynastic period, between 3500 and 3000 B.C.E., trade along the Nile River resulted in a shared culture and way of life. Towns grew into small kingdoms whose rulers constantly warred with one another, attempting to grab more land and extend their power. The big consumed the small; by 3000 B.C.E., the towns had been absorbed into just two kingdoms: Upper Egypt in the south and Lower Egypt in the north. These two then united, forming what historians term the **Old Kingdom**. (See **Map 1.5**.)

THE KINGS AND THE GODS IN THE OLD KINGDOM In the new capital city of Memphis, the Egyptian kings became the focal points of religious, social, and political life. While in Mesopotamia, kings were regarded as the gods' representatives on Earth, Egyptian kings were acknowledged as gods who ruled Egypt on behalf of the other gods. Hence, Egyptians in the Old Kingdom called their king "the good god" (the label *pharaoh* was not used until the New Kingdom) and told tales that emphasized the divinity of the king. In one such story, the god Osiris, ruler of Egypt, was killed and chopped into bits

Old Kingdom In ancient Near Eastern history, the period in Egyptian history from ca. 2680–2200 B.C.E., formed by the unification of the kingdoms of Upper Egypt and Lower Egypt.

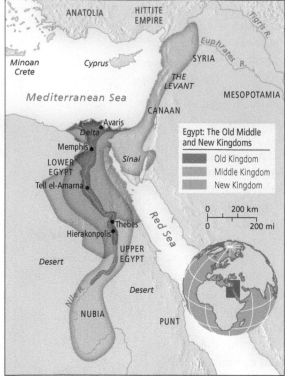

MAP 1.5 EGYPT: THE OLD, MIDDLE, AND NEW KINGDOMS
As this map shows, Egyptian power expanded from its base along the Nile delta, first southward along the Nile River, and then, through trade and conquest, into southwest Asia. Egypt's control of mineral resources, especially gold, turquoise, and copper, played an important role in its commercial prosperity. How did the New Kingdom compare to its predecessors? How does this map help explain the rivalry between New Kingdom Egypt and the Hittite Empire?

ma'at Ancient Egyptian concept of the fundamental order established by the gods.

 Read the Document

Workings of *Ma'at*: The Tale of an Eloquent Peasant

by his evil brother, Seth. Osiris's son, Horus, avenged his father by defeating Seth and reclaiming the Egyptian throne. All Egyptian kings, then, embodied Horus during their reign.

The story of Osiris, Seth, and Horus not only emphasized the divinity of the king, it also stressed the central theme of the Egyptian worldview: the struggle between the forces of chaos and of order. Seth embodied the forces of evil and disorder. In defeating Seth, Horus overcame chaos and restored what the Egyptians called *ma'at* to the world. The word *ma'at* has no English equivalent; in various contexts, it can mean truth, wisdom, justice, or stability. *Ma'at* was the way the gods had made the world—everything in its proper place, everything the way the gods wanted it to be. The king's essential task was to maintain **ma'at**, to keep things in order and harmony. The king's presence meant that cosmic order reigned and that the kingdom was protected against forces of disorder and destruction.

Like the Mesopotamians, the Egyptians believed in many gods, but in Egypt the gods were not prone to punish men and women without reason. Because the Nile River flooded regularly and predictably, each year leaving behind rich soil deposits, the natural world seemed far less harsh and erratic to the Egyptians. They thus regarded their gods as largely helpful. Ordinary Egyptians tended to pray to minor household gods, such as Tauret, portrayed as a pregnant hippopotamus who protected women during childbirth. Official religion, however, centered on the major state gods, worshiped and housed in monumental temples across the kingdom. The sun god Re was one of the most important Egyptian deities. Re journeyed across the sky every day in a boat, rested at night, and returned in the morning to resume his eternal journey. By endlessly repeating the cycle of rising and setting, the sun symbolized the harmonious order of the universe that Re established. Evil, however, in the form of Apopis, a serpent god whose coils could trap Re's boat like a reed in the Nile, constantly threatened this order. Re's cosmic journey could continue only if *ma'at* was maintained.

THE PYRAMIDS One spectacular feature of Egyptian religion in the Old Kingdom was the construction of pyramids. These elaborate monuments reflected Egyptian emphasis on the afterlife. The earliest pyramids, erected around 2680 B.C.E., were elaborate temples in which priests worshiped statues of the king surrounded by the enormous mud-brick monument. The pyramid contained compartments where the king could dwell in the afterlife in the same luxury he enjoyed during his life on Earth. King Djoser (2668–2649 B.C.E.) built the first pyramid complex, and the world's first monumental stone building, at Saqqara near Memphis. Known today as the Step Pyramid (pictured on p. 31), this structure rests above Djoser's burial place and rises high into the air in six steps, which represent a ladder to Heaven.

In the centuries after Djoser's reign, kings continued building pyramids for themselves and smaller ones for their queens, with each tomb becoming more architecturally sophisticated. The walls grew taller and steeper and contained hidden burial chambers and treasure rooms. The Great Pyramid at Giza, built around 2600 B.C.E. by King Khufu (or Cheops), was the largest human-made structure in the ancient world. It consists of more than two million stones that weigh an average of two and a half tons each. Covering 13 acres, it reaches over 480 feet into the sky.

Building the pyramid complexes was a long and costly task. In addition to the architects, painters, sculptors, carpenters, and other specialists employed on the site throughout the year, stone masons supervised the quarrying and transport of the colossal building blocks. Peasants, who were organized into work gangs and paid and fed

DJOSER'S STEP PYRAMID Djoser ascended to the throne of Egypt around 2668 B.C.E. and immediately ordered his vizier Imhotep to oversee the construction of his tomb. Up until this point, Egyptians constructed pyramids out of mud-brick, but Imhotep deviated from tradition and chose stone.

by the king, provided the heavy labor when the Nile flooded their fields every year. As many as 70,000 workers out of a total population estimated at 1.5 million sweated on the pyramids every day. Entire cities sprang up around pyramid building sites to house the workmen, artisans, and farmers. The construction of elaborate pyramids stopped after 2400 B.C.E., probably because of the expense, but smaller burial structures continued to be built for centuries.

THE SOCIAL AND POLITICAL ORDER IN THE OLD KINGDOM The king and the royal family stood at the top of the Old Kingdom's social and political hierarchy. As a god on Earth, the king possessed absolute authority. All of Egypt—all the land, every resource, every person—theoretically belonged to the king. Yet royal Egyptians were not free to act in any way they might choose. As we have seen, maintaining *ma'at*—ensuring that things remained in divine order—was central to the Egyptian worldview. For Egyptian kings, maintaining *ma'at* meant following carefully regulated rituals at almost all times. The rules that governed royalty differed from those for commoners. Kings, for example, had many wives and frequently married their daughters and sisters, whereas ordinary Egyptians were monogamous (a man took only one wife) and married outside the family.

Below the royal family stood the nobility, made up of priests, court officials, and provincial governors. Men in these ranks carried out the king's orders. Egypt, like the Mesopotamian empires, was a redistributive economy. The kings' officials collected Egypt's produce and redistributed it throughout the kingdom. The job of keeping records of the kings' possessions and supervising food production fell to the scribes, who were trained in **hieroglyphic** writing. *Hieroglyphs* (literally "sacred carvings")

hieroglyphic Ancient Egyptian system of writing that represented both sounds and objects.

📖 Read the Document

Praise of the Scribe's Profession:
An Egyptian Letter

represented both sounds (as in our alphabet) and objects (as in a pictorial system). Learning the hundreds of signs for literary or administrative purposes took years of schooling. It was worth the effort, however, for knowledge of hieroglyphs gave scribes great power. For 3,000 years, these royal bureaucrats kept the machinery of Egyptian government running despite the rise and fall of dynasties.

Ordinary Egyptians fell into three categories: skilled artisans, peasants, and slaves. Craftsmen and skilled workers such as millers and stone masons stood below the nobility on the social ladder. Employed in large workshops owned by the king or nobility, the craftsmen served the privileged classes above them. Below them were the peasants, who not only farmed, but also labored on public works such as temples, roads, and irrigation projects. As in medieval Europe, these peasants were tied to the land: They could not leave the estates that they farmed for the king or nobility, and if the land was sold, they were passed on to the new owner as well. Slaves occupied the bottom of the social ladder. They toiled on monumental building projects as well as within the temples and royal palaces. Slavery, however, was not dominant in the Egyptian economy. Free Egyptians did most of the work.

Free Egyptian women—whether from the nobility or the skilled artisans—possessed clear rights. They could buy and sell property, make contracts, sue in court, and own their own businesses. In a marriage, the husband and wife were regarded as equals. Women dominated certain occupations, such as spinning and weaving, and even worked as doctors.

WHERE IS *MA'AT*? THE COLLAPSE OF THE OLD KINGDOM Around 2200 B.C.E. the Old Kingdom collapsed, perhaps because terrible droughts lowered the level of the Nile. Famine followed. *Ma'at*—the divine harmony and order that stood at the center of the Egyptian worldview—had disappeared. For 200 years, anarchy and civil war raged in Egypt during what historians call the First Intermediate Period.

The chaos and disorder of the First Intermediate Period resulted in a significant religious and cultural shift. The optimism that had characterized Egyptian culture gave way to uncertainty and even pessimism as Egyptians wondered how to restore *ma'at* in a world so out of balance:

> Whom can I trust today?
> Hearts are greedy,
> And every man steals his neighbor's goods.[14]

In their quest to make sense out of the chaos, Egyptian writers began to emphasize rewards in the afterlife as recompense for righteous action here on Earth. In the Old Kingdom, Egyptians had sought to act justly in accordance with *ma'at* because they were confident that right action would be rewarded in the here and now. In the new climate of turmoil and hunger, however, they found comfort in the idea that although the good suffered in their earthly life, they would be rewarded in the life to come. During this period, the Egyptians developed the concept of a final judgment—the earliest known instance of such an idea in human history. After death, a person's heart would be weighed in the balance against *ma'at*. Those who tipped the scales—those who failed the test—would be consumed by the Devourer, a god with a crocodile's head. But those who passed would live like gods in the afterlife. (See *Different Voices* in this chapter.)

📖 Read the Document

Elders' Advice to Their Successors

THE MIDDLE KINGDOM The First Intermediate Period ended when the governors of Thebes, a city in Upper Egypt, set out to reunify the kingdom. In 2040 B.C.E., Mentuhotep II (r. 2040–2010 B.C.E.) established a vigorous new monarchy, initiating the **Middle Kingdom**. (See Map 1.5.) He and his successors restored *ma'at* to Egypt: They rebuilt the power of the monarchy, reestablished centralized control, and repaired Egypt's commercial and diplomatic links to southwest Asia. Prosperity and stability returned.

Middle Kingdom In ancient Near Eastern history, refers to the period of Egyptian history from 2040 to 1720 B.C.E.

Yet the Middle Kingdom was not a reincarnation of the Old Kingdom. The chaos of the First Intermediate Period modified political ideas and social relations. The king was no longer an omnipotent god. Capable of making mistakes and even of being afraid, the Middle Kingdom monarch appeared in texts as a lonely figure, seeking to serve as a good shepherd to his people. With this new concept of kingship came a slightly altered social order, with the nobility possessing more power and autonomy than in the Old Kingdom.

New developments also marked religion. With the return of *ma'at*—with life on Earth more prosperous and stable—Egyptians began to see the final judgment as more of a problem that needed to be solved than as a source of comfort. How could one enjoy life and yet be assured of living like a god for eternity, rather than being consumed by the Devourer? To be sure that they passed the final judgment, Egyptians had themselves buried with special scarabs. A scarab is a small figure of a dung beetle, but these funeral scarabs featured human heads and carried magic incantations or charms. This powerful magic prevented the heart from testifying against the individual when it was weighed in the final judgment. In other words, it was a kind of false weight, a finger on the scales, a way to deceive the gods and ensure passage to the afterlife.

ENCOUNTERS WITH OTHER CIVILIZATIONS While Egypt's position between two deserts guaranteed its military security, it did not isolate Egypt from the rest of the ancient world. During both the Old and Middle Kingdoms, Egyptian kings forged an economic network that included trading cities in the Levant, Minoan Crete (see Chapter 2), the southern Red Sea area called Punt, and Mesopotamia. To protect the trade routes along which raw materials and luxury goods were imported, rulers did not hesitate to use force. They also, however, used diplomacy to stimulate trade.

Egyptian interactions with Nubia (modern Sudan) were particularly important. Rich in gold and other natural resources, Nubia also benefited from its location at the nexus of trade routes from central and eastern Africa. Agents of Egyptian rulers, called Keepers of the Gateway of the South, tried to protect this trade by keeping the peace with the warlike Nubian tribes. Slowly, Egyptian monarchs made their presence more permanent. King Mentuhotep II, whose reign marked the start of the Middle Kingdom, not only reunified Egypt but also gained control of Lower Nubia. This expansion of Egyptian control ensured the free flow of Nubian resources northward. Around 1900 B.C.E., King Amenemhet built 10 forts at strategic locations where trade routes from the interior of Africa reached the Nile River. These forts reinforced Egyptian access to Nubian gold, ivory, and other natural resources.

Attracted by Egypt's stability and prosperity, peoples from different lands settled in the Nile Valley. They took Egyptian names and assimilated into Egyptian culture. The government settled these immigrants, as well as war captives, throughout the kingdom where they could mix quickly with the local inhabitants. This willingness to accept newcomers into their kingdom lent Egyptian civilization even more vibrancy.

Immigrants from Canaan (modern-day Lebanon, Israel, and parts of Jordan and Syria) played a significant role in Egyptian history toward the end of the Middle Kingdom. Around 1720 B.C.E., centralized state control began to deteriorate (for reasons that remain unclear), and Canaanites began to seize political control over the regions in which they had settled. A century of political decentralization and chaos—the Second Intermediate Period—ensued, with even larger groups of Canaanite immigrants settling in Egypt's Delta region:

> Foreigners have become people [i.e., Egyptians] everywhere. . . .
> See now, the land is deprived of kingship by a few men who ignore custom.[15]

By approximately 1650 B.C.E., one of these Canaanite groups had established control over the entire northern delta region and forced the Egyptian rulers there to pay them tribute. The era of Hyksos rule had begun. Although *Hyksos* meant "rulers of

Different Voices

Explaining Evil in Ancient Times

T *he gap that separates twenty-first-century Western readers from the inhabitants of ancient Mesopotamia or Egypt is huge, and yet some of their questions sound familiar: Why do the good and the just suffer? Where do we turn for hope when life seems hopeless? The two documents that follow offer different responses to evil times. The first is an excerpt from a lengthy poem inscribed on four tablets during the Akkadian Empire in Mesopotamia. The Akkadian era was generally prosperous, but as this document shows, daily survival remained difficult for many. The second document comes from the tumultuous intermediate period following the collapse of Egypt's Old Kingdom. The writer may have been king of one of the fragmented states that emerged as the Old Kingdom disintegrated. In* The Instructions for Merikare, *he shares with his son the lessons he has learned in a world gone mad.*

I. From Mesopotamia: I Will Praise the Lord of Wisdom

I turn around, but it is bad, very bad;
My ill luck increases and I cannot find what is right.
I called to my god, but he did not show his face,
I prayed to my goddess, but she did not raise her head.
Even the diviner with his divination could not make
   a prediction,
And the interpreter of dreams with his libation could not
   elucidate my case. . . .
What strange conditions everywhere!
When I look behind [me], there is persecution, trouble.
Like one who has not made libations to his god,
Nor invoked his goddess when he ate,
Does not make prostrations nor recognize [the necessity
   of] bowing down,
In whose mouth supplication and prayer are lacking,
Who has even neglected holy days, and ignored festivals . . .
Like one who has gone crazy and forgotten his lord,
Has frivolously sworn a solemn oath by his god, [like such
   a one] do I appear.
For myself, I gave attention to supplication and prayer;
My prayer was discretion, sacrifice my rule.
The day for worshipping the god was a joy to my heart;
The day of the goddess's procession was profit and gain to me.
The king's blessing—that was my joy. . . .
I wish I knew that these things would be pleasing to one's god!
What is good for oneself may be offense to one's god,
What in one's own heart seems despicable may be proper
   to one's god.
Who can know the will of the gods in heaven?
Who can understand the plans of the underworld gods?
Where have humans learned the way of a god?
He who was alive yesterday is dead today. . . .
As for me, exhausted, a windstorm is driving me on!
Debilitating Disease is let loose upon me;
An Evil Wind has blown [from the] horizon,

Headache has sprung up from the surface of the underworld. . . .
Feebleness has overcome my whole body,
An attack of illness has fallen upon my flesh.

II. From Egypt: The Instruction for Merikare

DO JUSTICE WHILST THOU ENDUREST UPON THE EARTH. Quiet the weeper; do not oppress the widow; supplant no man in the property of his father; and impair no officials at their posts. Be on thy guard against punishing wrongfully. Do not slaughter: it is not of advantage to thee. . . .

THE COUNCIL [OF GODS] WHICH JUDGES THE DEFICIENT, thou knowest they are not lenient on that day of judging the miserable. . . . they regard a lifetime as (but) an hour. A man remains over after death, and his deeds are placed beside him in heaps*. However, existence yonder is for eternity, and he who complains of it is a fool. (But) as for him who reaches it without wrongdoing, he shall exist yonder like a god, stepping out freely like the lords of eternity.

. . . .

Well directed are men, the cattle of the god. He made heaven and earth according to their desire, and he repelled the water-monster. He made the breath of life (for) their nostrils. . . . He has slain the treacherous of heart among them, as a man beats his son for his brother's sake. For the god knows every name.

For Discussion

1. What picture of Akkadian religious practice can we draw from the first document?
2. In this excerpt from *I Will Praise the Lord of Wisdom*, the anonymous author files a sort of cosmic complaint. What grievance does he present?
3. In the second excerpt, what advice does the king offer to his son Merikare? What does he want his son to understand?
4. How does *The Instruction for Merikare* demonstrate the new religious concepts that the Egyptians developed in response to the disappearance of political stability and economic prosperity during the First Intermediate Period?
5. Each of these documents reveals timeless existential concerns, but how do they point to the specific historical contexts in which they were written?

SOURCE: I. James B. Pritchard (ed.), *The Ancient Near East: Supplementary Texts and Pictures Relating to the Old Testament*, 597–598. Copyright © 1968 Princeton University Press, 1996 renewed Princeton University Press. Reprinted by permission of Princeton University Press. II. "The Instruction for King Meri-kare." James B. Pritchard, *Ancient Near Eastern Texts Relating to the Old Testament* (Princeton: Princeton University Press, 1950), p. 415 (right column), p. 417 (right column).

*"his deeds are placed beside him in heaps": the Council of Gods weighs his wrongdoing.

foreign lands" in Egyptian, the Hyksos dynasty (ca. 1650–1540 B.C.E.) quickly assimilated Egyptian culture. They used Egyptian names and symbols, worshiped Egyptian gods, and employed native Egyptians to staff their bureaucracies and keep their state records—in Egyptian hieroglyphs.

But the Hyksos, and the Canaanite immigrant community from which they emerged, not only absorbed Egyptian ways, they also transformed them. Canaanite immigrants brought with them into Egypt a vital skill: the ability to make bronze. An alloy of copper and tin, bronze is much harder and lasts much longer than either copper or tin alone. From about 3500 B.C.E. when people living in northern Syria and Iraq began making bronze, the technology spread slowly throughout southwest Asia. Archaeologists talk about the "Early Bronze Age" (roughly 3500–2000 B.C.E.), the "Middle Bronze Age" (ca. 2000–1550 B.C.E.), and the "Late Bronze Age" (ca. 1500–1100 B.C.E.). It was in the Middle Bronze Age, then, that Canaanite immigrants introduced bronze to Egypt. Bronze meant new possibilities in agriculture, craft production—and war.

In particular, bronze made possible the horse-drawn light chariot. This advanced military technology was already revolutionizing warfare throughout southwest Asia, Anatolia, and Greece when the Hyksos brought it to Egypt. Unlike earlier chariots, the Bronze Age model featured only two wheels fixed to an axle for easier maneuvering. Bronze spokes made the wheels more durable. Two men wearing bronze chain-mail armor rode into battle on each chariot, one driving the horses, the other shooting bronze-tipped arrows at the enemy. Troops of trained charioteers and bowmen easily outmaneuvered the traditional massed infantry forces and inflicted terrible casualties on them from a distance.

Chariot warfare reshaped the economic policies and foreign relations of Egypt, its rivals, and its allies. Imperial systems of governing and revenue collection became more sophisticated and centralized as rulers sought to meet the expenses of training and supplying armies of charioteers by expanding their economic resources. As a result, empires flourished as never before. Archaeologists thus see the period after approximately 1500 B.C.E. as a new era, the "Late Bronze Age," a period of unprecedented imperial stability and international exchange. In Chapter 2, we will examine the international structures of this period in detail. In the following section, we continue the story of Egypt as it reemerged as a great power.

The New Kingdom: The Egyptian Empire in the Late Bronze Age

Egypt's **New Kingdom** began about 1550 B.C.E., when King Ahmose I (r. ca. 1550–ca. 1525 B.C.E.) expelled the Hyksos from Egypt. During the New Kingdom, Egypt's kings first took the title **pharaoh**, which means "great house"—or master of all Egyptians. As Map 1.5 shows, Ahmose's new dynasty not only reasserted the monarch's authority and rebuilt the power of the central state, it also pushed Egypt's territorial boundaries into Asia as far as the Euphrates River.

BUILDING AN EMPIRE: MILITARY CONQUEST AND TERRITORIAL EXPANSION A large standing army made the New Kingdom conquests possible. Trained in the new chariot warfare and equipped with the composite bow (long known in Mesopotamia, but introduced into Egypt during the New Kingdom), Egypt's army was a mighty fighting force. One man in every 10 was forced into military service. Egyptian officers supplemented these troops with both mercenaries hired abroad and soldiers recruited in conquered regions of Palestine and Syria.

Egyptian attitudes toward non-Egyptians also encouraged the imperial expansion of the New Kingdom. Egyptians divided the world into two groups: themselves (whom they referred to as "The People") and everyone else. Egyptians believed that forces of chaos

New Kingdom In ancient Near Eastern history, the period in Egyptian history from 1550 to 1150 B.C.E. During the New Kingdom, Egyptian kings first took the title of pharaoh and established an empire that reached to the Euphrates River.

pharaoh Title for the Egyptian king, used during the New Kingdom period.

resided in foreign lands where the pharaoh had not yet imposed his will. Thus, it was the pharaoh's responsibility to crush all foreign peoples and bring order to the world.

In their drive to establish order in the world, Egyptian rulers in the New Kingdom clashed with kingdoms in Anatolia and Mesopotamia. Under the dynamic leadership of Thutmose I (r. 1504–1492 B.C.E.), the armies of Egypt conquered southern Palestine. A coalition of Syrian cities slowed further advance, but by the end of the reign of the great conqueror, Thutmose III (r. 1458–1425 B.C.E.), Egypt had extended its control over the entire western coast (see Map 1.5). Thutmose III led his armies into Canaan 17 times and strengthened the empire's hold on it and Syria. Canaan proved an economic asset, both because of its own natural resources and because it was a vital trading center with ties to Mesopotamia and beyond.

The New Kingdom also regained control over Nubia about 1500 B.C.E. To strengthen their grip on the area, pharaohs encouraged Egyptians to establish communities along the Nile River there. These Egyptian colonies exploited the fertile river lands in Nubia for the benefit of the pharaoh.

KEEPING AN EMPIRE: ADMINISTRATIVE AND DIPLOMATIC INNOVATION The Egyptians amassed a vast empire with military might. They maintained it with administrative skill and diplomatic innovation. In the New Kingdom, the pharaoh's bureaucracy divided Egypt into two major administrative regions: Upper Egypt in the south, governed from the city of Thebes, and Lower Egypt in the north, ruled from the city of Memphis. Regional administrators raised taxes and drafted men to fight in the army and work on the pharaoh's building projects. The chief minister of state, the **vizier**, superintended the administration of the entire kingdom. Every year he decided when to open the canal locks on the Nile to irrigate farmers' fields. He supervised the Egyptian treasury and the warehouses into which produce was paid as taxes.

New Kingdom pharaohs also relied on diplomacy to control their vast realm. They corresponded frequently with their provincial governors, the leaders of their vassal states, and the rulers of other great states. These letters testify that the Egyptian monarchs used trade privileges and political benefits as much as military coercion to control restless subordinates and interact with neighboring realms.

CONTINUITY IN THE NEW KINGDOM During the New Kingdom, many of the characteristics of life under the Old and Middle Kingdom continued unchanged. The basic social hierarchy remained intact, with village-based peasants laboring on the land owned by the royal family, priests of the major temples, and nobility. Both the pharaoh's government and the major temples continued to administer the redistributive economy by collecting taxes in the form of produce and paying the peasants who labored on their building projects and estates from their storehouses. The temple of the god Amun at Karnak, for example, controlled over 100,000 workers.

In the New Kingdom, as in the Old and Middle Kingdoms, monumental architecture remained a focal point of political and religious life. Amenhotep III (r. 1388–1350 B.C.E.) constructed both an enormous palace for himself and a gigantic burial temple, with a large open solar court as its sanctuary and two 64-foot-high statues of the pharaoh flanking the entryway. Ramesses II (r. 1279–1212 B.C.E.) ornamented his long reign by building the Great Temple at Abu Simbel in Nubia. Four 65-foot-high statues of the pharaoh guard the entrance to the temple. The sanctuary penetrates over 200 feet into the mountainside, where four gigantic statues of the four gods sit. Twice a year (on February 21 and October 21), the rising sun shines directly through the entrance and falls right on three of the statues; the fourth, the god of the underworld, remains in the shadows.

Women maintained their position in Egyptian society in the New Kingdom. They had complete equality with men in matters of property, business, and inheritance.

vizier The chief minister of state in New Kingdom Egypt, the vizier supervised the administration of the entire kingdom.

Watch the Video

Ramesses II: Abu Simbel

Some women held priesthoods. The most powerful, the "God's Wife of Amun," was often a member of the royal family. This priestess had administrative responsibilities as well as the obligation to perform religious rituals.

CHANGE IN THE NEW KINGDOM While there was much continuity between the New Kingdom and its predecessors, at two points in its history the New Kingdom took a new direction. In the first, Egypt came under the rule of a remarkable woman; in the second, of a religious visionary.

In 1479 B.C.E. the pharaoh Thutmose II (ca. 1491–1479 B.C.E.) died. His son—by a subordinate wife—and successor, Thutmose III, was a child, so Thutmose II's chief wife and half-sister, Hatshepsut, became regent for the child-king. While Hatshepsut at first kept the titles often associated with the pharaoh's wife, such as "God's Wife," within two years she claimed the title of pharaoh. Evidence indicates that women had ruled Egypt on four earlier occasions, but these women may have been only regents and so not recognized as kings. In contrast, Hatshepsut clearly claimed to be, and was acclaimed as, pharaoh.

Because pharaohs had always been men, all of the images of kingly power were male, and the elaborate royal rituals presumed a male ruler. Hatshepsut adapted her image to these expectations. For example, in most inscriptions she is referred to by masculine titles and pronouns, and most of her statues depict her as a man, complete with a ceremonial beard. On some statues, however, Hatshepsut does appear as a woman, and in some inscriptions she is called "Daughter [rather than Son] of Re."

Hatshepsut ruled for over 20 years. Like most male pharaohs, she waged war when necessary, including a major campaign in Nubia, but most of her reign was peaceful. When she died about 1458 B.C.E., Thutmose III took the throne. Late in his 30-year reign, he ordered that Hatshepsut's name be chiseled off monuments throughout Egypt and all her statues be destroyed. Why he did so is a mystery. Because Thutmose waited so long to try to erase the evidence of Hatshepsut's rule, it seems unlikely that he was angry at her for becoming king. A more convincing explanation is that Thutmose

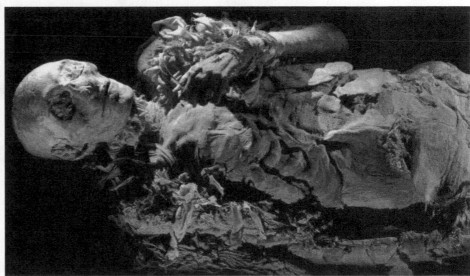

HATSHEPSUT: IMAGE AND REALITY Although she was a woman, tradition required that Hatshepsut be depicted as a man, as in this statue where she wears the pharaoh's customary beard. In 2007, archaeologists discovered Hatshepsut's mummy. Research revealed that the queen was between ages 45 and 60 when she died, that she had cancer, and that she was quite obese.

SOURCE: Head from an Osiride Statue of Hatshepsut. Egypt, New Kingdom, 18th dynasty, joint reign of Hatshepsut and Thutmose III. Ca. 1473–1458 B.C.E. From Deir-el-Bahri, Thebes. Limestone, H. 124.5 cm (49 in.). Rogers Fund, 1931 (31.3.157). The Metropolitan Museum of Art, New York, NY, U.S.A. Image © The Metropolitan Museum of Art/Art Resource, NY.

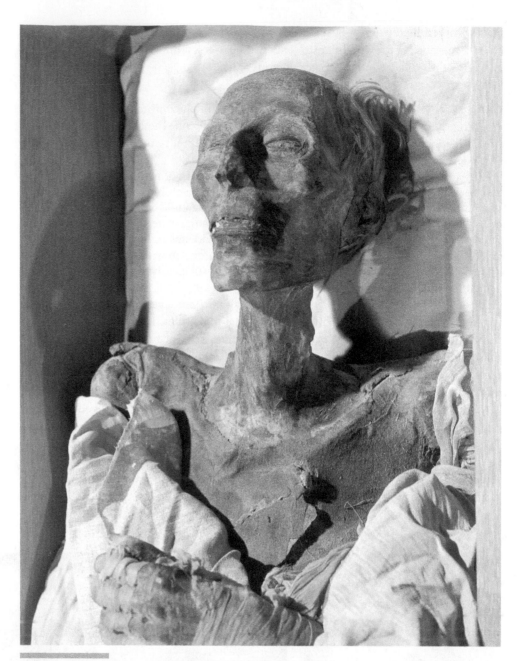

MUMMY OF RAMESSES II Both a science and an art, mummification preserved the body of King Ramesses II (r. 1279–1213 B.C.E.) for more than 3,000 years. Using a metal hook, embalmers extracted the brains through the nostrils. Sometimes they filled the skull with linen cloth and resin. Through an incision below the ribs, they removed all the organs except for the heart, which represented a person's life and would be examined by the gods on Judgment Day. The embalmers then dried the corpse by packing it with natrum, a natural compound of sodium carbonate and bicarbonate. After adding hairpieces and artificial eyes, the embalmers applied a layer of resin over the face and body, followed by a coat of paint—red for men and yellow for women.

was attempting to fulfill his basic duty as Egypt's king: to maintain *ma'at*. Hatshepsut's reign may have seemed too disorderly, too much of a change from the proper way of doing things. And so, to inform the gods that Egypt had returned to "proper" male kingship, Thutmose III ordered Hatshepsut erased from history.

Thutmose may have regarded the memory of Hatshepsut's reign as a danger to *ma'at*. It was, however, a stable era, in contrast to the second point at which the New Kingdom took a short, sharp change in direction. During the reign of Amenhotep IV (r. 1351–1334 B.C.E.), Egypt experienced a religious revolution. His father, Amenhotep III (r. 1388–1351 B.C.E.), had emphasized worship of Aten, the solar disc associated with the sun god Re, during his years on the throne. Building on this emphasis, Amenhotep IV changed his own name to Akhenaten ("one useful to Aten") and declared that Aten was not just the supreme god, but the only god.

Akhenaten attacked the worship of other gods, dismissed priests, closed temples, and appropriated their wealth and lands for himself. He forbade the celebration of ancient public festivals to the other gods and even the mention of their names, which his agents chiseled from monuments and buildings. Full of religious enthusiasm, Akhenaten and his queen, Nefertiti, abandoned the capital of Thebes and built a new city where no temple had ever stood. The modern name for this site is Tell el-Amarna and so historians refer to this period of religious ferment as the Amarna Period.

Because Akhenaten forbade the worship of other gods, some historians have argued that the Egyptians in the Amarna Period were the first people in history to develop **monotheism**, the idea of a single, all-powerful god. Yet this ignores the importance of pharaoh worship in Akhenaten's new religion. Akhenaten insisted that he and Nefertiti be worshiped as gods. Rather than inventing monotheism, then, Akhenaten may have been trying to restore the Old Kingdom conception of the king as a divine being.

Whatever Akhenaten's intentions or personal beliefs, his religious revolution proved short-lived. Because ordinary Egyptians were unwilling to abandon the many traditional gods who played an important role in their daily lives, the priests whose power Akhenaten had undermined succeeded in arousing opposition to the reforms. After Akhenaten's death, the royal court returned to Memphis. The new pharaoh, Tutankhamun (r. 1334–1325 B.C.E.), rebuilt the temples destroyed by Akhenaten's agents and returned the revenue that Akhenaten had appropriated from the priests. Egypt turned back to its traditional religious beliefs and practices, and *ma'at* was restored.

In the twelfth century B.C.E., however, Egypt slipped into a long decline. Drought, poor harvests, and inflation ruined the Egyptian economy, while weak rulers struggled to hold the kingdom together. But as we will see in Chapter 2, however, domestic developments alone do not explain the collapse of the New Kingdom.

monotheism The belief in only one god, first attributed to the ancient Hebrews. Monotheism is the foundation of Judaism, Christianity, Islam, and Zoroastrianism.

 Read the Document

Papyrus of Ani: The Egyptian Book of the Dead

THE SUN GOD BLESSES AKHENATEN AND NEFERTITI In this panel that once decorated an altar, the Sun God Aten beams his blessing down onto Akhenaten and his wife, Nefertiti, as they play with their daughters.

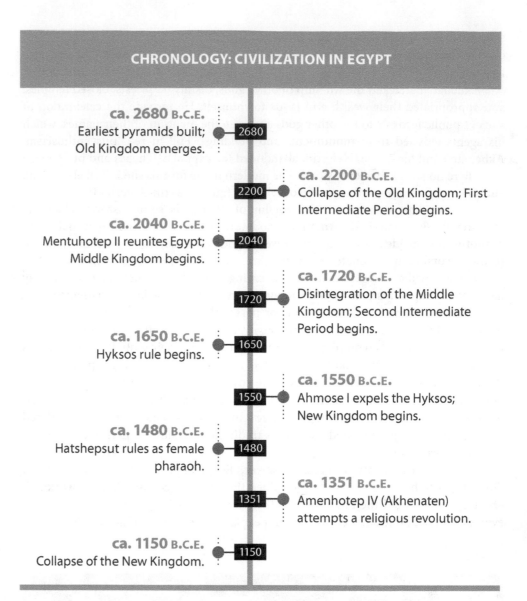

CHRONOLOGY: CIVILIZATION IN EGYPT

ca. 2680 B.C.E.
Earliest pyramids built;
Old Kingdom emerges.

2680

2200

ca. 2200 B.C.E.
Collapse of the Old Kingdom; First
Intermediate Period begins.

ca. 2040 B.C.E.
Mentuhotep II reunites Egypt;
Middle Kingdom begins.

2040

1720

ca. 1720 B.C.E.
Disintegration of the Middle
Kingdom; Second Intermediate
Period begins.

ca. 1650 B.C.E.
Hyksos rule begins.

1650

1550

ca. 1550 B.C.E.
Ahmose I expels the Hyksos;
New Kingdom begins.

ca. 1480 B.C.E.
Hatshepsut rules as female
pharaoh.

1480

1351

ca. 1351 B.C.E.
Amenhotep IV (Akhenaten)
attempts a religious revolution.

ca. 1150 B.C.E.
Collapse of the New Kingdom.

1150

Around 1150 B.C.E., the interconnected societies of Anatolia, Mesopotamia, and the eastern Mediterranean coast, as well as Egypt, experienced economic hardship and political fragmentation. The prosperity and stability of the Late Bronze Age abruptly disappeared. In the next chapter we will look closely at the factors that shaped this period of prosperity, the developments that brought it to an end, and the kingdoms that emerged in its aftermath.

CONCLUSION

Civilization and the West

During the millennia covered in this chapter, early Europeans such as Ötzi the Ice Man learned to control and capitalize on nature in many ways—cultivating crops, domesticating animals, and smelting copper. Linked by trade networks, their villages were growing larger and their societies more stratified and specialized. Even so, most of Europe did not make the leap into civilization during the third and second millennia B.C.E., and "the West" did not yet exist. The idea of "Western civilization" as both a geographic and cultural designation emerged much later, with the Greeks (see Chapter 3) who used the term *Europe* to designate the West—and who, like us, were often unclear about the West's actual boundaries.

Yet in areas that we often regard as outside the boundaries of the West, in Iraq and in Egypt, Western civilization had its beginnings. From the ancient Mesopotamian and Egyptian civilizations, the West inherited such crucial components as systems of writing and numeracy, and the core of its legal traditions. These civilizations also left a treasury of religious stories and ideas that, adapted and revised by a small, relatively powerless people called the Hebrews, became the foundational ethic of Western civilization. That development, within the context of the collapse of the International Bronze Age, is one of the main themes of Chapter 2.

MAKING CONNECTIONS

1. Each of the cultures studied in this chapter developed a distinctive architectural form: the megalith, the ziggurat, and the pyramid. What do they tell us about the societies that built them?
2. Sargon was the first empire builder in history. How did he do it? Why did he do it? How did his methods of empire building compare to those of later Mesopotamian and Egyptian empire makers?
3. How and why did Mesopotamian and Egyptian cultural and religious patterns differ? Which is the more striking, the differences between them or the parallels?

TAKING IT FURTHER

For suggested readings, see page R-1.

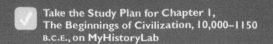
Chapter Review

Defining Civilization, Defining Western Civilization

1.1 What is the link between the food-producing revolution of the Neolithic era and the emergence of civilization?

When hunter-gatherers began farming and herding, food surpluses previously unknown in those societies allowed more newborns to live past infancy. The resulting population growth contributed to the spread of human settlements, and allowed for economic specialization and the development of social, political, and religious hierarchies, all of which are key ingredients for civilization.

Mesopotamia: Kingdoms, Empires, and Conquests

1.2 What changes and continuities characterized Mesopotamian civilization between the emergence of Sumer's city-states and the rise of Hammurabi's Babylonian Empire?

Although punctuated by the rise and fall of kingdoms and empires, Mesopotamian culture maintained a remarkable continuity over thousands of years. Constant features included the redistributive economic system that used the agricultural labor of the masses to sustain the religious and political hierarchy, and a religion marked by efforts to appease the many gods who, like the Tigris and Euphrates Rivers, were unpredictable and often destructive. Tales of these gods, written in the Akkadian language were adapted and passed on through the many Mesopotamian empires.

Egypt: The Empire of the Nile

1.3 What distinctive features characterized Egyptian civilization throughout its long history?

Both Egypt's sheltered geographic position and the predictability of the Nile River contributed to a civilization characterized by remarkable prosperity, stability, and continuity. Egyptians saw their kings as divine-like beings whose role was to ensure *ma'at*, the basic order and balance of the world. Both slaves and freemen labored to build the monumental architecture that displayed the dominance of the kings and made manifest Egyptians' faith in their gods. Empire-building was also an important Egyptian characteristic, as Egyptian rulers expanded their political dominion both southward into Africa and eastward toward Mesopotamia. Like its Hittite and Mesopotamian rivals, Egypt was a redistributive economy, with village-based peasants laboring on the land owned by the royal family, priests of the major temples, and nobility.

Chapter Time Line

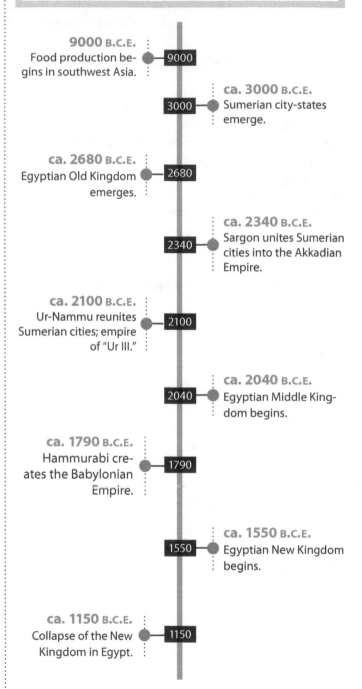

9000 B.C.E. Food production begins in southwest Asia. — 9000

3000 — **ca. 3000 B.C.E.** Sumerian city-states emerge.

ca. 2680 B.C.E. Egyptian Old Kingdom emerges. — 2680

2340 — **ca. 2340 B.C.E.** Sargon unites Sumerian cities into the Akkadian Empire.

ca. 2100 B.C.E. Ur-Nammu reunites Sumerian cities; empire of "Ur III." — 2100

2040 — **ca. 2040 B.C.E.** Egyptian Middle Kingdom begins.

ca. 1790 B.C.E. Hammurabi creates the Babylonian Empire. — 1790

1550 — **ca. 1550 B.C.E.** Egyptian New Kingdom begins.

ca. 1150 B.C.E. Collapse of the New Kingdom in Egypt. — 1150

2

The Age of Empires: The International Bronze Age and Its Aftermath, ca. 1500–550 B.C.E.

In 1984, scuba-diving **archaeologists** began to excavate the wreck of a merchant ship that sank about 1300 B.C.E. at Uluburun, off the southern coast of Turkey. Its cargo included ostrich eggshells, elephant tusks, a trumpet carved from a hippopotamus tooth from Egypt, a ton of scented resin from southwest Asia, and pomegranates packed in finely painted storage jars from the island of Cyprus. The ship's hold also contained 354 flat copper bars, each weighing about 50 pounds, and several bars of tin.

The Uluburun ship's cargo highlights two defining features of the **Late Bronze Age** (1500–1100 B.C.E.). First, the ship carried copper and tin, the metals needed to make bronze, one of the most desired commodities of this era. Because substantial deposits of tin and copper were rarely found in the same region, merchants—such as those who contracted with the Uluburun ship owner—traded over long distances and across political boundaries to obtain both ores. In turn, monarchs devoted military and diplomatic resources to fostering and protecting this trade, the foundation of much of their prosperity and power. Thus, a second defining feature of the Late Bronze Age was its unprecedented degree of international

LEARNING OBJECTIVES

2.1 ((	2.2 ((	2.3 ((
What elements made up the international system of the Late Bronze Age and why did it collapse?	What developments shaped southwest Asian and Mediterranean societies after the collapse of the International Bronze Age?	What beliefs and institutions shaped Hebrew civilization and its legacy?

((Listen to Chapter 2 on MyHistoryLab

HOUSE OF THE ADMIRAL (Detail)
Created about 1500 B.C.E., this lively wall painting is about 22 feet long and a foot and a half high and comes from the so-called House of the Admiral on the island of Thera, midway between Crete and Greece. The scenes of busy maritime activity outside a harbor town provide a glimpse of the international connections that created the "International Bronze Age."

◉ Watch the Video Series on MyHistoryLab

Learn about some key topics related to this chapter with the *MyHistoryLab Video Series:*
Key Topics in Western Civilization

Late Bronze Age The period from 1500 to 1100 B.C.E., characterized by an unprecedented degree of international trade and diplomatic exchange.

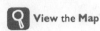 **View the Map**

International Trade Routes in the Bronze Age

trade and diplomatic exchange. The Uluburun ship could not have stopped at so many ports and picked up such a diverse cargo had monarchs not worked together to construct a stable international structure. Trade networks, an international diplomatic system, and cultural exchanges made the Late Bronze Age the "International Bronze Age."

The International Bronze Age collapsed suddenly and somewhat mysteriously between (roughly) 1200 and 1100 B.C.E. Like a wrecked cargo ship, once-vibrant cultures sank into a dark age of invasions, migrations, and political fragmentation. In the aftermath of these turbulent events, two of the most powerful empires the world has ever known, the Neo-Assyrian and the Neo-Babylonian, rose to dominate the ancient world. Regarding themselves as the heirs of the Sumerian, Akkadian, and Old Babylonian civilizations examined in Chapter 1, the rulers of these new empires consciously sought to preserve and pass on Mesopotamian traditions. Thus, the continuity of Mesopotamian culture remained unbroken, despite the political tumult of these centuries.

While mighty empires dominated the International Bronze Age and its aftermath, for the history of the West the most important development of this period occurred on the fringes of empire, amidst a relatively small and powerless people. Called the Israelites or the Hebrews, these people developed the world's first monotheistic religion and created the ethical framework of Western civilization.

A key question for this chapter, then, is how did the varied encounters of the International Bronze Age and its aftermath shape not only diplomatic and trade relations but also cultural assumptions and values?

The Dynamism of the International Bronze Age

> **2.1** What elements made up the international system of the Late Bronze Age and why did it collapse?

Trade in not only tin and copper for the making of bronze but also luxury goods and princess brides, ships and chariots, and even architectural styles and religious ideas created the International Bronze Age—and numerous sources for the historian to study. Rulers used the wealth generated by trade to erect palaces and temples, the remains of which provide archaeological evidence. These rulers also employed numerous scribes who recorded their economic agreements, diplomatic maneuvers, and military accomplishments. Inscribed on clay tablets rather than written on perishable parchment or paper, many of these documents survived across the millennia. In 1887, for example, an Egyptian peasant woman uncovered a collection of over 370 cuneiform tablets, the diplomatic and imperial correspondence of the pharaohs from the mid-fourteenth century B.C.E. These Amarna Letters, as they are called (because they were found at Tell El-Amarna), include correspondence between the pharaoh and rulers of other empires, and communications sent to the pharaoh by the leaders of his vassal states in Canaan. Written in Akkadian (the Mesopotamian language used for international communication), the Amarna Letters offer detailed evidence about the international system of the Late Bronze Age.

Zones of Power Within the International Bronze Age

The economic and diplomatic network of the International Bronze Age covered five separate but interconnected zones. **Map 2.1** highlights these zones: to the south, the New Kingdom in Egypt; to the north, the Hittite Empire in Anatolia; to the east, the Assyrian and Babylonian empires in Mesopotamia; to the west, the eastern Mediterranean kingdoms of the Minoans on Crete and the Mycenaeans on mainland Greece; and finally, several small kingdoms along the Syrian–Canaanite coast.

THE HITTITE KINGDOM OF HATTI In Chapter 1, we explored the history of the first zone of power in the International Bronze Age: New Kingdom Egypt. The second zone of power lay in the rich plateau of Anatolia (modern Turkey). By about 1650 B.C.E., an **Indo-European** people called the Hittites had established control over this region. "Indo-European" is a linguistic term: Armenian, Persian, and a majority of European languages share similarities in vocabulary and grammar inherited from an Indo-European parent language. Distinguished, then, from the Semitic and other peoples of southwest Asia by the language they spoke, the Hittites' origins remain obscure. Some scholars argue that they originated in northern India. Others believe that

2.1

2.2

2.3

Read the Document

Ancient Egyptian and Hittite Voices

View the Map

Map Discovery: Bronze Age Trade

Indo-European Parent language of a majority of modern European languages as well as modern Armenian and Persian; sometimes used to refer to the people who spoke this language.

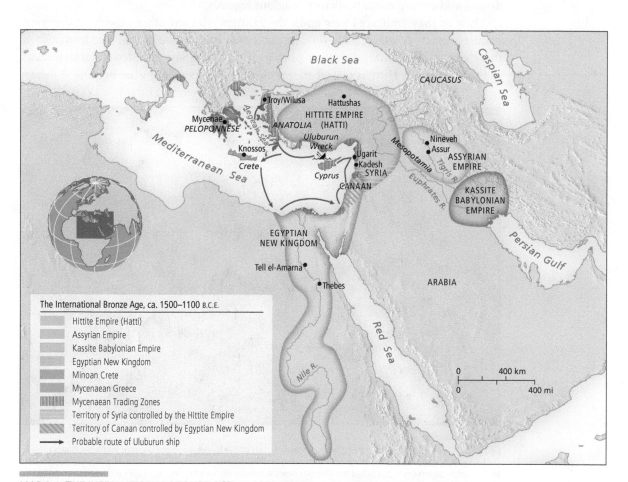

MAP **2.1** THE INTERNATIONAL BRONZE AGE, CA. 1500–1100 B.C.E. For 500 years, networks of commerce and diplomacy tied together the distinct cultures of Egypt, Greece, Anatolia, and southwest Asia. What were the five zones of power that shaped the International Bronze Age?

Indo-Europeans traveled from a homeland in the Caucasus to populate not only Anatolia but also modern-day India, Europe, and Iran. Still other scholars contend that Indo-Europeans existed in Anatolia from prehistory on.

Whatever their origins, by 1650 B.C.E. the Hittites had established a prosperous kingdom in central Anatolia called Hatti. The once-prominent idea that the Hittites invented the process of smelting iron and that their power rested on this secret skill has now been debunked. But even without iron, Hittite power gradually expanded from Anatolia into western Mesopotamia and Syria, and, by the fourteenth century B.C.E., into Canaan.

This expansion meant that the Hittite Empire and New Kingdom Egypt were soon competing for the same territories. Competition erupted into outright war at a number of points and finally produced an epic yet curiously indecisive military encounter: the Battle of Kadesh of 1274 B.C.E. (See *Encounters and Transformations* in this chapter.) Drained by this battle and those that succeeded it, Pharaoh Ramesses II and Hittite King Hattusili III turned to a diplomatic solution: They agreed that the Hittites would control northern Syria while Egypt kept its Canaanite territories. This treaty transformed long-term enemies into allies and marked a crucial step in stabilizing international relations.

Imperial expansion brought many diverse peoples under Hittite rule and reshaped Hittite religious practice. The Hittites rightly called their country "the land of a thousand gods." To unify its peoples, the Hittite monarchy transported its subjects' gods to its capital city of Hattusha and built many temples for them. Called the "Great King," the Hittite monarch played the role of chief priest of all the gods worshiped by the many different communities under his control. The new gods were simply added to the Hittite pantheon, regardless of any overlap or duplication of function. Thus, Hittite religion contained numerous sun gods, father gods, warrior deities, and fertility goddesses, and countless contradictory religious legends.

Just as they embraced new gods, the Hittites adopted other aspects of different cultures—such as architecture, diet, medical practices, and folklore—and transmitted these cultural borrowings to other peoples. By passing ancient Mesopotamian ideas to the Greeks, the Hittites played an important role in shaping what became Western

GODS ON PARADE This bas-relief of a procession of gods of the Underworld comes from Yazilikaya (literally "inscribed rock"), a rock sanctuary in modern Turkey that in Hittite times housed an elaborate religious site dedicated to the Hittite Storm God (also called the Weather God). A natural alcove of rocks, Yazilikaya comprises two roofless chambers that feature numerous carved rock reliefs. In the larger chamber, 64 gods join in a procession that culminates in the meeting of the Storm God with his consort the Sun Goddess. In Hittite myth, the Storm God's rains caused the Sun Goddess to conceive.

civilization. The Greek myth of Hercules likely resulted from this process of cultural transmission. The survival of the *Epic of Gilgamesh* in Hittite archives reveals that the Hittites adopted this Mesopotamian story (see Chapter 1), which they then passed on, via trade and conquest, to the Greeks. Over centuries of cultural transformation, Gilgamesh, the quintessential Mesopotamian hero, became Hercules. Similarly, Mesopotamian mathematical concepts probably made their way into Greek (and, hence, Western) culture via the Hittites.

Some scholars argue that the Hittites also deserve credit for creating the concept of history. In the Hittite kingdom, official proclamations often contained lengthy introductions that set the subject of the proclamation—a decree, perhaps, or a treaty—in context by reciting the past events that made it necessary or possible. These historical narratives demonstrate that the Hittites believed human beings could and should learn from history. Hittite kings, for example, were willing to acknowledge the incompetence or sins of past kings (something unthinkable in Egyptian annals in which the god-king could do no wrong), and to link such misbehavior to current misfortunes. Hittite historical accounts show that the Hittites sought to understand the present in terms of the past and saw history as the result of human action as well as divine whim.

Read the Document

Hittite Law Code: Excerpts from the Code of the Nesilim

KASSITE BABYLON AND ASSYRIA The third zone of power during the International Bronze Age lay in Mesopotamia. Around 1600 B.C.E. people known as Kassites infiltrated Mesopotamia as raiders, soldiers, and laborers. Their language and precise place of origin are unknown, but by 1400 B.C.E. they had gained control of most of southern Mesopotamia. For the next 250 years, Kassite monarchs maintained order and prosperity in Babylonia, establishing the longest ruling dynasty in ancient southwest Asian history.

During these centuries, Babylonia enjoyed a golden age. Kassite kings unified Babylonia's many cities through a highly centralized administration that controlled both urban centers and the countryside. The Kassite kings gained a reputation for fair rule by giving land to individuals of all ranks and by spending lavishly on temples, public buildings, and canals throughout the kingdom. Political stability and economic prosperity enabled Kassite Babylonia to become a renowned center of literature and learning. Seeking to overcome their outsider origins, Kassite kings claimed the Mesopotamian cultural legacy as their own. They ordered their scribes to copy and thus preserve Sumerian and Akkadian works.

Babylonia's chief rival for dominance in the Mesopotamian region during the International Bronze Age lay to the north: Assyria. Around 1360 B.C.E., the Assyrian kingdom began a new phase of expansion that culminated in the reign of the mighty Tukulti-Ninurta I (r. 1244–1208 B.C.E.), who led his armies to victory over Babylonia itself. By the time of Tukulti-Ninurta's death, Assyria controlled all the lands from northern Syria to southern Iraq.

THE MEDITERRANEAN CIVILIZATIONS: MINOAN CRETE AND MYCENAEAN GREECE
The fourth zone of power in the International Bronze Age lay to the east, with the Mediterranean civilizations of Minoan Crete and Mycenean Greece. Although not as large and powerful as Egypt's New Kingdom or the Mesopotamian empires of Kassite Babylon and Assyria, these seafaring civilizations played a vital role in the international system that shaped the Late Bronze Age. They were also the predecessors of ancient Greece.

Minoan civilization emerged about 2600 B.C.E. when small urban communities on the island of Crete began to trade with Egypt and to import copper and tin from the eastern Mediterranean. By 1700 B.C.E., the Minoans had developed a magnificent palace-centered culture. These palaces served as political, economic, and religious centers. Unlike the symmetrical monumental buildings of Mesopotamia and Egypt, Minoan palaces were so sprawling that the Greeks later termed them "labyrinths." Ordinary Minoans lived in houses built around the palace. Some of these palace-centered communities were actually small cities. Knossos, for example, housed approximately 25,000 people.

Minoan prosperity rested on its sea trade and the export of luxury goods—jewelry, painted vases, and delicate figures carved in the deep blue gemstone called lapis lazuli. The Minoans developed a merchant navy that traded with Greece, Egypt, and the coastal communities of the eastern Mediterranean. High-prowed and sturdy, Minoan vessels were well-suited for sailing the Mediterranean Sea.

Although their language was evidently Indo-European, the Minoans learned their pictographic script from the Egyptians. Called "Linear A," Minoan script has yet to be fully deciphered. As a result, what we know about the Minoans comes from art and architecture, rather than texts. The lack of military fortifications around Minoan palaces—in contrast to the strong defenses that ringed other Late Bronze Age centers— and the many images of women on the wall paintings from Minoan palaces have provoked speculation about Minoan social life. Some scholars argued that Minoan society was unusually peace-loving and **matriarchal** (female-dominated). Later discoveries of weapons collections and the strong evidence for the existence of bull worship—a practice usually linked with patriarchal societies—call these arguments into question. The dominance of female images in the paintings more likely points to an emphasis on fertility, while the lack of defensive fortifications probably indicates that the Minoans possessed a navy strong enough to make them feel secure on their island home.

This security ended abruptly and mysteriously. Minoan prosperity and power disappeared around 1400 B.C.E. Archaeologists do not know whether invaders caused the collapse of Minoan power or whether Minoan Crete was destroyed by a natural disaster, perhaps a tidal wave linked to a volcanic eruption on the nearby island of Thera.

In the wake of the Minoan collapse, the balance of economic power in the eastern Mediterranean shifted to the mainland of Mycenaean Greece. The term *Mycenaean* refers both to the kingdom of Mycenae (located in the Peloponnese, the southern peninsula of mainland Greece) and, more generally, to the culture of Greece during the

matriarchal A social or cultural system in which family lineage is traced through the mother and/or in which women hold significant power.

 View the **Map**

Map Discovery: Greece in the Bronze Age

LEAPING THE BULL Scholars used to think that this Minoan mural ca. 1500 B.C.E. depicted a sporting event, perhaps similar to the contests staged between animals and men in the Roman Colosseum centuries later. Scientists now tell us that it is impossible to somersault over a charging bull, so perhaps the mural has religious or astrological significance. What is clear is the undeniable Minoan artistry, able to communicate power and grace across the millennia.

Encounters and Transformations
A Diplomatic Revolution

To greedy and ambitious rulers, the lands stretching from western Syria down the Canaanite corridor (today's Lebanon, Israel, and Palestine) offered numerous temptations—timberlands, agricultural fields and pasture lands, hills heavy with metals, and port cities with international commercial connections. In the thirteenth century B.C.E., this region became the site of an important encounter between the Hittite and Egyptian empires, one that transformed not only Great Power alignments for the next century, but also diplomacy itself.

During the fourteenth century B.C.E., the Hittite Empire had expanded southward. By the turn of the century, however, Egypt under the New Kingdom had regained enough power to challenge Hittite control of Syria and Canaan. For two decades, the two empires jostled for advantage. Then, Ramesses II (1279–1212 B.C.E.) succeeded to the throne of New Kingdom Egypt. Determined to push the Hittites out of Canaan and Syria, Ramesses spent five years gathering troops for battle. In 1274 B.C.E. he led his army northward. Muwatalli II (ca. 1295–1272) awaited him with a Hittite and mercenary army of 37,000 infantry and 3,500 chariotry. The stage was set for a decisive battle between the two empires.

As the Egyptians under Ramesses drew near to the Syrian city of Kadesh, they captured two supposed deserters from the Hittite army. These men reported that Muwatalli, alarmed by Ramesses's advance, had retreated with his army about 200 miles to the north. Delighted with the news, Ramesses decided to press on to Kadesh with just one division in the hopes of capturing the city before the Hittites moved south again. This decision left the Egyptian army strung out over several miles. Moreover, the "deserters" were actually Muwatalli's spies: Ramesses had fallen into a carefully set trap. The Hittite army launched a surprise attack on Ramesses's poorly situated forces.

Panic-stricken, the Egyptians broke—but then Ramesses himself led a chariot charge. Inspired by the pharaoh's personal bravery (or so Ramesses's account of the battle insisted), his men rallied. In addition, both Hittite lack of discipline—Hittite soldiers turned to plunder the Egyptian camp rather than press their advance—and the lucky arrival of a force of allied Canaanite charioteers helped swing the day in the Egyptians' favor. Yet Egypt did not win the battle. Muwatalli lost almost all of his chariots, but the next day his infantry withstood Ramesses's attacks. Deciding enough was enough, Ramesses turned around and went home. Once back in Egypt, he boasted of a great victory. Although no such victory had occurred, Ramesses's less-than-accurate version of the battle was inscribed on pillars across the land.

The struggle over Syria and Canaan continued. Over the next several years, Ramesses and his army fought a number of battles against the forces of Muwatalli and his successors. Neither, however, possessed the strength to annihilate the other because the Battle of Kadesh had depleted the resources of both Great Powers. And while they were busy draining each other dry, Assyria was amassing military power and economic strength. This new player could seize control of the entire game if the two seasoned veterans did not switch strategy.

In 1258 B.C.E., Ramesses II and the Hittite King Hattusili III (ca. 1267–1237 B.C.E.) signed an innovative treaty. Ramesses abandoned claims to northern Syria and Hattusili acknowledged Egyptian control over Canaan. Yet the treaty did more than end the fighting. It also created an alliance: The two powers agreed to aid one another in case of invasion or rebellion. The treaty demonstrated that diplomatic ties could serve Great Power interests. This diplomatic innovation survived long after both the Hittite Empire and the New Kingdom had disappeared into history.

For Discussion

Despite Ramesses's grandiose claims to the contrary, Egypt did not win a great victory in the Battle of Kadesh. Why, then, is this battle seen as historically significant?

International Bronze Age. Mycenae dominated the Peloponnese, but did not rule all of Greece. Instead, the Mycenaean kingdoms traded with and warred against each other.

In the century before the Minoan collapse, the Mycenaeans interacted extensively with Minoan Crete and adapted many of its cultural practices, including its palace-centered economy and a script related to Linear A. Called "**Linear B,**" it is the earliest written form of Greek. Unfortunately, the surviving palace records, written on clay tablets, all relate to economic matters—landholding records, lists of broken equipment, inventories of available storage space, and the like. None of the tablets contains a story or religious hymn or battle chronicle.

Although we have no literary record of Mycenaean values or beliefs, the archaeological evidence, particularly Mycenaean burial sites, reveals a prosperous and militaristic culture. Mycenaean merchants extended Minoan commercial routes as far west as Spain and northern Italy. The line between trading and raiding was never very solid, however, and the Mycenaeans earned a well-deserved reputation for piracy.

 View the **Map**

Map Discovery: Mycenean Trade and Contacts

"**Linear B**" The earliest written form of Greek, used by the Mycenaeans.

CITY-STATES AND COASTAL COMMUNITIES: SYRIA AND CANAAN As Map 2.1 shows, the final zone of power in the International Bronze Age consisted of the regions of Syria and Canaan (or Palestine). The political fragmentation of this region and its key location made it the battleground on which the Hittite, Mesopotamian, and Egyptian empires fought for supremacy. Often reduced to pawns in imperial power plays, smaller states throughout Syria and Canaan nevertheless played an active role in fostering trading relations, shaping diplomatic patterns, and initiating cultural innovation.

The city-state of Ugarit, for example, appears frequently in Late Bronze Age texts. A port city, Ugarit controlled a kingdom of about 2,000 square miles blessed with rich natural resources. The fertile plain offered arable land for grape vines, olive trees, and grains, while the surrounding hill forests provided timber for shipbuilding and construction. Ugarit's greatest asset was a natural harbor that made the city a hub of international trade. Merchant ships, such as the one that sank at Uluburun, sailed to Ugarit from across the Mediterranean, while caravans laden with goods arrived from Mesopotamia, the Hittite lands, and Canaan. People from all these places settled in Ugarit, whose population was estimated at about 6,000–8,000 inhabitants. Perhaps another 25,000 people lived as farmers in about 150 villages in the Ugarit countryside. Its natural resources and strategic location, however, made Ugarit a natural target for acquisitive empires. By the thirteenth century B.C.E., the Hittite emperor chose the occupant of Ugarit's throne.

Ugarit was fairly typical of the city-states of Syria and Canaan during the International Bronze Age. In scattered cities throughout the region, urban culture thrived as a result of the flourishing international trade (and heavy exploitation of the rural agricultural populations). Continued prosperity, however, demanded that Syrian and Canaanite rulers walk a diplomatic tightrope, allying first with this empire and then with that, negotiating for survival in an age of imperial might.

TROY: A CITY OF LEGEND The five zones of power that we have delineated provide the parameters of the International Bronze Age. Scattered among these zones were small city-states and kingdoms, sometimes swallowed up by one of the large empires, sometimes independent. One of these, the Anatolian city-state of Troy, has captured the popular imagination for 3,000 years, ever since it was immortalized as the site of the Trojan War in Homer's epic poem, the *Iliad*, which recounts the final year of the tragic clash between the Greeks and the Trojans. According to the *Iliad*, the war began when Paris of Troy kidnapped the beautiful Helen, queen of the Greek city-state of Sparta, and ended with the total destruction of Troy.

 Read the Document

Homer: Debate among the Greeks at Troy

The *Iliad* was put into written form about 750 B.C.E., yet most scholars agree that it came out of an oral tradition extending back to the Late Bronze Age. The name "Troy" does not appear in Bronze Age documents, but many archaeologists argue that a conflict between Mycenae and a city-state called Wilusa in ancient texts may have sparked the oral tradition that became Homer's story of the war between the Greeks and Trojans—although if so, the point of contention was probably something dull, such as the question of safe passage for merchant ships, rather than the raging passion stirred up by a beautiful queen.

Archaeologists have identified the likely site of Troy/Wilusa on the northwestern Anatolian coast. Excavations there reveal that Troy prospered in the Late Bronze Age. Numerous distinct layers of occupation and construction tell us that generations of inhabitants rebuilt the city time and time again from about 3000 to 1000 B.C.E. Like the Troy of Homer's story, Troy VI (the sixth layer of occupation) was a grand city. It featured monumental gateways and a royal palace compound containing many mansions. But sometime around 1300 B.C.E., the city was destroyed—not by an enemy army, as in the legend of Troy, but probably by an earthquake. Troy's inhabitants rapidly rebuilt, but this new city (Troy VIIa) was smaller and poorer, not at all like the glorious civilization of Homer's tale.

So is Homer's Troy purely fiction? Perhaps . . . but perhaps not. We know that around 950 B.C.E. something decimated the city (Troy VIIb3) and left it a pile of rubble.

THE "DEATH MASK OF AGAMEMNON" This thin gold mask, about 11 inches long, was found at the citadel of Mycenae in the tomb of a ruler who died about 1550 B.C.E. Heinrich Schliemann, whose excavations were the first to show that Troy did exist in history as well as legend, mistakenly jumped to the conclusion that it was the death mask of King Agamemnon, who led the Greek forces during the Trojan War, as told in Homer's *Iliad*.

Enemy raids could have caused Troy's final destruction. Possibly the memory of these events fused with earlier tales of the grand civilization of Troy VI and its conflicts with Mycenaean Greeks and eventually took the form of Homer's *Iliad*. Like the *Epic of Gilgamesh*, the *Iliad* is a verbal version of an archaeological site, with many different layers of "occupation."

The Club of the Great Powers

Historians have used the label "the Club of the Great Powers" to describe the international network that shaped the Late Bronze Age. As the word *club* indicates, these Great Powers interacted closely and, in so doing, developed concepts and tools of international diplomacy and interchange that survived long after the Great Powers themselves had collapsed.

GREAT POWER RELATIONS AND EXCHANGES Great Power rulers knew who was in their club, who was leveraging for entrance, and who was vulnerable for expulsion. In the beginning of the Late Bronze Age, for example, Assyria was still too small and weak to be a member. By around 1330 B.C.E., however, Assyrian power was expanding and King Assur-Uballit I decided it was time to join the Great Powers' Club. He sent lavish gifts and a letter to the pharaoh that dared address the Egyptian ruler as an equal: "Up to now, my predecessors had not written: today I write to you."[1] In many ways, Great Power rulers acted as if they all belonged to the same extended (if somewhat dysfunctional) family. They addressed each other as "Brother," exchanged boastful letters, and traded gifts to celebrated enthronements, military conquests, and marriages (often to each others' daughters and sisters).

The gift exchanges among the Great Powers were highly formalized. Rulers did not hesitate to correct colleagues who failed to abide by the rules. For example, the Hittite king, Hattusili III, lectured the king of Assyria when he failed to send a suitable gift:

> It is the custom that when kings assume kingship, the kings, his equals in rank, send him appropriate gifts of greeting, clothing befitting kingship, and fine oil for his anointing. But you did not do this today.

Abiding by the rules of gift exchange was more than a matter of reciprocal greed. First, these exchanges signaled that each ruler recognized the legitimacy of the other, and so helped maintain the stability of international relations. Second, the rules of gift-giving were, for Great Power rulers, part of the definition of "civilization," and therefore one of the characteristics that differentiated them from barbarians. To be a member of the Club of Great Powers was to be a part of the civilized world. And third, gift-giving served as a disguised form of trade. One king would send a "gift" to another, and then demand a "gift" of equal value in return. In this way, luxury goods and other items in high demand circulated throughout the International Bronze Age economy. Egypt, for example, was the source of most of the Near Eastern gold supply as well as ivory, ebony, and alabaster.

Gift exchanges were confined to the Great Power kings and their queens, but Great Power rulers also actively fostered and protected trade in its wider forms. Much of their correspondence concerned the safety of caravan routes and shipping lanes. A ruler was responsible for the security of his realm. If bandits attacked a merchant's caravan, the ruler of the region in which the attack occurred was expected to make restitution. Trade was important to Great Power rulers both for the wealth it produced and for the taxes it generated. Moreover, international trade brought together the tin and copper needed to make bronze.

CONQUEST AND CLIENT STATES We saw in Chapter 1 that bronze was the key component of the light chariot, the central military technology of International Bronze Age empires. Because of the expense of maintaining armies of trained charioteers, Great Power rulers were constantly on the lookout for new sources of income. In addition to relying on trade to generate revenue, rulers depended on the spoils they claimed from military conquests and the tribute they collected from client states. War in the International Bronze Age was thus a business venture.

After conquest, most states became vassals or client-states of the conquering Great Power. Client-states provided their Great Power overlord with annual tribute and often with auxiliary troops. The relationship between a client-state and a Great Power was clearcut. A Great Power monarch writing to the ruler of one of his client-states would begin, "My servant." A client king's salutation to his overlord made the relationship even plainer:

> My king, my lord, my sun god, I prostrate myself at the feet of my lord, my sun god, seven times and seven times.[2]

COMMONALITIES AMONG THE GREAT POWER CULTURES The Egyptian, Hittite, Assyrian, Babylonian, and Minoan-Mycenean societies occupied different agricultural spaces; the fertility of the Nile delta, for example, contrasted with the aridity of most of Anatolia. They also possessed different histories, religions, and customs. Nevertheless, the Great Power societies in the International Bronze Age shared the same basic socio-economic structures and militaristic values.

Archaeologists and historians use the term **palace system** to describe Late Bronze Age societies. In this system, wealth and power concentrated in the hands of the small ruling elite, who lived separated from the laboring masses in monumental fortified palaces. Sometimes constituting entire cities, these palaces were set apart from the neighborhoods of ordinary people. In Assur, capital city of the Assyrian Empire, for example, all the palaces and temples stood within the walled inner city, far from the areas where the rest of the city's populace lived.

The Minoan palace at Knossos exemplifies the International Bronze Age palace system. The palace occupied three acres. At its center stood a courtyard surrounded by hundreds of rooms that served as living quarters for the political and religious elite, administrative headquarters, and shrines for religious worship. Frescoes (plaster painted while it is still wet) of sea creatures, flowers, acrobats, and scenes of daily life adorned the walls. The residents enjoyed indoor plumbing and running water, comforts that most people in the West would not enjoy until the nineteenth century C.E.

Two distinct social hierarchies delineated International Bronze Age societies: the palace dependents and the free people in the villages. The first group comprised the military officers, religious officials, scribes, craftsmen, and agricultural laborers within the palace system. Paid with rations, in the case of lower ranked laborers and craftsmen, and with royal land grants in the upper ranks, they ensured the continuity of imperial administration and the luxurious lifestyle of the royal family. At Knossos, the palace dependents' rations were stored in warehouses that could hold more than a quarter million gallons of wine or olive oil. The regularity of such rations meant that the palace dependents were probably better off than the free villagers in the country-side. Obliged to pay taxes and to labor on royal building projects for a part of every year, these villagers practiced mixed farming, scraping out a living growing grains, cultivating fruit trees, and grazing sheep and goats. In bad times, they were forced to borrow from wealthier neighbors. If they could not pay back the debt, they were forced into slavery.

At the top of all Bronze Age societies stood the royal family, the members of which lived in luxury beyond the comprehension of most of their subjects—and of most of us today. Thirty royal graves uncovered at Mycenae contain skeletons nearly six feet tall—taller than the average Mycenaean and clear evidence that the kings enjoyed better nutrition than their subjects. The many gold and silver drinking vessels and pieces of jewelry found in the graves further demonstrate the luxury in which not only Mycenaean but all Bronze Age rulers lived.

All Late Bronze Age cultures glorified military conquest and so placed the warrior high on the social scale. Kings personally led annual military campaigns; hence, battle accounts dominate royal chronicles. In Mycenaea, the graves of warriors contain not only their bodies, but also their armor, weapons, and even their chariots. The burial of such prized items indicates the prestige of the warrior class. To be manly was to be a warrior, as this account of a Hittite ritual for inducting troops into the army makes clear:

> They bring the garments of a woman, a distaff [for spinning cloth] and a mirror, they break an arrow and you speak as follows: "Is not this that you see here garments of a woman? We have them here for [the ceremony of taking] the oath. Whoever breaks these oaths and does evil to the king and the queen and the princes, let these oaths change him from a man into a woman!" . . . Let them break the bows, arrows, and clubs in their hands and let them put in their hands distaff and mirror![3]

palace system Late Bronze Age social system that concentrated religious, economic, political, and military power in the hands of an elite, who lived apart from most people in monumental fortified compounds.

THE INTERNATIONAL MONUMENTAL STYLE Many Late Bronze Age kings constructed new capital cities as a way to proclaim their power to their people and to their potential rivals at home and abroad. In constructing these palaces and cities, kings borrowed from each other's cultures to such a degree that a single "international style" in monumental building emerged, as these Hittite and Mycenaean fortress gates illustrate. The entrance gate to the Hittite capital of Hattusha and the gate into the citadel of Mycenae both feature massive stone lions, the symbol of royal strength in many Bronze Age societies.

Crisis and Collapse: The End of the International Bronze Age

The diplomatic, cultural, and economic connections between Egypt, southwest Asia, Anatolia, and Greece broke between 1200 and 1100 B.C.E. These civilizations plummeted into a dark age marked by invasions, migrations, and the collapse of stable governments. On the Greek mainland, the Greek language and some religious beliefs endured, but the population declined by an estimated 75 percent; the crafts, artistic styles, and architectural traditions of Mycenaean life were forgotten. Drought, famine, and invasion dominate the surviving records. A later text, *The Epic of Erra*, recalled this era as a time of horror:

> Sealand shall not spare Sealand . . . nor Assyrian Assyrian.
> Nor shall Elamite spare Elamite, nor Kassite Kassite . . .
> Nor country country, nor city city,
> Nor shall tribe spare tribe, nor man man, nor brother brother, and they shall slay one another.[4]

THE SEA PEOPLES What happened to cause the end of the International Bronze Age? Ancient texts point to raids and invasions by wandering migrants as a key cause. Around 1100 B.C.E., for example, the king of Ugarit warned the king of another Syrian kingdom, "The ships of the enemy have been coming. They have been burning down my villages and have done evil things to the country."[5] Egyptian accounts, which called these invaders the **Sea Peoples**, described their coming in dramatic terms:

> No land could stand before their arms. . . . They desolated its people, and its land was like that which had never come into being. They were coming forward into Egypt, while the flame was prepared for them.[6]

Who were these "Sea Peoples" and were they responsible for the collapse of the International Bronze Age system? Scholars have yet to reach agreement on an answer to this key question. One set of explanations focuses on events in Mycenaean Greece and the Hittite Empire. We know that warfare among the many Mycenaean kingdoms resulted in the breakdown of its palace-centered economic system by about 1150 B.C.E. Searching for the means of survival, many Greeks migrated. Approximately 50 years later, a deadly combination of famine, civil war, and international invasion triggered the collapse of the Hittite imperial government. As in Mycenaea, economic chaos followed and desperate peasants fled.

The fall of the Mycenaean kingdoms and the Hittite Empire contributed to destabilizing migrations throughout the eastern Mediterranean. Displaced groups plundered cities and brought destruction to the entire eastern Mediterranean as they moved southward. By 1170 B.C.E., the Egyptian Empire had lost control of Syria and Canaan, and Ugarit fell. Groups of raiders settled on the Mediterranean coast and extended their power inland. Organized political life in Canaan soon disintegrated.

SYSTEMIC INSTABILITY The story of the Sea Peoples is dramatic and compelling; it does not, however, fully explain the sudden end of the International Bronze Age. A second set of explanations for this collapse focuses on the internal instability of the Late Bronze Age palace system and its exploitation of agricultural laborers. Struggling to survive, peasants took out loans, and then, when they were unable to pay their debts, were forced into slavery. Facing enslavement, many peasants fled to mountainous regions or inaccessible marshes, places where they could eke out a living outside the palace system. They became *habiru*. The term *habiru* is often translated as "robber," "bandit," or "mercenary," and many of the habiru were one or all of those things, forced into such a life by the harshness of the socioeconomic order. For Great Power governments, the *habiru* were a constant problem, not only because of the threat of criminality and social disorder, but more fundamentally, because the flight of peasants worsened agricultural labor shortages and so threatened to undercut the entire palace system.

By the twelfth century B.C.E., this key weakness in the palace system helped destroy it. Many areas appear to have suffered from a lengthy drought, which heightened demands on laborers and escalated the numbers of *habiru*. In turn, those left behind found the demands placed on them even more arduous—and so even more peasants

Sea Peoples Name given by the Egyptians to the diverse groups of migrants whose attacks helped bring the International Bronze Age to an end.

View the Map

Map Discovery: The Sea Peoples

habiru Peasants who existed outside the palace system of the Late Bronze Age; often seen as bandits.

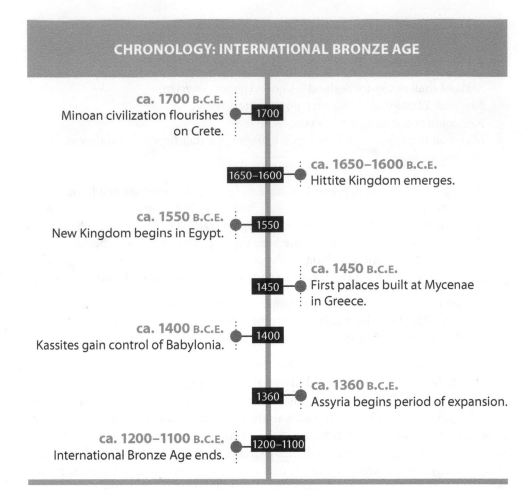

CHRONOLOGY: INTERNATIONAL BRONZE AGE

ca. 1700 B.C.E.
Minoan civilization flourishes on Crete.
— 1700

1650–1600 —
ca. 1650–1600 B.C.E.
Hittite Kingdom emerges.

ca. 1550 B.C.E.
New Kingdom begins in Egypt.
— 1550

1450 —
ca. 1450 B.C.E.
First palaces built at Mycenae in Greece.

ca. 1400 B.C.E.
Kassites gain control of Babylonia.
— 1400

1360 —
ca. 1360 B.C.E.
Assyria begins period of expansion.

ca. 1200–1100 B.C.E.
International Bronze Age ends.
— 1200–1100

fled. Moreover, when bands of Sea Peoples appeared, many *habiru* were more than happy to join them in ransacking the palaces and temples, the symbols of their oppression. While ancient texts tend to portray the Sea Peoples as outside invaders, recent archaeological and historical research demonstrates that many of them were already settled in the lands they attacked—they were, in other words, rebels rather than invaders, and their rebellion helped to destroy the International Bronze Age.

Recovery and Rebuilding: Empires and Societies in the Aftermath of the International Bronze Age

2.2 | What developments shaped southwest Asian and Mediterranean societies after the collapse of the International Bronze Age?

After the collapse of the International Bronze Age, the peoples of southwest Asia and the Mediterranean gradually rebuilt their world. Three important changes distinguished this new era from what had come before. First, the sophisticated international diplomatic and economic networks of the Late Bronze Age had disappeared, as had principal players in that network. Second, the disruption of Late Bronze Age trade routes resulted in an important metallurgical shift. No longer able to obtain both the tin and the copper necessary to create bronze, people began turning to a resource more plentiful and nearer to hand: iron. Ancient peoples had long been familiar with iron, but unforged iron is not very durable. Sometime after 1200 B.C.E., however, metalsmiths figured out how to smelt iron: By repeatedly heating the metal in a charcoal furnace, and then cold-hammering it, they created carbon steel, a sturdy metal that could outfight bronze. The **Iron Age** was born. By 1000 B.C.E. iron was widely used throughout the Mediterranean region, and by the ninth century B.C.E., throughout Mesopotamia and Egypt. As we will see, iron enabled the kings of Neo-Assyria and Neo-Babylonia to field armies far larger than ever before—and so to rule empires of unprecedented size.

A third change that distinguishes this era from the Late Bronze Age was the use of the domesticated camel for transport and travel. Camels began to appear in Near Eastern artwork and texts around 1100 B.C.E., although they had probably been domesticated centuries before. Because they can travel on little water, camels opened up desert routes to merchants. Rather than having to take roundabout roads that skirted the desert, they could opt for the direct—therefore, quicker and more profitable—route. As the camel trade became a significant factor in ancient economies, the Arab peoples began to play a larger role in southwest Asian cultures, usually as objects of fear. The ability of Arab raiders to plunder a caravan or to sack a city and then to disappear into the desert became legendary.

Before and Between the Empires

In the so-called "Dark Age" between the collapse of the International Bronze Age and the reemergence of Assyria as an imperial power (roughly 1100–950 B.C.E.), the weakening or disappearance of Great Powers allowed smaller kingdoms and city-states in Mesopotamia and the Levantine Corridor to flourish. As we will see later in this chapter, this period of transition saw the Israelite or Hebrew culture emerge in Canaan. **Map 2.2** shows that the Hebrew states of Israel and Judah rested within a network of Iron Age kingdoms and city-states. For over 600 years, these states formed shifting coalitions and alliances with and against each other and eventually the resurgent Assyrian and Babylonian empires as well.

NEW PEOPLES OF THE LAND: THE ARAMEANS Within the kaleidoscope of peoples, tribes, and migrants that surged through Syria and the Levant, the Arameans played a dominant role. Originally semi-nomadic pastoralists from northern Syria, Aramean tribes expanded into Assyrian and Babylonian territories during the waning years of the Late Bronze Age. Their raids helped weaken these kingdoms and loosen their hold on their empires. During the subsequent Iron Age, Arameans spread throughout the Near East; by the ninth century B.C.E. Aramean tribes dominated the whole of inland Syria and much of the Mesopotamian countryside, where Aramaic became the language of ordinary people.

The most important Aramean state was Aram-Damascus, centered on the city of Damascus (see Map 2.2). Occupied long before the Arameans emerged in the region, Damascus may be the oldest continuously inhabited city in the world. Damascus prospered and grew powerful during the Iron Age in part because of its location as a key trading post along one of the most economically vital "highways" in the ancient world: the camel caravan route from the Arabian desert to the Mediterranean Sea.

NEW PEOPLES OF THE SEA: THE PHOENICIANS Like the Arameans, the Phoenicians entered the historical record in the final centuries of the Late Bronze Age. Egypt's Late Bronze Age empire included Phoenician city-states along the northern Syrian coast (what is now Lebanon). In the tumult that accompanied the collapse of the International Bronze Age, these cities gained their independence. By 1000 B.C.E., the Phoenicians had developed a dynamic maritime civilization, based in eastern Mediterranean

Iron Age Historical period following the Bronze Age; marked by the prevalent use of iron.

🔍 **View the Map**

Empires of the Ancient Near East

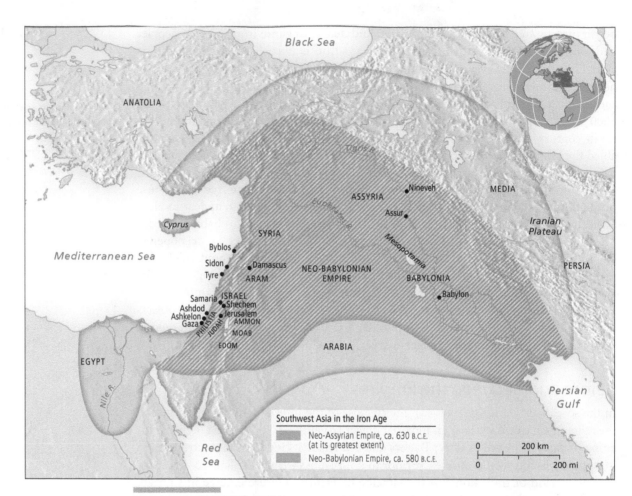

MAP **2.2** SOUTHWEST ASIA IN THE IRON AGE The economic and social crisis that accompanied the end of the International Bronze Age brought with it surges of migration, resulting in new peoples settling throughout southwest Asia and the coalescence of indigenous peoples into new tribal groups. Free (for a time) of Great Power control, Syria and Canaan splintered into small kingdoms and city-states. What were some of these smaller kingdoms and city-states? How did the rise of the Neo-Assyrian and Neo-Babylonian Empires change both the political map and the political realities of southwest Asia?

port cities such as Byblos, Tyre, and Sidon. By following old Minoan and Mycenaean trade routes, the port cities created a large commercial sphere of influence.

The Phoenicians, however, ventured beyond these old Bronze Age routes, even sailing into the Atlantic Ocean, as **Map 2.3** shows. The most dramatic Phoenician voyage occurred when Pharoah Necho II (610–595 B.C.E.) hired a Phoenician crew to circumnavigate the African continent—almost 2,000 years before Europeans would do so. Their sailing experience explains why the Phoenicians were probably the first peoples to develop the *bireme*, a ship with two sets of oars that could, therefore, achieve more speed and power when used in battle.

When the writers of the Hebrew Bible wanted to demonstrate the fabled wealth of King Solomon, they wrote that he contracted with King Hiram of Tyre for luxury goods and that he imported timber from Byblos. These biblical references to Phoenician city-states highlight Phoenician commercial dominance in the Iron Age. Renowned for their artisanal skills, the Phoenicians traded in weapons, jewelry, woodcraft, and the prized reddish-purple cloth for which the Phoenicians were named. (The word *Phoenician*, a Greek coinage, translates as "people of the purple cloth.") Map 2.3 shows that the search for metal ores also motivated much of Phoenician exploration and commerce.

To protect and expand their trade, the Phoenicians established overseas trading posts that grew into self-governing Phoenician colonies. These colonies extended as

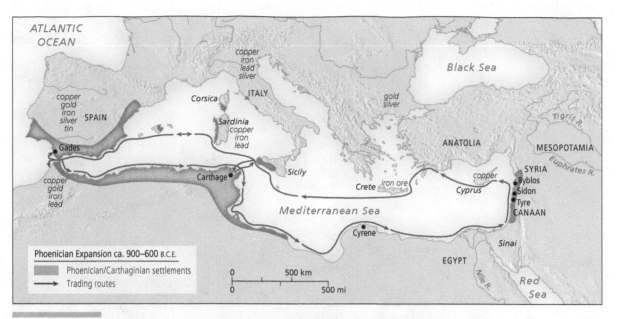

MAP **2.3** PHOENICIAN EXPANSION, CA. 900–600 B.C.E. Impelled by the quest for commerce—and particularly for control of the lucrative metals trade—Phoenicians developed a commercial empire across the Mediterranean Sea. Initially, the Phoenician settlements were only trading posts, but in many areas, these expanded into colonial settlements. By 600 B.C.E. Carthage had become the chief Phoenician city in the western Mediterranean. It controlled the resources of north Africa and parts of Spain. Why was the metals trade so important in this era? How did the Phoenicians serve as economic and cultural conduits, linking Asian, African, and European regions?

far as the coast of Spain, but the most important was Carthage ("New City") on the northern coast of modern Tunisia. Because of its magnificent harbor and strategic location, Carthage controlled trade between the eastern and western Mediterranean.

Their economic connections with lands that would later become the center of Western civilization meant that the Phoenicians served as cultural conduits between Near Eastern civilizations and Europe. Through trade and colonization, Phoenicians brought Asian and Egyptian artistic styles, many of them Bronze Age survivals, to western Mediterranean lands. One of the most important of these survivals was the phonetic alphabet. The principle of the phonetic alphabet seems to have been discovered around 1900 B.C.E. by Canaanites working in Egypt. The Canaanites simplified the complex Egyptian hieroglyphic system, keeping fewer than 30 signs, each representing a single consonant. The resulting "Proto-Canaanite" alphabet evolved into the alphabet used by the Phoenicians, who spread this efficient system of writing throughout the Mediterranean world, where the Greeks and then the Romans adopted it. In this way it became the source of all alphabets and writing in the West.

Read the Document

Mission to Byblos: The Report of Wenamun

CANAANITE CULTURES AND CONTINUITIES With the collapse of Egyptian imperial control at the end of the International Bronze Age, Canaan entered a period of instability, with semi-nomadic peoples moving through the region and new states coalescing. Map 2.2 shows that by around 1000 B.C.E., political power was dispersed among the coastal city-states of the Philistines and the small inland kingdoms of Ammon, Moab, and Edom, as well as Israel and Judah (discussed in the next section).

Many archaeologists argue that the Philistines originated as Aegean "Sea Peoples" who made their way to the Canaanite coast after living for some time in Egypt. One of the names of these peoples, the Peleset, may be the origin of the name "Palestine." By 1000 B.C.E. the Philistines inhabited five coastal city-states, each governed by a king. Loosely joined in a confederation, the Philistines became a major Canaanite power.

In contrast to the Philistines, most of the inhabitants of the Iron Age inland kingdoms were, archaeologists believe, indigenous Canaanites. They worshiped variations

TABLET AND PARCHMENT; CUNEIFORM AND ALPHABET This Neo-Assyrian relief from the Southwest Palace at Nineveh (ca. 630–620 B.C.E.) shows Assyrian scribes making an inventory of the booty from a military campaign against Babylonia. Significantly, one scribe holds a clay tablet and is writing in Akkadian cuneiform, whereas the second scribe is writing in Aramaic (and therefore in a phonetic alphabet script) on papyrus. By the seventh century B.C.E. both papyrus and parchment were widely used, but few of these fragile documents have survived.

of the pre-Bronze Age Canaanite gods El and Ba'al and their wives, the fertility goddesses Asherah and Ashtart (Astarte). Iron Age Canaanites also continued the ancient practice of worshiping their gods through non-figural sacred objects, such as standing stones, obelisks, and special trees. These sacred objects were often located on hilltops (called the "high places" in the Hebrew Bible or Old Testament). The core of Canaanite religious life remained, as it had been for millennia, the quest for fertility, both human and agricultural. The effort to ensure the birth of healthy children and abundant harvests accounts for the sensational features of Canaanite religious practices, such as cultic prostitution, in which the sexual union of the worshiper and priest or priestess reenacted the union of Ba'al and Ashtart, and child sacrifice, in which a couple offered their baby to the gods.

Empire Strikes Back: Neo-Assyrian and Neo-Babylonian Dominance

The independence of the small kingdoms and city-states of southern Anatolia, Syria, and Canaan did not last. Beginning in about 1000 B.C.E., the Assyrian and then the Babylonian imperial regimes began to regain control over their territories, reestablish their commercial power, and reconquer neighboring lands.

NEO-ASSYRIAN IMPERIALISM Even during the worst period of Aramean incursions and economic breakdown, Assyrian rulers never lost control of the Assyrian heartland, the rich agricultural region north and east of the city of Assur. As Map 2.2 shows, from about 1000 B.C.E. on, Assyria began again to exert control over the lands around this central zone. The reign of Ashurnasirpal II (883–859 B.C.E.) marked a key step in Assyrian imperial resurgence. Ashurnasirpal II campaigned throughout Syria and the Levant, gradually picking off the smaller city-states. He reasserted Assyrian power all the way to the Mediterranean coast, with the Phoenician city-states voluntarily paying tribute and accepting vassal status rather than facing the onslaught of the Assyrian military machine. Reviving and expanding Hittite imperial practice, Ashurnasirpal used mass deportations to punish conquered peoples, terrify potential enemies, and supply labor for monumental building projects such as his new, more glorious capital city.

Subsequent Assyrian monarchs extended and consolidated Ashurnasirpal's conquests. During the reign of Tiglath-Pileser III (r. 745–727 B.C.E.), the empire expanded rapidly. Ascending to the throne after four decades of rebellions and epidemics, Tiglath-Pileser reorganized the army and deployed it to quell rebellious subjects, annex parts of Canaan, and make himself king of Babylon. His achievements ushered in a century of Assyrian dominance—even, for a time, over Egypt. The Neo-Assyrian Empire was the first in history to control the Tigris, Euphrates, and Nile River valleys.

Administering such a large empire posed problems, especially in the realm of communication. Provincial governors ruled on the king's behalf, but if the king's orders took months to arrive, provinces could develop dangerous autonomy. To solve this problem, the Assyrians developed an early version of express mail. They erected road stations at intervals of about 20 to 30 miles (a day's march) along every major route (called "royal roads"). At these stations, the king's messengers would find supplies and fresh horses and mules for their chariots, so that they could travel from one end of the empire to the other in a matter of days.

The Assyrians fielded a standing army that was massive for the age—at least 100,000 men. All Assyrian men were required to serve in the military (although the wealthy could pay for substitutes), but the government also conscripted soldiers from the peoples it conquered. To pay for this army and for royal building projects, the Assyrian state imposed high taxes on its peoples, demanded tribute from its vassal states, and plundered the lands it conquered. Annual military campaigns, therefore, were an economic necessity.

Assyria's military successes rested in part on its innovative approach to fighting. The Assyrians invented mobile battering rams and siege towers to assault enemy cities, and pontoon bridges to transport heavy equipment across rivers. They also created the world's first cavalry unit. Ranks of highly skilled horsemen proved more adept than even the light chariot at breaking an infantry line, and unlike chariot forces, could conduct reconnaissance and fight in mountainous regions.

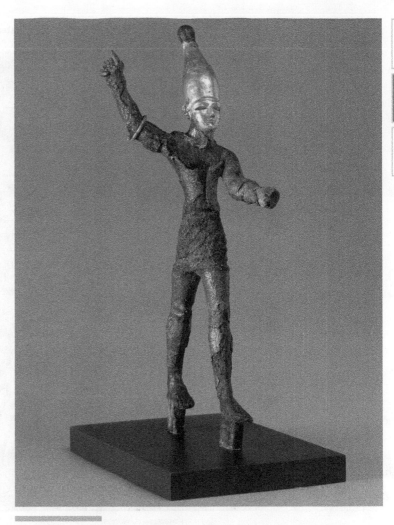

CULTURAL CONTINUITIES: BA'AL ACROSS THE CENTURIES This thirteenth-century B.C.E. bronze statuette of the Canaanite god Ba'al comes from Ugarit. The worship of Ba'al was a feature of Canaanite religion throughout both the Bronze and Iron Ages. A gold foil overlay distinguishes the head and face, and silver on the chest, arms, and legs perhaps represents armor.

Source: Réunion des Musées Nationaux/Art Resource, NY.

ASSYRIAN MILITARY INNOVATIONS: THE CAVALRY Ashurnasirpal II (883–859 B.C.E.) chose what had once been a minor provincial town, Kalhu, as the site of his new capital city. Proclaiming his greatness with monumental architecture, Ashurnasirpal built the Northwest Palace, a magnificent stone structure decorated with massive stone reliefs celebrating the king's triumphs. This photograph of a segment of one of those reliefs shows one of the most important Assyrian military innovations: use of cavalry troops.

With its great size and its innovative technologies, the Assyrian army developed a deserved reputation for terror. If a city or region resisted Assyrian control, its inhabitants met with no mercy. The Assyrians tortured, raped, mutilated, and skinned alive their defeated enemies. The survivors of these brutal conquests were then rounded up, forced to march for hundreds of miles, and dumped in strange lands to serve as an Assyrian labor source. By treating resistors and rebels with such cruelty, the Assyrians avoided having to fight very often: News of Assyrian atrocities spread to neighboring areas, which quickly and understandably surrendered to avoid such a fate. Hence, historians have described the Assyrian policy as "calculated frightfulness."[7]

Despite its ferocity, the Neo-Assyrian Empire played a crucial role in preserving and transmitting ancient Mesopotamian culture for future generations. Although the Assyrians ruled over Babylonia during the eighth and seventh centuries B.C.E. and even sacked the city of Babylon during the reign of Sennacherib (704–681 B.C.E.), they also recognized their cultural debt to Babylon and to its Akkadian and Sumerian predecessors. They treasured this cultural legacy and sought to collect and preserve scientific and literary works. During the Neo-Assyrian period, the final editions of the Akkadian creation story (the *Enuma Elish*) and the *Epic of Gilgamesh*—the versions that we know today—were written down.

The most remarkable effort in cultural collecting occurred during the reign of Asshurbanipal (668–627 B.C.E.). A warrior like all Assyrian kings, Asshurbanipal also

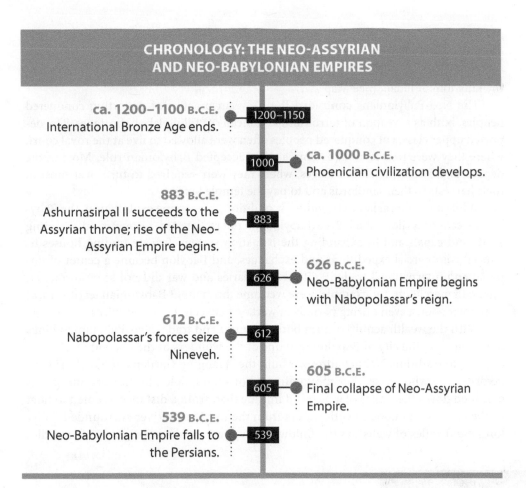

CHRONOLOGY: THE NEO-ASSYRIAN AND NEO-BABYLONIAN EMPIRES

ca. 1200–1100 B.C.E.
International Bronze Age ends.

1200–1150

1000

ca. 1000 B.C.E.
Phoenician civilization develops.

883 B.C.E.
Ashurnasirpal II succeeds to the
Assyrian throne; rise of the Neo-
Assyrian Empire begins.

883

626

626 B.C.E.
Neo-Babylonian Empire begins
with Nabopolassar's reign.

612 B.C.E.
Nabopolassar's forces seize
Nineveh.

612

605

605 B.C.E.
Final collapse of Neo-Assyrian
Empire.

539 B.C.E.
Neo-Babylonian Empire falls to
the Persians.

539

fancied himself a scholar. At his palace in the city of Nineveh he aimed to build a library that would contain every bit of Mesopotamian literature and learning produced up to his time. In perhaps the first known instance of what librarians call "collection development," Asshurbanipal sent representatives throughout the empire to purchase—or confiscate—tablets and texts. Back in Nineveh scribes copied and catalogued these tablets, and then shelved them in rooms divided by subject area. Classified documents such as spy reports and records of secret state affairs were stored in the deepest, least accessible rooms. Over 30,000 tablets, containing perhaps 10,000 different texts (many of them mere fragments), survive from Asshurbanipal's library.

Mighty as it was, the Assyrian Empire came to a sudden end. In the final decades of the seventh century B.C.E., a series of succession crises and revolts fatally weakened the empire. "Calculated frightfulness" produced such bitter resentment that subject peoples rebelled. The most significant of these rebels was the Babylonian king Nabopolassar in southern Mesopotamia (r. 626–605 B.C.E.). The self-described "son of a nobody," Nabopolassar fought for 10 years to free Babylon from Assyrian control. He then took the war into Assyria itself. In 616 B.C.E., after a three-month siege, Nineveh fell to the invaders. The victorious Nabopolassar proclaimed,

> I slaughtered the land of Subartu [Assyria]. . . . The Assyrian, who since distant
> days had ruled over all the peoples, and with his heavy yoke had brought injury
> to the people of the Land, his feet from Akkad I turned back, his yoke I threw off.

For some years Assyrians fought on with the assistance of Egyptian forces, but by 605 B.C.E., when Nabopolassar died, the Neo-Assyrian Empire had entirely collapsed.

THE NEO-BABYLONIAN EMPIRE Nabopolassar became the founder of the Neo-Babylonian (or Chaldean) Empire, which lasted until 539 B.C.E. Conflict with Egypt

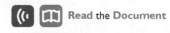 **Read the Document**

The Babylonian Chronicles:
The Fall of Nineveh Chronicle

dominated the early years of the empire as the two Great Powers scrambled to fill the power vacuum left by Assyria's collapse. In the course of this conflict, the brilliant general Nebuchadnezzar II (r. 604–562 B.C.E.) seized Syria, the Phoenician city-states, and the kingdom of Judah. (See Map 2.2.)

The Neo-Babylonians continued the Assyrian practice of deporting conquered peoples, both as a weapon of terror and as a means of filling labor shortages. The deported upper classes of conquered peoples often were allowed to live at the royal court, where they were treated well, as long as they accepted Babylonian rule. Most of the deportees, however, lived in villages, where they were required to turn over most of their harvests to their landlords and to pay the temple taxes.

While agricultural laborers endured conditions of extreme exploitation, the Babylonian economy flourished. Neo-Babylonian rulers devoted resources to restoring roads and canals and to expanding the irrigation system. Private trading houses financed commercial expeditions and exchanges, and Babylon became a center of imperial and international trade. Political boundaries and war did not seem to matter. Egyptian merchants, for example, were welcome throughout Babylonian territories, as were their goods, even during periods of warfare between the two empires.

With the wealth acquired from both conquest and trade, Neo-Babylonian kings made their capital city of Babylon into one of the wonders of the ancient world. According to tradition, Nebuchadnezzar built the "Hanging Gardens of Babylon" for a favorite wife who missed her mountainous homeland. Splendid flowers and plants cascaded down the slopes of a terraced hillside that, from a distance, seemed to float in the air. A moat flooded with waters from the Euphrates River surrounded Babylon's eight miles of walls. As the following illustrations show, brightly colored tiles

THE ISHTAR GATE The magnificently tiled Ishtar Gate provided a dramatic entrance to Babylon, capital city of the Neo-Babylonian Empire. Babylonian artists used brightly colored tiles to create complex three-dimensional depictions of animals and warriors. The gate now rests in a museum in Berlin. An artist's reconstruction shows what the gate may have looked like during the empire's heyday.

decorated the Ishtar Gate, which opened onto a grand avenue leading to the temple of Marduk, Babylon's greatest god.

In addition to their architectural achievements, the Neo-Babylonians compiled an impressive record in astronomical research and observation. Confident that such research could uncover the will of the gods, Babylonian astronomers recorded the movements of the stars, the planets, and the moon. They kept a continuous log of observations between 747 B.C.E. and 61 C.E., an astonishing achievement. By 500 B.C.E., they had accumulated so much astronomical data that they could perform complex mathematical computations to predict eclipses of the moon and sun. These astronomers' calculations, which Persians and Greeks would later adopt, helped lay the foundation of Western science. The Neo-Babylonians also gave the West the names of many constellations, the zodiac, and many mathematical models of astronomical phenomena.

The Neo-Babylonians looked not only to the stars but also to the past to orient themselves in their world. Like the rulers of the Neo-Assyrian Empire, the kings of Babylon regarded themselves as heirs and custodians of a long and valuable cultural tradition. Although Aramaic was now the language of everyday life, Akkadian remained the language of state affairs, and Babylonian kings even sought to revive archaic expressions and script. They also worked to preserve artworks from past generations and to restore ruined temples and palaces. King Nabonidus (555–539 B.C.E.) has been called "the first archaeologist" because of his restoration of holy places in Sumer and Akkad and his interest in collecting and identifying ancient artifacts, which he kept in a museum in his daughter's palace in Ur.

Nabonidus was also a deeply religious man, the son of a priestess to the moon goddess Sin. During his reign, Nabonidus's devotion to Sin alienated many Babylonians, who believed that he jeopardized Babylonian prosperity by neglecting the worship of Marduk. This alienation at least partly explains why, in 539 B.C.E., the Neo-Babylonian Empire quickly fell under Persian control. The end of the Neo-Babylonian dynasty, however, did not destroy Babylon's economic networks or cultural traditions. Both continued to flourish under Persian rule, which we will examine in Chapter 3.

The Civilization of the Hebrews

2.3   What beliefs and institutions shaped Hebrew civilization and its legacy?

One of the most influential civilizations in the West has been that of the Hebrews, a people who originated in Canaan in the tumultuous era at the end of the Late Bronze Age. The history of the Hebrews—or Israelites—took shape within the context of the events we have examined in this chapter: the International Bronze Age and its collapse, the emergence of several small states in Canaan and Syria, and the resurgence of the Assyrian and Babylonian empires after 1000 B.C.E.

The Early History of the Hebrews

The history of the early Hebrews is one of the most controversial subjects in the study of the ancient Near East. Our primary textual source for this history is the Hebrew Bible, or what Christians call the Old Testament. Drawn from a variety of oral and written sources, and composed many centuries after the events they describe, the Hebrew biblical texts condense a complex process of migration, settlement, and religious development. These texts are not historical narratives, in the sense that twenty-first century readers understand history. Some scholars, in fact, argue that these texts can tell us little about early Hebrew history. They point out that the books that make up the Hebrew Bible were first written down in the seventh and sixth centuries B.C.E., some 400 to 600 years after many of the events that they describe. According to these scholars, the apparent history in these texts is almost entirely fictional, a myth of origins composed to give meaning, solace, and identity to an oppressed people. The majority of scholars, however, argue that although the biblical texts first achieved written form centuries after the events they narrate, these documents were based on oral traditions, some of which go back to the original episodes. The biblical texts, then, are not "history" but, when checked against the archaeological evidence, can be used as an important source for uncovering that history.

The people who became the Hebrews first appear in the historical record in Canaan around 1200 B.C.E. at the end of the Late Bronze Age. Archaeological evidence points to a dramatic growth in the numbers of small settlements in the hill country of inland Canaan, on the margins of established urban society. Certain features distinguish these hamlets from others in the area. The houses were grouped in clusters of three or four, with common walls and courtyards. These material remains confirm the portrait of early Israelite culture that we receive from the Hebrew Bible: a largely self-sufficient agricultural society, with a strong emphasis on family and community life.

But from where did these new hill-dwellers come? Many centuries later, the biblical book of Exodus explained that a leader called Moses led them from slavery in Egypt to freedom in Canaan. The archaeological and linguistic evidence, however, indicates that these "proto-Israelites" were indigenous Canaanites, most likely a coalescence of semi-nomadic peoples and urban refugees who fled to the hills to escape the economic disarray and political tumult that accompanied the collapse of the International Bronze Age. Yet we need not discard the Exodus narrative entirely. Sea Peoples raided Egypt in the thirteenth century B.C.E. and many of these peoples wound up in Canaan and Syria. One of these groups, then, may have mixed with indigenous Canaanites to form what became the Hebrews; their story, told and retold, may have come to stand for the identity of the entire group.

Israel: From Monarchy to Exile

With the collapse of the Late Bronze Age empires, a power vacuum existed in Canaan. The Philistines and the Israelites competed for advantage. The Philistines controlled the Mediterranean coastal plain in Canaan and pushed relentlessly at the Hebrews living in the inland hills. According to traditions recorded in the Bible, the desperate Hebrews decided that a king would give them stronger leadership. Such a turn to kingship marked a sharp break in Hebrew culture. If historians are correct in locating early Hebrew origins at least in part in the flight of oppressed city-dwellers to the hill country, then much of Hebrew identity was rooted in opposition to centralized political power. In the biblical texts, anti-royalism—resistance to kingship and the corresponding exploitation of the agricultural masses—constitutes a powerful and repeated theme.

THE UNITED MONARCHY According to the biblical record, the Israelites chose Saul to be their first king around 1020 B.C.E. Some 20 years later, a popular warrior named David (ca. 1005–970 B.C.E.) succeeded Saul, defeated the Philistines, and built a prosperous, centralized kingdom with Jerusalem, an old Canaanite city, as its capital. (See Map 2.2.) David created a royal court complete with a harem; established a census as the basis for tax collection, military conscription, and forced labor; and set up a centralized bureaucracy run by professional soldiers, administrators, and scribes. (See *Justice in History* in this chapter.)

The Bible tells us that David's son Solomon (ca. 970–931 B.C.E.) raised Israel to the pinnacle of its power and prosperity. One of Solomon's greatest achievements was the construction of a grand temple in Jerusalem. Built with the technical assistance of Phoenician architects and artisans and the forced labor of Solomon's subjects, the Jerusalem temple became the focal point of Israel's religious worship. Highlighting Solomon's wealth and his wisdom, the biblical text paints a picture of a monarch forging long-distance economic and diplomatic relationships throughout the ancient world. He married foreign princesses to cement diplomatic agreements, controlled the trade routes running from Egypt and Arabia to Syria, and established economic ties with kingdoms as far away as that of Sabaea (Sheba) in Yemen.

Like almost every aspect of early Hebrew history, however, this history of what we now call the United Monarchy is extremely controversial. No other ancient texts bear witness to the monarchies of David and Solomon, and scholars disagree about the meaning of the archaeological evidence. Three main sets of explanations exist. A minority of scholars contends that David and Solomon never existed at all. A larger group of specialists argues that the biblical story of the United Monarchy blends tenth-century B.C.E. realities and later events. In this view, the historical David and Solomon were relatively poor, rough tribal chieftains of the tenth century (B.C.E.), while the kingly details of the biblical narrative reflect the conditions of the seventh and sixth centuries B.C.E. The mainstream of historical scholarship, however, insists that the United Monarchy did exist in the tenth century. Extra-biblical textual and archaeological evidence testifies that by the tenth century B.C.E., Canaan was politically divided among small kingdoms—including, it seems likely, the United Monarchy of Israel.

THE DIVIDED MONARCHY The monarchy built by David and Solomon did not last long. The Bible tells us that after Solomon died, the northern Israelites rebelled. Dissatisfied with Solomon's policies of high taxes and forced labor, they refused to acknowledge the kingship of Solomon's son and broke away to form a separate northern kingdom. They kept the name "Israel" for this northern state, but moved its capital to the city of Shechem (and later, Samaria). Solomon's successors retained the throne in Jerusalem and ruled over the smaller southern kingdom that remained, now called Judah (see Map 2.2). Solomon's death thus ushered in the period of the Divided Monarchy or the "successor kingdoms."

The fate of the Divided Monarchy became entangled with the rise of the Neo-Assyrian and Neo-Babylonian empires. Judah, as the smaller and poorer of the two kingdoms, was less attractive to invaders and therefore more politically stable. David's descendants remained on the throne throughout Judah's history and enjoyed relatively strong support from their people. In contrast, Israel experienced a number of revolutions and succession shifts, often a result of the meddling of outside powers. The northern state entered its period of greatest strength around 885 B.C.E., when an army commander named Omri (ca. 885–875 B.C.E.) seized power. Omri's son and successor Ahab (ca. 873–852 B.C.E.) built on his father's legacy to make Israel into one of the most formidable powers in Canaan.

View the Atlas Map

Israel and Judah Eighth Century B.C.E.

INTO EXILE The emergence of the Neo-Assyrian Empire, however, meant Israel's independence could not last. As we saw earlier in this chapter, in 745 B.C.E. Tiglath-Pileser III succeeded to the throne and expanded the Assyrian Empire. In just over a decade, Israel, like many of the smaller Syrian and Canaanite kingdoms, found itself an Assyrian vassal. And, like so many of the peoples under Assyrian control, the Israelites quickly grew weary of imperial demands. In 722 B.C.E., Israel's King Hoshea (ca. 731–722 B.C.E.) led a rebellion against Assyrian domination. In keeping with their policy of "calculated frightfulness," the Assyrians responded with brutality. The following year they wiped Israel off the map by annexing the territory outright and dividing it into four Assyrian provinces. Nearly 30,000 Israelites were deported to Mesopotamia. Today known as the Lost Ten Tribes of Israel, these deportees eventually forgot their cultural identity in their new homes and disappeared from history. Many of the remaining inhabitants of Israel took refuge in Judah (nearly doubling its population).

Although the destruction of its larger, more powerful northern neighbor increased Judah's regional importance, this small state survived during the age of empires only as an imperial vassal, first, of the Neo-Assyrians, then the Egyptians, Neo-Babylonians, and

Persians. Judahite kings who attempted to shrug off vassal status had little success. King Hezekiah (ca. 727–697 B.C.E.), for example, made the mistake of joining a Canaanite–Phoenician coalition against the mighty Assyrian monarch, Sennacherib. When the Assyrian army surrounded Jerusalem, Hezekiah surrendered and pledged his loyalty to his Assyrian overlord. The costs of survival were high: According to Sennacherib,

> Hezekiah himself, overwhelmed by the terror-inspiring splendor of my lordship . . . sent me in Nineveh, my lordly city, . . . elephant hides, ivory tusks, ebony-wood, boxwood, all kinds of valuable treasures, as well as his daughters, concubines, male and female musicians. He sent a personal messenger to deliver the tribute and render homage as a slave.[8]

Hezekiah's successors were not so fortunate. In 586 B.C.E., when King Zedekiah (ca. 597–586 B.C.E.) led another revolt, Babylonian forces burned Jerusalem to the

ASSYRIAN TORTURE TACTICS This Assyrian relief shows Assyrian soldiers impaling prisoners from Judah. In 701 B.C.E. the emperor Sennacherib and his army marched into Judah to put down a rebellion. They besieged the city of Lachish and then brutally tortured its inhabitants. They later besieged Jerusalem, but King Hezekiah's surrender saved the capital city.

ground and demolished Solomon's temple, the spiritual and political center of Judah. About 20,000 people were deported to Babylon, an event called the **Babylonian Exile.**

Unlike the inhabitants of Israel, however, the Hebrews deported from Judea retained their cultural and religious identity during their years in exile—and some were able to return to Judah. In 538 B.C.E., King Cyrus of Persia, now ruler of the Neo-Babylonian Empire as well, permitted all peoples exiled by the Babylonians to return to their homelands. Two generations later the Judahites finished building a new temple in Jerusalem, called the Second Temple. For the next 500 years this restored temple worship was the center of Hebrew religious life. Historians call the Hebrews who lived after the completion of the Second Temple *Jews* and their religion *Judaism*.

The Hebrew Religious Legacy

Were it not for this religion, Western civilization textbooks would barely mention Israel under the United Monarchy or the successor kingdoms of Israel and Judah. Like Ammon or Moab, Israel and Judah were minor Canaanite states, fairly insignificant players in the imperial power game. But unlike Ammon and Moab, Israel and Judah possessed and passed on a powerful religious legacy, one that shaped the very heart of Western cultural identity.

EARLY SYNCRETISM Early Hebrew religious practice, like all of early Hebrew history, remains controversial. The existing evidence indicates that as they coalesced as a people in the hill country of Canaan, the proto-Israelites combined Canaanite religious practices with the worship of the god Yahweh (written as "Jehovah" or "the Lord" in

Babylonian Exile The period of Jewish history between the destruction of Solomon's temple in Jerusalem by Babylonian armies in 587 B.C.E., and 538 B.C.E, when Cyrus of Persia permitted Jews to return to Palestine and rebuild the temple.

📖 Read the Document
Judaism Overview

2.1

2.2

2.3

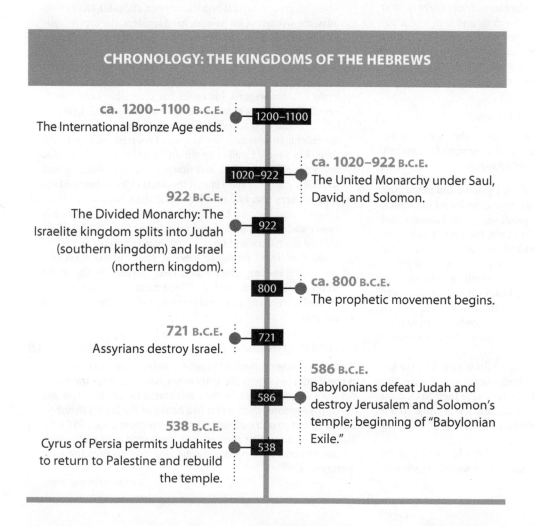

CHRONOLOGY: THE KINGDOMS OF THE HEBREWS

ca. 1200–1100 B.C.E.
The International Bronze Age ends.
1200–1100

1020–922
ca. 1020–922 B.C.E.
The United Monarchy under Saul, David, and Solomon.

922 B.C.E.
The Divided Monarchy: The Israelite kingdom splits into Judah (southern kingdom) and Israel (northern kingdom).
922

800
ca. 800 B.C.E.
The prophetic movement begins.

721 B.C.E.
Assyrians destroy Israel.
721

586
586 B.C.E.
Babylonians defeat Judah and destroy Jerusalem and Solomon's temple; beginning of "Babylonian Exile."

538 B.C.E.
Cyrus of Persia permits Judahites to return to Palestine and rebuild the temple.
538

syncretism The practice of blending foreign religious beliefs with an indigenous religious system; a common practice throughout the Roman Empire.

Yahwism The worship of Yahweh ("Jehovah"); the form of early Israelite religious belief.

English Bibles), a deity likely brought to Canaan by migrants from Midian, a desert region north of the Arabian peninsula. Belief in Yahweh became central to Hebrew identity but the early Israelites also continued to worship the head Canaanite god El, his consort Asherah, and the fertility deity Ba'al.

By the time of the United Monarchy, **syncretism**—the practice of fusing foreign beliefs to an indigenous system—molded Israelite religion into what we call **Yahwism** (the worship of Yahweh). The Israelites now identified early Canaanite shrines to El as places where Yahweh revealed himself to his people. Yahwism also adopted Canaanite liturgical practices, such as the celebration of the harvest (Succoth, in later Judaism) and the New Year (Rosh Hashanah), and the Canaanite belief in cherubim—winged, semi-divine beings with human heads and the bodies of bulls or lions that frequently guarded the thrones of gods and kings.

Different Voices
Holy War in the Ancient World

T he peoples of the ancient world drew no distinction between religion and politics. No king could rule without the gods' blessing and warfare served not only to expand the king's territory but also to glorify the gods and to demonstrate the divine power that upheld the political and social order. The accounts of "holy war" in these excerpts cannot be read as journalists' reports or historians' reconstructions. They are religious texts that allow us glimpses of the deepest motivations and aspirations of the societies that produced them.

I. The Annals of Assurnasirpal II of Assyria

One of the most famous Assyrian documents, The Annals of Assurnasirpal II, *provides detailed year-by-year records of the military campaigns of King Assurnasirpal (r. ca. 883–859).*

Assur, my great lord, who called me by name and made great my kingship over the kings of the four quarters [of the world], had made my name exceeding great, and . . . had commanded me to conquer, to subdue and to rule; trusting in Assur, my lord, I marched by difficult roads over steep mountains with the hosts of my army, and there was none who opposed me. . . .

While I was staying in the land of Kutmuhi, they brought me the word: "The city of Suru of Bit-Halupe has revolted . . . and Ahia-baba, the son of a nobody . . . they have set up as king over them." With the help of . . . the great gods who have made great my kingdom, I mobilized [my] chariots and armies and marched. . . .

To the city of Sura of Bit-Halupe I drew near, and the terror of the splendor of Assur, my lord, overwhelmed them. The chief men and the elders of the city, to save their lives, came forth into my presence and embraced my feet, saying: "If it is thy pleasure, slay! If it is thy pleasure, let live! That which thy heart desireth, do!"

Ahiababa, the son of nobody . . . I made captive. In the valor of my heart and with the fury of my weapons I stormed the city. All the rebels they seized and delivered them up. My officers I caused to enter into his palace and his temples. His silver, his gold . . . a great hoard of copper, alabaster, tables with inlay, the women of his palaces, his daughters, the captive rebels together with their possessions, the gods together with their possessions, precious stone from the mountains, his chariots with equipment, his horses . . . garments of brightly colored wool and garments of linen, goodly oil, cedar, and fine-scented herbs . . . his wagons, his cattle, his sheep, his heavy spoil, which like the stars of heaven could not be counted, I carried off. . . . I built a pillar over against his city gate, and I flayed all the chief men who had revolted, and I covered the pillar with their skins; some I walled up within the pillar, some I impaled upon the pillar on stakes, and others I bound to stakes round about the pillar; . . . and I cut off the limbs of the officers, of the royal officers who had rebelled. Ahiababa I took to Nineveh, I flayed him, I spread his skin upon the wall of Nineveh. My power and might I established over the land of Lake. . . . I increased the tribute and taxes and imposed upon them. . . .

At that time I fashioned a heroic image of my royal self, my power and my glory I inscribed thereon, in the midst of his palace I set it up. I fashioned memorial steles and inscribed thereon my glory and prowess, and I set them up by his city gate.

II. The Book of Numbers: The Israelites' War Against Midian

The Old Testament's Book of Numbers (titled in the Hebrew Bible, In the Wilderness) *tells the story of the Israelites after their exodus from Egypt and before their settlement in Canaan. Like the rest of the Pentateuch (the first five books of the Bible), Numbers is likely based on oral traditions first written down about 950* B.C.E. *This early account was then revised, expanded, and edited over subsequent centuries, probably achieving final form in the sixth century* B.C.E.

(continued on next page)

(continued from previous page)

While Israel dwelt in Shittim the people began to play the harlot with the daughters of Moab. These invited the people to the sacrifices of their gods, and the people ate and bowed down to their gods. So Israel yoked himself to Ba'al of Pe'or. And the anger of the Lord was kindled against Israel. *[The Lord sends a plague.]* . . . those that died by the plague were twenty-four thousand.

And the Lord said to Moses, "Harass the Midianites and smite them; for they . . . beguiled you in the matter of Pe'or." . . . And Moses said to the people, "Arm men from among you for the war, that they may go against Midian, to execute the Lord's vengeance on Midian. You shall send a thousand from each of the tribes of Israel to the war." So there were provided . . . twelve thousand armed for war. And Moses sent them to the war, a thousand from each tribe, together with Phinehas the son of Eleazar the priest. . . . They warred against Midian, as the Lord commanded Moses, and slew every male. . . . And the people of Israel took captive the women of Midian and their little ones; and they took as booty all their cattle, their flocks, and all their goods. All their cities in the places where they dwelt, and all their encampments, they burned with fire. . . . Then they brought the captives and the booty and the spoil to Moses, and to Eleazar the priest, and to the congregation of the people of Israel, at the camp on the plains of Moab by the Jordan at Jericho.

Moses, and Eleazar the priest, and all the leaders of the congregation, went forth to meet them outside the camp. And Moses was angry. . . . Moses said to them, "Have you let all the women live? Behold, these caused the people of Israel . . . to act treacherously against the Lord in the matter of Pe'or, and so the plague came among the congregation of the Lord. Now therefore, kill every male among the little ones, and kill every woman who has known man by lying with him. But all the young girls who have not known man by lying with him, keep alive for yourselves." . . . And Moses and Eleazar the priest received the gold from the commanders . . . and brought it into the tent of meeting, as a memorial for the people of Israel before the Lord.

SOURCES: I. D. D. Luckenbill, *Ancient Records of Assyria and Babylonia*, Vol. I (Chicago, IL: University of Chicago Press, 1926), 141, 144–145; II. Numbers 25: 1–3, 9, 16–18; Numbers 31: 3–18, 52–54.

For Discussion

1. How does the first excerpt illustrate the Assyrian policy of "calculated frightfulness"?
2. Compare these accounts: What motivated these holy wars? Who received credit and why? What do the differences between these accounts reveal about these different cultures?

ASTARTE WORSHIP IN JUDAH Archaeologists uncovered these small statues (called Astarte figurines after the most important Canaanite fertility goddess) in the remains of a number of private houses in what was the kingdom of Judah. Dating from about 800–600 B.C.E., these figurines provide evidence for the continuation of Canaanite religious practices among the Hebrews.

prophetic movement An important phase in the development of what became Judaism. In the ninth century B.C.E., Hebrew religious reformers, or prophets, demanded the transformation of religious and economic practices to reflect ideals of social justice and religious purity.

THE PROPHETIC MOVEMENT In the ninth century B.C.E., Yahwism took a new turn, a revolutionary move of marked significance for Western history. In the years after the formation of the monarchy, the gap between rich and poor widened. The centralization and growth of the state increased the tax burden on peasants, many of whom fell into debt and lost their land. They cried out for justice and a return to what they remembered as a more egalitarian society. From these roots emerged the **prophetic movement**, a call for social justice and religious purity that eventually transformed Yahwism into the world's first monotheistic religion.

The prophet Elijah led the initial movement. He and his followers demanded that Israelites worship *only* Yahweh, and thus called for purifying Yahwism of Canaanite religious beliefs and practices. Speaking on behalf of the downtrodden with words they believed Yahweh had given to them, these social critics condemned the religious and moral corruption of landowners and kings. They linked the worship of Yahweh (and only Yahweh) to a social ideal of community, in which exploitation of the poor was seen as a sin against Yahweh's plan for humanity.

Over the next century, prophets such as Amos, Hosea, Isaiah, and Micah continued to denounce the economic inequalities of Israel and Judah and to call for the worship of only Yahweh. They also began to articulate a vision of religion as a heartfelt spiritual practice resulting in social action, rather than a matter of placating the gods through ritual. In a revolutionary statement, Micah presented Yahweh as rejecting typical religious worship:

> With what shall I come before the Lord, and bow myself before God on high? . . .
> Will the Lord be pleased with thousands of rams, with ten thousands of rivers of oil?
> Shall I give my first-born for my transgression, the fruit of my body for the sin of my soul?
> He has showed you, O man, what is good; and what does the Lord require of you but to do justice, and to love kindness, and to walk humbly with your God?[9]

YAHWEH ALONE: THE EMERGENCE OF MONOTHEISM The destruction of the northern kingdom of Israel in 721 B.C.E. persuaded many within Judah of the truth of the prophets' message. They concluded that Yahweh had chosen the Assyrians as his means of punishing Israel for its sins. A mood of religious reform spread throughout the southern state. King Hezekiah sought to purify Judah's religious practice by destroying the shrines and sacred sites dedicated to Ba'al and Asherah, and by centralizing the worship of Yahweh in the Temple in Jerusalem.

Hezekiah's successor, Manasseh (697–642 B.C.E.), tried to reverse his father's reforms and return to traditional practices, but this counter-reformation proved short-lived. Manasseh's successor was assassinated after only two years on the throne, clearing the way for the boy king, Josiah (640–609 B.C.E.), during whose reign the most thorough-going reform of Hebrew religion occurred. In 622 B.C.E., when Josiah was 26 years old, workers repairing the Temple uncovered a scroll called the "Book of the Law" (an early version of what we know as Deuteronomy, the fifth book of the Bible), ostensibly written by Moses and containing the basic principles by which the Hebrews should live. Deuteronomy in its earliest written form dates not from the time of Moses (i.e., 1300s B.C.E.), but from the 600s (B.C.E.). Inspired by this supposed "archaeological find," Josiah implemented a host of reforms, all of them based on the central theme of Deuteronomy: the "Covenant," or sacred contract, between Yahweh and the Israelites. According to the terms of this Covenant, Yahweh designated Israel as his chosen people, and in return, the Israelites were to worship only him and to seek to abide by his law.

Stirred by this religious reformation, one of Josiah's subjects used the ideal of the Covenant to reinterpret the Hebrew past by writing the "Deuteronomistic History," an early version of the biblical books of Joshua, Judges, Samuel, and Kings. This history projects the vision of Yahweh as the true God of Israel back onto the earliest days of the Hebrew people, and recasts the story of the Israelites as a struggle between the true followers of Yahweh and those who strayed to worship other gods. In its narrative, the History emphasized the intertwined concepts of Land and Law: Yahweh had given his chosen people the land of Israel, but on the condition that they worshiped him as his law, spelled out in Deuteronomy, demanded.

Josiah's religious reformation ended in 609 B.C.E. when Egyptian forces captured and killed him. Within decades Judah had fallen to Babylonian conquest, Jerusalem was destroyed, and the period of the Babylonian Exile had begun. As they struggled to make sense of these horrific events, the Hebrew exiles took the final step toward monotheism. Grappling with the lessons of their history and the meaning of their religious faith now that the Temple was destroyed, they came to a revolutionary understanding of the divine. They came to see Yahweh as unbounded by time and space, not confined to a temple. The one and only God, he ruled not only Israel and Judah, but all people in all places and in all time—and even beyond time. This idea of the one eternal and transcendent God would have a powerful impact on Western culture.

The Babylonian Exile also resulted in a number of other important developments in Hebrew religion. First, the fear of losing their identity as Hebrews as they lived in a foreign land amid foreign gods led to a new emphasis on religious purity. Hebrew leaders developed a complex code of ethical and ritual requirements designed to reinforce the separate identity of the Hebrew people. For example, Hebrews could no longer marry non-Hebrews and they had to observe strict dietary laws.

This new emphasis on purity resulted in significant but contradictory changes for Hebrew women. On the one hand, they found their religious role more restricted: Childbirth and menstruation made women "unclean" and therefore unfit for public worship. On the other hand, many of the dietary and ritualistic requirements took place within the home, in the family context, and so gave women central responsibility in sustaining Hebrew identity.

A second important religious development during the Babylonian Exile was the compilation of the basic texts of the Hebrew Bible. During this era Hebrew leaders added to Deuteronomy a number of texts written earlier or preserved in oral tradition. Edited and compiled, these texts with Deuteronomy became the **Pentateuch** or the **Torah**—the first five books of the Bible. Exiled Hebrews also produced a second edition of the Deuteronomistic History, one that particularly emphasized the central role of the now-destroyed Temple and its priesthood in the life of the Israelites.

By emphasizing the priesthood and Temple sacrifices, the editors of this later version of the Deuteronomistic History (who probably were themselves priests) tried to make correct religious practice the key to Hebrew faith and identity. This stress on religious ritual, however, ignored the social concerns that the prophets had placed at the heart of Yahweh's Law. The period of the Exile, then, saw a continuation of the prophetic movement, as new prophets arose to challenge the priestly emphasis on right ritual and instead demanded social justice. The prophet Ezekiel, for example, depicted Yahweh as a shepherd with a special love for the weakest in his flock:

> I myself will be the shepherd of my sheep . . . says the Lord God. . . . Behold, I judge between sheep and sheep. Is it not enough for you to feed on the good pasture, that you must tread down with your feet the rest of your pasture; and to drink of clear water, that you must foul the rest with your feet? . . . Behold, I, I myself will judge between the fat sheep and the lean sheep.[10]

The tension between the prophetic call for social justice, implemented through practical action, and the priestly demand for religious purity, demonstrated through ritual practices, would never be fully reconciled, either in Judaism or in the monotheistic religions of Christianity and Islam, which, like Judaism, drew on ancient Hebrew roots.

Pentateuch The first five books of the Hebrew Bible.

Torah Most commonly, the first five books of the Hebrew Bible; also used to refer to the whole body of Jewish sacred writings and tradition.

THE HEBREW LEGACY From those Hebrew roots grew many characteristic features of Western civilization. The notion of the "chosen people" shaped not only Christian theology but also modern expressions of nationalism. "Manifest destiny"—the idea that the United States had the right and responsibility to extend its political control across the North American continent—is rooted in this ancient Hebrew idea. Western culture also draws on the Hebrew ideal of the Law. In Hebrew tradition, Yahweh's Law stands supreme: Every king, even God's chosen ruler, will be judged on how well he implements God's Law and how fairly he treats God's people. This idea provides the seeds of the key Western legal and political principle that no ruler or leader stands beyond the law. The summary of Yahweh's Law found in the Ten Commandments remains for many the foundation of Western ethics, while the Hebrew Bible still provides some of the most powerful and poetic narratives in the Western tradition.

Most important, the belief in an all-powerful, all-encompassing God who transcends space and time, and yet intervenes in human history to take care of his people, has had a powerful influence on Western societies. Seeing the hand of God in history allowed Western cultures to adopt a notion of human history as linear, as meaningful movement through time, rather than an endless repetition or a steady degradation, and so helped make possible the idea of progress. Similarly, the concept of a transcendent

Justice in History

Crime and Punishment in a King's Court

Around 990 B.C.E., "in the spring of the year, the time when kings go forth to battle," Israel's King David sent his troops against the Ammonites. Although a renowned warrior, David stayed behind in Jerusalem. One afternoon he took a walk on his roof after he woke from his nap. (An afternoon siesta was then, like now, common in Mediterranean cultures, and the roof constituted the coolest part of the building.) From his rooftop David saw a woman bathing, "and the woman was very beautiful." When the king discovered that the woman was Bathsheba, wife of Uriah the Hittite[*] who was serving in the war against Ammon, he ordered her brought to him. In the spare vocabulary of the biblical text, David "took her, and she came to him, and he lay with her." This action set in motion a sequence of events that ultimately divided the Israelite kingdom.

The story of David and Bathsheba is part of the "Court History of David," found in the Old Testament books of II Samuel and I Kings.[**] Some scholars insist that the Court History originates from the time of King Josiah in the seventh century B.C.E. Other scholars, however, date the earliest version of the Court History to Solomon's reign in the tenth century B.C.E. and argue that this first version was then combined with other stories during Josiah's religious reformation (and then revised again after the Babylonian Exile). But no matter what its origins, the History reflects the values that propelled Josiah's reforms and promotes a revolutionary idea of social justice.

David, the handsome warrior and popular hero whom the Lord chose to lead his people, sowed the seeds of national tragedy. A few weeks after his sexual encounter with Bathsheba, the king received a message from her: "I am with child." Caught in adultery, David scrambled to cover up his crime. Assuming that Uriah, like most soldiers on leave, would want sex, David ordered Bathsheba's husband home from the battlefield. If Uriah slept with Bathsheba, then everyone would assume he was the baby's father. But the Hittite soldier refused to violate the rules of purity that required a soldier engaged in holy war to abstain from sex. Even when David invited him to dinner and plied him with so much wine that he became drunk, Uriah resisted the temptation to bed his lovely wife.

Frustrated, David sent Uriah back to the battle, along with a message for his commander, Joab: "Set Uriah in the forefront of the hardest fighting, and draw back from him, that he may be struck down and die." Joab obeyed. Uriah and several of Israel's mightiest fighters died in a hard-fought engagement with the Ammonites. Shortly after, David added Bathsheba to his stable of wives. The king thought he had gotten away with murder. But, the Court History tells us, "the thing that David had done displeased Yahweh."

---

[*]"Hittite" here does not refer to the Hittite Empire, which disintegrated over one century earlier, but rather to a small Canaanite kingdom or tribe.

[**]II Samuel 9–20 and I Kings 1–2 of the Christian Old Testament.

(continued on next page)

A short time later, Yahweh's prophet, Nathan, arrived at court and told the king a story:

> There were two men in a certain city, the one rich and the other poor. The rich man had very many flocks and herds; but the poor man had nothing but one little ewe lamb, which he had bought. And he brought it up, and it grew up with him and with his children; it used to eat of his morsel, and drink from his cup, and lie in his bosom, and it was like a daughter to him. Now there came a traveler to the rich man, and he was unwilling to take one of his own flock or herd to prepare for the wayfarer who had come to him, but he took the poor man's lamb, and prepared it for the man who had come to him.

Infuriated by this injustice, David insisted, "As the Lord lives, the man who has done this deserves to die." Nathan replied, "You are the man."

Nathan's parable forced David to see himself as the selfish rich man who stole everything, including life itself, from Uriah. David recognized his crime and confessed, "I have sinned against Yahweh." But his confession did not mean he could evade the consequences of his actions. Nathan warned, "The sword shall never depart from your house. . . . Thus says Yahweh, 'Behold, I will raise up evil against you out of your own house.'"

David and Bathsheba's baby boy soon sickened and died. Bathsheba's second son by David, Solomon, inherited his father's throne, but only after the royal household endured a series of tragedies, including incestuous rape, murder, a civil war that forced David to flee his capital city, and the deaths of two more of David's sons (with a third executed by Solomon shortly after he took power). Solomon's reign may have marked the high point of the Hebrew monarchy, but his decision to continue the heavy taxation and forced labor policies of his father meant that resentment against the Davidic royal house festered among the people. This resentment finally burst into rebellion after Solomon's death and divided the kingdom.

By linking these unfolding tragedies to David's crime, the Court History revealed an idea of justice new to the ancient world. Because the kingdom belonged to Yahweh, not to David or any of his sons, Yahweh's Law applied to all. Although a mighty king, David was expected to obey the same laws that governed the behavior of an ordinary peasant. His failure to do so shattered his family, weakened his reign, and tarnished his legacy.

This emphasis on actions and consequences highlights a second important feature of the Court History: the importance of human action in a world under Yahweh's control. Although the History contains no miracles, no angels, no points of supernatural intervention in the natural world, the tragedies that unfold do not just happen by chance. Yahweh is in charge. Yet David and his sons are not pawns in a divine chess game. Their choices have consequences. What each person does matters. Justice, then, is individual as well as social, a working of Yahweh's will for the world in both communal and personal life.

For Discussion

1. How does the idea of kingship and justice revealed in the Court History differ from that of other Bronze and Iron Age monarchies?
2. How does the concept of justice revealed in this story strengthen and/or challenge the values that underlay the prophetic movement?

Taking It Further

Michael Dever, *What Did the Biblical Writers Know and When Did They Know It?* Grand Rapids, MI: Wm. B. Eerdmans Publishing Co., 2002. A clear and engaging introduction to the sources of the books of the Old Testament.

Israel Finkelstein and Neil Asher Silberman. *David and Solomon: In Search of the Bible's Sacred Kings and the Roots of the Western Tradition*. New York: Free Press, 2006. A more radical approach to the historical accuracy of the biblical picture of the United Monarchy than Dever's.

God contributed to the Western scientific tradition. Because God transcends rather than permeates the natural world, nature itself is not sacred. Human beings can study it; they can also use it, manipulate it, and transform it.

Read the Document

Suffering Explained

CONCLUSION

International Systems, Ancient Empires, and the Roots of Western Civilization

The International Bronze Age marked an early but crucial phase in the formation of Western civilization. Within a geographical area centered on the eastern Mediterranean but stretching far beyond its shores, a network of political, commercial, and cultural ties emerged among cities and kingdoms that had lived in relative isolation from each other. Long before it was possible to identify what we now call the West, the exchange of commodities, the spread of religious ideas, the growth of common political traditions, the dissemination of scientific and technological techniques, and the borrowing of one language from another created a complex pattern of cultural diffusion over a vast geographical area.

When the international system of the Late Bronze Age collapsed, these elements did not all disappear. The cultural inheritance of the Sumerians and Akkadians passed on to the Neo-Assyrian and Neo-Babylonian empires, consciously preserved in libraries and literary collections. The diplomatic innovations, most clearly seen in the treaty between Ramesses II and Hattusili III in 1258 B.C.E., became an important feature of international affairs. The proto-Canaanite alphabet survived, to be passed on to the Western world by the Phoenicians via the Greeks. And most important of all, in the midst of the collapse of Great Powers and the rise of new empires, a small, seemingly insignificant people with a still controversial origin encountered the divine in ways that continue today to influence, comfort, challenge, and transform peoples of the West and around the world.

MAKING CONNECTIONS

1. Review the key characteristics of Mesopotamian culture outlined in Chapter 1. Compare and contrast these characteristics with those of the Great Power cultures of the International Bronze Age and the later Neo-Assyrian and Neo-Babylonian societies. What is more important, cultural continuity or cultural transformation?

2. Consider this argument: "Empires dominated southwest Asia in the millennium from 1500 to 500 B.C.E.—and yet the developments of greatest significance for Western history and culture occurred not in the imperial systems, but in the smaller states, in the areas on the periphery of power." In what ways is this argument accurate? In what ways must it be modified or rejected?

3. How does the history of the Hebrews illuminate the central patterns of southwest Asian history in the period after the collapse of the International Bronze Age?

TAKING IT FURTHER

For suggested readings, see page R-1.

On MyHistoryLab

✓ **Take the Study Plan for Chapter 2, The Age of Empires: The International Bronze Age and Its Aftermath, ca. 1500–550 B.C.E., on MyHistoryLab**

Chapter Review

The Dynamism of the International Bronze Age

2.1 What elements made up the international system of the Late Bronze Age and why did it collapse?

Complex economic and diplomatic networks connected five geographic areas, known as zones of power. Called the "Club of Great Powers" by historians, they developed shared concepts and tools of international exchange and diplomacy. The end of the Late International Bronze Age was likely caused by a combination of factors, including large-scale migrations in the wake of the collapse of: the Mycenean and Hittite kingdoms, prolonged drought conditions, and growing numbers of laborers fleeing the heavy economic demands of the palace system.

Recovery and Rebuilding: Empires and Societies in the Aftermath of the International Bronze Age

2.2 What developments shaped southwest Asian and Mediterranean societies after the collapse of the International Bronze Age?

The end of the Great Powers' sophisticated diplomatic and economic networks meant that smaller city-states and kingdoms, with their shifting coalitions and alliances, were allowed to grow and thrive. The rise of the Neo-Assyrian and Neo-Babylonian empires, however, put an end to this period of small-state independence. Changing political partnerships cut off the supply of resources to create bronze, and forced ancient peoples to explore the use of iron and to develop new trade routes, both overseas and on land.

The Civilization of the Hebrews

2.3 What beliefs and institutions shaped Hebrew civilization and its legacy?

As Hebrew civilization evolved out of polytheism through Yahwism to monotheism, it also developed in tension between the prophetic emphasis on social justice and the priestly insistence on proper ritual, and between communal ideals and an all-powerful monarchy. The Western legal principle that no leader stands beyond the law can be traced back to the Hebrew ideal that every king is judged on how well he implements God's Law and how fairly he treats his people.

Chapter Time Line

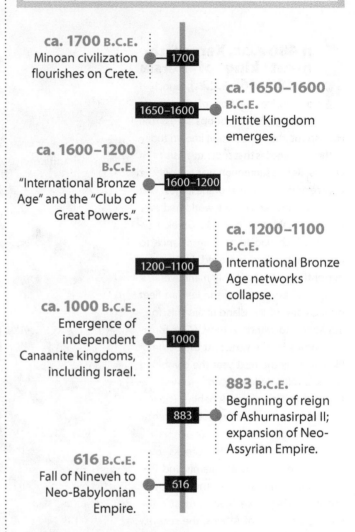

ca. 1700 B.C.E. Minoan civilization flourishes on Crete. — 1700

ca. 1650–1600 B.C.E. Hittite Kingdom emerges. — 1650–1600

ca. 1600–1200 B.C.E. "International Bronze Age" and the "Club of Great Powers." — 1600–1200

ca. 1200–1100 B.C.E. International Bronze Age networks collapse. — 1200–1100

ca. 1000 B.C.E. Emergence of independent Canaanite kingdoms, including Israel. — 1000

883 B.C.E. Beginning of reign of Ashurnasirpal II; expansion of Neo-Assyrian Empire. — 883

616 B.C.E. Fall of Nineveh to Neo-Babylonian Empire. — 616

3 Greek Civilization

I n 480 B.C.E. Xerxes, the great king of Persia (r. 485–465 B.C.E.), launched a massive invasion of Greece by leading 150,000 troops across the Hellespont, the narrow strait known today as the Dardanelles that separates Asia from Europe. Xerxes's intention was to conquer Greece and make it part of the largest and most powerful empire the world had ever known. Against all odds 31 Greek city-states, which had formed an alliance to repel the invaders, prevailed. In September of that year the highly maneuverable Athenian navy defeated the Persian fleet off the coast of the island of Salamis, forcing Xerxes to withdraw most of his forces to Anatolia for the winter. At the Battle of Plataea early the next year the combined Greek armies, led by Sparta, routed the troops that Xerxes had left behind. The surviving Persians were driven out of Greece, never to return.

The victories of the Greeks over the Persian colossus at Salamis and Plataea mark a milestone in the history of the West. They gave Greece, most notably the city-state of Athens, the security within which it could develop its political institutions as well as its philosophy,

LEARNING OBJECTIVES

3.1 ((·
How did Greek city-states develop their culture and political institutions during the Archaic Age?

3.2 ((·
How did the Persian Empire bring the peoples of the Near East together in a stable realm, and what elements of Persian religion and government have influenced Western thought?

3.3 ((·
What were the intellectual, social, and political innovations of Greece in the Classical Age?

((· Listen to Chapter 3 on MyHistoryLab

THE BATTLE OF SALAMIS, 480 B.C.E. This victory of the Athenian navy over Persia ended a major threat to Greek independence. This nineteenth-century painting of the battle accurately depicts the closeness of naval engagements in ancient times.

◉ Watch the Video Series on MyHistoryLab

Learn about some key topics related to this chapter with the *MyHistoryLab Video Series: Key Topics in Western Civilization*

3.1

3.2

3.3

science, literature, and art. The resulting achievements of Greek civilization, which continued to interact with those of other states in the Mediterranean region, became the bedrock of Western civilization.

It would be misleading, however, to celebrate the Greek victory over Persia as a triumph of the West over the East. The location of Greece in Europe and Persia in Asia suggests such a contrast. But as we have seen, the terms *the West* and *the East* refer to more than geography; they also designate a constellation of cultural traditions. Some of the political, religious, and scientific traditions that we identify as Western can be traced back to the Persian Empire; many of them were the products of cultural encounters between Greece and Persia.

This chapter will discuss the growth of Greek civilization in the context of its relationship with the Persian Empire. The main question it will address is:

What role did both Persia and Greece play in the making of the West?

Greece Rebuilds, 1100–479 B.C.E.

3.1	How did Greek city-states develop their culture and political institutions during the Archaic Age?

As we saw in Chapter 2, Greek civilization entered a period of economic and political decline at the end of the International Bronze Age. The years from about 1100 to 750 B.C.E, known as the Dark Age, were followed by a period of economic growth at home and encounters with Phoenicians and Persians abroad. The revival of Greece during the Archaic Age, which lasted until 479 B.C.E, set the stage for Greece's cultural achievements during its Classical Age.

During the Dark Age, Greece endured economic, political, and cultural stagnation that contrasted with the wealth and splendor of the Mycenaean states that had flourished during the Bronze Age. Few new settlements were established on the Greek mainland, and urban life disappeared. Maritime trade declined sharply and the economies controlled by the palaces collapsed. Because there was no longer a need for scribes to record inventories, Linear B writing disappeared. A serious decline in agriculture led to a steep decrease in food production and population.

A slow economic recovery began in the Greek world about 850 B.C.E., when the population began to grow and trade became brisker. Because of the harsh living conditions on the mainland during the Dark Age, many Greeks moved to a region called Ionia on the coasts and islands of western Anatolia. Relatively isolated from other Greek communities, these pioneers developed their own dialect of the Greek language. By 800 B.C.E. the Ionian Greeks were regularly interacting with the Phoenicians in the eastern Mediterranean.

Writing and Poetry During the Archaic Age

Between about 750 and 650 B.C.E., fresh ideas poured into Greece from the Near East through contact with the Phoenicians and other peoples. Encounters with Near Eastern poets, merchants, artisans, refugees, doctors, slaves, and spouses brought innovations to Greece. These included new economic practices (such as charging interest on loans), new gods and goddesses (such as Dionysos, the god of wine), and inventions of convenience (such as parasols to provide shade).

The most valuable import from the Phoenicians was the alphabet. As we saw in Chapter 2, the Phoenicians, who had been using an alphabet of 22 letters for at least three centuries, introduced the system to Greece around 750 B.C.E. The adoption of the alphabet, to which the Greeks added vowels, was one of the developments that marked the beginning of the Archaic Age. Because an alphabet records sounds, not words, it can be adjusted easily for any language. Greeks soon recognized the potential of the new system and learned to write and read, first for business and then for pleasure. They began to record their oral traditions, legends, and songs. At the same time, they began to compose a new literature and write down their laws.

Two of the greatest works of Western literature, the *Iliad* and the *Odyssey,* were soon written down in the new alphabet. A Greek poet named Homer, who probably lived around 750 B.C.E., is credited with composing these poems, but they were not entirely his invention. In writing the poems, Homer drew on oral tales about the legendary Trojan War that wandering poets had been reciting for centuries. The poets had elaborated on the stories so many times that they lost their historical accuracy. Nevertheless, many details in the poems, especially about weapons and armor no longer used in Homer's day, suggest that the earliest versions of the poems were first recited in the Bronze Age and may be loosely based on events of that time.

The *Iliad* and the *Odyssey* were part of a larger body of stories that told how an army of Greek warriors sailed to Troy, a wealthy city on the northwest coast of Anatolia, to recover a beautiful Greek princess, Helen, who had been abducted by a Trojan prince. After 10 years of savage fighting, the Greeks finally stormed Troy and won the war, though their greatest fighters had died in battle. When the surviving heroes returned to Greece, they were met with treachery and bloodshed.

Homer's genius lay in his retelling of these old stories. He did not relate the entire saga of the Trojan War because he knew that his audiences were familiar with it. Instead, he selected certain episodes, and in fresh ways he emphasized aspects of human character and emotion in the midst of violent conflict. In the *Iliad,* for example, he describes how the hero Achilles, the mightiest of all the Greeks fighting at Troy, grows angry when his commander in chief, Agamemnon, steals his favorite concubine. In a rage, Achilles withdraws from the battle and returns to fight only to avenge his best friend, who had been killed by Hector, the main Trojan hero. Achilles eventually slays Hector, but does not relinquish his fury until Hector's father, Priam, the king of Troy, begs him to return his son's corpse for proper burial. Achilles relents and weeps, his humanity restored after so much killing. In Homer's hands, the story of Achilles's anger becomes a profound investigation into human alienation and redemption.

📖 **Read the Document**

Homer *Iliad* (Eighth Century B.C.E.)

polis A self-governing Greek city-state.

acropolis The defensible hilltop around which a polis grew. In classical Athens, the Acropolis was the site of the Parthenon (Temple of Athena).

CHART OF THE DEVELOPMENT OF THE ALPHABET
This chart shows how the first five letters of the Phoenician alphabet developed into the first five letters of the English alphabet.

Political Developments During the Archaic Age

Greeks in the Archaic Age also experimented with new forms of social and political life. They developed a new style of community called the **polis** (plural *poleis*), or city-state. A polis was a self-governing community consisting of an urban center with a defensible hilltop, called an **acropolis**, and all the surrounding land farmed by citizens of the polis. Greek cities varied in size from a few square miles to several hundred. All contained similar institutions: an assembly in which the male citizens of the community gathered to discuss—and in some instances decide—public business; a council of male elders (usually aristocrats) who advised on public matters and in many cities made laws; temples to gods who protected the polis and on whose goodwill the community's prosperity depended; and an open area in the center of town called an **agora**, which served as a market and a place for informal discussions.

Living in a polis provided an extremely strong sense of community. A person could be a citizen of only one polis, and every citizen was expected to place the community's interests above all other concerns. Even the women, who were citizens but not permitted to play a role in public life, felt powerful ties to their polis. While only citizens had full membership in a polis, enjoying the greatest rights and bearing the greatest responsibilities, every city had noncitizens from other communities. Some of these noncitizens had limited rights and obligations, whereas slaves had no rights at all.

THE OLYMPIC GAMES AND GREEK UNITY During the Archaic Age Greeks also began to develop a sense of Greek unity that had been absent during the Dark Age. Athletic contests called panhellenic games, so named because they drew participants from the entire Greek world, became one of the means by which Greeks cultivated this new sense of Greek identity. The panhellenic games became a mainstay of aristocratic Greek culture in the Archaic Age. As many as 150 cities regularly offered aristocratic men the chance to win glory through competition in chariot-racing, discus-throwing, wrestling, footracing, and other field events. Through sports the Greeks found a common culture that allowed them to express their Greek identity and honor the gods at the same time because the games were also religious festivals.

The **Olympic Games**, which originated in 776 B.C.E., carried the most prestige. Every four years Greek athletes from southern Italy to the Black Sea gathered in the sacred grove of Olympia in the central Peloponnese to take part in games dedicated to Zeus, the chief Greek god. The rules required the poleis to call truces to any wars, even if they were in the middle of battle, and allow safe passage to all athletes traveling to Olympia. Records show the naming of champions at Olympia from 776 B.C.E to 217 C.E. The Roman emperor Theodosius I, who was a Christian, abolished the games in 393 C.E. because they involved the worship of Greek gods.

COLONIZATION AND THE SETTLEMENT OF NEW LANDS A population boom during the Archaic Age forced Greeks to emigrate because the rocky soil of the mainland could not provide enough food. From about 750 to 550 B.C.E., cities such as Corinth and Megara on the mainland and Miletos in Ionia established more than 200 colonies around the Mediterranean and Black Seas.

Greek emigrants sailed to foreign shores. Many colonists settled on the Aegean coast north into the Black Sea region, which offered plentiful farmlands. The important settlement at Byzantium controlled access to the agricultural wealth of these Black Sea colonies. Greeks established many new cities in Sicily and southern Italy as well as on the southern coast of France and the eastern coast of Spain. By 600 B.C.E. Greeks had founded colonies in North Africa in the region of modern Libya and on the islands of Cyprus and Crete. Greek merchants also set up a trading community on the Syrian coast and another in the Egyptian delta, with the pharaoh's permission (see **Map 3.1**).

Although all Greek colonies maintained formal religious ties with their mother city-states, or *metropoleis,* they were self-governing and independent. Some colonies grew rich and populous enough to establish their own colonies. Because the Greek colonists seized territory by force and sometimes slaughtered the local inhabitants, relations with the people already living in these lands were often tense.

The Greek adoption of coinage spurred commercial activity. Coinage first replaced barter as a medium of exchange in the kingdom of Lydia in western Anatolia about 630 B.C.E. Minted from precious metals—gold, silver, copper, bronze—and uniform in weight, coins helped people standardize the value of goods, a development that revolutionized commerce. During the sixth century B.C.E., Greeks living in Ionia and on the Greek mainland began to mint their own coins. Each polis used a distinctive emblem to mark its currency. When Athens became the dominant economic power in

agora An open area in the town center of a Greek polis that served as a market and a place for informal discussion.

View the Image

Greek Athletics

Olympic Games Greek athletic contests held in Olympia every four years between 776 B.C.E and 217 C.E.

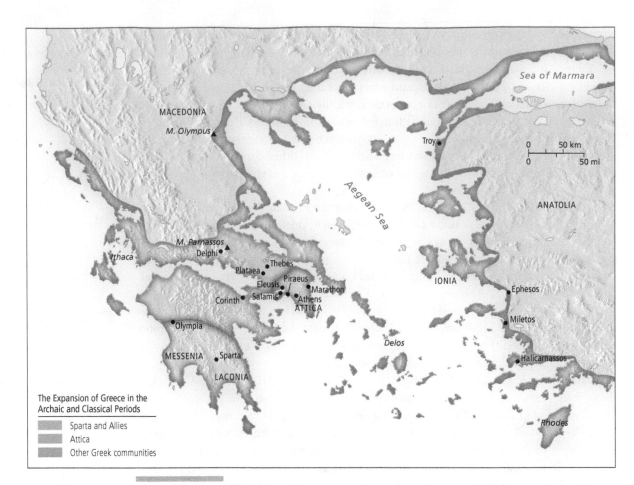

MAP **3.1** THE EXPANSION OF GREECE IN THE ARCHAIC AND CLASSICAL AGES During the Archaic and Classical Ages, Greek cities spread from Greece to the shores of the Black Sea and as far west as Italy and southern France. This map shows the Greek heartland: the mainland, the islands of the Aegean Sea, and Ionia. Although never unified politically in the Archaic and Classical Ages, the people in these cities spoke Greek, worshiped the same gods, and shared a similar culture. What prevented them from uniting politically?

the Aegean during the second half of the fifth century B.C.E., Athenian silver coinage became the standard throughout the Greek world and far beyond.

Greek colonization played a critical role in shaping Western civilization by creating wealthy centers of Greek culture in Italy and the western Mediterranean. Sometimes overshadowed in the historical record by city-states of the Greek mainland, such as Athens, Sparta, and Corinth, the impressive new poleis spread Greek civilization, language, literature, religion, and art far beyond Greece itself. The colony of Syracuse in Sicily, for example, grew to be larger than any city in Greece. Greek communities deeply influenced local cultures and made a significant impact on Etruscan and Roman civilization in Italy, as we will see in Chapter 5.

THE HOPLITE REVOLUTION The new wealth flowing through the Greek world facilitated the introduction of a new type of fighting force known as **hoplites**. These were units of well-armed, well-drilled infantry that entered the battlefield in massed ranks, four to eight deep, in a formation called a **phalanx**. Inspired by military developments in Assyria, Greek city-states came to realize that large infantry units were more effective than individual aristocratic warriors. Hoplite warfare required more soldiers than the aristocracy could provide, so the poleis had to recruit them from among the general population. Because the new recruits had to be wealthy enough to purchase their own armor and swords, hoplites generally came from the middle ranks of society.

In hoplite warfare each man relied for protection on the man to his right, whose shield protected his own sword arm. Cooperation was all-important, for if the line

hoplites Greek soldiers in the Archaic Age who could afford their own weapons. Hoplite tactics made soldiers fighting as a group dependent on one another. This contributed to the internal cohesion of the polis and eventually to the rise of democracy.

phalanx The military formation favored by hoplite soldiers. Standing shoulder to shoulder in ranks often eight men deep, hoplites moved in unison and depended on one another for protection.

broke, the individual soldier became more vulnerable. Hoplite fighting generated a sense of common purpose that had political consequences, as hoplites demanded a political voice in the communities for which they fought. Their growing confidence challenged aristocratic families who traditionally controlled community decision-making. Military organization thus contributed to political change.

THE RISE OF THE TYRANTS In many poleis new political leaders arose to champion the cause of the hoplite citizenry. These political leaders were known as **tyrants**, a word borrowed from the Near East that did not bear the negative connotation of cruel and arbitrary rule that it carries today. Originally the word *tyrant* meant someone who seized power in a polis rather than acquiring it by heredity, election, or some legal process. Tyrants were typically aristocrats, but they found their political support among the hoplites and the poor who felt left out of the political life of the community. Tyrants usually served the interests of the community as a whole, not just the aristocrats. They promoted overseas trade, built harbors, protected farmers, and began public works projects to employ citizen workers and to beautify their cities. They also cultivated alliances with tyrants in other poleis to establish peace and prosperity. Most important, the tyrants' authority enabled a broad range of citizens to participate in government for the first time.

But tyrannies contained a fatal flaw. The power of the tyrant was handed down from father to son, and the successors rarely inherited their fathers' qualities of leadership. As a result, tyrannies often became oppressive and unpopular, especially among the hoplites and poor who had supported the tyrants in the first place. Few tyrannies lasted more than two generations.

The most famous of the early Greek tyrannies arose in the large and immensely wealthy and powerful polis of Corinth in the mid-seventh century B.C.E. For many years an aristocratic family, the Bacchiads, had dominated Corinth. In 657 B.C.E., however, the tyrant Cypselus, who had been born into this family, seized power with popular support. He ruthlessly suppressed his aristocratic rivals but maintained his popularity with the people. Disenchantment, however, set in with the rule of Cypselus's son, Periander, who succeeded his father in 625 B.C.E. Periander's brutal methods of rule, which included the systematic execution or banishment of his political opponents and the murder of his wife, lost him the support of the people. Soon after his succession by a third tyrant, in 585 B.C.E., Corinth replaced the tyranny with an aristocratic form of government.

tyrants Rulers in Greek city-states, usually members of the aristocracy, who seized power illegitimately rather than acquiring it by heredity or election. Tyrants often gained political support from the hoplites and the poor.

CORINTH: CITADEL AT THE CROSS-ROADS One of the reasons for the legendary wealth of Corinth was its strategic position dominating the narrow land passage between the Peloponnese and mainland Greece and the crossing of ships over the Isthmus.

oligarchy A government consisting of only a few people rather than the entire community.

democracy A form of government in which citizens devise their own governing institutions and choose their leaders; began in Athens, Greece, in the fifth century B.C.E.

helots The brutally oppressed subject peoples of the Spartans. Tied to the land they farmed for Spartan masters, they were treated little better than beasts of burden.

Contrasting Societies of the Archaic Age

The two most important poleis on the Greek mainland, Sparta and Athens, developed very different political and social systems during the Archaic Age. Both city-states experienced hoplite revolutions, and both resisted the rule of tyrants, but they nonetheless developed in different directions. Sparta became an **oligarchy**, which means government by a few. Athens, on the other hand, developed into a **democracy**, a word meaning rule by the people. Democracy is a form of political organization in which the people share equally in the government of their communities, devise their own political institutions, and select their own leaders.

SPARTA: A MILITARIZED SOCIETY Cut off from the rest of Greece by mountain ranges to the west and north, Sparta dominated the Peloponnese, the southernmost part of Greece. Until about 700 B.C.E. Spartans lived much like other Greeks except that their hoplites, who called themselves "the Equals," achieved political power without the aid of tyrants. Sparta was formally a monarchy, ruled by two hereditary kings, each from one of the city-state's prominent aristocratic families. The two kings were equal in authority, which meant that one could veto the decisions of the other, except in time of war, when one of the kings was chosen commander in chief. Effective political power in this polis, however, resided in the *gerousia*, a council of 28 elders whom the assembly of Spartan citizens, known as the *damos*, elected for life. The damos, which comprised only hoplites, had little effective power. It elected the members of the gerousia by acclamation and could only vote to accept or reject policies that this council proposed.

Rapid expansion in the Peloponnese prompted Spartans to develop a highly militarized society, especially after 700 B.C.E., when the Spartans conquered Messenia, a fertile region in the western Peloponnese. To control the Messenians, who vastly outnumbered them, the Spartans reduced the Messenians to the status of **helots** or serfs. Technically free, helots were nevertheless bound to the land and forced to farm it for the Spartans who owned it. If a Spartan master sold the land to another Spartan, the helots stayed with the land. Helots paid half of their produce to their Spartan masters, who could and did kill them with impunity. Controlling the helots through terror became the Spartans' preoccupation.

In Sparta's social hierarchy free subjects stood one level above the helots. They included merchants, manufacturers, and other businessmen who lived in communities throughout Spartan territories. Free subjects paid taxes and served in the army when necessary, but they were not Spartan citizens.

The male and female citizens of Sparta stood at the top of the social pyramid. The greatest responsibility of all Spartan citizens was to fulfill the military needs of the polis. From early childhood, boys trained to become soldiers and girls trained to become the wives and mothers of soldiers. Boys left home at age 7 to live in barracks, where they mastered the skills of battle. They were periodically beaten to make them able to endure pain without flinching. Their comrades-in-arms played a more important role in their lives than their own families. Young married Spartan men were not permitted to live with their wives, but had to sneak away from their barracks at night to visit them.

Contempt for pain and hardship, blind obedience to orders, simplicity in word and deed, and courage were the chief Spartan virtues. Cowardice had no place in this society. Before sending their men to war, wives and mothers warned, "Come home with your shield—or on it!" Sparta's armies won a reputation as the most ferocious fighting force in all of Greece.

After its conquest of Messenia, Sparta organized the Peloponnesian League, an informal alliance of most of the other poleis in the Peloponnese, which it dominated. Spartans avoided wars far from home, but they and their allies joined with the Athenians and other Greeks in resisting Persia's aggression against Greece, as we will see shortly.

ATHENS: TOWARD DEMOCRACY Athens, the best known polis of ancient Greece, made an incalculably rich contribution to the political, philosophical, artistic, and literary traditions of Western civilization. The first democracy in the ancient world, Athens developed principles of government that remain alive today. Athens's innovative form of government and the flowering of its intellectual life stemmed directly from its response to tyranny and Persian aggression.

In the eighth and seventh centuries B.C.E., the Athenians settled Attica, the territory surrounding their city, rather than sending colonists abroad. In this way, Athens gained more land—about 1,000 square miles, the size of Rhode Island—and a larger population than any other polis on the Greek mainland. By the beginning of the sixth century, aristocrats controlled most of the wealth of Attica, and many of the Athenian peasants became heavily indebted to them. They risked being sold into slavery abroad if they could not repay their debts.

To forestall civil war between the debt-ridden peasantry and the aristocracy, both segments of the population of Attica agreed to let Solon, an Athenian statesman known for his practical wisdom, reform the political system. In 594 B.C.E. Solon (ca. 650–570 B.C.E.) enacted several reforms that limited the authority of the aristocracy and enabled all male citizens to participate more fully in public life. These reforms created the institutions from which democracy eventually developed. Solon cancelled debts, eliminated debt-slavery, and bought the freedom of Athenians who had been enslaved abroad. Taking advantage of a rise in literacy, Solon directed scribes to record his new laws on wooden panels for the whole community to read. This policy diminished aristocratic control of the interpretation of Athenian law and ensured that the laws would be enforced fairly for all Athenian citizens, regardless of their status.

Solon next organized the population into four political groups based on wealth. Only men in the two richest groups could hold the highest administrative office of *archon* and be elected to the highest court, traditionally a base of aristocratic authority. The third group could hold lower political office. The fourth group, the landless *thetes*, who could not afford hoplite weapons, did not hold any offices in the polis. All four groups, however, were represented in the council or **boule** of 400 male citizens (100 from each class), which served as an advisory body for the general assembly of all male citizens. Finally, men of any class could serve on a new court that Solon established. Women, slaves, and foreigners had no voice in government at all.

The changes introduced by Solon did not end social discontent or achieve political stability. Small farmers continued to become impoverished despite his cancellation of agricultural debt; many of them lost their land to their creditors. Solon's political compromises satisfied no one. The aristocracy felt that Solon had given away too much of their power, whereas the merchants, shopkeepers, and artisans who occupied the third political group were unhappy because they had not received more political power. Most of the elected offices remained in the hands of the aristocracy.

Capitalizing on this widespread discontent, a nobleman named Peisistratus (ca. 590–528 B.C.E.) seized power in 561 and ruled Athens as a tyrant from 547 until his death in 528 B.C.E. Like other tyrannies in Greece, Peisistratus's regime initially enjoyed wide support. He alleviated the plight of the small landowners by giving them land that he had seized from aristocrats. He sponsored building works, supported religious festivals, encouraged trade and economic development, and supported the arts. He initiated a vigorous tradition of Athenian intellectual life by inviting artists and poets to come to Athens from all over Greece. His sons, however, abused their power, and jealous aristocrats, assisted by Sparta, toppled the family's rule in 510. Peisistratus's surviving son fled to Persia.

Two years later, the assembly selected a nobleman named Cleisthenes to reorganize Athenian political institutions. By cleverly rearranging the basic political units of Attica into 10 artificial tribes, Cleisthenes unified this territory and made Athens the center of all important political activity. Building upon Solon's reforms, he set the basic

boule A council of 400 male citizens established by Solon in Greece in the sixth century B.C.E. It served as an advisory body for the general assembly of all male citizens.

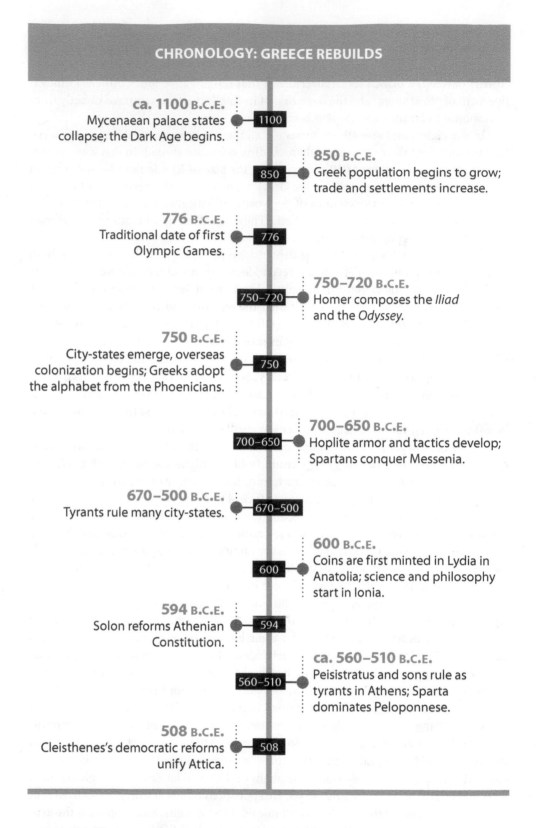

CHRONOLOGY: GREECE REBUILDS

ca. 1100 B.C.E.
Mycenaean palace states collapse; the Dark Age begins.
1100

850 B.C.E.
850
Greek population begins to grow; trade and settlements increase.

776 B.C.E.
Traditional date of first Olympic Games.
776

750–720 B.C.E.
750–720
Homer composes the *Iliad* and the *Odyssey*.

750 B.C.E.
City-states emerge, overseas colonization begins; Greeks adopt the alphabet from the Phoenicians.
750

700–650 B.C.E.
700–650
Hoplite armor and tactics develop; Spartans conquer Messenia.

670–500 B.C.E.
Tyrants rule many city-states.
670–500

600 B.C.E.
600
Coins are first minted in Lydia in Anatolia; science and philosophy start in Ionia.

594 B.C.E.
Solon reforms Athenian Constitution.
594

ca. 560–510 B.C.E.
560–510
Peisistratus and sons rule as tyrants in Athens; Sparta dominates Peloponnese.

508 B.C.E.
Cleisthenes's democratic reforms unify Attica.
508

institutions of democracy in place with a new boule of 500 male citizens, in which each of the tribes chose 50 members by lot. The boule heard proposals from citizens and on this basis made up the agenda for the assembly, which consisted of all adult male citizens. All these male citizens could also hold public office. In this way Cleisthenes broke the power of aristocratic families and set up the lasting, fundamental structures of Athenian democracy.

📖 **Read the Document**

Aristotle: The Creation of the Democracy in Athens

The Greek Encounter with Persia

3.2 How did the Persian Empire bring the peoples of the Near East together in a stable realm, and what elements of Persian religion and government have influenced Western thought?

Persian history began about 1400 B.C.E., when small groups of herdsmen started migrating into western Iran from areas north of the Caspian Sea. Over 500 years these settlers slowly coalesced into two closely related groups, the Medes and the Persians.

By about 900 B.C.E., the Medes had established mastery over all the peoples of the Iranian plateau, including the Persians. In 612 B.C.E., with the assistance of the Babylonians, the Medes conquered the Assyrians. They then pushed into central Anatolia (modern Turkey), Afghanistan, and possibly farther into Central Asia. In the sixth century, under the leadership of Cyrus the Great (r. 550–530 B.C.E.), Persia broke away from Median rule and soon conquered the kingdom of the Medes. Under the guidance of this brilliant monarch and his successors, the Persians acquired a vast empire. They followed a monotheistic religion, Zoroastrianism, and governed their subjects with a combination of tolerance and firmness.

Cyrus the Great and Persian Expansion

After ascending to the Persian throne Cyrus (r. ca. 550–530 B.C.E.) embarked on a dazzling 20-year career of conquest. His military genius and organizational skills transformed the small kingdom into a giant multiethnic empire that stretched from India to the Mediterranean Sea. Cyrus's swift victory over the Medes put Persia at the center of the Near East and thrust it into encounters with a diverse array of peoples.

Cyrus, who took the title of Great King, expanded his empire in several stages. In 546 B.C.E. he conquered Anatolia, where he first came into contact with Greeks. After his victories over these Greek cities, he installed loyal Greek rulers. Next he defeated the kingdom of Babylonia in 539 B.C.E., thus gaining control of Mesopotamia. Then he overran Afghanistan and fortified it against the raids of the Scythian nomads who lived on the steppe lands to the north. These fierce warriors posed a perpetual threat to the settled territories of Persia.

After Cyrus died in 530 B.C.E., his son Cambyses II (r. 529–522 B.C.E.) continued his father's policy of expansion by subduing Egypt and the wealthy Phoenician port cities of the Levant. Control of Phoenician naval resources enabled Persia to extend its empire overseas to Cyprus and the islands of the Aegean. Within barely 30 years, Persia had become the mightiest empire in the world, with territorial possessions spanning Europe, the Near East, and North Africa (see **Map 3.2**).

To ensure that they could easily communicate with their subjects, the Great Kings of Persia developed an elaborate system of roads that their Assyrian predecessors had begun to link their provinces. Officials maintained supply stations at regular intervals along these roads. The chief branch of this system, called the Royal Road, stretched between Anatolia and the Persian homeland in Iran. Persian roads not only facilitated the transportation of soldiers and commercial goods from one part of the empire to another, but they also made possible the flow of ideas and the transmission of cultural traditions.

The key to maintaining power over such a diverse empire lay in the Persian government's treatment of its many ethnic groups. The highly centralized Persian government wielded absolute power, but it rejected the brutal model of the Assyrian and Babylonian imperial system in favor of a more tolerant approach. After conquering Babylonia Cyrus allowed peoples exiled by the Babylonians, including the Hebrews, to return to their homelands. Subject peoples could worship freely and enjoy local

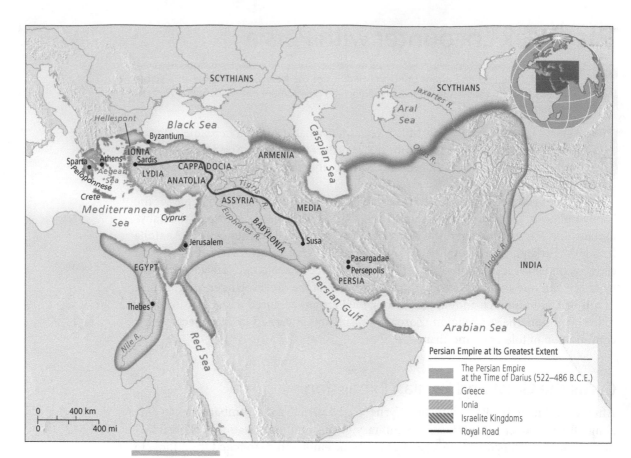

MAP **3.2** THE PERSIAN EMPIRE AT ITS GREATEST EXTENT The Persian Empire begun by Cyrus about 550 B.C.E. grew to include all of the Middle East as far as India, Egypt, and northern Greece. This multiethnic, multireligious empire governed its many peoples firmly but tolerantly. How did Persia try to hold this vast empire together?

autonomy if they acknowledged the political supremacy of the Great King. (See *Different Voices* in this chapter.)

ZOROASTRIANISM: AN IMPERIAL RELIGION The Great Kings of Persia and the Persian people followed **Zoroastrianism**, a monotheistic religion that still has followers around the world today. Its founder, the prophet Zarathustra, known more commonly by his Greek name Zoroaster, lived and preached sometime between 1400 and 900 B.C.E. His message spread throughout Iran for many centuries before it became Persia's chief faith.

Persians transmitted Zoroaster's teachings, known collectively as the *Avesta*, through oral tradition until scribes recorded them in the sixth century C.E. According to Zoroaster, Ahura Mazda (Lord Wisdom), the one and only god of all Creation, is the cause of all good things in the universe. He represents wisdom, justice, and proper order among all created things. Another supernatural being, Angra Mainyu (or Ahriman), the spirit of destruction and disorder, opposes Ahura Mazda and threatens his benevolent arrangement of creation. The conflict between good and evil supernatural powers means that Zoroastrianism is a **dualistic** but not a polytheistic religion, because Angra Mainyu does not possess divine status.

In Zoroastrian belief, Ahura Mazda will eventually triumph in this struggle with the forces of evil, leaving all creation to enjoy a blissful eternity. Until then, the cosmic fight between Ahura Mazda's forces of light and Angra Mainyu's forces of darkness gives meaning to human existence and lays the foundation for a profoundly ethical way of life. Ahura Mazda requires humans to contribute to the well-being of the world. Everyone must choose between right and wrong actions.

Zoroastrianism The monotheistic religion of Persia founded by Zoroaster that became the official religion of the Persian Empire.

dualistic A term used to describe a philosophy or a religion in which a rigid distinction is made between body and mind, good and evil, or the material and the immaterial world.

Different Voices
Liberty and Despotism in Ancient Persia

During the Persian Wars (490–479 B.C.E.), Greeks developed an image of Persia as a despotic state that denied its subjects the liberty that Greeks enjoyed in their poleis. The voices of Cyrus the Great King of Persia in the sixth century B.C.E. and the Greek historian Herodotus in the fifth century B.C.E. reveal how misleading those stereotypes could be. On the day of his coronation as king of Babylon in 539 B.C.E., Cyrus issued a proclamation assuring the Babylonian people that he would rule peacefully, repeal the oppressive burdens imposed on them by the tyrant Nabonidus, and restore the images of the Babylonian and Sumerian gods that Nabonidus had banished from their sanctuaries. Cyrus appeals to Marduk, the Babylonian god, to legitimize his rule. It is misleading to consider this proclamation the "first charter of human rights," a claim based on an inaccurate translation made in 1971. Nonetheless, Cyrus, known as "The Lawgiver," did use this opportunity to guarantee Babylonians freedom of religious worship and end the despotic rule of Babylon's last king.

The Greek historian Herodotus, who grew up in Ionia while it was under Persian control, also challenged the prevailing Greek stereotype of Persian despotism. In this excerpt from The Histories, Herodotus claimed that Persia had discussed the merits and drawbacks of the three forms of government—monarchy, oligarchy, and democracy—when Darius I (r. 522–486 B.C.E.) succeeded Cyrus as Great King. Darius decided in favor of maintaining monarchical rule, but he reputedly defended his position on the grounds that the king had given Persians their "freedom" and only he could preserve that liberty.

Cyrus Ends the Despotism of a Babylonian Tyrant

When I went as harbinger of peace i[nt]o Babylon I founded my sovereign residence within the royal palace amid celebration and rejoicing. Marduk, the great lord, bestowed on me as my destiny the great magnanimity of one who loves Babylon, and I every day sought him out in awe. My vast troops marched peaceably in Babylon, and the whole of [Sumer] and Akkad had nothing to fear. I sought the welfare of the city of Babylon and all its sanctuaries. As for the population of Babylon [. . . , w]ho as if without div[ine intention] had endured a yoke not decreed for them, I soothed their weariness, I freed them from their bonds(?). Marduk, the great lord, rejoiced at [my good] deeds, and he pronounced a sweet blessing over me, the king who fears him, . . . From [Shuanna] I sent back to their places . . . the gods who lived therein, and made permanent sanctuaries for them. I collected together all of their people and returned them to their settlements, and the gods of the land of Sumer and Akkad which Nabonidus—to the fury of the lord of the gods—had brought into Shuanna, at the command of Marduk, the great lord, I returned them unharmed to their cells, in the sanctuaries that make them happy. May all the gods that I returned to their sanctuaries, every day before Marduk and Nabu, ask for a long life for me, and mention my good deed.

SOURCE: http://www.britishmuseum.org/explore/highlights/article_index/c/cyrus_cylinder_-_translation.aspx. Excerpts from the translation of the *Cyrus Cylinder* by Irving Finkel are used by permission. Copyright © by The Trustees of the British Museum.

Herodotus Recounts Persia's Rejection of Democracy

Otanes recommended that the management of public affairs should be entrusted to the whole nation. "To me," he said, "it seems advisable, that we should no longer have a single man to rule over us—the rule of one is neither good nor pleasant. . . . How indeed is it possible that monarchy should be a well-adjusted thing, when it allows a man to do as he likes without being answerable? Such license is enough to stir strange and unwonted thoughts in the heart of the worthiest of men. Give a person this power, and straightway his manifold good things puff him up with pride . . . leading on to deeds of savage violence. . . . He sets aside the laws of the land, puts men to death without trial, and subjects women to violence. The rule of the many, on the other hand . . . is free from all those outrages which a king is wont to commit. . . . I vote, therefore, that we do away with monarchy, and raise the people to power."

Megabyzus spoke next, and advised the setting up of an oligarchy: "In all that Otanes has said to persuade you to put down monarchy," he observed, "I fully concur; but his recommendation that we should call the people to power seems to me not the best advice. For there is nothing so void of understanding, nothing so full of wantonness, as the unwieldy rabble. It were folly not to be borne, for men, while seeking to escape the wantonness of a tyrant, to give themselves up to the wantonness of a rude unbridled mob. . . . Let the enemies of the Persians be ruled by democracies; but let us choose out from the citizens a certain number of the worthiest, and put the government into their hands. For thus both we ourselves shall be among the governors, and power being entrusted to the best men, it is likely that the best counsels will prevail in the state." . . .

After him Darius came forward, and spoke as follows: "All that Megabyzus said against democracy was well said, I think; but about oligarchy he did not speak advisedly; for take these three forms of government—democracy, oligarchy, and monarchy—and let them each be at their best, I maintain that monarchy far surpasses the other two. What government can possibly be better than that of the very best man in the whole state? . . . Contrariwise, in oligarchies, where men vie with each other in the service of the commonwealth, fierce enmities are apt to arise between man and man, each wishing to be leader, and to carry his own measures; whence violent quarrels come, which lead to open strife, often ending in bloodshed. Then monarchy is sure to follow; and this too shows how far that rule surpasses all others. . . .

Lastly, to sum up all in a word, whence, I ask, was it that we got the freedom which we enjoy? Did democracy give it us, or oligarchy, or a monarch? As a single man recovered our freedom for us, my sentence is that we keep to the rule of one.

SOURCE: Herodotus, *The Histories*, trans. by George Rawlinson III. 80-1. (New York: Dutton, London: Dent, 1962). Reprinted by permission of Everyman's Library, Random House UK.

(continued on next page)

(continued from previous page)

For Discussion

1. Was the edict issued by Cyrus in 539 B.C.E. really a charter of human rights? What practical political considerations might have led him to issue this edict?

2. Did Darius's criticism of democracy and defense of monarchy have any merit, or were they merely rhetorical justifications of Darius's own desire for power?

View the Closer Look

Zoroastrianism: An Ancient Religion in Modern Times

At the Day of Judgment, sinners who have not listened to Ahura Mazda's instructions, such as those succumbing to the "filth of intoxication," will suffer eternal torment in a deep pit of terrible darkness. Those who have lived ethical lives will live forever in a world purged of evil. In a period of transformation called "the Making Wonderful," the dead will be resurrected, and all will live together in the worship of Ahura Mazda.

The Great Kings of Persia believed themselves to be Ahura Mazda's earthly representatives, responsible for fighting the forces of disorder in their world. Zoroastrianism thus provided an ideological support for the Persian Empire's wars of conquest and rule. The Great Kings lavishly supported the Zoroastrian church, and its priests, called magi, established the faith as the empire's official religion. They built grand temples with sacred fires throughout the empire. Although the Persian Empire tolerated other religions, Zoroastrianism became the official religion that supported the Great Kings.

Zoroastrian beliefs played an important role in shaping the three great Western religions: Judaism, Christianity, and Islam. The Zoroastrian belief that a powerful spirit of evil opposed God contributed to the Jewish belief in Satan, who appears in the later books of the Hebrew Bible as a demon with a distinct personality. In the first century C.E. Christians transformed Satan, whom they also called the Devil, into a cosmic force of evil. The Christian belief in a final struggle against the Devil, followed by the establishment of the kingdom of God on Earth, also originated in Zoroastrianism. The Zoroastrian idea of a final judgment, followed by an afterlife in Heaven or Hell, became a central concept in Christianity and Islam, although it was later downplayed within Judaism.

Persia Under Darius the Great

In 522 B.C.E. Darius, a Persian nobleman related to the royal family, seized the imperial throne by murdering one of the sons of Cyrus the Great. Assuming the status of the new Great King, Darius I inaugurated a new period of territorial expansion and cultural activity that lasted until the Macedonian conqueror Alexander the Great overwhelmed Persia in 330 B.C.E.

Darius controlled an efficient administration. He expanded and improved Persia's roads, set up a postal system, and standardized measures and coinage. He also reorganized Cyrus's system of provincial government, dividing the empire into 20 provinces called satrapies. Each province paid an annual sum to the central government based on its productivity. From the provincial capitals the governors, Persian noblemen called satraps, collected these taxes, gathered military recruits, and oversaw the bureaucracy.

View the Closer Look

Persepolis: A Royal City

By 513 B.C.E. Darius had greatly expanded his empire. On his northeastern frontier he annexed parts of India as far as the Indus River. To facilitate commerce he built a canal in Egypt that linked the Mediterranean and Red Seas. His conquests on the northwestern frontier of the Persian Empire, however, had the greatest impact on Western civilization because they brought Persia into direct contact with the Greeks. Eager to conquer Greece, Darius sent troops across the Hellespont to establish military bases in the north of Greece. Such incursions along the Greek frontier were only a small part of Darius's grand imperial strategy, but to the Greeks the growing Persian

DARIUS THE GREAT GIVING AN AUDIENCE In this carved panel from the Treasury of the Palace at Persepolis, the Great King Darius I (r. 522–486 B.C.E.) is shown receiving a dignitary. Darius is seated on his throne and holds a staff of office. Subject kings from all over the Persian Empire also came to court to pay their respects and bring tribute.

presence caused profound anxiety. The stage was set for the confrontation between the Persians and the Greeks, a conflict that demonstrated the limits of Persian imperialism.

Around 510 B.C.E. Darius conquered the Ionian Greek poleis. The Persians ruled their new subjects with a light hand, but the Ionian Greeks nevertheless revolted in 499 B.C.E. and asked Sparta and Athens for military assistance. The Spartans, who were further away from Ionia, refused, but the Athenians sent an expeditionary force that helped the rebels burn Sardis, a Persian provincial capital. The Persians crushed the rebellion in 494 B.C.E., but they did not forget Athens's intervention in it.

The Persian Wars, 490–479 B.C.E.

In 490 B.C.E., after four years of meticulous planning, a Persian army crossed the Aegean Sea in the ships of their Phoenician subjects. They landed at the beach of Marathon, some 26 miles from Athens. The area around Marathon was the traditional stronghold of the family of Peisistratus, the former Athenian tyrant. The Persians planned to install Peisistratus's son Hippias as the new tyrant of Athens.

To save their city, the Athenians marched to Marathon, and with the aid of troops from a neighboring polis (Spartan reinforcements arrived too late) defeated the Persians. The surprising Greek victory demonstrated that a force of heavily armed hoplites could defeat a more numerous but more lightly armored body of Persian infantry. Pride in this Greek victory also unified Athenians by making it unpopular to advocate a treaty or an alliance with Persia, as many had done before the battle.

After Marathon, Athens embraced even more dramatic reforms. A new political leader, Themistocles (ca. 523–ca. 458 B.C.E.), persuaded his fellow citizens to spend the proceeds from a rich silver mine in Attica on a new navy and port. By 480 B.C.E. Athens possessed nearly 200 warships, called **triremes**. With three banks of oars manned by the poorest citizens of the polis, who were paid to row them, the triremes transformed Athens

triremes Greek warships with three banks of oars. Triremes manned by the poorest people of Athenian society became the backbone of the Athenian Empire.

91

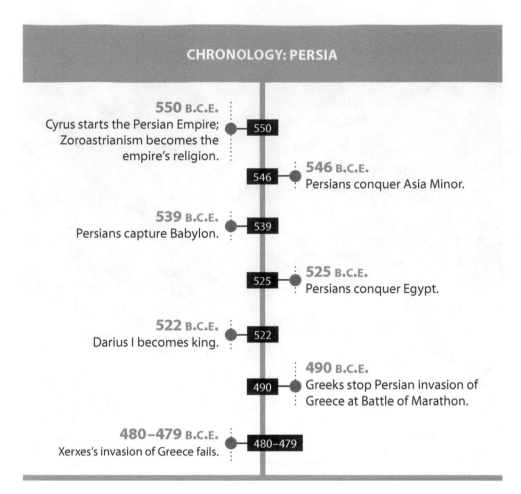

CHRONOLOGY: PERSIA

550 B.C.E.
Cyrus starts the Persian Empire; Zoroastrianism becomes the empire's religion.

550

546

546 B.C.E.
Persians conquer Asia Minor.

539 B.C.E.
Persians capture Babylon.

539

525

525 B.C.E.
Persians conquer Egypt.

522 B.C.E.
Darius I becomes king.

522

490

490 B.C.E.
Greeks stop Persian invasion of Greece at Battle of Marathon.

480–479 B.C.E.
Xerxes's invasion of Greece fails.

480–479

into a naval powerhouse. The entire male citizen body of Athens, not just the aristocrats and hoplites, could now be called to arms. The Athenian navy embodied Athenian democracy in action in that every male citizen had an obligation to defend his homeland.

Marathon dealt a blow to the Persians' pride that they resolved to avenge, but a major revolt in Egypt and Darius's death in 486 B.C.E. prevented them from invading Greece again for nearly a decade. In 480 B.C.E., Xerxes I, the new Great King, launched a massive invasion of Greece. He brought an overwhelming force of some 150,000 soldiers, a navy of nearly 700 mostly Phoenician vessels, and ample supplies. His troops crossed from Asia into Europe by means of a bridge of boats over the Hellespont, while the navy followed by sea in order to supply the troops. They intended to smash Athens.

Terrified by the size of the Persian army, fewer than 40 of the more than 700 Greek poleis joined the defensive coalition that had formed in anticipation of the invasion. Under the leadership of Sparta, the Greek allies planned to hold back the Persian land force in the north, while the Athenian navy would attack the invaders at sea. Leonidas, the Spartan king, led the coalition. A Greek force under his command stopped the Persians at the pass of Thermopylae until a traitor revealed an alternate path through the mountains that allowed the Persians to attack the Greeks from the rear. On the last day of the battle Leonidas, his entire force of 300 Spartans, and perhaps 1,200 allies died fighting.

Their sacrifice was not in vain. Thermopylae gave the Athenians precious time to evacuate their city and station their highly maneuverable fleet in the narrow straits of Salamis, just off the Athenian coast. In a stunning display of naval skill, the Athenian triremes defeated the Persian navy in a single day of heavy fighting. Xerxes returned to Persia, although he left a large army in central Greece.

Early in 479 B.C.E. a combined Greek army once again stopped the Persians at the Battle of Plataea, north of Attica. In this battle a large contingent of Spartans led the

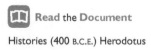

Read the Document

Histories (400 B.C.E.) Herodotus

LEONIDAS MONUMENT, THERMOPYLAE This monument celebrating the heroism of Leonidas and the Spartans at the Battle of Thermopylae in 480 B.C.E. was commissioned in 1955 by King Paul of Greece.

decisive final charge. The surviving Persian troops were driven out of Greece. That same year, the combined Greek naval force again defeated the Persian navy off the Ionian coast. Xerxes gave up the attempt to conquer Greece.

The Classical Age of Greece, 479–336 B.C.E.

3.3 What were the intellectual, social, and political innovations of Greece in the Classical Age?

The defeat of mighty Persia by a handful of Greek cities shocked the Mediterranean world. Xerxes's failure did not seriously weaken Persia, but it greatly strengthened the Greeks' own position in the Mediterranean and enhanced what we would now call their self-image. After the defeat of the Persians, the Greeks exhibited immense confidence in their ability to shape their political institutions and to describe and analyze their society and the world around them. The emboldened Athenians created a powerful empire that made them the dominant power in the Greek world while democratic institutions flourished in the polis. Yet Athens's very success sowed the seeds of its demise. After alienating many of the other Greek poleis, Athens lost the long and bitter Peloponnesian War with Sparta.

The distinguishing feature of the Classical Age was its remarkable creativity, especially in drama, science, history writing, philosophy, and the visual arts. Despite the turmoil of the Persian and Peloponnesian Wars, Greek society remained rigidly hierarchical with strictly defined gender roles and many slaves who did much of the heavy work. The structures of Greek society provided many male citizens with leisure time for debating public affairs in a democratic fashion, attending plays, and speculating about philosophical issues. The numerous Greek gods became the subject of much Greek art. Greeks worshiped these gods in temples in the Classical style, which the Romans and other Western peoples later imitated. None of the Greek cities produced as many creative men as Athens, which makes its experience as an empire and a democracy particularly revealing.

The Rise and Fall of the Athenian Empire

With the Persian threat to Greece nearly eliminated, Athens began a period of rapid imperial expansion. This aggressive foreign policy eventually backfired. It created resentment among the other Greek city-states that led to war and the collapse of the Athenian Empire.

FROM DEFENSIVE ALLIANCE TO EMPIRE After the Battle of Plataea, the Greek defensive alliance set out to evict the Persians from the Ionian coast. The Spartans soon grew disillusioned with this campaign and withdrew their troops, leaving Athenians in charge. In the winter of 478 B.C.E., Athens reorganized the alliance, creating the **Delian League**, named for the small island of Delos where the members of the league met. Athens contributed approximately 200 warships to continue attacks against the Persians, while the other members supplied either ships or funds to pay for them. The league ultimately gathered a naval force of 300 ships. By 469 B.C.E. it had driven the last Persians from the Aegean.

With the Persians ousted, several poleis tried to leave the league, but the Athenians forced them to remain in it. The Athenians were rapidly turning the Delian League into an Athenian Empire organized for their own benefit. In subsequent decades the Athenians established garrisons in many cities of the league and intervened in their political life by imposing heavy taxes and financial regulations. Several revolts broke out, but no polis in the empire could overcome Athens's might. In 460 B.C.E. Athens sent approximately 4,000 men and 200 warships to assist an Egyptian revolt against Persia, but Persia destroyed the expedition. Sobered by this debacle, the Athenians moved the treasury of the Delian League from Delos to Athens, claiming that they were protecting it from Persian retaliation. In fact, the Athenians spent the league treasury on public buildings in Athens, including the Parthenon. Athens had become indifferent to the original purpose of the league, but the revenues it generated by exploiting the other cities in the league simultaneously enabled democracy to flourish in Athens itself.

Delian League The alliance among many Greek cities organized by Athens in 478 B.C.E. in order to fight Persian forces in the eastern Aegean Sea. The Athenians gradually turned the Delian League into the Athenian Empire.

WARFARE AT SEA In the Classical world, navies relied on long-rowed vessels with bronze battering rams to attack enemy ships. This painting of a war galley was made about 550 B.C.E. and shows soldiers, oarsmen, and a man at the helm. Athenians perfected the war galley. Their ships could reach a speed of more than nine nautical miles per hour for short distances.

DEMOCRACY IN THE AGE OF PERICLES The chief designer of the Athenian Empire was Pericles (ca. 490–429 B.C.E.), an aristocrat who dominated Athenian politics from 461 B.C.E. until his death. During the so-called "Age of Pericles," Athenian democracy at home and empire abroad reached their peak.

During the Age of Pericles, Athens had about 40,000 male citizens. Only free men over age 18 could participate in the city's political life. Women, foreigners, slaves, and other imperial subjects had no voice in public life.

The representative council of 500 men established by Cleisthenes continued to administer public business. The citizen assembly met every 10 days and probably never had more than 5,000 citizens in attendance, except on the most important occasions. The assembly decided issues of war, peace, and public policy by majority vote. Because men gained political power through debate in the assembly, a politician's rhetorical skills were crucial in convincing voters.

Ten officials called *generals* were elected every year by popular vote to handle high affairs of state and direct Athens's military forces. Generals typically were aristocrats of proven expertise. Pericles, for example, was reelected general almost continually for more than 20 years.

The vast increase in public business required to run the empire multiplied the number of administrators. By the middle of the fifth century, Athens had about 1,500 officials in its bureaucracy. Boards of assessors determined how much money the members of the Delian League had to pay. Legal disputes among cities in the league forced Athens to increase the number of its courts. Because of the constant need for jurors and other officeholders, Pericles began paying wages for public service, the first such policy in history. Jurors were chosen by lot, and trials lasted no more than a day to expedite cases, save money, and prevent jury tampering.

Pericles also gave women a more important role in Athenian society. Before 451 B.C.E. children born to Athenian men and their foreign wives became full citizens. Pericles allowed citizenship only if both parents were Athenian citizens. As a result, Athenian women took pride in giving birth to the polis's only legitimate citizens. Nevertheless, Athenian female citizens could not speak or vote in the assembly, hold public office, or serve on juries.

Read the Document

Pericles' Funeral Oration by Thucydides, ca. 420 B.C.E.

THE PELOPONNESIAN WAR AND THE COLLAPSE OF ATHENIAN POWER Sparta and its allies felt threatened by growing Athenian power. Between 460 and 431 B.C.E., Athens and a few allies skirmished intermittently with Sparta and the Peloponnesian League it dominated. Full-scale war broke out between the two poleis in 431 B.C.E., dragging on until 404 B.C.E. (see **Map 3.3**). In the early stages of the conflict, which was called the Peloponnesian War, the Spartans repeatedly invaded Attica in the hope of defeating Athenian forces in open battle.

Thanks to Athens's fortifications, the Athenians endured these invasions. Safe behind their fortifications, they relied on their navy to deliver food and supplies from cities in the Athenian Empire. They also launched attacks against Spartan territory from the sea. Although plague struck the overcrowded city in 430 B.C.E., killing almost one-third of the population including Pericles, the Athenians fought on.

In 421 B.C.E., Sparta and Athens agreed to a 50-year truce, but a mere six years later war broke out again. The reckless policies of Alcibiades (ca. 450–404 B.C.E.), a young Athenian general, started a new round of warfare. A nephew of Pericles, Alcibiades lacked his uncle's wisdom. In 415 B.C.E. he persuaded the Athenians to send an expeditionary force of 5,000 hoplites to invade Sicily and seize the rich resources of the city of Syracuse for the war effort. Just as the fleet was about to sail, Alcibiades's enemies accused him of profaning a religious festival, and he fled to Sparta. After two years of heavy fighting, the Athenian expedition ended in utter disaster. Every Athenian ship was captured, and Athenian soldiers were killed or sold into slavery.

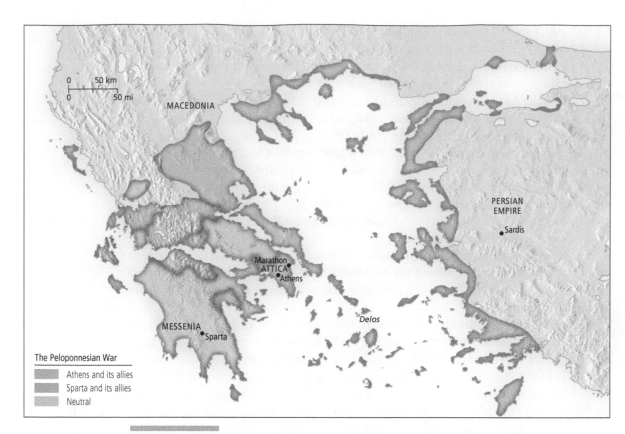

MAP **3.3** THE PELOPONNESIAN WAR During this long conflict that lasted from 431 to 404 B.C.E., the forces of Athens and its allies struggled with Sparta and its allies for control of mainland Greece. Though Sparta defeated the Athenian Empire, Athens survived as an influential force in Greek social, political, and economic life. How did the struggle for financial resources influence the outcome of the war?

The Peloponnesian War dragged on for another 10 years, but Athens never recovered from the catastrophic loss of men and ships in Sicily. At the suggestion of Alcibiades, the Spartans established a permanent military base within sight of Athens, which enabled them to control Attica. When 20,000 slaves in the Athenian silver mines escaped to freedom under the Spartans, Athens lost its main source of revenue. The final blow came when Lysander, the Spartan commander in chief, used money from Persia to build a navy strong enough to challenge Athenian sea power. At the Battle of Aegospotami on the Hellespont, Lysander's navy destroyed every Athenian ship. Athens surrendered in 404 B.C.E.

The victorious Spartan forces pulled down Athens's long walls stretching to Piraeus, but they refused to burn the city to the ground as some of its enemies demanded, because Athens had been Sparta's valiant ally in the Persian Wars. Instead, the Spartans set up an oligarchy in place of democracy. Led by the "Thirty Tyrants," a violent and conservative political faction, the oligarchy soon earned the hatred of Athenian citizens. Within a year the Athenians overthrew the tyrants and restored democracy.

Social and Religious Life in the Classical Age

During the Classical Age, the Greek poleis developed a way of life in which gender and social status determined one's position in society and politics. Greek men and women lived very different lives, guided by strict rules of behavior. A hierarchy of gender roles determined a person's access to public space, legal rights, and opportunities to work. In this emphatically patriarchal society, only men held positions of public authority, controlled wealth and inheritance, and participated in political life. Women were restricted to domestic activities that mostly took place out of sight of nonfamily members. At the bottom of society slaves of both sexes were completely subject to their masters.

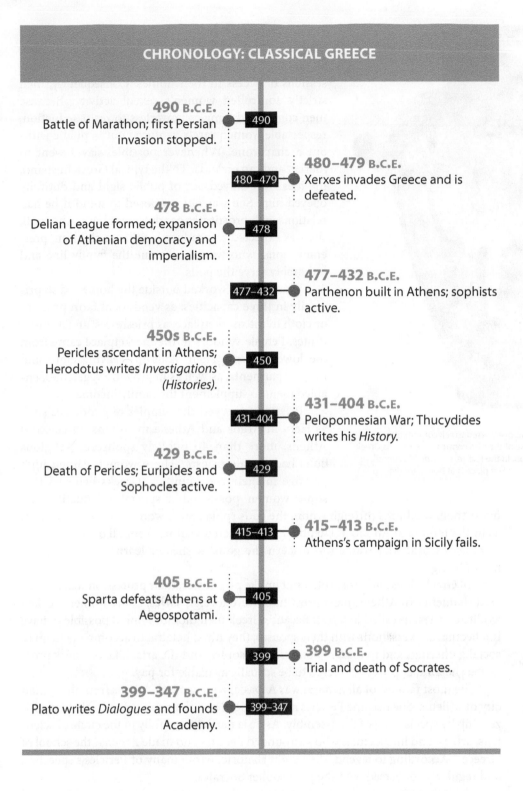

CHRONOLOGY: CLASSICAL GREECE

490 B.C.E.
Battle of Marathon; first Persian
invasion stopped.

490

480–479

480–479 B.C.E.
Xerxes invades Greece and is
defeated.

478 B.C.E.
Delian League formed; expansion
of Athenian democracy and
imperialism.

478

477–432

477–432 B.C.E.
Parthenon built in Athens; sophists
active.

450s B.C.E.
Pericles ascendant in Athens;
Herodotus writes *Investigations
(Histories).*

450

431–404

431–404 B.C.E.
Peloponnesian War; Thucydides
writes his *History.*

429 B.C.E.
Death of Pericles; Euripides and
Sophocles active.

429

415–413

415–413 B.C.E.
Athens's campaign in Sicily fails.

405 B.C.E.
Sparta defeats Athens at
Aegospotami.

405

399

399 B.C.E.
Trial and death of Socrates.

399–347 B.C.E.
Plato writes *Dialogues* and founds
Academy.

399–347

GENDER ROLES Greek women were expected to marry early in puberty, typically to men at least 10 years older than they were. Through marriage legal control of women passed from father to husband. In the case of divorce, which only men could initiate, the husband had to return his wife's dowry to her father. Most Greek houses were small and usually divided into two parts. In the brighter front rooms husbands entertained their male friends at dinner and enjoyed social interaction with other males. Wives spent most of their time in the more secluded part of the house, supervising the household slaves if there were any, raising children, dealing with their mothers-in-law, and weaving cloth.

GREEK MALE VIEW OF WOMEN In male-dominated Greek communities men idealized passive women. This Athenian vase of the fifth century B.C.E. reflects Greek men's view of a properly subordinate woman. In the image, the wife bids goodbye to her young husband, who is going off to war. Her place is at home, tending to chores until his return.

  Read the Document

Education and the Family
in Sparta, ca. 100 C.E.

hetairai Elite courtesans in ancient Greece who provided intellectual as well as sexual companionship.

Greek men feared that their wives would commit adultery, which carried the risk of illegitimate offspring and implied that husbands could not control their possessions or access to their homes. Consequently, men strictly controlled women's sexual activity. Because men considered females powerless to resist seduction, respectable women rarely ventured out in public without a chaperone. Whenever possible, slaves went to market and ran errands. To the typical Greek husband, the ideal wife stayed out of public sight and dutifully obeyed him. She was not supposed to mind if he had relations with prostitutes or adolescent boys. Above all, she was expected to produce legitimate children, preferably sons, who would continue the family line and honorably serve the polis.

Women who worked outside the home did so primarily in three capacities: as vendors of farm produce or cloth in the marketplace, as priestesses, and as prostitutes. Female vendors in the marketplace came from the lower classes. Their skills in weaving cloth and making garments, as well as in growing vegetables, enabled them to supplement the family income.

Priestesses served the temples of goddesses such as Hera in Argos and Athena in Athens. In classical Athens, more than 40 publicly sponsored religious cults had female priests. These women gained high prestige in their communities. Greeks believed that some women possessed a special spirituality that made them mediums through whom the gods spoke. Such women served as oracles, as in the temple of Apollo at Delphi. They attracted visitors from all over the Mediterranean world who wanted to discern the gods' wishes or learn what the future might bring.

All Greek cities had prostitutes, but unlike priestesses, their profession was considered shameful. In Athens, most prostitutes were foreign slaves. Some women worked as elite courtesans called **hetairai**. Because Greek men did not think it possible to have intellectual conversations with their spouses, they hired hetairai to accompany them to social gatherings and to discuss politics, philosophy, and the arts. Like ordinary prostitutes, hetairai also were expected to be sexually available for pay.

The most famous of all hetairai was Aspasia, who came to Athens from the Ionian city of Miletus. She became Pericles's companion, and their son gained Athenian citizenship by special vote of the assembly. Aspasia participated fully in the circle of scientists, artists, and intellectuals who surrounded Pericles and made Athens "the school of Greece." According to legend, she taught rhetoric, wrote many of Pericles's speeches, and regularly conversed with the philosopher Socrates.

The Athenian orator Demosthenes famously summed up Greek attitudes toward women with these words: "We have hetairai for the sake of pleasure, regular prostitutes to care for our physical needs, and wives to bear legitimate children and be loyal custodians of our households."[1]

In classical Greece, where men considered women intellectually and emotionally inferior, some men, especially prominent members of society, believed that the best sort of friendship was found in male relationships and took adolescent boys as lovers. In these relationships, which were publicly acknowledged, the older man often assumed the role of mentor to his younger companion. Some poleis institutionalized such relationships. In the city of Thebes, for example, the elite "Sacred Band" of 150 male couples led the city's hoplites into battle during the fourth century B.C.E. These men were considered the best warriors because they would not endure the shame of showing cowardice to their lovers. The Sacred Band could defeat even Spartan warriors.

SLAVERY: THE SOURCE OF GREEK PROSPERITY Slaves had no political, legal, or personal rights. Masters could kill them without serious penalty and could demand sexual favors at any time. Slavery existed in every polis and at every social level. The slave population expanded in the period after 600 B.C.E. as poleis prospered and demands for labor increased.

Most information about Greek slavery comes from Athens, which was the first major slave society that is well documented. Between about 450 and 320 B.C.E., Athens had a total population of perhaps 250,000 people, one-third of whom were enslaved. The proportion of slaves to free people was similar in other poleis. In the Archaic Age the Athenian aristocracy had begun to rely on slave labor to work their large landed estates. Most of these slaves had fallen into bondage for debt, but after Solon made the enslavement of Athenian citizens illegal in 594 B.C.E., the wealthy bought slaves outside Attica. Many slaves were captured during the Persian Wars, but most slaves were either the children of slaves or purchased from the thriving slave trade in non-Greek peoples from around the Aegean.

Slaves performed many tasks. The city of Athens owned public slaves who served as a police force, as executioners, as clerks in court, and in other capacities. Most slaves, however, were privately owned. Some were highly skilled artisans and businessmen who lived apart from their owners but were required to pay them a high percentage of their profits. Most Greek households had male and female slaves who performed menial tasks such as cooking and cleaning. Some rich landowners owned gangs of slaves who worked in the fields. Others rented slaves to the polis to labor in the silver mines, where they were worked to death under hideous conditions.

Slavery did not necessarily last until a person's death. For example, a few slaves were freed by their owners. Others saved enough money from their trades to buy their freedom. Freed slaves could not become citizens, however. Instead, they lived as resident foreigners in the polis of their former masters and often maintained close ties of loyalty and obligation to them.

Slavery was so widespread in Athens because it was profitable. The Athenian political system evolved to permit and support the exploitation of slaves to benefit the citizen class. The slaves were primarily responsible for the prosperity of Athens and gave the aristocrats the leisure to engage in intellectual pursuits and create the rich culture that became part of the core of Western civilization.

Read the Document

Aristotle on Slavery
(Fourth Century B.C.E.)

RELIGION AND THE GODS Religion permeated Greek life. Greeks worshiped many gods, whom they asked for favors and advice. Every city kept a calendar of religious observances established for certain days. Festivals marked phases in the agricultural year, such as the harvest or sowing seasons, and initiation ceremonies marked a person's transition from childhood to adulthood.

Above all, Greeks gave their devotion to the gods who protected their city. For instance, during the annual Panathenaea festival in Athens, the entire population, citizens and noncitizens alike, honored the city's patron goddess Athena with a grand procession and sacrifices. Every fourth year, the celebration was expanded to include athletic and musical competitions. In a joyous parade, the citizens would convey a robe embroidered with mythological scenes to the statue of Athena in her temple, called the Parthenon, or House of the Virgin Goddess, that stood on the Acropolis in the center of the city.

Although every polis had its own set of religious practices, people throughout the Greek world shared ideas about the gods. Like the Greek language, these shared religious beliefs gave Greeks a common identity. They also distinguished them from so-called barbarians who worshiped strange gods in ways the Greeks considered uncivilized.

Most Greeks believed that immortal and powerful gods and goddesses were all around them. These deities often embodied natural phenomena such as the sun and moon, but Greeks attributed human personalities and desires to them. Because these divine forces touched every aspect of daily life, human interactions with them were unavoidable and risky, for the gods could be as harmful as they were helpful to humans.

The Greeks believed that the 12 greatest gods lived on Mount Olympus in northern Greece as a large, dysfunctional family. Zeus was the father of some of the gods and king of them all. Hera was his sister and wife. Aphrodite was the goddess of sex and love. This jealous clan also included Apollo, god of the sun, prophecy, and medicine; Poseidon, god of the sea; and Athena, the goddess of wisdom. Greek mythology developed a set of stories about the Olympian gods that have passed into Western literature and art.

In addition to their home on Mount Olympus, the gods also maintained residences in cities. Temples served as the gods' living quarters. Worship at Greek temples consisted of offerings and sacrifices. Outside, in the open air, worshipers offered the gods small gifts, such as a small bouquet of flowers, a pinch of incense, or a small grain cake. On especially important festivals the Greeks sacrificed live animals to their gods on altars in front of the temples. Priests and priestesses supervised these rituals. The god inside the temple supposedly watched the priests prepare the sacrifice, heard the sacrificial animals bleat as their throats were slit, and listened to women howl as blood poured from the beasts. Finally, the god smelled the aroma of burning meat as the victim was cooked over the flames. Satisfied, the god awaited the next sacrifice while the cooked meat was usually distributed to the worshipers.

The Greeks also took pains to discern the future. Religious experts analyzed dreams and predicted the future based on the examination of the internal organs of sacrificed animals. Greeks and non-Greeks alike traveled to consult the priestess of Apollo, the so-called Oracle of Delphi, at a shrine in central Greece. If the god chose to reply to a query, he spoke through the mouth of his oracle, a priestess who would lapse into a trance. Priests recorded and explained the oracle's utterances, which could have more than one interpretation. When King Croesus of Lydia (r. 560–547 B.C.E.) supposedly asked the oracle what would happen if he went to war with the Persians, Apollo told him that "a great kingdom will fall." Croesus never dreamed it would be his own.

Cultural and Intellectual Life in Classical Greece

In the Classical Age, Greeks investigated the natural world and explored the human condition with astonishing freshness and vigor. Their legacy in drama, science, philosophy, and the arts has inspired people for many subsequent centuries. The term *renaissance,* which is applied to several cultural movements in later periods, refers to attempts to recapture the intellectual vitality of the Greek Classical Age and of the Romans, which drew heavily from it.

DRAMA Greek men and women examined their society's values through public dramatic performances. Athenian drama had its origins in an annual festival dedicated to Dionysus, the god of wine, which Peisistratus, the tyrant of Athens, introduced in 535 B.C.E. Plays, which included choral dancing, became part of these festivals, and authors entered their work in competition for a prestigious prize. Dramatic productions soon became a mainstay of Greek life. In their plays, usually set in the mythical past, the playwrights explored issues relevant to contemporary society. Above all, Greeks who attended the plays could expect to be educated and entertained. Fewer than 50 plays of the hundreds that were written during the Greek classical period have survived, but they count among the most powerful examples of Western literature.

In tragedies Athenian men watched stories about the terrible suffering underlying human society. In many of these plays a fatal personal flaw beyond one's ability to control led to the destruction of an important aristocrat or ruler. With an unflinching gaze, playwrights examined conflicts between violent passion and reason and between the laws of the gods and those of human communities. Their dramas depicted the terrible consequences of vengeance, the brutality of war, and the relationship of the individual to the polis. In the plays of the three great Athenian tragedians—Aeschylus, Sophocles, and Euripides—the audience learned vital lessons through the sufferings of the characters.

Aeschylus (525–456 B.C.E.) believed that the gods were just and that suffering stemmed directly from human error. His most powerful works include a trilogy called the *Oresteia*. These three plays express the notion that a polis can survive only when courts made up of citizens punish criminals, rather than leaving justice to family vendettas.

In the plays of Sophocles (ca. 496–406 B.C.E.), humans are free to act, but they are trapped by their own weaknesses, their history, and the will of the gods. In *Antigone*, a young woman buries her outlaw brother in accordance with divine principles but in defiance of her city's laws against burying rebels, knowing that she will be executed for her brave act. The misguided king who made the law and ordered her death realizes too late that a polis will prosper only if human and divine laws come into proper balance. In *Oedipus the King,* Oedipus unknowingly kills his father and marries his mother. When he learns what he has done, he blinds himself. Although he knows that fate caused his tragedy, he understands that he was the one who committed the immoral acts.

The plays of Euripides (ca. 484–406 B.C.E.) portray humans struggling against their fates. In these works, the gods have no human feeling and are capable of bestial action against humans. Euripides showed remarkable sympathy for women, who often fall victim to war and male deceit in his plays. At the end of *The Trojan Women,* the despairing Trojan queen Hecuba stands amid the smoldering ruins of her vanquished city, lamenting the cruel life as a slave that awaits her: "Lead me, who walked soft-footed once in Troy, lead me a slave where earth falls sheer away by rocky edges, let me drop and die withered away with tears."[2]

In addition to the tragedies, Greeks delighted in irreverent comedies. Performances of comedy probably began in the seventh century B.C.E. as lewd sketches associated with Dionysos, the god of wine and fertility. The playwright Aristophanes of Athens (ca. 450–388 B.C.E.) proved a master at presenting comedy as social commentary. No person, god, or institution escaped his mockery. Although committed to Athenian democracy, Aristophanes had no patience for hypocritical politicians or self-important intellectuals. His comic plays are full of raunchy sex, sarcasm, puns, and allusions to contemporary issues. Audiences howled at the fun, but these plays always carried a thought-provoking message. *The Birds* is an apt example. In this satire, Aristophanes tells the story of two down-on-their-luck Athenians who flee the city looking for peace and quiet. On their trek they have to deal with an endless stream of Athenian bureaucrats and frauds, whom Aristophanes mercilessly skewers. Finally the travelers seize power over the Kingdom of the Birds—and then transform it into a replica of Athens. This satire of Athenian imperialism shows Athenians helpless to avoid their own worst instincts.

 Read the Document

Aristophanes Argues Against the War, 411 B.C.E.

SCIENTIFIC THOUGHT Greek science began about 600 B.C.E. in the cities of Ionia, when a handful of men began to ask new questions about the natural world. Living on the border with Near Eastern civilizations, these Greek thinkers encountered the vigorous Babylonian scientific and mathematical traditions that still flourished in the Persian Empire. Carefully observing the natural world and systematically recording data, these men began to reconsider traditional Greek explanations for natural phenomena. They rejected the idea that gods arbitrarily inflicted floods, earthquakes, and other disasters on humanity. Instead, they looked for natural causes of such phenomena. To these investigators, the natural world was orderly, knowable through careful inquiry, and therefore ultimately predictable. These scientists inquired about the physical composition of the natural world, tried to identify the general principles that explained why change occurs, and began to think about proving their theories logically.

Thales of Miletus (ca. 625–547 B.C.E.), the first of these investigators, theorized that the Earth was a disk floating on water. When the Earth rocked in the water, he proposed, the motion caused earthquakes. Thales traveled to Egypt to study geometry and established the height of the pyramids by calculating the length of their shadows. Perhaps influenced by Egyptian and Babylonian teachings, he believed that water gave rise to everything else. His greatest success as an astronomer came when he predicted a solar eclipse in 585 B.C.E.

One of Thales's students, Anaximander (ca. 610–547 B.C.E.), wrote a pioneering essay about natural science called *On the Nature of Things*. Anaximander became the first Greek to create a map of the inhabited world. He also argued that the universe was rational and symmetrical. In his view, it consisted of Earth as a flat disk at its center, held in place by the perfect balance of the limitless space around it. Anaximander also believed that change occurred on Earth through tension between opposites, such as hot versus cold and dry versus wet.

A third great thinker from Miletus, Anaximenes (ca. 545–525 B.C.E.), suggested that air is the fundamental substance of the universe. Through different processes, air could become fire, wind, water, earth, or even stone. His conclusions, along with those of Thales and Anaximander, may seem odd and unsatisfactory today, but these men were pioneers in the scientific exploration of the natural world. Their willingness to remove the gods from explanations of natural phenomena, and their effort to defend their theories, established the foundations of modern scientific inquiry and observation.

These Milesian thinkers sparked inquiry in other parts of the Greek world. Heraclitus of Ephesus (ca. 500 B.C.E.) argued that fire, not gods, provided the true origin of the world. Leucippus of Miletus (fifth century B.C.E.) and Democritus of Abdera (ca. 460–370 B.C.E.) proposed that the universe consisted of an endless number of minute particles called atoms that floated everywhere. When the atoms collided or stuck together, they produced the elements of the world we live in, including life itself. These atomists had no need for gods to explain the natural world.

HISTORY The Western tradition of writing history has its roots in the work of Herodotus (ca. 484–420 B.C.E.), who grew to adulthood in the Ionian city of Halicarnassus. Herodotus sought to find the general causes of human events, not natural phenomena. He called his work *Investigations* (the original Greek meaning of the word *history*), and he attempted to explain the Persian Wars, which he considered the greatest wars ever fought.

Gods appear in Herodotus's narrative but do not cause events to occur. Instead, Herodotus attempted to show that humans always act in accordance with the general principle of reciprocity; that is, people predictably respond in equal measure to what befalls them. He described reciprocal violence in legends, such as that of the Trojan War, and recounted the conquest of Lydia by Cyrus the Great in the sixth century. He tells how the Greeks became involved in Persian affairs and finally triumphed over Persian aggression.

Herodotus traveled widely and made the description and analysis of foreign cultures an integral part of his "investigations." He frequently visited Athens, where he read portions of his history of the Persian War to appreciative audiences. He also went to Egypt, Babylonia, and other foreign lands, gathering information about local religions and customs. Herodotus relished the differences among cultures, and his narrative brims with vivid descriptions of exotic habits in far-off lands.

Although he considered Greeks superior to other peoples, Herodotus raised basic questions about cultural encounters that still engage us today. Are one culture's customs better than another's? Can we evaluate a foreign culture on its own terms or are we doomed to view the world through our own eyes and experiences?

Western civilization also owes an incalculable debt to Thucydides of Athens (d. ca. 400 B.C.E.). His brilliant *History of the Peloponnesian War* is perhaps the single most influential work of history in the Western tradition because it provides a model for analyzing the causes of human events and the outcomes of individual decisions. In it he combines meticulous attention to detail with a broad moral vision. To Thucydides, the Peloponnesian War was a tragedy. At one time under the leadership of Pericles, Athens epitomized all that was good about a human community. Its culture and political achievement had made it the "school of Greece." Unfortunately Athenians, like all humans, possessed a fatal flaw—the unrelenting desire to possess more. Never satisfied, they followed unprincipled leaders after Pericles's death, embarking on foolhardy adventures that eventually destroyed them.

In Thucydides's analysis, humans, not the gods, are entirely responsible for their own triumphs and defeats. As an analyst of the destructive impact of uncontrolled power on a society, Thucydides has no match. Even more than Herodotus, he set the standard for historical analysis in the West.

PHILOSOPHY The Greeks believed that their communities could prosper only when governed by just political institutions and fair laws. They questioned whether political and moral standards were rooted in nature or whether humans had invented them and preserved them as customs. They wondered whether absolute standards should guide polis life or whether humans are the measure of all things. No one has answered these questions satisfactorily to this day, but one of the legacies of classical Greece is that they were asked.

During the fifth century B.C.E., a group of teachers known as **Sophists**, or wise men, traveled throughout the Greek-speaking world. They shared no common doctrines, and they taught everything from mathematics to political theory with the hope of instructing people to lead better lives. The best-known Sophist was Protagoras (ca. 485–440 B.C.E.), who questioned the existence of gods and absolute standards of truth. All human institutions, he argued, were created through human custom or law and not through nature. Thus, because truth is relative, a person should be able to defend either side of an argument persuasively.

Socrates (469–399 B.C.E.) challenged the Sophists' notion that there were no absolutes to guide human life. He tried to help his fellow Athenians understand the basic moral concepts that governed their lives by relentlessly questioning them. Because Socrates wrote nothing himself, we know of his ideas chiefly through the accounts of his student, Plato (ca. 428–347 B.C.E.), who made his teacher the central figure in his own philosophical essays. (See *Justice in History* in this chapter.)

Plato established a center called the Academy in Athens for teaching and discussion, and earned a towering reputation among Greek philosophers. Like Socrates, he rejected the notion that truth and morality are relative concepts. Plato taught that absolute virtues such as goodness, justice, and beauty do exist, but on a higher level of reality than human existence. He called these eternal, unchanging absolutes **Forms**. In Platonic thought, the Forms constitute reality. Like shadows that provide only an outline of an object, what we experience in daily life merely approximates this reality.

3.1

3.2

3.3

Read the Document

Herodotus on the Egyptians
(Fifth Century B.C.E.)

Read the Document

Thucydides on Athens
(Fifth Century B.C.E.)

Sophists Professional educators who traveled throughout the ancient Greek world, teaching many subjects. Their goal was to teach people the best ways to lead better lives.

Forms In the philosophical teachings of Plato, these are eternal, unchanging absolutes such as Truth, Justice, and Beauty that represent true reality, as opposed to the approximations of reality that humans encounter in everyday life.

SYMPOSIUM At drinking parties called *symposia,* men would gather to enjoy an evening meal, complete with dancing girls, musicians, and wine. After dinner they often discussed serious issues, including philosophy and ethics. This cup, painted in Athens about 480 B.C.E., shows a young man reclining on a couch while a young woman dances for his pleasure.

Plato's theories about the existence of absolute truths and how humans can discover them continue to shape Western thought. In particular, Platonic theory emphasizes how the senses deceive us and how the truth is often hidden. We can discover truth only through careful, critical questioning rather than through observation of the physical world. As a result, Platonic thought emphasizes the superiority of theory over scientific investigation.

According to Plato, humans can gain knowledge of the Forms because we have souls that are small bits of a larger eternal Soul that enters our bodies at birth, bringing knowledge of the Forms with it. Our individual bits of Soul always seek to return to their source, but they must fight the constraints of the body and physical existence that obstruct their return. Mortals can aid the Soul in its struggle to overcome the material world by using reason to seek knowledge of the Forms. This rational quest for absolutes, Plato argued, is the particular responsibility of the philosophers, but all of us should embark on this search.

In his great political work, *The Republic,* Plato described how people might construct an ideal community based on the principles he had established. In this ideal state, educated men and women called the Guardians would lead the polis because they alone were capable of comprehending the Forms. They would supervise the brave Auxiliaries who defended the city. At the bottom of society were the Workers who produced the basic requirements of life, but were the least capable of abstract thought.

 Read the Document

Plato, *The Republic,*
The Philosopher-King

Justice in History
The Trial and Execution of Socrates the Questioner

In 399 B.C.E. the people of Athens tried and executed Socrates, their fellow citizen, for three crimes: not believing in Athenian gods, introducing new gods, and corrupting the city's young men. The charges were paradoxical, because Socrates had devoted his life to investigating how to live ethically and morally. Although Socrates could have escaped, he chose to die rather than betray his fundamental beliefs. Socrates wrote nothing down, yet his ideas and the example that he set by his life and death make him one of the most influential figures in the history of Western thought.

Born in Athens in 469 B.C.E., Socrates fought bravely during the Peloponnesian War. Afterward he openly defied the antidemocratic Thirty Tyrants whom the Spartans had installed in Athens. Socrates did not seek a career in politics or business. Instead he spent his time thinking and talking, which earned him a reputation as an eccentric. His friends, however, loved and respected him.

Socrates did not give lectures. Instead, he questioned people who believed they knew the truth. By asking them such questions as "What is justice? Beauty? Courage?" and "What is the best way to lead a good life?" Socrates revealed that they—and most people—did not truly understand their basic assumptions. Socrates did not claim to know the answers, but he did believe in the relentless application of rational argument to elicit answers. This style of questioning, known as the Socratic method, infuriated complacent men because it made them seem foolish. But it delighted people interested in taking a hard look at their most cherished beliefs.

Socrates attracted many followers. His brightest student was the philosopher Plato, to whom Socrates was not only a mentor but a hero. Plato wrote a number of dialogues, or dramatized conversations, in which Socrates appears as a questioner, pursuing the truth about an important topic. Four of Plato's dialogues—*Euthyphro, Apology, Crito,* and *Phaedo*—involve Socrates's trial and death.

The trial began when three citizens named Lycon, Meletus, and Anytus accused Socrates before a jury of 501 men. After hearing the charges, Socrates spoke in his own defense, but instead of showing remorse, he boldly defended his method of questioning. Annoyed by Socrates's stubbornness, the jury convicted him.

Athenian law permitted accusers and defendants to suggest alternative penalties. When the accusers asked for death, Socrates responded with astonishing arrogance. He suggested instead that Athens pay him for making the city a better place. Outraged by this response, the jury chose death by an even wider margin. Socrates accepted their verdict calmly.

While Socrates sat in prison waiting for his execution, a friend named Crito offered to help him escape. Socrates refused to flee. He told Crito that only a man who did not respect the law would break it, and that such a man would indeed be a corrupting influence on the young. Socrates pointed out that he had lived his life as an obedient Athenian citizen and would not break the law now. Human laws may be imperfect, he admitted, but they allow a society to function. Private individuals should never disregard them. To the end he remained a loyal citizen.

On his final day, with his closest friends around him, Socrates drank a cup of poison and died bravely. Plato wrote, "This is the way our dear friend perished. It is fair to say that he was the bravest, the wisest, and the most honorable man of all those we have ever known."[3]

Historians and philosophers have discussed Socrates's case since Plato's time. Were the accusations fair? What precisely was his crime? In the matter of corrupting Athens's youth, there is no doubt that at least two of his most fervent young followers, Alcibiades and Critias, had earned terrible reputations. Alcibiades had betrayed his city in the Peloponnesian War. Critias was one of the most violent of the Thirty Tyrants. Many Athenians suspected Socrates of

SOCRATES ON TRIAL Many sculptors made portraits of Socrates in the centuries after his death. Though Socrates was viewed as a hero who died for his beliefs, this sculptor did nothing to glamorize him. Socrates was famous for the beauty of his thoughts—and the ugliness of his face.

(continued on next page)

influencing them, even though these men represented everything he opposed.

Charges of impiety were harder to substantiate, but Athenians took them seriously. Socrates always participated in Athenian religious life. But during his defense he admitted that his religious views were not exactly the same as those of his prosecutors. His claim to have a divine *daimon* or "sign" who sat on his shoulder and gave him advice was eccentric though not actually sacrilegious. Many Athenians thought this daimon was a foreign god rather than Socrates's metaphor for his own mental processes.

The reasons for Socrates's prosecution lie deeper than the official charges indicate. His trial and execution emerged from an anti-intellectual backlash arising from the frustrations of Athens's defeat in the Peloponnesian War and in the Thirty Tyrants' rule. Even though Athenians had restored democracy, deep-seated resentments sealed Socrates's fate. In many societies throughout history, especially democratic ones like that of Athens that grant freedom to explore new ideas, people who fear change and creativity often attack artists, intellectuals, and innovators in times of stress. Athenians resented Socrates because he challenged them to think. He wanted them to live better lives, and they killed him.

For Discussion

1. What does this trial reveal about the nature of Athenian justice?
2. What does this trial tell us about the attitude of Athenians toward philosophy?
3. Was the execution of Socrates a failure or a logical consequence of Athenian democracy?

Taking It Further

Brickhouse, Thomas C., and Nicholas D. Smith. *Socrates on Trial.* 1989. A thorough analysis of Socrates's trial.

Stokes, Michael. *Plato: Apology, with Introduction, Translation, and Commentary.* 1997. The best translation, with important commentary.

Plato and his student Aristotle (384–322 B.C.E.) were the two greatest thinkers of classical Greece. Aristotle founded his own school in Athens, called the Lyceum. Unlike Plato, Aristotle did not envision the Forms as separate from matter. In his view, form and matter are completely bound together. For this reason, we can acquire knowledge of the Forms by observing the world around us and classifying what we find. Following this theory, Aristotle investigated many subjects, including animal and plant biology, aesthetics, psychology, and physics. His theories regarding mechanics (the study of motion) and his argument that the sun and planets revolve around the Earth acquired great authority among ancient and medieval thinkers and were not effectively challenged until the Scientific Revolution of the late sixteenth and seventeenth centuries.

Aristotle's political ideas were equally influential. Unlike Plato, who described an ideal state, Aristotle analyzed the political communities that actually existed in his day, the Greek poleis. This empirical approach to politics, which paralleled his study of the natural world, led him to conclude that human beings were by nature "political animals" who had a natural tendency to form political communities. By living in such societies they learned about justice, which was essential to the state and was its guiding principle. Aristotle's view that the people themselves, not the gods, established the state was immensely important in the history of Western thought. It has survived in modern democracies, especially in the United States, where the Constitution proclaims that the people themselves established the government and determined how it should be structured.

THE ARTS: SCULPTURE, PAINTING, AND ARCHITECTURE Like philosophers and dramatists during the Classical Age, Greek sculptors, painters, and architects pursued ideal beauty and truth. Classical artists believed the human body was beautiful and was the most appropriate subject of their attention. They also valued the human capacity to represent in art the ideals of beauty, harmony, and proportion found in nature. Greek men celebrated their ability to make rational judgments about what was beautiful and to create art that embodied those judgments.

To create a statue that was an image of physical perfection, sculptors copied the best features of several human models while ignoring their flaws. They strove to depict the muscles, movement, and balance of the human figure in a way that was both lifelike in its imitation of nature and yet idealized in the harmony and symmetry of the torso

THE ERECHTHEUM, LOCATED ON THE NORTH SIDE OF THE ACROPOLIS The Erechtheum was a temple to the goddess Athena in her oldest form as Athena Polias, the protector of the city.

and limbs. This balance between realism and idealism, as well as the belief that the human male body came closest to perfection and that men embodied the most admirable virtues, explains the proliferation of male statues—many of them nude—throughout the Greek world.

View the **Image**

Myron the Discus Thrower

Greek painters explored movement of the human body as well as colors and the optical illusion of depth. The figures that they depicted on vases and walls became increasingly lively and realistic as the Classical Age unfolded. Artists portrayed every sort of activity from religious worship to erotic fun, but regardless of the subject, they shared a similar goal: to create a lifelike depiction of the human figure.

In a similar effort to capture ideals of perfection, Greek architects designed their buildings, especially temples, to be symmetrical and proportional. They used mathematical ratios that they observed in nature to shape their designs. The buildings they created show a grace, balance, and harmony that have inspired architects for more than two millennia.

The temple of the goddess Athena in Athens, called the Parthenon, stood as the greatest triumph of classical Greek architecture. Built on the Acropolis of Athens, the temple symbolized Athens's imperial glory. Using funds appropriated from the Delian League, Athenians built the huge temple between 447 and 432 B.C.E. and dedicated it to the city's divine protector. The architects Ictinus and Callicrates achieved a superb

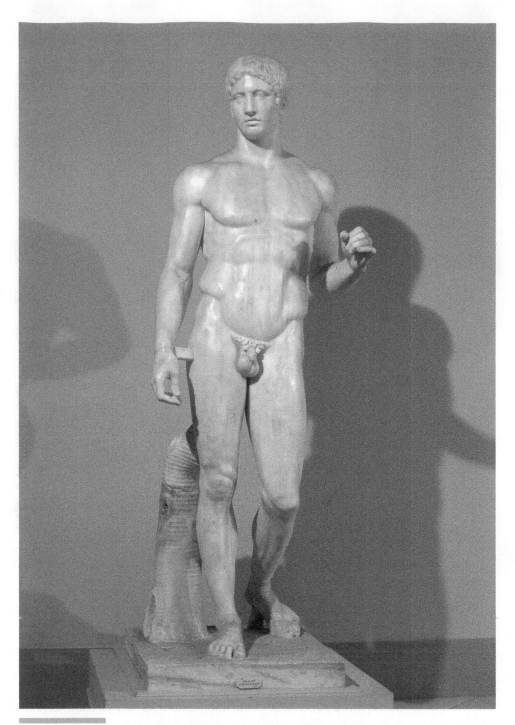

THE MALE NUDE IN GREEK SCULPTURE: POLYCLITUS'S SPEAR-CARRIER This Roman replica of a bronze statue of a warrior, probably the hero Achilles from the *Iliad,* by the Greek sculptor Polyclitus of Argos, reflects the desire of Greek artists to depict the ideal man. The spear-carrier's anatomy is perfectly proportioned, and his muscles indicate discipline and preparation for battle. He is the perfect male citizen, balanced and controlled yet poised to fight. The original statue has not survived.

example of structural harmony, perfectly balancing all the building's elements according to mathematical proportions copied from nature. For the Parthenon's sacred inner room, Phidias, a friend of Pericles, sculpted a statue of Athena made of gold and ivory over a wooden core and decorated it with gems and other precious metals. The temple also displayed an elaborate series of carved and brightly painted marble panels depicting the mythology of Athena. The Parthenon remained nearly intact until 1687 C.E., when powder kegs stored inside exploded, causing irreparable damage and leaving the structure much the way it appears today.

CONCLUSION

The Cultural Foundations of the West

Under the leadership of Athens, Greek city-states made the most enduring contributions of the ancient world to Western civilization. The influence of Greek philosophy, literature, science, art, and architecture remains evident even today in Europe and the lands Europeans settled. The most distinctive contribution of the Greeks to politics, the theory and practice of democracy, also thrives in many parts of the Western world. None of these political and cultural legacies of Greece, however, has come down through the ages without modification, alteration, and mixture with other non-Greek or nonclassical traditions. Greek culture underwent a process of modification in the Mediterranean lands, especially in Italy and in Asia during the Hellenistic period, as we will see in Chapter 4. The Greco–Roman culture that emerged from that process of cultural encounter and exchange has undergone further adaptation, revival, and modification in Europe during the past two thousand years.

This process of cultural encounters between Greek and non-Greek peoples in the ancient world becomes even more complicated when we consider the cultural exchanges that took place between Persia and Greece. Many of these encounters occurred as Persians transmitted older Near Eastern traditions of science, mathematics, astronomy, and religion to the Greeks and the people of the western Mediterranean, North Africa, and eventually Europe. An even more durable Persian influence on the West occurred after a Macedonian ruler, Alexander the Great, conquered Greece and then defeated the Persian Empire in the fourth century B.C.E. Alexander promoted Greek culture in the lands he conquered, but he also assumed the powers of the Persian Great King, which were antithetical to the principles of Athenian democracy. Alexander combined a theory of divinely authorized absolute monarchy with a tradition of Persian imperial rule that had a lasting impact on Western civilization. To the complex and sometimes contradictory political and cultural encounters of the Hellenistic age we now turn.

MAKING CONNECTIONS

1. Like modern-day Iran, Persia is usually considered part of Asia or the East. What role did ancient Persia play in the development of the West?
2. What were the lasting contributions of Greek civilization to the West?
3. Why did the three great poleis of Greece—Corinth, Athens, and Sparta—follow different paths of political development?
4. What were the differences between Athenian and Spartan women?

TAKING IT FURTHER

For suggested readings see page R-1.

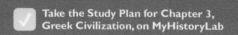
Chapter Review

Greece Rebuilds, 1100–479 B.C.E.

3.1 How did Greek city-states develop their culture and political institutions during the Archaic Age?

Encounters with people from the Near East led to the adoption of an alphabet, which Greeks used to record oral traditions and laws, and eventually to develop a new literature that includes some of the greatest works in the Western tradition. The establishment of the polis, or city-state, emphasized a strong sense of community among the Greeks who inhabited them, and the Olympic Games fostered a sense of Greek identity across city-states. The colonization that was a result of the population boom of the Archaic Age led to new commercial activity and the adoption of coinage, which in turn offered the means to develop advances in military technique and fighting.

The Greek Encounter with Persia

3.2 How did the Persian Empire bring the peoples of the Near East together in a stable realm, and what elements of Persian religion and government have influenced Western thought?

The Persians acquired a vast empire that they governed with a combination of tolerance and firmness. Conquered peoples were allowed to worship and live freely as long as they acknowledged the political supremacy of the king. An elaborate system of roads allowed for not only commercial trade and military transport, but also the transmission of cultural ideas and traditions. Their monotheistic religion, Zoroastrianism, played an important role in shaping the three great Western religions: Judaism, Christianity, and Islam.

The Classical Age of Greece, 479–336 B.C.E.

3.3 What were the intellectual, social, and political innovations of Greece in the Classical Age?

The social structures of Greek society, including strict gender roles and the institution of slavery, gave many male citizens the leisure time for attending plays, speculating about philosophical issues, and debating democratic ideals. Marked by creativity in drama, science, history writing, philosophy, and the visual arts, the cultural innovations of the Classical Age continue to influence the Western world even today. The Greek's legacy of the theory and practice of democracy continues to thrive in many parts of the world.

Chapter Time Line

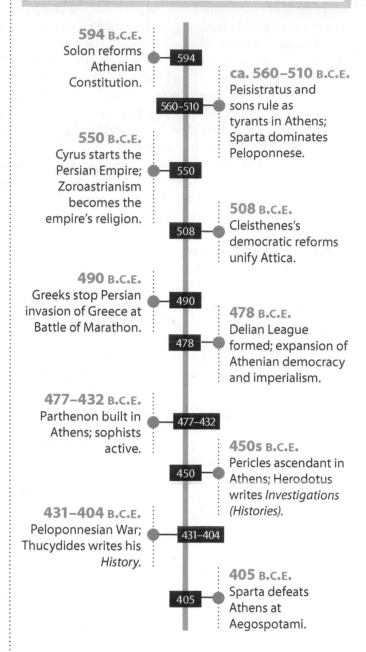

594 B.C.E. Solon reforms Athenian Constitution. — 594

ca. 560–510 B.C.E. Peisistratus and sons rule as tyrants in Athens; Sparta dominates Peloponnese. — 560–510

550 B.C.E. Cyrus starts the Persian Empire; Zoroastrianism becomes the empire's religion. — 550

508 B.C.E. Cleisthenes's democratic reforms unify Attica. — 508

490 B.C.E. Greeks stop Persian invasion of Greece at Battle of Marathon. — 490

478 B.C.E. Delian League formed; expansion of Athenian democracy and imperialism. — 478

477–432 B.C.E. Parthenon built in Athens; sophists active. — 477–432

450s B.C.E. Pericles ascendant in Athens; Herodotus writes *Investigations (Histories).* — 450

431–404 B.C.E. Peloponnesian War; Thucydides writes his *History.* — 431–404

405 B.C.E. Sparta defeats Athens at Aegospotami. — 405

4 Hellenistic Civilization

I n 323 B.C.E. an unprecedented succession of military victories by the young Macedonian monarch, Alexander the Great, came to an end. In the space of a mere 11 years Alexander had gained control of all of Greece and conquered the mighty Persian Empire. Slashing through what is today Iran and Afghanistan, he defeated the Indian ruler Poros and reached northwest India. Only then did his soldiers, suffering from fatigue and homesickness, refuse to advance farther. After consulting an omen that told him it was inauspicious to cross the rain-swollen River Beas, Alexander ordered a retreat. At Susa in southwest Iran he married his second and third wives (while still married to his first wife, Roxanna) and made plans for further conquests from India to the Atlantic. But Alexander's apparent ambition to establish a "universal monarchy" covering most of the known world was not to be realized. In June 323 B.C.E. he died, just two months shy of his thirty-third birthday. After his death his empire—the largest the world had ever known—collapsed and was divided into a number of smaller kingdoms, which acquired their own hereditary dynasties and continued the type of monarchical rule that Alexander had exercised.

The conquests of Alexander the Great marked the beginning of the Hellenistic period of Western civilization. Greeks called themselves *Hellenes*, and thus historians use the term **Hellenistic** to

CELT AND WIFE This dramatic statue epitomizes the mixing of cultures in the Hellenistic Age. The statue is a Roman copy in marble of a bronze original made at Pergamum in Anatolia by a Greek sculptor. The artist tells the tragic story of a defeated Celt (Gaul). Rather than be captured alive, he has just killed his wife and is at the precise moment of taking his own life. In typically Hellenistic style, the artist combines anatomical accuracy with psychological agony.

LEARNING OBJECTIVES

4.1 (((•
How did Alexander the Great create a large empire in which Greek civilization flourished in the midst of many diverse cultures?

4.2 (((•
What was the relationship between Greeks and non-Greeks in the lands that Alexander conquered and those with whom Greeks came into contact after his death?

4.3 (((•
What were the distinguishing features of Hellenistic society and culture, and what was the result of encounters between Greeks and non-Greeks?

4.4 (((•
What did Hellenistic thinkers contribute to philosophy and the scientific investigation of the natural world?

(((• Listen to Chapter 4 on MyHistoryLab

⊙ Watch the Video Series on MyHistoryLab

Learn about some key topics related to this chapter with the *MyHistoryLab Video Series: Key Topics in Western Civilization*

Hellenistic The word used to describe the civilization, based on that of Greece, that developed in the wake of the conquests of Alexander the Great.

barbarians A term used by Greeks to describe people who did not speak Greek and who were therefore considered uncivilized.

describe the complex cosmopolitan civilization, based on that of Greece, that developed in the wake of Alexander's conquests. This civilization offered a rich variety of goods, technologies, and ideas to those who knew the Greek language. Just as people throughout the world today study English because it is the primary language used in science and technology, global business, and international politics, people in the Hellenistic period used Greek as the common tongue in trade, politics, and intellectual life. Greek culture also became the standard by which civilized people identified themselves. Convinced of their intellectual and cultural superiority over inferior people—an idea promoted by the philosophy of Aristotle, Alexander's tutor—civilized people referred to those who did not speak Greek as **barbarians**, a term derived from the Greeks' description of these people's language as "ba-ba," meaning unintelligible to Greeks.

Hellenistic culture thrived within Alexander's successor kingdoms. It also spread far beyond the lands he conquered, mainly to the western Mediterranean, where it had a profound influence on the civilizations of North Africa and Europe, especially Rome. Romans, Jews, Persians, Celts, Carthaginians, and other peoples all absorbed elements of Greek culture—its philosophy, religion, literature, and art. Hellenism gave a common language of science and learning to diverse peoples speaking different languages and worshiping different gods. Hellenism thus provided a cultural unity to an area stretching from Europe in the west to Afghanistan in the east. Large parts of this cultural realm ultimately became what historians call the West.

The spread of Hellenistic culture over this vast area involved a series of cultural exchanges. Greek culture had great prestige and possessed a powerful intellectual appeal to non-Greek peoples, but it also threatened their local, traditional identities. Instead of simply accepting Greek culture, these non-Greek peoples engaged in a process of cultural adaptation and synthesis. In this way Hellenism, which throughout this period remained open to outside influences, absorbed foreign scientific knowledge, religious ideas, and many other elements of culture. These were then transmitted to the greater Hellenistic world. Some of the basic components of Western civilization originated in these cultural encounters between Greek and non-Greek peoples. These include the seven-day week, beliefs in Hell and Judgment Day, the study of astrology and astronomy, and technologies of metallurgy, agriculture, and navigation.

The Hellenistic era and the age of independent Hellenistic kingdoms came to a close in 30 B.C.E., when the Roman ruler Octavian brought an end to the Ptolemaic dynasty, which had ruled Egypt since the death of Alexander. Rome now controlled almost all the states that had been established in the lands that Alexander had conquered. The end of Ptolemaic Egypt therefore marked the end of the Hellenistic Age, but it did not put an end to the influence of Hellenism. As we will see in Chapter 5, Rome rose to power during the Hellenistic period and blended Greek culture with its own. The resulting Greco–Roman cultural synthesis, which Rome transmitted to the lands that it controlled, became the bedrock of Western civilization. This chapter will address the question:

How did Hellenism achieve its dominant position within the West?

The Impact of Alexander the Great

4.1 How did Alexander the Great create a large empire in which Greek civilization flourished in the midst of many diverse cultures?

The Hellenistic Age had its roots in Macedon, a kingdom to the north of Greece that was rich in timber, grain, horses, and fighting men. Most Macedonians lived in scattered villages and made a living by engaging in small-scale farming, raiding their neighbors, and trading over short distances. Relentless warfare against wild Thracian and Illyrian tribes to the north and east kept Macedonians constantly ready for battle.

Macedonians spoke a dialect of Greek, but their customs and political organization differed from those of the urbanized Greek communities that lay to their south. Unlike democratic Athens, Macedon had a hereditary monarchy. Cutthroat struggles for ascendancy in the royal family trained Macedonian kings to select the best moment to deliver a lethal blow to an enemy. Maintaining control over their territory was a constant problem for Macedon's kings because independent-minded nobles resented their rule. Only the army of free citizens could legitimize a king's reign. In return for their support, the soldiers demanded the spoils of war. As a result, Macedonian kings had to wage war continually to obtain that wealth and keep their precarious position on the throne.

The Rise of Macedon Under King Philip

Throughout most of the Classical Age of Greece these fierce Macedonian highlanders seemed like savages to the sophisticated Greeks. When cities started to appear in Macedon in the fifth century B.C.E., Macedonian noblemen began to emulate the culture of classical Greece. The members of the Macedonian royal family, for example, claimed the mythical Greek hero Heracles, son of the god Zeus, as their ancestor. This claim won them the right to compete in the Olympic Games, which were open only to Greeks. Macedonian kings also offered Greek playwrights and scholars large sums of money to lure them to their capital city of Pella.

In the political realm, however, Macedon shrewdly avoided involvement in Greek affairs. During the Persian Wars (490 B.C.E. and 480–479 B.C.E.), Macedonian kings pursued a cautious and profitable policy of friendship with the Persian invaders. During the convulsions of the Peloponnesian War (431–404 B.C.E.) and its turbulent aftermath, Macedon refrained from exploiting Athens, Sparta, and the other Greek cities as they bled to exhaustion. The lack of Greek entanglements, however, could not ease the tensions between kings and nobles in Macedon itself. In 399 B.C.E., Macedon slid into 40 years of anarchy. Just as Macedon was on the verge of disintegration, King Philip II (r. 359–336 B.C.E.) transformed the Macedonian kingdom.

A ruthless opportunist with a gift for military organization, the one-eyed Philip consolidated his power by eliminating his rivals, killing many of them in battle. He unified the unruly nobles who controlled different regions of Macedon by demonstrating the advantages of cooperation under his leadership. As Philip led the nobles to victory after victory over hostile frontier tribes and shared his plunder with them and with the common soldiers, the Macedonians embraced his leadership.

Philip created a new army in which the nobles had a special role as cavalry armed with heavy lances. Called the **Companions**, these cavalrymen formed elite regiments bound to their king by oaths of loyalty. Philip reorganized the infantry, or foot soldiers, who were recruited mainly from the rural peasantry, into phalanxes.

Companions Elite regiments of cavalrymen armed with heavy lances formed by Philip of Macedon in the fourth century B.C.E.

These Macedonian phalanxes, unlike those of the Greek hoplites, used long lances to hold off the enemy while the cavalry attacked the enemy formations from the rear. This new strategy, which Philip probably learned about when he was a hostage in Thebes, gave his armies an enormous tactical advantage over traditional Greek hoplite formations. After seizing the gold and silver mines of the north Aegean coast of Greece, Philip also had ample funds to hire additional armies of mercenaries to augment his Macedonian troops.

With Macedon firmly under his control, its borders secure, and his army eager for loot, Philip stood poised to strike at Greece. In 349 B.C.E. he seized several cities in northern and central Greece, inaugurating a decade of diplomacy, bribery, and threats as he maneuvered to dominate the rest of the Greek poleis.

Recognizing that Philip represented a threat to Greek liberty, the brilliant Athenian orator Demosthenes (384–322 B.C.E.) organized resistance among the city-states. In 340, when Philip attempted to seize the Bosporus, the narrow water link between the Aegean Sea and Athens's vital Black Sea trade routes, Demosthenes delivered a series of blistering speeches against Philip known as "the Philippics" and assembled an alliance of cities. In 338 B.C.E., however, Philip crushed the allied armies at the Battle of Chaeronea. Philip's 18-year-old son Alexander led the Companions in a cavalry charge that won the day for the Macedonians.

Philip then set up a coalition of Greek cities called the League of Corinth under his leadership. He also stationed Macedonian garrisons at strategic sites in Greece and forbade Greek cities to change their form of government without his approval. For the Greek poleis, the age of independence was over.

Philip next cast his eyes on the Persian Empire. In 337 B.C.E. he cloaked himself in the mantle of Greek culture and announced that he would lead his armies and those of the Greek cities against the Persians. His goal was to avenge Persia's invasion of Greece in the previous century. Philip's shrewd linking of classical Greek civilization with Macedonian military might now became a rallying cry for imperialist expansion under his direction. But as Philip laid plans for his assault on Persia in 336 B.C.E., one of his bodyguards assassinated him at the wedding of one of his daughters. Alexander, the son of Philip and Olympias, the king's bitterly estranged wife whom he had forced into exile the previous year, succeeded Philip as king and continued his father's plans to invade Persia. While Alexander honored his slain father, Olympias hung the sword that the assassin had used to kill him in the temple of Apollo and proceeded to murder Philip's son and daughter and his wife, Cleopatra Eurydice.

The Conquests of Alexander the Great

A man of immense personal charisma and political craftiness, Alexander (r. 336–323 B.C.E.) won the support of his soldiers by demonstrating fearlessness in combat and military genius on the battlefield. He combined a predatory instinct for conquest and glory with utter ruthlessness in the pursuit of power. These traits proved to be the key to his success. By the time of his death, Alexander had won military victories as far east as India, creating a vast empire. His successes made him a legend during his lifetime, and millions of his subjects worshiped him as a god. Historians consider him a pivotal figure in Western civilization because his conquests led to the spread of Hellenistic culture in lands that were to become important components of the West.

After brutally consolidating power in Macedon and Greece following his father's death, Alexander launched an invasion of Persia. With no more than 40,000 infantry and 5,000 cavalry, he crossed the Hellespont and marched into Persian territory in 334 B.C.E. The young Macedonian king won his first great victory over Persian forces at

ALEXANDER THE GREAT Detail of a Roman mosaic depicting Alexander the Great at the Battle of Issus, where he defeated the Persian army in 333 B.C.E. The empire he established by the time of his death in 323 B.C.E. defined the main boundaries of the Hellenistic world.

the Battle of the Granicus River, giving him control over Anatolia with its rich Greek coastal cities. He then marched into Syria, where he broke the main Persian army near the town of Issus in 333 B.C.E. Here, just as he had done at Granicus River, Alexander led the Macedonian cavalry's victorious charge into the teeth of the enemy. From this victory Alexander gained control of the entire eastern coast of the Mediterranean Sea and the Persian naval bases located there.

When Alexander captured the port city of Tyre in 332 B.C.E., Darius panicked and offered the young Macedonian his daughter in marriage and all of his empire west of the Euphrates River in return for peace. Alexander rejected the offer and marched into Egypt, where the inhabitants welcomed him as a liberator from their Persian masters and crowned him as Pharaoh. From Egypt he advanced into Mesopotamia, where he crushed Darius again on the battlefield at Gaugamela near the Tigris River.

When Alexander entered Babylon in triumph after Gaugamela, he again received an enthusiastic welcome as a liberator. From Babylon his forces ventured southeast to Persepolis, the Persian palace city, which fell in January 330 B.C.E. There Alexander ordered his soldiers to kill all the adult males, enslave the women, loot the palace's vast treasures, and burn it to the ground. The enormous wealth Alexander acquired from Persepolis and other Persian treasure centers paid for all of his military activities for the next seven years and invigorated the entire Macedonian economy. Darius III, the Great King of Persia (r. 335–330 B.C.E.), escaped to the east, but was soon murdered by his own nobles. The once-powerful Persian Empire, which covered one million square miles and had a population of 50 million people, lay in ruins.

Alexander had fulfilled his father's pledge to gain vengeance against Persia, but he had no intention of stopping his march of conquest (see **Map 4.1**). He pushed past the tribesmen of the harsh Afghan mountain ranges to penetrate central Asia. Then in 327 B.C.E. he entered what is today Pakistan through the Khyber Pass, the narrow route that separates central Asia from the south Asian subcontinent. At the Battle of the Hydaspes River, Alexander defeated the Indian king Poros, who had assembled a formidable army of 6,000 cavalry, 30,000 infantry, and 200 war elephants. But Alexander's exhausted armies refused to advance farther into India, and he was forced to retreat. The route he chose for his return westward passed through a scorching desert, where many of his soldiers died, and Alexander himself suffered nearly fatal wounds. While recuperating at Babylon in 323 B.C.E., where he had begun to plan more conquests, Alexander succumbed to fever after a drinking bout. He had never lost a battle.

In strategic locations through the lands he had conquered, Alexander established cities as garrisons for his troops. More than a dozen of these cities received the name *Alexandria* in his honor. Thousands of Greeks migrated east to settle in the new cities to take advantage of the expanded economic opportunities for trade and farming. These Greek settlers became the cultural and political elite of the new cities.

View the Map

The Conquests of Alexander the Great

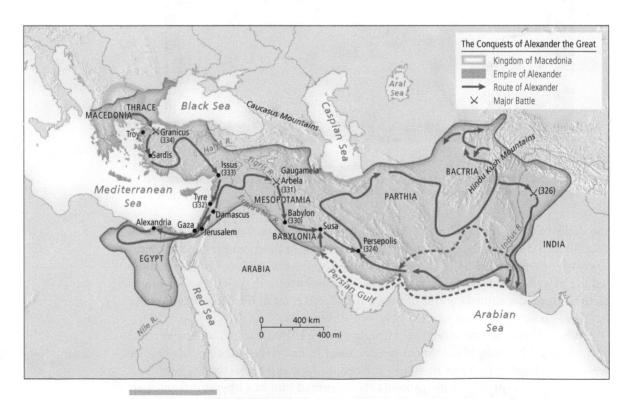

MAP **4.1** THE CONQUESTS OF ALEXANDER THE GREAT Alexander led troops from his Macedonian homeland as far east as the Indus Valley. He defeated the Persian Empire and incorporated it into his own empire. This map shows Alexander's march of conquest and the sites of his most important victories. Why was Macedonia unable to profit fully from these conquests?

CHRONOLOGY: ALEXANDER THE GREAT AND THE GREEK EAST

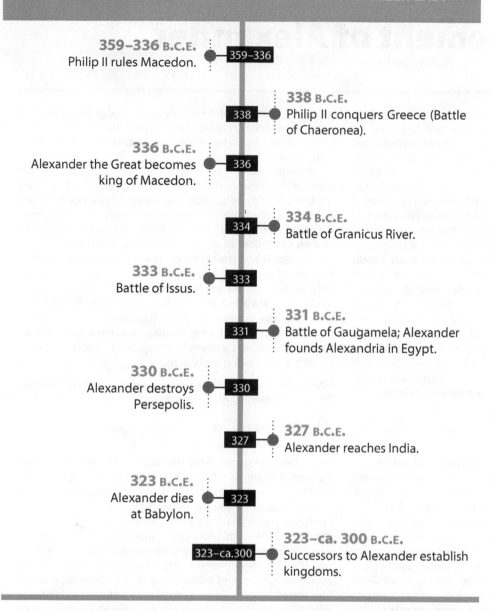

359–336 B.C.E.
Philip II rules Macedon.
`359–336`

`338`
338 B.C.E.
Philip II conquers Greece (Battle of Chaeronea).

336 B.C.E.
Alexander the Great becomes king of Macedon.
`336`

`334`
334 B.C.E.
Battle of Granicus River.

333 B.C.E.
Battle of Issus.
`333`

`331`
331 B.C.E.
Battle of Gaugamela; Alexander founds Alexandria in Egypt.

330 B.C.E.
Alexander destroys Persepolis.
`330`

`327`
327 B.C.E.
Alexander reaches India.

323 B.C.E.
Alexander dies at Babylon.
`323`

`323–ca.300`
323–ca. 300 B.C.E.
Successors to Alexander establish kingdoms.

Governing an empire of this size proved to be a difficult challenge. The Macedonian kingdom that Alexander led was geared to seizing land and plundering cities. It was another task entirely to create the infrastructure and discipline necessary for ruling an immense territory that had little linguistic or cultural unity. Alexander recognized that the only model of rule suitable to such a diverse empire was that which his Persian predecessors had devised: a Great King presiding over a hierarchy of nobles who governed Persian territory and some non-Persian provinces, and subject kings who ruled other non-Persian regions.

Necessity thus forced Alexander to bring his Macedonian troops and his new Persian subjects together in an uneasy balance. To that end, he persuaded his army to proclaim him "King of Asia"—that is, the new Great King. With his Companions he simply took over the government of the former Persian Empire from the top. He included a handful of loyal Persians in his administration by making them regional governors or **satraps**, while offering other Persian noblemen minor roles in his regime. These

satraps Persian provincial governors who collected taxes and oversaw the bureaucracy.

Different Voices

The Achievement of Alexander the Great

*T*he conquests of Alexander the Great lent themselves to different interpretations that depended to a large extent on whether one focused on the diffusion of Greek culture in Asia and Europe or on the brutal methods Alexander employed in subjecting different people to his rule. The Greek biographer Plutarch (ca. 46 C.E.–120 C.E.), writing during the Roman Empire, credited Alexander with facilitating the reception of Greek philosophy and culture in the lands that he conquered. In a speech celebrating these achievements Plutarch claimed that Alexander had gained a wider acceptance of Greek philosophy among the people whom he had conquered than the Greeks themselves had achieved during the Classical Age. One can attribute Plutarch's claim that Alexander promoted the unity of mankind to the rhetorical excesses of his speech. It is unlikely that Plutarch himself actually subscribed to such a noble interpretation of Alexander's relentless quest to establish a universal monarchy. The Jews, who had been conquered by Alexander, understandably had a far less positive view of his legacy. The Jewish author of the biblical book 1 Maccabees, written in the second century B.C.E., saw Alexander's reign as a period of violence and instability.

A Greek Biographer Celebrates the Cultural Achievement of Alexander the Great

But if you consider the effects of Alexander's instruction, you will see that he educated the Hyrcanians to contract marriages, taught the Arachosians to till the soil, and persuaded the Sogdians to support their parents, not to kill them, and the Persians to respect their mothers, not to marry them. Most admirable philosophy, which induced the Indians to worship Greek gods, and the Scythians to bury their dead and not to eat them! We admire the power of Carneades, who caused Clitomachus, formerly called Hashdrubal and a Carthaginian by birth, to adopt Greek ways. We admire the power that persuaded Diogenes the Babylonian, to turn to philosophy. Yet when Alexander was taming Asia, Homer became widely read, and the children of the Persians, of the Susianians and the Gedrosians sang the tragedies of Euripides and Sophocles. And Socrates was condemned by the sychophants in Athens for introducing new deities, while thanks to Alexander Bactria and the Caucasus worshipped the gods of the Greeks. Plato drew up in writing one ideal constitution but could not persuade anyone to adopt it because of its severity, while Alexander founded over 70 cities among barbarian tribes, sprinkled Greek institutions all over Asia, and so overcame its wild and savage manner of living. . . . Those who were subdued by Alexander were more fortunate than those who escaped him, for the latter had no one to rescue them from their wretched life, while the victorious Alexander compelled the former to enjoy a better existence. Alexander's victims would not have been civilized if they had not been defeated. . . . If, therefore, philosophers take the greatest pride in taming and correcting the fierce and untutored elements of men's character, and if Alexander has been shown to have changed the brutish customs of countless nations, then it would be justifiable to regard him as a very great philosopher. . . .

Believing that he had come as a god-sent governor and mediator of the whole world, he overcame by arms those he could not bring over by persuasion and brought men together from all over the world, mixing together, as it were, in a loving-cup, their lives, customs, marriages, and ways of living. He instructed all men to consider to be their native land and his camp to be their acropolis and their defense, while they should regard as kinsmen all good men, and the wicked as strangers. The difference between Greeks and barbarians was not a matter of cloak or shield, or of a scimitar or Median dress. What distinguished Greekness was excellence, while wickedness was the mark of the barbarian; clothing, food, marriage and the way of life they should all regard as common, being blended together by ties of blood and the bearing of children.

SOURCE: Plutarch, *On the Fortune or Virtue of Alexander*, in Michel Austin (ed.), *The Hellenistic World from Alexander to the Roman Conquest*, 2006, 57–58.

A Jewish Writer Describes the Misery Caused by Alexander the Great

After Alexander son of Philip, the Macedonian, who came from the land of Kittim, had defeated King Darius of the Persians and the Medes, he succeeded him as king; he had already become king of Greece. He fought many battles, conquered strongholds, and put to death the kings of the earth. He advanced to the ends of the earth, and plundered many nations. When the earth became quiet before him, he was exalted, and his heart was lifted up. He gathered a very strong army and ruled over countries, nations, and princes, and they became tributary to him. After this he fell sick and perceived that he was dying. So he summoned his most honored officers, who had been brought up with him from youth, and divided his kingdom among them while he was still alive. And after Alexander had reigned twelve years, he died. Then his officers began to rule, each in his own place. They all put on crowns after his death, and so did their descendants after them for many years; and they caused many evils on the earth.

SOURCE: *1 Maccabees 1–9.*

For Discussion

1. What criteria did Plutarch and the author of 1 Maccabees use to evaluate the achievement of Alexander the Great?
2. Did Alexander bring "civilization" to the lands he conquered?
3. How might the author of 1 Maccabees have responded to Plutarch's claim that Alexander brought men together from all over the world?

practical steps promised to bring order to the empire. By adopting the elaborate Persian ceremonial role of the Great King, Alexander demonstrated to his foreign subjects that his regime stood for security and continuity of orderly rule.

Alexander's proud Macedonian soldiers, however, ultimately stymied his efforts to achieve this balance. They refused to prostrate themselves before him, as Persian royal ceremony dictated. Alexander may well have thought of himself as a god, but his soldiers refused to worship him. Instead, they saw Alexander's recruitment of 30,000 Persian troops into their army as a threat to the traditional relations between Macedonian soldiers and their king. They also resented the marriages with the daughters of Persian noblemen that Alexander forced on them in order to unite Macedonians and Persians—although no Persian nobles received Greek or Macedonian wives. The Macedonian troops expected to keep all the spoils of victory for themselves. They wanted to be conquerors, not partners in a new government. They failed to understand that men of other cultures within the new empire might be equally loyal to Alexander and thus deserve a share of power and honor. Alexander's charismatic personality held his conquests together, but his death destroyed any dreams of cooperation between Persians and Greeks.

Alexander's adoption of the powers and symbolism of Persian kingship, even though it was unpopular with his Macedonian soldiers, was the product of an encounter between Macedonian and Persian styles of rule. The political culture that emerged from this encounter had a lasting influence on Western civilization. In contrast to the democratic and republican culture that had flourished in classical Athens, Alexander offered a model of royal and imperial rule that gave the king absolute power and identified that power, if not his own person, with that of the gods. Both traditions—democratic republicanism and divine-right absolutism—competed with each other throughout the history of the West. The competition became evident in classical Rome, which began as a republic but was later transformed into an empire in which the ruler had unrivalled power. The tension between the two ideologies persisted throughout the Middle Ages and into the Renaissance, when the Italian state of Florence revived the republican culture of ancient Greece and Rome at the same time that the duke of Milan revived the aspirations of the Roman Empire.

Hellenism in the East and West

4.2 What was the relationship between Greeks and non-Greeks in the lands that Alexander conquered and those with whom Greeks came into contact after his death?

The Hellenistic Successor States

Alexander left no adult heir, and the Macedonian nobles who served as his generals fought viciously among themselves to control his conquered territory. Eventually, these generals created a number of kingdoms out of lands Alexander had acquired (see **Map 4.2**). One general, Ptolemy (r. 323–286 B.C.E.), established the Ptolemaic dynasty in Egypt, which lasted until 30 B.C.E. Antigonus "the One-Eyed" (r. 306–301 B.C.E) gained control of the Macedonian homeland, where his descendants established the Antigonid dynasty, which survived until Rome overthrew the last of these monarchs in 167 B.C.E. The largest portion of Alexander's conquests, comprising the bulk of the old Persian Empire, fell to his general Seleucus (r. 312–281 B.C.E.). But the territory controlled by Seleucus's successors constantly shrank, and in the mid-third century B.C.E. the Parthians, a people from northeastern Persia, shook off Seleucid rule and created a vigorous new state in what is today Iran. By 150 B.C.E. the Seleucids ruled only Syria, Palestine, and a small portion of southeastern Anatolia.

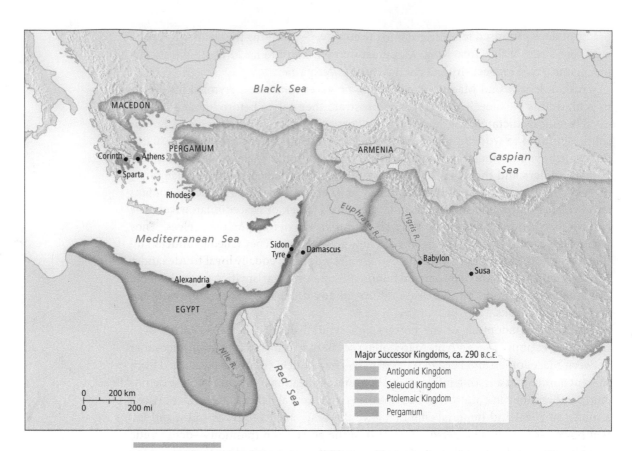

MAP **4.2** MAJOR SUCCESSOR KINGDOMS CA. 290 B.C.E.   After Alexander's death, his generals divided his empire into several kingdoms. This map shows the boundaries of the Antigonid, Seleucid, and Ptolemaic kingdoms about 290 B.C.E. The Antigonids acquired control of the old kingdom of Macedon in 294 B.C.E., although this control was not secured until the reign of Antigonus II (r. 276–239 B.C.E.). The city of Pergamum in Anatolia became a kingdom under Attalus I around 230 B.C.E. How did the rulers of these kingdoms maintain their power?

Following the example of Macedon itself, the Hellenistic successor states all maintained a monarchical form of government in which a king ruled the people with the support of the army and highly regimented bureaucracies. The leading administrators and bureaucrats were all Greeks and Macedonians. Indigenous people were not recruited into the ruling elite. Greek was the language of government and the elite in the successor kingdoms. The talented queen Cleopatra VII (r. 51–30 B.C.E.), who was the last descendant of Ptolemy to rule in Egypt, was the first of her line ever to speak Egyptian. Greek-speaking monarchs nonetheless knew that they needed to cultivate the goodwill of their non-Greek-speaking subjects. As one monarch asked in a Hellenistic political dialogue, "How can I accommodate myself to all the different races in my kingdom?" A subject answered: "By adopting the appropriate attitude to each, making justice one's guide."

The king towered over Hellenistic society, holding authority over all his subjects and bearing ultimate responsibility for their welfare. Following the example of Alexander, the Hellenistic monarch earned legitimacy by leading his troops into wars of conquest. The king embodied the entire community that he ruled. He was at once the ruler, father, protector, savior, source of law, and god of all his subjects. His garb reinforced his elevated position—the king arrayed himself in battle gear with a helmet or Macedonian sombrero, a crown, purple robes, a scepter, and a special seal ring. The monarch earned the loyalty of his subjects and glorified his own rule by founding cities, constructing public buildings, and rewarding his inner circle.

Ptolemy II, who ruled in Egypt from 283 to 246 B.C.E., exemplified these notions of Hellenistic kingship. Ptolemy expanded his dominions by conquering parts of Anatolia and Syria from the Seleucids. He also expanded the bureaucracy, refined the tax system, and funded new towns for his soldiers and veterans. With his support, merchants established new posts on the Red Sea, where they traded with merchants from India and other eastern lands. Ptolemy patronized the arts and sciences by building research institutes and libraries. He transformed Egypt's capital city of Alexandria, the port founded by Alexander in Egypt in 331 B.C.E., into the leading center of Greek culture and learning in the Hellenistic world. To reinforce his authority and majesty, Ptolemy II encouraged his subjects to worship him as a god the way earlier Egyptians had worshiped the pharaohs.

This worship of Hellenistic monarchs drew from indigenous traditions throughout the Near East, but in its Hellenistic form it had more political than religious significance. People worshiped their kings as a spontaneous expression of gratitude for the protection and peace that good government provided. For example, when the Antigonid king Demetrius "the Besieger" captured Athens in 308 B.C.E., the pragmatic Athenians sang a song in honor of their new master: "The other gods either do not exist or are far off, either they do not hear, or they do not care; but you are here and we can see you, not in wood and stone but in living truth."[1] Deification legitimized a king's rule and helped secure his subjects' loyalty.

Hellenistic monarchs depended on large professional armies to maintain their authority and defend their territories. These rulers fought wars over much larger territories than those that had led to squabbles among Greek city-states in previous centuries. The conquest of such territories required an increase in the size of field armies. The Athenian hoplites had numbered about 10,000 men in the fifth century B.C.E., but Hellenistic kings routinely mustered armies of between 60,000 and 80,000 men. Many soldiers came from military colonies that the kings established. In return for land, the men of these Greek-speaking colonies had to serve generation after generation in the king's army and police the native, non-Greek populations.

Encounters with Foreign Peoples

During the Hellenistic Age, Greeks encountered many foreign peoples; the effects of these interactions laid some of the foundations of the West. The encounters took place when Greeks explored regions in Africa and Europe where they had not penetrated before; when Hellenistic Babylonians, Egyptians, Persians, Afghans, and Hebrews resisted or adopted Hellenistic culture; and when Celtic peoples migrated to the boundaries of the Hellenistic world in Europe and Anatolia.

EXPLORING THE HELLENISTIC WORLD A spirit of inquiry—combined with a hunger for trade and profit—drove men to explore and map the unknown world during the Hellenistic Age (see **Map 4.3** on page 123). Explorers supported by monarchs ventured into the Caspian, Aral, and Red Seas. By the second century B.C.E., Greeks had established trading posts along the coasts of modern Eritrea and Somalia in east Africa, where merchants bought goods, particularly ivory, transported from the interior of Africa. Hellenistic

PTOLEMAIC KING OF EGYPT This golden ring depicts Ptolemy VI, who ruled Egypt from 176 to 145 B.C.E. Although he and his court spoke only Greek, he is depicted as a pharaoh wearing a double crown, the age-old symbol of Egyptian monarchy. The image on the ring demonstrated the integration of old and new political symbols in Egypt during the Hellenistic Age.

THE ROYAL LIBRARY OF ALEXANDRIA The cosmopolitan city of Alexandria, the capital of Egypt founded by Alexander in 331 B.C.E., became the leading center of Greek culture in the Hellenistic world. Its famous library, depicted here in a nineteenth-century German engraving, functioned as a major center of scholarship until the first century B.C.E.

people also craved pepper, cinnamon, cloves, and other spices and luxury goods from India, but Arab middlemen made direct trade between the Hellenistic world and India nearly impossible. One intrepid navigator named Eudoxus tried to find a sea route to India by sailing around Africa, but he never got farther southwest than the coast of Morocco.

The most ambitious and successful of all Hellenistic explorers was Pytheas of Marseilles (ca. 380–306 B.C.E.). Setting out from the Carthaginian city of Gades (the modern Spanish port of Cadiz) in about 310 B.C.E., he sailed north around Britain and reported the existence of either Iceland or Norway. He may have even reached the Vistula River in Poland by sailing through the Baltic Sea. Throughout his journeys Pytheas contributed much to navigational knowledge by recording astronomical bearings and natural wonders such as the northern lights. He is the first person known to have reported the midnight sun and polar ice.

As these explorers expanded geographical horizons, Greeks developed a condescending interest in the peoples of the world. Greeks considered themselves culturally superior to non-Greek-speaking peoples who lived beyond the borders of Hellenistic kingdoms, including Jews, Babylonians, Celts, steppe nomads, and sub-Saharan Africans. Greeks considered all of these peoples barbarians. Despite this prejudice,

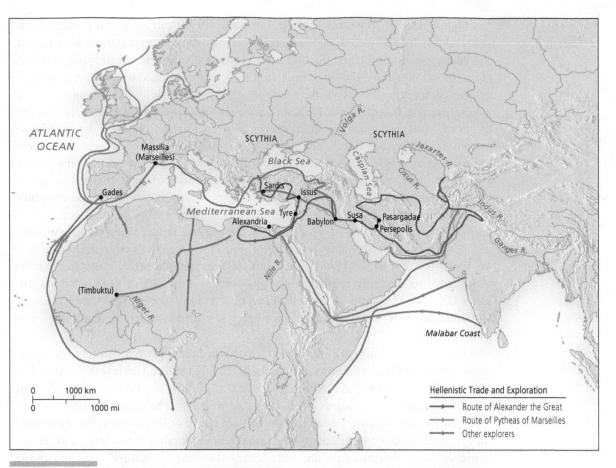

MAP **4.3** HELLENISTIC TRADE AND EXPLORATION During the Hellenistic Age, merchants traveled widely across the breadth of the Mediterranean and throughout the Near East. They sailed into the Persian Gulf and Indian Ocean on commercial ventures. Some explorers sailed along the east and west coasts of Africa as well as Europe's Atlantic coast, reaching Britain and the North Sea. What impact did these voyages have on the dissemination of Hellenistic culture?

educated men and women throughout the Hellenistic world enjoyed reading accounts in Greek of foreign peoples' customs, myths, natural history, and forms of government.

Knowledge about different peoples often came from non-Greek intellectuals who translated their accounts into Greek. For example, Berosus, a Babylonian priest, wrote a history of his people that also provided Greek readers with extensive astronomical knowledge. Manetho, an Egyptian priest, composed a history of his land. Hecataeus of Abdera, a Greek, wrote a popular history arguing that Egypt was the site of the origin of civilization. Most of what the West believed it knew about India until the Middle Ages derived from the reports of Megasthenes, a Seleucid diplomat who served as ambassador in India. Information about the histories and belief systems of their non-Greek neighbors entertained Greek intellectuals and helped Hellenistic rulers govern their conquered peoples.

RESISTANCE TO HELLENISTIC RULE Despite this curiosity among educated Greeks about foreign customs, barriers of mutual incomprehension, suspicion, and resentment separated Greeks from their subjects. Language was one such barrier. In most kingdoms, administrators conducted official business only in Greek. Few Greek settlers in the cities or even in isolated military colonies bothered to learn the local languages, and only a small percentage of the local populations learned Greek. Many communities ignored their Greek rulers completely. In Mesopotamia and Syria, Aramaic remained the dominant language, not Greek. Some non-Greeks, however, hoped to rise in the service of their Greek masters. They made an effort to learn Greek and assimilate into Hellenistic culture.

123

But their collaboration with Greek rulers alienated them from their own people and divided native societies into those who accepted Hellenistic culture and those who did not.

Many people conquered by the Greeks continued to practice their traditional religions. In Babylonia, age-old patterns of temple worship continued uninfluenced by Greek culture. Stunned by the loss of their empire, some aristocratic Persians found solace in Zoroastrianism, the traditional Persian religion. As we have seen in Chapter 3, Zoroastrianism teaches that the world is in the grip of an eternal struggle between the good forces of light, represented by the divine creator, Ahura Mazda, and the evil forces of darkness, represented by Angra Mainyu, the demonic destroyer. Persian Zoroastrianians considered Alexander to be Angra Mainyu's agent. In the aftermath of the Persian defeat, an important religious text (written in Greek, ironically) predicted that a warrior messiah would soon overthrow the Seleucid kings and restore Persia's true religion and rulers. A book known as the *Dynastic Prophecy* (ca. 300 B.C.E.) expressed similar hopes for Babylonians.

Resentful voices also rang out in Egypt. The *Demotic Chronicle* and *The Oracle of the Potter* (ca. 250 B.C.E.) maintained that the Ptolemies had brought the punishment of the gods to Egypt by displacing the pharaohs and interfering with religious customs. One day, the books assured readers, a mighty king would expel the conquerors. Not coincidentally, rebellions erupted in Egypt about the same time that these works gained popularity.

The Jewish response to Hellenism produced the best-known account of resistance, preserved in the First and Second Book of Maccabees in the Hebrew Bible. (See *Different Voices* in this chapter.) After Alexander's death, first the Ptolemies and then the Seleucids controlled Jerusalem and Jewish Palestine. The Ptolemaic monarchs at first tolerated Judaism and welcomed the rapid assimilation of Jerusalem's priestly aristocracy into Greek culture. Although traditional Jewish worship at the temple in Jerusalem continued, a gymnasium and other elements of Greek culture first appeared in Jerusalem during the rule of these Hellenized Jewish priests.

In 167 B.C.E., however, the Seleucid king Antiochus IV Epiphanes (r. 175–164 B.C.E.) tried to make the city more Hellenistic. When the Jews resisted, his soldiers put up statues of Greek gods in the Temple, an abomination in Jewish eyes. Initially, Antiochus had intended to advertise his own strength, not to suppress Judaism, but his plan backfired. A family of Jewish priests, the Maccabees, began a religious war of liberation. They drove the armies of Antiochus out of Palestine, purified the Temple in Jerusalem, and established an autonomous Jewish kingdom under their rule. Later, when Jewish writers sought to explain these actions to the Greek-speaking Jews of Alexandria, they described them in terms of resistance to Hellenism. However, the Maccabeans themselves soon adopted many Greek customs and used Greek names, causing deep rifts within Jewish society.

Read the Document

Maccabees: Resistance to Hellenization in the Hellenistic Period, ca. 100 B.C.E.

CELTS ON THE FRINGES OF THE HELLENISTIC WORLD In addition to the Greek culture that spread throughout the Mediterranean and Near East, Celtic civilization flourished in Europe during the Hellenistic Age. The Celts, who lived in tribes that were never politically unified on a large scale, shared common dialects, metal- and pottery-making techniques, and agricultural and home-building methods. They were the ancestors of many Europeans today.

Through trade and war, Celts influenced the northern margins of the Hellenistic world from Anatolia to Spain. Trade routes with the Celts from the Mediterranean were established as early as the eighth century B.C.E., but war often interrupted commerce. The military activities of Celtic tribes restricted the expansion of Hellenistic kingdoms in Macedon and Anatolia, thereby pressuring these kingdoms to strengthen their military capacities.

Archaeologists call the first Celtic civilization in central Europe **Hallstatt culture**, because of excavations of Celtic settlements in Hallstatt, Austria. Around 750 B.C.E., Hallstatt Celts started to spread from their homeland into Italy, the Balkans, Ireland,

Hallstatt culture The first Celtic civilization in central Europe; from about 750 to about 450 B.C.E., Hallstatt Celts spread throughout Europe.

Spain, and Anatolia, conquering local peoples on the way. These early Celts left no written records, so we know little of their political practices. The luxury goods and weapons they buried in graves, however, indicate a stratified society led by a warrior elite. Hallstatt sites were heavily fortified, suggesting frequent warfare. Men gained status through the competitive exchange of gifts, raiding, and valor in battle. In southern France, Celts encountered Hellenistic civilization at the Greek city of Massilia (modern Marseilles). There they participated in lively trade along the Rhône River for Greek luxury goods, including wine and drinking goblets.

In the mid-fifth century B.C.E. a new phase in Celtic civilization began. It is called **La Tène culture**, which takes its name from a site in modern Switzerland. More weapons were found in La Tène tombs than in the Hallstatt period, possibly indicating intensified warfare. La Tène Celts developed new centers of wealth and power, especially in the valleys of the Rhine and Danube Rivers. They also founded large, fortified settlements in these regions and in present-day France and England.

La Tène craftsmen benefited from new trade routes across the Alps to northern Italy, the home of Etruscan merchants and artisans (see Chapter 5). Etruscans traded bronze statuettes to the Celtic north, and they may have also introduced the two-wheeled fighting chariots found in aristocratic Celtic tombs. Greek styles in art reached the Celts through these Etruscan intermediaries, but Celtic artists developed their own distinctive style of metalwork and sculpture. Many Celtic communities began to use coinage, which they adopted from the Greeks.

For about a century relations between the Celtic and Mediterranean peoples centered on trade, but around 400 B.C.E. overpopulation in central Europe caused massive migrations of Celtic tribes (see **Map 4.4**). In 387 B.C.E. one migrating group of

La Tène culture A phase of Celtic civilization that lasted from about 450 to 200 B.C.E. La Tène culture became strong especially in the regions of the Rhine and Danube Rivers.

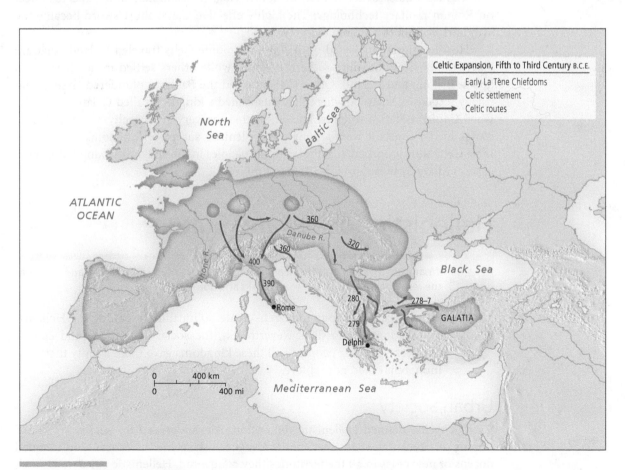

MAP **4.4** CELTIC EXPANSION, FIFTH TO THIRD CENTURY B.C.E. During the Hellenistic Age, Celtic peoples migrated into many parts of Europe and Asia Minor. This map shows their routes. What prevented Celts from uniting and forming an empire?

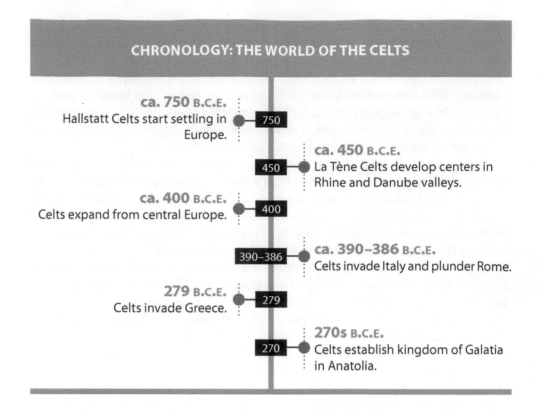

CHRONOLOGY: THE WORLD OF THE CELTS

ca. 750 B.C.E.
Hallstatt Celts start settling in Europe. — 750

ca. 450 B.C.E.
450 — La Tène Celts develop centers in Rhine and Danube valleys.

ca. 400 B.C.E.
Celts expand from central Europe. — 400

ca. 390–386 B.C.E.
390–386 — Celts invade Italy and plunder Rome.

279 B.C.E.
Celts invade Greece. — 279

270s B.C.E.
270 — Celts establish kingdom of Galatia in Anatolia.

Celts, called Gauls, sacked the city of Rome. Their invasion had an unexpected effect on Roman military technology: The highly effective Celtic short sword became the standard weapon of the Roman legions.

Hostile migrations lasted until 200 B.C.E. Some Celts traveled to lands that are Slavic today (Slovakia and southern Poland), while others settled in northern Italy, Spain, Britain, and Ireland. Other Celts invaded the Balkans, plundered Greece, and finally settled in Anatolia, where they established a kingdom called Galatia (from the word *Gauls*). Galatian soldiers, known for their bravery and cruelty, became mercenaries in the constant wars among the Hellenistic successor kingdoms. Ultimately, most Celts were absorbed, together with the peoples in the Hellenistic kingdoms in the eastern Mediterranean, into the Roman Empire.

Hellenistic Society and Culture

4.3 What were the distinguishing features of Hellenistic society and culture, and what was the result of encounters between Greeks and non-Greeks?

Chronic warfare among monarchs made political unity among the Hellenistic kingdoms impossible. Nevertheless, the social institutions and culture of Greek-speaking people in all these kingdoms gave them a unity that their monarchs could not achieve.

Urban Society

Greek city life defined Hellenistic civilization. Alexander and his successors seized dozens of Greek city-states scattered across the eastern Mediterranean and founded dozens of new cities in all the territories they conquered. Hellenistic cities were much more than garrisons established to enforce the conquerors' power. They continued traditions of learning, art, architecture, and citizen participation in public life that had flourished in the classical poleis. Most important, people in cities throughout the Hellenistic world spoke a standard version of Greek called **Koine** that gave them a sense of common identity.

On the surface, many of the institutions of the classical poleis remained the same: magistrates, councils, and popular assemblies ran the cities' affairs, and some form of democracy or election to office remained the norm in local government. Yet beneath the surface, the poleis had undergone radical changes. Because kings wielded absolute power, once-independent cities such as Athens and Corinth lost their freedom to make peace or wage war. Although they chose their own local governments, these cities now served as the bureaucratic centers that administered their rulers' huge kingdoms.

As we saw in Chapter 3, citizenship in the city-states of classical Greece was a carefully limited commodity that gave people a sense of identity, guaranteed desirable rights and privileges, and demanded certain responsibilities. The territories that any city-state controlled were relatively small, yet even Athens at the height of its empire in the fifth century B.C.E. never considered giving Athenian citizenship to all the people it ruled, even within Attica. In contrast, during the Hellenistic Age, large kingdoms containing many cities were the basic political units. People were both subjects of a king and citizens of their particular cities. To be sure, some philosophers played with the idea of a universal citizenship of all humankind, but there was no notion of a citizenship that all the people in one kingdom would share. Citizenship lost its political force because individual cities had lost their political autonomy. In a sharp break with earlier practice, important men sometimes gained the honor of citizenship in more than one city, which Greeks in the Classical Age would have found inconceivable.

To maintain the illusion of the cities' independence, Hellenistic kings permitted considerable autonomy in local government. Nonetheless, while democracies had developed in Greece during the Archaic and Classical periods to protect the interests of the poor as well as the rich, in the Hellenistic Age the wealthy dominated society and government, and the condition of the poor deteriorated. Rich men appointed or approved by the king controlled all the courts, held all the magistracies, and represented all the cities at the court of the kings, who in return showered these civic leaders with honors and rewards. Through land grants, tax immunities, and other favors, the monarchs developed networks of personal ties that bound civic leaders to them. In return, these urban elites served their king and spent their vast fortunes building magnificent temples, gymnasiums, and other structures for their fellow citizens.

Hellenistic kings and aristocrats turned their cities into showcases of art and design. Distinctive styles of building and ornamentation quickly spread from the east to Carthage, Rome, and other communities in the western Mediterranean. The most distinctive architectural innovations in the cities were vast palace complexes, which were built to accommodate the Hellenistic monarchs and their entourages in the successor kingdoms. Laying out streets on a grid plan became standard in the Mediterranean world, lending a sense of order to urban space. Stone theaters for plays and spectacles, council halls, and roofed colonnades called *stoas* sprang up everywhere, as did public baths with heated pools and gymnasium complexes with sports facilities, libraries, and lecture halls.

Hellenistic cities contained more diverse populations than had classical poleis. Alexandria, Egypt's largest and most cosmopolitan Greek city, boasted large communities of Macedonians, Greeks, Jews, Syrians, and Egyptians. Although these groups lived in different areas of the city and often fought violently with one another, they all participated to varying degrees in Alexandria's culture. For example, Alexandrian Jews who spoke Greek translated the Hebrew Bible into Greek, a version called the **Septuagint,** so that Jews who had lost their command of Hebrew could understand it. The Septuagint later provided early Christians, many of whom spoke and read Greek, with their knowledge of the Hebrew Bible, which Christians refer to as the Old Testament.

Koine The standard version of the Greek language spoken throughout the Hellenistic world.

Septuagint The Greek translation of the Hebrew Bible (Old Testament).

APHRODITE OF MELOS Aphrodite, the goddess of sexual love, displayed the perfection of the female form. This marble statue of her, which was found on the Greek island of Melos, was sculpted in the middle of the second century B.C.E. Popularly known by her Italian name, Venus di Milo, the goddess is half-nude. She rests on her right foot and seems to step forward toward the viewer. Originally one of her missing arms was probably raised to cover her breasts in a gesture of modesty. Her facial expression is serene. The garment draped loosely around her hips allowed the sculptor to explore the play of thin cloth over her thighs, expressing his delight in movement and physicality. More sedate than other voluptuous representations of Aphrodite from the Hellenistic period, this statue portrays a male vision of a perfect woman, highly sexual but also charmingly modest.

New Opportunities for Women

One measure of the status of women in a society is the level of female infanticide. Greek parents in the Classical Age routinely abandoned unwanted female babies, leaving them to die. Hellenistic families, however, particularly those of the Ptolemaic nobility, raised more baby girls than before. Greek women in Egypt and other Hellenized lands enjoyed full citizenship and held religious offices. Many owned land and property, paying taxes as men did, but they could only enter into business contracts of minimal value on their own.

Some aristocratic Hellenistic women wielded considerably more power than had been conceivable in the classical Greek period. The wives of Hellenistic kings were models of the new, more powerful Hellenistic woman. Inscriptions praise Hellenistic queens for demonstrating such traditional female virtues as piety and for producing sons. As public benefactors, these women built temples and public works, sponsored charioteers at the Olympic Games, and provided dowries for poor brides. Queens sometimes exerted real authority, at times supporting and commanding armies. For example, Arsinoë II (r. 276–270 B.C.E.), sister and wife of Ptolemy II, directed the Egyptian armies and navies of the Ptolemaic kingdom in their conquest of Phoenicia and much of the coast of Anatolia. Egyptian sources refer to her as Pharaoh, a royal title usually reserved for men, and she was often identified with the goddess Isis.

To a lesser extent, opportunities for non-aristocratic Greek women also increased during the Hellenistic Age. In Alexandria young women were taught dancing, music, reading and writing, and scholarship and philosophy. Often the daughters of scholars became scholars themselves. We know that non-aristocratic Greek women wrote about astronomy, musical theory, and literature, and many female poets competed for honors. In addition, a few Hellenistic women distinguished themselves as portrait painters, architects, and harpists. Despite these accomplishments, women still had fewer rights and opportunities than men, and they remained under the supervision of their male relatives. In Egypt, a woman could not travel overnight without her husband's permission.

Art and Architecture

Art and architecture during the Hellenistic period changed as Greek civilization was introduced into the successor kingdoms. Artists and architects continued to use classical motifs and themes, but instead of simply imitating classical models, they used them in new ways. This creative development of Greek classicism resulted from both the freedom that artists experienced working in a new environment and from the influences of native cultures. The most notable stylistic innovation of the Hellenistic age was the **baroque** style, which suggested movement rather than repose and often appealed to the emotions.

The baroque style was evident in many of the Hellenistic temple precincts, where the designers created sweeping vistas across carefully planned terraces and grand stairways. Some of the finest examples of Hellenistic baroque architecture have survived in Pergamum, a Greek city on the southern coast of modern Turkey, close to the Aegean Sea. To commemorate the victory of Pergamum over the Celts and the Seleucids, King Attalus I (241–197 B.C.E.) commissioned a series of monuments. The Acropolis in Athens provided the classical model for this work, but the commission of native craftsmen to create these monuments helps to explain their baroque features, most notably their vast scale and their many different focal points, which lead the viewer's eye across the façades of the buildings.

Hellenistic sculptors also took classical Greek forms in new directions. Turning away from representations of ideal perfection, Hellenistic artists delighted in exploring the movement of the human body and varieties of facial expression. Their subjects ranged from alluring love goddesses to drunks and haggard old boxers. Artists enjoyed portraying the play of fabrics across the human body to accentuate the contours of male and female flesh. The statue of Nike of Samothrace, probably carved on the island of Rhodes about 200 B.C.E., depicts this Greek goddess as if she has just landed on the bow of a ship, with her wings outstretched and her garment blowing in the wind. Sometimes painted in bright colors, these statues explored human frailty and homeliness as often as they celebrated beauty and lofty emotions. The statue of the Celt and his wife, also carved in Pergamum in the third century B.C.E. (see page 111), conveys not only physical movement, but also the depth of human emotions experienced by the man who is committing suicide.

Literature

Much Hellenistic literature has vanished, but surviving works give a glimpse of creativity and originality that often combined urbanity and scholarship. Hellenistic poets turned to frivolous themes because the repressive political climate discouraged them from questioning authority. Light comedy became immensely

4.1
4.2
4.3
4.4

baroque A dynamic style in art, architecture, and music that was intended to elicit an emotional response. Baroque buildings were massive, imposing structures with sweeping façades. The baroque style represented a development of Greek classicism in the Hellenistic period. In the seventeenth century the baroque style was closely associated with royal absolutism.

 View the Closer Look

Aspects of Hellenism in Gandharan Sculpture

PERGAMUM ALTAR OF ZEUS The buildings at Pergamum in northwest Anatolia (present-day Turkey) were constructed in the Hellenistic baroque style. They were based on classical Greek models but had sweeping facades that presented the viewer with multiple focal points. The Altar of Zeus at Pergamum, shown here in a twentieth-century reconstruction, is positioned on a massive stone podium with a 371-foot colonnade (a porch with a line of columns). Like many baroque buildings, the altar was opulently decorated. The two long friezes below the colonnade depict the life of the Greek mythological figure Telephos, son of Heracles, who was believed to be the founder of the city of Pergamum.

Justice in History
Divine Justice in the Hellenistic World

The widespread belief that personal misfortunes, such as illness, accidents, or destruction of one's property, indicated divine displeasure frequently led people in the Hellenistic world to confess their crimes. These offenses included secular crimes such as theft, slander, bodily injury, sorcery, and adultery, as well as religious crimes such as violating dietary rules, insulting the gods, or entering a sanctuary without cleansing the body or one's clothes. It did not matter whether the person had committed such an offense intentionally. The crucial factor was the sign of the gods' displeasure. When offenders became convinced of their guilt, they often went to the local sanctuary to discover the cause of the gods' anger and learn how they could atone for their misbehavior. Their objective was to receive signs from the gods through oracles or in dreams while they slept.

Inscriptions in the temple of the goddess Demeter at Knidos in Anatolia during the late second and first centuries B.C.E. reveal that the wronged party would sometimes initiate the judicial process by depositing an inscribed stone tablet at a sanctuary. The inscription would identify the alleged culprit and ask the gods to force the offender to come to the sanctuary to confess the crime. One of these inscriptions in a case of slander reads: "I dedicate to Demeter and Kore [another goddess, Demeter's daughter] the man who has made imputations against me, [claiming] that I made a poison against my own man; may he come up to the sanctuary of Demeter, with his entire family, burning [with fever] and confessing." Such inscriptions resembled the writing on "curse tablets" that people in the Hellenistic world occasionally inscribed to bring misfortune on an enemy. The purpose of these "confession inscriptions," however, was not to cause harm to another human being but to call the gods' attention to an act of injustice and to motivate those gods to pressure the guilty party to confess. The confessions were prayers for divine justice that would give the aggrieved party moral satisfaction or possibly revenge.

People suspected of crimes could also appeal to the gods to establish their innocence. When a woman named Tatias heard rumors that she had given her son-in-law a magical potion that had driven him insane, she went to the local sanctuary and "deposited curses in the temple." This public ceremony, which differed from the writing of a malevolent curse in private, was her way of demonstrating to the community that she was innocent. Unfortunately for Tatias, her relatives publicly annulled her curses, leaving her guilty in the eyes of society.

Ideally the only parties involved in this process were the accusers, the confessing criminals, and the gods, but the priests in the

TEMPLE OF APHRODITE This temple near Denizli, in modern-day Turkey, built in the first century B.C.E., was the preeminent temple of the goddess Aphrodite in Anatolia. People asking for divine assistance in eliciting confessions to crimes would often enter sanctuaries such as this.

sanctuary often played a crucial role in the process as well. They would receive or perhaps even solicit accusations from the victims of crime, assist in writing the confessions, and interpret the supposed signs of the divine will. In many cases they attempted to show that the afflictions that brought people to the sanctuary in the first place were punishments for their offenses. The priests did not, as historians once believed, inflict corporal punishment, but they did advise those who confessed how they might atone for their transgressions. Sometimes they interrogated an afflicted person who came to the sanctuary to determine the cause of the gods' wrath. Thus, the priests played a role usually assigned to judges in actual trials. The procedures followed in the sanctuaries were not trials in the proper sense of the word because they did not involve the testimony of witnesses or the delivering of verdicts. But the inscriptions often used legal language, which the priests probably suggested, and the procedure served the same purpose as a trial, which was to resolve conflict in society. Like trials, these proceedings involved encounters between the priest serving in a quasi-judicial capacity and the person who came to the sanctuary, as well as between that person and the god who was believed to have spoken through an oracle or a dream.

The involvement of priests in a process that resembled a trial of both secular and religious crimes reveals that Hellenistic societies drew no firm line between the secular and the religious spheres. Crimes that were prosecuted in the secular courts could also be dealt with in religious sanctuaries. Without the assistance of the priests, who controlled access to the sanctuaries and helped formulate the confessions, the process could not have functioned properly. The dedication of appeals and confessions to the gods also shows that the gods in these polytheistic societies were believed to play an active role not only in the resolution of problems of everyday life, but also in the administration of justice.

For Discussion

1. Why might a person in a Hellenistic kingdom go to a local sanctuary and later confess to a religious or secular offense?
2. How did Hellenistic religious beliefs influence prevailing notions of justice?

Taking It Further

Angelos Chaniotis, "Under the Watchful Eyes of the Gods," in S. Colvin (ed.), *The Greco-Roman East: Politics, Culture, Society* (2006). A study based on more than 140 confessions inscribed in stone.

popular, especially in the hands of the playwright Menander of Athens (ca. 300 B.C.E.). This clever author delighted audiences with escapist, frothy tales of temporarily frustrated love and happy endings. These plays, known now as New Comedy, developed from the risqué satires of classical Athens. They featured vivid street language and a cast of stock characters: crotchety parents, naive young men, silly young women, clever slaves, and wicked pimps.

Theocritus (ca. 300–ca. 260 B.C.E.), who came from the city of Syracuse in Sicily but wrote in Alexandria, invented a new genre called pastoral poetry. His verses described idyllic life in the countryside, but his rustic herdsmen reflected the sadness and tensions of city life. Of all the Hellenistic poets, Theocritus has had the most wide-ranging and enduring influence, providing a model for pastoral verse in Rome, Shakespeare's England, and even nineteenth-century Russia. The other great poet of Alexandria, Callimachus (ca. 305–240 B.C.E.), combined playfulness with extraordinary learning in works ranging from *Collections of Wonders of the World* to his moving love poems, the *Elegies*. His poetry provides the best example of the erudite style known as **Alexandrianism**, which demonstrated a command of meter and language and appealed more to the intellect than to the emotions.

The most accomplished historian of the Hellenistic period was Polybius (ca. 202–120 B.C.E.), a native of the Greek city of Megalopolis. Polybius devoted the latter part of his life to writing a history of Rome's meteoric rise to power within the Mediterranean region. As a work of literature, Polybius's *Histories* cannot compete with those of the great Greek historians Thucydides and Herodotus; his leaden style prevented him from capturing the drama of events. The strength of *Histories* lies in its comprehensive coverage of events in all the countries of the Mediterranean world and its adherence to high standards of accuracy and impartiality, both of which were noticeably absent in the works of his predecessors.

NIKE OF SAMOTHRACE This statue of Nike, the winged Greek goddess of victory, found on the Greek island of Samothrace, captures the sensation of her flight through the air by portraying her wings outstretched and the wind blowing the folds of her garment. The statue was situated on the sculpture of a bow of a ship, where Nike has just landed.

Alexandrianism A style of Hellenistic poetry that demonstrated a command of meter and language and appealed more to the intellect than the emotions.

  Read the Document

Polybius: Why Romans and Not Greeks Govern the World, ca. 140 B.C.E.

Hellenistic Philosophy and Science

4.4 What did Hellenistic thinkers contribute to philosophy and the scientific investigation of the natural world?

Hellenistic philosophers distinguished between three branches of their discipline: logic, the study of abstract reasoning; ethics, the study of how one should conduct one's life; and physics, the study of the natural world. In the Middle Ages educated people began to refer to physics as natural philosophy; since the eighteenth century they have identified this type of investigation as science.

COMEDY MOSAIC FROM POMPEII Many brilliant decorative mosaics have survived from the Hellenistic world. Often derived from Greek paintings that have been lost, these scenes give a vivid glimpse into everyday life. This mosaic is based on a scene from a comedy performed in a theater.

During the Hellenistic period all three branches of philosophy remained anchored in the works of Plato and Aristotle, but philosophy acquired its own distinctive features.

Philosophy: The Quest for Peace of Mind

The Hellenistic contribution to philosophy was most striking in the study of ethics. Three of the philosophical groups that emerged during this period—the Epicureans, the Stoics, and the Cynics—shared the common goal of acquiring an inner tranquility or peace of mind. According to Xenocrates (d. 314 B.C.E.), the head of the Platonic Academy in Athens, the purpose of studying philosophy "is to allay what causes disturbance in life." This quest for personal tranquility did not disregard the needs of other people. Its goal was to determine which ways of interacting with other people were right and which were wrong.

The first of these philosophical schools, the **Epicureans**, was founded by Epicurus of Samos (341–271 B.C.E.). Known by its meeting place in Athens, the Garden, this school was open to women and slaves as well as free men. Because Epicurus believed that "the entire world lives in pain," he urged people to gain tranquility through the rational choice of pleasure. The word *epicurean* today denotes a person of discriminating taste who takes pleasure in lavish eating and drinking, but the pleasure Epicurus sought was intellectual, a perfect harmony of body and mind. To

Epicureans Followers of the teachings of the philosopher Epicurus (341–271 B.C.E.). Epicureans tried to gain peace of mind by choosing pleasures rationally.

achieve this harmony, Epicurus recommended a virtuous and simple life, characterized by plain living and withdrawal from the stressful world of politics and social competition. Epicurus also reassured his students that they should fear neither death nor the gods. There was no reason to fear death because the soul was material; hence, there was no afterlife. Nor was there any reason to fear the gods, who lived happily, far from Earth, unconcerned with human activity. Freed from these fears, humans could find inner peace.

The main rival to Epicureanism was Stoicism, the school established by Zeno of Citium (ca. 335–ca. 263 B.C.E.) at Athens in 300 B.C.E. Taking its name from the Stoa Poikile (the Painted Portico) where Zeno and his successors taught, Stoicism remained influential well into the time of the Roman Empire. **Stoics** believed that all human beings have an element of divinity in them and therefore participate in one single indissoluble cosmic process. They could find peace of mind by submitting to that cosmic order, which Stoics identified with nature or fate. Thus, the word *stoic* today denotes a person who responds to pain or misfortune without showing emotion. Stoics believed that wise men did not allow the vicissitudes of life to distract them. Rather than calling for withdrawal from the world, like the Epicureans, Stoicism encouraged people to participate actively in public life. Because Stoicism accepted the status quo, many kings and aristocrats embraced it. They wanted to believe that their success formed part of a cosmic, divine plan.

Cynics took a different approach to gaining peace of mind. The word *cynic* today usually refers to a person who sneers at the sincerity of human motives and behavior. But the ancient Cynics, inspired by Antisthenes (ca. 445–360 B.C.E.), a devoted follower of Socrates, taught that the key to happiness was the rejection of all needs and desires. To achieve this goal, Cynics abandoned all possessions to lead a life of rigorous asceticism. Diogenes (ca. 412–324 B.C.E.), the chief representative of this philosophy, made his home in an empty barrel. Cynics showed contempt for the customs and conventions of society, including wealth, social position, and prevailing standards of morality. One prominent Cynic, Crates of Thebes (ca. 328 B.C.E.), caused a public scandal when he did the unthinkable: He took his wife, the philosopher Hipparchia, out for a meal in public instead of leaving her at home, where respectable women belonged. Some Cynics took the example of Diogenes to further extremes by satisfying, rather than denying, their simplest natural needs. Their behavior, which included public masturbation and defecation, gave them their name, which derived from the Greek word for dog. Their rejection of prevailing social values, coupled with their offensive public behavior, explains why their teachings failed to have a lasting impact.

ZENO OF CITIUM Zeno, the Athenian founder of Stoicism, argued that one should submit to the cosmic order, otherwise defined as nature or fate, in one's search for inner peace. Stoicism had considerable influence among Roman politicians and writers.

Explaining the Natural World: Scientific Investigation

While Athens remained the hub of philosophy in the Hellenistic Age, the Ptolemaic kings made Alexandria the center of scientific learning. There King Ptolemy I founded the Museum, an institution named after the Muses, goddesses of the arts and knowledge, that sponsored research and lectures on the natural world. Nearby, the royal Library housed hundreds of thousands of texts in an attempt to organize the entire body of knowledge of the world.

In addition to summarizing the work of previous scholars, scientists in Alexandria and throughout the Hellenistic world sought to describe the natural world as it actually was. This emphasis on scientific realism involved the rejection of some of the more speculative notions that had characterized classical Greek science. Theophrastus (ca. 371–287 B.C.E.), a disciple of Aristotle who is often considered the first scientist of the Hellenistic period, rejected the philosophical view of Aristotle that nature was static rather than dynamic and could be explained in terms of philosophical "first principles." Theophrastus's nine-volume *Enquiries into Plants* led him to the conclusion that plants had not devolved or "degenerated" from animals, as Aristotle had claimed.

In mathematics, Euclid (ca. 300 B.C.E.) produced a masterful synthesis of geometry in his work, *Elements,* which remained the standard geometry textbook until the twentieth century. Euclid demonstrated how one could attain knowledge of a subject by rational methods alone—by mathematical reasoning through the use of deductive proofs and theorems. Equally famous as a mathematician was Archimedes of Syracuse (ca. 287–212 B.C.E.), who calculated the value of *pi* (the ratio of a circle's circumference to its diameter) and measured the diameter of the sun. A sophisticated mechanical engineer, Archimedes reputedly said: "Give me a fulcrum and I will move the world." Archimedes put his scientific knowledge to work in wartime. During the Roman siege of Syracuse in 212 B.C.E., he reportedly built a huge reflecting mirror that focused the bright Sicilian sun on Roman warships, burning holes in their sails.

Knowledge of astronomy also advanced during the Hellenistic Age. In their research, Hellenistic investigators borrowed from the long tradition of observation of the heavens that Babylonian and Egyptian scholars had established. This intersection of Greek and Near Eastern astronomical work produced one of the richest new areas of knowledge in the Hellenistic world. For example, Heraclides of Pontus (ca. 388–312 B.C.E.) anticipated a heliocentric (sun-centered) theory of the universe when he observed that the planets Venus and Mercury orbit the sun, not Earth. Aristarchus of Samos (ca. 310–230 B.C.E.) established the idea that the planets revolve around the sun while spinning on their own axes. Eratosthenes of Cyrene (ca. 276–194 B.C.E.) made a calculation of the Earth's circumference that came within 200 miles of the actual figure.

The sun-centered view never won wide acceptance, however, because of fierce opposition from the followers of Aristotle, whose geocentric (Earth-centered) theories had become canonical. To support Aristotle's **cosmology** (a map of the universe), Hipparchus of Nicaea (ca. 190–127 B.C.E.) produced the first catalog of stars and insisted that they encircled the Earth. The geocentric view of the universe prevailed until the sixteenth century C.E., when the Polish astronomer Nicholas Copernicus, who had read the work of Heraclides and Aristarchus, provided mathematical data to support the sun-centered theory (see Chapter 17).

Medical theory and research also flourished in the great Hellenistic cities. Diocles, a Greek doctor of the fourth century B.C.E. who combined theory and practice, wrote the first handbook on human anatomy and invented a spoon-like tool for removing arrowheads from the human body. Doctors during this period believed that both human behavior and health were products of the balance of fluids, called humors, in the body. They argued about whether to categorize the humors as hot, cold, wet, and dry or as blood, phlegm, yellow bile, and black bile. Praxagoras of Cos (late fourth century B.C.E.) argued that the body contained more than a dozen kinds of humors. He also studied the relation of the brain to the spinal cord. Other doctors, such as Herophilus and Erasistratus, who lived in Alexandria in the fourth century B.C.E., systematically dissected human cadavers. They also may have practiced vivisection, operating on living subjects to study their organs. There is some evidence that they conducted

View the Image

Archimedes's Mirror

cosmology A theory concerning the structure and nature of the universe such as those proposed by Aristotle in the fourth century B.C.E. and Copernicus in the sixteenth century.

CHRONOLOGY: HELLENISTIC LITERATURE, SCIENCE, AND PHILOSOPHY

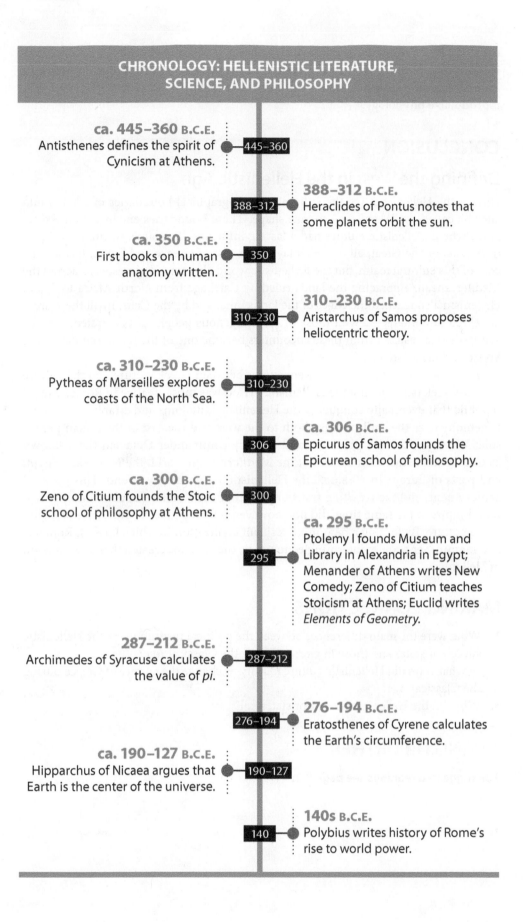

ca. 445–360 B.C.E.
Antisthenes defines the spirit of Cynicism at Athens.

`445–360`

`388–312`
388–312 B.C.E.
Heraclides of Pontus notes that some planets orbit the sun.

ca. 350 B.C.E.
First books on human anatomy written.

`350`

`310–230`
310–230 B.C.E.
Aristarchus of Samos proposes heliocentric theory.

ca. 310–230 B.C.E.
Pytheas of Marseilles explores coasts of the North Sea.

`310–230`

`306`
ca. 306 B.C.E.
Epicurus of Samos founds the Epicurean school of philosophy.

ca. 300 B.C.E.
Zeno of Citium founds the Stoic school of philosophy at Athens.

`300`

`295`
ca. 295 B.C.E.
Ptolemy I founds Museum and Library in Alexandria in Egypt; Menander of Athens writes New Comedy; Zeno of Citium teaches Stoicism at Athens; Euclid writes *Elements of Geometry*.

287–212 B.C.E.
Archimedes of Syracuse calculates the value of *pi*.

`287–212`

`276–194`
276–194 B.C.E.
Eratosthenes of Cyrene calculates the Earth's circumference.

ca. 190–127 B.C.E.
Hipparchus of Nicaea argues that Earth is the center of the universe.

`190–127`

`140`
140s B.C.E.
Polybius writes history of Rome's rise to world power.

experiments on condemned criminals who had not yet been executed, a practice outlawed today. Through dissection, whether of the dead or the living, these physicians learned a great deal about the human nervous system, the structure of the eye, and reproductive physiology.

CONCLUSION

Defining the West in the Hellenistic Age

During the Hellenistic Age the cultural and geographical boundaries of what would later be called the West began to take shape. These boundaries encompassed the regions where Hellenistic culture had a lasting influence. The lands within the empire of Alexander the Great, all of which lay to the east of Greece and Egypt, formed the core of this cultural realm, but the Hellenistic world also extended westward across the Mediterranean, embracing the lands ruled by Carthage from North Africa to Spain. Hellenism also reached the edges of the lands inhabited by the Celts. In all these areas Greek culture interacted with those of the indigenous peoples it penetrated, and the synthesis that resulted from these encounters became one of the main foundations of Western civilization.

As the next chapter shows, the encounter between Greek culture and the culture of non-Greek lands during the Hellenistic period was most creative in Rome, a small republic that eventually conquered the Hellenistic kingdoms and established its own hegemony over the lands that lay both to the west and the east of the Italian peninsula. When the Roman politician and military commander Octavian (later known as Caesar Augustus) won control of the Mediterranean world, the Near East, Egypt, and parts of Europe in 30 B.C.E., the Hellenistic Age came to an end. This political achievement, and the resulting transformation of the Roman Republic into the Roman Empire at the same time, did not, however, put an end to the influence of Hellenistic culture. By forging a new, more resilient civilization in which Greeks, Romans, and many other peoples intermingled in peace, the Romans created their own version of Hellenism.

MAKING CONNECTIONS

1. What were the main differences between the political institutions of the Hellenistic successor states and those in Greece during the Classical Age?
2. In what ways did Hellenistic culture modify or change the culture of Greece during the Classical Age?
3. Why did the Hellenistic successor states fail?

TAKING IT FURTHER

For suggested readings see page R-1.

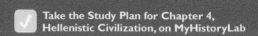
Chapter Review

The Impact of Alexander the Great

4.1 How did Alexander the Great create a large empire in which Greek civilization flourished in the midst of many diverse cultures?

A combination of diplomacy, bribery, and threats helped Phillip II position Macedonia to crush the allied armies of the city-states and set up a coalition of Greek cities under his leadership. Philip shrewdly linked classical Greek civilization with a rallying cry for imperialist expansion when he rallied the Greek people to avenge their invasion by Persia in the previous century. After Phillip's death, Alexander the Great honored his father's legacy by winning a series of victories in Asia. To hold together this vast kingdom, Alexander adopted the powers and symbolism of Persian kingship.

Hellenism in the East and West

4.2 What was the relationship between Greeks and non-Greeks in the lands that Alexander conquered and those with whom Greeks came into contact after his death?

Since the ruling elite was composed of Greeks and Macedonians and not indigenous peoples, Greek was the language of the government. To maintain the goodwill of their non-Greek subjects, Hellenistic monarchs founded cities, constructed public buildings, and maintained security by building and maintaining large professional armies. In return, kings were worshiped for the protection and peace that the government provided. While educated Greeks were curious about the cultures and traditions of the non-Greeks they encountered, few Greek settlers in new lands bothered to learn the local languages, and native resistance sometimes resulted when Greeks tried to force Hellenistic traditions on these cultures.

Hellenistic Society and Culture

4.3 What were the distinguishing features of Hellenistic society and culture, and what was the result of encounters between Greeks and non-Greeks?

Characterized by Greek city life, Hellenistic society emphasized the traditions of learning, visual arts, and citizen participation in public life. Cities, however, lost much of their independence in the Hellenistic successor kingdoms, and the wealthy acquired greater power and influence. Hellenistic cities had more diverse populations than in the classical Greek period, and the wealthy acquired a more dominant role in society and government. Some aristocratic women wielded greater power than in the classical period. Artists and architects continued to use classical motifs and themes but introduced the more highly ornamented baroque style.

Hellenistic Philosophy and Science

4.4 What did Hellenistic thinkers contribute to philosophy and the scientific investigation of the natural world?

The study of ethics was a lasting contribution of Hellenistic thinkers, as the different philosophical schools shared the common goal of acquiring an inner tranquility, or peace of mind. Scientists throughout the Hellenistic world placed an emphasis on scientific realism when it came to investigating the natural world, and the field of mathematics was marked by Euclid's demonstration of how knowledge can be attained by mathematical reasoning and Archimedes's calculation of the value of *pi*. Medical theory and research also flourished in the great Hellenistic cities.

Chapter Time Line

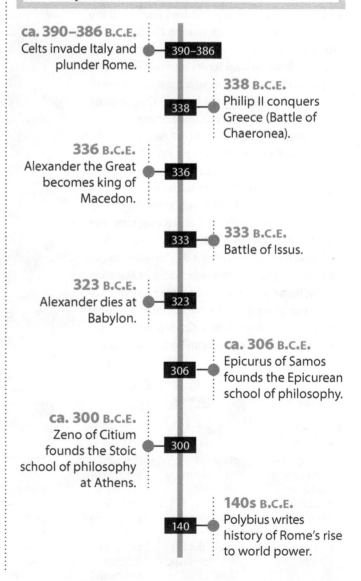

ca. 390–386 B.C.E. Celts invade Italy and plunder Rome. — 390–386

338 B.C.E. Philip II conquers Greece (Battle of Chaeronea). — 338

336 B.C.E. Alexander the Great becomes king of Macedon. — 336

333 B.C.E. Battle of Issus. — 333

323 B.C.E. Alexander dies at Babylon. — 323

ca. 306 B.C.E. Epicurus of Samos founds the Epicurean school of philosophy. — 306

ca. 300 B.C.E. Zeno of Citium founds the Stoic school of philosophy at Athens. — 300

140s B.C.E. Polybius writes history of Rome's rise to world power. — 140

5 The Roman Republic

I n 146 B.C.E. the Roman general Lucius Mummius led a large military force into the Greek city of Corinth, about 50 miles west-southwest of Athens. Mummius had just won a victory over the forces of the Achaean League, a confederation of Greek cities. Corinth was the most powerful city in this federation. Recognizing that their cause was hopeless, most Corinthians fled before the Romans reached the city gates, and Mummius entered the city unopposed. The Romans killed the men who remained, enslaved the women and children, plundered the city's treasures, and then burned Corinth to the ground. Thus ended a long chapter in the history of a Greek city known for its international trade, wealth, and the luxury in which many of its residents lived. The cities in the Achaean League came under the direct control of Rome and later became part of the Roman province of Achaea.

The sack of Corinth had a broader significance than the destruction of this once powerful Greek city. It marked the final step in the establishment of Rome as the dominant power in the Mediterranean world. The significance of this event was not lost on contemporaries. The Greek historian Polybius, who had tried to prevent the Achaean League from aligning itself with the kingdom of Macedon against Rome in 171 B.C.E., concluded his narrative of the rise of Rome in the Mediterranean with an account of this final blow to Greek independence. After the destruction of Corinth Rome continued its

VIEW OF THE FORUM FROM CAPITO-LINE HILL This view of the Forum was taken from the site of the temple of Jupiter, Rome's mightiest god. All victory processions after a successful war would have ended at this temple, where sacrifices were made. Now tourists visit the remains of buildings from which Rome ruled an international empire.

LEARNING OBJECTIVES

5.1 🔊
What type of government did Rome establish when it eliminated kingship?

5.2 🔊
How did the Roman Republic come to dominate the Mediterranean world during the Hellenistic Age?

5.3 🔊
How did the Roman encounter with Greek culture lead to the forging of a durable cultural synthesis?

5.4 🔊
How was Roman society structured, and what relationships existed within the Roman family?

5.5 🔊
Why did the Roman Republic end?

⊙ Watch the Video Series on MyHistoryLab

Learn about some key topics related to this chapter with the *MyHistoryLab Video Series: Key Topics in Western Civilization*

meteoric rise. Within little more than a century, Rome would gain control of the entire Mediterranean world, most of western Europe, and many of the Asian territories that Alexander the Great had conquered in the fourth century B.C.E. The lands that came under Roman rule would mark the geographical boundaries of what would later become the West. Rome also developed political and cultural traditions that became central to Western identity. These traditions were largely based on those of Greece, but they had a distinctive Roman imprint. The Greco–Roman culture that resulted from this encounter was then transmitted to the many lands that came under Roman rule. Greco–Roman culture, in which Latin, rather than Greek, was the dominant language in politics, diplomacy, commerce, and literature, thus became the most enduring foundation of Western civilization.

This chapter will address the question:

> **How did this small republic on the Italian peninsula rise to power within the Hellenistic world and thus lay the foundations of the geographical and cultural realm that we call the West?**

The Nature of the Roman Republic

| 5.1 | What type of government did Rome establish when it eliminated kingship? |

From Rome's Capitoline Hill a tourist today can look down on the Roman Forum and see a field of broken buildings and monuments. These remains lie at the heart of what was once an enormous empire extending from northern England to the Black Sea and from Morocco to Mesopotamia. On the western slope of the neighboring Palatine Hill, archaeologists have uncovered hut foundations from Rome's earliest occupants in the tenth century B.C.E. How the Roman Empire emerged from this crude village above a swamp remains one of the most remarkable stories in the history of the West.

During the Hellenistic Age, Rome expanded from a relatively small city-state with a republican form of government into a vast and powerful empire. As it conquered the peoples who ringed the Mediterranean—the Carthaginians, the Celts, and the Hellenistic kingdoms of Alexander's successors—Rome incorporated these newcomers into the political structure of the Republic (see **Map 5.1** on p. 147). Trying to govern these sprawling territories with institutions and social traditions suited for a city-state overwhelmed the Roman Republic and led to the establishment of a new form of government, the Roman Empire, by the end of the first century B.C.E.

Roman Origins and Etruscan Influences

Interaction with outsiders shaped the story of Rome from its beginning. Resting on low but easily defensible hills covering a few hundred acres above the Tiber River, Rome lies at the intersection of north-south and east-west trade routes that had been used

RAPE OF THE SABINE WOMEN In the legendary history of Rome, the first generation of Roman men acquired wives from the Italian tribe of Sabines, who inhabited the region around Rome. When the Sabines refused, the Romans supposedly abducted the Sabine women and then asked them to accept Roman husbands. The legend, which has no factual basis, was enshrined in the literary works of Livy and Plutarch. The word *rape* in this context refers to abduction, not sexual violation. The rape of the Sabine women became a popular subject for artists in the sixteenth and seventeenth centuries. This depiction of the rape was painted by Pietro da Cortona between 1627 and 1629.

in Italy since the Neolithic Age. Romans used these same routes to develop a thriving commerce with other peoples, many of whom they eventually conquered and absorbed.

Settlements began in Rome about 1000 B.C.E., but we know little about the lives of these first inhabitants. So small was the scale of village life that clusters of huts on the different hills may have constituted entirely different communities. What would one day be the Forum—the place of assembly for judicial and other public business—was a marsh that villagers used as protection and burial grounds.

Control of the Tiber River crossing and trade allowed Rome to grow quickly. Excavated graves from the eighth century B.C.E. reveal that a wealthy elite had already emerged. Women evidently shared the benefits of increased prosperity. One grave contained a woman buried with her chariot, a symbol of authority and status. During the seventh century Rome's population increased rapidly. Extended families or clans became a force in Roman life. Throughout this early period, according to Roman legend, kings ruled the city.

Historians think that Latin, the Roman language, was only one of at least 140 distinct languages and dialects spoken by Italy's frequently warring communities during the first four centuries of Rome's existence. During this period, Romans developed their military skills to defend themselves against their neighbors. Nevertheless, the Romans had amicable relations with some neighbors—particularly the Etruscans, who lived northwest of Rome.

In the seventh and sixth centuries B.C.E., Etruscan culture strongly influenced Rome. By 800 B.C.E. Etruscans, whose origins remain unknown although they may have migrated to Italy from Anatolia, were firmly established in Etruria (modern Tuscany), a region in central Italy between the Arno and Tiber Rivers. By the sixth century B.C.E. they controlled territory as far south as the Bay of Naples and east to the Adriatic Sea. The Etruscans maintained a loose confederation of independent cities that often fought against other Italian peoples.

Etruscans carried on a lively trade with Greek merchants, exchanging native iron ore and other resources for vases and other luxury goods. Commerce became the conduit through which Etruscans and later Romans absorbed many aspects of Greek culture. The Etruscans, for example, adopted the Greek alphabet and subscribed to many Greek myths, which they later transmitted to the Romans.

During the sixth century B.C.E., the Etruscans ruled Rome. Although the Etruscans and Romans spoke different languages, a common culture deriving from native Italian, Etruscan, and Greek communities gradually evolved, especially in religious practice. The three main gods of Rome—Jupiter, Minerva, and Juno—were first worshiped in Etruria. (The Greek equivalents were Zeus, Athena, and Hera.) Etruscan seers taught Romans how to interpret omens, especially how to learn the will of the gods by examining the entrails of sacrificed animals. Etruscans also gave the Romans a distinctive temple architecture that differed from that of the Greeks. Etruscan and later Roman temples had much deeper porticos, covered porches supported by colonnades.

Establishing the Roman Republic

By about 600 B.C.E. Romans had prospered sufficiently to drain the marsh that became the Forum. They also began to construct temples and public buildings, including the first Senate house, where the elders met to discuss community affairs. Under the rule of its kings, some of whom were of Etruscan origin, Rome became an important military power in Italy. Only free male inhabitants of the city who could afford their own weapons voted in the citizen assembly, which made public decisions with the advice of the Senate. Poor men could fight but not vote. Thus began the struggle between rich and poor that would plague Roman life for centuries.

About 500 B.C.E., when Rome had become a powerful city with perhaps 35,000 inhabitants, the Romans put an end to kingship and established a **republic**, a state in which political power resides in the people or their representatives rather than in a monarch. According to legend, in 509 B.C.E. Lucius Junius Brutus, a member of the ruling dynastic family, overthrew the tyrannical Etruscan king, Tarquin the Proud.

After the monarchy was abolished, Rome established several new institutions that structured political life for 500 years. An assembly comprising Rome's male citizens, called the Centuriate Assembly, managed the city's legislative, judicial, and administrative affairs. As in the Greek poleis, only men participated in public life. Each year, the assembly elected two chief executives called consuls, who could administer the law but whose decisions could be appealed to the assembly. In time, the assembly also elected additional officers to deal with legal and financial responsibilities. The Senate, comprising about 300 Romans who had held administrative offices, advised the consuls, though the senators had no formal authority. Priests performed religious ceremonies on behalf of the city. Hatred of kings, which became a staple of Roman political thought, prevented any one man from becoming too prominent. A relatively small group of influential families held real power within the political community by monopolizing the main offices and working behind the scenes. As we saw in Chapter 3, this kind of government is known as an oligarchy, or the rule of the few.

To celebrate the end of the monarchy, the people of Rome built a grand new temple to Jupiter on the Capitoline Hill, looking down on the Forum. They also established the community of Vestal Virgins, priestesses who served as caretakers of the sacred fire and hearth in the Temple of Vesta, one of Rome's most ancient religious sites. In such ways the welfare of Rome became a shared public concern.

Tensions between social groups shaped Roman political life during the Republic. At the top of the social hierarchy stood the **patricians**, a wealthy elite who traced their ancestry back to royal Rome. These families claimed to have toppled the monarchy. Because they monopolized the magistracies and the priesthoods, patricians occupied most of the seats in the Senate. Other rich landowners and senators with lesser pedigrees, as well as the prosperous farmers who made up the army's ranks, joined the patricians in resisting the **plebeians**, the general body of Roman citizens. The plebeians generally occupied the lower ranks of Roman society, although some of them managed to acquire

View the Map

Topographical Map: Ancient Rome, ca. Eighth Century B.C.E.

republic A state in which political power resides in the people or their representatives rather than in a monarch.

patricians In ancient Rome, patricians were aristocratic clans with the highest status and the most political influence.

plebeians The general body of Roman citizens.

Struggle of the Orders The political strife between patrician and plebeian Romans beginning in the fifth century B.C.E. The plebeians gradually won political rights and influence as a result of the struggle.

significant wealth. The plebeians demanded more political rights, such as a fair share of distributed public land and freedom from debt bondage. These efforts of poor Romans to acquire a political voice, called the **Struggle of the Orders**, accelerated during the fifth century B.C.E., when Rome experienced a severe economic recession.

The main weapon that the plebeians had in this struggle was the threat, realized on only three occasions, of literally leaving the city, thereby bringing economic life to a standstill and depriving the army of its soldiers. The first victory in the plebeians' struggle came in 494 B.C.E., when they won the right to elect two tribunes each year as their spokesmen. Tribunes could veto magistrates' decisions and so block arbitrary judicial actions by the patricians. In 471 B.C.E., a new Plebeian Assembly gave plebeians the opportunity to express their political views in a formal setting, although without the authority to enact legislation.

In 445 B.C.E., a new law permitted marriage between plebeians and patricians. This enabled wealthy plebeians to marry into patrician families. In 367 B.C.E., politicians agreed that one of each year's two consuls should be a plebeian. The plebeians now were fully integrated into Roman government. Moreover, Romans also limited the amount of public land that could be distributed to any citizen. The new arrangement prevented patricians from seizing the lion's share of conquered territories and enabled poor citizen soldiers to receive captured land. The last concession to the plebeians came in 287 B.C.E., when the decisions of the Plebeian Assembly became binding on the whole state.

When Polybius chronicled the meteoric rise of Rome to world power, he attributed the success of the Republic to its mixture of the three forms of government identified by Aristotle: monarchy, aristocracy, and democracy. In the Roman Republic, two consuls represented monarchy; the Senate represented aristocracy (those considered most fit to rule); and the assemblies, which included both patricians and plebeians, represented democracy. According to Polybius, this republican mixture of the three forms of government was supposed to prevent the evils that threatened to emerge from each: despotism from monarchy, oligarchy from aristocracy, and mob-rule from democracy. As it turned out, aristocracy tended to prevail in the Roman Republic because the two consuls were almost always rich senators and because patricians usually had the upper hand in the assemblies. It is true that the plebeians in the assembly could check the power of the patricians, and to that extent the Roman constitution was "balanced." But wealthy plebeians, who represented the "democratic" element in the Roman constitution, joined the patricians to form a new ruling elite. The government of the Roman Republic was therefore not as balanced as Polybius boasted. His description of that government, however, had a lasting impact on the efforts of later Western regimes to establish a form of government in which representatives of "the one," "the few," and "the many" all had a voice.

Roman Law

The conflict between the patricians and the plebeians during the early Republic resulted in the formulation of a body of law governing relations between individuals (private law) and between individuals and the government (public law). When the Republic was first established, legal disputes were settled by appealing to a body of unwritten customs that were believed to have originated in the distant past. When the application of these ancient customs in a specific case was unclear, a body of patricians known as the pontiffs would interpret the law. When plebeians began to participate in the political life of the Republic, they recognized that the patricians might interpret the law in favor of their social class. The assembly therefore demanded that the law be put in writing so that decisions by the pontiffs had to be based on an authoritative and publicly known text. Accordingly, a commission appointed in 451 B.C.E. produced a body of written law known as the **Law of the Twelve Tables,** which was inscribed on 12 bronze tablets and posted in the Forum. This legislation, which was supposedly modeled on the Athenian law of Solon, was actually a written summary of existing customary law, not new law being handed down for the first time.

Law of the Twelve Tables A Roman law code inscribed on 12 bronze tablets and published in 451 B.C.E. This summary of existing law was the first body of written law in Rome.

Justice in History

A Corrupt Roman Governor Is Convicted of Extortion

G overnors sent by the Roman Senate to rule the provinces wielded absolute power, which often corrupted them. One such man was Gaius Verres, who was convicted in 70 B.C.E. in a court in Rome for his flagrant abuse of power while governor of Sicily. The courtroom drama in which Verres was found guilty reveals one of the deepest flaws of the Roman Republic: the unprincipled exploitation of lands under Roman control. It also reveals one of Rome's greatest strengths: the presence of men of high ethical standards who believed in honest government and fair treatment of Roman subjects. The trial and its result reveal republican Rome at its best and worst.

While governor from 73 to 71 B.C.E., Verres had looted Sicily with shocking thoroughness. In his pursuit of gold and Greek art, Verres tortured and sometimes killed Roman citizens. His outraged victims employed the young and ambitious lawyer Marcus Tullius Cicero (106–43 B.C.E.) to prosecute Verres. They could not have chosen a better advocate.

The prosecution of Verres marks the beginning of Cicero's illustrious career as one of the most active politicians and certainly the greatest orator of the Republic. Cicero also stands as one of the most influential political philosophers of Western civilization, one who hated the corruption of political life and opposed tyranny in any form. His many literary works have influenced political thinkers from antiquity to the present.

In the Roman Republic, only senators and equestrians, the two ranks of the Roman aristocracy, between ages 30 and 60 could serve on juries for civil crimes such as those Verres committed. All adult male citizens had the right to bring a case to court, but women had less freedom to do so. After swearing oaths of good faith, accusers would read the charges in the presence of the accused, who in turn agreed to accept the decision of the court.

When a trial actually began, the prosecutor was expected to be present, but the accused could decline to attend. The prosecution and the defense both produced evidence, then cross-examined witnesses. Because a Roman lawyer could discuss any aspect of the defendant's personal or public life, character assassination became an important—and amusing—rhetorical tool.

After deliberating, the jury delivered its verdict and the judge gave the penalty required by law, generally fines or periods of exile. No provisions for appeal existed, but the assembly could grant a pardon by means of a legislative act.

Cicero worked this system to his advantage in his prosecution of Verres. He quashed an attempt to delay the trial until 69 B.C.E., when the president of the court would be a crony of Verres. Then, with a combination of ringing oratory and irrefutable evidence of Verres's crimes, Cicero made his case. The following excerpt from his speech shows Cicero's mastery of persuasive rhetoric:

Judges: At this grave crisis in the history of our country, you have been offered a peculiarly desirable gift. . . . For you have been given a unique chance to make your Senatorial Order less unpopular, and to set right the damaged reputation of these courts. A belief has taken root which is having a fatal effect on our nation—and which to us who are senators, in particular, threatens grave peril. This belief is on everyone's tongue, at Rome and even in foreign countries. It is this: That in these courts, with their present membership, even the worst criminal will never be convicted provided that he has money. . . . And at this very juncture Gaius Verres has been brought to trial. Here is a man whose life and actions the world has already condemned—yet whose enormous fortune, according to his own loudly expressed hopes, has already brought him acquittal! Pronounce a just and scrupulous verdict against Verres and you will keep the good name which ought always to be yours. . . . I spent fifty days on a careful investigation of the entire island of Sicily; I got to know every document, every wrong suffered either by a community or an individual. . . .

For three long years he so thoroughly despoiled and pillaged the province that its restoration to its previous state is out of the question. . . . All the property that anyone in Sicily still has for his own today is merely what happened to escape the attention of this avaricious lecher, or survived his glutted appetites. . . . It was an appalling disgrace for our country.

. . . In the first stage of the trial, then, my charge is this. I accuse Gaius Verres of committing acts of lechery and brutality against the citizens and allies of Rome, and many crimes against God and man. I claim that he has illegally taken from Sicily sums amounting to forty million sesterces. By the witnesses and documents, public and private, which I am going to cite, I shall convince you that these charges are true.[1]

Cicero's speech was persuasive, and the jury found Verres guilty. Verres went into exile in Marseilles to avoid his sentence, but he did not avoid punishment altogether. Justice—relentless and ironic—caught up with him years later during the civil wars that followed Julius Caesar's death in 44 B.C.E. Mark Antony, who was also a connoisseur of other people's wealth, wanted Verres's art collection for himself and so put Verres's name on a death list to obtain it. The former governor of Sicily was murdered in 43 B.C.E.

In his prosecution of Verres, Cicero delivered more than an indictment of one corrupt man. He revealed some of the deepest flaws of the Roman Republic. The trial inspired short-term reforms, but not until the reign of Emperor Caesar Augustus (r. 27 B.C.E.–14 C.E.) did Roman administration of provincial populations become more just.

SOURCE: From *Selected Works: Against Verres 1; Twenty-Three Letters; The Second Philippic Against Antony; On Duties, 111; On Old Age* by Cicero, translated by Michael Grant (Penguin Classics 1960, second revised edition, 1971.) Copyright © 1960, 1965, 1971 by Michael Grant. Reproduced by permission of Penguin Books, Ltd.

(continued on next page)

(continued from previous page)

For Discussion

1. What does the trial of Verres reveal about weaknesses in the Roman Republic?
2. Cicero's speech illustrates his disdain for corruption and tyranny. What are the tensions between personal morality and the requirements of governing a large empire?

Taking It Further

Gruen, Erich S. *The Last Generation of the Roman Republic.* Berkeley: University of California Press, 1974. A magisterial analysis of the republic's decline, with emphasis on legal affairs.

Rawson, Elizabeth. *Cicero: A Portrait.* Ithaca: Cornell University Press, 1975. This book gives a balanced account of Cicero's life.

natural law A law that is believed to be inherent in nature rather than established by human beings.

The original text of the Law of the Twelve Tables has not survived, but references in later legal documents provide a fairly good idea of its broad outlines. It covered such matters as the proper protection of women ("Women shall remain under the guardianship [of a man] even when they have reached legal adulthood") and debt bondage ("Unless he pays his debt or someone stands surety for him in court, bind him in a harness, or in chains . . ."). The value of the text to the plebeians resided not so much in the substance of the law, which was in many respects unfavorable to them, but in the legal procedures it spelled out. With the law now published, citizens discovered how to start a legal proceeding, which in civil cases (those involving property) meant they would bring the charge before a magistrate, who would then appoint a private citizen to examine witnesses and reach a decision. Only in serious criminal cases, such as homicide, would the magistrate take the initiative in prosecuting the case by himself. Because the Roman Republic did not have a large bureaucracy, the Twelve Tables encouraged citizens to settle cases among themselves, even in criminal cases involving serious physical injury.

The Twelve Tables governed civil and criminal disputes among Roman citizens. The frequency of disputes involving noncitizens, especially as Rome acquired distant lands, led to the establishment of another body of law, the *jus gentium* or law of nations. Because this law was based on what was considered to be the law of all civilized people, it was often equated with **natural law**, a system of justice believed to be inherent in nature rather than prescribed by human beings. The *jus gentium* became, in effect, the first body of international law.

Roman law developed significantly during the later years of the Roman Republic and the empire, and in the sixth century C.E. the Roman emperor Justinian promulgated a massive legal code known as the *Corpus Juris Civilis* (Body of Civil Law). This legal code later became the foundation of the legal systems of most European countries. But Romans never failed to recognize that the Law of the Twelve Tables lay at the core of this comprehensive legal code. Thus, the law written down at the behest of plebeians in the early Roman Republic became the foundation of the legal culture of the West.

Roman Territorial Expansion

5.2 How did the Roman Republic come to dominate the Mediterranean world during the Hellenistic Age?

Under the Republic, Rome conquered and incorporated all of Italy, the vast Carthaginian Empire in North Africa, Spain, and many of the Celtic lands to the north and west of Italy (see **Map 5.2** on p. 150). As a result of these conquests, the Roman state had to change the methods of government established in the fifth century B.C.E.

The Italian Peninsula

The new political and military institutions that developed in Rome enabled the Romans to conquer the entire Italian peninsula by 263 B.C.E. In the process the Romans learned the fundamental lessons necessary for ruling larger territories abroad. Romans began to expand their realm by allying with neighboring cities in Italy. For centuries, Rome and the other Latin-speaking peoples of Latium (the region of central Italy where Rome was situated) had belonged to a loose coalition of cities called the Latin League. Citizens of these cities shared close commercial and legal ties and could intermarry without losing citizenship rights in their native cities. More important, they forged close military alliances with one another.

In 493 B.C.E. Rome led the Latin cities in battle against fierce hill tribes who coveted Latium's rich farmlands. From the success of this venture, Rome learned the value of political alliances with neighbors. Rome and its allies next confronted the Etruscans. In 396 B.C.E. the Romans overcame the Etruscan city of Veii through a combination of military might and shrewd political maneuvering. From this experience, the Romans discovered the uses of careful diplomacy.

A temporary setback to Rome's expansion occurred in 389 B.C.E., when a raiding band of Celts from the north of Italy defeated a Roman army and plundered the city of Rome. Only after a generation did Romans recover from this disaster and reassert their preeminence among their allies. Still, they had learned that tenacity and discipline enabled them to endure even a serious military defeat.

The next major step in Rome's expansion came in 338 B.C.E., when Roman troops suppressed a three-year revolt of its Latin allies, who had come to resent Rome's overlordship. The peace settlement of this **Latin War** set the precedent for Rome's future expansion: Rome gave defeated peoples either partial or full citizenship depending on the treaty it struck with each community. (See *Encounters and Transformations* in this chapter.) The conquered allies were permitted to retain their own customs and were not forced to pay tribute. Rome asked for only two things in return: loyalty and troops. All allied communities had to contribute soldiers to the Roman army in wartime. With the huge new pool of troops, Rome became the strongest power in Italy.

In return for their military service and support of Rome, the newly incorporated citizens, especially wealthy landowners from the allied communities, received a share of the profits of war. They also received the guarantee of Roman protection from

Latin War A war that the Latin peoples of Italy waged against the Roman Republic between 340 and 338 B.C.E.

RUINS OF ROMAN THEATER IN AOSTA, ITALY The Greek city of Aosta in southern Italy, which flourished during the Hellenistic period, fell to Rome in the third century B.C.E. Romans built theaters in many of the cities they conquered.

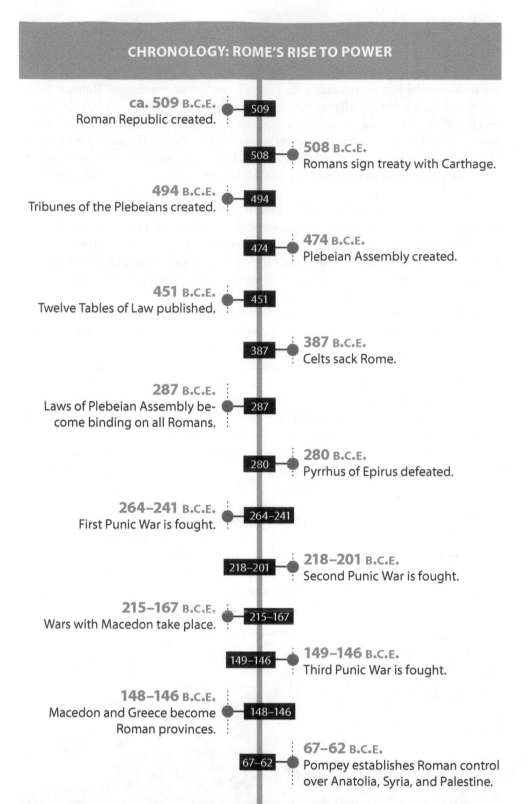

CHRONOLOGY: ROME'S RISE TO POWER

ca. 509 B.C.E.
Roman Republic created.

509

508

508 B.C.E.
Romans sign treaty with Carthage.

494 B.C.E.
Tribunes of the Plebeians created.

494

474

474 B.C.E.
Plebeian Assembly created.

451 B.C.E.
Twelve Tables of Law published.

451

387

387 B.C.E.
Celts sack Rome.

287 B.C.E.
Laws of Plebeian Assembly become binding on all Romans.

287

280

280 B.C.E.
Pyrrhus of Epirus defeated.

264–241 B.C.E.
First Punic War is fought.

264–241

218–201

218–201 B.C.E.
Second Punic War is fought.

215–167 B.C.E.
Wars with Macedon take place.

215–167

149–146

149–146 B.C.E.
Third Punic War is fought.

148–146 B.C.E.
Macedon and Greece become Roman provinces.

148–146

67–62

67–62 B.C.E.
Pompey establishes Roman control over Anatolia, Syria, and Palestine.

internal dissension or outside threats. Those communities not granted full Roman citizenship could hope to earn it if they served Roman interests faithfully. Some communities joined the Roman state willingly. Others, particularly the Samnites of south central Italy, resisted bitterly, but to no avail.

Romans then became embroiled in the affairs of Greek cities of the "toe" and "heel" of the boot-shaped Italian peninsula. Some of these Greek cities invited King

Pyrrhus of Epirus (r. 318–275 B.C.E.), a Hellenistic adventurer from the western Balkans, to wage war against Rome on their behalf. Pyrrhus invaded southern Italy with 25,000 men and 20 elephants. Though he defeated Roman armies in two great battles in 280 B.C.E., he lost nearly two-thirds of his own troops and withdrew from Italy. "Another victory like this and I'm finished for good!" he said to a comrade, giving rise to the expression "a Pyrrhic victory," which is a win so costly that it is ruinous. Without Pyrrhus's protection, the Greeks in southern Italy could not withstand Rome's legions, and by 263 B.C.E. Rome ruled all of Italy.

The Struggle with Carthage

By the third century B.C.E., imperial Carthage dominated the western Mediterranean region. From the capital city of Carthage located on the North African coast near modern Tunis, Carthaginians held rich lands from modern Algeria to Morocco, controlled the natural resources of southern Spain, and dominated the sea lanes of the western Mediterranean. Phoenician traders had founded Carthage in the eighth century B.C.E., and the city's energetic merchants carried on business with Greeks, Etruscans, Celts, and eventually Romans.

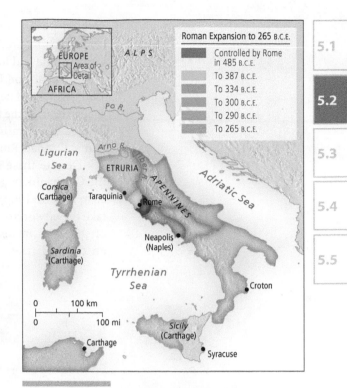

MAP **5.1** ROME'S EXPANSION IN ITALY Rome acquired control of Italy gradually over the course of more than 200 years. By 265 B.C.E. it had control of almost the entire Italian peninsula. How did Rome acquire these various lands?

Hellenistic culture influenced Carthage as it did other Mediterranean and Near Eastern cities. During the Classical Age, Carthaginian trade with the Greek cities in Sicily, and probably with Greek artisans in North Africa, introduced many aspects of Greek culture to Carthage. For example, Carthaginians worshiped the Greek goddess of agriculture, Demeter, and her daughter, Kore (also called Persephone), in an elegant temple. By the fourth century B.C.E. the Carthaginian Empire was playing an integral role in the economy of the Hellenistic world by exporting agricultural products, raw materials, metal goods, and pottery.

Rome and Carthage were old acquaintances. At the beginning of the Republic, the two had signed a commercial treaty. More than two centuries of wary respect and increasing trade followed. But in 264 B.C.E., just as Rome established power throughout the Italian peninsula, a war between Greek cities in Sicily drew Rome and Carthage into conflict. When a Carthaginian fleet went to help a Greek city in Sicily, another city, controlled by soldiers of Italian descent, asked Rome for assistance in dislodging the Carthaginians. The Senate refused, but the Plebeian Assembly, eager for the spoils of war, voted to intercede. Rome invaded Sicily, setting off the First Punic War, so called because the word *Punic* comes from the Latin word for *Phoenician*.

The First Punic War between Rome and Carthage for control of Sicily lasted from 264 to 241 B.C.E. During this time the Romans, who persisted in the conflict despite costly defeats, learned how to fight at sea, cutting off the Carthaginian supply lines to Sicily. In 241 B.C.E. Carthage signed a treaty in which it agreed to surrender Sicily and the surrounding islands and to pay a war indemnity over the course of a decade. Roman treachery, however, wrecked the agreement. While the Carthaginians struggled to suppress a revolt of mercenary soldiers, Rome seized Corsica and Sardinia, over which Carthage had lost effective control, and demanded larger reparations. Roman bad faith stoked Carthaginian desire for revenge.

War did not resume for another two decades. Under the able leadership of Hamilcar Barca (270–228 B.C.E.), Carthage developed resources in Spain, while Rome campaigned against Celts in north Italy and fierce tribes on the Adriatic coast. During these years trade between Rome and Carthage expanded. The growth of Carthaginian power in Spain, however, led to renewed conflict with Rome. The Second Punic War (218–201 B.C.E.)

erupted when Hamilcar's son, Hannibal (247–182 B.C.E.), 25 years old and eager for vengeance, ignored a Roman warning and captured Saguntum, a Spanish town with which Rome had formal ties of friendship. In a daring move, Hannibal then launched a surprise attack on Italy from the north by marching from Spain and crossing the Alps. With an army of nearly 25,000 men and 18 elephants, he crushed the Roman armies sent against him. In the first major battle, at the Trebia River in the Po Valley, 20,000 Romans died. At Lake Trasimene in Etruria in 217 B.C.E., another 25,000 Romans fell. In the same year at Cannae, Rome lost 50,000 men in its worst defeat ever.

Despite these staggering losses, the Romans persevered and eventually defeated the Carthaginian general. They succeeded, first of all, because Hannibal lacked sufficient logistical support from Carthage to capitalize on his early victories to besiege and take the city of Rome. Second, most of Rome's allies in Italy remained loyal. They had often seen Romans prevail in the past and knew that the Romans took fierce revenge on disloyal friends. Thus, the Roman policy of including and protecting allies

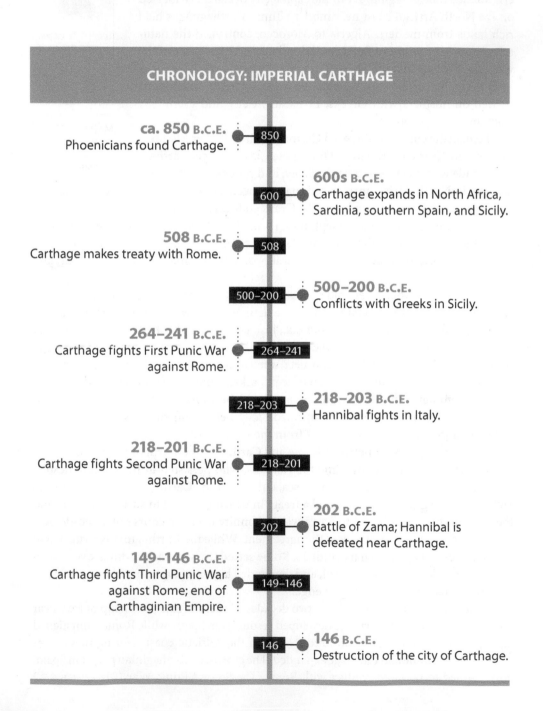

CHRONOLOGY: IMPERIAL CARTHAGE

ca. 850 B.C.E.
Phoenicians found Carthage.
850

600s B.C.E.
600
Carthage expands in North Africa, Sardinia, southern Spain, and Sicily.

508 B.C.E.
Carthage makes treaty with Rome.
508

500–200
500–200 B.C.E.
Conflicts with Greeks in Sicily.

264–241 B.C.E.
Carthage fights First Punic War against Rome.
264–241

218–203
218–203 B.C.E.
Hannibal fights in Italy.

218–201 B.C.E.
Carthage fights Second Punic War against Rome.
218–201

202
202 B.C.E.
Battle of Zama; Hannibal is defeated near Carthage.

149–146 B.C.E.
Carthage fights Third Punic War against Rome; end of Carthaginian Empire.
149–146

146
146 B.C.E.
Destruction of the city of Carthage.

paid off. A third reason for Hannibal's defeat was the indomitable Roman spirit. Finally, no matter how many times they were defeated, the Romans simply refused to stop fighting.

The turning point in the war came when Roman commanders adopted a new strategy. After incurring so many defeats, the army dared not face Hannibal in open battle. Instead, Quintus Fabius Maximus (d. 202 B.C.E.), the Roman commander in Italy, avoided direct confrontation on the battlefield and used guerilla tactics to pin down Hannibal in Italy, thereby earning the nickname "the Delayer." At the same time Publius Cornelius Scipio, later called Africanus (237–187 B.C.E.), took command of the Roman forces in Spain. Within a few years he defeated the Carthaginian forces there, preventing reinforcements from reaching Hannibal. In 204 B.C.E., Scipio led Roman legions into Africa, forcing Carthage to recall Hannibal from Italy to protect the city.

At the Battle of Zama near Carthage in 202 B.C.E., fortune finally deserted Hannibal. Scipio triumphed, and Hannibal fled into exile. Hannibal had won every battle but his last. Though Scipio did not destroy Carthage, the city lost all of its overseas territories to Rome.

Because the battles against Hannibal had been so costly, many vengeful Romans wanted the total destruction of Carthage. In particular, the statesman Marcus Porcius Cato (234–149 B.C.E.), who ended every public utterance with the demand "Carthage must be destroyed!", goaded Romans to resume war with their old adversary. The Third Punic War (149–146 B.C.E.) resulted in the destruction of Carthage. Survivors were enslaved, and the city was burned to the ground. Its territories became the Roman provinces of Africa.

Roman casualties in the struggle against Carthage resulted in a temporary change in the position of women in Roman society. Roman losses in the Battle of Cannae were so great that according to the historian Livy, "There was not one matron who was not bereaved." The inheritance of the slain soldiers' wealth by widows and children increased the fortunes of many Roman women, some of whom openly displayed their newfound wealth. In 215 B.C.E., to help pay the staggering cost of the war, the government passed the Oppian Law, which restricted the amount of gold that any single woman or widow could hold and forbade them to wear certain articles of clothing. In 195 B.C.E. a group of wealthier Roman women demonstrated in favor of repealing the Oppian Law. The women's participation in these demonstrations—the first of their kind in the West—marked the growing independence of women in the Republic.

View the Map

Map Discovery: The Punic Wars

The Macedonian Wars

By the end of the Punic Wars, Rome had also become involved in the affairs of the Hellenistic kingdoms of the East. Initially reluctant to take direct control of these regions, Roman leaders gradually assumed responsibility for maintaining order in the region and eventually established absolute control over the entire eastern Mediterranean region.

Rome waged three wars against Macedon between 215 and 167 B.C.E. that resulted in Rome's gaining mastery of Macedon and Greece. The First Macedonian War (215–205 B.C.E.) began when the Macedonian king, Philip V (r. 221–179 B.C.E.), made an alliance with Hannibal after the Roman defeat at the Battle of Cannae. The results of the conflict were inconclusive. Rome entered a second war with Macedon (201–196 B.C.E.) because Philip and the Seleucid king Antiochus III of Syria (r. 223–187 B.C.E.) had agreed to split the eastern Mediterranean between them. The poleis of Greece begged Rome for help, and Rome responded by ordering Philip to cease meddling in Greek affairs. Philip refused, and Roman forces easily defeated him with the support of Greek cities. In 196 B.C.E. the Roman general Titus Quinctius Flamininus declared the cities of Greece free and withdrew his forces.

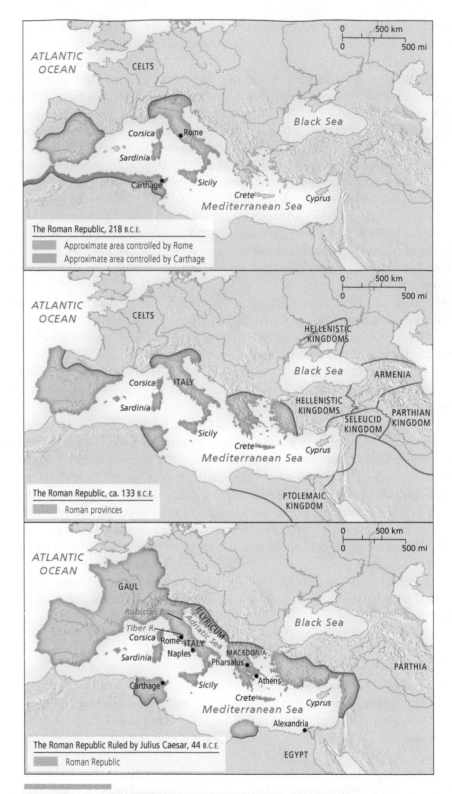

MAP **5.2** ROMAN CONQUEST DURING THE REPUBLIC Armies of the Roman Republic conquered the Mediterranean world during the Hellenistic Age, overcoming the Carthaginian Empire, the Hellenistic successor kingdoms, and many Celtic peoples in Spain and Gaul. What was the key to Roman military success?

These cities were not truly free, however. Rome installed oligarchic governments, on whose support the Romans could rely. These unpopular regimes reflected the class distinctions of Rome itself. When Antiochus III sent an army to free Greece from Roman control, Rome defeated him in 189 B.C.E. Rome imposed heavy reparations but took no territory, preferring to protect the newly freed Greek cities of Anatolia and Greece from a distance.

Encounters and Transformations
Roman Citizenship

In the early Roman Republic, citizenship, as in classical Athens, was a privilege granted to relatively few men. Roman citizens had the full protection of the law and could vote and hold political office. All legitimate male children of Roman citizens acquired the status of their fathers at birth. Neither slaves nor women possessed the rights of citizenship, but freed slaves acquired a limited form of citizenship upon their emancipation, and the sons of freed slaves became citizens.

The nature of Roman citizenship changed as the result of Roman encounters with the inhabitants of the territories in Italy that Rome conquered and absorbed into the Roman state. At the end of the Latin War (340–338 B.C.E.) Rome granted a limited form of citizenship to the former members of the Latin League that had attempted to acquire independence from the Republic. These new citizens acquired rights of property and the right to migrate to a different city within the lands the Republic controlled, but they could not enter into a lawful marriage with full Roman citizens. This form of limited citizenship, known as Latin right, gradually became a legal category that was extended beyond former members of the Latin League.

Citizens of states that were allied with Rome, known as *socii*, could acquire certain legal rights of citizenship in exchange for military service. Dissatisfaction with such arrangements was one of the causes of the Social War of 91–88 B.C.E. During this war the Senate passed a law, known as *Lex Julia*, that granted citizenship to all Italian and *socii* states that were not involved in the war or who would be willing to cease hostilities. Thus, the offer of citizenship became a tool of Roman military and foreign policy. At the end of the war Rome extended full Roman citizenship to all *socii* and those possessing Latin Right.

The *Lex Julia* marked a significant step in establishing the principle that one acquired citizenship by birth in a territory or state. This *lex solis* (law of territory) eventually became the main basis for determining nationality and citizenship in the West, although it has often had to accommodate the *lex sanguinis* (law of blood), in which one acquires citizenship from a parent or other relative. Both principles, for example, have a role in determining citizenship in the United States today. The original form of Roman citizenship, as a privilege granted to certain individuals, continued to determine the status of "freemen" in European cities until the nineteenth century, but the basis of Western nationality that prevails today has deep roots in the Roman law of citizenship passed in the first century B.C.E.

For Discussion

1. How did military and diplomatic needs change the Roman law of citizenship?
2. To what extent does the definition of American citizenship today reflect the Roman inheritance?

Rome's policy of control from a distance changed after a third war with Macedon (172–167 B.C.E.), when a new Macedonian king tried to supplant Rome as protector of Greece. After a smashing victory, Rome divided Macedon into four separate republics and forbade marriage and trade among them. Roman troops ruthlessly stamped out all opposition, destroying 70 cities and selling 150,000 people into slavery. The same fate awaited the Achaean cities that turned against Rome, most notably Corinth, whose destruction at the hands of the Roman general Mummius was described at the beginning of this chapter.

The Culture of the Roman Republic

5.3 How did the Roman encounter with Greek culture lead to the forging of a durable cultural synthesis?

During five centuries of republican rule, Rome created a new cultural synthesis by mixing elements of its own culture with that of Greece. The resulting synthesis, which Rome later disseminated throughout its empire, became a major foundation of Western identity. Much of the Greek culture that Rome assimilated and modified originated in the Hellenistic period, and the main impetus of this cultural exchange was Roman territorial expansion within the Hellenistic world.

The Encounter Between Hellenistic and Roman Culture

Romans had interacted with Greek culture for centuries, first indirectly through Etruscan intermediaries, and then through direct contact with Greek communities in southern Italy and Sicily. During the second century B.C.E., when Rome acquired the eastern Mediterranean through its wars with Macedon and the Seleucids, Hellenism's intellectual influence on Rome accelerated. In addition to fine statues and paintings, Greek ideas about literature, art, philosophy, and rhetoric poured into Rome after the Macedonian wars.

This Hellenistic legacy challenged many Roman assumptions about the world. But there was a paradox in how Roman patricians reacted to Hellenism. Many noblemen in Rome felt threatened by the novelty of Hellenistic ideas. They preferred to maintain their conservative traditions of public life and thought. They wanted to preserve the image of a strong and independent Roman culture, untainted by foreign influences. Thus, during the second century B.C.E., Romans occasionally tried to expel Greek philosophers from Rome because they worried that Greek ideas might undermine traditional Roman values. Yet many Roman aristocrats also admired the sophistication of Greek political thought, art, and literature and wished to participate in the Hellenistic community.

Consequently many members of the Roman elite learned Greek, but refused to speak it while on official business in the East. While Latin remained the language spoken in the Senate house, senators hired Greek tutors to instruct their sons at home in philosophy, literature, history, and rhetoric, and Greek intellectuals found a warm welcome from Rome's upper class. Cato the Censor, the senator who had insisted that Rome destroy Carthage, embodied the paradox of maintaining public distance from Greek culture while privately cherishing it. He cultivated an appearance of forthrightness and honesty, traditional Roman values that he claimed were threatened by Greek culture. He publicly denounced Greek oratory as unmanly,

CIRCULAR TEMPLE This circular temple from the city of Rome near the Tiber River dates to the late second century B.C.E. It is the earliest surviving marble temple in Rome. The plan of the temple and the original marble of the columns and much of the rest of the building came from Greece.

while drawing upon his deep knowledge of Greek rhetoric and literature to write his speeches praising Roman culture.

Before their exposure to the Hellenistic world in the second century B.C.E., Romans had little interest in literature. Their writing consisted mainly of inscriptions of laws and treaties on bronze plaques hung from the outer walls of public buildings. Families kept records of the funeral eulogies of their ancestors, while priests maintained simple lists of events and religious festivals. By about 240 B.C.E., Livius Andronicus, a former Greek slave, began to translate Greek dramas into Latin. In 220 B.C.E., a Roman senator, Quintus Fabius Pictor, wrote a history of Rome in Greek—the first major Roman prose work.

Hellenistic culture also had a major impact on Roman drama. Two Roman playwrights, Plautus (ca. 250–184 B.C.E.) and Terence (ca. 190–159 B.C.E.), took their inspiration from Hellenistic New Comedy and injected humor and wit into Roman literature. Their surviving works, which were always set in the Greek world, offer entertaining glimpses into the pitfalls of everyday life while also reinforcing the patrician values of the rulers of Rome's vast new domains.

Art and Architecture

The massive infusion of Hellenistic art to Rome following the Macedonian wars inevitably affected public taste. The most prestigious works of art decorated public shrines and spaces throughout the city. Many others went to private collectors, including Gaius Verres, the corrupt governor of Sicily who plundered the artistic treasures of that province when he was governor between 73 and 71 B.C.E. (See *Justice in History* in this chapter.) Ironically Cicero, who prosecuted Verres, was himself an avid collector of Greek art. The mania for Greek art became so intense that Greek artists soon moved to Rome to enjoy the patronage of wealthy Romans.

In Rome these artists often produced copies of Greek originals. In many cases only these Roman copies have survived. If it had not been for the Greek artists in Rome, therefore, many treasures of Greek art would have been lost to posterity. The encounter between Greece and Rome was not, however, limited to the imitation of Greek works. In portrait sculpture, for example, a realistic style developed in Rome that unflinchingly depicted all the wrinkles of experience on a person's face. In this way the venerable Roman tradition of making ancestral masks merged with Greek art.

The development of Roman architecture during the Republic tells a similar story. The early Roman works of architecture were essentially copies of Greek originals, complete with the three orders of Doric, Ionic, and Corinthian capitals on the columns. The main contributions that Romans made to architecture were structural, as in the construction of arches, vaults, and domes, rather than in artistic design. In the first century B.C.E., however, the magnificent temple of Fortune at Praeneste, a town near Rome, combined Italian and Hellenistic concepts in a genuinely Greco–Roman style. By the end of the Republic, Romans had gained enough confidence to adopt the intellectual heritage of Greece and use it to serve their own ends without fear of seeming "too Greek."

Philosophy and Religion

Many educated Romans found Greek philosophy attractive. The theory of matter advanced by the Hellenistic philosopher Epicurus, whose ethical philosophy we discussed in Chapter 4, gained wide acceptance among Romans. Epicurus believed that everything has a natural cause: that "nothing comes from nothing." Romans learned about Epicurus's theories of matter and the infinity of the universe from the poem, *On the Nature of the Universe,* by the Roman poet Lucretius (d. ca. 51 B.C.E.), who wrote in Latin. The Hellenistic ethical philosophy that held the greatest appeal to Romans, however, was Stoicism, because it encouraged an active public life. Stoic emphasis on mastering human difficulties appealed to patrician Romans' sense of duty and dignity. Cicero, in particular, combined Stoic ideas in a personal yet fully Roman way. He stressed moral behavior in political life while urging the attainment of a broad education. Cicero's high-minded devotion to the Republic won him the enmity of unscrupulous politicians. He was murdered in 43 B.C.E. after making public speeches accusing Mark Antony of being a threat to republican freedom.

The encounter between Roman and Hellenistic religion provides a striking example of the Greco–Roman cultural synthesis. Contact with Greek civilization during the Hellenistic period led to the development of a closer correspondence between many Roman and Greek gods. Thus, the powerful Roman god Jupiter acquired many of the characteristics of the Greek god Zeus. The Roman god of war, Mars, resembled the Greek god Ares, and the Roman goddess of hunting, Diana, acquired many of the attributes of Artemis. But the mythical personalities and activities of Roman gods were never the same as those of their Greek counterparts. Jupiter, for example, was not as sexually voracious as Zeus, while the Roman goddess Venus combined many of the features of the Greek goddess Aphrodite with those of the Etruscan deity Turan. All in all, Roman gods were much better behaved and more dignified than the group that Homer bequeathed to the Greeks.

Romans also recognized the local gods of the territories they conquered and absorbed. A decision by the Roman Senate to import the image of the foreign nature

ROMAN AND GREEK COLUMNS The Theater of Marcellus in Rome, completed in the late first century B.C.E., used columns with Doric, Ionic, and Corinthian capitals modeled on those in Greek architecture. Three of these columns with Corinthian capitals are shown to the left. Doric capitals, modeled on those of the Greek Parthenon, shown to the right, were often used in Roman architecture. In the classical revival of the eighteenth century C.E., the Doric order connoted seriousness of purpose, and in the United States it symbolized republican virtue.

goddess Cybele to Rome in 204 B.C.E. illustrates the ease with which Rome acquired new deities. The cult of Cybele, known as the Great Mother, flourished in the Hellenistic kingdom of Pergamum, where devotees worshiped her in the form of an ancient and holy rock. During the war with Hannibal, the Senate imported the rock to Rome to inspire and unify the city. A committee of leading citizens brought the sacred boulder to a new temple on the Palatine Hill amid wild rejoicing. When the ship carrying the rock got stuck in the Tiber River, legend has it that a noble lady, Claudia Quinta, towed the ship with her sash. Not only did Rome defeat Hannibal soon after the arrival of Cybele's sacred stone, but the move cemented Roman relations with Pergamum.

The recognition of imported gods resulted in a proliferation of Roman deities. In 27 B.C.E. the government constructed a new temple, the Pantheon (literally a "temple of all the gods"), to honor the hundreds of gods that the people recognized. With so many different gods, the Republic developed a policy of tolerating a wide variety of religious practices. This leniency, however, had its limits. The governing class viewed with suspicion any religious practice that was not conducted publicly, threatened public order, or challenged conventional standards of morality. In 186 B.C.E. the consuls received reports that a new cult of the god Dionysos, whom the Romans called Bacchus, had spread from Erturia to Rome, conducting nocturnal orgies. The members of this cult were allegedly engaging in "the promiscuous intercourse of free-born men and women" and

STATUE OF CYBELE, THE GREAT MOTHER Romans worshiped the Great Mother (*Magna Mater*) after her cult was introduced in Rome during the Second Punic War against Hannibal. People had worshiped this goddess throughout the eastern Mediterranean since remote antiquity. This statue represents her majestic power.

"debaucheries of every kind." They also were accused of "poison and secret murders" that went undetected because the "loud shouting and the noise of drums and cymbals" drowned out the cries of the victims. The government responded to these reports, which were almost certainly exaggerated, by demanding the arrest of the participants, declaring that no religious ceremonies should take place in private, and forbidding such assemblies in the future.

View the Image

The Interior of the Dome of the Pantheon, Rome

Rhetoric

The Roman passion for oratory, exemplified in the speeches of Cicero, also reflected the Roman adoption of a Greek tradition. As we saw in Chapter 3, Athenians developed the art of oratory to a high level. Romans had great admiration for this Greek tradition and imitated Athenian oratorical style. To some extent, Romans suffered from an inferiority complex regarding their oratorical skills. The great Roman rhetorician Quintilian (35–100 C.E.) admitted that Roman orators could never be as elegant or as subtle as the Greeks, but he argued that they could be "blunter" and "weightier." By emphasizing the power of persuasive speech, employed mainly in politics and law, Romans developed a style of oratory that was more effective, if not as sophisticated, as that of Greece.

As in many other areas of culture, the Roman achievement in oratory proved to be more durable than that of the Greeks, mainly because Romans developed a tradition of rhetorical instruction that had a lasting influence on Western education. Learning how to give classical orations became a skill once again during the Renaissance of the

Read the Document

Letters to Cicero, Fourteenth Century

TABLE 5.1 ROMAN GODS AND THEIR GREEK COUNTERPARTS

Roman God	Greek God	Association
Apollo	Apollo	the sun, prophecy, medicine
Bacchus	Dionysos	wine, agriculture, festivity
Ceres	Demeter	plants, maternal love
Diana	Artemis	hunting, the moon, fertility
Jupiter	Zeus	light, the sky
Juno	Hera	women
Mars	Ares	war
Mercury	Hermes	trade
Minerva	Athena	wisdom
Neptune	Poseidon	the sea
Victoria	Nike	Victory
Pan	Pan	herds, forests
Proserpina	Persephone or Kore	Fertility
Pluto	Hades	the underworld and the dead
Venus	Aphrodite	love, sex, beauty

fifteenth and sixteenth centuries, especially in Italy, which revived the Greco–Roman culture that had flourished in the Roman Republic. Educators in Renaissance Europe, as in ancient Rome, placed a premium on one's ability to inspire citizens to political or military action. Rhetoric, the art of persuasion, became more important, at least for members of the educated elite, than the attainment of philosophical wisdom. Thus, the knowledge of and training in rhetoric became one of the cultural legacies that the Roman Republic bequeathed to the West.

Social Life in Republican Rome

5.4 How was Roman society structured, and what relationships existed within the Roman family?

Under the Republic a few influential families dominated political life, sometimes making decisions about war and peace from which they could win wealth and prestige. The Roman Republic remained strong because these ruling families took pains to limit the power any one man or extended political family could attain.

Patrons and Clients

The ruling families of Rome established political networks that extended their influence throughout Roman society. These relationships depended on the traditional Roman institution of **patrons and clients**. By exercising influence on behalf of a social subordinate, a powerful man (the patron) would bind that man (the client) to him in anticipation of gaining future support. In this way complex webs of personal interdependency influenced the entire Roman social system. The patron-client system operated at every level of society. It was customary for a man of influence to receive his clients at his home the first thing in the morning. In a modest household the discussion between patron and client might involve everyday business such as shipping fish, arranging a marriage, or making a loan. But in the mansion of a Roman patrician a patron might be more interested in forging a political alliance. When several patron-client groups joined forces, they became significant political factions under the leadership of one powerful patron.

patrons and clients In ancient Roman society, a system in which a powerful man (the patron) would exercise influence on behalf of a social subordinate (the client) in anticipation of future support or assistance.

Pyramids of Wealth and Power

Like its political organization, Rome's social organization demonstrated a well-defined hierarchy. By the first century B.C.E. a new, elite class of political leaders had emerged in Rome, composed of both the original patrician families and wealthy plebeians who had attained membership in the Senate through their service in various public offices. The men of this leadership class dominated the Senate and formed the inner circle of government. From their ranks came most of the consuls. They set foreign and domestic policy, led armies to war, held the main magistracies, and siphoned off the lion's share of the Republic's resources.

Beneath this elite group came the equestrian class. Equestrians normally abstained from public office but were often tied to political leaders by personal obligation. They were primarily well-to-do businessmen who prospered from the financial opportunities that Rome's territorial expansion provided. For example, during the Republic, equestrian businessmen could bid on contracts to collect taxes from the provinces. The man awarded such a contract had few restraints on the methods by which he raised the revenue. After paying the treasury the amount agreed upon in the contract, he could keep any surplus as profit. Many equestrians accumulated fortunes in this way.

Next in rank came the large body of citizens who were known as plebeians. As we have seen, this group had acquired political representation and influence, but the Plebeian Assembly had gradually come under the control of politicians who were the clients of patrician patrons. These wealthy plebeian politicians, who had become members of a new ruling elite, had little interest in the condition of other plebeians, who now had no direct means to express their political will. Army service kept many plebeians who had small farms away from their land for long periods of time. Consequently, many plebeian farmers went bankrupt. Rich investors seized this opportunity to create huge estates by grabbing the bankrupt farms and replacing the free farmers with slaves. Sometimes impoverished plebeians became dependent tenant farmers on land they had once owned themselves. As a result, these plebeians increasingly turned to leaders who promised to protect them and give them land.

Rome's Italian allies had even fewer rights than the plebeians, despite their service in the Roman armies. Although millions of allies inhabited lands controlled by Rome, only a privileged few of the local elites received Roman citizenship. The rest could only hope for the goodwill of Roman officials.

At the bottom of the Roman hierarchy were slaves. By the first century B.C.E., about two million slaves captured in war or born in captivity lived in Italy and Sicily, amounting to about one-third of the population. Like Greeks, Romans considered slaves to be pieces of property, "talking tools," whom their owners could exploit at will. Freed slaves owed legal obligations to their former masters and were their clients. The brutal inequities of this system led to violence. The slave gangs who farmed vast estates in Sicily revolted first. In 135 B.C.E. they began an ill-fated struggle for freedom that lasted three years and involved more than 200,000 slaves.

Thirty years later another unsuccessful outburst began in southern Italy and Sicily because slave owners refused to comply with a senatorial decree to release any slaves who once had been free allies of Rome. During this outburst, 30,000 slaves took up arms between 104 and 101 B.C.E. The most destructive revolt occurred in Italy from 73 to 71 B.C.E. An army of more than 100,000 slaves led by the Thracian gladiator Spartacus (gladiators were slaves who fought for public entertainment) battled eight Roman legions, totaling about 50,000 men, before being crushed by the superior Roman military organization.

((• 🕮 **Read the Document**

Slaves in the Roman Countryside, ca. 150 B.C.E.–50 C.E.

The Roman Family

A Roman *familia* typically included not just the husband, wife, and unmarried children, but also their slaves and often freedmen and others who were dependent on the household. Legitimate marriages required the agreement of both husband and wife. Women usually married at puberty, as had been the practice in classical Athens, and men did so in their twenties. In most families only two or three children survived infancy. It was fairly common and socially acceptable for men to live with unmarried women (concubines) before they were married or after their wives had died, but not while they were married. Married men seeking extramarital sex generally turned to their slaves or engaged the services of prostitutes, a practice that was legal in republican Rome.

The Roman family mirrored the patterns of authority and dependency found in the political arena. Just as a patron commanded the support of his clients regardless of their status in public life, so the male head of the household directed the destiny of all his subordinates within the *familia*. A man ruled his *familia* with full authority over the purse strings and all of his descendants until he died. The head of the family, the *paterfamilias,* theoretically held power of life and death over his wife, children, and slaves, though few men exercised such power. In practice, women and grown children often enjoyed considerable independence, and patrician women often influenced political life, though always from behind the scenes.

Upper-class Romans placed great value on the continuity of the family name, family traditions, and control of family property through the generations. For these reasons they often adopted males, even of adult age, to be heirs, especially if they had no legitimate sons of their own. Legitimate offspring always took the name of their father, and in case of divorce, which could be easily obtained, continued to live with him. Illegitimate offspring stayed with their mother.

With few exceptions Roman women remained legally dependent on a male relative. In the most common form of marriage, a wife remained under the formal control of the *paterfamilias* to whom she belonged before her marriage—in most cases, her father. In practice this meant that she retained control of her own property and the inheritance she had received from her father. A husband in this sort of marriage would have to be careful to avoid angering his wife's father or brothers, and so he might treat his wife more justly. Another, older form of marriage brought the wife under the full control of her husband after the wedding. She had to worship the family gods of her husband's household and accept his ancestors as her own. If her husband died, one of his male relatives became her legal protector.

Slaves could not achieve the stability of family life through the generations that free Romans desired. Former female slaves (freedwomen) remained tied to their former masters with bonds of dependency and obligation. Roman law did not recognize marriage between slaves. Some Roman handbooks, explaining how to use slaves to maximum advantage, advocated letting slaves establish conjugal arrangements. Owners could, however, shatter such unions by selling either of the enslaved partners or their offspring.

The End of the Roman Republic

5.5   Why did the Roman Republic end?

The inequalities of wealth and power in Roman society eventually destroyed the Republic. The rapid acquisition of territories and the enormous wealth that the Roman elite accumulated from overseas conquest heightened those differences. Those who profited the most from imperial rule—politicians, governors, generals, and businessmen—fiercely resisted reformers' efforts to achieve a more equitable distribution of resources. The ruling elite sought personal glory and political advantage even if it came at the Republic's expense. Their quest for political prominence through military adventure, coupled with flaws in Rome's political institutions, eventually overwhelmed the republican constitution and brought about a revolution—a decisive, fundamental change in the political system.

The Gracchi

During the second century B.C.E., more and more citizen farmers in Italy lost their farms to powerful landholders, who replaced them with gangs of slaves. Some members of the political elite feared the danger inherent in these developments. If citizen farmers could no longer meet the property requirements for military service and pay for their own weapons, as they were required to do, Rome would lose its supply of recruits for its legions.

Two young brothers, Tiberius and Gaius Gracchus, attempted reforms. Although their mother was a patrician (the daughter of Scipio Africanus), she had married a wealthy plebeian. Thus, the brothers were legally plebeian, and they sought influence through the tribunate, an office limited to plebeians. As a tribune, Tiberius Gracchus (162–133 B.C.E.) convinced the Plebeian Assembly to pass a bill limiting the amount of public land that one man could possess. Excess land from wealthy landholders was to be redistributed in small lots to poor citizens. While the land redistribution was in progress, conservative senators ignited a firestorm of opposition to Tiberius Gracchus. He responded by running for a second term as a tribune, which was a break with precedent. Fearing revolution, a clique of senators in 133 B.C.E. clubbed Tiberius to death. Land redistribution did not cease, but a terrible precedent of public violence had been set.

A decade later, when Tiberius's brother Gaius Gracchus became a tribune in 123 B.C.E., he turned his attention to the problem of extortion in the provinces. With no checks on their authority, many corrupt governors who came from the ranks of the Senate forced provincials to give them money, valuable goods, and crops. Gaius Gracchus attempted to stop these abuses. To dilute the power of these corrupt provincial administrators and to win the political support of equestrians in Rome, he permitted equestrian tax collectors to operate in the provinces and to serve on juries that tried extortion cases. Gaius also tried to speed up land redistribution. But when he attempted to give citizenship to Rome's Italian allies to prevent Romans from confiscating their land, he lost the support of the Roman people, who did not wish to share the benefits of citizenship with non-Romans. In 121 B.C.E. Gaius committed suicide rather than allow himself to be murdered by a mob sent by his brother's senatorial foes.

The ruthless suppression of the Gracchus brothers and their supporters lit the fuse of political and social revolution in Rome. By attempting to effect change through the Plebeian Assembly, the Gracchus brothers unwittingly paved the way for less scrupulous politicians to seek power by falsely claiming to represent the interests of the poor. Their violent deaths signaled the end of political consensus among the oligarchy. Rivalry among the elite combined with the desperation of the poor was an explosive blend, with the army as the potentially decisive factor. If an unscrupulous politician were to join forces with poverty-stricken soldiers, the Republic would be in peril.

Gaius Marius (157–86 B.C.E.) became the first Roman general to use the army for political ends. He rose to power when the angry Roman poor made him their champion. Despite his equestrian origins, this experienced general won the consulship in 107 B.C.E. A special law of the Plebeian Assembly put him in command of the legions fighting King Jugurtha of Numidia in North Africa; and he brought the war to a quick and successful conclusion. Then he crushed Germanic tribes seeking to invade Italy.

In organizing his armies Marius made radical changes. He eliminated the property requirement for enlistment, thereby opening the ranks to the poorest citizens in the countryside and in Rome. These soldiers swore an oath of loyalty to their commander in chief, who in return promised them farms after a victorious campaign. Marius's reforms put generals in the middle of the long-running political struggle between the Senate and the Plebeian Assembly, the two institutions authorized to allocate lands won in war.

Marius achieved great personal power, but he did not use it against the institutions of the Republic. When he left Italy because of his unpopularity among the elite, the Roman Republic lurched ahead to its next major crisis: a revolt of the Italian allies.

War in Italy and Abroad

In 90 B.C.E. Rome's loyal allies in Italy could no longer endure being treated as inferiors when it came to distribution of land and booty. They launched a revolt against Rome known as the **Social War** (from the Latin word *socii,* which means "allies"). The confederation of allies demanded not independence but participation in the Roman Republic. They wanted full citizenship rights because they had been partners in Rome's wars and thus felt entitled to share in the fruits of victory. The allies lost the war, but soon afterward Rome granted citizenship to all Italians. These new citizens tilted the political scales away from the wealthy in Rome toward the population of Italy in general.

The Social War in Italy was followed by wars abroad. The patrician Lucius Cornelius Sulla (138–78 B.C.E.), consul in 88 B.C.E., was setting out with an army to put down a serious provincial revolt in Anatolia when the Plebeian Assembly turned command of his troops over to Marius, whose military reforms had aided the poor. In response, Sulla marched from southern Italy to Rome and placed his own supporters in positions of authority in the Senate, the Plebeian Assembly, and the magistracies.

Only a year later, however, while Sulla was still in Anatolia, Marius and the other consul, Cinna, won back political control of Rome. They declared Sulla an outlaw and killed many of his supporters in what became known as the Marian massacres. When Sulla returned to Italy in 82 B.C.E., at the head of a triumphant and loyal army, he seized Rome after a battle in which about 60,000 Roman soldiers died. He then murdered

Social War The revolt of Rome's allies against the Republic in 90 B.C.E., in which they demanded full Roman citizenship.

View the **Closer Look**   A Roman Warship

A ROMAN WARSHIP This relief depicts a Roman battleship. Rome became a naval power later in its history when it defeated Carthage and went on to rule the Mediterranean.

Different Voices
The Catiline Conspiracy

In 63 B.C.E. Lucius Sergius Catilina, known in English as Catiline, staged a conspiracy to bring down the government of the Roman Republic. Catiline was a member of a patrician family whose fortunes had declined. He had a distinguished military career, but the Senate dismissed him on trumped up charges of debauchery in 71 B.C.E. The conspiracy originated after he failed to become consul once again in 64 B.C.E. The conspirators planned to murder a large number of senators and assassinate Cicero, who was serving as consul that year. That plot failed. Catiline was killed in a battle with republican forces, and four co-conspirators were executed.

The account of the conspiracy by the Roman historian Sallust (ca. 86–35 B.C.E.) involves an analysis of the social and moral decline that proved fertile ground for Catiline in plotting to overthrow the government. Cicero was more concerned with exposing Catiline's bad character. In his first oration denouncing Catiline, Cicero attacked the man for his perfidy.

A Roman Historian's Analysis of the Catiline Conspiracy

At this period the empire of Rome appears to me to have been in an extremely deplorable condition; for though every nation, from the rising to the setting of the sun, lay in subjection to her arms, and though peace and prosperity, which mankind think the greatest blessings, were hers in abundance, there yet were found, among her citizens, men who were bent, with obstinate determination, to plunge themselves and their country into ruin; for, notwithstanding the two decrees of the senate, not one individual, out of so vast a number was induced by the offer of reward to give information of the conspiracy; nor was there a single deserter from the camp of Catiline. So strong a spirit of disaffection had, like a pestilence, pervaded the minds of most of the citizens.

Nor was this disaffected spirit confined to those who were actually concerned in the conspiracy; for the whole of the common people, from a desire of change, favored the projects of Catiline. This they seemed to do in accordance with their general character; for, in every state, they that are poor envy those of a better class, and endeavor to exalt the factious; they dislike the established condition of things, and long for something new; they are discontented with their own circumstances, and desire a general alteration; they can support themselves amidst revolt and sedition, without anxiety, since poverty does not easily suffer loss.

As for the populace of the city, they had become disaffected from various causes. In the first place, such as everywhere took the lead in crime and profligacy, with others who had squandered their fortunes in dissipation, and, in a word, all whom vice and villainy had driven from their homes, had flocked to Rome as a general receptacle of impurity. In the next place, many, who thought of the success of Sulla, when they had seen some raised from common soldiers into senators, and others so enriched as to live in regal luxury and pomp, hoped, each for himself, similar results from victory, if they should once take up arms. In addition to this, the youth, who, in the country, had earned a scanty livelihood by manual labor, tempted by public and private largesses, had preferred idleness in the city to unwelcome toil in the field. To these and all others of similar character, public disorders would furnish subsistence. It is not at all surprising, therefore, that men in distress, of dissolute principles and extravagant expectations, should have consulted the interest of the state no further than as it was subservient to their own. Besides, those whose parents, by the victory of Sulla, had been proscribed, whose property had been

CICERO ATTACKS CATILINE In this nineteenth-century representation of a session of the Roman Senate, Cicero gives one of his orations against Catiline, who is sitting alone to the right. From a fresco in Palazzo Madama, Rome, house of the Italian Senate.

SOURCE: Gaius Sallustius Crispus, *Conspiracy of Catiline*, Translated by J. S. Watson. New York: Harper & Brothers, 1867.

(continued on next page)

(continued from previous page)

5.1

5.2

5.3

5.4

5.5

confiscated, and whose civil rights had been curtailed, looked forward to the event of a war with precisely the same feelings.

All those, too, who were of any party opposed to that of the senate, were desirous rather that the state should be embroiled, than that they themselves should be out of power. This was an evil, which, after many years, had returned upon the community to the extent to which it now prevailed.

Cicero, First Oration Against Catiline

When, O Catiline, do you mean to cease abusing our patience? How long is that madness of yours still to mock us? When is there to be an end of that unbridled audacity of yours, swaggering about as it does now? Do not the nightly guards placed on the Palatine Hill—do not the watches posted throughout the city—does not the alarm of the people, and the union of all good men—does not the precaution taken of assembling the senate in this most defensible place—do not the looks and countenances of this venerable body here present, have any effect upon you? Do you not feel that your plans are detected? Do you not see that your conspiracy is already arrested and rendered powerless by the knowledge which every one here possesses of it? What is there that you did last night, what the night before—where is it that you were—who was there that you summoned to meet you—what design was there which was adopted by you, with which you think that any one of us is unacquainted?

Shame on the age and on its principles! The senate is aware of these things; the consul sees them; and yet this man lives. Lives! aye, he comes even into the senate. He takes a part in the public deliberations; he is watching and marking down and checking off for slaughter every individual among us. And we, gallant men that we are, think that we are doing our duty to the Republic if we keep out of the way of his frenzied attacks.

You ought, O Catiline, long ago to have been led to execution by command of the consul. That destruction which you have been long plotting against us ought to have already fallen on your own head.

SOURCE: *The World's Famous Orations,* 1906.

For Discussion

1. On what grounds did Sallust and Cicero condemn Catiline's conspiracy?
2. If Catiline had the support of the various groups of Romans that Sallust identified, why did his conspiracy fail?

3,000 of his political opponents. The Senate named Sulla dictator in 81 B.C.E., thereby giving him complete power. With the support of the Senate, whose authority he hoped to restore, Sulla restricted the power of tribunes to propose legislation because they had caused so much political instability for 50 years. After restoring the peace and the institutions of the state, and after becoming consul in 80 B.C.E, Sulla surprised many people by resigning the following year. Like Marius, Sulla was unwilling to destroy the Republic's institutions for the sake of his own ambition. It was enough for him to have restored peace and the preeminence of the Senate. Nevertheless, he had set a precedent for using armies in political rivalries. In the next 50 years the Senate conspicuously failed to restrain generals backed by their armies, thereby contributing to the collapse of the Republic.

The First Triumvirate

Three men provoked the Roman Republic's final downward spiral: Pompey (Gnaeus Pompeius, 106–48 B.C.E.), Marcus Licinius Crassus (ca. 115–53 B.C.E.), and Gaius Julius Caesar (100–44 B.C.E.). Pompey, the general who suppressed a revolt in Spain, and Crassus, the wealthiest man in Rome who had been one of Sulla's lieutenants, joined forces to crush the slave revolt of Spartacus in 71 B.C.E. Backed by their armies, they then became consuls for 70 B.C.E., even though Pompey was legally too young and had not yet held the prerequisite junior offices.

During their consulships, Pompey and Crassus made modest changes to Sulla's reforms. They permitted the tribunes to propose laws again and let equestrians serve on juries. After their year in office they retired without making further demands. Pompey continued his military career. In 67 B.C.E. he received a special command to clear pirates from the Mediterranean to protect Roman trade. The following year Pompey crushed the ongoing rebellion in Anatolia and reorganized the Near East, creating new provinces and more client kingdoms subservient to Rome.

When Pompey returned to Rome, he asked the Senate to grant land to his victorious troops. The Senate, jealous of his success and afraid of the power he would gain as the patron of so many veteran troops, refused. To gain land for his soldiers and have his political arrangements in the Near East ratified, Pompey made an alliance with two men even more ambitious than he: his old ally Crassus and Gaius Julius Caesar, the ambitious descendant of an ancient but poor patrician family. The three formed an informal alliance known as the **First Triumvirate**. No man or institution could oppose their combined influence. Caesar obtained the consulship in 59 B.C.E., despite the objections of many senators. By using illegal means that would return to haunt him, he directed the Senate to ratify Pompey's arrangements in the Near East and grant land to his troops. He resolved the financial problems of Crassus's clients, the equestrian tax collectors, at public expense.

As a reward for his efforts, the perpetually debt-ridden Caesar arranged to receive the governorship of the Po Valley and Illyricum for five years after his consulship

First Triumvirate The informal political alliance made by Julius Caesar, Pompey, and Crassus in 60 B.C.E. to share power in the Roman Republic. It led directly to the collapse of the Republic.

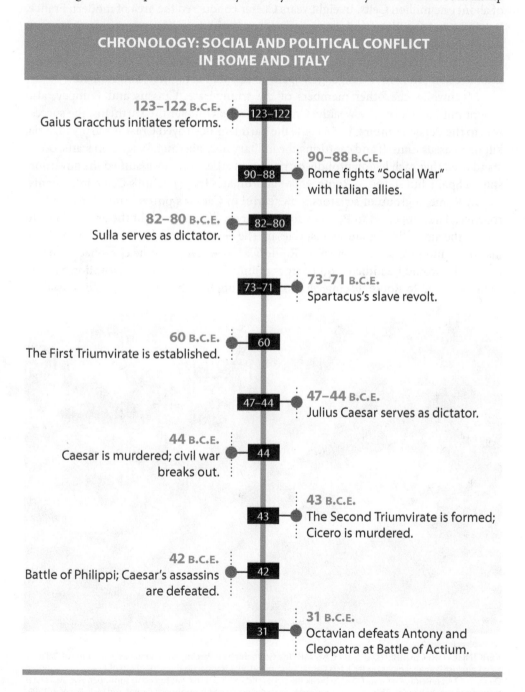

CHRONOLOGY: SOCIAL AND POLITICAL CONFLICT IN ROME AND ITALY

123–122 B.C.E.
Gaius Gracchus initiates reforms.
123–122

90–88 B.C.E.
Rome fights "Social War" with Italian allies.
90–88

82–80 B.C.E.
Sulla serves as dictator.
82–80

73–71 B.C.E.
Spartacus's slave revolt.
73–71

60 B.C.E.
The First Triumvirate is established.
60

47–44 B.C.E.
Julius Caesar serves as dictator.
47–44

44 B.C.E.
Caesar is murdered; civil war breaks out.
44

43 B.C.E.
The Second Triumvirate is formed; Cicero is murdered.
43

42 B.C.E.
Battle of Philippi; Caesar's assassins are defeated.
42

31 B.C.E.
Octavian defeats Antony and Cleopatra at Battle of Actium.
31

ended. Later he extended that term for 10 years. During this time, he planned to enrich himself at the expense of the provincials. As he set out for his governorship, however, he was given command of Transalpine Gaul (northwest of the Alps), where the German chieftain Ariovistus threatened Roman security. This change enabled Caesar to operate militarily in all of Gaul—and ultimately to conquer it.

Julius Caesar and the End of the Republic

Caesar's determination to conquer Gaul lay in his pursuit of personal political power. He knew that he could win glory, wealth, and prestige in Rome by conquering new lands, and to that end he promptly began a war (58–50 B.C.E.) against the Celtic tribes of Transalpine Gaul. A military genius, Caesar chronicled his ruthless tactics and victories in his *Commentaries on the Gallic War*, as famous today for its vigorous Latin as for its unflinching glimpse of Roman conquest, which resulted in the death or enslavement of about one million Celts. In eight years Caesar conquered the area of modern France, Belgium, and the Rhineland, turning these territories into Roman provinces. He even briefly invaded Britain. His intrusion into Celtic lands led to their eventual Romanization. The French language developed from the Latin spoken by Roman conquerors, as did the other "Romance" languages: Spanish, Italian, Portuguese, and Romanian.

Meanwhile, the other members of the triumvirate, Crassus and Pompey, also sought military glory. The wealthy Crassus failed to conquer the Parthians, the successors to the Persian Empire. In 53 B.C.E. the Parthians destroyed Crassus's army in Syria, killing Crassus himself and capturing the military insignia (metal eagles on staffs, called standards) that each legion proudly carried into battle. Pompey assumed the governorship of Spain, but stayed in Rome while subordinates fought Spain's Celtic inhabitants.

In Rome, a group of senators grew fearful of Caesar's power, ambitions, and arrogance. They appealed to Pompey for assistance, and he brought the armies loyal to him to the aid of the Senate against Caesar. The Senate then asked Caesar to lay down his command in Gaul and return to Rome. Caesar knew that if he complied with this request he would be indicted on charges of improper conduct or corruption as soon as he returned to Rome. Facing certain conviction, he refused to return for a trial. In

VERCINGETORIX SURRENDERS TO CAESAR The Gallic chieftain Vercingetorix, who raised an army of Gallic tribes against Roman legions under Julius Caesar's command, was trapped in the stronghold of Alesia, near modern Dijon, in 52 B.C.E. Reinforcements failed to break the siege, and Vercingetorix was forced to surrender. Five years later he was publicly beheaded. This scene of Vercingetorix throwing down his weapons was painted by L. Royer in 1899.

COIN FROM THE LATE ROMAN REPUBLIC The front of this silver coin depicts the god Janus (after whom the month of January is named), who looked in two directions. The reverse depicts a Roman galley.

49 B.C.E. he left Gaul and marched south with his loyal troops against the forces of the Senate in Rome. Recognizing the magnitude of his gamble ("The die is cast!" he said when he crossed the Rubicon River, the legal boundary between Gaul and the Roman territory under the direct control of the consuls), he deliberately plunged Rome into civil war. Because of his victories in Gaul and his generosity to the people of Rome, Caesar could pose as the people's champion while seeking absolute power for himself. Intimidated by Caesar's forces and public support, Pompey withdrew to Greece, but Caesar overtook and defeated him there at Pharsalus in 48 B.C.E. When Pompey fled to Egypt, high officials in the Ptolemaic court murdered him to win Caesar's favor.

It took Caesar more than two years to complete his victory over Pompey's supporters and return to Italy in 45 B.C.E. Back in Rome, Caesar had himself proclaimed dictator for life and assumed complete control over the government, flagrantly disregarding the traditions of the Republic. Because he did not live to fully implement his plan, Caesar's long-term goals for the Roman state remain unclear, but he probably intended to establish some version of Hellenistic monarchy.

Once in power, Caesar permanently ended the autonomy of the Senate. He enlarged this body from 600 (its size at the time of Sulla) to 900 men, and then filled it with his supporters. He also established military colonies in Spain, North Africa, and Gaul to provide land for his veterans and to secure those territories. He adjusted the chaotic republican calendar by adding one day every fourth year, creating a year of 365.25 days. The resulting "Julian" calendar lasted in western Europe until the sixteenth century C.E. Caesar regularized gold coinage and urban administration and planned a vast public library. At his death, plans for a major campaign against Parthia were underway, suggesting that conquest would have remained a basic feature of his rule.

View the Map

Map Discovery: Career of Julius Caesar

Caesar seriously miscalculated by assuming he could win over his enemies by showing them clemency and by making administrative changes that disregarded republican precedent. These changes earned Caesar the hatred of traditionalist senators who failed to recognize that the Republic was dead. On March 15, 44 B.C.E., a group of resentful and envious senators led by the idealistic Marcus Junius Brutus (85–42 B.C.E,) stabbed Caesar to death at a Senate meeting. The assassins claimed that they wanted to restore the Republic, but they had only unleashed another civil war.

Marcus Antonius (Mark Antony), who had been Caesar's right-hand man, stepped forward to oppose the conspirators. He was soon joined by Gaius Julius Caesar Octavianus (63 B.C.E.–14 C.E), Caesar's grandnephew and legal heir, who became known as Octavian. Though Octavian was only 19, he gained control of some of Caesar's legions and compelled the Senate to name him consul. Marcus Lepidus, commander of Caesar's cavalry, joined Mark Antony and Octavian to form the **Second Triumvirate** in 43 B.C.E. The new trio coerced the Senate into granting them power to rule Rome legally. By ruling without the active participation of the consuls and the Senate, the Second Triumvirate maintained Rome as a Republic in name only.

At the Battle of Philippi, a town in Macedonia, in 42 B.C.E., forces of the Second Triumvirate crushed the army of Brutus and the senators who had assassinated Caesar. But soon Antony, Octavian, and Lepidus began to struggle among themselves for absolute authority. Lepidus, who had taken control of Spain and North Africa, was forced out of office in 36 B.C.E.; Antony and Octavian agreed to separate the spheres of influence. Octavian took Italy and Rome's western provinces, while Antony took the eastern provinces.

In Egypt, Antony joined forces with Cleopatra VII, the last Ptolemaic monarch to rule there. Both stood to gain from this alliance: Antony secured control of the resources of Egypt while Cleopatra got territory and influence. In response to this alliance, Octavian launched a vicious propaganda campaign. Posing as the conservative protector of Roman tradition, he accused Antony of surrendering Roman values and territory to an evil foreign seductress. The inevitable war broke out in 31 B.C.E. At the Battle of Actium in Greece, Octavian's troops and fleet defeated Antony and Cleopatra's land and naval forces. The couple fled to Alexandria, in Egypt, where they committed suicide a year later.

As we saw in Chapter 4, the death of Cleopatra and the end of the Egyptian Ptolemaic dynasty in 30 B.C.E. marked the end of the Hellenistic Age, which had begun with the creation of successor kingdoms after the death of Alexander the Great in 323 B.C.E. The Battle of Actium and the subsequent Roman conquest of Egypt also effectively marked the end of the Roman Republic. Although Octavian, who was given the title Caesar Augustus by the Senate in 27 B.C.E., would preserve the forms of the Republic, he acquired effective absolute power in both Rome and the vast empire that Rome controlled. The transition from Republic to Empire also raised the question, which frequently recurred in the history of the West, whether republican political institutions were compatible with imperial power. The history of Athens and Rome suggests that they were not.

Second Triumvirate In 43 B.C.E. Octavian (later called Caesar Augustus), Mark Antony, and Lepidus made an informal alliance to share power in Rome while they jockeyed for control. Octavian emerged as the sole ruler of Rome in 31 B.C.E.

View the Image

Statue of Caesar Augustus

CONCLUSION

The Roman Republic and the West

The Roman Republic made four great contributions to the geographical and cultural area that would later be identified as the West. The first was the institution of republican government. Although Rome made many changes in its political institutions over the course of more than 500 years, it bequeathed to the West a model of government that mixed features of the three forms of government identified by Aristotle and analyzed by Polybius: monarchy, aristocracy, and democracy. The Roman Republic served as a model of government for political communities in the West for the next two thousand years. Not least among them was the United States of America, which became a republic in the late eighteenth century when it declared its independence from Great

Britain. By vesting executive power in a president rather than a monarch, just as Rome had given executive power to consuls, and by dividing the legislature into a Senate and a House of Representatives, the new American republic drew inspiration from the history of the Roman Republic. The most important difference between the institutions of the two republics was that the aristocratic Roman Senate played a much greater role than its American counterpart in the government of the Republic. Although in theory the Roman Senate was mainly an advisory body that had little formal power, its influence over the consuls and other magistrates was considerable.

Second, the Roman Republic transmitted to the West the ideal of **civic virtue**, the belief that the success of a republic depended on its citizens' possession of personal traits that contributed to the common good. These traits included *gravitas* (which meant dignity, seriousness, and duty), piety, and justice. Aristotle had emphasized the importance of civic virtue in his claim that citizenship consisted in political duties rather than political rights. There was little discussion of civic virtue in the Hellenistic monarchies, but a revival and development of the concept took place in the Roman Republic. During the late years of the Republic, moral philosophers and historians blamed the loss of Roman liberty on the perceived loss of civic virtue. The idea of civic virtue modeled on that of republican Rome profoundly influenced the history of the West, especially during the Renaissance in the fifteenth and sixteenth centuries, the Enlightenment in the eighteenth century, and the early years of the United States in the late eighteenth and early nineteenth centuries.

The third legacy that Rome bequeathed to the West was its legal system. Based originally upon the Law of the Twelve Tables, and developed gradually through judicial interpretation and eventual codification in the late imperial period, Roman law became the basis of most Western legal systems. Roman law systems in the West were rivalled only by those that followed the English system of common law. Many of the legal traditions associated with both English and Roman law, however, including the participation of citizens in the legal process, originated in the Roman Republic.

The fourth and arguably the most important legacy of Rome to the West was Greco–Roman culture. This distinctive Roman version of Hellenism represented a creative synthesis of Greek and Roman culture. In art and philosophy Roman culture was largely derivative of that of Greece, but in architecture and literature it represented a creative adaptation of the cultures that Romans encountered. Greco–Roman culture also preserved a large body of Greek art and philosophy, much of which has survived only through Roman imitations and translations. Credit for the successful transmission of Greco–Roman culture to subsequent generations can be attributed to the long period of peace, the *Pax Romana*, which lasted from 31 B.C.E. to 180 C.E. To that period of Roman world dominance, the Roman Empire, we now turn.

 Read the Document

Polybius: Why Romans and Not Greeks Govern the World, ca. 140 B.C.E.

civic virtue The belief that the success of a republic depended on its citizens' possession of personal traits that contributed to the common good.

MAKING CONNECTIONS

1. The Roman Republic rose to power during the Hellenistic period. In what sense were its political institutions and culture Hellenistic?
2. To what extent did Roman territorial expansion lead to the fall of the Roman Republic?
3. How did Romans model their society on that of classical and Hellenistic Greece? How did they modify or reject that cultural inheritance?
4. Compare the political institutions of the Roman Republic with those of the United States of America in the late eighteenth century.

TAKING IT FURTHER

For suggested readings see page R-1.

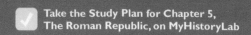
Chapter Review

The Nature of the Roman Republic

5.1 What type of government did Rome establish when it eliminated kingship?

Rome became a republic, a state in which political power resides in the people or their representatives rather than in a monarch. Tension between the elite and wealthy patricians and the plebeians, composed of rich landowners, the military, and the general populace, characterized Roman political life during the Republic.

Roman Territorial Expansion

5.2 How did the Roman Republic come to dominate the Mediterranean world during the Hellenistic Age?

New political and military institutions allowed Rome to conquer first the Italian peninsula, and then ally with neighboring cities in Italy. Building these alliances allowed the Romans to conquer nearby tribes, and later a combination of military might and diplomacy helped them defeat the powerful Etruscans. The attempt to assimilate conquered peoples included offering a limited form of citizenship in exchange for military service, and the growing army was then used to crush those, like Macedonia, who refused to submit to Rome's territorial ambitions. Victory over Carthage in the Third Punic War resulted in Rome's acquisition of all the territories ruled by Carthage.

The Culture of the Roman Republic

5.3 How did the Roman encounter with Greek culture lead to the forging of a durable cultural synthesis?

During the Roman territorial expansion within the Hellenistic world, Greek ideas about literature, art, philosophy, and rhetoric were adopted and adapted into Roman culture. Greek literature and art became the foundation of the Roman tradition in those areas, while elements of the Greek religion were transformed due to the Republic's toleration for a wide variety of religious practices. The educated elite emphasized the art of persuasion, or Rhetoric, over the attainment of philosophical wisdom, which became one of the Roman Republic's cultural legacies to the West.

Social Life in Republican Rome

5.4 How was Roman society structured, and what relationships existed within the Roman family?

At the top of the hierarchical structure of Roman society was an elite group of political leaders hailing from both pedigreed patrician families and some wealthy plebeians. Rich merchants from the equestrian class were next, and then general populace, or plebeians. As pieces of property, slaves were at the bottom of the hierarchy. The structure of the Roman family was similar, with the male head of the household exercising complete control over his family members. However, women and grown children often enjoyed considerable independence, and patrician women often wielded political power behind the scenes.

The End of the Roman Republic

5.5 Why did the Roman Republic end?

The inequitable distribution of resources in the Roman Republic eventually overwhelmed the republican constitution and caused a revolution. The rapid acquisition of territories allowed the ruling elite to become enormously wealthy, which only heightened the differences in wealth and power that characterized Roman society. This relentless pursuit of power and glory by the elite, coupled with flaws in Rome's political institutions, eventually caused a fundamental change in the political system.

Chapter Time Line

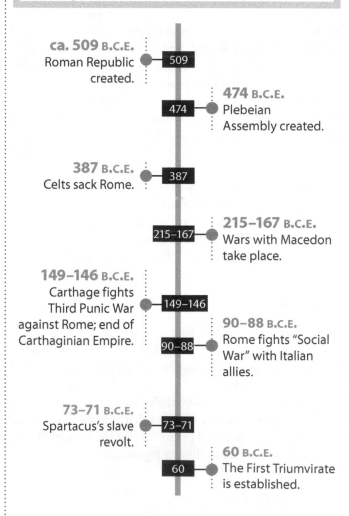

ca. 509 B.C.E. Roman Republic created. — 509

474 — **474 B.C.E.** Plebeian Assembly created.

387 B.C.E. Celts sack Rome. — 387

215–167 — **215–167 B.C.E.** Wars with Macedon take place.

149–146 B.C.E. Carthage fights Third Punic War against Rome; end of Carthaginian Empire. — 149–146

90–88 — **90–88 B.C.E.** Rome fights "Social War" with Italian allies.

73–71 B.C.E. Spartacus's slave revolt. — 73–71

60 — **60 B.C.E.** The First Triumvirate is established.

6

Enclosing the West: The Early Roman Empire and Its Neighbors, 31 B.C.E.–235 C.E.

n 155 C.E., Aelius Aristides, an aristocratic Greek writer who held Roman citizenship, visited Rome, where he gave a public oration in honor of the imperial capital. His words reveal what the Roman Empire meant to a wealthy, educated man from Rome's eastern provinces. According to Aristides, the trait "most worthy of consideration and admiration" in the Roman system was that "everywhere you have made citizens all those who are the more accomplished, noble and powerful people." A man might live thousands of miles from the city of Rome, and yet "neither does the sea nor a great expanse of intervening land keep one from being a citizen. . . . [Rome] has never refused anyone. But just as the earth's ground supports all men, so it too receives men from every land." Aristides's vision points to the key of the Romans' success—a willingness to assimilate their subjects into Rome's political and social life. Aristides believed that by transforming "non-Romans" into Romans, Rome's imperial expansion brought civilization to the world.

LEARNING OBJECTIVES

6.1 How did the Roman imperial system develop, and what roles did the emperor, Senate, army, and city of Rome play in this process?

6.2 How did provincial peoples assimilate to or resist Roman rule?

6.3 How did Romans interact with peoples living beyond the imperial borders?

6.4 What was the social and cultural response to the emergence and consolidation of the empire?

A HARBOR TOWN This first-century fresco, found in a Roman villa near Pompeii, offers us a glimpse of the lively seafaring trade that helped maintain the Roman Empire.

Listen to Chapter 6 on MyHistoryLab

⊙ Watch the Video Series on MyHistoryLab

Learn about some key topics related to this chapter with the *MyHistoryLab Video Series:*
Key Topics in Western Civilization

📖 Read the Document

Excerpt from *The Roman Oration*
by Aelius Aristides

Pax Romana Latin for "Roman
Peace," this term refers to the Roman Empire established by Augustus that lasted until the early third
century C.E.

Aristides's praise demonstrates Rome's success in creating a sense of common purpose among its citizens. During its first 250 years of existence, the empire brought cultural unity and political stability to an area stretching from the Atlantic Ocean to the Persian Gulf. The imperial regime brought peace to the Mediterranean world for more than two centuries. Historians call this era the ***Pax Romana***, the Roman Peace. But for the slaves whose labor fueled the economy and the small farmers whose taxes supported the state, Roman rule meant oppression and impoverishment.

This chapter analyzes the Roman Empire as three concentric circles of power—the imperial center, the provinces, and the frontiers and beyond. In the imperial center stood not only the emperor but also the Roman Senate, the chief legal and administrative institutions, and the city of Rome itself, an important model of the Roman way of life. In the second circle, provincial populations struggled with the challenges posed by the imposition of Roman rule and, in the process, helped construct a new imperial culture. The outermost circle of the empire, its frontier zones and the lands beyond, included Romans living within the empire's borders and the peoples who lived on the other side, but interacted with Rome through trade and warfare. By exploring what it meant to be a Roman in each of these circles, this chapter seeks to answer a key question:

How did the encounters between the Romans and the peoples they conquered transform the Mediterranean world and create a Roman imperial culture?

The Imperial Center

6.1 How did the Roman imperial system develop, and what roles did the emperor, Senate, army, and city of Rome play in this process?

After civil wars destroyed the Roman Republic, a new political system emerged. Rome's form of government changed from a republic, in which members of an oligarchy competed for power, to an empire, in which one man, the emperor, held absolute power for life. Roman culture was now anchored by an imperial system based on force (see **Map 6.1**).

Imperial Authority: Augustus and After

As we saw in Chapter 5, Julius Caesar's heir, Octavian (63 B.C.E.–14 C.E.), wrenched the state from the spiral of civil war and claimed that he had restored normal life to the Republic. In fact, Octavian destroyed the Republic while pretending to preserve it. In his own eyes, and those of a people weary of war, Octavian was the savior of *republican* Rome. Yet behind a façade of restored republican tradition, Octavian created a Roman version of a Hellenistic monarchy. By neutralizing his political enemies in the Roman Senate, vanquishing his military rivals, and establishing an iron grip on every

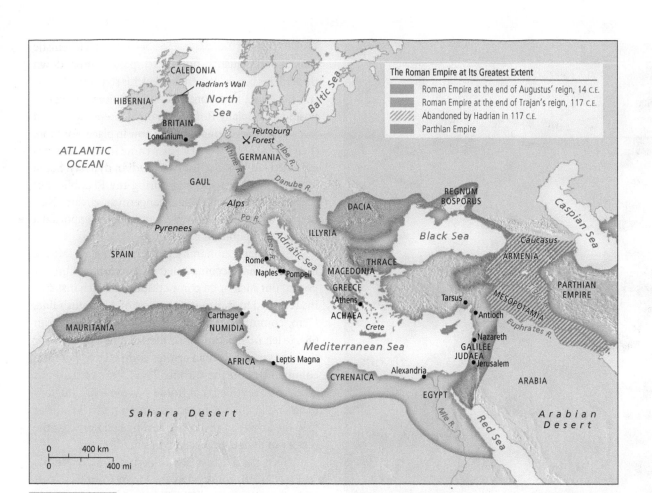

MAP 6.1 THE ROMAN EMPIRE AT ITS GREATEST EXTENT Stretching from the north of Britain to the Euphrates River, the empire brought together hundreds of distinct ethnic groups. When did the Empire reach its greatest extent? What forces compelled its contraction?

mechanism of power, Octavian succeeded where Julius Caesar and other republican politicians had failed: He achieved total mastery of the political arena at Rome. No one successfully challenged his authority.

To mask his tyranny, Octavian never wore a crown and modestly referred to himself as *Princeps,* or First Citizen. His position in Rome was all-powerful yet unobtrusive. In 27 B.C.E., as he boasted in the official account of his reign, he "transferred the Republic from his power into that of the Senate and the Roman people." This abdication was a sham and few people were fooled. Following Octavian's instructions, the Senate showered honors on him, including the name "Augustus" (which is how we will refer to him throughout the rest of this chapter). *Augustus* means "the revered" and implied an exalted, godlike authority. (It became the title of all subsequent emperors.) Augustus "accepted" the Senate's plea to remain consul and agreed to control the frontier provinces where the most troops were stationed, including Spain, Gaul, Germany, and Syria. The senators rejoiced, calling Augustus "sole savior of the entire empire."

In 23 B.C.E. Augustus renounced the consulship and was voted the powers of tribune for life. A tribune's power gave Augustus the right to conduct business in the Senate and veto legislation. It also conferred immunity from arrest and punishment. He could now legally interfere in all political and military affairs in the provinces. Augustus personally controlled Egypt, the richest province, as successor to the pharaohs, and soldiers swore an oath of allegiance to him. Other generals led legions into battle, but always in his name. Other magistrates officially administered the state, but no one was chosen without his approval.

 Read the Document

Augustus on His Accomplishments

AUGUSTUS: A COMMANDING PRESENCE This statue of Augustus dating to 19 B.C.E. depicts him as a warrior making a gesture of command. His face is ageless, the carving on his armor celebrates peace and prosperity, and his posture is balanced and forceful.

Julio-Claudian dynasty Established by Octavian Augustus, this hereditary monarchy drawn from members of his extended family ruled Rome until 68 C.E.

Antonine Age Almost one hundred years of political stability in the Roman Empire, inaugurated when Nerva adopted Trajan as his son and heir.

THE PROBLEM OF SUCCESSION Like a Hellenistic monarch, Augustus hoped to pass power down through his family. When he died, his stepson Tiberius (r. 14–37 C.E.) took control of the empire without opposition. Officially Rome remained a republic, but in fact a hereditary monarchy was now in place. For more than half a century, every ruler came from Augustus's extended family—the **Julio–Claudian dynasty**. Some senators muttered about restoring the Republic, but this remained an idle—and dangerous—dream. Neither the army nor the people would have supported a Senate-led republican rebellion.

Hereditary monarchy promised to stave off the instability that accompanied open competition for power. But such open competition, and such instability, returned to Rome after the last of Augustus's line, Nero, committed suicide in the face of rebellion in 68. He left no heir, and four men claimed power over the next year, as Roman armies competed to put their commanders on the throne. This "Year of the Four Emperors" revealed that Rome was more of a military dictatorship than a hereditary monarchy: Whoever held the loyalty of the armies controlled Rome, as the history of the next two centuries made clear.

The general Titus Flavius Vespasianus, or Vespasian (r. 69–79), emerged as the victor from the "Year of the Four Emperors." The Flavian dynasty that he established lasted just 25 years, until the death of his last son, Domitian (r. 81–96). A conscientious and able monarch, Domitian nevertheless ruled with an openly autocratic style. He created a reign of terror among Rome's elite until a group of senators murdered him.

To avoid another succession crisis, the Senate cooperated with the army in choosing a new emperor, the elderly senator Nerva (r. 96–98). They hoped that this respected man who had no sons would ensure orderly government, and so he did. Under pressure from the military, Nerva adopted the general Trajan (r. 98–117) as his son and heir. He thus inaugurated the era historians call the **Antonine Age**. For almost a century (96–180), Rome enjoyed competent rule because Nerva's practice of adopting highly qualified successors continued. After Trajan adopted Hadrian (r. 117–138), Hadrian in turn adopted Antoninus Pius (r. 138–161), and Antoninus adopted Marcus Aurelius (r. 161–180) as his successor. The Roman historian Tacitus (ca. 55–120) praised these emperors for establishing "the rare happiness of times, when we may think what we please, and express what we think."

This time of peace ended with another imperial murder. Unlike his immediate predecessors, Marcus Aurelius had a son. So he abandoned the custom of picking a qualified successor, and instead was followed to the throne by his incompetent, cruel, and eventually insane son, Commodus (r. 180–192). Conspirators within the imperial palace arranged to have Commodus strangled in 192, triggering another civil war.

A senator from North Africa, Septimius Severus, emerged victorious from this conflict and assumed the imperial throne (r. 193–211). Septimius Severus exemplified the ascent of provincial aristocrats to the highest levels of the empire. The Severan dynasty lasted until 235. Septimius Severus was popular with the army—he raised its pay for the first time in more than 100 years. But when the last emperor of his

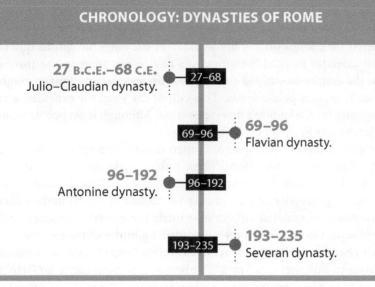

CHRONOLOGY: DYNASTIES OF ROME

27 B.C.E.–68 C.E.
Julio–Claudian dynasty.
27–68

69–96
69–96
Flavian dynasty.

96–192
Antonine dynasty.
96–192

193–235
193–235
Severan dynasty.

dynasty, Severus Alexander (r. 222–235), attempted to bribe the German tribes instead of fighting them, his own troops killed him because they wanted the cash for themselves. Again, the murder of an emperor provoked civil war. Fifty years of political and economic crises followed the end of the Severan dynasty. As we will see in Chapter 7, the imperial structure that emerged after this time of crisis differed significantly from the Augustan model.

THE EMPEROR'S ROLE: THE NATURE OF IMPERIAL POWER Under the Augustan imperial system, the emperor had four main responsibilities. First, he protected and expanded imperial territory. Only the emperor determined foreign policy, made treaties with other nations, and waged war, whether to protect the empire from its enemies or expand the empire with aggressive campaigns of conquest.

Second, the emperor administered justice and provided good government. In theory all citizens could appeal directly to him for justice. The emperor and his staff also responded to questions on points of law and administration from provincial governors and other officials who ruled in the emperor's name. Emperors provided emergency relief after natural disasters, looked after the roads and infrastructure of the empire, and financed public works in many provincial cities. During his long reign Augustus—the wealthiest individual in the empire—used his personal fortune to pay his soldiers, erect public buildings, and sponsor public spectacles such as gladiatorial contests.

The emperor's third responsibility stemmed from his religious role. As *Pontifex Maximus,* or High Priest, the emperor supervised the public worship of the gods of Rome, particularly Jupiter. Emperors and subjects alike believed that to fulfill Rome's destiny to rule the world, they needed to make regular sacrifices to the gods.

Finally, the emperor became a symbol of unity for the peoples of the empire. Inevitably, the emperor seemed more than human, even worthy of worship, for he was the guarantor of peace, prosperity, and victory for Rome, and had more power than any other living person.

Worship of the emperor began with Augustus. He was reluctant to call himself a god because Roman tradition opposed such an idea, but he permitted his spirit to be worshiped as a sort of *paterfamilias* or head of a universal family of peoples of the empire. He also referred to himself as the "son of a god"—in this case Julius Caesar, whom the Senate had declared divine. After Augustus, imperial worship became more pronounced, although few emperors, such as Domitian, emphasized their divinity during their lifetimes. Most were content to be worshiped after death. On his death-bed, Vespasian managed to joke, "I guess I'm becoming a god now."

In Rome's eastern provinces such as Egypt, where people for thousands of years had considered their kings divine, the worship of the emperor spread quickly. Each city's official calendar marked the emperor's day of ascension to the throne. Soon, cities across the empire worshiped the emperor on special occasions through games, speeches, sacrifices, and public feasts. This cult of the emperor provided a common focus of allegiance for the empire's diverse peoples. Although most people would never see their ruler, he was in their prayers every day.

He was also in their public spaces. Emperors built and restored roads, temples, harbors, aqueducts, and fortifications. These public works demonstrated the emperor's unparalleled patronage and concern for the public welfare. In turn, local aristocrats emulated his generosity by financing lavish building projects in their own cities.

Other elements of material culture also made the imperial presence real for the emperor's subjects. Coins, for example, provided a glimpse of the emperor's face and a phrase that characterized some aspect of his reign. Slogans such as "Restorer of the World," "Concord with the Gods," and "The Best Ruler—Sustenance for Italy" brought the ruler's message into every person's pocket. Statues of the emperor served a similar purpose. (One statue in Carthage in North Africa had a removable head, so that when a new emperor ascended the throne, the town leaders could save money by replacing only the head instead of the whole statue.)

Emperors also used military victories to celebrate their reigns. In the Republic, conquest had brought wealth and glory to generals. In the new imperial system, only the emperor could take credit for victory. Imperial propaganda described the emperor as eternally triumphant.

The City of Rome

The city of Rome stood as a monument to the authority of the emperor. Augustus boasted that he had found Rome built of brick and left it made of marble. Though an exaggeration, this claim reveals the effect of monarchy on Rome's urban fabric. Every emperor wanted to leave his mark on the city as a testimony to his generosity and power. As Rome grew, it became the model for cities throughout the empire. Its public spaces and buildings provided a stage for imperial rule (see **Map 6.2**).

The center of political and public life in Rome was the Roman Forum, a field filled with imposing buildings that housed the treasury and records office, law courts, and the Senate House. Roman law, inscribed on gleaming bronze tablets and placed on the outer walls of these buildings, testified to the principles of justice and order that formed the framework of the Roman state. Basilicas, colonnaded halls in which Romans conducted public business ranging from finance to trials, crowded against the sides of the Forum.

Because public and religious life were intertwined, the Forum also contained temples

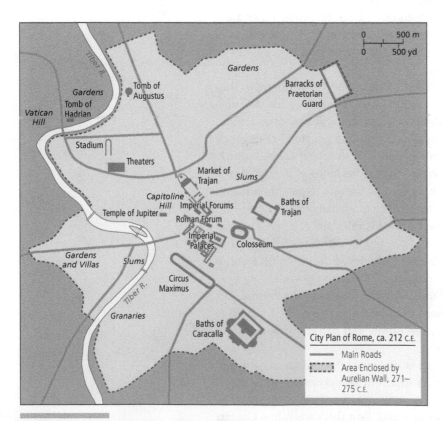

MAP **6.2** THE CITY OF ROME, CA. 212 C.E. This diagram shows the main public buildings of the imperial capital. Most cities elsewhere in the empire imitated this urban plan. How does the city plan illustrate the realities of power in imperial Rome?

of the gods who controlled Rome's destiny. Statues to the goddesses Victory and Concord stood in the Senate, while the huge marble temple of Jupiter "Best and Greatest," Rome's chief god, looked down on the Forum from the Capitoline Hill.

The Forum highlighted the emperor's power. Emperors built triumphal arches there. After a victorious military campaign, emperors and their troops paraded through the Forum on the Sacred Way, passed under the arches, and finished at the temple of Jupiter. Delighted crowds watched defeated kings pass by in chains and marveled at floats piled with loot and slaves carrying paintings depicting the war.

The emperor's might was on display throughout the city. Emperors spent gigantic sums on stadiums and additional forums. The huge arena called the Colosseum, built by Vespasian and his son Titus (r. 79–81), provided a spot in the heart of the city where 50,000 spectators could cheer the slaughter of men and animals.

Emperors also built and maintained luxurious public baths. Eleven aqueducts provided Rome with 300 million gallons of water every day for these baths, the city's many fountains, and those houses that had indoor plumbing.

To erect their monumental buildings, the Romans developed new architectural techniques. They were the first to build extensively in concrete (and may have invented it), which allowed them to develop new methods of construction such as the vault. The Pantheon, built by Hadrian in 126, is the largest ancient roofed building still standing today. With a diameter of 142 feet, its dome has no interior supports.

Emperors built their palaces on the Palatine Hill, which looked down on the Forum, and mansions covered nearby hills. Wealthy citizens lived in luxury that would not be equaled in the West for centuries. In contrast, the impoverished majority of Rome's inhabitants lived in filthy slums in the valleys between Rome's seven hills or along the Tiber River, where they crowded into apartment buildings up to six stories high. Lacking solid foundations, apartment buildings often collapsed and could become firetraps. (It is hardly a surprise, then, that Augustus established the first professional fire department in Western history.)

The Agents of Control

The emperor stood at the heart of the empire, but the imperial center included other agents of control, the most important of which were the Roman Senate and the army.

View the Closer Look

The Roman Colosseum

TRAJAN'S FORUM Built between 107 and 112, Trajan's Forum included libraries of Greek and Latin texts, an enormous basilica, a multistoried marketplace, and a marble column 125-feet high on which was carved the story of his conquest of Dacia (modern Romania).

THE ROMAN SENATE: FROM AUTONOMY TO ADMINISTRATION The Empire retained most of the basic machinery of government inherited from the Republic—but it operated in conformity with the emperor's wishes. The emperor, not the Senate, now controlled military, financial, and diplomatic policy. Free political debate was silenced. Because he wanted to avoid the competition for power that had destroyed the Republic, Augustus eliminated his opponents and filled the Senate with loyal supporters. Nevertheless, to maintain the illusion that he had saved rather than destroyed the Republic and because senators as a class were the wealthiest, most influential men in Rome, Augustus took pains to show respect for the Senate.

Deprived of its autonomy, the Senate became an administrative arm of imperial rule. Senators served as provincial governors, army commanders, judges, and financial officers. They managed the water and grain supplies of the city of Rome, and some of them served on the emperor's advisory council. Senators learned to serve the empire faithfully, even if they disliked the emperor personally.

Emperors often brought able new men into the Senate from the provinces. This practice gave provincial elites a stake in the imperial enterprise. By the end of the third century more than half of Rome's 600 or so senators came from outside Italy.

While the emperor's relationship with the Senate was of primary importance, other social ranks were also prominent in imperial administration. Many members of the equestrian class served in government positions. Emperors also employed freedmen and even slaves on their administrative staffs and benefited from their loyalty and competence.

THE ROMAN ARMY AND THE POWER OF THE EMPEROR The Roman army was another crucial component of imperial rule. The army could make or depose an emperor—something that every ruler understood. Without the army's support, Augustus would never have succeeded in remaking the Republican regime into his imperial system.

Augustus created a highly efficient professional army that served as the bulwark of the empire for nearly 250 years. His first step was to reduce the army from 60 legions to between 25 and 30 legions, so that the legionary troops now totaled 150,000 citizens. To solidify their loyalty, Augustus established regular terms of service and ample retirement benefits for veterans and their families.

auxiliary Soldiers in the Roman imperial army who were drawn from subject peoples. Auxiliaries received Roman citizenship after their term of service.

Soldiers drawn from subject peoples who were not citizens served as **auxiliary** troops. After completing their years of service, auxiliaries received Roman citizenship—an important incentive for recruitment. The combined legions and auxiliaries brought the military strength of the Roman army to 300,000 men.

Legionaries enlisted for 20 years of active service (with another five in reserve), but only about half survived to retirement. Short life expectancy rather than death in battle kept the survival figure low, although regular rations and medical care may have helped soldiers live longer than civilians. A soldier with special skills, such as literacy, could rise through the ranks and become an officer. For those who survived their service, Augustus established military colonies in Italy and the provinces. He rewarded more than 100,000 veterans with land. Later emperors continued this practice.

The imperial army epitomized Roman imperial values. It maintained a high degree of organization, discipline, and training—characteristics on which Romans prided themselves. To the Romans, strict military discipline distinguished their soldiers from disorganized barbarians. Military punishments were ferocious. For example, if a soldier fell asleep during sentry duty, his barrack mates were required to beat him to death. But tight discipline and vigorous training produced effective fighters. To keep in fighting shape, troops constantly drilled in weaponry, camp building, and battle formations. A Roman soldier was expected to march 20 miles in four hours—while carrying his 40-pound pack and swimming across rivers encountered along the way.

Life in the Roman Provinces: Assimilation, Resistance, and Romanization

| 6.2 | How did provincial peoples assimilate to or resist Roman rule? |

Beyond the city of Rome and the imperial center lay the second concentric circle of power, the Roman Empire's provinces. In these regions some people assimilated readily to Roman ways, while others resisted. Unlike the Greeks of the Classical Age, Romans in the imperial era were willing to assimilate the peoples they conquered into Rome's political and cultural life. Formal grants of Roman citizenship gave many people the legal rights and privileges of being Roman.

The Army: A Romanizing Force

The army played an important role in **Romanization**, the process by which subject peoples adopted and adapted Roman cultural and political practices. Provincial recruits learned Roman ways during their service. Latin, the language of command and army administration, provided another common bond to men whose mother tongues reflected the empire's ethnic diversity.

> **Romanization** The process by which conquered peoples absorbed aspects of Roman culture, especially the Latin language, city life, and religion.

Each of the legions with a contingent of auxiliary troops was stationed as a permanent garrison in a province with an elaborate logistical infrastructure to provide weapons, food, and housing. Camp architecture and fortifications, as well as weapons, armor, and tactics, followed the same conventions across the empire, thus reinforcing the army's role as a Romanizing force. Generals and staff officers often had postings in different provinces during their careers and so developed a sense of shared enterprise.

Retired Roman soldiers who settled in the provinces also served as a Romanizing force. Until the end of the second century c.e., soldiers could not legally marry during their military service, but many men reared families anyway with local women. Sons born to such unions frequently followed their fathers into the army. At retirement, most soldiers stayed near the bases in which they had been stationed. Many towns arose full of former military personnel and their friends, families, and small businesses. These towns helped transmit Roman culture and values to provincial peoples.

Occupation, Administration, and Commerce

Romanization was neither quick nor unopposed. Revolts against Roman authority often followed soon after a subject people's initial defeat, while freedom was still a living memory. Roman force, however, usually—but not always—proved overwhelming.

One such uprising occurred in Britain. After the conquest of Britain in 43 c.e., several British kingdoms supplied troops to the Roman army in return for protection and a degree of autonomy. But in 60 Emperor Nero annexed one such kingdom, the Iceni. Emboldened by their new dominance, the Roman agents abused Queen Boudicca and raped her daughters. The queen then led the Iceni into open rebellion. With the aid of neighboring tribes who also resented the Romans, Boudicca destroyed a legion and leveled several cities. Resistance, however, ended quickly in 61 after Roman forces routed Boudicca's troops, and the queen took her own life. The Britons, like many other peoples before and after them, learned that resistance to Rome was futile.

The tension between Roman armies and provincial populations never entirely disappeared, but gradually the top layers of conquered populations became Romanized. They adapted Roman customs and in some cases entered Roman politics. Romanization transformed the provinces from occupied zones where shattered communities obeyed foreign masters to imperial territories in which variations of Roman culture flourished, and provincial elites came to think of themselves as Romans.

The Romanization of conquered peoples coincided with the absorption of conquered territories into the Roman provincial system. A governor ruled each province: He and a small staff administered justice, supervised tax collection, and orchestrated the flow of goods back to Rome. This structure of government created an administrative-military class that drew its members from the senatorial and the equestrian orders. In the service of the emperor, these men climbed the ladder of success through appointments in different provinces. Gnaeus Julius Agricola (40–93) is an apt example. The father-in-law of the historian, Tacitus, Agricola had a brilliant military career. As governor of Britain, however, he co-opted the defeated elites into the Roman way of life. (See *Different Voices* in this chapter.)

Transport and commercial networks connected the provinces to Rome. Soldiers marched on the 40,000 miles of paved roads crisscrossing the empire, but because transporting goods by land remained more expensive than moving them by water, rivers and the Mediterranean were the primary arteries of trade. With pirates quelled by Roman fleets, shipping flourished. Improved harbors, ports, and canals further encouraged long-distance trade.

View the Map

Trade Routes of the Roman Empire

The Cities

The Roman way of life manifested itself most noticeably in cities. Provincial cities became "little Romes." They served the empire by funneling wealth from its massive hinterland into imperial coffers. As centers for tax collection and law courts, cities were where the imperial administrators interacted with provincial aristocrats, who dominated the local population. More than 1,000 cities eventually dotted the imperial map (see **Map 6.3**).

In the West where urban traditions were largely absent, the Romans created new cities, such as Lugdunum (Lyons) in France and Eburacum (York) in Britain. These new urban centers imitated the city of Rome in their physical and architectural layout. All of them had a forum in their center, flanked by a council house (modeled on the Roman Senate), basilicas, and temples. The cities provided all the amenities and requirements of Roman urban life, such as bathhouses, brothels, arenas for gladiatorial combat and wild beast hunts, and slave markets. Main streets in the towns led to the Roman road system.

Such cities were an important Romanizing force. Local elites started to speak Latin, identify local gods with Roman gods, adopt Roman architecture and styles of art, and enjoy the Roman way of life. Often these elites also received the reward of Roman citizenship. Some even entered the Roman Senate.

Common patterns characterized urban life throughout the empire. Women held no administrative office and had no role in public decision making, although wealthy

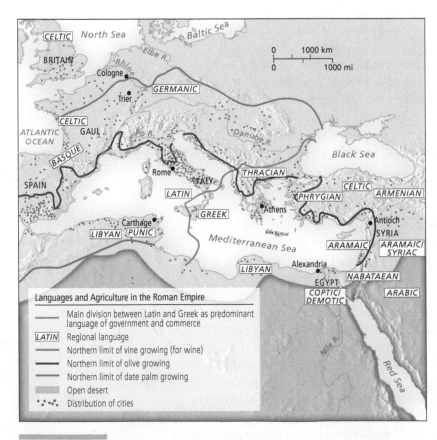

MAP **6.3** LANGUAGES AND AGRICULTURE IN THE ROMAN EMPIRE The 50 million inhabitants of the Roman Empire spoke many different languages and lived in a variety of climates and agricultural zones. Which of the divisions noted on this map were the most important and why? What does the distribution of cities reveal about the extent and limits of Roman power?

LITTLE ROMES Built in the early third century C.E., the amphitheater at the Tunisian town of El-Djem (the ancient city of Thysdrus) was one of the largest in the empire. Like the Colosseum in Rome, which it imitated, this arena sat thousands of spectators at gladiatorial fights and other entertainments.

View the Image

Roman Ruins at Conimbriga, Portugal

women sometimes presided as priestesses in civic religious observances. The male citizens of each city voted on local issues and elected town officials. A city council modeled on the Roman Senate presided over each city's affairs. A handful of the community's wealthiest men served in the city council or as magistrates and priests. The councils managed the grain supply, arranged for army recruitment, supervised the marketplaces, administered justice in local law courts, and, most important of all, collected taxes for the central government. In imitation of the emperor, councilors paid out of their own pockets for the upkeep of public works, aqueducts, and baths, and funded religious festivals and public amusements.

The Countryside

As Roman culture came to predominate in urban centers, the division between city and countryside widened. Provincial urban elites benefited from efficient and orderly government. In contrast, rural inhabitants, who formed most of the empire's population, faced economic exploitation and threats to their ways of life.

Despite the growth of trade, the Roman Empire was an agrarian state, and peasants performed the agricultural labor that drove the empire's economy. Some peasants rented their lands from landlords to whom they owed payment in the form of produce, money, or labor. If they failed to pay the rent, they could be punished or enslaved. Other peasants owned small farms sufficient to maintain their families, perhaps with the assistance of seasonal wage laborers or a few slaves. These landowning peasants faced the threat that a more powerful landowner might seize their fields by force. When this happened, peasants had little hope of getting their land back. The imperial system favored the wealthy and worked to the disadvantage of the rural poor. Rabbi Hanina ben Hama, who lived in Palestine about 240, stated bluntly that the empire established cities "to impose upon the people forced labor, extortion and oppression." Famine and natural disasters also posed a constant threat. A bad harvest could mean that peasants would have to sell their land or starve.

Despite these hardships, the peasantry managed to produce enough food to maintain the imperial system, especially the army. Indeed, agricultural productivity during this era was remarkable, considering the low yields of farms, the difficulty and expense of transportation, and the rudimentary technology. Some historians estimate that Europe did not see a comparable level of agricultural productivity again until the seventeenth century.

Food staples in the Mediterranean region included olives, grains, beans, and wine. Pasta had not yet appeared in Italy, and the tomato was unknown in Europe before the sixteenth century, when it was imported from the Americas. Wheat, often cooked in water to make porridge, was the Roman staple. Only the wealthy could afford to eat meat often. Most people relied on cheese, beans, and vegetables such as cabbage, garlic, and onions to supplement their wheat rations. The Romans did not have sugar, but most Romans seemed to enjoy sweets: They ate quantities of dates and honey.

Terrain, climate, and local farming customs determined the type of agriculture practiced. In Sicily and parts of southern Italy, chain gangs of slaves working on vast estates planted and harvested the crops. Migrant workers labored in the olive groves and wheat fields of Spain and North Africa, while seasonal movement of grazing animals predominated in the hilly regions of Italy and the Balkans.

Law, Citizenship, and Romanization

In the early empire, Roman law set Romans apart from the bulk of the population who followed their own laws. For example, Jews lived according to Jewish law or Athenians by Athenian law, as long as they paid their taxes to the emperor and did not cause trouble. If a Jew or an Athenian held Roman citizenship, however, he could also enjoy the rights and benefits of Roman law in addition to being the citizen of his native city. A Roman citizen possessed legally defined rights, including the guarantee of freedom from enslavement. Male citizens had the right to compete for public magistracies, vote in public assemblies, serve in the legions, and make an appeal in a criminal trial. No matter where they lived, Roman citizens took pride in their legal tradition and rights of citizenship.

Antonine Decree In 212 C.E. the emperor Aurelius Antoninus, called Caracalla, issued a decree that granted citizenship to all the free inhabitants of the Roman Empire. The decree enabled Roman law to embrace the entire population of the empire.

Then, in 212, Emperor Caracalla (r. 211–217) issued what became known as the **Antonine Decree**, which granted citizenship to virtually all free men and women within the empire, perhaps to increase the tax base. Legal uniformity further strengthened provincial loyalty to Rome.

Roman law made three important contributions to Western legal practices. First, the Romans created a standard feature of Western legal systems: the distinction between civil and criminal law. In Rome, civil law dealt with all aspects of family life, property and inheritance, slavery, and citizenship. It thus defined relations among different classes of Roman society and enabled courts to judge disputes among citizens. Criminal law addressed theft, homicide, sexual crimes, treason, and offenses against the government.

Second, Roman law influenced Western traditions of legal codification and interpretation. By the second century C.E., professional jurists (legal experts) directed imperial legal affairs under the supervision of the emperor. Far more than just imperial administrators, jurists such as Ulpian (d. 228) were legal scholars. They collected and analyzed earlier laws and judges' opinions, and wrote hundreds of commentaries that shaped the interpretation of Roman law for centuries, were passed on to the lawyers of medieval Europe, and still influence legal traditions. One such interpretative tradition is that under the principle of what the Romans called "equity," or fairness, judges should consider the spirit or intent rather than simply the letter of the law. According to Ulpian, "Law is the art of the good and the fair." On the basis of equity, Roman jurists argued that an accuser bears the burden of proof. A defendant does not have to prove he or she is innocent. Rather, he or she must be proven guilty.

Third, the Roman concept of "the law of nature" influenced Western ideas of justice. This concept stemmed in part from Stoicism (see Chapter 4), with its ideal of an underlying order to all things. From this ideal came the idea that certain principles of justice are part of nature itself, and thus that human laws should conform to natural law. Building on this Roman concept, later thinkers insisted that all human beings have inalienable rights and should be treated equally under the law.

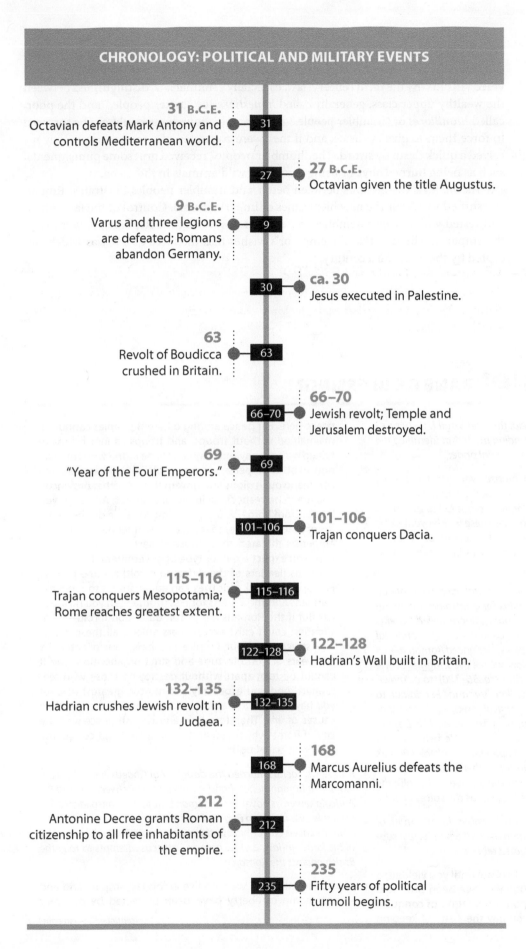

31 B.C.E.
Octavian defeats Mark Antony and controls Mediterranean world.

31

27

27 B.C.E.
Octavian given the title Augustus.

9 B.C.E.
Varus and three legions are defeated; Romans abandon Germany.

9

30

ca. 30
Jesus executed in Palestine.

63
Revolt of Boudicca crushed in Britain.

63

66–70

66–70
Jewish revolt; Temple and Jerusalem destroyed.

69
"Year of the Four Emperors."

69

101–106

101–106
Trajan conquers Dacia.

115–116
Trajan conquers Mesopotamia; Rome reaches greatest extent.

115–116

122–128

122–128
Hadrian's Wall built in Britain.

132–135
Hadrian crushes Jewish revolt in Judaea.

132–135

168

168
Marcus Aurelius defeats the Marcomanni.

212
Antonine Decree grants Roman citizenship to all free inhabitants of the empire.

212

235

235
Fifty years of political turmoil begins.

Equality under the law did not, however, exist in the Roman imperial age. Roman citizens had more rights than noncitizens, but not all Roman citizens had the same rights. In the first century C.E. laws began to reflect the differences in wealth that divided citizens. By the third century, law, especially criminal law, distinguished between the wealthy upper class, generally called *honestiores* or "better people," and the poor, called *humiliores* or "humbler people." For example, *honestiores* could not be tortured to force them to give evidence, and if they were convicted of a capital crime, they received a quick death by sword. The "humbler people" received gruesome punishments, such as being burned alive or being thrown to wild animals in the arena.

As the legal distinctions between better and humbler peoples illustrates, Roman law shifted to mirror the new hierarchies of imperial Rome. Control of the law, which had rested with citizen assemblies and magistrates during the Republic, now lay with the emperor. The idea that the emperor's wishes had the force of law was widely accepted by the early third century.

Different Voices

Roman Rule: BANE OR BLESSING?

In his epic poem, the Aeneid, the poet Virgil (70–19 B.C.E.) provided Rome with a founding myth that identified the central features of Roman imperial pride:

Other men will shape molten bronze with greater artistry; . . . others will plead cases with more skill, . . . and will predict the rising constellations. You, Roman, do not fail to govern all people with your supreme authority. These will be your skills: to establish law and order within a framework of peace, to be merciful to those who submit, to crush in war those who are arrogant.

As this quotation shows, Roman cultural identity centered on the belief that Romans had a genius for governing and therefore that the spread of Roman rule brought unparalleled benefits not only to Rome, but to those Rome conquered. Yet thoughtful Romans were aware that many peoples experienced Roman rule as oppressive. In the selections that follow, we see the struggles of one such Roman, the great historian Tacitus (ca. 55–120), to acknowledge the complex implications of the "Pax Romana." In addition to writing history, Tacitus climbed the political ranks, becoming consul under Nerva (r. 96–98) and governor of Asia about 112. Despite his political successes, Tacitus was a pessimist. He believed that the transformation from republic to empire had weakened Rome's moral character. Perhaps it is not surprising, then, that he was able to put himself in the position of not only the conqueror, but also the conquered. In the following excerpts, he gives us the voices of both.

A. In this section of his Histories, Tacitus describes the aftermath of a failed revolt in Gaul in 70. The Roman general who has just suppressed the revolt addresses the defeated rebels:

Tyranny and war always existed in Gaul until you yielded to our authority. And we, although we have been provoked many times, have imposed upon you by right of conquest only this one demand: that you pay the costs of keeping peace here. For peace among different peoples cannot be maintained without troops, and troops cannot be maintained without pay, and pay cannot be found without taxation. In other respects, we are equals. You yourselves often command our legions and govern this and other provinces. You are in no respect excluded or shut out. Although you live far from Rome, you enjoy as much as we do the benefits of praiseworthy emperors; on the other hand, the cruel emperors threaten most those closest to them. . . . Perhaps you expect a milder type of government if Tutor and Classicus [leaders of the defeated revolt] assume power? Perhaps you think that they can equip armies to repel the Germans and the Britons for less tribute than you now pay us? But if the Romans are driven out—God forbid—what situation could exist except wars among all these races? The structure of our Empire has been consolidated by 800 years of good fortune and strict organization, and it cannot be torn apart without destroying those who tear it apart. And you especially will run the greatest risk, for you have gold and natural resources, which are the chief causes of war. Therefore love and cherish peace and the city of Rome which you and I, conquered and conqueror, hold with equal rights.

B. In 77 C.E. Tacitus married the daughter of Gnaeus Julius Agricola (40–93), a Roman general and administrator. Between 78 and 85, Agricola served as governor of Roman Britain and consolidated Roman rule over northern England and southern Scotland (which the Romans called Caledonia). In this excerpt from Tacitus's biography of his father-in-law, a chief named Calgacus attempts to rally the British against the Romans:

Up until this day, we who live in this last strip of land and last home of liberty have been protected by our very

(continued on next page)

(continued from previous page)

remoteness. . . . Beyond us, there are no tribes, nothing except waves and rocks and, more dangerous than these, the Romans, whose oppression you have in vain tried to escape by obedience and submission. Plunderers of the world they are, and now that there is no more territory left to occupy their hands which have already laid the world waste, they are scouring the seas. If the enemy is rich, they are greedy; if the enemy is poor, they are power-hungry. Neither east nor west has been able to sate them. Alone of all men they covet rich nations and poor nations with equal passion. They rob, they slaughter, they plunder— and they call it "empire." Where they make a waste-land, they call it "peace."

C. In this section, Tacitus describes Agricola's policies of occupation.

For, to accustom to rest and repose through the charms of luxury a population scattered and barbarous and therefore inclined to war, Agricola gave private encouragement and public aid to the building of temples, courts of justice and dwelling houses, praising the energetic and reproving the indolent. Thus an honourable rivalry took the place of compulsion. He likewise provided a liberal education for the sons of the chiefs, and showed such a preference for the natural powers of the Britons over the industry of the Gauls that they who lately disdained the tongue of Rome now coveted its eloquence. Hence, too, a liking sprang up for our style of dress and the toga became fashionable. Step by step they were led to things which dispose to vice, the lounge, the bath, the elegant banquet. All this in their ignorance they called civilization, when it was but a part of their servitude.

For Discussion

1. How do Selections B and C illustrate the process of Romanization?
2. In two of the excerpts presented, Tacitus, like other ancient historians, quotes what he thought *might have been said*. How believable are these speeches? What sort of conclusions can we draw from them?
3. Tacitus used his historical writings to criticize many of the features of the Roman Empire. If history is written to promote a political objective, is it invalid?

SOURCE: A. Tacitus, *Histories,* 4.74; quoted in JoAnn Shelton, *As the Romans Did: A Sourcebook in Roman Social History* (Oxford: Oxford University Press, 1998), p. 288. B. Tacitus, *A Biography of Agricola,* 29–31; quoted in Shelton, p. 287. C. Tacitus, *A Biography of Agricola,* 21; from the *Complete Works of Tacitus,* edited by Moses Hadas, translated by Alfred John Church and William Jackson Brodribb (New York: The Modern Library, 1942).

The Frontier and Beyond

6.3   How did Romans interact with peoples living beyond the imperial borders?

In Virgil's *Aeneid,* Jupiter promises Rome "imperial rule without limit." But by the time of Hadrian's reign (117–138), the limits of the empire were clear. The third concentric circle of the Roman world consisted of the frontier—the outermost regions of the empire and the non-Roman world beyond. For the Romans, the lines drawn between the Roman Empire and the non-Roman world symbolized a cultural division between civilization and barbarism. Romans used this distinction to define their place in the world and to justify their conquests.

Like the generals of the Republic and the Hellenistic kings, Augustus set out to conquer as much land as possible to win glory and to demonstrate his power. He solidified Rome's control over Gaul and added large parts of the Danube River basin to the empire. His successors continued to add new lands to the empire. Britain fell to Rome in 43, and by 117 Trajan had annexed modern Romania, Mesopotamia, and parts of Arabia. At this point, the empire reached its greatest extent.

After Trajan, emperors turned their attention from conquest to consolidation. Trajan's successor, Hadrian, abandoned Mesopotamia and reorganized Rome's frontier with a series of fortifications, including the wall that still crosses the north of Britain and bears his name. His successors continued to fortify both the borders of the empire. By the early third century, regularly spaced military bases and fortresses dotted the empire's northern border while fleets patrolled the Rhine and Danube. In the East, another line of defenses extended from the Black Sea to the Nile. In North Africa, fortifications indicated the limits of cultivable land along the Sahara.

HADRIAN'S WALL Hadrian's massive fortification epitomizes the second-century-C.E. military concept of the fortified frontier. Stretched across northern Britain, it separated the Roman provinces to its south from the "barbarians" to the north.

Rome and the Parthian Empire

One of Rome's most formidable rivals was the Parthian (or Persian) Empire. Stretching from the Euphrates River to Pakistan, Parthia replaced the successor states of Alexander the Great in the mid-third century B.C.E. (see Chapter 4). The Parthian Empire was a powerful state that combined elements of Persian and Hellenistic culture. It survived until 224, when another Persian dynasty, the Sasanian, overthrew the last Parthian king.

The Romans knew the Parthians as fierce warriors. Parthia's specially bred battle horses, famous as far away as China, made heavily armed Parthian cavalrymen and archers worthy opponents of Rome's legions. Augustus—and most of the Roman emperors after him—shifted between war and diplomacy with Parthia. Trajan's conquest of Armenia and the Parthian provinces of Mesopotamia in 115–116 could not be sustained because they overextended Rome's resources.

The rivalry between Parthia and Rome, however, did not prevent commercial and technological exchanges. Romans prized Parthian steel and leather, and learned Parthian techniques of irrigation. In turn, Roman engineers and masons constructed roads and dams in Persia. Caravan routes that brought goods from India to Rome crossed Parthian territory. Most important, the Romans adopted the use of heavily armed cavalry from Parthia. By the fourth century, these units constituted the core of Roman military might.

Roman Encounters with Germanic Peoples

The peoples living north of the Rhine and Danube Rivers, not the Parthians, posed the greatest threat to Rome. Called "Germans" by the Romans, these peoples never used that term or thought of themselves as one group. Numbering in the millions, most of them spoke their own dialects and did not understand the language of other tribes. Led by aristocratic warriors, they often fought among themselves.

In the early years of Augustus's reign, Roman legions conquered large portions of "Germania" between the Rhine and Elbe Rivers. A revolt in 9 C.E. drove out the Romans, however, and Roman civilization never took root in the interior of northern Europe east of the Rhine. (See *Encounters and Transformations* in this chapter.) The Rhine and Danube Rivers became the boundary between Rome and its northern enemies. Most of Rome's legions were stationed along this key dividing line.

Tribes along the northern border sometimes fragmented into pro- and anti-Roman factions and occasionally formed loose confederations to invade the empire. For example, the *Marcomanni*, meaning "men of the borderlands," constituted one of these hostile confederations during the reign of Marcus Aurelius (161–180). Seeking booty, this confederation attacked the empire with more than 100,000 men.

During long periods of peace, the people on either side of the border interacted with one another through military service and trade. Germanic aristocrats developed a taste for Mediterranean luxuries, including wine and jewelry. Some lived in villas in imitation of Roman aristocrats. Germanic men served in the Roman army as auxiliary troops. Discharged after the standard 25 years of service, many of these men returned to their homes with Roman money in their purses, a smattering of Latin, and knowledge of the riches and power of the empire.

By 200, the weight of different peoples pressing on Rome's northern borders began to crack the imperial defenses. With the end of the Severan dynasty in 235, the empire entered 50 years of disasters. Invading groups from north of the Rhine and Danube Rivers pushed as far south as central Italy in search of plunder. The Romans ultimately repelled the invaders and restored the empire's security, but as we will see in the next chapter, the restored empire differed radically from the system Augustus inaugurated.

 View the Closer Look Marcus Aurelius and the Impending Invasion

THE EQUESTRIAN STATUE OF MARCUS AURELIUS IN PIAZZA DEL CAMPIDOGLIO IN ROME During his reign from 161–180 C.E., Marcus Aurelius campaigned against the barbarians that attempted to penetrate Rome's northern frontier.

Economic Encounters Across Continents

The Roman Empire was part of an almost global economic web. One Roman account from the first century C.E., *Voyage Around the Red Sea* (author unknown), describes a vast commercial network. Trade routes linked the Mediterranean basin, the East African coast, the Persian Gulf, and the Red Sea with southeast Asia and China.

ENCOUNTERS WITH CHINA Chinese documents from the first century C.E. mention ambassadors sent to Rome who reached as far as the Persian Gulf, and in 166, Roman merchants who claimed they were ambassadors from Emperor Marcus Aurelius went to China, but the two empires never established formal ties.

Silk, not diplomatic links, bound Rome and China together. Superior to wool and linen in texture and in its ability to retain colored dyes, silk was one of the most desired commodities in Roman society. The Chinese possessed a monopoly on silk production (until the sixth century C.E., when Western monks finally succeeded in smuggling the eggs of silkworms and the seeds of mulberry trees out of China).

In the Republican era, silk was so rare that even the wealthiest Romans could afford only small pieces, which they tended to wear as brooches. Then, during the age of Augustus, Romans learned to use the monsoon winds to travel from ports on the

Encounters and Transformations
The Battle of Teutoburg Forest

In September of 9 C.E., the Roman commander in Germania, Publius Quinctilius Varus, received word of an uprising some miles from his army's camp. The report came from Arminius, chief of one of the largest and most powerful German tribes. Arminius had fought for years in the Roman army as an auxiliary commander. His service to Rome earned him Roman citizenship and the rank of equestrian. Thus, when Arminius warned Varus of the rebellion, Varus believed him.

Already heading toward winter camp, Varus detoured into unfamiliar territory to quell the rebellion. After marching for hours, the troops at the head of the two-mile-long column of 18,000 men found themselves on a narrow track between a wooded hill and a bog. Here Arminius and his men, hidden amid the trees, attacked. The Romans were trapped. Packed so tightly that they could not lift their shields or fling their javelins, the soldiers could hardly defend themselves. Within hours, Arminius and his German troops annihilated three legions, along with six auxiliary infantry cohorts and three auxiliary cavalry units. Varus himself committed suicide.

The Battle of Teutoburg Forest, as the encounter between Varus's legions and Arminius's followers came to be known, transformed Roman imperial expectations and established the empire's boundaries in western Europe. Ever since Caesar's conquest of Gaul in 51 B.C.E., Roman forces had endeavored to move north and eastward into Germania. Moreover, in the decades before this momentous battle, Romans had come to view their army as unbeatable, particularly against "barbarians" such as the Germans. Varus's defeat changed all that. In panic, Roman troops abandoned the camps and fortresses that they had built beyond the Rhine. Most of these were never rebuilt. Except for brief punitive expeditions, Roman soldiers never again penetrated deep into Germania.

In 17 C.E. Augustus's successor Tiberius (r. 14–37) formally abandoned any effort to expand the empire across the Rhine. The Rhine River became an important cultural and political dividing line between the Roman and Germanic worlds. To the west and south of this line, Roman rule meant that people drank wine, followed Roman law, and spoke Latin—and eventually, the "Romance" (from "Roman") languages that derive from Latin. East of the Rhine, however, beer-drinking Germany followed a different cultural direction.

Yet Rome influenced that direction. In the decades *before* Varus's defeat, Germanic societies changed as they responded to the imposition of Roman rule over Gaul and the Rhineland. Inter-tribal exchanges and alliances increased—thus enabling these societies to coordinate a surprise attack on three of Rome's finest legions. Germanic societies also grew more hierarchical and militaristic, with mounted warriors gaining in wealth, power, and status. Arminius's victory accentuated these developments. Thus, the Battle of Teutoburg Forest not only halted the expansion of the Roman Empire in western Europe, it also accelerated the transformation of Germanic society that previous Germanic-Roman encounters had already begun.

For Discussion

How was the encounter of Arminius's followers and Varus's troops in 9 C.E. itself the product of a previous "encounter" and "transformation"? And what "transformation" followed the encounter in the Teutoburg Forest?

Red Sea coast of Egypt across the Indian Ocean to the west coast of India, a journey that took about 40 days. In India, merchants exchanged glass, gold, wine, copper, and other items for silk. By the time this trade occurred, the price of the silk would have multiplied several times, as payments were made to each middleman along the 5,000-mile "Silk Road" that ran from northern China across the sweltering deserts, towering mountains, and treacherous salt flats of central Asia and down through modern Afghanistan to the Indian coast (see **Map 6.4**). Yet silk was so precious that a successful journey guaranteed a Roman merchant a profit 100 times larger than his original investment.

Roman demand for silk, spices (especially pepper), and other luxury items from the Far East produced a trade imbalance. As early as the first century C.E., the Roman statesman and natural scientist Pliny the Elder (23–79) griped, "And by the lowest reckoning India, China, and the Arabian Peninsula take from our Empire many thousands of pounds of gold every year—that is the sum which our luxuries and our women cost us." Many historians view the drain of hard currency to the East to pay for luxury goods as a key economic weakness of the empire.

ENCOUNTERS WITH AFRICA Coins found in the interior of Africa suggest that the Romans may have had commercial dealings with peoples there. To the Romans, however, "Africa" was one of their provinces bordering the Mediterranean Sea—the region we know as North Africa today—not the vast continent that lay to the south, beyond the Sahara Desert. Only in the European Middle Ages would the name *Africa* come to stand for the entire continent.

The Romans knew little about sub-Saharan Africa. In 146 B.C.E., the Roman general Scipio Aemilianus sent the historian Polybius on an expedition down the west coast of Africa, which got as far as Senegal and a place Scipio called Crocodile River. In the first century C.E., a Roman military expedition that marched south from a base

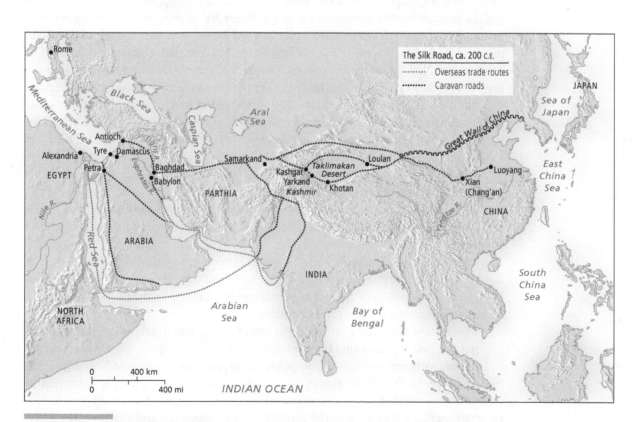

MAP **6.4** THE SILK ROAD   The Silk Road linked Asian cultures and economies to those on the continent of Europe for hundreds of years. Why was the first-century C.E. development of sea routes to supplement the overland parts of the journey a significant development? What products made their way across these continents—and why?

in North Africa in pursuit of some raiders may have reached Chad. One hundred years later, an intrepid Roman officer named Julius Maternus traveled south for four months, reaching a place "where the rhinoceroses gather." He emerged in the Sudan, where he found the Nile and returned home.

The Romans used the word *Aethiopians* ("the People with Burned Faces") to refer to the peoples who lived south of the Sahara. Most of their knowledge of these peoples came from the Egyptians, who regularly traded for ivory, gold, and slaves with peoples living in what the Egyptians called Nubia (in modern Sudan), where sophisticated and powerful kingdoms had existed for centuries.

Society and Culture in the Imperial Age

6.4	What was the social and cultural response to the emergence and consolidation of the empire?

The central theme of Roman politics after Augustus—the illusion of continuity masking fundamental change—also characterized imperial society and culture. The basic social structure of the Republic survived the shift to empire, but important changes occurred. While writers and poets praised Rome's greatness, they also explored the ambivalence of life under stable but autocratic rule. The spread of religious cults promising salvation hinted that many people under Roman rule found life less than stable and looked outside the political sphere for safety.

Upper and Lower Classes

In the Roman Empire, aristocrats remained at the top of the social pyramid, enjoying the greatest wealth, power, and prestige. Three social groups, or orders, possessed aristocratic status. The first order, the senators of Rome, occupied the top of the social pyramid. The rank of senator was not hereditary, but Augustus encouraged the sons of senators to follow in their fathers' footsteps and hold the offices that gave entry into the Senate. He also offered financial incentives to senators to have children and perpetuate their family line. Despite these efforts, most of the oldest Roman senatorial families had died out by the end of the first century C.E.; new families from Rome and the provinces took their place. All senators, and their descendants for three generations, had the right to wear a broad purple stripe on their togas.

Below the rank of senators stood the larger order of equestrians. Many equestrians continued to follow business careers as they had during the Republic, but the expansion of the empire gave them new opportunities for public service. Equestrians staffed many of the posts in the diplomatic, fiscal, and military services, and some entered the Senate.

The third aristocratic order was the curiales, members of local elites who served in the councils of every provincial city. Like senators and equestrians, they were expected to be wealthy, as well as of respectable birth and good moral character. Yet many sons of wealthy freedmen became city councilors.

These three aristocratic orders represented only about 1 percent of the empire's population. Below them came the common people—Rome's poor but free underclass of citizens. Although excluded from political life, commoners received benefits from imperial rule. In the city of Rome, adult male citizens received a daily allotment of free grain, olive oil, and pork. Ordinary Romans also received a steady diet of free entertainment, such as gladiatorial combats in the Colosseum and chariot races in the Circus Maximus. The satirist Juvenal (ca. 55–140) described life in the city of Rome as a matter of "bread and circuses": free food and free entertainment.

Ordinary urban Romans needed bread and circuses to compensate not only for their loss of political power, but also for their poor living conditions. Crowded into slums with little light or ventilation, the poor lived in misery. Disease kept birth rates and life expectancies low. Probably more than a quarter of all infants died within their first five years, and a third of those who survived were dead by age 10. The average life expectancy for Roman men was 45 years and the average for women 34.

Poor people lived in similarly wretched conditions in every Roman city, but without the daily distributions of grain. Most rural Romans were farmers, who provided most of the troops in the Roman army.

Slaves and Freedmen

Slavery was a fact of life in every ancient society. When Augustus took control of Rome, slaves constituted 35 to 40 percent of the population of Italy. These millions of slaves held the lowest status in a society in which social and legal status meant everything. Ancient slavery was not based on race or skin color. Most slaves had been captured in war. Others, born of a slave mother, were enslaved from birth.

Ownership of slaves reflected a person's status. The emperor and wealthy aristocrats owned tens of thousands of slaves who labored on their estates throughout the empire. Artisans, teachers, shopkeepers, and freedmen, in contrast, might own a slave or two. Because slaves could earn money, even some slaves owned slaves.

Slaves used for domestic service or in commerce and crafts were the lucky ones. Many male slaves worked on plantations, or "latifundia," as part of slave gangs. They often labored in chains and slept in underground prisons. The male slaves sent to work in the mines, some of whom were convicts, experienced even worse conditions. Female slaves were spared the horrors of working in the fields and mines, but they were valued far less than male slaves.

Violence lay at the heart of the institution of slavery. Masters could physically or sexually abuse slaves with impunity. A slave's testimony in court was valid only if extracted by torture. In the face of such brutality, slaves had few options. They could try to escape, but if caught, they were branded on the forehead. No slave revolt succeeded in imperial or republican Rome.

Slaves, however, might obtain their freedom through manumission. Through this carefully regulated legal procedure, a master granted freedom to a slave as a reward for faithful service, good behavior, or even out of affection. Of course, manumission also worked to the best interests of the owner: The hope of freedom kept slaves docile. Moreover, Roman law established limits to manumission. No more than 100 slaves could be freed at the death of an owner, and the slave had to be at least 30 years old and the owner at least 25.

Former slaves made up only about 5 percent of Rome's population, but their enterprise and ambition made the freedmen an important class. Many worked in business or as skilled laborers, teachers, and doctors. A freedman had only partial citizen rights, but his or her children became full Roman citizens, who could freely marry other citizens.

Slavery remained a part of Mediterranean economic and social life until the early Middle Ages; however, in the second century C.E., the economic role of slaves diminished. As emperors concentrated on consolidating rather than expanding the empire, the supply of slaves from warfare dwindled and their cost rose. Slave owning may have become less economically viable.

((• 📖 **Read** the Document

Slaves in the Roman Countryside

Women in the Roman Empire

Women in the senatorial and equestrian ranks possessed more freedom than was usual in the ancient world, in part because of a gradual shift in marriage customs. By 250, the form of marriage by which a woman passed from the control of her father to

LADIES AND THEIR HAIRDRESSER A skilled slave styles the hair of a trio of wealthy women in this first century fresco from Pompeii.

that of her husband had nearly died out. Instead, a married woman legally remained under the control of her father or guardian. Because their husbands no longer controlled their dowries, this legal change gave women more freedom. Some women used this freedom to move into the public sphere, taking part in banquets, attending gladiatorial battles at the Colosseum and races at the Circus Maximus, and presiding over literary salons. Women owned property, made investments, and became public benefactors. Many high-ranking women were educated in the liberal arts and lived cultivated lives. Their portraits—carved in stone or painted on walls—reveal a restrained elegance. The portraits of wives and daughters of emperors even appeared on coins.

At the highest level of society, some women possessed political power, though expressed behind the scenes. Livia (58 B.C.E.–29 C.E.), married to Augustus for 52 years, wielded enormous political influence during his and her son Tiberius's reigns. The Emperor Hadrian may have received his throne in part because of the influence of his cousin Trajan's wife, Plotina (d. 121). At her funeral, Hadrian admitted, "She often made requests of me, and I never once refused her."

Most women, of course, were not immortalized in stone or coin and had no political power. We have scanty evidence about the lives of non-aristocratic women in the Roman Empire. We do, however, know of women moneylenders, shopkeepers, and investors. Some women became doctors or artists. Most women probably married and gave birth to three or four children.

Although literary evidence demonstrates that many aristocratic Roman men cherished their daughters, female infanticide remained common. The expected ratio of female to male births is 105 to 100. In second-century C.E. Rome, however, the rate was 100 to 131. Unwanted babies—not only girls but also the sick and malformed, and some born outside marriage—were left by the roadside to die or to be reared by strangers.

Literature and Empire

The prosperity and stability of the Roman Empire allowed the literary arts to flourish. Wealthy patrons, including the emperor, sponsored publications and provided an audience for new works. Yet imperial rule also limited free expression. Roman writers confronted the tensions of living in a society that had exchanged freedom for stability.

The career of the philosopher Seneca (ca. 4 B.C.E.–65 C.E.) illustrates the constraints facing writers in the imperial era. Seneca intended his writings to give advice to rulers. Influenced by Stoicism (see Chapter 4), he acknowledged how hard it was to live a moral life. Seneca's integrity and rhetorical brilliance earned him the unenviable task of being Nero's tutor when the emperor was still an impressionable 12-year-old. For eight years Seneca guided Nero, and the empire enjoyed good government. As Nero matured, however, he found other, less decent advisers. Seneca, appalled by his student's descent into corruption, was accused of plotting to kill Nero. To avoid execution, he killed himself.

HISTORY-WRITING IN AN AGE OF AUTOCRACY The work of the historian Livy (59 B.C.E.–12 C.E.) illustrates the fine line writers in this autocratic society walked. In his history Livy presented Rome's rise to world mastery as a series of moral and patriotic lessons. He showed how Rome's military and moral strength catapulted it to world power. Although proud of Rome's greatness, Livy believed that with power came decadence. He did not gloss over the ruthlessness with which Augustus waged the civil war that destroyed the Republic, nor did he veil his criticism of what he perceived as Rome's moral and political decline. Livy's open criticism displeased Augustus, yet the emperor did not punish the historian, perhaps because Livy also expressed the hope that Augustus would restore Rome's glory.

The historian Tacitus (ca. 55–ca. 120) belonged to a later generation. While Livy experienced the tumultuous transition from republic to empire, Tacitus lived and wrote when the imperial system was firmly in place. Although his own career flourished under both the tyrannical Domitian and the just Trajan, Tacitus hated political oppression. He never abandoned his love for the best of Roman ideals. In the *Agricola*, his biography of his father-in-law, Tacitus affirmed that good men could serve their country honorably, even under bad rulers such as Nero. The *Agricola* thus inadvertently revealed an important accomplishment of Augustus's imperial system: It had tamed Rome's aristocrats, transforming them into an efficient governing class.

IMPERIAL POETRY Poets, too, had to adapt to life in an autocracy. The tragic career of Ovid (43 B.C.E.–17 C.E.) demonstrated the risks of offending an emperor. Ovid's love poems had made him the darling of Rome. But his lighthearted descriptions of Roman sexual life violated Augustus's efforts to restore traditional family values, while his book *Metamorphoses*, with its themes of change and impermanence in Greek and Roman mythology, indirectly challenged the ideal of a stable state under Augustus's leadership. In 8 C.E., Ovid's erotic poem, "The Art of Love," along with a sexual scandal involving Augustus's granddaughter, earned him the hostility of the emperor. Augustus exiled Ovid to a village on the Black Sea where the poet remained for the rest of his life.

Horace (65–8 B.C.E.), son of a wealthy freedman, escaped Ovid's fate by avoiding political and sexual entanglements and maintaining close ties to Augustus. His poetry on public themes praised the emperor for bringing peace and the hope of a moral life to the world. Throughout his work, Horace urged appreciation of life's temporary joys. In his most famous verse, he sings,

> Be wise, taste the wine, and since our time is brief, be moderate in your aspirations. Even as we speak, greedy life slips away from us. Grasp each day (*carpe diem*) and do not pin your hopes on tomorrow.

Virgil also earned Augustus's favor. At Augustus's request Virgil composed the *Aeneid*, an epic poem that legitimized and celebrated the emperor's reign. The *Aeneid* tells the story of Aeneas, a Trojan prince who founds the city of Rome. Through a series of cinematic "flash-forwards," Virgil presented the entire history of the Roman people as culminating in the reign of Augustus. Yet Virgil was not just an imperial propagandist as the ending of the *Aeneid* shows. Tempted by his love for the Carthaginian queen Dido to abandon his mission of founding Rome, Aeneas overcomes his personal desire to fulfill his mission: He abandons Dido, who then commits suicide. At the end of the poem, Aeneas stands victorious—but he has sacrificed everything. Virgil makes his readers wonder about the costs of public service.

Juvenal also exposed the weaknesses of the imperial age. One of the most quotable of Roman poets, Juvenal's satires mocked overeducated women, duplicitous Greeks, and boring provincials. His favorite target, however, was daily life in Rome. His descriptions of the city's noise, smells, flimsy housing, crowded streets, and pervasive criminality emphasized the wide gap in lifestyles between privileged and ordinary folk, and so highlighted the corruption of republican ideals.

Read the Document

Juvenal, A Satirical View of Women

Science in the Roman Empire

The Hellenistic scientific tradition (see Chapter 4) flourished under Roman rule. Using the division of spheres into units of 60 first developed by the Sumerians and perfected by the Babylonians, Claudius Ptolemy (ca. 90–170) codified the Hellenistic theory that the sun revolves around the Earth. Western astronomers used Ptolemy's maps of the heavens for nearly 1,500 years, while his *Geography* remained the basis of cartography until the sixteenth century.

Roman medicine shaped Western practices for more than 1,500 years. The physician Galen (131–201) sought to make medicine a science. He insisted on the importance of dissection for understanding the body and stressed the need for experimentation. For most of his career, Galen worked in Rome, but he served for four years as physician to the gladiators in Pergamum in Anatolia, where he was able to study firsthand the impact of trauma on the human body.

Galen's main influence on Western medicine, however, was negative. Galen believed that an imbalance in the body's four "humors," or basic bodily fluids (blood, black bile, yellow bile, and phlegm), produced disease. Too much blood, for example, meant fever. To restore the balance, Galen taught, the physician should restore the balance by applying leeches or cutting open a vein, and thereby drain the patient of "excess" blood. A strong purgative or emetic to induce vomiting or diarrhea could drain "excess" bile. Bloodletting and purging, and the humoral theory on which they were based, remained central in Western medical practice into the early nineteenth century. Unfortunately, these treatments weakened or killed innumerable patients.

Religious Life

Because the imperial regime made no effort to regulate religion, people throughout the empire freely worshiped many gods and maintained their traditional rituals. Nevertheless, this era witnessed significant religious change, including the transformation of Judaism and the emergence of Christianity.

POLYTHEISM IN THE EMPIRE Syncretism, the practice of equating gods and fusing their cults, was a common feature of imperial religious life and helped unify the empire. The Romans often identified foreign gods with their own deities. Romans did not care that other peoples might worship Jupiter, Juno, or any other Roman god in different ways or give the gods different attributes.

Each city in the empire had its own gods, but some religious cults transcended their places of origin. Feeling lost in the sprawl of the empire's cities, slaves, freedmen, and the urban poor turned to religions that offered both community and salvation. Religions that promised victory over death or liberation from the abuses and pain of daily existence spread across the empire.

The goddess Isis, for example, who originated in Egypt, offered freedom from fate to her many followers. Her story revolved around the death and resurrection of her husband, Osiris (also called Serapis). Her worshipers believed that they, too, would experience life after death. Moreover, Isis—often depicted holding her baby son, Horus—represented the universal mother and so promised compassionate nurture. In *The Golden Ass,* the Roman writer Apuleius (ca. 125–170) described the goddess's protective power. Full of eroticism and magic, the story tells of Lucius, a young Romeo, who turns into a donkey after he is caught spying on a gorgeous witch. Lucius stumbles through misadventures until Isis restores him to human form. Lucius thanks her for caring "for the troubles of miserable humans with a sweet mother's love" and becomes her priest.

MUMMY WRAPPING FROM EGYPT A painted linen cloth, wrapped around a mummy in an Egyptian burial during the second century C.E., shows the Egyptian god Osiris (on the left) and the jackal-headed god Anubis (on the right). Between them is the dead man, dressed in Roman clothing. His portrait has been carefully painted and added separately. The wrapping and portrait demonstrate the continuity of ancient Egyptian religion during Roman imperial rule.

Another religion that promised salvation to its initiates was that of Mithras, a sun god. According to his followers, Mithras was killed by his enemies on December 21, the winter solstice, and rose from the dead on December 25. By worshiping Mithras, his followers believed they too could achieve life after death. Limited to men, worship of Mithras took place in underground chambers in which small groups celebrated a ceremonial meal that evoked Mithras's memory, recited lessons about the journey of the soul after death, and sacrificed to the god. Because this religion stressed courage and duty, it particularly attracted soldiers.

Worship of the Unconquered Sun (Sol Invictus) also spread throughout the empire. Originating in Syria, this deity was associated with Helios-Apollo, the Greco–Roman sun god, and with Mithras. When Elagabalus, the high priest of the Syrian sun god (El-Gabal), became Roman emperor (r. 218–222), he built a huge temple dedicated to his god in Rome, and designated December 25, the birth and resurrection day of Mithras, as a special day of worship to the deity. Within 50 years, the Unconquered Sun became the chief god of official worship.

THE ORIGINS OF RABBINIC JUDAISM Roman rule reshaped Judaism and the history of the Jewish people. In 37 B.C.E., the Roman Senate appointed Herod the Great (37–4 B.C.E.), a Roman ally from southern Palestine, as "King of the Jews." Despite this grand

MITHRAS SLAYS THE BULL Designed around 200 C.E., a wall painting from a shrine at Marino, south of Rome, shows the god Mithras in the sacred act of sacrificing a bull. Limited to men only, the worship of Mithras occurred throughout the empire. Scholars are unsure of the symbolic meaning of the dog, scorpion, and snake shown in this painting.

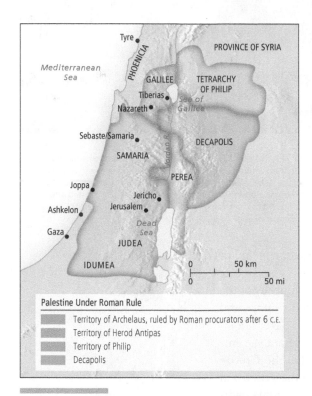

MAP **6.5** PALESTINE UNDER ROMAN RULE Herod the Great (73 B.C.E.–4 B.C.E.) ruled Palestine as a client king of Rome. After he died, however, the kingdom was divided among three of his sons. Just two years later, the Romans deposed Archelaus, the son who had inherited Judea, and assumed direct rule over his territories. How does this map illustrate the varieties of Roman administrative arrangements for governing the vast empire? How does it help explain why both Herod the Great and Herod Antipas play a role in the Gospel accounts of Jesus of Nazareth's birth, life, and death?

title, Herod ruled at the Romans' behest. Most Jews never regarded him as their rightful king. After Herod's death, his kingdom was divided among his three sons, but in 6 C.E., Augustus annexed the largest and most important of these kingdoms: Judea. The annexation of Judea meant that the Romans now directly controlled the city of Jerusalem, the spiritual center of Jewish life (see **Map 6.5**). Inept governors and heavy taxation caused Judea's economy to decline, famines and banditry became common, and a divide opened up among the Jews. The landed elite benefited from Roman rule. Ordinary Jews, however, viewed their leaders as collaborators with a godless power. They followed the scribes and rabbis ("my master" in Hebrew). These men of learning, who devoted their lives to copying religious texts and interpreting the scriptures, had little stake in Roman rule.

Sixty years of Roman mismanagement and the Jewish desire for independence led to revolt in Judea in 66. Jews formed their own government, appointed regional military commanders, abolished debt, and issued their own coinage. Internal divisions, however, weakened the rebellion. Imperial forces captured Jerusalem in 70, destroyed the Temple, and enslaved an estimated two million people.

Yet Judaism and the Jews survived. A new kind of religious life developed. Since the sixth century B.C.E., communities of Jews had lived outside Palestine, but after the Romans ransacked Judea, the **Diaspora** ("dispersion of population") characterized Jewish life. Jerusalem ceased to be the focus of Judaism's religious ceremony, although not of Jewish religious thought and hope. Animal sacrifice centered in the Temple disappeared. The rabbi replaced the priest

ARCH OF TITUS This marble relief from the Arch of Titus represents the loot from the Temple of Jerusalem carried in the triumphal parade in Rome after Titus crushed the Jewish revolt of 66–70. Soldiers display the Great Menorah, one of the holiest symbols of Judaism.

as religious instructor and community guide. Trained in the Jewish law, rabbis interpreted and taught the Torah and settled disputes. Synagogues developed into centers where Jews celebrated the Sabbath and prayed together.

The **Mishnah** emerged from this era. A collection of opinions, decisions, and homilies from both oral tradition and texts written to explain the Jewish law, the Mishnah was completed around 220. Each of the Mishnah's 63 books deals with a particular aspect of law, from ritual purity to crime. Among the moral principles the Mishnah stresses, saving life was paramount. To save a life, any person could break any Jewish religious law, except those forbidding idolatry, adultery, incest, or murder. Saving one life symbolized saving humanity.

THE EMERGENCE OF CHRISTIANITY Over a century before the Mishnah was compiled, the new religion of Christianity grew from Jewish roots. Beginning around 28 C.E., Jesus of Nazareth (ca. 4 B.C.E.–ca. 30 C.E.), a Jew from Galilee in northern Palestine, traveled through Palestine with a band of followers, urging men and women to join together in God's Kingdom before the imminent end of this world (see Map 6.5). Jesus's followers believed him to be the messiah, an important figure in Jewish prophetic writings. In Jewish belief, the messiah's coming would inaugurate a new age of blessing for God's people.

Sometime between 30 and 33 C.E., Jesus entered Jerusalem to preach his message. Roman authorities convicted him as a revolutionary and crucified him—the usual capital punishment for noncitizens in the empire. Jesus's followers, however, insisted that he rose from the dead and ascended into heaven, and that his spirit remained on Earth and guided their lives. Eventually called "Christians" (from the Greek word *Christ,* meaning "messiah" or "anointed one"), these men and women expected that Jesus would soon return and launch a new age of righteousness. They shared their possessions in common and—in a shocking violation of Roman and Jewish emphasis on family life—downplayed family and social ties. As the decades passed without Jesus's return, however, they focused on building their communities and preserving their distinctive faith.

But what defined this faith? Jesus's first followers were Jews who regarded him as a rabbi, a prophet, and eventually the messiah—all Jewish religious concepts. But as

Diaspora Literally "dispersion of population"; usually used to refer to the dispersion of the Jewish population after the Roman destruction of the Temple in Jerusalem in 70 C.E.

Mishnah Completed around 220, a collection of homilies and decisions to explain Jewish law.

 Read the Document

Judaism

Read the Document

Excerpt from the Gospel According to Luke

Read the **Document**

Christianity

orthodox In Christianity, the term indicates doctrinally correct belief.

heresy A teaching or belief not considered orthodox.

New Testament The collection of texts that, together with the Hebrew Bible, or Old Testament, comprise the Christian Bible. New Testament texts include the Epistles (letters of Paul of Tarsus to early Christians), the Gospels (stories of Jesus Christ's life, death, and resurrection), and other early Christian documents.

View the **Closer Look**

Early Christian Symbols

Christianity spread to non-Jews, and as Christians adjusted their expectations of Jesus's return, diverse and often clashing understandings of Jesus emerged.

In this process of religious debate and development, the work and teaching of Paul of Tarsus (d. ca. 65) were crucial. An educated Jew, Paul traveled throughout Anatolia and Greece, founding and developing Christian communities. Even more important, he wrote letters, or Epistles, that circulated among these communities. Written in the 50s, these letters taught that Jesus was not only the Jewish messiah, but also the Son of God who died on the cross as part of the divine plan. In Paul's letters, Jesus's brutal death became a loving sacrifice: By enduring the punishment that sinful men and women deserved, the sinless Son of God gave his followers eternal life in heaven after they died on Earth.

Paul's version of Jesus's teaching became the foundation of **orthodox** Christianity. *Orthodox* means "right belief," and from the mid-third century on, Christians who promoted beliefs about Jesus that differed from those defined as orthodox faced the charge of **heresy**. *Heresy* literally translates as "choice." A heretic was someone who chose to believe wrong things. But in the 200 years after Jesus's death, orthodox Christianity did not yet exist, and neither did the **New Testament** (the collection of texts that, together with the Old Testament or Hebrew Bible, comprise the Christian Bible). Because Jesus himself wrote nothing, different groups with different ideas could each claim to be his true followers.

While Paul, for example, taught that non-Jewish Christian men did not need to be circumcised (a key Jewish initiation rite) and that non-Jews need not follow Jewish dietary restrictions, others of Jesus's followers insisted that all Christians had to abide by all Jewish laws. Still other early Christians, called Marcionites, rejected not only Jewish laws and customs, but also the Jewish Scriptures and even the Jewish God. In their view, Jesus was not the Jewish messiah, but rather the chosen messenger of a loving God who came to Earth to save people from the vengeful God of the Jews.

An even more divisive issue than the relationship of Christians to Judaism was the question of Jesus's divinity. "Adoptionist" Christians saw Jesus as fully human, a man that God adopted to be his special son and to carry out his mission, while "docetic" Christians argued that Jesus only appeared to possess a material body but was in fact divine and not human at all. A third group of Christians believed Jesus was fully God and fully human. In 325 (see Chapter 7), this third view became orthodox

Justice in History
The Trial of Jesus in Historical Perspective

I n 30 c.e. imperial authorities in Jerusalem in the Roman province of Judea tried and executed a Jewish teacher known as Jesus of Nazareth. Although an insignificant event at the time, the trial of Jesus and its interpretation has had a profound impact on Western civilization.

Information about Jesus's trial comes from the New Testament books of Matthew, Mark, Luke, and John. These narratives, called the Gospels, were written 30 to 60 years after Jesus's death. They relate that during three years of teaching and miracles in Galilee and Judea, Jesus earned the resentment of the Jewish religious leadership by disregarding aspects of Jewish

religious law. According to the Gospels, when Jesus entered the Temple precinct in Jerusalem, he angered the Jewish elites by denouncing their hypocrisy and overturning the tables of money changers. The priests then conspired to kill him. They paid one of Jesus's followers to reveal his whereabouts. Soldiers arrested Jesus on the night either before or of the Passover feast and brought him to the house of Caiaphas, the Jewish High Priest. There Jesus either had a private hearing before the High Priest and his father-in-law (according to the Gospel of John) or a trial before the Sanhedrin, the highest Jewish court. According

(continued on next page)

to the Gospels of Matthew, Mark, and Luke, the Sanhedrin found Jesus guilty of blasphemy for claiming to be the messiah, the Son of God.

Lacking the authority under Roman rule to put Jesus to death, the Jewish leaders brought him before Pontius Pilate, the Roman governor, and demanded that he execute Jesus. Pilate hesitated, but the priests persuaded him by insisting that Jesus threatened the emperor's authority by claiming to be king of the Jews. Pilate's soldiers crucified Jesus, but according to the Gospels, the blame for Jesus's death lay with the Jews who demanded his execution. In all four Gospels, Jewish crowds in Jerusalem cry out, "Crucify him!" to a reluctant Pilate.

The Gospel accounts of Jesus's arrest, trial, and crucifixion pose problems for historians. Parts of these narratives conflict with what scholars understand about the conduct of trials by Jewish authorities and Roman administrators. For example, the historical evidence that we have indicates that the Sanhedrin did not hold trials at night. It did not meet in the house of the High Priest, nor convene on a feast day or the night before a feast.

Far more important than these issues, however, is the question of the crime of blasphemy. In first-century Judaism, the messiah was expected to be a kingly figure—but not God. If Jesus did identify himself as the messiah, he would not have been guilty of blasphemy. Some scholars, however, point out that the Jewish leaders would have regarded Jesus's claim to sit in God's presence (and thus to share in God's rule) as blasphemous.

Jesus's blasphemy remains unclear, but there is little debate about the importance of Jesus's confrontation with the Jewish elites in the Temple. Jesus committed a dangerous act by denouncing the priests in Jerusalem. These men, especially the High Priest himself, owed their power to the Roman overlords and were responsible for maintaining order. Many Jews in the Temple elite saw Jesus as an agitator who threatened their authority. According to Matthew, Mark, and Luke, the Temple guards, not Roman soldiers, arrested Jesus and brought him before the Sanhedrin. The Romans had appointed all 71 members of the court, including Caiaphas, who led it. These men knew that if they could not control Jesus, the Romans would replace them. The court could not execute Jesus, but it could send him before Roman magistrates on a charge that the Romans would prosecute—stirring up rebellion.

Jesus's popularity with the common people and the disturbance in the Temple precinct would have aroused Roman suspicion. Moreover, if Jesus had claimed to be the messiah, he was guilty of insurrection from a Roman standpoint, for the term had royal connotations, and no one within the empire could be called a king without the emperor's permission. Roman officials usually responded to real or imagined threats to the political order by crucifixion. In the eyes of Pontius Pilate, a cautious magistrate, Jesus was a threat to public order, and so deserved execution. Pilate would not have been reluctant to kill him.

Why, then, do the Gospels tend to shift the blame for Jesus's death from Pilate to the Jewish community? The Gospels began to be written down amid growing hostility and suspicion between Jews and Christians. Moreover, after Roman armies destroyed the Temple in the Jewish rebellion of 66–70, Christians wanted to disassociate themselves from Jews. They hoped to persuade Roman authorities to think of them not as rebels, but as followers of a lawful religion. Such concerns may have shaped the Gospel writers' tendencies to emphasize the role of Jewish leaders instead of Pilate in Jesus's death.

The Gospels also relate that before he died, Jesus predicted the destruction of the Temple. Many early Christians came to believe that the fall of the Temple and the savage repression of the Jewish rebellion were divine punishment for the Jews who had caused Jesus's death. These interpretations of Jesus's trial and execution, and of the destruction of the Jewish community in Palestine, helped poison Christian–Jewish relations for two millennia. From the first century through the twentieth, important segments of the Christian community blamed "the Jews" for Jesus's crucifixion.

For Discussion

1. What does Jesus's trial show about Roman methods of provincial administration—and about the limitations of these methods? Who had power in Judea?
2. In Christian theology, Jesus died for the sins of the world. In theological terms, then, all sinners—all human beings—bear responsibility for his death. Why does it matter if the Gospels blame Jesus's crucifixion on Jews instead of Romans?

Taking It Further

Borg, Marcus, and N.T. Wright. *The Meaning of Jesus: Two Visions.* 2007. Two leading New Testament scholars present their interpretations of the historical Jesus.

Crossan, John Dominic. *Who Killed Jesus: Exposing the Roots of Anti-Semitism in the Gospel Story of the Death of Jesus.* San Francisco: HarperSanFrancisco, 1997. An engaging and controversial investigation.

Sherwin-White, A. N. *Roman Society and Roman Law in the New Testament.* Eugene, OR: Wipf and Stock Publishers, 2004. A leading historian puts the New Testament in its Roman context.

doctrine, but in the first and second centuries, the Christian understanding of Jesus was far from set.

The question of Christianity's relationship with the material world also remained open in these centuries, as the emergence of **Gnostic** versions of Christianity illustrates. Gnostic beliefs varied widely (and not all Gnostics embraced Christianity), but in general Gnosticism taught that men and women are really spiritual beings who belong to God's realm, the world of the good, the world of the spirit. In contrast, the material world (including the human body) is not God's creation, but a fundamentally evil prison in which human spirits are trapped. In the Gnostic view, few humans recognize or *know* these truths. *Gnostic* comes from the Greek word

Gnostic Religious doctrine that emphasizes the importance of *gnosis*, or hidden truth, as a way of releasing spiritual reality from the prison of the essentially unreal or evil material world.

CHRIST AS THE GOOD SHEPHERD Carved in the second century c.e., this statue depicts Jesus as a good shepherd, a frequent motif in early Christian art. An image drawn from both the Hebrew Bible and Greek representations of the god Apollo, the Good Shepherd illustrates the blending of Greek and Hebrew ideas in Christianity.

 Read the Document

Gnostic Teachings of Jesus, According to Irenaeus

 Read the Document

Perpetua, The Autobiography of a Christian Martyr

gnosis, for knowledge. Gnosticism taught that only a few men and women possess the secret knowledge that will allow them to escape from the evil of this world and return to their rightful spiritual home. In Gnostic Christianity, then, Jesus is a kind of cosmic riddler who came not to save the world, but to save his few from the world. Gnosticism tended to promote disengagement from worldly affairs and detachment from physical needs and desires. While the solidification of orthodoxy in the third century meant that Gnostic Christians were labeled heretics, the question of the proper Christian attitude toward worldly concerns and bodily desires divides believers even today.

CHRISTIANITY WITHIN THE ROMAN WORLD Christianity drew many of its first converts from the urban "middle classes"—merchants, artisans, business owners—but it also appealed to socially marginalized groups, such as women, noncitizens, and slaves. Indeed, Jesus's message was revolutionary in the way it overturned boundaries of class, gender, and ethnicity. After Jesus's death, Paul encouraged a communal life in which all followers of Jesus were equal in the eyes of God. As he wrote to a small Christian community in Galatia in Anatolia, "For in Christ Jesus . . . there is no longer Jew or Greek, there is no longer slave or free, there is no longer male or female; for all of you are one in Christ Jesus."

Many of Christianity's core concepts, such as its ideas about personal salvation, the equality of individual men and women before God, and the redemption of humanity from sin, distinguished it from the empire's polytheistic faiths. Most strikingly, Christianity firmly rejected the existence of multiple gods and sought to convince followers of other religions that they stood in error. This conversionist impulse (called *proselytizing*), in addition to Christians' withdrawal from the public life of Roman culture, earned them suspicion—and sometimes death.

Until the mid-third century, persecutions of Christians tended to be local affairs, sparked by the hostility of a city magistrate or provincial governor. In 64, however, Emperor Nero blamed Christians for a fire that consumed central Rome. (Popular legend blamed him, equally wrongly.) Hundreds of Christians died in the arena before cheering crowds.

Christians called those who died rather than renounce their beliefs **martyrs**, or witnesses for their faith. The early Christian leader Tertullian (ca. 160–240) chided his Roman persecutors, "We multiply whenever we are mown down by you; the blood of Christians is [like] seed." But in 235 (the end date of this chapter), Christianity remained a minority movement within the Roman Empire.

CONCLUSION

Rome Shapes the West

The map of the Roman Empire outlined the heart of the regions included in the West today. Rome was the means by which cultural and political ideas developed in Mediterranean societies and spread into Europe. This quilt of lands and peoples was acquired mostly by conquest. An autocratic government stitched the pieces together. Although Roman authorities permitted no dissent, they allowed provincial peoples to become Roman. Being Roman meant that one had specific legal rights of citizenship, not that one belonged to a particular race or ethnic group. Thus, in addition to conquering the empire and patrolling its borders, the Roman army brought a version of Roman society to subject peoples. By imitating Roman styles of architecture and urban life, the cities, too, spread Roman civilization. Moreover, the elites of these cities helped funnel the resources of the countryside into the emperor's coffers, and so sustained the imperial system.

Rome's civilization, including its legal system, its development of cities, and its literary and artistic legacy, became the basis of much of Western civilization. The legal precedents Roman jurists established remain valid in much of Europe. Latin and Greek literature of the early Roman Empire has entertained, instructed, and inspired Western readers for nearly 2,000 years. Until recently all educated people in the West could read Latin, and many could read Greek. Many of our public buildings and memorial sculptures adhere to Roman models. The Roman Empire was the most important and influential model of an imperial system for Europeans until modern times. Of equal importance, the monotheism and ethical teachings of Judaism and Christianity have shaped Western culture.

> **martyr** In Christian tradition, believers who chose to die rather than to renounce or deny their Christian beliefs.

MAKING CONNECTIONS

1. Evaluate this argument: "Behind a carefully crafted façade of restored Republican tradition, Octavian created a Roman version of a Hellenistic monarchy, like those of Alexander the Great's successors in the eastern Mediterranean." What are the characteristics of a Hellenistic monarchy? Which of these characteristics did the Augustan system of imperial rule share? Why did Augustus seek to maintain the "façade of restored Republican tradition"?
2. How did the relationship between the Jewish population of Palestine and the Roman imperial government in the first century C.E. shape the early history of Christianity?

TAKING IT FURTHER

For suggested readings, see page R-1.

On MyHistoryLab

Chapter Review

The Imperial Center

6.1 How did the Roman imperial system develop, and what roles did the emperor, Senate, army, and city of Rome play in this process?

While Rome officially remained a Republic, a hereditary monarchy resulted when Augustus eliminated his enemies in the Roman Senate and defeated his military rivals. The role of the emperor included protecting and expanding territory, administering justice, supervising the public worship of Roman gods, and being a symbol of unity for the empire. The politically impotent Senate acted as an administrative arm of the emperor, and a loyal and large imperial army was crucial to maintaining his power. Finally, the city of Rome, including public works that demonstrated his power, was a testament to the authority of the emperor.

Life in the Roman Provinces: Assimilation, Resistance, and Romanization

6.2 How did provincial peoples assimilate to or resist Roman rule?

Provincial peoples were assimilated into imperial life when they joined the army as provincial recruits and adopted and adapted Roman culture. Revolts by conquered peoples were common soon after defeat, but were also short-lived and unsuccessful. New urban centers became smaller versions of Rome, where gradually the local elites learned Latin, worshiped Roman gods, adopted Roman visual arts, and were sometimes granted citizenship.

The Frontier and Beyond

6.3 How did Romans interact with peoples living beyond the imperial borders?

From commercial and technological exchanges with Parthia, to the trade of luxury items with China and contact with the Germanic and African peoples, a combination of trade, skirmishes, and cultural transmission marked Roman interaction with the peoples beyond their borders.

Society and Culture in the Imperial Age

6.4 What was the social and cultural response to the emergence and consolidation of the empire?

While the basic social structure of the empire appeared the same, with an elite group of the wealthy at the top of society and the lower classes living in poverty and squalor, a gradual shift in marriage customs gave women in the upper classes more autonomy and power. The arts continued to flourish despite imperial restrictions, with literature reflecting some of the inequalities of Roman life. The rise of religious cults, including Christianity with its message of personal salvation and equality of individuals, attested to the spread of social unrest and the fact many people under Roman rule were looking outside the political sphere for safety.

Chapter Time Line

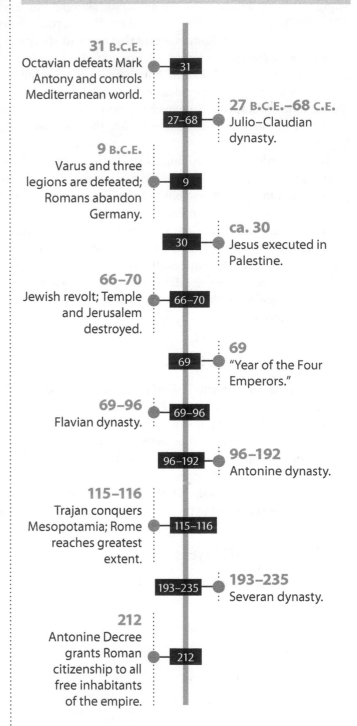

31 B.C.E. Octavian defeats Mark Antony and controls Mediterranean world. — 31

27 B.C.E.–68 C.E. 27–68 — Julio–Claudian dynasty.

9 B.C.E. Varus and three legions are defeated; Romans abandon Germany. — 9

ca. 30 30 — Jesus executed in Palestine.

66–70 Jewish revolt; Temple and Jerusalem destroyed. — 66–70

69 69 — "Year of the Four Emperors."

69–96 Flavian dynasty. — 69–96

96–192 96–192 — Antonine dynasty.

115–116 Trajan conquers Mesopotamia; Rome reaches greatest extent. — 115–116

193–235 193–235 — Severan dynasty.

212 Antonine Decree grants Roman citizenship to all free inhabitants of the empire. — 212

7 Late Antiquity: The Age of New Boundaries, 250–600

The events of the last week of August in 410 stunned the Roman World. A small army of landless warriors—no more than a few thousand men—led by their king, Alaric, forced their way into the city of Rome and plundered it for three days. For more than a year, Alaric had been threatening the city in an attempt to extort gold and land for his people. When his attempts at extortion failed, he attacked the city directly. Because Alaric's followers, the Visigoths, were Christian, they spared Rome's churches and took care not to violate the nuns. But that left plenty of loot—gold, silver, and silk—for them to cart away, and they did not hesitate to plunder the tombs of pagan emperors, including the Mausoleum of Augustus.

For these warriors and their families, who had first invaded the Roman Empire from their homelands in southern Russia 30 years earlier, pillaging the most opulent city in the Mediterranean world was a profitable interlude in a long struggle to secure a permanent home. For the Romans, however, the looting of Rome was an unfathomable disaster. They could scarcely believe that their capital city, the gleaming symbol of world rule, had fallen to an army of people they considered barbarian thugs. "If Rome is

View the **Closer Look** Tetrarchy: The Division of the Roman Empire Under Diocletian

THE TETRARCHS To depict their solidarity and readiness for war, the tetrarchs or co-emperors are presented as soldiers in military uniform, holding their swords with one hand and clasping their colleague's shoulder with the other. Each pair of figures shows one junior emperor and one senior emperor, who has more worry lines in his forehead as a sign of his greater responsibilities.

LEARNING OBJECTIVES

7.1 How did the Roman Empire successfully reorganize following the instability of the third century?

7.2 How did Christianity become the dominant religion in the Roman Empire, and how did it affect Roman society?

7.3 How did Christianity transform communities, religious experience, and intellectual traditions inside and outside the Roman Empire?

7.4 How and why did the Roman Empire in the West disintegrate?

Listen to Chapter 7 on MyHistoryLab

Watch the Video Series on MyHistoryLab

Learn about some key topics related to this chapter with the *MyHistoryLab Video Series: Key Topics in Western Civilization*

late antiquity The period between about 250 and 600, which bridged the classical world and the Middle Ages.

sacked, what can be safe?" lamented the Christian theologian Jerome when he heard the news in far-off Jerusalem. His remark captured the outrage and astonishment felt by Roman citizens everywhere, Christian and non-Christian alike, who believed that their empire was divinely protected and would last forever.

How did the Visigoths manage to sack Rome? The answer is rooted in the radical and debilitating transformations of the Roman Empire during late antiquity, the period between about 250 and 600, which bridged the classical world and the Middle Ages. **Late antiquity** can be divided into three stages. The first stage consisted of the half-century crisis from 235 to 284 of near-fatal civil war, foreign invasion, and economic crisis. During the second stage Rome experienced nearly 100 years of political reform and economic revival that stabilized it during the fourth century. Yet during the fifth century, the third stage of late antiquity, the political unity of the Mediterranean world ended. The Roman Empire collapsed in the West, and new Germanic kingdoms developed in Italy, Gaul, Britain, Spain, and North Africa. In contrast, the Roman Empire in the East, centered on its new capital city of Constantinople (modern Istanbul), managed to survive and prosper. Until their empire fell to the Turks 1,000 years later in 1453, the inhabitants of this eastern realm considered themselves Romans. In both Constantinople (where Roman political administration was maintained) and the new kingdoms of the West (where it was not), Rome's cultural legacy continued in the Greek and Latin languages and some forms of Roman law.

During late antiquity Christianity emerged as the dominant religion throughout the Roman Empire. From there it spread beyond the imperial borders, bringing new notions of civilization to the peoples of northern Europe, North Africa, and the Middle East. Henceforth, Western civilization was for most people a Christian civilization, and the borders that separated peoples were not just political ones, as in the ancient world, but religious ones. The encounter between the Roman Empire and Christianity raised this question:

How did their mutual interactions transform both the culture of the empire and the practice of Christianity?

Crisis and Recovery in the Third Century

7.1 How did the Roman Empire successfully reorganize following the instability of the third century?

Between 235 and 284, the Roman Empire staggered from political and economic turmoil. The institutions of the army and the office of the emperor, which had made the Roman Empire the dominant power in the Mediterranean, seemed incapable of standing up to new threats. Generals competed for the throne, chronic civil war shook the empire's very foundation, and invaders hungry for land and plunder broke through the weakened imperial borders. However, by the end of the third century, Emperor Diocletian arrested the disintegration with drastic administrative and social reforms.

The Breakdown of the Imperial Government

After the assassination of Emperor Severus Alexander in 235, military coup followed military coup as ruthless generals with nicknames like "Sword-in-Hand" competed for the throne. In the latter half of the third century, not one of more than four dozen emperors and would-be emperors died a natural death. Most emperors held power for only a few months. Preoccupied with merely staying alive and on the throne, they neglected the empire's borders, leaving them vulnerable to attack.

This had dire consequences. Invaders attacked both eastern and western provinces. To the Romans' deep shame, Emperor Valerian was captured in battle by the Great King of Persia in 260. War bands from across the Rhine River reached as far south as Italy, forcing Emperor Aurelian to build a great wall around the city of Rome in 270. Other cities across the empire constructed similar defenses. As a consequence of the political turmoil in the empire, the seat of power shifted from Rome to provincial cities. Unlike their predecessors, the soldier-emperors of this era, who came mostly from frontier provinces, had little time to cultivate the support of the Roman Senate. Instead, they held court in cities close to the embattled frontiers. Towns far from Rome, such as York in Britain or Trier in Gaul, had long functioned as military bases and supply distribution centers. Now they served as imperial capitals whenever the emperor resided there. Some cities and provinces took advantage of the weakened government to try to break away from Roman control.

The Restoration of the Imperial Government

Near the end of the third century, Emperor Diocletian (r. 284–305) rescued the empire from its chaotic condition. Drawing on his brilliant organizational talents, he launched a succession of military, administrative, and economic reforms that had far-reaching consequences. Not since the reign of Augustus three centuries earlier had the Roman Empire been so transformed.

After ruling alone for two years, Diocletian recognized that the enormous responsibilities of imperial government overburdened a single emperor. So he divided the

SUBJUGATION OF VALERIAN Persian kings built their tombs in a cliff six miles north of Persepolis, the old Persian royal center. Here at Naqsh-i Rustam, a carving depicts the Great King Shapur I (239–272) on horseback holding the arm of his prisoner, the Roman emperor Valerian. The previous Roman emperor, Philip (known as "the Arab"), kneels in supplication.

THE WALLS OF ROME Emperor Aurelian built a 12-mile circuit of walls around Rome in the 270s to protect the city from Germanic invaders. The walls, 20 feet high and 12 feet thick, had 18 major gates. That Rome should need protective walls would have been unthinkable during the early days of the Roman Empire.

tetrarchy The government by four rulers established by the Roman emperor Diocletian in 293 C.E. that lasted until 312. During the tetrarchy many administrative and military reforms altered the fabric of Roman society.

administration of the empire into two parts. In 286 he chose a co-ruler, Maximian, to govern the western half of the empire from Rome, while he continued to rule in the east. Then, in 293, Diocletian and Maximian further subdivided the empire by appointing two junior-level emperors. Each of these four co-emperors maintained a separate administrative system and his own army.

Through this system of shared government called the **tetrarchy** or rule of four, Diocletian hoped not only to make the imperial government more efficient, but also to put an end to the bloody cycle of imperial assassinations. Although he had gained the throne by murdering his predecessor, he knew that the empire's survival depended on a reliable succession strategy. To that end, Diocletian dictated that the junior emperors were to step into the senior emperors' places when the seniors retired. Then these new senior emperors were to select two new talented and reliable men to be junior emperors and become their eventual replacements. As supreme power was handed down from capable ruler to capable ruler, the constant cycle of assassinations and civil wars would be broken. Diocletian further subdivided the empire into almost 100 provinces. By focusing the responsibilities of provincial governors on smaller regions, Diocletian encouraged more efficient administration. He grouped these provinces into dioceses, each administered by a vicar who supervised the provincial governors. When Christianity later became legal in the empire, it borrowed the diocese as its principal administrative unit.

To restore Roman military power, Diocletian reorganized the Roman army, raising its total size to about 400,000 men for all of the empire, an increase of 50,000 soldiers, making it a huge army for its time. To protect the empire from invaders, he stationed most of these troops along the borders and built new military roads. In this way, forces of heavily armed cavalry could race to trouble spots if enemies broke through the frontiers. Diocletian also sought to reduce the army's involvement in political affairs. Although he was a soldier himself, he recognized that the army had played a disruptive role in earlier decades by constantly engaging in civil wars. He created many new

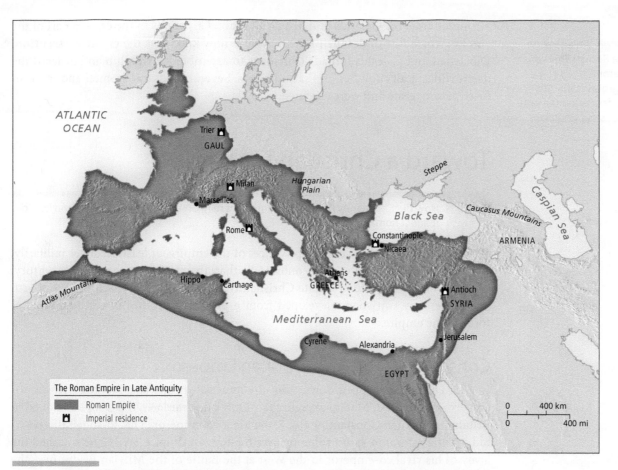

MAP **7.1** THE ROMAN EMPIRE IN LATE ANTIQUITY Following the reforms of Diocletian, the Roman Empire enjoyed a century of stable government, with the same borders as in earlier centuries. From this map, which areas of the West were most influenced by Roman civilization and which the least?

legions led by commanders who were loyal to him, but he reduced the size of each legion to limit its commander's power and to increase its maneuverability. With these military reforms in place, Diocletian was able to secure the empire's borders and suppress revolts (see **Map 7.1**).

Maintaining the expanded civilian and military apparatus created by the tetrarchy, especially in an era of rampant inflation, created new challenges. Diocletian had to make full use of the empire's financial resources and promote economic reforms. To halt the declining value of money, he attempted to freeze wages and prices by imperial decree. He also increased taxes and endeavored to make tax collection more effective by instituting a regular—and deeply resented—census to register all taxpayers. Although senators, army officers, and other influential citizens continued to be undertaxed or not taxed at all, the new tax system generated enough revenues to fund the enormous machinery of government.

The greatest tax burden fell on those least able to pay it: the peasants. The law required these agricultural workers to remain where the census registered them. Sons were supposed to follow their fathers. This attempt to maintain the agricultural tax base was successful, but it lessened social mobility, and the gap between rich and poor continued to grow. Many poor peasants turned to a few rich and powerful men for protection against the ruthless imperial tax collectors. In return, these peasants granted ownership of their farms to these wealthy patrons. The peasants, called *coloni*, continued to work the land but they gave up their freedom for security.

Diocletian's attempts to strengthen the empire led to religious persecution. He believed that failure to worship the traditional Roman gods had angered the deities and brought hardship to the empire. (See *Justice in History* in this chapter.) In 303, he and

Great Persecution An attack on Christians in the Roman Empire begun by Emperor Galerius in 303 C.E. on the grounds that their worship was endangering the empire. Several thousand Christians were executed.

his junior emperor Galerius initiated an attack on Christians in the eastern part of the empire, which was under their rule. In what is now known as the **Great Persecution**, Diocletian and Galerius forbade Christians to assemble for worship and ordered the destruction of all churches and sacred books. Several thousand women and men refused to cooperate and were executed.

Toward a Christian Empire

7.2 How did Christianity become the dominant religion in the Roman Empire, and how did it affect Roman society?

Diocletian left the eastern provinces of the empire, at least, stronger militarily, administratively, and economically than they had been for nearly a century. His attempt to eradicate Christianity, however, was a failure. In the fourth century Christians developed from a persecuted minority to the dominant force in the empire.

Constantine: The First Christian Emperor

In 305, Diocletian stepped down from the imperial throne and insisted that his co-emperor in the West, Maximian, retire too. Only one year later, the troops stationed in Britain proclaimed Constantine (ca. 280–337) a co-emperor. The 20-something-year-old general set out to assert sole rule over the Roman Empire. In 312 he smashed the army of his rival co-emperor in the West at the Battle of the Milvian Bridge over the Tiber River at Rome. Twelve years later he defeated the last tetrarch ruling in the East. Constantine then rejoined the western and eastern halves of the empire together with himself as absolute ruler. Thus, both the divided rule of the empire and the system of succession through co-emperors that Diocletian implemented came to an end.

In other ways, however, Constantine continued along Diocletian's reformist path. Under Constantine the empire's eastern and western sectors retained separate administrations. He retained Diocletian's emphasis on a large field army and heavily armored cavalry. The imperial bureaucracy and army remained immense, so taxes remained high. Under Diocletian coins had been losing their value, which contributed to the rampant inflation of prices and made the burden of taxes on the poor ever harder to sustain. To remedy the situation, Constantine reformed the coinage system. He recognized that the existing coins had become so debased they were effectively worthless, so he created a new gold coin—the *solidus,* which had a fixed gold content. The solidus stabilized the economy by restoring the value of currency. The new coin ended the inflationary spiral that had contributed so much to the political and social turmoil of the third century. It remained the standard coin in the Mediterranean world for 800 years.

Unlike Diocletian, Constantine embraced the new religion of Christianity. Most emperors had associated themselves with a divine protector. In fact, Constantine had chosen the sun god Apollo as his first divine companion. But the night before the pivotal Battle at the Milvian Bridge in 312, Constantine experienced a vision of the cross upon which Jesus had been crucified. After triumphing in battle, Constantine interpreted his vision as a sign from the Christian God who brought him the victory.

Because monotheistic Christianity repudiated rival gods and alternative forms of worship, Constantine's conversion led to the eventual triumph of Christianity throughout the empire. Constantine did not order his subjects to accept Christianity or forbid polytheist worship. He did, however, encourage widespread and public

THE COLOSSUS OF CONSTANTINE These fragments are all that remain of the colossal statue of Emperor Constantine, which stood 40-feet high in the apse of the Basilica of Maxentius in the Roman Forum. The co-emperor Maxentius began the basilica in 307 to glorify himself with a gigantic statue. After Constantine defeated Maxentius at the Battle of the Milvian Bridge in 312, Constantine had the head replaced with his own facial image. The emperor's head with its disproportionately large eyes that look toward heaven perhaps symbolized the Christian emphasis on the world to come over the transience of human life.

practice of his new faith. Before Constantine, Christian worship had often been conducted in the privacy of homes, but he lavished funds on church buildings. He obtained the gold for his new solidus coinage by looting the treasures that had been stored for centuries in polytheist temples. Now encouraged by the emperor, Christianity quickly gained strength and became a potent challenge to traditional modes of religious expression.

To create an entirely Christian new Rome, Constantine founded a second capital city, Constantinople, the "City of Constantine," on the site of the Greek city Byzantium in 324. Constantine's choice of location revealed a shrewd eye for strategy. The city lay at the juncture of two military roads that linked Europe and Asia and controlled communications between the Mediterranean and the Black Seas. From this strategic spot the emperor monitored the vast resources of the empire's eastern provinces. Like Diocletian, Constantine recognized that the wealth and power of the empire lay in the East.

📖 **Read** the Document

Eusebius of Caesarea, selections from
The Life of Constantine

🔍 **View** the Map

Spread of Christianity

Constantine's capital became a strongly fortified city. In response to the threat of attack by pirates, Emperor Theodosius II erected massive defensive walls around the city in 413. In future centuries these fortifications would protect the city—and indeed, the empire—from ruin on many occasions. With a new Senate formed on the model of that of the city of Rome, a steady supply of grain from Egypt to feed the capital's inhabitants, and plenty of opportunities for trade, Constantinople attracted people from all over the empire. The city rapidly grew in size, reaching perhaps several hundred thousand inhabitants by the early sixth century.

The Spread of Christianity

Before the fourth century Christianity had grown through missionaries who established congregations in most cities of the empire. After Constantine, successive emperors encouraged Christianity, which mushroomed throughout the empire through the spread of bishops who became local figures of great prestige. With imperial support, church leaders Christianized the look of cities by building churches and attacking polytheist temples.

THE RISE OF THE BISHOPS Part of the success of Christianity was due to the sophistication of its internal organization. In the early centuries of Christianity a distinction developed between the laity—the ordinary worshipers—and the priests, who led the worship, administered the sacraments, and acted as pastors for the laity. In imitation of the Roman urban administration, Christians developed their own administrative hierarchy. Just as an imperial official directed each city's political affairs with a staff of assistants, so each city's Christian community came to be led by a chief pastor, called a bishop, who in turn had a staff of subordinate priests and deacons. Just as a provincial governor controlled the political affairs of all of the cities and rural regions in his province, so the bishop of the main city of a province held authority over the other bishops and priests in the province. This main or head bishop came to be called a *metropolitan* (because he resided in the chief city, the metropolis, of the province) in the East, an *archbishop* in the West. This hierarchy of metropolitans/archbishops, bishops, priests, and deacons linked the scattered communities of believers together into what emerged as the Christian Church.

With this administrative structure, the Church grew quickly, and bishops became important authorities in their cities. A bishop supervised the religious life of his *see* or diocese, a unit based on Diocletian's administrative reforms. A diocese comprised not only the city itself, but also its surrounding villages and agricultural regions. Such supervision involved explaining Christian principles and teaching the Bible. Bishops soon became far more than religious teachers. As the Church grew wealthy from the massive donations of emperors such as Constantine and the humbler offerings of pious women and men throughout the empire, bishops used these resources to help the poor. The bishops cared for the general welfare of orphans, widows, sick people, prisoners, and travelers. When famine struck southern Gaul in the fifth century, for example, the bishop of Lyons sent so much food from his church estates that grain barges jammed the Rhône and Saône Rivers and carts full of grain clogged the roads going south.

Constantine permitted bishops to act as judges in civil actions, which made them agents of the imperial government. This policy soon entangled them in secular politics because litigants could choose to be tried before a bishop rather than a civil judge. The decisions of a bishop had the same legal authority as those rendered by civil judges. Using the rhetorical skills they had learned in Roman schools, bishops were also the advocates for their cities before provincial governors or the imperial court. In many ways they usurped the role of the traditional urban aristocracy. For example, when the people of Antioch in Syria rioted and smashed a statue of the emperor, the local bishop, not a local aristocrat, intervened to prevent imperial troops from massacring the city's people.

In the West, Rome became the most important see. Like all bishops, the bishop of Rome came to be called the "pope"—the papa or father of his flock. In his case the title stuck and eventually referred only to him. By the mid-fifth century the emperor formally recognized the pope's claim to have preeminence over other bishops. Two factors explain why the office of the bishop of Rome evolved into the **papacy**. First, together with Jerusalem, Rome was a site of powerful symbolic importance to Christians because the Apostle Peter, considered the first among Jesus's disciples, and Paul of Tarsus, the traveling teacher who took a leading role in spreading Christianity beyond its Jewish origins, died as martyrs in Rome. Second, early Christians considered Peter to have been the first bishop of Rome who passed on his authority to all subsequent popes in what is called the Doctrine of the Petrine Succession.

Popes claimed to be the chief bishops of the Christian world. They insisted that their spiritual authority took precedence over that of rival bishops in other important cities, especially Constantinople. The bishops (called patriarchs) of Constantinople often quarreled bitterly with the pope over matters of faith and politics. The tensions among these bishops led to divisions between the eastern and western parts of the empire that have lasted until the present day.

Through the authority of the bishops, the Church began functioning almost as an administrative arm of the government, although it still had its own internal organization. Indeed, when Roman rule collapsed in western Europe in the fifth century, the Church stepped in to fill the vacuum of public leadership.

CHRISTIANITY AND THE CITY OF ROME Christianity transformed the appearance of Roman cities. Constantine set an example of public and private spending on churches, hospitals, and monastic communities that conformed to Christian values. One of the great churches that Constantine built in Rome was called "Saint Paul Outside the Walls." This imposing structure marked the supposed burial spot of Paul of Tarsus. Constantine also financed the construction of another grand church on the presumed site of Peter's martyrdom and burial, in an obscure cemetery on what was called the Vatican hill, just outside Rome's wall. St. Peter's Basilica was an imposing structure, with five aisles punctuated with marble columns. Its altar rested over Peter's grave. (Today the papal basilica of St. Peter stands on that same spot, in the heart of the Vatican, the city-state of the pope.) The construction of these churches signaled that Jesus's apostles Peter and Paul had replaced Rome's mythical founders Romulus and Remus as the city's sacred patrons. With the construction of Christian churches, spending and construction on traditional buildings such as temples, bathhouses, and public entertainment facilities such as the circuses declined. At the prompting of Rome's bishops, other public buildings, such as the large basilicas used for public business, including legal trials, were turned into churches.

With the proliferation of new Christian churches in Rome and other cities came new religious festivals and rituals, such as the anniversaries of the martyrdom of saints. Sometimes a Christian holiday (holy day) competed with a non-Christian holiday. For example, Rome's churchmen designated December 25 as the birthday of Christ to challenge the popular festival of the Unconquered Sun, which fell on the same day. By the early sixth century, the Church had filled the calendar with days devoted to Christian ceremonies. Christmas and Easter (which commemorates the resurrection of Jesus) and days for commemorating specific martyrs supplanted traditional Roman holidays. These festivals thus changed the patterns of urban community life throughout the empire. Not all of the traditional Roman holidays disappeared, however. Those that Christians considered harmless continued to be observed as civic holidays. These included New Year's Day, the accession days of the emperors, and the days that celebrated the founding of Rome and Constantinople.

One additional development in the Christian shaping of time was the use of the letters A.D. as a dating convention. A.D. stands for *anno domini*, or "in the year of our Lord," referring to the year of Jesus's birth. The convention began in 531, when a monk

7.1

7.2

7.3

7.4

papacy The administrative and political institutions controlled by the Pope (Father), the bishop of the city of Rome. The papacy began to gain strength in the sixth century in the absence of Roman imperial government in Italy.

Read the Document

Pope Leo I on Bishop Hilary of Aries

BASILICA OF SAINT PAUL OUTSIDE THE WALLS The church of Saint Paul Outside the Walls was built by Emperor Constantine on the supposed burial spot of Paul of Tarsus. Like other late antique churches, Saint Paul's followed the plan of a Roman public building, a basilica, but added an altar in the semicircular apse at one end. The fifth-century mosaics of the triumphal arch portray the Apocalypse described in the prophecies of John the Revelator. In the middle is an image of Christ flanked by the 24 doctors of the church. At the left of the arch is Saint Paul pointing downward to his tomb.

in Rome established a simple system for determining the date of Easter every year. He began his calendar with the birth of Jesus in the year one (zero was unknown in Europe at this time) and started counting from there. Although he was probably a few years off in his determination of the year of Jesus's birth, his system came into general use by the tenth century. In many modern secular societies where belief in Christianity is not universal, the abbreviation A.D. has been replaced by C.E.—meaning "in the Common Era"—to designate years.

OLD GODS UNDER ATTACK Before Christianity became the dominant religion in the Roman Empire, people prayed to gods of all sorts. Different deities met different needs, and the worship of one did not preclude worship of another. To Christians, this diverse range of religious expression was intolerable. They labeled all polytheistic worship with the derogatory term **pagan** from the Latin word *paganus*, which meant "hillbilly," a reflection of the urban bias of early Christianity and the failure of Christianity to spread among country people.

After converting to Christianity in 312, Constantine ordered the end of the persecution of Christians. Although Christianity did not become the "official" religion of the empire for nearly a century, tolerance for non-Christian beliefs and practices began to fade. In the fourth century, imperial laws forbade sacrificing animals on the altars outside the old gods' temples. State funding for polytheistic worship gradually stopped. Instead of temples, emperors built churches with money collected from the

pagan The Christian term for polytheist worship (worshiping more than one god). In the course of late antiquity, the Christian Church suppressed paganism, the traditional religions of the Roman Empire.

taxpayers. Bishops and monks, often in collusion with local administrators, led attacks on polytheist shrines and holy places.

Because polytheism was not a single, organized religion, it offered no systematic opposition to government-supported attacks, but there were influential opponents to the Christianization of the empire. In sharp contrast to the pious Christian court at Constantinople, the conservative aristocracy of the city of Rome clung hard to the old gods. In 384, their spokesman begged the emperor for tolerance. Quintus Aurelius Symmachus argued that Rome's greatness had resulted from the observance of ancient rites. His pleas fell on deaf ears. Emperor Theodosius I (r. 379–395) and his grandson Theodosius II (r. 402–450) forbade all forms of polytheistic worship, and non-Christian practice lost the protection of the law. By the mid-fifth century, the aristocracy of the city of Rome had accepted Christianity. (See *Justice in History* in this chapter.)

Many less influential people also struggled to maintain ancient forms of worship, but the pace of conversion accelerated in the fifth and sixth centuries. Emperor Justinian (r. 527–565) sponsored programs of forced conversion in the countryside of Anatolia, where many of his subjects still followed ancient ways. Eradicating polytheism in the Roman Empire meant far more than substituting one religion for another. In the pre-Christian world, polytheism lay at the heart of every community, influencing every activity, every habit of social life. To replace the worship of the old gods required a true revolution in social and intellectual life. Completing that revolution became the challenge of the new Christian communities.

New Christian Communities and Identities

7.3 How did Christianity transform communities, religious experience, and intellectual traditions inside and outside the Roman Empire?

Christianity solidified community loyalties and allegiances by providing a shared belief system and new opportunities for participation in religious culture. Yet Christianity also opened up new divisions and gave rise to new hostilities over conflicting interpretations of the doctrines of the faith. Because Christians spoke Greek, Latin, Coptic, Syriac, Armenian, and other languages, different religious interpretations and rituals sometimes took hold among different language groups, creating distinct communities.

FEMALE PRIEST This foot-high ivory panel shows a female priest making a sacrifice at an altar to an unnamed god or goddess. *Symmachorum* means "of the family of the Symmachi," an aristocratic Roman clan in which some members defended the old gods in the face of Christianity. Unlike the polytheist cults of late antiquity, Orthodox Christians did not allow women to serve as priests.

📖 **Read the Document**

Paulus Orosius, from *Seven Books of History Against the Pagans*

211

The Creation of New Communities

Christianity fostered the growth of large-scale communities of faith by providing a well-defined set of beliefs and values. These basic beliefs and values had to be integrated with daily life and older ways of thinking. Thus, Christianity required followers to study and interpret the Bible. It also demanded allegiance to one God and a complex set of doctrines.

CHRISTIAN DOCTRINE AND HERESY Despite the institutionalization of the Church through the office of bishops, the theological controversies that had shaped Christianity from its very start continued and new controversies emerged. Councils of bishops met frequently to try to resolve doctrinal differences and produce statements of the faith that all parties could accept.

The persistent question was who was or is Jesus? Was he a man, God, or some combination of both? Like Jews, the followers of Christ believe that one God created and governs Heaven and Earth. If Jesus were just a man, as the adoptionist Christians discussed in Chapter 6 thought, then monotheism is preserved. If Jesus were a man that God adopted to be his special son and to carry out his mission, then Jesus was no different in his nature from any other man and could be subject to sin and error. If, however, Jesus were God who only appeared to possess the body of a man, as the docetic Christians believed, then other problems arose. For example, if Christ were entirely divine, then who did he pray to? This emphasis on Jesus's divinity made his death on the cross and his resurrection irrelevant, for God could not suffer and die. It also severed the links between Jesus and his human followers by emphasizing that Jesus was entirely "transcendent" or "other," entirely beyond human comprehension or human limitations.

A group of theologians developed the doctrine of the Trinity during the second and third centuries as an answer to these persistent questions about the nature of Jesus. They argued that the one God was to be understood as existing in three distinct "persons," each fully and absolutely God—God the Father, God the Son, and God the Holy Spirit—the Holy Trinity. This solution, however, did not entirely resolve the controversies. Church leaders continued to argue about the precise relation of the three persons within the Trinity. Were the Son and the Holy Spirit of the same essence as the Father? Were they equally divine? Did the Father exist before the Son?

These questions about the nature of the Trinity just continued the adoptionist–docetic debate in a different form, which came to be called the Arian–Athanasian dispute. The **Arians** followed Arius of Alexandria (ca. 250–336), a priest steeped in Greek philosophy. Arians asserted that God the Father created Jesus, so Jesus could not be equal to or of the same essence as God the Father. Arians argued that the Trinitarian idea that Jesus was both fully divine and fully human was illogical. The Athanasians, followers of Bishop Athanasius of Alexandria (293–373), were horrified by what they saw as the Arians' attempt to degrade Jesus's divinity. They argued that Christian truths were beyond human logic and that Jesus was fully God, equal to and of the same substance as God the Father, yet also fully human.

The Arian–Athanasian dispute resulted in perhaps the most influential of the many church meetings held in late antiquity: the Council of Nicaea. As the first general council, Nicaea signaled the beginning of an empire-wide Church. In 325, Emperor Constantine summoned the quarrelling bishops to Nicaea, a town near Constantinople, to reach a decision about the relationship among the divine members of the Holy Trinity. The bishops produced the Nicene Creed, which is still recited in Christian worship today. The creed, in agreement with Athanasian belief, states that God the Son (Jesus Christ) is identical in nature and essence to God the Father. In 451 the Council of Chalcedon reinforced the Nicene Creed. The assembled bishops agreed that Jesus was both fully human and fully divine, and that these two natures were entirely distinct

Arians Christians who believe that God the Father is superior to Jesus Christ his Son. Most of the Germanic settlers in western Europe in the fifth century were Arians.

though united. Their position became the interpretation accepted to this day by Orthodox, Catholic, and Protestant Christians.

COMMUNITIES OF FAITH AND LANGUAGE The doctrinal differences between Christian groups helped cement different communal and even ethnic identities in late antiquity. Three geographic zones of Christians emerged that held different interpretations of Christian doctrine, each a testament to the remarkable variety of Christian cultures.

A central zone based in Constantinople and including North Africa, the Balkans, and much of western Europe contained Christians called **Chalcedonians**, or orthodox. (In the Latin-speaking western provinces, they were also called Catholics.) These believers followed the decision of the Council of Chalcedon that defined Christ's divine and human natures as equal but entirely distinct. Christ was both God and man at the same time, but his divine and human natures did not mix. In late antiquity, the emperors in Constantinople and the popes in Rome—as well as most of the population of the Roman Empire—were Chalcedonian Christians.

Although the Christians in this first zone agreed on fundamental matters of doctrine, they differed culturally by producing Bibles, delivering sermons, and conducting religious ceremonies in their native languages—Latin in the western part of the central zone; mostly Greek (but also Syriac, Armenian, and Coptic) in the eastern part of the central zone. About 410, the monk Jerome finished a new Latin translation of the Bible that replaced earlier Latin versions. This translation, called the **Vulgate**, became the standard Bible in European churches until the sixteenth century.

The Western Church's use of Latin kept the door open for the transmission of all Latin texts into a world defined by Christianity. This ensured the survival of Roman legal, scientific, and literary traditions, even after Roman rule had evaporated in western Europe. Latin also forged a common bond among different political communities of the empire's western sector, where it served as an international language

Chalcedonians Christians who followed the doctrinal decisions and definitions of the Council of Chalcedon in 451 C.E. stating that Christ's human and divine natures were equal, but entirely distinct and united in one person "without confusion, division, separation, or change." Chalcedonian Christianity came to be associated with the Byzantine Empire and is called Greek Orthodoxy. In western Europe it is known as Roman Catholicism.

Vulgate The Latin translation of the Bible produced about 410 by the monk Jerome. It was the standard Bible in western Christian churches until the sixteenth century.

THE VIENNA GENESIS The Greek text written in silver ink at the top of the page tells the story of Susanna at the Well from the book of Genesis in the Bible. Though the illustration at the bottom of the page tells a biblical story, certain details reflect conditions in late antiquity, such as fortified cities and the growing importance of camels in travel and commerce. The seated, semi-nude female in the lower left is derived from polytheist religion. She personifies the stream from which the more modestly dressed Susanna gathers water.

Latin Christendom The parts of medieval Europe, including all of western Europe, united by Christianity and the use of Latin in worship and intellectual life. Latin served as an international language among the ruling elites in western Europe, even though they spoke different languages in their daily lives.

Monophysites Christians who do not accept the Council of Chalcedon (see Chalcedonians). Monophysites believe that Jesus Christ has only one nature, equally divine and human.

among ruling elites, even though they spoke different languages in their daily lives. Thus, Church-based Latin served as a powerful unifying and stabilizing influence. The Latin language combined with Christianity to spur the development of **Latin Christendom**—the many peoples and kingdoms in western Europe united by their common religion and shared language of worship and intellectual life.

In the eastern provinces of the Roman Empire, Christianity had a different voice. There a Greek-based Church developed. Greek was the language of imperial rule and common culture in that region, and Greek became the language of the Eastern Christian Church. In addition to the New Testament, which had been originally written in Greek, eastern Christians used a Greek version of the Hebrew Bible (the Old Testament) called the Septuagint, which Greek-speaking Jews had prepared in Alexandria in the second century B.C.E. for their own community. The Septuagint combined with the Greek New Testament to become the authoritative Christian Bible throughout most of Rome's eastern provinces.

In a second zone in the eastern Mediterranean and beyond were Anti-Chalcedonians, usually known by the derogatory term of **Monophysites** (literally "one nature"). They did not accept the teaching of the Council of Chalcedon about the combination of the divine and the human in Christ as being "in two natures." Instead, they believed that Christ had one nature in which the human evolved into the divine. In Christ, human nature "dissolved like a drop of honey in the sea." He had a human body and a human "living principle," but the divine took over his thinking. Three anti-Chalcedonian communities had developed by the end of late antiquity—in Armenia in the Caucasus mountain region of eastern Anatolia; in Egypt, among the native Egyptian speakers, called Copts; and among the inhabitants of Syria who spoke Syriac. A vast literature of biblical interpretation, sermons, commentaries, and church documents was gradually created in the languages of each of these communities.

In addition to the Chalcedonian and anti-Chalcedonian regions in late antiquity, a third zone of Christians consisted of the Arians. As described earlier, Arians believed that Jesus was not equal to or of the same substance as God the Father because God had created Jesus. Arians saw themselves as more rigidly monotheistic than Chalcedonian Christians, whose belief in the Trinity they regarded as bordering on polytheism. Most of the people who followed Arian Christianity were the Goths and other Germanic settlers who converted to Christianity in the fourth century, when they still lived north of the Danube River and in southern Russia. When they invaded the Roman Empire in the fifth century, they seized political control of Rome's western provinces. While the Goths were still north of the Danube, a missionary named Ulfila devised a Gothic alphabet and used it to translate the Bible from Greek into Gothic, an early version of German. A Christian Gothic culture thrived in the western zone despite its minority status.

In these three zones, variations of the Christian faith expressed in different languages formed the seedbed of ethnic communities, some of which still flourish, such as the Armenians, Copts, and Greek-speaking Orthodox Christians. Yet the spread of Christianity weakened other local groupings. As language-based Christian communities spread inside and outside the empire, many local dialects and languages disappeared. Only the languages in which Christianity found textual expression survived.

THE MONASTIC MOVEMENT Near the end of the third century, a new Christian spiritual movement took root in the Roman Empire. Known today as **asceticism**, this movement called for Christians to subordinate their physical needs and desires to a quest for spiritual union with God. Asceticism both challenged the emerging connection between the political and Christian authorities and rejected the growing wealth of the Church.

The life of an Egyptian Christian, Antony, provided a model for future ascetics. Around 280 he sold all his property and walked away from his crowded village near the

asceticism The Christian practice of severely suppressing physical needs and daily desires in an effort to achieve a spiritual union with God. Asceticism is the practice that underlies the monastic movement.

Nile into the desert in search of a higher spirituality. A few decades later, Athanasius, the Bishop of Alexandria who had argued against the Arians, composed a biography, the *Life of Antony,* telling how Antony overcame all the temptations the Devil could conjure up, from voluptuous naked women to opportunities for power and fame. Vividly describing the struggle between asceticism ("the discipline") and the lures of everyday life ("the household"), Athanasius's work became one of the most influential books in Western literature. It inspired thousands of men and women to imitate Antony by rejecting the ties of the household and material world. Asceticism appealed to those who desired an alternative to political and especially family life with its coercive parental authority, marriage, sexuality, and children. These all distracted from the contemplation of God.

Ascetic discipline required harsh and often violent treatment of the body. The first ascetics, called anchorites (meaning "withdrawal") or hermits (meaning "of the desert"), lived alone in the most inaccessible and uncomfortable places they could find, such as a cave, a hole in the ground, or on top of a pillar. In addition to praying constantly in their struggle to overcome the Devil and empty themselves of human desires so that God could enter and work through them, these men and women starved and whipped themselves, rejecting every comfort, including human companionship.

Over time, however, many Egyptian ascetics began to construct communities for themselves. The result was the **monastic movement**. Because these communities, called monasteries, often grew to hold 1,000 or more members, they required organization and guidance. Leaders emerged to provide clear instructions for regulating monastic life and offer spiritual guidance to the members of the monasteries. (The male inhabitants of monasteries were called monks, or solitary men. Women were called nuns.)

Drawing from the ideas of these earlier monastic rules written in Greek, Benedict of Nursia (ca. 480–547) wrote a Latin *Rule* that became the foundation of monasticism in western Europe. Benedict built a monastery on Monte Cassino near Naples in 529. While he emphasized voluntary poverty and a life devoted to prayer, he placed more stress on labor. Fearing that the Devil could tempt an idle monk, Benedict wanted his monks to keep busy. He therefore ordered that all monks perform physical labor for parts of every day when they were not sleeping or praying.

In the western Roman Empire, monasticism played a central role in preserving classical learning and thus allowing its integration into Christian culture in later centuries. Much of the credit for preserving the classical intellectual tradition lay with the monasteries founded by Benedict. These monks, called the Benedictine order, established monasteries throughout western Europe, modeled on Benedict's original monastery of Monte Cassino. Benedict himself was wary of classical teaching, but he wanted the monks and nuns under his supervision to be able to read religious books. At least basic education in literacy had to become part of monastic life. The Benedictine definition of "manual labor" expanded to include copying ancient manuscripts, which supplied the libraries in the monasteries and preserved Latin literature.

MONASTICISM AND WOMEN The monastic movement opened new avenues for female spirituality and offered an alternative to marriage and childbearing. By joining monastic communities and leaving the routines of daily life behind, women could escape the obligations of the male-dominated society. As Christian monasticism spread, ascetic women began to create communities of their own. They lived as celibate sisterhoods of nuns, dedicated to spiritual quest and service to God.

The wives or daughters of wealthy and powerful families were typically the founders of female monastic communities. Such women wielded an authority and influence that would not have been available to them otherwise. For example, Melania the Younger (383–439), the daughter of a wealthy Roman senatorial family, decided to sell her vast estates and spend the proceeds in religious pursuits. When the Roman Senate objected to the breaking up of Melania's family estates, she appealed to the

monastic movement In late antiquity, Christian ascetics organized communities where men and women could pursue a life of spirituality through work, prayer, and asceticism. Called the monastic movement, this spiritual quest spread quickly throughout Christian lands.

 Read the Document

Benedict of Nursia, *The Rule*

empress, who interceded with the legal authorities to enable her to dispose of her property. (Melania's slaves also objected because they did not want to be sold separately to raise cash for her religious projects, but she ignored them.) Melania spent her fortune building monasteries in the Holy Land of Palestine. Most women could not afford to make such dramatic gestures, but they could imitate Melania's accomplishment on a modest scale.

Despite the piety of women such as Melania, an increasingly negative view of women emerged in the writings of late antique churchmen. Christian writers branded women as disobedient, sexually promiscuous, innately sinful, and naturally inferior to men. They interpreted Genesis, the first book of the Bible, to mean that women bore a special curse. In their reading of the Genesis account, Eve, the first woman, seduced Adam, the first man. For this reason late antique Christians blamed Eve—and women collectively—for humanity's expulsion from the Garden of Eden and for all the woes human beings had suffered since. Yet Christians also believed that God would save the souls of women as well as men, and they honored Mary for her role in bringing Jesus, and therefore salvation, into the world. (See *Different Voices* in this chapter.)

JEWS IN A CHRISTIAN WORLD Until Christianity became the official religion of the Roman Empire, Jews had been simply one among hundreds of religious and ethnic groups who lived under Roman rule. Although polytheist Romans considered Jews eccentric because they worshiped only one god and refused to make statues of him, they still respected the Jewish people's faith. Before the fourth century, Jews had enjoyed full citizenship rights, practiced all professions, and belonged to all levels of society.

Christianity slowly erased all this. As we saw in Chapter 6, relations between Christians and Jews grew more hostile after the Jewish rebellion and the destruction of Jerusalem by the Roman army in 70. Christian theology mirrored this growing hostility. Christians taught that the Diaspora (the dispersion of Jews around the world after Jerusalem's destruction) was God's way of punishing the Jews for failing to accept Jesus as their messiah and for crucifying Jesus Christ.

Beginning in the fourth century, Roman laws began to discriminate against Jews, forbidding them to marry Christians, own Christian slaves, or accept converts to Judaism. With the support of Christian imperial officials, Church leaders sometimes forced entire communities of Jews to convert to Christianity on pain of death. Although organized resistance among scattered Jewish communities was impossible, many Jews refused to accept the deepening oppression. Their resistance ranged from acts of violence against Jews who had converted to Christianity to armed revolt against Roman authorities.

Individual Jewish communities continued to administer their own affairs under the leadership of rabbis—men who served as teachers and interpreters of Jewish law. We saw in Chapter 6 that the Mishnah, the final codification of Jewish oral law, was completed by the end of the third century. Rabbis incorporated the Mishnah into the **Talmud**, which included commentaries on the law, ethics, and Jewish history. The influential Jerusalem Talmud was compiled about 400, the Babylonian Talmud a century later. Rabbis and their courts now dominated Jewish communities. These learned men established academies of legal study in Roman Palestine and Persian Babylonia, where their interpretations guided everyday Jewish life.

In rabbinic Judaism women continued to play an important role in the household, especially since Judaism emphasized the importance of moral behavior and religious practice rather than dogma. As a result, as wives and mothers, Jewish women had a more positive role in the practice of their religion than women did in Christianity, which considered married women and men morally inferior to celibate nuns and monks. Some Jewish women served as leaders of synagogues in late antiquity, but in public life as opposed to private life, rabbinic Judaism subordinated women. For example, Jewish women did not receive an education at the Jewish academies. Excluded

Talmud Commentaries on Jewish law. Rabbis completed the Babylonian Talmud and the Jerusalem Talmud by the end of the fifth century C.E.

GREEK ZODIAC IN A SYNAGOGUE In late antiquity, Jews living in Palestine sometimes decorated their synagogues with mosaic floors depicting the zodiac. Although these mosaics appeared in synagogues and often contained Hebrew writing, the scenes and style of the mosaics were typical of Greek and Roman art. This blending demonstrates that members of the Jewish congregation also participated in the general non-Jewish culture of the province.

from the formal process of interpreting holy texts, Jewish women did not acquire highly prized religious knowledge.

Instead, men expected them to conform to submissive roles as daughters, wives, and mothers, much as women in other religious communities were expected to do.

Access to Holiness: Christian Pilgrimage

In late antiquity, Christians began to make religious journeys, or **pilgrimages**, to visit sacred places, especially those housing holy objects, known as **relics**. Christians believed these relics were inherently holy because they were physical objects associated with saints and martyrs or with Jesus himself. The most highly valued relics were bones from the venerated person. Christians believed that merely by touching something of a holy person, one could share in that holiness, which could cure them of an illness, heighten their spiritual awareness, or help them achieve eternal life.

The mortal remains of Christian martyrs provided the first relics for pilgrims; however, after the persecution of Christians ceased in 312, believers began to venerate the bodies of great bishops and ascetic monks and nuns. From the fourth century onward, Christians regularly dug up skeletons of saints, chopped them up, and

pilgrimages Religious journeys made to holy sites in order to encounter relics.

relics In Christian belief, relics are sacred objects that have miraculous powers. They are associated with saints, biblical figures, or some object associated with them. They served as contacts between Earth and Heaven and were verified by miracles.

Different Voices

Christian Attitudes Toward Sexuality, Contraception, and Abortion

C hurchmen were hostile to sexuality and considered celibacy the superior way for Christians to live. There were numerous reasons for this hostility, but most of all Christians expected Christ to return at any moment, which made any pursuit except for spiritual purification seem irrelevant. In addition, one of the attractions of early Christianity was liberation from coercive family ties, which distracted believers from their higher obligations to God. Yet as time passed and Christ did not return, churchmen began to recognize the necessity for Christians to produce children for the faith to grow. The result was a double ethic that exalted celibacy and yet placed special obligations on those who were married to bear children. The following excerpts illustrate this double ethic. The first document, attributed to Saint Patrick from the mid-fifth century, shows how an Irish woman's decision to live a celibate life subjected her to persecution from non-Christians who thought her obligation was to bear children. The second comes from a sermon by Caesarius, bishop of Arles from 502 to 542.

St. Patrick

And there was also a blessed lady of native Irish birth and high rank, very beautiful and grown up, whom I baptized; and a few days later she found some reason to come to us and indicated that she had received a message from an angel of god, and the angel had urged her too to become a virgin of Christ and to draw near to God. Thanks be to God. . . . she most commendably and enthusiastically took up that same course that all virgins of God also do—not with their fathers' consent; no, they endure persecution and their own parents' unfair reproaches, and yet their number grows larger and larger. . . . But it is the women kept in slavery who suffer especially; they even have to endure constant threats and terrorization.

Caesarius of Arles

No woman should take drugs for purposes of abortion, nor should she kill her children that have been conceived or are already born. If anyone does this, she should know that before Christ's tribunal she will have to plead her case in the presence of those she has killed. Moreover, women should not take diabolical draughts with the purpose of not being able to conceive children. A woman who does this ought to realize that she will be guilty of as many murders as the number of children she might have borne. I would like to know whether a woman of nobility who takes deadly drugs to prevent conception wants her maids or tenants to do so. Just as every woman wants slaves born for her so that they may serve her, so she herself should nurse all the children she conceives, or entrust them to others for rearing. Otherwise, she may refuse to conceive children or, what is more serious, be willing to kill souls which might have been good Christians. Now, with what kind of a conscience does she desire slaves to be born of her servants, when she herself refuses to bear children who might become Christians?

For Discussion

1. What do these documents reveal about Christian views about women?
2. How do Caesarius's reasons for opposing contraception and abortion differ from the arguments of those who oppose these practices today?

SOURCES: *St. Patrick: His Writing and Muirchu's Life*, edited and translated by A.B.E. Hood, Arthurian Period Sources, vol. 9 (London: Phillimor, 1978), p. 50. *Saint Caesarius of Arles, Sermons*, vol. 1 (sermons 1-80), translated by Sister Mary Mageleine Mueller, O.S.F. (New York: Fathers of the Church, Inc., 1956), pp. 221–22.

distributed the pieces to churches. The more important the holy person, the fiercer the competition for the bones and other objects associated with him or her. Churches in the largest cities of the empire, such as Rome, Constantinople, Alexandria, and Jerusalem, acquired fine collections. Residents of Constantinople believed that the Virgin Mary's robe, kept in a church inside the city, drove away enemies when it was carried in procession along the battlements.

Emperors and important bishops acquired the greatest and most powerful relics of all—those that had reportedly touched Jesus himself. These included the crown of thorns he wore when crucified, the cross on which he died, and the nails that fastened him to the wood. Relics reminded Christians that the martyrdom of his followers symbolically repeated Jesus's own death. Hence, they constructed church altars, where followers celebrated the Eucharist (the rite in which bread and wine are offered as Jesus's body and blood in memory of his death) over the graves or relics of martyrs.

Traveling to touch a relic was the primary motive for a pilgrimage. Palestine became a frequent destination of Christian pilgrims because it contained the most sacred sites and relics associated with events described in the Bible and particularly with Jesus's life and death. Between the fourth and seventh centuries, thousands of earnest

Christian pilgrims flocked to Palestine to visit holy sites and pray for divine assistance and forgiveness for their sins. Helena, the mother of Emperor Constantine, made pilgrimage fashionable. In the early fourth century, she visited Jerusalem, where she reportedly found remnants of the cross on which Jesus was crucified, and identified many of the sites pertaining to Jesus's life. Inspired by his mother's journey, Constantine funded the construction of lavish shrines and monasteries at these sites and guest houses for pilgrims. Practically overnight Palestine was transformed from a provincial backwater to the spiritual focus of the Christian world. Religious men and women—rich and poor, old and young, sick and healthy—streamed to Palestine and Jerusalem.

Palestine did not have a monopoly on holy places, however. Pilgrims traveled to places throughout the Roman world wherever saints had lived and died and where their relics rested. Pilgrimages contributed to the growth of a Christian view of the world in three ways. First, because pilgrimage was a holy enterprise, Christian communities gave hospitality and lodging to religious travelers. This fostered a shared sense of Christian community among people from many lands. Second, Christians envisioned a Christian "map" dominated by spiritually significant places. Travel guides that explained this "spiritual geography" became popular among pilgrims. Most of all, pilgrims who returned home, enriched in their faith and perhaps cured in mind or spirit, inspired their home communities with news of a growing Christian world directly linked to the biblical lands they heard about in church.

Christian Intellectual Life

During the first three centuries after Jesus's death, when Christians were marginalized and at times persecuted, many Church leaders criticized classical learning. Churchmen argued that the learning of pagan intellectuals was false wisdom, that it distracted Christians from what was truly important—contemplation of Jesus Christ and the eternal salvation he offered—and therefore that it corrupted young Christians. Tertullian (ca. 160–240), for example, argued for the separation of Christianity from the learning and culture of the non-Christian world: "What has Athens to do with Jerusalem? What is there in common between the philosopher and the Christian?" Christians like Tertullian mistrusted the human intellect and stressed the need to focus on the divine revelation of the Christian Scriptures.

After Constantine's conversion, influential voices in the Church began to answer these questions. To them, classical learning no longer seemed as threatening as it had before. Many Church leaders now came from the empire's urban elite, where they had absorbed classical learning. Christian officials grudgingly approved secular education because they recognized that the traditional curriculum was useful for administering the Church and for the law. Training in classical rhetoric, grammar, and literature became an integral part of upper-class Christian life. By the fifth century, traditional schooling for Christians was accepted as a useful if risky enterprise. As Basil the Great (ca. 330–379), bishop of Caesarea in Cappadocia (in modern Turkey), explained to young men about to embark on their studies, classical learning had both benefits and dangers. Although pagan learning, he advised, had some spiritual value, the charm of words could poison the Christian's heart.

Augustine of Hippo (354–430) most fully took up the challenge of classical learning to Christianity. By examining the most troubling philosophical and historical questions in light of the scriptures, Augustine became the most influential Church Father among Latin-speaking Christians. The **Church Fathers** were writers from both the Greek- and Latin-speaking worlds who sought to reconcile Christianity with classical learning.

Born to parents of modest means, Augustine attended traditional Roman schools as a youth, an education that made him thoroughly familiar with the classics and

Church Fathers Writers in late antiquity from both the Greek- and Latin-speaking worlds who sought to reconcile Christianity with classical learning.

prepared him for a high position in public life. After his conversion to Christianity, Augustine became the influential bishop of the city of Hippo Regius in North Africa. He recounted his spiritual experiences and conversion in the *Confessions* (397), an autobiography written in his middle age. Drawing on the ideas of the Greek philosopher Plato and on Christian scriptures, Augustine in the *Confessions* meditated on the meaning of life, especially on sin and redemption. Augustine showed that intellect alone was incapable of bringing about the spiritual growth that he desired. God needed to intervene. For his spiritual conversion to be complete, Augustine believed he had to cleanse himself of the desires of the flesh, which led him to renounce sexuality completely. Using his episcopal office as a platform from which to defend Christianity from polytheist philosophers and to define all aspects of the Christian life, Augustine displayed a sincere respect for Roman cultural and intellectual accomplishments—especially rhetoric and history. But he always believed Christianity was superior. For

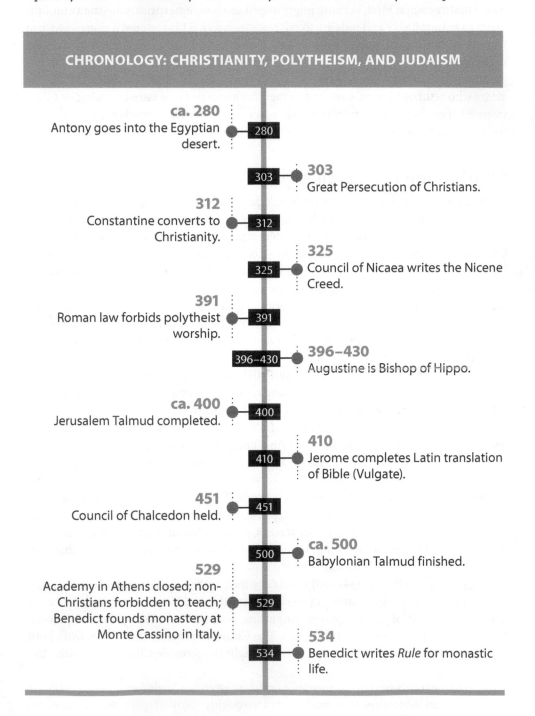

CHRONOLOGY: CHRISTIANITY, POLYTHEISM, AND JUDAISM

ca. 280 — 280
Antony goes into the Egyptian desert.

303 — **303**
Great Persecution of Christians.

312 — 312
Constantine converts to Christianity.

325 — **325**
Council of Nicaea writes the Nicene Creed.

391 — 391
Roman law forbids polytheist worship.

396–430 — **396–430**
Augustine is Bishop of Hippo.

ca. 400 — 400
Jerusalem Talmud completed.

410 — **410**
Jerome completes Latin translation of Bible (Vulgate).

451 — 451
Council of Chalcedon held.

500 — **ca. 500**
Babylonian Talmud finished.

529 — 529
Academy in Athens closed; non-Christians forbidden to teach; Benedict founds monastery at Monte Cassino in Italy.

534 — **534**
Benedict writes *Rule* for monastic life.

Augustine, the most dangerous enemy of all true Christians was "antiquity, mother of all evils"—the source of false beliefs.

In his book *The City of God*, completed in 423, Augustine developed a new interpretation of history. Augustine's historical theory disconnected Christian ideas of human destiny from the fate of the Roman Empire. In his view, the Roman Empire was just one among many that had existed and that would exist before Jesus's return. According to Augustine, the only dates humanity should view as spiritually significant were Jesus's time on Earth and the End of Days sometime in the future. Only God knew the significance of all events in between.

Augustine's theory proved timely. Within a few years of his death, the Vandals seized North Africa and the Roman Empire lost control of all of its provinces in western Europe. Augustine thus gave Roman Christians a new perspective with which to view this loss: Rome had contributed to world civilization and to the growth of the Christian Church, but now Christianity would grow on its own without the support of Roman emperors.

After the collapse of the Roman Empire in the western provinces, the challenge for Christian thinkers came less from reconciling Christianity with the power of classical learning than from keeping classical learning alive at all. Outside the monasteries, traditional schooling in the classics survived only as long as cities could afford to pay for teachers. In most of the towns of the western provinces of the empire, schools gradually disappeared during the fifth century as a result of the Germanic invasions. In the eastern provinces they survived until the seventh century, then faded away.

NEOPLATONISM AND CHRISTIANITY Greek and Roman philosophy remained influential in the late antique period. One branch of this tradition, called **Neoplatonism**, is associated with the thought of Plotinus (205–270), a non-Christian philosopher. His teachings greatly influenced Christianity, an example of how classical and Christian thought intertwined in late antiquity. Plotinus, who taught in Rome, traced his intellectual roots primarily to the works of Plato (ca. 429–327 B.C.E.). He also drew ideas from Aristotle (384–322 B.C.E.), Stoic philosophers (third century B.C.E.), and their followers.

Plotinus argued that all things that exist, whether intangible ideas or tangible matter, originate in a single force called the One. Humans could reunite their souls with the One by overcoming their passions and physical desires that were governed by the body. Many Neoplatonists believed that by gaining the help of the gods through magical rites and studying divine revelations, the human soul could reconnect with the One and realize its fullest potential. Neoplatonism had many similarities to Gnosticism, which was discussed in Chapter 6 and which also guided some early Christians. The Gnostics, however, emphasized magic in a way that the sober, philosophical Neoplatonists such as Plotinus thought was the work of "imbeciles."

Neoplatonism appealed to many Christians. For them, the One was God, and the Bible provided the divine revelations that could lead to the salvation of the human soul and reunification with God. Gregory of Nyssa (331–395) in the Greek East and Augustine in the Latin West were only two of the many churchmen who incorporated Neoplatonism into their own works in the later fourth century. After Christian and non-Christian Neoplatonists argued over whether the identity of "the One" could be equated with the Christian God, Emperor Justinian closed Plato's Academy in Athens in 529 and forbade non-Christians to teach philosophy.

Nevertheless, Neoplatonic thought helped shape the Christian doctrine of the immortality of the human soul. It also reinforced the ascetic ideal practiced by monks and nuns. Thus, contempt for the material, temporal world and the physical body took deep root in Christian culture.

Neoplatonism A philosophy based on the teachings of Plato and his successors that flourished in late antiquity, especially in the teachings of Plotinus. Neoplatonism influenced Christianity in late antiquity. During the Renaissance Neoplatonism was linked to the belief that the natural world was charged with occult forces that could be used in the practice of magic.

📖 **Read the Document**

Bishop Synesius of Cyrene, *Letter to His Brother*

The Breakup of the Roman Empire

7.4 How and why did the Roman Empire in the West disintegrate?

During the fifth century, the Roman Empire split into two parts: the Latin-speaking provinces in western Europe, and the largely Greek- and Syriac-speaking provinces in the East. As the Roman government lost control of its western domains, independent Germanic kingdoms emerged. The eastern provinces remained under the control of the Roman emperor, whose capital city was not Rome, but Constantinople. The definitive split of the Roman Empire marked the end of late antiquity. In future centuries the legacy of the Roman Empire survived in the West through Latin culture and Latin Christianity. In the East, it survived as a political reality until its final collapse 1,000 years later in 1453.

The Fall of Rome's Western Provinces

Why Roman rule remained strong in the eastern Mediterranean while collapsing in western Europe is one of the most hotly debated subjects in history. Most Christians of the time attributed the collapse of Roman rule to God's anger at the stubborn persistence of polytheist worship. Polytheists, for their part, blamed Christians for destroying the temples of the gods who had protected Rome in the past. In later centuries, the explanations varied. Edward Gibbon, an eighteenth-century writer whose *Decline and Fall of the Roman Empire* has influenced all historians of Rome and remains one of the most widely read history books of all time, criticized the Catholic Church for diverting able men away from public service and into religious life. Other historians attributed Rome's collapse in the West to enormous waves of savage barbarian invasions. The reason the Romans lost their western provinces is, however, more complicated and less dramatic than any of these one-dimensional explanations.

LOSS OF IMPERIAL POWER IN THE WEST The end of Roman rule in western Europe came in a haphazard and gradual fashion as the cumulative result of unwise decisions, weak leadership, and military failure. During the first century, the Romans established the northern limits of their empire in Europe along the Rhine and Danube Rivers. From that time forward, Roman generals and emperors withstood invasions of many different northern tribes looking for plunder and new lands. The Roman legions maintained a relatively stable northern frontier through diplomacy as well as military might. Since the time of Augustus, Roman emperors had permitted newcomers to settle on Roman lands. Until the fourth century, the empire had always been able to absorb the settlers.

In the fourth century, the sudden appearance of the Huns, a fierce nomadic people from central Asia, in southern Russia set in motion events that helped bring about the collapse of Roman rule in western Europe. Unlike the settled farmers who lived in Europe, the Huns were nomads who herded their flocks over the plains (or *steppes*) that stretched from southern Russia to central Asia. Able to travel vast distances quickly on their rugged horses, the highly mobile Huns overran adversaries from settled agricultural communities. The Huns also earned a reputation for ferocity. Living under the specter of starvation, they lusted after the great riches and easy lifestyles they observed in the urbanized empires of Rome and Persia.

In 376, in what is now south Russia, an army of Huns drove a group of Visigoths from their farmlands. The Visigoth refugees gained permission from the Roman Emperor Valens to cross the Danube and settle in the Balkans in return for supplying troops to the Roman army. In the past, Roman rulers had frequently made this sort of arrangement. The Roman officials in charge of this resettlement, however, exploited the refugees by charging them exorbitant fees for food and supplies. In 378 the Visigoths revolted. At the Battle of Adrianople in Thrace they killed Valens and destroyed an entire Roman army.

The Visigoths' successful rebellion wounded the empire, but not fatally. Rome's response to the disaster, however, sowed the seeds for a loss of imperial power in the west. Necessity forced the new emperor, Theodosius the Great, to permit Visigothic soldiers to serve in the Roman army under their own Visigothic commanders. But allowing independent military forces of dubious loyalty to operate freely within the empire was a terrible mistake. The consequences of Theodosius's decision became all too clear in the mid-390s when Alaric, the new Visigothic king, began to plunder Roman cities in the Balkans and Greece. As discussed at the beginning of this chapter, in 401 Alaric and his troops sacked Rome for three days. Senators and citizens could only watch as the Visigoths rampaged through their streets.

The Visigoths' sack of Rome not only dealt a psychological blow to the empire's inhabitants, it also led indirectly to the loss of many of Rome's western provinces. To fight Alaric, Rome's armies withdrew from the empire's northwestern defenses, leaving the frontier in Britain and along the Rhine vulnerable. In Britain, Rome abandoned its control entirely after an ambitious general, styling himself Constantine III, led Britain's last legions across the English Channel in 407 in an unsuccessful attempt to grab the imperial throne. This left Britain defenseless, vulnerable to groups of Germanic tribesmen known as the Saxons already settled on British soil.

Elsewhere the chaos spread. Although the invading bands were small, the imperial government in the West no longer possessed the administrative capacity to marshal its military resources and push the invaders out. In December 406, the Rhine River froze, enabling migrating Germanic tribes to enter the empire with little opposition. Small bands of these marauding tribes roamed through Gaul, while the Vandals and their allies raided their way through Spain. In 429 the Vandals crossed to North Africa, where they soon established an independent kingdom. By 450 the Visigoths had formed a kingdom of their own in Gaul and Spain.

Overwhelming numbers of savage tribesmen did not invade the empire. In fact, their numbers were puny. For example, only 40,000 Vandals controlled North Africa, which had a population of several million Romans. And although the Germans plundered and pillaged, they could not hold on to imperial lands and settle there without the active cooperation of Roman administrators who thought they could bargain with the tribesmen. Once they put down roots, however, the Germanic invaders consolidated their strength and established their rule. By then, Roman authorities lacked both the organization and the strength to expel them.

Even though most of the western provinces had fallen to invaders by 450, the Romans held on to Italy for a while longer. The city of Rome remained the home of the Senate, while the emperor of the western provinces resided in Ravenna, a town on Italy's northeast coast. Warlords, however, held the real power in Italy, although they were formally subordinate to the emperor. These soldiers were usually not Romans by birth, but they adopted Roman culture and fought for Rome. In 476 one of these warlords, a Germanic general named Odovacar, deposed the last emperor in the west, a boy named Romulus Augustulus, and named himself king of Italy. For many historians the year 476 used to symbolize the end of the Roman Empire in the west. In fact, however, 476 is a date of little significance. The Romans' control of their western provinces had slipped away decades earlier (see **Map 7.2**).

CULTURAL ENCOUNTERS AFTER THE END OF ROMAN RULE By the mid-fifth century, when most fighting between Germanic invaders and Romans had ended, the two sides, as rulers and ruled, began an era of intense encounters. In Britain the Germanic invaders were polytheists who snuffed out the Christians. Yet legends hint at a fierce resistance against the invaders. The stories about King Arthur that have captivated English-speaking

Read the Document

Ammianus Marcellinus on the Huns

7.1

7.2

7.3

7.4

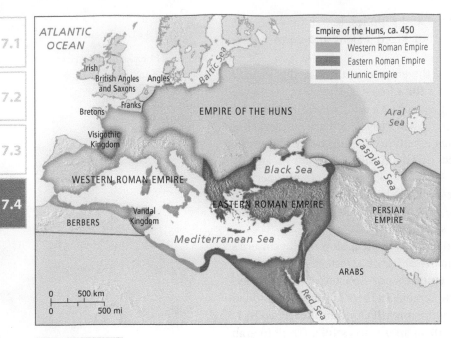

MAP **7.2** EMPIRE OF THE HUNS During late antiquity, the Huns established a powerful empire based in the Hungarian plain. These fierce horsemen terrified the settled peoples of the Roman world, but their empire broke up within a generation. Does the division of the Roman Empire into western and eastern halves indicate strength or weakness? Why?

Read the Document

Sidonius Apollinaris, *Rome's Decay* and *A Glimpse of the New Order*

Read the Document

Excerpt from *The Governance of God* (5th Century C.E.) Salvian

audiences since the Middle Ages are based on memories of valiant resistance to the Saxon invaders in the mid-fifth century.

In Gaul, North Africa, Italy, and Spain, the new settlers followed Arian Christianity. The Roman inhabitants, on the other hand, followed Chalcedonian (Catholic) Christianity and thus saw the invaders as heretics. Although this religious difference caused friction between the two peoples, it also worked to their mutual advantage. Roman law forbade marriage with Arian Christians, so the conquerors remained a distinctive minority in their new domains. This enabled them to maintain a separate Arian clergy and separate churches.

Of all the former empire's western provinces, Italy prospered the most under Germanic rule, particularly under the long reign of Theodoric the Ostrogoth (r. 493–526). Theodoric murdered Odovacar, the German warrior who had deposed the last Roman emperor in the West, to obtain the throne of Italy. In politics, Theodoric sought to create mutual respect between Ostrogoths and Romans by maintaining two separate administrations—one for his Ostrogoths, the other for the Romans—so that both communities could manage their own affairs under his supervision. He also included aristocratic Romans among his closest advisers and most trusted administrators. Even in his religious policies Theodoric pursued mutual tolerance. As an Arian Christian, he supported the separate Arian clergy, but he also maintained excellent ties with the pope, leader of the Roman Christians. Theodoric united Visigothic kingdoms in Gaul with his own in Italy, ultimately wielding great influence throughout western Europe. Italy prospered under his rule, and the communities of Ostrogoths and Romans lived together amicably.

Although Theodoric had paid formal homage to the emperor in Constantinople, during his rule the western provinces' links to the Roman Empire in the East began to weaken. Most of the invaders, including Theodoric's Ostrogoths, continued their traditional practice of pledging obedience to a local chieftain. This tradition began to erode loyalty to the far-off Roman emperor in Constantinople. By pledging themselves to a Germanic king, men gained a place in the "tribe" of their new chieftain.

Roman culture did not abruptly end with the last vestiges of Roman rule. It remained a vital presence in most regions, but it took different forms in the lands now ruled by Germanic leaders. In Britain, Roman culture perhaps fared the worst and little of it survived into later ages. There the Germanic language of the Saxon invaders and their Anglo allies took hold and began developing into the English spoken today. In Gaul, Italy, and Spain, the Germanic settlers quickly learned Latin. Over time these Latin-based "Romance" (based on the Roman speech) languages grew into the early versions of French, Italian, Catalan, Spanish, and Portuguese. Latin continued as the language of literacy, and the settlers borrowed heavily from Roman literary forms. Writing in Latin, they produced histories of their tribal kingdoms in imitation of Roman historians. They also developed law codes composed in Latin influenced by Roman models.

The Survival of Rome's Eastern Provinces

Despite the profound alterations wrought by Christianity and Rome's loss of the western provinces, the Roman Empire endured in the eastern Mediterranean without interruption. Constantinople, the imperial city founded by Constantine in 324, became the center of a remodeled empire that merged Christian and Roman characteristics. Historians call the remodeled Roman Empire in the East the **Byzantine Empire**, after Byzantium, the original Greek name of Constantinople.

CHRISTIANITY AND LAW UNDER JUSTINIAN The most important amalgamation of Christian and Roman traditions took place during the reign of Emperor Justinian (r. 527–565). Born in the Balkans, Justinian was the last emperor in Constantinople to speak Latin as his native language. He combined a powerful intellect, an unshakable Christian faith, and a driving ambition to reform the empire. He defied convention by marrying Theodora, a strong-willed former actress, and included her in imperial decision making once he became emperor.

Justinian inaugurated changes that highlighted his role as a Christian emperor. First, he emphasized the position of the emperor at the center of society in explicitly Christian

7.1

7.2

7.3

7.4

Byzantine Empire The eastern half of the Roman Empire, which lasted from the founding of Constantinople in 324 to its conquest by the Ottoman Turks in 1453.

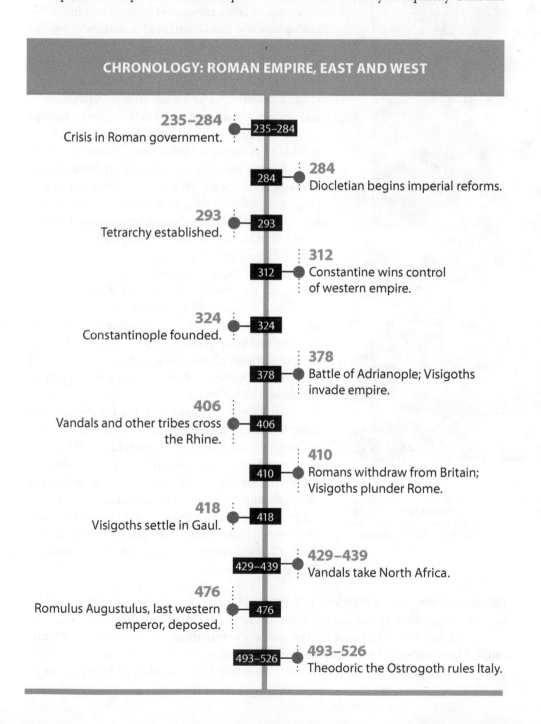

CHRONOLOGY: ROMAN EMPIRE, EAST AND WEST

235–284
Crisis in Roman government.

284
Diocletian begins imperial reforms.

293
Tetrarchy established.

312
Constantine wins control of western empire.

324
Constantinople founded.

378
Battle of Adrianople; Visigoths invade empire.

406
Vandals and other tribes cross the Rhine.

410
Romans withdraw from Britain; Visigoths plunder Rome.

418
Visigoths settle in Gaul.

429–439
Vandals take North Africa.

476
Romulus Augustulus, last western emperor, deposed.

493–526
Theodoric the Ostrogoth rules Italy.

DIPTYCH OF A CONSUL This ivory panel celebrates a Roman consul at Constantinople in the sixth century. In his right hand he holds the *mappa*, a ceremonial cloth that symbolizes his office. Behind him stand personifications of Rome (on his left) and Constantinople (on his right). Such panels were given as gifts when consuls took office. This one demonstrates Roman traditions continuing in the new world of Byzantium.

  Read the Document

Prologue of the *Corpus Juris Civilis*, ca. 530

terms. He was the first emperor to use the title "Beloved of Christ," and he amplified the emperor's role in Church affairs. Justinian considered it his duty as emperor to impose uniform religious belief throughout the empire by enforcing the decrees of the Council of Chalcedon as he interpreted them. In the East this meant stamping out the survival of polytheist worship and struggling to find a common ground with the anti-Chalcedonians. After Justinian reconquered some of the western domains of the empire, he had to deal with the Arian Vandals and Ostrogoths living there. In the East Justinian suppressed polytheism, but he never reached an agreement with the anti-Chalcedonian communities in Syria and Egypt. After the armies of Islam conquered these regions in the following century, the Christian churches there fell out of imperial control (see Chapter 8). In the West the bishops of North Africa and Italy resented Justinian's attempts to determine doctrine. As a result, a bitter division arose between Christian churches in the eastern and western Mediterranean over the rights of bishops to resist imperial authority on religious matters.

Justinian attempted to create a Christian society by using Roman law coupled with military force. Unlike rulers of Rome's early empire, who permitted subject peoples to maintain their own customary laws, Justinian suppressed local laws throughout his realm. He envisioned all of his subjects obeying only Roman law—law that he defined and that God approved. (Justinian was sure that if God did not approve of his legislative changes, God would not allow him to continue as emperor.)

Thus, in his God-given mission as emperor-legislator, Justinian reformed Roman law. To simplify the vast body of civil law, he ordered his lawyers to sort through all the laws that had accumulated over the centuries and determine which of them should still be enforced.

Justinian's codification of the law, which was completed in 534, and associated legal texts are now collectively called the *Corpus Juris Civilis*. The body of Roman law passed down to later generations primarily through this compilation. At the end of the eleventh century, scholars in Italy discovered manuscripts of Justinian's legal works in church libraries, and interest in Roman law revived. Thus, the *Corpus Juris Civilis* became a pillar of Latin-speaking European civilization.

RECONQUERING PROVINCES IN THE WEST Once he had reorganized the empire's legal system, Justinian turned his attention to Rome's fallen western provinces. He wanted to reestablish imperial control over these territories, now ruled by Germanic kings. Once the empire was restored to its former glory, Justinian's plan was to impose his version of Christian orthodoxy upon the Arian Vandals and Ostrogoths in his western domains. He would also force them to live under his version of Roman law and government.

In 533, Justinian sent a fleet of 10,000 men and 5,000 cavalry under the command of his general Belisarius to attack the Vandal kingdom in North Africa. It fell quickly, and within a year Belisarius celebrated a triumph in Constantinople. Encouraged by this easy victory, Justinian set his sights on Italy, where the Ostrogothic ruling family was embroiled in political infighting. This time Justinian underestimated his opponents. The Ostrogoths, who had won the support of the Roman population in Italy, mounted a fierce resistance to Belisarius's invasion in 537. Justinian failed to support Belisarius with adequate funds and soldiers. Bitter fighting dragged on for two decades. Justinian's armies eventually wrestled Italy back under imperial control, but the protracted reconquest had disastrous consequences. The years of fighting devastated Italy, and the financial burden drained the empire's resources (see **Map 7.3**).

One of the reasons Justinian's reconquest of Italy took decades was the visitation of a lethal plague that struck the empire in 542 and migrated swiftly to Italy, North Africa, and Gaul. The first onslaught took the lives of about 250,000 people, half the population of Constantinople. An estimated one-third of the empire's inhabitants died. With the population devastated, Justinian's army could not recruit the soldiers it needed to fight on several fronts.

The plague also weakened the economy. In many provinces, farms lay deserted and city populations shriveled. Commercial ties between the eastern and western

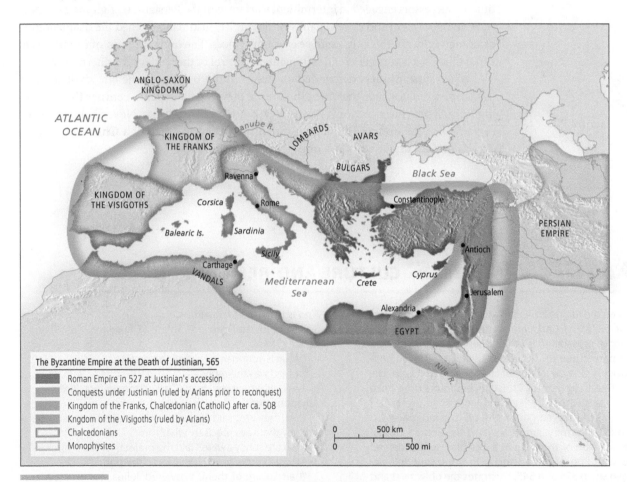

MAP **7.3** THE BYZANTINE EMPIRE AT THE DEATH OF JUSTINIAN, 565 When Justinian died in 565, Italy, North Africa, and part of Spain that had been lost in the fifth century had been restored, temporarily, to imperial rule. Under the dynamic Sasanian dynasty, the Persian Empire fought many wars with the Romans. Neither empire had an advantage because they were roughly the same size and possessed equivalent resources of wealth and manpower. Compare this map with Maps 7.1 and 7.2. What do these comparisons show about the decline of the Roman Empire?

Mediterranean declined. In the western provinces, economies became more "local" and self-sufficient.

THE STRUGGLE WITH PERSIA Although Justinian's greatest military successes were in the western Mediterranean, his most dangerous enemy was the Persian Empire (formerly Parthia) on his eastern flank. This huge, multiethnic empire, under the rule of the Sasanian dynasty (ca. 220–633), had been Rome's main rival throughout late antiquity. The tension stemmed chiefly from competition over Armenia, which was a rich source of troops, and Syria, which possessed enormous wealth. Though wars between Romans and Persians were frequent, neither side could win permanent superiority over the other.

Justinian fought several brutal wars with Persia. He gave top priority to this struggle by supplying it with more than half of his troops, led by his best generals. He also provided more financial resources to the struggle in the East than to the wars of reconquest in the West. Chosroes I (r. 531–579), the aggressive and ambitious Great King of Persia, proved a worthy adversary for Justinian. Chosroes repeatedly invaded the Byzantine Empire, causing great damage. In 540, for example, he sacked Antioch, the wealthiest city in Syria. Because war with Persia was extraordinarily expensive, Justinian bought peace by paying thousands of pounds of gold to the Persian monarch. Even this cost less than continuing to fight every year.

By the time of Justinian's death, the two empires had established an uneasy coexistence, but the basic animosity between them remained unresolved. For the next half century, Justinian's successors engaged in intermittent warfare with the Persians. By fighting expensive wars on the western and eastern flanks of his empire, Justinian hastened the disintegration of Roman imperial rule outside the eastern provinces. The overextension of resources ensured that Constantinople could not maintain control of the western Mediterranean.

When new invaders descended on Italy and the Balkans in the late sixth century, the Empire did not have the strength to resist them. In the seventh century the remaining Roman provinces in North Africa, Egypt, and Syria were lost. Nevertheless, in what remained of the Roman Empire, Justinian succeeded in creating a Christian–Roman society, united under one God, one emperor, and one law.

Justice in History
Two Martyrdoms: CULTURE AND RELIGION ON TRIAL

Between the reigns of Diocletian (r. 284–305) and Justinian (r. 527–565), Christians went from being a religious minority persecuted by the imperial government to a majority that persecuted non-Christians with the Roman government's backing. One thing did not change during this period, however. Whether polytheist or Christian, emperors used force to compel their subjects to believe and worship in prescribed ways, hoping to keep the empire in the gods' good graces. To ensure religious conformity, emperors used the Roman judicial system. A comparison of the trials of a Christian soldier named Julius in 303 with Phocas, an aristocrat in Constantinople accused of paganism in 529 and 545, illustrates the objectives and methods of the Roman government's religious prosecution.

In 303 officials brought a veteran soldier named Julius before the prefect Maximus. The following excerpt comes from a description of the trial:

"Who is this?" asked Maximus.

One of the staff replied: "This is a Christian who will not obey the laws."

"What is your name?" asked the prefect.

"Julius," was the reply.

"Well, what say you, Julius?" asked the prefect. "Are these allegations true?"

"Yes, they are," said Julius. "I am indeed a Christian. I do not deny that I am precisely what I am."

"You are surely aware," said the prefect, "of the emperors' edicts which order you to sacrifice to the gods?"

"I am aware of them," answered Julius. "I am indeed a Christian and cannot do what you want; for I must not lose sight of my living and true God.". . .

"If you think it a sin," answered the prefect Maximus, "let me take the blame. I am the one who is forcing you,

(continued on next page)

(continued from previous page)

so that you may not give impression of having consented voluntarily. Afterwards you can go home in peace, you will pick up your ten-year bonus, and no one will ever trouble you again. . . . If you do not respect the imperial decrees and offer sacrifice, I am going to cut your head off."

"That is a good plan," answered Julius, "Only I beg . . . that you execute your plan and pass sentence on me so that my prayers may be answered. . . . I have chosen death for now so that I might live with the saints forever."

The prefect Maximus then delivered the sentence as follows: "Whereas Julius has refused to obey the imperial edicts, he is sentenced to death."[1]

After Constantine's conversion to Christianity in 312, Christian officials began to attack polytheism with the government's support. Emperor Justinian launched three major persecutions of polytheists. In the first episode of persecution in 528–529, one year after Justinian ascended to the throne, a handful of government officials were charged with worshiping pagan gods.

One of these men was Phocas the Patrician, an aristocratic lawyer with an illustrious career in the emperor's service. After serving at court, he was sent to Antioch to rebuild the city after a ruinous earthquake in 527. He was arrested during that first episode of persecution. Cleared of charges of practicing paganism in 529, Phocas continued to enjoy Justinian's trust and earn further promotions. In 532 he served for a year as Praetorian Prefect, the emperor's most powerful official with responsibility for administering the empire. Phocas raised revenue for the construction of the new Cathedral of Holy Wisdom in Constantinople and spent his personal funds in supporting smaller churches and ransoming hostages captured by Byzantium's enemies. Justinian next made him a judge and sent him on a mission to investigate the murder of a bishop. Part of Justinian's confidence in Phocas came from the fact that he was deeply learned and competent. Phocas and other victims had a deep commitment to traditional Roman culture. But that very commitment led to their downfall. Their "paganism" was not the furtive worship of old gods like Zeus or Apollo. Rather, Phocas was considered a pagan because he was loyal to classical

JUSTINIAN This mid-sixth-century ivory panel depicts Emperor Justinian in a standard pose of Roman emperors. The panel sends the message that Justinian rules the world with the approval and support of God.

philosophy, literature, and rhetoric, without any Christian overlay or interpretation.

Then, in 545–546, during the second wave of persecution, despite his publicly recognized activities in support of the Church and his faithful service to Justinian, Phocas was arrested again, one of many doctors, teachers, and government officials suddenly charged with paganism. Constantinople endured a time of terror. Officials accused of worshiping the old gods in secret were driven from public office, had their property confiscated by the emperor, and were executed. In a panic, some of the accused took their own lives. Phocas was one of them. Rather than undergo the humiliation of public execution, he committed suicide. The furious emperor ordered that Phocas's body be buried in a ditch like an animal, without prayer or ceremony of any sort.

Phocas thus missed the third purge of 562, when polytheists were arrested throughout the empire, paraded in public, imprisoned, tried, and sentenced. Zealous crowds threw thousands of non-Christian books into bonfires.

The official reason for persecuting Christians such as Julius was relatively simple: Christians broke the law by refusing to make sacrifices to the Roman gods. But why did Christian governments also later use such a heavy hand in persecuting polytheists? Men like Phocas who were attacked as pagans were highly educated in the traditional learning of the Greco–Roman world. Indeed, it was this learning that was really on trial. For Justinian, this sort of classical learning had no place in a Christian empire.

For Discussion

Why did both polytheist and Christian governments of Rome persecute adherents of nonofficial religions?

Taking It Further

Helgeland, John. *Christians in the Military: The Early Experience.* 1985, 64–65. An introduction to the persecutions of Christians in the Roman army and their depiction in Christian literature.

Maas, Michael. *John Lydus and the Roman Past: Antiquarianism and Politics in the Age of Justinian.* 1992. This book explains how Justinian's policies about religion also involved an encounter with the empire's classical heritage.

CONCLUSION

The Age of New Boundaries

During late antiquity the transformation of the Roman world into new political configurations with new boundaries helped create a new conception of the West. Henceforth, the West was closely associated with the legacy of Roman civilization filtered through the lens of Christianity. The most lasting development of the period came from the encounter between the civilization of the Roman Empire and Christianity, which before the fourth century had been the faith of a persecuted minority. As Christianity became the dominant religion throughout the Roman Empire, it was itself transformed, not the least through the attempts to reconcile Christian revelation with classical learning. Christian thinkers assimilated much of classical culture, and with the support of the Roman emperors, Christianity became the official religion. During this process of assimilation, Christians disagreed among themselves over how they explained the divinity of Jesus Christ, and these disagreements led to distinctive strains of Christian belief.

The Roman Empire itself was irreparably split into two parts, which became the foundations for two distinctive Christian civilizations. After Roman rule in the West collapsed, Germanic rulers established new kingdoms in the old Roman provinces. Some of these kingdoms spoke Romance languages derived from Latin, and all of them used Latin for religious worship, learning, and the law. From the western provinces of the Roman Empire during late antiquity, Latin civilization spread to parts of central, eastern, and northern Europe that had never been part of the Roman Empire. In the eastern Mediterranean, the Roman Empire survived as the Byzantine Empire (discussed in Chapter 8) and became the home of Orthodox Christianity. In Byzantium, Greek remained the dominant tongue of daily life, learning, and Christian worship.

When Islam emerged as a powerful religious and political entity at the end of the late antique period, as we will discuss in Chapter 8, classical learning and Roman institutions also influenced its adherents. But the Muslim and Christian empires became enemies, a tendency that created the most lasting divisions among the peoples who had once been citizens of the Roman Empire.

MAKING CONNECTIONS

1. Besides the Bible, what were the significant influences on early Christianity?
2. What were the differences between Roman and Germanic ideas of rulership in late antiquity?
3. Why did the Roman Empire survive in the East and not the West in late antiquity?

TAKING IT FURTHER

For suggested readings, see page R-1.

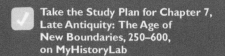
Chapter Review

Crisis and Recovery in the Third Century

7.1 How did the Roman Empire successfully reorganize following the instability of the third century?

Military, administrative, and economic reforms imposed organization on the previously chaotic Roman Empire. A system of shared government spread the heavy administrative responsibilities from one emperor to four, and ended the cycle of imperial assassinations by instituting a reliable succession strategy. New roads granted a significantly larger army the mobility to face invaders along the frontiers, and increased taxes and a regular census to register all taxpayers made the taxation system more profitable and efficient.

Toward a Christian Empire

7.2 How did Christianity become the dominant religion in the Roman Empire, and how did it affect Roman society?

After Constantine's conversion, successive emperors continued to encourage Christianity until it was finally the dominant religion in the empire. The internal organization of Christianity, including a clear distinction of power between the laity and the priests, imitated Roman urban administration and encouraged bishops to become important figures in Roman cities. These cities were transformed by public and private spending on churches, hospitals, and monastic communities that conformed to Christian values, and new religious festivals and rituals slowly replaced celebrations for polytheistic worship. Eventually, tolerance for any religions except Christianity waned.

New Christian Communities and Identities

7.3 How did Christianity transform communities, religious experience, and intellectual traditions inside and outside the Roman Empire?

Christianity supported the development of communities of faith by providing a well-defined set of beliefs and values that had to be integrated with daily life and older ways of thinking. At the same time, Roman laws began to discriminate against Jews as religious life in the empire became increasingly narrow. While Christians were historically wary of secular learning, training in classical rhetoric, grammar, and literature became an integral part of upper class Christian life, and monasticism played a central role in preserving classical learning.

The Breakup of the Roman Empire

7.4 How and why did the Roman Empire in the West disintegrate?

Poor decisions, weak leadership, and military failure contributed to the end of the Roman Empire. Permitting independent military forces of dubious loyalty to operate freely within the empire, and the inability of the imperial government to deal with multiple small invading bands of invaders, resulted in a tenuous hold over the West. The active cooperation of Roman administrators who thought they could bargain with the invading Germanic leaders led to these tribesmen settling down and consolidating their rule. Eventually, Roman authorities simply lacked the military strength and organization necessary to expel them.

Chapter Time Line

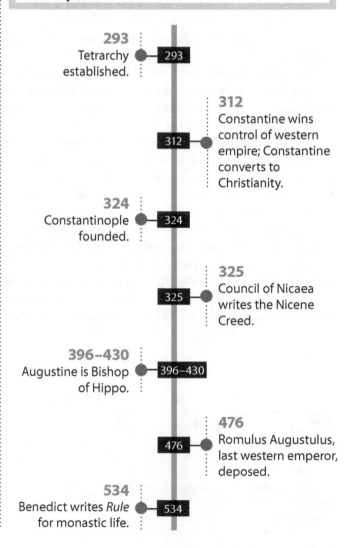

293
Tetrarchy established.

— 293

312
Constantine wins control of western empire; Constantine converts to Christianity.

— 312

324
Constantinople founded.

— 324

325
Council of Nicaea writes the Nicene Creed.

— 325

396–430
Augustine is Bishop of Hippo.

— 396–430

476
Romulus Augustulus, last western emperor, deposed.

— 476

534
Benedict writes *Rule* for monastic life.

— 534

8 Medieval Empires and Borderlands: Byzantium and Islam

I n 860 fierce Rus tribesmen aboard a fleet of sleek ships with prows shaped like dragons' heads raided the Byzantine villages along the shores of the Black Sea and then advanced to the gates of Constantinople, ready for pillage and rape. Panic gripped the inhabitants of the city. The Patriarch of Constantinople called on the people to repent of their sins to avoid God's wrath; when the Rus unexpectedly departed, the people of Constantinople interpreted it as an act of divine intervention.

Strategically located where the Black Sea meets the Sea of Marmara, Constantinople was the shining capital of the Byzantine Empire—and the largest and richest city in the world. Its Greek-speaking inhabitants considered the Rus savages, prone to the worst kinds of violence. Like so many other barbarian peoples, the Rus who were Vikings living in what is now Ukraine and Russia could not speak Greek, were not Christians, and did not recognize the authority of the Byzantine emperor, which the Greeks believed came directly from God. The leaders of Constantinople tried to keep these barbarians under control by signing treaties, which stipulated that no more than 50 Rus could enter the city at one time and they all had to leave by autumn. In exchange for civilized behavior, the Rus received free baths, food, provisions for a month, and equipment for their return to their homeland. By the ninth century the Rus had established a regular pattern. Each spring, after spending the winters

LEARNING OBJECTIVES

8.1 ((•
How did the Roman Empire's eastern provinces evolve into the Byzantine Empire?

8.2 ((•
How did Islam develop in Arabia, and how did its followers create a vast empire so quickly?

((• Listen to Chapter 8 on MyHistoryLab

THE CATHEDRAL OF HOLY WISDOM (HAGHIA SOPHIA) When Justinian entered his newly completed cathedral of Holy Wisdom (Haghia Sophia) in Constantinople in 537, he boasted, "Solomon, I have outdone you!" He meant that his church was bigger and more splendid than the Jerusalem Temple built by the biblical King Solomon. For centuries, Haghia Sophia was the largest building in Europe. In 1453 the church became a mosque. The large round banners display passages from the Qur'an.

👁 Watch the Video Series on MyHistoryLab

Learn about some key topics related to this chapter with the *MyHistoryLab Video Series:*
Key Topics in Western Civilization

8.1

8.2

along the river valleys of the north collecting tribute from the Slavic tribes, the Rus set off in their boats, risking dangerous rapids and waterfalls on the Dnieper River and ambush from hostile tribes, to reach the Black Sea and the splendid emporium of the world, Constantinople, which they called simply the "Great City."

Accustomed to winter treks, grubby villages, and constant danger, they were dazzled by the sight of the Great City, with its half million inhabitants and 12 miles of fortifications. The gilded cupolas of its churches, the marble palaces of the aristocrats and emperor, and the cavernous wharves and warehouses of its merchants amazed these tribesmen. The people of Constantinople were equally astonished—and frightened—by the sun-worn, fur-clad Rus.

The Rus came to Constantinople to trade. The merchants of Constantinople traded Byzantine and Chinese silks, Persian glass, Arabic silver coins (highly prized by the Rus), and Indian spices for honey, wax, slaves, and musty bales of furs from Scandinavia and what is now northern Russia. Despite their sense of superiority, the Byzantines needed the barbarians. In the merchant stalls of Constantinople, traders from many cultures met, haggled, and came to know something of one another. None perhaps were more unlike the other than the rough Rus and the refined Byzantines, but their mutual desires for profit kept them in a persistent, if tentative, embrace. These repeated interactions among diverse peoples who traded, competed, and fought with one another offer clues for understanding the medieval world, also known as the Middle Ages.

The term *Middle Ages* refers to the period between the ancient and modern civilizations from about the fifth to fifteenth centuries. Medieval culture rested on the foundations of three great civilizations: the Greek Christianity of Byzantium; the Arabic-speaking Islamic caliphates of the Middle East, North Africa, and Spain; and the Latin Christian kingdoms of western and northern Europe. The dynamic interactions among these three civilizations, distinguished by religion and language, lay at the heart of medieval culture. From the seventh to the eleventh centuries, the most energetic and creative of these three civilizations was the Islamic world, whose armies threatened both Byzantium and the Latin Christian kingdoms. In the century after the death of its founder, the prophet Muhammad, in 632, Islam's followers burst from their home in Arabia to conquer an empire stretching from Spain to central Asia. Especially during the tenth and eleventh centuries, this Islamic empire produced important philosophical and scientific work and supported a thriving economy.

The most distinctive feature of the medieval period was that all these civilizations rested on monotheistic religions that shared basic beliefs about God. All struggled to eliminate polytheism either by persuasion or force. However, because each of these medieval civilizations defined itself as an exclusive community of faith, cultural boundaries developed between them that are still visible today. This chapter examines two of these civilizations, Byzantium and Islam. Chapter 9 discusses the Latin Christian kingdoms. The most important question raised by the two civilizations discussed here is this:

How did their different versions of monotheism sustain them as empires?

Byzantium: The Survival of the Roman Empire

I n late antiquity Constantinople and Rome had symbolized the two halves of the Roman Empire. Once joined in a common Christian culture, eastern and western Christians gradually grew apart, so that by the late ninth century, they began to constitute separate civilizations, one Byzantine and the other Latin. There were still cultural exchanges between them as merchants, pilgrims, and scholars crossed back and forth, but the two civilizations had ceased to understand one another. They held different opinions about religious matters, such as the dating of Easter, the rituals of the liturgy, the role of images in worship, and the extent of the pope's authority. They also spoke different languages. In the East, Greek was the language of most of the population, and Latin had been largely forgotten by the end of the sixth century. In the West, Latin or local dialects of it prevailed. Except in southern Italy and Sicily, few Westerners knew Greek.

Eastern Europe became an unstable borderland on the flanks of Byzantium inhabited by polytheist farmers and nomads. Rival missionaries practicing Greek and Latin forms of Christianity competed there for converts and allies. Greek missionaries were the most successful in converting the Slavic peoples to Orthodox Christianity, a faith that survived among the Slavs even after the collapse of Byzantium itself.

An Embattled Empire

After the reign of Emperor Justinian (r. 527–565), the Byzantine Empire was gradually reduced to a regional power struggling for survival against many enemies. In the west the Byzantines faced the Germanic kingdom of the Lombards who eroded the imperial rule over Italy that Justinian had reestablished. The threats in the Balkans came from nomadic tribes from the Eurasian steppes, such as the Avars, Slavs, and Bulgars, who permanently settled there within the empire. These peoples became the ancestors of some of the current inhabitants of the region, such as modern Bulgarians, Croats, and Serbs. To the east the Byzantines confronted their old rival, the Persian Empire. Defeating Persia in a series of wars from 603 to 629 took such a huge toll that Byzantium was too exhausted to resist a new threat out of the Arabian peninsula from the armies of Islam. The encounters between these diverse enemies and Byzantium were usually hostile, and their encirclement of Byzantium forced Byzantine administration and military policy to change and adapt.

The Byzantine emperors after Justinian tried to hold on to the western provinces by reorganizing the administration of North Africa and Italy into two new units called *exarchates*—the Exarchate of Carthage (which also administered southern Spain) and the Exarchate of Ravenna. Because of their long distance from Constantinople and the immediate press of the local problems they confronted, the two exarchates were somewhat independent from the rest of the Byzantine Empire. The exarchs (or governors) held both civilian and military authority in these territories—a break from Roman practice, which had kept these two spheres separate. This joint command signaled the gravity of the problems the exarchs faced.

This administrative overhaul did not save Byzantium's western territories. Southern Spain fell to the Visigoths in the 630s, and Muslim armies took Carthage in 698. In 751 the Lombards captured Ravenna and put an end to the exarchate, although Byzantine rule survived in southern Italy until the eleventh century.

The Byzantine hold on eastern Europe also proved fragile. In much of the Balkan peninsula from the late sixth through ninth centuries, Byzantine weakness created a power vacuum that made the settled inhabitants who were Christians and still considered themselves subjects of the Roman Empire vulnerable to polytheist invaders. Like so many others before and after them, raiders and migrants poured out of the Eurasian steppes, a band of grasslands that spread some 5,000 miles from what is now Hungary and Ukraine in Europe into central Asia. Nomads could easily cross the grasslands on horseback. Interactions with the Avars, Slavs, Bulgars, and Rus contributed to the contraction of Byzantine territory and influence.

The nomadic Avars, who suddenly appeared in the sixth century on the plains of present-day Hungary from the steppes north of the Black Sea, had a bone-chilling reputation for ferocity. From Hungary they raided central Europe and the Balkans. These tenacious warriors dominated the region until the early ninth century and threatened Byzantium and the new kingdoms taking shape in Italy, Germany, and France.

The Avars created an empire by forcing conquered peoples to serve in their armies. Some of these peoples were Slavs. Between about 400 and 600, Slavic societies had formed from a blend of many cultures and ethnic groups. The Slavic communities that developed in eastern Europe between the Baltic Sea and the Balkans lay outside Byzantium's borders. Their Avar conquerors ruled by brute force, and most Slavs could not win back their independence. However, a few Slavic communities managed to overthrow Avar rule. In the second half of the sixth century, bands of Slavs began to migrate south across the Danube River into the Balkans. Collaborating with marauding Avars, the Slavs settled in sparsely populated frontier lands in what is now Croatia and Serbia. As the Slavs pushed south, many Byzantines abandoned their cities to the invaders. By 600, Slavic and Avar groups had seized most Byzantine lands from the Danube to Greece.

By the ninth century, these tribes began to convert to one or another form of Christianity, and the patterns of those conversions have had lasting consequences. The tribes in eastern Europe were fragmented politically, which mirrored the intricate distribution of ethnic and linguistic groups. State-building was especially complicated because much of the region had never been under Roman rule and lacked the legacies of Roman cities, institutions, and law that made the survival of Byzantium possible and the Germanic kingdoms of western Europe viable. Conversion patterns exacerbated eastern European fragmentation because the religious dividing line between those who adhered to Roman Catholicism and those who followed Orthodox Christianity cut directly through the region. Religion, like ethnicity and language, became a source of disunity rather than cohesion.

Fast on the heels of the Avars and Slavs from the steppes came the nomadic peoples called the Bulgars, who established rule over the largely Slavic inhabitants of the Balkans by the eighth century. The Bulgars destroyed the surviving old Roman cities there, expelled what Christians remained, and attacked the Byzantine Empire. In 811, after annihilating a Byzantine army, the Bulgarian khan (the head of a confederation of clans) Krum (r. 803–814) lined the skull of the slain Byzantine emperor with silver and turned it into a drinking cup. With this symbolic act of debasement, the Bulgarians gained a fierce reputation as enemies of Christianity and Byzantium.

In 865, however, Khan Boris I (r. 852–889) accepted the Orthodox Christianity of his former enemies in Byzantium. His conversion illustrates the politics of the period. During the ninth century Christianity began to acquire a powerful allure among the polytheistic tribes. Their acceptance of Christianity opened the possibility for diplomatic ties and alliances with the Christian powers. For Boris, therefore, conversion was a way to ward off Byzantine hostility and make peace. For four years, Boris negotiated with Rome, Constantinople, and German missionaries, all of whom sought to convert the Bulgars. In the end, Boris got what he wanted—a Bulgarian Orthodox Church that recognized the ultimate authority of the patriarch of Constantinople but was essentially autonomous.

The autonomy of the Bulgarian Church was further guaranteed later in the ninth century by the adoption of a Slavic liturgy rather than a Latin or Greek liturgy. This was made possible by the missionary work in neighboring Moravia of Cyril (ca. 826–869) and his brother Methodius (815–885), who had invented an alphabet to write the Slavic language. They translated a Greek church liturgy into a version of the Slavic language now known as Old Church Slavonic. The acceptance of the Slavonic liturgy gradually led the ethnically and linguistically mixed peoples of Bulgaria to identify with Slavic culture and language. From a string of monasteries established by the Bulgarians, the Old Church Slavonic liturgy spread among the Serbs, the Romanians, and eventually the Russians, creating cultural ties among these widespread peoples that have survived to the present.

As we saw at the beginning of this chapter, Byzantium also faced assault from the northern Rus. The Rus established a headquarters at Kiev on the Dnieper River and extended their domination over the local Slav tribes. From among the merchant-warriors of the Rus arose the forebears of the princes of Kiev, who by the end of the tenth century ruled a vast steppe and forest domain through a loose collective of subject principalities. The term *Rus* (later *Russian*) came to be applied to all the lands the princes of Kiev ruled.

Kievan Rus reached its zenith under Vladimir the Great (r. 978–1015) and his son Iaroslav the Wise (r. 1019–1054). A ruthless fighter, Vladimir consolidated into a single state the provinces of Kiev and Novgorod, a city in the far north that had grown rich from the fur trade. Born a polytheist, Vladimir had seven wives and took part in human sacrifices. However, when offered a military alliance with Byzantium in 987, he abandoned his wives, married the Byzantine emperor's sister, and converted to Orthodox Christianity. He then forced the inhabitants of Kiev and Novgorod to be baptized and cast their idols into the rivers. The Byzantine Church established administrative control over the Rus Church by appointing an Orthodox archbishop for Kiev. The liturgy was in Old Church Slavonic, which provided a written language and the stimulus for the literature, art, and music at the foundations of Russian culture. Iaroslav employed scribes to translate Greek religious books into Old Slavonic and founded new churches and monasteries across the Kievan state (see **Map 8.1**). The religious and political connection between the Rus and Byzantium shaped Russian history and limited the eastward spread of Latin Christianity (Roman Catholicism).

📖 **Read the Document**

Ibn Fadlan's *Account of the Rus*

Byzantine Civilization

In addition to assaults from so many directions, the Byzantine Empire faced turmoil from within. The loss of territories caused economic suffering, and religious controversies at times alienated the population from the government. But despite terrible losses, Byzantium endured. Three institutions held the empire together: the emperor, who set policies and safeguarded his subjects' welfare; the army, which defended the frontiers; and the Orthodox Church, which provided spiritual guidance.

IMPERIAL ADMINISTRATION AND ECONOMY Based at Constantinople, the emperor stood at the center of Byzantine society. His authority reached to every corner of the empire. This supreme ruler governed with the assistance of a large bureaucracy that he tightly controlled. In this hierarchical bureaucracy, elaborate titles and different clothing indicated different ranks. Only the emperor or members of his family, for example, could wear the color purple, a symbol of royalty. High dignitaries wore silk garments of distinctive colors encrusted with jewels. The higher the official, the more gems he was permitted to display. Bureaucrats and courtiers (members of the emperor's personal retinue) lined up in elaborate processions in order of their importance, as indicated by the color of their clothing and shoes. Through these ceremonies the emperor displayed the government to the people. Such processions were not just political propaganda.

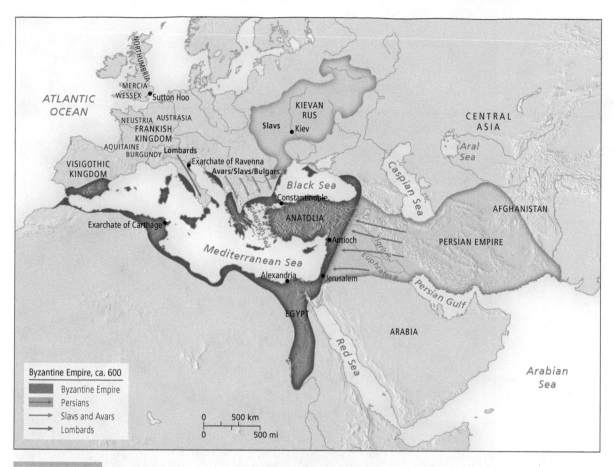

MAP **8.1** THE BYZANTINE EMPIRE, CA. 600 By 600 the Byzantine Empire consisted of Anatolia, Greece, part of the Balkans, Syria, Egypt, and some territories in North Africa and Spain. Until the rise of Islam, the Persian Empire remained Byzantium's greatest enemy. What parts of the Mediterranean were most influenced by Byzantine civilization?

They made the constitution of the empire evident through the hierarchic order of the procession. They also indicated the politics of the court as favored courtiers moved to a higher-ranked position in the procession, and those out of favor moved to a lower-ranked place or disappeared from the procession altogether.

Men fortunate or talented enough to obtain an office in the imperial government acquired wealth and influence. For this reason leading provincial families sent their sons to Constantinople to obtain positions in the bureaucracy. Through this method of recruitment, Constantinople remained in close touch with the outlying regions of the empire. This system gave provincial families a stake in the success of the empire and the provinces a voice in the capital. However, it was also vulnerable to corruption. Many men obtained their positions by bribing court officials. Other officeholders owed their jobs to family influence rather than talent. But even a corrupt system can be an effective form of government because official corruption made loyalty to the emperor more rewarding than opposition to him.

From his position at the head of this elaborate hierarchy, the emperor also controlled Byzantium's economy. The stable imperial coinage spurred a flourishing cash-based economy. Official monopolies controlled the production and distribution of specific commodities such as silk. These monopolies protected the interests of the emperor and those he favored by stifling competition. As long as the monopolies flourished, the government had a source of revenue through taxation.

By the end of the seventh century, however, when the rich provinces of Egypt and Syria and the wealthy cities of Alexandria, Antioch, Carthage, and others had fallen to the Arabs, the Byzantine economy stumbled. Thousands of refugees from

KING DAVID PLATE Nine silver plates made in Constantinople about 630 illustrate scenes from the career of the biblical King David. The largest plate (about 20 inches in diameter) shows David battling the giant Goliath. Though the subject matter is biblical, the style of representing clothing, human bodies, and spatial relationships comes directly from the classical tradition. The subject connected Byzantium's struggles with Persia to the Bible's heroic king.

SOURCE: Byzantine, early seventh century. Dish: David and Goliath. Silver, Syrian workmanship. D. 19 1/2 in. Found in Karavas, near Kyrenia, Cyprus, 1902. The Metropolitan Museum of Art, Gift of J. Pierpont Morgan, 1917.

lands conquered by Muslims streamed into the empire and strained its resources. In conquered Byzantine provinces, Muslim rulers set up their own monopolies and prevented Byzantine merchants from participating in long-distance commerce. Cut off from foreign markets, Byzantines stopped manufacturing goods for export and building new houses and churches. By 750, the standard of living in most Byzantine cities except Constantinople had fallen.

THE MILITARY SYSTEM OF THE THEMES In response to the many external threats, Byzantine society was reorganized for constant war. Emperors relied on their armies to protect Constantinople, the nerve center of the shrinking Byzantine state, and to defend the borders against invaders. By about 650 in Anatolia, which became the empire's main source of recruits for the army, emperors abandoned the late Roman system of relying on the provincial governors to protect the frontiers. To replace the old provinces, emperors created four military districts called *themes*. Each of the themes had its own army and administration commanded by a general chosen by the emperor. The themes' armies developed strong local identities and prided themselves on their military skills, a legacy the Byzantine Empire had inherited from the Roman legions. These military forces kept the empire from collapsing despite devastating losses to Islamic armies throughout the seventh century.

By 750 the themes had developed considerable autonomy from Constantinople and were the basis of further reorganization of the agricultural economy and procedures for recruitment. Soldiers and sailors who were once paid in cash from the emperor's tax revenues now were granted land on which to support themselves. Fighting men had to provide their own weapons from their income as farmers, and the theme system enabled the parts of the empire to function without direct support from the imperial treasury. The theme system created defensive flexibility for the empire. While it could no longer launch large-scale offensive conquests, Byzantium could at least attempt to defend its borders.

Over time the four original themes were subdivided and new ones added in other regions until, by the end of the eleventh century, there were 38 themes. The military strength of the empire came to depend on the theme system in which free, tax-paying soldier-farmers lived in villages under the supervision of a military commander who was also civil administrator. These soldier-farmers usually fought in their own districts, which meant they were defending their homes and families. As a result, they provided a formidable bulwark against invaders.

The Byzantine borders were especially harassed by Muslim enemies; however, from the first thrust of Muslim armies against Byzantium's frontier in the seventh century until its fall to the Turks in 1453, Constantinople held on. While the Persian Empire fell to Arab armies by the 630s, Byzantium survived. That fact is perhaps the most important measure of the success of Byzantium's military reorganization.

One of the lasting cultural fruits of these conflicts was legends of great heroes. These legends began as stories recited in verse to entertain Byzantine aristocrats whose ancestors had fought the Arabs. Several of these oral legends were eventually refashioned into popular epic poems. One such poem, *Digenes Akritas,* described the heroic feats of soldiers during the late eighth century on the eastern frontier of the empire, where Byzantines and Arabs both fought and cooperated. The father of the poem's hero was an Arab commander who abducted the daughter of a Byzantine general, married her, and converted to Christianity. The son of this mixed marriage was Digenes ("two-blooded"), a man of two peoples and two religions, who became a border fighter (an "akritas"). This greatest Byzantine hero, who lived between two cultures, was the poetic embodiment of the engagement between Byzantium and Islam. The legends surrounding *Digenes Akritas* had a profound influence on Greek literature. Later writers retold its stories again and again.

THE CHURCH AND RELIGIOUS LIFE Constantinople boasted so many churches and sacred relics that by 600 the Byzantines had begun to think of it as a holy city, protected by God and under the special care of the Virgin Mary. Churchmen taught that Constantinople was a "New Jerusalem" that would be at the center of events at the End of Days when God would bring history to an end and judge humanity.

One of the institutional pillars of the Orthodox Church in Byzantium was the clergy. They were organized hierarchically like the imperial bureaucracy. The patriarch, or chief bishop, of Constantinople headed several thousand clergymen in the capital and directed church affairs throughout the empire. Emperors generally controlled the appointment of patriarchs, and often the two worked closely together. The patriarch helped impose religious unity throughout the empire by controlling the network of bishops based in cities near and far. Each city's bishop supervised the veneration of the saints' relics housed in its churches. (Byzantines believed that sacred relics protected their communities, just as their polytheistic ancestors believed the gods had provided protection in the pre-Christian past.) Because bishops usually came from the city's elite, they were influential local leaders, responsible for administering many public policies, not just religious ones.

Monasteries played a significant role in the empire's life. Men and women went to separate monasteries to live a spiritual life, praying for their own salvation and that of

📖 Read the Document

Liutprand of Cremona, *Report of His Mission to Constantinople,* 968

icons The Christian images of God and saints found in Byzantine art.

others. People who needed help, such as orphans, the elderly, battered wives, widows, and the physically and mentally ill, found refuge in monasteries. Monks and nuns distributed food and clothing to the poor. Donors gave lavishly to fund these activities, and many monasteries grew wealthy through these gifts.

During the seventh and eighth centuries, Christian instruction under the supervision of the Church replaced the traditional Roman educational system. Pious Christians developed a suspicion of classical learning, with its references to ancient gods and to customs the Church condemned. Those few Byzantines who learned how to read did so by studying the Bible, not the classics of Greek antiquity. As a result of this general decline in learning, the Church monopolized culture and thought. Knowledge of classical literature, history, and science disappeared except in Constantinople, and even there the academic community was tiny.

ICONS AND THE ICONOCLASTIC CONTROVERSY The Orthodox Church created unity of faith and culture, but that unity was broken in the eighth century by controversy within the Church itself. As enemies tore at the borders of the empire, Byzantines wondered why God was punishing them. Their answer was that somehow they were angering God. Convinced that only appeasing God could save them, Emperor Leo III (r. 717–741) took action. To make Byzantium a completely Christian empire, he forcibly converted communities of Jews. His most important move, however, was to challenge the use of **icons**, the images of Christ and saints found everywhere in Byzantine worship.

Centuries before, the first Christians had refused to make images of Christ and other holy individuals. They had two reasons for banning such representations. First, the Hebrew Bible forbids creating representations of God, and they considered this prohibition still in effect for Christians. Second, they thought that Christians might start to worship their images the way that polytheists worshiped statues in their temples. "When images are put up, the customs of the pagans do the rest," wrote one church leader in the fourth century.

Despite such warnings, many Christians responded aesthetically to the beautiful polytheist statues and images that filled their cities. Christian sculptors and painters started to create a distinctive Christian art that combined religious images with the styles and techniques of classical art. After Constantine put an end to the persecution of Christians, this new art flourished. Artists routinely portrayed Christ and the saints in churches. During the sixth and seventh centuries, Byzantines used religious images with greater zeal than ever before. By 600, for example, the emperor placed a large image of Christ above the Bronze Gate, the main entrance to the imperial palace in Constantinople. Smaller icons became intensely popular in churches, homes, and monasteries.

Byzantine theologians defended icons as doorways through which the divine presence could make itself accessible to believers. Churchmen cautioned that God or saints do not actually reside within the icons, and so believers should not worship the images themselves. Rather, they should consider icons as openings to a spiritual world, enabling believers to encounter a holy presence. Thus, Byzantines treated icons with love and respect. Monks and nuns were particularly zealous in their veneration of icons.

However, by the eighth century, some Byzantine theologians thought icon veneration had gone too far and sought to revive the early Christian prohibitions against religious images. They advised Emperor Leo that icon veneration should be halted because uneducated believers confused the image of the icon with what it represented and worshiped icons as polytheists worshiped idols. When a volcanic eruption destroyed the island of Santorini in the Aegean, Leo concluded that these advisers were correct and that God was angered by icon veneration. In 726 Leo ordered the destruction of holy images (except for crucifixes) throughout the empire, but public resistance forced him to move carefully. For example, when he ordered workers to remove the image of Christ from the Bronze Gate at the imperial palace, the people of Constantinople rioted. Four years later, Leo renewed the general prohibition. The destruction of icons, known as **iconoclasm** (image breaking), divided Byzantine society until 842.

The veneration of icons was such a vital part of popular religious life that Leo found it difficult to enforce iconoclasm outside Constantinople. Revolts broke out in Greece and southern Italy when imperial messengers sought to destroy images. The iconoclastic controversy also affected international politics. Outraged by the emperor's prohibition of icons, which he considered heresy, Pope Gregory III, the dominant religious figure in the West, excommunicated Leo. In retaliation Leo deprived the papacy of religious authority over southern Italy, Sicily, and the Balkan coast of the Adriatic Sea, authority the popes had exercised since the fourth century. The popes never forgave the emperor because with the loss of religious authority came the loss of the principal source of papal revenues. This conflict contributed to a growing rift between Greek Orthodox and Latin Christianity. In the future, instead of relying on the Byzantine emperors for military protection, the Roman popes turned north to the Franks. The Iconoclastic Controversy created a lasting shift that allied the Roman pope with the kingdoms of western Europe.

iconoclasm The destruction of religious images in the Byzantine Empire in the eighth century.

 Read the Document

Epitome of the Iconoclastic Seventh Synod 754

RESTORATION OF THE ICONS This sixteenth-century Cretan icon commemorates when Empress Theodora established an annual festival in 843 to mark the end of Iconoclasm. The image of the Virgin Mary at the top is the Virgin Hodegetria, the protector of the city of Constantinople.

Macedonian Renaissance During the Macedonian dynasty's rule of Byzantium (867–1056), aristocratic families, the Church, and monasteries devoted their immense riches to embellishing Constantinople with new buildings, mosaics, and icons. The emperors sponsored historical, philosophical, and religious writing.

After years of turmoil, two Byzantine empresses who were influenced by monks and who sympathized with their subjects' religious convictions restored icons to churches. In 787, the Empress Irene called a general church council that reversed Leo's condemnation of icons. After Irene was deposed in 802 iconoclasm revived, but in 843 Empress Theodora introduced a religious festival for commemorating images, which Orthodox Christians still celebrate annually. The Iconoclastic Controversy may have widened the gap between Greek Orthodoxy and Latin Christianity, but its resolution created even greater religious unity within the Byzantine world. A common religious culture also provided solace and a spiritual connection to Byzantium for many Christians who found themselves in the former Byzantine territories that Islamic rulers had conquered.

THE BYZANTINE PORTRAIT This ivory plaque shows Emperor Constantine VII Porphyrogenitus (r. 913–959) being crowned by Christ. It was probably made in 944 to commemorate Porphyrogenitus's becoming the sole ruler of the empire. Under the emperor's left hand the inscription reads, "Emperor of the Romans."

The Macedonian Renaissance

Byzantium's losses to external enemies were reversed during the Macedonian dynasty (867–1056), the term for a line of emperors from the Balkans that lasted six generations. Before the Macedonians, instability characterized the Byzantine imperial system because when an emperor died, powerful families struggled over who would become the new emperor. But after Basil I (r. 867–886), the first Macedonian, murdered his way to the throne, his family retained power by naming emperors' sons as co-emperors and encouraging the principle of dynastic succession.

Under the Macedonian emperors, Byzantine armies and fleets fought Muslims on several fronts. In the east the Byzantines pushed into Syria and Palestine almost to Jerusalem. A large part of the Mesopotamian river valley fell into their hands. They annexed the kingdom of Georgia and part of Armenia. In the Mediterranean, the Byzantines retook the islands of Crete and Cyprus and kept the Muslims from southern Italy, although they were unable to prevent the conquest of Sicily, which became a center of Muslim culture.

The economy of Constantinople thrived. Home to more than half a million people by the tenth century, the city became a great marketplace where traders exchanged goods from as far away as China and the British Isles. It was also a center for the production of luxury goods, especially the highly prized silk cloth and brocades traded throughout Europe, Asia, and North Africa. Aristocratic families, the Church, and monasteries became immensely rich and embellished the city with magnificent buildings, mosaics, and icons, creating the **Macedonian Renaissance**.

The Macedonian dynasty released creative energies by restoring the religious unity that the Iconoclastic Controversy had compromised. The most original work was religious, embodied in sermons, theological scholarship, and especially hymns; however, thanks to generous imperial patronage, Constantinople also became a center for philosophical study and the writing of history for the first time since the seventh century. The accumulation and study of ancient Greek manuscripts created an important cultural link between the ancient and medieval worlds.

The patriarch Photius (ca. 810–ca. 893) was one of the most eminent scholars in the history of Byzantium. Photius maintained a huge library, which became a center for the study of ancient Greek literature. He wrote important works, including the *Library,* an encyclopedic compendium of classical and Byzantine writers both religious and secular. Photius's summaries and analyses of these writers have remained especially vital because many of these books have subsequently been lost. Photius was also deeply involved in Church politics and was twice deposed from office because of political intrigue in Constantinople. His selection as patriarch by Emperor Michael III in 858 while still a layman met with strong opposition from the Roman pope. A bitter critic of the Latin Christians—Photius and the pope each excommunicated the other—Photius is often blamed for widening the gap between the two main branches of Christianity.

Under the Macedonian dynasty elaborate court ceremonies magnified the quasi-sacred office of the emperor. The historian Emperor Constantine VII Porphyrogenitus (r. 913–959) wrote the *Book of Ceremonies,* which became a model for royal ceremony in kingdoms from Spain to Russia. The *Book of Ceremonies* disseminated Byzantine concepts of rulership, which suggested that the emperor, like Christ, had two natures. One of these natures was human and fallible, but the other was derived from God, which gave the properly consecrated ruler divine authority over his subjects. Hence, Byzantine emperors were anointed with holy oil in a ceremony that was similar to the ordination of priests. The divine authority of monarchs represented by the emperor's or king's anointment became a central feature of political thought during the Middle Ages.

Even under the Macedonians, Byzantium remained under the threat of invasions. The empire's success in meeting these threats depended on two factors—the political stability guaranteed by the Macedonian dynasty, and the organization and recruitment of the army through the military districts of the themes. In the early eleventh century, however, the dynasty weakened and the army deteriorated.

When Emperor Basil II (r. 976–1025) died, Byzantine power and prosperity were at their peak, but he left no direct male heirs. His nieces and their husbands ruled until 1056, largely because Byzantines believed that the peace and prosperity of the empire depended on the dynasty. Basil's successors, however, were not strong leaders. Administration of the empire was highly centralized, with a tangled bureaucracy that supervised everything from diplomatic ceremony to the training of artisans. Without energetic leadership, the Byzantine bureaucracy degenerated into routine and failed to respond to new challenges.

The early Macedonian emperors' success in checking invasions had been largely the result of Byzantium's superior military capacities, guaranteed by the systematic organization of the army in the themes and the strength of the economy. As discussed earlier, the success of the themes depended on a system in which free, tax-paying soldier-farmers fought in their own districts, defending their homes and families. However, by the eleventh century deteriorating economic conditions threatened the independence of these soldier-farmers. Every time a crop failed or drought or famine struck, starving soldier-farmers in the themes were forced to surrender their land and their independence to one of the aristocrats who offered them food. As these great landowners acquired more land, the small farmers who were the backbone of the army began to disappear or lose their freedom. Because only free landholders could perform military service, the concentration of land in the hands of a few was disastrous for the army. Qualified soldiers with the land to support them became rare.

The late Macedonian emperors lacked the will to prevent this trend, and the army increasingly depended on foreign mercenaries. These emperors found themselves in a bind. Their income largely depended on their monopoly over industry and trade, but that control meant that land was the only profitable alternative form of investment for aristocrats. Opening up the economy might have hurt their own incomes, and so the emperors failed to do what was necessary to protect the empire. The situation was bleak; however, over succeeding centuries, enemies ate away at Byzantium until its final collapse in 1453.

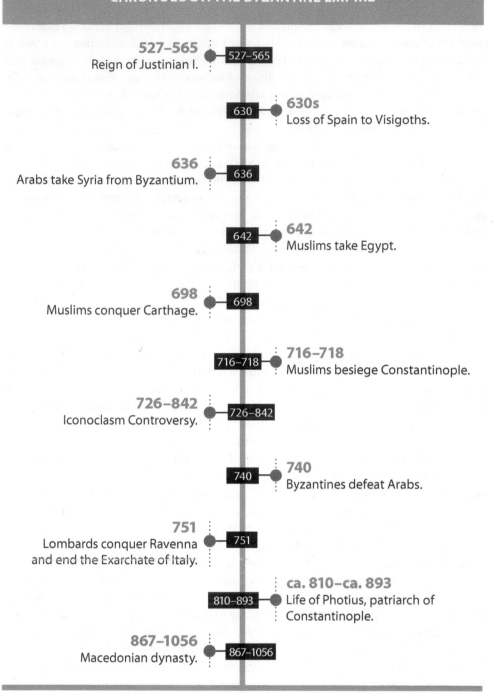

CHRONOLOGY: THE BYZANTINE EMPIRE

527–565
Reign of Justinian I. — 527–565

630 — **630s**
Loss of Spain to Visigoths.

636
Arabs take Syria from Byzantium. — 636

642 — **642**
Muslims take Egypt.

698
Muslims conquer Carthage. — 698

716–718 — **716–718**
Muslims besiege Constantinople.

726–842
Iconoclasm Controversy. — 726–842

740 — **740**
Byzantines defeat Arabs.

751
Lombards conquer Ravenna
and end the Exarchate of Italy. — 751

810–893 — **ca. 810–ca. 893**
Life of Photius, patriarch of
Constantinople.

867–1056
Macedonian dynasty. — 867–1056

The New World of Islam

8.2 How did Islam develop in Arabia, and how did its followers create a vast empire so quickly?

The Muslim armies that battered Byzantium created a new civilization that transformed the Mediterranean world and created an empire that stretched from Spain to central Asia (see **Map 8.2**). Today there are more than one billion Muslims around the globe. This growing faith has left an indelible stamp not only on the West but also on the rest of the world.

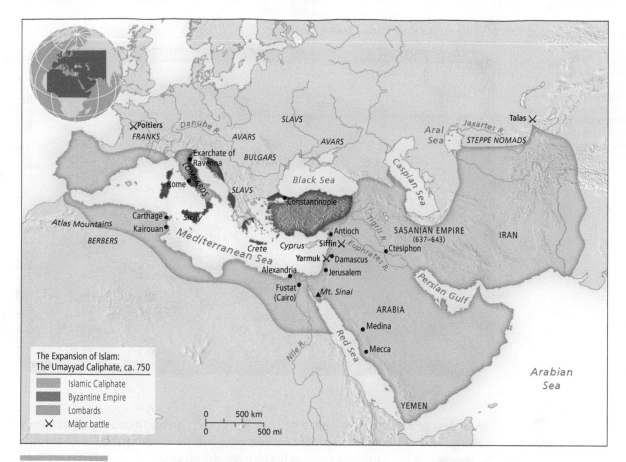

MAP **8.2** THE EXPANSION OF ISLAM: THE UMAYYAD CALIPHATE, CA. 750 By about 750 the Umayyad caliphate had reached its greatest extent. It provided political unity to territories stretching from central Asia to Spain. Islam became the dominant religion in this vast empire. Compare this map with Map 8.1. In what places did Islamic culture supplant Byzantine culture?

Islam originated in the early seventh century among the inhabitants of the Arabian peninsula. Arabs were tribal people. Many of them were nomads herding camels, goats, and sheep. (See *Encounters and Transformations* in this chapter.) In south Arabia, other Arabs farmed, lived in towns, and developed extensive commercial networks. Each tribe claimed descent from a common male ancestor. Tribal chiefs led by their own personal prestige and by the common consent of the tribesmen. Arab tribes, however, performed many of the functions of a state, which included protecting the lives and property of their members.

The Rise of Islam

Islam is based on the Qur'an and the sayings of the prophet Muhammad (ca. 570–632). Muhammad was born to the powerful Hashimite clan of the Quraysh tribe in the cosmopolitan and wealthy west Arabian trading city of Mecca. Mecca was the site of the Ka'aba, a sacred stone where polytheist Arabs worshiped many gods. As a young man Muhammad married a widowed businesswoman, Khadija, and worked as a caravan merchant, earning a reputation as a skilled arbitrator of disputes among tribes.

At about age 40, Muhammad reported that while he was meditating in solitude an angel appeared before him, saying, "Muhammad, I am Gabriel and you are the Messenger of God. Recite!" According to Muhammad's account, the angel gave him a message to convey to the people of Mecca. Muhammad's message was a call to all Arabs to worship the one true God (the god of Abraham) and to warn of the fires of hell if people failed to answer that call. Muhammad continued to recite his revelations

THE KA'ABA IN MECCA In pre-Islamic times, Arabs worshiped a large, black stone at the Ka'aba shrine in the center of Mecca. When Muhammad established Islam in Mecca in 629, he rejected the polytheist past and transformed the Ka'aba into the holiest place in the Islamic world, revered as the House of God. Muslims from all over the world make pilgrimages to the Ka'aba. These journeys foster a shared religious identity among them, no matter where their homelands lie.

View the **Closer Look**   The Ka'ba in Mecca

for the rest of his life. They were written down as the Qur'an (meaning "recitation"), the holy book of Islam. Though Muhammad won followers among friends and family, the people of Mecca initially rejected his monotheist message.

In 622, Muhammad and his followers moved from Mecca to Medina, 200 miles to the north, where feuding tribes had invited him to settle their disputes. Muhammad's emigration to Medina, known as the *Hijra,* is the starting date of the Muslim calendar. The event marks a turning point in the development of Islam. For the first time Muhammad and his followers lived as an independent community. Accepted by his disciples as the prophet of God, Muhammad strictly regulated the internal affairs of his new community and its relations with outsiders, creating a society that was political as well as religious. At the center of this Islamic community lay the **mosque,** the place where his followers gathered to pray and hear Muhammad recite the Qur'an.

mosque A place of Muslim worship.

Initially, Muhammad enjoyed good relations with the Jews who controlled the markets in Medina. He and his followers even abided by Jewish rituals, such as turning toward Jerusalem while praying. But as his influence among the Arab tribes grew, he became involved in disputes with the Jewish tribes who refused to accept him as a prophet. Alienated from the Jews, Muhammad changed the direction of prayer to Mecca, expelled some Jewish tribes from Medina, and massacred the men and enslaved the women and children of others. With Jewish opposition eliminated and control of Medina secured, Muhammad led an army against Mecca, which surrendered in 630.

Using force and negotiation, Muhammad drew many Arab tribes into his new religious community. His authority rested both on his ability as a military leader who raided caravans and defeated enemy tribes and on his reputation as a prophet. By the time he died, he had unified most of Arabia under Islam.

MUHAMMAD'S TEACHINGS Islam teaches that Allah (which means "God" in Arabic) revealed his message to Muhammad, the last in a line of prophets that included Abraham, Moses, and David, all pivotal biblical figures in the Jewish tradition, who transmitted divine instruction to humanity. Muslims also revere Jesus Christ as a prophet, but not as the son of God. Thus, Islam shares some of the beliefs of Judaism and Christianity.

Encounters and Transformations

Ships of the Desert:
CAMELS FROM MOROCCO TO CENTRAL ASIA

A remarkable thing happened when the Arab followers of the dynamic new religion of Islam encountered the humble camel, which had been the beast of burden in Arabia and the Near East for at least 2,000 years. The ancient caravan trade that transported goods on the backs of camels brought the Arabs into contact with a vast stretch of the world from Spain to China. In the exchanges that took place along the caravan routes, Islamic religious ideas were widely disseminated, and Arab merchants enriched Muslim cities. The camel also helped make Arab armies formidable in battle, which meant that Islam spread rapidly through conquest.

As the desert dwellers knew, camels were highly efficient for transporting people and goods, especially in arid regions, because of their bodies' capacity to conserve water. Able to drink as much as 28 gallons at a time, camels can last nine days without water and travel great distances. The fat in their humps allows them to survive for even longer without food. Camels are more efficient as pack animals than carts pulled by oxen or mules because they can traverse roadless rough terrain and cross rivers without bridges. They require fewer people to manage them on a journey than do wheeled vehicles.

Arabs developed the "North Arabian saddle," which enabled a rider to grasp the camel's reins with one hand while slashing downward at enemy troops with a sword in his other hand. Warriors on camels could attack infantry with speed and force. Camel-breeding Arab tribesmen, empowered by their new military technology, seized control of the lucrative spice trade routes and became an economic, military, and political force by exploiting and guarding the wealth of the caravans.

After Muhammad established his community in Mecca in 630, Islam literally "took off" on camelback. Tribesmen-warriors on camels spread Islam first throughout Arabia and the Middle East, and then to central Asia and across North Africa into Spain. Camels played a significant role in the expanding Islamic economy because they made long-distance trade extremely profitable. The transformations the camel brought were most evident in areas where the famous Roman roads had been a primary conduit of land trade. Thousands of miles of roads connected the provinces of the Roman Empire and let troops march easily from one front to another. However, the camels of Arabia changed that. Because these "ships of the desert" did not need paved roads, caravan routes did not have to stick to the Roman road systems, and merchants bypassed them altogether. New trade routes across the desert and other harsh terrains well suited to camels quickly developed from Morocco to central Asia, and paved roads started to disappear. Because camels could easily walk on narrow paths, the broad streets and wide markets suited to carts and wagons that typified Greek and Roman cities also fell out of use. Bazaars with narrow, winding lanes appropriate to camel traffic replaced them. Carts and wheeled vehicles all but vanished in these lands. There were also cultural consequences. In particular, caravan traffic linked China more closely to the Middle East and brought Chinese goods and ideas to the West.

For Discussion

How might the history of the West have differed if camel caravans had not replaced the system of Roman roads?

THE CAMEL CARAVAN This photograph shows a string of camels crossing sand dunes in the desert, carrying heavy loads, just as camel caravans would have in antiquity.

Pillars of Islam The five basic principles of Islam as taught by Muhammad.

Muhammad taught his followers basic principles that eventually came to be called the five **Pillars of Islam**. *Islam* means "submission," and by performing these acts of faith, Muslims ("those who submit to God") demonstrate obedience to the will of God. First, all Muslims must acknowledge that there is only one God and that Muhammad is his prophet. Second, they must state this belief in prayer five times a day. On Fridays, the noon prayers must be recited in the company of other believers if possible. Muslims may say their prayers anywhere. Third, Muslims must fast between sunrise and sunset during Ramadan, the ninth month of the Muslim calendar. Fourth, Muslims must donate money and food to the needy. Islam expects its followers to be kind to one another, especially to orphans and widows, and to work for the good of the entire Islamic community. Fifth, Muslims must make a pilgrimage to Mecca at least once in their lives if it is possible. As the focus of prayer and pilgrimage, Mecca quickly became the center of the Muslim world. The Qur'an affirmed Mecca's special role in Islam:

> Announce the Pilgrimage to the people. They will come to you on foot and riding along distant roads on lean and slender beasts, in order to reach the place of advantage (the Ka'aba) for them, and to pronounce the name of God on appointed days over cattle he has given them as food; then eat the food and feed the needy and the poor. (Qur'an 22:26)

With the spread of Islam to Persia, Asia, and parts of Europe in the seventh and eighth centuries, Muslims from different lands encountered one another in Mecca, developing a shared Islamic identity.

While the Qur'an contains many examples of proper behavior for the community to follow, Muslims also looked to Muhammad's example as a guide. Muhammad taught his followers to struggle for the good of the Muslim community. This struggle is called *jihad*. Islam teaches that the duty of *jihad* should be fulfilled by the heart, the tongue, the hand, and the sword. The *jihad* of the heart consists of a spiritual purification by battling the Devil and avoiding temptations to do evil. *Jihad* of the tongue requires believers to propagate the faith and of the hand to correct moral wrongs. *Jihad* of the sword is to wage holy war against unbelievers and enemies of Islam who can avoid attack by converting or paying special taxes, called the *jizya*. (See *Different Voices* in this chapter.) Most modern Muslim scholars understand *jihad* as waging war with one's inner self, the *jihad* of the heart, but some have revived the concept of *jihad* of the sword to support military struggle.

 Read the Document

The Qur'an

caliphate The Islamic imperial government that evolved under the leadership of Abu Bakr (r. 632–634), the successor of the prophet Muhammad. The sectarian division within Islam between the Shi'ites and Sunnis derived from a disagreement over how to determine the hereditary succession from Muhammad to the caliphate, which combined governmental and some religious responsibilities.

THE SUCCESSION CRISIS AFTER MUHAMMAD: SUNNIS AND SHI'ITES Muhammad had demonstrated a talent for leadership during his lifetime, but he did not designate his successor. His death in 632 therefore caused a crisis. Would the Islamic community stay united under a single new leader? After many deliberations, Muslim elders chose the prophet's father-in-law, Abu Bakr, to lead them. Abu Bakr (r. 632–634) became the first caliph, or successor to Muhammad. The Islamic government that evolved under his leadership, the **caliphate**, combined religious and political responsibilities.

Most Muslims supported Abu Bakr, but a minority opposed him. One group claimed that Muhammad's son-in-law and cousin, Ali, should have become the first caliph. Other Arab tribes rejected Islam itself. They claimed their membership in the Islamic community had been valid only when Muhammad was alive. Abu Bakr crushed them in a struggle called the Wars of Apostasy (a word meaning "renunciation of a previous faith"). By the time he died in 634, Abu Bakr had brought most of Arabia back under his control, but disputes between his followers and those of Ali led to a permanent split within Islam between the minority Shi'ites, who followed Ali, and the majority Sunnis, who followed Abu Bakr. While the Shi'ites and Sunnis both considered

Different Voices
Christian and Muslim Justifications for Holy War

A ugustine of Hippo (d. 430) was perhaps the most influential early Christian theologian. Early Christian thought was strongly pacifist as the New Testament clearly commands: "I say unto you, that you resist not evil: but if anyone strike you on the right cheek, turn to him the left also" (Luke 6:29). In contrast, Augustine developed a justification for Christian violence. Although he quoted biblical examples, his argument derives from the ancient Roman conception of just war. His case is a good example of the blending of biblical and Roman ideas characteristic of early Christianity.

Augustine of Hippo on Just War

[The] account of the wars of Moses will not excite surprise or abhorrence, for in wars carried on by divine command, he showed not ferocity but obedience; and God, in giving the command, acted not in cruelty, but in righteous retribution, giving to all what they deserved, and warning those who needed warning. What is the evil in war? Is it the death of some who will soon die in any case, that others may live in peaceful subjection? This is mere cowardly dislike, not any religious feeling. The real evils in war are love of violence, revengeful cruelty, fierce and implacable enmity, wild resistance, and the lust of power, and such like; and it is generally to punish these things, when force is required to inflict the punishment, that, in obedience to God or some lawful authority, good men undertake wars, when they find themselves in such a position as regards to conduct of human affairs, that right conduct requires them to act, or to make others act, in this way.

The sacred book of Islam, the Qur'an, consists of the prophet Mohammed's recitations of his visions of Allah. These excerpts about war and the relations of Muslims with other faiths have the status in Islam of the direct words of God.

The Qur'an on Religious War

Sura 2

190. You shall fight in the cause of god against those who attack you, but do not aggress. God does not love the aggressors.

191. You may kill those who wage war against you, and you may evict them whence they evicted you, for oppression is worse than murder. Do not fight them at the sacred mosque, unless they attack you therein. If they attack you, you may kill them. This is the just retribution for such disbelievers.

Sura 3

113. They are not all the same; among the followers of the scripture [that is, Jews and Christians as well as Muslims], there are those who are righteous. They recite God's revelations through the night, and they fall prostrate.

Sura 5

13. Also those who said, "We are Christians," we took their covenant. But they disregarded some of the commandments given to them. Consequently, we condemned them to animosity and hatred among themselves, until the day of resurrection. God will then inform them of everything they had done.

Sura 60

9. God enjoins you only from befriending those who fight you because of religion, evict you from your homes, and band together with others to banish you. You shall not befriend them. Those who befriend them are the transgressors.

SOURCE: S. J. Allen and Emilie Amt, eds. *The Crusades: A Reader.* 2003, 7, 10–13. Copyright © 2003 by S. J. Allen and Emilie Amt. Reprinted with permission of the publisher, the University of Toronto Press.

For Discussion

1. What makes war acceptable for a Christian or a Muslim?
2. How do Augustine's justifications for war compare with those of the Qur'an?
3. How does the Qur'an distinguish between Islam and Christianity?

the caliphate a hereditary office restricted to members of Muhammad's Hashimite clan of the Quraysh tribe, the Shi'ites believed that only direct descendants of Muhammad through his daughter Fatima and son-in-law Ali should rule the Islamic community. The Sunnis, in contrast, devised a more flexible theory of succession that allowed them later to accept even non-Arab caliphs.

During the wars among Muslims after the death of Muhammad, Abu Bakr created a highly trained Muslim army eager to spread the faith. Under the leadership of the second caliph, Umar (r. 634–644), Muslim forces invaded the rich territories of the Byzantine and Persian Empires. They seized Syria in 636. The next year they crushed the main Persian army, weakened from a long war with Byzantium, and captured the Persian capital,

Ctesiphon. Within a decade Islamic troops had conquered Egypt and all of Persia as far east as India. Meanwhile, Muslim fleets, manned by Egyptian and Syrian sailors, seized Cyprus, raided in the eastern Mediterranean. Muslim armies were racing across North Africa when civil war broke out among the Arabs in 655 and temporarily halted their advance.

Two groups struggled to control the caliphate during this six-year civil war. On one side were Muhammad's son-in-law Ali, who had become caliph in 656, and his supporters, the Shi'ites. On the other side was the wealthy Umayyad family, who opposed him and whose supporters were Sunnis. (See *Justice in History* in this chapter.) In 661 the Umayyads arranged Ali's assassination and took control of the caliphate, establishing a new dynasty, the Ummayads, that would last until 750. The Umayyads made Damascus in Syria their new capital city, which shifted Islamic power away from Mecca. The Shi'ites continued to oppose the Umayyads, but they remained a minority except in Persia and Iraq.

The Umayyad Caliphate

The Umayyad dynasty produced brilliant administrators and generals. At the end of the civil war, these talented leaders consolidated their control of conquered territories and established peace in the empire. Then they resumed wars of conquest; in less than a century, however, they built an empire that reached from Spain to central Asia.

THE "HOUSE OF WAR" As we saw in Chapter 6, the Romans distinguished themselves from uncivilized "barbarians" who had not yet come under Roman rule. In a similar fashion, Muslims viewed the world as consisting of two parts: the "House of Islam," which contained the territories they controlled, and the "House of War," which included all non-Muslim lands, which they hoped to conquer. By 700, Muslim armies had conquered North Africa as far as the Atlantic Ocean.

In 711, the Umayyads invaded Spain and easily overthrew the Arian Christian Visigothic kingdom. From Spain they attacked France, but in 732, Charles Martel "the Hammer," leading a Frankish army, stopped their advance at the Battle of Poitiers. After this defeat, the Umayyad armies retreated to their territories in Spain.

Umayyad caliphs also attempted to conquer the Christian kingdom of Nubia south of Egypt to obtain its gold and spread Islam. The Nubians repelled several Muslim invasions, however, and a peace treaty was signed between the Umayyad caliphate and Nubian kingdoms. This treaty was without parallel because the Nubians belonged to the "House of War." But what the Arabs failed to achieve through conquest, they gradually gained through immigration. By the fourteenth century, Muslim emigrants had Islamized Nubia. While struggling with the Nubians, Umayyad armies also attacked Byzantine territories, sometimes reaching as far as Constantinople, which they besieged but were never able to capture.

Umayyad armies moved eastward with equal speed and success. They reached modern Pakistan and India and captured the caravan city of Samarkand in central Asia, which was a hub on the trade route to China. In 751, just after the murder of the last Umayyad caliph, Muslim armies defeated Chinese troops at the Battle of Talas in central Asia. One consequence of this encounter between Arabs and Chinese was the introduction of paper from China into the Islamic world, from which it gradually spread to Christian Europe.

Like the Battle of Poitiers, which marked the limit of the Umayyads' expansion into western Europe, the Battle of Talas established the limit of Muslim military conquests into central Asia. For the next four centuries, these borders would define the Islamic world.

View the Map

Interactive Map: The Spread of Islam

Justice in History
"Judgment Belongs to God Alone":
ARBITRATION AT SIFFIN

On a spring day in 657, two Muslim armies confronted each other at Siffin, a village on the Euphrates River in Mesopotamia. Men who had been long-time rivals, the Caliph Ali (r. 656–661) and Muawiya, the governor of Syria, commanded the armies. Their rivalry stemmed from Muawiya's refusal to accept Ali's authority as caliph. The Battle of Siffin became a defining moment in the development of the Islamic state. Basic Islamic ideas about divine judgment were put to the test, leading to passionate debate about how God makes his judgment known to Muslims.

Ali had taken power after the assassination of Caliph Uthman, in 656. The murder went unpunished, but many people considered Ali responsible because as caliph he appointed officials known to have taken part in the murder and because he had never disavowed the crime. Uthman belonged to the influential Umayyad clan, and his supporters and family felt obliged to avenge his death. Chief among Ali's opponents was Muawiya, a leading Umayyad, who had a strong army and powerful support in Syria.

Muawiya's and Ali's quarrel also involved tensions within the Muslim community. The earliest converts to Islam and their descendants believed that their association with Muhammad entitled them to greater status than the many new non-Arab converts to Islam, most of whom supported Ali, enjoyed. The early converts supported Muawiya as did tribal leaders who opposed the caliph's growing authority.

The newer converts to Islam also had complaints. In their view, the earliest Muslims, including the Umayyad clan, enjoyed unfair privileges in the Islamic community even though all Muslims were supposed to be equals.

When Ali and Muawiya confronted each other at Siffin, they hesitated to fight because many of their soldiers recoiled from shedding the blood of other Muslims. As one of Ali's followers said,

> It is one of the worst wrongs and most terrible trials that we should be sent against our own people and they against us. . . . Yet, if we do not assist our community and act faithfully toward our leader, we deny our faith, and if we do that, we abandon our honor and extinguish our fire.[1]

So for three months, the armies only skirmished.

Finally, in July 657, real fighting broke out. Ali encouraged his men with these words: "Be steadfast! May God's spirit descend on you, and may God make you firm with conviction so that he who is put to flight knows that he displeases his God. . . ."

The battle came to a sudden halt when Muawiya's soldiers held up pages of the Qur'an on the ends of their spears and appealed for arbitration. Ali's men demanded that their leader settle his differences with Muawiya peacefully through arbitration.

Arab tribes frequently used third-party arbitrators to mediate their conflicts. Muhammad himself had been a skilled mediator before Islam was revealed to him. However, the arbitration between Ali and Muawiya failed, and the two men and their armies separated without having reached an agreement. For the next four years, Ali continued to rule as caliph, but his authority declined because many Arabs interpreted his willingness to go to arbitration as a sign of the weakness of his cause.

In contrast, Muawiya's power grew. He claimed the caliphate for himself and began to make deals with the tribal leaders. In 661 the Ummayyads arranged Ali's assassination, and Muawiya became caliph.

That the arbitration at Siffin occurred at all had lasting consequences. A small but influential faction of Ali's followers argued that God was the only true arbitrator. They believed that Ali should have refused arbitration and submitted to God's judgment through battle. These Muslims wanted to fight Muawiya to find out what God wanted. This splinter group became known as the Kharijites or "secessionists" because they seceded from Ali's followers. The Kharijites expressed their view of justice in the phrase "Judgment belongs to God alone."

The Kharijites also maintained that Ali was not only wrong to accept human arbitration, but that he and his supporters had thereby committed an unpardonable sin and should no longer be considered Muslims. The Kharijites claimed that they were the only true Muslims. Although their numbers were small,

THE QUR'AN Muslim artists devised elaborate Arabic scripts to enhance the beauty of the Qur'an, the holiest text of their faith. This page of the Qur'an is an example of the ninth-century Islamic School script from Tunisia.

(continued on next page)

(continued from previous page)

they established independent communities within the Islamic Empire until they disappeared from the historical record in the tenth century.

Other Muslims who disagreed with the Kharijites proclaimed that neither the Kharijites nor any other human being could know whether sinners were still Muslims in the eyes of God. In their opinion, believers would discover God's judgment on these matters only at the End of Days, when God will judge all humanity.

For Discussion

During this early Islamic Empire, how did different beliefs about how God makes his judgment known influence the Islamic sense of the forms human justice should take?

Taking It Further

W. M. Watt. *The Formative Period of Islamic Thought.* 1973. This account discusses the formation of sects and political groups in early Islamic history.

GOVERNING THE ISLAMIC EMPIRE The Umayyads developed a highly centralized regime that changed the political character of the Muslim community. The first Umayyad caliph, Muawiya (r. 661–680), established a hereditary monarchy to ensure orderly succession of power. This was a major change in the caliphate. Unlike the first four caliphs, who ruled by virtue of their prestige (as did Arab tribal chiefs) and more importantly by the consent of the community, the Umayyads made the caliphate an authoritarian institution. Because of this, some soldiers protested that the Umayyads had turned "God's servants into slaves," corrupted the faith, and seized the property of God. A second civil war broke out (683–692) between these protestors and the Umayyads, but the Umayyads emerged victorious.

To control their vast empire, Umayyad rulers had to create a new administrative system that both borrowed from and supplanted Byzantine and Persian institutions. The Umayyads designed new provinces that replaced old Byzantine and Persian administrative units. The Umayyads also created a professional bureaucracy based in Damascus to meet their expanding financial needs and ensure that the taxes collected in the provinces reached the central treasury. Most of the administrators had served the Byzantine or Persian Empires and were non-Muslims, although many converted to Islam. These officials provided administrative continuity between the conquered empires and the caliphate.

After the Umayyads made Arabic the official language of their empire, it gradually replaced the languages of the conquered peoples. Only in Persia (now Iran) did Persian, which later evolved into modern Farsi, survive as a widely spoken language, and even there Arabic was the language of government. In the Umayyad caliphate, Arabic functioned as Latin had done in the Roman Empire: It provided a common language for diverse subject peoples. By 800 Arabic had become the essential language of administration and international commerce from Spain to central Asia.

The rapid expansion of Islam created problems for Umayyad rulers eager to consolidate their power. Arab armies had conquered enormous territories, but Arabs were only a small minority among the huge non-Muslim majority. The Umayyads established garrison cities to hold down local populations. Just as Greek colonists followed in the footsteps of Alexander the Great in the fourth century B.C.E., many Arab settlers from the Arabian peninsula migrated to newly conquered lands. They established themselves first in the garrison towns where government officials were based and then in major cities, such as Alexandria, Jerusalem, and Antioch. Some immigrants came from nomadic tribes that adopted a settled way of life for the first time. Others were farmers from the highlands of Yemen, who brought sophisticated irrigation systems and agricultural techniques to their new homes.

Arabs also founded new cities. In Egypt they built Fustat, which would later become Cairo. In North Africa, they established Kairouan in Tunisia. In Mesopotamia they created Basra, an important port on the Persian Gulf and Kufa on the Euphrates River. Though built on a smaller scale than the major urban centers of the Roman and Persian Empires, most new Arab cities drew from Hellenistic town planning. They

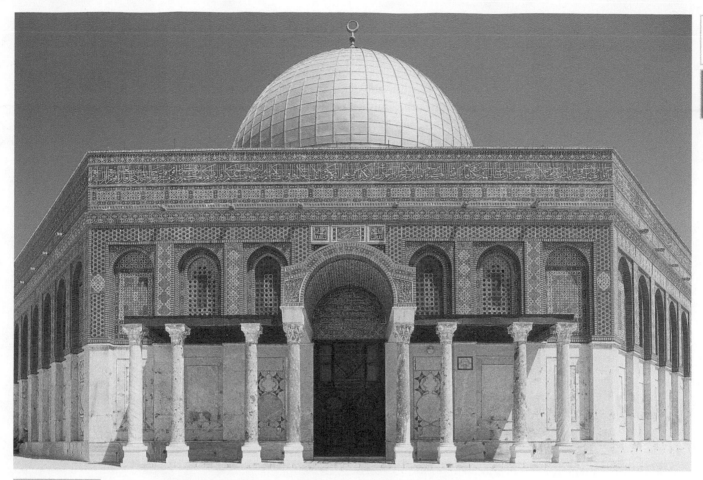

THE DOME OF THE ROCK IN JERUSALEM The Dome of the Rock, an eight-sided building with a gilded dome, dominates Jerusalem's skyline. Completed in 692 on the Temple Mount (the site of the Jewish Temple destroyed by the Romans in 69 C.E.), the building encloses a rock projecting from the floor. During the sixteenth century, the story began to circulate that when Muhammad ascended to heaven, his winged horse took one leap from Mecca to the rock and then sprang skyward.

had a square shape, walls with gates on all four sides, towers, and a central plaza. In the heart of these cities, Umayyad caliphs built a mosque to emphasize the central role of Islam in community life and to celebrate their own authority. The magnificent mosques in Damascus, Jerusalem, and other cities were intended to surpass the grand Christian churches in prestige.

Patterns of daily activity also changed under Muslim rule. With Islam now dominating public life, cities ceased to celebrate Greco–Roman culture. Theaters fell out of use because there was no Arabic tradition of publicly performed drama and comedy. The exercise fields, sports buildings, libraries, schools, and gymnasiums surviving from the Classical Age were also abandoned or adapted for other purposes. Revenues once earmarked for gymnasiums and public buildings now went to local mosques. These centers of Islamic urban culture replaced the forums and agoras of the Roman and Greek world as the chief public space for men. Mosque schools provided education for the community. Muslims gathered at mosques for public festivals and, of course, for religious worship. In their capacity as administrative centers, mosques provided courtrooms, assembly halls, and treasuries for the community. Judges, tax collectors, bureaucrats, and emissaries from the caliph conducted their affairs in the mosque precinct.

During the Umayyad caliphate, most Muslims were farmers and artisans who lived in prosperous villages. Many of these small communities stood on the vast estates of rich landowners who controlled the workers' labor. The caliphate also sponsored huge land reclamation projects on the edges of the desert in Syria and Mesopotamia.

Officials of the imperial government drew revenues directly from the villages that sprang up in these new farmlands.

BECOMING MUSLIMS Islam sharply defined the differences between Muslims and their non-Muslim subjects. Muslim conquerors understood themselves as a community of faith. Only those who converted to Islam could fully participate in the Islamic community. Their ethnicity did not matter. The Qur'an states that "there is no compulsion in religion," meaning that monotheists (Jews, Christians, and Zoroastrians) cannot be forced to convert to Islam. These monotheists were required to accept Islamic political authority, pay a special tax, and accept other restrictions. But polytheists could not be tolerated and had the choice of conversion to Islam or death.

Under the Umayyads, 10 percent of the total population in the caliphate were Muslim. Most of the first converts had probably been Christians, Jews, and Zoroastrians who willingly accepted Islam. Other converts were slaves in the households of their Muslim owners whose willingness to convert is less easy to determine. Still others were villagers who migrated to garrison cities and converted to share in the spoils of conquest—and avoid the taxes non-Muslims had to pay. Their eagerness to convert so threatened the tax base that some Muslim officials refused to acknowledge their conversion and sent them back to their villages.

Conversion to Islam increased as Muslim armies fought their way across North Africa. In the huge area that stretches from Egypt to the Atlantic Ocean, the Muslims conquered many polytheist ethnic groups whom the Arab conquerors collectively called Berbers. Faced with the choice of conversion or death, many Berbers joined the victorious Muslim armies. Islam unified the Berber populations and brought them into a wider Islamic world. With the aid of these additional troops, Islamic power spread even more quickly across North Africa and into Spain.

PEOPLES OF THE BOOK How do empires govern subject peoples? Do subjects have the same privileges and obligations as their rulers? Can they freely enter into the society of their masters? Previous chapters showed how the Egyptians, Assyrians, Persians, Hellenistic Greeks, and Romans answered these questions. Though their solutions differed, none of these great empires considered the religions of their subjects when deciding their place in society.

By distinguishing their subjects on religious, not ethnic, grounds, the Umayyad caliphate took a different approach to governing their subject peoples. Jews, Christians, and Zoroastrians constituted the main religions among conquered peoples. Islamic law called them "Peoples of the Book" because each of these religious communities had a sacred book and they lived as *dhimmis*, non-Muslims protected by the Muslim state. They had lower status than Muslims, but they were free to practice their religion; however, they could not make converts. Islamic law forbade their persecution or forcible conversion. For this reason, large communities of Jews, Christians, and Zoroastrians lived peacefully under Muslim rule.

Several Christian communities, separated by old controversies about doctrinal issues, coexisted within the Islamic Empire because the caliphate was indifferent to which Christian doctrine they followed. Followers of the Chalcedonian Orthodox Church changed the language of prayer from Greek to Syriac and then to Arabic. Though these Christians had no direct political ties with Constantinople, they followed the Byzantine emperors' Chalcedonian Orthodoxy (see Chapter 7). Thus, their church was called the Melkite, or Royal, Church. The Melkite Church is still the largest Christian community in the Middle East today. Anti-Chalcedonian (Monophysite) Christians formed the Jacobite Church in the late sixth century. The Jacobite Bible and prayers are in Syriac. The Nestorian Church, comprising Christians who emphasized Jesus's humanity rather than the combination of his humanity and divinity, also flourished under Muslim rule. Nestorian missionaries established communities in India, central

Asia, and China. The variety of Christian communities in the caliphate was greater than in Byzantium and the Latin Christian kingdoms where laws enforced conformity to the dogmas of one particular Church, Orthodox or Catholic.

Jewish communities also flourished throughout Umayyad lands, notably in southern Spain and Mesopotamia. Jews found their subordinate but protected status under Islam preferable to the open persecution they suffered in many Christian kingdoms. In Persia, Zoroastrian communities fared less well under Islamic rule. As they were slowly forced into remote regions, their numbers dwindled. In the tenth century, many Zoroastrians migrated to India, where they are known today as *Farsis*, a word that means "Persians."

COMMERCIAL ENCOUNTERS To strengthen their rule, the Umayyads transformed the economic system of the empire. From the time of their first conquests, Muslim rulers derived revenues primarily from the huge amounts of gold and silver taken in war, taxes, and contributions Muslims made to support widows and orphans. To increase their revenues, Umayyad rulers introduced a land tax for Muslim landowners, in imitation of Byzantine and Persian taxation. Even the proud Arab tribesmen, for whom paying taxes was humiliating because it implied subordination, had to pay taxes, though less than non-Muslims paid. With land tax revenues, the Umayyads could afford a standing professional army. This further reduced the fighting role of Arab tribes, enabling caliphs to cement their authority more firmly.

The peace the empire brought led to the rapid expansion of long-distance trade. Although merchants could travel safely from Morocco to central Asia and earn great profits, such expeditions were expensive. The Qur'an approved of mercantile trading, and Islamic law permitted letters of credit, loans, and other financial instruments that made commerce over huge distances possible long before Christian Europe had such sophisticated commercial tools.

Umayyad rulers further stimulated international commerce by creating a new currency that imitated Persian and Byzantine coinage. The Persian silver *drahm* (a word derived from the Greek *drachma*) inspired the Umayyad *dirham,* which became the standard coin throughout the caliphate by the 780s. Muslim merchants, and businessmen as far away as western Europe, Scandinavia, and Russia, paid for goods with silver dirhams. For gold coinage the Umayyads minted the *dinar* (a word derived from a Roman coin, the *denarius*). Like the dirham, the dinar also became a standard coin in the caliphate and distant lands. Merchants could depend on the value of this currency wherever they did business.

Umayyad caliphs also encouraged maritime trade. Alexandria in Egypt became the chief Mediterranean port for Arab commercial shipping. The Umayyads maintained peace in the Persian Gulf and the Indian Ocean. Arab merchants sailed to India and the city of Guangzhou in southern China, following the sea routes Persian navigators had established. Arab traders also sailed down the coast of East Africa to obtain slaves and natural resources such as ivory and gold from the interior. In later centuries Muslim navigators reached Malaysia, Indochina, Indonesia, and the Philippines.

The Abbasid Caliphate

After the last Umayyad caliph died in a battle in 750, the Abbasid clan, who were descendants of Muhammad's uncle, seized the caliphate and tried to exterminate the Umayyad family. The only Umayyad to escape, Abd al-Rahman I (r. 756–788), fled to Spain where he founded what would later become the caliphate of Córdoba.

The Abbasid caliphate (750–945) quickly altered the character of the Muslim world. In 762–763, the Abbasids built a new capital in Baghdad where they were exposed to the ceremonial and administrative traditions of Persia, which helped expand the intellectual horizons of the caliphs, their courtiers, and bureaucrats.

The Abbasid caliphs expanded their control over society, but they were far from despots. The caliph was first and foremost an emir—that is, the commander of a professional army. He was also responsible for internal security, which meant suppressing rebellions, supervising officials, and making sure taxes were honestly collected. But he did not interfere with other public institutions, such as mosques, hospitals, and schools. The principal exception was the office of market inspector, through which the caliph guaranteed fair business practices. In this commitment to the integrity of markets and trade, the Islamic caliphate was more advanced than either Byzantium, where privileged monopolies dominated the economy, or the Latin states of Europe, where a market economy hardly existed.

The period of Abbasid greatness lasted about a century (754–861), and its literature reflects its eclectic nature. The famous *Arabian Nights,* stories written down for the caliph Harun al-Rashid (r. 786–809), were based on Hellenistic, Jewish, Indian, and Arab legends. The *Arabian Nights* and the rich tradition of Arabic poetry, which often recounted tales of thwarted love, in turn influenced the western Christian poetry of romantic love. Harun al-Rashid began the grand project of translating into Arabic the literature of ancient Greece and texts from Syria, India, and Persia.

Philosophical and scientific inquiry thrived under Caliph al-Mamun (r. 813–833), who had an astronomical observatory built in Baghdad and appreciated the work of al-Kindi (d. ca. 870), the first outstanding Islamic philosopher. Al-Kindi grappled with questions specific to Islam but also with the works of Aristotle and problems in astrology, medicine, optics, arithmetic, cooking, and metallurgy. This made him well-known outside the Islamic world. The work of Arabic translators in the ninth and tenth centuries created a crucial cultural link between the ancient and medieval worlds. The Muslims supplied Arabic translations of ancient Greek and Syriac texts to a later generation of Jews and Christians in Spain, who translated them into Latin. These second- and third-hand Latin translations of ancient philosophy and science became the core of the university curriculum in western Europe during the twelfth century.

Abbasid political power ended in 945 when a clan of rough tribesmen from northwest Persia seized Baghdad. The Abbasid caliphs remained in office as religious and ceremonial figureheads; despite occasional attempts to reinvigorate the caliphate, its power as a ruling institution was over. However, the caliphate remained a vital symbol of Islamic unity and survived as a formal institution until 1924.

Read the Document

Harun al-Rashid and the Zenith of the Caliphate

Islamic Civilization in Europe

During the eighth and ninth centuries, the Muslim armies chipped away at Christian territories in Europe. Unlike their fellow Muslims in the Middle East and North Africa, most of the Muslims in Europe conducted themselves more as raiders than conquerors. They plundered and pillaged but did not stay long or attempt a mass conversion of Christians to Islam. These raids, however, made urban life impossible, and many Mediterranean cities almost disappeared. To survive, populations fled into the countryside, where families could live off the land and find protection with one of the local lords who built castles for defense.

The significant exceptions to the pattern of raiding were in Sicily and Spain. Between 828 and 965, Muslim armies conquered Sicily. Arab farmers and merchants migrated there from North Africa, and Islam spread among the general population although most Sicilians remained Christian. In Spain, Muslim conquests in the early eighth century brought the peninsula into the orbit of Islam except for small Christian states in the extreme north.

Sicily and Spain became the principal borderlands through which Arabic learning and science filtered into Catholic Europe. These borderlands became zones of intense cultural interaction, where several languages were spoken and where Christians and

Jews were allowed to observe their own faiths. Although small, Muslim Sicily and Spain were among the most dynamic places in Europe during the eighth to early eleventh centuries. No Christian city in western Europe could rival Córdoba, capital of Muslim Spain, in size and prosperity. Even within the Muslim world, only Baghdad could compare to it. A German nun visiting Córdoba during the tenth century thought the city embodied "the majesty and adornment of the world, the wondrous capital . . . radiating in affluence of all earthly blessings."[2]

The caliphate of Córdoba became the most important intellectual capital in western Europe, renowned for the learning of its Muslim and Jewish scholars. Córdoba's fame derived from the extensive authority and magnificent building projects encouraged by Caliph Abd al-Rahman III (r. 912–961) and his three successors. With an ethnically mixed population of more than 100,000, Córdoba boasted 700 mosques, 3,000 public baths, 5,000 silk looms, and 70 libraries. The caliph's library housed more than 400,000 volumes. The streets of the city were paved and illuminated at night, the best houses enjoyed indoor plumbing, and the rich had country villas as vacation retreats. (Rome did not erect streetlamps for another 1,000 years.) Besides the great mosque, which was one of the most famous religious monuments in Islam, the architectural centerpiece of the city was Madinat az-Zahra, a 400-room palace that Abd al-Rahman III built for his favorite concubine, Zahra. Adorned with marble and semiprecious stones from Constantinople, the palace took 20 years to build and housed 13,000 household servants in addition to the diplomats and courtiers who attended the caliph.

GREAT MOSQUE OF CÓRDOBA The great mosque of Córdoba was one of the wonders of the world during the tenth century. Because Islam prohibited the depiction of the human body, mosques were embellished with geometrical forms and quotations from the Qur'an. The repetition of multiple arches creates an intricate pattern that changes as the viewer moves about in the space.

The influence of the golden age of Córdoba in the tenth century can be found in the legacy of the poets, scientists, physicians, astronomers, and architects who thrived under the caliphs' patronage. Despite tensions between Muslims and Jews, many of the intellectuals in the caliphs' court were Arabized Jews. Typical of the many non-Muslims who served Arab rulers, Hasdai ibn Shaprut (915–970), who was probably a Jew, became famous for his medical skills, in particular his antidotes for poisons. In the caliphs' court the demand for his cures was strong, because several princes had fallen victim to conspiracies hatched in the palace harem or had been poisoned by their lovers. The trust that Hasdai gained from his medical skills led the caliph to appoint him to deal with sensitive customs and diplomatic disputes. Both Muslim and Christian rulers considered Jews such as Hasdai politically neutral, making them prized as diplomatic envoys. The Jew Samuel ibn Nagrela (993–1055) became vizier (chief minister) of the neighboring Muslim kingdom of Granada. An able Hebrew poet, biblical commentator, and philosopher, he also commanded Muslim armies. Nagrela's career reflected the value Muslims placed on learning and talent.

During the early eleventh century, succession disputes led to the murder of several caliphs, and the caliphate of Córdoba splintered into small states. The disunity of Muslim Spain provided opportunities for the stubborn little Christian states of the

📖 Read the Document

Ibn Khaldun, from the *Muqaddimah*

north to push against the frontiers of their opulent Muslim neighbors. The kingdom of Navarre under Sancho III (r. 1004–1035) was the first to achieve dramatic success against the Muslims. After his death his conquests were divided into the kingdoms of Navarre, Aragon, and Castile. During the reign of Alfonso VI (r. 1065–1109), Castile became the dominant military power in Spain. Forcing Muslims to pay him tribute

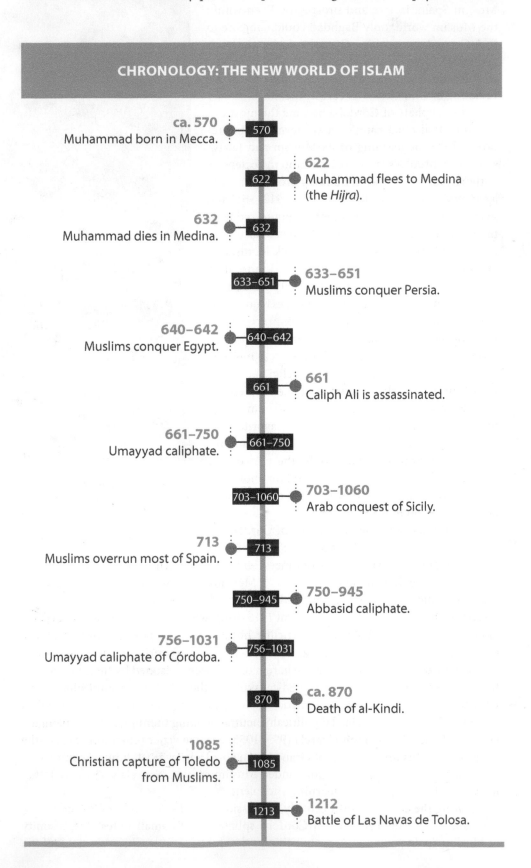

CHRONOLOGY: THE NEW WORLD OF ISLAM

ca. 570 | 570 |
Muhammad born in Mecca.

| 622 | **622**
Muhammad flees to Medina (the *Hijra*).

632 | 632 |
Muhammad dies in Medina.

| 633–651 | **633–651**
Muslims conquer Persia.

640–642 | 640–642 |
Muslims conquer Egypt.

| 661 | **661**
Caliph Ali is assassinated.

661–750 | 661–750 |
Umayyad caliphate.

| 703–1060 | **703–1060**
Arab conquest of Sicily.

713 | 713 |
Muslims overrun most of Spain.

| 750–945 | **750–945**
Abbasid caliphate.

756–1031 | 756–1031 |
Umayyad caliphate of Córdoba.

| 870 | **ca. 870**
Death of al-Kindi.

1085 | 1085 |
Christian capture of Toledo
from Muslims.

| 1213 | **1212**
Battle of Las Navas de Tolosa.

and helped by French knights eager for plunder and French monks ardent for converts, Alfonso launched a campaign known as the **Spanish Reconquest** that led to the capture of the city of Toledo in 1085. The center of Spanish Christianity before the Muslim conquests, Toledo provided Alfonso with a glorious prize that made him famous throughout Christian Europe (see **Map 8.3**).

The loss of Toledo so shocked the Muslim states in Spain that they asked for help from a sect of North African warriors called the Almoravids. The Almoravids defeated Alfonso VI and temporarily halted the Spanish Reconquest in 1086. But in 1212 at the Battle of Las Navas de Tolosa, the Christian kingdoms united to defeat the Muslims. Within two generations most Spanish Muslim cities, including Córdoba in 1236, fell to Christian armies. A few remnants of Muslim power hung on in Spain until 1492.

CONCLUSION

Three Cultural Realms

The death of the Byzantine Emperor Justinian I in 565 marked the last time one imperial ruler would control most of the territory from Spain to Syria. The Persian Empire still menaced Byzantium's eastern frontier, and except for Italy and some coastal areas of Spain, Germanic kings ruled western Europe. During the next two centuries, western Europe, the Mediterranean world, and the Middle East as

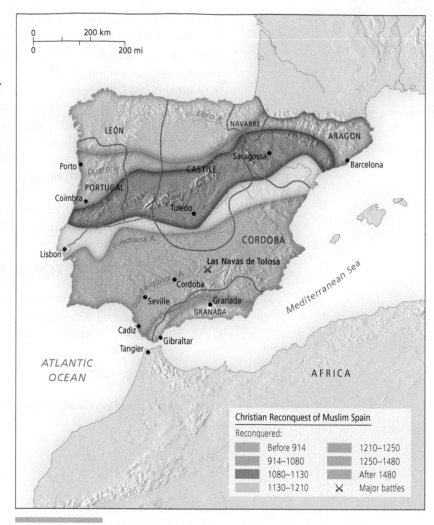

MAP 8.3 CHRISTIAN RECONQUEST OF MUSLIM SPAIN The Spanish Reconquest refers to the numerous military campaigns by the Christian kingdoms of northern Spain to capture the Muslim-controlled cities and kingdoms of southern Spain. This long, intermittent struggle began with the capture of Toledo in 1085 and lasted until Muslim Granada fell to Christian armies in 1492. What effects might this long series of engagement have had on the mentality of the Spanish Christians?

far as India and central Asia were reconfigured politically and culturally. Part of that reconfiguration came about as new peoples migrated into central Europe and the Balkans from the steppe frontiers. As threatening as they were, these new arrivals were eventually absorbed into the civilizations of the West through conversions to Christianity. By ca. 750, three new realms had come into sharp focus: the Christian Byzantine Empire based at Constantinople; the vast Umayyad caliphate created by Muhammad's Islamic followers; and, as Chapter 9 examines, Latin Christendom in western Europe, which was fragmented politically but united culturally by Christianity. Each of these regions was constituted as a community of religious faith, which had, at best, a limited toleration of other faiths. The cultural foundations they established and the divisions that emerged among them still shape the West today.

These three cultural realms of the West each borrowed from the heritage of ancient Rome, especially its network of cities, which survived most completely in the Mediterranean and the Middle East in the Byzantine and Islamic Empires. The religious traditions of antiquity, especially the emphasis on monotheism in Judaism, influenced each of the three realms. They each adapted parts of Roman law and reshaped it to suit changing needs and new cultural influences. The heritage of Rome remained strongest in Byzantium. But between the sixth and eleventh centuries, these three cultural realms came to be distinguished by the language that dominated intellectual and religious life

Spanish Reconquest Refers to the numerous military campaigns by the Christian kingdoms of northern Spain to capture the Muslim-controlled cities and kingdoms of southern Spain. This long, intermittent struggle began with the capture of Toledo in 1085 and lasted until Granada fell to Christian armies in 1492.

and by the forms of monotheism each practiced. In Byzantium the Greek language and Orthodox Christianity with its elaborate ceremonies defined the culture. By the end of the Umayyad caliphate in 750, the Arabic language and many Islamic beliefs and practices were becoming standard over a wide area. In western Europe, many languages were spoken, but Latin became the universal language of the Church and government.

The end of the Umayyad caliphate saw the limit of Muslim expansion in western Europe and central Asia. After that the Byzantine Empire struggled for survival. In Chapter 9 we will see how the kingdom of the Franks arrested Muslim incursions into western Europe. However, the very survival of many western European kingdoms was put to the test during the ninth and tenth centuries by yet more invasions and migrations from the Eurasian steppes and Scandinavia. By the end of the eleventh century, Latin Christianity had gathered sufficient cohesion and military strength to launch a vast counterstroke against Islam in the form of the Crusades.

MAKING CONNECTIONS

1. How did the Byzantine Empire manage to hold off so many enemies for so long?
2. Why did Islam split between Sunnis and Shi'ites?
3. Should Muslim countries be considered part of the West?

TAKING IT FURTHER

For suggested readings, websites, and films, see page R-1.

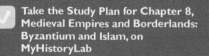

Chapter Review

Byzantium: The Survival of the Roman Empire

8.1 How did the Roman Empire's eastern provinces evolve into the Byzantine Empire?

Eastern and western Christians gradually grew apart until they were separate civilizations, one Byzantine and the other Latin. Besides difference of language, they held different opinions about religious matters, such as the rituals of the liturgy, the role of images in worship, and the authority of the pope. Eventually, the Byzantine Empire was reduced to a regional power struggling for survival against many enemies.

The New World of Islam

8.2 How did Islam develop in Arabia, and how did its followers create a vast empire so quickly?

Through forced conversion, negotiation, and by strictly regulating the internal affairs of the community and its relations with outsiders, Muhammad grew his new religious community and unified most of Arabia under Islam. After his death, the Umayyad dynasty's talented leaders consolidated their control of conquered territories and established peace in the empire before resuming wars of conquest. Immigration of Muslims throughout Arabia also contributed to the spread of Islam.

Chapter Time Line

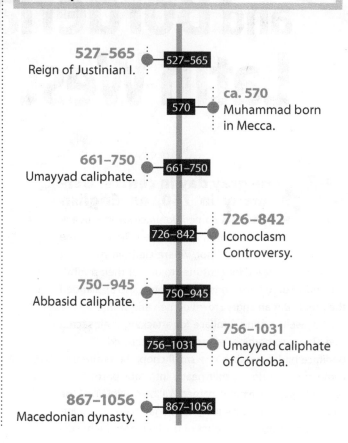

527–565 Reign of Justinian I. — 527–565

ca. 570 — 570 Muhammad born in Mecca.

661–750 Umayyad caliphate. — 661–750

726–842 — 726–842 Iconoclasm Controversy.

750–945 Abbasid caliphate. — 750–945

756–1031 — 756–1031 Umayyad caliphate of Córdoba.

867–1056 Macedonian dynasty. — 867–1056

9 Medieval Empires and Borderlands: The Latin West

One gray day in central Germany in 740, an English monk named Boniface swung his axe at an enormous oak tree. This was the sacred Oak of Thor, where German men and women had prayed for centuries to one of their mightiest gods. Some local Christians cheered and applauded the monk. But an angry crowd of men and women gathered as well, cursing Boniface for attacking their sacred tree. Then something extraordinary occurred. Though Boniface had only taken one small chop, the entire tree came crashing down, split neatly into four parts. Boniface's biographer, a monk named Willibald, explained the strange event as God's judgment against "pagan" worshipers. In Willibald's account of the incident, the hostile crowd was so impressed by the miracle that they immediately embraced Christianity. As the news spread, more and more Germans converted, and Boniface's fame grew. According to Willibald, "The sound of Boniface's name was heard through the greater part of Europe. From the land of Britain, a great host of monks came to him— readers, and writers, and men trained in other skills."[1]

Boniface played a leading role in spreading Christianity among the peoples of northern Europe. The Christian

THE IMAGE OF A MAN (*IMAGO HOMINIS*) In this eighth-century manuscript, the image of a man symbolizes the evangelist Matthew. The other three evangelists, Mark, Luke, and John, were symbolized by a lion, bull, and eagle, all fixed signs of the zodiac, created by ancient polytheist astronomers. The adaptation of Christianity to pagan symbolism conveyed the message that Christianity represented the fulfillment of ancient wisdom.

LEARNING OBJECTIVES

9.1 ((	9.2 ((	9.3 ((	9.4 ((
How did Latin Christendom build on Rome's legacy and how did Christianity spread?	How did the Carolingian Empire contribute to establishing a distinctive western European culture?	How did Latin Christianity consolidate itself after the collapse of the Carolingian Empire?	What were the causes and consequences of the Crusades?

((Listen to Chapter 9 on MyHistoryLab

◉ Watch the Video Series on MyHistoryLab

Learn about some key topics related to this chapter with the *MyHistoryLab Video Series: Key Topics in Western Civilization*

missionaries who traveled to lands far beyond the Mediterranean world brought Latin books and established monasteries. Through Christianity and the literacy disseminated from these monastic centers, the monks established cultural ties among the new Germanic converts to Roman learning. Historians refer to the Christianized Germanic kingdoms on the continent and Britain as *Latin Christendom* because they celebrated the Christian **liturgy** in Latin and accepted the pope's authority in Rome. Even though they no longer celebrate the liturgy in Latin as they did in the Middle Ages, Roman Catholics today continue to revere the pope and the traditions of medieval Latin Christianity.

As discussed in Chapter 8, Latin Christianity and Orthodox Christianity gradually grew apart during the Middle Ages, primarily over theological differences and disputes about who held the ultimate authority in the Church. These two issues preoccupied the clergy and bishops. For most lay Christians, however, the crucial differences were over liturgy and language. The liturgy consists of the forms of worship—prayers, chants, and rituals. In the Middle Ages there was a great deal of variety in the Christian liturgy, and a number of languages were used, but followers of the Roman church gradually came to identify themselves with the Latin liturgy and the Latin language. As a result, the diverse peoples of medieval western Europe began to be called the "Latin people."

The Latin Christendom that came to dominate western Europe joined the Greek Orthodox and Arabic Muslim civilizations that constituted the three pillars of the West during the Middle Ages. Recurrently pressing across the frontiers of the Greek Orthodox and Latin Christian civilizations were wave after wave of barbarian peoples coming from the Eurasian steppes and Scandinavia. The Avars, Rus, most Slavs, and Bulgars who threatened Byzantium became Orthodox Christians. The raiders and invaders who entered the western half of the Roman Empire—the Germanic tribes, the Magyars, some Slavs, and the Vikings—eventually became Latin Christians. Their conversions took place through missionary efforts and military expeditions that forced the conquered to convert. By the end of the eleventh century few polytheists could still be found in Europe. With the exception of the Muslim pockets in Spain and Sicily and isolated communities of Jews, Christianity had become the dominant faith.

In this crucial phase in forming Western civilization from about 350–1100, new political formations in western Europe made possible greater political cohesion that brought together ethnically and linguistically diverse peoples under obedience to an emperor or king. As in Byzantium and the Islamic caliphates, the empires and kingdoms of the Latin West enforced or encouraged uniformity of religion, spread a common language among the ruling elite, and instituted systematic principles for governing. The Carolingian Empire, which lasted from 800 to 843 and controlled much of western Europe, reestablished the Roman Empire in the West for the first time in more than 300 years and sponsored a revival of interest in Roman antiquity called the Carolingian Renaissance. The Carolingian Empire's collapse was followed by a period of anarchy as Europe faced further incursions of hostile invaders. During the eleventh century, however, the Latin West recovered in dramatic fashion. By the end of the century the Latin kingdoms were strong enough to engage in a massive counterassault against Islam, in part in defense of fellow Christians in Byzantium. These campaigns against Islam, known as the Crusades, produced a series of wars in the Middle East and North Africa that continued throughout the Middle Ages. However, the consequences of the Crusades, which poisoned relations among Christians and Muslims, have lasted well into modern times, long after the active fighting ceased. The transformations in this period raised this question:

liturgy The forms of Christian worship, including the prayers, chants, and rituals to be said, sung, or performed throughout the year.

How did Latin Christianity help strengthen the new kingdoms of the Latin West so that they were eventually able to deal effectively with both barbarian invaders and Muslim rivals?

The Birth of Latin Christendom

9.1 How did Latin Christendom build on Rome's legacy and how did Christianity spread?

By the time the Roman Empire collapsed in the West during the fifth century, numerous Germanic tribes had settled in the lands of the former empire. These tribes became the nucleus for the new Latin Christian kingdoms that emerged by 750 (see **Map 9.1**).

Germanic Kingdoms on Roman Foundations

The new Germanic kingdoms of Latin Christendom created a new kind of society. They borrowed from Roman law while establishing government institutions, but they also relied on their own traditional methods of rule. Three elements helped unify these kingdoms. First, in the Germanic kingdoms personal loyalty rather than legal rights unified society. Kinship obligations to a particular clan of blood relatives rather than citizenship, as in the Roman Empire, defined a person's place in society and his or her relationship to rulers. Second, Christianity became the dominant religion in the kingdoms. The common faith linked rulers with their subjects. And third, Latin served as the language of worship, learning, and diplomacy in these kingdoms. German

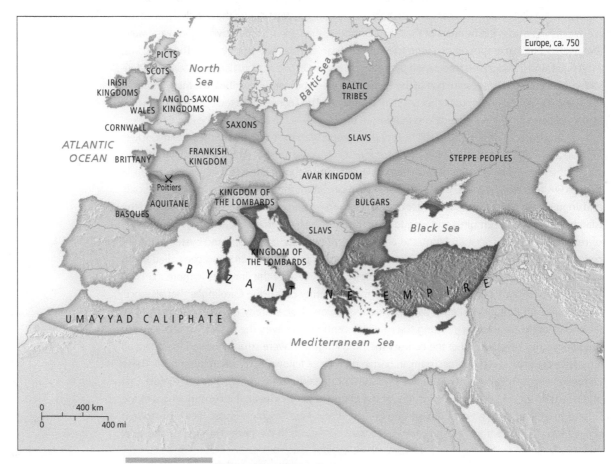

MAP **9.1** EUROPE, CA. 750 By about 750 the kingdom of the Franks had become the dominant power in western Europe. The Umayyad caliphate controlled Spain, and the Lombard kingdom governed most of Italy. The Byzantine Empire held power in Greece, as well as its core lands in Asia Minor. Based on this map, who were the dominant powers in the West: the Latin Christians of western Europe, the Greek Christians of the Byzantine Empire, or the Muslims of the Umayyad caliphate?

kingdoms based on Roman foundations appeared in Anglo-Saxon England, Frankish Gaul, Visigothic Spain, and Lombard Italy.

ANGLO-SAXON ENGLAND Roman civilization collapsed more completely in Britain during the fifth century than it did on the European continent, largely because of Britain's long distance from Rome and the small number of Romans who had settled there. About 400, the Roman economic and administrative infrastructure of Britain fell apart, and the last Roman legions left the island to fight on the continent. Raiders from the coast of the North Sea called Angles and Saxons (historians referred to them as Anglo-Saxons) took advantage of Britain's weakened defenses and launched invasions. They began to probe the island's southeast coast, pillaging the small villages they found there and establishing permanent settlements of their own.

Because the small bands of Anglo-Saxon settlers fought as often among themselves as they did against the Roman Britons, the island remained fragmented politically during the first few centuries of the invaders' rule. But by 750, three warring kingdoms managed to seize enough land to coalesce and dominate Britain: Mercia, Wessex, and Northumbria.

FRANKISH GAUL Across the English Channel from Britain lay the Roman province of Gaul. From the third to the seventh century the kingdom of the Franks, centered in Gaul, produced the largest and most powerful kingdom in western Europe. One family among the Franks, called the Merovingians, gradually gained preeminence. A crafty Merovingian war chief named Childeric ruled a powerful band of Franks from about 460 until his death in 481. With the support of his loyal soldiers, Childeric laid the foundation for the Merovingian kingdom. His energetic and ruthless son Clovis (r. 481–511) made the Franks one of the leading powers in the western provinces of the old Roman Empire. Clovis aggressively expanded his father's power base through the conquest of northern Gaul and neighboring territories. He murdered many of his relatives and other Frankish chieftains whom he considered rivals. In 486 Clovis overcame the last Roman stronghold in northern Gaul.

Around 500 the polytheist Clovis converted to Latin Christianity. About 3,000 warriors, the core of his army, joined their king in this change to the new faith. Clovis had a practical reason to convert. He intended to attack the Visigothic kingdom in southern Gaul. The Visigoths followed Arian Christianity, but their subjects, the Roman inhabitants of the region, were Latin Christians. By converting to Latin Christianity, Clovis won the support of many of the Visigoths' subjects. With their help, he crushed the Visigothic king Alaric II in 507. Clovis now controlled almost all of Gaul as far as Spain.

Read the Document

Gregory of Tours, Sixth Century

In the eighth century, however, the Merovingian kings became so ineffectual that real power passed to the man in charge of the royal household called the "Mayor of the Palace." One of these mayors, Charles Martel "the Hammer" (r. 719–741), established his personal power by regaining control over regions that had slipped away from Merovingian rule and by defeating an invading Muslim army at Poitiers in 732. Martel's son, Pepin the Short (r. 741–768), succeeded his father as Mayor of the Palace, but dethroned the last of the Merovingian monarchs and in 751 made himself king of the Franks. Pepin relied on the pope to legitimize his coup; in exchange, the Franks guaranteed the pope's safety. Thus began the vital alliance between the Frankish monarchy and the popes in Rome.

VISIGOTHIC SPAIN The Franks were never able to conquer Spain, where a Visigothic kingdom emerged. As in all the Germanic kingdoms, religion was a unifying force. Originally Arians, Visigoth kings converted to Latin Christianity in the late sixth century, and Visigothic Spain became a Latin Christian kingdom. The kings began to imitate the Byzantine emperors with the use of elaborate court ceremonies and frequent church councils as assemblies that enforced their will. Thus, the key to their success was the ability to employ the Church's spiritual authority to enhance the king's secular authority. However, the autocratic instincts of the Visigoth kings alienated many of the substantial landowners who were easily lured by the promises of Muslim invaders to treat them more favorably.

In 711 invading armies of Muslims from North Africa vanquished the last Visigothic king. As a result, most of Spain became part of the Umayyad caliphate. Many Christians from the upper classes converted to Islam to preserve their property and offices. Some survivors of the Visigoth kingdoms held on in the northwest of Spain, where they managed to keep Christianity alive.

LOMBARD ITALY Between 568 and 774, a Germanic people known as the Lombards controlled most of northern and central Italy. They were called *Langobardi,* or "Long Beards," from which the name *Lombard* derives. The Lombard king, Alboin (r. ca. 565–572), took advantage of the weakness of the Byzantine Empire and invaded Italy in 569. Alboin's army contained soldiers of different ethnic backgrounds. That lack of unity made it impossible for Alboin to build a strong, lasting kingdom.

The Lombard kings also faced two formidable external enemies—the Byzantine forces who remained in the Exarchate of Ravenna and the Franks. In 751 the Lombards' ruler defeated the Exarchate, leading to the Byzantine abandonment of Ravenna. Internal political disputes, however, prevented the Lombards from capitalizing on their victory over the Byzantines. Just two decades later the Frankish king Charlemagne invaded Italy and crushed the Lombards.

Different Kingdoms, Shared Traditions

With the exception of England, where Anglo-Saxon invaders overwhelmed the Roman population, the leaders of the new Germanic kingdoms faced a common problem: How should the Germanic minority govern subject peoples who vastly outnumbered them? These rulers solved this problem by blending Roman and Germanic traditions. For example, kings served as administrators of the civil order in the style of the Roman emperor, issuing laws and managing a bureaucracy. They also served as war leaders in the Germanic tradition, leading their men into battle in search of glory and loot. As the Germanic kings defined new roles for themselves, they discovered that Christianity could bind all their subjects together into one community of believers. The merging of Roman and Germanic traditions could also be traced in the law, which eventually erased the distinctions between Romans and Germans, and in the ability of women to own property, a right far more common among the Romans than the Germans.

CIVIL AUTHORITY: THE ROMAN LEGACY In imitation of Roman practice, the monarchs of Latin Christendom designated themselves as the source of all law and believed that they ruled with God's approval. Kings controlled all appointments to civil, military, and religious office. Accompanied by troops and administrative assistants, they also traveled throughout their lands to dispense justice, collect taxes, and enforce royal authority.

Frankish Gaul provides an apt example of how these monarchs adopted preexisting Roman institutions. When Clovis conquered the Visigoths in Gaul, he inherited the nearly intact Roman infrastructure and administrative system that had survived the collapse of Roman imperial authority. Merovingian kings (as well as Visigoth rulers in Spain and Lombards in Italy) found it useful to maintain parts of the preexisting system and kept the officials who ran them. For instance, Frankish kings relied on the bishops and counts in each region to deal with local problems. Because Roman aristocrats were literate and had experience in Roman administration on the local level, they often served as counts. Based in cities, these officials presided in local law courts, collected revenues, and raised troops for the king's army. Most bishops also stemmed from the Roman aristocracy. In addition to performing their religious responsibilities, bishops aided their king by providing for the poor, ransoming hostages who had been captured by enemy warriors from other kingdoms, and bringing social and legal injustices to the monarch's attention. Finally, the kings used dukes, most of whom were Franks, to serve as local military commanders, which made them important patrons of the community. Thus, the civil and religious administration tended to remain the responsibility of the Roman counts and bishops, but military command fell to the Frankish dukes.

WAR LEADERS AND WERGILD: THE GERMANIC LEGACY The kingdoms of Latin Christendom developed from war bands led by Germanic chieftains. By rewarding brave warriors with land and loot taken in war, as well as with revenues skimmed from subject peoples, chieftains created political communities of loyal men and their families, called **clans or kin groups**. Though these followers sometimes came from diverse backgrounds, they all owed military service to the clan chiefs. Because leadership in Germanic society was hereditary, networks of loyalty and kinship expanded through the generations. The various political communities gradually evolved into distinct ethnic groups led by a king. These ethnic groups, such as the Lombards and the Franks, developed a sense of shared history, kinship, and culture.

Kinship-based clans stood as the most basic unit of Germanic society. The clan consisted of all the households and blood relations loyal to the clan chief, a warrior who protected them and spoke on their behalf before the king on matters of justice. Clan chieftains in turn swore oaths of loyalty to their kings and agreed to fight for him in wars against other kingdoms. The clan leaders formed an aristocracy among the Germanic peoples. Like the Roman elites before them, the royal house and the clan-based aristocracy consisted of rich men and women who controlled huge estates. The new Germanic aristocrats intermarried with the preexisting Roman elites of wealthy landholders, thus maintaining control of most of the land. These people stood at the very top of the social order, winning the loyalty of their followers by giving gifts and parcels of land. Under the weight of this new upper class, the majority of the population, the ordinary farmers and artisans, slipped into a deepening dependence. Most peasants could not enter into legal transactions in their own name, and they had few protections and privileges under the law. Even so, they were better off than the slaves who toiled at society's very lowest depths. Valued simply as property, these men, women, and children had virtually no rights in the eyes of the law.

Though this social hierarchy showed some similarities to societies in earlier Roman times, the new kingdoms' various social groups were defined by law in a fundamentally different way. Unlike Roman law, which defined people by citizenship rights and obligations, the laws of the new kingdoms defined people by their **wergild**. A Germanic concept, *wergild* referred to what an individual was worth in case he or she suffered some grievance at the hands of another. If someone injured or murdered someone else, wergild was the amount of compensation in gold that the wrongdoer's family had to pay to the victim's family.

In the wergild system, every person had a price that depended on social status and perceived usefulness to the community. For example, among the Lombards service to the king increased a free man's worth—his wergild was higher than that of a peasant. In the Frankish kingdom, if a freeborn woman of childbearing age was murdered, the killer's family had to pay 600 pieces of gold. Noble women and men had higher wergild than peasants, while slaves and women past childbearing age were worth very little.

UNITY THROUGH LAW AND CHRISTIANITY Within the kingdoms of Latin Christendom, rulers tried to achieve unity by merging Germanic and Roman legal principles

clans or kin groups The basic social and political unit of Germanic society consisting of blood relatives obliged to defend one another and take vengeance for crimes against the group and its members.

wergild In Germanic societies, the term referred to what an individual was worth in case he or she suffered an injury. It was the amount of compensation in gold that the wrongdoer's family had to pay to the victim's family.

and by accepting the influence of the Church. Religious diversity among the peoples in their kingdoms made this unity difficult to establish. As discussed in Chapter 7, many of the tribes that invaded the Roman Empire during the fifth century practiced Arian Christianity. They kept themselves apart from the Latin Christians by force of law. For example, they declared marriage between Arian and Latin Christians illegal.

These barriers began to collapse when Germanic kings converted to the Latin Christianity of their Roman subjects. Some converted for reasons of personal belief or because their wives were Latin Christians. Others decided to become Latin Christians to gain wider political support. For instance, when Clovis converted about 500, laws against intermarriage between Arians and Latin Christians in Gaul disappeared. More and more Franks and Romans began to marry one another, blending the two formerly separate communities into one and reinforcing the strength of the Latin Church. By 750 most of the western European kingdoms had officially become Latin Christian, though substantial pockets of polytheist practice survived and communities of Jews were allowed to practice their faith.

Germanic kings adopted Latin Christianity, but they had no intention of abandoning their own Germanic law, which differed from Roman law on many issues, especially relating to the family and property. Instead, they offered their Roman subjects the opportunity to live under the Germanic law that governed the king. Clovis's *Law Code* or *Salic Law,* published sometime between 508 and 511, illustrated this development. The *Law Code* applied to Franks and to any other non-Roman peoples in his realm who chose to live according to Frankish law. Because the Romans dwelling in the Frankish kingdom technically still followed the laws of Byzantium, Clovis did not presume to legislate for them. Romans could follow their own law if they wished, or they could follow his laws and become Franks. By 750, however, most Romans had chosen to abandon their legal identity as Romans and live according to Frankish law, and the distinction between Roman and Frank lost all meaning. A similar process occurred in the other Germanic kingdoms. This unification of peoples under one law happened without protest, a sign that various groups had blended politically, religiously, and culturally.

GERMAN AND ROMAN WOMEN Roman law influenced more than just local administration in Latin Christendom. It also prompted Germanic rulers to reconsider the question of a woman's right to inherit land. In the Roman Empire, women had inherited land without difficulty. Indeed, perhaps as much as 25 percent of the land in the entire empire had been owned by women. In many Germanic societies, however, men could inherit land and property far more easily than women. Attitudes about female inheritance began to shift when the Germanic settlers established their homes in previously Roman provinces—and began to marry Roman women who owned property. However, the position of women varied a great deal among the Germanic tribes. Lombard law was much more restrictive for women than Frankish law where even a slave woman could become a queen.

By comparing the law codes of the new kingdoms over time, historians have detected the impact of Roman customs on Germanic inheritance laws. By the late eighth century, women in Frankish Gaul, Visigothic Spain, and even Lombard Italy could inherit land, though often under the restriction that they had to eventually pass it on to their sons. Despite these limitations, the new laws transformed women's lives. A woman who received an inheritance of land could live more independently, support herself if her husband died, and have a say in the community's decisions. Among the Merovingian Franks, women enjoyed especially high levels of respect. They participated in public assemblies and even appeared in law courts as advocates. They were so prominent that churchmen repeatedly admonished them to stay out of public affairs because it was unseemly. However, women's roles in household management, even of large estates and entire kingdoms, was unquestioned.

Most women, however, like most men, did not possess large estates or any landed property for that matter. Women managed and worked in the inner economy of the household; this included grinding grain with the hand-held rotary mill, cooking, baking, brewing, and especially making cloth. A number of crafts remained the exclusive preserve of women, as indicated by the Old English suffix "-ster," which indicated the feminine. A *webster* was a female weaver, a *brewster* a female brewer, for example. The term *spinster* survives in modern English to indicate an unmarried woman, who in the early Middle Ages would have worked at spinning.

The Spread of Latin Christianity in the New Kingdoms of Western Europe

As Latin Christianity spread as the official religion through the new kingdoms, churchmen decided that they had a moral responsibility to convert all the people of these kingdoms and beyond. They sent out missionaries to explain the religion to nonbelievers and challenge the worship of polytheist gods.

Meanwhile, bishops based in cities directed people's spiritual lives, instilling the moral and social conventions of Christianity through sermons delivered in church. Monks such as Boniface, who introduced this chapter, traveled from their home monasteries in Ireland, England, and Gaul to spread the faith to Germanic tribes east of the Rhine. Monasteries became centers of intellectual life, and monks replaced urban aristocrats as the keepers of books and learning.

THE GROWTH OF THE PAPACY In theory, the Byzantine emperors still had political authority over the city of Rome and its surrounding lands during this violent time. However, strapped for cash and troops, these distant rulers proved unequal to the task of defending the city from internal or external threats. In the resulting power vacuum, the popes stepped in to manage local affairs and became, in effect, princes who ruled over a significant part of Italy.

Gregory the Great (r. 590–604) stands out as the most powerful of these popes. The pragmatic Gregory wrote repeatedly to Constantinople, pleading for military assistance that never came. Without any relief from the Byzantines, Gregory had to look elsewhere for help. Through clever diplomacy, Gregory successfully cultivated the goodwill of the Christian communities of western Europe by offering religious sanction to the authority of friendly kings. He negotiated skillfully with his Lombard and Frankish neighbors to gain their support and establish the authority of the Roman Church. He encouraged Christian missionaries to spread the faith in England and Germany. In addition, he took steps to train educated clergymen for future generations, in this way securing Christianity's position in western Europe.

Gregory set the stage for a dramatic increase in papal power. As his successors' authority expanded over the next few centuries, relations between Rome

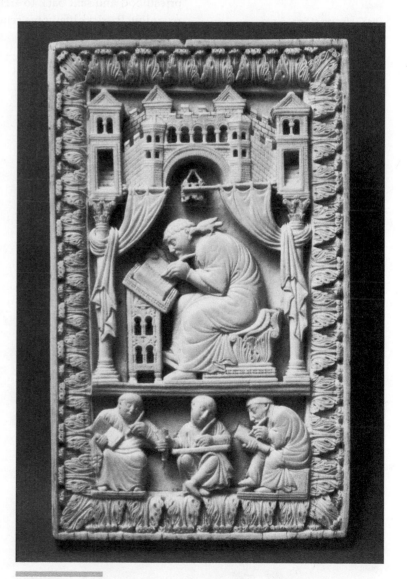

POPE GREGORY THE GREAT AND THREE SCRIBES In this tenth-century ivory depicting the influential sixth-century Pope Gregory, writing symbolizes his power and influence. During the early Middle Ages, the Church alone kept literacy and writing alive in the West.

SOURCE: St. Gregory writing with scribes, Carolingian, Franco-German School, ca. 850–875 (ivory). Kunsthistorisches Museum, Vienna, Austria/Bridgeman Art Library.

and the Byzantine emperors slowly soured, especially during the Iconoclastic Controversy discussed in Chapter 8. By the early eighth century the popes abandoned the fiction that they were still subject to the Byzantines and sought protection from the Frankish kings.

CONVERTING THE IRISH Though the Romans had conquered most of Britain during the imperial period, they never attempted to bring Ireland into their empire. Thus, the island off Britain's west coast had had only minimal contact with Christianity. Little is known of how Christianity came to Ireland. There were probably missionaries who traveled with traders from the Roman Empire, but the earliest firm date is 431 when Palladius was supposedly sent to administer to those in Ireland who were already Christians. The figure of Patrick (d. ca. 492 or 493) dominates the subsequent missionary history of Ireland, largely because his later biographers improbably gave him credit for converting all the Irish to Christianity. A ninth-century record describes Patrick's capture from a Roman villa in Britain by Irish raiders, who sold him into slavery in Ireland. He managed to escape and return to Britain, where he was ordained into the priesthood and sent back to Ireland as a missionary. A great deal of confusion exists regarding Patrick's life; some scholars argue that the traditional story of Patrick actually merges the experiences of the two missionaries Palladius and Patrick. Nevertheless, by the end of the fifth century, Christianity had a firm foothold in Ireland.

But Ireland was still an entirely rural place. Elsewhere in the West, Christianity spread out into the countryside from cities, with bishops administering the local church from their city cathedrals. Ireland, however, lacked cities in which to build churches and housing for bishops. No one living in Ireland knew Latin, Greek, or any of the other languages into which the Bible had been translated. And no schools existed where churchmen might teach the Gospel to new converts.

Irish churchmen found solutions to these problems in monasteries, places where priests could receive training and men and women from the surrounding homesteads and hamlets could learn to read Latin and absorb the basics of Christian education. The Irish scholars produced by these monasteries gained a high reputation for their learning across western Europe. They produced magnificently illustrated manuscripts in their libraries. These books brought Irish art to all the lands where Irish missionaries traveled.

CONVERTING THE ANGLO-SAXONS Irish missionaries established new monasteries in England and on the European continent. Columba (521–597), for instance, founded one on the island of Iona, off Scotland's western coast. From this thriving community missionaries began to bring Christianity to the peoples of Scotland. The offshoot monastery of Lindisfarne in northern England also became a dynamic center of learning and missionary activity. During the seventh century, missionaries based there carried Christianity to many other parts of England.

📖 **Read the Document**

The Confession of Saint Patrick

THE BOOK OF KELLS The Book of Kells consists of an ornately illustrated manuscript produced by Irish monks about 800 C.E. The book contains the four Gospels of the New Testament in Latin and is one of the masterpieces of early medieval art. This highly decorated page shows the opening "Q" of *quoniam*, the first word in the Latin Gospel of Luke.

They also began converting the people of Frisia on the North Sea, in the area of the modern Netherlands.

Pope Gregory the Great (r. 590–604) understood that the first step in creating new Christian communities was to convert as many people as possible to the faith. Deep learning about the religion could come later. To that end he instructed missionaries to permit local variations in worship and to accommodate harmless vestiges of pre-Christian worship practices. "Don't tear down their temples," Gregory advised, "put a cross on the roofs!"

Following Gregory's pragmatic suggestion, missionaries in England accepted certain Anglo-Saxon calendar conventions that stemmed from polytheist worship. For example, in the Anglo-Saxon calendar, the weekdays took their names from old gods: Tuesday derived from Tiw, a war god; Wednesday from Woden, king of the gods; Thursday from Thor, god of thunder; and Friday from Freya, goddess of agriculture. Anglo-Saxon deities eventually found their way into the Christian calendar as well. Eostre, for example, a goddess whose festival came in April, gave her name to the Christian holiday Easter.

Despite their common commitment to Latin Christianity, the Irish and Roman monks working throughout England disagreed strongly about proper Christian practice. For instance, they argued over how to perform baptism, the ritual of anointing someone with water to admit him or her into the Christian community. They bickered about how monks should shave the tops of their heads to show their religious vocation, and they squabbled about the correct means of calculating the date of Easter. These disputes threatened to create deep divisions among England's Christians. The overall conflict finally found resolution in 664 in the Anglo-Saxon kingdom of Northumbria, where monastic life flourished. At a council of monks and royal advisers called the Synod of Whitby, the Northumbrian monarch commanded that the Roman rather than Irish version of Christianity would prevail in his kingdom. His decision eventually was accepted throughout England.

View the Map

Spread of Latin Christianity in Western Europe

MONASTIC INTELLECTUAL LIFE The missionaries from Rome were members of the vigorous monastic movement initiated by Benedict of Nursia (ca. 480–547) from his monastery at Monte Cassino in Italy (see Chapter 7). These monks followed Benedict's *Rule,* a guidebook for the management of monastic life and spirituality. In the *Rule,* Benedict had written that individual monks should live temperate lives devoted to spiritual contemplation, communal prayer, and manual labor. So that their contemplations might not depart from the path of truth, Benedict had encouraged monks to seek guidance in the Bible, in the writings of the renowned theologians, and in works of spiritual edification. For Benedict, contemplative reading constituted a fundamental part of monastic life. Thus, monks had to be literate in Latin. They needed training in the Latin classics, which required books.

Medieval monasteries set aside at least two rooms—the **scriptorium** and the library—to meet the growing demand for books. In the scriptorium, scribes laboriously copied Latin and Greek manuscripts as an act of religious devotion. Monastery libraries were small in comparison with the public libraries of classical Rome, but the volumes were cherished and carefully protected. Because books were precious possessions, these libraries set forth strict rules for their use. Some librarians chained books to tables to prevent theft. Others pronounced a curse against anyone who failed to return a borrowed book. Nevertheless, librarians also generously lent books to other monasteries to copy.

scriptorium The room in a monastery where monks copied books and manuscripts.

Monks preferred to read texts with a Christian message, so these books were the most frequently copied. In many monasteries, however, monks preserved non-Christian texts as well. By doing so, they helped to keep knowledge of Latin and classical learning alive. Indeed, many of the surviving works by authors of the Classical Age were copied and passed on by monks in the sixth and seventh centuries. Without

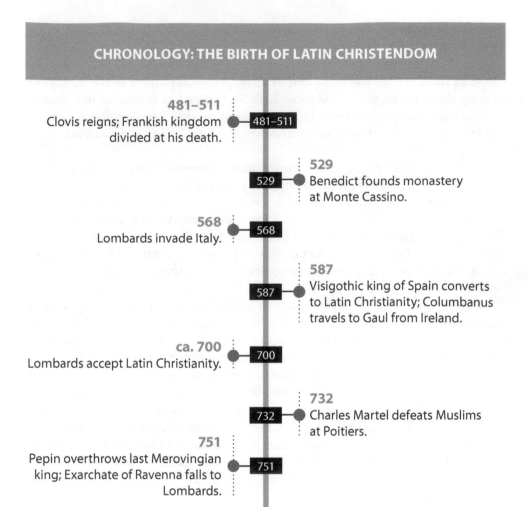

CHRONOLOGY: THE BIRTH OF LATIN CHRISTENDOM

481–511
Clovis reigns; Frankish kingdom divided at his death. | 481–511

529 | **529**
Benedict founds monastery at Monte Cassino.

568
Lombards invade Italy. | 568

587 | **587**
Visigothic king of Spain converts to Latin Christianity; Columbanus travels to Gaul from Ireland.

ca. 700
Lombards accept Latin Christianity. | 700

732 | **732**
Charles Martel defeats Muslims at Poitiers.

751
Pepin overthrows last Merovingian king; Exarchate of Ravenna falls to Lombards. | 751

the monasteries and scriptoria, knowledge today of the literature of the classical world would be greatly reduced.

Monks did far more than merely copy ancient texts, however. Some wrote original books of their own. At the English monastery at Jarrow, for example, Bede (d. 735) became the most distinguished scholar in eighth-century Europe. He wrote many books, including the *History of the English Church and People.* This work provided an invaluable source of information about the early Anglo-Saxon kingdoms.

Monks carried books with them when they embarked on missionary journeys. They also acquired new books during their travels. For instance, Benedict Biscop, the founder of the monasteries of Wearmouth (674) and Jarrow (682) in England, made six trips to Italy. Each time he brought back crates of books on all subjects, including works written by classical authors whom monks studied with interest. Other Anglo-Saxon missionaries transported this literary heritage to the monasteries they founded in Germany during the eighth century. As monks avidly read, copied, wrote, and transported books of all sorts, knowledge and intellectual discourse flourished in the monasteries.

Monks shared their expanding knowledge with Christians outside the monastery walls. They established schools at monasteries where boys (and, in some places, girls) could learn to read and write. In Italy some public schools survived from antiquity, but elsewhere most of the very few literate people who lived between 550 and 750 gained their education at monastery schools. The men trained in these schools played an important role in society as officials and bureaucrats. Their skills in reading and writing were necessary for keeping records and writing business and diplomatic letters.

Read the Document

Bede, Conversion of England (582)

The Carolingians

9.2 How did the Carolingian Empire contribute to establishing a distinctive western European culture?

Among the successor kingdoms to the Roman Empire in the West, discussed in the previous section, none was more powerful militarily than the Merovingian kingdom of the Franks. The Merovingian dynasty, however, was plagued by factions, royal assassinations, and do-nothing kings. When Pepin the Short deposed the last of the Merovingian kings in 751, he made himself king of the Franks and inaugurated the Carolingian dynasty.

Both the weak Merovingians and the strong Carolingians illustrated how the problem of succession from one king to another could destabilize early medieval monarchies. The kingdom was considered the private property of the royal family, and according to Frankish custom, a father was obliged to divide his estates among all his legitimate sons. As a result, whenever a king of the Franks died, the kingdom was divided up. When Pepin died in 768, the kingdom was divided between his sons, Charlemagne and Carloman. When Carloman died suddenly in 771, Charlemagne ignored the inheritance rights of Carloman's sons and may even have had them killed, making himself the sole ruler of the Franks.

The Leadership of Charlemagne

Charlemagne's (r. 768–814) ruthlessness with his own nephews epitomized the leadership that made him the mightiest ruler in western Europe and gave him the nickname of Charles the Great. An unusually tall and imposing figure, Charlemagne was a superb athlete and swimmer, a lover of jokes and high living, but also a deeply pious Christian. One of his court poets labeled him "The King Father of Europe." No monarch in European history has enjoyed such posthumous fame.

During his reign, Charlemagne engaged in almost constant warfare, especially against polytheistic Germanic tribes that he compelled to accept Christianity after their defeat. He went to war 18 times against the Saxons, whose forced conversion only encouraged subsequent rebellions. Three factors explain Charlemagne's persistent warfare. He believed he had an obligation to spread Christianity. He also needed to protect his borders from incursions by hostile tribes. Perhaps most important, however, was his need to satisfy his followers, especially the members of the aristocracy, by providing them with opportunities for plunder and new lands. As a result of his many wars, Charlemagne established a network of subservient kingdoms that owed tribute to him (see **Map 9.2**).

The extraordinary expansion of the Carolingian Empire represented a significant departure from the small, loosely governed kingdoms that had prevailed after the Roman Empire's collapse. Charlemagne's empire covered all of western Europe except for southern Italy, Spain, and the British Isles. His military ambitions brought the Franks into direct confrontation with other cultures—the polytheistic German, Scandinavian, and Slavic tribes; the Orthodox Christians of Byzantium; and the Muslims in Spain. These confrontations were usually hostile and violent, characterized as they were by the imposition of Frankish rule and Latin Christian faith.

CORONATION OF CHARLEMAGNE AS EMPEROR On Christmas Day 800, in front of a large crowd at St. Peter's Basilica in Rome, Pope Leo III (r. 795–816) presided over a ceremony in which Charlemagne was crowned emperor. Historians have debated exactly what happened, but according to the most widely accepted account, the assembled throng acclaimed Charlemagne emperor, and the pope prostrated himself

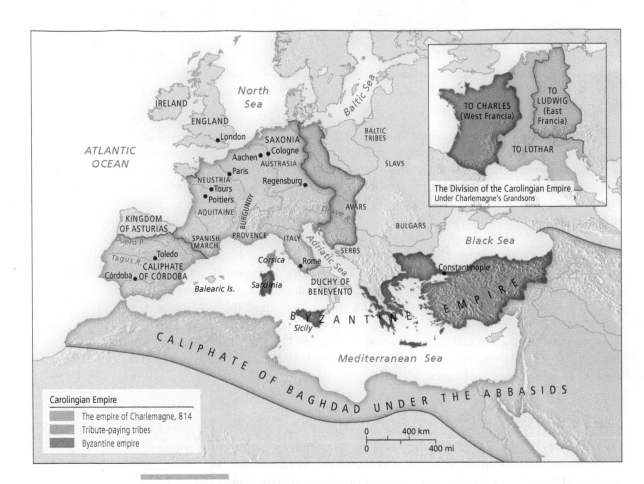

MAP **9.2** CAROLINGIAN EMPIRE Charlemagne's conquests were the greatest military achievement of the early Middle Ages. The Carolingian armies successfully reunified all western European territories of the ancient Roman Empire except for southern Italy, Spain, and Britain. However, the empire was fragile due to Frankish inheritance laws that required all legitimate sons to inherit lands from their fathers. By the time of Charlemagne's grandsons the empire began to fragment. By comparing this map with Map 9.1, determine what were the areas most under the influence of Latin Christianity as a result of the spread of the Carolingian Empire?

before the new emperor in a public demonstration of submission. Charlemagne's biographer Einhard later stated that the coronation came as a surprise to the king. Certainly there were dangers in accepting the imperial crown because the coronation was certain to antagonize Byzantium, where there already was a Roman emperor. To the Byzantines, Charlemagne was nothing more than a barbarian usurper of the imperial crown. In their minds the pope had no right to crown anyone emperor. Instead of reuniting the eastern and western halves of the ancient Roman Empire, the coronation of Charlemagne drove them further apart. Nevertheless, Charlemagne became the first Roman emperor in the West since the fifth century.

The coronation exemplified two of the most prominent characteristics of the Carolingians. The first was the conscious imitation of the ancient Roman Empire, especially the Christian empire of Constantine. Charlemagne conquered much of the former territory of the western Roman Empire, and the churches built during his reign were modeled after the fourth- and fifth-century basilicas of Rome. The second characteristic of Carolingian rule was the obligation of the Frankish kings to protect the Roman popes, an obligation that began under Charlemagne's father Pepin. In exchange for Frankish protection, the popes offered the Carolingian monarchs the legitimacy of divine sanction.

CAROLINGIAN RULERSHIP Even under the discerning and strong rulership of Charlemagne, the Carolingian Empire never enjoyed the assets that had united the ancient

Roman Empire for so many centuries. The Carolingians lacked a standing army and navy, professional civil servants, properly maintained roads, regular communications, and a money economy—a stark contrast with Byzantium and the Muslim caliphates, which could also boast the splendid capital cities of Constantinople, Damascus, Baghdad, and Córdoba. However, Charlemagne governed very effectively without a capital, spending much of his time ruling from the saddle.

Such a system of government depended more on personal than institutional forms of rule. Personal loyalty to the Carolingian monarch, expressed in an oath of allegiance, provided the strongest bonds unifying the realm, but betrayals were frequent. The Carolingian system required a monarch with outstanding personal abilities and unflagging energy, such as Charlemagne possessed; a weak monarch, however, threatened the collapse of the entire empire. Until the reign of Charlemagne, royal commands had been delivered orally, and there were few written records of what decisions had been made. As Charlemagne's decrees (called "capitularies") gradually came to be written out, they began to strengthen and institutionalize governmental procedures. In addition, Charlemagne's leading adviser, Alcuin, insisted that all official communications be stated in the appropriate Latin form, which would help prevent falsification because only the members of Charlemagne's court were well enough educated to know these proper forms.

One of the weaknesses of the previous Merovingian dynasty had been the decentralization of power, as local dukes appropriated royal resources and public functions for themselves. To combat this weakness, Charlemagne followed his father's lead in reorganizing government around territorial units called **counties**, each administered by a count. The counts were rewarded with lands from the king and sent to areas where they had no family ties to serve as a combined provincial governor, judge, military commander, and representative of the king. Traveling circuit inspectors reviewed the counts' activities on a regular basis and remedied abuses of office. On the frontiers of their sprawling kingdom, the Franks established special territories called **marches**, which were ruled by margraves with extended powers necessary to defend vulnerable borders.

In many respects, however, the Church provided the most vital foundations for the Carolingian system of rulership. As discussed in Chapter 7, the last years of the ancient Roman Empire the administration of the Church was organized around the office of the bishop. By the late seventh century this system had almost completely collapsed, as many bishoprics were left vacant or were occupied by royal favorites and relatives who lacked qualifications for church office. Because Carolingian monarchs considered themselves responsible for the welfare of Christianity, they took charge of the appointment of bishops and reorganized church administration into a strict hierarchy of archbishops who supervised bishops who, in turn, supervised parish priests. Pepin and Charlemagne also revitalized the monasteries and endowed new ones, which provided the royal court with trained personnel—scribes, advisers, and spiritual assistants. Most laymen of the time were illiterate, so monks and priests wrote the emperor's letters for him, kept government records, composed histories, and promoted education. All these tasks were essential for Carolingian rule.

THE CAROLINGIAN RENAISSANCE In addition to organizing an efficient political administration, Charlemagne sought to make the royal court an intellectual center. He gathered around him prominent scholars from throughout the realm and other countries. Under Charlemagne's patronage, these scholars were responsible for the flowering of culture that is called the Carolingian Renaissance.

The **Carolingian Renaissance** ("rebirth") was one of a series of revivals of interest in ancient Greek and Latin literature. Charlemagne understood that both governmental efficiency and the propagation of the Christian faith required the intensive study of Latin, which was the language of the law, learning, and the Church. The Latin

counties Territorial units devised by the Carolingian dynasty during the eighth and ninth centuries for the administration of the empire. Each county was administered by a count who was rewarded with lands and sent to areas where he had no family ties to serve as a combined provincial governor, judge, military commander, and representative of the king.

marches Territorial units of the Carolingian Empire for the administration of frontier regions. Each march was ruled by a margrave who had special powers necessary to defend vulnerable borders.

Carolingian Renaissance The "rebirth" of interest in ancient Greek and Latin literature and language during the reign of the Frankish emperor Charlemagne (r. 768–814). Charlemagne promoted the intensive study of Latin to promote governmental efficiency and to propagate the Christian faith.

canon law The collected laws of the Roman Catholic Church. Canon law applied to cases involving the clergy, disputes about church property, and donations to the Church. It also applied to the laity for annulling marriages, legitimating bastards, prosecuting bigamy, protecting widows and orphans, and resolving inheritance disputes.

 View the **Closer Look**

A Multicultural Book Cover

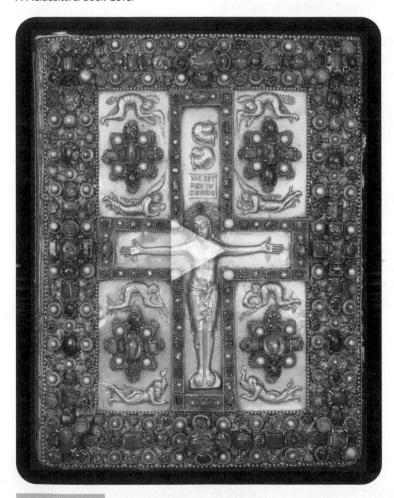

CAROLINGIAN RENAISSANCE ART This exquisite book cover for the Lindau Gospels is thought to have been produced at the Royal Abbey of St. Denis under the reign of Charles the Bald, grandson of Charlemagne, around 870. The images reflect several cultural influences, including Greek, Roman, Byzantine, Celtic, and Germanic, and they present a magnificent crucifixion iconography. Christ, true to Byzantine theology, is not shown suffering the agony of the cross but, instead, is depicted as serene, triumphant, and determined.

of everyday speech had evolved considerably since antiquity. During Charlemagne's time, spoken Latin had already been transformed into early versions of the Romance languages of Spanish, Italian, Portuguese, and French. Distressed that the poor Latin of many clergymen meant they misunderstood the Bible, Charlemagne ordered that all prospective priests undergo a rigorous education and recommended the liberal application of physical punishment if a pupil was slow in his lessons. The lack of properly educated teachers, however, ensured that the Carolingian reforms did not penetrate very far into the lower levels of the clergy, who taught by rote the rudiments of Christianity to the illiterate peasants.

Charlemagne's patronage was crucial for the Carolingian Renaissance, which took place in the monasteries and the imperial court. Many of the heads of the monastic scriptoria wrote literary works of their own, including poetry and theology. The Carolingian scholars developed a beautiful new style of handwriting called the Carolingian minuscule, in which each letter was carefully and clearly formed. Texts collected by Carolingian librarians provided the foundation for the laws of the Church (called **canon law**) and codified the liturgy, which consisted of the prayers offered, texts read, and chants sung on each day of the year.

The man most fully responsible for the Carolingian Renaissance was the English poet and cleric Alcuin of York (ca. 732–804), whom Charlemagne invited to head the palace school in Aachen. Charlemagne himself joined his sons, his friends, and his friends' sons as a student, but Charlemagne struggled in his classes. Despite many years of practice he still could not learn to form letters. Nevertheless, under Alcuin's guidance the court became a lively center of discussion and exchange of knowledge. They debated issues such as the existence of Hell, the meaning of solar eclipses, and the nature of the Holy Trinity. After 15 years at court, Alcuin became the abbot of the monastery of St. Martin at Tours, where he expanded the library and produced a number of works on education, theology, and philosophy.

A brilliant young monk named Einhard (ca. 770–840), who studied in the palace school, quickly became a trusted friend and adviser to Charlemagne. Based on 23 years of service to Charlemagne and research in royal documents, Einhard wrote the *Life of Charlemagne* (830–833), which describes Charlemagne's family, foreign policy, conquests, administration, and personal attributes. In Einhard's vivid Latin prose, Charlemagne comes alive as a great leader, a lover of hunting and fighting, who unlike his rough companions possessed a towering sense of responsibility for the welfare of his subjects and the salvation of their souls. In Einhard's biography, Charlemagne appears as an idealist, the first Christian prince in medieval Europe to imagine that his role was not just to acquire more possessions but to better humankind.

Charlemagne's rule and reputation have had lasting significance for western Europe. Around 776 an Anglo-Saxon monk referred to the vast new kingdom of the Franks as the Kingdom of Europe, reviving the Roman geographical term *Europa*. Thanks to the Carolingians, Europe became more than a geographical expression. It became the geographical center of a new Christian civilization that supplanted the Roman civilization of the Mediterranean and transformed the culture of the West.

The Division of Western Europe

None of Charlemagne's successors possessed his personal skills, and without a permanent institutional basis for administration, the empire was vulnerable to fragmentation and disorder. When Charlemagne died in 814, the imperial crown passed to his only surviving son, Louis the Pious (r. 814–840). Louis's most serious problem was dividing the empire among his own three sons, as required by Frankish inheritance laws. Disputes among Louis's sons led to civil war, even before the death of their father; while they were fighting, the administration of the empire was neglected.

After years of fighting, the three sons—Charles the Bald (d. 877), Lothair (d. 855), and Louis the German (d. 876)—negotiated the Treaty of Verdun, which divided the Carolingian Empire. Charles the Bald received the western part of the territories, the kingdom of West Francia. Louis the German received the eastern portion, the kingdom of East Francia. Lothair obtained the imperial title as well as the central portion of the kingdom, the "Middle Kingdom," which extended from Rome to the North Sea (see Map 9.2). In succeeding generations, the laws of inheritance created further fragmentation of these kingdoms, and during the ninth and tenth centuries the descendants of Charlemagne died out or lost control of their lands. By 987 none were left.

The Carolingian Empire lasted only a few generations. Carolingian military power, however, had been formidable, providing within the Frankish lands an unusual period of security from hostile enemies, measured by the fact that few settlements were fortified. After the empire's collapse, virtually every surviving community in western Europe required fortifications, represented by castles and town walls. Post-Carolingian Europe became fragmented as local aristocrats stepped into the vacuum created by the demise of the Carolingians—and it became vulnerable, as a new wave of raiders from the steppes and the North plundered and carved out land for themselves.

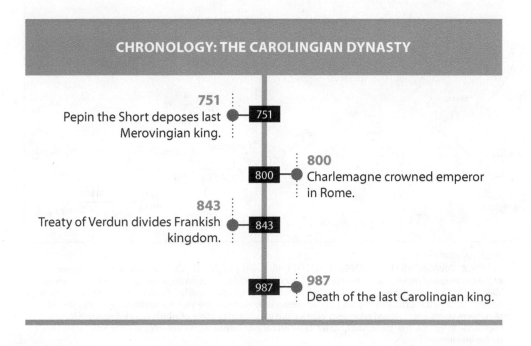

CHRONOLOGY: THE CAROLINGIAN DYNASTY

751 — 751 — Pepin the Short deposes last Merovingian king.

800 — 800 — Charlemagne crowned emperor in Rome.

843 — 843 — Treaty of Verdun divides Frankish kingdom.

987 — 987 — Death of the last Carolingian king.

Invasions and Recovery in the Latin West

9.3 How did Latin Christianity consolidate itself after the collapse of the Carolingian Empire?

Despite Charlemagne's campaigns of conquest and conversion, the spread of Christianity throughout western Europe remained uneven and incomplete. By 900, Latin Christianity was limited to a few regions that constituted the heartland of western Europe—the Frankish lands, Italy, parts of Germany that had been under Carolingian rule, the British Isles, and a fringe in Spain. Moreover, the heartland was vulnerable because during the ninth and tenth centuries, hostile polytheistic tribes raided deep into the tightly packed Christian core of western Europe (see **Map 9.3**). Despite these attacks Christianity survived, and the polytheist tribes eventually accepted the Christian faith. These conversions were not always the consequence of Christian victories in battle, as had often been the case during late antiquity and the Carolingian period. More frequently, they resulted from organized missionary efforts by monks and bishops.

The Polytheist Invaders of the Latin West

Some of the raiders during the eighth to eleventh centuries plundered what they could from the Christian settlements of the West and returned home. Others seized lands,

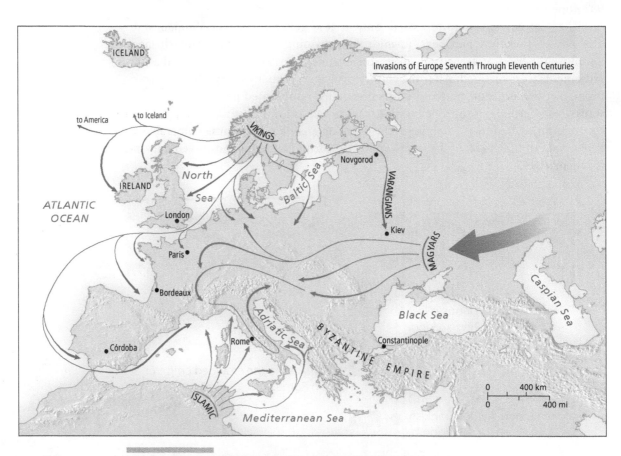

MAP 9.3 INVASIONS OF EUROPE, SEVENTH THROUGH ELEVENTH CENTURIES After the division of the Carolingian Empire, Britain and northern France, in particular, came under severe pressure from invading Viking bands from Scandinavia. The Varangians were a Viking tribe that invaded Kievan Rus and the territories of Novgorod. From the east came the Magyars, who eventually settled in the vast Hungarian plain. From the south there were persistent raids and conquests from various Islamic states, some of which established a rich Muslim civilization in Europe. (For these, see Chapter 8.) Which parts of Europe were most affected and which least affected by the invasions?

settled down, and established new principalities. The two groups who took advantage of the weakness of the Latin West most often during this period were the Magyars and Vikings.

The original homeland of the Magyars, later known as the Hungarians, was in the central Asian steppes. Gradually driven by other nomads to the western edge of the steppes, the Magyars crossed en masse in 896 into the middle of the Danube River basin, occupying sparsely settled lands that were easily conquered. Mounted raiding parties of Magyars ranged far into western Europe. Between 898 and 920 they sacked settlements in the prosperous Po River valley of Italy and then descended on the remnant kingdoms of the Carolingian Empire. Wherever they went they plundered for booty and took slaves for domestic service or sale. The kings of western and central Europe were powerless against these fierce raiders, who were unstoppable until 955 when the Saxon king Otto I destroyed a band of marauders on their way home with booty. After 955, Magyar raiding subsided.

The definitive end of Magyar forays, however, may have had less to do with Otto's victory than with the consolidation of the Hungarian plain into its own kingdom under the Árpád dynasty. Both Orthodox and Latin missionaries vied to convert the Magyars, but because of western political alliances they accepted Latin Christianity. On Christmas Day 1000, the Árpád king Stephen I (r. 997–1038) received the insignia of royalty directly from the pope and was crowned king. To help convert his people, King Stephen laid out a network of bishoprics and lavishly endowed monasteries.

The most devastating of the eighth- to eleventh-century invaders of western European settlements were the Vikings, also called Norsemen or Northmen. During this period, Danish, Norwegian, and Swedish Viking warriors sailed on long-distance raiding expeditions from their homes in Scandinavia. Every spring the long Viking dragon ships sailed forth, each carrying 50–100 warriors avid for loot. Propelled by a single square sail or by oarsmen when the winds failed or were blowing in the wrong direction, Viking ships were unmatched for seaworthiness and regularly sailed into the wild seas of the North Atlantic. The shallow-draft vessels could also be rowed up the lazy rivers of Europe to plunder monasteries and villages far into the interior.

Historians continue to debate the causes for the enormous Viking onslaught. Higher annual temperatures in the North may have stimulated a spurt in population that encouraged raiding and eventually emigration. But the primary motive seems to have been an insatiable thirst for silver, which was deemed the essential standard of social distinction in Scandinavian society. As a result, monasteries and cathedrals with their silver liturgical vessels were especially prized sources of plunder for Viking raiding parties. In 793, for example, Vikings pillaged the great English monastery at Lindisfarne for its silver—and largely destroyed it in the process.

By the middle of the ninth century, the Vikings began to maintain winter quarters in the British Isles and on the shores of the Carolingian kingdoms—locations that enabled them to house and feed ever-larger raiding parties. These raiders soon became invading armies that took land and settled their families on it. As a result, the Vikings moved from disruptive pillaging to permanent occupation, which created a lasting mark on Europe. Amid the ruins of the Carolingian Empire, Viking settlements on the Seine River formed the beginnings of the duchy of Normandy ("Northman land"), whose soldiers in the eleventh century would conquer England, Sicily, and much of southern Italy.

The most long-lasting influence of the Vikings outside Scandinavia was in the British Isles and North Atlantic. In 865 a great Viking army conquered large parts of northeastern England, creating a loosely organized network of territories known as the Danelaw. The Danish and Norse conquests in the British Isles left deep cultural residues in local dialects, geographical names, personal names, social structure, and literature. The most enduring example in Old English, the earliest form of spoken and written English, remains the epic of *Beowulf*, which recounts the exploits of a great Scandinavian adventurer in combat with the monster Grendel, Grendel's mother, and a fiery dragon.

Watch the Video

The Viking Ship Museum in Oslo

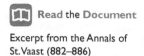

Read the Document

Excerpt from the Annals of St. Vaast (882–886)

VIKING SHIP This is a reconstructed Viking ship. It would have been propelled by a single square sail or rowed by oarsmen. Horses and warriors crowded into the ship. The tiller was mounted on the starboard side toward the stern. Stern-mounted rudders, which gave the helmsman much greater control of the direction of the ship, were gradually introduced during the twelfth century.

Read the Document

Saga of Erik the Red (985)

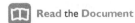

Read the Document

Speculum Princips, "The Animal Life of Greenland and the Character of the Land in Those Regions"

lord During the Middle Ages, a lord was someone who offered protection to dependents, known as vassals, who took an oath of loyalty to him. Most lords demanded military services from their vassals and sometimes granted them tracts of land known as fiefs.

vassals During the Middle Ages, men voluntarily submitted themselves to a lord by taking an oath of loyalty. Vassals owed the lord certain services—usually military assistance—and sometimes received in exchange a grant of land known as a fief.

280

In the North Atlantic, Vikings undertook long voyages into the unknown across cold rough seas. Beginning about 870, settlers poured into unsettled Iceland. Using Iceland as a base, they ventured farther and established new colonies in Greenland. In Iceland the adventures of these Viking warriors, explorers, and settlers were celebrated in poetry and sagas; those of Erik the Red and the Greenlanders recount hazardous voyages to the coasts of Canada. These Europeans arrived in North America 500 years before Christopher Columbus. In 930 the fiercely independent Icelanders founded a national parliament, the *althing*, an institution at which disputes were adjudicated through legal procedures rather than combat. The *althing* still functions as the parliament of the Republic of Iceland.

After the mid-ninth century, the kings of Scandinavia (Norway, Denmark, and Sweden) began to assert control over the bands of raiders who had constituted the vanguard of the Viking invasions. By the end of the tenth century, the great age of Viking raiding by small parties ended. The Scandinavian kings established firm hold over the settled population and converted to Christianity, bringing their subjects with them into the new faith. Hence, the descendants of the Viking raiders settled down to become peaceable farmers and shepherds.

The Rulers in the Latin West

As a consequence of the disintegration of the Carolingian order and the subsequent invasions, people during the ninth and tenth centuries began to seek protection from local warlords who assumed responsibilities once invested in royal authorities. Some of these warlords became the founders of what would become the kingdoms of the Latin West. They provided protection and a modicum of order in a period of anarchy caused by weak or failed governments.

LORDS AND VASSALS The society of warlords derived from Germanic military traditions in which a great chief attracted followers who fought alongside him. The relationship was voluntary and egalitarian. By the eighth century, however, the chief had become a **lord** who dominated others, and his dependents were known as **vassals**.

The bond of loyalty between lord and vassal was formalized by an oath. In the Carolingian period the vassal proved his loyalty to the lord by performing an act of homage, which made the vassal the "man" of the lord. The act of homage was a ritual in which the kneeling vassal placed his clasped hands between the hands of the lord and made a verbal declaration of intent, usually something such as, "Sir, I become your man." In return for the vassal's homage or *fealty*, as it came to be called, the lord swore to protect the vassal. The oath established a personal relationship in which the lord reciprocated the vassal's loyalty and willingness to obey the lord with protection and in some cases with a land grant called a **fief**. Lords frequently called on their vassals for military assistance to resist invaders or to fight with other lords. The fief supplied the vassal with an income to cover the expenses of armor and weapons and of raising and feeding horses, all of which were necessary to be an effective mounted soldier, known by the twelfth century as a **knight**. Historians called this connection between lord-vassal relations and the holding of a fief **feudalism**. The privileges for lords and vassals and their hold on fiefs lasted for many centuries, well into the eighteenth century in some parts of Europe. The long persistence of feudalism was one of the most important themes in the history of the West.

During the ninth and tenth centuries, after the collapse of public authority during the invasions and the dissolution of the Carolingian Empire, the lords often became the only effective rulers in a particular locality. Lords came to exercise many of the powers of a king, such as adjudicating disputes over property or inheritance and punishing thieves and murderers. (See *Justice in History* in this chapter.)

The mixture of personal lord-vassal obligations, property rights conveyed by the fief, and legal jurisdiction over communities caused endless complications. The king's vassals were also lords of their own vassals, who in turn were lords over lesser vassals down to the level of simple knight. In theory, such a system created a hierarchy of authority that descended down from the king, but reality was never that simple. In France, for example, many of the great lords possessed as much land as the king, which made it very difficult for the king to force them to enact his will. Many vassals held different fiefs from different lords, which created a confusion of loyalties, especially when two lords of the same vassal went to war against one another.

Women could inherit fiefs and own property of their own, although they could not perform military services. They often managed royal and aristocratic property when men were absent or dead, decided how property would be divided up among heirs, and functioned as lords when receiving the homage of male vassals. The lineage and accomplishments of prominent ladies enhanced their husbands' social prestige. A number of aristocratic families traced their descent from the female line, if it was more prestigious than the male line, and named their children after the wife's illustrious ancestors.

Lord-vassal relationships infiltrated many medieval social institutions and practices. Because most vassals owed military service to their lords, medieval armies were at least partially composed of vassal-knights who were obliged to fight for their lord for a certain number of days (often 40) per year. Vassals were required to provide their lord with other kinds of support as well. When summoned, they had to appear at the lord's court to offer advice or sit in judgment of other vassals who were their peers. When the lord traveled, his vassal was required to provide food and shelter in the vassal's castle, sometimes for a large entourage of family and retainers who accompanied the lord. Vassals were obliged to pay their lord certain fees on special occasions, such as the marriage of the lord's daughter. If the lord was captured in battle, his vassals had to pay the ransom.

THE WESTERN EUROPEAN KINGDOMS AFTER THE CAROLINGIANS At a time when the bonds of loyalty and support between lords and vassals were the only form of protection from invaders and marauders, lordship was a stronger social institution than the vague obligations all subjects owed to their kings. To rule effectively, a king was

fief During the Middle Ages, a fief was a grant of land or some other form of income that a lord gave to a vassal in exchange for loyalty and certain services (usually military assistance).

knight During the Middle Ages, a knight was a soldier who fought on horseback. A knight was a vassal or dependent of a lord, who usually financed the knight's expenses of armor and weapons and of raising and feeding horses with a grant of land known as a fief.

feudalism A term historians use to describe a social system common during the Middle Ages in which lords granted fiefs (tracts of land or some other form of income) to dependents, known as vassals, who owed their lords personal services in exchange. Feudalism refers to a society governed through personal ties of dependency rather than public political institutions.

Justice in History
Revealing the Truth: OATHS AND ORDEALS

N o participant in a lawsuit or criminal trial today would dream of entering the courtroom without an accompanying pile of documents to prove the case. In modern society we trust written over oral evidence because we are aware of how easily our memories can be distorted. In an early medieval court, however, the participants usually arrived with nothing more than their own sworn testimony and personal reputations to support their cause. Papers alleging to prove one thing or another meant little in a largely illiterate society. Unable to read and perhaps aware that the few who could read might deceive them, most people trusted what they had personally seen and heard. Count Berthold of Hamm expressed the opinion of many when, after being presented with documents opposing his claim to a piece of land, he "laughed at the documents, saying that since anyone's pen could write what they liked, he ought not to lose his rights over it."

To settle disputes, medieval courts put much more faith in confession or in eyewitness testimony than in documents. In 1124 Pope Calixtus II pronounced that "we put greater faith in the oral testimony of living witnesses than in the written word."

Under normal trial procedures, a man would give his oath that what he was saying was true. If he was an established and respected member of the community, he would also have a number of "oath-witnesses" testify for his reliability, although not to the truth or falsehood of his evidence. The court would also hear from witnesses in the case. This system worked well enough when two local men, known in the community, were at odds. But what happened when there was a trial involving a person who had a bad reputation, was a known liar, or was a stranger? What would happen in a case with no witnesses?

In these instances, medieval courts sometimes turned to trial by ordeal—subjecting the accused to a painful test—to settle the matter. The judicial ordeal was used only as a last resort, as a German law code of 1220 declared: "It is not right to use the ordeal in any case, except that the truth may be known in no other way." The wide range of situations and people handed over to the ordeal makes clear that in the eyes of the medieval courts, the ordeal was a fallback method when all else failed to reveal the truth.

There were several types of trial by ordeal. The most common was trial by fire. The accused would plunge his or her arm into a cauldron of boiling water to retrieve a coin or a jewel, or alternately would pick up a red-hot iron and walk nine paces. A variation of this method was to walk over hot coals or red-hot plowshares. After the accused suffered this ordeal, his or her hand or foot would be bound for three days and then examined. If the wound was healing "cleanly," meaning without infection, the accused was declared innocent. If not, he or she was adjudged guilty. Another common form of the ordeal was immersion in cold water, or "swimming," made famous in later centuries by its use in witch trials. The accused would be thrown into a river or lake. If the water "rejected" her and she floated, then she was guilty. If the water "embraced" her and she sank, then she was innocent. The obvious complication that a sinking person, even though innocent, may have also been a drowning person did not seem to deter use of trial by water.

The ordeal was especially widespread in judging crimes such as heresy and adultery and in assigning paternity. In 1218, Inga of Varteig carried the hot iron to prove that her son, born out of wedlock, was the son of deceased King Hakon III, which if true would change the line of succession in Norway. The ordeal was also used to decide much more pedestrian matters. In 1090, Gautier of Meigné claimed a plot of land from the monks of Saint Auban at Angers, arguing that he had traded a horse in return for the property. He too carried a hot iron to prove his claim.

The belief that an ordeal could effectively reveal guilt or innocence in a judicial matter was based on the widespread conviction that God constantly and actively intervened in earthly affairs and that his judgment could be seen immediately. To focus God's attention on a specific issue, the participants performed the ordeal in a ritual

TRIAL BY ORDEAL This fifteenth-century painting by Dieric Bouts (ca. 1415–1475) was commissioned by the city of Louvain in 1468 for a large project on the theme of the Last Judgment. It shows the widow of a murdered count holding a hot iron in her left hand and her husband's severed head in her right. Emperor Otto III judges her guilt for the murder on the basis of her willingness to undergo the hot-iron ordeal.

(continued on next page)

(continued from previous page)

manner. A priest was usually present to invoke God's power and to bless the implements employed in the ordeal. In one typical formula, the priest asked God "to bless and sanctify this fiery iron, which is used in the just examination of doubtful issues." Priests would also inform the accused, "If you are innocent of this charge … you may confidently receive this iron in your hand and the Lord, the just judge, will free you." The ritual element of the judicial ordeal emphasized the judgment of God over the judgment of men.

During the eleventh and twelfth centuries, the use of the ordeal waned. The recovery of Roman law, the rise of literacy and written documents in society at large, and a greater confidence in the power of courts to settle disputes all contributed to the gradual replacement of the ordeal with the jury trial or the use of torture to elicit a confession from the accused. In England the common law began to entrust the determination of the truth to a jury of peers who listened to and evaluated all the testimony. The jury system valued the opinions of members of the community over the reliability of the ordeal to reveal God's judgment. These changes mark a shift in medieval society toward a growing belief in the power of secular society to organize and police itself, leaving divine justice to the afterlife. But the most crucial shift came from within the Church itself, which felt its spiritual mission compromised by the involvement of priests in supervising ordeals. In 1215 the Fourth Lateran Council forbade priests from participating, and their absence made it impossible for the ordeal to continue as a formal legal procedure.

For Discussion

1. Why was someone's reputation in the community so significant for determining the truth in a medieval trial? How do reputations play a role in trials today?
2. What do oaths and the trial by ordeal reveal about the relationship between human and divine justice during the Middle Ages?

Taking It Further

Bartlett, Robert. *Trial by Fire and Water: The Medieval Judicial Ordeal.* 1986. Associates the spread of the trial by ordeal with the expansion of Christianity. The best study of the ordeal.

van Caenegen, R. C. *An Historical Introduction to Private Law.* 1992. A basic narrative from late antiquity to the nineteenth century that traces the evolution of early medieval trial procedures.

---

obliged to be a strong lord, in effect to become the lord of all the other lords, who in turn would discipline their own vassals. Achieving this difficult goal took several steps. First, the king had to establish a firm hand over his own lands, the royal domain. With the domain supplying food, material, and fighting men, the king could attempt the second step—establishing control over lords who lived outside the royal domain. To hold sway over these independent-minded lords, kings sometimes employed force but frequently offered lucrative rewards by giving out royal prerogatives to loyal lords. These prerogatives included the rights to receive fines in courts of law, to collect taxes, and to perform other governmental functions. As a result, some medieval kingdoms, such as France and England, began to combine in the hands of the same people the personal authority of lordship with the legal authority of the king, creating feudal kingship.

The final step in the process of establishing royal authority was to emphasize the sacred character of kingship. With the assistance of the clergy, kings emulated the great Christian emperors of Rome, Constantine and Justinian. Medieval kings became quasi-priests who received obedience from their subjects because commoners believed kings represented the majesty of God on Earth. The institution of sacred kingship gave kings an additional weapon for persuading the nobles to recognize the king's superiority over them.

Under the influence of ancient Roman ideas of rulership, some kings began to envision their kingdoms as something grander than private property. As the Germanic king and later emperor Conrad II (r. 1024–1039) put it, "If the king is dead the kingdom remains, just as the ship remains even if the helmsman falls overboard."[2] The idea slowly began to take hold that the kingdom had an eternal existence separate from the mortal person of the king and that it was superior to its component parts—its provinces, tribes, lords, families, bishoprics, and cities. This profound idea reached its fullest theoretical expression many centuries later. Promoting the sacred and eternal character of kingship required monarchs to patronize priests, monks, writers, and artists who could formulate and express these ideas.

EAST FRANCIA: THE GERMAN EMPIRE The kingdoms of East and West Francia, which arose out of the remnants of the Carolingian Empire, produced kings who attempted to expand the power of the monarchy and enhance the idea of kingship. East Francia largely consisted of Germanic tribes, each governed by a Frankish official called a duke. After 919 the dukes of Saxony were elected the kings of East Francia, establishing the foundations for the Saxon dynasty. With few lands of their own, the Saxon kings maintained their power by acquiring other duchies and controlling appointments to high church offices, which went to family members or loyal followers. The greatest of the Saxon kings, Otto I the Great (936–973), combined deep Christian piety with formidable military ability. More than any other tenth-century king, he supported the foundation of missionary bishoprics in polytheist Slavic and Scandinavian lands, thereby pushing the boundaries of Christianity beyond what they had been under Charlemagne. The pope crowned Otto emperor in 962, reviving the Roman Empire in the West, as Charlemagne had done earlier. Otto and his successors in the Saxon dynasty attempted to rule a more restricted version of the western empire than had Charlemagne. By the 1030s the Saxon kingdom had become the German Empire, consisting of most of the Germanic duchies, north-central Italy, and Burgundy. In later centuries these regions collectively came to be called the Holy Roman Empire.

As had been the case under Charlemagne, effective rulership in the new German Empire included the patronage of learned men and women who enhanced the reputation of the monarch. Otto and his able brother Bruno, the archbishop of Cologne, initiated a cultural revival, the **Ottonian Renaissance**, which centered on the imperial court. Learned Irish and English monks, Greek philosophers from Byzantium, and Italian scholars found positions there. Among the many intellectuals patronized by Otto, the most notable was Liutprand of Cremona (ca. 920–972), a vivid writer whose unabashed histories reflected the passions of the troubled times. For example, his history of contemporary Europe vilified his enemies and was aptly titled *Revenge*.

Ottonian Renaissance Under the patronage of the Saxon Emperor Otto I (936–973) and his brother Bruno, learned monks, Greek philosophers from Byzantium, and Italian scholars gathered at the imperial court, stimulating a cultural revival in literature and the arts. The writers and artists enhanced the reputation of Otto.

WEST FRANCIA: FRANCE Like East Francia, West Francia included many groups with separate ethnic and linguistic identities, but the kingdom had been Christianized much longer because it had been part of the Roman Empire. Thus, West Francia, although highly fragmented, possessed the potential for greater unity by using fully established Christianity to champion the king's authority.

Strengthening the monarchy became the crucial goal of the Capetian dynasty, which succeeded the last of the Carolingian kings. Hugh Capet (r. 987–996) was elevated as king of West Francia in an elaborate coronation ceremony in which the prayers of the archbishop of Reims offered divine sanction to the new dynasty. The archbishop's involvement established an important precedent for the French monarchy: Thereafter, the monarchy and the church hierarchy were closely entwined. From this mutually beneficial relationship, the king received ecclesiastical and spiritual support while the upper clergy gained royal protection and patronage. The term *France* at first applied only to Capet's feudal domain, a small but rich region around Paris, but through the persistence of the Capetians, West Francia became so unified that France came to refer to the entire kingdom.

The Capetians were especially successful in soliciting homage and services from the great lords of the land—despite some initial resistance. Hugh and his successors distinguished themselves by emphasizing that unlike other lords, kings were appointed by God. Shortly after his own coronation, Hugh had his son crowned—a strategy that ensured the succession of the Capetian family. Hugh's son, Robert II, the Pious (r. 996–1031), was apparently the first to perform the "king's touch": curing certain skin diseases with the power of his touch. The royal coronation cult and the king's touch established the reputation of French kings as miracle workers.

ANGLO-SAXON ENGLAND Anglo-Saxon England had never been part of the Carolingian Empire, but because it was Christian, England shared in the culture of the Latin West. England suffered extensive damage at the hands of the Vikings. After England was almost overwhelmed by a Danish invasion during the winter of 878–879, Alfred the

Great (r. 871–899) finally defeated the Danes as spring approached. As king of only Wessex (not of all England), Alfred consolidated his authority and issued a new law code. Alfred's successors cooperated with the nobility more effectively than the monarchs in either East or West Francia and built a broad base of support in the local units of government, the hundreds and shires. The Anglo-Saxon monarchy also enjoyed the support of the Church, which provided it with skilled servants and spiritual authorization.

During the late ninth and tenth centuries, Anglo-Saxon England experienced a cultural revival under royal patronage. King Alfred proclaimed that the Viking invasions had been God's punishment for the neglect of learning, without which God's will could not be known. Alfred accordingly promoted the study of Latin. He also desired that all men of wealth learn to read the language of the English people. Under Alfred a highly sophisticated literature appeared in Old English. This literature included poems, sermons, commentaries on the Bible, and translations of important Latin works. The masterpiece of this era was a history called the *Anglo-Saxon Chronicle*. It was begun during Alfred's reign but maintained over several generations.

During the late tenth and early eleventh centuries, England was weakened by another series of Viking raids and a succession of feeble kings. In 1066 William, the duke of Normandy and a descendant of Vikings who had settled in the north of France, defeated King Harold, the last Anglo-Saxon king. William seized the English throne. William the Conqueror opened a new era in which English affairs became deeply intertwined with those of the duchy of Normandy and the kingdom of France.

The Conversion of the Last Polytheists

As the core of the Latin West became politically stronger and economically more prosperous during the tenth and eleventh centuries, Christians made concerted attempts to convert the invaders, especially the polytheistic tribes in northern and eastern Europe. Through conversion, Latin Christianity dominated northern Europe up to the Kievan Rus border where Orthodox Christianity adopted from Byzantium triumphed.

CHRISTIAN CHURCH IMITATES POLYTHEIST TEMPLE The stave church was a type of wooden church built in northern Europe during the Middle Ages. Most of the surviving examples in Scandinavia are generally assumed to be modeled on polytheist temples. The Borgund church in Norway pictured here dates from about 1150.

Among the polytheistic tribes in Scandinavia, the Baltic Sea region, and parts of eastern Europe, the first Christian conversions usually took place when a king or chieftain accepted Christianity. His subjects were expected to follow. Teaching Christian principles and forms of worship required much more time and effort, of course. Missionary monks usually arrived after a king's conversion, but these monks tended to take a tolerant attitude about variations in the liturgy. Because most Christians were isolated from one another, new converts tended to practice their own local forms of worship and belief. Missionaries and Christian princes discovered that the most effective way to combat this localizing tendency was to found new bishoprics. Especially among the formerly polytheist tribes in northern and eastern Europe, the foundation of bishoprics created cultural centers of considerable prestige that attracted members of the upper classes. Those educated under the supervision of these new bishops became influential servants to the ruling families, further enhancing the stature of Christian culture.

Christian conversion especially benefited women through the abandonment of polygamous marriages, which were common among the polytheist peoples. As a result, aristocratic women played an important role in helping convert their peoples to Christianity. That role gave them a lasting influence in the churches of the newly converted lands, both as founders and patrons of convents and as writers on religious subjects. By the end of the fourteenth century organized polytheistic worship had disappeared in Scandinavia.

From the middle of the tenth century, a line of newly established Catholic bishoprics ensured that the Poles, Bohemians (Czechs), and Magyars (Hungarians) looked to the West and the pope for their cultural models and religious leadership. Poland,

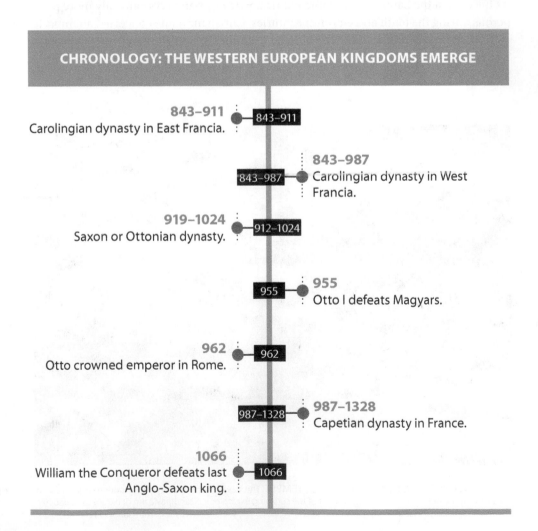

CHRONOLOGY: THE WESTERN EUROPEAN KINGDOMS EMERGE

843–911
Carolingian dynasty in East Francia.
843–911

843–987
Carolingian dynasty in West Francia.
843–987

919–1024
Saxon or Ottonian dynasty.
912–1024

955
Otto I defeats Magyars.
955

962
Otto crowned emperor in Rome.
962

987–1328
Capetian dynasty in France.
987–1328

1066
William the Conqueror defeats last Anglo-Saxon king.
1066

especially, favored Latin Christianity, an association that helped create strong political and cultural ties to western Europe. The Poles inhabited a flat plain of forested land with small clearings for farming. First exposed to missionaries tied to Saint Methodius, Poland resisted Christianity until Prince Mieszko (ca. 960–992) created the most powerful of the Slav states and accepted Latin Christianity in 966 in an attempt to build political alliances with Christian princes. Mieszko formally subordinated his country to the Roman pope with the Donation of Poland (ca. 991). Thus began Poland's long and special relationship with the papacy. At Mieszko's death, the territory of Poland approximated what it is today.

((• 📖 **Read the Document**

Social Conditions in the Ninth Century

9.1

9.2

9.3

9.4

The West in the East: The Crusades

9.4 What were the causes and consequences of the Crusades?

On a chilly November day in 1095 in a bare field outside Clermont, France, Pope Urban II (r. 1088–1099) delivered a landmark sermon to the assembled French clergy and laypeople eager to hear the pope. In stirring words Urban recalled that Muslims in the East were persecuting Christians and that the holy places in Palestine had been ransacked. He called upon the knights "to take up the cross" to defend their fellow Christians in distress.

Urban's appeal for a crusade was stunningly successful. When he finished speaking, the crowd chanted back, "God wills it." The news of Urban's call for a holy war in the East spread like wildfire. All across France and the western part of the German Empire knights prepared for the journey to Jerusalem. Unexpectedly and probably contrary to the pope's intentions, the poor and dispossessed also became enthused about an armed pilgrimage to the Holy Land. The zealous Peter the Hermit (ca. 1050–1115) preached the Crusade among the poor and homeless and gathered a huge unequipped, undisciplined army, which left for Jerusalem well in advance of the knights. Most of Peter the Hermit's People's Crusade starved or were enslaved long before they arrived in Constantinople. The Byzantine emperor was unwilling to feed the few who did arrive and shipped them off to Turkish territory where the Turkish army annihilated nearly all of them.

Urban's call for a crusade gave powerful religious sanction to the western Christian military expeditions against Islam. From 1095 until well into the thirteenth century, recurrent, large-scale crusading operations attempted to take, retake, and protect Christian Jerusalem (see **Map 9.4**), while the idea of going on a crusade lasted long after the thirteenth century into modern times.

The Origins of Holy War

The original impulse for the **Crusades** was the threat that Muslim armies posed to Christian peoples, pilgrims, and holy places in the eastern Mediterranean. By the middle of the eleventh century the Seljuk Turks, who had converted to Islam, were putting pressure on the Byzantine Empire. In 1071, after the Seljuks defeated the Byzantine army at Manzikert, all of Asia Minor lay open to Muslim occupation. Pope Urban's appeal for a crusade in 1095 came in response to a request for military assistance from the Byzantine emperor Alexius Comnenus, who probably thought he would get yet another band of Western mercenaries to help him reconquer Byzantine territory lost to the Seljuks. Instead, he got something utterly unprecedented—a massive volunteer army of perhaps 60,000 soldiers devoted less to cooperating with their Byzantine Christian brethren than to wresting as much territory as possible in the eastern Mediterranean from both Muslim and Byzantine hands.

Crusades Between 1095 and 1291, Latin Christians heeding the call of the pope launched eight major expeditions and many smaller ones against Muslim armies in an attempt to gain control of and hold Jerusalem.

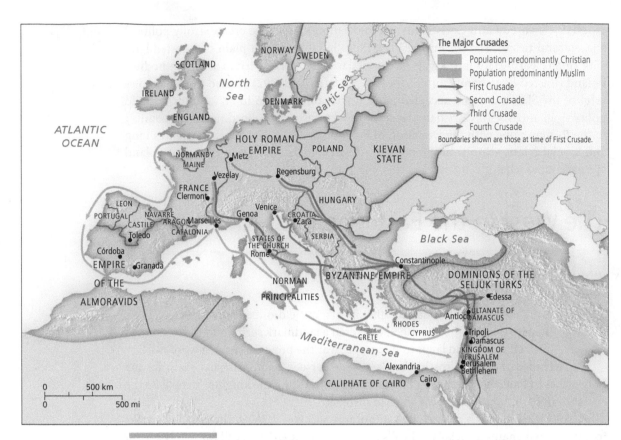

MAP **9.4** THE MAJOR CRUSADES During the first three Crusades, Christian armies and fleets from western Europe attacked Muslim strongholds and fortresses in the Middle East in an attempt to capture and hold Jerusalem. The Fourth Crusade never arrived in the Middle East, as it was diverted to besiege Constantinople. Based on this map, where were the borders between Christian and Muslim populations?

Pope Urban made a special offer in his famous sermon at Clermont to remit all penance for sin for those who went on the Crusade. Moreover, a penitential pilgrimage to a holy site such as Jerusalem provided a sinner with a pardon for capital crimes such as murder. Urban's offer muddled the long-standing difference between a pilgrim and a crusader. Until this point, a pilgrim was always unarmed, while a crusader carried weapons and was willing not just to defend other pilgrims from attack, but to launch an assault on those he considered heathens. The innovation of the Crusades was to create the idea of armed pilgrims who received special rewards from the Church. The merger of a spiritual calling and military action was strongest in the knightly orders—Templars, Hospitallers, and Teutonic Knights. The men who joined these orders were soldiers who took monastic vows of poverty, chastity, and obedience. But rather than isolating themselves to pray in a monastery, they went forth, sword in hand, to conquer for Christ. These knightly orders exercised considerable political influence in Europe and amassed great wealth.

In the minds of crusader-knights, greed probably jostled with fervent piety. Growing population pressures and the spread of primogeniture (passing landed estates on to the eldest male heir) left younger sons with little to anticipate at home and much to hope for by seeking their fortunes in the Crusades. Nevertheless, crusaders testified to the sense of community they enjoyed by participating in "the common enterprise of all Christians." Fulcher of Chartres recalled the unity displayed by crusaders from so many different countries: "Who has ever heard of speakers of so many languages in one army. . . . If a Breton or a German wished to ask me something, I was utterly without words to reply. But although we were divided by language, we seemed to be like brothers in the love of God and like near neighbors of one mind." The exhilarating experience of brotherhood in the love of God motivated many crusaders.

Different Voices

Christian and Muslim Accounts of the Atrocities Crusaders Committed During the Fall of Jerusalem in 1099

B oth Christians and Muslims were convinced that God was on their side during the Crusades. However, leaders on both sides had to find a way to convince people about the justness of their cause and the necessity to take up arms. The problem was to find a way to persuade people to risk their lives and fortunes on behalf of co-religionists and the abstract idea of holy war. One way to do that was to emphasize the atrocities of war. The Christian massacres of Muslims in Jerusalem after the city fell in 1099 became symbolic for both sides. Crusaders also burned Jews alive when they took refuge in their synagogue. Although even the Christian eyewitnesses did not deny the massacres, they indicated different things about God's will to the Christians than to the Muslims and Jews.

Raymond of Aguilers served as chaplain for a crusade and was an eyewitness of the siege and fall of Jerusalem. Abu L-Musaffar Al-Abiwardi was not in Jerusalem but was living in Baghdad at the time. His poem probably reflects the appeals for assistance that the Muslims living in Palestine sent to the caliphs of Baghdad.

A Christian Priest Reports and Interprets the Massacres

[After the surrender of the walls and towers of Jerusalem] some of our men (and this was more merciful) cut off the heads of their enemies; others shot them with arrows, so that they fell from the towers; others tortured them longer by casting them into the flames. Piles of heads, hands, and feet were to be seen in the streets of the city. It was necessary to pick one's way over the bodies of men and horses. But these were small matters compared to what happened at the Temple of Solomon [the Al-Aqsa Mosque], a place where religious services are ordinarily chanted. What happened there? If I tell the truth, it will exceed your powers of belief. So let it suffice to say this much, at least, that in the Temple and porch of Solomon, men rode in blood up to their knees and bridle reigns. Indeed, it was a just and splendid judgment of God that this place should be filled with the blood of the unbelievers, since it had suffered so long from their blasphemies. The city was filled with corpses and blood....

Now that the city was taken, it was well worth all our previous labors and hardships to see the devotion of the pilgrims at the Holy Sepulcher. How they rejoiced and exulted and sang a new song to the Lord! For their hearts offered prayers of praise to God, victorious and triumphant, which cannot be told in words. A new day, new joy, new and perpetual gladness, the consummation of our labor and devotion, drew forth from all new words and new songs. This day, I say, will be famous in all future ages, for it turned our labors and sorrows into joy and exultation; this day, I say, marks the justification of all Christianity, the humiliation of paganism, and the renewal of our faith.

SOURCE: From *The First Crusade: The Accounts of Eyewitnesses and Participants*, trans. A. C. Krey (Princeton: Princeton University Press, 1921), pp. 257–262.

A Muslim Appeal for Jihad Against the Crusaders

Sons of Islam, behind you are battles in which heads rolled at your feet.

. . .

Must the foreigners feed on our ignominy, while you trail behind you the
    train of a pleasant life, like men whose world is at peace?
When blood has been spilt, when sweet girls must for shame hide their lovely
    faces in their hands?
When the white swords' points are red with blood, and the iron of the brown
    lances is stained with gore!
At the sound of sword hammering on lance young children's hair turns white.
This is war, and the man who shuns the whirlpool to save his life shall grind
    his teeth in penitence.
This is war, and the infidel's word is naked in his hand, ready to be sheathed
    Again in men's necks and skulls.
This is war, and he who lies in the tomb at Medina [Muhammad] seems to raise his voice
    and cry: "O sons of Hasim! [Muhammad's great-grandfather, the "destroyer of evil"]
I see my people slow to raise the lance against the enemy: I see the Faith
    resting on feeble pillars.
For fear of death the Muslims are evading the fire of battle, refusing to believe
    that death will surely strike them." . . .

SOURCE: From E. J. Costello and F. Gabrieli, *Arab Historians of the Crusades*, ed. F. Gabrieli (Berkeley: University of California Press, 1969), p. 12.

For Discussion

1. How does Raymond of Aguilers justify the Christian atrocities on the Temple Mount? How does Abu L-Musaffar Al-Abiwardi appeal to his fellow Muslims?
2. What is more important in these appeals to war, serving God or defending co-religionists?
3. Since the Crusades, appeals for holy war have been a recurrent feature of relations between Muslims and Christians. How would you argue against these ideas of holy war?

Crusading Warfare

The First Crusade (1095–1099) was strikingly successful, but it was as much the result of Muslim weakness as Christian strength. Two factors depleted Arab Muslims' ability to resist the crusaders. First, the Arab states that controlled access to Jerusalem were already weakened from fighting the Seljuk Turks. Second, Muslims were divided internally. Theological divisions between Sunni and Shi'ite Muslims prevented the Muslim caliphs from uniting against the Christians.

In 1099, after a little more than a month's siege, the crusaders scaled the walls of Jerusalem and took possession of the city, which was also holy to Muslims and Jews and largely inhabited by them. (See *Different Voices* in this chapter.) The triumph of the First Crusade led to the establishment of the Latin principalities, which were devoted to maintaining a Western foothold in the Holy Land. The Latin principalities included all of the territory in contemporary Lebanon, Israel, and Palestine.

The subsequent crusades never achieved the success of the first. In 1144 Muslims captured the northernmost Latin principality, the county of Edessa—a warning to Westerners of the fragility of a defensive system that relied on a few scattered fortresses strung along a thin strip of coastline. In response to the loss of Edessa, Christians launched the Second Crusade (1147–1149). This ambitious offensive on several fronts failed in the East where the crusaders gained little ground. In the West, however, it was a great success because northern European crusaders helped the king of Portugal retake

JESUS CHRIST LEADING THE CRUSADERS The rider on the white horse is Jesus, who holds the Gospels in his right hand and the sword of righteousness in his teeth. The crusading knights bearing banners and shields emblazoned with the cross follow him. The figure in the upper left-hand corner represents St. John the Evangelist, whose writings were understood to prophesy the Crusades. This manuscript illumination dates from ca. 1310–1325.

SIDON CRUSADER SEA CASTLE, LEBANON This crusader castle survives on the coast of Lebanon in what was once a Latin Christian principality constructed to defend the Holy Land. The fortified port of Sidon anchored the thin strip of Christian territories along the Mediterranean coast of the Middle East.

Lisbon from the Muslims. In 1187, the sultan of Egypt and Syria, Saladin (1137–1193), recaptured Jerusalem for Islam. In response to this dispiriting loss, the Third Crusade (1189–1192) assembled the most spectacular army of European chivalry ever seen, led by Europe's three most powerful kings: German emperor Frederick Barbarossa, Philip Augustus of France, and Richard the Lion-Heart of England. Yet the Third Crusade's results were far from spectacular: After Frederick drowned wading in a river en route and Philip went home, Richard the Lion-Heart negotiated a truce with Saladin.

In 1199, Pope Innocent III called for the Fourth Crusade with the goal of recapturing Jerusalem. However, the Frankish knights and Venetian fleet diverted to intervene in a disputed imperial succession in Byzantium. Rather than fighting Muslims, Christian knights fought fellow Christians. In 1204 they besieged and captured Constantinople. The Westerners then divided the Byzantine Empire, set up a Latin regime that lasted until 1261, and neglected their oaths to reconquer Jerusalem. The Fourth Crusade dangerously weakened the Byzantine Empire by making it a prize for Western adventurers. None of the subsequent Crusades achieved lasting success in the Middle East. (See *Encounters and Transformations* in this chapter.)

The Significance of the Crusades

Despite the capture of Jerusalem during the First Crusade, the crusaders could not maintain control of the city. For more than two centuries, they wasted enormous efforts on what proved to be a futile enterprise. Neither did any of the Latin principalities in the Middle East survive for more than two centuries. The crusaders who resided in these principalities were obliged to learn how to live and trade with their Muslim neighbors, but few of them learned Arabic or took seriously Muslim learning. The strongest Islamic cultural and intellectual influences on Christian Europe came through Sicily and Spain rather than via returning crusaders.

Encounters and Transformations
Legends of the Borderlands:
ROLAND AND EL CID

From the eighth to the fifteenth centuries, Muslim and Latin Christian armies grappled with one another in the borderlands between their two civilizations in the Iberian peninsula, the territory now called Spain. The borderlands, however, were more than just places of conflict. During times of peace, Christians and Muslims traded with and even married one another, and in the confused loyalties typical of the times, soldiers and generals from both faiths frequently switched sides. These borderland clashes produced legends of great heroes, which once refashioned into epic poems created a lasting memory of Muslim and Christian animosity.

The Song of Roland, an Old French epic poem that dates from around 1100, tells a story about the Battle of Roncesvalles, which took place in 779. The actual historical battle had been a minor skirmish between Charlemagne's armies and some local inhabitants in Spain who were not Muslims at all, but *The Song of Roland* transformed this sordid episode into a great epic of Christian-Muslim conflict. In the climax of the poem, the Christian hero Roland, seeking renown for his valor, rejected his companion Oliver's advice to blow a horn to alert Charlemagne of a Muslim attack. The battle was hopeless; when the horn was finally sounded it was too late to save Roland or Oliver. Roland's recklessness made him the model of a brave Christian knight.

In the subsequent Spanish border wars, the most renowned soldier was Rodrigo Díaz de Vivar (ca. 1043–1099), known to history as El Cid (from the Arabic word for "lord"). He is remembered in legend as a heroic knight fighting for the Christian Reconquest of the peninsula, but the real story of El Cid was much more self-serving. El Cid repeatedly switched allegiances to the

THE DEATH OF ROLAND Here the dying Roland holds the horn he failed to blow in time to be rescued. No legend from the borderlands between Christianity and Islam had a greater influence on European Christian society than that of Roland.

Muslims. Even when a major Muslim invasion from North Africa threatened the very existence of Christian Spain, El Cid did not come to the rescue and instead undertook a private adventure to carve out a kingdom for himself in Muslim Valencia.

Soon after El Cid's death and despite his inconstant loyalty to Castile and Christianity, he was elevated to the status of the great hero of Christian Spain. The popularity of the twelfth-century epic poem, *The Poem of My Cid,* transformed this cruel, vindictive, and utterly self-interested man into a model of Christian virtue and self-sacrificing loyalty.

The medieval borderlands created legends of heroism and epic struggles that often stretched the truth. The borderlands were a wild frontier, not unlike the American frontier, into which desperate men fled to hide or to make opportunities for themselves. However, the lasting significance of the violent encounters that took place in these borderlands was not the nasty realities but the heroic models they produced. Poetry transformed reality into a higher truth that emphasized courage and faithfulness. Because these poems were memorized and recited in the vernacular languages of Old French and Castilian (now Spanish), they became a model of aristocratic values in medieval society and over the centuries a source for a national literary culture. Thus, becoming French or Spanish meant, in some respects, rejecting Islam, which has created a lasting anti-Muslim strain in western European culture.

For Discussion

How did transforming the accounts of battles between Christians and Muslims into heroic poems change how these events would be remembered among Christians?

CHRONOLOGY: THE CRUSADES

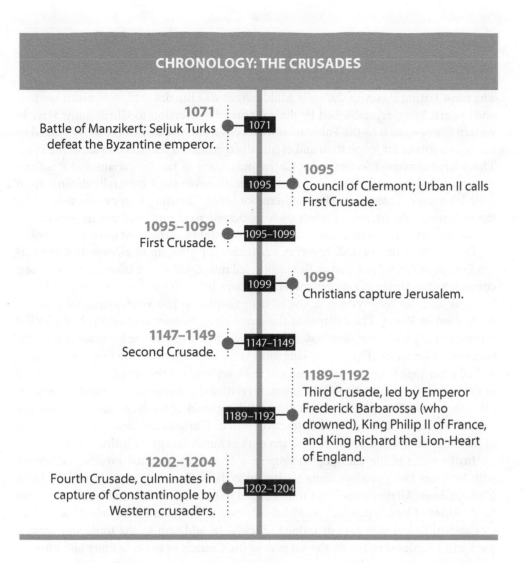

1071
Battle of Manzikert; Seljuk Turks defeat the Byzantine emperor.

1095
Council of Clermont; Urban II calls First Crusade.

1095–1099
First Crusade.

1099
Christians capture Jerusalem.

1147–1149
Second Crusade.

1189–1192
Third Crusade, led by Emperor Frederick Barbarossa (who drowned), King Philip II of France, and King Richard the Lion-Heart of England.

1202–1204
Fourth Crusade, culminates in capture of Constantinople by Western crusaders.

The most important immediate consequence of the Crusades was not the tenuous Western possession of the Holy Land, but the expansion of trade and economic contacts the expeditions facilitated. No one profited more from the Crusades than the Italian cities that provided transportation and supplies to the crusading armies. The Crusades helped transform Genoa, Pisa, and Venice from small ports of regional significance into hubs of international trade. Genoa and Venice established their own colonial outposts in the eastern Mediterranean, and both vied to monopolize the rich commerce of Byzantium. The new trade controlled by these cities included luxury goods such as silk, Persian carpets, medicine, and spices—all expensive, exotic consumer goods found in the bazaars of the Middle East. Profits from this trade helped galvanize the economy of western Europe, leading to an era of exuberant economic growth during the twelfth and thirteenth centuries.

The crusading ideal survived long after Europeans quit going on actual Crusades. When Columbus sailed west in 1492, he imagined he was engaged in a kind of Crusade to spread Christianity. Even as late as the twentieth century, some Latin American countries continued to collect a tax to finance Crusades.

CONCLUSION

An Emerging Unity in the Latin West

The most lasting legacy of the early Middle Ages was the distinction between western and eastern Europe, established by the patterns of conversion to Christianity. Slavs in eastern Europe, such as the Poles, who were converted to Latin Christianity looked to Rome as a source for inspiration and eventually considered themselves part of the West. Those who converted to Orthodox Christianity, such as the Bulgarians and Russians, remained Europeans certainly but came to see themselves as culturally distinct from their Western counterparts. The southern border of Christian Europe was defined by the presence of the Islamic caliphates, which, despite recurrent border wars with Christian kingdoms, greatly contributed to the cultural vitality of the West during this period.

During this same period, however, a tentative unity began to emerge among western European Christians, just as Byzantium fell into decline and Islam divided among competing caliphates. That ephemeral unity was born in the hero worship of Charlemagne and the resurrection of the Roman Empire in the West, symbolized by his coronation in Rome. The collapse of the Carolingian Empire created the basis for the European kingdoms that dominated the political order of Europe for most of the subsequent millennium. These new kingdoms were each quite distinctive, and yet they shared a heritage from ancient Rome and the Carolingians that emphasized the power of the law on the one hand and the intimate relationship between royal and ecclesiastical authority on the other. The most distinguishing mark of western Europe became the practice of Latin Christianity, a distinctive form of Christianity identifiable by the use of the Latin language and the celebration of the church liturgy in Latin.

In the wake of the Carolingian Empire, a system of personal loyalties associated with lordship and vassalage came to dominate the military and political life of Latin Christendom. All medieval kings were obliged to build their monarchies on the social foundations of lordship, which provided cohesion in kingdoms that lacked bureaucracies and sufficient numbers of trained officials. In addition to the lords and vassals, the Latin kingdoms relied on the support of the Church to provide unity and often to provide the services of local government. By the end of the eleventh century, emerging western Europe had recovered sufficiently from the many destructive invaders and had built new political and ecclesiastical institutions that enabled it to assert itself on a broader stage.

MAKING CONNECTIONS

1. Why were the kingdoms of Latin Christendom usually so weak?
2. How did the Carolingian Empire rise above those weaknesses? Why did it eventually fall prey to them?
3. Was military conflict between Christians and Muslims inevitable in the Crusades?

TAKING IT FURTHER

For suggested readings, see page R-1.

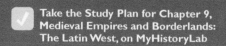
Chapter Review

The Birth of Latin Christendom

9.1 How did Latin Christendom build on Rome's legacy and how did Christianity spread?

Germanic kings acted as administrators in the style of Roman emperors by issuing laws and managing bureaucracy. The merging of Roman and Germanic traditions can also be traced in the law, and in the ability of women to own property, a right more common among the Romans than the Germans. Latin served as the language of worship, learning, and diplomacy. Conversion efforts on behalf of missionaries and intermarriage between Romans and Anglo-Saxons led to Christianity becoming the dominant religion in the kingdoms.

The Carolingians

9.2 How did the Carolingian Empire contribute to establishing a distinctive western European culture?

Charlemagne organized an efficient political administration that strengthened and institutionalized governmental procedures, and he also reorganized church administration into a strict hierarchy. Both new and revitalized monasteries provided the royal court with scribes, advisers, and spiritual assistants, and a revival of interest in ancient Greek and Latin literature marked the age.

Invasions and Recovery in the Latin West

9.3 How did Latin Christianity consolidate itself after the collapse of the Carolingian Empire?

Local warlords assumed responsibilities once invested in royal authorities and provided protection and order in a period of anarchy. Roman ideas of rulership influenced those leaders to expand the power of the monarchy and enhance the idea of kingship. The spread of Christianity to the edges of the continent was a result of organized missionary efforts by monks and bishops.

The West in the East: The Crusades

9.4 What were the causes and consequences of the Crusades?

The threat that Muslim armies allegedly posed to Christian peoples, pilgrims, and holy places in the eastern Mediterranean was the original cause of the Crusades; Pope Urban's appeal for a holy war in the east came as a response to the Byzantine emperor's request for military aid. Despite the successful capture of Jerusalem in the First Crusade, crusaders could neither maintain control of the city nor of the Latin principalities they established in the Middle East. Instead, for more than two centuries they wasted enormous efforts on a futile enterprise.

Chapter Time Line

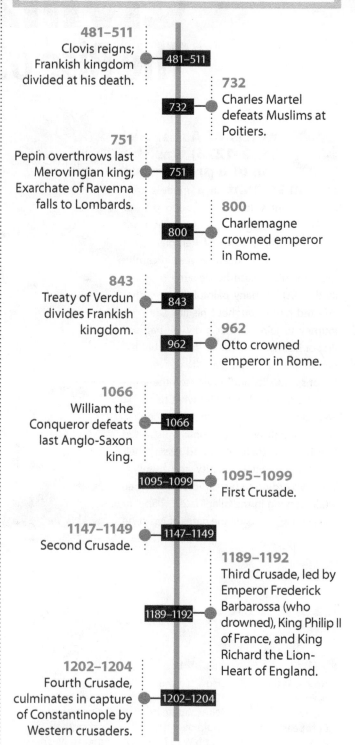

481–511
Clovis reigns; Frankish kingdom divided at his death.
481–511

732
732
Charles Martel defeats Muslims at Poitiers.

751
Pepin overthrows last Merovingian king; Exarchate of Ravenna falls to Lombards.
751

800
800
Charlemagne crowned emperor in Rome.

843
Treaty of Verdun divides Frankish kingdom.
843

962
962
Otto crowned emperor in Rome.

1066
William the Conqueror defeats last Anglo-Saxon king.
1066

1095–1099
1095–1099
First Crusade.

1147–1149
Second Crusade.
1147–1149

1189–1192
1189–1192
Third Crusade, led by Emperor Frederick Barbarossa (who drowned), King Philip II of France, and King Richard the Lion-Heart of England.

1202–1204
Fourth Crusade, culminates in capture of Constantinople by Western crusaders.
1202–1204

10

Medieval Civilization:
The Rise of Western Europe

Francis of Assisi (ca. 1182–1226) was the son of a prosperous merchant in a modest-sized town in central Italy. As a young man of 20, Francis joined the Assisi forces in a war with the nearby town of Perugia. Taken prisoner, he spent nearly a year in captivity. After his release he became seriously ill, the first of many painful illnesses that afflicted him throughout his life. During a journey to join another army, he had the first of his many visions or dreams that led him to give up fighting and to convert to a life of spirituality and service to others. Initially he searched about for what to do. He went on a pilgrimage to Rome as a beggar, and although lepers personally disgusted him he gave them alms and kissed their hands as an act of charity and humility. Then, according to his earliest biographer, while praying in the dilapidated chapel of San Damiano outside the gates of Assisi, he

ST. FRANCIS RENOUNCES HIS WORLDLY GOODS St. Francis stripped off all his clothing in the town square and renounced his worldly possessions, a spiritual act signifying his rejection of the material world. Francis's angry father, the figure in left center, has to be restrained to prevent him from striking his son with his clenched fist. Meanwhile, the bishop covers Francis's nakedness.

LEARNING OBJECTIVES

10.1 ((•
How was the medieval western European economy and society organized around manors and cities?

10.2 ((•
How did the Catholic Church consolidate its hold over the Latin West?

10.3 ((•
How did the western European monarchies strengthen themselves?

10.4 ((•
What made western European culture distinctive?

((• Listen to Chapter 10 on MyHistoryLab

⊙ Watch the Video Series on MyHistoryLab

Learn about some key topics related to this chapter with the *MyHistoryLab Video Series:*
Key Topics in Western Civilization

10.1

10.2

10.3

10.4

received a direct command from the crucifix above the altar: "Go Francis, and repair my house which, as you see, is nearly in ruins."

At first, Francis understood this command literally and began to repair churches and chapels. To raise money he took some of the best cloth from his father's shop and rode off to a nearby town where he sold the cloth and the horse. Angered by the theft of his cloth, his father denounced him to the town's authorities. When Francis refused the summons to court, his father had him brought to the bishop of Assisi for interrogation. Before his father could explain the situation to the bishop, Francis "without a word stripped off his clothing even removing his pants and gave them back to his father." Stark naked, Francis announced that he was switching his obedience from his earthly to his heavenly father. The astonished bishop gave him a cloak to cover his nakedness, but Francis renounced all family ties and worldly goods to live a life of complete poverty. Henceforth, he seemed to understand the command to "repair my house" as a metaphor for the entire Church, which he intended to serve in a new way.

Dressed in rags, Francis went about town begging for food, preaching repentance in the streets, and ministering to outcasts and lepers. Without training as a priest or license as a preacher, Francis at first seemed like a devout eccentric or even a dangerous heretic, but his rigorous imitation of Jesus began to attract like-minded followers. In 1210 Francis and 12 of his ragged brothers showed up in the opulent papal court of Pope Innocent III to request approval for a new religious order. A less discerning man than Innocent would have sent the strange band packing or thrown them in prison as a danger to established society, but Innocent was impressed by Francis's sincerity and his willingness to profess obedience to the pope. Innocent's provisional approval of the Franciscans was a brilliant stroke, in that it gave the papacy a way to manage the widespread enthusiasm for a life of spirituality and purity.

The life of Francis of Assisi and the religious order he founded, the Friars Minor (Lesser Brothers), known as the Franciscans, epitomized the strengths and tensions of medieval Europe. Francis was a product of the newly prosperous towns of Europe, which began to grow at an unprecedented rate after about 1050. In the streets of towns such as Assisi that thrived on profits from the international cloth trade, the extremes of wealth and poverty were always on display. Rich merchants such as Francis's father lived in splendid comfort and financed an urban building boom that had not been seen in the West for more than 1,000 years. The most lasting manifestations of that building boom were the vast new cathedrals, the pride of every medieval city. At the same time wretchedly poor people, many of them immigrants from the overpopulated countryside—starving and homeless—lined the steps into the great churches begging for alms. Francis abhorred the immorality of this contrast between wealth and poverty. His reaction was to reject all forms of wealth, to give away all his possessions, and to disdain money as poison. He and his followers devoted themselves to the poor and abandoned. They became traveling street preachers who relied entirely on the charity of others for food and shelter. Francis's rejection of the material world was not just a protest against the materialist values of his times. It was a total denial of the self. To put it in modern terms, it was a rejection of all forms of egotism and pride, combined with a revolutionary commitment to equality.

The late eleventh through thirteenth centuries were revolutionary in other ways. Based on the efforts of the knights who fought in the Crusades, the European merchants, and the great theologians of the Church, the Catholic West began to assert itself militarily, economically, and intellectually both in Byzantium and against the Muslim world. As a result, western Europeans more sharply distinguished themselves from the Orthodox and Muslim worlds. The West became more exclusively Latin and Catholic.

Internal developments within Europe made possible this consolidation of a distinctive Western identity and projection of Western power outside Europe. The agricultural revolution that began in the eleventh century stimulated population growth and urbanization. Fed by more productive farms, the expanding cities began to produce industrial goods, such as woolen cloth, that could be sold abroad in exchange for luxury goods from the Middle East and Asia. A number of vigorous kings created political stability in the West by consolidating their authority through financial and judicial bureaucracies. The most effective of these kings used a variety of strategies to force the most dangerous element in society, the landed aristocrats, to serve the royal interest. At the same time, the West experienced a period of creative ferment unequaled since antiquity. The Roman Catholic Church played a central role in encouraging intellectual and artistic activity, but there was also a flourishing literature in the vernacular languages such as French, German, and Italian. All these developments led to this question:

How did western European civilization mature during the eleventh through thirteenth centuries?

Two Worlds: Manors and Cities

10.1 How was the medieval western European economy and society organized around manors and cities?

After the end of the destructive Magyar and Viking invasions of the ninth and tenth centuries, the population of western Europe recovered dramatically. Technological innovations created the **agricultural revolution** that increased the supply of food. With more food available, people were better nourished than they had been in more than 500 years, and the population began to grow. In the seventh century all of Europe was home to only 14 million inhabitants. By 1300 the population had exploded to 74 million. From the seventh to the fourteenth centuries, then, the population grew many times over, perhaps as much as 500 percent.

The Medieval Agricultural Revolution

In the year 1000, the vast majority of people lived in small villages or isolated farmsteads. Peasants literally scratched out a living from a small area of cleared land around the village by employing a light scratch plow that barely turned over the soil. The farms produced mostly grain, which was consumed as bread, porridge, and ale or beer. Vegetables were rare; meat and fish, uncommon. Over the course of the century, the productivity of the land was greatly enhanced by a number of innovations that came into widespread use.

TECHNOLOGICAL INNOVATIONS The invention of new labor-saving devices ushered in the agricultural revolution. Farmers used water and windmills to grind grain, but others gradually adapted them to a wide variety of tasks, including turning saws to mill timber. In addition to these mechanical devices, the power of animals began to be used more efficiently. Metal horseshoes (until then, horses' hooves had been bound in cloth) gave horses better footing and traction. Perhaps even more important was the introduction of a new type of horse and ox collar. Older collars put pressure on the throat, which tended to choke the animal. The new collars transferred the pressure to the shoulders. With enhanced animal pulling power, farmers could plow the damp, heavy clay soils of northern Europe much more efficiently.

agricultural revolution Refers to technological innovations that began to appear during the eleventh century, making possible a dramatic growth in population. The agricultural revolution came about through harnessing new sources of power with water and windmills, improving the pulling power of animals with better collars, using heavy plows to better exploit the soils of northern Europe, and employing a three-field crop rotation system that increased the amount and quality of food available.

The centerpiece of the agricultural revolution was the heavy plow, called the *carruca*. It cut deeply and lifted the soil, aerating it and bringing minerals to the surface that were vital for plant growth. The *carruca*, however, required six or eight horses or oxen to pull it, and no single peasant family in the eleventh century could afford that many draft animals. Farmers had to pool their animals to create plow teams, a practice that required mutual planning and cooperation.

The introduction of the three-field system supplied the final piece in the agricultural revolution. In the three-field system farmers planted one field in the fall with grain and one in the spring with beans, peas, or lentils. The third field lay fallow. They harvested both fall and spring plantings in the summer, after which all the fields shifted. The three-field system produced extraordinary advantages: the amount of land under cultivation increased; beans planted in the spring rotation returned nitrogen to the soil; and the crop rotation combined with animal manure reduced soil exhaustion from excessive grain planting.

The agricultural revolution had a significant effect on society. First, villagers learned to cooperate—by pooling draft animals for plow teams, redesigning and elongating their fields to accommodate the new plow, coordinating the three-field rotation of crops, and timing the harvest schedule. To accomplish these cooperative ventures, they created village councils and developed habits of collective decision making that were essential for stable community life. Second, the system produced not only more food, but better food. Beans and other vegetables grown in the spring planting were rich in proteins.

A HEAVY CARRUCA PLOW At the center of the two-wheeled plow is a sturdy timber from which the coulter projects just in front of the plowshare, which is hidden by the earth. The surplus produced by the agricultural revolution made it possible for aristocrats to build huge and expensive castles such as the one in the background.

 Watch the Video

The Big Picture: The World in 1000 C.E.

MANORS AND PEASANTS The medieval agricultural economy bound landlords and peasants together in a unit of management called the **manor**. The lord of the manor usually owned his own large house or stone castle and served as the presiding judge of the villagers in the manor court. His wife, the *chatelaine* or lady of the manor, was his partner in management, and when the lord was away at war, which was often the case, she ruled the manor.

The peasants who worked the land of manors fell into three categories: serfs, freeholders, and cottagers. Lords did not own **serfs**, who were not slaves, but lords tied their serfs to the manor, which they could not leave. Serfs had certain legal rights denied to slaves, such as the right to a certain portion of what they produced, but the lord's will was law. Freeholders worked as independent farmers, owned their land outright, and did not have to answer to a lord. At the bottom of rural peasant society struggled numerous impoverished cottagers who had no rights to the land and farmed small, less desirable plots, often as squatters.

No matter what their official status, each family worked the land together with all family members performing tasks suitable to their abilities, strength, and age. The rigors of medieval farm labor did not permit a fastidious division of labor between women and men. Women did not usually drive the heavy plow, but they toiled at

manor A medieval unit of agricultural management in which a lord managed and served as the presiding judge over peasants who worked the land.

serfs During the Middle Ages, serfs were agricultural laborers who worked and lived on a plot of land granted them by a lord to whom they owed a certain portion of their crops. They could not leave the land, but they had certain legal rights that were denied to slaves.

other physically demanding tasks. During the critical harvest times, women and children worked alongside men from dawn to dusk. Young girls typically worked as gleaners, picking up the stalks and kernels that the male harvesters dropped or left behind, and girls took responsibility for weeding and cleaning the fields. Nearly all women from peasant girls to the household servants of the manor engaged themselves in the tasks of fabricating clothing from spinning thread and yarn, to weaving cloth, to sewing and tailoring.

THE GREAT MIGRATIONS AND THE HUNGER FOR LAND After the eleventh century most peasant families were considerably better off than their ancestors had been before the new technological innovations. Due to the agricultural revolution, nutritional levels improved so that famines decreased, and a "baby boom" led to dramatic population growth.

The effect of the baby boom meant that the amount of land available to farm was insufficient to support the expanding population of the manors. As more and more young people entered the workforce, they either sought opportunities in the cities or searched for land of their own. Both options meant that many young people and whole families had to migrate. The modern phenomenon of mass immigration is hardly new.

Where did all these people go? Migrants seeking to clear new lands for agriculture moved in three directions: Germans into lands of the Slavic tribes to the east, Scandinavians to the far north and the North Atlantic islands, and Christian Spaniards to the south into previously Muslim territories on the Iberian peninsula, slowly creating the outlines of what would become modern Spain. Between 1100 and 1300, these migrants brought as much as 40 percent more land under cultivation in Europe. The vibrant civilization discussed in the rest of this chapter was the direct consequence of the European demographic success.

TWELFTH-CENTURY MANOR MADE POSSIBLE BY THE HEAVY PLOW Aerial photograph of the manor of West Whelpington North (England), which was settled in the twelfth century, but whose inhabitants died out during the Black Death of the fourteenth century (see Chapter 11). Outlines of the individual families' farm gardens can be seen in the left center. On the lower right are the ridges and furrows of the elongated fields created by the use of the heavy plow.

The Growth of Cities

All across Europe during the twelfth and thirteenth centuries, cities exploded in size. Exact population figures are difficult to determine, and by our own modern standards most of these cities were modest in size—numbering in the tens of thousands rather than hundreds of thousands—but there is ample evidence of stunning growth. Between 1160 and 1300 Ghent expanded its city walls five times to accommodate all its inhabitants. During the thirteenth century the population of Florence grew by an estimated 640 percent.

THE CHALLENGE OF FREE CITIES The newly thriving cities proved troublesome for the lords, bishops, and kings who had legal authority over them. As the population grew and urban merchants, such as Francis of Assisi's father, became increasingly rich, the cities in which they lived enjoyed even greater resources in people and money than those available to the rural lords. In many places the citizens of the new enlarged towns attempted to rid themselves of their lords to establish self-rule or, at least, substantial autonomy for their city. In the cities of north-central Italy, for example, townsmen formed sworn defensive associations called **communes** (from *communis* meaning "shared"), which quickly became the effective government of the towns. The communes evolved into city-states, which seized control of the surrounding countryside. Perhaps as many as 100 or more cities in north-central Italy formed communes after 1070.

> **communes** Sworn defensive associations of merchants and workers that appeared in north-central Italy after 1070 and that became the effective government of more than a hundred cities. The communes evolved into city-states by seizing control of the surrounding countryside.

The Italian communes created the institutions and culture of self-rule. They were not fully democratic; nevertheless, in many of them a significant percentage of the male population, including artisans, could vote for public officials, hold office themselves, and have a voice in important decisions such as going to war or raising new taxes. They also emphasized the civic responsibilities of citizens to protect the weakest members of the community, to beautify the city with public buildings and monuments, and to defend it by serving in the militia and paying taxes. These cities created vital community institutions, some of which survive to this day. In the wake of the Crusades several north Italian communes, especially Venice, Genoa, and Pisa, became ports of international significance. Sailors from these cities had transported the crusading knights to the Holy Land, Egypt, Syria, and Byzantium. Even after the crusader kingdoms collapsed, these cities kept footholds in the eastern Mediterranean, some of which evolved into colonies. Through these trading cities western Europe became integrated into the international luxury trade, which they carried out with ships crisscrossing the Mediterranean Sea.

THE ECONOMIC BOOM YEARS The cities of the medieval West thrived on an economic base of unprecedented prosperity. What made possible the twelfth- and thirteenth-century economic boom? Four related factors explain the thriving medieval economy. We have already touched on the first two reasons: the agricultural revolution of the eleventh century, which enabled population growth; and the expansion of cities, which both facilitated the commercial boom and allowed city dwellers to be the primary beneficiaries of it.

The other two reasons were just as important: advances in transportation networks and the creation of new business techniques. Trade in grain, woolen cloth, and other bulk goods depended on the use of relatively cheap water transportation for hauling goods. Where there were neither seaports nor navigable rivers, drovers hauled goods cross-country by pack train, a very expensive enterprise. In Europe there were no land transportation routes or pack animals that rivaled the efficiency of the camel in the deserts of North Africa and the steppes of Asia. To address the problem and to facilitate transportation and trade, governments and local lords built new roads and bridges and repaired old Roman roads that had been neglected for 1,000 years.

A MEDIEVAL TOWN Carcassonne in southern France remains one of the best examples of a medieval walled city. Built on Roman foundations, the fortifications date from the eleventh to thirteenth centuries but were completely restored in the nineteenth century. In contrast to unfortified Roman cities, medieval towns required (as shown here) walls, fortified towers, and a moat for protection against bandits and the armies of rival towns and princes. The fortifications symbolized the insecurity of the prosperous towns. Carcassonne was a stronghold of the Cathars and subject to a long siege during the Albigensian Crusade (see the following text). After the defeat of the Cathars the walls were so effectively rebuilt that the city was considered impregnable.

The most lucrative trade was the international commerce in luxury goods. Because these goods were lightweight and high-priced, they could sustain the cost of long-distance transportation across land. Italian merchants virtually monopolized the European luxury trade. Camel caravans transported raw silk from China and Turkestan across Asia. Merchants sold the silk at trading posts on the shores of the Black Sea and in Constantinople to Italian merchants who shipped the goods across the Mediterranean, had the raw silk woven into cloth, and then earned enormous profits selling the shimmering fabrics to the ladies and gentlemen of the European aristocracy. Though small in quantity, the silk trade was of great value to international commerce because silk was so highly prized. One ounce of fine Chinese black silk sold on the London market for as much as a highly skilled mason would earn in a week's labor. Even the bulk commodities the Italians brought from the East were valuable enough to sustain the high transportation costs. Known by the generic term "spices," these included hundreds of exotic items: True spices such as pepper, sugar, cloves, nutmeg, ginger, saffron, mace, and cinnamon enhanced the otherwise bland cuisine; for dyeing cloth, blue came from indigo and red from madder root; for fixing the dyes the Genoese imported alum; and for pain relievers there were medicinal herbs including opiates. The profits from spices generated much of the capital in European financial markets.

Long-distance trade necessitated the creation of new business techniques. For example, the expansion of trade and new markets required a moneyed economy. Coins had almost disappeared in the West for nearly 400 years during the Early Middle Ages, when most people lived self-sufficiently on manors and bartered for what they could not produce for themselves. The few coins that circulated came from Byzantium or the Muslim caliphates. By the thirteenth century, Venice and Florence minted their own gold coins, which became the medium for exchange across much of Europe.

Merchants who engaged in long-distance trade invented the essential business tools of capitalism during this period. They created business partnerships, uniform accounting practices, merchants' courts to enforce contracts and resolve disputes, letters of credit (used like modern bankers' checks), bank deposits and loans, and insurance policies. The Italian cities established primary schools to train merchants' sons to write business letters and keep accounts—a sign of the growing professional character of business. Two centuries earlier an international merchant had been an itinerant peddler who led pack trains over dusty and muddy tracks to customers in small villages and castles. But by the end of the thirteenth century an international merchant could stay at home behind a desk, writing letters to business partners and ship captains and enjoying the profits from his labors in the bustling atmosphere of a thriving city.

At the center of the European market were the Champagne fairs in France, where merchants from northern and southern Europe met every summer to bargain and haggle (see **Map 10.1**). The Italians exchanged their silk and spices for English raw wool, Dutch woolen cloth, German furs and linens, and Spanish leather. From the Champagne fairs, prosperity spread into previously wild parts of Europe. Cities along the German rivers and the Baltic coast thrived through the trade of raw materials such as timber and iron, livestock, salt fish, and hides. The most prominent of the north German towns was Lübeck, which became the center of the Hanseatic League, a loose trade association of cities in Germany and the Baltic coast. Never achieving the level of a unified government, the league nonetheless provided its members mutual security and trading monopolies—which were necessary because of the weakness of the German imperial government.

Urban civilization, one of the major achievements of the Middle Ages, thrived from the commerce of the economic boom. From urban civilization came other achievements. All the cities built large new cathedrals to flaunt their accumulated wealth and to honor God. New educational institutions, especially universities, trained the sons of the urban, commercial elite in the professions. However, the merchants who commanded the urban economy were not necessarily society's heroes. The populace at large viewed them with deep ambivalence, despite the immeasurable ways in which they enriched society. Churchmen worried about the morality of making profits. Church councils condemned usury—the lending of money for interest—even though papal finances depended on it. Theologians promulgated the idea of a "just price," the idea that there should be a fixed price for any particular commodity. The just price was anathema to hardheaded merchants who were committed to the laws of supply and demand. Part of the ambivalence toward trade and merchants came from the inequities created in all market-based economies—the rewards of

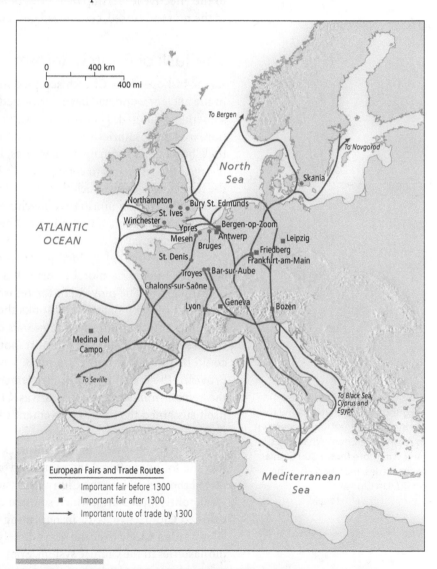

MAP **10.1** EUROPEAN FAIRS AND TRADE ROUTES Trade routes crisscrossed the Mediterranean Sea and hugged the Atlantic Ocean, North Sea, and Baltic Sea coastlines. Land routes converged in central France at the Champagne fairs. Other trade routes led to the large market cities in Germany and Flanders. What parts of Europe benefited the most from the economic boom? From this map, what parts were left out?

the market were unevenly distributed, both socially and geographically, as St. Francis's protest demonstrated. The prosperous merchants symbolized disturbing social changes, but they were also the dynamic force that made possible the intellectual and artistic flowering of the High Middle Ages.

The Consolidation of Roman Catholicism

10.2 How did the Catholic Church consolidate its hold over the Latin West?

The late eleventh through thirteenth centuries witnessed one of the greatest periods of religious vitality in the history of Roman Catholicism. Manifest by the Crusades (discussed in Chapter 9), the rise of new religious orders, remarkable intellectual creativity, and the final triumph over the surviving polytheistic tribes of northern and eastern Europe, the religious vitality of the era was due in no small part to the effective leadership of a series of able popes. They gave the Church the benefits of the most advanced, centralized government in Europe.

The Task of Church Reform

As the bishops of the Church accepted many of the administrative responsibilities that in the ancient world had been performed by secular authorities, their spiritual mission sometimes suffered. They became overly involved in the business of the world. In addition, over the centuries wealthy and pious people had made large donations of land to the Church, making many monasteries, in particular, immensely wealthy. Such wealth tempted the less pious to corruption, and the Roman popes were unlikely to eliminate the temptations from which they benefited. Even those popes who wanted to were slow to assemble the administrative machinery necessary to enforce their will across the unruly lands of Roman Catholicism. The impulse for reform derived in many respects from the material success of the Church and the monasteries.

The slow but determined progress of the popes from the eleventh to thirteenth centuries to enforce moral reform is the most remarkable achievement of the medieval papacy. The movement for reform, however, did not begin with the popes. It came out of the monasteries. Monks thought the best way to clean up corruption in the Church was to improve the morals of individuals. If men and women conducted themselves with a sense of moral responsibility, the whole institution of the Church could be purified. Monks and nuns, who set an example for the rest of the Church, provided the model for self-improvement for society at large. The most influential of the reform-minded monasteries was **Cluny** in Burgundy, established in 910. Cluny itself sustained the reform movement through more than 1,500 Cluniac monasteries throughout Europe.

From the very beginning Cluny was exceptional for several reasons. First, its aristocratic founder offered the monastery as a gift to the pope. As a result, the pope directed the activities of the Cluny monastery from Rome and kept it independent from local political pressures, which so often caused corruption. The Rome connection positioned Cluniacs to assist in reforming the papacy itself. Second, the various abbots who headed Cluny over the years closely coordinated reform activities of the various monasteries in the Cluniac system. Some of these abbots were men of exceptional ability and learning who had a European-wide reputation for their moral stature. Third, Cluny regulated the life of monks much more closely than did other monasteries, so the monks there were models of devotion. To the Cluniacs moral purity required complete renunciation of the benefits of the material world and a commitment to spiritual

Cluny A monastery founded in Burgundy in 910 that became the center of a far-reaching movement to reform the Church that was sustained in more than 1,500 Cluniac monasteries, modeled after the original in Cluny.

experiences. The elegantly simple liturgy in which the monks themselves sung the text of the mass and other prayers symbolized Cluniac purity. The beauty of the music enhanced the spiritual experience, and its simplicity clarified rather than obscured the meaning of the words. Because of these attractive traits, the Cluniac liturgy spread to the far corners of Europe.

The success of Cluny and other reformed monasteries provided the base from which reform ideas spread beyond the isolated world of monks to the rest of the Church. The first candidates for reform were parish priests and bishops. Called the *secular clergy* (in Latin *saeculum,* meaning "secular") because they lived in the secular world, they differed from the regular clergy (in Latin *regula,* those who followed a "rule") who lived in monasteries apart from the world. The lives of many secular clergy differed little from their lay neighbors. (*Laypeople* or *the laity* referred to all Christians who had not taken religious vows to become a priest, monk, or nun.) In contrast to celibate monks, who were sexually chaste, many priests kept concubines or were married and tried to bequeath church property to their children. In contrast to the Orthodox Church, in which priests were allowed to marry, the Catholic Church had repeatedly forbidden married priests, but the prohibitions had been ineffective until Cluniac reform stressed the ideal of the sexually pure priest. During the eleventh century bishops, church councils, and reformist popes began to insist on a celibate clergy.

The clerical reform movement also tried to eliminate the corrupt practices of simony and lay investiture. **Simony** was the practice of buying and selling church offices. **Lay investiture** took place when aristocrats, kings, or emperors installed churchmen and gave them their symbols of office ("invested" them). Through this practice, powerful lords controlled the clergy and usurped Church property. In exchange for protecting the Church, these laymen conceived of church offices as a form of vassalage and expected to name their own candidates as priests and bishops. The reformers saw as sinful any form of lay authority over the Church—whether the authority was that of the local lord or the emperor himself. As a result of this controversy, the most troublesome issue of the eleventh century became establishing the boundaries between temporal and spiritual authorities.

simony The practice of buying and selling church offices.

lay investiture The practice of nobles, kings, or emperors installing churchmen and giving them the symbols of office.

THE POPE BECOMES A MONARCH Religious reform required unity within the Church. The most important step in building unity was to define what it meant to be a Catholic. In the Middle Ages, Roman Catholicism identified itself in two ways. First, the Church insisted on conformity in rites. Rites consisted of the forms of public worship called the liturgy, which included certain prescribed prayers and chants, usually in Latin. Uniform rites meant that Catholics could hear the Mass celebrated in essentially the same way everywhere from Poland to Portugal, Iceland to Croatia. Conformity of worship created a cultural unity that transcended differences in language and ethnicity. When Catholics from far-flung locales encountered one another, they shared something meaningful to them all because of the uniformity of rites. The second thing that defined a Catholic was obedience to the pope. Ritual uniformity and obedience to the pope were closely interrelated because both the ritual and the pope were Roman. There were many bishops in Christianity, but as one monk put it, "Rome is . . . the head of the world."

Beginning in the late eleventh century the task of the popes became to make this theoretical assertion of obedience real—in short, to make the papacy a religious monarchy. Among the reformers who gathered in Rome was Hildebrand (ca. 1020–1085), one of the most remarkable figures in the history of the Church, a man beloved as saintly by his admirers and considered an ambitious, self-serving megalomaniac by many others. From 1055 to 1073 during the pontificates of some four popes, Hildebrand became the power behind the throne, helping enact wide-ranging reforms that enforced uniformity of worship and establishing the rules for electing new popes by the college of cardinals. In 1073 the cardinals elected Hildebrand himself pope, and he took the name Gregory VII (r. 1073–1085).

Gregory's greatness lay in his leadership over the internal reform of the Church. Every year he held a Church council in Rome where he decreed against simony and married priests. Gregory centralized authority over the Church itself by sending out papal legates, representatives who delivered orders to local bishops. He attempted to free the Church from external influence by asserting the superiority of the pope over all other authorities. Gregory's theory of papal supremacy led him into direct conflict with the German emperor, Henry IV (r. 1056–1106). The issue was lay investiture. During the eighth and ninth centuries weak popes relied on the Carolingian kings and emperors to name suitable candidates for ecclesiastical offices in order to keep them out of the hands of local aristocrats. At stake was not only power and authority, but also the income from the enormous amount of property controlled by the Church, which the emperor was in the best position to protect. During the eleventh century, Gregory VII and other reform-minded popes sought to regain control of this property. Without the ability to name his own candidates as bishops, Gregory recognized that his whole campaign for Church reform would falter. When Pope Gregory tried to negotiate with the emperor over the appointment of the bishop of Milan, Henry resisted and commanded Gregory to resign the papacy in a letter with the notorious salutation, "Henry, King not by usurpation, but by the pious ordination of God to Hildebrand now not Pope but false monk."

Gregory struck back in an escalating confrontation now known as the **Investiture Controversy**. He deposed Henry from the imperial throne and excommunicated him. **Excommunication** prohibited the sinner from participating in the sacraments and forbade any social contact whatsoever with the surrounding community. People caught talking, writing a letter, or even offering a drink of water to an excommunicated person could themselves be excommunicated. Excommunication was a form of social death, a dire punishment indeed, especially if the excommunicated person was a king. Both sides marshaled arguments from Scripture and history, but the excommunication was effective. Henry's friends started to abandon him, rebellion broke out in Germany, and the most powerful German lords called for a meeting to elect a new emperor. Backed into a corner, Henry plotted a clever counterstroke.

Early in the winter of 1077 Pope Gregory set out to cross the Alps to meet with the German lords. When Gregory reached the Alpine passes, however, he learned that Emperor Henry was on his way to Italy. In fear of what the emperor would do, Gregory retreated to the castle of Canossa, where he expected to be attacked. Henry surprised Gregory, however, by arriving not with an army, but as a supplicant asking the pope to hear his confession. As a priest Gregory could hardly refuse to hear the confession of a penitent sinner, but he nevertheless attempted to humiliate Henry by making him wait for three days, kneeling in the snow outside the castle. Henry's presentation of himself as a penitent sinner posed a dilemma for Gregory. The German lords were waiting for Gregory to appear in his capacity as the chief justice of Christendom to judge Henry, but Henry himself was asking the pope to act in his capacity as priest to grant absolution for sin. The priest in Gregory won out over the judge, and he absolved Henry.

Even after the deaths of Gregory and Henry, the Investiture Controversy continued to poison relations between the popes and emperors until the Concordat of Worms in 1122 resolved the issue in a formal treaty. The emperor retained the right to nominate high churchmen; however, in a concession to the papacy, the emperor lost the ceremonial privileges of investiture that conveyed spiritual authority. Without the ceremony of investiture, no bishop could exercise his office. By refusing to invest unsuitable nominees, the popes had the last word. Gregory VII's vision of papal supremacy over all kings and emperors persevered.

Investiture Controversy A dispute that began in 1076 between the popes and the German emperors over the right to invest bishops with their offices. The most famous episode was the conflict between Pope Gregory VII and Emperor Henry IV. The controversy was resolved by the Concordat of Worms in 1122.

excommunication A decree by the pope or a bishop prohibiting a sinner from participating in the sacraments of the Church and forbidding any social contact whatsoever with the surrounding community.

  Read the Document

Letter of Pope Gregory VII to the Bishop of Metz, 1081

HOW THE POPES RULED The most lasting accomplishment of the popes during the twelfth and thirteenth centuries derived less from dramatic confrontations with emperors than from the humdrum routine of the law. Beginning with Gregory VII, the papacy became the supreme court of the Catholic world by claiming authority over a vast range of issues. To justify these claims, Gregory and his assistants conducted massive research among old laws and treatises. These were organized into a body of legal texts called canon law.

Canon law came to encompass many kinds of cases, including all those involving the clergy, disputes about church property, and donations to the Church. The law of the Church also touched on many of the most vital concerns of the laity including annulling marriages, legitimating bastards, prosecuting bigamy, protecting widows and orphans, and resolving inheritance disputes. Most of the cases originated in the courts of the bishops, but the bishops' decisions could be appealed to the pope and cardinals sitting together in the papal consistory. The consistory could make exceptions from the letter of the law, called dispensations, giving it considerable power over kings and aristocrats who wanted to marry a cousin, divorce a wife, legitimate a bastard, or annul a will. By the middle of the twelfth century, Rome was awash with legal business. The functions of the canon law courts became so important that those elected popes were no longer monks but trained canon lawyers, men very capable in the ways of the world.

The pope also presided over the **curia**, the administrative bureaucracy of the Church. The cardinals in the curia served as ministers in the papal administration and visited foreign princes and cities as ambassadors or legates. Because large amounts of revenue were flowing into the coffers of the Church, the curia functioned as a bank. Rome became the financial capital of the West.

curia The administrative bureaucracy of the Roman Catholic Church.

In addition to its legal, administrative, and financial authority, the papacy also made use of two powerful spiritual weapons against the disobedient. Any Christian who refused to repent of a sin could be excommunicated, as Emperor Henry IV had been. The second spiritual weapon was the **interdict**, the suspension of the sacraments in a locality or kingdom whose ruler had defied the pope. During an interdict the churches closed their doors, creating panic among the faithful who could not baptize their children or bury their dead. The interdict, which encouraged a public outcry, could be a very effective weapon for undermining the political support of any monarch who ran afoul of the pope.

interdict A papal decree prohibiting the celebration of the sacraments in an entire city or kingdom.

THE PINNACLE OF THE MEDIEVAL PAPACY: POPE INNOCENT III The most capable of the medieval popes was Innocent III (r. 1198–1216). To him, the pope was the overlord of the entire world. He recognized the right of kings to rule over the secular sphere, but he considered it his duty to prevent and punish sin, a duty that gave him wide latitude to meddle in the affairs of kings and princes.

Innocent's first task was to provide the papacy with a strong territorial base of support so that the popes could act with the same freedom as kings and princes. Historians consider Innocent the founder of the Papal State in central Italy, an independent state that lasted until 1870 and survives today in a tiny fragment as Vatican City.

Innocent's second goal was keeping alive the crusading ideal. He called the Fourth Crusade, which went awry when the crusaders attacked Constantinople instead of conquering Jerusalem. He also expanded the definition of crusading by calling for a crusade to eliminate heresy within Christian Europe. Innocent was deeply concerned about the spread of new heresies, which attracted enormous numbers of converts, especially in the growing cities of southern Europe. By crusading against Christian heretics—the Cathars and Waldensians (see the following discussion)—Innocent authorized the use of military methods to enforce uniformity of belief.

The third objective was to assert the authority of the papacy over political affairs. Innocent managed the election of Emperor Frederick II. He also assumed the right to veto imperial elections. He excommunicated King Philip II of France to force him to

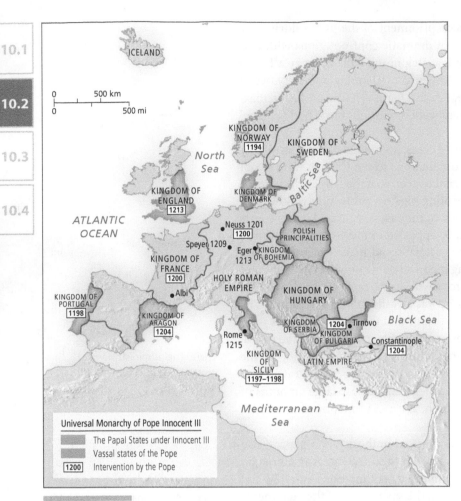

MAP **10.2** UNIVERSAL MONARCHY OF POPE INNOCENT III Besides his direct control of the Papal State in central Italy, Pope Innocent III made vassals of many of the kings of Catholic Europe. These feudal ties provided a legal foundation for his claim to be the highest authority in Christian Europe. Based on this map, what medieval countries were most influenced by the papal monarch?

take back an unwanted wife. And Innocent placed England under the interdict to compel King John to cede his kingdom to the papacy and receive it back as a fief, a transaction that made the king of England the vassal of the pope. Using whatever means necessary, he made papal vassals of the rulers of Aragon, Bulgaria, Denmark, Hungary, Poland, Portugal, and Serbia. Through the use of the feudal law of vassalage, Innocent brought the papacy to its closest approximation of a universal Christian monarchy (see **Map 10.2**).

Innocent's fourth and greatest accomplishment was to codify the rites of the liturgy and to define the dogmas of the faith. This monumental task was the achievement of the Fourth Lateran Council, held in Rome in 1215. This council, attended by more than 400 bishops, 800 abbots, and the ambassadors of the monarchs of Catholic Europe, issued decrees that reinforced the celebration of the sacraments as the centerpiece of Christian life. They included rules to educate the clergy, define their qualifications, and govern elections of bishops. The council condemned heretical beliefs, and it called for yet another Crusade. The council became the guidepost that has since governed many aspects of Catholic practice, especially with regard to the sacraments. It did more than any other council to fulfill the goal of uniformity of rites in Catholicism.

THE TROUBLED LEGACY OF THE PAPAL MONARCHY Innocent was an astute, intelligent man who in single-minded fashion pursued the greater good of the Church as he saw it. No one succeeded better than he in preserving the unity of the Catholic world in an era of chaos. His policies, however, were less successful in the hands of his less able successors. Their blunders undermined the pope's spiritual mission. Innocent's successors went beyond defending the Papal State and embroiled all Italy in a series of bloody civil wars between the Guelfs, who supported the popes, and the Ghibellines, who opposed them. The pope's position as a monarch superior to all others collapsed under the weight of immense folly during the pontificate of Boniface VIII (r. 1294–1303). His claims to absolute authority combined with breathtaking vanity and ineptitude corroded the achievements of Innocent III.

In 1302 Boniface promulgated the most extreme theoretical assertion of papal superiority over lay rulers. The papal bull, *Unam Sanctum*, decreed that "it is absolutely necessary for salvation that every human creature be subject to the Roman pontiff." Behind the statement was a specific dispute with King Philip IV of France (r. 1285–1314), who was attempting to try a French bishop for treason. The larger issue behind the dispute was similar to the Investiture Controversy of the eleventh century, but this time no one paid much attention to the pope. The loss of papal moral authority had taken its toll. In the heat of the confrontation, King Philip accused Pope Boniface of heresy, one of the few sins of which he was not guilty, and sent his agents to arrest the pope. Boniface died shortly after, and the papal monarchy died as well.

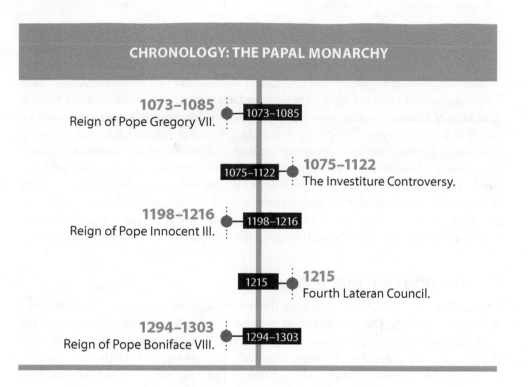

CHRONOLOGY: THE PAPAL MONARCHY

1073–1085
Reign of Pope Gregory VII.
`1073–1085`

`1075–1122`
1075–1122
The Investiture Controversy.

1198–1216
Reign of Pope Innocent III.
`1198–1216`

`1215`
1215
Fourth Lateran Council.

1294–1303
Reign of Pope Boniface VIII.
`1294–1303`

THE RELIGIOUS OUTCASTS: CATHARS AND WALDENSIANS In its efforts to defend the faith, the Church during the first half of the thirteenth century began to authorize bishops and other clerics to conduct inquisitions (formal inquiries) into specific instances of heresy or perceived heresy. The so-called heretics tended to be faithful people who sought personal purity in religion. During the thirteenth and early fourteenth centuries, inquisitions and systematic persecutions targeted the Cathars and Waldensians, who at first had lived peacefully with their Catholic neighbors and shared many of the same beliefs with them.

The name *Cathar* derives from the Greek word for purity. The Cathars were especially strong in northern Italy and southern France. Heavily concentrated around the French town of Albi, the Cathars were also known as Albigensians. They departed from Catholic doctrine, which held that God created the Earth, because they believed that an evil force had created all matter. To purify themselves, an elite few—known as "perfects"—rejected their own bodies as corrupt matter, refused to marry and procreate, and in extreme cases gradually starved themselves. These purified perfects provided a dramatic contrast to the more worldly Catholic clergy. For many, Catharism became a form of protest against the wealth and power of the Church. By the 1150s the Cathars had organized their own churches, performed their own rituals, and even elected their own bishops. Where they became deeply rooted, as in the south of France, they practiced their faith openly until Pope Innocent III authorized a crusade against them.

The Waldensians were the followers of Peter Waldo (d. ca. 1184), a merchant of Lyons, France, who like Francis of Assisi had abandoned all his possessions and taken a vow of poverty. Desiring to imitate the life of Jesus and live in simple purity, the Waldensians preached and translated the Gospels into their own language so that laypeople who did not know Latin could understand them. At first the Waldensians seemed similar to the Franciscans, but because of the Waldensians' failure to obtain licenses to preach as the Franciscans had done, they came to be depicted by Church authorities as heretics. In response, the Waldensians created an alternative church that became widespread in southern France, Rhineland Germany, and northern Italy.

Catholic authorities, who were often the objects of strong criticisms from the Cathars and Waldensians, grew ever more hostile to them. Bishops declared heretics liable to the same legal penalties as those guilty of treason, which authorized the political authorities to proceed against them. In 1208 Pope Innocent III called the Albigensian Crusade, the first of several holy wars launched against heretics in the south of France. The king of France was only too happy to fight the Albigensian Crusade because he saw it as a means of expanding royal power in a region of France where his authority was weak. To eradicate the remaining Cathars and Waldensians, several kings and popes initiated inquisitions. By the middle of the thirteenth century, Catholic authorities had either converted or exterminated the Cathars except for a few isolated pockets in the mountains. Inquisitorial campaigns nearly wiped out the Waldensians, but scattered groups have managed to survive to this day, mostly by retreating to the relative safety of the high Alps and later to the Americas. (See *Justice in History* in this chapter.)

Discovering God in the World

Even before the First Crusade, Catholic Europe began to experience an unprecedented spiritual awakening. The eleventh-century papal campaign to reform the morals of the clergy helped make priests both more respectable and better educated. A better-educated clergy in turn educated the laity more effectively. In large numbers Catholic Christians began to internalize the teachings of the Church. The most devout were drawn to dedicating their lives to religion. In England, for example, the number of monks increased tenfold from the late eleventh century to 1200. The newly expanding cities built loyalty and encouraged peaceable behavior through the veneration of civic patron saints. The most vital indication of spiritual renewal was the success of new religious orders, which satisfied a widespread yearning to discover the hand of God in the world.

THE PATRON SAINTS Saints are holy people whose moral perfection gives them a special relationship with the sacred. Ordinary Christians venerated saints to gain access to supernatural powers, protection, and intercession with God.

The relationship between Christian believers and the saints was profoundly intimate and intertwined with many aspects of life: Parents named their children after saints who became special protectors; every church dedicated itself to a saint; every town and city adopted a patron saint. And even entire peoples cherished a patron saint. For example, the Irish adopted Saint Patrick, who supposedly brought Christianity to the island.

A city gained protection from a patron saint by obtaining the saint's relics: the corpse, skeleton, part of the skeleton, or some object associated with the saint. These relics, verified by miracles, served as contacts between Earth and Heaven. The belief in the miraculous powers of relics created an enormous demand for them in the thriving medieval cities. But because the remains of the martyrs and early saints of the Church were spread across the Middle East and Mediterranean from Jerusalem to Rome, someone first had to discover the saint's relics and then transfer them to new homes in the churches of the growing western and northern European cities. Relics were bought or stolen, and there was ample room for fraud in passing off unauthentic bones to gullible buyers. During the Crusades the supply of relics greatly increased because the knights had access to the tombs of early Christian saints and martyrs.

During the twelfth and thirteenth centuries public veneration of saints began to undergo a subtle shift away from the cults of the local patron saints toward more universal figures such as Jesus and the Virgin Mary. The patron saints had functioned almost like the family deities of antiquity who served the particular needs of individuals and communities, but the papal monarchy encouraged uniformity throughout Catholicism.

Christians had always honored the Virgin Mary, but beginning in the twelfth century her immense popularity provided Catholics with a positive female image that contradicted the traditional misogyny and mistrust associated with Eve. Clerics and monks had long depicted women as deceitful and lustful in luring men to their moral ruin. In contrast, the veneration of the Virgin Mary promoted the image of a loving mother who would intervene with her son on behalf of sinners at the Last Judgment. Theologians still taught that the woman Eve had brought sin into the world, but the woman Mary offered help in escaping the consequences of sin.

The popularity of Mary was evident everywhere. The burgeoning cities of Europe dedicated most of the new cathedrals to her. Mary became a model with whom women could identify, presenting a positive image of femininity. In images of her suckling the Christ child, she became the perfect embodiment of the virtue of charity, the willingness to give without any expectation of reward. In contrast to the early Christian saints who were predominantly martyrs and missionaries, during the twelfth and thirteenth centuries saints exhibited sanctity more through nurturing others, especially by feeding the poor and healing the sick. Women embodied the capacity to nurture, and many more women became saints during this period than during the entire first millennium of Christianity. In 1100 fewer than 10 percent of all the saints were female. By 1300 the percentage had increased to 24 percent. During the fifteenth century about 30 percent were women.

THE NEW RELIGIOUS ORDERS By the eleventh century many men attracted to the religious life found the traditional orders too lax in their discipline and too worldly. In 1098 a small group of Benedictine monks removed themselves to an isolated wasteland to establish the Cistercian Order. The Cistercians practiced a very strict discipline. They ate only enough to stay alive. Each monk possessed only one robe. Unlike other orders, such as the Cluniacs, which required monks to attend frequent and lengthy services, the Cistercians spent more time in private prayer and manual labor. Their churches were bare of all decoration. Under the brilliant leadership of Bernard of Clairvaux (1090–1153), the Cistercians grew rapidly, as many men disillusioned with the sinful and materialistic society around them joined the new order. Bernard's asceticism led him to seek refuge from the affairs of the world, but he was also a religious reformer and activist, engaged with the important issues of his time. He even helped settle a disputed papal election and called for a crusade.

The Cistercians established their new monasteries in isolated, uninhabited places where they cleared forests and worked the land so that they could live in complete isolation from the troubled affairs of the world. Their hard work had an ironic result. By bringing new lands under the plow and by employing the latest technological innovations, such as water mills, many of the Cistercian monasteries produced more than was needed for the monks, and the sale of excess produce made the Cistercians rich. The economic success of the Cistercians helped them expand even more rapidly, especially into places previously untouched by monasticism in northeastern Europe. The rapid Cistercian push beyond the frontiers of Latin Europe helped disseminate the culture of Catholic Christianity through educating the local elites and attracting them to join

MOSAICS IN THE BASILICA OF ST. MARK IN VENICE Pilgrims learned of Venice's intimate association with its patron, St. Mark, from the magnificent mosaics that adorned the basilica's ceilings and walls. This scene shows a miracle that occurred after St. Mark's body was lost during a fire in the basilica. The leaders of Venice, shown on the left, spent days in prayer. In response, St. Mark opened a door in a column shown at the far right to reveal the place where his body was hidden. In between these two scenes, those who witnessed the miracle turn to one another in amazement. The leaders of Venice derived considerable prestige and political authority from their veneration of St. Mark.

THE TWO MARYS: THE MOTHER OF GOD AND THE REPENTANT PROSTITUTE Medieval thinking about women began with the fundamental dichotomy between Eve, the symbol of women as they are, and Mary, the ideal to which all women strived. Eve brought sin and sex into the world through her disobedience to God. Mary, the Virgin Mother, kept her body inviolate. Into the gap between the two natures of women emerged Mary Magdalene, who was considered in the twelfth century to have been a repentant prostitute even though there is no biblical evidence that she was. In contrast to the perpetually virginal ideal of Mary, the mother of Christ, the idea of Magdalene as a prostitute offered the possibility of redemption to all women. In this painting, the Virgin Mary suckles the Christ child in the middle, while Magdalene, shown on the left, makes an offering of her devotion.

friars "Brothers" who wandered from city to city and throughout the countryside begging for alms. Unlike monks who remained in a cloister, friars tried to help ordinary laypeople with their problems by preaching and administering to the sick and poor.

the Cistercians. By recruiting lay brothers, known as *converses*, the Cistercians made important connections with the peasants.

More than a century after the foundation of the Cistercians in France, the Spaniard Dominic and the Italian Francis formulated a new kind of religious order composed of mendicant **friars**. From the very beginning the friars wanted to distinguish themselves from monks. As the opening of this chapter indicated, instead of working in a monastery to feed themselves as did the Cistercians, friars ("brothers") wandered from city to city and throughout the countryside begging for alms (*mendicare* means "to beg"; hence, *mendicant friars*). Unlike monks who remained in a cloister, friars tried to help ordinary laypeople with their problems by preaching and administering to the sick and poor.

The Spaniard Dominic (1170–1221) founded the Dominican Order to convert Muslims and Jews and to combat heresy among Christians against whom he began his preaching mission while traveling through southern France. The ever-perceptive Pope Innocent III recognized Dominic's talents while he was visiting Rome and gave his new order provisional approval. Dominic believed the task of conversion could be achieved through persuasion and argument. To hone the Dominicans' persuasive skills, they created the first multigrade, comprehensive educational system. It connected schools located in individual friaries with more advanced regional schools that offered specialized training in languages, philosophy, and especially theology. Most Dominican friars never studied at a university but enjoyed, nevertheless, a highly sophisticated education that made them exceptionally influential in European intellectual life. Famed for their preaching skills, Dominicans were equally successful in exciting the illiterate masses and debating sophisticated opponents.

The Franciscan Order enjoyed a similar success. Francis of Assisi (1182–1226), whose story opened this chapter, deeply influenced Clare of Assisi (1194–1253), who founded a parallel order for women, the Poor Clares. Like the Franciscans, she and her followers enjoyed the "privilege of perfect poverty," which forbade the ownership of any property even by the community itself.

Both the Dominican and Franciscan Orders spread rapidly. Whereas the successful Cistercians had founded 500 new houses in their first century, the Franciscans established more than 1,400 in their first 100 years. Liberated from the obligation to live in a monastery, the mendicant friars traveled wherever the pope ordered them, making them effective agents of the papal monarchy. They preached crusades. They pacified the poor. They converted heretics and non-Christians through their inspiring preaching revivals. Even more effectively than the Cistercians before them, they established Catholic colonies along the frontiers of the West and beyond. They became missionary scouts looking for opportunities to disseminate Christian culture. In 1254 the Great Khan in Mongolia sponsored a debate on the principal religions of the world. There, many thousands of miles from Catholic Europe, was a Franciscan friar ready to debate the learned men representing Islam, Buddhism, and Confucianism.

THE FLOWERING OF RELIGIOUS SENSIBILITIES During the twelfth and thirteenth centuries, the widespread enthusiasm for religion exalted spiritual creativity. Experimentation pushed Christian piety in new directions, not just for aristocratic men, who dominated the Church hierarchy and the monasteries, but for women and laypeople from all social levels.

Catholic worship concentrated on the celebration of the Eucharist. The **Eucharist**, which was the crucial ritual moment during the Mass, celebrated Jesus's last meal with his apostles. The Eucharistic rite consecrated bread and wine as the body and blood of Christ. After the consecration, the celebrating priest distributed to the congregation the bread, called the host. Drinking from the chalice of wine, however, was a special privilege of the priesthood. More than anything else, belief in the miraculous change from bread to flesh and wine to blood, along with the sacrament of baptism, distinguished Christian believers from others. The Fourth Lateran Council in 1215 obligated all Christians to partake of the Eucharist at least once a year at Easter.

As simple as it was as a ritual observance, belief in the Eucharistic miracle presented a vexing and complex theological problem—why the host still looked, tasted, and smelled like bread rather than flesh, and why the blood in the chalice still seemed to be wine rather than blood. After the Fourth Lateran Council, Catholics solved this problem with the doctrine of **transubstantiation**. The doctrine rested on a distinction between the outward appearances (the "accidents" in theological terms) of the object, which the five senses could perceive, and the substance of an object, which they could not. When the priest spoke the words of consecration during the Mass, the bread and wine changed into the flesh and blood of Christ in substance ("transubstantiated"), but not in outward appearances. Thus, the substance of the Eucharist literally became God's body, but the senses of taste, smell, and sight perceived it as bread and wine.

Veneration of the Eucharist enabled the faithful to identify with Christ because believers considered the consecrated Eucharistic wafer to be Christ himself. By eating the host, they had literally ingested Christ, making his body part of their bodies.

Eucharist Also known as Holy Communion or the Lord's Supper, the Eucharistic rite of the Mass celebrates Jesus's last meal with his apostles when the priest-celebrant consecrates wafers of bread and a chalice of wine as the body and blood of Christ. In the Middle Ages the wafers of bread were distributed for the congregation to eat, but drinking from the chalice was a special privilege of the priesthood. Protestants in the sixteenth century and Catholics in the late twentieth century began to allow the laity to drink from the chalice.

transubstantiation A doctrine promulgated at the Fourth Lateran Council in 1215 that explained by distinguishing between the outward appearances and the inner substance how the Eucharistic bread and wine changed into the body and blood of Christ.

Justice in History
Inquiring into Heresy: THE INQUISITION
IN MONTAILLOU

In 1208 Pope Innocent III issued a call for a crusade against the Cathars or Albigensians. Fighting on behalf of French King Philip II, Simon de Montfort decisively defeated the pro-Cathar barons of southern France at Muret in 1213. Catharism retreated to the mountains, where a clandestine network of adherents kept the faith alive. The obliteration of these stubborn remnants required methods more subtle than the blunt instrument of a crusade. It required the techniques of inquisitors adept at interrogation and investigation.

Against the Cathar underground, the inquisition conducted its business through a combination of denunciations, exhaustive interrogations of witnesses and suspects, and confessions. Because its avowed purpose was to root out doctrinal error and to reconcile heretics to the Church, eliciting confessions was the preferred technique. But confessed heretics could not receive absolution until they informed on their friends and associates.

One of the last and most extensively documented inquisition cases against Catharism took place in Montaillou, a village in the Pyrenees Mountains, near the border of modern France and Spain. The Montaillou inquisition began in 1308, a century after the launch of the Albigensian Crusade and long after the heyday of Catharism.

BURNING OF THE HERETICAL BOOKS OF THE CATHARS In this fifteenth-century painting, St. Dominic, the figure with a halo on the left, gives a Catholic book to a Cathar priest dressed in blue. The Cathars attempt to burn the book, which miraculously floats unharmed above the flames.

However, the detailed records of the Montaillou inquisitors provide a revealing glimpse into Catharism and its suppression as well as the procedures of the inquisition. The first to investigate Montaillou was Geoffrey d'Ablis, the inquisitor of Carcassone. In 1308 he had every resident over age 12 seized and imprisoned. After the investigation, the villagers suffered the full range of inquisitorial penalties for their Cathar faith. The inquisitor's court sentenced some to life in prison, others to be burned at the stake. It forced many of those who were allowed to return to Montaillou to wear a yellow cross, the symbol of a heretic, sewn to the outside of their garments.

Unfortunately for these survivors, the most fearsome inquisitor of the age, Jacques Fournier, who was later elected Pope

Benedict XII, investigated Montaillou again from 1318 to 1325. Known as an efficient, rigorous opponent of heresy, Fournier forced virtually all the surviving adults in Montaillou to appear before his tribunal. When the scrupulous Fournier took up a case, his inquiries were notoriously lengthy and rigorous. Both witnesses and defendants spoke of his tenacity, skill, and close attention to detail in conducting interrogations. If Fournier and his assistants could not uncover evidence through interrogation and confession, they did not hesitate to employ informers and spies to obtain the necessary information. When Pierre Maury, a shepherd the inquisitors sought for many years, returned to the village for a visit, an old friend received him with caution: "When we saw you again we felt both joy and fear. Joy, because it was a long time since we had seen you. Fear, because I was afraid lest the Inquisition had captured you up there: if they had they would have made you confess everything and come back among us as a spy in order to bring about my capture."[1]

Fournier's success in Montaillou depended on his ability to play local factions against each other by encouraging members of one clan to denounce the members of another. Fournier's persistence even turned family members against one another. The clearest example of this convoluted play of local alliances and animosities, family ties, religious belief, and self-interest is the case of Montaillou's wealthiest family, the Clergues.

Bernard Clergue was the count's local representative, which made him a kind of sheriff; his brother Pierre was the parish priest. Together they represented both the secular and religious arms of the inquisition in Montaillou. In his youth, Pierre had Cathar sympathies, and he allegedly kept a heretical book or calendar in his home. Nevertheless, at some time before 1308, he and Bernard betrayed the local Cathars to the inquisition. In the proceedings that followed, they had the power to either protect or expose their neighbors and family members. When the inquisition summoned one of his relatives, Bernard warned her to "say you fell off the ladder in your house; pretend you

(continued on next page)

have broken bones everywhere. Otherwise it's prison for you."[2] Pierre relentlessly used his influence for his own and his family's benefit. A notorious womanizer, Pierre frightened women into sleeping with him by threatening to denounce them to the inquisition. Those he personally testified against were primarily from other prominent Montaillou families who represented a challenge to the Clergues' power. As one resident bitterly testified, "The priest himself cause[s] many inhabitants of Montaillou to be summoned by the Lord Inquisitor of Carcassone. It is high time the people of the priest's house were thrust as deep in prison as the other inhabitants of Montaillou."[3]

Despite the Clergues' attempted misuse of the inquisitorial investigation for their own purposes, the inquisitor Fournier persevered according to his own standards of evidence. In 1320 he finally had Pierre Clergue arrested as a heretic. The sly priest died in prison.

For Discussion

1. How did the methods of the inquisition help create outcasts from Catholic society? How did these methods help consolidate Catholic identity?

2. The primary function of the inquisition was to investigate what people believed. What do you think the inquisitors thought justice to be?

Taking It Further

Lambert, Malcolm. *The Cathars.* 1998. The best place to investigate the Cathar movement in the full sweep of its troubled history.

Le Roy Ladurie, Emmanuel. *Montaillou: The Promised Land of Error.* Translated by Barbara Bray. 1978. The best-selling and fascinating account of life in a Cathar village based on the records of Fournier's inquisition.

Moore, R. I. *The Formation of a Persecuting Society: Power and Deviance in Western Europe, 950–1250.* 1987. Places the harassment of heretics in the broader context of medieval persecutions.

Eucharistic veneration became enormously popular in the thirteenth century and the climax of dazzling ritual performance. Priests enhanced the effect of the miracle by dramatically elevating the host at the moment of consecration, holding it in upraised hands. Altar screens had special peepholes so that many people could adore the host at the elevation, and the faithful would rush from altar to altar or church to church to witness a succession of host elevations.

Many Christians became attracted to mysticism, the attempt to achieve union of the self with God. To the mystic, complete understanding of the divine was spiritual, not intellectual, an understanding best achieved through *asceticism*, the repudiation of material and bodily comforts. Both men and women became mystics, but women

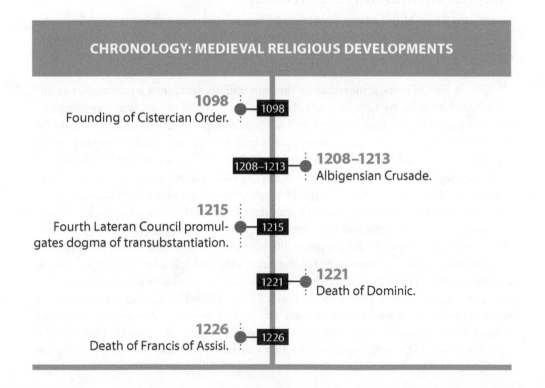

CHRONOLOGY: MEDIEVAL RELIGIOUS DEVELOPMENTS

1098
Founding of Cistercian Order.
1098

1208–1213
Albigensian Crusade.
1208–1213

1215
Fourth Lateran Council promulgates dogma of transubstantiation.
1215

1221
Death of Dominic.
1221

1226
Death of Francis of Assisi.
1226

concentrated on the more extreme forms of asceticism. For example, some women allowed themselves to be walled up in dark chambers to achieve perfect seclusion from the world and avoid distractions from their mystical pursuits. Others had themselves whipped, wore painful scratching clothing, starved themselves, or claimed to survive with the Eucharist as their only food. Female mystics, such as Juliana of Norwich (1342 to ca. 1416), envisioned a holy family in which God the Father was almighty, but the Mother was all wisdom. Some female mystics believed that Christ had a female body because he was the perfect nurturer, and they ecstatically contemplated spiritual union with him.

Mystics, however, were exceptional people. Most Christians contented themselves with the sacraments, especially baptism, penance, and the Eucharist; perhaps a pilgrimage to a saint's shrine; and a final attempt at salvation by making a pious gift to the Church on their deathbed.

Strengthening the Center of the West

During the twelfth and thirteenth centuries, the kingdoms of Catholic western Europe became the supreme political and economic powers in the Christian world, eclipsing Byzantium—an achievement that made them potent rivals to the Islamic states. One reason was stronger political unity. These kingdoms laid the foundations of the modern nation-states, which remain to this day the dominant forms of government around the globe. What happened in France and England during the twelfth and thirteenth centuries, therefore, represents one of the most important and lasting contributions of the West to world history.

The Monarchies of Western Europe

During the High Middle Ages, France and England began to exhibit the fundamental characteristics of unified kingdoms. Stable borders, permanent bureaucracies, sovereignty, and the rule of law were the foundations on which they became the most powerful kingdoms in Europe during the twelfth and thirteenth centuries (see **Map 10.3**).

The kings of France achieved unity through military conquests and shrewd administrative reforms. In the turbulent Middle Ages, dynastic continuity was a key ingredient in building loyalty and avoiding chaos. From Philip I (r. 1060–1108) to Philip IV (r. 1285–1314), France enjoyed not only a succession of extremely effective kings but a consistent policy that guaranteed the borders, built a bureaucracy, expanded the idea of royal sovereignty, and enforced the rule of law. By securing complete military and judicial control of the royal domain, the Ile-de-France, these kings provided the dynasty with a dependable income from the region's abundant farms and the thriving trade of Paris. To administer the domain and lands newly acquired by conquest, the French monarchy introduced new royal officials, the *baillis,* who were paid professionals, some trained in Roman law. Directly responsible to the king, they had full administrative, judicial, and military powers in their districts. The *baillis* laid the foundation for a bureaucracy that centralized French government. Louis IX (r. 1226–1270), who was canonized St. Louis in 1297 for his exemplary piety and justice, introduced a system of judicial appeals that expanded royal justice and investigated the honesty of the *baillis.* Philip IV, the Fair (r. 1285–1314), greatly expanded the king's authority and also managed to bring the Church under his personal control, making the French clergy largely exempt from papal

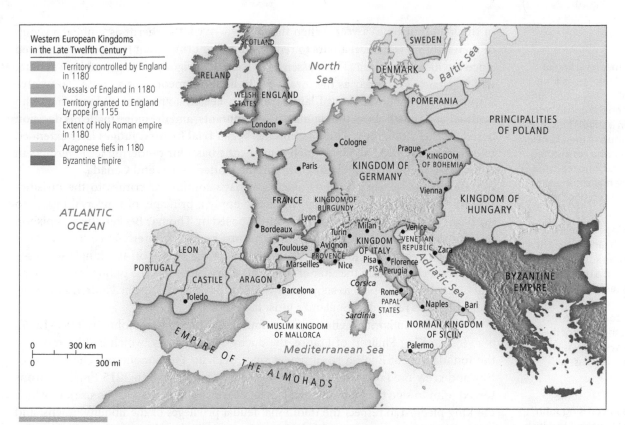

Western European Kingdoms in the Late Twelfth Century

- Territory controlled by England in 1180
- Vassals of England in 1180
- Territory granted to England by pope in 1155
- Extent of Holy Roman empire in 1180
- Aragonese fiefs in 1180
- Byzantine Empire

MAP 10.3 WESTERN EUROPEAN KINGDOMS IN THE LATE TWELFTH CENTURY The kings of England occupied Ireland as well as much of western France. France itself was consolidated around the Ile-de-France, the area around Paris. The kingdoms of Germany, Bohemia, Burgundy, and Italy were ruled by the German emperors. Based on this map, which countries had the potential for the greatest power in the twelfth century?

supervision. To pay for his frequent wars, Philip expelled the Jews after stripping them of their lands and goods and then turned against the rich Order of the Knights Templar, a crusader order that had amassed a fortune as the papal banker and creditor of Philip. He confiscated the Templars' lands and tortured the knights to extort confessions to various crimes in a campaign to discredit them. (See *Different Voices* in this chapter.) Philip was perhaps most effective in finding new ways to increase taxation. Under Philip, royal revenues grew tenfold from what they had been in the saintly reign of Louis IX.

England was even better unified than France. When the Duke of Normandy, William I the Conqueror (r. 1066–1087), seized England in 1066, he claimed the crown and all the land for himself. The new king kept about one-fifth of the land under his personal rule and parceled out the rest to the loyal nobles, monasteries, and churches. This policy ensured that every landholder in England held his property as a fief, directly or indirectly, from the king, a principle of lordship enforced by an oath of loyalty to the crown required of all vassals. About 180 great lords from among the Norman aristocracy held land directly from the king, and hundreds of lesser nobles were vassals of these great lords. William accomplished what other kings only dreamed about: He had truly made himself the lord of all lords. William's hierarchy of nobles transformed the nature of the English monarchy, giving the Norman kings far greater authority over England than any of the earlier Anglo-Saxon kings had enjoyed.

Building on the legacy of the conquest, King Henry II (r. 1154–1189) reformed the judiciary. His use of sheriffs to enforce the royal will produced the legends of Robin Hood, the bandit who resisted the nasty sheriff of Nottingham on behalf of the poor. But in reality the sheriffs probably did more good than harm in protecting the weak against the powerful. In attempting to reduce the jurisdiction of the nobles, Henry made it possible for almost anyone to obtain a writ that moved a case to a royal court. Henry introduced a system of itinerant **circuit court** judges who visited every shire

 **Read the Document**

The Battle of Hastings, 1066

circuit court Established by King Henry II (r. 1154–1189) to make royal justice available to virtually anyone in England. Circuit court judges visited every shire in England four times a year.

grand jury In medieval England after the judicial reforms of King Henry II (r. 1154–1189), grand juries were called when the circuit court judge arrived in a shire. The sheriff assembled a group of men familiar with local affairs who constituted the grand jury and who reported to the judge the major crimes that had been committed since the judge's last visit.

trial by jury When disputes about the possession of land arose after the late twelfth century in England, sheriffs assembled a group of 12 local men who testified under oath about the claims of the plaintiffs, and the circuit court judge made his decision on the basis of their testimony. The system was later extended to criminal cases.

Magna Carta In 1215 some English barons forced King John to sign the "great charter," in which the king pledged to respect the traditional feudal privileges of the nobility, towns, and clergy. Subsequent kings swore to uphold it, thereby accepting the fundamental principle that even the king was obliged to respect the law.

English Parliament Assembly usually consisting of representatives of the "commons," which consisted of townsmen and prosperous farmers who lacked titles of nobility, but whom the king summoned because he needed their money.

 **Read the Document**

The Magna Carta

in the land four times a year. When this judge arrived, the sheriff assembled a group of men familiar with local affairs to report the major crimes that had been committed since the judge's last visit. These assemblies were the origins of the **grand jury** system, which persists to this day as the means for indicting someone for a crime. To resolve disputes over the possession of land, sheriffs collected a group of 12 local men who testified under oath about the claims of the disputants, and the judge made his decision based on their testimony. These assemblies began **trial by jury**. Judges later extended to criminal cases trial by jury, which remains the basis for rendering legal verdicts in common-law countries, including Britain, the United States, and Canada.

Henry also subjected priests alleged to have committed crimes to the jurisdiction of the royal courts. The king wanted to apply a principle of universal justice to everyone in the realm, a principle fiercely opposed by Thomas Becket, the archbishop of Canterbury. Becket insisted the Church must be free of interference from secular authorities. When four knights—believing they were acting on the king's wishes—murdered Becket before the altar of the Canterbury cathedral, the public was outraged and blocked Henry's plan to subject the Church to royal justice. The Church soon canonized Becket, revered as England's most famous saint.

The royal authority Henry asserted foundered under King John (r. 1199–1216), who lost to King Philip II of France, the duchy of Normandy, which had been one of the foundations of English royal power since William the Conqueror. The barons of England grew tired of John's requests to pay for wars he lost. In 1215 English barons forced John to sign the **Magna Carta** ("great charter," in reference to its size), in which the king pledged to respect the traditional feudal privileges of the nobility, towns, and clergy. Contrary to widespread belief, Magna Carta had nothing to do with asserting the liberty of the common people or guaranteeing universal rights. It addressed only the privileges of a select few rather than the rights of the many. Subsequent kings, however, swore to uphold it, thereby accepting the fundamental principle that even the king must respect the law. After the Magna Carta the lord of all lords became less so. King Edward I (r. 1272–1307) began to call the **English Parliament** (from the French "talking together") in order to raise sums of money for his foreign wars. The English Parliament differed from similar assemblies on the Continent. It usually included representatives of the "commons," which consisted of townsmen and prosperous farmers who lacked titles of nobility, but whom the king summoned because he needed their money. As a result, a broader spectrum of the population joined parliament than in most other medieval kingdoms.

To the east the Holy Roman Empire suffered from the division between its principal component parts in Germany and northern Italy. Germany itself was an ill-defined region, subdivided by deep ethnic diversity and powerful dukes who ruled their lands with a spirit of fierce independence. As a result, emperors could not rule Germany directly, but only by demanding homage from the dukes who became imperial vassals. These feudal bonds were fragile substitutes for the kinds of monarchic institutions that evolved in France and England. The emperor's best asset was the force of his personality and his willingness to engage in a perpetual show of force to prevent rebellion. In northern Italy, the other part of the emperor's dominion, he did not even enjoy these extensive ties of vassalage and could rely only on vague legal rights granted by the imperial title and his ability to keep an army on the scene.

The century between the election of Frederick I (r. 1152–1190), known as Barbarossa or "red-beard," and the death of his grandson Frederick II (r. 1212–1250) represented the great age of the Holy Roman Empire, a period of relative stability preceded and followed by disastrous phases of anarchy and civil war. In the case of both of these emperors, lofty ambitions contrasted with the flimsy base of support and the failure to sustain judicial reforms, which prevented the centralization that took place in France and England. After Frederick II's death, his successors lost their hold on both Italy and Germany.

During the twelfth and thirteenth centuries, Spain and Poland, both of which would later become major European powers, were broken into small, weak principalities.

Different Voices
The Trial of the Knights Templar

The Knights Templar had been one of the most successful crusading orders, but after the end of the Crusades, their popularity declined. Nevertheless, they retained extensive properties given to finance their crusading expeditions. Deeply indebted to the Knights and in need of cash to finance his wars against England, King Philip IV of France seized upon rumors about a secret Templar initiation rite to justify arresting the prominent French Templars and confiscating their properties. Some Templars confessed under torture but later reversed themselves. The following documents describe the alleged secret rites of the Templars and summarize the testimony of some of those arrested. This notorious case not only illustrates how a ruthless king financed his kingdom, but how unsubstantiated rumors of homosexual practices could be used to destroy personal reputations and the order itself. The Crown burned many Templars at the stake, dissolved their order, and seized their property.

Royal Order for the Arrests of the Templars (September 14, 1307)

By the testimony of a great number of reliable witnesses, the brothers of the order of Knights Templar have been behaving as though they were wolves under sheep's clothing, and villainously trampling on the religion of our faith under the dress of religion.

They are again crucifying in these days our Lord Jesus Christ, by bringing him wounds more grievous than those he bore on the cross. For on initiation into their order, his image is presented to them, and they deny him three times with wretched and miserable blows, and with horrific cruelty spit three times in his face.

Then taking off their everyday clothes, they line up in the presence of the visitor or deputy who is receiving them for initiation. Next he kisses them; first at the bottom of the spine, secondly on the navel, and finally on the mouth, in accordance with the profane rite of their Order—but for shame on human dignity. Not fearing to break human law, they bind themselves with a vow of initiation to give themselves over, one to another, to that disgusting and terrifying vice of sexual intercourse—when asked and without excuse.

SOURCE: *Chronicles of the Crusades: Eyewitness Accounts of the Wars between Christianity and Islam,* trans. E. Hallam (London: Orion Publishing Co., 1989), p. 286. Reprinted by permission.

Pope Clement V Suppresses the Templars (March 22, 1312)

Many of the Templars accused of participating in the initiation rites, including the prominent knights Geoffrey of Charney and the Grand Master of the Templars James of Molay, denied under oath any homosexual practices among the knights. Nevertheless, Pope Clement V decided to condemn them. But it is evident from the papal bull that they still had supporters among the cardinals who were not convinced of the Templars' guilt.

There were therefore two opinions: some said that sentence should immediately be pronounced, condemning the order for the alleged crimes, and others objected that from the proceedings taken up to now the sentence of condemnation against the order could not justly be passed. After long and mature deliberation, having in mind God alone and the good of the Holy Land, without turning aside to right or to left, we elected to proceed by way of provisions and ordinance; in this way scandal will be removed, perils avoided, and property saved for the help of the Holy Land. We have taken into account the disgrace, suspicion, vociferous reports, and other attacks mentioned above against the order, also the secret reception into the order, and the divergence of many of the brothers from the general behavior, way of life and morals of other Christians. . . . We observe in addition that the above have given rise to grave scandal against the order, scandal impossible to allay as long as the order continues to exist. We note also the danger to faith and to souls, the many horrible misdeeds of so many brothers of the order, and many other just reasons . . .

SOURCE: *Decrees of the Ecumenical Councils,* trans. N.P. Tanner (Washington, D.C.: Georgetown University Press, 1990), Vol. 1, pp. 336–343.

For Discussion

1. Historians now consider the charges against the Templars fabrications. Why would these accusations of denying Christ and homosexual practices rather than others be fabricated to destroy the Templars?
2. In his suppression of the order, Pope Clement is especially concerned about causing scandal. Why might covering up a scandal be more important for the Church than finding out the truth of the allegations?

Medieval Culture: The Search for Understanding

10.4   What made western European culture distinctive?

Medieval intellectuals vastly expanded the range of Western culture. The most important cultural encounters came when thinkers read the books of ancient philosophers and faced challenging ideas that did not fit easily into their view of the world. The greatest medieval thinkers attempted to reconcile the reason of the ancients and the faith of the Christians by creating new philosophical systems. Lawyers began to look back to ancient Roman law for guidance about how to settle disputes, adjudicate crimes, and create governmental institutions. Muslim influences reinvigorated the Christian understanding of the sciences. Themes found in Persian love poetry found their way into the Christian notion of courtly love. Catholic western Europe experienced a cultural flowering through the spread of education, the growing power of Latin learning, and the invention of the university. Distinctively western forms developed in literature, music, drama, and above all the Romanesque and Gothic architecture of Europe's great cathedrals.

Revival of Learning

Some simple statistics reveal the magnitude of the educational revolution in medieval western Europe. In 1050 less than 1 percent of the population of Latin Christian Europe could read, and most of these literate people were priests who knew just enough Latin to recite the offices of the liturgy. Four hundred years later, as much as 40 percent of men living in cities were literate. Europeans embraced learning on a massive scale. How did this come about?

In 1050 only monasteries and cathedral schools provided an education. The curriculum was very basic, usually only reading and writing. Monastic education trained monks to read the books available in their libraries as an aid to contemplating the mysteries of the next world. In contrast, the cathedral schools, which trained members of the ecclesiastical hierarchy, emphasized the practical skills of rational analysis that would help future priests, bishops, and royal advisers solve the problems of this world.

By 1100 the number of cathedral schools had grown significantly and the curriculum expanded to include the study of the ancient Roman masters, Cicero and Virgil, who became models for clear Latin composition. These schools met the demand for trained officials from various sources—the thriving cities, the growing church bureaucracy, and the infant bureaucracies of the western kingdoms.

scholasticism A term referring to a broad philosophical and theological movement that dominated medieval thought and university training. Scholasticism used logic learned from Aristotle to interpret the meaning of the Bible and the writings of the Church Fathers, who created Christian theology in its first centuries.

SCHOLASTICISM: A CHRISTIAN PHILOSOPHY In the cathedral schools, the growing need for training in logic led to the development of scholasticism. **Scholasticism** refers to the use of logic learned from Aristotle to interpret the meaning of the Bible and the writings of the Church Fathers, who formulated Christian theology in its first centuries. The principal method of teaching and learning in the cathedral schools was the lecture. In the classroom the lecturer recited a short passage in Latin, presented the comments of other authorities on it, and drew his own conclusions. He then moved on to another brief passage and repeated the process. In addition to listening to lectures, students engaged in disputations in which they presented oral arguments for or against a particular thesis, a process called dialectical reasoning. The lecturers evaluated student disputants on their ability to investigate through logic the truth of a thesis. Disputations required several skills—verbal facility, a prodigious memory to produce apt citations on the spot, and the ability to think quickly. The process we know today as debate originated with these medieval disputations. Lectures and disputations became the core activities of the scholastics, who considered all subjects, however sacred, as appropriate for reasoned examination.

None of the scholastic teachers was more influential than the acerbic, witty, and daring Peter Abelard (1079–1142). Students from all over Europe flocked to hear Abelard's lectures at the cathedral school of Paris. Abelard's clever criticisms of the ideas of other thinkers delighted students. In *Sic et Non* ("Yes" and "No"), Abelard boldly examined some of the foundations of Christian truth. Employing the dialectical reasoning of a disputation, he presented both sides of 150 theological problems discussed by the Church Fathers. He left the conclusions open in order to challenge his students and readers to think further, but his intention was to point out how apparent disagreements among the experts masked a deeper level of agreement about Christian truth.

UNIVERSITIES: ORGANIZING LEARNING From the cathedral schools arose the first universities. The University of Paris evolved from the cathedral school where Abelard once taught. Initially the universities were little more than guilds (trade associations), organized by either students or teachers to protect their interests. As members of a guild, students bargained with their professors, as would other tradesmen, over costs and established minimum standards of instruction. The guild of the law students at Bologna received a charter in 1158, which probably made it the first university. Some of the early universities were professional schools, such as the medical faculty at Salerno, but true to their origins as cathedral schools, most emphasized theology over other subjects.

The medieval universities formulated the basic educational practices still in place today. They established a curriculum, examined students, conferred degrees, and conducted graduation ceremonies. Students and teachers wore distinctive robes, which are still worn at graduation ceremonies. Teachers were clergymen—that is, they "professed" religion, hence, the title of *professor* for a university instructor. In their first years students pursued the liberal arts curriculum, which consisted of the *trivium* (grammar, rhetoric, and logic) and the *quadrivium* (arithmetic, geometry, astronomy, and music). Arts and sciences faculties and distribution requirements in modern universities are vestiges of the medieval liberal arts curriculum.

Medieval universities did not admit women because the Church barred women from the priesthood and most university students trained to become priests. (Women did not attend universities in significant numbers until the nineteenth century.) The few women who did receive advanced educations relied on a parent or a private tutor, such as Abelard who tutored the young Heloise. But tutoring had its own dangers. The relationship of Abelard and Heloise resulted in a love affair, a pregnancy, and Abelard's castration at the hands of Heloise's relatives.

THE ANCIENTS: RENAISSANCE OF THE TWELFTH CENTURY The scholastics' integration of Greek philosophy with Christian theology represented a key facet of the **Twelfth-Century Renaissance**, a revival of interest in the ancients comparable in importance to the Carolingian Renaissance of the ninth century and the Italian Renaissance of the fifteenth. Between about 1140 and 1260, new Latin translations of the Greek classics arrived from Sicily and Spain, where Christians had close contacts with Muslims and Jews. Muslim philosophers translated into Arabic the Greek philosophical and scientific classics, which were readily available in the Middle East and North Africa. Jewish scholars who knew both languages then translated these Arabic versions into Latin. Later a few Catholic scholars traveled to Byzantium, where they learned enough Greek to make even better translations from the originals.

As they encountered the philosophy of the ancients, Muslim, Jewish, and Christian thinkers faced profoundly disturbing problems. The philosophical methods of reasoning found in Greek works, especially those by Aristotle, were difficult to reconcile with the principles of faith revealed in the Qur'an of Islam and the Hebrew and Christian Bibles. Religious thinkers recognized the superiority of Greek thought and worried that the power of philosophical reasoning undermined religious truth. As men of faith they challenged themselves to demonstrate that philosophy did not, if properly understood, contradict religious teaching. Some of them went even further to employ philosophical reasoning to demonstrate the truth of religion. They always faced opposition within their own religious faiths, however, especially from people who thought philosophical reason was an impediment to religious faith.

The most perceptive Muslim thinker to confront the questions raised by Greek philosophy was Averroës (1126–1198), who rose to become the chief judge of Córdoba

Twelfth-Century Renaissance
An intellectual revival of interest in ancient Greek philosophy and science and in Roman law in western Europe during the twelfth and early thirteenth centuries. The term also refers to a flowering of vernacular literature and the Romanesque and Gothic styles in architecture.

 View the Image

Illustration from the Properties of Things

and an adviser to the caliph. In *The Incoherence of the Incoherence* (1179–1180), Averroës argued that the aim of philosophy was to explain the true, inner meaning of religious revelations. This inner meaning, however, was not to be disclosed to the unlettered masses, who had to be told only the simple, literal stories and metaphors of Scripture. Although lively and persuasive, Averroës's defense of philosophy failed to stimulate additional philosophical speculation within Islam. Once far superior to that of the Latin Christian world, Islamic philosophy and science declined as Muslim thinkers turned to mysticism and rote learning over rational debate. In fact, Averroës received a more sympathetic hearing among Jews and Catholics than among Muslims.

Within Judaism, Moses Maimonides (1135–1204)—a contemporary of Averroës, also from Córdoba—was the most prominent thinker. His most important work in religious philosophy, *The Guide for the Perplexed* (ca. 1191), synthesized Greek philosophy, science, and Judaism. Widely read in Arabic, Hebrew, and Latin versions, the book stimulated both Jewish and Christian philosophy.

For medieval Catholic philosophers, one of the most difficult tasks was reconciling the biblical account of the divine creation with Aristotle's teaching that the universe was eternal. Even in this early clash between science and religion, creationism was the sticking point. Thomas Aquinas (1225–1274), whose philosophy is called **Thomism**, most effectively resolved the apparent conflict between faith and philosophy. A Dominican friar, Aquinas spent most of his career developing a school system for the Dominicans in Italy, but he also spent two short periods teaching at the University of Paris. Aquinas avoided distracting controversies and academic disputes to concentrate on his two great summaries of human knowledge—the *Summary of the Catholic Faith Against the Gentiles* (1261) and the *Summary of Theology* (1265–1274). In both of these massive scholastic works, reason fully confirmed Christian faith. Encyclopedias of knowledge, both books rigorously examined whole fields through dialectical reasoning.

Building on the works of Averroës, Aquinas solved the problem of reconciling philosophy and religion by drawing a distinction between *natural truth* and *revealed truth*. For Aquinas, natural truth meant the kinds of things anyone can know through the operation of human reason. Revealed truth referred to the things that one can know only through revelation, such as the doctrines of the Trinity and the incarnation of Christ. Aquinas argued that these two kinds of truths could not possibly contradict one another because both came from God. Apparent contradictions could be accommodated by an understanding of a higher truth. On the issue of Creation, for example, Aquinas argued that Aristotle's understanding of the eternal universe was inferior to the higher revealed truth of the Bible that God created the universe in seven days.

The most influential of the scholastic thinkers, Aquinas asserted that to achieve religious truth one should start with faith and then use reason to reach conclusions. He was the first to understand theology systematically in this way, and in doing so he raised a storm of opposition among Christians threatened by the difficulty of philosophical thinking. The theological faculties in universities at first prohibited Aquinas's writings. Nevertheless, his method remains crucial for Catholic theology to this day.

Just as scholastic theologians looked to ancient Greek philosophy as a guide to reason, jurists revived ancient Roman law, especially at the universities of Bologna and Pavia in Italy. In the law faculties, students learned the legal work of Emperor Justinian—the text of the *Corpus Juris Civilis,* together with the commentaries on it. The systematic approach of Roman law provided a way to make the legal system less arbitrary for judges, lawyers, bureaucrats, and advisers to kings and popes. Laws had long consisted of a contradictory mess of municipal regulations, Germanic customs, and feudal precepts. Under Roman law, judges had to justify their verdicts according to prescribed standards of evidence and procedure. The revival of Roman law in the twelfth century made possible the legal system that still guides most of continental Europe.

Thomism A branch of medieval philosophy associated with the work of the Dominican thinker, Thomas Aquinas (1225–1274), who wrote encyclopedic summaries of human knowledge that confirmed Christian faith.

Courtly Love

In addition to the developments in philosophy, theology, and the law, the Twelfth-Century Renaissance included a remarkable literary output of romances in the vernacular languages, the tongues spoken in everyday life. Poets called **troubadours** wrote romances—poems of love, meant to be sung to music—which reflected an entirely new sensibility about the relationships between men and women. Their literary movement is called **courtly love** or chivalry. The troubadours composed their poems in Provençal, one of the languages of southern France, and the princely courts of southern France provided the first audience. These graciously elegant poems show influences from Arabic love poetry and from Muslim mystical literature in which the soul, depicted as feminine, seeks her masculine God/lover. The troubadours secularized this theme of religious union by portraying the ennobling possibilities of the love between a woman and a man. In so doing, they popularized the idea of romantic love, one of the most powerful concepts in all of Western history, an ideal that still dominates popular culture to this day.

The ideal male depicted in courtly love poems was the knight-errant, a warrior who roamed in search of adventure. He was poor and free of ties to home and family, a man who lived a life of perfect freedom, but whose virtue led him to do the right thing. Knights took vows in the name of ladies, revealing that the courtly love ideal included a heavy dose of erotic desire. Besides self-denial, the most persistent chivalric fantasy was the motif of the young hero who liberates a virgin, either from a dragon or from a rioting mob of peasants.

The courtly love poems of the troubadours idealized women. The male troubadours, such as Chrétien de Troyes (1135–1183), placed women on a pedestal and treated men as the "love vassals" of beloved women to whom they owed loyalty and service. Female troubadours, such as Marie de France (dates unknown), did not place women on a pedestal but idealized emotionally honest and open relationships between lovers. From southern France, courtly love spread to Germany and elsewhere throughout Europe.

The Center of Medieval Culture: The Great Cathedrals

When tourists visit European cities today, they usually want to see the cathedrals. Mostly built between 1050 and 1300, these imposing structures symbolize the soaring ambitions and imaginations of their largely unknown builders. During the great medieval building boom, cities built hundreds of new cathedrals and thousands of other churches, sparing no expense and reflecting the latest experimental techniques in architectural engineering and

troubadours Poets from the late twelfth and thirteenth centuries who wrote love poems, meant to be sung to music, which reflected a new sensibility, called courtly love, about the ennobling possibilities of the love between a man and a woman.

courtly love An ethic first found in the poems of the late twelfth- and thirteenth-century troubadours that portrayed the ennobling possibilities of the love between a man and a woman. Courtly love formed the basis for the modern idea of romantic love.

10.1

10.2

10.3

10.4

⊙ **View the Closer Look**   The Joys and Pains of the Medieval Joust

THE MEDIEVAL JOUST This scene from a manuscript from ca. 1300–1340 idealizes the medieval joust, which served to keep the warring skills of noblemen sharp and provide popular entertainment.

323

ROMANESQUE ARCHITECTURE The rounded arches, the massive columns, the barrel vaults in the ceilings, and the small windows were characteristic of the Romanesque style. Compare the darkness of this interior of a Romanesque monastery in Tuscany, Italy, with the Gothic style of the Abbey Church of St. Denis, France, in the next illustration.

GOTHIC VAULTS The delicately ribbed ceiling vaults and vast expanses of stained glass in the Abbey Church of St. Denis, France, brings light into the church, in contrast with the obscurity of the Romanesque monastery in the previous illustration.

Romanesque A style in architecture that spread throughout western Europe during the eleventh and the first half of the twelfth centuries and was characterized by arched stone roofs supported by rounded arches, massive stone pillars, and thick walls.

View the Image

The Leaning Tower of Pisa

artistic fashion. These buildings became multimedia centers for the arts—incorporating architecture, sculpture, stained glass, and painting and providing a setting for the performance of music and drama. The medieval cathedrals took decades, sometimes centuries, to build at great cost and sacrifice.

The **Romanesque** style of cathedral-building spread throughout western Europe during the eleventh century and the first half of the twelfth century because the master masons who understood sophisticated stone construction techniques traveled from one building site to another, bringing with them a uniform style. The principal innovation of the Romanesque was the arched stone roofs, which were more aesthetically pleasing and less vulnerable to fire than the flat roofs they replaced. The rounded arches of these stone roofs, called *barrel vaults*, looked like the inside of a barrel. Romanesque churches employed transepts, which fashioned the church into the shape of a cross if viewed from above, the vantage point of God. The high stone vaults of Romanesque churches and cathedrals required the support of massive stone pillars and thick walls. As a result, windows were small slits that imitated the slit windows of castles.

The religious experience of worshiping in a Romanesque cathedral had an intimate, almost familiar quality to it. In such a building, God became a fellow townsman, an associate in the grand new project of making cities habitable and comfortable.

During the late twelfth and thirteenth centuries, the **Gothic** style replaced the Romanesque. The innovation of this style was the ribbed vault and pointed arches, which superseded the barrel vault of the Romanesque. These narrow pointed arches drew the viewer's eye upward toward God and gave the building the appearance of weightlessness that symbolized the Christian's uplifting reach for heaven. The neighborly solidity of the Romanesque style disappeared for a mystical appreciation of God's utter otherness, the supreme divinity far above mortal men and women. The Gothic style also introduced the innovation of the flying buttress, an arched construction on the outside of the walls that redistributed the weight of the roof. This innovation allowed for thin walls pierced by windows much bigger than possible with Romanesque construction techniques.

The result was stunning. The stonework of a Gothic cathedral became a skeleton to support massive expanses of stained glass, transforming the interior spaces into a mystical haven from the outside world. At different times of the day, the multicolored windows converted sunlight into an ever-changing light show that offered sparkling hints of the secret truths of God's creation. The light that passed through these windows symbolized the light of God. The windows themselves contained scenes that were an encyclopedia of medieval knowledge and lore. In addition to Bible stories and the lives of saints, these windows depicted common people at their trades, animals, plants, and natural wonders. Stained-glass windows celebrated not only the promise of salvation, but all the wonders of God's creation. They drew worshipers out of the busy cities in which they lived and worked toward the perfect realm of the divine.

In France, Germany, Italy, Spain, and England, cities made enormous financial sacrifices to construct new Gothic cathedrals during the economic boom years of the thirteenth century. Because costs were so high, many cathedrals, such as the one in Siena, Italy, remained unfinished, but even the incomplete ones became vital symbols of local identity.

10.1

10.2

10.3

10.4

Gothic A style in architecture in western Europe from the late twelfth and thirteenth centuries, characterized by ribbed vaults and pointed arches, which drew the eyes of worshipers upward toward God. Flying buttresses, which redistributed the weight of the roof, made possible thin walls pierced by large expanses of stained glass.

🔍 **View the Image**

Mont Saint Michel at Night

👁 **Watch the Video**

The Big Picture: The World in 1200 C.E.

FLYING BUTTRESSES OF CHARTRES CATHEDRAL The flying buttress did more than hold up the thin walls of Gothic cathedrals. The buttress created an almost lacelike appearance on the outside of the building, magnifying the sense of mystery evoked by the style.

CONCLUSION

Asserting Western Culture

During the twelfth and thirteenth centuries, western Europe matured into its own self-confident identity. Less a semi-barbarian backwater than it had been even in the time of Charlemagne, western Europe cultivated modes of thought that revealed an almost limitless capacity for creative renewal and critical self-examination. That capacity, first evident during the Twelfth-Century Renaissance, especially in scholasticism, is what has most distinguished the West ever since. These critical methods repeatedly caused alarm among some believers. However, this tendency to question basic assumptions is among the greatest achievements of Western civilization. The western European university system, which was based on teaching methods of critical inquiry, differed from the educational institutions in other cultures, such as Byzantium or Islam, that were devoted to passing on received knowledge. This distinctive critical spirit connects the cultures of the ancient, medieval, and modern West.

MAKING CONNECTIONS

1. What was the role of theology and philosophy in allowing the West to assert itself more forcefully?
2. Why was kingship the most effective form of political organization in the Middle Ages?
3. By the end of the thirteenth century, what distinguished Christian from Muslim culture?

TAKING IT FURTHER

For suggested readings, websites, and films, see page R-1.

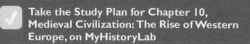
Chapter Review

Two Worlds: Manors and Cities

10.1 How was the medieval western European economy and society organized around manors and cities?

The medieval agricultural economy bound landlords and peasants together in a unit of management called the manor, a system where the lord of the manor presided over the villagers, including serfs, freeholders, and cottagers. The population growth that was a result of the agricultural revolution and its food surplus led to migrations to urban centers; at the same time, new transportation networks spurred the creation of business techniques that supported trade, including a moneyed economy. The population explosion in cities supported this commercial boom.

The Consolidation of Roman Catholicism

10.2 How did the Catholic Church consolidate its hold over the Latin West?

A movement toward reform against worldly pursuits required unity within the Church, which included building a Catholic identity based on conformity of religious rites and obedience to the pope. Monastic orders flourished as Catholic Christians internalized the teachings of the Church and devoted their lives to religion. The economic success of the monasteries encouraged expansion, as well as new traveling orders, which facilitated the spread of Catholic Christianity into the far corners of the Latin West.

Strengthening the Center of the West

10.3 How did the western European monarchies strengthen themselves?

During the High Middle Ages, France and England began to exhibit the fundamental characteristics of unified kingdoms when extremely effective kings instituted reforms to stabilize borders, build permanent bureaucracies, expand the concept of sovereignty, and enforce the rule of law.

Medieval Culture: The Search for Understanding

10.4 What made western European culture distinctive?

The invention of the medieval university established educational practices still in place today, and the integration of the ancient reason and Christian faith created new philosophical systems. Ancient Roman law provided guidance about how to settle disputes and create governmental institutions, while Muslim influences reinvigorated the Christian understanding of the sciences. Distinctively Western forms developed in literature, music, drama, and in the architecture of Europe's great cathedrals.

Chapter Time Line

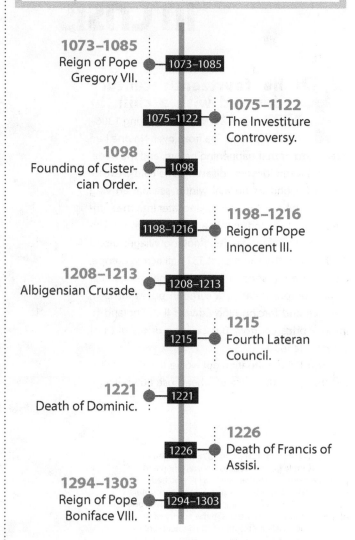

1073–1085 Reign of Pope Gregory VII. — `1073–1085`

1075–1122 `1075–1122` — The Investiture Controversy.

1098 Founding of Cistercian Order. — `1098`

1198–1216 `1198–1216` — Reign of Pope Innocent III.

1208–1213 Albigensian Crusade. — `1208–1213`

1215 `1215` — Fourth Lateran Council.

1221 Death of Dominic. — `1221`

1226 `1226` — Death of Francis of Assisi.

1294–1303 Reign of Pope Boniface VIII. — `1294–1303`

11

The Medieval West in Crisis

The fourteenth century dawned with a chill. In **1303 and then** again during 1306–1307, the Baltic Sea froze over. No one had ever heard of that happening before, and the freezing cold foretold worse disasters. The cold weather spread beyond its normal winter season, arriving earlier in the autumn and staying later into the summer. Then it started to rain and did not let up. The Caspian Sea began to rise, flooding villages along its shores. In the summer of 1314 all across Europe, crops rotted in sodden fields. The meager harvest came late, precipitating a surge in prices for farm produce and forcing King Edward II of England to impose price controls. But capping prices did not grow more food.

In 1315 the situation got worse. In England during that year, the price of wheat rose 800 percent.

THE OTTOMAN SULTAN In 1478 the Venetian painter, Gentile Bellini, went to Constantinople to paint the portrait of Sultan Mehmet II, who had conquered the Byzantine Empire. Hence, encounters between Christian Europe and the Turks became one of the most important themes in the history of the West. Although Islam prohibited the depiction of the human image, the Sultan apparently did not object to a Christian painting his portrait.

LEARNING OBJECTIVES

11.1 ((ᐧ	11.2 ((ᐧ	11.3 ((ᐧ	11.4 ((ᐧ	11.5 ((ᐧ	11.6 ((ᐧ
What caused the deaths of so many Europeans?	How did forces outside Europe, in particular the Mongol and Ottoman Empires, influence conditions in the West?	How did disturbances in the rudimentary global economy of the Middle Ages precipitate almost complete financial collapse and widespread social discontent in Europe?	How did incessant warfare transform the most powerful medieval states?	Why did the Church fail to provide leadership and spiritual guidance during these difficult times?	How did European culture offer explanations and solace for the otherwise inexplicable calamities of the times?

11.1

11.2

11.3

11.4

11.5

11.6

👁 Watch the Video Series on MyHistoryLab

Learn about some key topics related to this chapter with the *MyHistoryLab Video Series:*
Key Topics in Western Civilization

Preachers compared the ceaseless rains to the great flood in the Bible, and floods did come, overwhelming dikes in the Netherlands and England, washing away entire towns in Germany, turning fields into lakes in France. Everywhere crops failed.

Things got much worse. Torrential rains fell again in 1316, and for the third straight year the crops failed, creating the most severe famine in recorded European history. The effects were most dramatic in the far north. In Scandinavia agriculture almost disappeared, in Iceland peasants abandoned farming and turned to fishing and herding sheep, and in Greenland the European settlers began to die out. Already malnourished, the people of Europe became susceptible to disease and famine. Desperate people resorted to desperate options. They ate cats, rats, insects, reptiles, animal dung, and tree leaves. Stories spread that some ate their own children. In Poland the starving were said to cut down criminals from the gallows for food.

By the 1340s, nearly all of Europe west of Poland was gripped by a seemingly endless cycle of disease and famine. Then came the deadliest epidemic in European history, the Black Death, which killed at least one-third of the total population. The economy collapsed. Trade disappeared. Industry shriveled. Hopeless peasants and urban workers revolted against their masters, demanding relief for their families. Neither state nor Church could provide it. The two great medieval kingdoms of France and England became locked in a struggle that depleted royal treasuries and wasted the aristocracy in a series of clashes that historians call the Hundred Years' War. The popes left the dangerous streets of Rome for Avignon, France, where they were obliged to extort money to survive. After the pope returned to Rome, a group of French cardinals refused to go and elected a second pope, leading to the Great Schism when Europe was divided by allegiances to two different popes.

During the twelfth and thirteenth centuries the West had asserted itself against Islam through the Crusades and spread Catholic Christianity to the far corners of Europe. During the fourteenth and early fifteenth centuries, however, the West drew into itself due to war, epidemics, and conflicts with the Mongol and Ottoman Empires. As an additional shock, the Byzantine Empire, once the bastion of Orthodox Christianity, fell to the Muslim armies of the Ottomans. This chapter explores these encounters with death and turmoil, and asks this question:

How did the death and turmoil of fourteenth- and fifteenth-century Europe transform the identity of the West?

A Time of Death

11.1 What caused the deaths of so many Europeans?

The magnitude of Europe's demographic crisis is evident from the raw numbers. In 1300 the population of Europe was about 74 million—roughly 15 percent of its current population and about double the population of California today. Population size can be an elementary measure of the success of an economy to keep people alive; by this measure, Europe had been very successful up to about 1300. It had approximately doubled its population over the previous 300 years. After the 1340s, however, Europe's ability to sustain its population evaporated. Population fell to just

11.1

11.2

11.3

11.4

11.5

11.6

52 million. The demographic crisis of the fourteenth century was the greatest natural disaster in Western civilization since the epidemics of antiquity. How did it happen?

Famine

Widespread famine, caused by a crisis in agricultural production, began during the decade of 1310–1320. The agricultural revolution of the eleventh century had made available more food and more nutritious food, triggering the growth of the population during the Middle Ages. During the twelfth and thirteenth centuries, vast tracks of virgin forests were cleared for farming, especially in eastern Europe. After all the good bottomland was cleared, farmers moved to clear the more marginal land on hills and mountainsides. These clearings created soil erosion that contributed to the devastating floods of the 1310s. Thus, human actions facilitated the ecological catastrophe. By the fourteenth century no more virgin land was available for clearing, which meant that a still-growing population tried to survive on a fixed amount of farming land. Because of the limitations of medieval agriculture, the ability of farmers to produce food could not keep up with unchecked population growth. The propensity for famine was especially acute in heavily populated western Europe. In eastern Europe, the lower population and better balance between agriculture, animal husbandry, and fishing meant the population remained better fed and less susceptible to famine and disease.

At the same time there was probably a change in climate, known as the "Little Ice Age." The mean annual temperatures dropped just enough to make it impossible to grow crops in the more northerly parts of Europe and at high elevations such as the Alps. Before the fourteenth century, for example, grapes were grown in England to produce wine; however, with the decline in temperatures, the grape vineyards ceased to produce. Growing grapes in England became possible again only with global warming in the twenty-first century. The result of the Little Ice Age was twofold. First, there was less land available for cultivation as it became impossible to grow crops in marginal areas. Second, a harsher climate shortened the growing season, which meant that even where crops could still grow, they were less abundant.

The imbalance between food production and population set off a dreadful cycle of famine and disease. Insufficient food resulted in either malnutrition or starvation. Those who suffered from prolonged malnutrition were particularly susceptible to epidemic diseases, such as typhus, cholera, and dysentery. By 1300, children of the poor faced the probability of extreme hunger once or twice during the course of their childhood. In Pistoia, Italy, priests kept the *Book of the Dead*, which recorded the pattern: famine in 1313, famine in 1328–1329, famine and epidemic in 1339–1340 that killed one-quarter of the population, famine in 1346, famine and epidemic in 1347, and then the killing hammer blow—the Black Death in 1348 (see **Map 11.1**).

The Black Death

Black Death An epidemic disease, possibly bubonic plague, that struck Europe between 1348 and the 1350s killing at least one-third of the total population.

Following on the heels of the Great Famine, the **Black Death** arrived in Europe in the spring of 1348 with brutal force. In the lovely hilltop city of Siena, Italy, all industry stopped, carters refused to bring produce and cooking oil in from the countryside, and on June 2 the daily records of the city council and civil courts abruptly ended, as if the city fathers and judges had all died or rushed home in panic. A local chronicler, Agnolo di Tura, wrote down his memories of those terrible days:

> Father abandoned child, wife husband, one brother another; for this illness seemed to strike through the breath and sight. And so they died. And none could be found to bury the dead for money or friendship. Members of a household brought their dead to a ditch as best they could, without priest, without divine offices. Nor did the [death] bell sound. And in many places in Siena great pits were dug and piled deep with the multitude of dead. . . . And I,

11.1

11.2

11.3

11.4

11.5

11.6

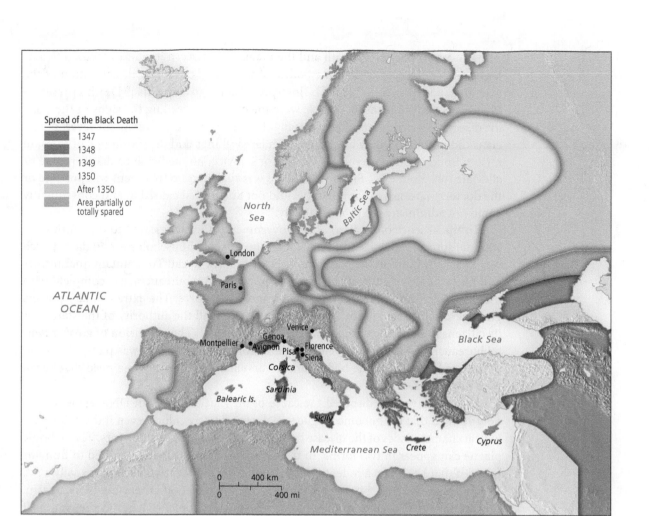

Spread of the Black Death

- 1347
- 1348
- 1349
- 1350
- After 1350
- Area partially or totally spared

MAP **11.1** SPREAD OF THE BLACK DEATH After the Black Death first appeared in the ports of Italy in 1347, it spread relentlessly throughout most of Europe, killing at least 20 million people in Europe alone. What does this map show about how rapidly the Black Death spread?

Agnolo di Tura, called the Fat, buried my five children with my own hands. And there were also those who were so sparsely covered with earth that the dogs dragged them forth and devoured many bodies throughout the city.[1]

During the summer of 1348 more than half of the Sienese died. The construction of Siena's great cathedral, planned to be the largest in the world, stopped and was never resumed due to a lack of workers. In fact, Siena, once among the most prosperous cities in Europe, never fully recovered and lost its economic preeminence.

No disease left more distinctive and disturbing signs on the body than the Black Death. According to one quite typical contemporary description: "all the matter which exuded from their bodies let off an unbearable stench; sweat, excrement, spittle, breath, so fetid as to be overpowering; urine turbid, thick, black or red. . . . "[2] In the introduction to *The Decameron,* Giovanni Boccaccio described what he had witnessed of the symptoms:

In the year 1348 after the fruitful incarnation of the Son of God, that most beautiful of Italian cities, noble Florence, was attacked by deadly plague. . . . The symptoms . . . began both in men and women with certain swellings in the groin or under the armpit. They grew to the size of a small apple or an egg, more or less, and were vulgarly called tumors. In a short space of time these tumors spread from the two parts named [to] all over the body. Soon after this the symptoms changed and black or purple spots appeared on the arms or thighs or any other part of the body, sometimes a few large ones, sometimes many little ones. These spots were a certain sign of death, just as the original tumor had been and still remained.[3]

11.1

11.2

11.3

11.4

11.5

11.6

The fear of the Black Death and the inability to discern its causes focused the attention of contemporaries on the bodies of the sick. Almost any discoloration of the skin or glandular swellings could be interpreted as a sign of the Black Death's presence. Physicians and surgeons, of course, were the experts in reading the signs of the body for disease. As victims and their distraught families soon discovered, however, physicians did not really know what the glandular swellings and discolorations of the skin meant. Boccaccio reported that "No doctor's advice, no medicine could overcome or alleviate this disease. . . . Either the disease was such that no treatment was possible or the doctors were so ignorant that they did not know what caused it, and consequently could not administer the proper remedy."[4]

In the absence of an alternative, government officials resorted to quarantines to stop the spread of the disease. They locked up infected households for 40 days, which was especially hard on the poor who needed to work to eat. To maintain quarantines and bury the dead, city councils created public health bureaucracies, complete with their own staff physicians, grave diggers, and police force. The extraordinary powers granted to the public health authorities helped expand the authority of the state over its citizens in the name of pursuing the common good. The expansion of governmental bureaucracy that distinguished modern from medieval states was partly the result of the need to keep human bodies under surveillance and control—a need that began with the Black Death.

Experts have long disputed the cause of the Black Death, but DNA evidence has now verified that the bubonic plague was the most likely culprit, even if the epidemiological characteristics of the disease have mutated over the past 700 years. The bubonic plague can appear in two forms. In the first form it is usually transmitted to humans by a flea that has bitten a rodent infected with the *Yersinia pestis* bacillus, usually a rat. The infected flea then bites a human victim. The infection enters the bloodstream, causing inflamed swellings called buboes (hence, "bubonic" plague) in the glands of the groin or armpit, internal bleeding, and discoloration of the skin, symptoms similar to those Boccaccio described. The second form of plague was the pneumonic type, which infected the lungs and spread by coughing and sneezing. Either form could be lethal, but the complex epidemiology of bubonic plague meant that the first form could not be transmitted directly from one person to another. After being infected, many victims probably developed pneumonia as a secondary symptom, which then spread quickly to others. As one contemporary physician put it, one person could seemingly infect the entire world. In some cases, the doctor caught the illness and died before the patient did.

The visitations of the bubonic plague in the late nineteenth and twentieth centuries, which have been observed by physicians trained in modern medicine, formed the basis for the theory linking the Black Death to the bubonic plague. Alexandre Yersin discovered the bubonic plague bacillus (*Yersinia pestis*) in Hong Kong in 1894 and traced its spread through rats and fleas. Most historians and epidemiologists think that something similar to this must have happened in 1348, but there are differences between the fourteenth- and twentieth-century plagues. The Black Death spread much more rapidly from person to person and place to place than the bubonic plague does in modern epidemics. For example, rats do not travel very far very fast, and in modern examples the bubonic plague has rarely spread more than 12 miles per year. In 1348, however, the Black Death traveled as far in a day as rat-borne bubonic plague does in a year. Many of the reported symptoms from the fourteenth century do not match the symptoms observed in modern plague victims. Moreover, the Black Death, unlike the bubonic plague, seems to have had a long incubation period before the first symptoms appeared. Because of the long incubation, those who had the disease transmitted it to others before they knew they were sick, which helps explain why the disease was so lethal despite attempts to quarantine those afflicted with it.

11.1

11.2

11.3

11.4

11.5

11.6

Thus, the bacillus has probably mutated, changing the epidemiology, or the bubonic plague that appeared during the Black Death was often confused with other epidemics that had other characteristics.

In Europe about 20 million people died, which would have been more than the combined populations of the six largest cities (New York, Los Angeles, Chicago, Houston, Philadelphia, and Phoenix) in the United States today. Across Europe life expectancy decreased from 43 years in 1300 to only 24 years by 1400. The deaths usually clustered in a matter of a few weeks or months after the disease first appeared in a particular locale. The death toll, however, varied erratically from place to place, ranging from about 20 to 90 percent. So great was the toll in southern and western Europe that entire villages were depopulated or abandoned. Paris lost half its population, Florence as much as four-fifths, and Venice two-thirds. In the seaport of Trapani, Italy, everyone apparently died or left. Living in enclosed spaces, monks and nuns were especially hard hit. All the Franciscans of Carcassonne and Marseille in France died. In Montpellier, France, only 7 of the 140 Dominicans survived. In isolated Kilkenny, Ireland, Brother John Clyn found himself left alone among his dead brothers, and he began to write a diary of what he had witnessed because he was afraid he might be the last person left alive in the world. (See *Different Voices* in this chapter.)

The Black Death kept coming back. In the Mediterranean basin where the many port cities formed a network of contagion, the plague reappeared between 1348 and 1721 in one port or another about every 20 years. Some of the later outbreaks were just as lethal as the initial 1348 catastrophe. Florence lost half its population in 1400; Venice lost a third in 1575–1577 and a third again in 1630–1631. Less exposed than the Mediterranean, northern Europe suffered less and saw the last of the dread disease in the Great Plague of London of 1665–1666. Most of Poland escaped without any signs of the disease, and east-central Europe in general was far less severely hit than western Europe, probably because the sparse population made the spread of contagion less likely.

Watch the Video

The Plague

THE TRIUMPH OF DEATH This detail from Francesco Traini's fresco, *The Triumph of Death,* in the Camposanto, Pisa, ca. 1350, depicts an elegant cavalcade of aristocrats on horseback peering in horror at the bodies of plague victims.

SOURCE: Cemetery, Pisa, Italy/Canali PhotoBank, Milan/SuperStock.

11.1

11.2

11.3

11.4

11.5

11.6

FLAGELLANTS During the Black Death many people believed God was punishing them for their sins. In order to expiate those sins, some young men performed flagellation, a practice once reserved for monks who whipped themselves as a form of penance. In order to control the practice among laymen, confraternities were formed in which collective flagellation was organized. The flagellants depicted here are formed into a procession displaying a holy banner and crucifix while one brother flogs two others.

A Cold Wind from the East

11.2 How did forces outside Europe, in particular the Mongol and Ottoman Empires, influence conditions in the West?

During the same period the West was suffering from deadly microbes, it also faced the mounted warriors of the distant Mongol tribes, whose relentless conquests drove them from Outer Mongolia across central Asia toward Europe. The Mongols and Turks were nomadic peoples from central Asia. Closely related culturally but speaking different languages, these peoples exerted an extraordinary influence on world history despite a rather small population. **Map 11.2** shows the place of origin of the Mongols and Turks and where they spread across a wide belt of open, relatively flat steppe land stretching from the Yellow Sea between China and the Korean peninsula to the Baltic Sea and the Danube River basin in Europe. Virtually without forests and interrupted only by a few easily traversed mountain ranges, the broad Eurasian steppes have been the great migration highway of world history from prehistoric times to the medieval caravans and the modern trans-Siberian railway.

As the Mongols and Turks charged westward out of central Asia on their fast ponies, they put pressure on the kingdoms of the West. Mongol armies hobbled Kievan Rus, and Turks destroyed Byzantium. As a consequence, the potential Orthodox allies in the East of the Catholic Christian West were weakened or eliminated. Converts to Islam, the Ottomans pushed into the Balkans. In contrast to the era of the twelfth-century Crusades, Catholic Europe found itself on the defensive against a powerful Muslim foe.

11.1

11.2

11.3

11.4

11.5

11.6

The Mongol Invasions

Whereas the Europeans became successful sailors because of their extensive coastlines and close proximity to the sea, the Mongols became roving horsemen because they needed to migrate several times a year in search of grass and water for their ponies and livestock. They also became highly skilled warriors because they competed persistently with other tribes for access to the grasslands.

Between 1206 and 1258, the Mongols transformed themselves from a collection of disunited tribes with a vague ethnic affinity to create the most extensive empire in the history of the world. The epic rise of the previously obscure Mongols was the work of a Mongol chief named Temujin, who succeeded in uniting the various quarreling tribes and transforming them into a world power. In 1206 Temujin was proclaimed Genghis Khan (ca. 1162–1227) ("Very Mighty King"), the supreme ruler over all the Mongols. Genghis broke through the Great Wall of China, destroyed the Jin (Chin) Empire in northern China, and occupied Beijing. His cavalry swept across Asia as far as Azerbaijan, Georgia, northern Persia, and Kievan Rus. Genghis Khan ordered that after his death his empire would be divided into four principalities or khanates for his sons and grandsons. They continued Mongol expansion. Eventually, Mongol armies conquered territories that stretched from Korea to Hungary and from the Arctic Ocean to the Arabian Sea.

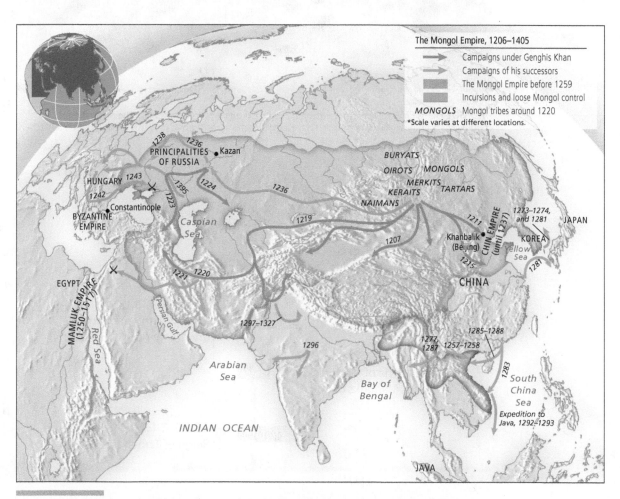

MAP **11.2** THE MONGOL EMPIRE, 1206–1405 The Mongols and Turks were nomadic peoples who spread out across Asia and Europe from their homeland in the region of Mongolia. The Mongol armies eventually conquered vast territories from Korea to the borders of Hungary and from the Arctic Ocean to the Arabian Sea. From the dates shown, how rapidly did the Mongol armies spread their rule?

11.1

11.2

11.3

11.4

11.5

11.6

MONGOL HORSEMAN Unlike the fourteenth-century European representations of the Mongols, this contemporary Chinese illustration accurately depicts the appearance, dress, and equipment of a Mongol Archer on horseback.

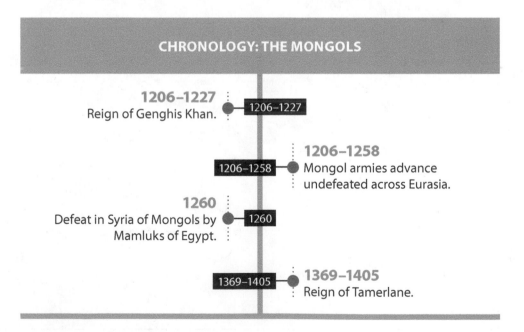

CHRONOLOGY: THE MONGOLS

1206–1227
Reign of Genghis Khan.
`1206–1227`

`1206–1258`
1206–1258
Mongol armies advance undefeated across Eurasia.

1260
Defeat in Syria of Mongols by Mamluks of Egypt.
`1260`

`1369–1405`
1369–1405
Reign of Tamerlane.

The Mongol success was accomplished through a highly disciplined military organization, tactics that relied on extremely mobile cavalry forces, and a sophisticated intelligence network. During the campaign against the Rus in the winter of 1223, the Mongol cavalry moved with lightning speed across frozen rivers. Although the Rus

11.1

11.2

11.3

11.4

11.5

11.6

forces outnumbered the Mongol armies and had superior armor, they were crushed in every encounter with the Mongols.

The Mongol armies employed clever tactics. First, they unnerved enemy soldiers with a hail of arrows. Then they appeared to retreat, only to draw the enemy into false confidence before the Mongol horsemen delivered a deadly final blow. European chroniclers at the time tried to explain their many defeats at the hands of the Mongols by reporting that the Mongol "hordes" had overwhelming numbers, but evidence clearly shows that their victories were the result not of superior numbers, but of superior discipline and the sophistication of the Mongol intelligence network. Once they had conquered a territory the Mongols secured the caravan routes across Asia, known as the Silk Road, creating the Mongol Peace. (See *Encounters and Transformations* in this chapter.) However, the Mongol Peace came at an enormous human cost. It is estimated that Ghenghis Khan's armies were responsible for the deaths of 40 million people or about 11.1 percent of the world's population, a death toll second only to World War II, which killed 66 million people. And Mongol armies may have been responsible for spreading the *Yersinia pestis* bacillus from its home in China, making the Mongols indirectly responsible for the Black Death.

Mongol power climaxed in 1260. In that year the Mongols suffered a crushing defeat in Syria at the hands of the Mamluk rulers of Egypt, an event that ended the Mongol reputation for invincibility. Conflicts and succession disputes among the various Mongol tribes made them vulnerable to rivals and to rebellion from their unhappy subjects. The Mongol Empire did not disappear overnight, but its various successor khanates never recaptured the dynamic unity forged by Genghis Khan. During the fourteenth century the Mongol Peace sputtered to an end.

In the wake of these upheavals, a warrior of Mongol descent known as Tamerlane (r. 1369–1405) created an army composed of Mongols, Turks, and Persians, which challenged the established Mongol khanates. Tamerlane's conquests rivaled those of Genghis Khan, but with very different results. His armies pillaged the rich cities that supplied the caravan routes. Thus, in his attempt to monopolize the lucrative trans-Eurasian trade, Tamerlane largely destroyed it. The collapse of the Mongol Peace broke the thread of commerce across Eurasia and stimulated the European search for alternative routes to China that ultimately resulted in the voyages of Christopher Columbus in 1492.

Read the Document

The Mongols: An Excerpt from the *Novgorod Chronicle*, 1315

The Rise of the Ottoman Turks

The Mongol armies were never very large, so the Mongols had always augmented their numbers with Turkish tribes. The result was that outside Mongolia, Turks gradually absorbed the Mongols. Turkish replaced Mongolian as the dominant language, and the Turks took over the government of the central Asian empires that had been scraped together by the Mongol conquests. In contrast to the Mongols, many of whom remained Buddhists, the Turks became Muslims and created an exceptionally dynamic, expansionist society of their own (see **Map 11.3**).

Among the Turkish peoples, the most successful state builders were the Ottomans. Named for Osman I (r. 1281–1326), who brought it to prominence, the Ottoman dynasty endured for more than 600 years, until 1924. The nucleus of the Ottoman state was a small principality in Anatolia (a portion of present-day Turkey), which in the early fourteenth century began to expand at the expense of its weaker neighbors, including the Byzantine Empire. The Ottoman state was built not on national, linguistic, or ethnic unity, but on a purely dynastic network of personal and military loyalties to the Ottoman prince, called the sultan. Thus, the vitality of the empire depended on the energy of the individual sultans. The Ottomans thought of themselves as *ghazis,* warriors for Islam devoted to destroying polytheists, including Christians. (To some Muslims, the Christian belief in the Trinity and veneration

11.1

11.2

11.3

11.4

11.5

11.6

Encounters and Transformations
The Silk Road

Nothing better facilitated encounters between East and West than the Silk Road. The label actually refers to a network of caravan trails connecting China with western Asia and Europe through the Taklimakan, one of the most inhospitable deserts on Earth. Travelers had little choice but to pick their way from oasis to oasis across central Asia. On the eastern and western edges of this vast territory the civilizations of China and the West developed, and the Silk Road connected them.

Many highly valuable commodities were transported along these routes besides silk, including ivory, gold, jewels, iron, furs, and ceramics (hence, the term "fine China" for the most precious ceramics). None of these commodities, however, captured the imagination of the West as much as silk, which had been transported from China across the Silk Road since Roman times (see Chapter 6). The importance of the Silk Road required peaceful political conditions to thrive, lest caravans be plundered. Perhaps the greatest era for the Silk Road came under the Chinese T'ang dynasty (618–907), which provided stability that allowed commerce to flower along the road. After the T'ang dynasty collapsed, the road was unsafe until the Mongol invasions in the thirteenth century.

The Mongol invasions completely altered the composition of Asia and much of eastern Europe—economically, politically, and ethnically. Once the Mongols had conquered new territories, they established the Mongol Peace by reopening the Silk Road across the Asian steppes, making trans-Eurasian trade possible and guaranteeing the safety of merchants. Thanks to the Mongols, European Christians began to traverse the Silk Road to China and to encounter directly the civilizations of the East. The Mongols were tolerant of religious diversity and welcomed the first Christian missionaries into China. A Roman Catholic archbishopric was founded in Beijing in 1307.

The most famous of the many merchants who traversed the Silk Road during the Mongol Peace were the Venetians from the Polo family, including Marco Polo, who arrived at the court of the Great Khan in China in 1275. Marco Polo's book about his travels offers a vivid and often remarkably perceptive account of the Mongol Empire during the Mongol Peace. It also illustrates better than any other source the cultural engagement of the Christian West with the Mongol East during the late thirteenth century. Although Marco Polo was a merchant who traveled

(continued on next page)

View the Closer Look   Mongols and Trade on the Silk Road

MARCO POLO TRAVELING BY CAMEL CARAVAN ON THE SILK ROAD This illustration is likely from a late fourteenth-century atlas. A Mongol escort provides security for the travelers.

11.1

11.2

11.3

11.4

11.5

11.6

(continued from previous page)

to make a profit, his book brought a great store of cultural information—some accurate, some fanciful—that stimulated the Western imagination about the East. Perhaps most revealing were his discussions of religion. Marco classified peoples according to their religion and evaluated religions with the eye of a western European Catholic. He was harshest about Muslims, but seemed more tolerant of "idolaters"; that is, Buddhists and Hindus, whose practices he found intriguing. He also reported on magical practices and reports of miracles. Because of the popularity of his book, Marco Polo's views of Asia became the principal source of knowledge in the West about the East until the sixteenth century.

For Discussion

What were the advantages and disadvantages of the Mongol Peace for the West?

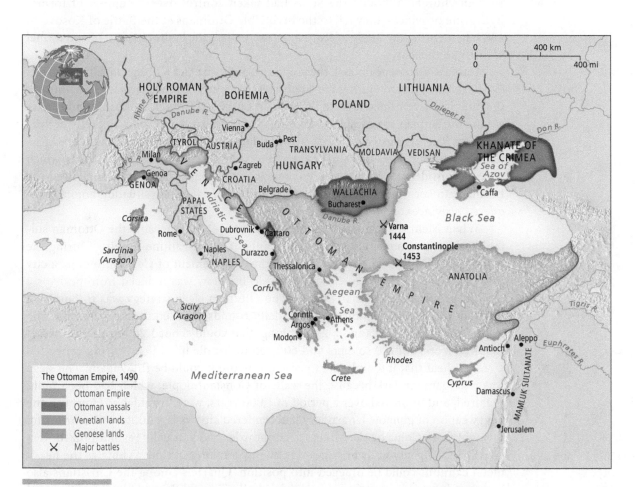

MAP **11.3** THE OTTOMAN EMPIRE The Ottoman state expanded from a small principality in Anatolia, which is south of the Black Sea. From there the Ottomans spread eastward into Kurdistan and Armenia. In the West they captured all of Greece and much of the Balkan peninsula. From this map, what was the strategic significance for trade and military power of the location of the Ottoman Empire?

of numerous saints demonstrated that Christians were not true monotheists.) During the fourteenth century, incessant Ottoman guerilla actions gradually chipped away at the Byzantine frontier.

The Byzantine Empire in the middle of the thirteenth century was emerging from a period of domination by Frankish knights and Venetian merchants who had conquered Constantinople during the Fourth Crusade in 1204. In 1261, the Byzantine emperor, Michael VIII Palaeologus (r. 1260–1282), recaptured the great city. The revived Byzantine Empire, however, was a pale vestige of what it once had been, and the Palaeologi emperors desperately sought military assistance from western Europe to defend themselves from the Ottomans. Dependent on mercenary

11.1

11.2

11.3

11.4

11.5

11.6

armies and divided by civil wars, the Byzantines offered only pathetic resistance to the all-conquering Ottomans.

From their base in Anatolia, the Ottomans raided far and wide, launching pirate fleets into the Aegean and gradually encircling Constantinople after they crossed over into Europe in 1308. By 1402 Ottoman territory had grown to 40 times its size a century earlier. During that century of conquests, the frontier between Christianity and Islam shifted. The former subjects of the Byzantines in the Balkans fell to the Ottoman Turks. Fragile Serbia, a bastion of Orthodox Christianity in the Balkans, broke under Ottoman pressure. First unified in the late twelfth century, Serbia established political independence from Byzantium and autonomy for the Serbian church. Although the Serbs had taken control over a number of former Byzantine provinces, they fell to the invincible Ottomans at the Battle of Kosovo in 1389. Lamenting the Battle of Kosovo has remained the bedrock of Serbian national identity to this day.

Serbia's western neighbors, the kingdoms of Bosnia and Herzegovina, deflated under Ottoman pressure during the late fifteenth century. Unlike Serbia, where most of the population remained loyal to the Serbian Orthodox Church, in Bosnia and Herzegovina the Serbian-speaking land-holding classes converted to Islam to preserve their property. The subjugated peasants, also Serbian-speaking, remained Orthodox Christians who turned over one-third of everything they raised to their Muslim lords, which created considerable resentment and religious tensions. The Ottomans allowed the Bosnians to keep their territorial identity and name, a unique situation among conquered provinces of the Ottoman Empire.

When Mehmed II, "The Conqueror" (r. 1451–1481), became the Ottoman sultan, he began to obliterate the last remnants of the Byzantine Empire. During the winter of 1451–1452, the sultan ordered the encirclement of Constantinople, a city that had once been the largest in the world but now was reduced from perhaps a million people to fewer than 50,000. The Ottoman siege strategy was to bombard Constantinople into submission with daily rounds from enormous cannons. The largest was a monster cannon, 29 feet long, that could shoot 1,200-pound stones. It required a crew of 200 soldiers and 60 oxen to handle it, and each firing generated so much heat that it took hours to cool off before it could be fired again. The siege was a gargantuan task because the walls of Constantinople, which had been built, repaired, and improved over a period of 1,000 years, were formidable. However, the new weapon of gunpowder artillery had rendered city walls a military anachronism. Brought from China by the Mongols, gunpowder had gradually revolutionized warfare. Breaching city walls in sieges was merely a matter of time as long as the heavy metal cannons could be dragged into position. Quarrels among the Christians also hampered the defense of Constantinople's walls. Toward the end, the Byzantine emperor was forced to melt down church treasures so "that from them coins should be struck and given to the soldiers, the sappers and the builders, who selfishly cared so little for the public welfare that they were refusing to go to their work unless they were first paid."[5]

The final assault came in May 1453 and lasted less than a day. When the city fell, the Ottoman army spent the day plundering, raping, and enslaving the populace. The last Byzantine emperor, Constantine XI, was never found amid the multitude of the dead. The fall of Constantinople ended the Christian Byzantine Empire, the continuous remnant of the ancient Roman Empire. But the idea of Rome was not so easily snuffed out. The first Ottoman sultans residing in Constantinople continued to be called "Roman emperors."

Although the western European princes had done little to save Byzantium, its demise shocked them. Now they were also vulnerable to the Ottoman onslaught. For the next 200 years the Ottomans used Constantinople as a base to threaten Christian Europe. Hungary and the eastern Mediterranean empire of Venice remained the last

Read the Document

Mehmed II (15th Century) Kritovoulos

11.1

11.2

11.3

11.4

11.5

11.6

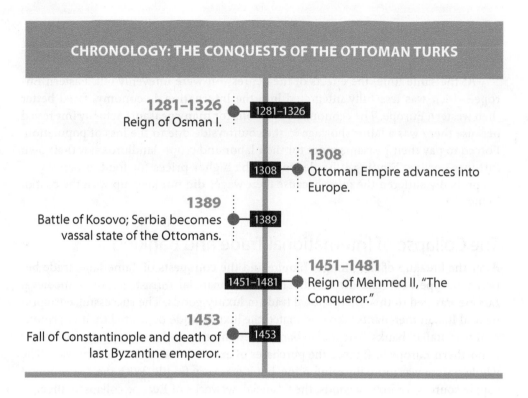

CHRONOLOGY: THE CONQUESTS OF THE OTTOMAN TURKS

1281–1326 | 1281–1326
Reign of Osman I.

1308 | **1308**
Ottoman Empire advances into Europe.

1389 | 1389
Battle of Kosovo; Serbia becomes vassal state of the Ottomans.

1451–1481 | **1451–1481**
Reign of Mehmed II, "The Conqueror."

1453 | 1453
Fall of Constantinople and death of last Byzantine emperor.

lines of defense for the West, and at various times in succeeding centuries the Ottomans launched expeditions against Europe, including two sieges of Vienna (1529 and 1683) and several invasions of Italy.

Hundreds of years of attacks by the Mongol and Ottoman Empires redrew the map of the West. Events in Europe did not and could not take place in isolation from the eastern pressures and influences. The Mongol conquest finished off Kievan Rus. Although Mongols burned down Moscow in the winter of 1238 and pillaged it in 1293, its remote, forested location offered some security from further attacks and occupation. As a result, Moscow and the Republic of Novgorod, which escaped the Mongol attacks entirely, replaced Kiev as the centers of power in what would become Russia. The Ottoman conquests also created a lasting Muslim presence within the borders of Europe, especially in Bosnia and Albania. In succeeding centuries Christian Europe and the Muslim Ottoman Empire would be locked in a deadly competitive embrace, but they also benefited from innumerable cultural exchanges and regular trade. Hostility between the two sides was recurrent but never inevitable and was broken by long periods of peaceful engagement. In fact, the Christian kingdoms of western Europe went to war far more often with one another than with the Turks.

 Read the Document

An Ambassador's Report on the Ottoman Empire (1555) Ogier Ghiselin de Busbecq

 Read the Document

Venetian Observations on the Ottoman Empire Late Sixteenth Century

Economic Depression and Social Turmoil

11.3 How did disturbances in the rudimentary global economy of the Middle Ages precipitate almost complete financial collapse and widespread social discontent in Europe?

Adding insult to injury in this time of famine, plague, and conquest, the West began to suffer a major economic depression during the fourteenth century. The economic boom fueled by the agricultural revolution and the revitalization of European cities during the eleventh century and the commercial prosperity of the twelfth and thirteenth centuries petered out in the fourteenth. The

11.1

11.2

11.3

11.4

11.5

11.6

causes of this economic catastrophe were complex, but the consequences were obvious. Businesses went bust, banks collapsed, guilds were in turmoil, and workers rebelled.

At the same time, the effects of the depression were unevenly felt. Eastern Europe, which was less fully integrated into the international economy, fared better than western Europe. The economic conditions for many peasants actually improved because there was a labor shortage in the countryside due to the loss of population. Forced to pay their peasants more for their labor and crops, landlords saw their own fortunes decline. Finding it harder to pay the higher prices for food, urban workers probably suffered the most because their wages did not keep up with the cost of living.

The Collapse of International Trade and Banking

After the breakup of the Mongol Empire and the conquests of Tamerlane, trade between Europe and Asia dwindled. The entire financial infrastructure of medieval Europe was tied to this international trade in luxury goods. The successful, entrepreneurial Italian merchants who dominated the luxury trade deposited their enormous profits in Italian banks. The Italian bankers lent money to the aristocracy and royalty of northern Europe to finance the purchases of exotic luxuries and to fight wars. The whole system was mutually reinforcing, but it was very fragile. With the disruption of supply sources for luxury goods, the financial networks of Europe collapsed, precipitating a major depression. By 1346, all the banks in Florence, the banking center of Europe, had crashed.

The luxury trade that brought exotic items from Asia to Europe represented only half of the economic equation. The other half was the raw materials and manufactured goods that Europeans sold in exchange, principally woolen cloth. The production of woolen cloth depended on a sophisticated economic system that connected shepherds in England, the Netherlands, and Spain with woolen cloth manufacturers in cities. The manufacture of cloth and other commodities was organized by **guilds**, which were professional associations devoted to protecting the special interests of a particular trade or craft and to monopolizing production and trade in the goods the guild produced. The rise of the guilds marked a shift from household manufactures performed by women, as was common in the early Middle Ages, to industrial production performed mostly by men in shops. Over time, many guilds attempted to restrict or prohibit female membership.

There were two types of guilds. The first type, merchant guilds, attempted to monopolize the local market for a particular commodity. There were spice guilds, fruit and vegetable guilds, and apothecary guilds. The second type, craft guilds, regulated the manufacturing processes of artisans such as carpenters, bricklayers, woolen-cloth manufacturers, glass blowers, and painters. These guilds were dominated by master craftsmen, who ran their own shops. Working for wages in these shops were the journeymen, who knew the craft but could not yet afford to open their own shops. Under the masters and journeymen were apprentices, who usually worked without pay for a specific number of years to learn the trade.

In many cities the guilds expanded far beyond the economic regulation of trade and manufacturing to become the backbone of urban society and politics. The masters of the guilds constituted part of the urban elite, and guild membership was often a prerequisite for holding public office. One of the obligations of city government was to protect the interests of the guildsmen, who in turn helped stabilize the economy through their influence in city hall. Guilds often organized festivals and sports competitions, endowed chapels, and provided funeral insurance for their members and welfare for the injured and widows of masters.

guilds Professional associations devoted to protecting the special interests of a particular trade or craft and to monopolizing production and trade in the goods the guild produced.

When the economy declined during the fourteenth century, the urban guilds became lightning rods for mounting social tension. Guild monopolies produced considerable conflict, provoking anger among those who were blocked from joining guilds, young journeymen who earned low wages, and those who found themselves unemployed due to the depression. These tensions exploded into dangerous revolts.

((• 📖 Read the Document

Guilds: Regulating the Craft, 1347

Workers' Rebellions

Economic pressures erupted into rebellion most dramatically among woolen-cloth workers in the urban centers in Italy, the Netherlands, and France. The most famous revolt involved the Ciompi, the laborers in the woolen-cloth industry of Florence, Italy, where guilds were the most powerful force in city government. The Ciompi, who performed the heaviest jobs such as carting and the most noxious tasks such as dyeing, had not been allowed to have their own guild and were therefore deprived of the political and economic rights of guild membership.

Fueling the Ciompi's frustration was the fact that by the middle of the fourteenth century woolen-cloth production in Florence dropped by two-thirds, leaving many workers unemployed. In 1378 the desperate Ciompi rebelled. A crowd chanting, "Long live the people, long live liberty," broke into the houses of prominent citizens, released political prisoners from the city jails, and sacked the rich convents that housed the pampered daughters of the wealthy. Over the course of a few months, the rebels managed to force their way onto the city council, where they demanded tax and economic reforms and the right to form their own guild. The Ciompi revolt is one of the earliest cases of workers demanding political rights. The disenfranchised workers did not want to eliminate the guilds' monopoly on political power. They merely wanted a guild of their own so that they could join the regime. That was not to be, however. After a few weeks of success, the Ciompi were divided and defeated.

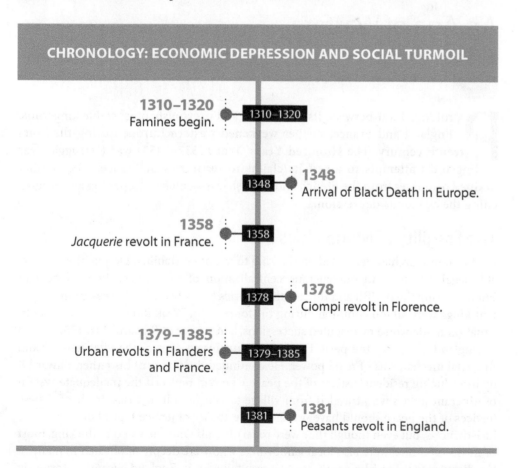

CHRONOLOGY: ECONOMIC DEPRESSION AND SOCIAL TURMOIL

1310–1320
Famines begin.

1348
Arrival of Black Death in Europe.

1358
Jacquerie revolt in France.

1378
Ciompi revolt in Florence.

1379–1385
Urban revolts in Flanders and France.

1381
Peasants revolt in England.

11.1

11.2

11.3

11.4

11.5

11.6

Shortly after the Ciompi revolt faded, troubles broke out in the woolen-cloth centers of Ghent and Bruges in Flanders and in Paris and Rouen in France. In these cases, however, the revolt spread beyond woolen-cloth workers to voice the more generalized grievances of urban workers. In Ghent and Bruges the weavers attempted to wrest control of their cities from the local leaders who dominated politics and the economy. In Paris and Rouen in 1380, social unrest erupted in resistance to high taxes and attacks by the poor on the rich.

Like urban workers, many rural peasants also rebelled during the troubled fourteenth century. In France in 1358 a peasant revolt broke out called the *Jacquerie*. Filled with hatred for the aristocracy, the peasants indulged in pillaging, murder, and rape, but they offered no plan for an alternative social system or even for their own participation in the political order, so their movement had no lasting effects. They were quickly defeated by a force of nobles.

Unlike the French *Jacquerie*, the peasants who revolted in England in 1381 had a clear political vision for an alternative society. The English rebels demanded the abolition of new taxes, lower rents, higher wages, and the end of serfdom, but to these they added a class-based argument against the aristocracy. Influenced by popular preachers, who told them that in the Garden of Eden there had been no aristocracy, the English rebels imagined an egalitarian society without ranks or hierarchy. However, the greatest peasant rebellion in medieval English history ended with broken promises and no tangible achievements.

None of the worker or peasant revolts of the fourteenth century met with lasting success. However, the rebellions revealed for the first time in the West a widespread impulse among the lower classes to question and protest the existing social and economic order. The tradition of worker protest became common and recurrent during subsequent centuries.

An Age of Warfare

11.4	How did incessant warfare transform the most powerful medieval states?

Prolonged war between its two largest and previously most stable kingdoms, England and France, further weakened western Europe during the fourteenth century. The **Hundred Years' War** (1337–1453) was a struggle over England's attempts to assert its claims to territories in France. The conflict drained resources from the French and English aristocracies, deepening and lengthening the economic depression.

Hundred Years' War Refers to a series of engagements (1337–1453) between England and France over England's attempts to assert its claims to territories in France.

The Fragility of Monarchies

Medieval monarchies depended on the king to maintain stability. Despite the remarkable legal reforms and bureaucratic centralization of monarchies in England and France during the twelfth and thirteenth centuries (see Chapter 10), weak or incompetent kings were all too common during the fourteenth. Weak kings created a perilous situation made worse by disputed successions. The career of Edward II (r. 1307–1327) of England illustrates the peril. Edward was unable to control the vital judicial and financial mechanisms of royal power. He continued the policy of his father, Edward I, by introducing resident justices of the peace who had replaced the inadequate system of itinerant judges who traveled from village to village to hear cases. In theory, these justices of the peace should have prevented the abuses of justice typical of aristocratic jurisdictions, but even though they were royal officials who answered to the king, most of those appointed were also local landowners who were deeply implicated in many of the disputes that came before them. As a result, justice in England became notoriously

11.1

11.2

11.3

11.4

11.5

11.6

corrupt and the cause of discontent. Edward II was so incompetent to deal with the consequences of corrupted justice that he provoked a civil war in which his own queen joined his aristocratic enemies to depose him.

The French monarchy was no better. In fact, the French king was in an even weaker constitutional position than the English monarch. In France the king had effective jurisdiction over only a small part of his realm. Many of the duchies and counties of France were quasi-independent principalities paying only nominal allegiance to the king, whose will was ignored with impunity. In these regions the administration of justice, the collection of taxes, and the recruitment of soldiers all remained in the hands of local lords. To explain why he needed to raise taxes, Philip IV, "The Fair" (r. 1285–1314), created a representative assembly, the Estates General, which met for the first time in 1302. Even so, he still had to negotiate with each region and town individually to collect the taxes. Given the difficulty of raising taxes, the French kings resorted to makeshift solutions that hurt the economy, such as confiscating the property of vulnerable Jewish and Italian merchants and debasing the coinage. Such a system made the finances of the kingdom of France especially shaky because the king lacked a dependable flow of revenue.

The Hundred Years' War

The Hundred Years' War revealed the fragility of the medieval monarchies. The initial cause of the war involved disputes over the duchy of Aquitaine. The king of England inherited the title of duke of Aquitaine, who was a vassal of the French crown, which meant that the English kings technically owed military assistance to the French kings whenever they asked for it. A long succession of English kings had reluctantly paid homage as dukes of Aquitaine to the king of France, but the unusual status of the duchy held by the king of England was a continuing source of contention.

The second cause of the war derived from a dispute over the succession to the French crown. When King Charles IV died in 1328, his closest surviving relative was none other than the archenemy of France, Edward III (r. 1327–1377), king of England. To the barons of France, the possibility of Edward's succession to the throne was unthinkable, and they excluded him because his relation to the French royal family was through his mother. Instead the barons elected to the throne a member of the Valois family, King Philip VI (r. 1328–1350). At first Edward reluctantly accepted the decision. However, when Philip started to hear judicial appeals from the duchy of Aquitaine, Edward changed his mind. He claimed the title of king of France for himself, sparking the beginning of more than a century of warfare (see **Map 11.4**).

The Hundred Years' War (1337–1453) was not a continuous formal war, but a series of occasional pitched battles, punctuated by long truces and periods of general exhaustion. Nineteenth-century historians invented the term *Hundred Years' War* to describe the prolonged time of troubles between the two countries. France, far richer and with three times the population, held the advantage over sparsely populated England, but the English were usually victorious because of superior discipline and the ability of their longbows to break up cavalry charges. As a rule, the English avoided open battle, preferring raids, sieges of isolated castles, and capturing French knights for ransom. For many Englishmen the objective of fighting in France was to get rich by looting. Because all the fighting took place on French soil, France suffered extensive destruction and significant civilian casualties from repeated English raids.

FROM ENGLISH VICTORIES TO FRENCH SALVATION In the early phases of the war, the English enjoyed a stunning series of victories. At the Battle of Sluys in 1340, a

11.1

11.2

11.3

11.4

11.5

11.6

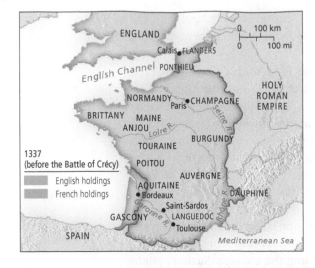

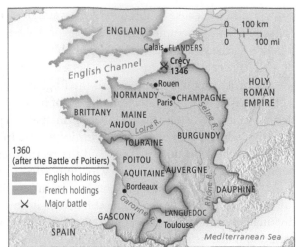

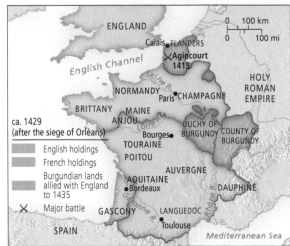

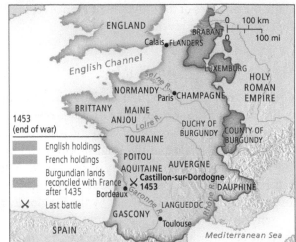

MAP **11.4** THE HUNDRED YEARS' WAR This map illustrates four phases of the Hundred Years' War. In the first phase (1337), England maintained a small foothold in the southwest of France. In the second phase (1360), England considerably expanded the territory around Aquitaine and gained a vital base in the north of France. In the third phase (ca. 1429), England occupied much of the north of France, and England's ally Burgundy established effective independence from French authority. In the fourth phase at the end of the war (1453), England had been driven from French soil except at Calais, and Burgundy maintained control over most of its scattered territories. What were the likely effects of the frequent changes of rulership for France?

small English fleet of 150 ships carrying the English invasion forces ran into a French blockade of more than 200 ships. In the heavy hand-to-hand combat, the English captured 166 French ships and killed some 20,000 men, so many that it was later said, "If fish could talk, they would speak French." At Agincourt in 1415, King Henry V (r. 1413–1422) and England's disease-racked army of 6,000 were cut off by a French force of about 20,000, yet in the ensuing battle the English archers repelled a hasty French cavalry charge and the fleeing, terrified horses trampled the French men-at-arms as they advanced. The English lost only a few hundred, but the French suffered nearly 10,000 casualties. After Agincourt, the French never again dared challenge King Henry in open battle, and were forced to recognize him as the heir to the French throne.

English victory appeared complete, but by 1422 Henry V was dead, leaving two claimants to the French throne. The English asserted the rights of the infant King Henry VI of England, son of King Henry V. Most of the French defended the claim of the Dauphin (the title of the heir to the throne) Charles, the only surviving son of the late King Charles VI of France. The Hundred Years' War entered a new phase with factions of the French aristocracy supporting the two rivals in a bloody series of engagements. The war was now as much a civil war as one between kingdoms.

11.1

11.2

11.3

11.4

11.5

11.6

ENGLISH LONGBOW ARCHERS English archers use the longbow at the Battle of Crecy in 1346. The English long-bow archers on the right are massacring the French crossbowmen on the left. Because of the cumbersome process of cranking back the bowstring between shots, the crossbow had a much slower shooting rate than a longbow.

By 1429 the English were again on the verge of final victory. They occupied Paris and Rheims, and their army was besieging Orleans. The Dauphin Charles was penni-less and indecisive. Even his own mother denied his legitimacy as the future king. At this point, a 17-year-old illiterate peasant from Burgundy, Joan of Arc (Jeanne d'Arc, ca. 1412–1431), following "divine voices," went to Orleans to lead the French armies. Under her inspiration Orleans was relieved, French forces began to defeat the En-glish, much of the occupied territory was regained, and the Dauphin was crowned King Charles VII (r. 1429–1461) in the cathedral of Rheims. After Joan failed to recap-ture Paris, however, her successes ceased. (See *Justice in History* in this chapter.) The final victory of the French came from the leadership of King Charles and the general exhaustion of the English forces.

Charles VII reorganized the French army and gradually chipped away at the English holdings in France, eventually taking away Aquitaine in 1453. The English lost all their possessions in France except Calais, which was finally surrendered in 1558. There was no peace treaty, just a fading away of war in France, especially after England stumbled into civil war—the War of the Roses (1455–1485).

View the Map

The Hundred Years' War

THE HUNDRED YEARS' WAR IN PERSPECTIVE The Hundred Years' War had broad consequences. First, nearly continuous warfare between the two most powerful king-doms in the West exacerbated other conflicts as well. Scotland, the German princes, Aragon, Castile, and most importantly Burgundy were drawn into the conflict, making the English-French brawl a European-wide war at certain stages. The squabble between France and England also made it much more difficult to settle the Great Schism that split the Church during the same period. Second, the war devastated France, which

11.1

11.2

11.3

11.4

11.5

11.6

Justice in History
The Trial of Joan of Arc

After only 15 months as the inspiration of the French army, Joan of Arc fell into the hands of the English, who brought her to trial at Rouen in 1431 for witchcraft. The English needed to stage a show trial to demonstrate to their own demoralized forces that Joan's remarkable victories resulted from witchcraft rather than military superiority. In the English trial, Joan testified that she was merely responding to spiritual voices she heard that commanded her to wear men's clothing. On the basis of her cross dressing, the ecclesiastical tribunal declared her a witch and a relapsed heretic. The court sentenced her to be burned at the stake.

From the beginning of her emergence onto the political scene, the voices Joan heard guided her every move. Joan claimed that she heard the voices of St. Catherine, St. Margaret, and the Archangel Michael. To Joan, these voices carried the authority of divine commands.

JOAN OF ARC Arrival of Joan of Arc at the Château de Chinon, March 6th 1428.

The problem the English judges faced was to demonstrate that the voices came from the Devil rather than from God. If they could prove that, then they had evidence of witchcraft and sorcery. Following standard inquisitorial guidelines, the judges knew that authentic messages from God would always conform to church dogma. Any deviation from official doctrines would constitute evidence of demonic influence. Thus, during Joan's trial the judges demanded that she make theological distinctions that were alien to her. When they wanted to know if the voices were those of angels or saints, Joan seemed perplexed and responded, "This voice comes from God. . . . I am more afraid of failing the voices by saying what is displeasing to them than answering you."[6] The judges kept pushing, asking if the saints or angels had heads, eyes, and hair. Exasperated, Joan simply replied, "I have told you often enough, believe me if you will."

The judges reformulated Joan's words to reflect their own rigid scholastic categories and concluded that her "veneration of the saints seems to partake of idolatry and to proceed from a pact made with devils. These are less divine revelations than lies invented by Joan, suggested or shown to her by the demon in illusive apparitions, in order to mock at her imagination while she meddled with things that are beyond her and superior to the faculty of her condition."[7] In other words, Joan was just too naive and uneducated to have authentic visions. But the English judges were on dangerous ground because during the previous 50 years there had been a number of notable female mystics, including St. Catherine of Siena and St. Bridget of Sweden, whose visions the pope had accepted as authentic. The English could not take the chance that they were executing a real saint. So they changed tactics.

If they could not convict her for bad theology, the English needed evidence for superstitious practices. In an attempt to do that, they drew up 70 charges against Joan. Many of these consisted of allegations of performing magic, such as chanting spells, visiting a magical tree at night, and invoking demons. They attempted to prove bad behavior by insinuating that a young man had refused to marry her on account of her immoral life. They asserted that her godmother was a notorious witch who had taught her sorcery. None of these ploys worked, however, because Joan consistently denied the charges. She did, however, admit to one allegation: she dressed as a man.

Some of the charges against her and many of the judges' questions concerned how she dressed:

> The said Joan put off and entirely abandoned women's clothes, with her hair cropped short and round in the fashion of young men, she wore shirt, breeches, doublet, with hose joined together, long and fastened to the said doublet by twenty points, long leggings laced on the outside, a short mantle reaching to the knee, or thereabouts, a close-cut cap, tight-fitting boots or buskins, long spurs, sword, dagger, breastplate, lance and other arms in the style of a man-at-arms.[8]

The judges explained to her that "according to canon law and the Holy Scriptures" a woman dressing as a man or a man as a woman is "an abomination before God."[9] She replied simply and consistently that "everything that I have done, I did by command of the voices" and that wearing male dress "would be for the great good of France."[10] When they asked her to put on a woman's dress in order to take the Eucharist on Easter Sunday, she refused, saying the miracle of the Eucharist did not depend on whether she wore a man's or a woman's clothing. On many occasions she had been asked to put on a woman's dress and refused. "And as for womanly duties, she said there were enough other women to do them."[11]

(continued on next page)

(continued from previous page)

After a long imprisonment and psychological pressure from her inquisitors, Joan confessed to charges of witchcraft, signed a recantation of her heresy, and agreed to put on a dress. She was sentenced to life imprisonment on bread and water. Why did she confess? Some historians have argued that she was tricked into confessing because the inquisitors really wanted to execute her but could not do so unless she was a *relapsed* heretic. To be relapsed she had to confess and then somehow return to her heretical ways. If that were the inquisitors' intention, Joan soon obliged them. After a few days in prison, Joan threw off the women's clothes she had been given and resumed dressing as a man.

Joan was willing to be burned at the stake rather than disobey her voices. Why? Historians will never know for sure, but dressing as a man may have been necessary for her to fulfill her role as a military leader. In her military career, Joan had adopted the masculine qualities of chivalry: bravery, steadfastness, loyalty, *and* a willingness to accept pain and death. She made herself believable by dressing as a knight. Joan's condemnation was much more than another example of men's attempt to control women.

Joan's transgressive gender identity threatened the whole system of neat hierarchical distinctions upon which Christian theology rested. To the theologians, everything in God's Creation had its own proper place and anyone who changed his or her divinely ordained position in society presented a direct affront to God.

For Discussion

1. In medieval ecclesiastical trials such as this one, what kinds of evidence were presented and what kind of justice was sought?
2. What did Joan's claim that she heard voices reveal about her understanding of what constituted the proper authority over her life?

Taking It Further

Joan of Arc. *In Her Own Words,* Translated by Willard Trask. 1996. The record of what Joan reputedly said at her trials.
Warner, Marina. *Joan of Arc: The Image of Female Heroism.* 1981. A highly readable feminist reading of the Joan of Arc story.

eventually regained control of most of its territory but still suffered the most from the fighting. During the century of war, the population dropped by half, due to the ravages of combat, pillage, and plague. Third, the deaths of so many nobles and destruction of their fortunes diminished the international luxury trade. Merchants and banks as far away as Italy went broke. In addition, the war disrupted the Flemish woolen industry causing further economic damage. Finally, the war helped make England more English. Before the war the Plantagenet dynasty in England was more French than English. The monarchs possessed extensive territories in France and were embroiled in French affairs. English aristocrats also had business in France, spoke French, and married their French cousins. After 1450 the English abandoned the many French connections that had stretched across the English Channel since William the Conqueror sailed from Normandy to England in 1066. Henceforth, the English upper classes cultivated English rather than French language and culture.

The Military Revolution

The "military revolution" first became evident during the Hundred Years' War but lasted well into the seventeenth century. It refers to changes in warfare that marked the transition from the late medieval to the early modern state. The heavily armored mounted knights, who had dominated European warfare and society since the Carolingian period, were gradually supplanted by foot soldiers as the most effective fighting unit in battle. Infantry units were composed of men who fought on foot in disciplined ranks, which allowed them to break up cavalry charges by concentrating firepower in deadly volleys. Infantry soldiers could fight on a greater variety of terrains than mounted knights, who needed level ground and plenty of space for their horses to maneuver. The effectiveness of infantry units made battles more ferocious but also more decisive, which was why governments favored them. Infantry, however, put new requirements on the governments that recruited them. Armies now demanded large numbers of well-drilled foot soldiers who could move in disciplined ranks around a battlefield. Recruiting, training, and drilling soldiers made armies much more complex organizations than they had been, and officers needed

11.1

11.2

11.3

11.4

11.5

11.6

to possess a wide range of management skills. Governments faced added expenses as they needed to arrange and pay for the logistical support necessary to feed and transport those large numbers. The creation of the highly centralized modern state resulted in part from the necessity to maintain a large army in which infantry played the crucial role.

Infantry used a variety of weapons. The English demonstrated the effectiveness of longbowmen during the Hundred Years' War. Capable of shooting at a much more rapid rate than the French crossbowmen, the English longbowmen at Agincourt protected themselves behind a hurriedly erected stockade of stakes and rained a shower of deadly arrows on the French cavalry to break up charges. In the narrow battlefield, which was wedged between two forests, the French cavalry had insufficient room to

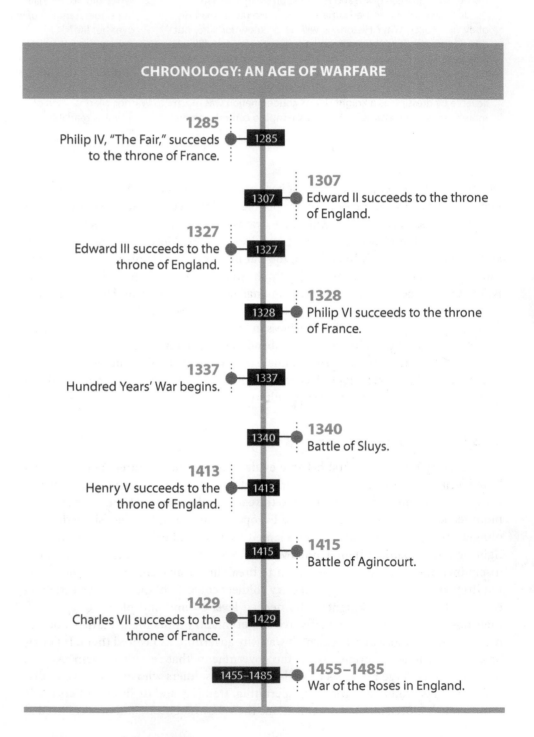

CHRONOLOGY: AN AGE OF WARFARE

1285
Philip IV, "The Fair," succeeds to the throne of France.
1285

1307
1307
Edward II succeeds to the throne of England.

1327
Edward III succeeds to the throne of England.
1327

1328
1328
Philip VI succeeds to the throne of France.

1337
Hundred Years' War begins.
1337

1340
1340
Battle of Sluys.

1413
Henry V succeeds to the throne of England.
1413

1415
1415
Battle of Agincourt.

1429
Charles VII succeeds to the throne of France.
1429

1455–1485
1455–1485
War of the Roses in England.

11.1

11.2

11.3

11.4

11.5

11.6

maneuver; when some of them dismounted to create more room, their heavy armor made them easy to topple over and spear through the underarm seam in their armor. Some English infantry units deployed ranks of pikemen who created an impenetrable wall of sharp spikes.

The military revolution of the fourteenth and fifteenth centuries also introduced gunpowder to European warfare. Arriving from China with the Mongol invasions, gunpowder was first used in the West in artillery. Beginning in the 1320s, besieging armies shot stone or iron against fortifications from huge wrought-iron cannons. By the early sixteenth century bronze muzzle-loading cannons were used in field battles. With the introduction during the late fifteenth century of the handgun and the harque-bus (a predecessor to the musket), properly drilled and disciplined infantrymen could deliver destructive firepower. Gunshots pierced plate armor, whereas arrows bounced off. The slow rate of fire of these guns, however, necessitated carefully planned battle tactics. Around 1500 the Spanish introduced mixed infantry formations that pursued "shock" and "shot" tactics. Spanish pikemen provided the shock, which was quickly followed by gunshot or missile fire. This combination of technology and technique enabled Spanish infantry formations to defeat cavalry even in the open field without defensive fortifications, an unprecedented feat. By the end of the fifteenth century, every army included trained infantry.

The military revolution precipitated a major shift in European society. The successful states were those that created the financial base and bureaucratic structures necessary to field a professional army composed of infantry units and artillery. Superior armies required officers capable of drilling infantry or understanding the science of warfare to serve as an artillery officer.

A Troubled Church and the Demand for Religious Comfort

11.5 Why did the Church fail to provide leadership and spiritual guidance during these difficult times?

In reaction to the suffering and widespread death during the fourteenth century, many people turned to religion for spiritual consolation and for explanations of what had gone wrong. But the spiritual authority of the Church was so dangerously weakened during this period that it failed to satisfy the popular craving for solace. The moral leadership that had made the papacy such a powerful force for reform during the eleventh through thirteenth centuries evaporated in the fourteenth. Many lay-people found their own means of religious expression, making the Later Middle Ages one of the most religiously creative epochs in Christian history.

The Babylonian Captivity of the Church and the Great Schism

Faced with anarchy in the streets of Rome as local aristocrats engaged in incessant feud-ing, seven consecutive popes chose to reside in the relative calm of Avignon, France. This period of voluntary papal exile is known as the **Babylonian Captivity of the Church** (1305–1378), a biblical reference recalling the captivity of the Jews in Babylo-nia (587–539 B.C.E.). The popes' presumed subservience to the kings of France during this period dangerously politicized the papacy, destroying its ability to rise above the petty squabbles of the European princes and to serve as a spiritual authority to all. Even though these French popes residing in France were never the French kings' lackeys,

Babylonian Captivity of the Church Between 1305 and 1378 seven consecutive popes volun-tarily chose to reside in Avignon, France, in order to escape anarchy in the streets of Rome. During this period the popes became subser-vient to the kings of France.

351

11.1

11.2

11.3

11.4

11.5

11.6

Different Voices
The Struggle over the Papal Monarchy

T he most extreme assertion of papal authority during the Middle Ages came from Pope Boniface VIII (1294-1303). In his decree Clericis Laicos of 1296, he asserted that any secular ruler whether emperor, king, or even minor officials of towns who taxed the Church or seized its property would incur a sentence of excommunication. In 1302 in the midst of a bitter conflict with the King of France, Boniface expanded that bold rejection of any jurisdictional claims by secular princes over the Church in the decree Unam Sanctam excerpted below.

From Pope Boniface VIII, *Unam Sanctam*

We are taught by the words of the Gospel that in this church and in her power there are two swords, a spiritual one and a temporal one. . . . But both then are in the power of the church, the material sword and the spiritual. But the one is exercised for the church, the other by the church, the one by the hand of the priest, the other by the hand of kings and soldiers, though at the will and sufferance of the priest. One sword ought to be under the other and the temporal authority subject to the spiritual power. . . . Therefore we declare, state, define and pronounce that it is altogether necessary to salvation for every human creature to be subject to the Roman Pontiff.

SOURCE: *The Middle Ages*, ed. Brian Tierney. 3rd ed. (New York: Alfred A. Knopf, 1978), vol. 1, pp. 321–22. © The McGraw-Hill Companies, Inc. Reprinted by permission.

Boniface's radical claim did not sit well with medieval princes any more than it would with governments today. Not only did King Philip IV of France send troops to Boniface's hideout in Anagni in an attempt to force his resignation, but within a few years of the pope's death, the papacy itself moved to France. During the fourteenth

century several theologians and political thinkers attempted to refute Boniface and to assert the authority of autonomous secular states. In this passage William of Ockham (1299–1350) defends the liberty of the emperor to act without papal interference and even questions the authority of a heretical or immoral pope over the Church itself. This passage is from Ockham's Dialogus.

From William of Ockham, *Dialogus*

Every people and every community and every body which can make law for itself without the consent or authority of anyone else can without the authority of anyone else elect certain persons to represent the whole community or body. . . . Moreover, if men so elected come together at one time, they constitute a general council, since a general council seems to be nothing else than an assembly of certain men who represent the whole of Christendom. Therefore, a general council can be convened without the authority of anyone whatever who is not a catholic and a believer, and, consequently, without the authority of a heretical pope.

SOURCE: *The Middle Ages*, ed. Brian Tierney. 3rd ed. (New York: Alfred A. Knopf, 1978), vol. 1, pp. 328. © The McGraw-Hill Companies, Inc. Reprinted by permission.

For Discussion

1. How does Boniface interpret the two swords metaphor of authority for the benefit of the clergy and the papacy? Does he leave any wiggle room for his opponents?

2. How does Ockham attack the claims of the popes that "it is altogether necessary to salvation for every human creature to be subject to the Roman Pontiff?" Is Ockham advocating democracy in this passage?

---

indulgences Certificates that allowed penitents to atone for their sins and reduce their time in purgatory. Usually these were issued for going on a pilgrimage or performing a pious act, but during the Babylonian Captivity of the Church (1305–1378) popes began to sell them, a practice Martin Luther protested in 1517 in an act that brought on the Protestant Reformation.

 View the Map

The Great Schism

Great Schism The division of the Catholic Church (1378–1417) between rival Italian and French claimants to the papal throne.

the enemies of the kings of France did not trust them. The loss of revenues from papal lands in Italy lured several popes into questionable financial schemes, which included accepting kickbacks from appointees to church offices, taking bribes for judicial decisions, and selling **indulgences**, certificates that allowed penitents to atone for their sins and reduce their time in Purgatory.

When Pope Urban VI (r. 1378–1389) announced his intention to reside in Rome, a group of disgruntled French cardinals returned to Avignon and elected a rival French pope. The Church was then divided over allegiance to Italian and French claimants to the papal throne, a period called the **Great Schism** (1378–1417). Toward the end of the schism there were actually three rival popes. During the Great Schism the kings, princes, and cities of Europe divided their allegiances between the rival candidates. Competing political alliances, not doctrinal differences, split the Church.

The **Conciliar Movement** attempted to create a mechanism for ending the Schism. The conciliarists, however, also sought to restrict the theoretical and practical authority of the papacy. They argued that a general meeting or *council* of the bishops of the Church had authority over the pope. A king could call such a council to undertake reforms, pass judgment on a standing pope, or order a conclave to elect a new one. Several general councils convened during the early fifteenth century to resolve the Schism and initiate reforms, but the intertwining of political and Church affairs made solutions difficult to achieve. The Council of Constance (1414–1417) finally succeeded in restoring unity to the Church and also in formally asserting the principle that a general council was superior to the pope and should be called frequently. The Council of Basel (1431–1449) approved a series of necessary reforms, but Pope Eugene IV (r. 1431–1447), who opposed conciliarism, never implemented them. The failure of even the timid reforms of the Council of Basel opened the way for the more radical rejection of papal authority during the Protestant Reformation of the sixteenth century.

The Search for Religious Alternatives

The popes' loss of moral authority during the Babylonian Captivity and the Great Schism opened the way for a remarkable variety of reformers, mystics, and preachers. Most of these movements were traditional in their doctrines, but some were heretical. The weakened papacy was unable to control them, as it had successfully done during the thirteenth-century Crusade against the Albigensians.

PROTESTS AGAINST THE PAPACY: NEW HERESIES For most Catholic Christians during the fourteenth century, religious life consisted of witnessing or participating in the seven sacraments, the formal rituals celebrated by duly consecrated priests usually within the confines of churches. After baptism, which was universally performed on infants, the most common sacraments for lay adults were penance and communion. Both of these sacraments emphasized the authority of the clergy over the laity and therefore were potential sources for resentment. The sacrament of penance required the layperson to confess his or her sins to a priest, who then prescribed certain penalties to satisfy the sin. At communion, it was believed, the priest changed the substance of an unleavened wafer of bread, called the Eucharist, into the body of Christ and a chalice of wine into Christ's blood, a miraculous process of transubstantiation (see Chapter 10). Priests and lay recipients of communion both ate the wafer, but the chalice was reserved for the priest alone. More than anything else, the reservation of the chalice for priests profoundly symbolized the privileges of the clergy. Because medieval Catholicism was primarily a sacramental religion, reformers and heretics tended to concentrate their criticism on sacramental rituals.

The most serious discontent about the authority of the popes, the privileges of the clergy, and the efficacy of the sacraments appeared in England and Bohemia (a region in the modern Czech Republic). An Oxford professor, John Wycliffe (1320–1384), criticized the power and wealth of the clergy, played down the value of the sacraments for encouraging ethical behavior, and exalted the benefits of preaching, which promoted a sense of personal responsibility. During the Great Schism, Wycliffe rejected the authority of the rival popes and asserted instead the absolute authority of the Bible, which he wanted to make available to the laity in English rather than in Latin, which most laypeople could not understand.

Outside England Wycliffe's ideas found their most sympathetic audience among a group of reformist professors at the University of Prague in Bohemia, where Jan Hus (1369–1415) regularly preached to a large popular following. Hus's most revolutionary act was to offer the chalice of consecrated communion wine to the laity, thus symbolically diminishing the special status of the clergy. When Hus also preached against indulgences, which he said converted the sacrament of penance into a cash transaction, Pope John XXIII excommunicated him. Hus attended the Council of Constance to defend his ideas. Despite the promise of a safe-conduct from the Holy Roman emperor (whose jurisdiction included Bohemia and Constance) that should have made him immune from arrest, Hus was imprisoned, his writings were condemned, and he was burned alive as a heretic.

Conciliar Movement A fifteenth-century movement that advocated ending the Great Schism and reforming church government by calling a general meeting or council of the bishops, who would exercise authority over the rival popes.

11.1

11.2

11.3

11.4

11.5

11.6

11.1

11.2

11.3

11.4

11.5

11.6

Modern Devotion A fifteenth-century religious movement that stressed individual piety, ethical behavior, and intense religious education. The Modern Devotion was promoted by the Brothers of the Common Life, a religious order whose influence was broadly felt through its extensive network of schools.

Wycliffe and Hus started movements that survived their own deaths. In England Wycliffe's followers were the Lollards and in Bohemia the Hussites carried on reform ideas. Both groups were eventually absorbed into the Protestant Reformation in the sixteenth century.

IMITATING CHRIST: THE MODERN DEVOTION In the climate of religious turmoil of the fourteenth and fifteenth centuries, many Christians sought deeper spiritual solace than the institutionalized Church could provide. By stressing individual piety, ethical behavior, and intense religious education, a movement called the **Modern Devotion** built on the existing traditions of spirituality and became highly influential. Promoted by the Brothers of the Common Life, a religious order established in the Netherlands, the Modern Devotion was especially popular throughout northern Europe. In the houses for the Brothers, clerics and laity lived together without monastic vows, shared household tasks, joined in regular prayers, and engaged in religious studies. (A similar structure was devised for women.) The lay brothers continued their occupations in the outside world, thus influencing their neighbors through their pious example. The houses established schools that prepared boys for church careers through constant prayer and rigorous training in Latin. Many of the leading figures behind the Protestant Reformation in the sixteenth century had attended schools run by the Brothers of the Common Life.

The Modern Devotion also spread through the influence of the best-seller of the late fifteenth century, the *Imitation of Christ,* written about 1441 by a Common Life brother, probably Thomas à Kempis. By emphasizing frequent private prayer and

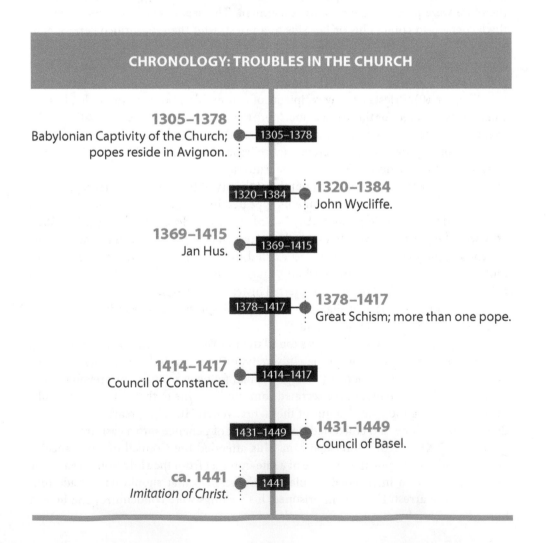

CHRONOLOGY: TROUBLES IN THE CHURCH

1305–1378
Babylonian Captivity of the Church; popes reside in Avignon. — 1305–1378

1320–1384 — 1320–1384
John Wycliffe.

1369–1415 — 1369–1415
Jan Hus.

1378–1417 — **1378–1417**
Great Schism; more than one pope.

1414–1417 — 1414–1417
Council of Constance.

1431–1449 — **1431–1449**
Council of Basel.

ca. 1441 — 1441
Imitation of Christ.

moral introspection, the *Imitation* provided a manual to guide laypeople in the path toward spiritual renewal that had traditionally been reserved for monks and nuns. There was nothing especially reformist about the *Imitation of Christ*, which emphasized the need for regular confession and communion. However, its popularity helped prepare the way for a broad-based reform of the Church by turning the walls of the monastery inside out, spilling out a large number of lay believers who were dedicated to becoming living examples of moral purity for their neighbors.

The Culture of Loss

11.1

11.2

11.3

11.4

11.5

11.6

11.6 How did European culture offer explanations and solace for the otherwise inexplicable calamities of the times?

During the fourteenth and early fifteenth centuries, the omnipresence of violence and death provoked widespread anxiety. This anxiety had many manifestations. Some people went on long penitential pilgrimages to the shrines of saints or to the Holy Land. During the fourteenth century the tribulations of the pilgrim's travels became a metaphor for the journey of life itself, stimulating creative literature. Still others tried to find someone to blame for calamities. The search for scapegoats focused on minority groups, especially Jews and Muslims.

Reminders of Death

In no other period of Western civilization has the idea of death so pervaded popular cultures as during the fourteenth and fifteenth centuries. The Reminders of Death was a theme found in religious books, literary works, and the visual arts. A contemporary book of moral guidance advised the reader that "when he goes to bed, he should imagine not that he is putting himself to bed, but that others are laying him in his grave."[12] Reminders of Death became the everyday theme of preachers, and popular woodcuts represented death in simple but disturbing images. The Reminders of Death tried to encourage ethical behavior in this life by showing that in everyone's future was neither riches, nor fame, nor love, nor pleasure, but only the decay of death.

The most famous Reminder of Death was the Dance of Death. First appearing in a poem of 1376, the Dance of Death evolved into a street play, performed to illustrate sermons that called for repentance. It also appeared in church murals, depicting a procession led by a skeleton that included representatives of the social orders, from children and peasants to pope and emperor. All danced to their inevitable deaths. At the Church of the Innocents in Paris, the inscription that accompanies the mural depicting the Dance of Death reads:

> Advance, see yourselves in us, dead, naked, rotten and stinking. So will you be. . . . To live without thinking of this risks damnation. . . . Power, honor, riches are nothing; at the hour of death only good works count. . . . Everyone should think at least once a day of his loathsome end [in order to escape] the dreadful pain of hell without end which is unspeakable.[13]

In earlier centuries, tombs had depicted death as serene: On top of the tomb rested an effigy of the deceased, dressed in the finest clothes with hands piously folded and eyes open to the promise of eternal life. In contrast, during the fourteenth century, tomb effigies began to depict putrefying bodies or naked skeletons, symbols of the futility of human status and achievements. These tombs were disturbingly graphic Reminders of Death. Likewise, poems spoke of the disgusting smell of rotting flesh, the livid color of plague victims, and the cold touch of the dead.

11.1

11.2

11.3

11.4

11.5

11.6

DANCE OF DEATH This late-fifteenth century painted engraving illustrates the fascination with death during the period. The skeletons dance and play musical instruments. The cadaver on the right holds his own entrails.

Late medieval society was completely frank about the unpleasant process of dying, unlike modern societies that hide the dying in hospitals and segregate mourning to funeral homes. Dying was a public event, almost a theatrical performance. The last rites of the Catholic Church and the Art of Dying served to assist souls in their final test before God and to separate the departed from their kin. According to the Art of Dying, outlined in numerous advice books and illustrations, the sick or injured person should die in bed, surrounded by a room full of people, including children. Christians believed that a dying person watched a supernatural spectacle visible to him or her alone as the heavenly host fought with Satan and his demon minions for the soul. The Art of Dying compared the deathbed contest to a horrific game of chess in which the Devil did all he could to trap the dying person into a checkmate just at the moment of death. In the best of circumstances, a priest arrived in time to hear a confession, offer words of consolation, encourage the dying individual to forgive his or her enemies and redress any wrongs, and perform the last rites.

Pilgrims of the Imagination

During the Middle Ages, a pilgrimage offered a religiously sanctioned form of escape from the omnipresent suffering and peril. Pious Christians could go on a pilgrimage to the Holy Land, Rome, or the shrine of a saint, such as Santiago de Compostela in Spain, Canterbury in England, or Częstochowa in Poland. The usual motive for a pilgrimage was to fulfill a vow or promise made to God, or to obtain an indulgence, which exempted the pilgrim from some of the time spent in punishment in Purgatory after death. The pilgrimage became the instrument for spiritual liberation and escape from difficulties. As a result, going on a pilgrimage became a compelling model for creative literature, especially during the fourteenth century. Not all of these great works

11.1

11.2

11.3

11.4

11.5

11.6

of literature were fictional pilgrimages, but many evoked the pilgrim's impulse to find a refuge from the difficulties of daily life or to find solace in the promise of a better life to come.

DANTE ALIGHIERI AND *THE DIVINE COMEDY* In *The Divine Comedy* an Italian poet from Florence, Dante Alighieri (1265–1321), imagined the most fantastic pilgrimage ever attempted, a journey through Hell, Purgatory, and Paradise. A work of astounding originality, *The Divine Comedy* remains the greatest masterpiece of medieval literature. Little is known about Dante's early life except that somehow he acquired expertise in Greek philosophy, scholastic theology (the application of logic to the understanding of Christianity, discussed in Chapter 10), Latin literature, and the newly fashionable poetic forms in Provençal, the language of southern France. Dante's involvement in the dangerous politics of Florence led to his exile under pain of death if he ever returned. During his exile Dante wandered for years, suffering grievously the loss of his home: "Bitter is the taste of another man's bread and . . . heavy the way up and down another man's stair" (*Paradiso,* canto 17). He sustained himself by writing his great poetic vision of human destiny and God's plan for redemption.

In the poem Dante himself travels into the Christian version of the afterlife. Dante's trip, initially guided by the Latin poet Virgil, the epitome of ancient wisdom, starts in Hell. As he travels deeper into Hell's harsh depths, a cast of sinful characters who inhabit the world of the damned warn Dante of the harmful values of this world. In Purgatory his guide becomes Beatrice, Dante's deceased beloved, who stands for the Christian virtues. In this section of the poem, he begins the painful process of spiritual rehabilitation

THE ART OF DYING In this death scene, the dying man receives extreme unction (last rites) from a priest. A friar holds a crucifix for him to contemplate. Above his head a devil and angel compete for his soul, while behind him Death lurks waiting for his moment.

11.1

11.2

11.3

11.4

11.5

11.6

in which he comes to accept the Christian image of life as a pilgrimage. In Paradise he achieves spiritual fulfillment by speaking with figures from the past who have defied death. Although the poem is deeply Christian, it displays numerous non-Christian influences. The passage through Hell, for example, derived from a long Muslim poem reconstructing Muhammad's *miraj*, a night journey to Jerusalem and ascent to heaven.

The lasting appeal of this long and difficult poem is a wonder. Underlying the appeal of *The Divine Comedy* is perhaps its optimism, which expresses Dante's own cure to his depressing condition as an exile. The power of Dante's poetry established the form of the modern Italian language. Even in translation the images and stories can intrigue and fascinate.

GEOFFREY CHAUCER AND *THE CANTERBURY TALES* Geoffrey Chaucer (ca. 1342–1400) was the most outstanding English poet prior to William Shakespeare. As a courtier and diplomat, Chaucer was a trusted adviser to three successive English kings. But he is best known for his literary output, including *The Canterbury Tales*.

In *The Canterbury Tales* a group of 30 pilgrims tell stories as they travel on horseback to the shrine at Canterbury. Chaucer's use of the pilgrimage as a framing device for telling the stories allowed him to bring together a collection of people from across the social spectrum, including a wife, indulgence hawker, miller, town magistrate, clerk, landowner, lawyer, merchant, knight, abbess, and monk. The variety of characters who told the tales allowed Chaucer to experiment with many kinds of literary forms, from a chivalric romance to a sermon. The pilgrimage combined the considerations of religious morality with the fun of a spring vacation. Many pilgrims were more concerned with the pleasures of this world than preparing for the next, which was the avowed purpose of going on a pilgrimage. In this intertwining of the worldly and the spiritual, Chaucer brought the abstract principles of Christian morality down to a level of common understanding.

CHRISTINE DE PISAN AND THE DEFENSE OF FEMALE VIRTUE The work of the poet Christine de Pisan (1364–1430) was not a spiritual pilgrimage like Dante's or Chaucer's but a thoughtful and passionate commentary on the tumultuous issues of her day. At age 15 Pisan married a notary of King Charles V of France, but by age 25 she was a widow with three young children. In order to support her family, she turned to writing and relied on the patronage of the royalty and wealthy aristocrats of France, Burgundy, Germany, and England.

Christine de Pisan championed the cause of women in a male-dominated society. Following the fashion of the times, she invented a new chivalric order, the Order of the Rose, whose members took a vow to defend the honor of women. She wrote a defense of women for a male readership and an allegorical autobiography. But she is most famous for the two books she wrote for women readers, *The Book of the City of Ladies* and *The Book of Three Virtues* (both about 1407). In these she recounted tales of the heroism and virtue of women and offered moral instruction for women in different social roles. In 1415 she retired to a convent where in the last year of her life she wrote a masterpiece of ecstatic lyricism that celebrated the early victories of Joan of Arc. Pisan's book turned the martyred Joan into the heroine of France.

Defining Cultural Boundaries

During the Later Middle Ages, systematic discrimination against certain ethnic and religious groups increased markedly in Europe. As European society enforced ever-higher levels of religious uniformity, intolerance spread in the ethnically mixed societies of the European periphery. Intolerance was marked in three areas: Spain with its mixture of Muslim, Jewish, and Christian cultures; the German borderlands in east-central

Europe, where Germans mingled with Slavs; and Ireland and Wales, where Celts came under the domination of the English. Within the heartland of Europe were other areas of clashing cultures—Switzerland, for example, where the folk culture of peasants and shepherds living in the isolated mountains collided with the intense Christian religiosity of the cities.

RELIGIOUS COMMUNITIES IN TENSION The Iberian peninsula was home to thriving communities of Muslims, Jews, and Christians. Since the eleventh century the aggressive northern Christian kingdoms of Castile and Aragon had engaged in a protracted program of Reconquest (*Reconquista*) against the Muslim states of the peninsula. By 1248 the Reconquest was largely completed, with only a small Muslim enclave in Granada holding out until 1492. The Spanish Reconquest placed former enemies in close proximity to one another. Hostilities between Christians and Muslims ranged from active warfare to tense stalemate, with Jews working as cultural intermediaries between the two larger communities.

During the twelfth and thirteenth centuries Muslims, called the Mudejars, who capitulated to the conquering Christians, received guarantees that they could continue to practice their own religion and laws. During the fourteenth century, however, Christian kings gradually reneged on these promises. In 1301 the king of Castile decreed that the testimony of any two Christian witnesses could convict a Jew or Muslim, notwithstanding any previously granted privileges that allowed them to be tried in their own courts. The Arabic language began to disappear in Spain as the Mudejars suffered discrimination on many levels. By the sixteenth century, the practice of Islam became illegal, and the Spanish state adopted a systematic policy to destroy Mudejar culture by prohibiting Muslim dress, customs, and marriage practices.

The Jews also began to feel the pain of organized, official discrimination. Christian preachers accused Jews of poisonings, stealing Christian babies, and cannibalism. When the Black Death arrived in 1348, the Jews of Aragon were accused of having poisoned the wells, even though Jews were dying just like Christians. Beginning in 1378, a Catholic prelate in Seville, Ferrant Martínez, commenced an anti-Jewish preaching campaign by calling for the destruction of all 23 of the city's synagogues, the confinement of Jews to a ghetto, the dislodging of all Jews from public positions, and the prohibition of any social contact between Christians and Jews. His campaign led to an attack on the Jews of Seville in 1391. Violence spread to other cities throughout the peninsula and the nearby Balearic Islands. Jews faced a stark choice: conversion or death. After a year of mob violence, about 100,000 Jews had been murdered and an equal number had gone into hiding or fled to more tolerant Muslim countries. The 1391 pogroms led to the first significant forced conversions of Jews in Spain. A century later in 1492, on the heels of the final Christian victory of the Reconquest, all remaining Jews in Spain were compelled to either leave or convert.

Violence against religious minorities occurred in many places, but besides Spain it was most systematic in German-speaking lands. Between November 1348 and August 1350, violence against Jews occurred in more than 80 German towns. Like the allegations in Aragon, the fear that Jews poisoned the wells led to massacres in German lands even *before* plague had arrived in these communities. The frequent occurrence of violence on Sundays or feast days suggests that preachers consciously or unconsciously encouraged the rioting mobs.

Jews had already been expelled from England in 1290 and France in 1306. The situation for Jews was better in Italy where the small population of Jews signed contracts with local towns offering them protection. This pattern of friction among ethnic communities was largely absent in Poland, however, where King Casimir III the Great (1333–1370) granted Jews special privileges and welcomed Jewish immigrants, many of them fleeing persecution elsewhere.

11.1

11.2

11.3

11.4

11.5

11.6

11.1

11.2

11.3

11.4

11.5

11.6

ETHNIC COMMUNITIES IN TENSION Other regions with diverse populations also witnessed discrimination and its brutal consequences. During the population boom of the twelfth and thirteenth centuries, German-speaking immigrants had established colonial towns in the Baltic and penetrated eastward, creating isolated pockets of German culture in Bohemia, Poland, and Hungary. During the fourteenth and fifteenth centuries, hostilities between the native populations and the colonizing Germans arose, particularly in Bohemia. One Czech prince offered 100 silver marks to anyone who brought him 100 German noses. The Teutonic Knights, who had been the vanguard of the German migrations in the Baltic, began to require German ancestry for membership. In German-speaking towns along the colonized borderlands of east-central Europe, city councils and guilds began to use ethnicity as a qualification for holding certain offices or joining a guild. The most famous example was the "German Paragraph" in guild statutes, which required candidates for admission to a guild to prove German descent. As the statutes of a bakers' guild put it, "Whoever wishes to be a member must bring proof to the councilors and the guildsmen that he is born of legitimate, upright German folk." Others required members to be "of German blood and tongue," as if language were a matter of biological inheritance.[14] German guildsmen were also forbidden to marry non-Germans.

In the Celtic fringe of the British Isles, too, discrimination became far more evident in the fourteenth century. In Ireland the ruling English promulgated laws that attempted to protect the cultural identity of the English colonists. The English prohibited native Irish from citizenship in town or guild membership. The Statutes of Kilkenny of 1366 attempted to legislate ethnic purity: They prohibited intermarriage between English and Irish and required English colonists to speak English, use English names, wear English clothes, and ride horses in the English way. They also forbade the English to play Irish games or listen to Irish music. A similar pattern appeared in Wales, where the lines dividing the Welsh and English communities hardened as the English community attempted to prevent its absorption into the majority culture.

CONCLUSION

Looking Inward

Unlike the more dynamic, outward-looking thirteenth century, Europeans during the fourteenth and early fifteenth centuries turned their attention inward to their own communities and their own problems. Europe faced one calamity after another, each crisis compounding the misery. The process of changing Western identities during this period can be seen in two ways.

First, as a result of the Western encounters with the Mongol and Ottoman Empires, the political and religious frontiers of the West shifted. These two empires redrew the map of the West by ending the Christian Byzantine Empire. With the Mongol invasions, the eastward spread of Christianity into Asia ended. The Ottoman conquests left a lasting Muslim influence inside Europe, particularly in Bosnia and Albania. The Ottoman Empire remained hostile to and frequently at war with the Christian West for more than 200 years.

Second, most Europeans reinforced their identity as Christians and became more self-conscious of the country in which they lived. At the same time Christian civilization was becoming eclipsed in parts of the Balkans, however, it revived in the Iberian peninsula, where the Muslim population (once the most extensive in the West) suffered discrimination and defeat. The northern Spanish kingdoms, for example, began to unify their subjects around a militant form of Christianity that was overtly hostile to Muslims and Jews. In many places in the West, religious and ethnic discrimination against minorities increased. A stronger sense of self-identification by country can

11.1

11.2

11.3

11.4

11.5

11.6

be most dramatically seen in France and England as a consequence of the Hundred Years' War.

Except for the very visible military conquests of the Mongols and the Ottomans, the causes of most of the calamities of the fourteenth century were invisible or unknown. No one recognized a climate change or understood the dynamics of the population crisis. No one understood the cause of the epidemics. Only a few merchants grasped the role of the Mongol Empire in the world economy or the causes for the collapse of banking and trade. Unable to distinguish how these forces were changing their lives, Europeans only witnessed their consequences. In the face of these calamities, European culture became obsessed with death and with finding scapegoats to blame for events that could not be otherwise explained. However, calamity also bred creativity. The search for answers to the question, "Why did this happen to us?" produced a new spiritual sensibility and a rich literature. Following the travails of the fourteenth century, moreover, there arose in the fifteenth a new, more optimistic cultural movement—the Renaissance. Gloom and doom were not the only responses to troubles. As we will see in the next chapter, during the Renaissance some people began to search for new answers to human problems in a fashion that would transform the West anew.

MAKING CONNECTIONS

1. Many of the responses to the calamities of the fourteenth century seem "irrational" to modern eyes. Why might people have reacted in these ways? If one-third of the population of the United States were to die from a mysterious disease in a matter of a few months, how do you think people would react today?
2. Calamities provoked fear. Who were the most likely victims of widespread fear?
3. How could the Church have better helped Christians deal with their suffering during this period?

TAKING IT FURTHER

For suggested readings, websites, and films, see page R-1.

Chapter Review

A Time of Death

11.1   What caused the deaths of so many Europeans?

A crisis in food production, caused by a combination of the limitations of medieval agriculture and climate change, resulted in widespread famine and a population susceptible to disease. Weakened and starving, 20 million people died in Europe from the Black Death, which, historians suspect, was a variation of the modern bubonic plague.

A Cold Wind from the East

11.2   How did forces outside Europe, in particular the Mongol and Ottoman Empires, influence conditions in the West?

Hundreds of years of attacks allowed the Mongol and Ottoman Empires to redraw the map of the West. The Ottoman conquests created a lasting Muslim presence within the borders of Europe. Consequently, the potential Orthodox allies in the East of the Catholic Christian West were weakened or eliminated.

Economic Depression and Social Turmoil

11.3   How did disturbances in the rudimentary global economy of the Middle Ages precipitate almost complete financial collapse and widespread social discontent in Europe?

Since the fragile financial system of medieval Europe was tied to the international trade for luxury goods, the trade's collapse, due to disrupted supply sources, caused a major depression. As the economy declined, social unrest spread when those with grievances ranging from low wages to unemployment targeted the urban guilds. These tensions exploded into dangerous revolts that eventually spread to rural areas.

An Age of Warfare

11.4   How did incessant warfare transform the most powerful medieval states?

Continuous war between England and France, its two most powerful kingdoms, further weakened western Europe and revealed the fragility of the medieval monarchies. The conflict drained resources from the French and English aristocracies, worsening the economic depression by diminishing the international luxury trade.

A Troubled Church and the Demand for Religious Comfort

11.5   Why did the Church fail to provide leadership and spiritual guidance during these difficult times?

Unrest in Rome prompted the voluntary exile to France of several popes, and this in turn caused many to view the papacy as beholden to France's kings. One result was the Great Schism, which led to first two and then three claimants to the papal throne, with rulers of Europe dividing their loyalty among them. The papacy was unable to rise above the squabbles of the European princes and serve as a spiritual and moral authority to all. Instead, an anxious populace turned to a variety of reformers, mystics, and preachers.

The Culture of Loss

11.6   How did European culture offer explanations and solace for the otherwise inexplicable calamities of the times?

European culture became obsessed with death and searched for meaning during a time of famine, plague, and unrest. This search for answers bred a new spiritual sensibility that included penitential pilgrimages, which in turn spawned a rich literature. Others looked for someone to blame for events that could not be otherwise explained, and the search for scapegoats focused on minority groups, especially Jews and Muslims.

Chapter Time Line

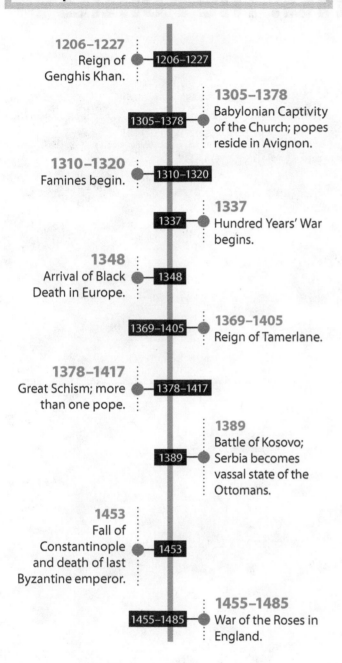

1206–1227
Reign of Genghis Khan.
| 1206–1227 |

1305–1378
Babylonian Captivity of the Church; popes reside in Avignon.
| 1305–1378 |

1310–1320
Famines begin.
| 1310–1320 |

1337
Hundred Years' War begins.
| 1337 |

1348
Arrival of Black Death in Europe.
| 1348 |

1369–1405
Reign of Tamerlane.
| 1369–1405 |

1378–1417
Great Schism; more than one pope.
| 1378–1417 |

1389
Battle of Kosovo; Serbia becomes vassal state of the Ottomans.
| 1389 |

1453
Fall of Constantinople and death of last Byzantine emperor.
| 1453 |

1455–1485
War of the Roses in England.
| 1455–1485 |

12 The Italian Renaissance and Beyond: The Politics of Culture

Niccolò Machiavelli (1469–1527) is best known as the father of modern political thought. His little book, *The Prince* (1513), became a classic because it unmasked the realities of political life. For 15 years he worked as a diplomat and political adviser, at the center of the action in his hometown of Florence. But in 1512 the regime there changed. Distrusted by the new rulers and suspected of involvement in an assassination plot, he was imprisoned, tortured, and exiled to his suburban farm. Impoverished, and miserable, Machiavelli survived by selling lumber from his woods to his former colleagues, who cheated him. To help feed his family he snared birds. For entertainment he played cards with the local innkeeper, a butcher, a miller, and two bakers. As he put it, "caught this way among these lice I wipe the mold from my brain (by playing cards) and release my feeling of being ill-treated by Fate."

In the evenings, however, Machiavelli transformed himself. He put on the elegant robes he had worn as a government official. And then, "dressed in a more appropriate manner I enter into the ancient courts of ancient men and am welcomed by them kindly." Machiavelli was reading the works of the ancient Greek and Roman historians, but he described it as a conversation: He asked the ancients about the reasons for their actions, and he found answers in their books. He

THE IDEALIZED BODY Michelangelo's statue of the biblical warrior King David transformed the young boy who slew the giant Goliath into a superman whose physical bearing was greater than any normal man. Michelangelo wanted to improve upon nature by altering the proportions of a natural man, making the head and hands significantly larger than normal.

LEARNING OBJECTIVES

12.1 ((•
How did the political and social climate of the Italian city-states help create Renaissance culture?

12.2 ((•
How did ancient culture influence the Renaissance?

12.3 ((•
How did the western European monarchies become more assertive and effective?

((• Listen to Chapter 12 on MyHistoryLab

◉ Watch the Video Series on MyHistoryLab

Learn about some key topics related to this chapter with the *MyHistoryLab Video Series:*
Key Topics in Western Civilization

12.1

12.2

12.3

recorded their answers in *The Prince*. For four hours, "I feel no boredom, I dismiss every affliction, I no longer fear poverty nor do I tremble at the thought of death: I become completely part of them."

Renaissance means "rebirth," and historians use the word to describe a movement that sought to imitate and understand the culture of antiquity. Machiavelli's evening conversations with the ancients perfectly expressed the sensibility of the Italian Renaissance. This bored, unhappy, disillusioned man found in the ancients the stimulating companions he missed in life. For him, the ancient past was more alive than the present. In this sense Machiavelli was very much a Renaissance man, because feeling part of antiquity is what the Renaissance was all about. Ancient examples of leadership promised to be a cure for the ills of a troubled time.

As we discussed in Chapter 11, during the fourteenth and fifteenth centuries, many Europeans experienced a sense of loss, a preoccupation with death, and pessimism about the human capacity for good. Yet in Florence during this same period, a cultural movement we call the Renaissance began to express a more optimistic view of life. The Renaissance emphasized the responsibilities of humans to improve their communities through social welfare, to beautify their cities, and to devote themselves to the duties of citizenship. Machiavelli—despite the bleak circumstances of his later life—was one of the Renaissance thinkers who thought the world could be set right through concerted political action. Like medieval thinkers he was pessimistic about human nature, but he believed that strong leadership and just laws could counteract human weakness. In this respect he differed from the medieval writers who thought the contemplative life of the monk was the highest calling to which a person could aspire.

The Renaissance came alive in Italy because the political structures of its city-states encouraged cultural experimentation. The idea that society could be reengineered according to the principles that made ancient Greece and Rome great first appeared in the early 1400s in Italy, but by 1500, the Renaissance had spread to much of western Europe.

The Italian Renaissance was not the first time the West experienced a revival of ancient learning and thought. In the ninth century, members of Emperor Charlemagne's court had reinvigorated education in Latin (Chapter 9). And in the twelfth century, a European-wide intellectual movement had led to the foundation of the universities, the reintroduction of Roman law, and the spread of scholastic philosophy and theology (Chapter 10). But unlike these earlier rediscoveries of classical learning, the Italian Renaissance helped refashion the concept of Western civilization. From the fifth to the fourteenth centuries, the West identified itself primarily through conformity to Latin Christianity or Roman Catholicism, which meant the celebration of uniform religious rituals in Latin and obedience to the pope. The Renaissance added a new element to this identity. Although by no means anti-Christian, Renaissance thinkers began to think of themselves as the heirs of pre-Christian cultures—Hebrew, Greek, and Roman. They began to imagine Western civilization identified by more than Christianity. Western civilization became the history of a common culture dating back to antiquity. Through reading the texts and viewing the works of art of the long-dead ancients, people during the Italian Renaissance gained historical and visual perspective on their own world and cultivated a critical attitude about both the past and their own culture.

Renaissance A term meaning "rebirth" used by historians to describe a movement that sought to imitate and understand the culture of antiquity. The Renaissance generally refers to a movement that began in Italy and then spread throughout Europe from about 1350 to 1550.

How then did the encounter during the Renaissance with the philosophy, literature, and art of the Ancient world transform the way Europeans thought?

Watch the Video

The Italian Renaissance

The Cradle of the Renaissance: The Italian City-States

12.1 How did the political and social climate of the Italian city-states help create Renaissance culture?

Compared with the rest of Europe and other world civilizations, Renaissance Italy had many politically autonomous city-states. The Netherlands and parts of the Rhine valley were as thoroughly urbanized, but only in Italy did cities have so much political power.

The evolution of the Italian city-states went through two distinct phases. The first phase established the institutions of self-government, the procedures for electing officials, and the theory of republicanism. During the eleventh and twelfth centuries, about 100 Italian towns became independent republics, also known as communes because they practiced a "communal" form of government. They developed the laws and institutions of self-government. The male citizens of these tiny republics gathered on a regular basis in the town square to debate important issues. To conduct the day-to-day business of government, they elected city officials from among themselves.

The governmental practices of these city-states produced the political theory of **republicanism**, which described a state in which government officials were elected by the people or a portion of the people. The theory of republicanism was first articulated in the Middle Ages by Marsilius of Padua (1270–1342) in *The Defender of the Peace*, a book that relied on the precedents established by the ancient Roman republic. Marsilius recognized two kinds of government—principalities and republics. Principalities relied upon the idea that political authority came directly from God and trickled down through kings and princes to the rest of humanity. According to this principle, government's job was to enforce God's laws. Marsilius, however, suggested that laws derive not from God, but from the will of the people, who freely choose their own form of government and can change it. In Marsilius's theory, citizens regularly expressed their will through voting.

In the second phase of the evolution, which occurred during the fourteenth century, most city-states abandoned or lost their republican institutions and came to be ruled by princes. This transformation was related to the economic and demographic turmoil created by the international economic collapse and the Black Death (see Chapter 11). Two of the largest republics, however, Florence and Venice, survived without losing their liberty to a prince. The Renaissance began in these two city-states (see **Map 12.1**). Their survival as republics helps explain the origins of the Renaissance. Renaissance culture, at least at first, required the freedom of a city-republic.

The Renaissance Republics: Florence and Venice

In an age of despotic princes, Florence and Venice were keenly aware of how different they were from most other cities, and they feared they might suffer the same fate as their neighbors if they did not defend their republican institutions and liberty. In keeping alive the traditions of republican self-government, these two cities created an environment of competition and freedom that stimulated creative ingenuity. Although neither of these cities were democracies or egalitarian, they were certainly more open to new ideas than cities ruled by princes. In both Florence and Venice, citizens prized discussion and debate, the skills necessary for success in business and politics. By contrast, in the principalities all cultural activity tended to revolve around and express the tastes of the ruler, who monopolized much of the wealth. In Florence and Venice a few great families called the *patriciate* controlled most of the property, but these patricians

republicanism A political theory first developed by the ancient Greeks, especially the philosopher Plato, but elaborated by the ancient Romans and rediscovered during the Italian Renaissance. The fundamental principle of republicanism as developed during the Italian Renaissance was that government officials should be elected by the people or a portion of the people.

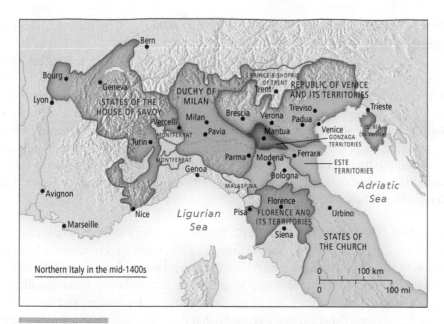

MAP **12.1** NORTHERN ITALY IN THE MID-FIFTEENTH CENTURY During the Renaissance the largest city-states, such as Milan, Venice, and Florence, gained control of the surrounding countryside and smaller cities in the vicinity, establishing regional territorial states. Among the large states, only Venice and Florence remained republics. Milan and Savoy were ruled by dukes. The Gonzaga family ruled Mantua and the Este family Modena and Ferrara. The states of the Church were ruled by the pope in Rome. What might be the strengths and weaknesses of a system of small city-states?

competed among themselves to gain recognition and fame by patronizing great artists and scholars. This patronage by wealthy men and women made the Renaissance possible. Because the tastes of these patricians dictated what writers and artists could do, understanding who these patricians were helps explain Renaissance culture.

FLORENCE UNDER THE MEDICI The greatest patron during the early Renaissance was the fabulously rich Florentine banker Cosimo de' Medici (1389–1464). Based on his financial power, Cosimo effectively took control of the Florentine republic in 1434, ushering in a period of unprecedented peace in the city and artistic splendor called the Medicean Age (1434–1494). Cosimo's style of rule was clever. Instead of making himself a prince, which most of the citizens of Florence would have opposed, he managed the policies of the republic from behind the scenes. He seldom held public office, but he made himself the center of Florentine affairs through shrewd negotiating, quiet fixing of elections, and generous distribution of bribes, gifts, and jobs. Cosimo's behind-the-scenes rule illustrated a fundamental value of Renaissance culture—the desire to maintain appearances. In this case, the appearance of a republic was saved, even as the reality of liberty was compromised.

Cosimo's patronage of intellectuals and artists mirrored a similar ambition to maintain appearances. It helped make him appear a great statesman similar to those of the ancient Roman republic, such as the orator and senator Cicero. Cosimo appreciated intelligence and merit wherever he found it. He frequented the discussions of prominent scholars, some of whom became his friends. He financed the acquisition of manuscripts of ancient Latin and Greek literature and philosophy. In return for his financial support, many Florentine scholars dedicated their works to Cosimo. His artistic patronage helped create the image of an open-handed and benevolent godfather for his community. Because he had not been elected to rule Florence, he needed to find a way to create a proper image that would justify his power. To do that, he decorated the private chapel in his palace with frescoes that depicted him accompanying the Magi, the wise men or kings who according to the Bible brought gifts to the baby Jesus. Thus, Cosimo made himself appear similar to those ancient kings who first recognized the divinity of Christ. This image of great wisdom and religious piety helped Cosimo justify the fact that he controlled elections and dictated policies.

Cosimo's grandson Lorenzo the Magnificent (r. 1469–1492) expanded Medici dominance in Florentine politics through "veiled lordship." Although Lorenzo never took the title of prince, he behaved like one by intervening publicly in the affairs of state. Unlike Cosimo's public patronage, Lorenzo's interest in the arts concentrated on building villas, collecting precious gems, and commissioning small bronze statues, things that gave him private pleasure rather than a public reputation. Although a fine poet and an intellectual companion of the most renowned scholars of his age, Lorenzo ignored the republican sensibilities of the Florentines with his princely style of rule and undermined public support for the Medici.

VENICE, THE COSMOPOLITAN REPUBLIC Venice was more politically stable than Florence. Situated in the midst of a vast lagoon, Venice's main streets consisted of broad channels in which great seagoing merchant ships were moored and canals choked with private boats for local transportation. To protect their fragile city from flooding, the Venetians recognized that they had to cooperate among themselves, and thus the imperative for survival helped create a republic that became a model of stability and ecological awareness. The Venetians, for example, created the world's first environmental regulatory agencies, which were responsible for hydrological projects, such as building dikes and dredging canals, and for forestry management to prevent soil erosion and the consequent silting up of the lagoon.

Venice was among the first European powers to possess overseas colonies. To guarantee its merchant ships access to the eastern Mediterranean and Constantinople, Venice conquered a series of ports along the Adriatic and in Greece. Its involvement in international trade and its distant colonies made Venice unusually cosmopolitan. Many Venetian merchants spent years abroad, and some settled in the colonies. Moreover, people from all over Europe flocked to Venice—Germans, Turks, Armenians, Albanians, Greeks, Slavs, and Jews—each creating their own neighborhoods and institutions. Venetian households owned Russian, Asian, Turkish, and African slaves, all of whom contributed to the diversity of the city.

The most influential foreign group in Venice consisted of the Greeks. Venice had long maintained close commercial and cultural ties with the Greek world. Many of Venice's churches were modeled after the huge basilicas of Constantinople, and many Venetian merchants spoke Greek. After the fall of the Byzantine Empire to the Ottoman Turks in 1453, Greek Christian refugees found a home in Venice and other Italian cities, including scholars who reintroduced Greek philosophy and literature to eager Italian readers. One of these scholars was John Bessarion (1403–1472), a Byzantine archbishop who compiled a library of Greek manuscripts that he left to the republic of Venice. Venice also became the leading center in western Europe for the publication of Greek books.

The defining characteristics of Venetian government were its social stability and liberty, traits that made it the envy of more troubled cities in Italy and republican-minded reformers throughout Europe, especially in England, the Netherlands, and Poland. Whereas the Florentine republic was notoriously unstable and subject to subversion by the Medici, Venice's republican constitution lasted from 1297 to 1797, making it the longest-surviving republic in history. It was, however, an exclusive republic. Out of a total population of nearly 150,000, only the political elite of 2,500 nobles could vote or hold high office. This elite and Venice's many wealthy religious institutions patronized Renaissance thinkers and artists.

At the top of Venetian society was the *doge,* a member of the nobility who was elected to the office for life. The most notable Renaissance doge was Andrea Gritti (r. 1523–1538). Gritti sometimes bent the laws in his favor, but he never manipulated elections or managed Venice's affairs as completely as Cosimo de' Medici did in Florence

View the Map

Venetian Colonial Empire

View the Closer Look

Mamluk Trade

THE MARCIANA LIBRARY Built by the architect Jacopo Sansovino, the Marciana Library was built to house the collection of Greek manuscripts given to the Republic of Venice by the exiled Greek archbishop John Bessarion. The Marciana, the oldest public library in the world, is still housed in this building and is open to scholars and university students.

a century before. Like the Medici, however, Gritti used his own financial resources and his personal influence to transform his city into a major center of Renaissance culture.

Gritti hired some of the most prominent European artists, musicians, and poets to come to Venice. These included the architect and sculptor Jacopo Sansovino (1486–1570). As official architect of the city, Sansovino transformed its appearance with his sculptures, palaces, and churches that imitated the styles of classical Greece and Rome. One of his most notable buildings was the Marciana Library, which was begun in 1537 to house Bessarion's collection of Greek manuscripts.

Princes and Courtiers

Although the Renaissance began in the relative freedom of republics, such as Florence, it soon spread to the Italian principalities. In contrast to the multiple sources of support for the arts and learning in the republics, patronage in the principalities was more constricted, confined to the ruler and members of his court. The term *prince* refers to rulers who possessed formal aristocratic titles, such as the Marquis of Mantua, the Duke of Milan, or the King of Naples. Most Renaissance princes came from local families who seized control of the government by force. Some, however, had been soldiers of fortune who had held on to a city as a spoil of war or had even overthrown a government that had once employed them to defend the city. Regardless of how a prince originally obtained power, his goal was to establish a dynasty, that is, to guarantee the rights of his descendants to continue to rule the city. Some dynasties—such as that of the d'Este family, which ruled Ferrara from 1240 to 1597—were well established and popular.

THE IDEAL PRINCE Federico II da Montefeltro (1422–1482), Duke of Urbino, achieved the glorious reputation that so many princes craved. Although he was illegitimate, his father sent him to study at the most fashionable school in Italy and to apprentice as a soldier under a renowned mercenary captain. In Renaissance Italy, an illegitimate boy could not inherit his father's property. Thus, he usually had two career options:

He could become a priest to obtain a living from the church, or he could become a mercenary and take his chances at war. Federico became a mercenary. From among the peasants of Urbino he recruited an army that he hired out to the highest bidder. He soon earned a European-wide reputation for his many victories and enriched the duchy with the income from mercenary contracts and plunder. When his half-brother was assassinated in 1444, Federico became the ruler of Urbino; by 1474 he obtained from the pope the title of duke. Federico epitomized the ideal Renaissance prince—a father figure to his subjects, astute diplomat, brilliant soldier, generous patron, avid collector, and man of learning.

Federico's rule was stern but paternalistic. He personally listened to his subjects' complaints and judged their disputes. His conquests tripled the size of his duchy and financed his building projects and collection of Latin manuscripts. Federico's personal library surpassed that of any contemporary university in Europe, and his wide-ranging reading showed his openness to the latest developments in learning. His greatest achievement, however, was the building of a vast palace, the best example of Renaissance architectural ideals. Because of Federico, the small mountainous duchy of Urbino acquired a cultural importance far greater than its size of 18,000 inhabitants warranted.

THE IDEAL PRINCESS Isabella d'Este (1474–1539), the Marchioness of Mantua, was the ideal Renaissance princess, known during her lifetime as "the first lady of the world." Enjoying an education that was exceptional for a woman in the fifteenth century, she grew up in the court at Ferrara, where she was surrounded by painters and poets and where she cultivated ambassadors and intellectuals. But her influence went far beyond that. When her husband was absent and after his death, she ruled Mantua by herself, earning a reputation as a negotiator and diplomat. An avid reader and collector, she knew virtually all the great artists and writers of her age.

THE IDEAL COURTIER The Renaissance republics developed a code of conduct for the ideal citizen that encouraged citizens to devote their time and energies to public service: to hold public office, pay taxes honestly, and beautify the city through patronage of the arts.

The Renaissance principalities also created a code for the ideal courtier. A courtier was a man or woman who lived in or regularly visited the palace of a prince. Courtiers performed all kinds of services for princes, such as taking care of the family's wardrobe, managing servants, educating children, providing entertainment, keeping accounts, administering estates, going on diplomatic missions, and fighting battles. To best serve the princely family, a courtier needed to cultivate many skills. Men trained in horsemanship, swordplay, and athletics to stay in shape for war. Women learned to draw, dance, play musical instruments, and engage in witty conversation. Both men

ISABELLA D'ESTE, THE IDEAL PRINCESS The Marchioness of Mantua, Isabella d'Este, was the most famous woman of the early sixteenth century. She set the fashions for all of Europe, but most important, she was a brilliant negotiator and ruler in her husband's absence.

SOURCE: Titian (ca. 1488–1576). Portrait Isabella d'Este (1474–1539), Margravine of Mantua, wife of Francesco Gonzaga, Margrave of Mantua. 1534. Oil on canvas, 102 64 cm. Kunsthistorisches Museum, Vienna, Austria. © Erich Lessing/Art Resource, NY.

and women needed to speak foreign languages to converse with visitors and diplomats. Men, and some of the women, also learned Latin and Greek, which were the foundations of a formal education.

The courtiers performed many of the essential functions in the princely states that elected officials did in the republics. To preserve the peace of the state, princes needed to prevent conflicts among the courtiers. Baldassare Castiglione (1478–1529), who wrote the most influential guide to how a courtier should behave, *The Book of the Courtier*, maintained that two general principles governed all courtly manners—nonchalance and ease:

> I have found quite a universal rule which . . . seems to me valid above all others, and in all human affairs whether in word or deed: and that is to avoid affectation in every way possible as though it were some very rough and dangerous reef; and . . . to practice in all things a certain nonchalance, so as to conceal all art and make whatever is done or said appear to be without effort and almost without any thought about it. . . .
>
> Therefore we may call that art true art which does not seem to be art; nor must one be more careful of anything than of concealing it, because if it is discovered, this robs a man of all credit and causes him to be held in slight esteem.[1]

In other words, Castiglione praised the ability to appear to be natural and effortless while doing something that required training and effort. The need to maintain appearances, which we saw in the disguised rule of Cosimo de' Medici in Florence, became a distinguishing trait of Italian Renaissance culture. *The Book of the Courtier* translated the ideals of civility so admired in Renaissance culture into a plan for human comportment. By using courtly manners, human beings governed the movements of the body according to an almost mathematical ideal of proportion.

COURTIERS WAITING ON A PRINCELY FAMILY On the right side of this fresco, male courtiers pose while waiting around in the court of the Gonzaga in Mantua. These elegant gentlemen epitomized the nonchalance and ease idealized in Baldassare Castiglione's *The Book of the Courtier*. On the left, the prince they serve receives a letter from a messenger. Other courtiers surround the prince, princess, and their family.

By studying *The Book of the Courtier* and its many imitators, which were translated into Latin, English, French, and Spanish, any literate young man or woman of talent and ambition could aspire to act and speak like an aristocrat. Many of its precepts of the courtly ideal were incorporated into the curriculum of schools.

THE PAPAL PRINCE The Renaissance popes combined the roles of priests and princes. They were the heads of the Church. They also had jurisdiction over the Papal States in central Italy. The Papal States were supposed to supply the pope with the income to run the Church, but when the popes had resided in Avignon (France) from 1305 to 1378 and during the Great Schism of 1378–1417, they had lost control of the Papal States. To reassert their control, popes had to force rebellious lords and cities into obedience. Julius II (r. 1503–1513) took his princely role so seriously that he donned armor and personally led troops in battle. The popes also fought with neighboring Italian states that had taken advantage of the weakness of the papacy.

These military adventures undermined the popes' ability to provide moral leadership. In addition, Pope Alexander VI (r. 1492–1503) ignored his priestly vows of celibacy and fathered four children by his favorite mistress. He financed his son Cesare Borgia's attempts to carve out a principality for himself in Italy. He also married off his daughter, Lucrezia Borgia, in succession to Italian princes who were useful allies in the pope's military ambitions. The enemies of the Borgia family accused them of all kinds of evil deeds, including poisoning one of Lucrezia's husbands, incest, and conducting orgies in the Vatican. Many of these allegations were false or exaggerated, but the papacy's reputation suffered.

Despite their messy engagement with politics, several Renaissance popes gained lasting fame as builders and patrons of the arts. They were embarrassed by the squalor of the city of Rome, which had become a neglected ruin. They sought to create a capital they felt worthy for Christendom. During the reign of Leo X (1513–1521), a son of Lorenzo the Magnificent, Rome became a center of Renaissance culture. Leo's ambition for the city can best be measured in his project to rebuild St. Peter's Basilica as the largest church in the world. He tore down the old basilica, which had been a major pilgrimage destination for more than 1,000 years, and planned the great church that still dominates Rome today.

The Contradictions of the Patriarchal Family

The princes and even the popes justified their authority, in part, on the principle that men should rule. Governments were based on the theory of the patriarchal family in which husbands and fathers dominated women and children. (See *Justice in History* in this chapter.) In advice books on family management, such as Leon Battista Alberti's *Four Books on the Family* (written in the 1430s), patriarchs were the sources of social order and discipline for all society. Although mothers or marriage brokers might arrange marriages, by law fathers or male guardians had to approve the arrangement. They sought beneficial financial and political alliances with other families. This gave older men an advantage in the marriage market because they were usually better off financially than younger ones. As a result, husbands tended to be much older than wives. In Florence in 1427, for example, the typical first marriage was between a 30-year-old man and an 18-year-old woman. Husbands were encouraged to treat their spouses with a kindly but distant paternalism. All women were supposed to be kept under strict male supervision. The only honorable role for an unmarried woman was as a nun.

However, reality often contradicted patriarchal theory. First, death from epidemic diseases, especially the Black Death, and separations due to marital strife, which were common even though divorce was not possible, made family life insecure. Second, the wide age gap meant that husbands were likely to die long before their wives. Thus many women became widows at a relatively young age with children still to raise.

Third, many men, especially international merchants and migrant workers, were away from their families for long periods. So regardless of the patriarchal theory that fathers should be in control, in reality they were often absent or dead. Mothers who were supposed to be modest, obedient to their husbands, and invisible to the outside world not only had to raise children alone but often had to manage their dead or absent husbands' business and political affairs. By necessity, many resilient, strong, and active women were involved in worldly affairs, and mothers had much more direct influence on children than fathers. Despite the theory of patriarchy, the families of Renaissance Italy were matriarchies in which mothers ruled.

The contradictions of family life and the tenuous hold many families had on survival encouraged examinations of family life in the culture of Renaissance Italy.

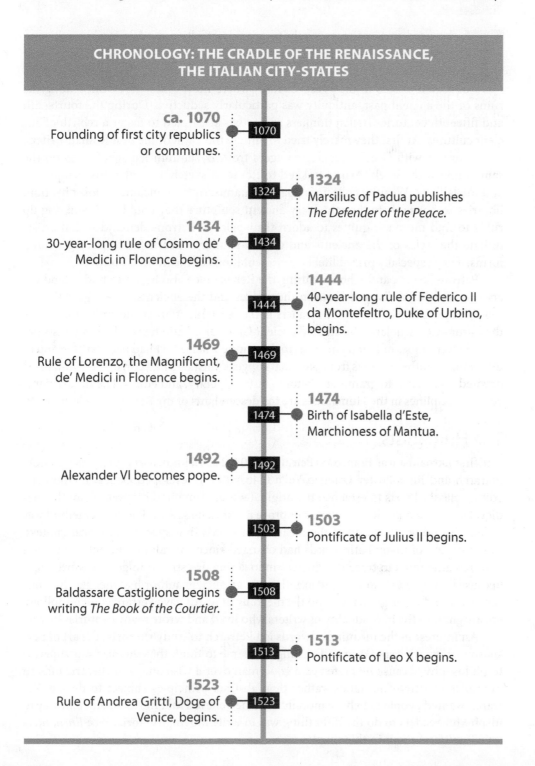

CHRONOLOGY: THE CRADLE OF THE RENAISSANCE, THE ITALIAN CITY-STATES

ca. 1070
Founding of first city republics or communes.
— 1070

1324 —
1324
Marsilius of Padua publishes
The Defender of the Peace.

1434
30-year-long rule of Cosimo de' Medici in Florence begins.
— 1434

1444 —
1444
40-year-long rule of Federico II da Montefeltro, Duke of Urbino, begins.

1469
Rule of Lorenzo, the Magnificent, de' Medici in Florence begins.
— 1469

1474 —
1474
Birth of Isabella d'Este, Marchioness of Mantua.

1492
Alexander VI becomes pope.
— 1492

1503 —
1503
Pontificate of Julius II begins.

1508
Baldassare Castiglione begins writing *The Book of the Courtier.*
— 1508

1513 —
1513
Pontificate of Leo X begins.

1523
Rule of Andrea Gritti, Doge of Venice, begins.
— 1523

Making fun of impotent old husbands married to unfulfilled young wives became a major theme in comic drama. Given the demographic ravages of the Black Death, preachers showed particular concern for the care of children; the chubby little cherubs that seem to fall from the sky in many Renaissance paintings show the universal craving for healthy children.

The Influence of Ancient Culture

12.2 How did ancient culture influence the Renaissance?

The need in Renaissance Italy to provide effective models for how citizens, courtiers, and families should behave stimulated a reexamination of ancient culture. The civilizations of ancient Greece and Rome had long fascinated the educated classes in the West. In Italy, where most cities were built among the ruins of the ancient past, antiquity was particularly seductive. During the fourteenth and fifteenth centuries Italian thinkers and artists attempted to foster a rebirth of ancient cultures. At first they merely tried to imitate the Latin of the best Roman writers. Then contact with Greek-speaking refugees from Byzantium led scholars to do the same thing with Greek. Artists trekked to Rome to sketch ancient ruins, sculptures, and medallions. Wealthy collectors hoarded manuscripts of ancient philosophy, built libraries to house them, bought every ancient sculpture they could find, and dug up ruins to find more antiquities to adorn their palaces. Patrons demanded that artists imitate the styles of the ancients and display similar concern for rendering natural forms. They especially prized lifelike representations of the human body.

Patrons, artists, and scholars during the Renaissance also began to understand the enormous cultural distance between themselves and the ancients, which gave them a sense of their place in history The leaders in the reexamination of ancient cultures were the **humanists**, scholars who studied ancient Greek and Latin texts. The humanists developed techniques of literary analysis to determine when a text had been written and to differentiate authentic texts from ones that copyists' mistakes had corrupted. Humanists devoted themselves to grammar, rhetoric, history, poetry, and ethics. The modern university disciplines in the Humanities are the descendants of the Renaissance humanists.

The Humanists

The first humanist was Francesco Petrarca (1304–1374), known in English as Petrarch. Petrarch and his follower Lorenzo Valla (1407–1457) developed critical methods by editing classical texts to establish the original words, a method different from the medieval scribe's temptation to alter or improve a text as he saw fit. Petrarch's method was called **philology**, the study of the meaning of words in a specific historical context. The meaning of many Latin words had changed since the fall of Ancient Rome, and Petrarch attempted to trace the changes in meaning. He strived to get the words right because he wanted to understand exactly what an ancient author had meant. This concern with finding original texts and the meaning of words gave Petrarch and his followers insight into the individuality of writers who lived and wrote many centuries before.

An interest in the meaning of words led Petrarch to study **rhetoric**, the art of persuasive or emotive speaking and writing. He came to think that rhetoric was superior to philosophy because he preferred a good man over a wise one, and rhetoric offered examples worthy of imitation rather than abstract principles subject to debate. Petrarch wanted people to behave morally. And he believed that the most efficient way to inspire his readers to do the right thing was to write moving rhetoric. (See *Encounters and Transformations* in this chapter.)

humanists During the Renaissance humanists were writers and orators who studied ancient Latin and sometimes Greek texts. Their principal interests were grammar, rhetoric, poetry, history, and ethics.

philology A method reintroduced by the humanists during the Italian Renaissance devoted to the comparative study of language, especially to understanding the meaning of a word in a particular historical context.

Read the Document

Petrarch: *Rules for the Successful Ruler,* ca. 1350

rhetoric The art of persuasive or emotive speaking and writing, which was especially valued by the Renaissance humanists.

Encounters and Transformations
Encounters with the Ancient World:
PETRARCH WRITES A LETTER TO CICERO'S GHOST

Petrarch was famous for his poetry, in both his native Italian and Latin. To improve his Latin style, he was always watching for anything by the Roman orator Cicero (106–43 B.C.E.). In 1345 Petrarch discovered a previously unknown collection of letters Cicero had written to his friend Atticus.

As Petrarch read the letters, however, he suffered a shock. Cicero had a reputation as the greatest Roman sage, a model of Latin style, philosophical sophistication, and ethical standards. But in the letters Petrarch found not sage moral advice, but gossip, rumors, and crude political calculations. Cicero looked like a scheming politician, a man of crass ambition rather than grand philosophical wisdom. Although Petrarch could never forgive Cicero for failing to live up to his philosophical ideals, he had discovered a man so human he could imagine having a conversation with him.

And a conversation was precisely what Petrarch set out to have. Cicero, however, had been dead for 1,388 years. So Petrarch wrote a letter to his ghost. Adopting Cicero's own elegant Latin, Petrarch attacked the Roman for going against the moral advice he had given others. Petrarch quoted Cicero back to Cicero, asking how he could be such a hypocrite: "I long had known how excellent a guide you have proved for others; at last I was to learn what sort of guidance you gave yourself. . . . Now it is your turn to be the listener."[2]

Petrarch lectured Cicero for his corruption and moral failures. The point of the exercise of writing a letter to a dead man was in part to practice good Latin style, but also to compare the ideals Cicero had avowed in his philosophical work and the way he really lived. Making comparisons is an elementary critical technique, and it became the hallmark of Petrarch's analysis. His letter made the ancients seem like other men who made mistakes and told lies. No longer a repository of timeless truths, the ancient world became a specific time and place. After his letter to Cicero, Petrarch wrote letters to other illustrious ancients in which he revealed their human qualities and shortcomings.

Petrarch's encounter with the ancients changed how he understood the past and humanity. The ancients were history in the most literal sense. They were long dead. But they were also human, capable of brave deeds and vulnerable to temptations, just the way Petrarch and his contemporaries were.

For Discussion

How did Petrarch's encounter with Cicero transform his view of his own culture? How can an encounter with another culture change how you view your own?

Renaissance humanists sought to resurrect a form of Latin that had been dead for more than 1,000 years and was distinct from the living Latin used by the Church, law courts, and universities—which they thought inferior to ancient Latin. In this effort, humanists acquired a difficult but functional skill that opened many employment opportunities to them and gave them public influence. They worked as schoolmasters, secretaries, bureaucrats, official historians, and ambassadors. Many other humanists were wealthy men who did not need a job but were fascinated with the way the new learning could be used to persuade other people to do what they wanted them to do.

Because humanists could be found on different sides of almost all important questions, the significance of their work lies less in what they said than in how they said it. They wrote about practically everything: painting pictures, designing buildings, planting crops, draining swamps, raising children, managing a household, and educating women. They debated the nature of human liberty, the virtues of famous men, the vices of wicked ones, the meaning of Egyptian hieroglyphics, and the cosmology of the universe.

How did the humanists' use of Latin words and grammar influence the understanding of this vast range of subjects? Each language organizes experience according to the needs of the people who speak it, and all languages make arbitrary distinctions, dividing up the world into different categories. People who study a foreign language run across these arbitrary distinctions when they learn that some expressions can never be translated exactly. When humanists read classical Latin texts, they encountered unfamiliar words, sentence patterns, and rhetorical models—the linguistic leftovers of ancient experience and culture. Humanists' recovery of what can be called the *Latin point of view* often altered their own perceptions and shaped their own cultural experiences in subtle ways.

For example, when a fifteenth-century humanist examined what the ancient Romans had written about painting, he found the phrase *ars et ingenium*. *Ars* referred to skills that could be learned by following established rules and adhering to models provided by the best painters. Thus, the ability of a painter to draw a straight line, to mix colors properly, and to identify a saint with the correct symbol were examples of *ars* or what we would call craftsmanship. The meaning of *ingenium* was more difficult to pin down, however. It referred to the inventive capacity of the painter, to his or her ingenuity. The humanists discovered that the ancients had made a distinction between the craftsmanship and the ingenuity of a painter. As a result, when humanists and their pupils looked at paintings, they began to make the same distinction and began to admire the genius of artists whose work showed ingenuity as well as craftsmanship. Ingenuity came to refer to the painter's ability to arrange figures in a novel way, to employ unusual colors, or to create emotionally exciting effects that conveyed piety, sorrow, or joy as the subject demanded. So widespread was the influence of the humanists that the most ingenious artists demanded higher prices and became the most sought after. In this way, creative innovation was encouraged in the arts, but it all started very simply with the introduction of new words into the Latin vocabulary of the people who paid for paintings. A similar process of establishing new categories altered every subject the humanists touched.

The humanist movement spread rapidly during the fifteenth century. Leonardo Bruni (ca. 1370–1444), who became the chancellor of Florence (the head of the government's bureaucracy), created **civic humanism** to defend the republican institutions and values of the city. By reading the ancient writers, Bruni rediscovered the ethics of public service. Civic humanists argued that the ethical man should devote himself to active service to his city rather than to passive contemplation in scholarly retreat or monastic seclusion.

Lorenzo Valla employed humanist scholarship to undermine papal claims to authority over secular rulers. The pope's theoretical authority depended on the so-called Donation of Constantine, according to which Emperor Constantine had transferred his imperial authority in Italy to the pope in the fourth century. By using philology, Valla demonstrated that many of the Latin words found in the Donation could not have been written before the eighth century. For example, the document used the word *satrap*, which Valla was confident a Roman at the time of Constantine would not have known. Thus, he proved that this famous document was a forgery. Valla's analysis of the Donation was one of the first uses of philology and historical analysis of documents to serve a political cause. As a result, many rulers and especially the popes saw the need to hire a humanist to defend their own interests.

The intellectual curiosity of the humanists led them to master many topics. This breadth of accomplishment contributed to the ideal of the "Renaissance Man (or "Renaissance Woman"), a person who sought excellence in everything he or she did. No one came closer to this ideal than Leon Battista Alberti (1404–1472). As a young man, Alberti wrote Latin comedies and satirical works that drew on Greek and Roman models, but as he matured he tackled more serious subjects. Although he was a bachelor and thus knew nothing firsthand about marriage, he drew upon the ancient writers to create the most influential Renaissance book on the family, which included sections on relations between husbands and wives, raising children, and estate management. He composed the first grammar of the Italian language. He dabbled in mathematics and wrote on painting, law, the duties of bishops, love, horsemanship, dogs, agriculture, and flies. He mapped the city of Rome and wrote the most important fifteenth-century work on the theory and practice of architecture. His interest in architecture, moreover, was not just theoretical. In the last decades of his life, Alberti dedicated much of his spare time to building projects that included restoring an ancient church in Rome, designing Renaissance façades for medieval churches, and erecting a palace for his most important patron. One of his last projects was the first significant work for making and deciphering secret codes in the West.

The humanists guaranteed their lasting influence through their innovations in education. Humanist education did not seek to train specialists or professionals, such

civic humanism A branch of humanism introduced by the Florentine chancellor Leonardo Bruni who defended the republican institutions and values of the city. Civic humanism promoted the ethic of responsible citizenship.

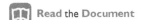 **Read** the **Document**

Lorenzo Valla Skewers the Supposed "Donation of Constantine," ca. 1440

as the theologians, lawyers, and physicians. Instead, humanists aimed to create well-rounded men (women were not usually accepted in humanist schools), critical thinkers who could tackle any problem that life presented. The curriculum emphasized the study of Greek and Latin and the best authors in those ancient languages. Command of good grammar, the ability to write and speak effectively, knowledge of history, and an appreciation for virtuous behavior were the goals of humanist education. It was a curriculum well suited for the active life of civic leaders, courtiers, princes, and churchmen. The influence of the humanist curriculum persists in the general education requirements of modern American universities, which require students, now of both sexes, to obtain intellectual breadth before they specialize in narrow professional training.

Historians have identified a few female humanists from the Renaissance. Because they were so unusual, learned humanist women were often ridiculed. Jealous men accused the humanist Isotta Nogarola (1418–1466) of promiscuity and incest, and other women insulted her in public. A famous male schoolmaster said that Isotta was too feminine in her writings and should learn how to find "a man within the woman."[3] Laura Cereta (1475–1506), who knew Greek as well as Latin and was adept at mathematics, answered the scorn of a male critic with rhetorical insult:

> I would have been silent, believe me, if that savage old enmity of yours had attacked me alone. . . . But I cannot tolerate your having attacked my entire sex. For this reason my thirsty soul seeks revenge, my sleeping pen is aroused to literary struggle, raging anger stirs mental passions long chained by silence. With just cause I am moved to demonstrate how great a reputation for learning and virtue women have won by their inborn excellence, manifested in every age as knowledge, the [purveyor] of honor. Certain, indeed, and legitimate is our possession of this inheritance, come to us from a long eternity of ages past.[4]

These few humanist women were among the first feminists. They advocated female equality and female education but also urged women to take control of their lives. Cereta maintained that if women paid as much attention to learning as they did to their appearances, they would achieve equality. But despite the efforts of female humanists, progress in women's education was slow. The universities remained closed to women until late in the nineteenth century. The first woman to earn a degree from a university only did so in 1678. It took another 200 years before many others could follow her example. (See *Different Voices* in this chapter.)

The humanists educated generations of wealthy young gentlemen whose appreciation of antiquity led them to collect manuscripts of ancient literature, philosophy, and science. These patrons also encouraged artists to imitate the ancients. What began as a narrow literary movement became the stimulus to see human society and nature through entirely new eyes. Some humanists, especially in northern Europe, applied the techniques of humanist scholarship with revolutionary results to the study of the Bible and the sources of Christianity.

Understanding Nature: Moving Beyond the Science of the Ancients

The humanists' initial concern was to imitate the language of the ancients. Most of them preferred to spend time reading rather than observing the world. In fact, their methods were ill-suited to understanding nature: When they wanted to explain some natural phenomenon such as the movement of blood through the body or the apparent movements of the planets and stars, they looked to ancient authorities for answers rather than to nature itself. Renaissance scientists searched for ancient texts about nature, and then debated about which ancient author had been correct. The humanists' most prominent contributions to science consisted of adopting the ideas of Muslim scientific writers and of recovering classical Greek texts. They circulated

Different Voices
The Battle of the Sexes

A busive writing about women was pervasive in Western literature. However, during the Renaissance the "women's question" raised the issue of whether education could improve women's lot in life. What distinguished this debate during the Renaissance was the active role women took in defending their own interests.

Although they wrote in the seventeenth century, Ferrante Pallavicino (1618–1644) and Arcangela Tarabotti (1604–1652) represented the culmination of the Italian Renaissance debate about women. Pallavicino pulled out the usual litany of the anti-woman argument. Tarabotti answered Pallavicino on every point.

Ferrante Pallavicino, Letter Addressed to "Ungrateful Woman"

I know how you mock my scorn: a woman never grieves unless she weeps tears of blood, and her normal tears are pure deceit in liquid form, the holding back of pretense. . . .

Your ingratitude has reached the limit in bad manners; it has taught me that there is nothing human in a woman but her face, with which she lies even when silent and warns how there is nothing to expect but falsity from a being who deceives at first sight. She shares the same genus of animal with man, appropriating for herself, however, all the bestial qualities that ensure, while differing from man in that she simply has no reason whatsoever: as a consequence, she acts like a brute animal. . . .

Unfortunate women are those without men to provide the support that remedies their own weakness! Without men they could not avoid being flung down at every moment, like the blind and the mad, into a thousand chasms. The women of Tartary (Mongolia and Turkey) understood this well: it was their custom never to allow their head to be covered by a more precious headdress than the form of a human foot, to signify that woman, brainless and witless, finds her greatest glory in her subjection to man. Representing themselves in the act of being trodden underfoot, they paid homage to their noblest part; they were not foolish like other women, adorning their heads with treasures from robbed tombs or weighed down with braided chains dotted with gems.

Arcangela Tarabotti, "Misogynists Named and Unnamed Are Condemned" from *Paternal Tyranny*

(Divine Omnipotence) wills (women) supreme authority over the male sex to be made manifest, as he is unworthy of any other treatment but prison and stripes (scars from whipping). So it is simply not true that man, like staves to the vine, supports the woman who otherwise would fall spineless; rather he approaches her to induce her to fall by countless ploys and be supported by him.

A clever mind wishing to operate in a sinister fashion easily manages to invent chimeras (an absurd creation of the imagination) that distort the true nature of things and force the strangest meanings from bits of arcane learning. And thus our most astute author wrongly interprets the custom of women of Tartary, who bore on their heads as their most precious ornament a human foot. The correct meaning is that woman, as quick and ready for noble deeds, runs with many feet along the path of virtue, keeping one united with her mind so she can walk securely on her way, without stumbling. She needs the extra assistance so as not to fall into the snares and traps set for her innocent nature without end by the cursed "genius" of the male sex, who is always opposed to doing good.

His interpretation, therefore, that there is no greater glory for a woman, a mindless creature with no sense, than to be subject to the male is obviously false. The contrary is true: that her greatest torment and suffering is to find herself subjected to the tyranny and inhumane whims of men.

SOURCE: Arcangela Tarabotti, *Paternal Tyranny*, edited and translated by Letizia Panizza. (Copyright © 2004 by The University of Chicago. Reprinted by permission of the University of Chicago Press.) 146–149, 158–162.

For Discussion

1. Do Pallavicino and Tarabotti argue through rhetoric or logic? What is the difference between the two ways of arguing?
2. How would you refute Pallavicino? How would you refute Tarabotti?

Latin translations of Arabic books and themselves translated the work of ancient Greek scientists into the more widely understood Latin. The Renaissance approach contrasted to the scientific method of today, in which scientists form a hypothesis and then determine whether it is correct by experimenting and observing the natural world as directly as possible.

The texts rediscovered and translated during the Renaissance, nevertheless, broadened the discussion of two subjects crucial to the scientific revolution of the late sixteenth and seventeenth centuries—astronomy and anatomy. In 1543 the Polish humanist Nicolaus Copernicus (1473–1543) resolved the complications in the system of the second-century astronomer Ptolemy. Whereas Ptolemy's writings had placed Earth at the center of the universe, Copernicus cited other ancient writers who put the sun in the center. Thus, the first breakthrough in theoretical astronomy was achieved not by making new observations, but by comparing ancient texts. Nothing was proven, however, until Galileo Galilei (1564–1642) turned his newly invented telescope to the heavens in 1610 to observe the stars through his own eyes rather than through an ancient text (see Chapter 17).

Andreas Vesalius (1514–1564) built upon recently published studies in anatomy from ancient Greece to write a survey of human anatomy, *On the Fabric of the Human Body* (1543), a book that encouraged dissection of corpses and anatomical observations. With Vesalius, anatomy moved away from relying exclusively on the authority of ancient books to encouraging medical students and physicians to examine the human body with their own eyes. Building upon Vesalius's work, Gabriele Falloppio (ca. 1523–1562) made many original observations of muscles, nerves, kidneys, bones, and most famously the "fallopian tubes," which lead from the ovaries to the uterus in the female reproductive system, which he described for the first time.

Besides recovering ancient scientific texts, the most important Renaissance contributions to science came secondhand from developments in the visual arts and technology. Florentine artists during the early fifteenth century applied mathematics and visual theory derived from Arabic texts to paintings. The goal was to make paintings more accurately represent reality by creating the visual illusion of the third dimension of depth on a two-dimensional rectangular surface, a technique known as *linear perspective* (see the next section, "Antiquity and Nature in the Arts"). These artists contributed to a more refined understanding of how the eye perceives objects, which led to experiments with glass lenses. A more thorough knowledge of optics made possible the invention of the telescope and microscope.

Invented in the 1450s in Germany, the printing press combined with the availability of cheap paper led to the printing revolution, which rapidly expanded the availability of books. Printed books made with moveable type had been made for centuries in China and Korea, but given the huge number of characters necessary, printed books were never very common. In Europe, however, the limited number of letters in the alphabet made printing much more feasible. Scientific books accounted for only about 10 percent of the titles of the first printed books, but the significance of printing for science was greater than the sales figures would indicate. Print meant that new discoveries and ideas reached a wider audience, duplication of scientific investigation could be avoided, illustrations were standardized, and scientists built upon each other's work. With the invention of the printing press, scientific work became closely intertwined with publishing, so that published scientific work advanced science, and scientific work that was not published went largely unnoticed. Leonardo da Vinci (1452–1519), the greatest Renaissance observer of nature, contributed nothing to science because he failed to publish his findings. Because he hid the drawing he made of an airplane in a secret notebook, he had no influence on the development of air travel. The fundamental principle of modern science and, in fact, of all modern scholarship is that research must be made available to everyone through publication.

View the **Closer Look**

The Copernican Universe

LEONARDO INVENTS A FLYING MACHINE AND PARACHUTE Leonardo da Vinci's notebooks are filled with numerous examples of his unprecedented inventions. In his drawings on the top he designed a flying machine similar to a modern helicopter and a parachute. On the bottom are modern models based on his drawings. Leonardo kept his inventions in his secret notebooks, which meant no one could follow up on his ideas.

Antiquity and Nature in the Arts

More than any other age in Western history, the Italian Renaissance is identified with the visual arts. The unprecedented numbers of brilliant artists active in a handful of Italian cities during the fifteenth and sixteenth centuries overshadow any other contribution of Renaissance culture.

Under the influence of the humanists, Renaissance artists began to imitate the sculpture, architecture, and painting of the artists from classical Greece and Rome. At first they merely tried to copy ancient styles and poses. Just as humanists recaptured antiquity by collecting, translating, and analyzing the writings of classical authors, so Renaissance artists made drawings of classical medals, sculpture, and architecture. Because artists believed that classical art was superior to their own, these sketches became valuable models from which other artists could learn. Two of the most influential Florentine artists, the architect Filippo Brunelleschi (1377–1446) and the sculptor Donatello (1386–1466), probably went to Rome together as young men to sketch the ancient monuments.

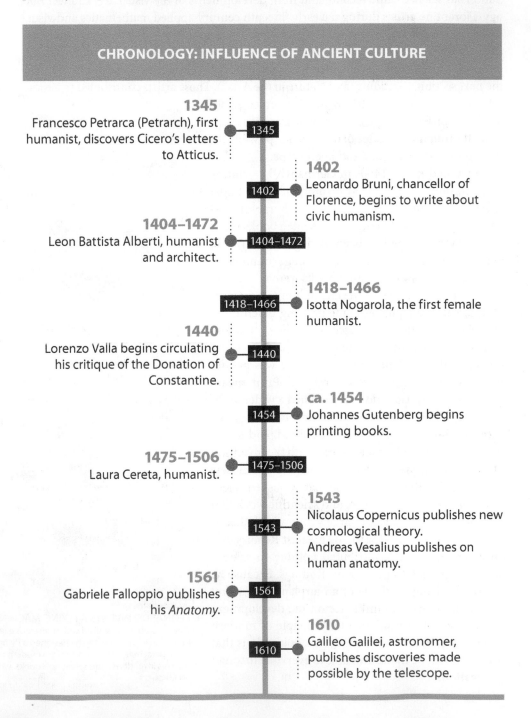

CHRONOLOGY: INFLUENCE OF ANCIENT CULTURE

1345
Francesco Petrarca (Petrarch), first humanist, discovers Cicero's letters to Atticus.

1402
Leonardo Bruni, chancellor of Florence, begins to write about civic humanism.

1404–1472
Leon Battista Alberti, humanist and architect.

1418–1466
Isotta Nogarola, the first female humanist.

1440
Lorenzo Valla begins circulating his critique of the Donation of Constantine.

ca. 1454
Johannes Gutenberg begins printing books.

1475–1506
Laura Cereta, humanist.

1543
Nicolaus Copernicus publishes new cosmological theory.
Andreas Vesalius publishes on human anatomy.

1561
Gabriele Falloppio publishes his *Anatomy*.

1610
Galileo Galilei, astronomer, publishes discoveries made possible by the telescope.

Renaissance artists, however, wanted not only to copy ancient styles, they also wanted to understand how the ancients had made their figures so lifelike. That led them to observe nature itself more directly, especially the anatomy of the human body. Renaissance art, then, was driven by the passionate desire of artists and their patrons to imitate both ancient works and nature. These twin desires produced a creative tension in their work because the ancients, whose works of art often depicted gods and goddesses, had idealized and improved on what they observed in nature. Renaissance artists sought to depict simultaneously the ideal and the real—an impossible goal, but one that sparked remarkable creativity.

The work of the most important painter of the early Renaissance in Florence, Masaccio (1401–ca. 1428), exemplified this blending of the idealized and the natural. In the Brancacci chapel, Masaccio depicted street scenes from Florence complete with portraits of actual people, including himself. These were examples of naturalism. On other figures in the scene called *The Tribute Money* (shown below)—Jesus, St. Peter, and St. John—he placed heads copied from ancient sculptures of gods. These were examples of idealized beauty, which were especially suitable for saints. The realistic figures helped viewers identify with the subject of the picture by allowing them to recognize people they actually knew. The idealized figures represented the saintly, whose superior moral qualities made them appear different from average people.

The Renaissance style evolved in Masaccio's hometown of Florence early in the fifteenth century. In 1401 the 24-year-old Brunelleschi entered a competition to design bronze panels depicting the biblical account of Abraham's willingness to sacrifice his son Isaac for the north doors of the Baptistery of Florence's cathedral. He lost to Lorenzo Ghiberti (1378–1455). Look at the illustrations on page 382. Ghiberti's panel shown on the right reveals the two characteristic elements of the early

THE TRIBUTE MONEY: COMBINING NATURAL AND IDEALIZED REPRESENTATIONS In this detail of a fresco of Christ and his apostles, Masaccio mixed naturalism and idealized beauty. The figure on the right with his back turned to the viewer is a tax collector, who is depicted as a normal human being. The head of the fourth figure to the left of him, who represents one of the apostles, was copied from an ancient statue that represents ancient ideals of beauty. Among the figures on the far left are portraits of Masaccio himself and his collaborator Masolino.

THE COMPETITION PANELS OF THE SACRIFICE OF ISAAC These two panels were the finalists in a competition to design the cast bronze doors on the north side of the Baptistery in Florence. Each demonstrates a bold new design that attempted to capture the emotional drama of the exact moment when an angel arrests Abraham's arm from sacrificing his son Isaac (Genesis 22:1–12). Both artists went on to be closely associated with the new style of the Renaissance. The panel on the left, by Filippo Brunelleschi, lost to the one on the right, by Lorenzo Ghiberti. Notice how the Ghiberti relief better conveys the drama of the scene by projecting the elbow of Abraham's upraised arm outward toward the viewer. As a result, the viewer's line of sight follows the line of the arm and knife directly toward Isaac's throat.

Renaissance style: idealization and naturalism. The head of Isaac is modeled after a classical Roman sculpture, and the figures and horse on the left of his panel are depicted as realistically as possible. In these elements, Ghiberti was imitating both antiquity and nature.

Ghiberti worked on the north doors for 21 years. He won such fame that when he finished he was immediately offered a new commission to complete panels for the east doorway. These doors, begun in 1425, took 27 years to finish. In the east doors, Ghiberti substituted a simple square frame for the Gothic frame of the north doors, thereby liberating his composition. In the illustration on page 383, which depicts the biblical story of the brothers Jacob and Esau, the background architecture of rounded arches and classical columns creates the illusion of depth. This illusion is achieved through **linear perspective**, that is, the use of geometrical principles to depict a three-dimensional space on a flat, two-dimensional surface. Linear perspective, a method for imitating the way nature appears to the human eye, was an achievement of the Florentine Renaissance, something never perfected before, neither in antiquity nor in the Islamic world, which supplied the Florentines with the theory of vision that made the innovation possible. In the panels of the east doors, Ghiberti created the definitive Renaissance interpretation of the ancient principles of the harmony produced by geometry. Michelangelo said that the doors were fit to serve as the "gates of paradise."

Most humanist theorists of painting linked artistic creativity with masculinity. By the sixteenth century, however, these theorists were proved wrong, as female painters

linear perspective In the arts, the use of geometrical principles to depict a three-dimensional space on a flat, two-dimensional surface.

View the Image

The Duomo Dominating Florence

LINEAR PERSPECTIVE In these square panels Ghiberti explored the full potential of the newly discovered principles of linear perspective. Notice how he created the illusion of a round arcade of columns.

rose to prominence. The most notable was Sofonisba Anguissola (ca. 1532–1625). Born into an aristocratic family, she received a humanist education along with her five sisters and brother. As a woman, she was prohibited from studying anatomy or drawing male models. So she specialized in portraits, often of members of her family, and self-portraits. She developed a distinctive style of depicting animated faces as in the portrait of her sisters playing chess shown on page 384. Her fame was so great that King Philip II of Spain hired her as his official court painter. Her example inspired other aristocratic women to take up painting.

The Renaissance Patron

All the Renaissance arts displayed the influence of patrons, the wealthy people who controlled the city-states and had been educated in humanist schools. Until the end of the sixteenth century, all painters, sculptors, and even poets worked for a patron. A patron, who could be an individual or a group, such as a religious order or a government, commissioned a work of art, such as an altar painting, portrait bust, statue, or palace. Patron and artist would agree on a contract, which might specify exactly what the artist was to do, what kinds of materials he was to use (almost all Renaissance artists were men), how much they could cost, how much he could rely on assistants, how much he had to do himself, and even how he was to arrange figures in the work. Michelangelo Buonarroti (1475–1564) sculpted *David,* which has become the most famous work of Renaissance art, to fulfill a contract that had been debated in a committee meeting of the government of Florence. Regardless of their talent, artists could never do whatever they wanted. They had to respond to the demand created by their patrons, who were the consumers of art. The Renaissance was not yet a consumer society as modern Western societies are; nonetheless, the desires of the wealthy upper classes created a growing demand for art.

Some patrons supported the career of an artist for an extended time. Princes, in particular, liked to take on an artist—give him a regular salary and perhaps even an

PORTRAITS IN RENAISSANCE ART Sofonisba Anguissola excelled at portrait painting. In this collective portrait of her three sisters and their nurse, she rejected the traditional props associated with women, such as pets or needlework, to show them engaged in the challenging intellectual game of chess. In this way Anguissola subverted female stereotypes.

official title—in exchange for having him do whatever the prince wanted. Thus, Duke Lodovico Sforza (1451–1508) brought Leonardo da Vinci to Milan, where Leonardo painted a portrait of the duke's mistress, devised plans for a giant equestrian statue of the duke's father, designed stage sets and carnival pageants, painted the interior decorations of the castle, and did engineering work.

Most patrons supported the arts to enhance their own prestige and power. Some, such as Pope Julius II, had exceptional influence on artists. He even persuaded Michelangelo, who saw himself as a sculptor, to paint the ceiling of the Sistine Chapel.

The Spread of the Renaissance

The Renaissance spread as other Europeans encountered the culture of Italy. Princes and aristocrats who studied or fought in Italy were the first to export Italian art and artists abroad. King Philip of Spain was just one of many sixteenth-century monarchs who lured Italian artists to his court. Perhaps no country was more enthralled with the Italian Renaissance than Poland, where many aristocrats who had studied in Italy built palaces and whole planned towns in imitation of Renaissance ideals. Even the Kremlin in Moscow was designed by Italian architects.

After the collapse of the Italian city-states during the Italian Wars (1494–1530), the growing power of the western European monarchies facilitated the spread of Renaissance culture outside of Italy. As we discuss next, the French invaded the Italian peninsula at the end of the fifteenth century and sparked years of warfare in Italy; however, King Francis I (r. 1515–1547) was impressed by what he saw. He had the first Renaissance-style chateau built in France and hired Italian artists, including Leonardo da Vinci, to bring Renaissance culture to his kingdom. Leonardo spent his last years living in a great chateau King Francis gave him.

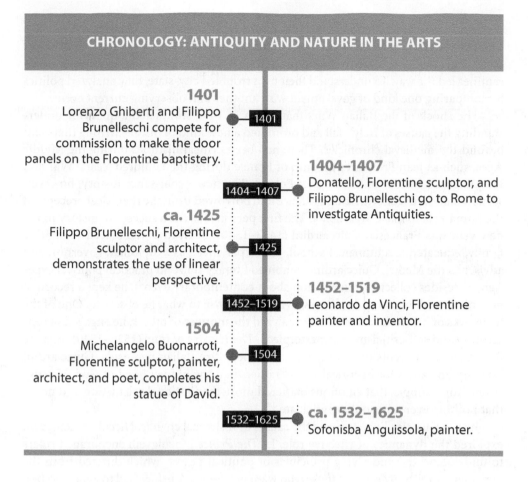

CHRONOLOGY: ANTIQUITY AND NATURE IN THE ARTS

1401
Lorenzo Ghiberti and Filippo Brunelleschi compete for commission to make the door panels on the Florentine baptistery.

1404–1407
Donatello, Florentine sculptor, and Filippo Brunelleschi go to Rome to investigate Antiquities.

ca. 1425
Filippo Brunelleschi, Florentine sculptor and architect, demonstrates the use of linear perspective.

1452–1519
Leonardo da Vinci, Florentine painter and inventor.

1504
Michelangelo Buonarroti, Florentine sculptor, painter, architect, and poet, completes his statue of David.

ca. 1532–1625
Sofonisba Anguissola, painter.

The Early Modern European State System

12.3 How did the western European monarchies become more assertive and effective?

The civic independence that had made the Italian Renaissance possible was challenged during the Italian Wars when France, Spain, and the Holy Roman Empire attempted to carve up the peninsula for themselves. The wars started in 1494 when the French king attempted to seize the kingdom of Naples. His invasion of Italy drew in rival monarchs from Spain and the Holy Roman Empire who could not tolerate French control of wealthy Italy and pitted the Italian city-states against one another as they attempted to save themselves from foreign conquest. These wars were a disaster for Italy. For nearly 40 years wave after wave of foreign armies crossed the Alps and turned Italy into a battleground. The low point was the sack of Rome in 1527 when German mercenaries plundered the city, destroyed works of art, and imprisoned the Medici pope. By 1530 the king of Spain had defeated his rival in France for control of Italy. All of the large cities except Venice came under Spanish domination.

The surrender of the rich city-states of Italy was the first sign of a transformation in the European system of states. Only the large monarchies of the West, such as France, Spain, and England, could muster the materiel and manpower necessary to put and keep a large army in the field. The Italian Wars revealed the outlines of the early modern European state system, which was built on the power of large countries ruled by kings. These kings amassed unprecedented resources that not only crushed Italy, but also enabled Europe to dominate much of the globe through colonies in the Americas, Asia, and Africa (see Chapter 13).

The Origins of Modern Historical and Political Thought

The revival of the monarchies of western Europe and the loss of the independence of the Italian city-states forced a rethinking of politics. As in so many other fields, the Florentines led the way. To understand their own troubled city-state, they analyzed politics by comparing one kind of government with another and observing current events.

The shock of the Italian Wars that began in 1494 stimulated a quest for understanding the causes of Italy's fall and prompted a new kind of history writing that went beyond the medieval chronicles. There had been critical histories during the Middle Ages, such as Jean Froissart's account of France during the Hundred Years' War and Jan Dlugosz's history of the kings of Poland. The new Renaissance history, however, set new standards for criticizing evidence and borrowed from the rhetorical precepts of the humanists to make arguments. The first person to write a successful history in the new vein was Francesco Guicciardini (1483–1540). Born to a well-placed Florentine family, educated in a humanist school, and experienced as a diplomat, governor, and adviser to the Medici, Guicciardini combined literary skill and practical political experience. Besides collecting information about contemporary events, he kept a record of how his own thoughts and values evolved in response to what he observed. One of the hallmarks of his work was that as he analyzed the motives of others, he engaged in self-scrutiny and self-criticism. His masterpiece, *The History of Italy* (1536–1540), was the first account of events that occurred across the entire Italian peninsula. Guicciardini saw human causes for historical events rather than the hidden hand of God. He suggested, for example, that emotions mattered more than rational calculation and noted that nothing ever turns out as anticipated.

Just as Guicciardini examined the causes of historical change, Niccolò Machiavelli explored the dynamics of effective rule. In *The Prince* Machiavelli encouraged rulers to understand the underlying principles of political power, which differed from the personal morality expected of those who were not rulers. A prince had to appear to be a moral person, but Machiavelli pointed out that the successful prince might sometimes have to be immoral to protect the state. How would the prince know when this might be the case?

Machiavelli's answer was that "necessity" forced political decisions to override normal morality. The prince "must consider the end result," which meant that his highest obligation was preserving the existence of the state that had been entrusted to him and providing security for all its citizens. This obligation took precedence even over his religious duty.

Through Guicciardini's analysis of human motivations and Machiavelli's attempt to discover what made certain actions necessary, historical and political thought moved in a new direction. The key to understanding history and politics was in the details of human events. To Guicciardini, these details provided clues to the psychology of leaders. To Machiavelli, they revealed the hidden mechanisms of chance and planning that governed not just political decisions, but all human events.

Read the Document

The Prince (1519), Machiavelli

Monarchies: The Foundation of the State System

The European state system was one of the most lasting achievements of the Renaissance. By the state system, historians referred to a complex of interrelated changes. First, governments established standing armies. As a result of the military revolution that brought large numbers of infantry to the field of battle and gunpowder cannons to besiege cities and castles, governments had to modernize their armies or face defeat. Since the ninth century, kings had relied on feudal levies in which soldiers were recruited to fulfill their personal obligation to a lord, but by the late fifteenth century, governments began to organize standing professional armies. These armies, however, were expensive because the soldiers had to be regularly paid and the new artillery was costly. Moreover, fortifications had to be improved to withstand the artillery. As a result, kings were desperate for new revenues.

The need for revenues led to the second development, the growth of taxation. Every European state struggled with the problem of taxation. The need to tax efficiently produced the beginnings of a bureaucracy of tax assessors and collectors. People resisted the new taxes, creating tension with the monarch.

This tension led to the third development. Monarchs attempted to weaken the resistance by abolishing the tax exemptions of local communities and ignoring regional assemblies and parliaments that were supposed to approve new taxes. During the twelfth and thirteenth centuries, effective government was local government, and kings could seldom interfere in the affairs of towns and regions. During the fifteenth century, however, to raise taxes and impose their will throughout the realm, kings everywhere tried to eliminate or erode the independence of towns and parliaments.

Fourth, monarchs tried to reduce the independence of the aristocracy and the Church. In the kingdoms of western Europe, the most significant threats to the king's power were the aristocrats. Kings struggled to co-opt these aristocrats or force them to submit. Most monarchs also sought to oblige churchmen to become agents of government policy. Monarchs were most successful in reducing the power of the aristocrats and the Church in France, England, and Spain. In eastern Europe, despite the attempts by kings to accomplish what their western cousins had done, the aristocracy remained in control. In Poland, Bohemia, and Hungary, the aristocrats elected the kings and kept royal power in check.

The fifth development in the evolution of the Renaissance Europe state system was the institution of resident ambassadors. During the Italian Wars, the kings of Europe began to exchange ambassadors who resided at foreign capitals and were responsible for informing their sovereign about conditions in the host country and representing their rulers' interests abroad. Resident ambassadors became the linchpins in a sophisticated information network that provided intelligence about the intentions and capabilities of other kings, princes, and cities. These ambassadors typically enjoyed a humanist education, which helped them adapt to strange and unpredictable situations, understand foreign languages, negotiate effectively, and speak persuasively. Ambassadors cultivated courtly manners, which smoothed over personal conflicts. For the new state system, gathering reliable information became as important as maintaining armies and collecting taxes. Although the Italian city states were the first in many of these developments, they were soon outstripped by the larger monarchies of the West.

France, with the largest territory and population (more than 16 million) in western Europe, had the potential to become the most powerful state in Europe. Under King Charles VII (r. 1422–1461), France created its first professional army. Equally important, the **Pragmatic Sanction of Bourges** (1438) guaranteed the virtual autonomy of the French Church from papal control, enabling the French king to interfere in religious affairs and exploit Church revenues for government purposes. A third important weapon in the development of the French national monarchy was the *taille*, an annual direct tax. During the final years of the Hundred Years' War, which ended in 1453, the Estates General (France's parliament) granted the king the right to collect the *taille*. After the war, Louis XI (r. 1461–1483) turned it into a permanent source of revenue for himself and his successors. Armed with the financial resources of the *taille*, Louis and his successors expanded the reach of the French monarchy.

In contrast to France, the kingdoms of Spain had never been major players in European affairs during the Middle Ages. The Iberian peninsula was home to several small kingdoms—Portugal, Castile, Navarre, and Aragon, which were all Christian, and Granada, which was Muslim. Each kingdom had its own laws, political institutions, customs, and language. Unlike France, these Christian kingdoms were poor, underpopulated, and preoccupied with the reconquest, the attempt to drive the richer Muslims from the peninsula. There was little reason to assume that this region would

Pragmatic Sanction of Bourges An agreement in 1438 that guaranteed the virtual autonomy of the French Church from papal control, enabling the French king to interfere in religious affairs and exploit Church revenues for government purposes.

Justice in History
Vendetta as Private Justice

During the fourteenth and fifteenth centuries, the official justice the law courts provided competed with the private justice of revenge. Private justice was based on the principle of retaliation. When someone was murdered or assaulted, the victim's closest male relatives were obliged to avenge the injury by harming the perpetrator or one of his relatives to a similar degree. A son was obliged to avenge the death of his father, a brother the injury of his brother. Because governments were weak, the only effective justice was often private justice or, as the Italians called it, *vendetta*. As the most significant source of disorder during the Renaissance, vendetta was a practice that all governments struggled to eradicate.

While criminals tried to cover their tracks, vendetta avengers committed their acts openly and even bragged about them. An act of revenge was carried out in public, so there would be witnesses, and often in a highly symbolic way to humiliate the victim. Private justice always sought to deliver a message.

An episode of revenge from the most sophisticated city in Europe on the eve of the Renaissance illustrates the brutality of private justice, especially the need to make a public example of the victim. After a period of disorder in 1342, the Florentines granted extraordinary judicial powers to a soldier of fortune, Walter of Brienne, known as the Duke of Athens. But Walter offended many Florentines by arresting and executing members of prominent families. In September 1342 a crowd led by these families besieged the government palace in Florence and captured the duke's most hated henchmen, the "conservator" and his son. An eyewitness reported what happened next:

> The son was pushed out in front, and they cut him up and dismembered him. This done, they shoved out the conservator himself and did the same to him. Some carried a piece of him on a lance or sword throughout the city, and there were those so cruel, so bestial in their anger, and full of such hatred that they ate the raw flesh.[5]

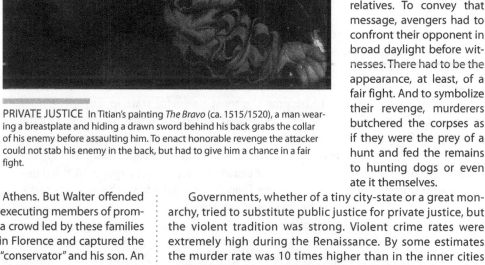

PRIVATE JUSTICE In Titian's painting *The Bravo* (ca. 1515/1520), a man wearing a breastplate and hiding a drawn sword behind his back grabs the collar of his enemy before assaulting him. To enact honorable revenge the attacker could not stab his enemy in the back, but had to give him a chance in a fair fight.

Another account from nearly 200 years later tells of the murder of Antonio Savorgnan, a nobleman who had killed a number of his enemies. Rather than attempting to have Antonio arrested as they could have, the murderers avenged their dead relatives through private justice. One eyewitness recounted that Antonio was attacked while leaving church, and then, "It was by divine miracle that Antonio Savorgnan was wounded: his head opened, he fell down, and he never spoke another word. But before he died, a giant dog came there and ate all his brains, and one cannot possibly deny that his brains were eaten."[6] This time a dog did the avengers' work for them.

In both of these accounts, the writers wanted readers to believe that the victim had been eaten, by humans or by a dog. The eating of a victim signaled that avengers were killing as an act of private justice, a legitimate act of revenge for the murder of close relatives. To convey that message, avengers had to confront their opponent in broad daylight before witnesses. There had to be the appearance, at least, of a fair fight. And to symbolize their revenge, murderers butchered the corpses as if they were the prey of a hunt and fed the remains to hunting dogs or even ate it themselves.

Governments, whether of a tiny city-state or a great monarchy, tried to substitute public justice for private justice, but the violent tradition was strong. Violent crime rates were extremely high during the Renaissance. By some estimates the murder rate was 10 times higher than in the inner cities of the United States today. As governments sought to control violence and the values of moderation spread, a different kind of private justice appeared—the duel. Traditionally, the duel had been a means for knights to resolve disputes; however, during the sixteenth century, duels became more

(continued on next page)

common, even among men who had never been soldiers. Duelists had to conform to elaborate rules: There had to be legitimate causes for a challenge to a duel, the combatants had to recognize each other as honorable men, the fight took place only after extensive preparations, judges who were experts on honor had to serve as witnesses, and the combatants had to swear to accept the outcome and not to fight one another again.

Dueling, in effect, civilized private justice. The complexity of the rules of dueling limited the violence and meant that fewer fights took place. Although dueling was always against the law, princes tended to wink at duels because they kept conflicts among their own courtiers under control. But governments became far less tolerant of other forms of private justice, especially among the lower classes. They attempted to abolish feuds and vendettas and insisted that all disputes be submitted to the courts.

For Discussion

1. Why was private justice a challenge to the emerging states of the Renaissance?
2. How did private justice reflect Renaissance values, such as the value of keeping up appearances?

Taking It Further

Muir, Edward. *Mad Blood Stirring: Vendetta in Renaissance Italy.* 1998. A study of the most extensive and long-lasting vendetta in Renaissance Italy. It traces the evolution of vendetta violence into dueling.

Weinstein, Donald. *The Captain's Concubine: Love, Honor, and Violence in Renaissance Tuscany.* 2000. An engaging account of an ambush and fight between two nobles over a woman who was the concubine of the father of one of the fighters and the lover of the other. It reveals the relationship between love and violence in Renaissance society.

become one of the greatest powers in Europe, the rival of France. The Renaissance made that possible.

That rise to power began with a wedding. In 1469 Isabella, who later would become queen of Castile (r. 1474–1504), married Ferdinand, who later would be king of Aragon (r. 1479–1516). The objective of this arranged marriage was to solidify an alliance between the two kingdoms, not to unify them, but in 1479 Castile and Aragon were combined into the kingdom of Spain. Of the two, Castile was the larger, with a population of perhaps six million, and wealthier. Together Isabella and Ferdinand, each still ruling their own kingdoms, at least partially subdued the rebellious aristocracy and built up a bureaucracy of well-educated middle-ranking lawyers and priests to manage the government.

The Christian kings of Iberia had long wanted to make the entire peninsula Christian. In 1492 the armies of Isabella and Ferdinand defeated the last remaining Iberian Muslim kingdom of Granada. While celebrating the victory over Islam, the monarchs made two momentous decisions. The first was to rid Spain of Jews as well as Muslims. Isabella and Ferdinand decreed that within six months all Jews had to either convert to Christianity or leave. To enforce conformity to Christianity among the converted Jews who did not leave, the king and queen authorized an ecclesiastical tribunal, the Spanish Inquisition, to investigate the sincerity of conversions. The second decision was Isabella's alone. She financed a voyage by a Genoese sea captain, Christopher Columbus, to sail west into the Atlantic in an attempt to reach India and China. Isabella seemed to have wanted to outflank the Muslim kingdoms of the Middle East and find allies in Asia. As we shall see in the next chapter, Columbus's voyage had consequences more far-reaching than Isabella's intentions, adding to the crown of Castile immense lands in the Americas.

Despite the diversity of their kingdoms, Isabella and Ferdinand made Spain a great power and established the framework for the diplomatic relations among European states for the next century and a half (see **Map 12.2**). They married their children into the royal houses of England, Portugal, Burgundy, and the Holy Roman Empire, creating a network of alliances that isolated France. As a result of these marriage alliances, their grandson, Charles V, succeeded to the Habsburg lands of Burgundy; inherited the crown of Spain; was elected Holy Roman Emperor, which included all of Germany; ruled over the Spanish conquests in Italy; and was the Emperor of the Indies, which included all of Spanish Central and South America and the Philippines. This

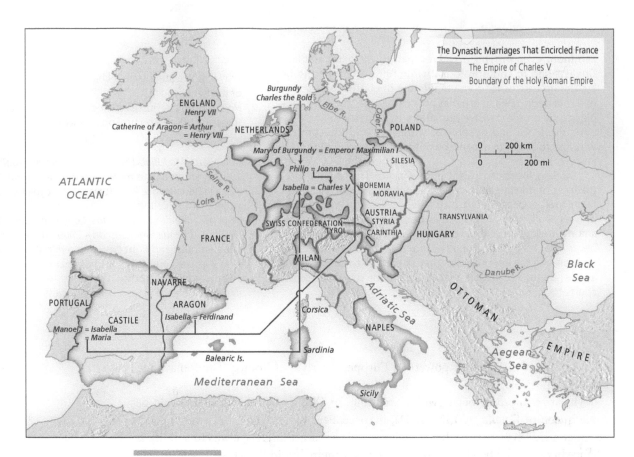

MAP **12.2** THE DYNASTIC MARRIAGES THAT ENCIRCLED FRANCE Through skillfully arranging the marriages of their sons and daughters, Ferdinand of Aragon and Isabella of Castile managed to completely surround the rival kingdom of France with a network of alliances. What does this map reveal about the function of royal marriages in the early modern state system?

was the greatest accumulation of territories by a European ruler since Charlemagne in the ninth century.

Unlike Spain, England had been one of the great medieval powers. However, at the end of the Hundred Years' War in 1453, the English crown was defeated and England was exhausted. Thousands of disbanded mercenaries flooded England and enlisted in feuds among aristocratic families. The mercenaries brought to England the violence they had practiced in the wars with France. Under the tensions caused by defeat and revolt, the royal family fractured into the two rival branches of Lancaster and York, which fought a vicious civil war, now known as the War of the Roses (1455–1485) from the red and white roses used to identify members of the opposing sides.

When Henry Tudor finally ended the civil wars and became King Henry VII (r. 1485–1509), there was little reason to believe that England could again become a major force in European events. Henry took years to become safe on his own throne. He revived the Court of Star Chamber as an instrument of royal will to punish unruly nobles who had long bribed and intimidated their way out of trouble with the courts. Because his own hand-picked councilors served as judges, Henry could guarantee that the court system became fairer and more obedient to his wishes. He confiscated the lands of rebellious lords, thereby increasing his own income, and he prohibited all private armies except those that served his interests. By managing his administration efficiently, eliminating unnecessary expenses, and staying out of war, Henry governed without the need to call on Parliament for increased revenues.

England was still a backward country with fewer than three million people. But by nourishing an alliance with newly unified Spain, Henry brought England back into

CHRONOLOGY: THE EARLY MODERN EUROPEAN STATE SYSTEM

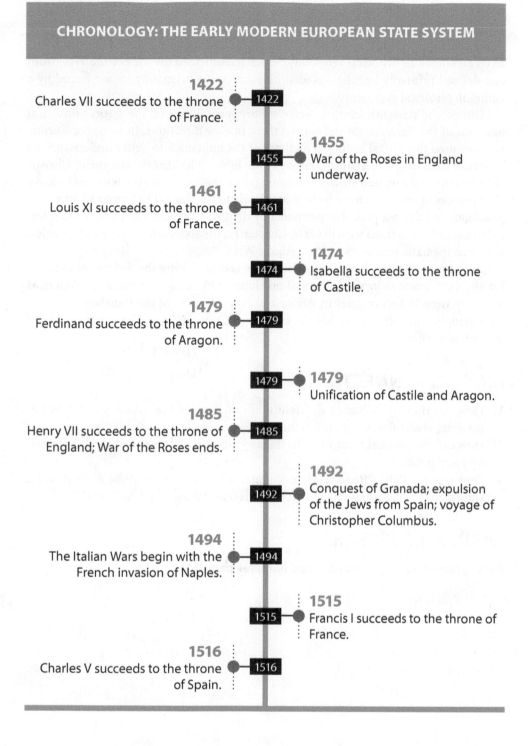

1422
Charles VII succeeds to the throne of France.
1422

1455
1455
War of the Roses in England underway.

1461
Louis XI succeeds to the throne of France.
1461

1474
1474
Isabella succeeds to the throne of Castile.

1479
Ferdinand succeeds to the throne of Aragon.
1479

1479
1479
Unification of Castile and Aragon.

1485
Henry VII succeeds to the throne of England; War of the Roses ends.
1485

1492
1492
Conquest of Granada; expulsion of the Jews from Spain; voyage of Christopher Columbus.

1494
The Italian Wars begin with the French invasion of Naples.
1494

1515
1515
Francis I succeeds to the throne of France.

1516
Charles V succeeds to the throne of Spain.
1516

European affairs. When his son Henry VIII succeeded to the throne, the Tudor dynasty was more secure than any of its predecessors and England more stable than it had ever been.

CONCLUSION

The Politics of Culture

The Renaissance began as an attempt to imitate the style of the best ancient Latin authors and orators. Within a generation, however, humanists and artists pushed this narrow literary project into a full-scale attempt to refashion human society on the model of ancient cultures. Reading about the ancients and looking at their works of art provoked comparisons with contemporary Renaissance society. The result was the development of a critical approach to the past and present. The critical approach fostered an enhanced historical sensibility, which transformed the idea of the West from one defined primarily by religious identification with Christianity to one forged by a common historical experience.

During the sixteenth century, western Europeans absorbed the critical-historical methods of the Renaissance and turned them in new directions. In northern Europe scholars used the critical historical methods of the humanists to better understand the historical sources of Christianity, especially the Bible. With that development, Christianity began to take on new shades of meaning, and many Christians attempted to make the practices of the Church conform more closely to the Bible. The humanist approach to religion led down a path that permanently divided Christian camps over the interpretation of Scripture. As we will see in Chapter 14, the sixteenth-century Reformation shattered the hard-won unity of the Catholic West.

As the next chapter shows, however, in the century before the Reformation Spanish and Portuguese sailors encountered previously unknown cultures in the Americas and only vaguely known ones in Africa and Asia. Because of the Renaissance, those who thought and wrote about these strange new cultures did so with the perspective of antiquity in mind.

MAKING CONNECTIONS

1. How did rhetoric influence different kinds of Renaissance activities, such as humanism, visual arts, and political theory?
2. How did the political turmoil of the Italian Wars stimulate new thinking about history and politics?
3. How was the Italian Renaissance encounter with the culture of the ancient world similar to other encounters discussed in this book? How was it different?

TAKING IT FURTHER

For suggested readings, websites, and films, see page R-1.

On MyHistoryLab

✓ Take the Study Plan for Chapter 12, The Italian Renaissance and Beyond: The Politics of Culture, on MyHistoryLab

Chapter Review

The Cradle of the Renaissance: The Italian City-States

12.1 How did the political and social climate of the Italian city-states help create Renaissance culture?

Most city-states abandoned their republican institutions after the turmoil created by the international economic collapse and widespread plague. However, two of the largest (Florence and Venice) survived as republics. This created an environment of competition and freedom that stimulated creative ingenuity.

The Influence of Ancient Culture

12.2 How did ancient culture influence the Renaissance?

Scholars, called humanists, developed techniques in literary analysis that allowed them to study ancient Greek and Latin texts. The texts rediscovered and translated included scientific work that broadened the scientific discussion of fields like astronomy and anatomy, and gave Renaissance artists the tools to apply mathematics and visual theory to visual arts.

The Early Modern European State System

12.3 How did the monarchies of western Europe become more assertive and effective during the late fifteenth and early sixteenth centuries?

Historical and political thought were transformed when key thinkers of the age attempted to understand history and politics through the details of human events. By creating a state system that included standing armies, regular taxation, and dependent and loyal aristocracy, rulers were able to create a more effective state system.

Chapter Time Line

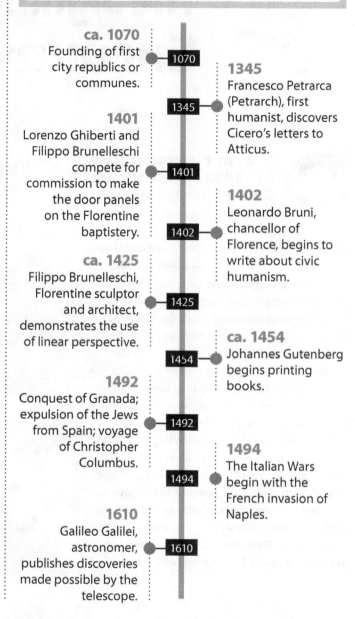

ca. 1070 Founding of first city republics or communes. — 1070

1345 Francesco Petrarca (Petrarch), first humanist, discovers Cicero's letters to Atticus. — 1345

1401 Lorenzo Ghiberti and Filippo Brunelleschi compete for commission to make the door panels on the Florentine baptistery. — 1401

1402 Leonardo Bruni, chancellor of Florence, begins to write about civic humanism. — 1402

ca. 1425 Filippo Brunelleschi, Florentine sculptor and architect, demonstrates the use of linear perspective. — 1425

ca. 1454 Johannes Gutenberg begins printing books. — 1454

1492 Conquest of Granada; expulsion of the Jews from Spain; voyage of Christopher Columbus. — 1492

1494 The Italian Wars begin with the French invasion of Naples. — 1494

1610 Galileo Galilei, astronomer, publishes discoveries made possible by the telescope. — 1610

13

The West and the World: The Significance of Global Encounters, 1450–1650

On a hot October day in 1492, Christopher Columbus and his men, dressed in heavy armor, clanked onto the beach of an island in the Bahamas. The captain and his crew had been at sea sailing west from the Canary Islands for five weeks, propelled by winds they thought would take them straight to Asia. As the ships under Columbus's command vainly searched among the islands of the Caribbean for the rich ports of Asia, Columbus thought he must be in India and thus called the natives he met "Indians." At another point he thought he might be among the Mongols of central Asia, which he described in his journal as the "people of the Great Khan." Both of Columbus's guesses about his location were incorrect, but they have left a revealing linguistic legacy: "Indians" for native Americans, and both "cannibals" and "Caribbean" from Columbus's inconsistent spellings of Khan. Columbus believed that the people he called the Cannibals or Caribs ate human flesh. But he got that information—also incorrect—from their enemies. Thus began one of the most lasting misunderstandings from Columbus's first voyage.

CHRISTOPHER COLUMBUS This near contemporary portrait of the mariner depicts him as a well-dressed Renaissance gentleman.

LEARNING OBJECTIVES

13.1	13.2	13.3	13.4
Why did the European incursions into sub-Saharan Africa lead to the forced migration of Africans to the Americas as slaves?	How did the arrival of Europeans in the Americas transform native cultures and life?	Why was the European encounter with Asian civilizations far less disruptive than those in Africa and the Americas?	How was the world tied together in a global biological and economic system?

 Listen to Chapter 13 on MyHistoryLab

◉ Watch the Video Series on MyHistoryLab

Learn about some key topics related to this chapter with the *MyHistoryLab Video Series: Key Topics in Western Civilization*

13.1

13.2

13.3

13.4

Historians know very little about the natives' first thoughts of the arrival of their foreign visitors, largely because within a few generations the Caribs almost completely died out. By the time someone was interested in hearing it, no one was left to pass down their story.

Western civilization at the end of the fifteenth century hardly seemed on the verge of encircling the globe with outposts and colonies. Its kingdoms had barely been able to reorganize themselves sufficiently for self-defense, let alone world exploration and foreign conquest. The Ottoman threat was so great that all of southern and eastern Europe was on the defensive. The hostilities between Turks and Christians blocked the traditional trade routes to Asia, which had stimulated the great medieval economic expansion of Europe. In comparison with the Ottoman Empire or Ming China, Europe's puny, impoverished states seemed more prone to quarreling among themselves than to seeking expanded horizons.

Nevertheless, by 1500 Europeans could be found fighting and trading in Africa, the Americas, and Asia. A mere 50 years later, Europeans had destroyed the two greatest civilizations in the Americas, begun the forced migration of Africans to the Americas through the slave trade, and opened trading posts throughout South and East Asia.

Before 1492 the West, identified by its languages, religions, agricultural technology, literature, folklore, music, art, and common intellectual tradition that stretched back to pre-Christian antiquity, was largely confined to Europe and the Middle East. Barely a century after Columbus's voyages, Western culture could be found in many distant lands, and western European languages and forms of Christianity were adopted by or forced upon other peoples. The West was now more of an idea than a place, a certain kind of culture that thrived in many different environments. As western Europeans came under the influence of the far-flung peoples they visited, they were themselves transformed as they began to discover the principle of cultural relativity and tolerate human differences. The European voyages integrated the globe biologically and economically. Microbes, animals, and plants that had once been isolated were now transported throughout the world. Because the Europeans possessed the ships for transport and the guns for coercion, they became the dominant players in international trade, even in places thousands of miles from the European homeland. The question raised by this first phase of the European global encounters is this:

How were both the West and the rest of the world transformed?

◉ **Watch the Video**

The Big Picture: The World in 1491

Europeans in Africa

13.1 Why did the European incursions into sub-Saharan Africa lead to the forced migration of Africans to the Americas as slaves?

Medieval Europeans had accumulated a substantial knowledge about North Africa, but except for Ethiopia they were almost completely ignorant of the region south of the Sahara Desert. By the fifteenth century, Muslim contacts with sub-Saharan Africa made it clear that the region was a source of gold and slaves. In search of these, Europeans, especially the Portuguese, began to journey down the west coast of Africa.

Sub-Saharan Africa Before the Europeans Arrived

For centuries highly developed, prosperous kingdoms had governed the interior of sub-Saharan Africa. During the fifteenth and sixteenth centuries when European contacts with the sub-Sahara dramatically expanded, however, the once-strong kingdoms were either in decline or engaged in protracted struggles with regional rivals. The Europeans arrived at precisely the moment when they could take advantage of the weaknesses produced by internal African conflicts.

The Muslim kingdom of Mali, a landlocked empire between the Upper Senegal and Niger Rivers, had long had a monopoly of the gold caravans that carried the coveted metal from the fabled city of Timbuktu across the Sahara to the gold-greedy Mediterranean. During the European Middle Ages Mali was the greatest empire in sub-Saharan Africa, but by 1400 it was in decline. Internal power struggles had split apart the once-vast empire. In 1482, when the Portuguese founded a gold-trading post at Elmina, they found the rulers of Mali much weaker than they had been 100 years before (see the trade routes and towns on **Map 13.1**).

Influenced by Mali, the forest kingdoms of Guinea were built on a prosperous urban society and extensive trading networks. European travelers compared the great city of Benin favorably with the principal European cities of the time. The towns of Guinea held regular markets, similar to the periodic fairs of Europe, and carefully scheduled them so they would not compete with each other. The staples of the long-distance trade routes in this region were high-value luxury goods, especially imported cloth, kola nuts (a mild stimulant popular in Muslim countries), metalwork such as cutlasses, ivory, and of course gold. However, civil wars weakened these kingdoms during the sixteenth century, opening the way for greater European influence.

Unlike the kingdoms of the western sub-Sahara, which tended to be Muslim, mountainous Ethiopia was predominantly Christian. In fact, Europeans saw Ethiopians as potential allies against Islam. Diplomatic contacts between Rome and Ethiopia intensified at the time of the Council of Florence in 1439, which attempted to unify all Christians in defense against Ottoman Turks. Learned Ethiopian churchmen became known in western Europe and created the impression that Ethiopia was an abundant land peopled by pious Christians. Portuguese visitors were duly impressed by the splendor of the emperor of Ethiopia, the Negus, who traveled with 2,000 attendants and 50,000 mules to carry provisions and tents. By the early sixteenth century, however, the Ethiopian kingdom had become overextended. In the 1520s and 1530s Muslims attacked deep into the Ethiopian heartland, raiding and burning the wealthy Ethiopian monasteries. The raids severely weakened the power of the Negus. Ethiopia survived, but competing Christian warlords weakened the central authority.

 Read the Document

Ibn Battuta, selections from the *Rihla*

 View the Image

View of the Guinea Coast

 Read the Document

The Land of Prester John (1540)
Francisco Alvarez

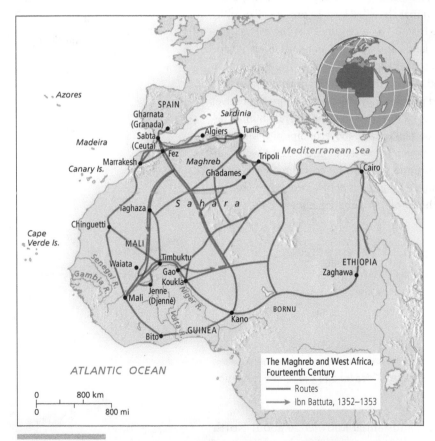

MAP **13.1** THE MAGHREB AND WEST AFRICA, FOURTEENTH CENTURY Long before the arrival of the Portuguese via sea routes, caravans of camels crisscrossed the Sahara Desert during the fourteenth century, linking the sources of gold in Mali with the Maghreb (the coast of northwest Africa) and the seaports of the Mediterranean. The greatest medieval Arabic traveler, Ibn Battuta (1304–1368/69), crossed the Sahara and spent more than a year in Mali. He left the most extensive account of medieval West Africa. What does the existence of these trade routes suggest about the strength of contacts between Africa and Europe before the Portuguese voyages?

European Voyages Along the African Coast

Gold brought Europeans to sub-Saharan Africa. European merchants traded European silver for African gold in the Maghreb, the collective name for the present-day regions of Morocco, Algeria, and Tunisia. The Maghreb was the northern terminus of the gold caravans from Mali. European merchants made handsome profits from the gold trade, but they recognized they could make even greater profits if they could cut out the middlemen of the Maghreb. The Europeans had little hope, however, of using the camel caravan routes across the Sahara because of the hostility of Muslim inhabitants who were wary about foreign interlopers, especially Christian ones.

The alternative for Europeans was to outflank the Muslims by a sea route. As early as the thirteenth century, European voyagers ventured down the west coast of Africa into uncharted waters, but such voyages soon ran into trouble. Adapted to the calm waters of the Mediterranean, European galleys were ill-suited for voyaging on the heavy seas of the Atlantic. Such ships were not only easily swamped, they also required the feeding of large crews of oarsmen. In addition, the long coastline of West Africa lacked protective harbors for refuge from storms. For Europeans to gain direct access to the gold of Mali, they needed to develop new kinds of ships.

NEW MARITIME TECHNOLOGY During the fifteenth century changes in the technology of ocean sailing surmounted the disadvantages of Mediterranean galleys. The location of the Iberian peninsula (the land of present-day Portugal and Spain) made possible the building of a hybrid ship that combined features of Mediterranean and Atlantic designs.

The new ship was the **caravel**. Iberians modified the older cog design, the dominant ship in the Atlantic, by adding extra masts and creating a new kind of rigging that combined the square sails of Atlantic ships, suitable for sailing in the same direction as the wind was blowing, with the triangular "lateen" sails of Mediterranean galleys, which permitted sailing into the wind. The result was a ship that could sail in a variety of winds, carry large cargoes, be managed by a small crew, and be defended by guns mounted in the castle superstructure. These hybrid three-mast caravels first appeared about 1450; for the next 200 years Europeans sailed ships of this same basic design on long ocean voyages to the very ends of the Earth.

> **caravels** Hybrid three-masted ships developed about 1450 in the Iberian peninsula by combining the rigging of square with triangular lateen sails. These ships could be sailed in a variety of winds, carry large cargoes, be managed by a small crew, and be defended by guns mounted in the castle superstructure.

Other late-medieval innovations also assisted European navigators. The compass, originally from China, provided an approximate indicator of direction. The astrolabe, borrowed from Muslim mariners, and naked-eye celestial navigation made it possible to estimate latitudes. Books of sailing directions, called portolanos, many of which were adapted from Islamic sources, included charts of ports and recorded the location of dangerous shoals and safe harbors for future voyages.

Technology alone, however, does not explain why Europeans set sail around the globe in this era. There had been great ocean navigating efforts before. For centuries, Polynesians successfully navigated their way across the Pacific Ocean in open canoes. The Vikings regularly crossed the North Atlantic from the tenth to fourteenth centuries, and the Chinese engaged in extensive exploratory voyages throughout the Indian Ocean earlier in the fifteenth century. The desire to profit from an expanded trade network and to outflank the Muslims who blocked the eastern trade routes motivated European voyages in the fifteenth and sixteenth centuries.

NEW COLONIALISM The search for greater profits created new kinds of colonies. Mediterranean colonies established during the Crusades of the twelfth and thirteenth centuries had relied on native inhabitants to produce commodities that the colonizers expropriated. These were either aristocratic colonies in which a few warriors occupied castles to dominate the native population or mercantile colonies built around a trading post for foreign merchants.

settler colony A colony authorized when a private person obtained a license from a king to seize an island or parcel of land and occupied it with settlers from Europe who exported their own culture to the new lands. Settler colonies first appeared among the islands of the eastern Atlantic and portions of the Americas.

plantation colony First appearing in the Cape Verde Islands and later in the tropical parts of the Americas, these colonies were established by Europeans who used African slave labor to cultivate cash crops such as sugar, indigo, cotton, coffee, and tobacco.

During the fifteenth century, Castile and Portugal founded colonies in the Canary Islands, the Madeira archipelago, the Azores, and the Cape Verde Islands. The climate of these islands was similar to that of the Mediterranean and invited the cultivation of typical Mediterranean crops, such as grains and sugar cane, but the islands lacked a native labor force for either an aristocratic or a mercantile colony. When Europeans arrived, the Canaries had few inhabitants and the other islands were uninhabited. In response to the labor shortage, two new types of colonies emerged, both of which were later introduced into the Americas.

The first new type of colony was the **settler colony**. The settler colony derived from the medieval, feudal model of government, in which a private person obtained a license from a king to seize an island or some part of an island. The king supplied financial support and legal authority for the expedition. In return, the settler promised to recognize the king as his lord and occasionally to pay a fee after the settlement was successful. The kings of Castile and Portugal issued such licenses for the exploitation of the Atlantic islands. The actual expeditions to colonize these islands were private enterprises, and adventurers from various parts of Europe vied for a license from any king who would grant them one. For example, the first European settlement in the Canary Islands was led by a Norman-French knight, who could not obtain sufficient support from the king of France and thus switched loyalties to the king of Castile.

After the arrival of the Europeans, all the natives of the Canaries, called the Guanches, were killed or died off from European diseases, creating the need for settler families from Europe to till the land and maintain the Castilian claim on the islands. These European peasants and artisans imported their own culture. They brought with them their traditional family structures, customs, language, religion, seeds, livestock, and patterns of cultivation. Wherever settler colonies were found, whether in the Atlantic islands or the New World, they remade the lands in the image of the Old World.

The second new type of colony was the **plantation colony**. Until the occupation of the Cape Verde Islands in the 1460s, the Atlantic island colonies had relied on European settlers for labor. However, the Cape Verdes attracted few immigrants, and yet the islands seemed especially well-suited for growing the lucrative sugar cane crop. The few permanent European colonists there tended to be exiled criminals who were disinclined to work. Because there was no indigenous population to exploit on the Cape Verdes, the Europeans began to look elsewhere for laborers. They voyaged to the African coast, where they bought slaves who had been captured by African slavers from inland villages. These slaves worked as agricultural laborers in the Cape Verdes sugar cane fields.

Thus, in the Cape Verdes began the tragic conjunction between African slavery and the European demand for sugar. That conjunction is what created the new type of European colonialism. When sugar began to replace honey as the sweetener of choice for Europeans, sugar cultivated by slaves in plantation colonies, first in the Atlantic islands and later in the West Indies and American mainland, met the almost insatiable demand. Over the next 300 years, this pattern for plantation colonies was repeated for other valuable agricultural commodities, such as indigo for dyes, coffee, and cotton, which were grown to sell in European markets. The first loop of what would eventually become a global trading circuit was now completed.

THE PORTUGUESE IN AFRICA The Portuguese launched the first European voyages along the African coast during the fifteenth century. The sponsor of these voyages was Prince Henry the Navigator (1394–1460). As governor of Algarve, the southernmost province of Portugal, Henry financed numerous exploratory voyages. Although the many voyages of Henry's sailors did not fulfill his dreams of conquest and enormous riches, his sailors discovered bases near the Senegal and Gambia Rivers for the Malinese gold trade. He and other members of his family also helped colonize Madeira and the Azores. As a source of sugar, Madeira became a valuable colony (see Maps 13.1 and **13.2**).

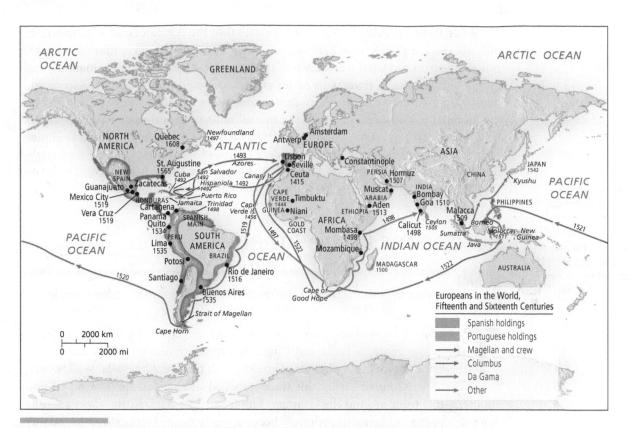

MAP 13.2 EUROPEANS IN THE WORLD, FIFTEENTH AND SIXTEENTH CENTURIES During the fifteenth and sixteenth centuries European sailors opened sea lanes for commerce across the Atlantic, Pacific, and Indian Oceans. Dates indicate the first arrival of Europeans. Notice the relative distances of these routes. Which parts of the world did the new sea lanes connect most easily to Europe?

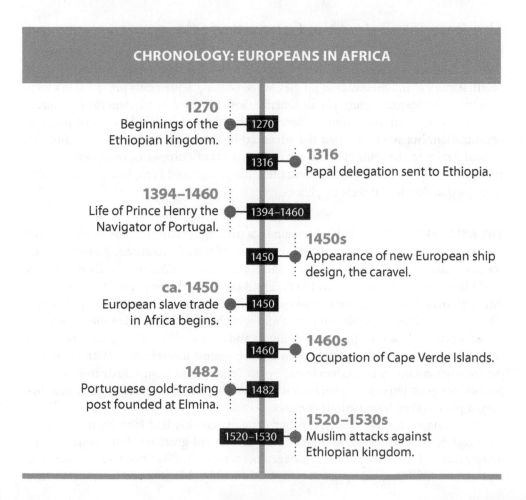

CHRONOLOGY: EUROPEANS IN AFRICA

1270
1270
Beginnings of the Ethiopian kingdom.

1316
1316
Papal delegation sent to Ethiopia.

1394–1460
1394–1460
Life of Prince Henry the Navigator of Portugal.

1450s
1450
Appearance of new European ship design, the caravel.

ca. 1450
1450
European slave trade in Africa begins.

1460s
1460
Occupation of Cape Verde Islands.

1482
1482
Portuguese gold-trading post founded at Elmina.

1520–1530s
1520–1530
Muslim attacks against Ethiopian kingdom.

After Henry's death, Portuguese exploration of the African coast accelerated. In only six years, a private merchant of Lisbon commissioned voyages that added 2,000 miles of coastline to what was known to the Portuguese. In 1482 the Portuguese royal family took control of trade with Africa and transformed what had been a loose and haphazard enterprise under private contractors into a lucrative source of revenue for the monarchy. The monarchy required that all sailings be authorized and all cargoes inventoried. To protect the trade, the Portuguese built a permanent fortress at Elmina near the mouth of the Volta River in modern Ghana in West Africa. Rather than establishing new settler or plantation colonies, the Portuguese on the African coast relied on **trading posts** that supplied gold, ivory, pepper, and slaves.

trading posts Areas built by European traders along the coasts of Africa and Asia as a base for trade with the interior. Trading posts or factories were islands of European law and sovereignty, but European authority seldom extended very far beyond the fortified post.

Europeans in the Americas

13.2 How did the arrival of Europeans in the Americas transform native cultures and life?

The first European voyagers to the Americas also coveted gold and sought an alternative route to India and China. Europeans relied on Asian sources for medicines, spices, and all kinds of luxury goods that were unavailable elsewhere. The desire to profit from this trade impelled men to take great risks to find an alternative route around the Ottoman Empire to East Asia. In the short run, the Americas proved to be an impediment because the two continents stood in the way of getting to Asia. But in the long run, the European voyages to the Americas brought consequences unimaginable to those who first began to sail west from Europe.

The Americas Before the Conquistadores

Prior to their contact with Europeans, the peoples of the Americas displayed remarkable cultural variety. Nomadic hunters spread across the sub-Arctic regions, western North America, and the Amazon jungles, while farming settlements prevailed in much of South America and eastern North America. Some of these North American cultures, such as the Anasazi and Iroquois, developed highly sophisticated forms of political organization, but none matched the advanced civilizations of Mesoamerica and the central Andes to the south. On the eve of the arrival of Europeans, two great civilizations, the Aztecs of central Mexico and the Incas of highland Peru, had built extensive empires that dominated their neighbors.

THE AZTEC EMPIRE OF MEXICO Mesoamerica (the region known today as Mexico and Central America) had been the home of a series of highly urbanized, politically centralized cultures: the Mayas (300–900), the Toltecs (900–1325), and finally the Aztecs (1325 to the Spanish conquest in 1522). The Aztecs found safety from incessant warfare with neighboring tribes on an island in Lake Texcoco, where they established the city of Tenochtitlán, now Mexico City. From their base at Tenochtitlán the Aztecs followed a brilliantly successful policy of divide and conquer, first allying with powerful neighbors to attack weaker groups, then turning against former allies. With the riches gained from conquest, the Aztecs transformed Tenochtitlán from a dusty town of mud houses to a great imperial capital built of stone with a grand botanical garden that displayed plants taken from various climates.

The Aztecs excelled in the perpetual state of war that had long been the dominant fact of life in Mexico; as a result, they attributed great religious value to war. They practiced the "flowery war," a staged occurrence during which states agreed to a predetermined time and place for a battle, the only objective of which was to take prisoners for temple sacrifice. Sustaining the gods' hunger for human sacrifices became the most notorious feature of Aztec religion. The Aztecs attributed their military successes to their tribal god, Huitzilopochtli, the giver of light and all things necessary for life. However, Huitzilopochtli could be nourished only with human blood, creating the need among the Aztec faithful to acquire human captives.

The rituals of sacrifice permeated Aztec society. An estimated 10,000 victims were sacrificed each year, with the number rising to 50,000 on the eve of the Spanish conquest. From the very first encounters, the paradox of Aztec culture baffled Europeans.

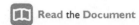 **Read the Document**

The Midwife Addresses the Woman Who Has Died in Childbirth–Anonymous

13.1

13.2

13.3

13.4

THE AZTEC RITE OF HUMAN SACRIFICE An Aztec priest in a cape prepares to cut the heart out of a sacrificial victim as assistants hold him down.

Despite their practice of human sacrifice, the Aztecs displayed refined manners, a sensitivity to beauty, and a highly developed religion. Whatever biases the Europeans brought with them about the "savages" of the New World, it was obvious that the Aztecs had created a great civilization.

THE INCAN EMPIRE OF THE ANDES At about the same time the Aztecs were thriving in Mexico, the Incas expanded their empire in Peru. Whereas the Aztecs created a loosely linked empire based on tribute payments, the Incas employed a more direct form of rulership. Around 1438 the first Incan emperor spread his rule beyond the valley of Cuzco. By the end of the fifteenth century, the Incas had begun to integrate by force the distinctive cultures of the various conquered regions. In this way, they created a mountain empire 200 miles wide and 2,000 miles long, stretching from modern Chile to Ecuador and comprising a population of about 10 million. From his capital at Cuzco, the Incan emperor lived in luxury and established an elaborately hierarchic political structure. His authority was carried through layers of aristocrats down to officials who were responsible for every 10 families in every village. These families supplied food and tribute for the empire, worked on roads and bridges, and served in the army. State-owned warehouses of food guaranteed the peasants freedom from starvation and provided for the sick and elderly. A superb network of roads and bridges covered more than 18,000 miles and made it possible to communicate with relays of runners who could cover as much as 140 miles a day. Troops could also be quickly dispatched to trouble spots via these roads.

Despite this well-organized imperial system, the Incan Empire became overly centralized because decisions could only be made by the emperor himself. Emperor Huayna Capac (r. 1493–1525) founded a second capital further south at Quito in an attempt to decentralize the overextended empire, but at his death a bitter civil war broke out between the northern and southern halves of the empire, led respectively by his rival sons. This war weakened Incan unity on the eve of the Spanish conquest.

View the Map

Expansion of the Inca Empire

The Mission of the European Voyagers

The European arrival in the Americas was the result of Christopher Columbus's (1451–1506) epic miscalculation. Born in Genoa to an artisan family, Columbus followed the destiny of so many of his compatriots by becoming a sailor. "From a very small age," he reported late in life, "I went sailing upon the sea."[1] He spent more than 40 years sailing everywhere sailors went. Columbus certainly had extensive experience as a seaman, but more crucial to understanding his mistake was his religious devotion. Columbus believed that he had been predestined to fulfill biblical prophecies. If he could reach China, he could outflank the Ottoman Turks and recapture Jerusalem from the Muslims who had held it since 1187. Columbus believed that the recapture of the Holy City would usher in the Second Coming of Christ. To persuade Queen Isabella of Castile to finance his voyage to China by sailing west, Columbus later admitted that he ignored navigational data and, instead, relied "entirely on holy, sacred Scripture and certain prophetic texts by certain saintly persons, who by divine revelation have had something to say on this matter."[2]

Europeans had long recognized that it was theoretically possible to reach China by sailing west. Most educated people, and certainly all those influenced by the Renaissance humanists, agreed the world was round. Sailors knew the world was round because they could see that the hull of a ship disappeared on the horizon before its masts did. The problem was not a theoretical one about the shape of the Earth but a practical one about getting around it. During Columbus's life the most widely accepted authority on the circumference of the Earth was the ancient Greek geographer Ptolemy, who had estimated that the distance across the Atlantic Ocean from Europe to Asia was more than 10,000 miles. No ship in Columbus's day could hope to sail that far without landfalls along the way for finding provisions and making repairs. In fact, Ptolemy had underestimated the size of the Earth by 25 percent.

Columbus, however, decided that Ptolemy had overestimated the distance. He also claimed that the wealthy islands of Japan lay farther east of the Asian continent than they actually do, thus further minimizing the distance of the voyage. When Columbus first proposed sailing west to Asia, King John II of Portugal consulted a committee of experts who quite correctly pointed out Columbus's miscalculations, which seem to have been more the result of wishful thinking and religious fervor than geographical expertise.

King John's rejection led Columbus to seek patronage elsewhere. Columbus applied to Queen Isabella of the newly unified Spain, whose own advisers at first recommended against the voyage for the same reasons the Portuguese experts had rejected the plan. However, when the Spanish defeated the Muslim kingdom of Granada in 1492, which completed the Christian reconquest of the Iberian peninsula, Isabella succumbed to the religious enthusiasm of the moment and relented. She offered Columbus a commission for the voyage in the hope that it would ensure a final Christian victory over Islam.

On August 3, 1492, Columbus set sail with three small ships—the Niña, Pinta, and Santa Maria—and a crew of 90 men and boys. After refitting in the Canary Islands, the modest convoy entered unknown waters guided only by Columbus's faith in finding China, which was, in fact, thousands of miles farther west than he thought it would be. At two in the morning on the moonlit night of October 12, a lookout spied land, probably Watling Island in the Bahamas.

In all, Columbus made four voyages across the Atlantic (1492, 1493, 1498, 1502), exploring the Caribbean Islands, the coast of Central America, and part of the coast of South America. He never abandoned the belief that he had arrived in Asia. His four voyages were filled with adventures. On the third voyage, he was arrested by the newly appointed Spanish governor of Hispaniola on false charges and sent home in chains for trial; on the fourth he was marooned for nearly a year on Jamaica after worms weakened the timbers of his ships. He garnered considerable wealth in gold found on his voyages, but he never received the titles and offices that Queen Isabella had promised him before his first voyage. (See *Justice in History* in this chapter.)

Soon after Columbus returned to Spain from his first voyage, the Spanish monarchs who had sponsored him tried to obtain a monopoly to explore the western Atlantic. They appealed to Pope Alexander VI, who was himself a Spaniard and sympathetic to their request. The pope ordered a line of demarcation drawn along a north-south line 100 leagues (about 300 miles) west of the Azores and Cape Verde Islands. Spain received all lands to the west of the line; Portugal obtained the lands to the east. This line of demarcation seemed to limit the Portuguese to Africa, which alarmed them and led to direct negotiations between the Portuguese and the Spaniards. The result of the negotiations was the Treaty of Tordesillas in 1494, which moved the line of demarcation to 370 leagues (about 1,110 miles) west of the Cape Verde Islands, a decision that granted to Portugal all of Africa, India, and Brazil.

Despite Columbus's persistent faith that he had found a route to the East Indies, other voyagers began to suspect, even before Columbus's death, that he had not found Asia at all and that other routes had to be explored. Another Italian, the Florentine Amerigo Vespucci (1454–1512), met Columbus, helped him prepare for the third voyage, and later made at least two voyages of his own across the Atlantic. From his voyages, Vespucci recognized something of the immensity of the South American continent and was the first to use the term *New World*. Because he coined the term and because the account of his voyages got into print before Columbus's, Vespucci's given name, Amerigo (America), came to be attached to the New World rather than Columbus's. By the 1520s, Europeans had explored the Americas extensively enough to recognize that the New World was nowhere near India or China.

📖 **Read the Document**

From *The Journal of Christopher Columbus* (1492)

Justice in History
The Trial of Christopher Columbus

On October 12, 1998, a court put Christopher Columbus on trial in Tegucigalpa, Honduras. The Honduran jury, which included two Catholic priests, found Columbus guilty on 10 charges, including kidnapping, rape, enslavement, invasion of peaceful lands, murder, torture, and genocide against the natives of the Americas. A life-size painting of the handcuffed explorer stood in for the defendant, who had been dead for nearly 500 years. The trial took place before a crowd of about 2,000 people, many from the indigenous Lenca people. According to the two priests on the jury, the original plan for the show trial had been to find Columbus guilty and then hold him prisoner until the Spanish government made reparation payments. However, as the jury began to deliberate, the crowd started chanting, demanding he receive capital punishment. Complying with the demands of the people, two Lenca warriors executed Columbus by firing a dozen arrows into the painting.

The Honduran trial was not the only one that has questioned Columbus's reputation in recent years. In the United States elementary school teachers have organized their classes for mock trials of the famous explorer. In New York City a fourth grade class charged Columbus with land theft, enslavement, torture, and murder. After a lively mock trial the class unanimously sentenced Columbus to jail time and ordered he undergo psychotherapy. In response, several Italian-American associations launched a campaign to preserve the Italian explorer's image as a hero. The figure of Columbus remains a powerful symbol of the encounters, so often violent and deadly, between the Europeans and the native peoples of the Americas.

A controversial figure even in his own time, Columbus was, in fact, arrested and put on trial by a royal judge on the island of Hispaniola in 1500. Columbus was an intrepid explorer, but even he admitted he was a poor administrator. He had established a Spanish colony on the island of Hispaniola (Haiti and Dominican Republic today), but after six years of his governorship, the island suffered recurrent rebellions, not only from the Indians but from the colonists as well. Part of the problem was that Columbus promised the colonists far more than he could deliver. He depicted the island as offering abundant gold that could

THE ARREST OF CHRISTOPHER COLUMBUS BY BOBADILLA This image represents what was one of the most famous incidents in the Columbus saga. The engraving shows Bobadilla, the figure in the center-left, wielding a baton, which symbolized his royal authority. In the center right is Columbus gesturing his dismay as irons are fitted to his ankles. Behind Bobadilla the rebels are shown welcoming Bobadilla as he crosses a gang plank. In the far right soldiers load Columbus onto a small boat to be towed out to the caravel anchored at sea ready to transport him back to Spain.

(continued on next page)

(continued from previous page)

be virtually picked off the ground and compliant Indians who would do the settlers' work for them. As a result, the colony attracted idlers and former convicts who quickly discovered that the island had a difficult environment and was inhabited by self-reliant Indians who were quite unwilling to become slaves of the Spaniards. When Columbus returned to Hispaniola on his third voyage in 1498, he discovered widespread abuse of the Indians and open rebellion against his governorship by the settlers on the southern part of the island. The arbitrary rule of Columbus and his brothers, who had been in charge during his absence, enraged the rebels. The rebels demanded the right to appeal to the Crown, a demand that raised a fundamental issue about how a colony so far from Spain could be ruled with respect to the law. Columbus himself recognized he was neither suited to be an administrator nor properly educated to act as a judge. He requested one be sent from Spain to help quell the rebellion and bring justice to the island.

Ferdinand and Isabella responded by appointing Francisco de Bobadilla, an aristocratic lawyer, to put down the rebellion and to investigate the numerous charges against Columbus. Bobadilla arrived in Hispaniola with a poor opinion of Columbus based on conversations in Spain with numerous men who had returned from the New World. Bobadilla arrived with the authority to take over the government of Hispaniola if he thought there was a legitimate case against Columbus. Columbus's son Ferdinand reported what happened next:

> On his arrival, Bobadilla, who was most anxious to remain in office, neither held a hearing nor took any evidence. Instead, early in October, 1500, he put the Admiral [Columbus] and his brother Diego in chains aboard ship under a strong guard; he forbade anyone publicly to mention them, on pain of very severe penalties. He then held a farcical inquest, taking testimony from their open enemies, the rebels, and showing public favor to and even egging on all who wished to speak ill of the prisoners. From the wicked and shameless things these people said, one had to be blind not to see that they were guided by prejudice rather than truth.[3]

Columbus considered himself a martyr. On board ship the captain offered to remove the chains, but Columbus refused, wanting to keep them on so that he could embarrass the king and queen when he arrived in their presence. Aboard ship he wrote a series of letters in which he reflected on his humiliation

and its causes. He admitted he had exceeded his authority by arbitrarily hanging colonists accused of rebellion, but he justified himself by arguing that he was attempting to bring order to a frontier inhabited by savages. Whereas after his first voyage he had depicted the Indians as peace loving and naturally good, he now changed his mind. The Indians, he said, were warlike and wild, incapable of conforming to civilized society. They were people of the Devil. He blamed them even more than the Spanish rebels who had actually caused his downfall. Ferdinand and Isabella freed Columbus from his shackles and the charges against him, but he never fully regained his authority as the governor of Hispaniola.

The trial of Columbus marked a moment of transformation in the European experience in the New World. Even Columbus had to admit he had not discovered a paradise, but an impoverished land whose inhabitants could barely feed themselves, let alone support invaders unwilling to work. His own attitudes toward the native inhabitants switched to match the bigotry of the other settlers who treated the Indians with contempt. The creaky Spanish legal system showed how ill equipped it was for bringing justice to a distant colony. The experience of 1499–1500 on Hispaniola would be repeated time and again in the Spanish conquests in America. The most brutal men in Spanish society found ways to disregard authority, to abuse the natives, and to subvert justice largely because there was no one capable of stopping them. The fantasy world of a terrestrial paradise Columbus had created in his mind began to collapse around him.

For Discussion

1. Who was right, Columbus or Bobadilla? Why? Should Columbus be held responsible for his false representation of Hispaniola and for his poor governorship?
2. What do Columbus's troubles reveal about the strengths and weaknesses of the Spanish colonial system?
3. What do mock trials of historical figures such as Columbus seek to accomplish? Are they successful?

Taking It Further

Fernández-Armesto, Felipe. *Columbus*. 1991. Among the many studies of Columbus this may be the most trustworthy and balanced.

The Life of the Admiral Christopher Columbus by his Son Ferdinand. Translated and Annotated by Benjamin Keen. 1959. A fascinating account of events from Columbus's point of view.

Explorers followed two distinct strategies for finding a sea route to East Asia. The first strategy was the Portuguese pursuit of routes to the south and east around Africa. Between 1487 and 1488, Bartholomew Dias (ca. 1450–1500) reached the Cape of Good Hope at the southern tip of the African continent. This discovery made it evident that passage to India could be achieved by sailing south, rounding the tip of Africa, and crossing the Indian Ocean. Political and financial problems in Portugal, however, prevented a follow-up to Dias's voyage for 10 years. Between 1497 and 1499, Vasco da Gama (ca. 1460–1524) finally succeeded in sailing from Lisbon to India around the Cape of Good Hope. As a consequence of the route opened by da Gama, the Portuguese were the first Europeans to establish trading posts in Asia. They reached the Malabar Coast of India in 1498 and soon found their way to the Spice Islands and China. By the middle of the sixteenth century, the Portuguese had assembled a string of more than 50 trading posts and forts from Sofala on the east coast of Africa to Nagasaki in Japan.

The second strategy for reaching Asia consisted of Spanish attempts to pursue Columbus's proposed route west. The problem faced by those sailing under the Spanish flag was to find a way around the barrier presented by the American continents. A Portuguese sailor named Ferdinand Magellan (ca. 1480–1521) persuaded the king of Spain to sponsor a voyage to Asia sailing west around South America. That venture (1519–1522), which began under Magellan's command, passed through the strait named after him at the tip of South America and crossed the Pacific in a voyage of extreme hardship. His men suffered from thirst and hunger and died of scurvy. Magellan himself was killed by natives in the Philippines. After three years at sea, 18 survivors from the original 240 in Magellan's fleet reached Seville, Spain, having sailed around the world for the first time. Contemporaries immediately recognized the epic significance of the voyage, but the route opened by Magellan was too long and arduous for the Spanish to employ as a reliable alternative to the Portuguese route around Africa.

In the course of three centuries (about 1480–1780), European navigators linked the previously isolated routes of seaborne commerce, opened all the seas of the world to trade, and encountered many of the cultures and peoples of the world. Within the Indian Ocean and the western Pacific, the Europeans faced stiff competition from Arab and Chinese merchant sailors. But for the first 100 years or so, the Portuguese and Spanish effectively maintained a monopoly over the global trade routes back to Europe. Gradually English, Dutch, and French sailors also made their way around the globe. In the Americas, inadvertently made known to Europeans by Christopher Columbus, the Spanish immediately began settlements and attempted to subdue the indigenous populations.

◉ Watch the Video

The "Achievement" of Columbus

SPANISH CONQUISTADORES LAND ON AN ISLAND IN THE NEW WORLD The armored Spaniards are met by the naked inhabitants who offer them jewels and gold. As one of their first acts, the Spaniards erect a cross, symbolizing the Christian conquest of the New World.

The Fall of the Aztec and Incan Empires

Following the seafaring captains, such as Columbus and Magellan, came the **conquistadores**, who actually conquered the new-found land. They were Spanish adventurers, usually from impoverished minor noble families, who sought fortune and royal recognition through exploration and conquest. Spain was a poor land with few opportunities for advancement, a bleak situation that made the lands of the New World a powerful lure to many men seeking a fortune. Embroiled in almost continuous warfare in Europe, the Spanish crown was also perennially strapped for cash, which meant the king of Spain was highly motivated to encourage profitable foreign conquests. Many of the conquistadores launched their own expeditions with little or no legal authority, hoping to acquire sufficient riches to impress the king to give them official sanction for additional conquests. Those who did acquire legal authority from the crown received the privilege to conquer new lands in the name of the king of Spain and to keep a portion of those territories for themselves. In return they were obliged to turn over to the king one-fifth—the "royal fifth"—of everything of value they acquired, an obligation enforced by a notary sent along with the conquistadores to keep a record of valuables that were found. The conquistadores also extended Spanish sovereignty over new lands and opened the way for missionaries to bring millions, at least nominally, into the Christian fold.

The king required all conquistadores to read a document, called the **requerimiento**, to the natives before making war on them. Derived from the Muslim declaration of *jihad* or holy war, this Spanish Christian document briefly explained the principles of Christianity and commanded the natives to accept them immediately along with the authority of the pope and the sovereignty of the king of Spain. If the natives refused, the conquistador warned that they would be forced through war to subject themselves "to the yoke and obedience of the Church and of Their Highnesses. We shall take you and your wives and your children, and shall make slaves of them, and as such shall sell and dispose of them as Their Highnesses may command. And we shall take your goods, and shall do you all the mischief and damage that we can."[4] The *requerimiento* revealed the conflicting motives behind the Spanish conquest. On the one hand, the Spanish were sincerely interested in converting the natives to Christianity. On the other, the conquistadores tried to justify their actions by suggesting that the natives had brought the attack on themselves by refusing to obey the Spanish king.

HERNÁN CORTÉS AND THE CONQUEST OF MEXICO Among the first and most successful of the conquistadores was Hernán Cortés (1485–1547). Cortés arrived on the Yucatán peninsula of present-day Mexico in February 1519, beginning a conquest that culminated in the collapse of the Aztec Empire and the Spanish colonization of Mexico. Cortés followed a policy with the natives of divide and conquer, making alliances with peoples who resented Aztec domination and then using their warriors on the front lines of his battles where they absorbed most of the losses. If after a reading of the *requerimiento* the native chieftains did not immediately surrender, Cortés's men attacked them, breaking through their lines on horses, which the natives had never seen before.

Cortés's greatest achievement was the conquest of the Aztec capital. After a number of bloody battles, he set off with only 450 Spanish troops, 15 horses, and 4,000 native allies to seize Tenochtitlán, a city of at least 300,000 and defended by thousands of warriors. As Cortés approached, Montezuma II was slow to set up a strong defense, because he suspected Cortés might be the white god, Quetzalcóatl, who according to prophecies would arrive one day from the east. The result was disastrous for the Aztecs. Montezuma knew his reign was doomed unless he could gain the assistance of other gods to drive Quetzalcóatl away. Thus, rather than an ardent military campaign, the king's defense primarily took the form of human sacrifices to please the gods. By the time Tenochtitlán finally surrendered, the shiny jewel

conquistadores Spanish adventurers in the Americas who explored and conquered the lands of indigenous peoples, sometimes without legal authority but usually with a legal privilege granted by the king of Spain who required that one-fifth of all things of value be turned over to the king. The conquistadores extended Spanish sovereignty over new lands.

requerimiento A document read by conquistadores to the natives of the Americas before making war on them. The document briefly explained the principles of Christianity and commanded the natives to accept them immediately along with the authority of the pope and the sovereignty of the king of Spain. If the natives refused, they were warned they would be forced to accept Christian conversion and subjected to Spain anyway.

📖 Read the Document

Excerpts from the "Account of Alva Ixtlilxochiltl" (1519)

CORTÉS ARRIVES IN MEXICO The figure on the right is the native woman La Malinche, who served as Cortés's mistress and translator, a position often occupied by native women who served as mediators between the indigenous and Spanish cultures. She is interpreting for the bearded Hernán Cortés at his meeting with Montezuma II (seated on left) at Tenochtitlán in November 1519.

that had so impressed the Spanish when they first glimpsed it from the surrounding mountains lay in smoldering ruins.

By 1522 Cortés controlled a territory in New Spain—as Mexico was renamed—larger than Old Spain itself. Aztec culture and its religion of human sacrifice disappeared as Franciscan friars arrived to evangelize the surviving population.

FRANCISCO PIZARRO AND THE CONQUEST OF PERU A small contingent of Spanish conquistadores also managed to conquer the vast Incan Empire in Peru. In 1531 Francisco Pizarro (ca. 1478–1541) left Panama with a small expedition of 180 men and 30 horses. He sailed to northern Peru and sent out spies who discovered that the Incan emperor, Atahuallpa, could be found in the highland city of Cajamarca. When Pizarro and his forces arrived there, the central square was empty, but Atahuallpa was encamped nearby with a large army. Pizarro invited Atahuallpa to come for a parlay, but instead treacherously took him captive. The news of the capture plunged the overly centralized Incan Empire into a crisis because no one dared take action without the emperor's orders. In an attempt to satisfy the Spaniards' hunger for riches and to win his freedom, Atahuallpa had a room filled with gold and silver for the conquistadores, but the treasure merely stimulated their appetite for more. In July 1533 Pizarro executed the emperor, and by the following November he had captured the demoralized Incan capital of Cuzco.

The conquest of Peru gave the Spanish access to untold wealth. Through the collection of the royal fifth, gold and silver flowed into the royal coffers in Spain. The discovery in 1545 of the fabulous Peruvian silver mine of Potosí (in what is now southern Bolivia) coincided with the introduction of the mercury amalgamation process that separated silver from ore. Mercury amalgamation enabled the Spaniards to replace surface gathering of silver ore with tunneling for ore, a procedure that led to greatly elevated yields of precious metals. For a century the silver of Peru helped otherwise impoverished Spain become the most powerful kingdom in Europe.

Spanish America: The Transplanting of a European Culture

With the defeat of the Aztec and Incan Empires, the process of transplanting Spanish society to the Americas began in earnest. The arrival of Europeans was a catastrophe for most native peoples, some of whom—in the Caribbean, northern Argentina, and central Chile—completely disappeared through the ravages of conquest and diseases. Spanish became the language of government and education, and Latin the language of religion. Nevertheless, many native languages and cultural traditions survived. Spanish America became not only the first outpost of Western civilization outside of Europe, but also the home of new hybrid cultures and ethnicities.

The basic form of economic and social organization in Spanish America was the **encomienda** system, created as an instrument to exploit native labor. An encomienda was a royal grant awarded for military or other services that gave the conquistadores and their successors the right to gather tribute from the Indians in a defined area. In return, the encomendero (the receiver of the royal grant and native tribute) was theoretically obliged to protect the natives and teach them the rudiments of the Christian faith. Because the encomiendas were very large, only a small number of Spanish settlers were actually encomenderos. In greater Peru, which included modern Peru, Ecuador, and Bolivia, there were never more than 500 encomenderos. By the seventeenth century these encomiendas had evolved to become great landed estates called **haciendas**.

There were only a few prosperous encomenderos, but the stories about those who rose from rags to riches in the New World were so compelling that during the sixteenth century alone more than 200,000 Spaniards migrated there. They came from every part of the Iberian peninsula, from every class except the peasantry, and they practiced a wide variety of trades. There were nobles, notaries, lawyers, priests, physicians, merchants, artisans, and sailors, as well as vagabonds prone to crime and rebellion. In effect, these immigrants duplicated the Spanish Catholic society in the New World, complete with its class divisions and tensions, except that the native population or African slaves substituted for the peasants. Included among the immigrants were an unknown number of Jews who hid their faith and who escaped the rigors of the Spanish Inquisition by fleeing to the Americas, where they were less likely to suffer persecution.

Only one in ten of Spanish immigrants was a woman, and for a long time the colonies suffered from a shortage of Spanish women. Although native Americans were usually excluded from Spanish society, many native women who were the mistresses or wives of Spaniards became partially assimilated to European culture and helped pass it on to their offspring. These women knew both languages, which made them valuable interpreters, and were familiar with both cultures, which enabled them to explain native customs to the Spanish. The progeny of European men and Indian women constituted the *mestizo,* or genetically mixed, population.

THE ENCOUNTER OF THREE CULTURES On this wooden bottle painted in the Incan style about 1650, an African drummer leads a procession, followed by a Spanish trumpeter and an Incan official. The mixing of cultures that occurred after the arrival of the Spanish and Portuguese distinguished the Americas from other civilizations.

encomienda The basic form of economic and social organization in early Spanish America, based on a royal grant awarded to a Spaniard for military or other services that gave the grantee and his successors the right to gather tribute from the Indians in a defined area.

haciendas Large landed estates that began to be established in the seventeenth century and replaced encomiendas throughout much of Spanish America.

The king of Spain was represented in the Americas by two viceroys, the highest colonial officials. One in Mexico City governed the West Indies, the mainland north of Panama, Venezuela, and the Philippines. The other in Lima, Peru, had authority over all of Spanish South America, excluding Venezuela. However, the vast territory of Spanish America and the enormous cultural diversity within it precluded any rigorous centralized control either from Spain or from the viceroys' capitals.

In Spanish America the church was a more effective presence than the state. Driven by the same religious fervor as Columbus, Catholic missionaries trekked into the farthest reaches of Spanish America, converting the native populations to Christianity with much more success than in Africa or Asia. Greed had enticed the conquistadores, but an ardent desire to spread the gospel of Christianity spurred the missionaries. The most zealous missionaries were members of religious orders—Franciscans, Dominicans, and Jesuits—who were distinguished from the parish priests by their autonomy and special training for missionary work.

Church officials generally assumed that it took 10 years for the transition to a settled Christian society, a policy that meant that Christianity arrived in two stages. First, members of a religious order evangelized the population by learning the native language, then preaching and teaching in it. They also introduced the celebration of the Catholic sacraments. Once churches were built and Christianity was accepted by the local elite, the missionaries moved on to be replaced, in the second stage, by parish priests who expected to stay in one place for their entire lives. In the border regions, evangelizing never ceased and members of the missionary orders stayed on until the end of colonial times. (See *Encounters and Transformations* in this chapter.)

 View the Closer Look   Dominican Baptizing an Indian

FIRST BAPTISM OF THE INDIANS BY THE DOMINICANS In this painting, which shows French dominance in North America, a French Dominican baptizes an American Indian from the French Territory of New France, which spanned much of North America at its peak in 1712.

Encounters and Transformations

Between Indian and Christian:
CREATING HYBRID RELIGION IN MEXICO

A s conquest passed into colonialism during the sixteenth century, Christian missionaries began to exert a profound influence on Indian moral and religious practices. However, as the Indians accepted Christianity they adapted it to meet their needs and to fit into their culture. As a result, native Americans created a new hybrid religion that combined both Christian and Indian elements, as Indian uses of the cross and adoption of flagellation illustrate.

As his army marched across Mexico, Cortés replaced native idols with Christian crosses. Missionaries later placed crosses in churches, encouraged making the sign of the cross a ritual practice, and introduced the wearing of miniature crosses as a kind of personal talisman that offered protection from illness and evil influences. Mayas readily adopted the Christian cross because they already had a symbol similar to it. However, the Maya at first misunderstood what the missionaries meant about the cross and took the example of Christ too literally. Some Maya actually performed crucifixions, usually of children, whose hands were nailed or tied to the cross and whose hearts were torn out in a vestige of pre-Christian practices. There are also reports of pigs and dogs sacrificed on crosses. Even though the Maya had missed the point of Christ's singular sacrifice, they had understood the power behind the Christian symbol, which the Spaniards had used in their conquest of the Maya, and they wanted some of that power for themselves.

When the Franciscan friars arrived in Mexico City in 1524, they introduced the practice of flagellation, which imitated Christ's whipping at the hands of Roman soldiers and served as a means of penance for sins. The friars employed self-flagellation

as a tool for impressing the natives. Fray Antonio de Roa encouraged conversions through dramatic flagellations, called "a general discipline." After a collective flagellation in which the Indians who had converted to Christianity imitated Fray Roa, he proceeded out of the church, naked from the waist up, with a cord around his neck, and shoeless. He walked over hot coals, and then delivered a sermon about how much greater the pains of Hell would be than those from the burning coals. After the sermon he doused his whole body with boiling water.

During the sixteenth century the Indians themselves began to practice flagellation, especially during processions conducted during Holy Week (the week before Easter). The natives flogged themselves with such evident enthusiasm that the friars had to intervene to prevent the Indians from seriously harming themselves. On many occasions during the colonial period, the Indians used self-flagellation as a means of rousing their fellows in protest against Spanish domination. Flagellation became not just a form of penance, but a means for arousing the passions of spectators, which could be turned toward rallying Mexicans against the Spanish. Even now flagellation remains the most distinctive feature of the Mexican passion plays. By adapting European Christian rituals for purposes other than those intended by the Christian missionaries, the natives created a new hybrid religious culture that was distinctively Mexican.

HYBRID RELIGION Here a priest flagellates a naked Incan in Peru. Introduced by Christian missionaries, flagellation became one of the more extreme forms of religious practice among the newly converted Indians.

For Discussion

How did the native Mexican adaptations of Christianity compare to the popular medieval religious practices discussed in Chapter 11? Had the Mexicans become part of the Western culture simply by accepting Christianity?

Portuguese Brazil: The Tenuous Colony

In 1500 Pedro Cabral sighted the Brazilian coast, claiming it for Portugal under the Treaty of Tordesillas. While the Spaniards busied themselves with the conquest of Mexico and Peru, the Portuguese largely ignored Brazil, which lacked any obvious source of gold or temptingly rich civilizations to conquer. Instead, the Portuguese concentrated on developing their lucrative empire in Asia.

The impetus for the further colonization of Brazil was the growing European demand for sugar. The Brazilian climate was perfectly suited for cultivating sugar cane. Between 1575 and 1600, Brazil became the Western world's leading producer of sugar, luring thousands of poor young men from Portugal and the Azores who took native women as wives, thereby producing a distinctive *mestizo* population. Sugar cane production required backbreaking, dangerous labor to clear the land, to weed, and especially to cut the cane. To help work the vast coastal plantations the Portuguese attempted to enslave the Tupí-Guaraní natives, but European diseases soon killed them off.

The Portuguese increasingly looked to Africans to perform the hard labor they were unwilling to do themselves. As a result, the Brazilian demand for slaves intensified the Portuguese presence in West Africa and the African presence in Brazil. In the search for even more slaves, Portuguese slave buyers enlarged their area of operations in Africa south to Angola, where in 1575 they founded a trading post. This post became the embarkation point for slave traders who sailed directly to Brazil and sold slaves in exchange for low-grade Brazilian tobacco, which they exchanged for more slaves when they returned to Angola.

As in Spanish America, Portuguese authorities felt responsible for converting the natives to Christianity. In Brazil, the Jesuits took the lead during the last half of the sixteenth century by establishing a school for the training of missionaries on the site of the present city of São Paulo. Once converted, natives were resettled into villages called **aldeias**, which were similar to Spanish missions. The Jesuits attempted to protect the natives against the white colonists who wanted to enslave them, creating a lasting conflict between the Jesuit fathers and local landowners. Both Jesuits and colonists appealed to the king to settle their dispute. Finally, the king gave the Jesuits complete responsibility for all Indians in aldeias, but he allowed colonists to enslave Indians who had not been converted or who were captured in war. The Portuguese connected Christian conversion with settlement in aldeias, which meant that any unsettled native was, by definition, a heathen. Nevertheless, these restrictions on enslaving Indians created a perceived labor shortage and further stimulated the demand for African slaves.

More rural and more African than Spanish America, Brazil during its colonial history remained a plantation economy in which the few dominant white European landowners were vastly outnumbered by their African slaves. In certain areas a racially mixed population created its own vibrantly hybrid culture that combined native, African, and European elements, especially in the eclectic religious life that fused Catholicism with polytheistic forms of worship. Although Brazil occupied nearly half of the South American continent, until the twentieth century most of the vast interior was unexplored by Europeans and unsettled except by the small native population.

North America: The Land of Lesser Interest

Compared with Central and South America, North America outside Mexico held little attraction for Europeans during the sixteenth century. During the reign of Queen Elizabeth I (r. 1558–1603), English efforts finally turned to establishing colonies in the Americas. Two prominent courtiers, Humphrey Gilbert and his stepbrother, Walter Raleigh, sponsored a series of voyages intended to establish an English colony called

aldeias Settlements for natives who had converted to Christianity in Brazil. In these settlements the Jesuit fathers protected the natives from enslavement.

Virginia in honor of Elizabeth, "The Virgin Queen." The English interest in colonization was made possible by Elizabeth's success in strengthening the monarchy, building up the fleet, and encouraging investments in New World colonies. In 1585 the first English colonists in the Americas landed on Roanoke Island off the coast of North Carolina, but they were so poorly prepared that this attempt and a second one in 1587 failed. The inexperienced and naive English settlers did not even make provisions for planting crops.

The successful English colonies came a generation later. Learning from past mistakes, the colonists of Jamestown in Virginia, who landed in 1607, brought seeds for planting, built fortifications for protection, and established a successful form of self-government. From these modest beginnings, the English gradually established

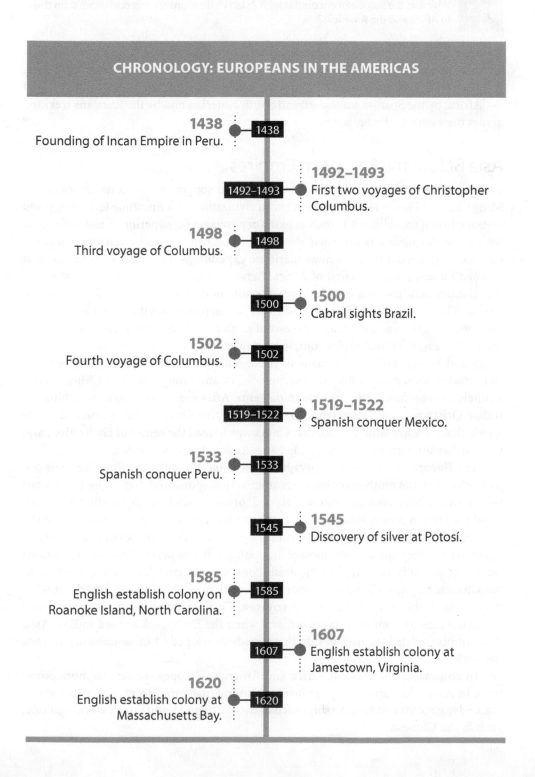

CHRONOLOGY: EUROPEANS IN THE AMERICAS

1438
Founding of Incan Empire in Peru.

1492–1493
First two voyages of Christopher Columbus.

1498
Third voyage of Columbus.

1500
Cabral sights Brazil.

1502
Fourth voyage of Columbus.

1519–1522
Spanish conquer Mexico.

1533
Spanish conquer Peru.

1545
Discovery of silver at Potosí.

1585
English establish colony on Roanoke Island, North Carolina.

1607
English establish colony at Jamestown, Virginia.

1620
English establish colony at Massachusetts Bay.

vast plantations along the rivers of Virginia. There they raised tobacco to supply the new European habit of smoking, which had been picked up from native Americans. In 1620 religious refugees from England settled in Massachusetts Bay; however, in contrast to Central and South America, North America by 1650 remained only marginally touched by Europeans and played a very minor role in European economic interests.

Europeans in Asia

13.3 Why was the European encounter with Asian civilizations far less disruptive than those in Africa and the Americas?

ndia, the Malay peninsula, Indonesia, the Spice Islands, and China were the ultimate goal of the European voyagers during the fifteenth and sixteenth centuries. They were eventually reached by many routes—by the Portuguese sailing around Africa, by the Spanish sailing around South America, and by the Russians trekking across the vastness of Siberia.

Asia Before the European Empires

The greatest potential rival to the Europeans who sought access to Asian trade was Ming China (1368–1644), a highly advanced civilization with maritime technology and organizational capability to launch exploratory voyages far superior to Europe's. Even before the Portuguese began their slow progress down the west coast of Africa, the Chinese organized a series of huge maritime expeditions into the Indian Ocean that reached far down the east coast of Africa. Between 1405 and 1433 the Chinese established diplomatic contacts and demanded tribute in dozens of kingdoms in India and Africa. The size and ambition of these fleets far surpassed anything that sailed from Europe at this time, and the massive crews of as many as 27,500 men (compared to Columbus's crew of 90) included a complement of scholars to communicate with foreign kings and highly skilled technicians to make repairs to the fleet. The Chinese fleets took trade goods, such as silk, tea, and porcelains, and brought back to China strange animals, hostage kings, and possible trade items. After nearly 30 years of searching the Indian Ocean ports, the Ming emperors concluded that China already possessed all the goods that were available abroad, that China was indeed the center of civilization, and that further investments in oceangoing expeditions were unwarranted.

The European and Chinese voyages of the fifteenth century differed in their objectives and in the motives of the governments that sponsored them. The Europeans were mostly privateers seeking personal profit or captains who enjoyed official government backing in return for a portion of the profits. The economic motive behind the European voyages made them self-sustaining because the Europeans sailed only to places where they could make money. In contrast, the imperial Chinese expeditions were only partially motivated by the desire for economic gain. The official purpose of the Chinese voyages was to learn about the world; once the Chinese found out what they wanted, they ceased the official voyages. Chinese merchant traders continued to ply the seas on their own, however, and when the Europeans arrived in East Asia, they simply inserted themselves into this already developed Chinese-dominated trade network.

In contrast to the trade in Africa and America, Europeans failed to monopolize trade in Asia. The Europeans were just one among many trading groups, some working under government sponsorship, such as the Portuguese, and others working alone, such as the Chinese.

The Trading Post Empires

For 300 years after establishing the first trading posts in Asia, Europeans had little influence there in comparison to the Americas. In 1497–1499 Vasco da Gama opened the most promising route for the Portuguese around Africa to South and East Asia. But the sailing distances were long, limiting the number of people who could be transported to Asia. In contrast to the Americas, the Asian empires were well equipped to defend themselves against European conquest. Because Europeans lacked the support system, which in the Americas the colonial system provided, few Europeans settled in Asia, and even missionary work proved much more difficult than in the Americas.

Unlike Brazil, where the Portuguese established colonial plantations, in Asia they established trading posts along the coasts of India, China, and the Spice Islands. When the Portuguese first arrived at a location with a safe harbor and easy access to the hinterland, they built a fort and forced, bribed, or tricked the local political authority, usually a chieftain, to cede the land around the post to Portugal. The agents sent to trade in Asia were called *factors* and their trading posts were called **factories**. But they were not factories in the modern sense of sites for manufacturing. They were safe places where merchants could trade and store their merchandise. The factors lived in the factories with a few other Portuguese traders, a small detachment of troops, and servants recruited from the local population. Nowhere did Portuguese authority extend very far into the hinterland. The traditional political structures of local chieftains remained, and the local elites usually went along with the arrangement because they profited by reselling European wares, such as cloth, guns, knives, and many kinds of cheap gadgets. The factors acquired silks, gold, silver, raw cotton, pepper, spices, and medicines. Some of these outposts of the Portuguese Empire survived until late in the twentieth century, but their roots remained exceedingly shallow. Even in places such as East Timor, an island in Indonesia, and Macao on the south China coast, which were Portuguese outposts for more than four centuries, only a small native elite ever learned the Portuguese language or adapted to European culture.

The European trading posts in Asia proved very lucrative. Consider the search for the spice nutmeg. In an account published in 1510, an Italian traveler, Ludovico di Varthema, described the previously unknown nutmeg trees, which he found growing in the Banda Islands, a small archipelago some 1,000 miles east of Java. These were the only places in the world where nutmeg grew. Besides adding flavor to foods, nutmeg was believed to possess powers to cure all kinds of diseases and to induce a hallucinatory euphoria. The demand for nutmeg was so great and the supply so limited that exporting it yielded enormous profits. At one time, nutmeg was the most valuable commodity in the world after gold and silver. In the early seventeenth century the markup on a pound of nutmeg transported from the Banda Islands to Europe was 60,000 percent. It is no wonder European traders were willing to risk their lives on long, dangerous sea voyages to obtain nutmeg and other spices.

In return for raw materials such as nutmeg, European merchants typically traded manufactured goods, and they made every effort to ensure that other European powers were excluded from competing in this trade in Asia. Crucial to enforcing the system was a network of factories and a strong navy, which was primarily used against other European and occasionally Muslim interlopers. Through the trading post empires, commercial rivalries among European states extended abroad to Asia. Competition over these trading posts foreshadowed the beginnings of a global economy dominated by Europeans. It also demonstrated the Europeans' propensity to transform European wars into world wars.

In addition to trade, the Portuguese and other European powers sought to spread Christianity. To accomplish conversions, missionaries resorted to persuasion, because without the backing of a full-scale conquest as in the Americas, resorting to force was usually not an option. The missionaries frequently drew the ire of local rulers, who viewed the converts as traitors—a situation that led to the persecution of some of the

factories Trading posts established by European powers in foreign lands.

new Christians. To accomplish their task of conversion, Christian missionaries had to learn the native languages and something of the native culture and religion. In this effort, the Jesuits were particularly dedicated. They sent members of their order to the Chinese imperial court, where they lived incognito for decades, although they made few converts. Jesuits also traveled to Japan, where they established an outpost of Christianity at Nagasaki. With the exception of the Spanish Philippines, which was nominally converted to Catholicism by 1600, Christian missionaries in Asia were far less successful than in the Americas. Perhaps one million Asians outside the Philippines had been converted during this period, but many of these conversions did not last. Christians were most successful in converting Buddhists and least effective among Muslims, who almost never abandoned their faith.

By the end of the sixteenth century, Portuguese and Spanish shipping in Asian waters faced recurrent harassment from the English, French, and Dutch. The Dutch drove the Portuguese from their possessions in Ceylon, India, and the Spice Islands, except for East Timor. But none of these sixteenth-century European empires was particularly effective at imposing European culture on Asia in a way comparable with the Americas. In the Spanish Philippines, for example, few natives spoke Spanish, and there were fewer than 5,000 Spanish inhabitants as late as 1850. European states competed among themselves for trade and tried to enforce monopolies, but the Europeans remained peripheral to Asian culture until the late eighteenth and early nineteenth centuries, when the British expanded their power in India and colonized Australia and New Zealand.

The expansion of the Russian Empire into Asia depended not on naval power but on cross-country expeditions. The heartland of the Russian Empire was Muscovy, the area around Moscow, but the empire would eventually spread from the Baltic Sea to the Pacific Ocean. After 1552 Russians began to push across the Ural Mountains into Siberia. They were lured by the trade in exotic furs; these were in great demand among the upper classes of northern Europe, both to keep warm and as fashion statements. The Russians' search for furs was equivalent to the Spanish search for gold; like gold, fur attracted adventurous and desperate men. Following the navigable rivers and building strategic forts along the way, expeditions collected furs locally and then advanced deeper into the frozen wilds of Siberia. Several of the great aristocratic families

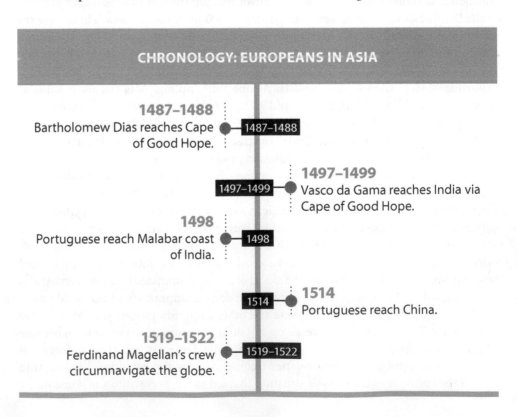

CHRONOLOGY: EUROPEANS IN ASIA

1487–1488
Bartholomew Dias reaches Cape of Good Hope. — 1487–1488

1497–1499 — **1497–1499**
Vasco da Gama reaches India via Cape of Good Hope.

1498
Portuguese reach Malabar coast of India. — 1498

1514 — **1514**
Portuguese reach China.

1519–1522
Ferdinand Magellan's crew circumnavigate the globe. — 1519–1522

of Russia acquired enormous wealth from the Siberian fur trade, which was so lucrative that Russian trappers kept pushing farther and farther east. In this quest for furs, expeditions reached the Pacific coast in 1649, by which time Russia had established a network of trading posts over all of northern Asia.

The significance of the European trading post empires is based less in the influence of Europe on Asia than in the influence of Asia on Europe. Asian products from spices and opium to silk cloth and oriental rugs became commonplace items in middle- and upper-class European households. European collectors became fascinated with Chinese porcelains, lacquered boxes, and screen paintings. At the same time, Asian tourists began to visit Europe, a tradition begun when four Japanese converts to Christianity arrived in Lisbon in 1586 and made a celebrated tour of Europe.

The Beginnings of the Global System

13.4 How was the world tied together in a global biological and economic system?

As a result of the European voyages of the fifteenth and sixteenth centuries, a network of cultural, biological, and economic connections formed along intercontinental trading routes. For many thousands of years, Europe, northern Africa, and Asia had been in contact with one another, but the system that formed during the sixteenth century encompassed most of the globe, including sub-Saharan Africa and the Americas. Unlike earlier international trading systems that linked Europe and Asia, the new global system was dominated by Europeans. Today's global economy, based on cellular telephones, the Internet, air transportation, and free trade, is merely an extension and elaboration of the system that first appeared on a global scale during the sixteenth century. This system transformed human society by bringing into contact what had previously been separate and isolated—regional cultures, biological systems, and local economies.

The Columbian Exchange

The most dramatic changes were at first produced by the trade of peoples, plants, animals, microbes, and ideas between the Old and New Worlds—a process known as the **Columbian Exchange**. For the native Americans, the importation of Europeans, Africans, and diseases had devastating consequences—threatening indigenous religions, making native technology irrelevant, disrupting social life, and destroying millions of lives. For Europeans, the discovery of previously unknown civilizations profoundly shook their own understanding of human geography and history. Neither the ancient philosophers nor the Bible, which was understood to be an accurate history of humankind since the creation of the world, had provided a hint about the peoples of the Americas.

Columbian Exchange The trade of peoples, plants, animals, microbes, and ideas between the Old and New Worlds that began with Columbus.

THE SLAVE TRADE Slavery and the slave trade had existed long before the Europeans expanded the practice. All of the ancient civilizations had been slave societies with as many as one-third of the population in bondage. During the Middle Ages a small number of slaves were employed as domestic servants and concubines in the Christian cities of the Mediterranean, and in Muslim countries large numbers of slaves were found in harems, used as laborers, and even trained as soldiers. During the wars between Christians and Muslims, victors habitually enslaved captives. In the sixteenth and seventeenth centuries Barbary pirates in the Mediterranean captured approximately 850,000 white Europeans during sea raids and forced them into slavery in Muslim North Africa. Large-scale transportation of black Africans began during the ninth and tenth centuries, when Muslim traders took tens of thousands from the island of Zanzibar off the east coast of Africa to lower Iraq, where they performed the heavy labor of draining swamps and cutting sugar cane. Slavery was also widespread in Islamic West Africa. Mali depended heavily on slave labor, and in Muslim Ghana slaves constituted about one-third of the population. Thus, the enslavement of Africans by Africans was well established when the Europeans arrived.

The slave trade flourished only when and where it was profitable. The necessary conditions for profitability were a strong demand for labor-intensive agricultural commodities, a perceived shortage of local labor, a supply of people who could be captured elsewhere, and a moral and legal climate that permitted slavery. These conditions were all present in the late fifteenth and sixteenth centuries. The population of Europe developed a taste for exotic products such as sugar, tobacco, coffee, and indigo dye. The European colonizers who sought to supply the demand for these goods needed agricultural workers, first for the colonies in the Atlantic islands and then for plantations in the Americas where European diseases decimated the indigenous population, creating a labor shortage. Europeans also found it difficult to enslave the native peoples, who knew the territory and could easily escape.

The flourishing demand for labor was supplied by the population of Africa. Once Europeans started to buy up slaves in the coastal trading posts, enterprising African chieftains sent out slave-hunting expeditions. As a consequence, the slave-trading states of the Guinea coast gained power at the expense of their neighbors and spread the web of the slave trade deep into the African interior. The slave hunters sold captives to the Europeans for transportation across the Atlantic. Following the Portuguese in the trade came the Dutch, English, French, and Danes, who eventually established their own trading posts to obtain slaves.

In addition to the economic incentive for slavery, both Christianity and Islam provided a moral justification and legal protection for it. Enslaving others was considered legitimate punishment for unbelievers. Of all the Western religions, only Judaism demonstrated a consistent moral resistance to the slave trade because Jewish identity depended heavily on remembering the biblical account of the enslavement of the ancient Hebrews in Egypt. Notable exceptions were the few Jewish plantation owners in Surinam, who did use slave labor. The problem for Christian and Muslim slavers was that when a slave converted to Christianity or Islam, the pretext for enslavement disappeared. To solve this problem, Christians created a new rationalization by connecting slavery to race. As the African slave trade expanded during the seventeenth and eighteenth centuries, Europeans began to associate slavery with "blackness," which was considered inferior to "whiteness." Among Muslims, the justification for enslavement remained a religious one, and when a slave converted to Islam he or she was, at least theoretically, supposed to be freed.

Due to slavery large parts of the Americas were transformed into outposts of sub-Saharan African cultures. Blacks came to outnumber native Americans and constituted the majority of the colonial population in most of the Caribbean and broad parts of coastal Central America, Venezuela, Guyana, and Brazil. Much of the male population of Angola was transported directly to Brazil, a forced migration that resulted in a dramatic excess of females over males in the most heavily depopulated areas of Angola. During the nearly 400 years of the European slave trade (ca. 1519–1867), about 11 million Africans were shipped to the Americas.

The slave ships that sailed the infamous Middle Passage across the Atlantic were so unhealthy, with Africans "stacked like books on a shelf," that a significant portion of the human cargo died en route. The physical and psychological burdens that slavery placed on its victims can scarcely be imagined, in large part because few slaves were ever allowed to learn to read and write, and thus direct records of their experiences are rare. Documents from ship surgeons, overseers, and slave masters, however, indicate that slaves were subjected to unhealthy living conditions, backbreaking work, and demoralization.

Despite these crushing hardships and even within the harsh confines of white-owned plantations, black slaves created their own institutions, family structures, and cultures.

BIOLOGICAL EXCHANGES How did a few thousand Europeans so easily conquer the civilizations of the Americas, populated by millions of people? After all, the Aztecs, Incas, and others put up a stubborn resistance to the conquistadores, and yet the Europeans triumphed time after time. The answer: epidemics. Along with their gunpowder weapons, the conquistadores' most effective allies were the invisible microbes of Old World diseases, such as smallpox. A native of the Yucatán peninsula recalled the better days before the conquest:

> There was then no sickness; they had no aching bones; they had then no high fever; they had then no smallpox; they had then no burning chest; they had then no abdominal pain; they had then no consumption; they had then no headache. At that time the course of humanity was orderly. The foreigners made it otherwise when they arrived here.[5]

The toll that epidemic disease had on the natives soon after their initial contact with Europeans stunned nearly every chronicler of the New World conquests. Between 1520 and 1600, Mexico suffered 14 major epidemics; Peru suffered 17. By the 1580s the populations of the Caribbean islands, the Antilles, and the lowlands of Mexico and Peru had almost completely died off. Historians estimate the deaths in the tens of millions. The pre-conquest population of Mexico, which has been estimated at about 19 million, dropped in 80 years to 2.5 million. Even the infrequent contacts between European fishermen and fur traders with natives on the coast of what is now Canada led to rapid depopulation.

The most deadly culprit was smallpox, but measles, typhus, scarlet fever, and chicken pox also contributed to the devastation. All of these were dangerous and even life-threatening conditions to Europeans and Africans alike; however, from exposure, people of the Old World had either died young or survived the illness with a resistance to infection from the disease. In contrast, native Americans had never been exposed to

View the Image

Diagram of the Slave Ship Brookes

13.1

13.2

13.3

13.4

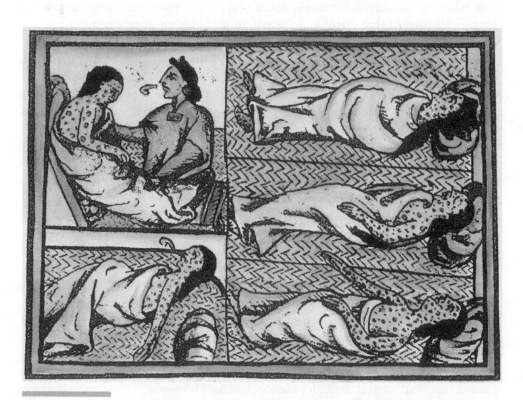

BIOLOGICAL EXCHANGES A medicine man treats dying Aztecs during a smallpox epidemic in Mexico.

Columbian question The debate among historians and epidemiologists about whether syphilis or its ancestor disease originated in the Americas and was brought to the Old World after Columbus's voyages.

Watch the Video

The Columbian Exchange

Read the Document

José de Acosta, The Columbian Exchange (1590)

these diseases and as a population completely lacked immunities to them. As a result, all it took was for one infected person to arrive from the Old World to kill off many millions in the New World. After Cortés's men were first driven from Tenochtitlán, a Dominican friar reported that a new ally appeared: "When the Christians were exhausted from war, God saw fit to send the Indians smallpox, and there was a great pestilence in the city. . . ."[6] The Spaniards' immunity to the very diseases that killed off so many Indians reinforced the impression that the Europeans were favored agents of the gods or gods themselves.

In exchange, the New World gave the Old World syphilis, or at least contemporary Europeans thought so. Historians and epidemiologists have long debated what they call the **Columbian question** about the origins of syphilis. Some argue that syphilis or a venereal disease that might be classified as its ancestor came back from the New World with Columbus's sailors, but others assert that syphilis was widespread in the Old World long before 1492. Scholars still do not know the answer to the Columbian question, but it is true that after 1492 there were epidemic outbreaks of sexually transmitted diseases, leading many to assume an American origin.

The exchange of other forms of life was less obviously disastrous. Following the European settlers came a flood of European animals and plants. With the conquistadores came pigs, cattle, goats, sheep, donkeys, and horses—all previously unknown in the New World. Pigs that escaped from the first Spanish ships to land in Florida were the ancestors of the ubiquitous wild razorback pigs of the southern United States. Vast areas of Mexico and Peru depopulated of humans were repopulated with enormous herds of sheep. The cattle herded by the present-day gauchos of Argentina derive from Iberian stock. The characteristic Latin American burro came from Europe as did the horse, which came to be so prized by the plains Indians of North America. Sheep, cattle, and horses, in particular, completely changed the way of life of the native American peoples.

From Europe came the lucrative plantation crops of sugar, cotton, rice, and indigo, crops that required a large supply of field hands. European varieties of wheat, grapes, and olives soon appeared as major crops in Mexico and elsewhere. In exchange, the Americas offered new crops to the Old World such as tobacco, cocoa, paprika, American cotton, pumpkins, beans, tomatoes, maize (corn), and potatoes. European peasant farmers discovered that maize and the potato provided an attractive substitute for wheat. In many places, the potato replaced wheat as the staple in the diet of the poor. By yielding more calories per acre than wheat or virtually any other traditional grain, the potato made it possible to support more people on a given amount of land. With the spread of the potato as a food source, European populations began to increase rapidly, a trend that created population pressures, which in turn stimulated additional European migrations to the Americas.

THE PROBLEM OF CULTURAL DIVERSITY Before Columbus sailed west, Europeans possessed two systems of thought that seemed to explain everything to them—the Aristotelian and the Christian. The ancient Greek philosopher Aristotle and his commentators provided a systematic explanation of geography and cosmology based on what they knew of the world. They had named the continents, described their peoples, and estimated the size of the globe. Particularly in the European universities, Aristotle was still considered practically infallible, the primary source of all human knowledge. But Aristotle had not even imagined the Americas, and that fact raised the possibility that he was wrong on other matters as well. He knew nothing of the llama, the potato, or syphilis—common knowledge to even the most ignorant conquistador. Aristotle had assumed that the heat of the equatorial zone was so great that no one could live there, but the Spanish had found great civilizations thriving astride the equator. In 1570, when Joseph de Acosta felt a chill in the tropics on his way to America, he observed, "what could I else do then but laugh at Aristotle's Meteors and his Philosophy."[7] Travelers to the New World began to realize that the ancients had not known half the truth about the world.

For Jews and Christians, the Bible remained the unchallenged authority on the origins of the whole world, but the New World created numerous problems for biblical interpretation. The book of Genesis told of the Creation and the great flood, which had destroyed all people and all animals except those saved in Noah's ark. The New World brought into question that vision of a single creation and cleansing flood simply because it could not explain why the plants and animals of the Americas were so different. If the only animals on Earth were those Noah preserved, then why were they different on the two sides of the Earth? About the New World a French writer asked, "How falls it out that the nations of the world, coming all of one father, Noah, do vary so much from one another, both in body and mind?"[8] Thinkers argued either that there must have been more than one creation or that the great flood must not have covered the entire Earth. However, these solutions tacitly recognized that a literal reading of the words of Scripture could not produce a satisfactory account of the history of the world.

The greatest conceptual challenges to Christian Europe were the New World peoples themselves. If these people were not the children of God's Creation, then how did they get there? If they were God's children, then why were they so different from Europeans? In the terms available to sixteenth-century thinkers, there were three possible ways to answer these questions. One was to assume that the native Americans were subhumans, demons, or some strange form of animal life. This answer was the most convenient one to those who sought to exploit the natives. Often with little or no foundation, these Europeans believed that the natives practiced devil worship, incest, sexual promiscuity, polygamy, sodomy, and cannibalism—all signs of their demonic nature. In this extreme form of European belief, the natives did not even possess a human soul and were neither capable of converting to Christianity nor worthy of human rights.

A second answer to why the peoples of the New World were so different sprung from a belief that the natives were complete innocents. The native peoples lived in a kind of earthly Paradise, unspoiled by the corruption of European society. Some of the early English explorers of Virginia found the natives "most gentle, loving and faithful, void of any guile or treason," and one missionary found them "all the more children of God owing to their very lack of capacity and skill."[9] A tiny number of unconventional theological thinkers hypothesized that the native Americans had been created before the Hebrews as reported in the Bible, and, therefore, had not been subject to the Fall of Man and still lived in the earthly Paradise.

The most influential spokesman during the sixteenth century for this idea of native innocence was the powerful advocate of human rights Bartolomé de Las Casas (1474–1566). Throughout his career, Las Casas forcefully argued against the enslavement and ill treatment of the native Americans, which he chronicled in his most important published work, *A Short Account of the Destruction of the Indies* (1542). He saw the natives as innocents who needed to be guided rather than forced to accept Christianity and should not be enslaved. (See *Different Voices* in this chapter.)

The third response to the question of how to explain the New World peoples neither dehumanized them nor assumed them innocent but simply recognized their differences as the natural consequence of human diversity. Advocates of this position proposed toleration. Deciding whether a particular people were bad or good raised questions about the criteria for making such judgments, and these questions introduced the principle of cultural relativism. **Cultural relativism** recognized that many (but not necessarily all) standards of judgment are specific to particular cultures rather than fixed truths established by natural or divine law. Cultural relativists attempt to understand why other people think and act the way they do. Such an approach can be traced to a small group of sixteenth-century European thinkers who tried to make sense of the new discoveries. Perplexed by the cultural diversity he had observed in the New World, Peter Martyr D'Anghiera (1457–1526), a pious priest and astute historian of Spanish explorations, noted that different peoples made judgments on the basis of

View the Image

How the Savages Roast Their Enemies, 1575

View the Image

Spanish Mistreatment of the Indians

cultural relativism A mode of thought first explored during the sixteenth century to explain why the peoples of the New World did not appear in the Bible. Cultural relativism recognized that many (but not necessarily all) standards of judgment are specific to particular cultures rather than the fixed truths established by natural or divine law.

421

Different Voices
Debate over the Treatment of Indians

B *artolomé de las Casas and Juan Ginés de Sepúlveda engaged in a famous debate in Valladolid, Spain, in 1550 over the legitimacy of the Spanish conquest of the Americas. Emperor Charles V organized the debate to determine whether the Indians were capable of self-government. Las Casas had actual experience in the New World, having served as a bishop in Mexico. Lacking any personal experience in the Americas, Sepúlveda relied on the reports of others. Las Casas was shocked by the brutal treatment of the natives and argued the Indians needed protection. Instead of enslaving Indians, Las Casas advocated enslaving Africans, an argument he later regretted. In contrast, Sepúlveda argued the Indians were "natural slaves."*

Bartolomé de las Casas, A Short Account of the Destruction of the Indies (1542)

God made all the peoples of this area, many and varied as they are, as open and as innocent as can be imagined. The simplest people in the world—unassuming, long-suffering, unassertive, and submissive—they are without malice or guile, and are utterly faithful and obedient both to their own native lords and to the Spaniards in whose service they now find themselves. Never quarrelsome or belligerent or boisterous, they harbour no grudges and do not seek to settle old scores; indeed, the notions of revenge, rancour, and hatred are quite foreign to them. . . .

They are innocent and pure in mind and have a lively intelligence, all of which makes them particularly receptive to learning and understanding the truths of our Catholic faith and to being instructed in virtue; indeed, God has invested them with fewer impediments in this regard than any other people on earth. Once they begin to learn of the Christian faith they become so keen to know more, to receive the Sacraments, and to worship God, that the missionaries who instruct them do truly have to be men of exceptional patience and forbearance; and over the years I have time and again met Spanish laymen who have been so struck by the natural goodness that shines through these people that they frequently can be heard to explain: "These would be the most blessed people on earth if only they were given the chance to convert to Christianity."

SOURCE: Bartolomé de las Casas, *A Short Account of the Destruction of the Indies*, edited and translated by Nigel Griffin, copyright 1991 by Nigel Griffin, introduction by Anthony Pagden (Penguin Classics 1992). Trans. and notes copyright © 1992 by Nigel Griffin. Introduction copyright © 1992 by Anthony Pagden. Reproduced by permission of Penguin Books Ltd.

Juan Ginés de Sepúlveda, *The Second Democrates* (1547)

The man rules over the woman, the adult over the child, the father over his children. That is to say, the most powerful and most perfect rule over the weakest and most imperfect. This same relationship exists among men, there being some who by nature are masters and others who by nature are slaves. Those who surpass the rest in prudence and intelligence, although not in physical strength, are by nature the masters. On the other hand, those who are dim-witted and mentally lazy, although they may be physically strong enough to fulfill all the necessary tasks, are by nature slaves. It is just and useful that it be this way. We even see it sanctioned in divine law itself, for it is written in the Book of Proverbs: "He who is stupid will serve the wise man." And so it is with the barbarous and inhumane peoples (the Indians) who have no civil life and peaceful customs. It will always be just and in conformity with natural law that such people submit to the rule of more cultured and humane princes and nations. Thanks to their virtues and the practical wisdom of their laws, the latter can destroy barbarism and educate these (inferior) people to a more humane and virtuous life. And if the latter reject such rule, it can be imposed upon them by force of arms. Such a war will be just according to natural law. . . .

And you must realize that prior to the arrival of the Christians, they did not live in that peaceful kingdom of Saturn (the Golden Age) that the poets imagine, but on the contrary they made war against one another continually and fiercely, with such fury that victory was of no meaning if they did not satiate their monstrous hunger with the flesh of their enemies. . . . These Indians are so cowardly and timid that they could scarcely resist the mere presence of our soldiers. Many times thousands upon thousands of them scattered, fleeing like women before a very few Spaniards, who amounted to fewer than a hundred. . . .

Until now we have not mentioned their impious religion and their abominable sacrifices, in which they worship the Devil as God, to whom they thought of offering no better tribute than human hearts. . . . Interpreting their religion in an ignorant and barbarous manner, they sacrificed human victims by removing the hearts from the chests. They placed these hearts on their abominable altars. With this ritual they believed that they had appeased their gods. They also ate the flesh of the sacrificed men. . . .

War against these barbarians can be justified not only on the basis of their paganism but even more so because of their abominable licentiousness, their prodigious sacrifice of human victims, the extreme harm that they inflicted on innocent persons, their horrible banquets of human flesh, and the impious cult of their idols.

SOURCE: From Pike, Frederick B. *Latin American History: Select Problems,* 1/e. Copyright © 1969 Wadsworth, a part of Cengage Learning, Inc. Reproduced by permission. www.cengage.com/permissions.

For Discussion

1. How did las Casas and Sepúlveda differ in their understanding of the basic nature of the Indians? How did these differing understandings shape their opposing arguments?
2. How reliable are these accounts of the native peoples of the Americas?
3. What was at stake for the definition of the West in these debates?

EXECUTION OF NATIVE AMERICANS In this illustration for one of Bartolomé de Las Casas's books condemning Spanish policy in America, conquistadors assisted by a priest are shown burning an Indian chieftain of Cuba alive. In the background mounted soldiers chase down native Cubans.

different criteria: "The Ethiopian thinks the black color to be fairer than the white, and the white man thinks otherwise. The bearded man supposes he is more comely than he that wants a beard. As appetite therefore moves, not as reason persuades, men run into these vanities, and every province is ruled by its own sense. . . ."[10] What others thought fundamental moral truths, Martyr considered manifestations of superficial cultural differences. The discovery in the New World that non-Christians could lead moral lives, love their families, practice humility and charity, and benefit from highly developed religious institutions shook the complacent sense of European superiority.

CONCLUSION

The Significance of the Global Encounters

The world was forever changed by the European voyages from about 1450 to 1650. The significance of these encounters lay not so much in the Europeans' geographical discoveries as in the scale of permanent contact these voyages made possible among previously isolated peoples of the world. The European voyages of the fifteenth and sixteenth centuries created the global capitalist system.

As a result of the European slaving enterprises on the coast of West and Central Africa, millions of Africans were uprooted, transported in chains to a strange land, and forced to toil in subhuman conditions on plantations. There they grew crops for the increasingly affluent European consumers and generated profits often used to buy more slaves in Africa, parts of which became depopulated in the process. Until well into the nineteenth century, every cup of coffee, every puff of tobacco, every sugar candy, and every cotton dress of indigo blue came from the sweat of a black slave.

Many of the native Americans lost their lives, their land, and their way of life as a result of European encounters. In the Americas, native peoples suffered from the invasion of Old World microbes even more than from the invasion of Old World conquerors. The destruction of the Aztec and Incan Empires were certainly the most dramatic, but everywhere native peoples struggled to adapt to an invasion of foreign beings from a foreign world.

Asia was far less altered by contact with Europeans. The most thorough European conquest in Asia—the Russians in Siberia—was of the least populated region of the entire continent. European civilization remained on the cultural periphery of Asia. But European access to Asian luxury goods remained a crucial component in the expanding global economy that became one of the first fruits of European capitalism.

Coming to terms with the variety of world cultures became a persistent and absorbing problem in Western civilization. Most Europeans retained confidence in the inherent superiority of their civilization, but the realities of the world began to chip away at that confidence, and economic globalization profoundly altered Western civilization itself. Westerners began to confront the problem of understanding "other" cultures and in so doing changed themselves. The West came to mean less a place in Europe than a certain kind of culture that was exported throughout the world through conversion to Christianity, the acquisition of Western languages, and the spread of Western technology.

MAKING CONNECTIONS

1. What motivated the European voyagers and conquistadores to take such great risks?
2. Compare and contrast the European treatment of Africans with that of the natives of the New World.
3. The European global encounters of the fifteenth and sixteenth centuries produced one of the greatest disasters in human history. Agree or disagree. What are your reasons?

TAKING IT FURTHER

For suggested readings, websites, and films, see page R-1.

On MyHistoryLab

Take the Study Plan for Chapter 13,
The West and the World: The Significance
of Global Encounters, 1450–1650,
on MyHistoryLab

Chapter Review

Europeans in Africa

13.1 Why did the European incursions into sub-Saharan Africa lead to the forced migration of Africans to the Americas as slaves?

European travels to the interior of sub-Saharan Africa coincided with the decline of once-strong African kingdoms that were weakened by internal struggles with regional rivals. Europeans soon realized there was a ready supply of gold and slaves, both of which were required to maintain and develop plantation colonies that required agricultural labor.

Europeans in the Americas

13.2 How did the arrival of Europeans in the Americas transform native cultures and life?

When Spanish adventurers seeking fortune and glory began arriving in the Americas, some native peoples completely disappeared due to the resulting conflict and the rampant spread of disease. While many native languages and cultural traditions survived, the institution of Spanish as the language of government and education, and Latin as the language of religion, had a negative effect on the remarkable cultural variety displayed by the peoples of the Americas prior to their contact with Europeans.

Europeans in Asia

13.3 Why was the European encounter with Asian civilizations far less disruptive than those in Africa and the Americas?

Europeans were just one among many trading groups in Asia. In contrast to the Americas, the Asian empires were well equipped to defend themselves against European conquest, and few Europeans settled there since Asia lacked the support of the colonial system of the Americas.

The Beginnings of the Global System

13.4 How was the world tied together in a global biological and economic system?

As a result of the European voyages of the fifteenth and sixteenth centuries, a network of cultural, biological, and economic connections formed along intercontinental trading routes. This system transformed human society by bringing into contact what had previously been separate and isolated regional cultures, biological systems, and local economies.

Chapter Time Line

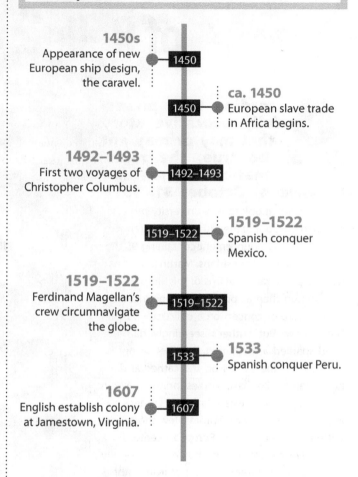

1450s
Appearance of new European ship design, the caravel.
1450

ca. 1450
1450
European slave trade in Africa begins.

1492–1493
First two voyages of Christopher Columbus.
1492–1493

1519–1522
1519–1522
Spanish conquer Mexico.

1519–1522
Ferdinand Magellan's crew circumnavigate the globe.
1519–1522

1533
1533
Spanish conquer Peru.

1607
English establish colony at Jamestown, Virginia.
1607

14 The Reformations of Religion

According to a powerfully evocative story that may or may not be true, the reformation began on **Halloween, October 31, 1517.** An obscure monk-turned-university-professor nailed to the door of the cathedral in Wittenberg, Germany, an announcement containing 95 theses or debating propositions. Martin Luther had no hint of the ramifications of this simple act—as common then as posting an announcement for a lecture or concert on a university bulletin board now. But Luther's seemingly harmless deed sparked a revolution. Whether or not he ever posted the theses on the cathedral door, he certainly did have copies printed. Within weeks, all Germany was ablaze over Luther's daring attack on the pope. Within a few short years Wittenberg became the European center for a movement to reform the Church. As the pope and high churchmen resisted Martin Luther's call for reform, much of Germany and eventually most of northern Europe and Britain broke away from the Catholic Church. The **Protestant Reformation** dominated European affairs from 1517 until 1560.

LEARNING OBJECTIVES

14.1 ((	14.2 ((	14.3 ((	14.4 ((
What caused the religious rebellion that began in German-speaking lands and spread to much of northern Europe?	How did the Lutheran Reformation create a new kind of religious culture?	How and why did Protestant denominations multiply to such an extent in northern Europe and Britain?	How did the Catholic Church respond to the unprecedented threat to its dominance of religious authority in the West?

((Listen to Chapter 14 on MyHistoryLab

Albertus Durerus Noricus
ipsum me propys sic effin
gebam coloribus aetatis
anno XXVIII.

THE IMITATION OF CHRIST In Albrecht Dürer's self-portrait at age 28, he literally shows himself imitating Christ's appearance. The initials AD are prominently displayed in the upper left-hand corner. They stand for Albrecht Dürer, but also for *anno domini*, "the year of our Lord."

SOURCE: Albrecht Dürer, "Self-Portrait." 1500. Oil on panel. 26 1/4" × 19 1/4" (66.7 × 49 cm). Alte Pinakothek, Munich. SCALA/Art Resource, NY.

👁 Watch the Video Series on MyHistoryLab

Learn about some key topics related to this chapter with the *MyHistoryLab Video Series: Key Topics in Western Civilization*

14.1

14.2

14.3

14.4

Martin Luther succeeded because he expressed in print what many felt in their hearts—that the Church was failing in its most fundamental obligation to help Christians achieve salvation. In contrast, many Catholics considered the Protestants dangerous heretics whose errors made salvation impossible. Moreover, for the many Catholics who had long recognized the need for reforms in the Church and been diligently working to achieve them, the intemperate Martin Luther only made matters worse.

The division between Protestants and Catholics split the West into two distinctive religious cultures. The result was that the hard-won unity of the West, which had been achieved during the Middle Ages through the expansion of Christianity to the most distant corners of the European continent and through the leadership of the papacy, was lost. Catholics and Protestants continued to share a great deal of the Christian tradition, but fateful issues divided them: their understanding of salvation, the function of the sacraments in promoting pious behavior, the celebration of the liturgy in Latin, and obedience to the pope.

The fundamental conflict during the Reformation was about religion, but religion can never be entirely separated from politics or society. The competition among the kingdoms and the social tensions within the cities of central and northern Europe magnified religious controversies. The Reformation raised this question:

Protestant Reformation Period that dominated European affairs between 1517 and 1560 when the movement for religious reform begun by Martin Luther led Germany, Britain, and most of northern Europe to break away from the Catholic Church.

How did encounters between Catholics and Protestants permanently transform religious unity into religious division in the West?

Causes of the Reformation

14.1 What caused the religious rebellion that began in German-speaking lands and spread to much of northern Europe?

The Protestant Reformation was the culmination of nearly 200 years of turmoil within the Church. During the fourteenth and fifteenth centuries the contradiction between the Church's divine mission and its obligations in this world hampered its moral influence. On the one hand, the Church taught that its mission was otherworldly, the source of spiritual solace and the guide to eternal salvation. On the other hand, the Church was thoroughly of this world. It owned vast amounts of property, maintained a far-reaching judicial bureaucracy to enforce canon (Church) law, and was headed by the pope, who was also the territorial prince of the Papal State in central Italy. Whereas from the eleventh to the thirteenth centuries the popes had been the source of moral reform and spiritual renewal in the Church, by the fifteenth century the popes had become part of the problem. The problem was not so much that they had become corrupt, but they were unable to respond effectively to the demands of ordinary people who were increasingly concerned with their own salvation and the effective government of their communities.

Three developments, in particular, contributed to the demand for religious reform: the search for the freedom of private religious expression; the print revolution; and the northern Renaissance interest in the Bible and other sources of Christian knowledge.

The Search for Freedom

As we saw in Chapter 11, a series of events during the fourteenth century weakened the authority of the popes and led believers to look elsewhere for spiritual leadership and consolation. Between 1305 and 1378 seven popes in a row abandoned Rome and chose to reside in the relative calm of Avignon, France. The period came to be called the Babylonian Captivity of the Church, a pejorative term that reflected the widespread opinion outside France that the popes had become subservient to the kings of France and were financially corrupt. During the Great Schism (1378–1417), rival Italian and French popes divided the Church and eroded papal authority even further.

While the papacy's moral authority declined, lay Christians were drawn to new forms of worship. Particularly influential was the Modern Devotion, encouraged by the *Imitation of Christ* written about 1441. The Modern Devotion channeled believers' desire to transcend this world of evil and pain by emphasizing frequent private prayer and moral introspection. The *Imitation* provided a kind of spiritual manual that helped laypeople follow the same path toward spiritual renewal that traditionally had been reserved for monks and nuns. The goal was to imitate Christ so thoroughly that Christ entered the believer's soul. In a self-portrait as shown on page 426 influenced by the Modern Devotion, Albrecht Dürer (1471–1528) resembles Christ himself.

The religious fervor that drew many Christians to such profound forms of religious expression further alienated many from the papacy. They began to see the pope as a thieving foreigner who extorted money that could be better spent locally. German communities, in particular, protested against the financial demands and the questionable practices of the pope and higher clergy. Some bishops neglected their duties regarding the spiritual guidance of their flock. Some never resided in their dioceses (the district under the bishop's care), knew nothing of the problems of their people, and were concerned only with retaining their incomes and lavish living standards. Living amid the pleasures of Rome, these high clergymen were in no position to discipline parish priests, some of whom also ignored their moral responsibilities by living openly with concubines and even selling the sacraments. Although immorality of this sort was probably not widespread, a few notorious examples bred enormous resentment among the laity.

In an effort to assert control over the church in their own communities, city officials known as magistrates attempted to stem the financial drain and end clerical abuses. They restricted the amount of property ecclesiastical institutions could own, tried to tax the clergy, made priests subject to the town's courts of law, and eliminated the churchmen's exemption from burdensome duties, such as serving in the town militia or providing labor for public works. On the eve of the Reformation—especially in the cities of Germany and the Netherlands—magistrates had already begun to assert local control over the Church, a tendency that prepared the way for the Protestants' efforts. For many laypeople, the overriding desire was to obtain greater spiritual and fiscal freedom from the Church hierarchy.

The Print Revolution

Until the mid-fifteenth century, the only way in the West to reproduce any kind of text—a short business record or a long philosophical book—was to copy it laboriously by hand. As medieval scribes made copies on parchment, however, they often introduced errors or "improved" the original text as they saw fit. Thus, two different copies of the same text could read differently. Parchment books were also very expensive; a book as long as the Bible might require the skins of 300 sheep to make the parchment sheets and hundreds of hours of labor to copy the text. The high cost meant that books were limited to churchmen and to the very rich. Few Christians ever actually read the Bible simply because Bibles—like all books—were so rare.

Two fifteenth-century inventions revolutionized the availability of books. First, moveable metal type was introduced around 1450; after that time, printed books first began to appear. Perhaps the very first was a Bible printed by Johannes Gutenberg (ca. 1398–1468) in Mainz, Germany. Equally important, cheap manufactured paper replaced expensive sheepskins. These two developments reduced the cost of books to a level that made them available even to artisans of modest incomes.

The demand for inexpensive printed books was astounding. During the first 40 years of print, more books were produced than had been copied by scribes during the previous 1,000 years. By 1500, presses in more than 200 cities and towns had printed six million books. Half of the titles were on religious subjects, and because the publishing industry (then as now) produced only what people wanted to buy, the predominance of religion reveals what was on the minds of the reading public.

The buyers of printed books included, of course, the traditionally literate classes of university students, churchmen, professionals, and aristocratic intellectuals. Remarkably, however, there was also an enormous demand among people for whom books had previously been an unimaginable luxury. During the fourteenth and fifteenth centuries literacy rates had steadily risen, although they varied a great deal across Europe. The knowledge of what was in books, however, spread widely beyond the literate few because reading for most people in the fifteenth and sixteenth centuries was an oral, public activity. In parish churches, taverns, and private houses the literate read books out loud to others for their entertainment and edification.

The expansion of the university system during this period also created more demand for books. Between 1300 and 1500 the number of European universities grew from 20 to 70. The universities also developed a new way of reading. During the fifteenth century the Sorbonne in Paris and Oxford University decreed that libraries were to be quiet places, an indication of the spread of silent reading among the most highly educated classes. Compared with the tradition of reading aloud, silent reading was faster and more private. The silent reader learned more quickly and also decided independently the meaning of what had been read. Once many cheap books were available to the silent readers among the best educated, the interpretation of texts, especially the notoriously difficult text of the Bible, could no longer be easily regulated.

It is difficult to imagine that the Reformation could have succeeded without the print revolution. Print culture radically changed how information was disseminated and gave people new ways to interpret their experiences. Between 1517 and 1520, Martin Luther wrote some 30 tracts, mostly in a riveting colloquial German. Three hundred thousand copies were printed and distributed throughout Europe. No other author's ideas had ever spread so fast to so many.

The Northern Renaissance and the Christian Humanists

As discussed in Chapter 12, the humanists were devoted to rediscovering the lost works of antiquity and imitating the style of the best Greek and Latin authors of the ancient world. As the humanists examined these ancient texts, they developed the study of philology, of how the meanings of words change over time. These endeavors stimulated a new kind of approach to the sources of Christianity. The humanist Lorenzo Valla (ca. 1407–1457), for example, questioned the accuracy of the Vulgate, the Latin translation of the Bible accepted by the Church.

The humanists who specialized in subjecting the Bible to philological study were called the **Christian humanists**. In examining the sources of Christianity, their goal was not to criticize Christianity or the Church but to understand the precise meaning of its founding texts, especially the Bible and the writings of the Church fathers, who wrote in Greek and Latin and commented on the Bible during the early centuries of Christianity. The Christian humanists first sought to correct what they saw as mistakes in interpreting Christian doctrine. Their second goal was to improve morals.

Christian humanists During the fifteenth and sixteenth centuries, these experts in Greek, Latin, and Hebrew subjected the Bible to philological study in an attempt to understand the precise meaning of the founding text of Christianity.

429

northern Renaissance A movement in northern Europe that built on the foundations of the Italian Renaissance, especially to subject the Bible and the sources of Christianity to critical scrutiny.

They believed that the path to personal morality and to Church reform lay in imitating "the primitive church," which meant the practices of Christianity at the time of Jesus and the apostles. Most of the Christian humanists came from northern Europe. They constituted the most influential wing of the **northern Renaissance**, a movement that built on the foundations of the Italian Renaissance. Through their efforts, the Christian humanists brought the foundations of Christianity under intense scrutiny during the early sixteenth century.

Exploiting the potential of the relatively new printing industry, the Dutchman, Desiderius Erasmus (ca. 1469–1536), became the most influential and inspiring of the Christian humanists. During times of war, Erasmus eloquently called for peace. He also

ALBRECHT DÜRER, THE KNIGHT, DEATH, AND THE DEVIL This engraving of 1513 illustrates Erasmus's *Handbook for the Militant Christian* by depicting a knight steadfastly advancing through a frightening landscape. A figure of death holds an hourglass, indicating that the knight's time on Earth is limited. A devil follows behind him threateningly. His valiant horse and loyal dog represent the virtues that a pious Christian must acquire.

SOURCE: Albrecht Dürer, "Knight, Death and the Devil". Engraving. (MM14997 B). The Metropolitan Museum of Art, Harris Brisbane Dick Fund, 1943. (43.106.2)

published a practical manual for helping children develop a sense of morality, and he laid out easy-to-follow guidelines for spiritual renewal in the *Handbook for the Militant Christian*. The artist Albrecht Dürer transformed the theme of that book into a visual allegory shown on page 430. Erasmus's penchant for moral criticism reached the level of high satire in his masterpiece, *The Praise of Folly* (1514). In it he attacked theologians preoccupied by silly questions, such as whether the Resurrection could take place at night; he lampooned corrupt priests who took money from dying men to read the last rites; he ridiculed gullible pilgrims who bought phony relics as tourist souvenirs; and he parodied the vanity of monks who thought the color of their robes more important than helping the poor. Erasmus also translated the Greek New Testament into a new Latin version. His critical studies were the basis of many new translations of the Hebrew and Greek Bible into vernacular languages, including the popular English translation, the King James Bible.

Erasmus's friend, the Englishman Thomas More (1478–1535), is best known for his book *Utopia* (1516). More's little book established the genre of utopian fiction, which described imaginary, idealized worlds. It depicted an imaginary island found in the New World, "Utopia," a double entendre in Greek meaning both "nowhere" and "good place." The Utopians were monotheists who, although not Christians, intuitively understood pure religion and lived a highly regulated life. Utopia represented More's understanding of how a society that imitated the primitive church might appear. In particular he promoted communism based on the passage in Scripture that states believers in Christ "were of one heart and soul, and no one claimed private ownership of any possessions, but everything they owned was held in common" (Acts 4:32). More shared some of Erasmus's ideas about the critical study of Scripture and a purer Church, but unlike Erasmus he was no pacifist.

Erasmus and More remained loyal Catholics. As a chancellor of the English government, More ruthlessly persecuted Protestants. Nevertheless, the work of these two men helped popularize some of the ideas that came to be associated with the Protestant reformers. To them, the test for the legitimacy of any religious practice was twofold. First, could it be found in the Bible? Second, did it promote moral behavior? By focusing attention on the sources of Christianity, the Christian humanists emphasized the deep disparity they perceived between the Christianity of the New Testament and the state of the Church in their own time.

The Lutheran Reformation

14.2 How did the Lutheran Reformation create a new kind of religious culture?

The Protestant Reformation began with the protests of Martin Luther against the pope and certain Church practices. Like Erasmus and More, Luther used the Bible as the litmus test of what the Church should do. If a practice could not be found in the Bible, Luther thought, then it should not be considered Christian. But unlike Erasmus and More, he also introduced theological innovations that made compromise with the papacy impossible.

Luther and his followers, however, would not have succeeded without the support of local political authorities who had their own grievances against the pope and the Holy Roman Emperor, a devout defender of the Catholic faith. The Lutheran Reformation first spread in Germany with the assistance and encouragement of those local authorities—the town magistrates and the territorial princes. Under the sponsorship of princes and kings, Lutheranism spread from Germany into Scandinavia.

Martin Luther and the Break with Rome

Martin Luther (1483–1546) suffered a grim childhood and uneasy relationship with his father, a miner who wanted his son to become a lawyer. During a break from the University of Erfurt, where he was studying law, Luther was thrown from his horse in a storm and nearly died. That frightening experience impelled him to become a monk, a decision that infuriated his father because it meant young Luther abandoned a promising professional career. By becoming a monk, Luther replaced the control of his father with obedience to his superiors in the Augustinian Order. They sent him back to the University of Erfurt for advanced study in theology and then transferred him from the lovely garden city of Erfurt to Wittenberg in Saxony, a scruffy town "on the edge of beyond," as Luther described it. At Wittenberg Luther began to teach at an undistinguished university, far from the intellectual action. Instead of lamenting his isolation, Luther brought the world to his university by making it the center of the religious reform movement.

As a monk, Luther had been haunted by a deep lack of self-worth:

> In the monastery, I did not think about women, or gold, or goods, but my heart trembled, and doubted how God could be gracious to me. Then I fell away from faith, and let myself think nothing less than that I had come under the Wrath of God, whom I must reconcile with my good works.[1]

Obsessed by the fear that no amount of charitable good works, prayers, or religious ceremonies would compensate for God's contempt of him, Luther suffered from anxiety attacks and prolonged periods of depression. He understood his psychic turmoil and shaky faith as any monk would—the temptations of the Devil, who was a very powerful figure for Luther.

Over several years, while preparing and revising his university lectures on St. Paul, Luther gradually worked out a solution to his own spiritual crisis by reexamining the theology of penance. The sacrament of penance provided a way to confess sins and receive absolution for them. If a penitent had lied, for example, he could seek forgiveness for the sin by feeling sorry about it, confessing it to a priest, and receiving a penalty, usually a specified number of prayers. Penance took care of only those penalties the Church could inflict on sinners. God's punishment for sins would take place in Purgatory (a place of temporary suffering for dead souls) and at the Last Judgment. But Catholic theology taught that penance in this world would reduce punishment in the next. In wrestling with the concept of penance, Luther long meditated on the meaning of a difficult passage in St. Paul's epistle to the Romans (1:17): "The just shall live by faith." Luther came to understand this passage to mean that eternal salvation came not from performing the religious good works of penance, but from faith, which was a gift from God. That gift was called "grace" and was completely unmerited. Luther called this process of receiving God's grace **justification by faith** alone, because the ability to have faith in Christ was a sign that one had received God's grace.

Luther's emphasis on justification by faith alone left no room for human free will in obtaining salvation, because Luther believed that faith could come only from God's grace. This did not mean that God controlled every human action, but it did mean that humans could not will to do good. They needed God's help. Those blessed with God's grace would naturally perform good works. This way of thinking about God's grace had a long tradition going back to St. Augustine, the Church father whose work profoundly influenced Luther's own thought. In fact, many Catholic thinkers embraced a similar position, but they did not draw the same conclusions about free will that Luther did. Luther's interpretation of St. Augustine on free will separated Lutheran from Catholic theology. Based on his rejection of free will, Luther condemned all but two of the Church sacraments as vain works that deluded people into thinking they could earn salvation by performing them. He retained communion and baptism because they were

justification by faith Refers to Martin Luther's insight that humanity is incapable of performing enough religious good works to earn eternal salvation. Salvation is an unmerited gift from God called grace. Those who receive grace are called the Elect.

clearly authorized by the Bible, but disputes over the meaning of these two sacraments created divisions within the Protestant Reformation movement itself. Luther and other Protestants, moreover, changed the ceremonies of communion, allowing the laity to partake of the wine, which the Catholics had reserved for priests alone. The woodcut by Lucas Cranach illustrates the Lutheran ritual of communion.

For Luther, this seemingly bleak doctrine of denying the human will to do good was liberating. It freed him from his persistent fears of damnation. He no longer had to worry whether he was doing enough to please God or could muster enough energy to fight the Devil. All he had to do was trust in God's grace. After this breakthrough, Luther reported that "I felt myself to be born anew, and to enter through open gates into paradise itself. From here, the whole face of the Scriptures was altered."[2]

THE 95 THESES In 1517 Luther became embroiled in a controversy that led to his and his followers' separation from the Roman Catholic Church. In order to finance the building of a new St. Peter's Basilica in Rome, Pope Leo X had issued a special new "indulgence," a particular form of penance whereby a sinner could remove years of punishment in Purgatory after death by performing a good work here on Earth. For example, pilgrims to Rome or Jerusalem often received indulgences, concrete measures

COMMUNION IN BOTH KINDS In this woodcut by Lucas Cranach the Elder, Lutheran ministers offer both the communion wine and bread to the laity. Catholics reserved the wine for the priests, which set them apart from the laity. Changes in the rituals of the Eucharist or communion were among the most divisive issues separating Catholic from Protestant.

of the value of their penances. Indulgences formed one of the most intimate bonds between the Church and the laity because they offered a means for the forgiveness of specific sins.

During the fourteenth century popes in need of ready cash had begun to sell indulgences. But Pope Leo's new indulgence went far beyond the promise of earlier indulgences by offering a one-time-only opportunity to escape penalties in Purgatory for all sins. Moreover, the special indulgence could apply not only to the purchaser, but to the dead already in Purgatory. The new indulgence immediately made all other indulgences worthless because it removed all penalties for sin whereas others removed only some.

Frederick the Wise, the Elector of Saxony (a princely title indicating that he was one of those who elected the emperors of the Holy Roman Empire) and the patron of Martin Luther's university, prohibited the sale of Pope Leo's special indulgence in Electoral Saxony, but it was sold just a few miles away from Wittenberg, across the border in the domain of Archbishop Albrecht of Mainz. Albrecht needed the revenues that the sale of indulgences would bring because he was in debt. He had borrowed enormous sums to bribe Pope Leo to allow him to hold simultaneously three ecclesiastical offices—a practice that was against Church law. To help Albrecht repay his debts, the pope allowed Albrecht to keep half of the revenue from the indulgence sale in his territories. Wittenbergers began to trek over the border to Albrecht's lands to listen to the sales pitch of a shameless indulgence hawker, the Dominican John Tetzel (1470–1519). Tetzel staged an ecclesiastical version of a carnival barker's act in which he harangued the crowd about their dead parents who could be immediately released from the flames of Purgatory for the sacrifice of a few coins. He allegedly ended his sermons with the notorious jingle,

As soon as the coin in the coffer rings,
Right then the soul to heaven springs.[3]

A group of the Wittenbergers who heard Tetzel asked Martin Luther for his advice about buying the indulgence. Luther responded less as a pastor offering comforting advice to his flock than as a university professor keen for debate. He prepared in Latin 95 theses—arguments or talking points—about indulgences that he announced he was willing to defend in an academic disputation. Luther had a few copies printed and, as we saw at the beginning of this chapter, probably posted one on the door of Wittenberg Cathedral. The **95 theses** were hardly revolutionary in themselves. They argued a simple point that salvation could not be bought and sold, a proposition that was sound, Catholic theology, and they explicitly accepted the authority of the pope even as they set limits on that authority. On that point, Luther followed what the Church councils of the fifteenth century had decreed. Luther's tone was moderate. He simply suggested that Pope Leo may have been misled in issuing the new indulgence. No one showed up to debate Luther, but someone translated the 95 theses into German and printed them. Within a few weeks, the previously unknown professor from an obscure university was the talk of the German-speaking lands.

The Dominicans counterattacked. Tetzel himself drew up opposing theses, which provoked a public clamor that Luther had tried to avoid. In 1519 at Leipzig before a raucous crowd of university students, Luther finally debated the theses and other issues with Johann Eck, a professor from the University of Ingolstadt. When Eck cleverly backed him into a logical corner, Luther refused to retreat. He insisted that the Bible was the sole guide to human conscience, and he questioned the authority of both popes and councils when they departed from the Bible. This was the very teaching for which earlier heretics had been burned at the stake. At this point Luther had no choice but to abandon his allegiance to the Church to which he had dedicated his life. By this time, Luther also had a large following in Wittenberg and beyond. The core of this group, who called themselves "evangelicals," consisted of university students, younger humanists, and well-educated, reform-minded priests and monks.

95 theses Propositions about indulgences Martin Luther announced he was willing to defend in debate. The publication of the 95 theses in 1517 started the Protestant Reformation.

 Read the Document

Martin Luther's "Ninety-Five Theses," 1517

THE PATH TO THE DIET OF WORMS In the wake of the Leipzig debate, Luther abandoned his moderate tone and launched an inflammatory pamphlet campaign. All were available in Luther's acerbic German prose, which delighted readers. *Freedom of a Christian* (1520) argued that the Church's emphasis on good works had distracted Christians from the only source of salvation—God's grace, which was manifest in the faith of the Christian. It proclaimed the revolutionary doctrine of the **priesthood of all believers**, which reasoned that those of pure faith did not need a priest to stand between them and God, a doctrine that undermined the authority of the Catholic clergy over the laity. The most inspirational pamphlet, *To the Christian Nobility of the German Nation* (1520), called upon the German princes to reform the Church and to defend Germany from exploitation by the corrupt Italians who ran the Church in Rome. When Pope Leo ordered Luther's books burned and demanded Luther retract his writings, Luther responded with a defiant demonstration in which he and his students burned the pope's decree and all of the university library's books of Church law. The die was cast.

The pope demanded that Luther be arrested, but Luther's patron, the Elector Frederick, answered by defending the professor. Frederick refused to make the arrest without first giving Luther a hearing at the Imperial Diet (parliament), which was set to meet at the town of Worms in 1521. Assembled at the Diet of Worms were haughty princes, grave bishops, and the resplendent young emperor Charles V (r. 1519–1558), who was presiding over his first Imperial Diet. The emperor ordered Luther to disavow his writings, but Luther refused to do so. For several days the Diet was in an uproar, divided by friends and foes of Luther's doctrines. Just before he was to be condemned by the emperor, Luther disappeared, and rumors flew that he had been assassinated. For days no one knew the truth. The truth was that Frederick the Wise had kidnapped Luther for his own safety and hid him in the castle at Wartburg, where for nearly a year he labored in quiet seclusion translating Erasmus's version of the New Testament into German. (See *Justice in History* in this chapter.)

The Appeal of Luther's Message

In its early phases the Reformation spread most rapidly among the educated urban classes. During the sixteenth century, 50 of the 65 German imperial cities, at one time or another, officially accepted the Protestant Reformation. Most of the 200 smaller

priesthood of all believers
Martin Luther's doctrine that all those of pure faith were themselves priests, a doctrine that undermined the authority of the Catholic clergy over the laity.

Ego sum Papa.

33. Ego sum Papa! (Ich bin der Papst!)
Anonyme, zeitgenössische Karikatur des lasterhaften Papstes Alexander VI.
Nach einem französischen Holzschnitt

ANTI-CATHOLIC PROPAGANDA This woodcut, titled *I Am the Pope*, satirizes the papacy by depicting Pope Alexander VI as a monster. Alexander was infamous for allegedly conducting orgies in the Vatican. This kind of visual propaganda was an effective way to undermine support for the papacy.

View the **Closer Look**   A Saint at Peace in the Grasp of Temptation

SAINT ANTHONY TORMENTED BY DEMONS This engraving by Martin Schongauer is based on the story of St. Anthony, a pious Christian of the third century, who was assailed by demons in the Egyptian desert as he tried to live his life in isolation and meditation. St. Anthony's serene expression in the face of this violent assault represents the power of Christian faith over adversity and temptation.

German towns with a population of more than 1,000 also experienced some form of the Protestant movement. During the 1520s and 1530s, the magistrates (mayors and other officeholders) of these towns took command of the Reformation movement by seizing control of the local churches. The magistrates implemented Luther's reform of worship, disciplined the clergy, and stopped the drain of revenues to irresponsible bishops and the distant pope.

The German princes of the Holy Roman Empire had their own reasons to resent the power of the Church. They wanted to appoint their own nominees to ecclesiastical offices and to diminish the legal privileges of the clergy. Despite his steadfast

Catholicism, Emperor Charles V was in no position to resist their demands. During most of his reign, Charles faced a two-front war—against France and against the Ottoman Turks. Charles desperately needed the German princes' military assistance. At the first Imperial Diet of Speyer in 1526, Charles allowed the princes to decide whether they would enforce the edict of the Diet of Worms against Luther and his followers. To preserve the empire from external enemies, the emperor was forced to allow its internal division along religious lines.

Luther's message especially appealed to women, and he promoted a "sexual revolution" that was truly transformative for attitudes about marriage. In the early days of the movement, many women felt that Luther's description of "the priesthood of all believers" included them. Women understood Luther's phrase "the freedom of a Christian" as freeing them from the restrictive roles that had traditionally kept them silent and at home. Moreover, Luther and the other major reformers saw positive religious value in the role of wife and mother. Abandoning the Catholic Church's view that celibate monks and nuns were morally superior to married people, Luther declared marriage holy and set an example by taking a wife, the ex-nun Katherina von Bora. In countless popular images of them, Martin and Katherina became the model married couple. Luther encouraged other priests and nuns to marry because he considered celibacy as the work of Satan. The wives of the reformers often became partners in the Reformation, taking particular responsibility for organizing charities and ministering to the poor.

In the early phases of the Reformation, women preached and published on religious matters. These women demanded to be heard in churches and delivered inspiring sermons. Marie Dentière, a former abbess of a French convent who joined the Reformation cause, asked, "Do we have two Gospels, one for men and the other for women? . . . For we [women] ought not, any more than men, hide and bury within the earth that which God has . . . revealed to us women?"[4] Most women were soon disappointed because their preaching and writing threatened the male authorities. In some places laws were passed that prohibited women from discussing religious questions. In England, women were even prevented from reading the Bible aloud to others. The few women who were able to speak and act openly in public were either queens or the wives of prominent reformers. Most women confined their participation in the Reformation to the domestic sphere, where they instructed children, quietly read the Bible, and led prayer circles.

One of the attractions of Protestantism was that it allowed divorce, which was prohibited by Catholic Church law. However, the reform leaders were quite reluctant to grant women the same rights as their husbands in obtaining a divorce. During the early years of the Reformation, there were many marriages in which one spouse followed the old faith and the other the new. But if the woman converted and her husband did not, the Protestant reformers counseled that she should obey her husband even if he forced her to act contrary to God's will. She could pray for his conversion but could not leave or divorce him. Most women were forced to remain married regardless of their feelings. A few exceptional women left their husbands anyway and continued to proclaim their religious convictions to the world. One such woman, Anne Askew from England, was tortured and executed for her beliefs.

THE GERMAN PEASANTS' REVOLT The Reformation also appealed to many peasants because it offered them a simplified religion and, most important, local control of their churches. The peasants of Wendelstein, a typical South German village, had been complaining about the conduct of its priests for some time. In 1523, they hired a "Christian teacher" and told him in no uncertain terms: "We will not recognize you as a lord, but only as a servant of the community. We will command you, not you us, and we order you to preach the gospel and the word of God purely, clearly, and truthfully—without any human teachings—faithfully and conscientiously."[5] These villagers understood the

Justice in History

Here I Stand: LUTHER AT THE DIET OF WORMS

T he Elector Frederick the Wise chose to defend Martin Luther, saving him from arrest and possible execution. Nevertheless, Frederick probably did not fully agree with Luther's positions. He claimed to have never exchanged more than 20 words with Luther. For Frederick, the issue was a matter of law and his own personal authority, not of religion, even though he was a pious man. As Luther's lord and the patron of the University of Wittenberg, Frederick felt the obligation to protect his own subject from outside interference, especially from distant Rome.

Luther's case had already been lost in the papal court of Rome with the issuing of a formal ban against him, but Frederick saw some hope by appealing to the new emperor, Charles V, who would be presiding over the Imperial Diet when it met at the city of Worms. The oath the emperor had taken at his coronation obligated him to follow the letter of the law. Two clauses in the imperial constitution, which was revised for Charles's coronation, applied to the Luther case. One guaranteed that no German could be tried outside of Germany. The other stated that no one could be condemned without just cause and a formal hearing. No matter what the emperor's personal views, as a constitutional monarch he could neither pack Luther off to Rome in chains nor refuse to grant a review of the charges against him.

In addition, the old jurisdictional conflicts between the emperor and the pope, which went back to the Investiture Controversy of the eleventh century (see Chapter 10), prevented Charles from accepting too readily the pope's authority in the case. For the same reason the papal party, led by Rome's representative to the Diet of Worms, Aleander, rejected the very idea that Luther should receive a judicial hearing before the Diet. Aleander argued that Emperor Charles should simply implement the Church's decision to condemn the wayward professor. The inexperienced young emperor faced violently conflicting advice from those for and against Luther, but after considerable deliberation he accepted Frederick's position. Luther deserved a hearing. Martin Luther set off for Worms with the full expectation that he was going to his own execution.

When Luther arrived in Worms in a two-wheeled cart with a few companions, he was met by a huge crowd of 2,000 partisans who accompanied him through the streets. The city of Worms was tense. Posters defending Luther were plastered everywhere, and rough-looking Spanish soldiers swaggered about intimidating Luther's followers. The day after his arrival the imperial marshal brought Luther before the electors, members of the Diet, and the emperor, who declared, "That fellow will never make a heretic of me." Piled on a table in front of the emperor were Luther's books. An official named Eck (but not the same Johann Eck of the Leipzig debate) conducted the interrogation. He asked the monk if the books were his. Luther said they were and that he had written even more. "Do you defend them all, or do you care to reject a part?" To everyone's surprise the combative theology professor asked for more time to think things over.

Late the following afternoon Luther returned and Eck put the question to him again. This time he had an answer: "Most serene emperor, most illustrious princes, most clement lords, if I have not given some of you your proper titles I beg you to forgive me. I am not a courtier, but a monk. You asked me yesterday whether the books were mine and whether I would repudiate them. They are all mine, but as for the second question, they are not all of one sort."

Luther had made a clever distinction, one that gave him the opportunity to make a speech rather than answer simply yes or no. First, he pointed out that some of the books quoted Scripture and dealt with fundamental Christian truths. He could hardly damn himself by repudiating what all Christians held true. A second group of books complained about "the desolation of the Christian world by the evil lives and teaching of the papists." To this provocative statement, the emperor blurted out, "No." Luther went on to decry the "incredible tyranny" to which the papacy had subjected Germany. This appeal to German nationalist sentiment awakened many in the Diet to his cause even if they disagreed with him on doctrinal matters. The

LUTHER BEFORE THE EMPEROR AT THE DIET OF WORMS IN 1521 Luther's courageous stand at the Imperial Diet became one of the most dramatic moments in the Luther story. The young Emperor Charles V is seated on a throne at the left, flanked by the Electors and cardinals. In front of him is a table containing Luther's books. The image captures the episode when Luther was asked whether he would repudiate his books or not.

(continued on next page)

(continued from previous page)

third group of books attacked individuals, and although Luther admitted his attacks may have crossed a line for a university professor, he insisted that he could not repudiate these writings either without encouraging future tyrants. Finally, he declared that if he could be convinced of his errors on the grounds of Scripture he would be the first to throw his books into the flames. Eck, however, was not satisfied and demanded a plain answer, "Do you or do you not repudiate your books and the errors which they contain?"

Luther's recorded reply became one of the great moments in the history of religious liberty: "Since then Your Majesty and your lordships desire a simple reply, I will answer. . . . Unless I am convicted by Scripture and plain reason—I do not accept the authority of popes and councils, for they have contradicted each other—my conscience is captive to the Word of God. I cannot and I will not recant anything, for to go against conscience is neither right nor safe. God help me. Amen." The first printed account of Luther's speech added a final phrase, "Here I stand, I can do no other." Whether he ever spoke it or not, "Here I stand," became the motto of the Lutheran defiance of papal and imperial authority.[6]

The Diet of Worms issued an edict condemning Luther and his writings, making future compromises impossible. Luther himself, however, had managed to ignite the national fervor of the Germans, and it was they who kept Luther and the movement he started alive.

For Discussion

1. What were the legal issues involved in Luther's hearing before the Diet of Worms?
2. Did the law of the empire serve justice in the case of Luther?
3. What did the ruling imply for the future relationship between Church and state on religious questions?

Taking It Further

Bainton, Roland H. *Here I Stand: A Life of Martin Luther.* 1950. Although dated, the book is still useful for an account of the legal issues involved in Luther's trial.

Oberman, Hieko A. *Luther: Man Between God and the Devil.* Translated by Eileen Walliser-Schwarzbart. 1989. Less detailed on the trial than Bainton, it is the best overall biography of the reformer.

Reformation to mean that they could take control of their local church and demand responsible conduct from the minister they hired. However, other peasants understood the Reformation in more radical terms as licensing social reforms that Luther himself never supported. Their enthusiasm for Luther's message took on a strong Apocalyptic character. Luther himself thought that the end of the world, the **Apocalypse** in the language of the Bible, was at hand and that what was depicted in the Bible explained what was happening in his own day. Luther's strong sense of the end times encouraged his peasant followers to seize the moment before Christ's Second Coming to cleanse the world of evil by rebelling against the injustices they faced in their daily lives.

Apocalypse In the language of the Bible, the end times which would lead into Christ's Second Coming.

In June 1524 a seemingly minor event sparked a revolt of peasants in many parts of Germany. When an aristocratic lady demanded that the peasants in her village abandon their grain harvest to gather snails for her, they rebelled and set her castle on fire. Over the next two years, the rebellion spread as peasants rose up against their feudal lords to demand the adoption of Lutheran reforms in the Church, a reduction of feudal privileges, the abolition of serfdom, and the self-government of their communities. Their rebellion was unprecedented. It was the largest and best-organized peasant movement ever in Germany, a measure of the powerful effect of the Protestant reform message. Like the Reformation, the revolt was the culmination of a long period of discontent; however, unlike the Reformation, it was a tragic failure.

These peasants were doing exactly what they thought Luther had advocated when he wrote about the "freedom of the Christian." They interpreted his words to mean complete social as well as religious freedom. However, Luther had not meant anything of the sort. To him, the freedom of the Christian referred to inner, spiritual freedom, not liberation from economic or political bondage. Instead of supporting the rebellion begun in his name, Luther and nearly all the other reformers backed the feudal lords and condemned in uncompromising terms the violence of the peasant armies. In *Against the Thieving, Murderous Hordes of Peasants* (1525), Luther expressed his own fear of the lower classes and revealed that despite his acid-tongued attacks on the pope, he was fundamentally a conservative thinker who was committed to law and order. He urged that the peasants be hunted down and killed like rabid dogs. And so they were. Between 70,000 and 100,000 peasants died, a slaughter

14.1

📖 Read the Document

Swabian Peasants, "The Twelve Articles"

14.2

14.3

14.4

far greater than the Roman persecutions of the early Christians. To the peasants, Luther's conservative position on social and economic issues felt like betrayal, but it enabled the Lutheran Reformation to retain the support of the princes, which was essential for its survival.

Lutheran Success

Soon after the crushing of the Peasants' Revolt, the Lutheran Reformation faced a renewed threat from its Catholic opponents. In 1530 Emperor Charles V bluntly commanded all Lutherans to return to the Catholic fold or face arrest. Enraged, the Lutherans refused to comply. The following year the Protestant princes formed a military alliance, the Schmalkaldic League, against the emperor. Renewed trouble with France and the Turks prevented a military confrontation between the league and the emperor for 15 years, giving the Lutherans enough breathing space to put the Reformation on a firmer basis in Germany by training ministers and educating the laity in the new religion. In the meantime Lutheranism spread beyond Germany into Scandinavia, where it received support from the kings of Denmark and Sweden as it had among the princes of northern Germany.

After freeing himself from foreign wars, Charles V turned his armies against the Protestants. However, in 1552 the Protestant armies defeated him, and Charles was forced to relent. In 1555 the **Religious Peace of Augsburg** established the principle of *cuius regio, eius religio*, which means "he who rules determines the religion of the land." Protestant princes were permitted to retain all church lands seized before 1552 and to enforce Protestant worship, but Catholic princes were also allowed to enforce Catholic worship in their territories. Those who disagreed with their ruler's religion would not be tolerated. Their options were to change religion or to emigrate elsewhere. With the Peace of Augsburg the religious division of the Holy Roman Empire became permanent.

The following year, Emperor Charles, worn out from ceaseless warfare, the anxieties of holding his vast territories together, and nearly 40 years of trying to stamp out Protestantism, abdicated his throne and retired to a monastery, where he died in 1558.

Religious Peace of Augsburg In 1555 this peace between Lutherans and Catholics within the Holy Roman Empire established the principle of *cuius regio, eius religio*, which means "he who rules determines the religion of the land." Protestant princes in the Empire were permitted to retain all Church lands seized before 1552 and to enforce Protestant worship, but Catholic princes were also allowed to enforce Catholic worship in their territories.

The Diversity of Protestantism

> **14.3** How and why did Protestant denominations multiply to such an extent in northern Europe and Britain?

The term *Protestant* originally applied only to the followers of Luther who *protested* the decisions of the second Imperial Diet of Speyer in 1529, which attempted to force them back into the Catholic fold. In time, though, the term came to describe much more than that small group. Protestantism encompassed innumerable churches and sects, all of which refused to accept the pope's authority. Many of these have survived since the Reformation, some disappeared in the violence of the sixteenth century, and others have sprung up since, especially in North America, where Protestantism has thrived.

The varieties of Protestantism can be divided into two types. The first was the product of the **Magisterial Reformation**, which refers to the churches that received official government sanction. These included the Lutheran churches (Germany and Scandinavia); the Reformed and Calvinist churches (Switzerland, Scotland, the Netherlands, and a few places in Germany); and the Anglican Church (England, Wales, parts of Ireland, and later in England's colonies). The second was the product of the **Radical Reformation** and included the movements that failed to gain official recognition and were at best tolerated, at worst persecuted. This strict division into Magisterial and Radical Protestantism broke down in eastern Europe, where the states did not enforce religious conformity (see **Map 14.1**).

Magisterial Reformation Refers to Protestant churches that received official government sanction.

Radical Reformation Refers to Protestant movements that failed to gain official government recognition and were at best tolerated, at worst persecuted, during the sixteenth century.

The Reformation in Switzerland

The independence of Switzerland from the Holy Roman Empire meant that from the beginning of the Reformation local authorities could cooperate with the reformers without opposition from the emperor. The Swiss Confederation bound together 13 fiercely proud regions, called cantons. Except for the leading cities of Zürich, Basel, and Geneva, Switzerland remained an impoverished land of peasants who could not fully support themselves from the barren mountainous land. To supplement their meager incomes, young Swiss men fought as mercenaries in foreign armies, often those of the pope. Each spring, mercenary captains recruited able-bodied Swiss men from the mountain villages. The Swiss men left the women behind to tend the animals and farms. By summer, the villages were emptied of all men except the old and invalid. Each fall at the end of the fighting season, the survivors of that season's campaign trudged home, always bringing bad news to a fresh group of widows. The strain created by the mercenary's life stimulated the desire for sweeping reforms in Switzerland.

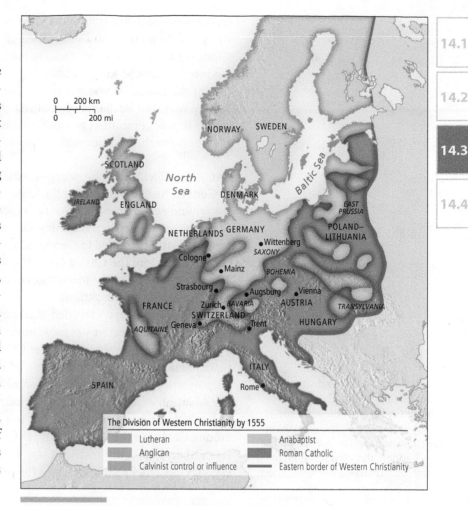

MAP 14.1 THE DIVISION OF WESTERN CHRISTIANITY BY 1555 The West, which had been culturally unified by Christianity for more than 1,000 years, split apart during the sixteenth century. These religious divisions persist to this day. In what parts of Europe did the Protestant Reformation most completely alter the religious makeup of the population?

ZWINGLI'S ZÜRICH Ulrich Zwingli (1484–1531) had served as a chaplain with the Swiss mercenaries under the pope in Italy. In 1520, after being named the People's Priest of Zürich, Zwingli criticized his superior bishop for recruiting local young men to die in the papal armies. That same year he began to call for reform of the Church, advocating the abolition of the Roman Catholic mass, the marriage of priests, and the closing of monasteries. One of the novel features of Zwingli's reform was the strict emphasis on preaching the Word of Scripture during Church services, in contrast with the emphasis on ritual in the traditional Catholic liturgy. Zwingli ordered the removal of all paintings and statues from churches because they distracted parishioners from concentrating on the preaching. The Zwinglian Reformation began independently of the Lutheran Reformation and created a separate reform center from which reform ideas spread throughout Switzerland, southern Germany, and England.

Two features distinguished the Zwinglian from the Lutheran Reformation. One was Zwingli's desire to have reformed ministers participate in governmental decisions. In Lutheran Germany, church and state supported each other, but they remained legally separate, and the prince alone had the authority to determine the religion of the land. In Zürich, the moral Christian and the good citizen were one and the same, and Zwingli worked with the magistrates of the city council, who step-by-step legalized the Reformation and enforced conformity through its police powers.

Luther and Zwingli also differed in their understanding of the nature of the Eucharist, the communion sacrament that reenacted Christ's Last Supper with his apostles. Luther believed that Christ's body was spiritually present in the communion bread. "You will receive," as he put it, "as much as you believe you receive."[7] This emphasis

View the Map

The Swiss Confederation

on the inner, spiritual state of the believer was very characteristic of Luther's introspective piety. In contrast to Luther, Zwingli could not accept the idea of the presence of Almighty God in a humble piece of bread. To Zwingli, the Eucharistic bread was just a symbol that stood for the body of Christ. The problem with the symbolic interpretation of the Eucharist was that the various reformers could not agree with Zwingli on exactly what the Eucharist symbolized. As early as 1524, it became evident that each reformer was committed to a different interpretation, and these different interpretations became the basis for different Protestant churches.

CALVIN'S GENEVA In the next generation the momentum of the Reformation shifted to Geneva, Switzerland, under the leadership of John Calvin (1509–1564). Trained as a lawyer and exiled from his home in France in 1533 for his reformist views, Calvin spent several years wandering, searching for a quiet retreat, and collaborating with other reformers. After he settled in Geneva in 1536, Calvin spent the rest of his life transforming the town into the City of God. The linchpin of the Genevan reform was the close cooperation between the magistrates of the city council and the clergy in enforcing the moral discipline of the citizens.

Calvin's theology extended the insights of Luther and Zwingli to their logical conclusions. This pattern is most obvious in Calvin's understanding of justification by faith. Luther had argued that the Christian could not earn salvation through good works and that faith came only from God. Calvin reasoned that if an all-knowing, all-powerful God knew everything in advance and caused everything to happen, then the salvation of any individual was predetermined or, as Calvin put it, "predestined." Calvin's doctrine of **predestination** was not new. In fact, it had long been discussed among Christian theologians. But for Calvin two considerations made it crucial. First was Calvin's certainty that God was above any influence from humanity. The "majesty of God," as Calvin put it, was the principle from which everything else followed.

predestination The doctrine promoted by John Calvin that since God, the all-knowing and all-powerful being, knew everything in advance and caused everything to happen, then the salvation of any individual was predetermined.

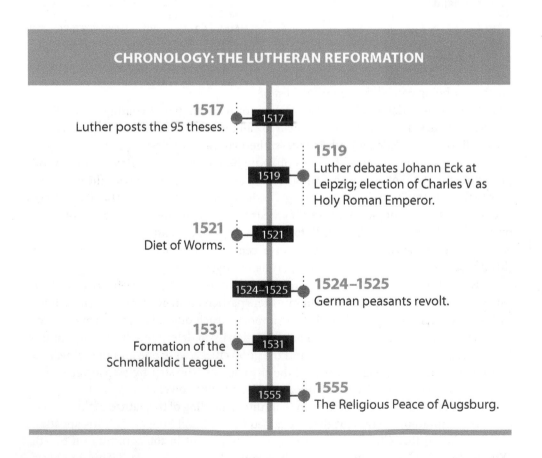

CHRONOLOGY: THE LUTHERAN REFORMATION

1517 Luther posts the 95 theses.

1519 Luther debates Johann Eck at Leipzig; election of Charles V as Holy Roman Emperor.

1521 Diet of Worms.

1524–1525 German peasants revolt.

1531 Formation of the Schmalkaldic League.

1555 The Religious Peace of Augsburg.

Second, Calvin and other preachers had noticed that in a congregation attending a sermon, only a few paid attention to what was preached, while the vast majority seemed unable or unwilling to understand. The reason for this disparity seemed to be that only the Elect, as the Bible decreed, could truly follow God's Word. The Elect were those who had received God's grace and would be saved. The Elect were known only to God, but Calvin's theology encouraged the converted to feel the assurance of salvation and to accept a "calling" from God to perform his will on Earth. God's **calling** gave Calvinists a powerful sense of personal direction, which committed them to a life of moral activity, whether as preacher, wife, or shoemaker.

Calvin composed an elegant theological treatise, the *Institutes of the Christian Religion,* first published in six chapters in 1535 but constantly revised and expanded until it reached 80 chapters in the definitive 1559 edition. Calvin the lawyer wrote a tightly argued and reasoned work, like a trial attorney preparing a case. In Calvin's theology the parts fit neatly together like a vast, intricate puzzle. Calvin's work aspired to be a comprehensive reformed theology that would convince through reasoned deliberation, and it became the first systematic presentation of Protestant doctrine. Whereas Luther spun out his sometimes contradictory ideas in a series of often polemical pamphlets, Calvin devoted himself to perfecting his comprehensive theology of Protestantism. (See *Different Voices* in this chapter.)

Given its emphasis on building a holy community, Calvinism helped transform the nuclear family into a social unit for training and disciplining children. Because women were responsible for educating children, they had to be literate. Calvinist women and men were both disciplined and liberated—disciplined to avoid physical and material pleasures, liberated from the necessity to do good works but guided by God's grace to do them anyway. Calvinism spread far beyond its Swiss home, becoming the dominant form of Protestantism in France, the Netherlands, Scotland, and New England.

calling The Calvinist doctrine that God calls the Elect to perform his will on Earth. God's calling gave Calvinists a powerful sense of personal direction.

ICONOCLASM IN THE NETHERLANDS Protestants sometimes initiated reform by vandalizing churches through acts of iconoclasm—the removing, breaking, or defacing of religious statues, paintings, and symbols such as crucifixes. In this engraving the men on the left of the church haul down statues. Note that one statue is already lying on the ground. On the right side of the church, men are breaking the stained glass windows with clubs. Reformers justified iconoclasm because the money for images could be better spent feeding the poor and because they thought paintings and sculptures distracted parishioners from listening to preaching.

Different Voices

A Catholic Cardinal Challenges John Calvin

In 1539 Cardinal Jacopo Sadoleto wrote a letter to the magistrates and citizens of Geneva inviting them to return to the Catholic Church. A few months later the reformer John Calvin replied to Sadoleto. Although both letters are polemical in tone, they isolate the significant differences between the two faiths. In these excerpts from the two letters, Sadoleto and Calvin show how Catholics and Protestants had a very different understanding of what constituted "the Church."

Sadoleto's Letter to the Genevans, March 18, 1539

The point in dispute is whether is it more expedient for your salvation, and whether you think you will do what is more pleasing to God, by believing and following what the Catholic Church throughout the whole world, now for more than 1,500 years, or (if we require clear and certain recorded notice of the facts) for more than 1,300 years approves with general consent; or innovations introduced within these 25 years, by crafty or, as they think themselves, acute men; but men certainly who are not themselves the Catholic Church? For, to define it briefly, the Catholic Church is that which in all parts, as well as at the present time in every region of the world, united and consenting in Christ, has been always and everywhere directed by the one Spirit of Christ; in which Church no dissension can exist; for all its parts are connected with each other, and breathe together. But should any dissension and strife arise, the great body of the Church indeed remains the same, but an abscess is formed by which some corrupted flesh, being torn off, is separated from the spirit which animates the body, and no longer belongs in substance to the body ecclesiastic. I will not here descend to the discussion of single points, or load your ears with a multitude of words and arguments. . . . [Then he proceeds to do just that] I will say nothing of the Eucharist, in which we worship the most true body of Christ. . . . Nor will I speak of confession of sins to a priest, in which confession that which forms the strongest foundation of our safety, viz., true Christian humility, has both been demonstrated by Scripture, and established and enjoined by the Church; this humility these men have studied calumniously to evade, and presumptuously to cast away. Nor will I say anything either of the prayers of the saints to God for us, or of ours for the dead, though I would fain know what these same men would be at when they despise and deride them. Can they possibly imagine that the soul perishes along with its body? This they certainly seem to insinuate, and they do it still more openly when they strive to procure for themselves a liberty of conduct set loose from all ecclesiastical laws, and a license for their lusts.

Calvin's Reply to Sadoleto, September 1, 1539

You are mistaken in supposing that we desire to lead away the people from that method of worshipping God which the Catholic Church always observed. You either labor under a delusion as to the term *church*, or, at least, knowingly and willingly give it a gloss. I will immediately show the latter to be the case, though it may also be that you are somewhat in error. First, in defining the term, you omit what would have helped you in no small degree to the right understanding of it. When you describe it as that which in all parts, as well as at the present time in every region of the earth, being united and consenting in Christ, has been always and everywhere directed by the one Spirit of Christ, what comes of the Word of the Lord [i.e., the Bible], that clearest of all marks, and which the Lord himself, in pointing out the Church, so often recommends to us? For seeing how dangerous it would be to boast of the Spirit without the Word, He declared that the Church is indeed governed by the Holy Spirit, but in order that that government might not be vague and unstable, He annexed it to the Word. For this reason Christ exclaims that those who are of God hear the Word of God—that His sheep are those which recognize His voice as that of their Shepherd, and any other voice as that of a stranger (John X. 27). For this reason the Spirit, by the mouth of Paul declares (Eph. ii. 20) that the Church is built upon the foundation of the Apostles and Prophets. Also, that the Church is made holy to the Lord, by the washing of water in the Word of life. In short, why is the preaching of the gospel so often styled the kingdom of God, but because it is the scepter by which the heavenly King rules His people?

SOURCE: From *A Reformation Debate:* John Calvin and Jacopo Sadoleto. Ed. by John C. Olin (New York: Fordham University Press, 2000), copyright © 2000, Fordham University Press.

For Discussion

1. How do the definitions of the Church in these two writers differ?
2. What is at stake in the differences between these definitions? In other words, who gains and who loses from the Catholic versus the Calvinist definition?
3. Notice how Sadoleto suggests the Calvinists "imagine the soul perishes along with its body." What does this mean? If true, what would it mean for the Christian notion of eternal salvation?
4. Notice how often Calvin refers to the Word, that is Scripture. What does he achieve by emphasizing Scripture over all other sources of authority?

The Reformation in Britain

Great Britain, as the island kingdom is known today, did not exist in the sixteenth century. The Tudor dynasty, which began in 1485 with Henry VII (see Chapter 12), ruled over England, Wales, and Ireland, but Scotland was still a separate kingdom with its own monarch and church institutions. These countries had distinctive political traditions, cultures, and languages; as a result, their Reformation experiences differed considerably. The Tudors imposed the Reformation as a matter of royal policy, and they were mostly successful in England and Wales. But they hardly made a dent in the religious culture of Ireland, which was a remarkable exception to the European pattern of conformity to the religion of the ruler. There the vast majority of the population remained Catholic. Scotland, also an exception to the rule, wholeheartedly accepted the Protestant Reformation against the will of its Catholic queen and most of the clergy.

THE TUDORS AND THE ENGLISH REFORMATION In 1527 the rotund, self-absorbed, but crafty King Henry VIII (r. 1509–1547) announced that he had come to the pious conclusion that he had gravely sinned by marrying his brother's widow, Catherine of Aragon. By this time the couple had been married for 18 years, their only living child was the princess Mary, and at age 42 Catherine was unlikely to give birth to more children. Henry let it be known that he wanted a son to secure the English throne for the Tudor dynasty. He also had his eye on the most engaging woman of the court, Anne Boleyn, who was less than half Catherine's age. In the past, popes had usually been cooperative when a powerful king needed an annulment, but Pope Clement VII (r. 1523–1534) was in no position to oblige Henry. At the time of the marriage, the papal curia had issued a dispensation for Henry to marry his brother's widow, a practice that is prohibited in the Bible. In effect, Henry was asking the papacy to admit it had made a mistake. In addition, at the moment when Henry's petition for divorce arrived, Clement was under the control of Catherine's nephew, the Emperor Charles V, whose armies had recently captured and sacked the city of Rome. In 1531 Henry gave up trying to obtain papal approval and divorced Catherine anyway. Eighteen months later he secretly married Anne. England's compliant Archbishop Thomas Cranmer (1489–1556) pronounced the marriage to Catherine void and the one to Anne valid. But the marriage to Anne did not last. When she failed to produce a male heir, Henry had her arrested, charged with incest with her brother and adultery with other men. She was convicted and beheaded.

The English separation from the Roman Catholic Church took place in 1534 through the Acts of Supremacy and Succession. The separation has often been understood as a by-product of Henry's capricious lust and the plots of his brilliant minister, Thomas Cromwell (ca. 1485–1540). It is certainly true that Henry's desire to rid himself of Catherine led him to reject papal authority and to establish himself as the head of the Church of England. It is also certainly true that Henry was an inconstant husband: Of his six wives, two were divorced and two beheaded. However, historians do not explain the English Reformation simply as the consequence of royal whim or the machinations of a single minister.

The English Reformation began as a declaration of royal independence from papal supervision rather than an attempt to reform the practices of the Church. Under Henry VIII the English Reformation could be described as Catholicism without the pope. Protestant doctrine, at first, had little role in the English Reformation, and Henry himself had sharply criticized Martin Luther in a treatise probably ghost-written by Thomas More. Royal supremacy established control over the Church by granting to the king supervising authority over liturgical rituals and religious doctrines. Thomas Cromwell, who worked out the practical details for parliamentary legislation, was himself a Protestant, and no doubt his religious views emboldened him to reject papal authority. But the principal theorist of royal supremacy was a Catholic, Thomas Starkey (ca. 1499–1538). A sojourn in Italy had acquainted Starkey with Italian Renaissance political theory, which emphasized concepts of civic liberty. In fact, many English Catholics found royal supremacy acceptable as long as it meant only abandoning submission to the pope in distant Rome. Those who opposed cutting the connection to Rome suffered for their opposition, however. Bishop John Fisher (ca. 1469–1535) and

Read the Document

The Act of Supremacy, 1534

445

Read the Document

Anonymous, "The Execution of Archbishop Cranmer," 1556

Sir Thomas More, the humanist author of *Utopia* and former chancellor of England, were executed for their refusal to go along with the king's decision.

With this display of despotic power, Henry seized personal control of the English church and then closed and confiscated the lands of the monasteries. He redistributed the monastic lands to the nobility in an effort to purchase their support and to make money for the crown. Henry's officials briefly flirted with some Protestant reform but largely avoided theological innovations. On the local level many people embraced the Reformation for their own reasons, often because it gave them a sense of control over the affairs of their community. Others went along simply because the power of the king was too strong to resist.

Henry's six wives bore three surviving children. As each succeeded to the throne, the official religion of England gyrated wildly. Because his youngest child, Edward, was male, Henry designated him successor to the throne. His two daughters, Mary and Elizabeth, were to succeed only if Edward died without an heir, which he did. Only 10 years old when he followed his father to the throne, King Edward VI (r. 1547–1553) was the pawn of his Protestant guardians, some of whom pushed for a more thorough Protestant Reformation in England than Henry had espoused. After Edward's premature death, his half-sister, Queen Mary I (r. 1553–1558), daughter of Henry and Catherine of Aragon, attempted to bring England back to obedience to the pope. Her unpopular marriage to Philip II of Spain and her failure to retain the support of the nobles, who were the foundation of Tudor government, damaged the Catholic cause in England.

Mary's successor and half-sister, Elizabeth Tudor, the daughter of Henry and Anne Boleyn, was an entirely different sort. Queen Elizabeth I (r. 1558–1603), raised as a Protestant, kept her enemies off balance and her quarrelsome subjects firmly in hand with her charisma and shrewd political judgments. Elizabeth became one of the most successful monarchs ever to reign anywhere. Without the considerable talents of Elizabeth, England could easily have fallen into civil war over religion—as the Holy Roman Empire and France did and as England itself did some 40 years after her death.

Between 1559 and 1563, Elizabeth repealed the Catholic legislation of Mary and promulgated her own Protestant laws, collectively known as the Elizabethan Settlement, which established the Church of England, known as the Anglican Church (Episcopalian in the United States). Her principal adviser, William Cecil (1520–1598), implemented the details of the reform through reasonable debate and compromise rather than by insisting on doctrinal purity and rigid conformity. The touchstone of the Elizabethan Settlement was the 39 Articles (finally approved by Parliament in 1571), which articulated a moderate version of Protestantism. It retained the ecclesiastical hierarchy of bishops as well as an essentially Catholic liturgy translated into English.

The Church of England under Elizabeth permitted a wide latitude of beliefs, but it did not tolerate "recusants," those who as a matter of principle refused to attend Church of England services. These were mostly Catholics who set up a secret network of priests to serve their sacramental needs and whom the government considered dangerous agents of foreign powers. Many others were militant Protestants who thought the Elizabethan Settlement did not go far enough in reforming religion. The most vocal and influential of the Protestant dissenters were the Puritans, Calvinists who demanded a church purified of what they thought were remnants of Roman Catholicism.

SCOTLAND: THE CITADEL OF CALVINISM While England groped its way toward moderate Protestantism, neighboring Scotland became one of the most thoroughly Calvinist countries in Europe. In 1560 the parliament of Scotland overthrew Roman Catholicism against the will of Mary Stuart, Queen of Scots (1542–1587). The wife of the French king, Mary was absent in France during the crucial early phases of the Reformation and returned to Scotland only after her husband's death in 1561. Despite her Catholicism, Mary proved remarkably conciliatory toward the Protestants by putting royal funds at the disposal of the new Reformed Kirk (Church) of Scotland. But the Scottish Calvinists never trusted her, and their mistrust would bring about her doom when they rebelled against her and drove her into exile in England. There Queen Elizabeth had her imprisoned and eventually executed because she remained a dangerous symbol for Catholics in England and Scotland.

The Scots Confession of 1560, written by a panel of six reformers, established the new church. John Knox (ca. 1514–1572) breathed a strongly Calvinist air into the church through his many polemical writings and the official liturgy he composed in 1564, the *Book of Common Order*. Knox emphasized faith and individual Christian conscience over ecclesiastical authority. Instead of the episcopal structure in England, which granted bishops the authority over doctrine and discipline, the Scots Kirk established a Presbyterian form of organization, which gave organizational authority to the pastors and elders of the congregations, all of whom had equal rank. As a result the Presbyterian congregations were independent from any central authority.

The Radical Reformation

The magisterial reformers in Germany, Switzerland, England, and Scotland managed to obtain official sanction for their religious reforms, often at the cost of some compromise with governmental authorities. As a result of those compromises, radicals from among their own followers challenged the magisterial reformers and demanded faster, more thorough reform. In most places the radicals represented a small minority, perhaps never more than 2 percent of all Protestants. But their significance outstripped their small numbers, in part because they forced the magisterial reformers to respond to their arguments and because their enemies attempted to eradicate them through extreme violence.

The radicals divided into three categories: Anabaptists, who attempted to construct a holy community on the basis of literal readings of the Bible; Spiritualists, who abandoned all forms of organized religion to allow individuals to follow the inner voice of the Holy Spirit; and Unitarians, who advocated a rational religion that emphasized ethical behavior over ceremonies.

ANABAPTISTS: THE HOLY COMMUNITY For Anabaptists, the Bible was a blueprint for reforming not just the church, but all of society. Because the Bible reported that Jesus was an adult when he was baptized, the Anabaptists rejected infant baptism and adopted adult baptism. (**Anabaptism** means to rebaptize.) An adult, they believed, could accept baptism as an act of faith, unlike an oblivious infant. Anabaptists saw the sacraments of baptism and communion as symbols of faith, which had no purpose or meaning unless the recipient was already a person of faith. Adult baptism reserved for the Elect allowed the creation of a pure church, isolated from the sinfulness of the world.

Because they did not want the Elect to have to compromise with the sinful, Anabaptists advocated the complete separation of church and state. Anabaptists sought to obey only God and completely rejected all established religious and political authorities. They required adherents to refuse to serve in government offices, swear oaths, pay taxes, or serve as soldiers. Anabaptists sought to live in highly disciplined "holy communities," which excommunicated errant members and practiced simple services based on scriptural readings. Because the Anabaptist communities consisted largely of uneducated peasants, artisans, and miners, a dimension of economic radicalism colored the early Anabaptist movement. For example, some Anabaptist radicals advocated the elimination of all private property and the sharing of wealth. On the position of women, however, Anabaptists were staunchly conservative, denying women any public role in religious affairs and insisting that they remain under the strict control of their fathers and husbands. By subordinating women, they thought they were following the Bible, but so did their more egalitarian opponents. Literal readings of the Bible proved slippery.

Anabaptism Meaning "to rebaptize"; refers to those Protestant radicals of the sixteenth century who rejected infant baptism and adopted adult baptism. Anabaptists treated the Bible as a blueprint for reforming not just the Church but all of society, a tendency that led them to reject the authority of the state, to live in self-governing "holy communities," and in some cases to practice a primitive form of communism.

Because the Anabaptists promoted a radical reorganization of society along biblical lines, they provoked a violent reaction. In Zürich, the city council decreed that the appropriate punishment for all Anabaptists was to be drowned in the local river where they had been rebaptizing themselves. By 1529 it became a capital offense in the Holy Roman Empire to be rebaptized; during the sixteenth century perhaps as many as 5,000 Anabaptists were executed for the offense, a persecution that tended to fragment the Anabaptists into isolated, secretive rural communities.

During a brief period in 1534 and 1535, an extremely radical group of Anabaptists managed to seize control of the northern German city of Münster. An immigrant Dutch tailor, John of Leiden, set up a despotic regime in Münster that punished with death any sin, even gossiping or complaining. John of Leiden introduced polygamy and collective ownership of property. He set an example by taking 16 wives, one of whom he beheaded for talking back, stomping on her body in front of the other frightened wives. As the besieging armies closed in, John forced his followers to crown him king and worship him. After his capture, John was subjected to an excruciating torture; as a warning to others, his corpse was displayed for many years hanging in an iron cage.

The surviving Anabaptists abandoned the radicalism of the Münster community and embraced pacifism and nonviolent resistance. However, even these peaceful souls suffered persecution. "God opened the eyes of the governments by the revolt at Münster," as the Protestant reformer Heinrich Bullinger put it, "and thereafter no one would trust even those Anabaptists who claimed to be innocent."[8] A Dutchman, Menno Simons (1496–1561), tirelessly traveled about the Netherlands and Germany, providing solace and guidance to the isolated survivors of the Münster disaster. His followers, the Mennonites, preserved the noblest features of the Anabaptist tradition of quiet resistance to persecution. Both the Mennonites and the Amish in North America are direct descendants of sixteenth- and seventeenth-century Anabaptist groups. Under Mennonite influence, Thomas Helwys founded the first Baptist church in England in 1612. As the leader of the English Baptists, Helwys wrote an unprecedented appeal for the absolute freedom of religion. In it he defended the religious rights of Jews, Muslims, and even atheists as well as all varieties of Christians. For his views he was imprisoned, where he died.

SPIRITUALISTS: THE HOLY INDIVIDUAL Whereas the Anabaptists radicalized the Swiss Reformation's emphasis on building a godly community, the **Spiritualists** radicalized Luther's commitment to personal introspection. Perhaps the greatest Spiritualist was the aristocratic Caspar Schwenckfeld (1490–1561), who was a friend of Luther's until he broke with the reformer over what he considered the weak spirituality of established Lutheranism. Schwenckfeld believed that depraved humanity was incapable of casting off the bonds of sin, which only a supernatural act of God could achieve. An intense conversion experience revealed this separation from sinfulness and granted spiritual illumination to the believer. Schwenckfeld called this illumination the "inner Word," which he understood as a living form of the Scriptures that the hand of God wrote directly on the believer's soul. Schwenckfeld also prized the "outer Word," that is, the Scriptures, but he found the emotional experience of the inner Word more powerful than the intellectual experience that came from reading the Bible. Spiritualists reflected an inner peace evident in their calm physical appearance, lack of anxiety, and mastery of bodily appetites—a state Schwenckfeld called the "castle of peace."

The most prominent example of the Spiritualist tendency in the English-speaking world is the Quakers, who first appeared in England a century after the Lutheran Reformation. The Quakers, or Society of Friends, interpreted the priesthood of all believers to mean that God's spirit, which they called the Light of Christ, was given equally to all men and women. This belief led them to abandon a separately ordained ministry

spiritualists A tendency within Protestantism, especially Lutheranism, to emphasize the power of personal spiritual illumination, called the "inner Word," a living form of the Scriptures written directly on the believer's soul by the hand of God.

and to replace organized worship with meetings in which any man, woman, or child could speak, read Scripture, pray, or sing, as the spirit moved them. The Quakers' belief in the sacredness of all human beings also inclined them toward pacifism and egalitarianism. In no other religious tradition have women played such a prominent role for so long. From the very beginning of the movement, female Friends were prominent in preaching the Quaker gospel. In Quaker marriages, wives were completely equal to their husbands—at least in religious matters.

UNITARIANS: A RATIONALIST APPROACH In the middle of the sixteenth century numerous sects that rejected the divinity of Christ emerged as part of the Radical Reformation. They were called Arians, Socinians, Anti-Trinitarians, or **Unitarians** because of their opposition to the Christian doctrine of the Trinity. Since 325, when the Council of Nicaea established the Trinity as official Christian dogma, Christians had accepted that the one God has three identities: God the Father, God the Son, and God the Holy Spirit. The doctrine of the Trinity made it possible for Christians to believe that at a particular moment in history, God the Son became the human being Jesus Christ. The Church Fathers at Nicaea embraced Trinitarian doctrine in response to Arians who accepted Jesus as a religious leader, but denied that he was fully divine and "co-eternal" with God the Father. During the intellectual tumult of the Reformation, radicals revived various forms of the Arian doctrine. The Italian Faustus Socinus (1539–1604) taught a rationalist interpretation of the Scriptures and argued that Jesus was a divinely inspired man, not God-become-man. Born in Siena, Italy, Socinus's rejection of the doctrine of the Trinity made life dangerous for him in Italy, and he escaped to Poland where he found the freedom to proclaim his views. Socinus's ideas remain central to Unitarianism and form the core theology of the Polish Brethren.

Catholics and magisterial Protestants alike were extremely hostile to Unitarians, who tended to be well-educated humanists and men of letters. Unitarian views thrived in advanced intellectual circles in northern Italy and eastern Europe, but the most famous critic of the Trinity was the brilliant, if eccentric, Spaniard Michael Servetus (1511–1553). Trained as a physician and widely read in the literature of the occult, Servetus published influential Anti-Trinitarian works and daringly sent his provocative works to the major Protestant reformers. Based on a tip from the Calvinists in Geneva, the Catholic inquisitor-general in Lyons, France, arrested Servetus, but he escaped from prison during his trial. While passing through Geneva on his way to refuge in Italy, he was recognized while attending a church service and again imprisoned. Although no law in Geneva allowed capital punishment, Servetus was convicted of heresy and burned alive.

Unitarians A religious reform movement that began in the sixteenth century and rejected the Christian doctrine of the Trinity. Unitarians (also called Arians, Socinians, and Anti-Trinitarians) taught a rationalist interpretation of the Scriptures and argued that Jesus was a divinely inspired man, not God who became a man, as other Christians believed.

The Free World of Eastern Europe

Because eastern Europe offered a measure of religious freedom and toleration unknown elsewhere in sixteenth-century Europe, it attracted refugees from the oppressive princes of western Europe, none of whom tolerated more than one religion in their territories if they could help it. Religious toleration was made possible by the relative weakness of the monarchs in Bohemia, Hungary, Transylvania, and Poland-Lithuania, where the great landowning aristocrats exercised nearly complete freedom on their estates. The Reformation radicalized many aristocrats who dominated the parliaments, enabling Protestantism to take hold even against the wishes of the monarch.

In Bohemia (now in the Czech Republic), the Hussite movement in the fourteenth century had rejected papal authority and some of the sacramental authority of the priesthood long before the Protestant Reformation. After the Lutherans and Calvinists attracted adherents in Bohemia, the few surviving Hussites and the new Protestants formed an alliance in 1575, which made common cause against the Catholics.

In addition to this formal alliance, substantial numbers of Anabaptists found refuge from persecution in Bohemia and lived in complete freedom on the estates of tolerant landlords who were desperate for settlers to farm their lands.

The religious diversity of Hungary was also remarkable by the standards of the time. By the end of the sixteenth century, much of Hungary's population had accepted some form of Protestantism. Among the German-speaking city dwellers and the Hungarian peasants in western Hungary, Lutheranism prevailed, whereas in eastern Hungary Calvinism was dominant.

No other country was as tolerant of religious variety as Transylvania (now in Romania), largely because of the weak monarchy, which could not have enforced religious uniformity even if the king had wanted to do so. In Transylvania, Unitarianism took hold more firmly than anywhere else. In 1572 the tolerant ruler Prince István Báthory (r. 1571–1586) granted the Unitarians complete legal equality to establish their own churches along with Catholics, Lutherans, and Calvinists—the only place in Europe where equality of religions was achieved. Transylvania was also home to significant communities of Jews, Armenian Christians, and Orthodox Christians.

The sixteenth century was the golden age of the Polish-Lithuanian Commonwealth, the largest territorial unit in Europe. From the Lutheran cities in the German-speaking north to the vast open plains of Great Poland, religious lines often paralleled ethnic or class divisions: Calvinism took hold among the independent-minded nobility while the vast majority of peasants remained loyal to Orthodoxy or Catholicism. Nevertheless, the Commonwealth escaped the religious wars that plagued the Holy Roman Empire. King Sigismund August (r. 1548–1572) declared to the deputies in the Polish parliament, "I am not king of your consciences," and inaugurated extensive toleration of Protestant churches. Fleeing persecution in other countries, various Anabaptist groups and Unitarians found refuge in Poland. Jews also began to flock to Poland in the sixteenth century where they would eventually create the largest gathering of Jews in Europe.

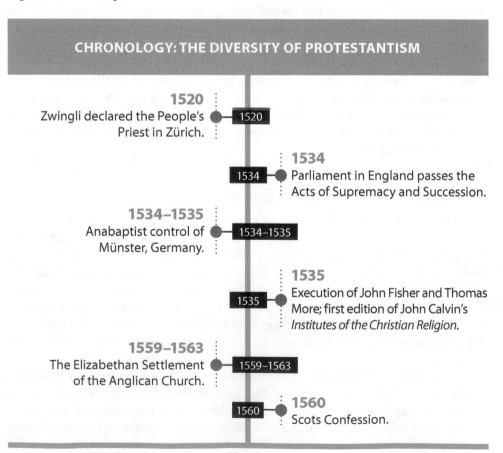

CHRONOLOGY: THE DIVERSITY OF PROTESTANTISM

1520
Zwingli declared the People's Priest in Zürich.
`1520`

`1534`
1534
Parliament in England passes the Acts of Supremacy and Succession.

1534–1535
Anabaptist control of Münster, Germany.
`1534–1535`

`1535`
1535
Execution of John Fisher and Thomas More; first edition of John Calvin's *Institutes of the Christian Religion.*

1559–1563
The Elizabethan Settlement of the Anglican Church.
`1559–1563`

`1560`
1560
Scots Confession.

The Catholic Reformation

14.4 How did the Catholic Church respond to the unprecedented threat to its dominance of religious authority in the West?

The Catholic Reformation, also known as the Counter Reformation, profoundly revitalized the Catholic Church. The **Catholic Reformation** was a series of efforts to purify the Church. These were not just a reaction to the Protestant Reformation but evolved out of late medieval spirituality, driven by many of the same impulses that stimulated the Protestants.

Catholic Reformation A series of efforts during the sixteenth century to purify the Church that evolved out of late medieval spirituality and that included the creation of new religious orders, especially the Society of Jesus.

The Religious Orders in the Catholic Reformation

The new Catholic religious orders of the sixteenth century exhibited a religious vitality that had little to do with the Protestant threat. In fact, none of the new orders began near the centers of Protestantism, such as Germany. Italy, which remained strongly Catholic, produced the largest number of new orders, followed by Spain and France.

JESUITS: THE SOLDIERS OF GOD Officially organized in 1540, the Society of Jesus elected Ignatius Loyola (1491–1556) the first General of the Society. Loyola's dynamic personality and intense spirituality gave the new order its distinctive commitment to moral action in the world. Loyola began his career as a courtier to King Ferdinand of Aragon and a soldier. The Society of Jesus preserved some of the values Loyola had acquired as a courtier-soldier—social refinement, loyalty to authority, sense of duty, and high-minded chivalry.

Loyola's personal contribution to religious literature was the *Spiritual Exercises* (1548), which became the foundation of Jesuit practice. Republished in more than 5,000 editions in hundreds of languages, the *Exercises* prescribe a month-long retreat devoted to a series of meditations in which the participant mentally experiences the spiritual life, physical death, and miraculous resurrection of Christ. Much of the power of the *Exercises* derives from the systematic employment of each of the five senses to produce a defined emotional, spiritual, and even physical response. Participants in the *Exercises* seem to hear the blasphemous cries of the soldiers at Christ's crucifixion, feel the terrible agony of his suffering on the cross, and experience the blinding illumination of his resurrection from the dead. Those who participated in the *Exercises* considered the experience life-transforming and usually made a steadfast commitment to serve the Church. As a result, the Jesuit order grew rapidly. At Loyola's death in 1556 there were about 1,000 Jesuits, but by 1700 there were nearly 20,000, and many young men who wished to join had to be turned away because there were insufficient funds to train them.

The Jesuits, like Franciscans and Dominicans, distinguished themselves from other religious orders by ministering to others. They did not wear clerical clothing, and on foreign missions they devoted themselves to learning the language and culture of the peoples they hoped to convert. Jesuits became famous for their loyalty to the pope, and some took a special fourth vow (in addition to the three traditional vows of poverty, chastity, and obedience) to go on a mission if the pope requested it. Many traveled as missionaries to distant parts of the globe, such as China and Japan. In Europe and the Americas, the Jesuits established a vast network of colleges. These colleges offered free tuition, which made them open to the poor, and combined a thorough training in languages, humanities, and sciences with religious instruction and moral guidance. They became especially popular because the Jesuit fathers were much more likely to pay personal attention to their students than professors in the

Read the Document

Rules for Thinking with the Church (1535), Ignatius Loyola

Watch the Video

The Global Mission of the Jesuits

established universities. In Europe the Jesuit college system transformed the culture of the Catholic elite. These colleges attracted the sons of the aristocrats and the wealthy who absorbed from the Jesuit instructors the values of Renaissance humanism and the Catholic Reformation.

WOMEN'S ORDERS: "AS IF THEY WERE DEAD" Creating a ministry that was active in the world was much more difficult for the female orders than for the Jesuits and the other male orders. Women who sought to reinvigorate old orders or found new ones faced hostility from ecclesiastical and civic authorities, who thought women had to be protected by either a husband or the cloister wall. Women in convents were supposed to be entirely separated from the world, "as if they were dead."

The most famous model for convent reform was provided by Teresa of Avila (1515–1582), who wrote a strict new rule for the Carmelites. The new rule required mortifications of the flesh and complete withdrawal from the world. Teresa described her own mystical experiences in her *Autobiography* (1611) and in the *Interior Castle* (1588), a compelling masterpiece in the literature of mysticism. Teresa advocated a very cautious brand of mysticism, which was checked by regular confession and skepticism about extreme acts of self-deprivation. For example, she recognized that a nun who fell into an apparent rapture after extensive fasting was probably just having hallucinations from the hunger.

Many women who willingly chose the religious life thrived in a community of women where they were liberated from the rigors of childbearing and freed from direct male supervision. These women could devote themselves to cultivating musical or literary talents to a degree that would have been impossible in the outside world. Nuns created their own distinctly female culture, producing a number of learned women and social reformers who had considerable influence in the arts, education, and charitable work such as nursing.

Paul III, The First Catholic Reformation Pope

Despite the many earlier attempts at reform and the Protestant threat, the Catholic Church was slow to initiate its own reforms because of resistance among bishops and cardinals of the Church hierarchy. More than 20 years after Luther's defiant stand at the Diet of Worms in 1521, Pope Paul III (r. 1534–1549) finally launched a systematic counterattack. As a member of the powerful Farnese family, who had long treated church offices as their private property, Paul seemed an unlikely reformer. But more than any other pope, Paul understood the necessity to respond to Protestantism. It was Pope Paul, for example, who formally approved the Jesuits and began to employ them as missionary soldiers for the Church. To counter Protestantism, Pope Paul III also used three other tools: the Roman Inquisition, the *Index of Forbidden Books*, and, most importantly, the Council of Trent.

In 1542, on the advice of an archconservative faction of cardinals, Paul III reorganized the Roman Inquisition, called the Holy Office. The function of the Inquisition was to inquire into the beliefs of all Catholics primarily to discover indications of heresies, such as those of the Protestants. Jews, for example, were exempt from its authority, although Jews who had converted or been forced to convert to Christianity did fall under the jurisdiction of the Inquisition. There had been other inquisitions, but most had been local or national. The Spanish Inquisition was controlled by the Spanish monarchs, for example. In contrast, the Holy Office came under the direct control of the pope and cardinals and termed itself the Universal Roman Inquisition. Its effective authority did not reach beyond northern and central Italy, but it set the tone for the entire Catholic Reformation Church. The Inquisition subjected defendants to lengthy interrogations and stiff penalties, including prison sentences and even execution in exceptional cases.

THE ECSTASY OF ST. TERESA Teresa of Avila eloquently expressed the intimate connection between physical and spiritual experiences that was a common feature of Catholic mysticism. Often afflicted by an intense pain in her side, Teresa reported a vision of an angel who thrust a lance tipped with fire into her heart. This "seraphic vision," which became the subject of Gianlorenzo Bernini's famous sculpture in Santa Maria della Vittoria in Rome (1645–1652), epitomized the Catholic Reformation sensibility of understanding spiritual states through physical feelings. In Teresa's case, her extreme bodily deprivations, paralysis, and intense pain conditioned how she experienced the spiritual side of her nature. Many have seen an erotic character to the vision, which may be true, but the vision best demonstrates a profound psychological awareness that bodily and spiritual sensations cannot be precisely distinguished.

14.1

14.2

14.3

14.4

THE INQUISITION CRITICIZES A WORK OF ART This painting, now called the *Supper in the House of Levi*, originally depicted the Last Supper when Christ introduced the mass to his apostles. Because there are many figures in it who are not mentioned in the biblical account and the supper appears as if it were a Renaissance banquet, the Inquisitors asked the artist, Paolo Veronese, to answer questions about his intended meaning. Ordered to remove the offending figures, Veronese instead changed the name of the painting to depict the less theologically contro-versial supper in the house of Levi.

SOURCE: Paolo Veronese, "The Feast in the House of Levi." 1573. Oil on Canvas. 18'2" × 41' (5.54 × 12.8 m). Galleria dell' Accademia, Venice. SCALA/ Art Resource, NY

A second effort to stop the spread of Protestant ideas led to the *Index of Forbid-den Books,* first drawn up in 1549 in Venice, the capital of the publishing industry in Italy. The *Index* censored or banned many books that the Church considered detrimen-tal to the faith and the authority of the Church. Most affected by the strictures were books about theology and philosophy, but the censors also prohibited or butchered books of moral guidance, such as the works of Erasmus, and classics of literature, such as Giovanni Boccaccio's *The Decameron.* The official papal *Index* of 1559 prohibited translations of the Bible into vernacular languages such as Italian because laypeople required a trained intermediary in the person of a priest to interpret and explain the Bible. The Church's protective attitude about biblical interpretation clearly distinguished the Catholic from the Protestant attitude of encouraging widespread Bible reading. It remained possible to buy certain heretical theological books "under the counter," but possessing such books could be dangerous if agents of the Inquisition conducted a raid.

The Council of Trent

By far the most significant of Pope Paul III's contributions to the Catholic Reformation was his call for a general council of the Church, which began to meet in 1545 in Trent on the border between Italy and Germany. The Council of Trent established principles that guided the Catholic Church for the next 400 years.

Between 1545 and 1563 the council met under the auspices of three different popes in three separate sessions, with long intervals of as much as 10 years between sessions. The objective of these sessions was to find a way to respond to the Protestant criticisms of the Church, to reassert the authority of the pope, and to launch reforms to guarantee a well-educated and honest clergy.

THE DEATH OF THE VIRGIN The Council of Trent enjoined artists to use their art to teach correct doctrine and to move believers to true piety. Religious art had to convey a message simply, directly, and in terms that unlettered viewers could understand. The best Catholic art employed dramatic theatrical effects in lighting and the arrangement of figures to represent deep emotional and spiritual experiences. The Italian painter Caravaggio (1573–1610) most thoroughly expressed the ideal of dramatic spirituality envisioned by the Council. In this image of the death of Virgin Mary, the overhanging drapery evokes a stage curtain as do the lighting effects. The gestures of the apostles and Mary Magdalene imitate those of actors. However, the realism of the scene went too far and got Caravaggio into trouble. The dead Virgin is dressed in red, the color of prostitutes, not her usual blue; in fact, Caravaggio used as his model a dead prostitute who had drowned in the Tiber River. In addition, the realism of the corpse offended many.

The decrees of the Council of Trent, which had the force of legislation for the entire Church, defied the Protestants by refusing to yield any ground on the traditional doctrines of the Church. The decrees confirmed the efficacy of all seven of the traditional sacraments, the reality of Purgatory, and the spiritual value of indulgences. In order to provide better supervision of the Church, bishops were ordered to reside in their dioceses. Trent decreed that every diocese should have a seminary to train priests, providing a practical solution to the problem of clerical ignorance.

The Council of Trent represented a dramatic reassertion of the authority of the papacy, the bishops, and the priesthood. Yet it had no effect whatsoever in luring Protestants back into the Catholic fold.

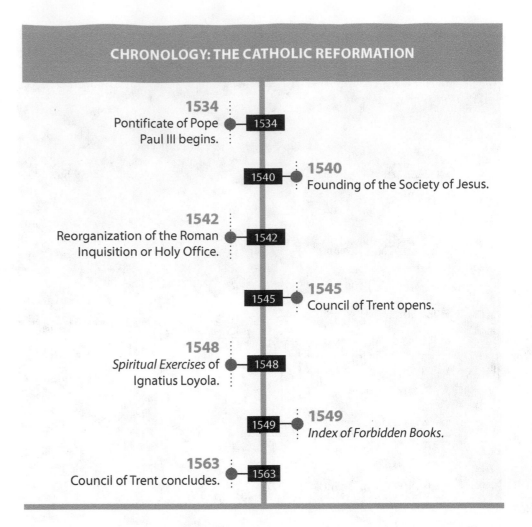

CHRONOLOGY: THE CATHOLIC REFORMATION

1534
Pontificate of Pope
Paul III begins.
1534

1540
1540 Founding of the Society of Jesus.

1542
Reorganization of the Roman
Inquisition or Holy Office.
1542

1545
1545 Council of Trent opens.

1548
Spiritual Exercises of
Ignatius Loyola.
1548

1549
1549 *Index of Forbidden Books.*

1563
Council of Trent concludes.
1563

CONCLUSION

Competing Understandings

The Reformation permanently divided the West into two discordant religious cultures of Protestant and Catholic. The religious unity of the West achieved during the Middle Ages had been the fruit of many centuries of diligent effort by missionaries, monks, popes, and crusading knights. That unity was lost through the conflicts between, on the one hand, reformers, city magistrates, princes, and kings who wanted to control their own affairs and, on the other hand, popes who continued to cling to the medieval concept of the papal monarchy. In the West, Christians no longer saw themselves as dedicated to serving God in the same way as all other Christians. Instead, Catholics and Protestants emphasized their differences.

The differences between these two cultures had lasting implications for how people understood and accepted the authority of the Church and the state, how they conducted their family life, and how they formed their own identities as individuals and as members of a larger community. Chapter 15 will explore all of these themes.

The division also had tragic consequences. From the late sixteenth century to the late seventeenth century, European states tended to create diplomatic alliances along this ideological and religious divide, allowed disputes about doctrine to prevent peaceful reconciliation, and conducted wars as if they were a fulfillment of God's plan. Even after the era of religious warfare ended, Protestant and Catholic cultures remained ingrained in all aspects of life, influencing not just government policy but painting, music, literature, and education. This division reshaped the West into a place of intense religious and ideological conflict, which by the eighteenth century drove many thoughtful people to reject the traditional forms of Christianity altogether and to advocate religious toleration and the separation of Church and state, ideas that were barely conceivable in the sixteenth century.

MAKING CONNECTIONS

1. How did the critical and historical approach of the humanists alter thinking about religion?
2. Compare Catholic and Protestant religious cultures as they were formulated in the sixteenth century.
3. Why did the Protestant Reformation cause so much opposition and even violence?

TAKING IT FURTHER

For suggested readings, websites, and films, see page R-1.

Chapter Review

Causes of the Reformation

14.1 What caused the religious rebellion that began in German-speaking lands and spread to much of northern Europe?

The search for freedom of religious expression, combined with the decline of the pope's moral authority and the perception of the Church as greedy and untrustworthy, was one cause of the religious rebellion. The print revolution was another, as it dramatically changed how quickly information could be disseminated. Finally, the Christian humanists' focus on the original sources of Christianity emphasized the disconnection they perceived between the Christianity of the Bible and the state of the Church in their own time.

The Lutheran Reformation

14.2 How did the Lutheran Reformation create a new kind of religious culture?

Because Luther believed that faith could come only from God's grace, there was no room for human free will in obtaining salvation. Those blessed with God's grace would naturally perform good works, and this interpretation of free will is what separated Lutheran from Catholic theology.

The Diversity of Protestantism

14.3 How and why did Protestant denominations multiply to such an extent in northern Europe and Britain?

In places like Switzerland, which consisted of a population weary of the strain of mercenary life, the idea of religious reform was welcomed. Since the country was independent from the Holy Roman Empire, local authorities were able to cooperate with the reformers. Calvinism was widely adopted in parts of both Switzerland and Scotland; in addition, the reformation in Britain, which began as a declaration of royal independence from the papacy, waxed and waned depending on the king or queen sitting on the throne.

The Catholic Reformation

14.4 How did the Catholic Church respond to the unprecedented threat to its dominance of religious authority in the West?

Pope Paul III formally approved new religious orders like the Jesuits, and encouraged them to act as missionary soldiers for the Church. He also reorganized and strengthened the Roman Inquisition, an organization dedicated to discovering heretics; used the *Index of Forbidden Books* to censor or ban books deemed threatening; and, most importantly, called for the Council of Trent, which established principles that guided the Catholic Church for the next 400 years.

Chapter Time Line

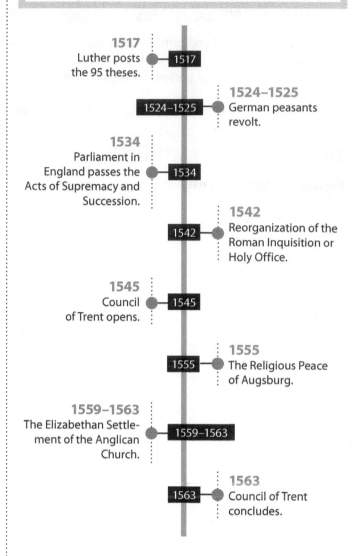

1517
Luther posts the 95 theses. — 1517

1524–1525 — **1524–1525**
German peasants revolt.

1534
Parliament in England passes the Acts of Supremacy and Succession. — 1534

1542 — **1542**
Reorganization of the Roman Inquisition or Holy Office.

1545
Council of Trent opens. — 1545

1555 — **1555**
The Religious Peace of Augsburg.

1559–1563
The Elizabethan Settlement of the Anglican Church. — 1559–1563

1563 — **1563**
Council of Trent concludes.

15 The Age of Confessional Division

O n July 10, 1584, Catholic extremist François Guion, with a brace of pistols hidden under his cloak, surprised William the Silent, the Prince of Orange, as he was leaving the dining hall of his palace and shot him at point-blank range. William led the Protestant nobility in the Netherlands, which was in revolt against the Catholic king of Spain. Guion masqueraded as a Protestant for seven years in order to ingratiate himself with William's party, and before the assassination he consulted three Catholic priests who confirmed the religious merit of his plan. Spain's representative in the Netherlands, the Duke of Parma, had offered a reward of 25,000 crowns to anyone who killed William; at the moment of the assassination four other potential assassins were in Delft trying to gain access to the Prince of Orange.

PROCESSION OF THE CATHOLIC LEAGUE During the last half of the sixteenth century, Catholics and Protestants in France formed armed militias or leagues. Bloody confrontations between these militias led to prolonged civil wars. In this 1590 procession of the French Catholic League, armed monks joined soldiers and common citizens in a demonstration of force.

LEARNING OBJECTIVES

15.1	15.2	15.3	15.4	15.5
How did the expanding population and Price Revolution exacerbate religious and political tensions?	How did religious and political authorities attempt to discipline the people?	Why did people in the sixteenth century think witches were a threat?	How did religious differences provoke violence and start wars?	How did the countries of eastern Europe during the late sixteenth century become enmeshed in the religious controversies that began in western Europe during the early part of the century?

(((Listen to Chapter 15 on MyHistoryLab

Watch the Video Series on MyHistoryLab

Learn about some key topics related to this chapter with the *MyHistoryLab Video Series: Key Topics in Western Civilization*

The murder of William the Silent exemplified an ominous figure in Western civilization—the religiously motivated assassin. There had been many assassinations before the late sixteenth century, but those assassins tended to be spurred by the desire to gain political power or to avenge a personal or family injury. Religion hardly ever supplied a reason. In the wake of the Reformation, however, killing a political leader of the opposing faith to serve God's plan became all too common. The assassination of William illustrated patterns of violence that have since become the *modus operandi* of the political assassin—the use of deception to gain access to the victim, the vulnerability of leaders who wish to mingle with the public, the lethal potential of easily concealed handguns (a new weapon at that time), the corruption of politics through vast sums of money, and the obsessive hostility of religious zealots against their perceived enemies. The widespread acrimony among the varieties of Christian faith created a climate of religious extremism during the late sixteenth and early seventeenth centuries. The extremists made religious toleration virtually impossible.

Religious extremism was just one manifestation of an anxiety that pervaded European society at the time—a fear of hidden forces controlling human events. In an attempt to curb that anxiety, the European monarchs formulated their politics based on the **confessions** of faith, or statements of religious doctrine, peculiar to Catholics or the various forms of Protestantism. During this age of confessional division, European countries polarized along confessional lines, and governments persecuted followers of minority religions, whom they saw as threats to public security. Anxious believers everywhere were consumed with pleasing an angry God; when they tried to find God within themselves, however, many Christians seemed only to find the Devil in others.

The religious controversies of the age of confessional division redefined the West. During the Middle Ages, the West came to be identified with the practice of Roman Catholic Christianity. The Renaissance added to that identity an appreciation of pre-Christian history going back to Greek and Roman Antiquity. The Reformation of the early sixteenth century eroded the unity of Christian Europe by dividing the West into Catholic and Protestant camps. This division was especially pronounced in western Europe, but less so in eastern Europe where weak kingdoms were unable to create confessional states. During the late sixteenth and seventeenth centuries, governments reinforced religious divisions and attempted to unify their peoples around a common set of beliefs.

confessions The formal sixteenth-century statements of religious doctrine: the Confession of Augsburg for Lutherans, the Helvetic Confessions for Calvinists, the Thirty-Nine Articles for Anglicans, and the decrees of the Council of Trent for Catholics.

How did the encounter between the confessions and the state transform Europe into religiously driven camps?

The Peoples of Early Modern Europe

15.1 How did the expanding population and Price Revolution exacerbate religious and political tensions?

During the tenth century if a Rus had wanted to see the sights of Paris—assuming he had even heard of Paris—he could have left Kiev and walked under the shade of trees all the way to France, so extensive were the forests and so sparse the human settlements of northern Europe. By the end of the thirteenth century, the wanderer from Kiev would have needed a hat to protect him on the shadeless journey. Instead of human settlements forming little islands in a sea of forests, the forests were by then islands in a sea of villages and farms, and from almost any church tower the sharp-eyed traveler could have seen other church towers, each marking a nearby village or town. At the end of the thirteenth century, the European continent had become completely settled by a dynamic, growing population, which had cleared the forests for farms.

During the fourteenth century all of that changed. A series of crises—periodic famines, the catastrophic Black Death, and a general economic collapse—left the villages and towns of Europe intact, but a third or more of the population was gone. In that period of desolation, many villages looked like abandoned movie sets, and the cities did not have enough people to fill in the empty spaces between the central market square and the city walls. Fields that had once been put to the plow to feed the hungry children of the thirteenth century were neglected and overrun with bristles and brambles. During the fifteenth century a general European depression and recurrent epidemics kept the population stagnant.

In the sixteenth century the population began to rebound as European agriculture shifted from subsistence to commercial farming. The sudden swell in human numbers brought dramatic and destabilizing consequences that contributed to pervasive anxiety.

The Population Recovery

During a period historical demographers call the "long sixteenth century" (ca. 1480–1640), the population of Europe began to grow consistently again for the first time since the late thirteenth century. As shown in **Figure 15.1**, in 1340 on the brink of the Black Death, Europe had about 74 million inhabitants, or 17 percent of the world's total. By 1400 the population of all of Europe had dropped to 52 million, or 14 percent of the world's total. Over the course of the long sixteenth century, Europe's population grew to 77.9 million, just barely surpassing the pre–Black Death level.

Figure 15.2 depicts some representative population figures for the larger European countries during the sixteenth century. Two important facts emerge from these data. The first is the much greater

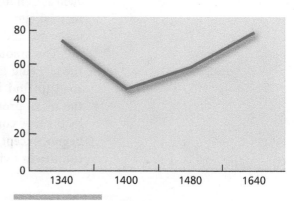

FIGURE **15.1** EUROPEAN POPULATION IN MILLIONS

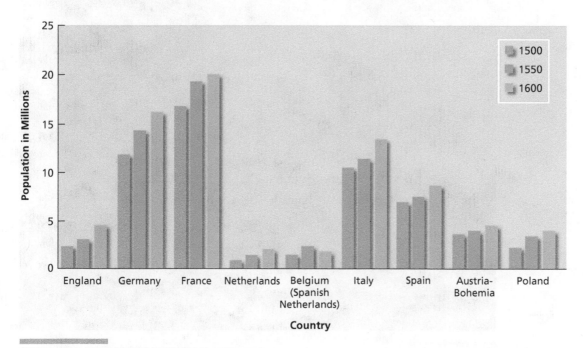

FIGURE **15.2** EUROPEAN POPULATION, 1500–1600

SOURCE: Jan de Vries, "Population," In *Handbook of European History 1400–1600: Late Middle Ages, Renaissance and Reformation*, Vol. 1: *Structures and Assertions* (eds.), Thomas A. Brady, Jr., Heiko A. Oberman, and James D. Tracy (1994), Table 1, 13. Copyright © 1994 by Brill Academic Publishers. Reproduced with permission of Brill Academic Publishers via Copyright Clearance Center.

rate of growth in northern Europe compared with southern Europe. England grew by 83 percent, Poland grew by 76 percent, and even the tiny, war-torn Netherlands gained 58 percent. During the same period Italy grew by only 25 percent and Spain by 19 percent. These trends signal a massive, permanent shift of demographic and economic power from the Mediterranean countries of Italy and Spain to northern, especially northwestern, Europe. The second fact to note from these data is the overwhelming size of France, which was home to about a quarter of Europe's population. Once France recovered from its long wars of religion, its demographic superiority overwhelmed competing countries and made it the dominant power in Europe, permanently eclipsing its chief rival, Spain.

What explains the growth in the population? To a large extent, the transformation from subsistence to commercial agriculture in certain regions of Europe made it possible. Peasants who practiced subsistence farming consumed about 80 percent of everything they raised, and what little was left over went almost entirely to the landlord as feudal dues and to the church as tithing—the obligation to give to God one-tenth of everything earned or produced. Peasant families lived on the edge of existence. During the sixteenth century, subsistence agriculture gave way to commercial crops, especially wheat, which was sold in town markets and the great cities such as London, Antwerp, Amsterdam, Paris, Milan, Venice, and Barcelona. As commercial agriculture spread, the population grew because the rural population was better fed and more prosperous.

The amount of land available, however, could not provide enough work for the growing farm population. As a result, the landless were forced to take to the road to find their fortunes. These vagabonds, as they were called, exemplified the social problems that emerged from the uneven distribution of wealth created by the new commerce. Because large-scale migrations to the Americas had not yet begun, except from Spain, the landless had few options other than to seek opportunities in a city.

THE RISE OF COMMERCIAL AGRICULTURE During the sixteenth century commercial agriculture began to produce significant surpluses for the expanding population of the cities. This scene depicts a windmill for grinding grain and a train of wagons hauling produce from the country to be marketed in a city.

The Thriving Cities

By the 1480s cities began to grow, but the growth was uneven with the most dramatic growth occurring in the cities of the North, especially London, Antwerp, and Amsterdam. The surpluses of the countryside, both human and agricultural, flowed into the cities during the sixteenth century. Compared with even the prosperous rural villages, the cities seemed incomparably rich. Half-starved vagabonds marveled at shops piled high with food (white bread, fancy pies, fruit, casks of wine, roasting meats); they wistfully passed taverns full of drunken, laughing citizens; and they begged for alms in front of magnificent, marble-faced churches.

Every aspect of the cities exhibited dramatic contrasts between the rich and poor, who lived on the same streets and often in different parts of the same houses. Around 1580 Christian missionaries brought a native American chief to the French city of Rouen. Through an interpreter he was asked what impressed him the most about European cities, which were so unlike the villages of North America. He replied that he was astonished that the rag-clad, emaciated men and women who crowded the streets did not grab the plump, well-dressed rich people by the throat.

City officials recognized the social problems caused by the disparities in wealth. Every city maintained storehouses of grain and regulated the price of bread and the size of a loaf so that the poor could be fed. The impulse to feed the poor was less the result of humanitarian motives than fear of a hungry mob. Cities guarded carefully against revolts and crime. Even for petty crime, punishment was swift, sure, and gruesome. The beggar who stole a loaf of bread from a baker's cart had his hand amputated on a chopping block in the market square. A shabbily dressed girl who grabbed a lady's glittering trinket had her nose cut off so that she could never attract a man. A burglar was tortured, drawn, and quartered, with his severed head impaled on an iron spike at the town gate as a warning to others.

However talented or enterprising, new arrivals to the city had very limited opportunities. They could hardly start up their own business because all production was strictly controlled by the guilds, which were associations of merchants or artisans organized to protect their interests. Guilds rigidly regulated their membership and required an apprenticeship of many years. Guilds also prohibited technological innovations, guaranteed certain standards of workmanship, and did not allow branching out into new lines. Given the limited opportunities for new arrivals, immigrant men and women begged on the streets or took charity from the public dole. The men picked up any heavy-labor jobs they could find. Both men and women became servants, a job that paid poorly but at least guaranteed regular meals.

Among the important social achievements of both Protestant and Catholic Reformations were efforts to address the problems of the destitute urban poor, who constituted at least a quarter of the population, even in the best of times. In Catholic countries such as Italy, Spain, southern Germany, and France, there was an enormous expansion of credit banks, which were financed by charitable contributions in order to provide small loans to the poor. Catholic cities established convents for poor young women who were at risk of falling into prostitution and for women who had retired from the sex trade. Catholic and Protestant cities established orphanages, hospitals for the sick, hospices for the dying, and public housing. Both Catholic and Protestant cities attempted to distinguish between the "honest" poor—those who were disabled and truly deserving—and the "dishonest" poor who were thought to be malingerers. Protestant cities established poorhouses, which segregated the poor, subjected them to prisonlike discipline, and forced the able-bodied to work.

The more comfortable classes of the cities enjoyed large palaces and luxurious lifestyles. They hired extensive staffs of servants, feasted on meat and fine wines, and purchased exotic imports such as silk cloth, spices from the East, and, in the Mediterranean cities, slaves from eastern Europe, the Middle East, or Africa. Rich merchants

Price Revolution After a long period of falling or stable prices that stretched back to the fourteenth century, Europe experienced sustained price increases between about 1540 and 1640, causing widespread social and economic turmoil.

maintained their status by marrying within their own class, monopolizing municipal offices, and educating their children in the newly fashionable humanist schools. The wealthy of the cities were the bastions of social stability. They possessed the financial resources and economic skills to protect themselves from the worst consequences of economic instability, especially the corrosive wave of price inflation that struck the West after about 1540.

The Price Revolution

Price inflation became so pervasive during the last half of the sixteenth century that it contributed to the widespread fear that hidden forces controlled events. After a long period of falling or stable prices that stretched back to the fourteenth century, Europe experienced sustained price increases, beginning around 1540, in what historians called the **Price Revolution**. The inflation lasted a century, forcing major economic and social changes that permanently altered the face of Western society. During this period overall prices across Europe multiplied five- or sixfold.

What caused the inflation? The basic principle is simple. The price paid for goods and services is fundamentally the result of the relationship between *supply* and *demand*. If the number of children who need to be fed grows faster than the supply of grain, the price of bread goes up. This happens simply because mothers who can afford it will be willing to pay a higher price to save their children from hunger. If good harvests allow the supply of grain to increase at a greater rate than the demand for bread, then prices go down. Two other factors influence price. One is the *amount of money in circulation.* If the amount of gold or silver available to make coins increases, there is more money in circulation. When more money is circulating, people can buy more things, which creates the same effect as an increase in demand—prices go up. The other factor is called the *velocity of money in circulation,* which refers to the number of times money changes hands to buy things. When people buy commodities with greater frequency, it has the same effect as increasing the amount of money in circulation or of increasing demand—again, prices go up.

The precise combination of these factors in causing the great Price Revolution of the sixteenth century has long been a matter of considerable debate. Most historians would now agree that the primary cause of inflation was population growth, which increased demand for all kinds of basic commodities, such as bread and woolen cloth for clothing. As Europe's population finally began to recover, it meant that more people needed and desired to buy more things. This explanation is most obvious for commodities that people need to survive, such as grain to make bread. These commodities have what economists call *inelastic demand;* that is, consumers do not have a great deal of discretion in purchasing them. Everybody has to eat. The commodities that people could survive without if the price is too high are said to have *elastic demand,* such as dancing shoes and lace collars. In England between 1540 and 1640 overall prices rose by 490 percent. More telling, however, is that the price of grain (inelastic demand) rose by a stunning 670 percent, whereas the price of luxury goods (elastic demand) rose much less, by 204 percent. Thus, inflation hurt the poor, who needed to feed their children, more than the rich, whose desires were more elastic.

Monetary factors also contributed to inflation. The Portuguese brought in significant amounts of gold from Africa, and newly opened mines in central Europe increased the amount of silver by fivefold as early as the 1520s. The discovery in 1545 of the fabulous silver mine of Potosí (in present-day Bolivia) brought to Europe a flood of silver, which Spain used to finance its costly wars. As inflation began to eat away at royal incomes, financially strapped monarchs all across western Europe debased their currency because they believed, mistakenly, that producing more coins containing less silver would buy more. In fact, the minting of more coins meant each coin was worth less and would buy less. In England, for example, debasement was a major source of inflation during the 1540s and 1550s.

The Price Revolution severely weakened governments. Most monarchs derived their incomes from their own private lands and taxes on property. As inflation took hold, property taxes proved dangerously inadequate to cover royal expenses. Even frugal monarchs such as England's Elizabeth I (r. 1558–1603) were forced to take extraordinary measures, in her case to sell off royal lands. Spendthrift monarchs faced disaster. Spain was involved in the costly enterprise of nearly continuous war during the sixteenth century. To pay for the wars, Charles V resorted to a form of deficit financing in which he borrowed money by issuing *juros,* which provided lenders an annuity yielding between 3 and 7 percent on the amount of the principal. By the 1550s, however, the annuity payments of the *juros* consumed half of the royal revenues. Charles's son, Philip II, inherited such an alarming situation that in 1557, the year after he assumed the throne, he was forced to declare bankruptcy. Philip continued to fight expensive wars and borrow wildly, and thus failed to get his financial house in order. He declared bankruptcy again in 1575 and 1596. Philip squandered Spain's wealth, impoverishing his own subjects through burdensome taxes and contributing to inflation by borrowing at high rates of interest and debasing the coinage. Although the greatest military power of the sixteenth century, Spain sowed the seeds of its own decline by fighting on borrowed money.

Probably the most serious consequence of the Price Revolution was that the hidden force of inflation caused widespread human suffering. During the late sixteenth and early seventeenth centuries, people felt their lives threatened, but they did not know the source and so they imagined all kinds of secret powers at work, especially supernatural ones. The suspicion of religious differences created by the Reformation provided handy, if utterly false, explanations for what had gone wrong. Catholics suspected Protestants, Protestants suspected Catholics, both suspected Jews, and they all worried about witches. Authorities sought to relieve this widespread anxiety by looking in all the wrong places—disciplining the populace, hunting for witches, and battling against enemies from the opposite side of the confessional divide.

Disciplining the People

15.2 How did religious and political authorities attempt to discipline the people?

The first generation of the Protestant and Catholic Reformations had been devoted to doctrinal disputes and to either rejecting or defending papal authority. Subsequent generations of reformers faced the formidable task of building the institutions that would firmly establish a Protestant or Catholic religious culture. Leaders of all religious confessions, whether Lutheran, Calvinist, Catholic, or Anglican, attempted to revitalize the Christian community by disciplining nonconformists, enforcing moral rigor, and attacking popular culture. Discipline required cooperation between church and secular authorities, but it was not entirely imposed from above. Many people wholeheartedly cooperated with moral correction and even encouraged reformers to go further. Others actively or resentfully resisted it.

Establishing Confessional Identities

Between 1560 and 1650 religious confessions reshaped European culture. A confession consisted of the adherents to a particular statement of religious doctrine—the Confession of Augsburg for Lutherans, the Helvetic Confessions for Calvinists, the Thirty-Nine Articles for Anglicans, and the decrees of the Council of Trent for Catholics.

The process of establishing confessional identities did not happen overnight. During the second half of the sixteenth century, Lutherans turned from the struggle to survive within the hostile Holy Roman Empire to building Lutheranism wherever it was the chosen religion of the local prince. They had to recruit clergy and provide each clergyman with a university education, which was made possible by scholarship endowments from the Lutheran princes of the empire. Once established, the Lutheran clergy became a branch of the civil bureaucracy, received a government stipend, and enforced the will of the prince. Calvinist states followed a similar process; however, where they were in a minority, as in France, Calvinists had to go it alone, and the state often discriminated against them. In those places confessional identities were established in opposition to the state and the dominant confession. Catholics responded with their own aggressive plan of training new clergymen, educating the laity, and reinforcing the bond between church and state. Just as with the Lutheran princes, Catholic princes in the Holy Roman Empire associated conformity to Catholicism with loyalty to themselves, making religion a pillar of the state.

Everywhere in western Europe (except for Ireland, the Netherlands, a few places in the Holy Roman Empire, and for a time France) the only openly practiced religion was the religion of the state. The eastern European states of Poland, Bohemia, Hungary, and Transylvania offered greater religious freedom.

Regulating the Family

One matter on which Calvinists, Lutherans, and Catholics agreed was that the foundation of society should be the authority fathers had over their families. This principle of patriarchy, as discussed in Chapter 12, was a traditional *ideal*. The *reality* of high mortality from disease, however, destabilized family life during the fifteenth and sixteenth centuries. Unstable families often lacked fathers and senior males, making it difficult if not impossible to sustain patriarchy in daily life. The confessions that emerged from the Reformation attempted to combat this trend by reinforcing patriarchy. According to an anonymous treatise published in 1586 in Calvinist Nassau, the three pillars of Christian society were the church, the state, and the household. This proposition made the father's authority parallel to the authority of the clergy and king. To enforce patriarchy, ecclesiastical and secular authorities regulated sexuality and the behavior of children. The authorities' goal seems to have been to encourage self-discipline as well as respect for elders. Self-discipline reached into all aspects of life from sexual behavior to table manners. (See *Encounters and Transformations* in this chapter.)

Despite the near universal acceptance of the theory of patriarchy, the reality of the father's and husband's authority varied a great deal. Since the early Middle Ages in northwestern Europe—in Britain, Scandinavia, the Netherlands, northern France, and western Germany—couples tended to wait to marry until their mid- or late twenties, well beyond the age of sexual maturity. The couple had to be economically independent before they married, which meant both had to accumulate savings or the husband needed to inherit from his deceased father before he could marry. When they did finally marry, they established their own household separate from either of their parents. Husbands were usually only two or three years older than their wives, and that proximity of age tended to make those relationships more cooperative and less authoritarian than the theory of patriarchy might suggest. By contrast, in southern Europe, men in their late twenties or thirties married teenaged women over whom they exercised authority by virtue of the age difference. In eastern Europe, both spouses married in their teens and resided in one of the parental households for many years, which placed both spouses for extended periods under the authority of one of their fathers.

Justice in History
The *Auto-da-Fé:* THE POWER OF PENANCE

Performed in Spain and Portugal from the sixteenth to eighteenth centuries, the *auto-da-fé* merged the judicial processes of the state with the sacramental rituals of the Catholic Church. An *auto* took place at the end of a judicial investigation conducted by the inquisitors of the Church after the defendants had been found guilty of a sin or crime. The term ***auto-da-fé*** means "act of faith," and the goal was to persuade or force a person who had been judged guilty to repent and confess. Organized through the cooperation of ecclesiastical and secular authorities, *autos-da-fé* brought together an assortment of sinners, criminals, and heretics for a vast public rite that dramatized the essential elements of the sacrament of penance: *contrition,* by which the sinner recognized and felt sorry for the sin; *confession,* which required the sinner to admit the sin to a priest; and *satisfaction* or *punishment,* by which the priest absolved the sinner and enacted some kind of penalty. The *auto-da-fé* transformed penance, especially confession and satisfaction, into a spectacular affirmation of the faith and a manifestation of divine justice.

The *auto* symbolically anticipated the Last Judgment. By suffering bodily pain in this life the soul might be relieved from worse

Auto-da-Fé Lisbon

punishments in the next. Officers of the Inquisition forced the sinners, convicts, and heretics, now considered penitents, to march in a procession that went through the streets of the city from the cathedral to the town hall or place of punishment. These processions would typically include some 30 or 40 penitents, but in moments of crisis they could be far larger. In Toledo in 1486 there were three *autos*—one parading 750 penitents and two displaying some 900 each.

A 1655 *auto* in Córdoba illustrates the symbolic character of the rites. Soldiers carried torches to light the pyre for those to be burnt. Following them in a procession came three bigamists who wore on their heads conical miters or hats painted with representations of their sin, four witches whose miters depicted devils, and three criminals with harnesses around their necks to demonstrate their status as captives. The sinners carried unlit candles to represent their lack of faith. Criminals who had escaped arrest were represented in the procession by effigies made in their likeness; for those who had died before punishment, effigies were carried in their coffins. The marching sinners appeared before their neighbors and fellow citizens stripped of

the normal indicators of status, dressed only in the emblems of their sins. Among them walked a few who wore the infamous *sanbenitos,* a kind of tunic or vest with a yellow strip down the back, and a conical hat painted with flames. These were the *relajados,* the unrepentant or relapsed sinners.

The procession ended in the town square at a platform on which the sinners performed their public penances as on the stage of a theater. Forced to their knees, priests asked the penitents to confess and to plead for readmission into the bosom of the church. For those who did confess, a herald announced the sentence that would rescue them from the pains of Purgatory and the flames of the *auto.* The sentence required them to join a penitential procession for a certain number of Fridays, perform self-flagellation in public, or wear a badge of shame for a prescribed period of time. Those who failed to confess faced a more immediate sentence.

The most horrendous scenes of suffering awaited the *relajados.* If holdouts confessed prior to the reading of the sentence, then the *auto* was a success, a triumph of the Christian faith over its enemies. Therefore, priests attempted everything that they could to elicit confessions, including haranguing, humiliating, and torturing the accused until their stubborn will broke. If the accused finally confessed after the herald read the sentence, then the executioner would strangle them before burning, but if they held out to the very end, the executioner lit the flames while they were still living. From the ecclesiastics' point of view, the refusal to confess was a disaster for the entire Church because the flames of the pyre opened a window into Hell. They would certainly prefer to see the Church's authority acknowledged through confession than to see the power of Satan manifest in such a public fashion.

Eyewitnesses reported that crowds watched the violence of the *autos-da-fé* with silent attention in a mood of deep dread, not so much of the inquisitors, it seems, as for the inevitability of the final day of divine judgment that would arrive for them all. The core assumption of the *auto-da-fé* was that bodily pain could save a soul from damnation. As one contemporary witness put it, the inquisitors removed "through external ritual [the sinners'] internal crimes." Church authorities assumed that the public ritual framework for the sacrament of penance would have a salutary

(continued on next page)

(continued from previous page)

effect on those who witnessed the *auto* by encouraging them to repent before they too faced divine judgment.

For Discussion

1. How did the *auto-da-fé* contribute to the formation of an individual and collective sense of being a Catholic?
2. In the *auto-da-fé*, inflicting physical pain was more than punishment. How was pain understood to have been socially and religiously useful?

Taking It Further

Flynn, Maureen. "Mimesis of the Last Judgment: The Spanish *Auto da fé*," *Sixteenth Century Journal* 22 (1991): 281–297. The best analysis of the religious significance of the *auto-da-fé*.

Flynn, Maureen. "The Spectacle of Suffering in Spanish Streets," In Barbara A. Hanawalt and Kathryn L. Reyerson (eds.), *City and Spectacle in Medieval Europe* (1994). In this fascinating article Flynn analyzes the spiritual value of physical pain.

auto-da-fé Meaning literally a "theater of faith," an *auto* was practiced by the Catholic Church in early modern Spain and Portugal as an extended public ritual of penance designed to cause physical pain among the sinful and promote fear of God's judgment among those who witnessed it.

The marriage pattern in northwestern Europe required prolonged sexual restraint by young men and women until they were economically self-sufficient. In addition to individual self-control, sexual restraint required social control by church and secular authorities. Their efforts seem to have been generally successful. For example, in sixteenth-century Geneva, where the elders were especially wary about sexual sins, the rates of illegitimate births were extremely low. The elders were particularly concerned to discipline women and keep them subservient. In 1584 in another Swiss town, Calvinist elders excommunicated Charlotte Arbaleste and her entire household because she wore her hair in curls, which the elders thought were too alluring.

Northwestern European families also tended to be smaller, as married couples began to space their children through birth control and family planning. These self-restrained couples practiced withdrawal, the rhythm method, or abstinence. When mothers no longer relied on wet nurses and nursed their own infants, often for long periods, they also reduced their chances of becoming pregnant. Thus, limiting family size became the social norm in northwestern Europe, especially among the educated and urban middle classes. Protestant families tended to have fewer children than Catholic families, but Catholics in this region also practiced some form of birth control, even though Church law prohibited all forms except abstinence.

The moral status of marriage also demonstrated regional variations during the early modern period. Protestants no longer considered husbands and wives morally inferior to celibate monks and nuns, and the wives of preachers in Protestant communities certainly had a respected social role never granted to the concubines of priests. But the favorable Protestant attitude toward marriage did not necessarily translate into a positive attitude toward women. In Germany the numerous books of advice, called the Father of the House literature, encouraged families to subordinate the individual interests of servants, children, and the mother to the dictates of the father, who was advised to be fair but must always be obeyed. Even if a wife was brutally treated by her husband, she could neither find help from authorities nor expect a divorce.

THE DOMESTIC IDEAL During the late sixteenth and seventeenth centuries, idealized depictions of harmonious family life became very popular, especially in the Netherlands. This painting by Pieter De Hooch is a prime example of the simple pleasures of domesticity. A young child helps her mother who is peeling apples next to the warm fireplace.

Encounters and Transformations
The Introduction of the Table Fork:
THE NEW SIGN OF WESTERN CIVILIZATION

Sometime in the sixteenth century, western Europeans encountered a new tool that initiated a profound and lasting transformation in Western society: the table fork. Before the table fork, people dined in a way that, to our modern sensibilities, seems disgusting. Members of the upper classes indulged themselves by devouring meat in enormous quantities. Whole rabbits, lambs, and pigs roasted on a spit were placed before diners. A quarter of veal or venison or even an entire roast beef, complete with its head, might be heaved onto the table. Diners used knives to cut off a piece of meat that they then ate with their hands, allowing the juices to drip down their arms. They used the long sleeves of their shirts to wipe meat juices, sweat, and spittle from their mouths and faces. These banquets celebrated the direct physical contact between the body of the dead animal and the bodies of the diners themselves who touched, handled, chewed, and swallowed it.

During the sixteenth century, puritanical reformers who were trying to abolish the cruder aspects of popular culture also promoted new table manners. New implements made certain that diners did not come into direct physical contact with their food before they placed it in their mouths. In addition to napkins—which came into widespread use to replace shirt sleeves for wiping the mouth—table forks appeared on upper-class tables. It became impolite to transfer food directly from the common serving plate to the mouth. Food first had to go onto each individual's plate and then be cut into small portions and raised to the mouth. A French treatise of 1672 warned that "meat must never be touched . . . by hand, not even while eating."[1]

This prohibition had nothing to do with cleanliness because bacteria were not discovered until the end of the nineteenth century. The use of the table fork had more to do with civility than hygiene. Certain foods, such as bread or many fruits such as cherries, were and still are always eaten with the hands. In determining when to use a fork it was not cleanliness that mattered, but the kind of food consumed. Forks enabled sixteenth-century diners to avoid their growing sense of discomfort with the textures and juices of meats that reminded them of an animal's flesh and blood.

Forks, then, enabled cultured people to distance themselves from the dead animal that they were eating. More generally, the spreading use of the fork was part of a set of changes linked to growing revulsion with the more physical aspects of human nature, such as reproduction—or the killing and consumption of animals. Just as sixteenth-century church authorities sought to regulate sexuality, so table manners regulated meat eating.

THE INTRODUCTION OF THE TABLE FORK During the late sixteenth century the refinement of manners among the upper classes focused on dining. No innovation was more revolutionary than the spread of the use of the table fork. Pictured here is the travel cutlery, including two table forks, of Queen Elizabeth I.

Paradoxically, the civility that resulted from the use of the table fork both created and eroded social divisions. Eating meat with a fork became one more way for those in the upper social ranks to distinguish themselves from the "uncivilized" masses below. Yet everyone—regardless of their social origins—could learn how to use a fork. A clerk or governess could disguise a humble background simply by learning how to eat properly. Gradually—very gradually—behavior replaced birth as a marker of "good breeding." In the end, the transformations that occurred in Western society because of its encounter with the table fork—the blurring of class distinctions and creation of a universal code of manners—were so gradual and subtle that few of us who use a table fork daily are even aware of its profound significance.

For Discussion

How do manners, both good and bad, communicate messages to other people? Why is it important to have good manners?

Discipline also played a large role in raising children. The *Disquisition on the Spiritual Condition of Infants* (1618) pointed out that because of original sin, babies were naturally evil. The godly responsibility of the father was to break the will of his evil offspring, taming them so that they could be turned away from sin toward virtue. The very title of a 1591 Calvinist treatise revealed the strength of the evil-child argument: *On Disciplining Children: How the Disobedient, Evil, and Corrupted Youth of These Anxious Last Days Can Be Bettered.* The treatise advised that the mother's role should be limited to her biological function of giving birth. In order to break the will of their infants, mothers were encouraged to wean them early and turn them over for a strict upbringing by their fathers. It directed fathers to be vigilant so that their wives did not corrupt the children, because women "love to accept strange, false beliefs, and go about with benedictions and witches' handiwork."[2]

Hunting Witches

15.3 Why did people in the sixteenth century think witches were a threat?

witch-hunt Refers to the dramatic increase in the judicial prosecution of alleged witches in either Church or secular courts from the middle of the sixteenth to the middle of the seventeenth centuries.

magic Learned opinion described two kinds of magic: natural magic, which involved the manipulation of occult forces believed to exist in nature, and demonic magic, which called upon evil spirits to gain access to power. It was widely accepted as a reality until the middle of the seventeenth century.

The most catastrophic manifestation of the widespread anxiety of the late sixteenth and seventeenth centuries was the great **witch-hunt**. The judicial prosecution of alleged witches in either Church or secular courts dramatically increased about the middle of the sixteenth century and lasted until the late seventeenth, when the number of witchcraft trials rapidly diminished and stopped entirely in most of Europe.

Throughout this period, people accepted the reality of two kinds of **magic**. The first kind was natural magic, such as the practice of alchemy or astrology, which involved the manipulation of occult forces believed to exist in nature. The fundamental assumption of natural magic was that everything in nature is alive. The trained magician could coerce the occult forces in nature to do his bidding. During the Renaissance many humanists and scientific thinkers were drawn to natural magic because of its promise of power over nature. Natural magic, in fact, had some practical uses. Alchemists, for example, devoted themselves to discovering what they called the "philosopher's stone," the secret of transmuting base metals into gold. In practice this meant that they learned how to imitate the appearance of gold, a very useful skill for counterfeiting coins or reducing the content of precious metals in legal coins. Natural magic did not imply any kind of contact with devils. Most practitioners of natural magic desired to achieve good, and many considered it the highest form of curative medicine.

Many people of the sixteenth and seventeenth centuries also believed in a second kind of magic—demonic magic. The practitioner of this kind of magic—usually but not always a female witch—called upon evil spirits to gain access to power. Demonic magic was generally understood as a way to work harm by ritual means. Belief in the reality of harmful magic can be found in the Bible and had been widespread for centuries, but only in the fifteenth century did ecclesiastical and secular authorities, convinced that large groups of people were engaging in such heretical practices, prosecute them in large numbers. By the sixteenth century the Protestants' literal readings of the Bible and the disorienting conflicts of the Reformation contributed to fears about witches.

People in many different places—from shepherds in the mountains of Switzerland to Calvinist ministers in the lowlands of Scotland—thought they perceived the work of witches in human and natural events. The alleged practice of witchcraft took two forms: *maleficia* (doing harm by magical means) and *diabolism* (worshiping the devil).

There were many kinds of *maleficia,* including coercing an unwilling lover by sprinkling dried menstrual blood in his food, sickening a pig by cursing it, burning a barn after marking it with a hex sign, bringing wasting diarrhea to a child by reciting a spell, and killing an enemy by stabbing a wax statue of him.

Midwives and women who specialized in healing were especially vulnerable to accusations of witchcraft. The intention behind a particular action they might have performed was often obscure, making it difficult to distinguish between magic designed to bring beneficial results, such as the cure of a child, and *maleficia* designed to bring harmful ones. With the high infant mortality rates of the sixteenth and seventeenth centuries, performing magical rituals for a sick baby could be very risky. The logic of witchcraft beliefs implied that a bad ending must have been caused by bad intentions.

While some people certainly attempted to practice *maleficia,* the second and far more serious kind of ritual practice associated with demonic magic, diabolism, certainly never took place. The theory behind diabolism was that the alleged witch made a pact with the Devil, by which she received her magical power, and worshiped him as her god.

The most influential witchcraft treatise, *The Hammer of Witches* (1486), had an extensive discussion of the ceremony of the pact. After the prospective witch had declared her intention to enter his service, Satan appeared to her, often in the alluring form of a handsome young man who offered her rewards, including a demonic lover, called an *incubus.* To obtain these inducements, the witch was obligated to renounce her allegiance to Christ, usually signified by stomping on the cross. The Devil then rebaptized the witch, guaranteeing that her soul belonged to him. To signify that she was

View the **Closer Look** Women and Witchcraft

BURNING OF A WITCH Authorities burned a young woman accused of witchcraft, Anne Hendricks, in Amsterdam in 1571.

Different Voices
Were There Really Witches?

Even during the height of the witch-hunt the existence of witches was controversial. Most authorities assumed that the Devil worked evil on Earth and that hunting witches, therefore, was an effective means of defending Christians. These authorities used the church and secular courts to interrogate alleged witches, sometimes supplemented by torture, to obtain confessions and the identities of other confederate witches. These authorities considered the hunting of witches part of their duty to protect the public from harm. Others accepted the reality of witchcraft but doubted the capacity of judges to determine who was a witch. A few doubted the reality of witchcraft altogether.

Johann Weyer (1515?–1588) was a physician who argued that most witches were deluded old women who suffered from depression and needed medical help rather than legal punishment. The Devil deceived them into thinking they had magical powers, but because Weyer had a strong belief that only God had power over nature, he did not credit the Devil or witches with any special powers. No one else during the sixteenth century disputed the reality of the powers of witches as systematically as he. Jean Bodin (1529?–1596) was one of the greatest legal philosophers of the sixteenth century. Although he was once skeptical of the reality of witchcraft, he changed his mind after witnessing several cases in which women voluntarily confessed to performing evil acts under the guidance of Satan. He considered witchcraft a threat to society and condemned Weyer's soft-hearted view.

Johann Weyer's Letter to Johann Brenz (1565)

Witches have no power to make hail, storms, and other evil things, but they are deceived by the devil. For when the devil, with the permission and decree of God, can make hail and storms, he goes to his witches and urges them to use their magic and charms, so that when the trouble and punishment come, the witches are convinced that they and the devil have caused it. Thus, the witches cannot make hail and other things, but they are deluded and blinded by the devil himself to whom they have given themselves. In this way they think that they have made hail and storms. Not on that account but for their godless lives should they be punished severely. . . .

Our witches have been corrupted in their phantasy by the devil and imagine often that they have done evil things that didn't even happen or caused natural occurrences that actually did not take place. In their confessions, especially under torture, they admit to doing and causing many things which are impossible for them and for anyone. One should not believe them when they confess that they have bound themselves to the devil, given themselves to his will, promised to follow his evil goals, just as we do not believe their confession that they make hail and storms, disturb and poison the air, and other impossible deeds. . . .

Even if an old woman, in deep depression, gives herself to the devil, one should not immediately condemn her to the fire but instead have regard for her confused, burdened, and depressed spirits and use all possible energy to convert her that she may avoid evil, and give herself to Christ. In this way we may bring her to her senses again, win her soul, and save her from death. . . .

Jean Bodin, On the Demonic Madness of Witches (1580)

The judgment which was passed against a witch in a case to which I was called on the last day of April, 1578, gave me occasion to take up my pen in order to clarify the subject of witches—persons who seem strange and wondrous to everyone and incredible to many. The witch whom I refer to was named Jeanne Harvillier, a native of Verbery near Compiegne. She was accused of having murdered many men and beasts, as she herself confessed without questioning or torture, although she at first stubbornly denied the charges and changed her story often. She also confessed that her mother presented her at the age of twelve years to the devil, disguised as a tall black man, larger than most men and clothed in black. The mother told him that as soon as her daughter was born she had promised her to him, whom she called the devil. He in turn promised to treat her well and to make her happy. And from then on she had renounced God and promised to serve the devil. And at that instant she had had carnal copulation with the devil, which she had continued to the age of 50, or thereabouts, when she was captured. She said also that [the] devil presented himself to her when she wished, always dressed as he had been the first time, booted and spurred, with a sword at his side and his horse at the door. And no one saw him but her. He even fornicated with her often without her husband noticing although he lay at her side. . . .

Now we have shown that ordinarily women are possessed by demons more often than men and that witches are often transported bodily but also often ravished in an ecstasy, the soul having separated itself from the body, by diabolical means, leaving the body insensible and stupid. Thus, it is completely ridiculous to say that the illness of the witches originates in melancholy, especially because the diseases coming from melancholy are always dangerous. . . . Thus, Weyer must admit that there is a remarkable incongruity for one who is a doctor, and a gross example of ignorance (but it is not ignorance) to attribute to women melancholy diseases which are as little appropriate for them as are the praiseworthy effects of a tempered melancholy humor. This humor makes a man wise, sober, and contemplative (as all of the ancient philosophers and physicians remark), which are qualities as incompatible with women as fire with water. And even Solomon, who as a man of the world knew well the humor of women, said that he had seen a wise man for every 1,000 men, but that he had never seen a wise woman. Let us therefore abandon the fanatic error of those who make women into melancholics.

SOURCE: Robert M. Kingdon (ed.), *Transition and Revolution: Problems and Issues of European Renaissance and Reformation History* (Minneapolis: Burgess Publishing Company, 1974), 221–232. Reprinted by permission.

For Discussion

1. How can the uncoerced confessions of women to witchcraft be explained?
2. Why would an otherwise intelligent observer such as Jean Bodin be so willing to believe in the reality of the power of witches?

one of his own, the Devil marked her body in a hidden place, creating a sign, which could easily be confused with a birthmark or blemish. To an inquisitor or judge, a mark on the skin that did not bleed and was insensitive to pain when pierced with a long pin often confirmed the suspicion that she was a witch.

After making the pact witches allegedly gathered in large numbers to worship the devil at nocturnal assemblies known as sabbaths. The Devil was believed to have given them the power to fly to these gatherings. At these assemblies, so it was claimed, witches killed and ate babies, danced naked, and had promiscuous sexual relations with other witches and demons. The belief that witches attended sabbaths, which judicial authorities confirmed by forcing them to confess under severe torture, explains why witch-hunting took a high toll in human life. Between 1450 and 1750, approximately 100,000 people in Europe were tried for witchcraft, and about 50,000 were executed. Approximately half of the trials took place in the German-speaking lands of the Holy Roman Empire, where the central judicial authorities exercised little control over the determination of local judges to secure convictions. Prosecutions were also extensive in Switzerland, France, Scotland, Poland, Hungary, and Transylvania. Relatively few witches were executed in Spain, Portugal, Italy, Scandinavia, the Netherlands, England, and Ireland.

The determination of both Catholics and Protestants to discipline deviants of all sorts and to wage war against the Devil intensified the hunt for witches. The great majority of trials occurred between 1560 and 1650, when religious tensions were strong and economic conditions severe. The trials rarely occurred in a steady flow, as one would find for other crimes. In many cases the torture of a single witch would lead to her naming many alleged accomplices, who would then also be tried. This would lead to a witch panic in which scores and sometimes hundreds of witches would be tried and executed. Eighty percent of accused witches were women, especially those who were unmarried or widowed, but men and even young children could be accused of witchcraft as well. The hunts came to an end when judicial authorities recognized that no one was safe, especially during witch panics, and when they realized that legal evidence against witches was insufficient for conviction. The Dutch Republic was the first to ban witch trials in 1608. (See *Different Voices* in this chapter.)

The Confessional States

15.4 How did religious differences provoke violence and start wars?

The Religious Peace of Augsburg of 1555 provided the model for a solution to the religious divisions produced by the Reformation. According to the principle of *cuius regio, eius religio* (he who rules determines the religion of the land), each prince in the Holy Roman Empire determined the religion to be followed by his subjects; those who disagreed were obliged to convert or emigrate. Certainly, forced exile was economically and personally traumatic for those who emigrated, but it preserved what was almost universally believed to be the fundamental principle of successful rulership—one king, one faith, one law. In other words, each state should have only one church. Except in the states of eastern Europe and a few small troubled principalities in the Holy Roman Empire, few thought it desirable to allow more than one confession in the same state. A policy of religious toleration seemed inconceivable to all but a tiny minority of intellectuals.

The problem with this political theory of religious unity was the reality of religious divisions created by the Reformation. In some places there were as many as three active confessions—Catholic, Lutheran, and Calvinist—in addition to the minority sects, such as the Anabaptists and the Jewish communities. The alternative to religious

fanatic Originally referring to someone possessed by a demon, during the sixteenth century a fanatic came to mean a person who expressed immoderate enthusiasm in religious matters or who pursued a supposedly divine mission, often to violent ends.

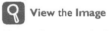

View the Image

Heretic Burning at the Stake

Huguenots The term for French Calvinists, who constituted some 10 percent of the population by 1560.

unity would have been religious toleration, but hardly anyone in a position of authority was willing to advocate that. John Calvin expelled advocates of religious toleration, and Martin Luther was aggressively hostile to those who disagreed with him on seemingly minor theological points. After 1542 with the establishment of the Universal Inquisition, the Catholic Church was committed to exposing and punishing anyone who professed a different faith, with the exception of Jews in Italy, who were under papal protection. Geneva and Rome became competing missionary centers, each flooding the world with polemical tracts and specially trained missionaries willing to risk their lives by going behind the enemy lines to console their co-religionists and evangelize for converts.

Religious passions ran so high that during the late sixteenth century a new word appeared to describe a personality type that may not have been entirely new but was certainly much more common—the **fanatic**. Originally referring to someone possessed by a demon, *fanatic* came to mean a person who expressed immoderate enthusiasm in religious matters, a person who pursued a supposedly divine mission, often to violent ends. Fanatics from all sides of the religious divide initiated waves of political assassinations and massacred their opponents. François Guion, the assassin of William the Silent, whose story began this chapter, was in many ways typical of fanatics in his steadfast pursuit of his victim and his willingness to masquerade for years under a false identity. During the sixteenth and seventeenth centuries, no religious community had a monopoly on fanatics. They served the pope as well as the Protestant churches.

Wherever there were significant religious minorities within a state, the best that could be hoped for was a condition of anxious tension, omnipresent suspicion, and periodic hysteria (see **Map 15.1**). The worst possibility was civil war in which religious affiliations and political rivalries intertwined in such complicated ways that finding peaceful solutions was especially difficult. Between 1560 and 1648 several religious civil wars broke out, including the French Wars of Religion, the Dutch revolt against Spain, the Thirty Years' War in Germany, and the English Civil War. (The latter two will be discussed in Chapter 16.)

The French Wars of Religion

When King Henry II (r. 1547–1559) of France died unexpectedly from a jousting accident, he left behind his widow, the formidable Catherine de' Medici (1519–1589), and a brood of young children—including his heir, Francis II (r. 1559–1560), who was only 15. Henry II had been a peacemaker. In contrast, Catherine and her children, including three sons who successively ascended to the throne, utterly failed to keep the peace. For some 40 years France was torn apart by a series of desperate civil wars.

THE HUGUENOTS: THE FRENCH CALVINIST COMMUNITY By 1560 Calvinism had made significant inroads into predominantly Catholic France. Pastors sent from Geneva had been especially successful in the larger provincial towns, where their evangelical message appealed to enterprising merchants, professionals, and skilled artisans. One in ten of the French had become Calvinists, or **Huguenots** as French Protestants were called. The political strength of the Huguenots was greater than their numbers might indicate, because between one-third and one-half of the lower nobility professed Calvinism. Calvinism was popular among the French nobility for two reasons. One involved the imitation of social superiors. The financial well-being of any noble depended on his patron, an aristocrat of higher rank who had access to the king and who could distribute jobs and lands to his clients. When a high aristocrat converted to Protestantism, he tended to bring into the new faith his noble clientele, who converted through loyalty to their patron or through the patron's ability to persuade those who were financially dependent on him. As a result of a few aristocratic conversions in southwest France, Calvinism spread through "a veritable religious spider's web,"[3] as one contemporary put it.

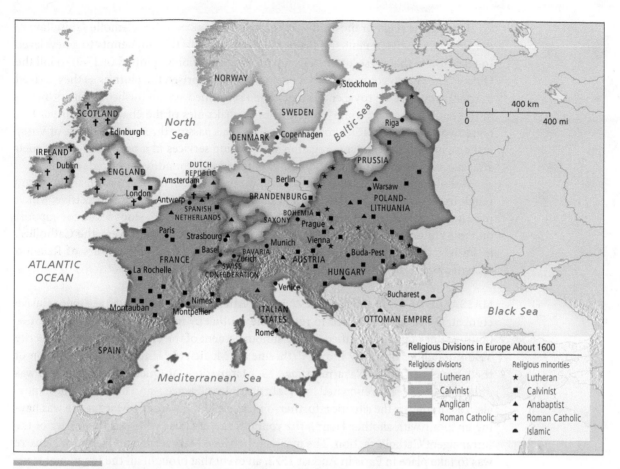

MAP **15.1** RELIGIOUS DIVISIONS IN EUROPE ABOUT 1600   After 1555 the religious borders of Europe became relatively fixed, with only minor changes in confessional affiliations to this day. What does the distribution of religious minorities suggest about the potential for religious conflict? Which states might have the greatest potential for violence on the basis of religious differences?

A second reason for the spread of Calvinism was the influence of aristocratic women. The sister of King Francis I of France (r. 1515–1547), Marguerite of An-goulême (1492–1549), married the King of Navarre (an independent kingdom situated between France and Spain) and created a haven in Navarre for Huguenot preachers and theologians. Her example drew other aristocratic ladies to the Huguenot cause, and many of the Huguenot leaders during the French Wars of Religion were the sons and grandsons of these early female converts. Marguerite's daughter, Jeanne d'Albret, sponsored Calvinist preachers for several years before she publicly announced her own conversion in 1560. Her son, Henry Bourbon (Henry of Navarre), became the principal leader of the Huguenot cause during the **French Wars of Religion** and the person responsible for eventually bringing the wars to an end.

THE ORIGINS OF THE RELIGIOUS WARS   Like all civil wars, the French Wars of Religion exhibited a bewildering pattern of intrigue, betrayal, and treachery. Three distinct groups constituted the principal players. The first group was the royal family, consisting of Queen Catherine de' Medici and her four sons by Henry II—King Francis II (r. 1559–1560), King Charles IX (r. 1560–1574), King Henry III (r. 1574–1589), and Duke Francis of Alençon (1554–1584)—and her daughter, Marguerite Valois (1553–1615). The royal family remained Catholic but on occasion reconciled themselves with the Huguenot opposition, and Marguerite married into it. The second group was the Huguenot faction of nobles led by the Bourbon family who ruled Navarre. The third group was the hard-line Catholic faction led by the Guise family. These three groups vied for supremacy during the successive reigns of Catherine de' Medici's three sons.

French Wars of Religion   A series of political assassinations, massacres, and military engagements between French Catholics and Calvinists from 1560 to 1598.

During the reign of the sickly and immature Francis II, the Catholic Guise family dominated the government and raised the persecution of the Huguenots to a new level. In response to that persecution, a group of Huguenot nobles plotted in 1560 to kill the Guises. The Guises got wind of the conspiracy and surprised the plotters as they arrived in small groups at the royal chateau of Amboise. Some were ambushed, some drowned in the Loire River, and some hanged from the balconies of the chateau's courtyard. A tense two years later in 1562, the Duke of Guise was passing through the village of Vassy just as a large Huguenot congregation was holding services in a barn. The duke's men attacked the worshipers, killing some 740 of them and wounding hundreds of others.

Following the massacre at Vassy, civil war broke out in earnest. For nearly 40 years religious wars sapped the strength of France. Most of the battles were indecisive, which meant neither side sustained military superiority for long. Both sides relied for support on their regional bases: The Huguenots' strength was in the southwest; the Catholics', in Paris and the north. Besides military engagements, the French Wars of Religion spawned political assassinations and massacres.

MASSACRE OF ST. BARTHOLOMEW'S DAY After a decade of bloody yet inconclusive combat, the royal family tried to resolve the conflict by making peace with the Protestants, a shift of policy signified by the announcement of the engagement of Marguerite Valois, daughter of Henry II and Catherine de' Medici, to Henry Bourbon, the son of the Huguenot King of Navarre. At age 19, Marguerite—or Queen Margot, as she was known—was already renowned for her brilliant intelligence—and for her wanton morals. To complicate the situation further, on the eve of the wedding Marguerite was having an affair with another Henry, the young Duke of Guise who was the leader of the intransigent Catholic faction. The marriage between Marguerite and Henry of Navarre was to take place in Paris in August 1572, an event that brought all the Huguenot leaders to the heavily armed Catholic capital for the first time in many years. The gathering of all their enemies in one place presented too great a temptation for the Guises, who hatched a plot to assassinate the Huguenot leaders. Perhaps because she had become jealous of the Huguenots' growing influence on her son, King Charles IX, Catherine suddenly switched sides and became implicated in the plot.

Catherine somehow convinced the weak-willed king to order the massacre of the Huguenot nobles gathered in Paris. On August 14, 1572, St. Bartholomew's Day, the people of Paris began a slaughter. Between 3,000 and 4,000 Huguenots were butchered in Paris and more than 20,000 were put to death throughout the rest of France. Henry of Navarre saved his life by pretending to convert to Catholicism, while most of his companions were murdered.

Catherine's attempted solution for the Huguenot problem failed to solve anything. Henry of Navarre escaped his virtual imprisonment in the royal household, set Marguerite up in an isolated castle, returned to Navarre and his faith, and reinvigorated Huguenot resistance.

The wars of religion continued until the assassination of King Henry III, brother of the late Charles IX. Both Charles IX and Henry III had been childless, a situation that made Henry Bourbon of Navarre the rightful heir to the throne, even though he was a Huguenot. Henry Bourbon became King Henry IV (r. 1589–1610). He recognized that predominantly Catholic France would never accept a Huguenot king, and so in 1593 with his famous quip, "Paris is worth a mass," Henry converted to Catholicism. Most Catholic opposition to him then collapsed. Once Henry became a Catholic he managed to have the pope annul his childless marriage to Marguerite so that he could marry Marie de' Medici and obtain her huge dowry. Affable, witty, generous, and exceedingly tolerant, "Henry the Great" became the most popular king in French history, reuniting the war-torn country by ruling with a very firm hand. With the **Edict of Nantes** of 1598, he allowed the Huguenots to build a quasi-state within the state, giving them the right to have their own troops, church organization, and political autonomy within

Edict of Nantes Promulgated by King Henry IV in 1598, the edict allowed the Huguenots to build a quasi-independent state within the kingdom of France, giving them the right to have their own troops, Church organization, and political autonomy within their walled towns, but banning them from the royal court and the city of Paris. King Louis XIV revoked the edict in 1685.

 Read the Document

The Edict of Nantes 1598

their walled towns, but banning them from the royal court and the city of Paris. The Edict of Nantes was a very limited act of religious toleration, but it probably went as far as was politically possible during the confessional strife of the late sixteenth century.

Despite his enormous popularity, Henry too fell victim to fanaticism. After surviving 18 attempts on his life, in 1610 the king was fatally stabbed by a Catholic fanatic, who took advantage of the opportunity presented when the royal coach unexpectedly stopped behind a cart loading hay. Catholics and Protestants alike mourned Henry's death and considered the assassin mad. Henry's brilliant conciliatory nature and the horrors of the religious wars had tempered public opinion.

Philip II, His Most Catholic Majesty

France's greatest rivals were the Habsburgs, who possessed vast territories in the Holy Roman Empire, controlled the elections for emperor, and had dynastic rights to the throne of Spain. During the late sixteenth century, Habsburg Spain took advantage of French weakness to establish itself as the dominant power in Europe. When Emperor Charles V (who had been both Holy Roman Emperor and king of Spain) abdicated his thrones in 1556, the Habsburg possessions in the Holy Roman Empire and the emperorship went to his brother, Ferdinand I, and the balance of his vast domain went to his son, Philip II (r. 1556–1598). Philip's inheritance included Spain, Milan, Naples, Sicily, the Netherlands, scattered

ST. BARTHOLOMEW'S DAY MASSACRE A Protestant painter, François Dubois, depicted the merciless slaughter of Protestant men, women, and children in the streets of Paris in 1572. The massacre was the most bloody and infamous in the French Wars of Religion and created a lasting memory of atrocity.

outposts on the north coast of Africa, colonies in the Caribbean, Central America, Mexico, Peru, and the Philippines. In 1580 Philip also inherited Portugal and its far-flung overseas empire, which included a line of trading posts from West Africa to the Spice Islands and the vast colony of unexplored Brazil.

This grave, distrustful, rigid man saw himself as the great protector of the Catholic cause and committed Spain to perpetual hostility toward Muslims and Protestants.

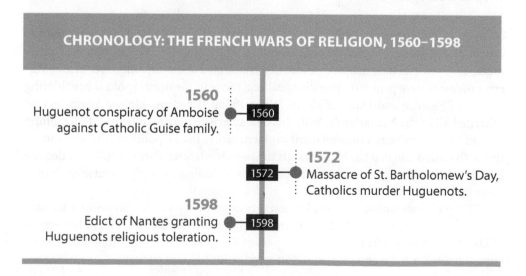

CHRONOLOGY: THE FRENCH WARS OF RELIGION, 1560–1598

1560 — 1560
Huguenot conspiracy of Amboise against Catholic Guise family.

1572 — **1572**
Massacre of St. Bartholomew's Day, Catholics murder Huguenots.

1598 — 1598
Edict of Nantes granting Huguenots religious toleration.

On the Muslim front he first bullied the Moriscos, the descendants of the Spanish Muslims. The Moriscos had received Christian baptism but were suspected of secretly practicing Islam. In 1568 Philip issued an edict that banned all manifestations of Muslim culture and ordered the Moriscos to turn over their children to Christian priests to educate. The remaining Moriscos were eventually expelled from the country in 1609.

Philip once said he would rather lose all his possessions and die a hundred times than be the king of heretics. (See *Justice in History* in this chapter.) His attitude toward Protestants showed that he meant what he said. Through his marriage to Queen Mary I of England (r. 1553–1558), Philip encouraged her persecutions of Protestants, but they got their revenge. After Mary's death her half-sister, Queen Elizabeth I, refused Philip's marriage proposal and in 1577 signed a treaty to assist the Protestant provinces of the Netherlands, which were in rebellion against Spain. To add insult to injury, the English privateer Sir Francis Drake (ca. 1540–1596) conducted a personal war against Catholic Spain by raiding the Spanish convoys bringing silver from the New World. In 1587 Drake's embarrassing successes culminated with a daring raid on the great Spanish port city of Cadiz, where, "singeing the king of Spain's beard," he destroyed the anchored Spanish fleet and many thousands of tons of vital supplies.

Philip retaliated by building a huge fleet of 132 ships armed with 3,165 cannons, which in 1588 sailed from Portugal to rendezvous with the Spanish army stationed in the Netherlands and launch an invasion of England. As the Invincible Armada, as it was called, passed through the English Channel, it was met by a much smaller English fleet, assembled out of merchant ships refit for battle. Unable to maneuver as effectively as the English in the fluky winds of the channel and mauled by the rapid-firing English guns, the **Spanish Armada** suffered heavy losses and was forced to retreat to the north, where it sustained further losses in storms off the coast of Scotland and Ireland. Barely more than half of the fleet finally straggled home. The defeat severely shook Philip's sense of invincibility.

The reign of Philip II illustrated better than any other the contradictions and tensions of the era. No monarch had at his grasp as many resources and territories as Philip, and yet defending them proved extremely costly. The creaky governmental machinery of Spain put a tremendous burden on a conscientious king such as Philip; even his unflagging energy and dedication to his duties could not prevent military defeat and financial disaster. Historians remember Philip's reign for its series of state bankruptcies and for the loss of the Dutch provinces in the Netherlands, the most precious jewel in the crown of Spain.

Spanish Armada A fleet of 132 ships, which sailed from Portugal to rendezvous with the Spanish army stationed in the Netherlands and launch an invasion of England in 1588. The English defeated the Armada as it passed through the English Channel. The defeat marked a shift in the power balance from Spain to England.

 Read the Document

John Hawkins Reports on the Spanish Armada (1588), John Hawkins

The Dutch Revolt

The Netherlands boasted some of Europe's richest cities, situated amid a vast network of lakes, rivers, channels, estuaries, and tidal basins that periodically replenished the exceptionally productive soil through flooding. The Netherlands consisted of 17 provinces, each with its own distinctive identity, traditions, and even language. The southern provinces were primarily French-speaking; those in the north spoke a bewildering variety of Flemish and Dutch dialects. When Philip II became king of Spain he also inherited all of the Netherlands. With his characteristic bureaucratic mentality, Philip treated Dutch affairs as a management problem rather than a political sore spot, an attitude that subordinated the Netherlands to Spanish interests. Foreign rule irritated the Dutch, who had long enjoyed ancient privileges including the right to raise their own taxes and muster their own troops.

Philip's harsh attitude toward Protestants upset the Netherlands' delicate balance among Catholic, Lutheran, Calvinist, and Anabaptist communities, as did the arrival of Huguenot refugees from the French Wars of Religion. In 1566 Calvinist fanatics occupied many Catholic churches and destroyed paintings and statues.

 View the Map

Revolt of the Netherlands, 1555

View the Closer Look

The Netherlands: A Historical Map

In response, Philip issued edicts against the heretics and strengthened the Spanish Inquisition. The Inquisition in Spain was an arm of the monarchy charged with ensuring religious conformity, but when introduced in the Netherlands, it became an investigating agency devoted to finding, interrogating, and, if necessary, punishing Protestants.

Philip also dispatched 20,000 Spanish troops under the command of the Duke of Alba (1508–1582), a veteran of the Turkish campaigns in North Africa and victories over the Lutheran princes in the Holy Roman Empire. Alba directly attacked the Protestants. He personally presided over the military court, the Council of Troubles, which became so notoriously tyrannical that the people called it the Council of Blood. As an example to others, he systematically razed several small villages where there had been incidents of desecrating Catholic images and slaughtered every inhabitant. Alba himself boasted that during the campaign against the rebels, he had 18,000 people executed, in addition to those who died in battle or were massacred by soldiers. Sixty thousand refugees, about 2 percent of the population, went into exile.

The Prince of Orange, William the Silent (1533–1584), organized the **Dutch Revolt** to resist Alba. Within a few short years, William the Silent seized permanent control of the provinces of Holland and Zealand, which were then flooded by Calvinist refugees from the southern provinces.

His policies a failure, Alba was recalled to Spain in 1573. After Alba's departure, no one kept control of the unpaid Spanish soldiers, who in mutinous rage turned against cities loyal to Spain, including Brussels, Ghent, and most savagely Antwerp, the rich center of trade. Antwerp lost 7,000 citizens and one-third of its houses to the "Spanish fury," which permanently destroyed its prosperity.

Alba's replacement, the shrewd statesman and general the Duke of Parma (r. 1578–1592), ultimately subdued the southern provinces, which remained a Spanish colony. The seven northern provinces, however, united in 1579, declared independence from Spain in 1581, and formally organized as a republic in 1588 (see **Map 15.2**). William the Silent became the *stadholder* (governor) of the new United Provinces; after his assassination in 1584 his 17-year-old son, Maurice of Nassau, inherited the same title.

The Netherlands' struggle for independence transformed the population of the United Provinces from mixed religions to staunch Calvinism. The alliance with England, which provided much-needed financial and moral support, reinforced the Protestant identity of the Dutch, and the failure of the Spanish Armada to land Parma's men in England guaranteed the survival of an independent Netherlands. The Dutch carried on a sporadic and inconclusive war against Spain until the end of the Thirty Years' War in 1648, when the international community recognized the independent United Provinces of the Netherlands, known as the Dutch Republic.

Dutch Revolt The rebellion against Spanish rule of the seven northern provinces of the Netherlands between 1579 and 1648, which resulted in the independence of the Republic of the United Provinces.

Literature in the Age of Confessional Division

Churches and monarchs everywhere demanded religious conformity in word and deed, a situation that would seem to stifle creativity, and yet the late sixteenth and early seventeenth centuries were among the most remarkable periods in the history of creative literature. Some literary figures did find their works banned and some had political or personal troubles with their monarch. But the controversies of the day seemed to have stimulated rather than inhibited great writers. Political and religious turmoil led them to rise above the petty religious squabbles that preoccupied so many of their contemporaries and to ask penetrating questions about the meaning of life. And

MAP **15.2** THE NETHERLANDS DURING THE DUTCH REVOLT, CA. 1580 During the late sixteenth century the northern United Provinces separated from the Spanish Netherlands. The independence of the United Provinces was not recognized by the other European powers until 1648. What might be the implications of the fact that the dividing line between French- and Flemish-speakers did not correspond to the political divisions?

CHRONOLOGY: SPAIN AND THE NETHERLANDS, 1568–1648

1568
Edict against Morisco culture.

1580
King Philip II inherits Portugal and the Portuguese Empire.

1584
Assassination of William the Silent.

1588
Defeat of the Spanish Armada, failed Spanish invasion of England; the seven northern provinces of the Netherlands become a republic.

1609
Expulsion of the Moriscos from Spain.

1648
Treaty of Westphalia recognizes independence of the Netherlands.

vernacular languages The native spoken languages of Europe, which became literary languages and began to replace Latin as the dominant form of learned expression during the sixteenth century.

importantly, they did so in their native languages. During this period the native or **vernacular languages** of western Europe became literary languages, replacing Latin as the dominant form of expression, even for the educated elite.

FRENCH LITERATURE DURING THE RELIGIOUS TURMOIL In France royal decrees in 1520 and 1539 substituted French for Latin in official legal and government documents. A century later, with the founding of the Académie Française, it became government policy to promote, protect, and refine the French language. The greatest masters of French prose during this crucial period were François Rabelais (ca. 1483–1553) and Michel de Montaigne (1533–1592).

Trained as a lawyer, Rabelais became a friar and priest but left the Church under a cloud of heresy to become a physician. Rabelais's satirical masterpiece, a series of novels recounting the fantastic and grotesque adventures of the giants Gargantua and Pantagruel, combined an encyclopedic command of humanist thought with stunning verbal invention that has had a lasting influence on humorous writers to this day. Rabelais's optimistic vision of human nature represented a startling contrast to the growing anxiety provoked by the religious controversies of his time. Rabelais's controversial work was banned, and he was briefly forced into exile.

It is ironic that Montaigne became a master of French prose. His mother was a Catholic of Spanish-Jewish origin, and the young Michel spoke only Latin for the first six years of his life because his German tutor knew no French. After a modestly successful legal career, Montaigne retired to the family chateau to discover himself by writing essays, a literary form well suited to reflective introspection. In his essays, Montaigne struggled with his lasting grief over the premature death from dysentery of a close friend, reflected on his own experience of the intense physical pain of illness, and diagnosed the absurd causes of the French Wars of Religion. Montaigne's essays were a profound series of meditations on the meaning of life and death, presented in a calm voice of reason to an age of violent fanaticism. In one essay, for example, he exposed the presumption of human beings: "The most vulnerable and frail of all creatures is man, and at the same time the most arrogant." Montaigne thought it presumptuous that human beings picked themselves out as God's favorite creatures. How did they know they were superior to other animals? "When I play with my cat, who knows if I am not a pastime to her more than she is to me?"[4] His own skepticism about religion insulated him from the sometimes violent passions of his era. His essay "On Cannibals" pointed to the hypocrisy of Christians who condemned the alleged cannibalism of the native Americans but justified the torture and murder of other Christians over some minor theological dispute. Montaigne argued that the capacity to understand and tolerate cultural and religious differences, not rigid adherence to biblical laws, defined a truly ethical, truly Christian person.

STIRRINGS OF THE GOLDEN AGE IN IBERIA The literary tradition in the Iberian peninsula thrived in several languages: Basque, Galician, Portuguese, Castilian, and Catalan. The greatest lyric poet of the peninsula, Luís Vaz de Camões (1524–1580), lost an eye in battle and was sent to the Portuguese East Indies after he killed a royal official in a street brawl. When he returned years later, he completed his epic poem *The Lusiads* (1572), a celebration of Vasco da Gama's discovery of the sea route to India, which became the national poem of Portugal. Camões modeled this work on the ancient epics, especially the *Aeneid,* the greatest Latin epic of ancient Rome, and even included the gods of Olympus as commentators on the human events of Camões's time. By connecting Portugal directly to the glories of the ancient empires, Camões elevated the adventures of his fellow Portuguese in Asia to an important moment in the history of the world.

The period when Spain was the dominant power in Europe coincided with the Golden Age of Spanish literature. Because Spain was unified around the crown of Castile, the Castilian language became the language we now call Spanish. The greatest literary figure was Miguel de Cervantes Saavedra (1547–1616), an impoverished son of an unsuccessful doctor with little formal education. Like Camões, Cervantes survived many adventures. He lost the use of his left hand at the naval Battle of Lepanto and spent five years languishing in a Turkish prison after his capture by Algerian pirates. The disabled veteran wrote plays for the Madrid theater and worked as a tax collector, but was still imprisoned several times for debts. Desperate to make money, Cervantes published a serial novel in installments between 1605 and 1615. It became the greatest masterpiece in Spanish literature, *Don Quixote.*

The prototype of the modern novel form, *Don Quixote* satirizes chivalric romances. Cervantes presented reality on two levels, the "poetic truth" of the master and dreamer Don Quixote and the "historic truth" of his squire and realist Sancho Panza. Don Quixote's imagination persistently ran away with him as he tilted at windmills, believing they were fierce dragons. It remained to Sancho Panza to point out the unheroic truth. Cervantes pursued the interaction between these two incongruous views of truth as a philosophical commentary on existence. For Cervantes there was no single, objective truth, only psychological truths revealed through the interaction of the characters, an idea that contrasted with the notion of dogmatic religious truth that dominated the time.

THE ELIZABETHAN RENAISSANCE During the reign of Elizabeth I (r. 1558–1603), the Renaissance arrived in England. The daughter of Henry VIII and Anne Boleyn, Elizabeth faced terrible insecurity as a girl. Her father had her mother beheaded, she was declared illegitimate, and her half-sister Mary imprisoned her in the Tower of London for treason. After she ascended to the throne in 1558, however, she proved to be a brilliant leader. Elizabeth prevented the kind of religious civil wars that broke out in France by establishing a moderate form of Protestantism as the official religion. She presided over the beginnings of England's rise as a major European power. Perhaps most remarkably, she became a patron and inspiration for England's greatest age of literature.

The principal figure of the Elizabethan Renaissance was a professional dramatist, William Shakespeare (1564–1616). In a series of theaters, including the famous Globe on the south side of the Thames in London, Shakespeare wrote, produced, and acted in comedies, tragedies, and history plays. Shakespeare's enormous output of plays, some of which made veiled allusions to the politics of Elizabeth's court, established him not only as the most popular dramatist of his time, but the greatest literary figure in the English language. The power of his plays derives from the subtle understanding of human psychology found in his characters and the stunning force of his language. For Shakespeare, as for Montaigne, the source of true knowledge was self-knowledge, which most people lacked. Pride and human authority prevented people from knowing themselves:

> But man, proud man,
> Drest [dressed] in a little brief authority,
> Most ignorant of what he's most assured,
> His glassy [dull] essence, like an angry ape,
> Plays such fantastic tricks before high
> heaven
> As make the angels weep.
> (*Measure for Measure* II, ii, 117)

Unlike most contemporary authors, Shakespeare wrote for a broad audience of paying theatergoers that included common workers as well as highly educated members of Elizabeth's court. This need to appeal to a large audience who gave instant feedback helped him hone his skills as a dramatist.

QUEEN ELIZABETH I OF ENGLAND Carried by her courtiers, Elizabeth presided over the greatest age of English literature.

States and Confessions in Eastern Europe

15.5 How did the countries of eastern Europe during the late sixteenth century become enmeshed in the religious controversies that began in western Europe during the early part of the century?

T he religious diversity of eastern Europe contrasted with the religious conformity of western Europe's confessional states. Whereas in western Europe the religious controversies stimulated writers to investigate deeply the human condition but made them cautious about expressing nonconforming religious opinions, writers and creative people in eastern Europe during this period were able to explore a wide range of ideas in a relatively tolerant atmosphere. Bohemia and Poland, in particular, allowed levels of religious diversity unheard of elsewhere. During the last decades of the sixteenth century and early decades of the seventeenth, however, dynastic troubles compromised the relative openness of the eastern states, enmeshing them in conflicts among themselves that had an increasingly strong religious dimension. In the Holy Roman Empire, the weakness of the mad Emperor Rudolf permitted religious conflicts to fester, setting the stage for the disastrous Thirty Years' War (1618–1648) that pitted Catholic and Protestant princes against one another.

Around the Baltic Sea, rivalries among Lutheran Sweden, Catholic Poland-Lithuania, and Orthodox Russia created a state of almost permanent war in a tense standoff among three very different political and religious states. The enormous confederation of Poland-Lithuania sustained the most decentralized, religiously diverse state anywhere in Europe. By the end of the century, it remained politically decentralized but had become an active theater of the Catholic Reformation where dynastic policy firmly supported the Roman Church. Russia began to strengthen itself under the authoritarian rule of the tsars, who began to transform it into a major European power.

The Dream World of Emperor Rudolf

In Goethe's *Faust,* set in sixteenth-century Germany, drinkers in a tavern sing:

> The dear old Holy Roman Empire,
> How does it hang together?

Good question. How did this peculiarly decentralized state—neither holy, nor Roman, nor an empire, as Voltaire would later put it—hang together? In the late sixteenth century the empire consisted of one emperor; seven electors; 50 bishops and archbishops, 21 dukes, margraves, and landgraves; 88 independent abbots and assorted prelates of the Church; 178 counts and other sovereign lords; about 80 free imperial cities; and hundreds of free imperial knights. The emperor presided over all, and the Imperial Diet served as a parliament, but the Holy Roman Empire was, in fact, a very loose confederation of semi-independent, mostly German-speaking states, many of which ignored imperial decrees that did not suit them. During the first half of the sixteenth century the empire faced a number of challenges—the turmoil within the empire created by Lutheranism, endless French enmity on the western borders, and the tenacious Ottoman threat on the eastern frontier. Only the universal vision and firm hand of Emperor Charles V kept the empire together. The universal vision and firm hand disappeared in the succeeding generations of emperors to be replaced by petty dynastic squabbles and infirm minds.

The crippling weakness of the imperial system became most evident during the reign of Rudolf II (r. 1576–1612). The Habsburg line had a strain of insanity going back to Joanna "The Mad," the mother of Emperors Charles V (r. 1519–1558) and Ferdinand I (r. 1558–1564), who happened to be Rudolf's two grandfathers, giving him a double dose of Habsburg genes. Soon after his election to the imperial throne, Rudolf moved his court from bustling Vienna to the lovely quiet of Prague in Bohemia. Fearful of noisy crowds and impatient courtiers, standoffish toward foreign ambassadors who presented him with difficult decisions, paranoid about scheming relatives, and prone to wild emotional gyrations from deep depression to manic grandiosity, Rudolf was hardly suited for the imperial throne. In fact, many contemporaries, who had their own reasons to underrate him, described him as hopelessly insane. Rudolf certainly suffered from moments of profound melancholy and irrational fears that may have had genetic or organic causes, but he was probably unhinged by the conundrum of being the emperor, a position that trapped him between the glorious universal imperial ideal and the ignoble reality of unscrupulous relatives and petty rivalries.

Incapable of governing, Rudolf transmuted the imperial ideal of universality into a strange dream world. In Prague he gathered around him a brilliant court of humanists, musicians, painters, physicians, astronomers, astrologers, alchemists, and magicians. These included an eclectic assortment of significant thinkers—the great astronomers Tycho Brahe and Johannes Kepler, the notorious occult philosopher Giordano Bruno, the theoretical mathematician and astrologer John Dee, and the remarkable inventor of surrealist painting Giuseppe Arcimboldo. Many of these figures became central figures in the Scientific Revolution, but Rudolf also fell prey to fast-talking charlatans. These included Cornelius Drebbel, who claimed to have invented a perpetual-motion machine. This weird court, however, was less the strange fruit of the emperor's hopeless dementia than the manifestation of a striving for universal empire. Rudolf sought to preserve the cultural and political unity of the empire, to eradicate religious divisions, and to achieve peace at home. Rudolf's court in Prague was perhaps the only place left during the late sixteenth century where Protestants, Catholics, Jews, and even radical heretics such as Bruno could gather together in a common intellectual enterprise. The goal of such gatherings was to discover the universal principles that governed nature, principles that would provide the foundations for a single unifying religion and a cure for all human maladies. It was a noble, if utterly improbable, dream.

While Rudolf and his favorite courtiers isolated themselves in their dream world, the religious conflicts within the empire reached a boiling point. Without a strong emperor, confessional squabbles paralyzed the Imperial Diets. In 1607, the Catholic Duke of Bavaria annexed Donauworth—a city with a Lutheran majority—to his own territories. Despite the illegality of the duke's action, Rudolf passively acquiesced, causing fear among German Protestants that the principles of the Religious Peace of Augsburg of 1555 might be ignored. The Religious Peace had allowed princes and imperial free cities, such as Donauworth, to determine their own religion. The Duke of Bavaria's violation of Donauworth's status as a free city jeopardized not only civic liberty but religious liberty. In the following decade, more than 200 religious revolts or riots took place. In 1609 the insane Duke John William of Jülich-Cleves died without a direct heir, and the most suitable claimants to the Catholic duchy were

EMPEROR RUDOLF II Among the many creative people in Emperor Rudolf's court was the Italian surrealist painter Giuseppe Arcimboldo, who specialized in creating images out of fruits, vegetables, flowers, and animals. This is a portrait of Emperor Rudolf.

two Lutheran princes. The succession of a Lutheran prince to this Catholic dukedom would have seriously disrupted the balance between Catholics and Protestants in Germany. Religious tensions boiled over. As Chapter 16 will describe, in less than a decade the empire began to dissolve in what became the Thirty Years' War.

The Renaissance of Poland-Lithuania

As the major power in eastern Europe, Poland-Lithuania engaged in a tug-of-war with Sweden over control of the eastern Baltic and almost constant warfare against the expansionist ambitions of Russia (see **Map 15.3**). Nevertheless, during the late sixteenth and early seventeenth centuries, Poland-Lithuania experienced a remarkable cultural and political renaissance inspired by influences from Renaissance Italy linked to strong commercial and diplomatic ties to the Republic of Venice and intellectual connections with the University of Padua. But perhaps the most remarkable achievement of Poland-Lithuania during this contentious time was its unparalleled level of religious toleration and parliamentary rule.

Very loosely joined since 1385, the Kingdom of Poland and the Grand Duchy of Lithuania formally united as the Polish-Lithuanian Commonwealth in 1569. The republican thought from Renaissance Italy directly influenced the political structure and values of the Commonwealth. Polish jurists studied law at the universities of Padua and Bologna where they learned to apply the civic values of Italy to the Polish context. Under these influences, the Polish constitution guaranteed that there would be no changes of the law, no new taxes, and no limitations on freedoms without the consent of the parliament, known as the Sejm. The novel feature of the Commonwealth

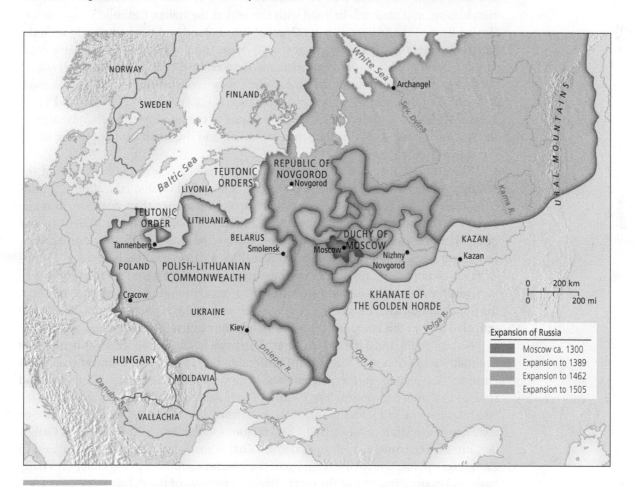

MAP **15.3** POLAND-LITHUANIA AND RUSSIA These countries were the largest in Europe in the size of their territories but were relatively underpopulated compared to the western European states. What might be the long-term implications for Poland-Lithuania of the expansion of Russia?

was how the nobles (*szlachta*) reserved power for themselves through their control of regional assemblies, which in turn dominated the Sejm. The *szlachta* consisted of between 6.6 and 8 percent of the population and nearly 25 percent of ethnic Poles. Elsewhere in Europe, except for Spain, the nobility accounted for no more than 1 to 3 percent of the population. Thus, a much higher percentage of the population of Poland-Lithuania enjoyed political rights than in any other country in Europe. In 1573 the Sejm introduced a highly limited monarchy for Poland. The Sejm elected the king and treated him, at best, as a hired manager. While the rest of Europe moved toward ever more authoritarian monarchies, Poland moved in the opposite direction toward broader political participation.

The Warsaw Confederation of 1573 prohibited religious persecution, making the Commonwealth the safest and most tolerant place in Europe. Poland-Lithuania contained an incomparable religious mixture of Roman Catholics, Lutherans, Calvinists, Russian Orthodox, Anabaptists, Unitarians, Armenians, and Jews. These communities, however, were strongly divided along geographic and social lines. Lutheranism was a phenomenon of the German-speaking towns, the peasants of Poland remained Catholic, those in Lithuania were Orthodox, and many of the nobles were attracted to Calvinism.

During the late sixteenth century, however, many Protestants in Poland returned or converted to the Roman Catholic faith. The key to the transformation was the changing attitude of the Polish *szlachta,* who had promoted religious diversity because they believed that religious liberty was the cornerstone of political liberty. The revival of Catholicism owed a great deal to Stanislaus Hosius (1504–1579), who had studied in Italy before he returned to Poland to become successively a diplomat, bishop, and cardinal. Imbued with the zeal of the Italian Catholic Reformation, Hosius invited the Society of Jesus (Jesuits) into Poland and worked closely with the papal *nuncios* (the diplomatic representatives of the pope), who organized a campaign to combat all forms of Protestantism. Between 1565 and 1586, 44 Polish nobles studied at the Jesuit college in Rome. When they returned, they took up the most influential church and government offices in Poland. Jesuit colleges sprouted up in many Polish towns, attracting the brightest sons of the nobility and urban bourgeoisie. A close alliance between the kings of Poland and the Jesuits enhanced the social prestige of Catholicism.

The cultural appeal of all things Italian also helped lure many members of the Polish nobility back to Catholicism. Through the spread of elite education, Catholicism returned to Poland largely through persuasion rather than coercion. But the transformation did not occur without violent repercussions. Lutheran, Calvinist, and Bohemian Brethren churches were burned. In Cracow armed confrontations between Protestant and Catholic militants led to casualties. In 1596 the Polish king and Catholic fanatics imposed Catholicism on the Orthodox in the eastern parts of the Commonwealth. Although allowed to retain their rites, Orthodox believers had to accept the pope's authority. Despite the growing religious hostility, Poland did not degenerate into civil war, as did France or the Netherlands over much the same issues.

Not all Poles and Lithuanians interpreted the Italian influence as affirming the Catholic Reformation. In 1580 Count Jan Zamoyski (1542–1605) founded the city of Zamość, designed as an ideal Renaissance city on the Italian model. Zamoyski had studied at Padua and returned to Poland determined to build his own Padua. He invited Armenians and Jews to inhabit the new town as citizens. A forceful advocate of civic freedom against royal authority and religious toleration, he built a Roman Catholic Church, a Calvinist chapel, an Armenian Orthodox church, and two synagogues. In Zamoyski's planned town the religions of the West encountered one another on a daily basis and exemplified one of the most attractive features of the Polish Renaissance.

Perhaps most remarkable was the position of Jews in Poland. During the early modern period Poland-Lithuania became the center of European Jewish culture. Jews

ZAMOŚĆ One of the finest examples of a Renaissance planned-town, Zamość in eastern Poland imitated the arcaded streets of Padua, Italy.

described Vilnius as the "new Jerusalem." Jews had their own parliament and sent nonvoting representatives to the Sejm, a form of unequal citizenship but a guarantee of certain rights without parallel elsewhere in Europe. Unlike other parts of Europe, in Poland-Lithuania Jews were not forced to assimilate or hide and were allowed to develop their own distinctive communities.

The Troubled Legacy of Ivan the Terrible

While Poland experimented with a decentralized confederation dominated by nobles that severely restricted the king's initiative, Russia did the opposite. During the late fifteenth and sixteenth centuries, the grand dukes of Moscow who became the tsars of Russia gradually expanded their power over the **boyars** (the upper-level nobles who dominated Russian society) and challenged Moscow's neighbors—Poland-Lithuania and the Republic of Novgorod.

Although well integrated into the European diplomatic community and engaged in trade with its western neighbors, Russia for more than 300 years had been under the "Tartar Yoke," a term describing the Mongolian tribes that overran the country, pillaging and depopulating it. Ivan III, "The Great" (1462–1505), succeeded in gradually throwing off the Tartar Yoke by refusing to continue to pay tribute to the Mongols.

Ivan's marriage to Zoë, the niece of the last Greek emperor of Constantinople, gave him the basis for claiming that the Russian rulers were the heirs of Byzantium and the exclusive protectors of Orthodox Christianity, the state religion of Russia. Following

boyars Upper-level nobles who dominated Russian society until the tsars began to supplant them in the fifteenth and sixteenth centuries.

487

THE MOSCOW KREMLIN The Kremlin in Moscow was the seat of government for the Russian tsars until 1712. Originally built in 1156, the present enclosure of the Kremlin dates from the sixteenth century and reflects the influence of Italian architects brought to Moscow as well as traditional Byzantine styles. This view shows the Cathedral of St. Michael the Archangel and the Bell Tower of Ivan the Great.

View the **Closer Look**

St. Basil's Cathedral, Moscow

View the **Map**

Interactive Map: The Rise of Moscow

the Byzantine tradition of imperial pomp, Ivan practiced Byzantine court ceremonies, and his advisers developed the theory of the Three Romes. According to this theory, the authority of the ancient Roman Empire had passed first to the Byzantine Empire, which God had punished with the Turkish conquest, and then to Moscow as the third and last "Rome." Ivan celebrated this theory by assuming the title of tsar (or "Caesar"). With his wife's assistance, he hired Italian architects to rebuild the grand ducal palace, the Kremlin.

With his capture of the vast northern territories of the Republic of Novgorod, Ivan expanded the Russian state north to the White Sea and east to the Urals. In 1478 Ivan sent his army to Novgorod, massacred the population, abolished the parliament, and burned the archive, ending the rich republican tradition of northern Russia. Ivan's invasion of parts of Lithuania embroiled Russia in a protracted conflict with Poland that lasted more than a century. Like his fellow monarchs in western Europe, Ivan began to bring the aristocrats under control by incorporating them into the bureaucracy of the state.

Ivan III's grandson, Ivan IV, "The Terrible" (1533–1584), succeeded his father at age three and became the object of innumerable plots, attempted coups, and power struggles among his mother, uncles, and the boyars. The trauma of his childhood years and a painful disease of the spine made him inordinately suspicious and prone to acts of impulsive violence. When at age 17 Ivan was crowned, he reduced the power of the dukes and the boyars. He obliged them to give up their hereditary estates. In return he redistributed lands to them with the legal obligation to serve the tsar in war. In

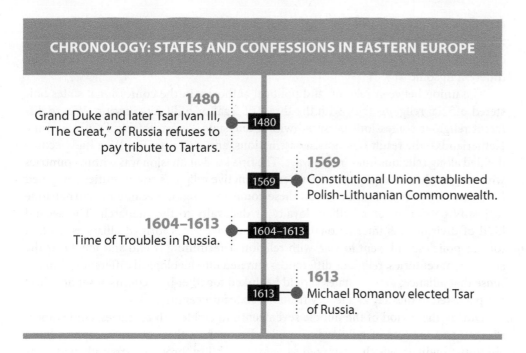

CHRONOLOGY: STATES AND CONFESSIONS IN EASTERN EUROPE

1480
Grand Duke and later Tsar Ivan III, "The Great," of Russia refuses to pay tribute to Tartars.
1480

1569
1569
Constitutional Union established Polish-Lithuanian Commonwealth.

1604–1613
Time of Troubles in Russia.
1604–1613

1613
1613
Michael Romanov elected Tsar of Russia.

weakening the boyars, Ivan gained considerable support among the common people and was even remembered in popular songs as the people's tsar. At first, he was a great reformer who introduced a code of laws and a church council. By setting aside half of the realm as his personal domain, he created a strong financial base for the army, which led to military successes in the prolonged wars against Poland-Lithuania and Sweden.

Nevertheless, Ivan distrusted everyone, and his struggle with the boyars led him to subvert his own reforms. He often arrested people on charges of treason, just for taking trips abroad. In a cruel revenge to his enemies among the boyars, he began a reign of terror in which he personally committed horrendous atrocities. His massacre in 1570 of the surviving inhabitants of Novgorod, whom he suspected of harboring Polish sympathies, contributed to his reputation as a bloody tyrant. During his reign, the Polish threat and boyar opposition to his rule revealed signs of the fragility of Russian unity.

Then, during the "**Time of Troubles**" (1604–1613), Russia fell into chaos. Boyar families struggled among themselves for supremacy, the Cossacks from the south led a popular revolt, and Poles and Swedes openly interfered in Russian affairs. Finally, the Time of Troubles ended when in 1613 the national assembly elected Tsar Michael Romanov, whose descendants ruled Russia until 1917. During the seventeenth century the Romanovs gradually restored order to Russia, eroded the independence of local governments, and introduced serfdom to keep the peasants on the land. By the end of the seventeenth century Russia was strong enough to reenter European affairs as a major power.

 **View the Image**

Ivan the Terrible

Time of Troubles The period from 1604 to 1613 when Russia fell into chaos, which ended when the national assembly elected Tsar Michael Romanov, whose descendants ruled Russia until they were deposed in 1917.

CONCLUSION

The Divisions of the West

During the late sixteenth and early seventeenth centuries, hidden demographic and economic pressures eroded the confidence and security of many Europeans, creating a widespread sense of unease. Most people retreated like confused soldiers behind the barricades of a rigid confessional faith, which provided reassurance that was unavailable elsewhere. To compensate for the absence of predictability in daily life, societies everywhere imposed strict discipline—discipline of women, children, the poor, criminals, and alleged witches. The frenzy for social discipline displaced the fear of those things that could not be controlled (such as price inflation) onto the most easily controllable people, especially the weak, the subordinate, and those perceived to be different in some way.

The union between religion and political authority in the confessional states bolstered official religious faith with the threat of legal or military coercion. Where different religious confessions persisted within one state—most notably France and the Netherlands—the result was riots, assassinations, and civil war. The West had become divided along religious lines in two ways. The first kind of division was within countries with religiously mixed populations, where distinctive religious communities competed for political power and influence. In these countries religion became the cornerstone to justify patriotism or rebellion, loyalty or disloyalty to the monarch. The second kind of division was international. The confessional states formed alliances, crafted foreign policies, and went to war, with religion determining friend and foe. Over the subsequent centuries, religious differences mutated into ideological differences, but the sense that alliances among states should be linked together by a common set of beliefs has persisted to this day as a legacy from the sixteenth century.

During the period of the middle seventeenth to eighteenth centuries, confessional identity and the fear of religious turmoil led monarchs throughout Europe to build absolutist regimes, which attempted to enforce stability through a strengthened, centralized state. The principles of religious toleration and the separation of church and state were still far in the future. They were made possible only as a consequence of the hard lessons learned from the historical turmoil of the late sixteenth and seventeenth centuries.

MAKING CONNECTIONS

1. Why was it so difficult to establish religious toleration in the sixteenth century?
2. A common emotion during the age of confessional division was fear. How do you explain the spread of collective fears?
3. How did religious fanatics perceive the world during this period?

TAKING IT FURTHER

For suggested readings, websites, and films, see page R-1.

Chapter Review

The Peoples of Early Modern Europe

15.1 How did the expanding population and Price Revolution exacerbate religious and political tensions?

When the farms of the countryside could no longer provide enough food or work for a growing population, the cities became crowded with the destitute looking for fortune. The inflation of the Price Revolution caused widespread human suffering when the price of grain was out of reach for the poor. An anxious and hungry people, already divided along religious lines, targeted both each other and the supernatural as the source of their misery.

Disciplining the People

15.2 How did religious and political authorities attempt to discipline the people?

Church and secular authorities worked together to impose order by establishing confessional identities, or institutions that would establish a particular religious culture, and attempting to regulate the family by reinforcing the ideal of a patriarchal family structure.

Hunting Witches

15.3 Why did people in the sixteenth century think witches were a threat?

During a time of religious tensions and economic upheaval, people believed they saw the work of the supernatural in both human and natural events. The determination of both Catholics and Protestants to discipline deviants of all sorts and to wage war against the Devil intensified the hunt for witches.

The Confessional States

15.4 How did religious differences provoke violence and start wars?

The existence of significant religious minorities within a state resulted in tension, suspicion, and periodic hysteria. The complicated ways that religious affiliations and political rivalries were intertwined made finding peaceful solutions difficult, and the outcome of these tensions was sometimes civil war.

States and Confessions in Eastern Europe

15.5 How did the countries of eastern Europe during the late sixteenth century become enmeshed in the religious controversies that began in western Europe during the early part of the century?

Religious conflicts compounded by dynastic troubles in the Holy Roman Empire set in motion the disastrous Thirty Years' War, and rivalries among Lutheran Sweden, Catholic Poland-Lithuania, and Orthodox Russia created a state of almost permanent war in a tense standoff among three very different political and religious states.

Chapter Time Line

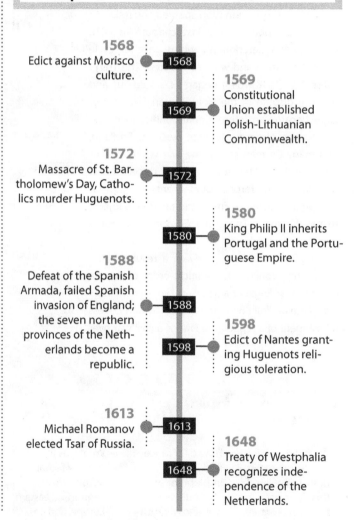

1568 Edict against Morisco culture. — 1568

1569 Constitutional Union established Polish-Lithuanian Commonwealth. — 1569

1572 Massacre of St. Bartholomew's Day, Catholics murder Huguenots. — 1572

1580 King Philip II inherits Portugal and the Portuguese Empire. — 1580

1588 Defeat of the Spanish Armada, failed Spanish invasion of England; the seven northern provinces of the Netherlands become a republic. — 1588

1598 Edict of Nantes granting Huguenots religious toleration. — 1598

1613 Michael Romanov elected Tsar of Russia. — 1613

1648 Treaty of Westphalia recognizes independence of the Netherlands. — 1648

16 Absolutism and State Building, 1618–1715

In 1651 Thomas Hobbes, an English philosopher living in exile in France, was convinced that the West had descended into chaos. As he looked around him, Hobbes saw nothing but political instability, rebellion, and civil war. The turmoil had begun in the late sixteenth century, when the Reformation sparked the religious warfare described in the last chapter. In 1618 the situation deteriorated when another cycle of political strife and warfare erupted. The Thirty Years' War (1618–1648) began as a religious and political dispute in the Holy Roman Empire but soon became an international conflict involving the armies of Spain, France, Sweden, England, and many German states. The war wreaked economic and social havoc in Germany, decimated its population, and forced governments throughout Europe to raise large armies and tax their subjects to pay for them. The entire European economy suffered as a result.

During the 1640s, partly as a result of that devastating conflict, the political order of Europe collapsed. In England a series of bloody civil wars led to the destruction of the monarchy and the establishment of a republic. In France a civil war over

THE FRONTISPIECE OF THOMAS HOBBES'S *TREATISE LEVIATHAN*, PUBLISHED IN LONDON IN 1651
The ruler is depicted as incorporating the bodies of all his subjects, as they collectively authorized him to govern.

LEARNING OBJECTIVES

16.1 What did absolutism mean, both as a political theory and as a practical program, and how was absolutism related to the growth of the power of the state?

16.2 How did France and Spain implement absolutism in the seventeenth century and how powerful did those states become?

16.3 What was the nature of royal absolutism in central and eastern Europe, and how did the policies of the Ottoman Empire and Russia help to establish the boundaries of the West during this period?

16.4 Why did absolutism fail to take root in England and the Dutch Republic during the seventeenth century?

(((Listen to Chapter 16 on MyHistoryLab

👁 Watch the Video Series on MyHistoryLab

Learn about some key topics related to this chapter with the *MyHistoryLab Video Series: Key Topics in Western Civilization*

16.1

16.2

16.3

16.4

constitutional issues drove the royal family from Paris. In Spain the king faced rebellions in four of his territories, while in Ukraine Cossacks staged a military uprising against the Polish-Lithuanian Commonwealth, killing more than one million people.

Hobbes proposed a solution to this multifaceted crisis. In *Leviathan* (1651), a theoretical treatise on the origin of political power, he argued that in the absence of a strong government society would degenerate into a constant state of war. In this dangerous world life would soon become, in Hobbes's famous words, "solitary, poor, nasty, brutish, and short."[1] The only way for people to find political stability would be to agree with their neighbors to form a political society by surrendering their independent power to a ruler who would make laws, administer justice, and maintain order. In this society the ruler would not share power with others. His subjects, having agreed to endow him with such extensive power, could not resist or depose him. The term used to designate the type of government Hobbes was recommending is **absolutism**. In the most general terms, absolutism means a political arrangement in which one ruler possesses unrivaled power.

During the seventeenth and early eighteenth centuries many European monarchs tried to introduce absolutism and increase the wealth and power of the states they ruled. These efforts always met with resistance. In most cases the rulers and their ministers prevailed, and Europe entered the "age of absolutism," which did not end until the outbreak of the French Revolution in 1789. The main question that this chapter addresses is:

absolutism A theory and form of government in the seventeenth and eighteenth centuries in which a ruler claimed unrivaled power.

Why did some European rulers achieve greater success than others in realizing these political objectives?

The Nature of Absolutism

16.1 What did absolutism mean, both as a political theory and as a practical program, and how was absolutism related to the growth of the power of the state?

Seventeenth-century absolutism had both a theoretical and a practical dimension. Theoretical absolutists included writers such as Hobbes who described the nature of power in the state and explained the conditions for its acquisition and continuation. Practical absolutists were the rulers who took concrete political steps to gain control over all other political authorities within the state.

The Theory of Absolutism

When seventeenth-century political writers referred to the monarch's absolute power, they usually meant that he did not share the power to make law with representative assemblies. Hobbes, for example, referred to the absolute ruler as "sole legislator," while the French magistrate Jean Bodin (1530–1596), one of the earliest proponents of absolutist theory, argued in *Six Books of a Commonwealth* (1576) that the most important power of an absolute ruler was the right to make law by himself.

Absolute rulers also claimed that they were above the law. This meant that when monarchs acted for reason of state, that is, for the benefit of the entire kingdom, they did not have to obey the law of their kingdoms. Nor could they be held legally accountable for their actions because they had no legal superior to judge them. Being above

divine right The theory that rulers received their power directly from God.

Read the Document

Jacques-Benigne Bossuet, *Politics Drawn from the Very Words of the Holy Scripture*

Estates General The legislative assembly of France in the Old Regime.

Cortes Legislative assemblies in the Spanish kingdoms.

diets Legislative assemblies in German territories.

standing armies Trained and equipped military forces that were not disbanded after the conclusion of war. Standing armies often helped maintain order and enforce governmental policy at home.

the law, however, did not mean monarchs could act arbitrarily, illegally, or despotically, even though some of them did so from time to time. Absolutist theorists claimed monarchs were obliged to respect the property rights of their subjects whenever they were not acting for reason of state. Under all circumstances monarchs were expected to follow the law of God.

Some absolutist theorists, although not Hobbes, claimed that rulers received their power directly from God. This theory of **divine right** supported royal absolutism, so the theorists claimed, because God would only invest the ruler he appointed with powers that resembled his own. The theory of divine right also supported the absolutist argument that subjects could not resist their monarch under any circumstances.

The Practice of Absolutism

In their quest for absolute power European monarchs employed three strategies. First, they sought to eliminate or weaken national legislative assemblies. In France, which historians consider the most absolutist state in seventeenth-century Europe, the monarchy stopped summoning its national legislature, the **Estates General**, in 1614. In Spain monarchs sought to reduce the powers of the legislative assemblies, the **Cortes**, of their various kingdoms, while in Germany many princes stopped consulting the **diets** of their territorial states.

The second strategy of absolutist rulers was to subordinate the nobility to the king and make them dependent on his favor. Monarchs who aspired to a position of unrivaled power in their kingdoms took steps to keep the nobility in line by suppressing aristocratic challenges to their authority and by appointing men from different social groups as their chief ministers. Yet the king could not afford to alienate these wealthy and high-ranking men, upon whom he still relied for running his government and maintaining order in the localities. Absolute monarchs, therefore, offered nobles special privileges, such as exemption from taxation, positions in the king's government, and freedom to exploit their peasants in exchange for their recognition of the king's absolute authority. In this way, nobles became junior partners in the management of the absolutist state.

The third strategy of absolute monarchs was to control the administrative machinery of the state and use it to enforce royal policy throughout their kingdoms. Absolute monarchs were by nature state builders. They established centralized bureaucracies that extended the reach of their governments down into the smallest towns and villages and out into the most remote regions of their kingdoms. The business conducted by these centrally controlled bureaucracies included the collection of taxes, the recruitment of soldiers, and the operation of the judicial system. Some absolute monarchs used the power of the state to impose and maintain religious conformity. As the seventeenth century advanced, they also used the same power to regulate the price of grain, stimulate the growth of industry, and relieve the plight of the poor. In these ways, absolutist policies had an impact on the lives of all royal subjects, not just noblemen and royal councilors.

Warfare and the Absolutist State

The growth of European states in the seventeenth century was closely related to the conduct of war. During the period from 1600 to 1721, European powers were almost constantly at war. To meet the demands of war, rulers began keeping men under arms at all times. By the middle of the seventeenth century, after the Thirty Years' War had come to an end, most European states had acquired such **standing armies**. These military forces not only served their rulers in foreign wars, but also helped to maintain order and enforce royal policy at home. Standing armies became one of the main props of royal absolutism.

European armies also became larger, in many cases tripling in size. In the 1590s Philip II of Spain had mastered Europe with an army of 40,000 men. By contrast, in the late seventeenth century Louis XIV of France needed an army of 400,000 men to become the dominant power on the continent. The increasing size of these forces partly stemmed from the introduction and extensive use of gunpowder in the fifteenth and sixteenth centuries. Gunpowder led to the widespread use of the musket, a heavy shoulder firearm carried by a foot soldier. The use of the musket demanded the recruitment and equipment of large armies of infantry, who marched in square columns with men holding long pikes (long wooden shafts with pointed metal heads) to protect the musketeers from enemy attacks. As the size of these armies of foot soldiers grew, the role of mounted soldiers, who had dominated medieval warfare, shrank.

Changes in military technology and tactics also necessitated more intensive military training. In the Middle Ages mounted knights had acquired great individual skill, but they did not need to work in precise unison with other men under arms (see "The Military Revolution" in Chapter 11). Seventeenth-century foot soldiers, however, had to learn to march in formation, to coordinate their maneuvers, and to fire without harming their comrades in arms. Therefore, they needed to be drilled. Drilling took place in peacetime as well as during war. The wearing of uniforms, which began when the state assumed the function of clothing its thousands of soldiers, gave further unity and cohesion to the trained fighting force.

The cost of recruiting, training, and equipping these mammoth armies was staggering. In the Middle Ages individual lords often had sufficient financial resources to assemble their own private armies. By the beginning of the seventeenth century the only institution capable of putting the new armies in the field was the state itself. The same was true for navies, which now consisted of heavily armed sailing ships, each of which carried as many as 400 sailors. To build these large armies and navies, as well as to pay the increasing cost of waging war itself (which rose 500 percent between 1530 and 1630), governments had to identify new methods of raising and collecting taxes. In times of war as much as 80 percent of state revenue went for military purposes.

The equipment and training of military forces and the collection and allocation of the revenue necessary to subsidize these efforts stimulated the expansion and refinement of the state bureaucracy. Governments employed thousands of new officials to supervise the collection of new taxes. To make the system of tax collection more efficient, governments often introduced entirely new administrative systems. Some states completely reorganized their bureaucracies to meet the demands of war. They created new departments to supervise the recruitment of soldiers, the manufacture of equipment and uniforms, the building of fleets, and the provisioning of troops in time of war.

The Absolutist State in France and Spain

16.2   How did France and Spain implement absolutism in the seventeenth century and how powerful did those states become?

The first two European monarchies to become absolutist states were France and Spain. The political development of these two countries, however, followed very different courses. The kingdom of France became a model of state building and gradually emerged as the most powerful country in Europe. The Spanish monarchy, on the other hand, struggled to introduce absolutism at a time when the overall economic condition of the country was deteriorating and its military forces were suffering a series of defeats.

The Foundations of French Absolutism

The first serious efforts to establish absolutism in France took place during the reign of Louis XIII (r. 1610–1643). When Louis was only eight years old, a Catholic assassin

regency Rule by relative of a monarch during a period when the monarch was too young to rule or otherwise incapacitated.

parlements The highest provincial courts in France, the most important of which was the Parlement of Paris.

intendants French royal officials who became the main agents of French provincial administration in the seventeenth century.

killed his father, Henry IV (1589–1610). Louis's mother, Marie de' Medici, assumed the leadership of the government during his youth. This period of **regency**, in which aristocratic factions vied for supremacy at court, exposed the main weakness of the monarchy, which was the rival power of the great noble families of the realm. The statesman who addressed this problem most directly was Louis's main councilor, Cardinal Armand Jean du Plessis de Richelieu (1585–1642), who became the king's chief minister in 1628. Richelieu directed all his energies toward centralizing the power of the French state in the person of the king.

Richelieu's most immediate concern was to bring the independent nobility to heel and subordinate their local power to that of the state. He suppressed several conspiracies and rebellions led by noblemen and restricted the independent power of the provincial assemblies and the eight regional **parlements**, which were the highest courts in the country. Richelieu's great administrative achievement was the strengthening of the system of the **intendants**. These paid crown officials, who were recruited from the professional classes and the lower ranks of the nobility, became the main agents of French local administration. Responsible only to the royal council, they collected taxes, supervised local administration, and recruited soldiers for the army.

Richelieu's most challenging task was increasing the government's yield from taxation, a task that became more demanding during times of war. Levying taxes on the French population was always a delicate process; the needs of the state conflicted with the privileges of various social groups, such as the nobles, who were exempt from taxation, and the estates of individual provinces, such as Brittany, that claimed the right to tax the people themselves. Using a variety of tactics, Richelieu managed to increase the yield from the *taille,* the direct tax on land, as much as threefold during the period from 1635 to 1648. He supplemented the *taille* with taxes on officeholding. Even then, the revenue was insufficient to meet the extraordinary demands of war.

CARDINAL RICHELIEU Triple portrait of Cardinal Richelieu, who laid the foundations of French absolutism.

Richelieu's protégé and successor, Jules Mazarin (1602–1661), continued his policies but was unable to prevent civil war from breaking out in 1648. This challenge to the French state, known as the *Fronde* (a pejorative reference to a Parisian game in which children flung mud at passing carriages), had two phases. The first, the Fronde of the Parlement (1648–1649), began when the members of the Parlement of Paris, the most important of all the provincial parlements, refused to register a royal edict that required them to surrender four years' salary. This act of resistance led to demands that the king sign a document limiting royal authority. The rebels put up barricades in the streets of Paris and forced the royal family to flee the city. The second and more violent phase was the Fronde of the Princes (1650–1653), during which Prince de Condé and his noble allies waged war on the government and even formed an alliance with France's enemy, Spain. Only after Condé's military defeat did the entire rebellion collapse.

The Fronde stands as the great crisis of the seventeenth-century French state. It revealed the strength of the local, aristocratic, and legal forces with which the king and his ministers had to contend. In the long run, however, these forces could not destroy the achievement of Richelieu and Mazarin. By the late 1650s the damage had been repaired and the state had resumed its growth.

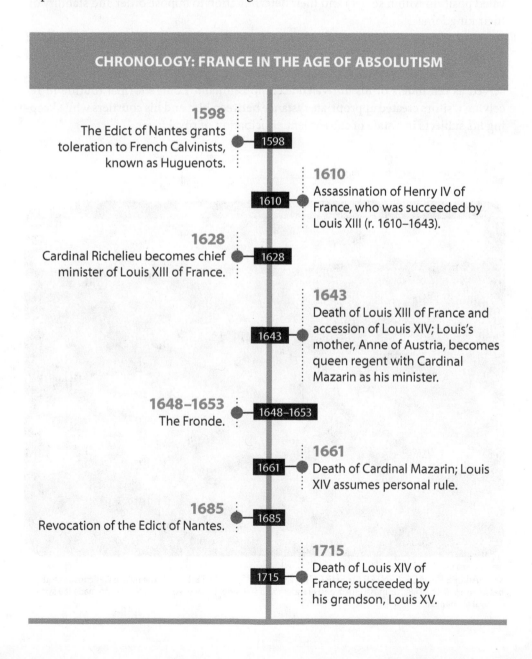

CHRONOLOGY: FRANCE IN THE AGE OF ABSOLUTISM

1598
The Edict of Nantes grants toleration to French Calvinists, known as Huguenots.

1598

1610
Assassination of Henry IV of France, who was succeeded by Louis XIII (r. 1610–1643).

1610

1628
Cardinal Richelieu becomes chief minister of Louis XIII of France.

1628

1643
Death of Louis XIII of France and accession of Louis XIV; Louis's mother, Anne of Austria, becomes queen regent with Cardinal Mazarin as his minister.

1643

1648–1653
The Fronde.

1648–1653

1661
Death of Cardinal Mazarin; Louis XIV assumes personal rule.

1661

1685
Revocation of the Edict of Nantes.

1685

1715
Death of Louis XIV of France; succeeded by his grandson, Louis XV.

1715

baroque A dynamic style in art, architecture, and music that was intended to elicit an emotional response. Baroque buildings were massive, imposing structures with sweeping façades. The baroque style represented a development of Greek classicism in the Hellenistic period. In the seventeenth century the baroque style was closely associated with royal absolutism.

Absolutism in the Reign of Louis XIV

The man who presided over the development of the French state for the next 50 years was the king himself, Louis XIV (r. 1643–1715), who assumed direct control of his government after the death of Mazarin in 1661. In an age of absolute monarchs, Louis towered over his contemporaries. His reputation as the most powerful ruler of the seventeenth century derives as much from the image he conveyed as from the policies he pursued. Artists, architects, dramatists, and members of his immediate entourage helped the king project an image of incomparable majesty and authority. Paintings and sculptures of the king depicted him in sartorial splendor, holding the symbols of power and displaying expressions of regal superiority that bordered on arrogance. At Versailles, about 10 miles from Paris, Louis constructed a lavishly furnished palace that became his main residence and the center of his court. The palace was built in the **baroque** style, which emphasized the size and grandeur of the structure while also conveying a sense of unity and balance among its diverse parts. The sweeping façades of baroque buildings gave them a dynamic quality that evoked an emotional response from the viewer. The baroque style, criticized by contemporaries for its exuberance and pomposity, appealed to absolute monarchs who wished to emphasize their unrivaled position within society and their determination to impose order and stability on their kingdoms.

Court life at Versailles revolved entirely around the king. Court dramas depicted Louis, who styled himself "the sun king," as Apollo, the god of light. The paintings in the grand Hall of Mirrors at Versailles, which recorded the king's military victories, served as reminders of his unrivaled accomplishments. Louis's formal routine in receiving visitors created appropriate distance between him and his courtiers while keeping his subjects in a state of subservient anticipation of royal favor.

View the **Closer Look**   Versailles

VERSAILLES PALACE, CENTER OF THE COURT OF LOUIS XIV AFTER 1682 The palace was constructed between 1669 and 1686. Its massiveness and grandeur and the order it imposed on the landscape made it a symbol of royal absolutism.

Louis's greatest political achievement was securing the complete loyalty and dependence of the old nobility. This he achieved first by requiring the members of these ancient families to come to Versailles for a portion of every year, where they stayed in apartments within the royal palace itself. At Versailles Louis involved them in the elaborate cultural activities of court life and in ceremonial rituals that emphasized their subservience to the king. He also excluded these nobles from holding important offices in the government of the realm, a strategy designed to prevent them from building an independent power base within the bureaucracy. Instead he recruited men from the mercantile and professional classes to run his government. This policy of taming the nobility and depriving them of central administrative power could work only if they received something in return. Like all the absolute monarchs of western Europe, Louis used the patronage at his disposal to grant members of the nobility wealth and privileges in exchange for their loyalty to the crown. In this way the monarchy and the nobility served each other's interests.

In running the actual machinery of government, Louis built upon and perfected the centralizing policies of Richelieu and Mazarin. After the death of Mazarin in 1661, the king, then 23 years old, became his own chief minister, presiding over a council of state that supervised the work of government. An elaborate set of councils at the highest levels of government set policy that department ministers then implemented. The provincial intendants became even more important than they had been under Richelieu and Mazarin, especially in providing food, arms, and equipment for royal troops. The intendants secured the cooperation of local judges, city councils, and parish priests as well as the compliance of the local population. If necessary they could call upon royal troops to enforce the king's policies, but for the most part they preferred to rely on the more effective tactics of negotiation and compromise with local officials. The system, when it worked properly, allowed the king to make decisions that directly affected the lives and beliefs of his 20 million subjects.

In the late seventeenth century the French state also became involved in the economic and financial life of the country. The minister most responsible for this increase in state power was Jean-Baptiste Colbert (1619–1683), a protégé of Mazarin who in 1661 became controller general of the realm. Born into a family of merchants, and despised by the old nobility, Colbert epitomized the type of government official Louis recruited into his service. Entrusted with the supervision of the entire system of royal taxation, Colbert increased royal revenues by reducing the cut taken by tax collectors.

Even more important, Colbert exploited the country's economic resources for the benefit of the state. The theory underlying this set of policies was **mercantilism**, which held that the wealth of the state depended on its ability to import fewer commodities than it exported. Its goal was to secure the largest possible share of the world's monetary supply. Colbert increased the size of France's merchant fleet, founded overseas trading companies, and levied high tariffs on France's commercial rivals. To make France economically self-sufficient, he encouraged the growth of the French textile industry, improved the condition of the roads, built canals throughout the kingdom, and reduced some of the burdensome tolls that impeded internal trade.

The most intrusive exercise of the power of the state during Louis XIV's reign was his decision to enforce religious uniformity. In 1598 the Edict of Nantes had given French Calvinists, known as Huguenots, the freedom to practice their religion. Louis considered the existence of this large Huguenot minority within his kingdom an affront to his sense of order. In 1685 therefore Louis revoked the Edict, thereby denying freedom of religious worship to about one million of his subjects. The army enforced public conversions to Catholicism and closed Protestant churches. Large numbers of Huguenots emigrated to the Netherlands, England, Germany, and North America.

16.1

16.2

16.3

16.4

📖 Read the Document

Louis de Rouvroy, duc de Saint-Simon, Mémoires

mercantilism The theory that the wealth of a state depends on its ability to import fewer commodities than it exports and thus acquire the largest possible share of the world's monetary supply. The theory encouraged state intervention in the economy and the regulation of trade.

Few exercises of absolute power in the seventeenth century caused more disruption in the lives of ordinary people than this attempt to realize Louis's ideal of "one king, one law, one faith."

Louis XIV and the Culture of Absolutism

A further manifestation of the power of the French absolutist state was Louis's success in influencing and transforming French culture. Kings had often served as patrons of the arts by providing income for artists, writers, and musicians and endowing cultural and educational institutions. Louis took this type of royal patronage to a new level, making it possible for him to control the dissemination of ideas and the very production of culture itself. During Louis's reign royal patronage, emanating from the court, extended the king's influence over the entire cultural landscape. The architects of the palace at Versailles, the painters of historical scenes that hung in its hallways and galleries, the composers of the plays and operas performed in its theaters, the sculptors who created busts of the king to decorate its chambers, and the historians and pamphlet writers who celebrated the king's achievements in print all benefited from Louis's direct financial support.

Much of Louis's patronage went to cultural institutions. He took over the Academy of Fine Arts in 1661, founded the Academy of Music in 1669, and chartered a theater company, the *Comédie Française,* in 1680. Two great French dramatists of the late seventeenth century, Jean-Baptiste Molière (1622–1673), the creator of French high comedy, and Jean Racine (1639–1699), who wrote tragedies in the classical style, benefited from the king's patronage. Louis even subsidized the publication of a new journal, the *Journal des savants,* in which writers advanced their ideas. In 1666 Louis extended his patronage to the sciences with the founding of the *Académie des Sciences,* which had the twofold objective of advancing scientific knowledge and glorifying the king. It also benefited the state by devising improvements in ship design and navigation.

Of all the cultural institutions that benefited from Louis XIV's patronage, the *Académie Française* had the most enduring impact on French culture. This society of literary scholars, founded in 1635, sought to standardize the French language and preserve its integrity. In 1694, 22 years after Louis became the academy's patron, the first official French dictionary appeared in print. This achievement of linguistic uniformity, in which words received authorized spellings and definitions, reflected the pervasiveness of Louis's cultural influence as well as the search for order that became the defining characteristic of his reign.

The Wars of Louis XIV, 1667–1714

Colbert's financial and economic policies, coupled with the military reforms of the Marquis de Louvois, laid the foundation for the creation of a formidable military machine. In 1667 Louis XIV began unleashing its full potential. With an army 20 times larger than the French force that had invaded Italy in 1494, Louis fought four separate wars against an array of European powers between 1667 and 1714. His goal in all these wars was territorial acquisition (see **Map 16.1**). In this case Louis set his sights mainly on the German and Spanish territories in the Rhineland along the eastern borders of his kingdom. Contemporaries suggested, however, that he was thinking in grander terms than traditional French dynastic ambition. Propagandists for the king in the late 1660s claimed that

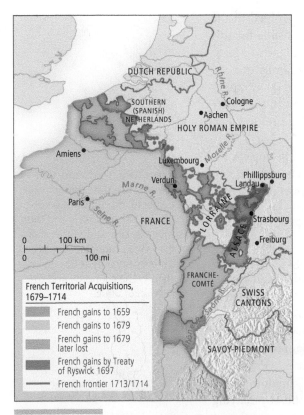

MAP 16.1 FRENCH TERRITORIAL ACQUISITIONS, 1679–1714 Louis XIV thought of the Rhine River as France's natural eastern boundary, and territories acquired in 1659 and 1697 allowed it to reach that limit. Why did France pursue this policy of expansion toward the Rhine?

Louis harbored visions of establishing a "universal monarchy" or an "absolute empire," reminiscent of the empires of ancient Rome, Charlemagne in the ninth century, and Charles V in the sixteenth century.

Louis never attained the empire of his dreams. After he launched an offensive against German towns along the Rhine River in 1688, Great Britain, the Dutch Republic, Spain, and Austria formed a coalition against him. Finally matched by the combined military strength of these allies, forced to wage war on many different fronts (including North America), and unable to collect enough taxes to pay for the war, France felt compelled to conclude peace in 1697. The Treaty of Ryswick marked the turning point in the expansion of the French state and laid the groundwork for the establishment of a **balance of power** in the next century, an arrangement whereby various countries form alliances to prevent any one state from dominating the others.

The Treaty of Ryswick, however, did not mark the end of French territorial ambition. In 1701 Louis went to war once again, this time as part of an effort to place a French Bourbon candidate, his grandson Duke Philip of Anjou, on the Spanish throne. The impending death of the mentally weak, sexually impotent, and chronically ill King Charles II of Spain (r. 1665–1700) without heirs had created a succession crisis. In 1698 the major European powers had agreed to a treaty that would divide Spanish lands between Louis and the Holy Roman Emperor, both of whom were Charles's brothers-in-law. By his will, however, Charles left the Spanish crown and all its overseas possessions to Philip. This bequest offered France more than it would have received on the basis of the treaty. If the will had been upheld, the Pyrenees Mountains would have disappeared as a political barrier between France and Spain, and France, as the stronger of the two kingdoms, would have controlled unprecedented expanses of European and American territory.

Dreaming once again of universal monarchy, Louis rejected the treaty in favor of King Charles's will. The British, Dutch, and Austrians responded by forming a Grand Alliance against France and Spain. After a long and costly conflict, known as the War of the Spanish Succession (1701–1713), the members of this coalition were able to dictate the terms of the Treaty of Utrecht (1713). Philip, who suffered from fits of manic depression and went days without dressing or leaving his room, remained on the Spanish throne as Philip V (r. 1700–1746), but only on the condition that the French and Spanish crowns would never be united. Spain ceded its territories in the Netherlands and in Italy to the Austrian Habsburg Monarchy and its strategic port of Gibraltar at the entrance to the Mediterranean to the British. Britain also acquired large parts of French Canada, including Newfoundland and Nova Scotia. The treaty thus dashed Louis's hopes of universal monarchy and confirmed the new balance of power in Europe.

The loss of French territory in North America, the strains placed on the taxation system by the financial demands of war, and the weakening of France's commercial power as a result of this conflict made France a less potent state at the time of Louis's death in 1715 than it had been in the 1680s. Nevertheless, the main effects of a century of French

balance of power An arrangement in which various countries form alliances to prevent any one state from dominating the others.

 View the Map

Map Discovery: The Treaty of Utrecht

LOUIS XIV Portrait of Louis XIV in military armor, with his plumed helmet and his crown on the table to the right. The portrait was painted during the period of French warfare. In the background is a French ship.

state building remained, including a large, well-integrated bureaucratic edifice that allowed the government to exercise unprecedented control over the population and a military establishment that remained the largest and best equipped in Europe.

Absolutism and State Building in Spain

The history of Spain in the seventeenth century is almost always written in terms of failure, as the country endured a long period of economic decline that began in the late sixteenth century. With a precipitate drop in the size of the population, the monarchy became progressively weaker under a series of ineffective kings. To make matters worse, the country suffered a series of military defeats, most of them at the hands of the French. As a result, Spain lost its position as the major European power (see **Map 16.2**). By the early eighteenth century Spain was a shadow of its former self, and its culture reflected uncertainty, pessimism, and nostalgia for its former imperial greatness. None of this failure, however, should obscure the fact that Spain, like France, underwent a period of state building during the seventeenth century, and that its government, like that of France, gravitated toward absolutism.

The Spanish monarchy in 1600 ruled more territory than did France, but its many principalities and small kingdoms possessed far more independence than even the most remote and peripheral French provinces. The center of the monarchy was the kingdom of Castile, with its capital at Madrid. This kingdom, the largest and wealthiest territory within the Iberian peninsula, had been united with the kingdom of Aragon in 1479 when King Ferdinand II of Aragon (r. 1479–1516), the husband of Queen

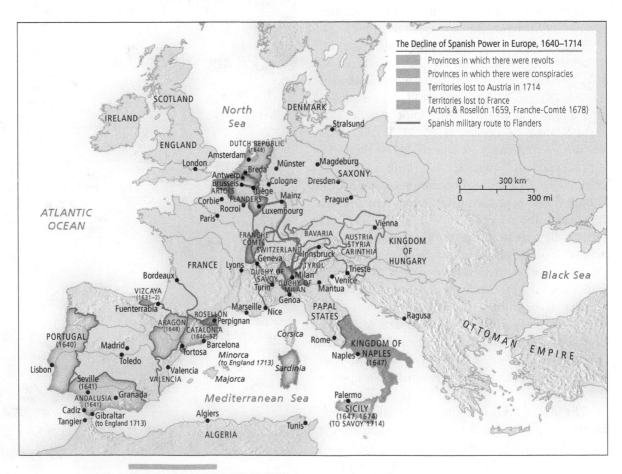

MAP **16.2** THE DECLINE OF SPANISH POWER IN EUROPE, 1640–1714 Revolts in the United Provinces of the Netherlands and Portugal account for two of the most significant losses of Spanish territory. Military defeat at the hands of the French in 1659 and Austria in 1714 account for the loss of most of the other territories. Why did Spain have less military success than France during these years?

Isabella of Castile (r. 1474–1504), ascended the throne. These two kingdoms, however, continued to exist as separate states after the union, each having its own representative institutions and administrative systems. Each of them, moreover, contained smaller, semiautonomous kingdoms and provinces that retained their own distinctive political institutions. Outside the Iberian peninsula the Spanish monarchy ruled territories in the Netherlands, Italy, and the New World.

The only institution besides the monarchy itself that provided any kind of administrative unity to all these Spanish territories in the seventeenth century was the Spanish Inquisition, a centralized ecclesiastical court with a supreme council in Madrid and 21 regional tribunals in different parts of Spain, Italy, and America.

The great challenge for the Spanish monarchy in the seventeenth century was to integrate the various kingdoms and principalities of Spain into a more highly centralized state and make the machinery of that state more efficient and profitable. The statesman who made the most sustained efforts at realizing these goals was the energetic and authoritarian Count-Duke of Olivares (1587–1645), the contemporary of Richelieu during the reign of the Spanish king Philip IV (1621–1665). Olivares faced a daunting task. As a result of decades of warfare, the Spanish monarchy in the 1620s was penniless, the kingdom of Castile had gone bankrupt, and the entire country had entered a period of protracted economic decline.

To deal with these deep structural problems, Olivares proposed a reform of the entire financial system, the establishment of national banks, and the replacement of the tax on consumption, the *millones*, with proportional contributions from towns and villages in Castile. He also tried to make all the Spanish kingdoms and principalities contribute to the national defense on a proportionate basis. His goal was to unify the entire peninsula in a cohesive Spanish national state, similar to that of France. This policy involved suppression of the historic privileges of the various kingdoms and principalities and the direct subordination of each area to the king. It was, in other words, a policy based on the principles of royal absolutism.

Olivares was unable to match the state-building achievement of Richelieu in France. Three factors explain his failure. The first was the opposition he confronted within Castile itself, especially from the cities represented in the Cortes, over the question of taxation. The second, a problem facing Spain throughout the seventeenth century, was military failure. Spanish losses to France during the final phase of the Thirty Years' War aggravated the financial crisis and prevented the monarchy from capitalizing on the prestige that usually attends military victory. The third and most serious impediment was opposition to the policy of subordinating the outlying Spanish regions to the kingdom of Castile. The kingdoms and provinces on the periphery of the country were determined to maintain their individual laws and liberties, especially the powers of their own Cortes. The problem became more serious when Olivares, in the wake of military defeat by the French and Dutch, put more pressure on these outlying kingdoms and provinces to contribute to the war effort. During the tenure of Olivares, Spain faced separatist revolts in Portugal, Catalonia, Sicily, and

DIEGO DE VELÁZQUEZ, PORTRAIT OF THE PRINCE BALTASAR CARLOS, HEIR TO THE SPANISH THRONE The depiction of the six-year-old prince on a rearing horse was intended to suggest military and political power at a time when the monarchy was losing both. The prince died in 1646, before he could succeed to the throne.

Germany and the Thirty Years' War, 1618–1648

Before 1648 the main political power within the geographical area known as Germany was the Holy Roman Empire. This large political formation was a loose confederation of kingdoms, principalities, duchies, ecclesiastical territories, and cities, each of which had its own laws and political institutions. The emperor, who was elected by a body of German princes, exercised immediate jurisdiction only in his own dynastic possessions and in the imperial cities. He also convened a legislative assembly known as the *Reichstag*, over which he exercised limited influence. The emperor did not have a large administrative or judicial bureaucracy through which he could enforce imperial law in the localities. The empire was not in any sense a sovereign state, even though it had long been a major force in European diplomacy. It had acquired and maintained that international position by relying on the military and financial contributions of its imperial cities and the lands controlled directly by the Habsburg emperors.

The Thirty Years' War permanently altered the nature of this intricate political structure. That war began as a conflict between Protestant German princes and the Catholic emperor over religious and constitutional issues. The incident that triggered it in 1618 was the so-called Defenestration of Prague, when members of the predominantly Protestant Bohemian legislature, known as the Diet, threw two imperial officials out a castle window as a protest against the religious policies of their recently elected king, the future emperor Ferdinand II. The Diet proceeded to depose Ferdinand, a Catholic, and elect a Protestant prince, Frederick V of the Palatinate, to replace him. The war soon broadened into a European-wide struggle over the control of German and Spanish territory, as the Danes, Swedes, and French successively entered the conflict against the emperor and his Spanish Habsburg relatives. For a brief period in the late 1620s England also entered the conflict against Spain. The war, which was fought mainly on German soil, had a devastating effect on the country. More than one million soldiers marched across German lands, sacking towns and exploiting the resources of local communities. Germany lost up to one-third of its population, while the destruction of property retarded the economic development of the country for more than 50 years.

 **Read the Document**

Thirty Years' War (1618), Rushworth

DEFENESTRATION OF PRAGUE, MAY 23, 1618 The Thirty Years' War was touched off when Protestant nobles in the Bohemian legislature threw two Catholic imperial governors out the window of a castle in Prague.

The political effects of the war were no less traumatic. By virtue of the Treaty of Westphalia, which ended the war in 1648, the empire was permanently weakened, although it continued to function until 1806 (see **Map 16.3**). The individual German territories within the empire developed more institutional autonomy than they had before the war. They became sovereign states, with their own armies, foreign policies, and central bureaucracies. Two of these German states became major European powers and developed their own forms of absolutism. The first was Brandenburg-Prussia, a collection of various territories in northern Germany that was transformed into the kingdom of Prussia at the beginning of the eighteenth century. The second state was the Austrian Habsburg Monarchy, which in the eighteenth century was usually identified simply as Austria. The Habsburgs had long dominated the Holy Roman Empire and continued to secure election as emperors after the Treaty of Westphalia. In the late seventeenth century, however, the Austrian Habsburg Monarchy acquired its own institutional identity, distinct from that of the Holy Roman Empire. It consisted of the lands that the Habsburgs controlled directly in the southeastern part of the empire and other territories, including the kingdom of Hungary, which lay outside the territorial boundaries of the empire.

The Growth of the Prussian State

In 1648, at the end of the Thirty Years' War, Prussia could barely claim the status of an independent state, much less an absolute monarchy. The core of the Prussian state was Brandenburg, which was an electorate because its ruler cast one of the ballots to

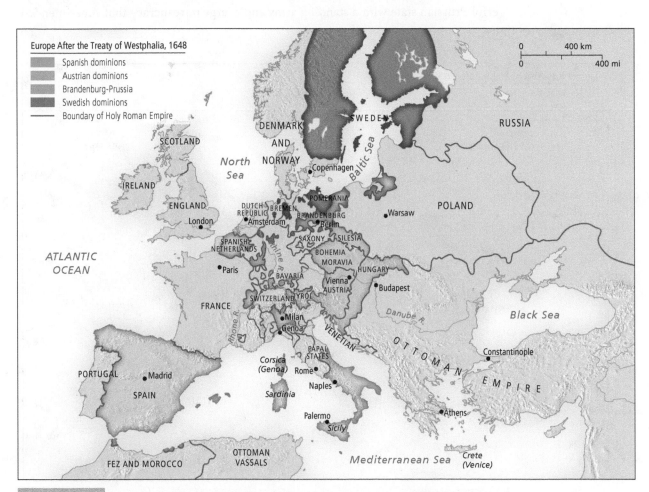

MAP **16.3** EUROPE AFTER THE TREATY OF WESTPHALIA, 1648 The Holy Roman Empire no longer included the Dutch Republic, which was now independent of Spain. Some of the lands of the Austrian Habsburg Monarchy and Brandenburg-Prussia lay outside the boundaries of the Holy Roman Empire. Italy was divided into a number of small states in the north, while Spain ruled Naples, Sicily, and Sardinia. Which European powers suffered the greatest losses of territory as a result of the Thirty Years' War?

Junkers The traditional nobility of Prussia.

elect the Holy Roman Emperor. The Hohenzollern family, which controlled the electorate, held lands that lay scattered throughout northern Germany and stretched into eastern Europe. The largest was Prussia, a Baltic territory lying outside the boundaries of the Holy Roman Empire. As ruler of these disparate and noncontiguous lands, the Elector of Brandenburg had virtually no state bureaucracy, collected few taxes, and commanded only a small army. Most of his territories, moreover, lay in ruins in 1648, having been devastated by Swedish and imperial troops at various times during the war.

The Great Elector Frederick William (r. 1640–1688) began the long process of turning this ramshackle structure into a powerful and cohesive German state (see **Map 16.4**). His son and grandson, King Frederick I (r. 1688–1713) and Frederick William I (r. 1713–1740), completed the transformation. The key to their success, as it was for all aspiring absolute monarchs in eastern Europe, was to secure the compliance of the traditional nobility, who in Prussia were known as **Junkers**. The Great Elector Frederick William achieved this end by granting the Junkers a variety of privileges, including exemption from import duties and the excise tax. The most valuable concession was the legal confirmation of their rights over their serfs. During the previous 150 years Prussian peasants had lost their freedom, becoming permanently bound to the estates of their lords and completely subject to the Junkers' arbitrary brand of local justice. The Junkers had a deeply vested interest in perpetuating this oppressive system of serfdom, and the lawgiver Frederick was able to provide them with the legal guarantees they required.

With the loyalty of the Junkers secure, Frederick William began building a powerful Prussian state with a standing army and a large bureaucracy that superintended

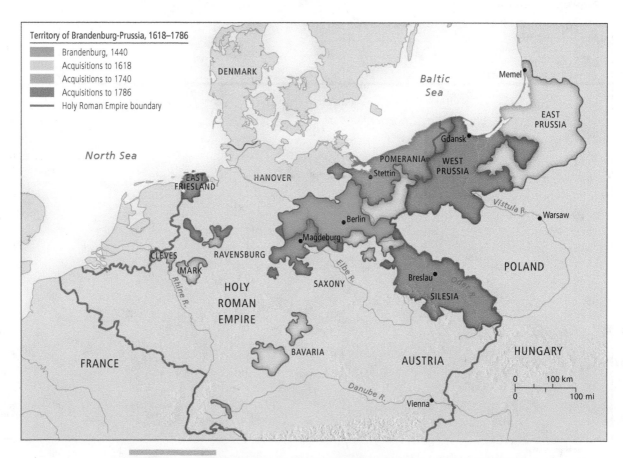

MAP **16.4** THE GROWTH OF BRANDENBURG-PRUSSIA, 1618–1786 By acquiring lands throughout northern Germany, Prussia became a major European power. The process began during the early seventeenth century, but it continued well into the eighteenth century. The Prussian army, which was the best trained fighting force in Europe in the eighteenth century, greatly facilitated Prussia's growth. What challenges did the Prussian government face in governing this state?

military and financial affairs. The army grew rapidly, rising to 30,000 men in 1690 and 80,000 by 1740. It consisted of a combination of carefully recruited volunteers, foreign mercenaries, and, after 1713, conscripts from the general population. Its most famous regiment, known as the Blue Prussians or the Giants of Potsdam, consisted of 1,200 men, each of whom was at least six feet tall. Commanded by officers drawn from the nobility and reinforced by Europe's first system of military reserves, this army quickly became the best trained fighting force in Europe. Prussia became a model military state, symbolized by the transformation of the royal gardens into an army training ground during the reign of Frederick William I.

As this military state grew in size and complexity, its rulers acquired many of the attributes of absolute rule. Most significantly, they became the sole legislators within the state. The main representative assembly in the electorate, the Diet of Brandenburg, met for the last time in 1652. Frederick William and his successors, however, continued to consult with smaller local assemblies, especially in the matter of taxation. The naming of Frederick I as king of Prussia in 1701 marked a further consolidation of royal power. His son's style of rule, which included physical punishment of judges whose decisions displeased him, suggested that the Prussian monarchy not only had attained absolute power, but could occasionally abuse it.

The Austrian Habsburg Monarchy

The Austrian Habsburgs were much less successful than the Hohenzollerns in building a centralized, consolidated state along absolutist lines. The various territories that made up the Austrian Habsburg Monarchy in the late seventeenth century were larger and more diverse than those that belonged to Prussia. Map 16.3 shows that in addition to the cluster of duchies that form present-day Austria, the Austrian Habsburg monarchy embraced two subordinate kingdoms. The kingdom of Bohemia, lying to the north, had struggled against Habsburg control for nearly a century and included the provinces of Moravia and Silesia. The kingdom of Hungary, lying to the southeast, included the large semiautonomous principality of Transylvania. The Habsburgs regained Hungary from the Ottoman Empire in stages between 1664 and 1718. In 1713 the monarchy also acquired the former Spanish Netherlands and the Italian territories of Milan and Naples.

The Austrian Habsburg monarchs of the seventeenth and early eighteenth centuries never succeeded in integrating these ethnically, religiously, and politically diverse lands into a unified, cohesive state similar to that of France. The main obstacle was a lack of a unified bureaucracy. The only centralized administrative institutions in this amalgam of kingdoms were the Court Chamber, which superintended the collection of taxes throughout the monarchy, and the Austrian army, which included troops from all Habsburg lands. Even these centralized institutions had difficulty operating smoothly. For all practical purposes, the Habsburgs had to rule their various kingdoms separately.

In governing its Austrian and Bohemian lands, this decentralized Habsburg monarchy nonetheless acquired some of the characteristics of absolutist rule. After defeating the Bohemians at the Battle of White Mountain in 1620 during the Thirty Years' War, Emperor Ferdinand II (r. 1618–1637) strengthened his authority not only in Bohemia, but over all the territories under his direct control. After punishing the rebels and exiling many of the Protestant nobility, he undertook a deliberate expansion of his legislative and judicial powers, and he secured direct control over all his administrative officials.

A policy of severe religious repression accompanied this increase in the emperor's authority. Ferdinand assumed that Protestantism served as a justification for rebellion, and he therefore decided that its practice could not be tolerated. He required that Protestants in all the emperor's territories take a Catholic loyalty oath, and he banned Protestant education.

Habsburgs were not so successful in trying to impose absolutism on Hungary in the late seventeenth and eighteenth centuries. Hungarians had a long tradition of limited, constitutional rule in which the national Diet exercised powers of legislation and taxation, just as Parliament did in England. Habsburg emperors made some limited inroads on these traditions but they were never able to break them. They also were unable to achieve the same degree of religious uniformity that they had imposed on their other territories. In Hungary the Habsburgs encountered the limits of royal absolutism.

The Ottoman Empire: Between East and West

In the seventeenth and early eighteenth centuries the southeastern border of the Habsburg monarchy separated the kingdom of Hungary from the Ottoman Empire. This militarized frontier marked not only the political boundary between two empires, but a deeper cultural boundary between East and West.

As we have seen in previous chapters, the West is not just a geographical area. It is also a cultural area; the people who inhabit this territory share many of the same religious, political, legal, and philosophical traditions. In the eyes of most Europeans, the Ottoman Turks, who posed a recurrent military threat to the Habsburg monarchy, did not belong to this Western world. Because the Ottoman Turks were Muslims, Europeans considered them enemies of Christianity, infidels who were bent on the destruction of Christendom. Ottoman emperors, known as sultans, were reputedly despots who ruled over their subjects as slaves. Western literature also depicted the sultans as cruel and brutal tyrants, the opposite of the ideal Christian prince. One French play of 1612 showed the mother of the sultan Mehmed the Conqueror (r. 1451–1481) drinking the blood of a victim.

These stereotypes of the Turks gave Europeans a sense of their own Western identity. Turks became a negative reference group with whom Europeans could compare themselves. The realities of Ottoman politics and culture, however, were quite different from their representations in European literature. Turkish despotism, the name Europeans gave to the Ottoman system of government, existed only in theory. Ever since the fourteenth century Ottoman writers had claimed for the sultan extraordinary powers, including the right to seize the landed property of his subjects at will. In practice, however, the sultan never exercised unlimited power. The spirit of Muslim law limited his prerogatives, and he shared power with the grand vizier, his chief executive officer. By the 1660s, when most European states had entered the age of absolutism, the sultan's power had become largely titular. Moreover, the Ottoman practice of tolerating non-Muslim religions within the empire made the sultans less absolutist than most of their seventeenth-century European counterparts. (See *Different Voices* in this chapter.)

Even the Ottoman Empire's high degree of administrative centralization did not extend to all the territories it ruled. Many of its provinces, especially those in the Balkans, enjoyed a considerable measure of autonomy, especially in the seventeenth century. The Balkans, which were geographically part of Europe, never experienced the full force of direct Turkish rule. As in most monarchies of western and central Europe, a complex pattern of negotiation between the central imperial administration and local officials characterized Ottoman rule. In Europe the Ottoman Empire bore the closest resemblance to the Spanish monarchy, which also ruled many far-flung territories. Like Spain, the Ottoman Empire declined in power during the seventeenth century and lost effective control of some of its outlying provinces.

Ottoman Turks and Europeans frequently went to war against each other, but their interactions with the West were not always hostile. The Turks had been involved in European warfare since the fifteenth century, and they had formed diplomatic alliances with the French against the Austrian Habsburgs on a number of occasions. Europeans and Ottomans often acquired military technology and administrative techniques from each other. Trade between European countries and the Ottoman Empire

Different Voices

Western Writers Evaluate the Ottoman Turks

*W*estern commentators displayed ambivalent feelings toward the Ottoman Turks in the seventeenth century. On the one hand, Westerners were impressed with the power of the Sultan, the size of the Ottoman Empire, the discipline of their soldiers, and the political obedience of their subjects to their sovereign. On the other hand, Westerners considered the Turks barbarous. Richard Knolles (1550–1610) reflected this ambivalence in the preface to his history of the Turks with an analysis of their greatness. He then condemned the ways in which this barbarous people violated international and natural law. Thomas Smith, a clergyman at Oxford University, agreed with Knolles that the Turks were a barbarous nation, but he attributed this trait to their lack of interest in education and their intolerance of other religions.

An English Writer Criticizes the Turks for Violating the Law

But to come nearer unto the causes of the Turks greatness, … first in them is to be noted an ardent and infinite desire of sovereignty, wherewith they have long since promised unto themselves the monarchy of the whole world, a quick motive unto their so haughty designs. Then, such a rare unity and agreement amongst them, as well in the manner of their religion (if it be so to be called) as in matters concerning their state (especially in all their enterprises to be taken in hand for the augmenting of their Empire) as that thereof they call themselves *Islami*, that is to say, men of one mind, or at peace among themselves; so as it is not to be marveled, if thereby they grow strong themselves, and dreadful to others. Join unto this their courage, conceived by the wonderful success of their perpetual fortune, their notable vigilance in taking the advantage of every occasion for the enlarging of their monarchy, their frugality and temperateness in their diet and other manner of living, their straight observing of their ancient military discipline, their cheerful and almost incredible obedience unto their princes and Sultans; such, as in that point no nation in the world was to be worthily compared unto them—all great causes why their empire hath so mightily increased and so long continued. . . .

And yet these great ones not contented by such commendable and lawful means still to extend or establish their far spreading empire, if that point once come in question, they stick not in their devilish policy to break and infringe the laws both of nations and nature. Their leagues grounded upon the law of nations, be they with never so strong capitulations concluded, or solemnity of oath confirmed, have with them no longer force than stands with their own profit, serving indeed but as snares to entangle other princes in, until they have singled out him whom they purpose to devour; the rest fast bound still looking on as if their own turn should never come, yet with no more assurance of their safety by their leagues than had the other whom they see perish before their faces. As for the kind law

of nature, what can be thereunto more contrary than for the father most unnaturally to embrue his hands in the blood of his own children and the brother to become the bloody executioner of his own brethren, a common matter among the Ottoman emperors? All which most execrable and inhumane murders they cover with the pretended safety of their state, as thereby freed from the fear of all aspiring competitors (the greatest torment of the mighty) and by the preservation of the integrity of their Empire, which they thereby keep whole and entire unto themselves, and so deliver it as it were by hand from one to another, in no part dismembered or impaired. By these and such like means is this barbarous empire (of almost nothing) grown to that height of majesty and power, as that it hath in contempt all the rest, being it self not inferior in greatness and strength unto the greatest monarchies that ever yet were upon the face of the earth, the Roman Empire only excepted.

SOURCE: Richard Knolles, *The General History of the Turks from the First Beginnings of That Nation to the Rising of the Ottoman Family*, 1603.

An English Clergyman Comments on the Learning and Religious Intolerance of the Turks

The Turks are justly branded with the character of a barbarous nation, which censure does not relate either to the cruelty and severity of their punishments . . . or to want of discipline . . . or to want of civil behavior among themselves . . . but to the intolerable pride and scorn wherewith they treat all the world besides.

Their temper and genius, the constitution of their government, and the principles of their education incline them to war, where valor and merit are sure to be encouraged, and have their due reward. They have neither leisure nor inclination to entertain the studies of learning or the civil arts, which take off the roughness and wildness of nature, and render men more agreeable in their conversation. And though they are forced to commend and admire the ingenuity of the Western Christians, when they see any mathematical instrument, curious pictures, map, or sea-charts, or open the leaves of any printed book, or the like; yet they look upon all this as a curiosity, that not only may be spared, but what ought to be carefully avoided, and kept out of their empire, as tending to soften men's minds, and render them less fit for arms, which they look upon as the best and truest end of life, to enlarge their greatness and their conquests.

But it is not so much their want of true and ingenuous learning which makes them thus intractable and rude to strangers as a rooted and inveterate prejudice against and hated of all others who are of a different religion. It is not to be

(continued on next page)

(continued from previous page)

expected that where this principle prevails, and is looked upon as a piece of religion and duty, they who embrace it should be guilty of any act of kindness and humanity; except when they are bribed to it with hope of reward and gain, or forced to it by the necessities of state, or wrought upon more powerfully, as it were against their wills by the resentments of some favors and kindnesses received, which may happen now and then in some of better natures and more generous tempers.

SOURCE: Thomas Smith, *Remarks Upon the Manners, Religion and Government of the Turks*, 1678.

For Discussion

1. Which characteristics of the Turks given in the two documents did the authors view as positive and which did they view as negative?
2. To what extent do these two descriptions of the Turks support the Western view that the Ottoman Empire was an "oriental despotism"?
3. These two writers based their assessments of the Turks upon reports from travelers. What value do such reports have as historical evidence?

Read the Document

Defeat of Ottoman Turks (1683), King John Sobieski

View the Map

Map Discovery: Expansion of Russia Under Peter the Great

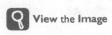

View the Image

Peter the Great

remained brisk throughout this period. Europe supplied hardware and textiles to the Turks while they in turn shipped coffee, tobacco, and tulips to European ports. Communities of Turks and other Muslims lived in European cities, while numerous European merchants resided in territories under Ottoman control.

These encounters between Turks and Europeans suggest that the militarized boundary between the Habsburgs and the Ottoman Empire was more porous than its fortifications suggested. Military conflict and Western contempt for Turks disguised a complex process of political and cultural interaction between the two civilizations. Europeans tended to think of the Ottoman Empire as "oriental," but it is more accurate to view it as a region lying between the East and the West.

Russia and the West

The other power that marked the boundary between East and West was the vast Russian Empire, which stretched from its boundary with Poland-Lithuania in the west to the Pacific Ocean in the east. Until the end of the seventeenth century, the kingdom of Muscovy and the lands attached to it seemed, at least to Europeans, part of the Asiatic world. Dominated by an Eastern Orthodox branch of Christianity, Russia drew very little upon the cultural traditions associated with western Europe. Unlike its Slavic neighbor Poland, Russia had not absorbed large doses of German culture. It also appeared to Europeans to be another example of "oriental despotism," a state in which the ruler, known as the tsar (the Russian word for Caesar), could rule his subjects at will, "not bound up by any law or custom."

During the reign of Tsar Peter I, known as Peter the Great (r. 1682–1725), Russia underwent a process of Westernization, bringing it more into line with the culture of European countries and becoming a major European power. This policy began after Peter visited England, the Dutch Republic, northern Germany, and Austria in 1697 and 1698. Upon his return he directed his officials and members of the upper levels of Russian society to adopt Western styles of dress and appearance, including the removal of men's beards. (Scissors were kept in the customs house for this purpose alone.) Beards symbolized the backward, Eastern Orthodox culture from whose grip Peter hoped to extricate his country. Young Russian boys were sent abroad for their education. Women began to participate openly in the social and cultural life of the cities, in violation of Orthodox custom. Smoking was permitted despite the Church's insistence that Scripture condemned it. The calendar was reformed and books were printed in modern Russian type. Peter's importation of Western art and the imitation of Western architecture complemented this policy of enforced cultural change.

Westernization also involved military and political reforms that changed the character of the Russian state. During the first 25 years of his reign Peter had found himself unable to achieve sustained military success against his two great enemies, the Ottoman Turks to the south and the Swedes to the west. During the Great Northern War with Sweden (1700–1721), Peter introduced a number of military reforms that eventually turned the tide against his enemy. Having learned about naval technology from the British and Dutch, he built a large navy. He introduced a policy of conscription, giving him a standing army of more than 200,000 men. A central council, established in 1711, not only directed financial administration but also levied and supplied troops.

This new military state also acquired many of the centralizing and absolutist features of western European monarchies. Efforts to introduce absolutism in Russia had begun during the reigns of Alexis (r. 1645–1676) and Fedor (r. 1676–1682), who had strengthened the central administration and brutally suppressed peasant rebellions. Peter built upon his predecessors' achievement. He created a new structure for managing the empire, appointing 12 governors to superintend Russia's 43 separate provinces. He brought the Church under state control. By establishing a finely graded hierarchy of official ranks in the armed forces, the civil administration, and the court, Peter not only improved administrative efficiency, but he also made it possible for men of non-aristocratic birth to attain the same privileged status as the old landowning nobility. He won the support of all landowners by introducing **primogeniture** (inheritance of the entire estate by the eldest son), which prevented the subdivision of their estates, and supporting the enserfment of the peasants. In dealing with his subjects Peter claimed more power than any other absolute monarch in Europe. Muscovites often told foreign visitors that the tsar treated them like slaves, punishing them at will and executing them without due process.[2] During the trial of his own son, Alexis, for treason in 1718, Peter told the clergy that "we have a sufficient and absolute power to judge our son for his crimes according to our own pleasure."[3]

The most visible sign of Peter's policy of westernization was the construction of the port city of St. Petersburg on the Gulf of Finland, which became the new capital of the Russian Empire. One of the main objectives of Russian foreign policy during Peter's reign was to secure access to the Baltic Sea, allowing Russia to open maritime trade with Europe and become a Western naval power. By draining a swamp on the estuary of the Neva River, Peter laid the foundations of a city that became the new capital of his empire. Construction began in 1703; within 20 years St. Petersburg had a population of 40,000 people. With his new capital city now looking westward, and an army and central administration reformed on the basis of Prussian and French example, Peter could enter the world of European diplomacy and warfare as both a Western and an absolute monarch. (See *Encounters and Transformations* in this chapter.)

primogeniture The legal arrangement by which the eldest son inherits the entire estate upon the death of the father.

 Read the Document

Peter the Great, "Correspondence with Alexis" (Russia), 1715

Resistance to Absolutism in England and the Dutch Republic

16.4 Why did absolutism fail to take root in England and the Dutch Republic during the seventeenth century?

Royal absolutism did not succeed in all European states. In Poland-Lithuania and Hungary, for example, where the nobility exercised considerable political power, legislative assemblies continued to meet throughout the seventeenth and eighteenth centuries. Both countries had long traditions of constitutional government, and the Poles elected their kings. In western Europe the kingdom of England and the northern provinces of the Netherlands also resisted efforts to

Encounters and Transformations
St. Petersburg and the West

The building of a new capital city, St. Petersburg, symbolized the encounter between Russia and the West during the reign of Peter the Great. Peter had seized the land on which the city was located, the marshy delta of the Neva River, from Sweden during the Northern War. The construction of the city, which first served as a fortress and then a naval base, occurred at a tremendous cost in treasure and human life. Using the royal powers he had significantly augmented earlier in his reign, Peter ordered more than 10,000 workers (and possibly twice that number) from throughout his kingdom to realize this ambitious and risky project. The harsh weather conditions, the ravages of malaria and other diseases, and the chronic shortages of provisions in a distant location resulted in the death of thousands of workers. Beginning in 1710 Peter ordered the transfer of central governmental, commercial, and military functions to the new city. The city became the site for Peter's Winter Palace, the residences of Russia's foreign ambassadors, and the headquarters of the Russian Orthodox Church. The Academy of Fine Arts and the Academy of Sciences were built shortly thereafter. During the 1730s Russia's first bourse, or exchange, fulfilled the prophecy of a British observer in 1710 that the city, with its network of canals, "might one day prove a second Amsterdam or Venice." Thus, St. Petersburg came to embody all the modernizing and westernizing achievements of Peter the Great.

The location of the new city and its architecture reflected Russia's encounter with the West. With access to the Baltic Sea, the new city, often described as "a window on the West," looked toward the European ports with which Russia increased its commerce and the European powers that Russia engaged in battle and diplomacy. The architects, stonemasons, and interior decorators that Peter commissioned came from France, Italy, Germany, and the Dutch Republic, and they constructed the buildings in contemporary European styles. The general plan of the city, drawn up by a French architect, featured straight, paved streets with stone paths that are now called sidewalks. St. Petersburg thus became a port through which Western influences entered Russia. The contrast with the old capital, Moscow, which was situated in the center of the country and embodied the spirit of the old Russia that Peter strove to modernize, could not have been clearer.

The construction of St. Petersburg played a central role in transforming Russia from a medieval kingdom on the fringes of Europe into a modern, Western power. It did not, however, eliminate the conflict in Russia between those who held the West up as the cultural standard that Russia should emulate and those who celebrated Russia's cultural superiority over the West. This conflict, which began in the eighteenth century, has continued to the present day. During the period of communism in the twentieth century, when St. Petersburg was renamed Leningrad and Moscow once again became the political capital of the country, the tradition that emphasized Russia's Eastern orientation tended to prevail. It was no coincidence that the collapse of communism and the disintegration of the Union of Soviet Socialist Republics in 1989 led to a renewed emphasis on Russia's ties with the West. The restoration of St. Petersburg's original name in 1991 and the celebration of its 300th anniversary in 2003 were further attempts to integrate Russia more fully into the West.

View the Image Winter Palace at St. Petersburg

PICTURE OF ST. PETERSBURG (1815) This view of St. Petersburg from the quay in front of the Winter Palace reveals the city's Western character. The buildings lying across the Neva River, including the bourse, were designed by European architects. The gondolas, seen in the foreground docking at the quay, enhanced St. Petersburg's reputation as "Venice of the North."

For Discussion

1. How did the founding of St. Petersburg contribute to the growth of the Russian state?
2. How did Peter the Great's absolute power facilitate the growth of the city?

Taking It Further

Whittaker, Cynthia Hyla (ed.). *Russia Engages the World, 1453–1825*. 2003. Includes essays on St. Petersburg and Russia's European Identity.

Hughes, Lindsey. *Russia in the Age of Peter the Great*. 1998. Includes chapters on Russia and the World and Russian government, society, and culture.

implement royal absolutism. In England this resistance to absolutism resulted in the temporary destruction of the monarchy in the middle of the seventeenth century and the permanent limitation of royal power after 1688. In the northern Netherlands, an even more resounding rejection of absolutism occurred. After winning their independence from absolutist Spain, the Dutch established a republic with a decentralized form of government that lasted the entire seventeenth and eighteenth centuries.

The English Monarchy

At different times in the seventeenth century English monarchs tried to introduce royal absolutism, but the political traditions of the country stood as major obstacles to their designs. The most important of these traditions was that the king could not make law or tax his subjects without the consent of Parliament, which consisted of the House of Lords (the nobility and the bishops) and the House of Commons, an elected assembly that included the lesser aristocracy, lawyers, and townsmen.

In the early seventeenth century some members of the House of Commons feared that this tradition of parliamentary government might come to an end. The first Stuart king, James I (r. 1603–1625), aroused some of these fears as early as 1604 when he called his first parliament. James thought of himself as an absolute monarch, and in a number of speeches and published works he emphasized the height of his independent royal power, which was known in England as the **prerogative**. James's son, Charles I (r. 1625–1649), gave substance to these fears of absolutism by forcing his subjects to lend money to the government during a war with Spain (1625–1629), imprisoning men who refused to make these loans, and collecting duties on exports without parliamentary approval. When members of the House of Commons protested against these policies, Charles dismissed Parliament in 1629 and decided to rule without summoning it again.

This period of nonparliamentary government, known as the **personal rule**, lasted until 1640. During these years Charles, unable to collect taxes by the authority of Parliament, used his prerogative to bring in new revenues, especially by asking all subjects to pay "ship-money" to support the outfitting of ships to defend the country against attack. During the personal rule the king's religious policy fell under the control of William Laud, who was named archbishop of Canterbury in 1633. Laud's determination to restore many of the rituals associated with Roman Catholicism alienated large numbers of the more zealous Protestants, known as Puritans, and led to a growing perception that members of the king's government were engaged in a conspiracy to destroy both England's ancient constitution and the Protestant religion.

The personal rule might have continued indefinitely if Charles had not once again faced the financial demands of war. In 1636 the king tried to introduce a new religious liturgy in his northern kingdom of Scotland. The liturgy included a number of rituals that the firmly Calvinist Scottish population considered Roman Catholic. The new liturgy so angered a group of women in Edinburgh that they threw their chairs at the bishop when he introduced it. In response to this affront to their religion, the infuriated Scots signed a National Covenant (1638) pledging to defend the integrity of their Church, abolished episcopacy (government of the church by bishops) in favor of a Presbyterian system of church government, and mobilized a large army. To secure the funds to fight the Scots, Charles was forced to summon his English Parliament, thereby ending the period of personal rule.

The English Civil Wars and Revolution

Tensions between the reconvened English Parliament and Charles led to the first revolution of modern times. The Long Parliament, which met in November 1640, impeached many of the king's ministers and judges and dismantled the judicial apparatus

prerogative The set of powers exercised by the English monarch alone, rather than in conjunction with Parliament.

personal rule The period from 1629 to 1640 in England when King Charles I ruled without Parliament.

of the 11 years of personal rule, including the courts that had been active in the prosecution of Puritans. Parliament declared the king's nonparliamentary taxes illegal and enacted a law limiting the time between the meetings of Parliament to three years.

This legislation did not satisfy the king's critics in Parliament. Their suspicion that the king was conspiring against them and their demand to approve all royal appointments created a poisoned political atmosphere in which neither side trusted the other. In August 1642 civil war began between the Parliamentarians, known as Roundheads

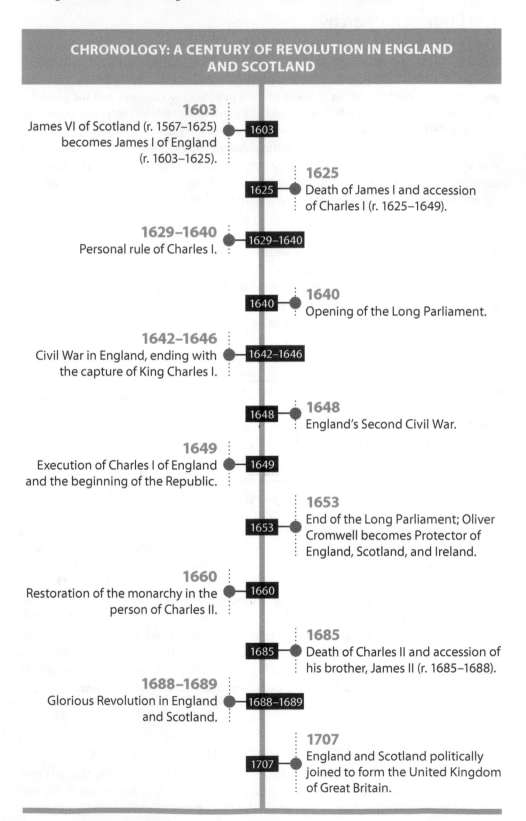

CHRONOLOGY: A CENTURY OF REVOLUTION IN ENGLAND AND SCOTLAND

1603
James VI of Scotland (r. 1567–1625) becomes James I of England (r. 1603–1625).

1603

1625
1625
Death of James I and accession of Charles I (r. 1625–1649).

1629–1640
Personal rule of Charles I.
1629–1640

1640
1640
Opening of the Long Parliament.

1642–1646
Civil War in England, ending with the capture of King Charles I.
1642–1646

1648
1648
England's Second Civil War.

1649
Execution of Charles I of England and the beginning of the Republic.
1649

1653
1653
End of the Long Parliament; Oliver Cromwell becomes Protector of England, Scotland, and Ireland.

1660
Restoration of the monarchy in the person of Charles II.
1660

1685
1685
Death of Charles II and accession of his brother, James II (r. 1685–1688).

1688–1689
Glorious Revolution in England and Scotland.
1688–1689

1707
1707
England and Scotland politically joined to form the United Kingdom of Great Britain.

because many of the artisans who supported them had close-cropped hairstyles, and the Royalists or Cavaliers, who often wore their hair in long flowing locks. Parliament, with the military support of the Scots and a well-trained, efficient fighting force, the New Model Army, won this war in 1646 and took Charles prisoner. The king's subsequent negotiations with the Scots and the English Presbyterians, who had originally fought against him, led to a second civil war in 1648. In this war, which lasted only a few months, the New Model Army once again defeated Royalist forces.

This defeat of the king's forces led to a revolution. Following the wishes of the army, Parliament set up a court that tried and executed the king in January 1649. (See *Justice in History* in this chapter.) Shortly thereafter the House of Commons abolished the monarchy itself, thus making England a republic. This revolutionary change in the form of English government, however, did not lead to the establishment of a democratic regime. Democracy, in which a large percentage of the adult male population could vote, was the goal of the Levellers, a political party that originated in the New Model Army and attracted considerable support in London. The Levellers called for annual parliaments, the separation of powers between the executive and legislative branches of government, and the introduction of universal suffrage for men. The army officers, however, resisted these demands, and after an unsuccessful mutiny in the army, the Leveller party collapsed. The defeat of the Levellers guaranteed that political power in the new English republic would remain in the hands of men who occupied the upper levels of English society, especially those who owned property in land.

The republican government established in 1649 did not last. Tensions between the army and Parliament, fueled by the belief that the government was not creating a godly society, resulted in the army's dissolution of the Long Parliament in 1653 and the selection of a small legislative assembly consisting of zealous Puritans who were nominated by the army. When this "Parliament of the Saints" broke down later that year, Oliver Cromwell (1599–1658), the commander in chief of the army and the most prominent member of the republican government after 1649, assumed the title of Lord Protector. The protectorate, in which Cromwell shared legislative power with Parliament, represented an effort to return to a more traditional form of government. Cromwell however, relied primarily on the army to maintain power, thereby alienating many of the members of the landed class. After Cromwell's death in 1658, renewed tension between the army and Parliament led to a period of political chaos. In 1660 the army and Parliament decided to restore the monarchy by inviting Charles, the son of Charles I, to return from exile. When he returned, not only the monarchy but also the House of Lords and the Church of England were restored. The revolution had officially come to an end.

Later Stuart Absolutism and the Glorious Revolution

Charles II (r. 1660–1685) and his brother James II (r. 1685–1688) were both absolutists who admired the political achievement of their cousin, Louis XIV of France. They realized, however that they could never return to the policies of their father, much less adopt those of Louis. Neither of them attempted to rule indefinitely without Parliament, as Charles I had. Instead they sought to destroy the independence of Parliament by packing it with their own supporters and using the prerogative to weaken the force of the parliamentary statutes to which they objected.

The main political crisis of Charles II's reign was the attempt by a group of members of Parliament, headed by the Earl of Shaftesbury (1621–1683) and known by their opponents as Whigs, to exclude the king's brother, James, from the throne on the grounds that he was a Catholic. Charles opposed this strategy because it violated the theory of hereditary divine right, according to which God sanctioned the right of the king's closest heir to succeed him. Those members of Parliament who supported

Justice in History
The Trial of Charles I

In January 1649, after the New Model Army had defeated Royalist forces in England's second civil war and purged Parliament of its Presbyterian members, the few remaining members of the House of Commons voted by a narrow margin to erect a High Court of Justice to try King Charles I. This trial, which resulted in Charles's execution, marked the only time in European history that a monarch was tried and executed while still holding the office of king.

The decision to try the king formed part of a deliberate political strategy. The men who arranged the proceeding knew that they were embarking upon a revolutionary course by declaring that the House of Commons, as the elected representative of the people, was the highest power in the realm. They also knew that the republican regime they were establishing did not command a large body of popular support. By trying the king publicly in a court of law and by ensuring that the trial was reported in daily newspapers (the first such trial in history), they hoped to prove the legitimacy of their cause and win support for the new regime.

The decision to bring the king to justice created two legal problems. The first was to identify a crime upon which the trial would be based. For many years members of Parliament had insisted that the king had violated the ancient laws of the kingdom. The charge read that he had "wickedly designed to erect an unlimited and tyrannical power" and had waged war against his people in two civil wars. His prosecutors claimed that those activities amounted to the crime of treason. The problem was that treason in England was a crime a subject committed against the king, not the king against his subjects. In order to try the king for this crime, his accusers had to construct a new theory of treason, according to which he had attacked his own political body, which they identified with the kingdom or the state.

The second problem was to make the court itself a legitimate tribunal. According to English constitutional law, the king possessed the highest legal authority in the land. He appointed his judges, and the courts represented his authority. Parliament could vote to erect a special court, but the bill authorizing it would become law only if the king agreed to it. In this case the House of Commons had set up the court by its own authority, and it had named 135 men, most of whom were army officers, to serve as its judges. The revolutionary nature of this tribunal was difficult to disguise, and Charles made its illegality the basis of his defense. When asked how he would plead, he refused, demanding to be told by what authority he had been brought into court.

The arguments presented by King Charles and John Bradshawe, the president of the court, regarding the legitimacy of the court reflected the main constitutional conflict in seventeenth-century England. On the one hand was the doctrine of divine-right absolutism, according to which the king received his authority from God. He was therefore responsible to God alone, not the people. His subjects could neither try him in a court of law nor fight him on the battlefield. "A king," said Charles, "cannot be tried by any superior jurisdiction on earth." On the other hand was the doctrine of popular sovereignty, which held that political power came from the people. As Bradshawe said in response to Charles's objection, "Sir, as the law is your superior, so truly Sir, there is something that is superior to the law, and that is indeed the parent or author of law, and that is the people of England." This trial, therefore, involved not only a confrontation between Charles and his revolutionary judges but an encounter between two incompatible political ideologies.

In 1649 the advocates of popular sovereignty triumphed over those of divine right. Charles was convicted as a "tyrant, traitor, murderer, and public enemy of the good people of this nation." The verdict was never in doubt, although only 67 of the 135 men originally appointed as judges voted to convict the king, and a mere 59 signed the death warrant. The trial succeeded only to the extent that it facilitated the establishment of the new regime. With Charles gone,

TRIAL OF CHARLES I AT WESTMINSTER HALL, JANUARY 1649 The king is sitting in the prisoner's box in the foreground, facing the commissioners of the High Court of Justice. His refusal to plead meant that a full trial could not take place.

(continued on next page)

the revolutionaries could move ahead with the abolition of the monarchy and the establishment of a republic. But in dramatic terms the trial was a complete failure. Charles, a small shy man with a nervous stammer, was expected to make a poor impression, but he spoke eloquently when he refused to plead, and he won support from spectators in the gallery. In the greatest show trial of the seventeenth century, the royal defendant stole the show.

When Charles's son, Charles II, was restored to the throne in 1660, Royalists finally had their revenge against the judges of this court. Those who could be found alive were hanged, disemboweled, and quartered. For those who were already dead, there was to be another type of justice. In 1661 Royalists exhumed the badly decomposed corpses of Bradshawe, Henry Ireton, and Oliver Cromwell, the three men who bore the largest responsibility for the execution of the king. The three cadavers were hanged and their skulls were placed on pikes on top of Westminster Hall.

This macabre ritual served as the Royalists' way of vilifying the memory of the judges of this illegal and revolutionary trial, and their unpardonable sin of executing an anointed king.

For Discussion

1. The men who brought King Charles to trial often spoke about bringing him to "justice." How is justice best understood in this context?
2. How does this trial reveal the limitations of divine-right absolutism in England?

Taking It Further

Peacey, Jason (ed). *The Regicides and the Execution of Charles I.* 2001. A collection of essays on various aspects of this episode and the men who signed the death warrant.

Wedgewood, C. V. *The Trial of Charles I.* 1964. Presents a full account and analysis of the trial.

Charles on this issue, called Tories, thwarted the designs of the Whigs in three successive parliaments between 1679 and 1681.

An even more serious political crisis occurred after James II succeeded to the throne in 1685. James began to exempt his fellow Catholics from the penal laws, which prevented them from worshiping freely, and from the Test Act of 1673, which denied them the right to hold political office. James began appointing Catholics to positions in the army, the central administration, and local government. These efforts to grant toleration and political power to Catholics revived the traditional English fears of absolutism and "popery." Not only the Whigs but also the predominantly Anglican Tories became alarmed at the king's policies. The birth of a Catholic son to James by his second wife, the Italian princess Mary of Modena, in June 1688 created the fear that the king's religious policy might continue indefinitely. A group of seven Whigs and Tories, including the Bishop of London, invited William III of Orange, the captain-general of the military forces of the Dutch Republic and James's nephew, to come to England to defend their Protestant religion and their constitution. William was married to James's eldest daughter, the Protestant Princess Mary, and as the king's nephew, he also had a claim to the throne himself.

Invading with an international force of 12,000 men, William gathered substantial support from the English population. When James's army defected, the king was forced to flee to France without engaging William's forces in battle. The Convention, a special parliament convened by William in 1689, offered the crown to William and Mary while at the same time securing their assent to the Declaration of Rights, a document that later became the parliamentary statute known as the Bill of Rights. This bill, which the English consider the cornerstone of their constitution, corrected many of the abuses of royal power at the hands of James and Charles, especially the practice of exempting individuals from the penalties of the laws made by Parliament. By proclaiming William king and by excluding Catholics from the throne, the Bill of Rights also destroyed the theory of hereditary divine right.

The events of 1688–1689 were decisive in defeating once and for all the absolutist designs of the Stuart kings and in guaranteeing that Parliament would form a permanent and regular place in English government. The Glorious Revolution also prompted the publication of a political manifesto, John Locke's *Two Treatises of Government* (1690). Locke, a radical Whig, had written the *Treatises* in the early 1680s as a protest against the absolutist policies of Charles II, but only after the abdication and flight of James II could he safely publish his manuscript. Like Hobbes, Locke argued that people

Read the Document

John Locke Justifies the Glorious
Revolution

left the state of nature and agreed to form a political society mainly to protect their property. Unlike Hobbes, however, Locke asserted that the people never relinquished their sovereignty and could replace a government that had violated the trust placed in it. Locke's treatises constituted an uncompromising attack on the system of royal absolutism, which he equated with slavery.

We have seen that the success of absolutism in continental European countries led to the expansion of state power. Paradoxically, the defeat of absolutism in England fostered the growth of the English state. As long as Parliament had remained suspicious of the Stuart kings, it had been reluctant to facilitate the growth of the state, which until 1688 was under direct royal control. Once the Glorious Revolution permanently restricted the king's power, and Parliament emerged as the highest power within the country, Members of Parliament (MPs) had less to fear from the executive branch of government. The inauguration of a long period of warfare against France in 1689 required the development of a large army and navy, the expansion of the bureaucracy, government borrowing on an unprecedented scale, and an increase in taxes. By 1720 the kingdom of Great Britain, which had been created by the parliamentary union of England and Scotland in 1707, could rival the French state in military power, wealth, and diplomatic prestige.

The Dutch Republic

In many respects the United Provinces of the Netherlands, known as the Dutch Republic, forms the most striking exception to the pattern of state building in seventeenth-century Europe. Formally established in 1588 during its revolt against Spanish rule, the Dutch Republic was the only major European power to maintain a republican form of government throughout the seventeenth century. As a state it also failed to conform to the pattern of centralization and consolidation that became evident in almost all European monarchies. Having successfully resisted the centralizing policies of a large multinational Spanish monarchy, the Dutch Republic never acquired much of a centralized bureaucracy of its own. The provinces formed little more than a loose confederation of sovereign republican states. Each of the provinces sent deputies to the States General, where unanimity was required on all important issues, such as the levying of taxes, the declaration of war, and the ratification of treaties.

Political power in the Dutch Republic lay mainly with the wealthy merchants and bankers who served as regents in the councils of the towns. The members of this bourgeois elite did not tend to seek admission to landed society in the way that successful English merchants often did. Nor were they lured into becoming part of an ostentatious court in the manner of the French nobility. Immersed in the world of commerce, they remained part of mercantile society and used their political power to guarantee that the Dutch state would serve the interests of trade.

The political prominence of Dutch merchants reflected the commercial character of the Dutch economy. Shortly after its truce with Spain in 1609, the Dutch cities, especially the port city of Amsterdam in Holland, began to dominate European and world trade. The Dutch served as middlemen and shippers for all the other powers of Europe, transporting grain from the Baltic, textiles from England, timber from Scandinavia, wine from Germany, sugar from Brazil and Ceylon, silk from Persia and China, and porcelain from Japan to markets throughout the world. The Dutch even served as middlemen for their archenemy Spain, providing food and manufactured goods to the Spanish colonies in the New World in exchange for silver from the mines of Peru and Mexico. As part of this process Dutch trading companies, such as the Dutch East India Company, began to establish permanent outposts in India, Indonesia, North America, the Caribbean, South America, and South Africa. Thus, a relatively small country with one-tenth the population of France became a colonial power.

To support their dynamic mercantile economy, Dutch cities developed financial institutions and techniques favorable to trade. An Exchange Bank in Amsterdam, which had a monopoly on the exchange of foreign currencies, eased international transactions. A stock market, also situated in Amsterdam, facilitated the buying and selling of shares in commercial ventures. Dutch merchants developed rational and efficient methods of bookkeeping. Even lawyers contributed to the success of Dutch commerce. In *The Freedom of the Sea* (1609), the great legal and political philosopher Hugo Grotius (1583–1645) defended the freedom of merchants to use the open seas for trade and fishing, thereby challenging the claims of European monarchs who wished to exclude foreigners from the waters surrounding their countries. Grotius, who also wrote *The Law of War and Peace* (1625), gained a reputation as the founder of modern international law.

One of the most striking contrasts between the Dutch Republic and the kingdom of France in the seventeenth century lay in the area of religious policy. Whereas in France the revocation of the Edict of Nantes represented the culmination of a policy enforcing religious uniformity and the suppression of Protestant dissent, the predominantly Calvinist Dutch Republic gained a reputation for religious toleration. The Dutch Reformed Church did not always deserve this reputation, but secular authorities, especially in the cities, proved remarkably tolerant of different religious groups. Amsterdam, which attracted a diverse immigrant population during its period of rapid growth, contained a large community of Jews, including the philosopher Baruch Spinoza (1632–1677). The country became the center for religious exiles and political dissidents, accommodating French Huguenots who fled their country after the repeal of the Edict of Nantes in 1685 as well as English Whigs (including the Earl of Shaftesbury and John Locke) who were being pursued by the Tory government in the 1680s.

This tolerant bourgeois republic also made a distinct contribution to European culture during the seventeenth century, known as its Golden Age. The Dutch cultural

THE AMSTERDAM STOCK EXCHANGE IN 1668 Known as the Bourse, this multipurpose building served as a gathering point for merchants trading in different parts of the world. The main activity was the buying and selling of shares of stock in trading companies during trading sessions that lasted for two hours each day.

REMBRANDT, SYNDICS OF THE CLOTHMAKERS OF AMSTERDAM (1662) Rembrandt's realistic portrait depicted wealthy Dutch bourgeoisie, who had great political as well as economic power in the Dutch Republic.

achievement was greatest in the area of the visual arts, where Rembrandt van Rijn (1606–1669), Franz Hals (ca. 1580–1666), and Jan Steen (1626–1679) belonged to an astonishing concentration of artistic genius in the cities of Amsterdam, Haarlem, and Leiden. Dutch painting reflected the religious, social, and political climate of this era. The Protestant Reformation had ended the tradition of devotional religious painting that had flourished during the Middle Ages, and the absence of a baroque court culture reduced the demand for royal and aristocratic portraiture and for paintings of heroic classical, mythological, and historical scenes. Instead, the Dutch artists of the Golden Age produced intensely realistic portraits of merchants and financiers, such as Rembrandt's famous *Syndics of the Clothmakers of Amsterdam* (1662). Realism became one of the defining features of Dutch painting, evident in the numerous street scenes, still lifes, and landscapes that Dutch artists painted and sold to a largely bourgeois clientele.

In the early eighteenth century the Dutch Republic lost its position of economic superiority to Great Britain and France, which developed even larger mercantile empires of their own and began to dominate world commerce. The long period of war against France, which ended in 1713, took its toll on Dutch manpower and wealth, and the relatively small size of the country and its decentralized institutions made it more difficult for it to recover its position in European diplomacy and warfare. As a state it could no longer fight above its weight, and it became vulnerable to attacks by the French in the nineteenth century and the Germans in the twentieth. But in the seventeenth century this highly urbanized and commercial country showed that a small, decentralized republic could hold its own with the absolutist states of France and Spain as well as with the parliamentary monarchy of England.

CONCLUSION

The Western State in the Age of Absolutism

Between 1600 and 1715 three fundamental political changes helped redefine the West. The first was the dramatic and unprecedented growth of the state. During these years all Western states grew in size and strength. They became more cohesive as they brought the outlying provinces of kingdoms more firmly under central governmental control. The administrative machinery of the state became more complex and efficient. The armies of the state could be called upon at any time to take action against internal rebels and foreign enemies. The income of the state increased as royal officials collected higher taxes, and governments became involved in the promotion of trade and industry and in the regulation of the economy. By the beginning of the eighteenth century one of the most distinctive features of Western civilization was the prevalence of these large, powerful, bureaucratic states. There was nothing like them in the non-Western world.

The second change was the introduction of absolutism into these Western states. With the notable exception of Poland and Hungary, rulers aspired to complete and unrivaled power. These efforts achieved varying degrees of success, and in two states, England and the Dutch Republic, they ended in failure. Nevertheless, during the seventeenth and eighteenth centuries the absolutist state became the main form of government in the West. For this reason historians refer to the period of Western history beginning in the seventeenth century as the age of absolutism.

The third change was the conduct of a new style of warfare by Western absolutist states. The West became the arena where large armies, funded, equipped, and trained by the state, engaged in long, costly, and bloody military campaigns. The conduct of war on this scale threatened to drain the state of its financial resources, destroy its economy, and decimate its civilian and military population. Western powers were not unaware of the dangers of this type of warfare. The development of international law and the attempt to achieve a balance of power among European powers represented efforts to place restrictions on seventeenth-century warfare. These efforts, however, were not completely successful, and in the eighteenth and nineteenth centuries warfare in the West entered a new and even more dangerous phase, aided by the technological innovations that the Scientific and Industrial Revolutions made possible. To the first of those great transformations, the revolution in science, we now turn.

MAKING CONNECTIONS

1. Absolutist rulers sought unrivaled power, but they frequently encountered resistance. Why were they often unable to achieve the power they desired?
2. The Thirty Years' War was a major turning point in German and European history. What impact did it have on the development of absolutist theory and the development of modern states?
3. Many American notions of liberty originated in seventeenth-century England. How did developments in the two English Revolutions of the seventeenth century contribute to the ideology of religious liberty?
4. How would you define the political and cultural boundaries of the West by the beginning of the eighteenth century?

TAKING IT FURTHER

For suggested readings see page R-1.

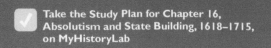
Chapter Review

The Nature of Absolutism

16.1 What did absolutism mean, both as a political theory and as a practical program, and how was absolutism related to the growth of the power of the state?

In theory, an absolute monarch was above the law when acting for reasons of state, but was expected to follow the law of God and to respect the property rights of his or her subjects. In practice, these same monarchs sought to increase the power of the state by eliminating or weakening legislative assemblies, making the nobility dependent on royal favor, and controlling the administrative machinery of the state to enforce and support their own policies, which often included warfare.

The Absolutist State in France and Spain

16.2 How did France and Spain implement absolutism in the seventeenth century and how powerful did those states become?

While the kingdom of France became a model of state building and gradually emerged as the most powerful country in Europe, the Spanish monarchy struggled to introduce absolutism at a time when the overall economic condition of the country was deteriorating and its military forces were suffering a series of defeats.

Absolutism and State Building in Central and Eastern Europe

16.3 What was the nature of royal absolutism in central and eastern Europe, and how did the policies of the Ottoman Empire and Russia help to establish the boundaries of the West during this period?

The aspiring absolute rulers of eastern and central Europe lacked a unified bureaucracy and were unable to solidify their power and integrate their diverse lands into a unified state. But they did secure the compliance of the nobility and were able to establish political systems and policies that shared many of the characteristics as states in western Europe, a fact that challenged the traditional European perception that the Ottoman and Russian Empires belonged entirely to an eastern, Asian world.

Resistance to Absolutism in England and the Dutch Republic

16.4 Why did absolutism fail to take root in England and the Dutch Republic during the seventeenth century?

Political and economic traditions were obstacles for rulers seeking to establish absolute monarchies in these states. When Charles I of England taxed his subjects without the consent of Parliament, civil war ensued. When James II tried to introduce absolutism in the 1680s, he was forced to abdicate. As the only state to maintain a republic in the seventeenth century, the Dutch Republic was a loose confederation of sovereign states, with little central bureaucracy and political power held by wealthy merchants and bankers, not the nobility.

Chapter Time Line

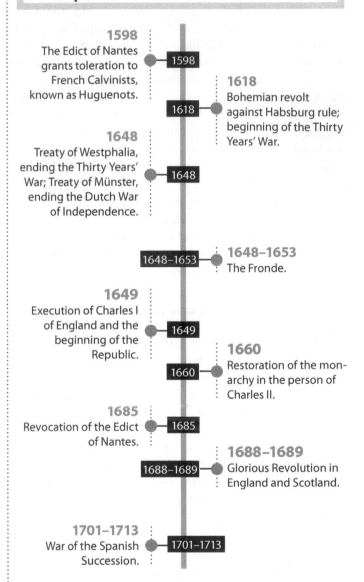

1598
The Edict of Nantes grants toleration to French Calvinists, known as Huguenots.
— 1598

1618
Bohemian revolt against Habsburg rule; beginning of the Thirty Years' War.
— 1618

1648
Treaty of Westphalia, ending the Thirty Years' War; Treaty of Münster, ending the Dutch War of Independence.
— 1648

1648–1653
The Fronde.
— 1648–1653

1649
Execution of Charles I of England and the beginning of the Republic.
— 1649

1660
Restoration of the monarchy in the person of Charles II.
— 1660

1685
Revocation of the Edict of Nantes.
— 1685

1688–1689
Glorious Revolution in England and Scotland.
— 1688–1689

1701–1713
War of the Spanish Succession.
— 1701–1713

17 The Scientific Revolution

I **n 1609 Galileo Galilei,** an Italian mathematician at the University of Padua, directed a new scientific instrument, the telescope, toward the heavens. Having heard that a Dutch artisan had put together two lenses in a way that magnified distant objects, Galileo built his own such device. Anyone who has looked through a telescope can appreciate his excitement. Objects that appeared one way to the naked eye looked entirely different when magnified by his new "spyglass," as he called it. The surface of the moon, long believed to be smooth, uniform, and perfectly spherical, now appeared full of mountains and craters. Galileo's spyglass showed that the sun, too, was imperfect, marred by spots that appeared to move across its surface. Such sights challenged traditional science, which assumed that "the heavens," the throne of God, were perfect and thus never changed. Traditional science was shaken even further when Galileo showed that Venus, viewed over many months, appeared to change its shape, much as the moon did in its phases. This discovery provided evidence for the relatively new

THE TELESCOPE The telescope was the most important of the new scientific instruments that facilitated discovery. This engraving depicts an astronomer using the telescope in 1647.

LEARNING OBJECTIVES

17.1 What were the achievements and discoveries of the Scientific Revolution?

17.2 What methods did scientists use during this period to investigate nature, and how did they think nature operated?

17.3 Why did the Scientific Revolution take place in western Europe at this time?

17.4 How did the Scientific Revolution influence philosophical and religious thought in the seventeenth and early eighteenth centuries?

17.5 How did the Scientific Revolution change the way in which seventeenth- and eighteenth-century Europeans thought of the place of human beings in nature?

👁 Watch the Video Series on MyHistoryLab

Learn about some key topics related to this chapter with the *MyHistoryLab Video Series: Key Topics in Western Civilization*

theory that the planets, including Earth, revolved around the sun rather than the sun and the planets around the Earth.

Galileo shared the discoveries he made not only with fellow scientists, but also with other educated members of society. He also staged a number of public demonstrations of his new astronomical instrument, the first of which took place on top of one of the city gates of Rome in 1611. To convince those who doubted the reality of the images they saw, Galileo turned the telescope toward familiar landmarks in the city. Interest in the new scientific instrument ran so high that a number of amateur astronomers acquired telescopes of their own.

Galileo's discoveries were part of what historians call the Scientific Revolution. This development changed the way Europeans viewed the natural world, the supernatural realm, and themselves. It led to controversies in religion, philosophy, and politics and changes in military technology, navigation, and business. It also set the West apart from the civilizations of the Middle East, Asia, and Africa and provided a basis for claims of Western superiority over the people in those lands.

The scientific culture that emerged in the West by the end of the seventeenth century was the product of a series of cultural encounters. It resulted from a complex interaction among scholars proposing different ideas of how nature operated. Some of these ideas originated in Greek philosophy. Others came from Christian sources. Still other ideas came from a tradition of late medieval science that had been influenced by the scholarship of the Islamic Middle East.

The main question this chapter seeks to answer is this:

How did European scientists in the sixteenth and seventeenth centuries change the way in which people in the West viewed the natural world?

The Discoveries and Achievements of the Scientific Revolution

17.1 What were the achievements and discoveries of the Scientific Revolution?

U nlike political revolutions, such as the English Revolution of the 1640s discussed in the last chapter, the Scientific Revolution developed gradually over a long period of time. It began in the mid-sixteenth century and continued into the eighteenth century. Even though it took a relatively long time to unfold, it was revolutionary in the sense that it transformed human thought, just as political revolutions have fundamentally changed systems of government. The most important changes in seventeenth-century science took place in astronomy, physics, chemistry, and biology.

Astronomy: A New Model of the Universe

The most significant change in astronomy was the acceptance of the view that the sun, not the Earth, was the center of the universe. Until the mid-sixteenth century, most natural philosophers—as scientists were known at the time—accepted the views of the ancient Greek astronomer Claudius Ptolemy (100–170 C.E.). Ptolemy's observations and calculations supported the cosmology of the Greek philosopher Aristotle (384–322 B.C.E.). According to

Ptolemy and Aristotle, the center of the universe was a stationary Earth, around which the moon, the sun, and the other planets revolved in circular orbits. Beyond the planets a large sphere carried the stars, which stood in a fixed relationship to each other, around the Earth from east to west once every 24 hours, thus accounting for the rising and setting of the stars. Each of the four known elements—earth, water, air, and fire—had a natural place within this universe, with the heavy elements, earth and water, being pulled down toward the center of the Earth and the light ones, air and fire, hovering above it. All heavenly bodies, including the sun and the planets, were composed of a fifth element, called ether, which unlike matter on Earth was thought to be eternal and could not be altered, corrupted, or destroyed.

This traditional view of the cosmos had much to recommend it, and some educated people continued to accept it well into the eighteenth century. The Bible, which in a few passages referred to the motion of the sun, reinforced the authority of Aristotle. And human observation seemed to confirm the motion of the sun. We do, after all, see the sun "rise" and "set" every day, so the idea that the Earth rotates at high speed and revolves around the sun contradicts the experience of our senses. Nevertheless, the Earth-centered model of the universe failed to explain many patterns that astronomers observed in the sky, most notably the paths followed by planets. Whenever ancient or medieval astronomers confronted a new problem as a result of their observations, they tried to accommodate the results to the Ptolemaic model. By the sixteenth century this model had been modified or adjusted so many times that it had gradually become a confused collection of planets and stars following different motions.

Faced with this situation, a Polish cleric, Nicolaus Copernicus (1473–1543), looked for a simpler and more plausible model of the universe. In *On the Revolutions of the Heavenly Spheres*, which was published shortly after his death, Copernicus proposed that the center of the universe was not the Earth but the sun. The book was widely circulated, but it did not win much support for the sun-centered theory of the universe. Only the most learned astronomers could understand Copernicus's mathematical arguments, and even they were not prepared to adopt his central thesis. In the late sixteenth century the great Danish astronomer Tycho Brahe (1546–1601) accepted the

Read the Document

On the Revolution of the Heavenly Spheres (1500s) Nicolaus Copernicus

TWO VIEWS OF THE PTOLEMAIC OR PRE-COPERNICAN UNIVERSE (*Left*) In this sixteenth-century engraving the Earth lies at the center of the universe and the elements of water, air, and fire are arranged in ascending order above the Earth. The orbit that is shaded in black is the firmament or stellar sphere. The presence of Christ and the saints at the top reflects the view that Heaven lay beyond the stellar sphere. (*Right*) A medieval king representing Atlas holds a Ptolemaic cosmos. The Ptolemaic universe is often referred to as a two-sphere universe: The inner sphere of the Earth lies at the center and the outer sphere encompassing the entire universe rotates around the Earth.

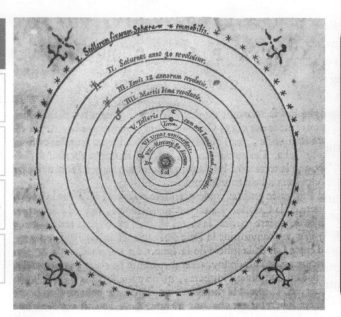

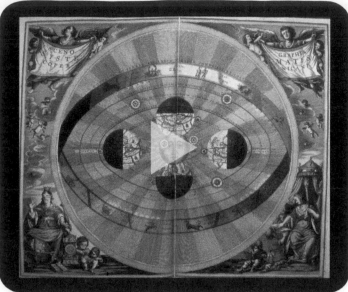

🔍 **View the Closer Look**

The Copernican Universe

TWO EARLY MODERN VIEWS OF THE SUN-CENTERED UNIVERSE (*Left*) The depiction by Copernicus. Note that all the orbits are circular, rather than elliptical, as Kepler was to show they were. The outermost sphere is that of the fixed stars. (*Right*) A late-seventeenth-century depiction of the cosmos by Andreas Cellarius in which the planets follow elliptical orbits. It illustrates four different positions of the Earth as it orbits the sun.

argument of Copernicus that the planets revolved around the sun but still insisted that the sun revolved around the Earth.

Significant support for the Copernican model of the universe among scientists began to materialize only in the seventeenth century. In 1609 a German astronomer, Johannes Kepler (1571–1630), using data that Brahe had collected, confirmed the central position of the sun in the universe. In *New Astronomy* (1609) Kepler also demonstrated that the planets, including the Earth, followed elliptical rather than circular orbits and that physical laws governed their movements. Not many people read Kepler's book, however, and his achievement was not fully appreciated until many decades later.

Galileo Galilei (1564–1642) was far more successful in gaining support for the sun-centered model of the universe. Galileo had the literary skill, which Kepler lacked, of being able to write for a broad audience. Using the evidence gained from his observations with the telescope, and presenting his views in the form of a dialogue between the advocates of the two competing worldviews, Galileo demonstrated the plausibility and superiority of Copernicus's theory.

The publication of Galileo's *Dialogue Concerning the Two Chief World Systems—Ptolemaic and Copernican* in 1632 won many converts to the sun-centered theory of the universe, but it lost him the support of Pope Urban VIII, who had been one of his patrons. The character in *Dialogue* who defends the Ptolemaic system is named Simplicio (that is, a simple—or stupid—person). Urban wrongly concluded that Galileo was mocking him. In 1633 Galileo was tried before the Roman Inquisition, an ecclesiastical court whose purpose was to maintain theological orthodoxy. The charge against him was that he had challenged the authority of Scripture and was therefore guilty of heresy, the denial of the theological truths of the Roman Catholic Church. (See *Justice in History* in this chapter.)

As a result of this trial, Galileo was forced to abandon his support for the Copernican model of the universe, and *Dialogue* was placed on the Index of Prohibited Books, a list compiled by the papacy of all printed works containing heretical ideas. Despite this setback, by 1700 Copernicanism commanded widespread support among scientists and the educated public. *Dialogue*, however, was not removed from the Index until 1822.

Physics: The Laws of Motion and Gravitation

Galileo made his most significant contributions to the Scientific Revolution in physics. In the seventeenth century the main branches of physics were mechanics (the study of motion and its causes) and optics (the study of light). Galileo formulated a set of laws governing the motion of material objects that challenged the accepted theories of Aristotle regarding motion and laid the foundation of modern physics.

According to Aristotle, whose views dominated science in the late Middle Ages, the motion of every object—except the natural motion of falling toward the center of the Earth—required another object to move it. If the mover stopped, the object fell to the ground or simply stopped moving. But this theory could not explain why a projectile, such as a discus or a spear, continued to move after a person threw it. Galileo's answer to that question was a theory of inertia, which became the basis of a new theory of motion. According to Galileo, an object continues to move or lie at rest until something external to it intervenes to change its motion. Thus, motion is neither a quality inherent in an object nor a force that it acquires from another object. It is simply a state in which the object finds itself.

Galileo also discovered that the motion of an object occurs only in relation to things that do not move. A ship moves through the water, for example, but the goods that the ship carries do not move in relationship to the moving ship. This insight explained to the critics of Copernicus how the Earth can move even though we do not experience its motion. Galileo's most significant contribution to mechanics was his formulation of a

SIR ISAAC NEWTON This portrait was painted by Sir Godfrey Kneller in 1689, two years after the publication of *Mathematical Principles of Natural Philosophy.*

CHRONOLOGY: DISCOVERIES OF THE SCIENTIFIC REVOLUTION

1543
Copernicus publishes *On the Revolutions of the Heavenly Spheres.*
1543

1609
1609
Johannes Kepler publishes *New Astronomy.*

1628
William Harvey publishes *On the Motion of the Heart and Blood in Animals.*
1628

1632
1632
Galileo publishes *Dialogue Concerning the Two Chief World Systems.*

1638
Galileo publishes *Discourses on the Two New Sciences of Motion and Mechanics.*
1638

1659
1659
Robert Boyle invents the air pump and conducts experiments on the elasticity and compressibility of air.

1687
Newton publishes *Mathematical Principles of Natural Philosophy.*
1687

mathematical law of motion that explained how the speed and acceleration of a falling object are determined by the distance it travels during equal intervals of time.

The greatest achievements of the Scientific Revolution in physics belong to English scientist Sir Isaac Newton (1642–1727). His research changed the way future generations viewed the world. As a boy Newton felt out of place in his small village, where he worked on his mother's farm and attended school. Fascinated by mechanical devices, he spent much of his time building wooden models of windmills and other machines. When playing with his friends he always found ways to exercise his mind, calculating, for example, how he could use the wind to win jumping contests. It became obvious to all who knew him that Newton belonged at a university. In 1661 he entered Cambridge University, where, at age 27, he became a chaired professor of mathematics.

Newton formulated a set of mathematical laws to explain the operation of the entire physical world. In 1687 he published his theories in *Mathematical Principles of Natural Philosophy*. The centerpiece of this monumental work was the **universal law of gravitation**, which demonstrated that the same force holding an object to the Earth also holds the planets in their orbits. This law represented a synthesis of the work of other scientists, including Kepler on planetary motion and Galileo on inertia. Newton paid tribute to the work of these men when he said, "If I have seen farther, it is by standing on the shoulders of giants." But Newton went further than any of them by establishing the existence of a single gravitational force and by giving it precise mathematical expression. His book revealed the unity and order of the entire physical world and thus offered a scientific model to replace that of Aristotle.

universal law of gravitation A law of nature established by Isaac Newton in 1687 holding that any two bodies attract each other with a force that is directly proportional to the product of their masses and indirectly proportional to the square of the distance between them. The law was presented in mathematical terms.

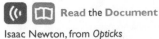 Read the Document

Isaac Newton, from *Opticks*

Chemistry: Discovering the Elements of Nature

The science today called chemistry originated in the study and practice of **alchemy**, the art of attempting to turn base metals into gold or silver and to identify natural substances that could be used in the practice of medicine. Alchemy has often been ridiculed as a form of magic that is the antithesis of modern science, but alchemists performed experiments that contributed to the growth of the empirical study of nature. The Swiss physician and alchemist Paracelsus (1493–1541), who rejected the traditional method of curing patients by altering the balance of fluids (such as blood and bile) in the body, occupies a significant place in the early history of chemistry. In his effort to find what he called a panacea, or a remedy for all diseases, Paracelsus treated his patients with chemicals, such as mercury and sulfur. In this way chemistry became an accepted part of medical science.

During the seventeenth century chemistry gained further recognition as a legitimate field of scientific research, largely as the result of the work of Robert Boyle (1627–1691). Boyle, who also had an interest in alchemy, destroyed the prevailing idea

alchemy The practice, rooted in a philosophical tradition, of attempting to turn base metals into precious ones. It also involved the identification of natural substances for medical purposes. Alchemy was influential in the development of chemistry and medicine in the sixteenth and seventeenth centuries.

Gulilmꝰ Faithorne ad viu: delin: et sculp:

ROBERTUS BOYLE AR.M:

PORTRAIT OF ROBERT BOYLE WITH HIS AIR PUMP IN THE BACKGROUND (1664) Boyle's pump became the center of a series of experiments carried on at the Royal Society in London.

that all basic constituents of matter share the same structure. He contended that the arrangement of their components, which he identified as corpuscles or atoms, determined their characteristics. He also conducted experiments on the volume, pressure, and density of gas and the elasticity of air. Boyle's most famous experiments, undertaken with an air pump, proved the existence of a vacuum. Largely as a result of Boyle's discoveries, chemists won acceptance as members of the company of scientists.

Biology: The Circulation of the Blood

The English physician William Harvey (1578–1657) made one of the great medical discoveries of the seventeenth century by demonstrating in 1628 that blood circulates throughout the human body. Traditional science had maintained that blood originated in the liver and then flowed outward through the veins. A certain amount of blood flowed from the liver into the heart, where it passed from one ventricle to the other and then traveled through the arteries to different parts of the body. During its journey this arterial blood was enriched by a special *pneuma* or "vital spirit" that was necessary to sustain life. When this enriched blood reached the brain, it became the body's "psychic spirits," which influenced human behavior.

Through experiments on human cadavers and live animals in which he weighed the blood that the heart pumped every hour, Harvey demonstrated that rather than sucking in blood, the heart pumped it through the arteries by means of contraction and constriction. The only gap in his theory was the question of how blood went from the ends of the arteries to the ends of the veins. This question was answered in 1661, when scientists, using a new instrument known as a microscope, could see the capillaries connecting the veins and arteries. Harvey, however, had set the standard for future biological research.

 Read the Document

William Harvey, *Address to the Royal College of Physicians*, 1628

The Search for Scientific Knowledge

17.2 What methods did scientists use during this period to investigate nature, and how did they think nature operated?

The natural philosophers who made these scientific discoveries worked in different disciplines, and each followed his own procedures for discovering scientific truth. In the sixteenth and seventeenth centuries there was no "scientific method." Many natural philosophers, however, shared similar views about how nature operated and the means by which humans could acquire knowledge of it. In searching for scientific knowledge, these scientists observed and experimented, used deductive reasoning, expressed their theories in mathematical terms, and argued that nature operated like a machine. These features of scientific research ultimately defined a distinctly Western approach to solving scientific problems.

Observation and Experimentation

The most prominent feature of scientific research in sixteenth- and seventeenth-century Europe was the observation of nature, combined with the testing of hypotheses by rigorous experimentation. This was primarily a process of **induction**, in which theories emerged only after the accumulation and analysis of data. It assumed a willingness to abandon preconceived ideas and base scientific conclusions on experience and observation. This approach is also described as empirical: **empiricism** demands that all scientific theories be tested by experiments based on observation of the natural world.

In *New Organon* (1620), the English philosopher Francis Bacon (1561–1626) promoted this empirical approach to scientific research. Bacon complained that all previous scientific endeavors, especially those of ancient Greek philosophers, relied

induction The process of reasoning that formulates general hypotheses and theories on the basis of specific observation and the accumulation of data.

empiricism The practice of testing scientific theories by observation and experiment.

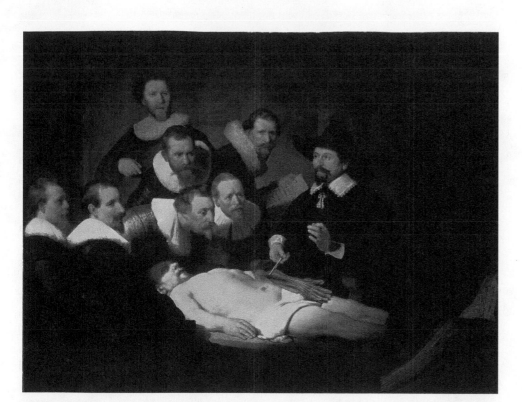

DISSECTION The Dutch surgeon Nicolaes Tulp giving an anatomy lesson in 1632. As medical science developed in the sixteenth and seventeenth centuries, the dissection of human corpses became a standard practice in European universities and medical schools. Knowledge of the structure and composition of the human body, which was central to the advancement of physiology, could best be acquired by cutting open a corpse to reveal the organs, muscles, and bones of human beings. The practice reflected the emphasis scientists placed on observation and experimentation in conducting scientific research.

too little on experimentation. In contrast, his approach involved the thorough and systematic investigation of nature, a process that Bacon, who was a lawyer and judge, compared to the interrogation of a person suspected of committing a crime. For Bacon, scientific experimentation was "putting nature to the question," a phrase that referred to questioning a prisoner under torture to determine the facts of a case.

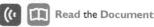 Read the Document

Francis Bacon, from *Novum Organum*

Deductive Reasoning

The second feature of sixteenth- and seventeenth-century scientific research was the use of **deductive reasoning** to establish basic scientific truths or principles. From these principles other ideas or laws could be deduced logically. Just as induction is linked to empiricism, so deduction is connected to **rationalism**. Unlike empiricism—the idea that we know truth through what the senses can experience—rationalism insists that the mind contains rational categories independent of sensory observation.

Unlike the inductive experimental approach, which found its most enthusiastic practitioners in England, the deductive approach had its most zealous advocates on the European continent. The French philosopher and mathematician René Descartes (1596–1650) became the foremost champion of this methodology. In his *Discourse on the Method* (1637), Descartes recommended that to solve any intellectual problem, a person should first establish fundamental principles or truths and then proceed from those ideas to specific conclusions.

Mathematics, in which one also moves logically from certain premises to conclusions by means of equations, provided the model for deductive reasoning. Although rational deduction proved to be an essential feature of scientific methodology, the limitations of an exclusively deductive approach became apparent when Descartes and

deductive reasoning The logical process by which ideas and laws are derived from basic truths or principles.

rationalism The theory that the mind contains rational categories independent of sensory observation; more generally that reason is the primary source of truth.

533

his followers deduced a theory of gravitation from the principle that objects could influence each other only if they actually touched. This theory, as well as the principle upon which it was based, lacked an empirical foundation and eventually had to be abandoned.

Mathematics and Nature

The third feature of scientific research in the sixteenth and seventeenth centuries was the application of mathematics to the study of the physical world. Scientists working in both the inductive and the deductive traditions used mathematics. Descartes shared with Galileo the conviction that nature had a geometrical structure and could therefore be understood in mathematical terms. The physical dimensions of matter, which Descartes claimed were its only properties, could of course be expressed mathematically. Galileo claimed that mathematics was the language in which philosophy was written in "the book of the universe."

Isaac Newton's work provided the best illustration of the application of mathematics to scientific problems. Newton used observation and experimentation to confirm his theory of universal gravitation, but he wrote his *Mathematical Principles of Natural Philosophy* in the language of mathematics. His approach to scientific problems, which became a model for future research, used examples derived from experiments and deductive, mathematical reasoning to discover the laws of nature.

The Mechanical Philosophy

Much of seventeenth-century scientific experimentation and deduction assumed that the natural world operated as if it were a machine made by a human being. This **mechanical philosophy** of nature appeared most clearly in the work of Descartes. Medieval philosophers had argued that natural bodies had an innate tendency to change, whereas artificial objects, that is, those constructed by humans, did not. Descartes, as well as Kepler, Galileo, and Bacon, denied that assumption. Mechanists argued that nature operated in a mechanical way, just like a piece of machinery. The only difference was that the operating structures of natural mechanisms could not be observed as readily as the structures of a machine.

Mechanists perceived the human body itself as a machine. Harvey, for example, described the heart as "a piece of machinery in which, though one wheel gives motion to another, yet all the wheels seem to move simultaneously." The only difference between the body and other machines was that the mind could move the body, although how it did so was controversial. According to Descartes, the mind was completely different from the body and the rest of the material world. Unlike the body, the mind was an immaterial substance that could not be extended in space, divided, or measured mathematically, the way one could record the dimensions of the body. Because Descartes made this sharp distinction between the mind and the body, we describe his philosophy as **dualistic**.

Descartes and other mechanists argued that matter was completely inert or dead. It did not possess a soul or any innate purpose. Its only property was "extension," or the physical dimensions of length, width, and depth. Without a spirit or any other internal force directing its action, matter simply responded to the power of the other bodies with which it came in contact. According to Descartes, all physical phenomena could be explained by reference to the dimensions and the movement of particles of matter. He once claimed, "Give me extension and motion and I will construct the universe."[1]

The view of nature as a machine implied that it operated in a regular, predictable way in accordance with unchanging laws of nature. Scientists could use reason to discover what those laws were and thus learn how nature performed under any

mechanical philosophy The seventeenth-century philosophy of nature, championed by René Descartes, holding that nature operated in a mechanical way, just like a machine made by a human being.

dualistic A term used to describe a philosophy or a religion in which a rigid distinction is made between body and mind, good and evil, or the material and the immaterial world.

circumstances. The scientific investigations of Galileo and Kepler were based on those assumptions, and Descartes made them explicit. The immutability of the laws of nature implied that the entire universe was uniform in structure, an assumption that underlay Newton's formulation of the laws of motion and universal gravitation.

The Causes of the Scientific Revolution

17.3 Why did the Scientific Revolution take place in western Europe at this time?

Why did the Scientific Revolution take place at this particular time, and why did it originate in western European countries? There is no simple answer to this question. We can, however, identify developments that inspired these scientific discoveries. Some of these developments arose out of earlier investigations conducted by natural philosophers in the late Middle Ages, the Renaissance, and the sixteenth century. Others emerged from the religious, political, social, and economic life of early modern Europe.

Developments Within Science

The three internal causes of the Scientific Revolution were the research into motion conducted by natural philosophers in the fourteenth century, the scientific investigations conducted by Renaissance humanists, and the collapse of the dominant conceptual frameworks, or paradigms, that had governed scientific inquiry and research for centuries.

LATE MEDIEVAL SCIENCE Modern science can trace some of its origins to the fourteenth century, when the first significant modifications of Aristotle's scientific theories began to emerge. The most significant of these refinements was the theory of impetus. Aristotle had argued that an object would stop as soon as it lost contact with the object that moved it. Late medieval scientists claimed that objects in motion acquire a force that stays with them after they lose contact with the mover. This theory of impetus questioned Aristotle's authority, and it influenced some of Galileo's early thought on motion.

Natural philosophers of the fourteenth century also began to recommend direct, empirical observation in place of the traditional tendency to accept preconceived notions regarding the operation of nature. This approach to answering scientific questions did not result in the type of rigorous experimentation that Bacon demanded three centuries later, but it did encourage scientists to base their theories on the facts that emerged from an empirical study of nature.

The contribution of late medieval science to the Scientific Revolution should not be exaggerated. Philosophers of the fourteenth century continued to accept Ptolemy's cosmology and the anatomical and medical theories of the Greek physician Galen (129–200 C.E.). The unchallenged position of theology as the dominant subject in late medieval universities also guaranteed that new scientific ideas would receive little favor if they challenged Christian doctrine.

RENAISSANCE SCIENCE Natural philosophers during the Renaissance contributed more than their late medieval predecessors to the rise of modern science. Many of the scientific discoveries of the late sixteenth and seventeenth centuries drew their inspiration from Greek scientific works that had been rediscovered during the Renaissance. Copernicus, for example, found the idea of his sun-centered universe in the writings of Aristarchus of Samos, a Greek astronomer of the third century B.C.E. whose work had been unknown during the Middle Ages. Similarly, the works of the ancient Greek philosopher Democritus in the late fifth century B.C.E. introduced the idea, developed

Neoplatonism A philosophy based on the teachings of Plato and his successors that flourished in Late Antiquity, especially in the teachings of Plotinus. Neoplatonism influenced Christianity in Late Antiquity. During the Renaissance Neoplatonism was linked to the belief that the natural world was charged with occult forces that could be used in the practice of magic.

paradigm A conceptual model or intellectual framework within which scientists conduct their research and experimentation.

by Boyle and others in the seventeenth century, that matter was divisible into small particles known as atoms. The works of Archimedes (287–212 B.C.E.), which had been virtually unknown in the Middle Ages, stimulated interest in the science of mechanics. The recovery and translation of previously unknown texts also made scientists aware that Greek scientists did not always agree with each other and thus provided a stimulus to independent observation and experimentation as a means of resolving their differences.

Renaissance revival of the philosophy of **Neoplatonism** (see Chapter 7) made an even more direct contribution to the birth of modern science. While most medieval natural philosophers relied on the ideas of Aristotle, Neoplatonists drew on the work of Plotinus (205–270 C.E.), the last great philosopher of antiquity who synthesized the work of Plato, other ancient Greek philosophers, and Persian religious traditions. Neoplatonists stressed the unity of the natural and spiritual worlds. Matter is alive, linked to the divine soul that governs the entire universe. To unlock the mysteries of this living world, Neoplatonists turned to mathematics, because they believed the divine expressed itself in geometrical harmony, and to alchemy, because they sought to uncover the shared essence that linked all creation. They also believed that the sun, as a symbol of the divine soul, logically stood at the center of the universe.

Neoplatonic ideas influenced seventeenth-century scientists. Copernicus, for example, took from Neoplatonism his idea of the sun sitting at the center of the universe, as "on a royal throne ruling his children, the planets which circle around him." From his reading in Neoplatonic sources Kepler acquired his belief that the universe was constructed according to geometric principles. Newton was fascinated by the subject of alchemy, and the original inspiration of his theory of gravitation probably came from his Neoplatonist professor at Cambridge, who insisted on the presence of spiritual forces in the physical world. Modern science resulted from an encounter between the mechanical philosophy, which held that matter was inert, and Neoplatonism, which claimed that the natural world was alive.

THE COLLAPSE OF PARADIGMS The third internal cause of the Scientific Revolution was the collapse of the intellectual frameworks that had governed scientific research since antiquity. In all historical periods scientists prefer to work within an established conceptual framework, or what the scholar Thomas Kuhn has referred to as a **paradigm**, rather than introduce new theories. Every so often, however, the paradigm that has governed scientific research for an extended period of time can no longer account for many different observable phenomena. A scientific revolution occurs when the old paradigm collapses and a new paradigm replaces it.[2]

The revolutionary developments we have discussed in astronomy and biology were partly the result of the collapse of old paradigms. In astronomy the paradigm that had governed scientific inquiry in antiquity and the Middle Ages was the Ptolemaic model, in which the sun and the planets revolved around the Earth. By the sixteenth century, however, new observations had so confused and complicated this model that, to men like Copernicus, it no longer provided a satisfactory explanation for the material universe. Copernicus looked for a simpler and more plausible model of the universe. His sun-centered theory became the new paradigm within which Kepler, Galileo, and Newton all worked.

In biology a parallel development occurred when the old paradigm constructed by Galen, in which the blood originated in the liver and traveled through the veins and arteries, also collapsed because it could not explain the findings of medical scholars. Harvey introduced a new paradigm, in which the blood circulated through the body. As in astronomy, Harvey's new paradigm served as a framework for subsequent biological research and helped shape the Scientific Revolution.

Developments Outside Science

Nonscientific developments also encouraged the development and acceptance of new scientific ideas. These developments include the spread of Protestantism, the patronage of scientific research, the invention of the printing press, and military and economic change.

PROTESTANTISM Protestantism played a limited role in causing the Scientific Revolution. In the early years of the Reformation, Protestants were just as hostile as Catholics to the new science. Reflecting the Protestant belief in the literal truth of the Bible, Luther referred to Copernicus as "a fool who went against Holy Writ." Throughout the sixteenth and seventeenth centuries, moreover, Catholics as well as Protestants engaged in scientific research. Indeed, some of the most prominent European natural philosophers, including Galileo and Descartes, were devout Catholics. Nonetheless, Protestantism encouraged the emergence of modern science in three ways.

First, as the Scientific Revolution gained steam in the seventeenth century, Protestant governments were more willing than Catholic authorities to allow the publication and dissemination of new scientific ideas. Protestant governments, for example, did not prohibit the publication of books that promoted novel scientific ideas on the grounds that they were heretical, as the papacy did in compiling the Index of Prohibited Books. The greater willingness of Protestant governments, especially those of England and the Dutch Republic, to tolerate the expression of new scientific ideas helps to explain why the main geographical arena of scientific investigation shifted from the Catholic Mediterranean to the Protestant North Atlantic in the second half of the seventeenth century. (See *Different Voices* in this chapter.)

Second, seventeenth-century Protestant writers emphasized the idea that God revealed his intentions not only in the Bible, but also in nature itself. They claimed that individuals therefore had a duty to study nature, just as it was their duty to read Scripture to gain knowledge of God's will. Kepler's claim that the astronomer was "as a priest of God to the book of nature" reflected this Protestant outlook.

Third, many seventeenth-century Protestant scientists believed that the millennium, a period of one thousand years when Christ would come again and rule the world, was about to begin. Millenarians believed that during this period knowledge would increase, society would improve, and humans would gain control over nature. Protestant scientists, including Boyle and Newton, conducted their research and experiments believing that their work would contribute to this improvement of human life after the Second Coming of Christ.

PATRONAGE Scientists could not have succeeded without financial and institutional support. Only an organizational structure could give science a permanent status, let it develop as a discipline, and give its members a professional identity. The universities, which today support scientific research, were not the main source of that support in the seventeenth century. They remained predominantly clerical institutions with a vested interest in defending the medieval fusion of Christian theology and Aristotelian science. Instead of the universities, scientists depended on the patronage of wealthy and influential individuals, especially the kings, princes, and great nobles who ruled European states. This group included Pope Urban VIII, ruler of the Papal States.

Patronage, however, could easily be withdrawn. Scientists had to conduct themselves and their research to maintain the favor of their patrons. Galileo referred to the new moons of Jupiter that he observed through his telescope as the Medicean stars to flatter the Medici family that ruled Florence. His publications were inspired as much by his obligation to glorify Grand Duke Cosimo II as by his belief in the sun-centered theory.

Academies in which groups of scientists could share ideas and work served as a second important source of patronage. One of the earliest of these institutions was the Academy of the Lynx-Eyed in Rome, named after the animal whose sharp

Different Voices
Copernicus and the Papacy

In dedicating his book, On the Revolution of the Heavenly Spheres (1543), to Pope Paul II (r. 1464–1471), Copernicus explained that he drew inspiration from ancient philosophers who had imagined that the Earth moved. Anticipating condemnation from those who based their astronomical theories on the Bible, he appealed to the pope for protection while showing contempt for the theories of his opponents. Paul II neither endorsed nor condemned Copernicus's work, but in 1616, the papacy suspended the book's publication because it contradicted Scripture.

Copernicus on Heliocentrism and the Bible

. . . I began to chafe that philosophers could by no means agree on any one certain theory of the mechanism of the Universe, wrought for us by a supremely good and orderly Creator . . . I therefore took pains to read again the works of all the philosophers on whom I could lay my hand to seek out whether any of them had ever supposed that the motions of the spheres were other than those demanded by the mathematical schools. I found first in Cicero that Hicetas had realized that the Earth moved. Afterwards I found in Plutarch that certain others had held the like opinion. . . .

Taking advantage of this I too began to think of the mobility of the Earth; and though the opinion seemed absurd, yet knowing now that others before me had been granted freedom to imagine such circles as they chose to explain the phenomena of the stars, I considered that I also might easily be allowed to try whether, by assuming some motion of the Earth, sounder explanations than theirs for the revolution of the celestial spheres might so be discovered.

Thus assuming motions, which in my work I ascribe to the Earth, by long and frequent observations I have at last discovered that, if the motions of the rest of the planets be brought into relation with the circulation of the Earth and be reckoned in proportion to the circles of each planet . . . the orders and magnitudes of all stars and spheres, nay the heavens themselves, become so bound together that nothing in any part thereof could be moved from its place without producing confusion of all the other parts and of the Universe as a whole. . . .

It may fall out, too, that idle babblers, ignorant of mathematics, may claim a right to pronounce a judgment on my work, by reason of a certain passage of Scripture basely twisted to serve their purpose. Should any such venture to criticize and carp at my project, I make no account of them; I consider their judgment rash, and utterly despise it.

SOURCE: From Nicolaus Copernicus, *De Revolutionibus Orbium Coelestium* (1543), trans. by John F. Dobson and Selig Brodetsky in *Occasional Notes of the Royal Astronomical Society, 2*(10), 1947. Reprinted by permission of Blackwell Publishing.

Papal Decree Against Heliocentrism, 1616

Decree of the Holy Congregation of his Most Illustrious Lord Cardinals especially charged by His Holiness Pope Paul V and by the Holy Apostolic See with the index of books and their licensing, prohibition, correction and printing in all of Christendom. . . .

This Holy Congregation has also learned about the spreading and acceptance by many of the false Pythagorean doctrine, altogether contrary to the Holy Scripture, that the earth moves and the sun is motionless, which is also taught by Nicholaus Copernicus's *On the Revolutions of the Heavenly Spheres* and by Diego de Zuñiga's *On Job*. This may be seen from a certain letter published by a certain Carmelite Father, whose title is *Letter of the Reverend Father Paolo Antonio Foscarini on the Pythagorean and Copernican Opinion of the Earth's Motion and Sun's Rest and on the New Pythagorean World System* . . . in which the said Father tries to show that the above mentioned doctrine of the sun's rest at the center of the world and the earth's motion is consonant with the truth and does not contradict Holy Scripture. Therefore, in order that this opinion may not creep any further to the prejudice of Catholic truth, the Congregation has decided that the books by Nicholaus Copernicus (*On the Revolutions of Spheres*) and Diego de Zuñiga (*On Job*) be suspended until corrected; but that the book of the Carmelite Father Paolo Antonini Foscarini be completely prohibited and condemned; and that all other books which teach the same be likewise prohibited, according to whether with the present decree it prohibits[,] condemns and suspends them respectively. In witness thereof this decree has been signed by the hand and stamped with the seal of the Most Illustrious and reverend Lord cardinal of St. Cecilia. Bishop of Albano, on March 5, 1616.

SOURCE: From *The Galileo Affair: A Documentary History,* ed. and trans. by Maurice A. Finocchiaro, copyright © 1989 by The Regents of the University of California, is reprinted by permission of the University of California Press.

For Discussion

1. Why did the papal authorities prohibit and condemn the work by Antonini Foscarini but only suspend those of Copernicus and Diego de Zuñiga?
2. How did Copernicus and the papal authorities differ about classical antiquity and the truth of Holy Scripture?

CHRONOLOGY: THE FORMATION OF SCIENTIFIC SOCIETIES

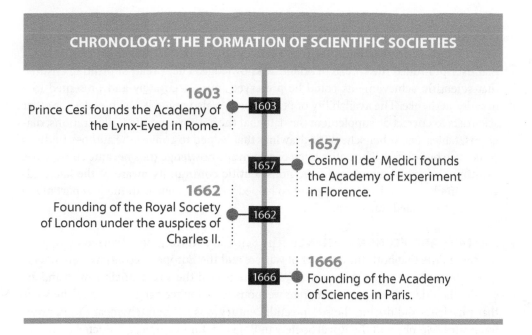

1603
Prince Cesi founds the Academy of the Lynx-Eyed in Rome.

`1603`

1657

`1657`
Cosimo II de' Medici founds the Academy of Experiment in Florence.

1662
Founding of the Royal Society of London under the auspices of Charles II.

`1662`

1666

`1666`
Founding of the Academy of Sciences in Paris.

vision symbolized the power of observation required by the new science. Founded in 1603 by Prince Cesi, the Academy published many of Galileo's works. In 1657 Cosimo II founded a similar institution in Florence, the Academy of Experiment. These academies offered a more regular source of patronage than scientists could acquire from individual positions at court, but they still served the function of glorifying their founders, and they depended on patrons for their continued existence. The royal academies established in the 1660s, however, especially the Royal Academy of Sciences in France (1666) and the Royal Society in England (1662), became in effect public institutions that operated with a minimum of royal intervention and made possible a continuous program of work.

The mission of the Royal Society in England was the promotion of scientific knowledge through experimentation. It also placed the results of scientific research at the service of the state. Members of the Royal Society, for example, did research on ship construction and military technology. These attempts to use scientific technology to strengthen the power of the state show how the growth of the modern state and the emergence of modern science were related.

THE FOUNDING OF THE FRENCH ACADÈMIE DES SCIENCES Like the Royal Society in England, the French Academy of Sciences was dependent upon royal patronage. Louis XIV, seen sitting in the middle of the painting, used the occasion to glorify himself as a patron of the sciences as well as the arts. The painting also commemorates the building of the Royal Observatory in Paris, which is shown in the background.

THE PRINTING PRESS Printing made it much easier for scientists to share their discoveries with others. During the Middle Ages, books were handwritten. Errors could creep into the text as it was being copied, and the number of copies that could be made of a manuscript limited the spread of scientific knowledge. The spread of printing ensured that scientific achievements could be preserved more accurately and presented to a broader audience. The availability of printed copies also made it much easier for other scientists to correct or supplement the data that the authors supplied. Illustrations, diagrams, tables, and other schematic drawings that helped to convey the author's findings could also be printed. The entire body of scientific knowledge thus became cumulative. Printing also made members of the nonscientific community aware of the latest advances in physics and astronomy and so helped to make science an integral part of the culture of educated Europeans.

MILITARY AND ECONOMIC CHANGE The Scientific Revolution occurred at roughly the same time that both the conduct of warfare and the European economy were undergoing dramatic changes. As territorial states increased the size of their armies and arsenals, they demanded more accurate weapons with longer range. Some of the work that physicists did during the seventeenth century was deliberately meant to improve weaponry. Members of the Royal Society in England, for example, conducted extensive scientific research on the trajectory and velocity of missiles, and so followed Francis Bacon's recommendation that scientists place their research at the service of the state.

The needs of the emerging capitalist economy also influenced scientific research. The study of mechanics, for example, led to new techniques to ventilate mines and raise coal or ore from them, thus making mining more profitable. Some of the questions discussed at the meetings of the Royal Society suggest that its members undertook research to make capitalist ventures more productive and profitable. The research did not always produce immediate results, but ultimately it increased economic profitability and contributed to the English economy in the eighteenth century.

The Intellectual Consequences of the Scientific Revolution

17.4 How did the Scientific Revolution influence philosophical and religious thought in the seventeenth and early eighteenth centuries?

The Scientific Revolution profoundly affected the intellectual life of educated Europeans. The discoveries of Copernicus, Kepler, Galileo, and Newton, as well as the assumptions on which their work was based, influenced what educated people in the West studied, how they approached intellectual problems, and what they thought about the supernatural realm.

Education

During the seventeenth and early eighteenth centuries, especially between 1680 and 1720, science and the new philosophy that was associated with it became an important part of university education. Outside academia, learned societies, public lectures, discussions in coffeehouses, and popular scientific publications spread the knowledge of science among the educated members of society. In this way science secured a permanent foothold in Western culture.

The spread of science did not go unchallenged. It encountered academic rivals committed not only to traditional Aristotelianism but also to Renaissance humanism. In the late seventeenth century, a conflict arose between "the ancients," who revered the wisdom of classical authors, and "the moderns," who emphasized the superiority of the new scientific culture. The most concrete expression of this conflict was the Battle of the Books, an intellectual debate that raged over the question of which group of thinkers had contributed more to human knowledge. No clear winner in this battle emerged, and the conflict between the ancients and the moderns was never completely resolved. The humanities and the sciences, while included within the same curriculum at many universities, are still often regarded as representing separate cultural traditions.

Skepticism and Independent Reasoning

The Scientific Revolution encouraged the habit of **skepticism**, the tendency to doubt what we have been taught and are expected to believe. This skepticism formed part of the method that seventeenth-century scientists adopted to solve philosophical problems. As we have seen, Descartes, Bacon, Galileo, and Kepler all refused to acknowledge the authority of classical or medieval texts. They preferred to rely upon the knowledge they acquired from observing nature and using their own rational faculties.

In *Discourse on the Method,* Descartes showed the extremes to which this skepticism could be taken. Descartes doubted the reality of his own sense perceptions and even his own existence until he realized that the very act of doubting proved his existence as a thinking being. As he wrote in words that have become famous, "I think, therefore I am."[3] Upon this foundation Descartes went on to prove the existence of God and the material world, thereby conquering the skepticism with which he began his inquiry. In the process, however, he developed an approach to solving intellectual problems that asked people to question authority and think clearly and systematically for themselves. The effects of this method became apparent in the late seventeenth century, when skeptics invoked Descartes's methodology to challenge both orthodox Judaism and Christianity. Some of the most radical of those opinions came from Baruch Spinoza (1632–1677), who grew up in Amsterdam in a community of Spanish and Portuguese Jews who had fled the Inquisition. Although educated as an Orthodox Jew, Spinoza also studied Latin and read Descartes and other Christian writers. From Descartes, Spinoza learned "that nothing ought to be admitted as true but what has

skepticism A tendency to doubt what one has been taught or is expected to believe.

17.1 17.2 17.3 **17.4** 17.5

CHRONOLOGY: THE IMPACT OF THE SCIENTIFIC REVOLUTION

1620
1620 Francis Bacon argues for the necessity of rigorous experimentation.

1633
1633 Galileo tried by the Roman Inquisition.

1637
1637 René Descartes publishes *Discourse on the Method.*

1670
1670 Baruch Spinoza publishes *A Treatise on Religion and Political Philosophy,* challenging the distinction between spirit and matter.

1686
1686 Bernard de Fontenelle publishes *Conversations on the Plurality of Worlds.*

been proved by good and solid reason." This skepticism and independence of thought led to his excommunication from the Jewish community at age 24.

Spinoza used Descartes's skepticism to challenge Descartes himself. He rejected Descartes's separation of the mind and the body and his radical distinction between the spiritual and the material. For Spinoza there was only one substance in the universe, which he identified with both God and nature. The claim that God and nature were two names for the same reality challenged not only the ideas of Descartes, but also the fundamental tenets of Christianity, including the belief in a personal God who had created the natural world by design and continued to govern it. In *A Treatise on Religion and Political Philosophy* (1670), Spinoza described "a universe ruled only by the cause and effect of natural laws, without purpose or design."

Spinoza's skeptical approach to solving philosophical and scientific problems revealed the radical intellectual potential of the new science. The freedom of thought that Spinoza advocated, as well as the belief that nature followed unchangeable laws

BARUCH SPINOZA Spinoza was one of the most radical thinkers of the seventeenth century. His identification of God with nature made him vulnerable to charges of atheism. His followers in the Dutch Republic, who were known as freethinkers, laid the foundations for the Enlightenment in the eighteenth century.

and could be understood in mathematical terms, served as important links between the Scientific Revolution and the Enlightenment of the eighteenth century. We will discuss those connections more fully in Chapter 19.

Science and Religion

The new science presented two challenges to traditional Christian belief. The first involved the apparent contradiction between the sun-centered theory of the universe and biblical references to the sun's mobility. Because the Bible was considered the inspired word of God, the Church took everything it said, including any passages regarding the operation of the physical world, as literally true. The Bible's reference to the sun moving across the sky served as the basis of the papal condemnation of sun-centered theories in 1616 and the prosecution of Galileo in 1633.

The second challenge to traditional Christian belief was the implication that if the universe functioned as a machine, on the basis of unchanging natural laws, then God played little part in its operation. God was akin to an engineer, who had designed the perfect machine, and therefore had no need to interfere with its workings. This position, which thinkers known as **deists** adopted in the late seventeenth and eighteenth centuries, denied the Christian belief that God was constantly active in the operation of the world. More directly, it rejected the possibility of miracles. None of the great scientists of the seventeenth century were themselves deists, but their acceptance of the mechanical philosophy made them vulnerable to the charge that they denied Christian doctrine.

Although the new science and seventeenth-century Christianity appeared to be on a collision course, some scientists and theologians insisted that there was no conflict between them. They argued that religion and science had different concerns. Religion dealt with the relationship between humanity and God. Science explained how nature operated. As Galileo wrote in 1615, "The intention of the Holy Ghost is to teach us how one goes to heaven, not how heaven goes."[4] Scripture was not intended to explain natural phenomena, but to convey religious truths that human reason could not grasp.

Another argument for the compatibility of science and religion was the claim that the mechanical philosophy, rather than relegating God to the role of a retired engineer, actually manifested God's unlimited power. In a mechanistic universe God was still the creator of the physical world and the maker of the laws by which nature operated. He was still all-powerful and present everywhere. According to Boyle and Newton, moreover, God played a supremely active role in governing the universe. Not only had he created the universe, but as Boyle argued, he also continued to keep all matter constantly in motion. This theory served the purpose of redefining God's power without diminishing it in any way. Newton arrived at a similar position in his search for an immaterial agent who would cause gravity to operate. He proposed that God himself, who he believed "endures always and is present everywhere," made bodies move according to gravitational laws. Throughout the early eighteenth century this feature of Newtonian natural philosophy served as a powerful argument for the active involvement of God in the universe.

As the new science became more widely accepted, many theologians, especially Protestants, accommodated scientific knowledge to their religious beliefs. Some Protestants welcomed the discoveries of science as an opportunity to purify the Christian religion by combating the superstition, magic, and ignorance that they claimed the Catholic Church had been promoting. Clergymen argued that because God worked through the processes of nature, scientific inquiry could lead to knowledge of God. Religion and science could illuminate each other.

Theologians and philosophers also began to expand the role that reason played in religion. The English philosopher John Locke (1632–1704) argued that reason should be the final judge of the existence of the supernatural and the true meaning of the Bible. This new emphasis on the role of reason in religion coincided with a rejection of the religious zeal that had prevailed during the Reformation and the wars of religion. Increasingly, political and ecclesiastical authorities condemned religious enthusiasm as dangerous and irrational.

deists Seventeenth- and eighteenth-century thinkers who believed that God created the universe and established immutable laws of nature but did not subsequently intervene in the operation of nature or in human affairs.

  Read the document

Galileo Galilei, *Letter to the Grand Duchess Christina*, 1615

Justice in History
The Trial of Galileo

The events leading to the trial of Galileo for heresy in 1633 began in 1616, when a committee of theologians reported to the Roman Inquisition that the sun-centered theory of Copernicus was heretical. Those who accepted this theory were declared to be heretics not only because they questioned the Bible itself, but because they denied the exclusive authority of the Catholic Church to interpret the Bible. The day after this report was submitted, Pope Paul V (r. 1605–1621) instructed Cardinal Robert Bellarmine (1542–1621), a theologian who was on good terms with Galileo, to warn him to abandon his Copernican views. Galileo had written extensively in support of the sun-centered thesis, especially in his *Letters on Sunspots* (1613) and his *Letter to the Grand Duchess Christina* (1615), although he had never admitted that the theory was proved conclusively. Then he was told not to hold, teach, or defend in any way the opinion that the sun was stable or the Earth moved. If he ignored that warning, he would be prosecuted as a heretic.

During the next 16 years Galileo published two books. The first, *The Assayer* (1623), attacked the views of an Italian philosopher regarding comets. The book won Galileo support, especially from the new pope, Urban VIII (r. 1623–1644), who was eager to be associated with the most fashionable intellectual trends. Urban took Galileo under his wing and made him the intellectual star of his court. Urban even declared that support for Copernicanism was rash but not heretical.

The pope's patronage may have emboldened Galileo to exercise less caution in writing his second book of this period, *Dialogue Concerning the Two Chief World Systems* (1632). Ostensibly an impartial presentation of the rival Ptolemaic and Copernican cosmologies, this book promoted Copernicanism in its own quiet way. Galileo sought proper authorization from ecclesiastical authorities to put the book in print, but he allowed it to be published in Florence before it received official approval from Rome.

The publication of *Dialogue* precipitated Galileo's fall from the pope's favor. Urban, accused of leniency with heretics, ordered the book taken out of circulation in the summer of 1632 and appointed a commission to investigate Galileo's activities. After receiving their report, he turned the matter over to the Roman Inquisition, which charged Galileo with heresy.

The Roman Inquisition had been established in 1542 to preserve the Catholic faith and prosecute heresy. Like the Spanish Inquisition, this Roman ecclesiastical court has acquired a reputation for being harsh and arbitrary, for administering torture, for proceeding in secrecy, and for denying the accused the right to know the charges before the trial. There is some validity to these criticisms, although the Inquisition did not torture Galileo or deny him the opportunity to defend himself. The most unfair aspect of the proceeding, and of inquisitorial justice in general, was that the same judges who had brought the charges against the accused and conducted the interrogation also decided the case. This meant that in a politically motivated trial such as Galileo's, the verdict was a foregone conclusion. To accept Galileo's defense would have been a sign of weakness and a repudiation of the pope.

Although the underlying issue in the trial was whether Galileo was guilty of heresy for denying the sun's motion and the Earth's immobility, the more technical question was whether by publishing *Dialogue* he had violated the prohibition of 1616. In his defense Galileo claimed he had only written *Dialogue* to present "the physical and astronomical reasons that can be advanced for one side or the other." He denied holding Copernicus's opinion to be true.

In the end the court determined that by publishing *Dialogue*, Galileo had violated the injunction of 1616. He had disseminated "the false opinion of the Earth's motion and the sun's stability," and he had "defended the said opinion already condemned." Even Galileo's efforts "to give the impression of leaving it undecided and labeled as probable" was still a serious error, because there was no way that "an opinion declared and defined contrary to divine Scripture may be probable." The court also declared that Galileo had obtained permission to publish the book in Florence without telling the authorities there that he was under the injunction of 1616.

Throughout the trial every effort was made to distance the pope from his former protégé. The papal court feared that because the pope had been Galileo's patron and had allowed him to develop his ideas, he himself would be implicated in Galileo's heresy. Information regarding the pope's earlier support for Galileo would not be allowed to surface during the trial. The court made sure, for example, that no one from the court of the Grand Duke of Tuscany in Florence, who had secured Galileo's appointment at the University of Padua and had defended him throughout this crisis, would testify for him. The trial tells us

THE TRIAL OF GALILEO, 1633 Galileo is shown here presenting one of his four defenses to the Inquisition. He claimed that his book *Dialogue Concerning the Two Chief World Systems* did not endorse the Copernican model of the universe.

SOURCE: Gérard Blot/Art Resource/Reunion des Musees Nationaux

(continued on next page)

(continued from previous page)

as much about Urban VIII's efforts to save face as about the Catholic Church's hostility to the new science.

The Inquisition required Galileo to renounce his views and avoid further defense of Copernicanism. After making this humiliating submission to the court, he was sent to Siena and later that year was allowed to return to his villa near Florence, where he remained under house arrest until his death in 1642.

For Discussion

1. Galileo was silenced because of what he had printed. Why had he published these works, and why did the Church consider his publications a threat?

2. Should disputes between science and religion be resolved in a court of law? Why or why not?

Taking It Further

Finocchiaro, Maurice (ed). *The Galileo Affair: A Documentary History.* 1989. A collection of original documents regarding the controversy between Galileo and the Roman Catholic Church.

Sharratt, Michael. *Galileo: Decisive Innovator.* 1994. A study of Galileo's place in the history of science that provides full coverage of his trial and papal reconsiderations of it in the late twentieth century.

The new emphasis on the reasonableness of religion and the decline of religious enthusiasm are often viewed as evidence of a trend toward the **secularization** of European life, a process in which religion gave way to more worldly concerns. In one sense this secular trend was undeniable. By 1700, theology had lost its dominant position at the universities and religion had lost much of its influence on politics, diplomacy, and economic activity.

Religion, however, had not lost its relevance. It remained a vital force in the lives of most Europeans. Many of those who accepted the new science continued to believe in a providential God and the divinity of Christ. Moreover, a small but influential group of educated people, following the lead of the French scientist and philosopher Blaise Pascal (1623–1662), argued that religious faith occupied a higher sphere of knowledge that reason and science could not penetrate. Pascal, the inventor of a calculating machine and the promoter of a system of public coach service in Paris, was an advocate of the new science. He endorsed the Copernican model of the universe and opposed the condemnation of Galileo. He introduced a new scientific theory regarding fluids that later became known as Pascal's law of pressure. But by claiming that knowledge of God comes from the heart rather than the mind, Pascal challenged the contention of Locke and Spinoza that reason was the ultimate arbiter of religious truth.

secularization The reduction of the importance of religion in society and culture.

Humans and the Natural World

> **17.5** How did the Scientific Revolution change the way in which seventeenth- and eighteenth-century Europeans thought of the place of human beings in nature?

The spread of scientific knowledge not only redefined the views of educated people regarding the supernatural, but also led them to reconsider their relationship to nature. This process involved three separate but related inquiries: to determine the place of human beings in a sun-centered universe, to investigate how science and technology had given human beings greater control over nature, and to reconsider the relationship between men and women in light of new scientific knowledge about the human mind and body.

The Place of Human Beings in the Universe

The astronomical discoveries of Copernicus, Kepler, and Galileo offered a new outlook about the position of human beings in the universe. The Earth-centered Ptolemaic cosmos that dominated scientific thought during the Middle Ages was also human-centered. Human beings inhabited the planet at the very center of the universe, and on that planet they enjoyed a privileged position. They were, after all, created in the image of God, according to Christian belief.

The acceptance of a sun-centered model of the universe began to change these views of humankind. Once it became apparent that the Earth was not the center of the universe, human beings began to lose their privileged position in nature. The Copernican universe was neither Earth-centered nor human-centered. Scientists such as Descartes continued to claim that human beings were the greatest of nature's creatures, but their habitation of a tiny planet circling the sun inevitably reduced the sense of their own importance. Moreover, as astronomers began to recognize the incomprehensible size of the cosmos, the possibility emerged that there were other habitable worlds in the universe, calling into further question the unique status of humankind.

In the late sixteenth and seventeenth centuries a number of literary works explored the possibility of other inhabited worlds and forms of life. Kepler's *Somnium, or Lunar Astronomy* (1634), a book that combined science and fiction, described various species of moon dwellers, some of whom were rational and superior to humans. The most ambitious of these books on extraterrestrial life was Bernard de Fontenelle's *Conversations on the Plurality of Worlds* (1686). This fictional work by a dramatist and poet who was also well versed in scientific knowledge became immensely popular throughout Europe and was more responsible than any purely scientific achievement for leading the general reading public to call into question the centrality of human beings in Creation.

The Control of Nature

The Scientific Revolution strengthened the confidence human beings had in their ability to control nature. By disclosing the laws governing the operation of the universe, the new science gave humans the tools they needed to make nature serve them more effectively than it had in the past. Francis Bacon, for example, believed that knowledge of the laws of nature could restore the dominion over nature that humans had lost in the biblical Garden of Eden. Bacon thought that nature existed for human beings to control and exploit for their own benefit. His famous saying, "knowledge is power," conveyed his confidence that science would give human beings this type of control. This optimism regarding human control of nature found support in the belief that God permitted such mastery, first by creating a regular and uniform universe and then by giving humans the rational faculties by which they could understand nature's laws.

Many seventeenth-century scientists emphasized the practical applications of their research, just as scientists often do today. Descartes, who used his knowledge of optics to improve the grinding of lenses, considered how scientific knowledge could drain marshes, increase the velocity of bullets, and use bells to make clouds give rain. In his celebration of the French Academy of Sciences in 1699, Fontenelle wrote that "the application of science to nature will constantly grow in scope and intensity and we shall go on from one marvel to the next; the day will come when man will be able to fly by fitting on wings to keep him in the air . . . till one day we shall be able to fly to the moon."[5]

The hopes of seventeenth-century scientists for the improvement of human life by means of technology remained in large part unfulfilled until the eighteenth century. Only then did the technological promise of the Scientific Revolution begin to be realized, most notably with the innovations that preceded or accompanied the Industrial Revolution (see Chapter 21). By the middle of the eighteenth century, the belief that science would improve human life became an integral part of Western culture. Faith in human progress also became one of the main themes of the Enlightenment, which will be discussed in Chapter 19.

Women, Men, and Nature

The new scientific and philosophical ideas challenged ancient and medieval notions about women's physical and mental inferiority to men but not other traditional ideas about gender roles.

Until the seventeenth century, a woman's sexual organs were thought to be imperfect versions of a man's, an idea that made woman an inferior version of man and, in some respects, a freak of nature. During the sixteenth and seventeenth centuries, scientific literature advanced the new idea that women's sexual organs were perfect in their own right and served distinct functions in reproduction. Aristotle's view that men made a more important contribution to reproduction than women also came under attack. Semen was long believed to contain the form of both the body and the soul, while a woman only contributed the formless matter on which the semen acted. By 1700, however, most scholars agreed that both sexes contributed equally to the process of reproduction.

Some seventeenth-century natural philosophers also questioned ancient and medieval ideas about women's mental inferiority to men. In making a radical separation between the mind and the human body, Descartes, for example, found no difference between the minds of men and women. As one of his followers wrote in 1673, "The mind has no sex."[6] A few upper-class women provided evidence to support this revolutionary claim of female intellectual equality. Princess Elisabeth of Bohemia, for example, carried on a long correspondence with Descartes during the 1640s and challenged many of his ideas on the relationship between the body and the soul. The English noblewoman Margaret Cavendish (1623–1673) wrote scientific and philosophical works and conversed with leading philosophers. In early eighteenth-century France, small groups of women and men gathered in the salons or private sitting rooms of the nobility to discuss philosophical and scientific ideas. In Germany women helped their husbands run astronomical observatories.

ASTRONOMERS IN SEVENTEENTH-CENTURY GERMANY Elisabetha and Johannes Hevelius working together with a sextant in a German astronomical observatory. More than 14 percent of all German astronomers were female. Most of them collaborated with their husbands in their work.

Although seventeenth-century science laid the foundations for a theory of sexual equality, it did not challenge other traditional ideas that compared women unfavorably with men. Most educated people continued to ground female behavior in the humors, claiming that because women were cold and wet, as opposed to hot and dry, they were naturally more deceptive, unstable, and melancholic than men. They also continued to identify women with nature itself, which had always been depicted as female. Bacon's use of masculine metaphors to describe science and his references to "man's mastery over nature" therefore seemed to reinforce traditional ideas of male dominance over women. His language also reinforced traditional notions of men's superior rationality.[7] In 1664 the secretary of the Royal Society, which excluded women from membership, proclaimed that the mission of that institution was to develop a "masculine philosophy."[8]

The new science thus strengthened the theoretical foundations for the male control of women at a time when many men expressed concern over women's "disorderly" and "irrational" conduct. In a world populated with witches, rebels, and other women who refused to adhere to conventional standards of proper feminine behavior, the adoption of a masculine philosophy was associated with the reassertion of patriarchy.

CONCLUSION

Science and Western Culture

Unlike many of the cultural developments in the history of the West, the Scientific Revolution owes very little to Eastern influences. During the Middle Ages the Islamic civilizations of the Middle East produced a rich body of scientific knowledge that influenced the development of medieval science in Europe, but by the time of the Scientific Revolution, Middle Eastern science no longer occupied the frontlines of scientific research. Middle Eastern natural philosophers had little to offer their European counterparts as they made their contributions to the Scientific Revolution.

China and India had also accumulated a large body of scientific knowledge in ancient and medieval times. When Jesuit missionaries began teaching Western science and mathematics to the Chinese in the sixteenth and seventeenth centuries, they learned about earlier Chinese technological advances, including the invention of the compass, gunpowder, and printing. They also learned that ancient Chinese astronomers had been the first to observe solar eclipses and comets. By the time the Jesuits arrived, however, Chinese science had entered a period of decline. When those missionaries returned home, they introduced Europeans to many aspects of Chinese culture but very few scientific ideas that European natural philosophers found useful.

None of these Eastern civilizations had a scientific revolution comparable to the one that occurred in the West in the late sixteenth and seventeenth centuries. For China the explanation probably lies in the absence of military and political incentives to promote scientific research at a time when the vast Chinese empire was relatively stable. In the Middle East the explanation is more likely that Islam during these years failed to give priority to the study of the natural world. In Islam nature was either entirely secular (that is, not religious) and hence not worthy of study on its own terms or so heavily infused with spiritual value that it could not be subjected to rational analysis. In Europe, however, religious and cultural traditions allowed scientists to view nature as both a product of supernatural forces and something that was separate from the supernatural. Nature could therefore be studied objectively without losing its religious significance. Only when nature was viewed as both the creation of God and at the same time as independent of God could it be subjected to mathematical analysis and brought under human control.

Scientific and technological knowledge became a significant component of Western culture, and in the eighteenth century Western science gave many educated Europeans a new source of identity. These people believed that their knowledge of science, in conjunction with their Christian religion, their classical culture, and their political institutions, made them different from, if not superior to, people living in the East.

The rise of Western science and technology played a role in the growth of European dominance over Africa, Asia, and the Americas. Science gave Western states the military and navigational technology that helped them gain control of foreign lands. Knowledge of botany and agriculture allowed Western powers to develop the resources of the areas they colonized and use these resources to improve their own societies. Some Europeans even appealed to science to justify their dominance of the people in the lands they settled and ruled. To this process of Western imperial expansion we now turn.

MAKING CONNECTIONS

1. Were the changes in astronomy, physics, chemistry, and biology in the sixteenth and seventeenth centuries revolutionary? In which field were the changes most significant?
2. Scientists today often refer to the scientific method. Was there a scientific method in the seventeenth century or did scientists employ various methods?
3. Why did the Scientific Revolution occur at this time? Did it owe its development more to internal or external developments?
4. What does the conflict between the supporter of a sun-centered theory and the Catholic Church suggest about the compatibility of science and religion in the seventeenth century?

TAKING IT FURTHER

For suggested readings see page R-1.

Chapter Review

The Discoveries and Achievements of the Scientific Revolution

17.1 What were the achievements and discoveries of the Scientific Revolution?

Discoveries in astronomy, physics, chemistry, and biology transformed human thought in the seventeenth century. The most significant change in astronomy was due to Kepler and Galileo supporting the Copernican model of the universe, which claimed that the sun, not the Earth, was the center of the universe. In the field of physics, Sir Isaac Newton offered a scientific model of the physical world based on the laws of motion and gravitation. In chemistry, the discovery of atoms by Robert Boyle advanced the idea that the arrangement of a subject's atoms determined its characteristics, and William Harvey's demonstration of how blood circulates through the human body set the standard for future research in biology and medicine.

The Search for Scientific Knowledge

17.2 What methods did scientists use during this period to investigate nature, and how did they think nature operated?

Scientists used an empirical or inductive approach, which demands testing all scientific theories through rigorous experiments based on observation of the natural world. They also used deductive reasoning to establish basic truths or principles, and from these premises then arrived at other logical conclusions or laws. Scientific research conducted in both traditions applied mathematics to the study of a natural world that was believed to operate as if it were a machine made by a human being.

The Causes of the Scientific Revolution

17.3 Why did the Scientific Revolution take place in western Europe at this time?

Within the realm of science, the research into motion conducted by natural philosophers in the fourteenth century, the scientific investigations by Renaissance humanists, and the collapse of the dominant conceptual frameworks, or paradigms, that had governed scientific inquiry and research for centuries were factors in the revolution of scientific thought. Outside of science, the spread of Protestantism; the patronage, or sponsorship, of scientific research; the invention of the printing press; and military and economic change all created a favorable environment for the development of new ideas.

The Intellectual Consequences of the Scientific Revolution

17.4 How did the Scientific Revolution influence philosophical and religious thought in the seventeenth and early eighteenth centuries?

Science and its associated philosophies became an important part of the university education system. Outside academia, scientific knowledge was spread by way of popular scientific publications and coffeehouse debate. Both of these trends helped popularize skepticism among educated people, an approach to solving philosophical and scientific problems that emphasizes independent thought. While religion remained a vital force in most people's lives, a trend of secularization, the process by which belief in religion is displaced by more worldly concerns, marked the end of the seventeenth century.

Humans and the Natural World

17.5 How did the Scientific Revolution change the way in which seventeenth- and eighteenth-century Europeans thought of the place of human beings in nature?

Three separate but related areas of inquiry led people to reconsider their relationship to nature. The newly accepted sun-centered model of the universe forced humans to question their status as unique and central to the universe, while the new science hinted at the potential to make the natural world serve people more effectively than in the past. Even long established differences in equality between the sexes were called into question when new scientific knowledge about the human body advanced the idea that female sex organs were perfect in their own right and served a crucial function in reproduction.

Chapter Time Line

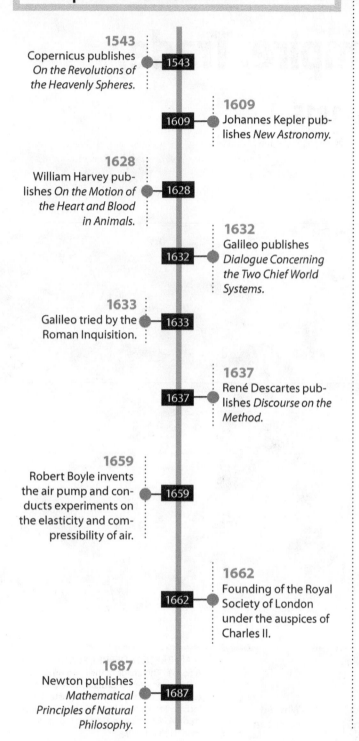

1543
Copernicus publishes
*On the Revolutions of
the Heavenly Spheres.*

1543

1609
Johannes Kepler pub-
lishes *New Astronomy.*

1609

1628
William Harvey pub-
lishes *On the Motion of
the Heart and Blood
in Animals.*

1628

1632
Galileo publishes
*Dialogue Concerning
the Two Chief World
Systems.*

1632

1633
Galileo tried by the
Roman Inquisition.

1633

1637
René Descartes pub-
lishes *Discourse on the
Method.*

1637

1659
Robert Boyle invents
the air pump and con-
ducts experiments on
the elasticity and com-
pressibility of air.

1659

1662
Founding of the Royal
Society of London
under the auspices of
Charles II.

1662

1687
Newton publishes
*Mathematical
Principles of Natural
Philosophy.*

1687

18 The West and the World: Empire, Trade, and War, 1650–1815

I n 1789 Olaudah Equiano, a freed slave living in Great Britain, wrote an account of his experiences in captivity. Equiano's narrative recounted his seizure in the Gambia region of Africa and his transportation on a slave ship to the British Caribbean colony of Barbados. He described the unmerciful floggings to which the Africans on his ship were subjected, the unrelieved hunger they experienced, and the insufferable heat and smells they endured in the hold of the ship. He witnessed the suicide of those who threw themselves into the sea

JEAN-BAPTISTE DEBRET, *PUNISHMENT OF A SLAVE* This image of the flogging of a slave in Brazil conveys the brutality of Atlantic slavery. The French painter Jean-Baptiste Debret included this engraving in his three-volume study, *A Pictureque and Historic Voyage to Brazil* (1834–1839).

SOURCE: Biblioteca Nacional, Rio de Janiero Brazil/The Bridgeman Art Library.

LEARNING OBJECTIVES

18.1 (((•	18.2 (((•	18.3 (((•	18.4 (((•	18.5 (((•
How did the composition of European empires change during this period?	In what ways did the wars waged by European powers involve competition for overseas possessions?	How did European empires create an Atlantic economy in which slavery was a major feature?	How did Western attitudes toward Asian peoples change during this period of empire-building?	Why did European powers lose control of some of their colonies between 1775 and 1825?

(((• Listen to Chapter 18 on MyHistoryLab

Watch the Video Series on MyHistoryLab

Learn about some key topics related to this chapter with the *MyHistoryLab Video Series: Key Topics in Western Civilization*

to avoid further misery. He was terrified that his white captors would eat him, and he wished for a merciful death.

Once the ship had reached its destination, the Africans were herded into pens where white plantation owners examined, purchased, and branded them. The most moving part of Equiano's narrative is his account of the cries he heard as family members were sold to different masters. "O you nominal Christians," wrote Equiano, "might not an African ask you, learned you this from your God? Is it not enough that we are torn from our country and friends to toil for your luxury and lust of gain? Must every tender feeling be sacrificed to your avarice?"[1]

Between 1650 and 1815 millions of African men and women took journeys similar to Equiano's. The forced emigration of black Africans from their homelands, their sale to white landlords, and their subjection to inhumane treatment number among the abiding horrors of Western civilization. To understand how these horrors could have occurred, especially at the hands of men who proclaimed a commitment to human freedom, we must study the growth of European empires during these centuries.

As European states grew in size, wealth, and military power in the sixteenth and seventeenth centuries, the most powerful of them acquired large overseas empires. By the end of the seventeenth century the British, French, and Dutch had joined the Portuguese and the Spanish as overseas imperial powers. As we discussed in Chapter 13, the first stage of empire-building, which lasted from 1500 until about 1650, had many different motives. The search for gold and silver, the mission to Christianize the indigenous populations, the desire of some colonists to escape religious persecution, the urge to plunder, the efforts of monarchs to expand the size of their dominions, and the desire to profit from international trade all figured in the process. In 1625 the English government recognized many of these motives when it declared the purpose of the colony of Virginia to be "the propagation of the Christian religion, the increase of trade, and the enlarging of the royal empire."[2]

During the second stage of empire-building, which lasted from about 1650 to 1815, the economic motive for acquiring overseas possessions became dominant. More than anything else, the desire for profit within a world economy shaped imperial policy. In the eyes of western European governments, all colonies were economic enterprises. They supplied the parent country, often referred to as the **metropolis**, with agricultural products, raw materials, and minerals. Overseas colonies also provided the metropolis with markets for its manufactured goods.

The main question that this chapter will address is:

metropolis The parent country of a colony or imperial possession.

How did the growth of these empires and the encounters between Europeans and non-Western peoples change the political, economic, and cultural history of the West?

European Empires in the Americas and Asia

18.1 How did the composition of European empires change during this period?

The main political units in Europe during this long period of history are usually referred to as **states**. A state is a consolidated territorial area that has its own political institutions and recognizes no higher authority. Thus, we refer to France, England (which became Great Britain after its union with Scotland

states Consolidated territorial areas that have their own political institutions and recognize no higher political authority.

553

empires Large political formations consisting of different kingdoms or territories outside the boundaries of the states that control them.

View the Map

Interactive Map of European Claims in America ca. 1750

Watch the Video

The Big Picture: The World in 1700 C.E. (Part I)

in 1707), Prussia, the Dutch Republic, and Portugal as states. As we have discussed in Chapter 16, most of these states acquired larger armies and administrative bureaucracies during the sixteenth and seventeenth centuries, mainly to meet the demands of war. Consequently, they became more highly integrated and cohesive political structures.

Many European states formed the center or core of much larger political formations known as **empires**. The main characteristic of empires in the seventeenth and eighteenth centuries was that they contained many different kingdoms or territorial possessions. The metropolis controlled these imperial territories, but did not fully integrate them into its administrative structure. Some of the territories that formed a part of these empires were located in Europe. The Austrian Habsburg monarchy, for example, had jurisdiction over a host of separate kingdoms and principalities in central and eastern Europe, including Hungary and Bohemia. The Spanish monarchy controlled many different kingdoms and provinces in the Iberian peninsula as well as territories in southern Italy and the Netherlands. On the eastern and southeastern periphery of Europe lay two other empires: the Russian and the Ottoman, which controlled vast expanses of land not only in eastern Europe, but also in Asia. As in previous centuries, the Russian and Ottoman Empires marked the ever-shifting boundaries between East and West.

Beginning in the fifteenth century, as the result of transoceanic voyages of exploration and the establishment of overseas colonies, western European states acquired, settled, or controlled territories in the Americas, Africa, and Asia. Mastery of these lands came much more quickly in the New World than in Asia. The indigenous peoples of North and South America whom Europeans encountered when they arrived were able fighters, but diseases introduced by the Europeans drastically reduced their numbers. European settlers, who had the added advantage of superior military technology, were able to gain the upper hand in battle, seize or purchase their lands, and force those who survived to retreat to less inhabited areas.

When Europeans started to develop extensive trading routes in Asia, however, that continent was already highly developed politically and militarily. Three Muslim empires—the Ottoman, the Safavid (Persia), and the Mughal (India)—and the neighboring Chinese Empire in East Asia occupied the mass of land from the Balkans to the Pacific Ocean. Only when these Asian empires began to fall apart, giving greater autonomy to the smaller, subordinate states within their boundaries, were Europeans able to exploit the situation, secure favorable trading arrangements with provincial rulers in Asia, and ultimately gain control over some Asian territories.

The Rise of the British Empire

The fastest-growing of the new European overseas empires during this period was that of Great Britain. England had begun its overseas empire in the late twelfth century, when it conquered the neighboring island of Ireland, but only in the seventeenth century did it begin to acquire lands in the New World and Asia. By 1700 the English empire in the Americas included colonies on the eastern North American seaboard, a vast territory in the northern part of Canada, and a cluster of islands in the Caribbean, most notably Barbados, Jamaica, and the Bahamas.

These Caribbean or West Indian colonies developed an economy that used slave labor, and therefore black slaves brought there from Africa soon outnumbered Europeans by a significant margin. In the colonies on the mainland of North America, however, most of the colonists were white, even in the southern colonies, where black slaves accounted for less than half the population.

Many English settlers, especially in the northern colonies, emigrated so that they might practice their religion without legal restraint. During the 1630s communities of English Protestants known as Puritans settled in New England. They objected to the control of the English Church by bishops, especially during the period from 1633 to 1641, when William Laud served as archbishop of Canterbury. Their main complaint was that the church services authorized by Laud too closely resembled those of Roman Catholicism. During the same years small groups of English Catholics, who were denied the right to practice their religion, took refuge in Maryland. In the late seventeenth century a dissenting Protestant sect known as Quakers (so called because their founder, George Fox, told them to quake at the word of the Lord), smarting under legislation that denied them religious freedom and political power, emigrated to Pennsylvania.

During the seventeenth century the English also established trading posts, known as factories, along the coast of India. They settled at Surat in 1612, Madras in 1639, Bombay in 1661, and Calcutta in 1690. These mercantile depots differed markedly from the colonies in the Caribbean and on the North American mainland. The number of British settlers in India, who were mostly members of the East India Company (which had a monopoly of British trade with India), remained small, and they did not establish large plantations. Consequently, they did not introduce slave labor.

As **Map 18.1** shows, the British also acquired influence and ultimately political control of the area from Southeast Asia stretching down into the South

SAMUEL SCOTT, *A THAMES WHARF* (1750s) British merchants conducted a brisk trade with Asia and the Americas in the eighteenth century.

Pacific. In the late seventeenth century the British began to challenge the Dutch and the Portuguese for control of the trade with Indonesia. In the second half of the eighteenth century, British merchants established a thriving trade with the countries on the Malay peninsula. In the late eighteenth century the British also began to explore the South Pacific, which remained the last part of the inhabited world that Europeans had not yet visited. (See *Justice in History* in this chapter.) In 1770 the British naval officer and explorer Captain James Cook (1728–1779) claimed the entire eastern coast of Australia for Britain, and in 1788 the British established a penal colony in the southeastern corner of the Australian continent at Botany Bay.

The Scattered French Empire

French colonization of North America and India paralleled that of Great Britain, but it never achieved the same degree of success. As the British were establishing footholds in the West Indies and the mainland of North America, the French acquired their own islands in the Caribbean and laid claim to large sections of Canada and the Ohio and Mississippi River valleys in the present-day United States. In the West Indies the French first drew their labor supply from servants indentured for periods of three years, but in the eighteenth century they began to follow the British and Spanish pattern of importing slaves to provide labor for the sugar plantations. In North America French settlers did not require a large labor supply, as their main economic undertakings were the fur trade and fishing, and so they did not introduce slaves to those areas.

The parallel between French and British overseas expansion extended to India, where in the early eighteenth century the French East India Company established factories at Pondicherry, Chandenagar, and other locations. Rivalry with the British also

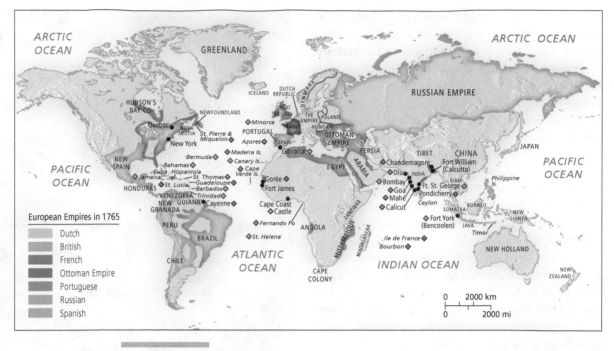

MAP **18.1** EUROPEAN EMPIRES IN 1763 This map shows the overseas possessions of Britain, France, the Dutch Republic, Spain, and Portugal. Russian overseas expansion into North America had not yet begun. How would you compare the strength of these empires? Was there a correlation between their geographical size and their power?

led the French to make alliances with native governors of Indian provinces, to assist them in a series of military conflicts with the British between 1744 and 1815. The British ultimately prevailed in this struggle, reducing the French presence in India to a few isolated factories by the early nineteenth century.

The waning of French influence in India coincided with a series of territorial losses in the New World. Defeats suffered at the hands of the British during the Seven Years' War (1756–1763) resulted in the transfer of French Canada and the territory east of the Mississippi River to Great Britain. During that conflict France also ceded the vast region of Louisiana between the Mississippi River and the Rocky Mountains to Spain. France regained Louisiana in 1801 but then promptly sold the entire territory to the United States in 1803. The following year the French Caribbean colony of Saint Domingue became independent, although France retained possession of its other West Indian colonies.

The Commercial Dutch Empire

The tiny Dutch Republic acquired almost all of its overseas possessions in the first half of the seventeenth century, at about the same time that the British and French were establishing their first colonies in Asia and the New World. The formation of the Dutch Empire went hand in hand with the explosive growth of the Dutch economy in the seventeenth century. At that time the Dutch Republic became the center of a global economy, and its overseas colonies in the New World, Asia, and Africa helped the Dutch Republic maintain its commercial supremacy. Dutch overseas settlements, just like Dutch port cities in the metropolis, were dedicated almost exclusively to serving the interests of trade.

The Dutch were more eager than other European powers to use military and naval power to acquire and fortify trading depots. They seized two trading posts from the Portuguese on the West African coast in 1637, and in 1641 they also acquired from Portugal the African islands of São Tomé and Principe. In 1654 they seized two small

THE DUTCH FACTORY OF BATAVIA IN INDONESIA, CA. 1665 The Dutch Republic dominated the Asian trade in the seventeenth century. Batavia (now Jakarta) was the most important of their settlements in Southeast Asia. The efforts of the Dutch to transplant their culture is evident in this building's Dutch style of architecture.

West Indian islands and plantation colonies on the Guiana coast of South America, mainly in present-day Surinam. From these settlements in Africa and the Caribbean the Dutch carried on trade with the Spanish, Portuguese, French, and British colonies. Through these ports the Dutch brought more than 500,000 slaves to Brazil, the Spanish colonies, and the French and British West Indies.

In addition to their African and Caribbean possessions, the Dutch established a presence in three other parts of the world. In the early seventeenth century they settled a colony in the Hudson River valley on the North American mainland. They named the colony New Netherland and its main port, at the mouth of the river, New Amsterdam. In 1664 the Dutch lost the colony to the English, who renamed the colony and the port New York. The second area was in Asia, where the Dutch East India Company established a fort at Batavia (now Jakarta in Indonesia) and factories in India, China, and Japan. These possessions allowed the Dutch to engage in trade throughout Asia. In the eighteenth century, however, the British began to take control of Dutch trading routes.

The third area was the southern tip of Africa, where in 1652 the Dutch settled a colony at the Cape of Good Hope, mainly to provide support for ships engaged in commerce with the East Indies. In this colony some 1,700 Dutch settlers, most of them farmers known as **boers**, developed an agricultural economy on plantations that employed slave labor. The loss of this colony to the British at the end of the eighteenth century reflected a more general decline of Dutch military and imperial strength.

 View the Image

View of Batavia, Indonesia 1764

boers Dutch settlers, most of them farmers, who settled in the Dutch colony established at the Cape of Good Hope in southern Africa.

The Vast Spanish Empire

Of the five western European overseas empires, the Spanish monarchy controlled the most land. At the height of its power in 1650, the Spanish Empire covered the western part of North America from California to Mexico and from Mexico down through Central America. It also included Florida and the Caribbean islands of Cuba,

Justice in History

The Trial of the Mutineers on the *Bounty*

I n December 1787 a British ship named the *Bounty*, under the captainship of William Bligh, left Portsmouth, England, on a momentous journey to Tahiti, an island in the South Pacific that Captain James Cook had first visited in 1769. The goal of the voyage of the *Bounty* was neither exploration nor colonial expansion, but to bring home breadfruit trees that Cook had discovered on his second trip to the island in 1773. The trees, so it was hoped, would be introduced to the West Indies as a source of food for the slaves and hence the survival of the plantation economy. The voyage of the *Bounty* was therefore part of the operation of the new global economy that European expansion had made possible. The total size of the crew, all of whom had volunteered for service, was 46. The master's first mate, who became the main leader of a mutiny against Bligh, was Fletcher Christian.

The mutiny did not take place until after the ship had remained at Tahiti for a number of months, loaded its cargo of more than one thousand breadfruit plants, and begun its return voyage. The main reason for the mutiny was Captain Bligh's abusive and humiliating language. Unlike many other officers who faced the task of maintaining order on their ships and commanding the obedience of their crews, Bligh did not flog his men. In that regard Bligh's behavior was mild. Instead, he went into tantrums and verbally abused them, belittling them and calling them scoundrels. Just before the mutiny Bligh called Fletcher Christian a cowardly rascal and falsely accused him of stealing from him. On the morning of April 28, 1788, Christian arrested Bligh at bayonet point, tied his hands behind his back, and threatened him with instant death if he should speak a word. Claiming that "Captain Bligh had brought all this on himself," Christian and his associates put Bligh and 18 other members of the crew into one of the ship's small launch boats and set them adrift, leaving them to reach a nearby island by their own power.

The mutineers sailed on to the island of Tubuai, where after a brief stay they split into two groups. Nine of them, headed by

THE MUTINEERS CASTING BLIGH ADRIFT IN THE LAUNCH, ENGRAVING BY ROBERT DODD (1790) This was the central act in the mutiny led by Fletcher Christian. Captain Bligh is standing in the launch in his nightclothes. Some of the breadfruit trees loaded on the ship at Tahiti can be seen on the top deck.

Christian and accompanied by six Tahitian men and 12 women, established a settlement on Pitcairn Island, where their descendents still reside today. The remaining 16 mutineers returned to Tahiti. All but two of these men were apprehended in 1791 by Captain Edwards of the H.M.S. *Pandora*, which had sailed to Tahiti to arrest and return them to England for trial. At the beginning of its return voyage the *Pandora* was shipwrecked, and four of the prisoners drowned. The rest reached England aboard another ship in 1792. They were promptly charged before a navy court-martial with taking the *Bounty* away from its captain and with desertion, both of which were capital offenses under the Naval Discipline Act of 1766.

The trial took place aboard a British ship, H.M.S. *Duke*, in Portsmouth Harbor in September 1792. The proceeding had all the markings of a state trial, a proceeding initiated by the government for offenses against the Crown. Mutiny and desertion represented challenges to the state itself. During the second period of imperial expansion navies became major instruments of state power. Even when ships were used for purposes of exploration rather than naval combat, they served the interests of the state. The captain of the ship represented the power of the sovereign at sea. Because of the difficulty of maintaining order in such circumstances, the captain was given absolute authority. He could use whatever means necessary, including the infliction of corporal punishment, to preserve order. To disobey or challenge the captain was interpreted as an act of rebellion.

The trial was based on the assumption that the mutiny was illegal and seditious. The only question was the extent of individual involvement in the act itself. The degree of involvement was measured by evidence of one's co-operation with Christian or his loyalty to Bligh. The mere fact that some men had remained with Christian on the *Bounty* did not prove that they had supported the mutiny. Four of those men gave little evidence of having voluntarily cooperated with Christian, and those four men were eventually acquitted. The testimony of Captain Bligh, who declared that those four crew

(continued on next page)

(continued from previous page)

members had been reluctant to put him in the launch boat, was decisive in securing their not-guilty verdicts.

The remaining six men were convicted and sentenced to die by hanging. Three of those men were eventually spared their lives. Peter Heywood and James Morrison were well connected to influential people in the navy and the government and received royal pardons. William Muspratt, one of only three mutineers to hire a lawyer, entered a protest against the procedures of the court. In a court-martial, unlike a criminal trial at the common law, a prisoner could not call witnesses in his own defense. At the time of his conviction Muspratt protested that he had been "debarred calling witnesses whose evidence I have reason to believe would have tended to prove my innocence." The difference between the two systems of criminal justice, he claimed, "is dreadful to the subject and fatal to me." On this ground Muspratt was reprieved.

The three men who were executed died as model prisoners, proclaiming the illegality of their rebellion. By securing their conviction and dramatizing it with a widely publicized hanging, the government had upheld its authority and thus reinforced the power of the Crown.

For Discussion

1. How would you characterize the different ideals of justice adhered to by the mutineers on the *Bounty* and the British admiralty court that tried them?
2. What does the journey of the *Bounty* tell us about the role of the British navy in the process of imperial expansion? What problems were inherent in using British ships for these purposes?

Taking It Further

Rutter, Owen (ed.). *The Court-Martial of the "Bounty" Mutineers.* 1931. Contains a full transcript of the trial.

Hispaniola, and Puerto Rico. It embraced almost all of South America except Brazil, which was under Portuguese control. In Asia the main Spanish possessions were the Philippine Islands, which served as the main base from which the Spanish engaged in trade with other Asian countries.

Spanish overseas possessions formed part of a much more authoritarian imperial system than those of the British. Like all mercantilist enterprises, the Spanish colonial empire served the purposes of trade. Until the eighteenth century a council known as the House of Trade, situated in Seville, exercised a monopoly over all colonial commerce. It funneled trade with the colonies from the southwestern Spanish port of Cadiz to selected ports on the eastern coasts of Spanish America, from which it was then redirected to other ports. The ships returned to Spain carrying the gold and silver from Mexican and Peruvian mines.

The Bourbon kings of Spain, who came to power in 1700, introduced political reforms that were intended to increase the volume of the colonial trade and prevent the smuggling that threatened to undermine it. On the one hand, they opened up the colonial trade to more Spanish and American ports and also permitted more trade within the colonies. On the other hand, the Bourbons, especially Charles III (r. 1759–1788), brought their overseas territories under more direct control of Spanish royal officials and increased the efficiency of the tax collection system. These **Bourbon reforms** made the empire more manageable and profitable, but they also created tension between the Spanish-born bureaucrats and the **creoles**, the people of Spanish descent who had been born in the colonies. These tensions eventually led in the early nineteenth century to a series of wars of independence from Spain that we shall discuss in a later section.

Bourbon reforms Measures introduced by the Bourbon kings of Spain in the eighteenth century to make the Spanish empire more manageable and profitable.

creoles People of Spanish descent who had been born in Spanish America.

The Declining Portuguese Empire

The Portuguese had been the first European nation to engage in overseas exploration and colonization. During the late fifteenth and sixteenth centuries, they had established colonies in Asia, South America, and Africa (see Chapter 13). By the beginning of the eighteenth century, however, the Portuguese Empire had declined in size and wealth in relation to its rivals. The Portuguese continued to hold a few ports in India, most notably the small island of Goa. They also retained a factory at Macao off the southeastern coast of China. In the New World the major Portuguese plantation colony was Brazil, which occupied almost half the land mass of South America and supplied Europe with sugar, cacao (from which chocolate is made), and other agricultural commodities.

18.1

◈ View the **Map**

Seventeenth-Century Portuguese Map
of the Indian Ocean

18.2

18.3

18.4

18.5

Closely linked to Brazil were the Portuguese colonies along and off the West African coast. These possessions were all deeply involved in the transatlantic trade, especially in slaves. The Portuguese also had a series of trading stations and small settlements on the southeastern coast of Africa, including Mozambique.

A relatively weak European power, Portugal did not fare well in the fierce military conflicts that ensued in South America and Asia over control of the colonial trade. Portugal's main military and economic competition came from the Dutch, who seized many of its Asian, African, and South American colonies, thereby acquiring many Portuguese trading routes. Most of those losses took place in Asia between 1600 and 1670. The Portuguese Empire suffered further attrition when the crown relinquished Bombay and the northern African port of Tangier to the English as part of the dowry for the Portuguese princess Catherine of Braganza when she married King Charles II of Great Britain in 1661.

Brazil remained by far the most important of the Portuguese possessions during the late seventeenth and eighteenth centuries. The colony suffered from an unfavorable balance of trade with Portugal, but it expanded in population and wealth during this period, especially after the discovery of gold and diamonds led to large-scale mining in the interior. The slave trade increased in volume to provide additional labor in the mines and on the sugar plantations. In the first quarter of the nineteenth century, as the British slave trade declined and came to an end, Portuguese ships carried 871,600 slaves to Brazil. Between 1826 and 1850 the number increased to an astonishing 1,247,700. As a result of this massive influx of Africans, slaves accounted for approximately 40 percent of the entire Brazilian population in the nineteenth century.

Like most other European countries, Portugal tightened the control of its imperial possessions during the second half of the eighteenth century. During the ministry of the dictatorial Marquis of Pombal from 1755 to 1777, the Portuguese government increased its control over all aspects of colonial life. Like the Bourbon reforms in Spanish America, this legislation created considerable resentment among the creoles. As in Spanish America, these tensions led to demands for Brazil's autonomy in the nineteenth century.

The Russian Empire in the Pacific

The only eastern European state that established an overseas empire during the eighteenth century was Russia. Between the fifteenth and the early eighteenth centuries Russia had gradually acquired a massive overland empire stretching from St. Petersburg in the west across the frigid expanse of Siberia to the Pacific Ocean. The main impulse of Russian expansion had been the search for exotic furs that were in high demand in the colder climes of Russia and northern Europe. During the reign of the empress Catherine the Great (r. 1762–1796), Russia entered a period of further territorial expansion. On its western frontier it took part in the successive partitions of Poland between 1772 and 1795, while to the south it held the Crimean region within the Ottoman Empire between 1783 and 1792.

In the late eighteenth and early nineteenth centuries Russia extended its empire overseas. Russian traders and explorers undertook numerous expeditions to Hawaii and other islands in the Pacific Ocean, sailing as far south as Mexico. They did not, however, establish colonies in these locations. Further expeditions brought Russia across the northern Pacific, where they encroached upon the hunting grounds of the native Aleuts in Alaska. The Russian-American Company, established in 1789, built trading posts along the Pacific seaboard from Alaska down to Fort Ross in northern California. These claims led to a protracted territorial dispute with Spain, which had established a string of missions and settlements on the California coast as far north as San Francisco. In this way the two great European empires of Russia and Spain, advancing from opposite directions, confronted each other on the western coast of North

America. Russian expansion into Alaska and California also led to territorial disputes with the United States, which was engaged in its own process of territorial expansion westward toward the Pacific during the nineteenth century.

Warfare in Europe, North America, and Asia

18.2	In what ways did the wars waged by European powers involve competition for overseas possessions?

Until the middle of the seventeenth century, European states engaged each other in battle almost exclusively within their own continent. The farthest their armies ever traveled was to the Near East to fight the Turks or to Ireland to conquer the native Celts. The acquisition of overseas empires and the disputes that erupted between European powers over the control of global trade brought those European conflicts to new and distant military theaters. Wars that began over territory in Europe were readily extended to America in one direction and to Asia in the other. The military forces that fought in these imperial battles consisted not only of metropolitan government troops but also colonists. These colonial forces were often supplemented by the troops drawn from the local population, such as when the French recruited native Americans to fight with them against the British in North America. This pattern of recruiting soldiers from the indigenous population, which began in the eighteenth century, became the norm during the third and final phase of empire-building in the nineteenth and early twentieth centuries.

Wars fought overseas placed a premium on naval strength. Ground troops remained important, both in Europe and overseas, but naval power increasingly proved to be the crucial factor. All of the Western imperial powers either possessed or acquired large navies. Great Britain and the Dutch Republic rose to the status of world powers on the basis of sea power, while the French strengthened their navy considerably during the reign of Louis XIV. The Dutch used their naval power mainly against the Portuguese and the British, while the British directed theirs against the French and the Spanish and also the Dutch. The overwhelming success that the British realized in these conflicts resulted in the establishment of British maritime and imperial supremacy.

Mercantile Warfare

An increasingly important motive for engaging in warfare in the late seventeenth and eighteenth centuries was the protection and expansion of trade. The theory that underlay and inspired these imperial wars was mercantilism. As discussed in Chapter 16, mercantilists believed that the wealth of a state depended on its ability to import fewer commodities than it exported and thus acquire the largest possible share of the world's monetary supply. Mercantilists encouraged domestic industry and placed heavy customs duties or tariffs on imported goods. Mercantilism was therefore a policy of **protectionism**, the shielding of domestic industries from foreign competition. Mercantilists also sought to increase the size of the country's commercial fleet, establish colonies to promote trade, and import raw materials from the colonies to benefit domestic industry. The imperial wars of the seventeenth and eighteenth centuries, which were fought over the control of colonies and trading routes, thus formed part of a mercantilist policy.

The earliest of these mercantile wars took place between the emerging commercial powers of England and the Dutch Republic in the third quarter of the seventeenth

protectionism The policy of shielding domestic industries from foreign competition through a policy of levying tariffs on imported goods.

century (1652–1654, 1664–1667, 1672–1675). The Dutch resented the passage of English laws, known as the Navigation Acts, which excluded them from trade with English colonies. The Dutch also claimed the right, denied to them by the English, to fish in British waters. Not surprisingly, many of the engagements in these Anglo-Dutch wars took place at sea and in the colonies. The most significant result of these conflicts was the Dutch loss of the port city of New Amsterdam, now renamed New York, to the English.

Shortly after the first Anglo-Dutch conflict, England went to war against Spain (1655–1657). Although this war pitted Protestants against a Catholic power, the two countries fought mainly over economic issues. The war resulted in the British acquisition of Jamaica, one of its most important Caribbean colonies, in 1655. When Britain tried to smuggle more goods than it was allowed by the Treaty of Utrecht (1713) into the Spanish trading post of Portobelo on the Isthmus of Panama, the Spanish retaliated by cutting off the ear of Robert Jenkins, an English captain. This incident led to the War of Jenkins' Ear in 1739. In 1762, during another war against Spain (as well as France), armed forces from Britain and the North American colonies seized the Cuban port of Havana, which Britain returned to Spain in exchange for Florida. The acquisition of Florida gave the British control of the entire North American eastern seaboard.

Anglo-French Military Rivalry

Anglo-Spanish conflict paled in comparison with the bitter commercial rivalry between Great Britain and France during the eighteenth century. Anglo-French conflict was one of the few consistent patterns of eighteenth-century European warfare. It lasted so long and had so many different phases that it became known as the second Hundred Years' War, a recurrence of the bitter period of warfare between England and France from the middle of the fourteenth century to the middle of the fifteenth century.

THE WARS OF THE SPANISH AND AUSTRIAN SUCCESSIONS, 1701–1748 This eighteenth-century Anglo-French rivalry had its roots in the War of the Spanish Succession (1701–1713). The war began as an effort to prevent France from putting Louis XIV's grandson, Philip, on the Spanish throne (see Chapter 16). By uniting French and Spanish territory, the proposed succession would have created a massive French-Spanish empire not only in Europe, but in the Western Hemisphere as well. This combination of French and Spanish territory and military power threatened to eclipse the British colonies along the North American coast and deprive British merchants of much of their valuable trade.

The ensuing struggle in North America, known in the British colonies as Queen Anne's War, was settled in Britain's favor by the Treaty of Utrecht in 1713. Philip V (r. 1700–1746) was allowed to remain on the Spanish throne, but French and Spanish territories in Europe and America were kept separate. Even more important, the French ceded their Canadian territories of Newfoundland and Nova Scotia to the British. The treaty, which also gave Britain the contract to ship slaves to the Spanish colonies for 30 years, marked the emergence of Britain as Europe's dominant colonial and maritime power.

The next phase of Anglo-French warfare, the War of the Austrian Succession (1740–1748), formed part of a European conflict that engaged the forces of Austria, Prussia, and Spain, in addition to those of Britain and France. In this conflict European dynastic struggles once again intersected with competition for colonial advantage overseas. The ostensible cause of this war was the impetuous decision by the new king of Prussia, the absolutist Frederick II, to seize the large German-speaking province of Silesia from Austria upon the succession of Maria Theresa (r. 1740–1780) as the ruler of the hereditary Habsburg lands (see **Map 18.2**). Frederick struck with

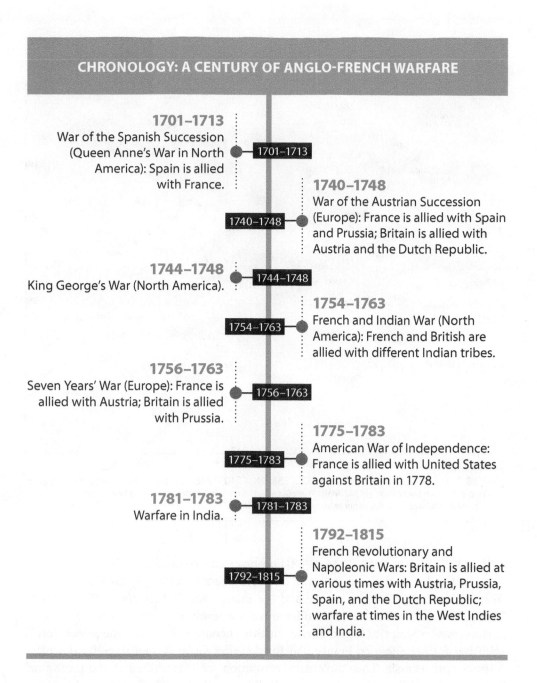

CHRONOLOGY: A CENTURY OF ANGLO-FRENCH WARFARE

1701–1713
War of the Spanish Succession (Queen Anne's War in North America): Spain is allied with France.

1701–1713

1740–1748
War of the Austrian Succession (Europe): France is allied with Spain and Prussia; Britain is allied with Austria and the Dutch Republic.

1740–1748

1744–1748
King George's War (North America).

1744–1748

1754–1763
French and Indian War (North America): French and British are allied with different Indian tribes.

1754–1763

1756–1763
Seven Years' War (Europe): France is allied with Austria; Britain is allied with Prussia.

1756–1763

1775–1783
American War of Independence: France is allied with United States against Britain in 1778.

1775–1783

1781–1783
Warfare in India.

1781–1783

1792–1815
French Revolutionary and Napoleonic Wars: Britain is allied at various times with Austria, Prussia, Spain, and the Dutch Republic; warfare at times in the West Indies and India.

1792–1815

devastating effectiveness, and by the terms of the treaty that ended the war he acquired most of the province.

Frederick's aggression enticed other European powers to join the conflict. Eager to acquire Habsburg territories in different parts of Europe, France and Spain both declared war on Austria. Britain then entered the war against France, mainly to keep France from acquiring Austria's possessions in the Netherlands.

The colonial phase of this war, known in British North America as King George's War, opened in 1744, when the French supported the Spanish in a war that Spain had been waging against Britain since 1739 over the Caribbean trade. Clashes between French and British trading companies in India also began in the same year. The main military engagement of this war was the seizure of the French port and fortress of Louisbourg on Cape Breton Island in Canada by 4,000 New England colonial troops and a large British fleet. At the end of the war, however, the British returned Louisbourg to the French in exchange for the factory of Madras in India, which the French had taken during the war.

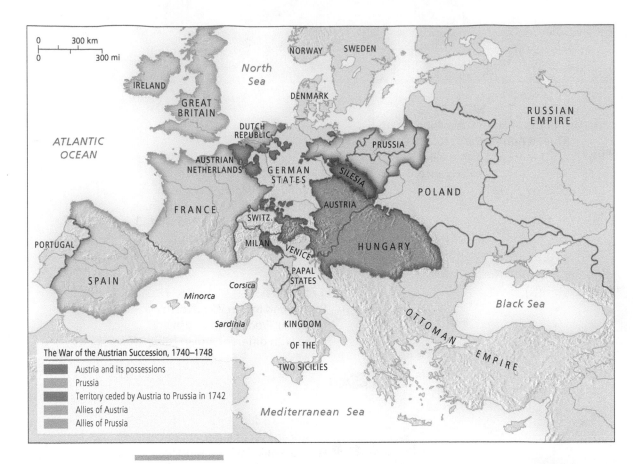

MAP **18.2** THE WAR OF THE AUSTRIAN SUCCESSION, 1740–1748 Austria lost Silesia to Prussia during the War of the Austrian Succession in 1742. Maria Theresa's efforts to regain the province in the Seven Years' War were unsuccessful. Why was Frederick eager to acquire and retain Silesia?

View the **Map**

Atlas Map: The Seven Years' War

View the **Image**

1755 Battle Between British and Indians

THE SEVEN YEARS' WAR, 1756–1763 European and colonial rivalries became even more entangled in the next outbreak of Anglo-French warfare, known as the Seven Years' War (1756–1763) in Europe and the French and Indian War (1754–1763) in North America. In Europe the conflict arose as a result of Maria Theresa's eventually unsuccessful attempt to regain Silesia. In this encounter, however, she joined forces with her former enemies, France and Russia, after Great Britain signed a defensive alliance with Prussia. This "diplomatic revolution" of 1756 shifted all the traditional alliances among European powers, but it did not affect Anglo-French rivalry in the colonies, which continued unabated.

The fighting in North America was particularly brutal and inflicted extensive casualties. In their struggle to gain control of eastern port cities and interior lands, the British and the French secured alliances with different Indian tribes. Among the many victims were some of France's Indian allies who contracted smallpox when British-American colonists sold them blankets deliberately contaminated with the disease—the first known use of germ warfare in the West.

This colonial war also had an Asian theater, in which French and British forces, most of them drawn from the trading companies of their respective countries, vied for mercantile influence and the possession of factories along the coast of the Indian Ocean. This conflict led directly to the British acquisition of the Indian province of Bengal in 1765.

The Treaty of Paris of 1763 ended this round of European and colonial warfare. In Europe Prussia managed to hold on to Silesia, although its army incurred heavy casualties and its economy suffered from the war. In North America all of French Canada east of the Mississippi, including the entire province of Quebec, with its predominantly

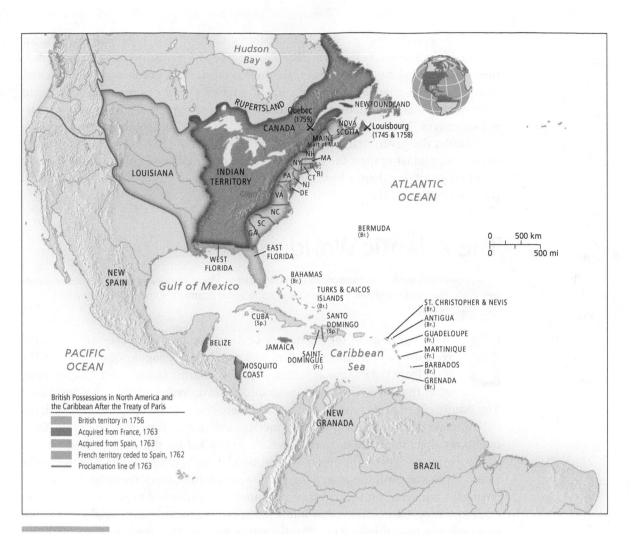

MAP **18.3** BRITISH POSSESSIONS IN NORTH AMERICA AND THE CARIBBEAN AFTER THE TREATY OF PARIS, 1763 The British acquisition of French territory marked a decisive moment in the expansion of the British Empire. What were the differences between the British colonies on the North American mainland and those in the Caribbean?

French population and French system of civil law, passed into British control (see **Map 18.3**). Even more important, the treaty secured British naval and mercantile superiority in the Atlantic, Caribbean, and Indian oceans. By virtue of its victories over France, Britain gained control of the lion's share of world commerce. This commercial superiority had profound implications for the economic development of Britain. Partly because of its ability to acquire raw materials from its colonies and to market its products throughout the world, Britain became the first country to experience the Industrial Revolution.

THE AMERICAN AND FRENCH REVOLUTIONARY WARS, 1775–1815 Despite the British victory over the French in 1763, the long conflict between the two countries continued into the early nineteenth century. During the American War of Independence (1775–1783), the North American colonists secured French military aid, a British fleet attacked the French colony of Martinique, and the French dispatched an expedition against the British at Savannah that included hundreds of Africans and **mulattos**, or people of mixed race, drawn from the population of the West Indies. In India further conflicts between the French and British occurred, mainly between 1781 and 1783. These simultaneous military engagements in various parts of the world turned this phase of Anglo-French conflict into the first truly global war.

mulattos People of mixed white and black race.

565

Anglo-French rivalry entered yet another phase between 1792 and 1815, during the era of the French Revolution (see Chapter 20). The British were able to maintain their military and naval superiority, although once again it required an alliance with many European powers and the creation of a new balance of power against France. Even during this later phase of this French-British rivalry the British pursued imperial objectives. They expanded their empire in India and consolidated their territory there under the governorship of Richard Wellesley (1760–1842). In 1795, in the midst of the war against France, the British also acquired the Dutch colony at the Cape of Good Hope, giving them a base for their claims to much larger African territories in the nineteenth century.

The Atlantic World

18.3 How did European empires create an Atlantic economy in which slavery was a major feature?

By the beginning of the eighteenth century, the territorial acquisitions of the five European maritime powers had moved the geographical center of the West from the European continent to the Atlantic Ocean itself. The Atlantic, rather than separating large geographical land masses, gave them a new unity. The boundaries of this new Western world were the four continents that bordered the Atlantic: Europe, Africa, North America, and South America. The main thoroughfares that linked them were maritime routes across the Atlantic and up and down its coasts. The main points of commercial and cultural contact between the four continents, until the end of the eighteenth century, were the coastal areas and ports that bordered on the ocean. Within this Atlantic world arose new patterns of trade and economic activity, new interactions between ethnic and racial groups, and new political institutions. The Atlantic world also became the arena in which political and religious ideas were transmitted across the ocean and transformed within new environments.

The Atlantic Economy

The exchange of commercial goods and slaves between the western coasts of Europe, the African coasts, and the ports of North and South America created a major economic enterprise (see **Map 18.4**). The ships that brought the slaves from Africa to the Americas used the profits gained from their transactions to acquire precious metals and agricultural products for the European market. They then returned to western European Atlantic ports, where the goods were sold.

The Atlantic economy was fueled by the demand of a growing European population for agricultural products that were unavailable in Europe and were more costly to transport from Asia. Sugar was the most important of these commodities, but tobacco, cotton, rice, cacao, and coffee also became staples of the transatlantic trade. (See *Encounters and Transformations* in this chapter.) For their part, North and South American colonists created a steady demand for manufactured goods, especially cutlery and metal tools produced in Europe.

Two of the commodities imported from the colonies, tobacco and coffee, were criticized for their harmful effects. "Tobacco, that outlandish weed," read one popular rhyme, "It spends the brain and spoils the seed." Critics also claimed that it had a hallucinatory effect. Coffee, a stimulant that originally came from the Middle East but later from Haiti and Brazil, was believed to encourage political radicalism, probably because the coffeehouses served as gathering places for political dissidents. Contemporaries also identified coffee's capacity to produce irritability and depression.

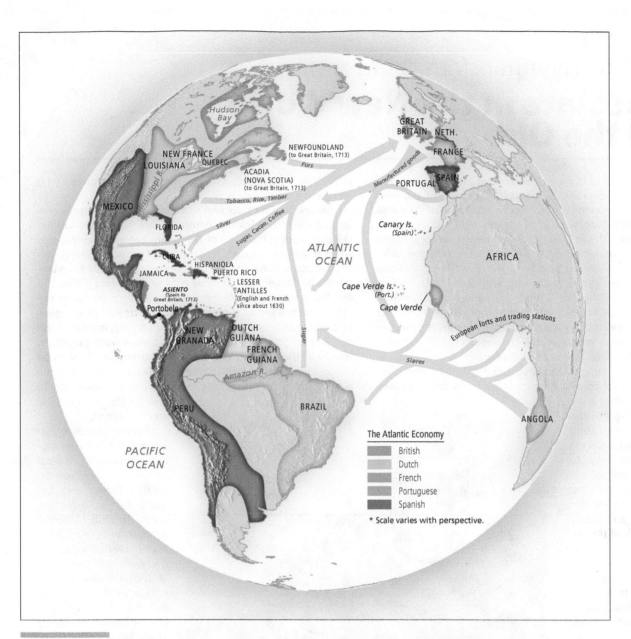

MAP **18.4** THE ATLANTIC ECONOMY IN THE MID-EIGHTEENTH CENTURY Commodities and African slaves were exchanged between the four continents of North America, South America, Europe, and Africa. What was the role of the slave trade in this global economy?

The Atlantic economy had its own rhythms but was also part of a global economy. As Europeans had expanded the volume of their imports from America, those markets were fully integrated into this world system. The system was capitalist in the sense that private individuals produced and distributed commodities for profit in a systematic way. European governments had an interest in this capitalist economy because as mercantilists they wanted their countries to acquire the largest possible share of world trade, but they did not control the actual operations of the marketplace. Their role was mainly to authorize individuals or trading companies to conduct trade in a particular geographical area.

The Atlantic Slave Trade

The slave trade became the linchpin of the Atlantic economy, and all five western European imperial powers—Britain, France, the Dutch Republic, Spain, and Portugal—participated in it. The trade arose to meet the demand of plantation owners in the

Encounters and Transformations
Chocolate in the New World and the Old

One product of the encounters that took place between Spaniards and the indigenous people of the New World was the widespread consumption of chocolate among western Europeans in the seventeenth century. Long before the Spanish Conquest of the sixteenth century, Aztecs and Mayans produced chocolate from the seeds of the cacao tree, which was indigenous to South America. They consumed chocolate mainly as a beverage and used it, like tobacco (another native American plant), in religious and political ceremonies and for medicinal purposes. Spanish colonists received gifts of chocolate from Indians and soon began to enjoy the pleasurable physiological effects of this commodity, which contains chemical agents that act like amphetamines.

By the beginning of the seventeenth century, chocolate made its way from colonial America across the Atlantic to Spain. Shortly thereafter it became available in other western European countries. Its widespread use prepared the way for the introduction of two other stimulants that came originally from the Middle East and Asia in the latter half of the seventeenth century: coffee and tea.

Because chocolate was grown in non-Christian lands where Spaniards believed that demons inhabited the landscape, and because it was associated with sexual pleasure, it met with harsh disapproval. Clerics denounced it—together with tobacco—as an inducement to vice and the work of Satan. Gradually, however, chocolate came to be viewed in purely secular terms as a commodity, without any religious significance.

The European demand for chocolate contributed to three major transformations of Western life. The first was the growth of the Atlantic trade and a global economy. Among the products that were shipped from the Americas to Europe in exchange for slaves and manufactured goods, cacao was second only to sugar in volume. In preconquest America cacao had often served as an exchange currency. Now it was assigned a specific value in the world marketplace. As the price of chocolate escalated, Spain established a monopoly over the trade, and thus integrated it into the mercantilist system.

Second, the introduction of chocolate into Europe transformed Western drinking patterns. There had been nothing like chocolate in the diets of Europeans before its arrival, and when it was introduced, new rituals of consumption developed. Cups with handles were designed specifically for drinking the hot beverage, the same cups later used for coffee and tea. Europeans adopted the Aztec custom of scooping the foam from the top of a chocolate drink. The European desire to sweeten chocolate, and also coffee and tea, increased the demand for sugar, which in turn encouraged the growth of slavery on the sugar plantations in the West Indies. Sweetened chocolate eventually began to be served as a candy, and by the nineteenth century chocolate candy became the main form in which the commodity was consumed.

Finally, chocolate became a part of the emerging bourgeois sexual culture of eighteenth-century France and England. Just as in preconquest Spanish America, it began to play a role in rituals of sexual seduction. It is no accident that boxes of chocolate are popular gifts on Valentine's Day and that the most well-known chocolate candy in the United States, Godiva, features the English noblewoman who rode naked through the streets of Coventry in 1140. The sustained exchange of a delectable commodity between the New World and the Old World thus contributed to a transformation of Western culture.

THE CHOCOLATE HOUSE (1787) Men and women drinking chocolate, tea, and coffee at the White Conduit House, Islington, London.

SOURCE: Thomas Rowlandson (1756–1827), "The Chocolate House," 1787. HIP/Art Resource, NY.

For Discussion

1. To what extent did the tastes of European consumers determine the nature of the Atlantic economy in the seventeenth and eighteenth centuries?
2. Why did political leaders and clerics differ in their views regarding the value of chocolate in the seventeenth and eighteenth centuries?

New World for agricultural labor. In the seventeenth century this demand became urgent when disease ravaged the indigenous Indian population and when indentured whites who had emigrated from Europe in search of a more secure future gained their freedom. Slave labor possessed considerable advantages over free labor. Plantation masters could discipline slaves more easily and force them to work longer hours. Slaves became a vital part of a plantation economy in which one authority, the plantation master, directed the growing, harvesting, and processing of sugar and agricultural commodities. The use of slave labor also allowed the economies of European countries, especially Britain, to develop. Those who had invested in the colonial trade received attractive returns on their investment, while agricultural profits acquired from crops produced by slaves encouraged the growth of domestic manufacturing.

The slave trade formed the crucial link in the triangular pattern of commercial routes that began when European vessels traveled to ports along the western coast of Africa. There they exchanged European goods, including guns, for slaves that African merchants had captured in the interior and had marched to the sea. At these ports European slave traders branded the slaves with initials indicating to which nation they belonged. Traders then packed them into ships that transported them across the Atlantic to the coast of South America, to the Caribbean, or as far north as Maryland. This was the notorious **Middle Passage**, the second leg of the triangular journey, which was completed when the ships returned to their points of origin loaded with the plantation products of America. Once they had arrived in the Americas, the slaves were sold to the owners of plantations in the tropical areas of the Caribbean and the south Atlantic and in the more moderate climates of the North American mainland.

The African slave trade conducted by Europeans differed from other forms of slavery in world history in three respects. The first was its size: it was the largest involuntary, transoceanic transportation of human beings in world history. Between 1500 and 1867 more than 12.5 million slaves were shipped from Africa to the New World. Deaths at sea reduced the number of slaves who actually arrived in the Americas to about 11 million. Nine out of every ten of these slaves were sent to Brazil or the Caribbean region, including the northern coast of South America.

The second distinctive feature of African slavery in the Americas was its racial character. In this respect it differed from the forms of slavery that had existed in ancient Greece, Rome, and medieval Europe, where people of different races and ethnicities had been enslaved. It also differed from Muslim slavery, which involved the captivity of white European Christians as well as black Africans. As the slave trade brought millions of black Africans into the Americas, slavery came to be equated with being black, and Europeans referred to the color of the slaves' skin as evidence that they were inferior to white people.

The third distinctive feature of the Atlantic slave trade was its commercial character. Its sole function was to provide slave traders with a profit and slave owners with

A SATIRE AGAINST COFFEE AND TOBACCO A seventeenth-century satirical depiction of two European women smoking tobacco and drinking coffee. Turkey, represented by the figure to the right, was the main source of coffee in the seventeenth century. An African servant, to the left, pours the coffee. Tobacco came from the Americas.

Read the Document

Willem Bosman, from *A New and Accurate Description of the Coast of Guinea Divided into the Gold, the Slave, and the Ivory Coasts*

Middle Passage The journey taken by European ships bringing slaves from Africa to the Americas.

Read the Document

King Louis XIV, "The Code Noir" (French), 1685

Read the Document

Venture Smith, from *A Narrative of the Life and Adventures of Venture*

a supply of cheap labor. Europeans defended the right of slave masters to own their slaves as they would other pieces of property. The Atlantic slave trade turned African slaves into commercial commodities and treated them in a manner that deprived them of all human dignity. To justify such treatment their owners insisted that they "were beasts and had no more souls than beasts."[3]

One harrowing incident on the British slave ship *Zong* reveals the way in which financial calculations determined the fate of slaves. The *Zong* set sail in 1781 from Africa with 442 African slaves on board. When the slaves began to fall ill and die from malnutrition and disease, the captain of the ship, Luke Collingwood, feared that the owners of the ship would suffer a financial loss. If, however, the slaves were to be thrown overboard on the pretext that the safety of the crew was in jeopardy, those who had insured the voyage would absorb the loss. Accordingly Collingwood tied 132 slaves together, two by two, and flung them into the sea. When the ship owners went to court to collect the insurance, they argued that slaves were no different from horses and that they had a perfect right to throw the slaves overboard to preserve the safety of the ship.

The slave trade itself became the object of intense competition, as each country tried to establish a monopoly over certain routes. During the seventeenth century the British managed to make inroads into the French slave trade, and eventually the British surpassed the Portuguese and the Dutch as well. By 1700 British ships were transporting more than 50 percent of all slaves to the Americas. The dominance that Britain established in the slave trade reinforced its growing maritime and commercial strength. With an enormous merchant marine and a navy that could support it, the British came to dominate the slave trade in the same way they came to dominate the entire world economy. Both revealed how far mercantile capitalism had triumphed in Britain and its overseas possessions.

In the late eighteenth century, however, a movement arose in all European countries to end both the slave trade and the institution of slavery itself. (See *Different Voices* in this chapter.) The movement drew much of its inspiration from religious zeal, especially among evangelical Protestants in Britain and Jesuits in Spain and Portugal. The movement gradually acquired widespread support. In Britain more than 300,000 people supported the cause of abolition by refusing to buy sugar—the largest consumer boycott the world had ever known. British capitalists also came to the conclusion that slavery was no longer economically advantageous. Goods produced by free labor, especially by machine, made slavery appear less cost-effective than in the past.

By the first decade of the nineteenth century opposition to slavery began to achieve limited success. In 1807 the British Parliament legislated an end to the trade within the British Empire, and in the following year the United States refused to allow any of its ports to accept slave ships. The Dutch ended their slave trade in 1814, the French in 1815, and the Spanish in 1838. The Portuguese continued to import slaves to Brazil until 1850.

Liberation of the slaves generally came later. The British dismantled the system within their empire between 1834 and 1838. Slavery persisted until 1848 in the French Caribbean, 1865 in the southern United States, 1886 in Cuba, and 1888 in Brazil.

Ethnic Diversity in the Atlantic World

European countries had always possessed some ethnic diversity, but the emigration of people from many different parts of Europe and Africa to America, followed by their intermarriage, created societies of much greater complexity. Even white European communities in the colonies were more ethnically diverse than in the metropolis. The British colonies, for example, attracted not only English, Scottish, and Irish settlers, but also Germans, French, and Swiss.

Different Voices
The Abolition of the Slave Trade

In 1787 Quobna Ottobah Cugoano (1757–1791), a former slave, published a treatise calling for the abolition of the African slave trade. Like the narrative written by Olaudah Equiano quoted at the beginning of this chapter, Cugoano's book described the horrors of the African slave trade that he himself had experienced. In this passage Cugoano deplored the effect that the slave trade had on his native Africa. In Great Britain the politician and philanthropist William Wilberforce (1759–1833) spearheaded the campaign to abolish the slave trade in the late eighteenth and early nineteenth centuries. His was a lonely voice when he gave his first speech to parliament on this subject in 1789, 18 years before Britain ended the slave trade. Wilberforce also discussed the deleterious effects of the slave trade on Africa.

A Former Slave Exposes the Effects of the Slave Trade on Africa

That base traffic of kid-napping and stealing men was begun by the Portuguese on the coast of Africa, and as they found the benefit of it for their own wicked purposes, they soon went on to commit further depredations. The Spaniards followed their infamous example, and the African slave trade was thought most advantageous for them, to enable themselves to live in ease and affluence by the cruel subjection and slavery of others. The French and English, and some other nations in Europe, as they founded settlements or colonies in the West Indies or in America, went on in the same manner, and joined hand in hand with the Portuguese and Spaniards to rob and pillage Africa and desolate the inhabitants of the western continent. But the European depredators and pirates have not only robbed and pillaged the people of Africa themselves; but, by their instigation, they have infested the inhabitants with some of the vilest combinations of fraudulent and treacherous villains, even among their own people, and have set up their forts and factories as a reservoir of public and abandoned thieves and as a den of desperadoes, where they may ensnare, entrap and catch men. So that Africa has been robbed of its inhabitants, its freeborn sons and daughters have been stolen, and kid-napped and violently taken away and carried into captivity and cruel bondage. And it may be said in respect to that diabolical traffic which is still carried on by the European depredators, that Africa has suffered as much and more than any other quarters of the globe.

SOURCE: Quobna Ottobah Cugoano, *Thoughts and Sentiments on the Evil and Wicked Traffic of the Slavery and Commerce of the Human Species* (London, 1787).

An English Politician Launches a Campaign to End the Slave Trade in 1789

What should we suppose must naturally be the consequence of our carrying on a slave trade with Africa? With a country vast in its extent, not utterly barbarous, but civilized in a very small degree? Does one suppose a slave trade would help their civilization? Is it not plain that she must suffer from it? ... that her barbarous manners must be made more barbarous; and that the happiness of her millions of inhabitants must be prejudiced with her intercourse with Britain? Does not everyone see that a slave trade, carried on around her coasts, must carry violence and desolation to her very center? That in a Continent just emerging from barbarism, if a trade in men is established, if her men are all converted into goods, and become commodities that can be bartered, it follows, they must be subject to ravage just as goods are; and this, too, at a period of civilization, when there is no protecting legislature to defend this their only sort of property, in the same manner as the rights of property are maintained by the legislature of every civilized country. ... In Africa it is the personal avarice and sensuality of their kings ... [T]hese two vices we stimulate in all these African princes, and we depend upon these vices for the very maintenance of the slave trade. ...

I must speak of the transit of the slaves in the West Indies. This I confess, in my opinion, is the most wretched part of the whole subject. So much misery condensed in so little room is more than the human imagination had ever before conceived. ... Let anyone imagine to himself 6 or 700 of these wretches chained two and two, surrounded with every object that is nauseous and disgusting, diseased, and struggling under every kind of wretchedness! How can we bear to think of such a scene as this? One would think it had been determined to heap upon them all the varieties of bodily pain, for the purposes of blunting the feelings of the mind. ... Exclusive of those who perish before they set sail, not less than 12½ percent perish in the passage. Besides these the Jamaica report tells you that not less than 4½ percent die on the shore before the day of sale, which is only a week or two from the time of landing. One third more die in the seasoning, and this in a country exactly like their own, where they are healthy and happy as some of the evidences would pretend. ... Upon the whole, however, there is a mortality of about 50 percent, and this amongst negroes who are not bought unless healthy at first, and unless (as the phrase is with cattle) they are sound in wind and limb.

SOURCE: From *Cobbett's Parliamentary History* 28, pp. 41–43.

For Discussion

1. How did Cugoano and Wilberforce differ in their views of Africa?
2. The slave trade in Britain was not abolished until 1807, 20 years after the publication of Cugoana's treatise and 18 years after Wilberforce began his parliamentary campaign. Why might other legislators in Britain have resisted their efforts?
3. Why was the mortality rate of slaves transported to the West Indies higher than those shipped to other destinations?

THE SLAVE SHIP BY J. M. W. TURNER (1840) The English painter J. M. W. Turner captured the horror of the incident that took place aboard the slave ship *Zong*, when the crew threw 132 slaves overboard in 1781.

SOURCE: Joseph Mallord William Turner (English 1775–1851), "Slave Ship (Slavers Throwing Overboard the Dead and Dying. Typhoon Coming On)." 1840. Oil on canvas. 90.8 x 122.6 (35 3/4 x 48 1/4 in). Henry Lillie Pierce Fund. 99.22. Courtesy, Museum of Fine Arts, Boston. Reproduced with permission. © 2006 Museum of Fine Arts, Boston. All Rights Reserved.

The ethnicity of colonial populations was more varied in Latin America than in North America. The higher proportion of African slaves, more frequent intermarriage among different groups, and the free status achieved by many blacks and mulattos created highly stratified societies. In these colonies divisions arose not only between the recently arrived Europeans and the creoles, but also among the various groups that Europeans considered socially inferior.

Volume of the Transatlantic Slave Trade from Africa, 1500–1867	
Year	Volume
1501–1525	13,600
1526–1550	50,300
1551–1575	60,500
1576–1600	152,000
1601–1625	352,770
1626–1650	315,500
1651–1675	489,000
1676–1700	719,000
1701–1725	1,088,000
1726–1750	1,471,200
1751–1775	1,925,300
1776–1800	2,009,000
1801–1825	1,877,000
1826–1850	1,771,200
1851–1867	225,800
Total	12,520,170

SOURCE: David Eltis and David Richardson, *Atlas of the Transatlantic Slave Trade*, 2010, p. 89.

The most complex social structure in the New World developed in Brazil. Portuguese bureaucrats stood at the top of the Brazilian social hierarchy, holding a social position just above a large and wealthy group of planter creoles. These two elite groups dominated a lower-class social hierarchy of **mestizos** (people of mixed white and Indian ancestry), indigenous people, mulattos, freed blacks, and slaves.

mestizos People of mixed white and Indian ancestry.

Encounters Between Europeans and Asians

18.4 How did Western attitudes toward Asian peoples change during this period of empire-building?

In Asia, European powers initially did not try to acquire and govern large territories and subjugate their populations, as they did in America. Europeans first came to Asia to trade, not to conquer or establish large colonies. Europeans did not engage in fixed battles with Asians, take steps to reduce the size of their populations, or force them to migrate, as they did in the New World. Nevertheless, during the period from 1650 to 1815 European powers established or greatly expanded their empires in Asia.

When Europeans used military force in Asia, it was almost always against rival European powers, not the indigenous population. When European countries did eventually use force against Asians, they discovered that victory was much more difficult than it had been in the New World. Indeed, Asian peoples already possessed or were acquiring sufficient military strength to respond to European military might. In China and Japan the possession of this military power prevented Europeans from even contemplating conquest or exploitation until the nineteenth century. Establishment of European hegemony in Asia, therefore, took longer and was achieved more gradually than in the Americas.

Political Control of India

Despite their original intentions, Europeans eventually began to acquire political control over large geographical areas in Asia and subject Asians to European rule. The first decisive steps in this process took place in India during the second half of the eighteenth century. Until that time the British in India, most of whom were members of the British East India Company, remained confined to the factories that were established along the Indian coast. We saw earlier that the main purpose of these factories was to engage in trade not only with Europe, but also with other parts of Asia. In conducting this trade the British had to deal with local Indian merchants and compete with the French, the Portuguese, and the Dutch, who had established factories of their own. They also found it advantageous to make alliances with the provincial governors, known as **nawabs**, who controlled the interior of the country. It became customary for each European power to have its own candidate for nawab, with the expectation that he would provide favors for his European patrons once he took office.

nawabs Native provincial governors in eighteenth-century India.

MILITARY CONFLICT AND TERRITORIAL ACQUISITIONS, 1756–1856 In 1756 this pattern of trading and negotiating resulted in armed military conflict in the city of Calcutta in the northeastern province of Bengal. The British had established a factory at Calcutta in 1690, and they continued to carry on an extensive trade there with Indian merchants, many of whom were Hindus. Bengal's nawab, the Muslim Siraj-ud-Daulah, had contempt for all Europeans, especially the British, and he was determined that he would not be beholden to any of them. In June 1756 he sent an army of 50,000 Muslims against Calcutta, burning and plundering the city and besieging the East India Company's Fort William, which was manned by 515 troops in the service of the company. The entire British population of the city, together with more than 2,000 Hindus, had taken refuge in the fort. After a long struggle, which resulted in the death of hundreds of Indians, the fort fell to the nawab's forces, and some of the British officers and magistrates, including the governor of Calcutta, fled by sea.

During this siege the shooting death of a Bengali guard led to an incident that became permanently emblazoned on the emerging imperial consciousness of the British people. In response to the shooting, officers in the nawab's army crammed the entire remaining British contingent, a total of 146 men and women, into the fort's lockup or prison, known as the Black Hole of Calcutta. Measuring 18' × 14', it was meant to hold only three or four prisoners overnight. The stench was so bad that many prisoners vomited on the people squeezed next to them. The insufferable heat and lack of water and air were stifling. Only 22 men and one woman survived until the next morning, when the nawab released them. The remainder either had been trampled to death or had asphyxiated.

The deaths of these British men and women in the Black Hole of Calcutta led the British to seek swift and brutal retribution against the nawab. In 1757, under the direction of the British military officer Robert Clive, a force of 800 British troops and 2,000 native Indian soldiers known as **sepoys** retook Calcutta and routed Siraj-ud-Daulah's army at the Battle of Plassey. The British executed Siraj-ud-Daulah and replaced him with a nawab more amenable to their interests. Eight years later the British East India Company secured the right to collect taxes and thus exercise political control over the entire province of Bengal. The enormous revenue from these taxes enabled the company to acquire a large army, composed mainly of sepoys. This force grew to 115,000 men by 1782. The British then used this army, equipped with Western military technology, to gain control of other provinces in India and defeat their French rivals in subsequent engagements during the early nineteenth century.

These further acquisitions of Indian territory led eventually to the establishment of British dominance throughout the South Asian subcontinent (see **Map 18.5**). New territories were brought under British control in the early years of the nineteenth century; during the tenure of Lord Dalhousie as governor-general of India from 1848 to 1856, the British annexed eight Indian states, including the great Muslim state of Oudh in 1856. The expansion of British control went hand in hand with the introduction of Western technology and literature, the English language, and British criminal procedure. After suppressing a mutiny of sepoys against British rule in 1857, the British government abolished the East India Company and assumed direct control of the entire South Asian continent.

sepoys Indian troops serving in the armed forces of the British East India Company.

Changing European Attitudes Toward Asian Cultures

European imperialism in Asia played a crucial role in the formation of Western identity. Until the seventeenth century Europeans thought of "the East" mainly as the Near East, an area that was largely subsumed within the Ottoman Empire. The Far East, comprising South Asia (India), East Asia (China, Japan), and Southeast Asia (Burma, Siam, Indonesia), generally did not enter into European perceptions of "the Orient." Europeans had little contact with this part of the world, and much of what they knew about it was shrouded in mystery. During this period Europeans viewed the Far East mainly as an exotic land, rich in spices, silk, and other luxury commodities.

As Western missionaries and merchants made more frequent contacts with Asian society, Europeans developed more informed impressions of these distant lands and peoples. Some of those impressions were negative, especially when they dealt with the political power of Asian rulers, but many other characterizations of the East were positive. Interest in and admiration for Indian and Chinese culture were most widespread during the middle years of the eighteenth century. More and more European scholars committed themselves

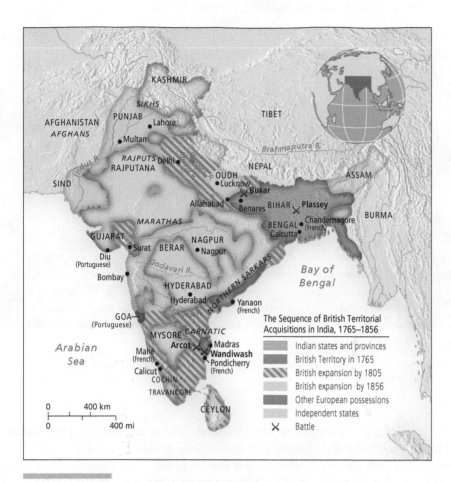

MAP **18.5** THE SEQUENCE OF BRITISH TERRITORIAL ACQUISITIONS IN INDIA, 1765–1856 British political control of large territories on the South Asian subcontinent began more than a century after the establishment of the first factories along the coast. Why did the East India Company acquire territories in India that it had not originally wished to govern?

to the systematic study of Asian languages, especially Chinese and Sanskrit. European writers and thinkers used Asian comparisons to reinforce their criticisms of the West. The French writer Voltaire (1694–1778), for example, regarded Asian cultures as superior to those of Europe in many respects. Voltaire also found the East unaffected by the superstition and the fanaticism that characterized Western Christianity, which he loathed. To him, the main philosophical tradition of China, Confucianism, which embodied a strict moral code, was a more attractive alternative. Eastern religion, especially Hinduism, also won admiration for its ethical content and its underlying belief in a single deity.

This mid-eighteenth-century admiration of Asian culture even extended to Chinese and Indian political institutions. Voltaire transformed the despotic Chinese Empire into an enlightened monarchy, while the French Jesuit priest Guillaume Thomas Raynal (1713–1796) idealized the "purity and equity" of the ancient Indian political system. The corruption of governments in Europe made native Asian political systems look good by comparison. In Britain there was more disrespect for the members of the East India Company, known as **nabobs**, than there was for native Indian officials.

This intellectual respect for Asian philosophy and politics coincided with a period of widespread Asian influences on Western art, architecture, and design. Eastern themes began to influence British buildings, such as in the Brighton Pavilion, designed by John Nash. Small cottages, known as bungalows, owed their inspiration to Indian models. French architects built pagodas (towers with the roof of each story turning upward) for their clients. Chinese gardens, which unlike classical European gardens were not arranged geometrically, became popular in England and France.

 **Read** the **Document**

Baron de Montesquieu, *Excerpt from The Spirit of the Laws*

nabobs Members of the British East India Company who made fortunes in India and returned to Britain, flaunting their wealth.

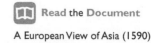 **Read** the **Document**

A European View of Asia (1590)

BRIGHTON PAVILION This building, designed by John Nash, reflected the incorporation of Eastern styles into English architecture, and was inspired by the description of Kubla Khan's palace in Samuel Taylor Coleridge's poem "Kubla Khan" (1816).

chinoiserie A French word for an eighteenth-century decorative art that combined Chinese and European motifs.

 Watch the Video

The Big Picture: The World in 1700 C.E. (Part II)

A new form of decorative art that combined Chinese and European motifs, known in France as ***chinoiserie***, became highly fashionable. Wealthy French people furnished their homes with Chinese wallpaper and hand-painted folding screens. The demand for Chinese porcelain, known in English simply as china, was insatiable. Vast quantities of this porcelain, technically and aesthetically superior to the stoneware produced in Germany and England, left China for the ports of western Europe.

Asian styles also influenced styles of dress and types of recreation. Indian and Chinese silks were in high demand, and Europeans preferred Indian cotton over that produced in the New World. A style of Indian nightwear known as pajamas became popular in England. A new sport, polo, which had originated in India, made its entry into the upper levels of European society at this time.

During the late eighteenth and early nineteenth centuries the high regard in which many Europeans held Asian culture began to wane. As the European presence in Asia increased, as the British began to exercise more control in India, and as merchants began to monopolize the Asian trade, Western images of the East became more negative. Europeans now tended to view Chinese philosophy not as a repository of ancient ethical wisdom, but rather irrational when compared with that of the West. Confucianism fell out of favor, and Eastern religion in general came to be regarded as being inferior to Christianity. European thinkers ranked Asian political systems below those of the more "advanced" countries of Europe. English writers claimed that the Chinese did not deserve their reputation for industry, ingenuity, and technological innovation.

Western ideas of racial difference reinforced Europeans' belief in their superiority over Asians. Europeans argued that differences in skin color and facial features reflected their superiority over the Chinese, dark-skinned South Asians, and Polynesians. Intellectual theories of race, which emerged in Europe during the late eighteenth century and were applied mainly to black Africans, provided a supposedly empirical and scientific foundation for these assumptions. Westerners used the color of South Asians' complexion, which had determined the position of a person in the Hindu caste system, to identify them as "coloreds." Chinese people, previously described in the West as white, were now referred to as being nonwhite or yellow.

The Crisis of Empire and the Atlantic Revolutions

18.5 Why did European powers lose control of some of their colonies between 1775 and 1825?

During the period from 1780 to 1825, European empires experienced a crisis that marked the end of the second stage of European overseas expansion. As a result of this crisis, British, French, and Spanish governments lost large segments of their empires in the Americas. New states were carved out of the older sprawling empires.

The crisis was to some extent administrative. Having acquired large expanses of territory overseas, European states faced the challenging problem of governing them from a distance. They not only had to rule large areas inhabited by non-European peoples (Indians and African slaves), but they also faced the difficulty of maintaining the loyalty of people of European descent who were born in the colonies. These creoles became the main protagonists in the struggles that led to the independence of the North American colonies from Britain in 1776 and the South American colonies from Spain a generation later.

In the French colony of Saint Domingue and in Britain's European colony of Ireland, different stories unfolded. In Saint Domingue, the location of the only successful revolution in the Caribbean region, the revolution was led not by white creoles but by people of color, including the slaves who worked on the plantations. In Britain's European colony of Ireland, where an unsuccessful revolution against British rule took place in 1798, the urge for independence came both from settlers of British descent and the native Irish population.

Q View the Map

European Colonial Territories Before and After 1800

The American Revolution, 1775–1783

The first Atlantic revolution began with the revolt of the 13 North American colonies in 1775 and resulted in the establishment of their independence from British rule in 1783. During the second half of the eighteenth century, tension arose between the British government and its transatlantic colonies. These overseas British colonies had developed traditions of self-government, but various governmental bodies responsible to the British Parliament continued to exercise control over their activities. The colonies had their own militias, but they also received protection from British troops when conflicts developed with the French.

The crisis that led to the American Revolution had its roots in the situation that emerged at the end of the French and Indian War. To maintain the peace of 1763, the British government stationed troops on the frontiers of the colonies.

It argued that because the troops were protecting the colonists, they should contribute financially to their own defense. To this end the government began imposing new taxes on the colonists. In 1765 the British Parliament passed the Stamp Act, which forced colonists to purchase stamps for almost anything that was printed. This piece of legislation raised the central constitutional issue of whether Parliament had the power to legislate for British subjects in lands that did not elect members of that Parliament. "Taxation without representation is tyranny" became the main rallying cry of the colonists. Opposition to the Stamp Act was so strong that Parliament repealed the act the following year, but it later passed a statute declaring that it had the authority to tax the colonists as it pleased. When the government imposed new taxes on the tea imported from Britain in 1773, colonists dressed as Indians threw the tea into Boston Harbor.

The government responded to this "Boston Tea Party" by passing a series of statutes, known in the colonies as the Intolerable Acts, in 1774. One of these acts specified

THE BOSTONIANS' PAYING THE EXCISE MAN OR TARRING AND FEATHERING (1774) This satirical engraving reflects the hatred of colonial Americans at the collection of taxes levied on them without their consent. The Boston Tea Party is depicted in the background. The colonists are forcing the tax collector to drink the tea on which he is trying to collect taxes.

 View the Closer Look

The British Surrender, Yorktown, Virginia 1781

that the port of Boston be closed until the colonists had repaid the cost of the tea. The Intolerable Acts led to organized resistance to British rule; in the following year, military conflict broke out at Lexington and Concord in Massachusetts. On July 4, 1776, 13 of the colonies on the North American mainland, stretching from New Hampshire to Georgia, approved a Declaration of Independence from Great Britain. A long revolutionary war, in which the colonists received assistance from France in 1778, ended with the defeat of British troops at Yorktown in 1781 and the recognition of the republic of the United States of America in the Treaty of Paris in 1783.

The case that the American colonists made for independence from Britain drew upon four distinct sources. First, the political theories of John Locke, who justified resistance against the Stuart monarchy at the time of the Glorious Revolution and who placed limits on legislative as well as executive power, became the main inspiration of the Declaration of Independence. Second, the Revolution found support in the customs and traditions embodied in the English common law, especially the principle that governments could not encroach upon property rights. Third, republican ideas, drawn from ancient Greece and Rome and revived at the time of the Renaissance, offered colonists a model of a community of virtuous men joined in a commitment to the body politic. Finally, the belief that all men had a natural right to life, liberty, and the pursuit of happiness provided a philosophical inspiration to the colonists' cause (see Chapter 19).

Read the Document

Thomas Paine, "Common Sense"

The Haitian Revolution, 1789–1804

The second successful revolution in the Atlantic world took place in the French Caribbean colony of Saint Domingue, known later as Haiti, which occupied the western portion of the island of Hispaniola. This revolution resulted in the establishment of the colony's independence, but the revolt was directed not so much against French rule as against the island's white planters. Just like their counterparts in Spanish and British Caribbean colonies, these planters, known in Haiti as *colons*, had little desire for national independence. They wished to remain within the protective custody of the French state. Because they formed a distinct minority of the total population, they did not think of themselves as constituting a separate national community. Successful resistance to imperial rule, moreover, would have required them to arm their slaves, which would have threatened their control of the black population.

The Haitian revolution began in 1789 when the people defined legally as free coloreds, most of whom were mulattos, rose up in protest against the refusal of the white planters, who were creoles, to give them representation in the revolutionary French National Assembly as well as in local assemblies in Saint Domingue. This rebellion led directly to a massive slave revolt in 1791. At that time slaves constituted about 90 percent of the population. Their uprising took place after the French National Assembly voted to abolish slavery in France, but not in the French colonies. In this revolt 12,000 African slaves, armed with machetes and reacting to their brutal treatment by their masters, destroyed a thousand plantations and killed hundreds of whites. Their tactics, which included cutting white planters in half, raping their wives and daughters, and decapitating their children, were matched by those of the planters, who retaliated by torturing blacks and hanging them in the streets.

Spanish and British armies, frightened that this slave rebellion would spread to their colonies, occupied Saint Domingue and massacred thousands of slaves, many of them after they surrendered. In 1795, however, the Spanish withdrew from Saint Domingue and ceded their portion of the island of Hispaniola to France. The British were likewise forced to leave the colony in 1798, having lost as many as 40,000 soldiers, most of them from disease. The man who had assumed the leadership of the slave revolt, the freed slave Toussaint L'Ouverture, then proceeded to conquer the entire island in 1801, abolish slavery, and proclaim himself the governor-general of an autonomous province.

In 1801 a French army of 20,000 men occupied Saint Domingue. The purpose was to make the colony the centerpiece of a restored French Empire, which was to include Florida, Louisiana, French Guiana, and the French West Indies. The French secured the surrender of L'Ouverture, but when it was learned that the French were planning to reintroduce slavery, two black generals, Jean-Jacques Dessalines and Henri Christophe, whom the French had enlisted to suppress the revolt, united freed blacks and slaves against the French forces. In 1803 these united forces drove the French out of the colony, and in 1804 they established the independent state of Haiti.

This new state of Haiti was far different from the United States, in that it was governed entirely by people of color and it banned slavery. It proclaimed racial equality by defining all Haitians as black. Haiti's new government destroyed the plantation system,

RÉVOLTE DES NOIRS A SAINT-DOMINGUE.

HAITIAN REVOLT AGAINST THE FRENCH In 1794, Haitian slaves led a successful revolt against the French. Former slaves that had risen in the military ranks, such as Toussaint L'Ouverture and Jean-Jacques Dessalines, led the revolt, in which guerilla warfare techniques were used to overcome the French.

redistributed the land among free blacks, and forbade foreigners to hold property. Deciding upon the form of government took time, however, because the new rulers of the country were divided between those who wished to establish a monarchy and those who favored a republic. Those divisions led to a prolonged civil war from 1807 until 1822, when the warring northern and southern provinces were integrated into a single republic.

The Haitian revolution was the most radical and egalitarian of the Atlantic revolutions of the late eighteenth and early nineteenth centuries. Its unqualified declaration of human equality and its abolition of slavery served as an inspiration to abolitionist movements in other countries, including the United States, throughout the nineteenth century. The destruction of the plantation system, however, transformed the country's economy. As a French possession Saint Domingue was quite possibly the richest colony in the world, producing about two-fifths of the world's sugar and half of its coffee. After the revolution, with its economy severed from that of France, the country could no longer compete successfully in the Atlantic economy.

The Irish Rebellion, 1798–1799

The success of the American Revolution directly inspired a revolution in the kingdom of Ireland. Unlike the residents of the 13 colonies in North America, the Gaelic people of Ireland had long thought of themselves as a distinct nation. The English, however, had begun a conquest of this Irish nation in the twelfth century, and during the next 500 years had struggled to rule it effectively. One of their methods was to settle English landlords on Irish lands. They had done this in the Middle Ages by giving large estates to English feudal lords, but those old Anglo-Irish families had gradually begun to think of themselves as Irish. After the Reformation they had remained Catholic, while most English people had become Protestant.

In the sixteenth century the English government began to settle colonies of English Protestants on plantations in various parts of Ireland. The purpose of this policy was to gain tighter control over the country and to promote the loyalty of Irish landowners to the English government. In the early seventeenth century James VI of Scotland (who had also become James I of England in 1603) had settled both Scottish Presbyterians, later known as the Scots Irish, and English Anglicans in the northern Irish province of Ulster. These Protestants of Scottish and English descent had become the core of the ruling establishment throughout Ireland, especially after the failure of Catholic rebellions in 1641–1649 and again in 1689–1690.

In the eighteenth century these Irish Protestants began to resent their subservient relationship to the British government. Just like the American colonists, they recognized the way in which the Irish economy was serving British rather than Irish interests, and they resented the control that Britain had over the Irish Parliament. A reform association known as the Society of United Irishmen, led by the Protestant Ulsterman Wolfe Tone, succeeded in building common ground between Protestants and Catholics. The United Irishmen demanded the repeal of the laws that denied Catholics the right to hold office and sit in the Irish Parliament.

The ideals of the United Irishmen drew on many different sources. A long tradition of Presbyterian republican radicalism found reinforcement in the ideals of the American Revolution. The Irish objected to paying tithes to the established Church of England and, like the American colonists in the 1760s, they resented paying taxes to support the British war against the French during the 1790s.

In 1798 the United Irishmen aligned themselves with lower-class Catholic peasants known as **Defenders**. These Irish groups then staged a rebellion against British rule with the intention of establishing an Irish republic. Like the American colonists, the Irish revolutionaries sought French aid, but it came too little and too late, and the rebellion failed. The revolt, which featured atrocities on both sides, left 30,000 people dead.

The British government recognized that its arrangement for ruling Ireland, in which the nationalist republican movement had originated, could no longer work. It decided therefore to bring about a complete union between Great Britain and Ireland. By the terms of this arrangement, which took effect in 1801, Ireland's Parliament ceased to meet. Instead, the Irish elected a limited number of representatives to sit in the British Parliament. Ireland thus became a part of the United Kingdom, which had been formed when England and Scotland were united in 1707. The proximity of Ireland to Britain, which made the prospect of Irish independence much more dangerous, was a major factor in making the British determined to hold on to this "internal colony." The forces of Irish nationalism could not be contained, however, and during the nineteenth century new movements for Irish independence arose.

Defenders Irish Catholic peasants who joined the United Irishmen in the rebellion against Britain in 1798.

National Revolutions in Spanish America, 1810–1824

The final set of revolutions against European imperial powers occurred between 1810 and 1824 in six Spanish American colonies. These struggles, like the American Revolution, turned colonies into new states and led to the building of new nations. The first of these revolutions began in Mexico in 1810, and others soon arose in Venezuela, Argentina, Colombia, Chile, and Peru. In these revolutions creoles played a leading role, just as they had in the American War of Independence. The main sources of creole discontent were the Bourbon reforms, which ironically had sought to make the Spanish Empire more efficient and thus preserve it. The reforms had achieved this goal, however, by favoring commercial interests at the expense of the traditional aristocracy, thereby reversing or threatening the position of many creole elites. The creoles also faced increasingly heavy taxation, as the Spanish government sought to make them support the expenses of colonial administration.

During the late eighteenth century Spanish creole discontent had crystallized into demands for greater political autonomy, similar to the objectives of British American colonists. South American creoles began to think of themselves as Spanish Americans and sometimes simply as Americans. Like British American colonists, they also read and found inspiration in the works of French political philosophers. Nevertheless, the Spanish creole struggle against imperial rule did not commence until some 30 years after the North American colonies had won their independence. One reason for this slow development of revolutionary action was that Spanish American creoles still looked to the Spanish government to provide them with military support against the threat of lower-class rebellion. Faced with this threat, which continued to plague them even after independence, creoles were reluctant to abandon the military and police support provided by the metropolis.

The event that eventually precipitated these wars for national independence was the collapse of the Spanish monarchy after the French army invaded Spain in 1808 (see Chapter 20). This development left the Spanish Empire, which had always been more centralized than the British Empire, in a weakened position. In an effort to reconstitute the political order in their colonies, creoles sought to establish greater autonomy. Once the monarchy was restored, this demand for autonomy led quickly to armed resistance. This resistance began in Mexico, but it soon spread throughout Spanish America and quickly acquired popular support.

The man who took the lead in these early revolts against Spanish rule was the fiery Venezuelan aristocrat Simón Bolívar (1783–1830). Bolívar led uprisings in his homeland in 1811 and 1814 and eventually defeated the Spanish there in 1819. Unlike most creoles, Bolívar was not afraid to recruit free coloreds and blacks into his armies. His hatred of European colonial governors knew few boundaries. At one point he reportedly commanded his soldiers to shoot and kill any European on sight. He vowed never to rest until all of Spanish America was free. Bolívar carried the struggle for liberation to Peru, which became independent in 1824, and created the state of Bolivia in

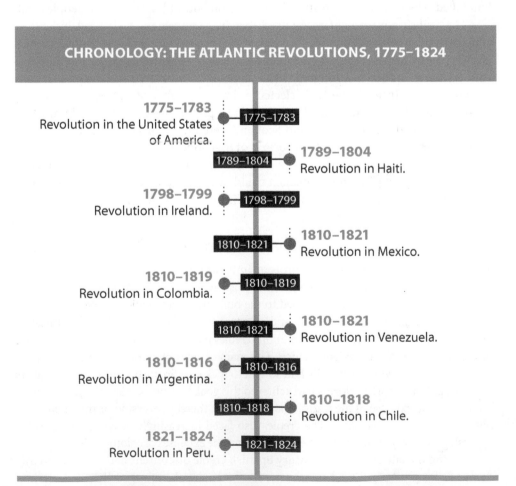

CHRONOLOGY: THE ATLANTIC REVOLUTIONS, 1775–1824

1775–1783
Revolution in the United States of America.
`1775–1783`

`1789–1804`
1789–1804
Revolution in Haiti.

1798–1799
Revolution in Ireland.
`1798–1799`

`1810–1821`
1810–1821
Revolution in Mexico.

1810–1819
Revolution in Colombia.
`1810–1819`

`1810–1821`
1810–1821
Revolution in Venezuela.

1810–1816
Revolution in Argentina.
`1810–1816`

`1810–1818`
1810–1818
Revolution in Chile.

1821–1824
Revolution in Peru.
`1821–1824`

1825. He was more responsible than any one individual for the liberation of Spanish America from Spanish rule. Independent states were established in Argentina in 1816, Chile in 1818, Colombia in 1819, and Mexico in 1821. By then the Spanish, who in the sixteenth century had the largest empire in the world, retained control of only two colonies in the Western Hemisphere: Puerto Rico and Cuba.

📖 **Read the Document**

Simón de Bolívar, "Address to Second National Congress" (Venezuela), 1819

CONCLUSION

The Rise and Reshaping of the West

During the second period of European empire-building, the West not only expanded geographically, but also acquired a large share of the world's resources. By dominating the world's carrying trade, and by exploiting the agricultural and mineral resources of the Americas, Western states gained control of the world economy. The slave trade, with all its horrors, formed an important part of this economy and served as one of the main sources of Western wealth.

Western economic power laid the foundations for Western political control. In Asia, European states assumed political control over territories slowly and reluctantly, as Britain's gradual and piecemeal acquisition of territory in India revealed. In the Americas, European powers acquired territory with relative ease, and European possessions in the New World soon became part of the West. By 1700, as we have seen, the geographical center of the West had become the Atlantic Ocean.

The American territories that were brought under European political control also became, at least to some extent, culturally part of the West. The European colonists who settled in the Americas preserved the languages, the religions, and many of the cultural traditions of the European countries from which they came. When some of the British and Spanish colonies in the Americas rebelled against European regimes in the late eighteenth and early nineteenth centuries, the identity of the colonists who led the resistance remained essentially Western. Even the political ideas that inspired national resistance to European regimes had their origins in Europe.

The assertion of Western political and economic power in the world cultivated a sense of Western superiority. The belief that Europeans, regardless of their nationality, were superior to those from other parts of the world originated in the encounters that took place between Europeans and both African slaves and the indigenous peoples in the Americas. In the late eighteenth century a conviction also developed, although much more slowly, that the West was culturally superior to the civilizations of Asia. This belief in Western superiority became even more pronounced when the economies of Western nations began to experience more rapid growth than those of Asia. The main source of this new Western economic strength was the Industrial Revolution, which will be the subject of Chapter 21.

MAKING CONNECTIONS

1. Why did Britain become the major European imperial power by the beginning of the nineteenth century?
2. Why did wars between European powers in the eighteenth century spread to the Americas and Asia?
3. How could Europeans who professed to believe in the dignity of human beings justify placing Africans in slavery?
4. Which of the Atlantic Revolutions was the most radical and why?
5. How did the growth of European empires contribute to a redefinition of the West?

TAKING IT FURTHER

For suggested readings see page R-1.

On MyHistoryLab

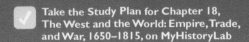

Take the Study Plan for Chapter 18,
The West and the World: Empire, Trade,
and War, 1650–1815, on MyHistoryLab

Chapter Review

European Empires in the Americas and Asia

18.1 How did the composition of European empires change during this period?

Britain gradually became the dominant imperial power in the eighteenth century as France, the Dutch Republic, Spain, and Portugal lost control of many of their colonies. The Spanish imperial system was more authoritarian than the British. Both Spain and Portugal introduced a series of reforms in the late eighteenth century, but they were unable to stem the decline of their empires. The Russian Empire continued to grow during this period, mainly in an eastward direction.

Warfare in Europe, North America, and Asia

18.2 In what ways did the wars waged by European powers involve competition for overseas possessions?

Wars waged by European powers, especially between Britain and France but also between Britain and both the Dutch and the Spanish, between 1650 and 1815, had both a European and an imperial dimension. European powers sought to gain or retain control over overseas colonies to increase their share of world trade and to import raw materials from the colonies to benefit domestic industry.

The Atlantic World

18.3 How did European empires create an Atlantic economy in which slavery was a major feature?

Driven by the demand for agricultural products unavailable in Europe, the Atlantic economy included the exchange of commercial goods and slaves overseas. As its center, the slave trade arose to meet the demand of plantation owners in the New World for cheap agricultural labor. Europeans purchased slaves from Africa in exchange for European goods and then transported the slaves to the Americas, where they used the profits from selling the slaves to acquire products from American plantations and mines. They completed the triangular journey by marketing these products in Europe.

Encounters Between Europeans and Asians

18.4 How did Western attitudes toward Asian peoples change during this period of empire-building?

As Western missionaries and merchants made more frequent contact with previously distant and mysterious Asian societies, Europeans developed their impressions of the Far East. European scholars studied Asian languages and explored philosophical traditions, and the aristocracy acquired Asian art. When trade intensified and the European presence in Asia increased, this high regard for Asian culture decreased, and Western images of the East became more negative.

The Crisis of Empire and the Atlantic Revolutions

18.5 Why did European powers lose control of some of their colonies between 1775 and 1825?

Governing large expanses of territory and peoples from overseas proved to be an administrative challenge exacerbated by the difficulty of maintaining the loyalty of those of European descent born in the colonies. These struggles turned colonies into new states and led to the building of new nations.

On MyHistoryLab

Take the Study Plan for Chapter 18,
The West and the World: Empire, Trade,
and War, 1650–1815, on MyHistoryLab

Chapter Time Line

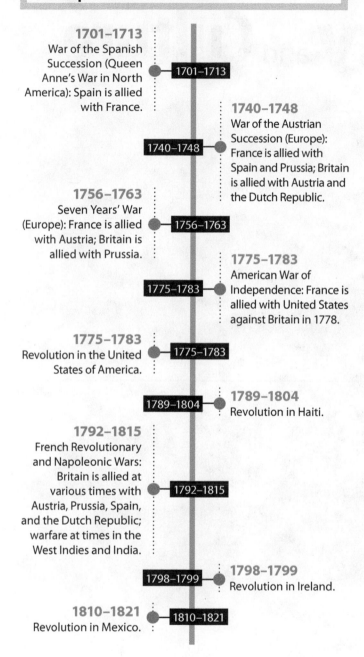

1701–1713
War of the Spanish Succession (Queen Anne's War in North America): Spain is allied with France.

1701–1713

1740–1748

1740–1748
War of the Austrian Succession (Europe): France is allied with Spain and Prussia; Britain is allied with Austria and the Dutch Republic.

1756–1763
Seven Years' War (Europe): France is allied with Austria; Britain is allied with Prussia.

1756–1763

1775–1783

1775–1783
American War of Independence: France is allied with United States against Britain in 1778.

1775–1783
Revolution in the United States of America.

1775–1783

1789–1804

1789–1804
Revolution in Haiti.

1792–1815
French Revolutionary and Napoleonic Wars: Britain is allied at various times with Austria, Prussia, Spain, and the Dutch Republic; warfare at times in the West Indies and India.

1792–1815

1798–1799

1798–1799
Revolution in Ireland.

1810–1821
Revolution in Mexico.

1810–1821

19 Eighteenth-Century Society and Culture

n 1745 Thomas Brown and 11 other men living on the estate of the Earl of Uxbridge, an English nobleman, were jailed for up to one year for shooting deer and rabbits on the earl's land. All 12 defendants were poor. Brown eked out a living as a coal miner in the earl's mines and rented a cottage and five acres of land from him. Like many of his fellow villagers, Brown supplemented his family's diet by shooting game from time to time, usually as he was walking to work through the earl's vast estate. This poaching violated a set of English parliamentary statutes known as the game laws, which restricted the shooting or trapping of wild animals to wealthy landowners.

LEARNING OBJECTIVES

19.1 ((•
What social groups belonged to the aristocracy and how did they exercise power and influence?

19.2 ((•
How did the rural peasantry and those who lived in the towns challenge the aristocracy in the eighteenth century?

19.3 ((•
What were the main features of Enlightenment thought and how did it present a threat to the old order?

19.4 ((•
What impact did the Enlightenment have on Western culture and politics?

FIRST LECTURE IN THE SALON OF MADAME GEOFFRIN, 1755 The speaker is lecturing on Voltaire's *The Orphan of China* before a predominantly aristocratic audience of men and women.

SOURCE: Lemonnier, Anicet Charles Gabriel (1743–1824), "Reading of Voltaire's tragedy 'L'orphelin de la Chine' at the salon of Madame Geoffrin." 1755. Oil on Canvas, 129 x 196 cm. D. Arnaudet. Chateaux de Malmaison et Bois-Preau, Rueil-Malmaison, France. RMN Reunion des Musees Nationaux/Art Resource, NY.

((• Listen to Chapter 19 on MyHistoryLab

⦿ Watch the Video Series on MyHistoryLab

Learn about some key topics related to this chapter with the *MyHistoryLab Video Series: Key Topics in Western Civilization*

The earl and other noblemen defended the game laws on the grounds that they were necessary to protect their property. The laws, however, served an even more important purpose of maintaining social distinctions between landowners and the common people. Members of the landed class believed that only they should have the right to hunt game and to serve deer, pheasants, and hares at lavish dinners attended by their social equals. For a poor person like Thomas Brown, who was described in a court document as "a rude disorderly man and a most notorious poacher," to enjoy such delicacies was a challenge to the social order.

This mid-eighteenth-century encounter between the Earl of Uxbridge and his tenants reflected the tensions that simmered beneath the calm surface of eighteenth-century European society. These tensions arose between the aristocracy, a small but wealthy governing elite, and the masses of tenants and laborers who formed the overwhelming majority of the population. The aristocracy occupied a dominant position in eighteenth-century society and politics. They controlled an enormous portion of their countries' wealth, much of it in land. They staffed the state bureaucracies, the legislative assemblies, the military officer corps, and the judiciaries of almost all European states.

By 1800 the social and political dominance of the aristocracy had begun to wane. Their legitimacy as a privileged elite was increasingly called into question. In a few countries political power began to pass from them to other social groups. This change began during a period of political stability between 1750 and the outbreak of the French Revolution in 1789.

The decline of the aristocracy was the result of a series of cultural encounters. In the first, aristocratic landowners confronted peasants and agricultural laborers who resented the repressive features of upper-class rule. In the second increasingly literate, politically active people who occupied the middle ranks of society, such as merchants and skilled artisans, criticized the aristocracy and demanded political reform. The third set of encounters was the cultural and intellectual movement known as the Enlightenment. Even though many of the Enlightenment's most prominent thinkers came from the ranks of the aristocracy, they advanced a set of political, social, economic, and legal ideas that inspired the creation of a more egalitarian society. This chapter will explore the following question:

How did these social and cultural encounters change the political and intellectual cultures of the West?

The Aristocracy

19.1 What social groups belonged to the aristocracy and how did they exercise power and influence?

During the eighteenth century a relatively small, wealthy group of men dominated European society and politics. This social and ruling elite is often referred to as the **aristocracy**, a term derived from a Greek word meaning the men best fit to rule. In the eighteenth and nineteenth centuries the term *aristocracy* also referred to the wealthiest members of society, especially those who owned land.

aristocracy A term that originally applied to those who were considered the most fit to rule and later identified the wealthiest members of society, especially those who owned land.

nobility Members of the aristocracy who received official recognition of their hereditary status, including their titles of honor and legal privileges.

Within the aristocracy those who received official recognition of their hereditary status, including their titles of honor and special legal privileges, were known as the **nobility**. In the Middle Ages the nobility consisted mainly of warriors who prided themselves on their courage and military skill. Over the course of many centuries these military functions became less important, although many noblemen, especially in central and eastern Europe, continued to serve as military officers in the armies of the state.

The aristocracy for the most part lived on their estates in the countryside, but they also spent time in the cities and towns, where many of them owned townhouses or even palaces. In cities that were centers of national government, such as Madrid and Berlin, aristocrats were prominent members of the royal court, and many of them served as royal judges. The aristocracy, therefore, maintained a visible and powerful presence in urban society.

By the eighteenth century most European aristocracies included a relatively small group of titled noblemen (such as dukes and counts) who possessed great wealth and political influence and a much larger group of lesser aristocrats, occasionally referred to as gentry, who did not necessarily have hereditary titles. In Spain a vast gulf separated a few hundred titled noblemen, the *titulos,* and thousands of sometimes poverty-stricken *hidalgos.* In Britain a few hundred titled noblemen, known as peers, took precedence over some 50,000 families that belonged to the gentry. In Poland the nobility, known as the *szlachta,* was divided between a tiny, powerful group of magnates and some 700,000 noblemen of more modest means who constituted more than 10 percent of the entire population.

The aristocracy was not completely closed to outsiders. Commoners could gain entrance to it, especially its lower ranks, on the basis of acquired wealth or government service. Lawyers, wealthy merchants, or accomplished state servants might accumulate wealth during their careers, use that wealth to purchase land, and then acquire a title of nobility. Many of the Russians who received titles of nobility in the early eighteenth century were commoners. In France many of the royal officials who belonged to the **nobility of the robe** in the eighteenth century could not trace their noble status back further than two generations.

nobility of the robe French noblemen whose families acquired their status by appointment to office.

Women of non-noble birth occasionally gained entry into aristocratic society by marriage. This usually occurred when a nobleman who was greatly in debt arranged to marry his son to the daughter of a wealthy merchant to secure the dowry from the father of the bride. The dowry became the price of the daughter's admission to the nobility.

In the sixteenth and seventeenth centuries the size of the aristocracy had grown faster than the general population as a result of economic prosperity and the expansion of the state bureaucracy. In the eighteenth century the size of the aristocracy stabilized and in many countries declined, as nobles took steps to restrict the number of newcomers from the lower orders. It was never a very large social group. The number of titled nobles was almost always less than 1 percent of the total population; even when lesser nobles or gentry were taken into account, their total numbers usually amounted to no more than 4 percent. Only in Poland and Hungary did the percentages climb to more than 10 percent.

class A social group with similar economic and political interests.

Because of the small size of this social group, many members of the aristocracy knew each other, especially those who had seats in the same political assembly or served together at court. The aristocracy was, in fact, the only real **class** in European society before the early nineteenth century, in the sense that they formed a cohesive social group with similar economic and political interests, which they were determined to protect.

The Wealth of the Aristocracy

The aristocracy was the wealthiest social group in all European countries, and during the eighteenth century many of its members became even wealthier. The most

MARRIAGE INTO THE NOBILITY This painting by William Hogarth, in a series titled *Marriage à la Mode,* depicts the negotiation of a marriage contract between an English earl and a wealthy London merchant. The earl, seated to the right and pointing to his family tree, is negotiating with the merchant sitting across the table. The marriage will take place between the earl's vain son, sitting to the far left, and the distracted daughter of the merchant, sitting next to him. The two individuals who are about to be married have no interest in each other. The earl has incurred large debts from building the large mansion depicted in the rear, and he intends to use the dowry to recover financially. By virtue of this transaction the daughter will enter aristocratic society.

SOURCE: © National Gallery, London/Art Resource, NY.

prosperous aristocratic families lived in stupendous luxury. They built magnificent homes on their country estates and surrounded them with finely manicured gardens. In the cities, where service at court demanded more of their time, they built spacious palaces, entertained guests on a lavish scale, and purchased everything from expensive clothes to artistic treasures. This ostentatious display of wealth confirmed their social importance and status.

Most of the income that supported the lifestyle of the aristocracy came directly or indirectly from land. In all European countries the aristocracy owned at least one-third of all the land, and in some countries, such as England and Denmark, they owned more than four-fifths of it. Even in the Italian states, where many of the nobility had come from families of merchants, they controlled large estates. Land provided the aristocracy with either feudal dues or rents from the peasants or laborers who lived and worked on their estates. Because noblemen did not engage in manual labor themselves, some social critics later condemned them as unproductive parasites living off the labor of others.

During the first half of the eighteenth century the collective wealth of the European aristocracy reached new heights. In eastern Europe that new wealth came mainly from the dramatic increase in the size of the population. With more serfs under their control, the landed nobility could increase the wealth they gained from these poor people's labor and feudal dues. In western Europe, most notably Britain and France, the members of the aristocracy increasingly participated in other forms of economic activity. They operated rural industries such as mining and forestry. They entered the financial world by lending money to the government. They became involved in urban building projects and in the economic development of overseas colonies. Some members of old noble families considered such commercial pursuits to be beneath their status, but by investing at a distance, nobles could give the impression that they were not actually engaged in the sordid transactions of the marketplace.

Although some historians have argued that the members of the eighteenth-century aristocracy were social and economic conservatives who were unable or unwilling to act in an entrepreneurial manner, aristocratic involvement in financial and commercial projects suggests a different conclusion. Even on their agricultural estates, many members of the aristocracy, both titled and untitled, adopted capitalist techniques to make their lands more productive. In England a nobleman, Charles Townshend, became widely known as "Turnip Townshend" when he introduced a crop rotation that included the lowly turnip. This type of agricultural entrepreneurship accounts for the accumulation of many aristocratic fortunes.

Size of the Aristocracy in European States in the Eighteenth Century			
Country	Date	Number of Nobles	Percent of the Population
Austria	1800	90,000	1.15%
France	1775	400,000	1.60
Great Britain and Ireland	1783	50,000	3.25
Hungary	1800	400,000	11.25
Poland	1800	700,000	11.66
Russia	1800	600,000	1.66
Spain	1797	402,000	3.80
Sweden	1757	10,000	0.50
Venice	1797	1,090	0.80

SOURCES: A. Corvisier, *Armies and Society in Europe, 1494–1789* (1976), 113, 115; J. Meyer, *Noblesses et pouvoirs dans l'Europe d'Ancien Régime* (1973); M. Reinard and A. Armenguard, *Histoire Générale de la Population Modiale* (1961); J. Dewald, *The European Nobility* (1996), 22–27.

The Political Power of the Aristocracy

The mid-eighteenth century also marked the apex of political power for the aristocracy in Europe. Having recovered from the economic and political turmoil of the mid-seventeenth century, when they experienced a temporary eclipse of their power, aristocrats pursued various strategies to increase or preserve their share of local and national political power. In England, where the Glorious Revolution had restricted royal power, the aristocracy gained political dominance. A small group of noblemen sat in the House of Lords, while the gentry formed the large majority of members of the House of Commons. After 1689 the English king could not rule without the cooperation of these two Houses of Parliament. The monarchy tried to control the proceedings of that assembly by creating parties of royal supporters within both houses. Because those parties were controlled by the king's ministers, who were themselves members of the nobility, the system allowed the aristocracy to dominate.

In absolute monarchies members of the aristocracy exercised political power by dominating the institutions through which the monarchy exercised its power. As we saw in Chapter 16, absolute monarchs appeased the aristocracy by giving them control over provincial government and recruiting them to occupy positions in the central bureaucracy of the state. In France, for example, noblemen of the robe, a privileged group of approximately 2,000 officials, dominated the state bureaucracy. In Russia tsars granted the nobility privileges to secure their assistance in running local government.

The aristocracy also exercised political power through the judiciary. Members of the aristocracy often served as judges of the law courts of their kingdoms. In England noblemen and gentry served as the judges of almost all the common law courts, hearing cases both at the center of government at Westminster and in the provinces. In France noblemen staffed the nine regional *parlements* that registered royal edicts and acted as a court of appeal in criminal cases. The nobility controlled the central tribunals of the German kingdoms and principalities. At the local level the aristocracy exercised either a personal jurisdiction over the peasants who lived on their lands or an official jurisdiction as magistrates, such as the justices of the peace in each English county.

The Cultural World of the Aristocracy

During the eighteenth century aristocracies in western European countries adopted a lifestyle that emphasized their learning, refinement, and appreciation of the fine arts. It had not always been that way. As late as the fifteenth century the aristocracy had a reputation for their indifference or even hostility to learning, and their conduct was often uncouth if not boorish. In eastern Europe a tradition of aristocratic illiteracy persisted into the eighteenth century. In western and central Europe, however, the pattern began to change in the sixteenth century, when members of the aristocracy started providing for the education of their children either at universities or in private academies. Even more important, aristocratic families began to acquire the manners and social graces that would be acceptable at court. By the eighteenth century the aristocracy, especially its upper ranks, became the backbone of what was then called "polite society."

The aristocracy also developed a sophisticated appreciation of high culture. Their homes housed large private collections of artwork that occasionally rivaled those of contemporary European monarchs. They were the main participants in the cultural life of European cities, especially Paris, London, Rome, Vienna, and Berlin. They formed the audiences of musical recitals, attended plays and operas in large numbers, and frequented the art galleries that were established in all the capitals of Europe. They also became the patrons of musicians, writers, and artists.

The homes of the eighteenth-century aristocracy reflected their preference for **classicism**, a style in art, architecture, music, and literature that emphasized proportion, adherence to traditional forms, and a rejection of emotion and enthusiasm. The classicism of the eighteenth century marked a step away from the more dynamic, imposing baroque style, which had flourished in the seventeenth century. Classicism celebrated the culture of ancient Greece and Rome. The revival of that culture in the eighteenth century in art and architecture is often referred to as **neoclassicism**. The residences of the eighteenth-century aristocracy built in the classical style were perfectly proportioned and elegant without being overly decorated. Their Greek columns and formal gardens, lined with statues of classical figures, served as symbols of their cultural heritage. The classical architecture of the eighteenth century reflected the quiet confidence of the aristocracy that they, like their Greek and Roman forebears, occupied a dominant position in society.

Eighteenth-century music, which is likewise referred to as classical, reflected a concern for formal design, proportion, and concise melodic expression. The two greatest composers of the eighteenth century, Franz Joseph Haydn (1732–1809) and Wolfgang Amadeus Mozart (1756–1791), whose music was played before predominantly aristocratic audiences, became the most famous composers in this tradition. Classical music appealed less to the emotions than either the baroque music of the seventeenth century or the romantic music of the nineteenth century. The dominance of classicism in music and architecture during the eighteenth century reflected broader cultural currents in European intellectual life, when science and philosophy placed the highest value on the rationality and order of all material and human life.

classicism A style in art, architecture, music, and literature that emphasizes proportion, adherence to traditional forms, and a rejection of emotion and enthusiasm.

neoclassicism The revival of the classical art and architecture of ancient Greece and Rome in the eighteenth century.

CHISWICK HOUSE This house was built by Lord Burlington as a library and reception hall on his estate near London about 1725. Symmetrical, balanced, and restrained, the building embodies many of the features of classicism. Chiswick House was modeled on the architecture of the Italian Andrea Palladio (1518–1580), who in turn drew his inspiration from the buildings of ancient Rome.

Challenges to Aristocratic Dominance

19.2 How did the rural peasantry and those who lived in the towns challenge the aristocracy in the eighteenth century?

Starting around the middle of the eighteenth century, the aristocracy endured increasingly acrimonious challenges to their power and criticisms of their values and lifestyles. They gradually lost the respect that they commanded from the lower ranks of society. By the end of the century many European aristocracies had suffered a loss of political power and an erosion of their privileges. A claim of nobility began to be viewed more as a sign of vanity than as a natural right to rule. The revolution that took place in France in the last decade of the eighteenth century, followed by the reform movements that developed in its wake throughout Europe in the early nineteenth century, brought the age of aristocracy to an end. Members of the aristocracy managed to regain some of what they had lost in the French Revolution, and they also showed their resourcefulness by accommodating themselves to the new order, but they never recovered the dominant position they had held in the eighteenth century.

Encounters with the Rural Peasantry

One set of challenges to the aristocracy came from the peasants and serfs who lived and worked on agricultural estates. This was the social group over whom the aristocracy exercised the most direct control. In central and eastern Europe, where the institution of serfdom persisted, aristocratic control over the rural masses was most oppressive. Landlords not only determined where serfs lived and when they married, but they also collected burdensome financial duties from the serfs. Royal edicts that eliminated some of the duties of serfdom in the late eighteenth century only partially relieved the plight of the rural masses.

In western Europe, where serfdom had for the most part given way to tenant ownership and leasehold tenure, the condition of the rural population was only marginally better than in Prussia, Austria, and Russia. After 1720, famines in western Europe became less common than in the late seventeenth century, making it possible for peasants to eke out an existence. However, other economic pressures, including the elimination of common pasture rights and an increase in taxation, continued to weigh heavily on them. Over the course of the eighteenth century the number of peasants owning small plots of land declined. Many of those who leased land were forced to sell it as landowners consolidated their holdings. Consequently, the number of landless laborers who worked for wages increased. By 1789 almost half the peasants in France had no land at all.

Under these circumstances the relationship between peasants and aristocratic landowners continued to deteriorate. The realities of the marketplace gradually eroded the paternalistic concern that the nobility had traditionally shown for the welfare of their serfs or tenants. As the relationship between landlord and peasant became predominantly economic, visual and personal contact between lord and peasant became less frequent. Landlords built their mansions away from the local village, and by surrounding their homes with acres of parkland and gardens they shielded themselves from the sight of the peasants working in the fields. The most direct contact a landlord made with the members of the lower classes was with the servants who worked in their homes.

As economic pressures on peasants mounted, conflicts between them and their landlords increased. In some countries, most notably France, peasants brought their grievances before village assemblies. These democratic institutions frequently succeeded in upholding peasants' demands, especially when royal officials in the provinces, who wished to collect their own taxes from the peasants, sided with them against the aristocracy.

Another option for the peasants was to file lawsuits against the lords, often with the assistance of the royal government. In Burgundy numerous peasant communities hired lawyers to take their **seigneurs** or lords to court to prevent the imposition of new financial dues or the confiscation of communal village land. In these lawsuits, which became common in the second half of the eighteenth century, peasants challenged not only the imposition of seigneurial dues but the very institution of aristocratic lordship. In 1765 one lawyer representing a peasant community argued that the rights claimed by landowners "derive from the violence of seigneurs" and had always been "odious." The language used in these cases inspired much of the rhetoric employed in the abolition of feudal privilege at the time of the French Revolution (see Chapter 20).

seigneur The lord of a French estate who received payments from the peasants who lived on his land.

Peasants occasionally took more direct action against their landlords. In eastern France the number of incidents of rural violence against the property of seigneurs who tried to collect new financial exactions increased toward the end of the eighteenth century. In Ireland a group known as the Whiteboys maimed cattle and tore down fences when landowners denied tenants their common grazing rights. Other forms of peasant action included poaching on the lands of landowners who claimed the exclusive right to hunt or trap game on their estates. The hunting activities of the tenants of the Earl of Uxbridge discussed at the beginning of this chapter were just one example of this type of lower-class resistance to aristocratic privilege.

In eastern Europe the deteriorating economic condition of the peasantry led to large-scale rebellion. Bohemia, Hungary, and Croatia, all of which lay within the boundaries of the Austrian Habsburg monarchy, witnessed large peasant revolts in the 1780s. The bloodiest of these rebellions occurred in the province of Transylvania in 1784, when 30,000 peasants butchered hundreds of noblemen and their families after those landowners had raised the dues owed to them as much as 1,000 percent.

The largest eastern European rural rebellion took place in Russia between 1773 and 1774. Pretending to be the murdered Tsar Peter III (d. 1762), the Cossack Emelian Pugachev (1726–1775) set out to destroy the Russian government of Catherine the Great and the nobility that served it. Pugachev assembled an army of 8,000 men, which staged lightning raids against government centers in the southern Urals. The most serious phase of this uprising took place when these troops marched into the agricultural regions of the country and inspired as many as three million serfs to revolt. Pugachev promised to abolish serfdom, end taxation, and eliminate the lesser aristocracy. The rebellion took a heavy toll, as the serfs and soldiers murdered some 3,000 nobles and officials. The Russian upper class feared that the rebellion would spread and destroy the entire social order, but government troops prevented that from happening by brutally suppressing the rising. They locked Pugachev in an iron cage and carried him to Moscow, where he was hanged, quartered, and burned.

Neither Pugachev nor the serfs who joined his rebellion envisioned the creation of a new social order. They still spoke in conservative terms of regaining ancient freedoms that had been lost. But this massive revolt, like others that resembled it, reflected the depth of the tension that prevailed between landlord and peasant, between nobleman and serf, in the apparently stable world of the eighteenth century. That tension served as one of the most striking and ominous themes of eighteenth-century social history.

The Social Position of the Bourgeoisie

In the cities and towns the most serious challenges to the aristocracy came not from the urban masses, who posed an occasional threat to all urban authorities, but from the **bourgeoisie**. This social group was more heterogeneous than the aristocracy. It consisted of untitled people of property who lived in the cities and towns. Prosperous merchants and financiers formed the upper ranks of the bourgeoisie, while members of the legal and medical professions, second-tier government officials, and emerging industrialists occupied a social niche just below them. The bourgeoisie also included some skilled artisans and shopkeepers who were far more prosperous than the large mass of urban laborers. The size of the bourgeoisie grew as the urban population of Europe expanded during the eighteenth century, even before the advent of industrialization. This social group was far more numerous in the North Atlantic countries of France, the Dutch Republic, and Britain than in the states of central and eastern Europe. In England the bourgeoisie accounted for about 15 percent of the total population in 1800, whereas in Russia they constituted no more than 3 percent.

Because it was possible for some members of the bourgeoisie to achieve upward social mobility and join the ranks of the aristocracy, the social and economic boundaries separating wealthy townsmen from the lower aristocratic ranks were often blurred. In French towns it was often difficult to distinguish between wealthy financiers and noble bureaucrats. Although the two groups received their income from different sources, they both belonged to a wealthy, propertied elite. The middle and lower ranks of the bourgeoisie, however, gradually emerged as a social group that acquired its own social, political, and cultural identity, distinct from that of the aristocracy.

Bourgeois identity originated in the towns, which had their own political institutions and their own social hierarchies. The bourgeoisie also possessed the means of effectively communicating with

bourgeoisie A social group, technically consisting of those who were untitled people of property living in the towns, that included prosperous merchants and financiers, members of the professions, and some skilled craftsmen known as "petty bourgeoisie."

JOSHUA REYNOLDS, MARY, DUCHESS OF RICHMOND (CA. 1765) At a time when most European noblewomen were attracting criticism for their luxury and vanity, this prominent English duchess was depicted as being engaged in the simple domestic task of needlepoint. Some members of the aristocracy were able to deflect criticism of their lifestyle by adopting the habits of the bourgeoisie.

SOURCE: Sir Joshua Reynolds (1723–1792), "Mary, Duchess of Richmond (1740–96)," 1746–67, oil on canvas. Private Collection/The Bridgeman Art Library.

each other and thus were capable of forming common political goals. Their high rates of literacy made them the core of the new political force of public opinion that emerged in the eighteenth century. The bourgeoisie were the main audience of the thousands of newspapers, pamphlets, and books that rolled off the presses. A "public sphere" of activity, in which politically conscious townsmen participated, became a peculiar feature of bourgeois society. During the eighteenth and early nineteenth centuries the bourgeoisie became the leaders of movements seeking political change. They organized and became the main participants in protests, demonstrations, petitioning drives, and efforts to overthrow established regimes.

The Bourgeois Critique of the Aristocracy

At the core of bourgeois identity lay a set of values that contrasted with those attributed to the aristocracy, especially the noblemen and noblewomen who gathered at court. Not all members of the bourgeoisie shared these values, nor did all members of the nobility embody those attributed to them. Nonetheless, the bourgeois critique of aristocratic society, which flourished mainly among the lower or middle bourgeoisie rather than the great merchants and financiers, contributed to the formation of bourgeois identity and helped to erode respect for the traditional aristocracy.

The bourgeois critique of the aristocracy consisted of three related claims. First, the bourgeoisie alleged that the aristocracy lived a life of luxury, hedonism, and idleness that contrasted with the values of the thrifty, sober, hardworking bourgeoisie. Unlike the aristocracy, the bourgeoisie did not display their wealth. Second, the bourgeoisie accused court nobles of sexual promiscuity and immorality and depicted their wives as vain flirts. There was some foundation to this charge, especially because the predominance of arranged marriages within the nobility had induced many noble husbands and wives to seek sexual partners outside marriage. By contrast, the bourgeoisie tended to enter into marriages in which both partners remained faithful to each other. Third, the bourgeoisie considered the members of the aristocracy participants in a decadent international culture that often ignored or degraded their own wholesome, patriotic values.

This bourgeois critique of the aristocracy had profound political implications. It contributed to bourgeois demands for the right to participate fully in the political process. These demands came not from wealthy financiers, merchants, and capitalists who had the opportunity to ascend into the ranks of the nobility, but from men of more modest means: holders of minor political offices, shopkeepers, and even skilled artisans. Criticism of aristocratic values and the demands for an expansion of the franchise received support from intellectuals who are usually identified with the movement known as the **Enlightenment**. Not all of these thinkers and writers came from the middle ranks of society. Many of them were, in fact, members of the aristocracy or the beneficiaries of aristocratic patronage. Nevertheless, their goal was to bring about the reform of society, and that inevitably led to a critique of aristocratic values and behavior.

Enlightenment An international intellectual movement of the eighteenth century that emphasized the use of reason and the application of the laws of nature to human society.

The Enlightenment

19.3   What were the main features of Enlightenment thought and how did it present a threat to the old order?

The Enlightenment was the defining intellectual and cultural movement of the eighteenth century. Contemporaries used the word *enlightenment* to describe their own intellectual outlook and achievements. For Immanuel Kant (1724–1804), the renowned German philosopher and author of *Critique of Pure Reason* (1781), enlightenment was the expression of intellectual maturity, the attainment of understanding solely by using one's reason without being influenced by

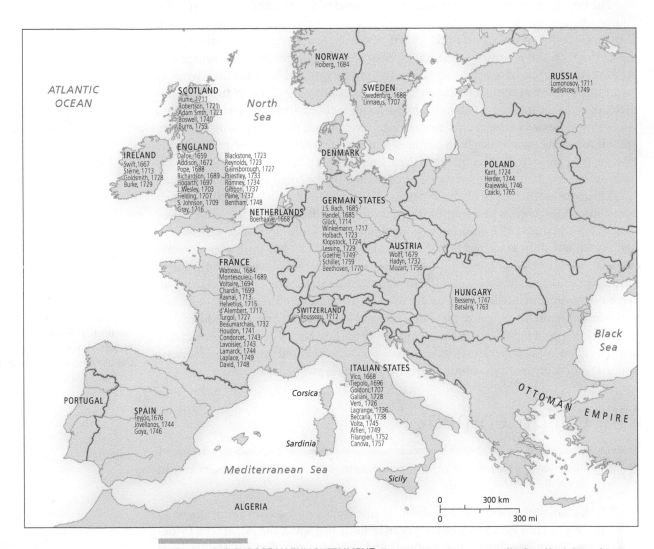

19.1

Read the Document

Immanuel Kant Defines the Enlightenment, 1784

19.2

19.3

philosophes The writers and thinkers of the Enlightenment, especially in France.

19.4

Republic of Letters An international community of Enlightenment writers and thinkers in the eighteenth century.

dogma, superstition, or another person's opinion. For Kant, enlightenment was both the process of thinking for oneself and the knowledge of human society and human nature that one achieved as a result. His famous exhortation, "Have the courage to know!" could serve as a slogan for the entire Enlightenment.

The Enlightenment is often referred to as a French movement, and it is true that the most famous of the European writers and thinkers of the Enlightenment, known as **philosophes**, were French. But French philosophes found inspiration in seventeenth-century English sources, especially the writings of Isaac Newton (1647–1727) and John Locke (1632–1704), while German, Scottish, Dutch, Swiss, and Italian writers made their own distinctive contributions to Enlightenment thought. The ideas of the Enlightenment also spread to the Americas, where they inspired movements for political reform and national independence. The men and women of the Enlightenment thought of themselves not so much as French, British, or Dutch, but as members of an international **Republic of Letters**, not unlike the international community of scholars that had arisen within the ancient Roman Empire and again at the time of the Renaissance. This cosmopolitan literary republic knew no geographical boundaries, and it was open to ideas from all lands (see **Map 19.1**). Its literary achievements, however, bore a distinctly Western stamp, and the ideas its members promoted became essential components of Western civilization.

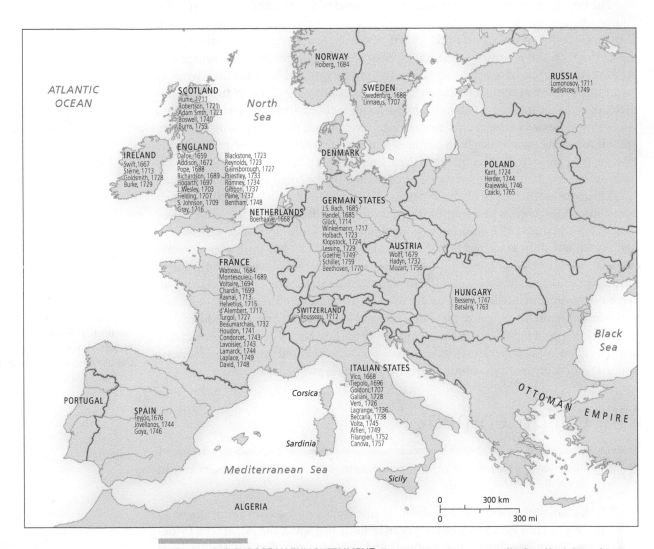

MAP **19.1** THE EUROPEAN ENLIGHTENMENT The map shows the countries of birth and birthdates of thinkers and writers of the Enlightenment. The greatest number came from France and Britain, but all European countries were represented. The map does not draw sharp distinctions between the territorial boundaries of European states because the men and women of the Enlightenment thought of themselves as belonging to an international "Republic of Letters" that knew no political boundaries. What were the values that these thinkers and writers shared?

Themes of Enlightenment Thought

Because the Enlightenment spanned the entire European continent and lasted for more than a century, it is difficult to establish characteristics that all its participants shared. The Enlightenment was more a frame of mind, an approach to obtaining knowledge, as Kant claimed, than a set of clearly defined beliefs. Enlightenment writers, however, emphasized several intellectual themes that gave the entire movement a certain degree of unity and coherence.

REASON AND THE LAWS OF NATURE The first theme that Enlightenment thinkers emphasized was the elevation of human reason to a position of paramount philosophical importance. Philosophes placed almost unlimited confidence in the ability of human beings to understand how the world operated. In previous ages philosophers had always found a place for human reason, but they also placed limits on it, especially when it came into conflict with religious faith. In the eighteenth century, however, philosophes placed greater emphasis on reason alone, which they believed to be superior to religious faith and the final arbiter of all philosophical and theological disputes.

Confidence in human reason underlay the effort of Enlightenment thinkers to discover scientific laws that governed not only the operation of the natural world, but also the functioning of human society. The belief that scientific laws governed human behavior was the most novel feature of Enlightenment thought. For example, the Scottish philosopher David Hume (1711–1776) proposed a science of the human mind in his *Treatise of Human Nature* (1739–1740) and a science of politics in *Political Discourses* (1752). The Scottish economist Adam Smith (1723–1790), who described the operation of economic life in *The Wealth of Nations* (1776), believed that the economy followed inviolable laws, just like those that governed the movement of the heavens. The Enlightenment thus gave birth to modern social science. Economics, political science, sociology, anthropology, and psychology all trace their origins as intellectual disciplines to this time. They are all based on the premise that reason can discover the laws or principles of human nature.

The search for natural laws governing all human life provides an explanation for the unprecedented interest of eighteenth-century writers in non-European cultures. During the Enlightenment, European writers subjected the peoples of the world to detailed description, classification, and analysis. The first thorough, scholarly studies of Indian, Chinese, and Arab cultures appeared in print during the middle and late eighteenth century. Egypt, which had been isolated from the West since the sixteenth century, became the subject of an extensive literature, especially after the French occupied the country in 1798. Books on societies that Europeans were encountering for the first time, including the indigenous peoples of northwestern Canada, Australia, and Tahiti, also became readily available in the bookshops of Paris and London.

RELIGION AND MORALITY The spread of scientific knowledge in the eighteenth century gave the thinkers of the Enlightenment a new understanding of God and his relationship to humankind. The Christian God of the Middle Ages and the Reformation period was an all-knowing, personal God who often intervened in the lives of human beings. He could be stern and severe or gentle and merciful, but he was always involved in the affairs of humankind, which he governed through Providence. The gradual recognition that the universe was of unfathomable size and that it operated in accordance with natural laws made God appear more remote. Most philosophes believed that God was still the creator of the universe and the author of the natural laws that governed it, but they did not believe that he was still actively involved in its operation. God was the playwright of the universe, but not its director. This belief that God had created the universe, given it laws, and then allowed it to operate in a mechanistic fashion is known as **deism**. In deism there was no place for the traditional Christian belief that God became human to redeem humankind from original sin.

View the Image

Title Page from Vico, *Principii di una Scienza Nuova*

deism The belief that God created the universe and established immutable laws of nature but did not subsequently intervene in the operation of nature or in human affairs.

597

Encounters and Transformations

The Enlightenment, Pacific Islanders, and the Noble Savage

When European explorers visited the Pacific islands for the first time in the late eighteenth century, they encountered peoples who had had no previous contact with the West. Enlightenment thinkers, who delighted in studying cultures that were different from their own, seized upon the descriptions of these people, especially the natives of Tahiti, as evidence of the real nature of human beings, before the advent of civilization. From this commentary emerged a picture of the noble savage, who was viewed as being closer to nature than contemporary Europeans. The most positive assessment of the primitive culture of the Pacific islanders appeared in Denis Diderot's *Supplement to the Voyages of Bougainville*, written in 1772 and published in 1796. Regarding the Tahitians, Diderot wrote:

> The life of savages is so simple, and our societies are such complicated machines! The Tahitian is close to the origin of the world, while the European is closer to its old age . . . they understand nothing about our manners or our laws, and they are bound to see in them nothing but shackles disguised in a hundred different ways. These shackles could only provoke the indignation and scorn of creatures in whom the most profound feeling is a love of liberty.

Diderot (1713–1784) admired these islanders' natural religion, their lack of sexual inhibitions, and their superior sense of morality and justice. His depiction of Tahitian society provided support for the argument of Jean-Jacques Rousseau in *Discourse on Inequality* (1754) that civilization itself had a profoundly negative effect on human society.

Western encounters with the noble savages in the "New World" of the Pacific presented an unprecedented challenge to the dominant Western view of the natural state of human beings. Neither Thomas More, who contrasted the evils of European society with the virtues of a fictional island society in *Utopia* (1516), nor Bartolome de las Casas, the Spanish priest who condemned conquistadors for their brutal treatment of native Americans, idealized human beings in a natural, uncivilized

DENIS DIDEROT Diderot's *Encyclopedia*, which he co-authored with D'Alembert, stands as a classic statement of the range and themes of Enlightenment thought. In *Supplement to the Voyages of Bougainville*, Diderot presented his radical ideas regarding religion and sexual morality.

state. The Christian belief that all people are born in a state of original sin prevented them from taking this position. Even John Locke, who described a peaceful state of nature in *Two Treatises of Government* (1690), referred to "the viciousness of man" in that state and contended that the inconveniences of the state of nature necessitated the formation of government. Only when Enlightenment thinkers, with their emphasis on natural law and their hostility to traditional Christianity, encountered Pacific peoples who were untouched by Western civilization did the image of the noble savage fully emerge. Interest in these uncivilized people was so great that Tahitian natives were transported to Paris and London where they became the darlings of literate society.

The idealization of primitive Pacific islanders by Enlightenment thinkers gave Westerners a standard by which they could gain a clearer sense of their own identity. As we saw in Chapter 16, the boundaries of the West became blurred in the early eighteenth century, as both the Ottoman Empire and Russia became more closely tied to Europe. Eighteenth-century descriptions of "uncivilized" Pacific islanders who had radically different customs from those of the West made it possible for Westerners to determine who they were by observing who they were not. For those philosophes who believed that these islanders were noble savages, this self-evaluation was not very favorable. It transformed earlier appeals for reform, such as those urged by More and Las Casas, into demands for a fundamental restructuring of society.

For Discussion

1. In what ways did Diderot's idealization of the culture of Pacific islanders challenge traditional Christianity?
2. How might a person who did not subscribe to the ideas of the Enlightenment have criticized Diderot's argument regarding the noble savage?

Taking It Further

Diderot, Denis. *Rameau's Nephew* and *D'Alembert's Dream*. 1976. These two works by Diderot, unpublished during his lifetime, provide further insights into Diderot's criticism of conventional morality, society, and religion.

Enlightenment thinkers, especially those who were deists, believed that human beings could use reason to discover the natural laws God had laid down at the time of creation. This inquiry included the discovery of the principles of morality, which no longer were to be grounded in the Bible. To observe the laws of God now meant not so much keeping his commandments, but discovering what was natural and acting accordingly. In a certain sense God was being remade in a human image and was being identified with the natural instincts of human beings. Religion had become equated with the pursuit of human happiness.

Because Enlightenment thinkers believed that God established natural laws for all humanity, doctrinal differences between religions became less important. In the Enlightenment view, all religions were valid to the extent that they led to an understanding of natural law. This denial of the existence of one true religion led to a demand for toleration of all religions, including those of non-Western peoples.

((•)) 📖 Read the Document

Voltaire, "On Universal Toleration"

Enlightenment thinkers were highly critical of the superstitious and dogmatic character of contemporary Christianity, especially Roman Catholicism. French philosophes in particular had little use for priests, whom they castigated relentlessly in their letters and pamphlets. They minimized the importance of religious belief in the conduct of human life and substituted rational for religious values. They had little respect for the academic discipline of theology. The German-born Parisian writer Baron d'Holbach (1723–1789), one of the few philosophes who could be considered an atheist (one who denied the existence of God), dismissed theology as a "pretended science." He claimed that its principles were "only hazardous suppositions, imagined by ignorance, propagated by enthusiasm or knavery, adopted by timid credulity, preserved by custom which never reasons, and revered solely because not understood."[1]

In *An Enquiry Concerning Human Understanding* (1748), David Hume epitomized the new religious outlook of the Enlightenment. Hume challenged the claim of the seventeenth-century rationalist philosopher René Descartes that God implants clear and distinct ideas in our minds, from which we are able to deduce other truths. Hume argued instead that our understanding derives from sense perceptions, not innate ideas. Even more important, he denied that there was any certain knowledge, thereby calling into question the authority of revealed truth and religious doctrine.

Hume's writing on religion reflected his skepticism. Raised a Presbyterian, he nevertheless rejected the revealed truths of Christianity on the ground that they had no rational foundation. The concept of Providence was completely alien to his philosophical position. An avowed agnostic, he expressed contempt for organized religion, especially Catholicism in France and Anglicanism in England. Organized religion, according to Hume, "renders men tame and submissive, is acceptable to the magistrate, and seems inoffensive to the people; till at last the priest, having firmly established his authority, becomes the tyrant and disturber of human society."[2]

PROGRESS AND REFORM Theories regarding the stages of human development, coupled with the

WILLIAM HOGARTH, CREDULITY, SUPERSTITION, AND FANATICISM (1762)
Hogarth was a moralist who embodied the rationalism and humanitarianism of the Enlightenment. In this engraving he exposes the effects of fanatical religion, witchcraft, and superstition. The sermon has whipped the entire congregation into a highly emotional state. The woman in the foreground is Mary Tofts, who was believed to have given birth to rabbits. The boy next to her, William Perry, who had allegedly been possessed by the Devil, vomits pins. The Protestant preacher's wig falls off, exposing the shaven head of a Roman Catholic monk. An unemotional Turk observes this scene from outside the window.

SOURCE: William Hogarth (1697–1764), "Credulity, Superstition, and Fanaticism," 1762, engraving. The Israel Museum, Jerusalem, Israel/Vera & Arturo Schwarz Collection of Dada and Surrealist Art/The Bridgeman Art Library.

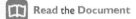 Read the Document

Marquis de Condorcet, Passage from *Sketch for a Historical Picture of the Progress of the Human Mind*

commitment of philosophes to the improvement and ultimate transformation of society, contributed to the Enlightenment belief in the progress of civilization. (See *Different Voices* in this chapter.) Until the eighteenth century the very notion of progress was alien to even the most highly educated Europeans. Programs of reform were almost always associated with the restoration of a superior golden age rather than the realization of something new and different. If movement took place, it was cyclical rather than progressive. In the eighteenth century, however, the possibility of improvement began to dominate philosophical and political discussion. The Enlightenment was largely responsible for making this belief in progress, especially toward the attainment of social justice, a prominent feature of modern Western culture.

Another source of the Enlightenment's belief in progress was the conviction that corrupt institutions could be reformed. State bureaucracies, established churches, and the institution of monarchy itself all became the targets of Enlightenment reformers. The judicial institutions of government were particularly susceptible to this type of reforming zeal. Campaigns arose to eliminate the administration of judicial torture and capital punishment. Philosophes hoped that these reforms would lead to the creation of a more humane, civilized society.

The Italian jurist Cesare Beccaria (1738–1794) provided the intellectual inspiration of the movement for legal reform. In his *Essay on Crimes and Punishments* (1764), Beccaria argued that punishment should be used not to exact retribution for crimes, but to rehabilitate the criminal and to serve the interests of society. "In order that every punishment may not be an act of violence committed by one or by many against a private member of society," wrote Beccaria, "it should be above all things public, immediate, and necessary, the least possible in the case given, proportioned to the crime, and determined by the laws."[3] Beccaria called for the abolition of capital punishment and the imprisonment of convicted felons. The prison, which prior to the eighteenth century had been little more than a jail or holding facility, now became a symbol of the improvement of society.

Voltaire and the Spirit of the Enlightenment

The philosophe who captured all the main themes and the spirit of the Enlightenment was the writer and philosopher François Marie Arouet (1694–1778), known universally by his pen name, Voltaire. Born into a French bourgeois family, Voltaire became one of the most prominent and prolific writers of the eighteenth century. Although he wrote for a fairly broad, predominantly bourgeois audience, and although he decried the injustices of aristocratic society, he was comfortable in the homes of the nobility and at the courts of European monarchs. Voltaire's main career was as an author. He wrote plays, novels, poems, letters, essays, and history. These writings revealed commitment to scientific rationality, contempt for established religion, and unflagging pursuit of liberty and justice.

Like many men of the Enlightenment, Voltaire developed a deep interest in science. He acquired much of his scientific knowledge from a learned noblewoman, Madame du Châtelet (1706–1749), a scientist and mathematician who translated the works of Newton into French. Madame du Châtelet became Voltaire's mistress, and the two lived together with her tolerant husband in their country estate in eastern France. The sexual freedom they experienced was characteristic of many Enlightenment figures, who rejected the Christian condemnation of sexual activity outside marriage and who justified their behavior on the basis of natural law and the pursuit of happiness. From Madame du Châtelet, Voltaire acquired not only an understanding of Newton's scientific laws, but also a commitment to women's education and equality.

Different Voices
The Enlightenment Debate over Progress

T he Enlightenment produced two radically different views of the course of human development. The more optimistic of these, expressed most clearly by the French mathematician and political reformer the Marquis de Condorcet (1743–1794), envisioned human beings gradually progressing toward perfection. The more pessimistic view, exemplified by the Swiss born philosopher and political theorist Jean-Jacques Rousseau, saw civilization as inherently corrupting and degenerative. Rousseau developed this pessimistic view in his historical analysis of the causes of social and economic inequality. His description of the state of nature offered a philosophical foundation for the Enlightenment's ideal of the noble savage. (See Encounters and Transformations in this chapter.)

The Marquis of Condorcet Celebrates the Progress of the Human Mind

All these causes of the improvement of the human species, all these means that assure it, will by their nature act continuously and acquire a constantly growing momentum. . . . [W]e could therefore already conclude that the perfectibility of man is unlimited, even though, up to now, we have only supposed him endowed with the same natural faculties and organization. What then would be the certainty and extent of our hopes if we could believe that these natural faculties themselves and this organization are also susceptible of improvement? This is the last question remaining for us to examine.

The organic perfectibility or degeneration of races in plants and animals may be regarded as one of the general laws of nature. This law extends to the human species; and certainly no one will doubt that progress in medical conservation [of life], in the use of healthier food and housing, a way of living that would develop strength through exercise without impairing it by excess, and finally the destruction of the two most active causes of degradation—misery and too great wealth—will prolong the extent of life and assure people more constant health and a more robust constitution. We feel that the progress of preventive medicine as a preservative, made more effective by the progress of reason and social order, will eventually banish communicable or contagious illnesses and those diseases in general that originate in climate, food, and the nature of work. It would not be difficult to prove that this hope should extend to almost all other diseases, whose more remote causes will eventually be recognized. Would it be absurd now to suppose that the improvement of the human race should be regarded as capable of unlimited progress? That a time will come when death would result only from extraordinary accidents or the more and more gradual wearing out of vitality, and that, finally, the duration of the average interval between birth and wearing out has itself no specific limit whatsoever? No doubt man will not become immortal, but cannot the span constantly increase between the moment he begins to live and the time when naturally, without illness or accident, he finds life a burden?

SOURCE: Marie Jean Antoine Nicolas Caritat, Marquis de Condorcet, Esquisse d'un tableau historique des progrès de l'esprit humain (Paris: Masson et Fils, 1822), pp. 279–285, 293–294, 303–305.

Rousseau on the Degeneration of Humankind (1754)

Many writers have hastily concluded that man is naturally cruel and requires civil institutions to make him more mild; whereas nothing is more gentle than man in his primitive state, as he is placed by nature at an equal distance from the stupidity of brutes and the fatal ingenuity of civilized man. Equally confined by instinct and reason to the sole care of guarding himself against the mischiefs which threaten him, he is restrained by natural compassion from doing any injury to others, and is not led to do such a thing even in return for injuries received. . . . The example of savages, most of whom have been found in this state, seems to prove that men were meant to remain in it, that it is the real youth of the world, and that all subsequent advances have been apparently so many steps towards the perfection of the individual, but in reality towards the decrepitude of the species.

Before the invention of signs to represent riches, wealth could hardly consist in anything but lands and cattle, the only real possessions men can have. But, when inheritances so increased in number and extent as to occupy the whole of the land, and to border on one another, one man could aggrandize himself only at the expense of another. . . . Thus, as the most powerful or the most miserable considered their might or misery as a kind of right to the possessions of others, equivalent, in their opinion, to that of property, the destruction of equality was attended by the most terrible disorders. Usurpations by the rich, robbery by the poor, and the unbridled passions of both, suppressed the cries of natural compassion and the still feeble voice of justice, and filled men with avarice, ambition and vice. Between the title of the strongest and that of the first occupier, there arose perpetual conflicts, which never ended but in battles and bloodshed. The new-born state of society thus gave rise to a horrible state of war; men thus harassed and depraved were no longer capable of retracing their steps or renouncing the fatal acquisitions they had made, but, laboring by the abuse of the faculties which do them honor, merely to their own confusion, brought themselves to the brink of ruin.

SOURCE: Jean-Jacques Rousseau, Discourse on Inequality (1754).

For Discussion

1. What is the basis of Condorcet's optimism that human beings are progressing toward perfection?
2. What is the basis of Rousseau's contention that the human species was degenerating?
3. Do you think modern Western society is progressing or deteriorating?

Justice in History

A Case of Infanticide in the Age of the Enlightenment

A mid-eighteenth-century trial of a young French woman charged with killing her newborn child provides a window into the life of women who occupied the lower rungs of French society, in contrast to those who frequented the court and met in salons. The trial also raises the larger question, debated during the Enlightenment, of whether the punishments prescribed for infanticide were proportionate to the crime.

In August 1742 Marie-Jeanne Bartonnet, a 21-year-old unmarried woman from a small French village in Brie, moved to Paris, where she took up residence with Claude le Queux, whom she had known in her youth, and Claude's sister. At that time Bartonnet was seven months pregnant. On October 22 Bartonnet caused a ruckus in the middle of the night when she went to the toilet and began groaning loudly and bleeding profusely. When her neighbors found her, and when she asked for towels for the blood, they suspected that she had had a miscarriage and called for a midwife. By the time the midwife arrived, it was clear that the delivery had already taken place and that the infant had fallen down the toilet to the cesspool five stories below. Suspecting that Bartonnet had killed the baby, the proprietress of the building reported her to the nearest judicial officer. The next day authorities returned to the building and found the dead infant in the cesspool. An autopsy revealed that either a blunt instrument or a fall had dented the child's skull. After a medical examination of Bartonnet revealed the signs of having just delivered a baby, she was arrested and imprisoned for the crime of infanticide.

Bartonnet came very close to being executed, but the strict procedures of French justice saved her from paying the ultimate price for her apparent crime. In the seventeenth and eighteenth

A WOMAN ACCUSED OF MURDER IN THE EIGHTEENTH CENTURY With the exception of infanticide—the crime for which Marie-Jeanne Bartonnet was tried and convicted—few women were tried for capital crimes in the eighteenth century. One exception was Sarah Malcolm, a 22-year-old Englishwoman, shown here in a portrait by William Hogarth (1733). Malcolm was executed for slitting the throat of a wealthy lady in London.

centuries French criminal justice had established clear criteria for determining the guilt or innocence of a person accused of a crime. These procedures involved a systematic interrogation of the accused (only rarely under torture), the deposition of witnesses, the evaluation of physical evidence, and the confrontation of the accused with the witnesses who testified against her. There also was a mandatory review of the case, which involved a further interrogation of the defendant, before the Parlement of Paris, the highest court in northern France.

The interrogations of Bartonnet did not give her judges much evidence on which they could convict her. When asked the name of the village where she had lived in Brie, she told her interrogators, "It's none of your business." She denied that she had even known she was pregnant, refused to name the man with whom she had had intercourse, and claimed that she had mistaken her labor pains for colic or diarrhea. She denied picking her baby off the floor of the toilet after the delivery and throwing it into the cesspool. When presented with the baby's corpse, she claimed she did not recognize it.

After this interrogation, Bartonnet was given the opportunity to challenge the testimony of the witnesses who had seen her the night of the delivery. The most damning testimony came from Madame Pâris, the wife of the proprietor, who had found Bartonnet on the toilet and thus could verify the circumstances of the clandestine delivery. Bartonnet's inability to challenge the testimony of Madame Pâris led directly to her initial conviction. After reviewing the entire dossier of evidence, the king's attorney recommended conviction for concealing her pregnancy, hiding her delivery, and destroying her child. French criminal procedure entrusted the decision of guilt or innocence to the judges themselves, and

(continued on next page)

(continued from previous page)

on November 27 they voted that Bartonnet should be executed by hanging.

Marie-Jeanne Bartonnet's fate, however, was not yet sealed. When her case was appealed to the Parlement of Paris, Bartonnet repeated her statement that she had gone to the toilet but did not know whether she had given birth. Even though her execution was warranted by terms of a law of 1557 that defined the crime of infanticide, the judges of this court voted to commute her sentence to a public whipping, banishment from the jurisdiction of the Parlement of Paris, and confiscation of her property. The basis of this decision appears to have been the absence of any proof that she had deliberately killed her baby. Indeed, its injuries could have been caused by its fall down the drain pipe into the cesspool. There was also the defendant's persistent refusal to make a confession. She may have been lying, but it is equally possible that once she had delivered the baby, which happened very quickly, she convinced herself that it had not happened.

Bartonnet's trial for infanticide stands at the end of a long period of intense prosecution of this crime. Trials of this sort declined as cities built foundling hospitals for abandoned infants and as moral criticism of illegitimacy was redirected from the pregnant mother to the father. The new legal values promoted at the time of the Enlightenment, moreover, made it less likely that any woman or man would be executed for this or any other crime.

For Discussion

1. As in many trials, the facts of this case can be used to support different claims of justice. If you had been the prosecutor in this trial, what position would you have taken to prove the crime of infanticide? If you had been defending Marie-Jeanne Bartonnet, what arguments would you have used in her defense?

2. In his *Essay on Crimes and Punishments* (1764), Beccaria recommended that punishments be determined strictly in accordance with the social damage committed by the crime. What would Beccaria have said about the original sentence of death in this case? What would he have said about the modified sentence handed down by the Parlement of Paris?

Taking It Further

Jackson, Mark (ed.). *Infanticide: Historical Perspectives on Child Murder and Concealment, 1550–2000* (Ashgate, 2002). A collection of essays on infanticide in various countries.

Wolfe, Michael (ed.). *Changing Identities in Early Modern France.* 1997. Gives a full account of Marie-Jeanne Bartonnet's trial for infanticide.

Voltaire lived with her until she died in 1749 while giving birth to a child that neither Voltaire nor her husband had fathered.

Voltaire's belief in a Newtonian universe—one governed by the universal law of gravitation—laid the foundation for his deism and his attacks on contemporary Christianity. In his *Philosophical Dictionary* (1764), he lashed out at established religion and the clergy, Protestant as well as Catholic. In a letter to another philosophe attacking religious superstition he pleaded, "Whatever you do, crush the infamous thing." In Voltaire's eyes Christianity was not only unreasonable, but also vulgar and barbaric. He condemned the Catholic Church for the slaughter of millions of indigenous people in the Americas on the grounds that they had not been baptized, as well as the executions of hundreds of thousands of Jews and heretics in Europe. All of these people were the victims of "barbarism and fanaticism."[4]

Voltaire's indictment of the Church for these barbarities was matched by his scathing criticism of the French government for a series of injustices, including his own imprisonment for insulting the regent of France. While living in England for three years, Voltaire became an admirer of English legal institutions, which he considered more humane and just than those of his native country. A tireless advocate of individual liberty, he became a regular defender of victims of injustice. One of the victims he defended was Jean Calas, a Protestant shopkeeper from Toulouse who had been tortured and executed for allegedly murdering his son because he had expressed a desire to convert to Catholicism. The boy had, in fact, committed suicide.

Voltaire showed a commitment to placing his knowledge in the service of humanitarian causes. In his most famous novel, *Candide* (1759), the character by that name challenged the smug confidence of Dr. Pangloss, the tutor who repeatedly claimed that they lived in "the best of all possible worlds." At the end of the novel Candide responded to this refrain by saying that "we must cultivate our garden." Voltaire, instead

Read the Document

Voltaire on the Relation of Church and State (Mid-Eighteenth Century)

MADAME DU CHÂTELET In her *Institutions de physique* (1740) this French noble-woman, the mistress of Voltaire, made an original and impressive attempt to give Newtonian physics a philosophical foundation.

View the Image

The Spirit of the Laws,
Montesquieu—Frontispiece

of being content with the current condition of humankind, was demanding that we work actively to improve society.

Enlightenment Political Theory

Enlightenment thinkers are known most widely for their political theories, especially those that supported the causes of liberty and reform. They did not share a common political ideology or agree on the most desirable type of political society, but they did share a belief that politics was a science that had its own natural laws. They also thought of the state in secular rather than religious terms. There was little place in Enlightenment thought for the divine right of kings. Nor was there a place for the Church in the government of the state. On other issues, however, there was little consensus. Three thinkers in particular illustrate the range of Enlightenment political thought: Montesquieu, Rousseau, and Paine.

BARON DE MONTESQUIEU: THE SEPARATION OF POWERS The most influential political writer of the Enlightenment was the French philosophe Charles-Louis de Secondat, Baron de Montesquieu (1689–1755). The son of a nobleman of the robe from Bordeaux, Montesquieu had a legal education and also developed an interest in science, history, and anthropology. In *Spirit of the Laws* (1748), Montesquieu argued that there were three forms of government: republics, monarchies, and despotisms, each of which had an activating or inspirational force. In republics that force was civic virtue, in monarchies it was honor, and in despotisms it was fear. In each form of government there was a danger that the polity could degenerate: The virtue of republics could be lost, monarchies could become corrupt, and despotisms could lead to repression. The key to maintaining moderation and preventing this degeneration of civil society was the law of each country.

Montesquieu used his knowledge of the British political system, which he had studied firsthand while living in England for two years, to argue that the key to good government was the separation of executive, legislative, and judicial power. He was particularly concerned about the independence of the judiciary. Montesquieu was unaware that legislative and executive powers actually overlapped in eighteenth-century Britain, but his emphasis on the importance of a separation of powers became the most durable of his ideas. It had a profound influence on the drafting of the Constitution of the United States of America in 1787.

JEAN-JACQUES ROUSSEAU: THE GENERAL WILL Also influential as a political theorist was the Swiss philosophe Jean-Jacques Rousseau (1712–1778), who as a young man moved from Geneva to Paris and became a member of a prominent intellectual circle. Rousseau did not conform to the model of the typical Enlightenment thinker. His distrust of human reason and his emotionalism separated him from Hume, Voltaire, and Diderot. That distrust laid the foundations for the romantic reaction against the Enlightenment in the early nineteenth century (see Chapter 22).

CHRONOLOGY: LITERARY WORKS OF THE ENLIGHTENMENT

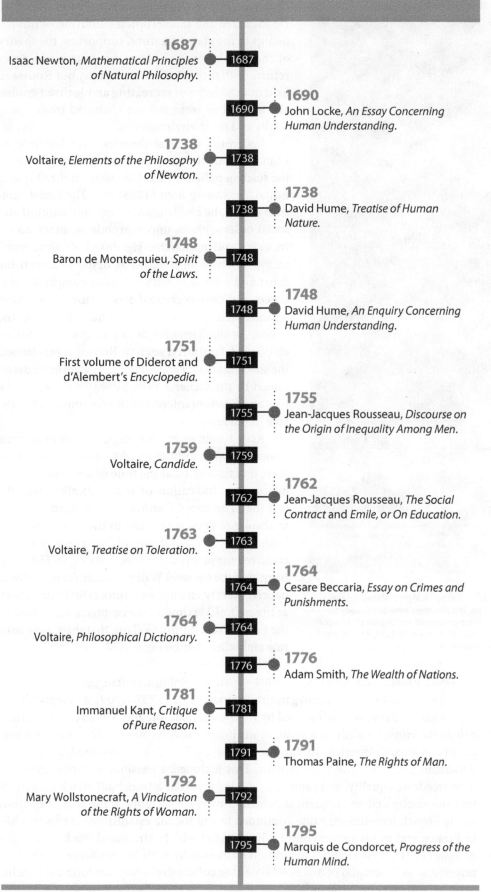

1687
Isaac Newton, *Mathematical Principles of Natural Philosophy.*

1687

1690
1690
John Locke, *An Essay Concerning Human Understanding.*

1738
Voltaire, *Elements of the Philosophy of Newton.*

1738

1738
1738
David Hume, *Treatise of Human Nature.*

1748
Baron de Montesquieu, *Spirit of the Laws.*

1748

1748
1748
David Hume, *An Enquiry Concerning Human Understanding.*

1751
First volume of Diderot and d'Alembert's *Encyclopedia.*

1751

1755
1755
Jean-Jacques Rousseau, *Discourse on the Origin of Inequality Among Men.*

1759
Voltaire, *Candide.*

1759

1762
1762
Jean-Jacques Rousseau, *The Social Contract* and *Emile, or On Education.*

1763
Voltaire, *Treatise on Toleration.*

1763

1764
1764
Cesare Beccaria, *Essay on Crimes and Punishments.*

1764
Voltaire, *Philosophical Dictionary.*

1764

1776
1776
Adam Smith, *The Wealth of Nations.*

1781
Immanuel Kant, *Critique of Pure Reason.*

1781

1791
1791
Thomas Paine, *The Rights of Man.*

1792
Mary Wollstonecraft, *A Vindication of the Rights of Woman.*

1792

1795
1795
Marquis de Condorcet, *Progress of the Human Mind.*

DIFFERENCES AMONG THE PHILOSOPHERS This satirical print shows Rousseau, to the left, and Voltaire engaged in heated debate. The two men were both major figures in the Enlightenment, but they differed widely in temperament and in their philosophical and political views. Rousseau was very much the rebel; unlike Voltaire, he distrusted reason and articulated highly egalitarian political principles.

SOURCE: Bibliotheque Nationale de France.

 Read the Document

Jean-Jacques Rousseau, *Emile*

Instead of celebrating the improvement of society as it evolved into higher forms, Rousseau had a negative view of the achievements of civilization. He idealized the uncorrupted condition of human beings in the state of nature, supporting the theory of the "noble savage." Human beings could never return to that original natural state, but Rousseau held out the hope of recreating an idealized golden age when they were not yet alienated from themselves and their environment.

Rousseau's political theories were hardly conventional, but they appealed to some segments of the reading public. In his *Discourse on the Origin of Inequality Among Men* (1755) and *The Social Contract* (1762), he challenged the existing political and social order with an uncompromising attack on aristocracy and monarchy. He linked absolute monarchy, which he referred to as despotism, with the court and especially with the vain, pampered, conceited, and over-decorated aristocratic women who wielded political influence with the king and in the salons. As an alternative to this aristocratic, monarchical, and feminized society, Rousseau proclaimed the sovereignty of the people. Laws were to be determined by the General Will, by which he meant the true and inherent interest of the community, not the vote of the majority.

As a result of his writings, Rousseau became associated with radical republican and democratic ideas that flourished at the time of the French Revolution. One indication of that radicalism was the fact that *The Social Contract* was banned not only in absolutist France, but also in the republics of the Netherlands and Switzerland. Rousseau was also criticized for justifying authoritarian rule. His argument that the General Will placed limits on individual civil liberty encouraged autocratic leaders, such as the radical Maximilien Robespierre at the time of the French Revolution, to claim that their dictatorial rule embodied that General Will.

THOMAS PAINE: THE RIGHTS OF MAN Of all the Enlightenment political theorists, the English publicist and propagandist Thomas Paine (1737–1809) was arguably the most radical. Paine was influenced by Rousseau, Diderot, and Voltaire, but his radicalism developed mainly as a result of his intense involvement in the political world of revolutionary America. In *Common Sense* (1776), Paine presented the case for American independence from Britain. This included a passionate statement of human freedom, equality, and rationality. It also involved a trenchant attack on hereditary monarchy and an eloquent statement for the sovereignty of the law. At the time of the French Revolution, Paine continued to call for the establishment of a republic in France and in his native country. In his most widely circulated work, *The Rights of Man* (1791), he linked the institution of monarchy with the aristocracy, which he referred to as "a seraglio of males, who neither collect the honey nor form the hive but exist only for lazy enjoyment."

The Rights of Man emphasized an idea that appeared in much Enlightenment writing. Like Locke, Diderot, and Rousseau, Paine spoke the language of natural rights. Until the Enlightenment, rights were considered legal privileges acquired by royal charter or by inheritance. One had a right, for example, to a particular piece of land or to elect representatives from one's county or town. Those rights could be surrendered under certain circumstances, such as when a person sold land. The new emphasis on natural law, however, led to the belief that simply by being a human being one acquired natural rights that could never be taken away. The American Declaration of Independence (1776), drafted by Thomas Jefferson, presented an eloquent statement of these God-given inalienable rights, which included "life, liberty and the pursuit of happiness."

Women and the Enlightenment

The emphasis that Enlightenment thinkers placed on natural law led to two very different views regarding the position of women in society. A large number of philosophes, including Diderot and Rousseau, argued that because women are different in nature from men, they should be confined to an exclusively domestic role as wives and mothers. Rousseau also insisted on the separate education of girls. This patriarchal argument supported the emerging theory of **separate spheres**, which held that men and women should conduct their lives in different social and political environments. The identification of women with the private, domestic sphere laid the foundation for the ideology of female domesticity, which became popular in bourgeois society in the nineteenth century. This ideal denied women the freedom that aristocratic women in France had acquired during the eighteenth century, especially those who belonged to polite society. It also continued to deny them civil rights. Eighteenth-century women could not vote and could not initiate lawsuits. They were not full members of civil society.

separate spheres The theory that men and women should conduct their lives in different social and political environments, confining women to the domestic sphere and excluding them from the public sphere of political involvement.

A small minority of Enlightenment thinkers rejected this theory of the separate spheres, demanding the full equality of men and women. The first of these appeals came from the Marquis de Condorcet, who published *On the Admission of Women to the Rights of Citizenship* in 1789. In this pamphlet Condorcet proposed that all women who owned property be given the right to vote. He later called for universal suffrage for all men and women on the grounds that they shared a common human nature.

Condorcet's English contemporary, Mary Wollstonecraft (1759–1797), also made an eloquent appeal for extending civil and political rights to women. In *A Vindication of the Rights of Woman* (1792), Wollstonecraft argued that girls should receive the same education as boys and learn how to support themselves. Only in this way could women take control of their lives and become the social and political equals of men. Thus, Wollstonecraft challenged the belief of Rousseau and other male Enlightenment thinkers that cultural and social differences between men and women were "natural."

  Read the Document

Mary Wollstonecraft, Introduction to *A Vindication of the Rights of Woman*

The Enlightenment and Sexuality

One facet of Enlightenment thought that had a profound effect on the position of women in society was the appeal for greater sexual permissiveness. Many philosophes, including Voltaire, Diderot, and Holbach, remained openly critical of the strict standard of sexual morality enforced by Christian churches. The basic argument of the philosophes was that sexual activity should not be restricted because it was pleasurable and a source of happiness. The arbitrary prohibitions imposed by the Church contradicted human nature. Enlightenment thinkers used European encounters with pagan natives of the South Pacific, who were reported to enjoy great sexual permissiveness, to reinforce this argument. Diderot appealed to the sexual code of the Tahitians in his attack on Christian sexual morality.

Many philosophes, including Voltaire, practiced what they preached and lived openly with women out of wedlock. Other members of wealthy society adopted an even more libertine lifestyle. The Venetian adventurer and author Giacomo Casanova (1725–1798), who was expelled from a seminary for his immorality, gained fame for his life of gambling, spying, and seducing hundreds of women. To one young Spanish woman, who resisted his advances to protect her virginity, he said: "You must abandon yourself to my passion without any resistance, and you may rest assured I will respect your innocence." Casanova's name soon became identified with sexual seduction.

The violent excesses to which this type of eighteenth-century sexual permissiveness could lead can be seen in the career of the Marquis de Sade (1740–1814). The author of licentious libertine narratives, including his own memoirs and an erotic novel, *Justine* (1793), de Sade described the use of violence in sexual encounters and thus gave rise to the word *sadism* to describe the pleasurable administration of pain. He spent 27 years in prison for his various sexual offenses.

It makes sense that noblemen like Casanova and de Sade would have adopted the libertine values of the Enlightenment thinkers. Somewhat more remarkable was the growth of public sexual permissiveness among all social groups, including the rather prim and proper bourgeoisie and the working poor. Erotic literature, such as John Cleland's *Memoirs of a Woman of Pleasure* (1749), and pornographic prints achieved considerable popularity in an increasingly commercialized society, while prostitution became more open and widespread. Voltaire and Diderot might not have approved of this literature or these practices, but the libertine, anti-Christian, materialist outlook of these philosophes helped to prepare the ground for their acceptance.

The Impact of the Enlightenment

19.4   What impact did the Enlightenment have on Western culture and politics?

The ideas of the Enlightenment spread to every country in Europe and the Americas. They inspired programs of reform and radical political movements. Enlightenment thought, however, did not become the property of the entire population. It appealed mainly to the educated and the relatively prosperous, and it failed to penetrate the lower levels of society.

The Spread of Enlightened Ideas

The ideas of the Enlightenment spread rapidly among the literate members of society, mainly by means of print. During the eighteenth century, print became the main medium of formal communication. The technology of printing allowed for the publication of materials on a scale unknown a century before. Pamphlets, newspapers, and books rolled off presses not only in the major cities, but in provincial towns as well. Literacy rates increased dramatically throughout western Europe. By 1750 more than half the male population of France and England could read basic texts. The foundation of public libraries in all the major cities of western Europe made printed materials more widely available. In many bookshops, rooms were set aside for browsing in the hope that readers would eventually purchase the books they consulted.

One of the most widely circulated publications of the Enlightenment was the *Encyclopedia* compiled by Denis Diderot and the mathematician Jean le Rond d'Alembert.

This massive 17-volume work, which was published between 1751 and 1765, contained thousands of articles on science, religion, politics, and the economy. The entries in the *Encyclopedia* were intended not only to promote knowledge, but also to advance the ideas of the Enlightenment. Included, for example, were two entries on natural law, which was described as being "perpetual and unchangeable." Other articles praised the achievements of science and technology and gave special attention to industrial crafts and trades. Underlying the entire enterprise was the belief that knowledge was useful, that it could contribute to the improvement of human life. In these respects, the *Encyclopedia* became the quintessential statement of the worldview of the Enlightenment, and its publication stands as a crowning achievement of the entire movement.

Encyclopedias, pamphlets, newspapers, and novels were not the only means by which the ideas of the Enlightenment spread. Literary societies and book clubs, which proliferated in the major cities of western Europe, encouraged the public reading and discussion of the latest publications. Scientific societies sponsored lectures on developments in physics, chemistry, and natural history. One of the most famous of these lectures demonstrated the power of electricity by charging a young boy, suspended from the ground, with static electricity. This "electrified boy," who was not harmed in the process, attracted objects from a stool placed below him. Lectures like this one attracted large crowds.

Equally important in the spread of the scientific and cultural ideas of the Enlightenment were museums, where an increasingly curious and educated public could view scientific and cultural artifacts, many of them gathered from around the world. The museums often sponsored exhibits and lectures. Paris became home to many of these museums in the 1780s, and they could be found in all the major cities of Europe by the end of the eighteenth century.

Enlightenment ideas also spread, although more informally, in the coffeehouses that sprang up in cities across Europe. These commercial establishments were open to everyone who could pay the fare, and therefore they proved immensely successful in facilitating the spread of ideas within the bourgeoisie. Newspapers were often read aloud at coffeehouses, and political debates often took place there.

Another set of institutions that promoted the ideas of the Enlightenment were the secret societies of men and women known as **freemasons**. Committed to the principles of liberty and equality, freemasons strove to create a society based on reason and virtue. Freemasonry first appeared in England and Scotland in the seventeenth century and then spread to France, the Dutch Republic, Germany, Poland, and Russia during the eighteenth century. Some of the most famous figures of the Enlightenment, including Voltaire, belonged to masonic lodges. In the 1770s there were more than 10,000 freemasons in Paris alone. In the lodges philosophes interacted with merchants, lawyers, and government leaders. The pope condemned the freemasons in 1738, and many civil authorities considered their ideas subversive.

The most famous informal cultural institutions of the Enlightenment were the **salons**, the private sitting rooms or parlors of aristocratic women where discussions of philosophy, science, literature, and politics took place. The salons of Madame Geoffrin and Madame du Deffand in Paris won international fame. The women who hosted these meetings invited the participants, entertained those who attended, and used their conversational skills to direct and facilitate the conversation. They also used their influence to secure aristocratic patronage of the young male writers and scientists whom they cultivated. Most of the prominent male figures of the French Enlightenment participated in these meetings, at least during the early years of their careers.

The salons became the target of contemporary criticism because they allowed women a place in public life and because they epitomized aristocratic culture. What mattered most in the salons, however, was not gender or social status, but quickness of wit, conversational skill, and intellectual appeal. Thus, the salon contributed to the creation of a society based on merit rather than birth alone.

19.1

19.2

19.3

19.4

Read the Document

Denis Diderot, Preliminary Discourse from the *Encyclopedia* (France), 1751

freemasons Members of secret societies of men and women that flourished during the Enlightenment. These societies were dedicated to the creation of a society based on reason and virtue and committed to the principles of liberty and equality.

salons Private sitting rooms or parlors of aristocratic French women where discussions of philosophy, science, literature, and politics took place in the eighteenth century.

The Limits of the Enlightenment

The ideas of the Enlightenment spread rapidly across Europe, but their influence was limited. The market for books by philosophes such as Voltaire and Rousseau was quite small. Diderot and d'Alembert's *Encyclopedia* sold a remarkable 25,000 copies by 1789, but that was exceptional, and libraries purchased a large number of them. Paine's *The Rights of Man* also reached a fairly broad audience, mainly because it was written in a simple direct style and its price was deliberately kept low. Most books on social and political theory and scholarly works on science did not sell very well. For example, Rousseau's *Social Contract* was a commercial failure.

Books on other topics had much better sales. Inspirational religious literature continued to be immensely popular, indicating the limits of Enlightenment secularism. Novels, a relatively new genre of fiction that appealed to the bourgeoisie, were almost as successful. Rousseau and Voltaire both used novels to advance their radical social views. In France, books that were banned because of their pornographic content or their satirical attacks on the monarchy, the clergy, or ministers in the government also proved to be best-sellers in the huge underground French book market.

Pseudoscientific popular literature also revealed the limited influence of the Enlightenment. The reading public did not show much interest in genuinely scientific books, but they did purchase thousands of copies of publications on such technological developments as hot-air balloons, which became a new fad in the 1780s, and on the monsters supposedly sighted in distant lands. They also bought books on **mesmerism**. The Viennese physicist and physician Franz Anton Mesmer (1734–1815), who moved to Paris in 1778, claimed that he had discovered a fluid that permeated and surrounded all bodies and was the source of heat, light, electricity, and magnetism. Sickness was caused by the obstruction to the flow of this fluid in the human body. To restore this flow, patients were massaged, hypnotized, or "mesmerized" with the intention of producing a convulsion or crisis that restored health. Mesmerism developed into a form of spiritualism in which its patients engaged in séances with spirits, and its practitioners dabbled in the occult. This pseudoscience, which the French Academy of Science rejected as a hoax, became the subject of numerous pamphlets and newspaper articles that fascinated the reading public.

Those who read books about mesmerism had only a tenuous connection with the learned world of the Enlightenment. Among those who were illiterate or barely literate, Enlightenment ideas made even fewer inroads. Throughout the eighteenth century, for example, uneducated villages continued to believe in magic and witchcraft and occasionally lynched neighbors suspected of causing misfortune by such means. Philosophes considered the belief in magic and witchcraft as superstitious and ignorant, but they were unable to change popular mentality.

More physical manifestations of popular culture included cockfighting and baiting bulls, bears, and badgers by tying them down and allowing dogs to attack them. These blood sports, which could attract thousands of spectators at a single event, resulted in the serious injury or death of the animals. Enlightenment thinkers and many others condemned this activity for its cruelty and barbarism and argued that just like the torture and execution of criminals, these pastimes had no place in polite society. Popular sports, however, could not be easily eradicated. They did not begin to disappear until the nineteenth century, often as the result of campaigns conducted by clergymen.

The Political Legacy of the Enlightenment

When we turn to Enlightened political ideas, we confront an even more difficult task of determining the extent of their impact. The main figures of the Enlightenment were intellectuals—men of letters who did not occupy positions of great political importance and who did not devote much thought to the challenging task of putting

mesmerism A pseudoscience developed by Franz Anton Mesmer in the eighteenth century that treated sickness by massaging or hypnotizing the patient to produce a crisis that restored health.

their theories into practice. Rulers often treated Enlightenment thinkers with suspicion, if only because they criticized established authority. Nevertheless, Enlightenment thought did make its mark on eighteenth-century politics in two strikingly different ways.

Enlightened Absolutism

The first was through the reforms enacted by rulers known as **enlightened despots**, although the term *despot* is misleading because these enlightened rulers were rarely despotic in the sense of exercising power cruelly and arbitrarily. Enlightened absolutists, as these monarchs are more properly called, used royal power to implement reforms that Enlightenment thinkers had proposed. The connection between Enlightenment and royal absolutism is not as unnatural as it might appear. It is true that philosophes tended to be critical of the **Old Regime**, the eighteenth-century political order dominated by an absolute monarch and a privileged nobility and clergy. But many of them, including Voltaire, had little sympathy with democracy, which they identified with irrational mob rule. These philosophes preferred to entrust absolute monarchs with the implementation of the reforms they advocated.

Rulers of central and eastern European countries were particularly receptive to Enlightenment thought. These monarchs had read widely in the literature of the Enlightenment and introduced Western intellectuals to their courts. The most famous of the enlightened absolutists was King Frederick II of Prussia, known as Frederick the Great (r. 1740–1786). A deist who wrote poetry and played the flute, Frederick was enamored of all things French. When the French philosophe d'Alembert visited his court, the king hosted a dinner at which he spoke only French, leaving many of the Prussian guests to sip their soup in stunned silence. Frederick corresponded extensively with Voltaire and invited him to take up residence at his French-style royal palace, "Sans Souci," at Potsdam. The relationship between king and philosopher, however, was often stormy, and when Frederick publicly burned a publication in which Voltaire had lampooned a royal favorite, Voltaire left Potsdam.

The departure of Voltaire did not weaken Frederick's determination to implement policies that reflected the ideals of the Enlightenment. The most noteworthy of these was the introduction of religious toleration throughout his predominantly Lutheran kingdom. Protestants of all denominations and Catholics (but not Jews) received the protection of the law and even benefited from royal patronage. Frederick also introduced legal reforms with the intention of realizing the Enlightenment ideal of making the law both rational and humane. He authorized the codification of Prussian law (an undertaking that was completed after his death in 1794), abolished judicial torture, and eliminated capital punishment. To provide for the training of future servants of the state, he began a system of compulsory education throughout the country. Like most enlightened rulers, Frederick never abandoned his commitment to absolute rule, which he strengthened by winning the support of the nobility. He also remained committed to the militaristic and expansionist policies of his father, Frederick William I. For him there was no contradiction between his style of rule and his commitment to Enlightenment ideals.

In neighboring Austria two Habsburg rulers, Maria Theresa (r. 1740–1780) and her son Joseph II (r. 1780–1790), pursued reformist policies that gave them the reputation of being enlightened monarchs. Most of Maria Theresa's reforms were of an administrative nature. Stunned by the Prussian invasion and occupation of the Habsburg province of Silesia in 1740, Maria Theresa set out to strengthen the Habsburg monarchy by gaining complete control over taxation and by reorganizing the military and civil bureaucracy. She also took steps to make the serfs more productive, mainly by restricting the work they performed on their lords' lands and by abolishing the feudal dues they paid.

These efforts won the applause of philosophes, but the policies of Maria Theresa that most clearly bore the stamp of the Enlightenment were her legal reforms. Inspired

enlightened despots The term assigned to absolute monarchs who initiated a series of legal and political reforms in an effort to realize the goals of the Enlightenment.

Old Regime The political order of eighteenth-century France, dominated by an absolute monarch and a privileged nobility and clergy.

Read the Document

Voltaire on Social Conditions in Eighteenth-Century France

19.1

19.2

19.3

19.4

Read the Document

Cesare Beccaria, *On Crimes and Punishments*

Read the Document

Catherine the Great's Constitution (1767)

by Beccaria and Montesquieu, she established a commission to reform the entire corpus of Austrian law. She promulgated a new code of criminal law in 1769, and seven years later she issued an edict abolishing judicial torture. Joseph continued this program of legal reform by reorganizing the entire central court system and by eliminating capital punishment. He also revealed the influence of the Enlightenment by granting religious toleration, first to Protestants and eastern Orthodox Christians in 1781, and then to Jews in 1782. With respect to social issues, he completed his mother's work of abolishing serfdom altogether.

The efforts of Catherine II of Russia (r. 1762–1796) to implement the ideas of the Enlightenment followed a different course from those of Maria Theresa and Joseph. The daughter of a German prince, Catherine received an education grounded in a traditional curriculum of history, geography, and Lutheran theology. In 1745 she was married to a distant cousin, Peter, who was in line to inherit the Russian throne from his aunt, the childless Empress Elizabeth (r. 1741–1762). After arriving in St. Petersburg Catherine not only studied Russian language, literature, and religion, but also read widely in western European sources, including the works of Enlightenment thinkers. She later corresponded with Voltaire and d'Alembert and employed the famous salon hostess Madame Geoffrin at her court. At Catherine's invitation Diderot visited St. Petersburg for six months.

Early in her reign, Catherine embarked on a program of reform similar to those of other enlightened absolutists. In 1767 she appointed a commission to codify Russian law on the basis of western European principles. Her recommendations to the commission included the abolition of torture and inhumane punishment and the establishment of religious toleration. She was eventually forced to disband the commission, whose members could not agree on a new code, but she later abolished torture and capital punishment on her own authority. Like Maria Theresa, she instituted administrative and educational reforms, including the introduction of primary schooling in the provinces. Catherine, who became known as Catherine the Great, also tried unsuccessfully to provide for the education of girls.

Catherine gained a reputation for being an enlightened European monarch, but she never fully embraced the ideals of the Enlightenment. She admitted that it was easier to subscribe to those ideals than to implement them. On the issue of serfdom, which most Enlightenment thinkers wished to see abolished, she would not yield. Catherine not only preserved that social system to secure the loyalty of the Russian nobility, but also extended it to Ukraine and parts of Poland after Russia incorporated those regions into the empire. Some philosophes called for the dissolution of large imperial structures, but Catherine expanded the Russian Empire by acquiring vast territories in Eastern Europe, East Asia, and Alaska.

Eventually Catherine disavowed the ideals of the Enlightenment altogether. After putting down the Pugachev rebellion in 1774, she began to question the desirability of social reform. The experience of the French Revolution in the 1790s (see Chapter 20) led her to repudiate Enlightenment reformism.

The Enlightenment and Revolution

While Enlightenment thought led to enlightened absolutism, it also led in the opposite direction. The second mark that Enlightenment thought made on eighteenth-century politics was the inspiration it gave to movements for reform and revolution in western Europe and the Americas. The emphasis placed by Enlightenment thinkers on individual liberty, natural rights, and political reform pressured monarchs and the traditional nobility either to make concessions or to relinquish power altogether. Very few philosophes were themselves revolutionaries, but their ideas contributed to the creation of a new political order.

The towering reputation of Voltaire during the French Revolution in 1789, as well as the anger of conservatives who exhumed and burned his bones after the revolution

CATHERINE THE GREAT Catherine II of Russia on the day she succeeded in taking the throne from her husband, Peter III, at Peterhof in 1762. Catherine, who despised her husband, joined a conspiracy against him right after his accession to the throne. Catherine, like Peter, had several lovers, and her two children, including the future emperor Paul, were reputedly conceived by members of the nobility.

SOURCE: Vigilius Erichsen (1722–82), "Equestrian Portrait of Catherine II (1729–96), the Great of Russia," oil on canvas. Musee des Beaux-Arts, Chartres, France/The Bridgeman Art Library.

had ended, suggests that this philosophe's passionate criticisms of the Old Regime and his pleas for human freedom played a significant role in the revolutionary developments of the 1790s. The same is true of the radical Rousseau, whose concept of the General Will served as the basis of a revolutionary ideology. Rousseau's democratic and republican ideas were used to justify some of the most important changes that took place during the revolution. Contemporaries either glorified or attacked him, depending on their political philosophy, for having actually caused the revolution. One book published in 1791 was titled *On Jean-Jacques Rousseau Considered as One of the First Authors of the Revolution.*

Yet another application of enlightened ideas to politics took place in the Americas. The advocates of colonial independence from their mother countries, such as Thomas Jefferson in Virginia and Símon Bolívar in Venezuela and Colombia, were all deeply influenced by the Enlightenment concepts of natural law, natural rights, liberty, and popular sovereignty. The Declaration of Independence, which was written by Jefferson, betrayed its debt to the Enlightenment in its reference to the inalienable rights of all men and to the foundation of those rights in "the law of nature and Nature's God." As discussed in Chapter 18, the American Revolution cannot be explained solely in terms of these Enlightenment ideas. The colonists found inspiration in many different sources, including English common law. But the American colonists did wish to create an entirely new world order, just as did many Enlightenment thinkers. They also adopted some of the most radical political ideas of the Enlightenment, which identified the people as the source of political power.

CONCLUSION

The Enlightenment and Western Identity

The Enlightenment was a distinctly Western phenomenon. It arose in the countries of western Europe and then spread to central and eastern Europe and to the Americas. Many traditions identified today as "Western values" either had their origin or received their most cogent expression in the Enlightenment. In particular, the commitment to individual liberty, civil rights, toleration, and rational decision making all took shape during this period.

It would be misleading to make a simple equation between the ideas of the Enlightenment and the Western intellectual tradition. The ideals of the Enlightenment have never been fully accepted within Western societies. Ever since the original formulation of Enlightenment ideas, conservatives have challenged those ideas on the grounds that they would lead to the destruction of religion and the social order. Those conservative criticisms became most vocal at the time of the French Revolution and during the early years of the nineteenth century.

Even though the values of the Enlightenment have never met with universal approval, they gave many Europeans a clear sense of their own identity with respect to the rest of the world. Educated people who prided themselves on being enlightened knew that their scientific, rational worldview was not shared by Asians, Africans, indigenous Americans, or South Pacific islanders. It did not matter whether Enlightenment thinkers had a positive view of those other cultures, like Voltaire or Rousseau, or a negative one, like Montesquieu. What mattered was that they shared a similar mental outlook and a commitment to individual liberty, justice, and the improvement of civilization. For all of them religious faith was less important, both as an arbiter of morality and as a source of authority, than it was in these other cultures. The men and women of the Enlightenment all looked to the law of their country as a reflection of natural law and as the guardian of civil liberty. Their writings helped their European and colonial audiences think of themselves as even more distinct from non-Western people than they had in the past.

MAKING CONNECTIONS

1. How might a nobleman in the eighteenth century have defended himself from the critiques leveled by members of the bourgeoisie?
2. In what ways did Enlightenment thinkers contribute to the decline of the aristocracy in the late eighteenth century?
3. What were the main issues over which philosophes disagreed? What were the issues that led Rousseau to disagree with Voltaire, Condorcet, and Mary Wollstonecraft?
4. How did the Enlightenment help to define the geographical limits of the West in the late eighteenth century?

TAKING IT FURTHER

For suggested readings see page R-1.

Chapter Review

The Aristocracy

19.1 What social groups belonged to the aristocracy and how did they exercise power and influence?

The nobility, who inherited their titles of honor and special privileges, and the gentry, those without hereditary titles, composed the aristocracy. As a group they pursued various strategies to increase or preserve their share of local and national political power. In England, the aristocracy was able to control Parliament, and in absolute monarchies nobles dominated institutions through which the monarchy exercised power, including the judiciary.

Challenges to Aristocratic Dominance

19.2 How did the rural peasantry and those who lived in the towns challenge the aristocracy in the eighteenth century?

In some countries, grievances were aired in village assemblies, and peasants sometimes sued landowners. In eastern Europe the deteriorating economic condition of the peasantry led to large-scale rebellion. In the cities, the literate bourgeoisie, a new political force of public opinion, condemned the aristocracy's life of luxury, hedonism, sexual promiscuity, and immorality.

The Enlightenment

19.3 What were the main features of Enlightenment thought and how did it present a threat to the old order?

A confidence in human reason and a new understanding of the vastness of the universe led Enlightenment thinkers to reconsider the image of an all-knowing and personal God of earlier times in favor of a more remote God who had little to do with how the world operated. Enlightenment belief in the progress of civilization and the idea that corrupt institutions were capable of reform threatened both the concepts of divine right of kings and the marriage of religion and state.

The Impact of the Enlightenment

19.4 What impact did the Enlightenment have on Western culture and politics?

Enlightenment thinkers were critical of the Old Regime of absolute monarchs and their privileged aristocracy, but did not advocate democracy. Instead, they preferred that enlightened absolutists use royal power to implement reforms. But the Enlightenment emphasis on individual liberty, natural rights, and political reform gave power to movements for reform and revolution, both in western Europe and in the Americas, where advocates of colonial independence were influenced by Enlightenment concepts.

Chapter Time Line

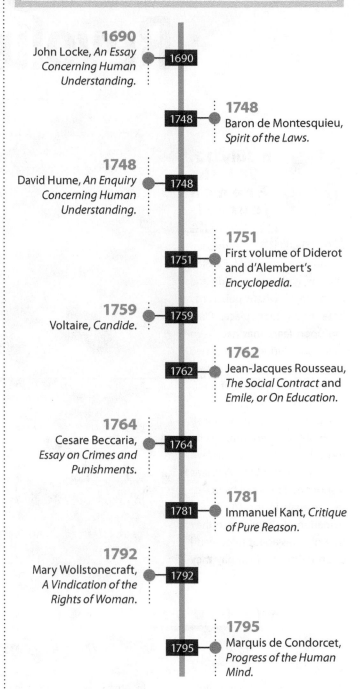

1690
John Locke, *An Essay Concerning Human Understanding.*
1690

1748
1748
Baron de Montesquieu, *Spirit of the Laws.*

1748
David Hume, *An Enquiry Concerning Human Understanding.*
1748

1751
1751
First volume of Diderot and d'Alembert's *Encyclopedia.*

1759
Voltaire, *Candide.*
1759

1762
1762
Jean-Jacques Rousseau, *The Social Contract* and *Emile, or On Education.*

1764
Cesare Beccaria, *Essay on Crimes and Punishments.*
1764

1781
1781
Immanuel Kant, *Critique of Pure Reason.*

1792
Mary Wollstonecraft, *A Vindication of the Rights of Woman.*
1792

1795
1795
Marquis de Condorcet, *Progress of the Human Mind.*

20 The Age of the French Revolution, 1789–1815

On July 12, 1789, the French journalist Camille **Desmoulins** addressed an anxious crowd of Parisian citizens gathered outside the Palais-Royal, where public debate often took place. Playing upon fears that had been mounting during the past two months, Desmoulins claimed that the government of Louis XVI was preparing a massacre of Parisians. "To arms, to arms!" Desmoulins cried out, as he roused the citizens to their own defense. That night Parisians responded to his call by invading arsenals in the city in anticipation of the violence they thought was about to descend upon them. The next day they

THE STORMING OF THE BASTILLE, JULY 14, 1789 Parisian citizens attacked the Bastille not because it was a symbol of the Old Regime, but because it contained weapons that they needed to protect themselves from royalist troops.

LEARNING OBJECTIVES

20.1
Why did the Old Regime collapse in 1789, and what revolutionary changes took place during the next two years?

20.2
How did a second more radical revolution in 1792 create a regime that instituted the Reign of Terror?

20.3
In what ways did the political events of the revolution change French culture?

20.4
Did the rule of Napoleon from 1799 to 1814 confirm or betray the achievements of the French Revolution?

20.5
In what ways did the French Revolution change the course of European and Western history?

((• Listen to Chapter 20 on MyHistoryLab

👁 Watch the Video Series on MyHistoryLab

Learn about some key topics related to this chapter with the *MyHistoryLab Video Series:*
Key Topics in Western Civilization

20.1

20.2

20.3

20.4

20.5

continued to seize weapons and declared themselves members of the National Guard, a volunteer militia of propertied citizens.

On the morning of July 14, crowds of Parisians moved toward an ancient fortress known as the Bastille, where royal troops were stationed. The Parisians feared that the troops in the Bastille would take violent action against them, and they also wanted to capture the ammunition stored inside the building, which served as an arsenal and a prison. Negotiations with the governor of the Bastille were interrupted when some of the militia, moving into the courtyard of the fortress, demanded the surrender of the troops. Both sides fired shots, and the exchange led to a full-scale assault upon the Bastille by the National Guard.

After three hours of fighting and the death of 83 people, the governor surrendered. His captors, bearing the arms they had seized, then led him to face charges before the officers of the city government. The crowd, however, crying for vengeance against their oppressors, attacked the soldiers and crushed some of them underfoot. The governor was stabbed hundreds of times, hacked to pieces, and decapitated. The chief magistrate of the city suffered the same fate for his reluctance to issue arms to its citizens. The crowd then placed the heads of the two men on pikes and paraded through the city.

The storming of the Bastille was the first of many violent episodes that occurred during the sequence of events called the French Revolution. That revolution brought about some of the most fundamental changes in European political life since the end of Roman rule. It heralded the destruction of the Old Regime, the eighteenth-century political order that had been dominated by an absolute monarch and a privileged nobility and clergy. It led to the submission of the Catholic Church to state control. A more radical phase of the revolution, beginning in 1792, resulted in the destruction of the French monarchy and the declaration of a republic. It also led to a period of state-sponsored terrorism in 1793 and 1794, during which one group of revolutionaries engaged in a brutal campaign to eliminate their real and imagined enemies.

The excesses of the revolution led to a conservative reaction, and after a long period of rule by Napoleon Bonaparte between 1799 and 1815, the French monarchy was restored, marking the end of the revolutionary period. The ideas of the revolution, however, especially its commitment to democratic republicanism and its concept of the nation, continued to dominate politics in the West for the next two hundred years. This chapter will address this question:

How did the French Revolution permanently change the political culture of the West?

The First French Revolution, 1789–1791

20.1 Why did the Old Regime collapse in 1789, and what revolutionary changes took place during the next two years?

The French Revolution consisted of two distinct revolutions. The first, which began in 1789, resulted in a destruction of royal absolutism and the drafting of a constitution. The second and more radical revolution began in 1792 with the abolition of the monarchy and the formation of the French Republic.

The Beginning of the Revolution

The immediate cause of the revolution was a financial crisis that bankrupted the monarchy and deprived it of its authority. The government of Louis XVI (r. 1774–1792) had inherited considerable debts as a result of protracted periods of warfare with Great Britain. The opening of a new phase of this warfare in 1778, when France intervened in the American War of Independence on the side of the United States, pushed the government further into debt and strained the entire French economy. As the crisis deepened the king proposed a direct tax on all landowners. The nobility, however, objected to this plan, which would have perpetuated the absolutist policies of the royal government.

The deterioration of the government's financial condition finally forced the king to yield. When tax returns dried up as the result of an agricultural crisis in the summer months of 1788, the government could no longer pay its creditors. In a desperate effort to save his regime, Louis announced that he would convene the Estates General, a national representative assembly that had not met since 1614.

The meeting of the Estates General was set for May 1789. During the months leading up to its opening, public debates arose over how the delegates should vote. The Estates General consisted of representatives of the three orders or social groups, known as estates, which made up French society: the clergy, the nobility, and the **Third Estate**. The Third Estate technically contained all the commoners in the kingdom (about 96 percent of the population), ranging from the wealthiest merchant to the poorest peasant. The elected representatives of the Third Estate were propertied nonnoble elements of lay society, including many lawyers and military officers.

Before the meeting a dispute arose among the representatives over whether the three groups would vote by estate, in which case the first two estates would dominate the assembly, or by head, in which case the Third Estate would have about the same number of representatives as the other two estates. Each side claimed that it was the best representative of the "nation," a term meaning the entire body of French people.

After the king indicated that he would side with the clergy and the nobility, the Third Estate took the dramatic step of declaring itself a National Assembly and asked members of the other estates to vote with them. When the king locked the Third Estate

Third Estate The component of the Estates General in Old Regime France that technically represented all the commoners in the kingdom.

  Read the Document

Emmanuel Joseph Sieyès, *What Is the Third Estate?*

JACQUES-LOUIS DAVID, THE OATH OF THE TENNIS COURT The oath taken by the members of the Third Estate not to disband until France had a constitution led to the creation of the National Assembly and the legislation that destroyed royal absolutism and feudalism.

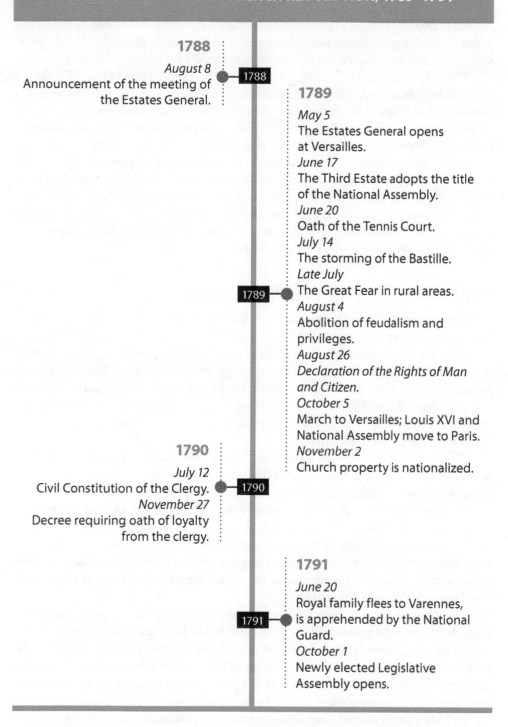

CHRONOLOGY: THE FIRST FRENCH REVOLUTION, 1789–1791

1788

August 8
Announcement of the meeting of the Estates General.

1788

1789

May 5
The Estates General opens at Versailles.
June 17
The Third Estate adopts the title of the National Assembly.
June 20
Oath of the Tennis Court.
July 14
The storming of the Bastille.
Late July
The Great Fear in rural areas.

1789

August 4
Abolition of feudalism and privileges.
August 26
Declaration of the Rights of Man and Citizen.
October 5
March to Versailles; Louis XVI and National Assembly move to Paris.
November 2
Church property is nationalized.

1790

July 12
Civil Constitution of the Clergy.
November 27
Decree requiring oath of loyalty from the clergy.

1790

1791

June 20
Royal family flees to Varennes, is apprehended by the National Guard.
October 1
Newly elected Legislative Assembly opens.

1791

out of their meeting place without explanation, the outraged members went to a nearby indoor tennis court and took a solemn oath (known as the Oath of the Tennis Court) that they would not disband until the country had been given a constitution. One week later the king ordered the nobility and the clergy to join the National Assembly.

As this political crisis was reaching a climax, a major social crisis, fueled by the high price of bread, caused a breakdown of public order. For many years French agriculture had experienced difficulty meeting the demands of an expanding population. A widespread harvest failure in 1788 reduced the supply even further. As the price of bread soared, demand for manufactured goods shrank, thus causing widespread unemployment among artisans. An increasing number of bread riots, peasant revolts,

Read the Document

"Petition of Women of the Third Estate"

and urban strikes contributed to a sense of panic at the very time that the government's financial crisis deepened. In Paris the situation reached a critical point in June 1789.

At that point the king, a man with little political sense, made the ill-advised decision to send 17,000 royal troops to Paris to restore order. The arrival of the troops gave the impression that the government was planning to attack the people of the city. In this atmosphere of public paranoia Parisians formed the National Guard and stormed the Bastille.

The fall of the Bastille unnerved the king. When he asked one of his aides, "Is it a revolt?" the aide replied, "No, sire, it is a revolution." The revolution had just begun. It moved into high gear two weeks later when the National Assembly responded to the outbreak of social unrest in the provinces. The scarcity of grain in the countryside gave rise to false rumors that the nobles were engaged in a plot to destroy crops and starve the people into submission. Peasants armed themselves and prepared to fight off the hired agents of the nobility. A widespread panic, known as the "Great Fear," gripped many parts of the country. Townspeople and peasants amassed in large numbers to defend themselves and save the harvest. In response to this panic, which reached its peak in the last two weeks of July, the National Assembly began to pass legislation that destroyed the Old Regime and created a new political order.

The Creation of a New Political Society

Between August 1789 and September 1790 the National Assembly took three revolutionary steps. First, it eliminated noble and clerical privileges. In August the assembly abolished the feudal dues that peasants paid their lords, the private legal jurisdictions of noblemen, the collection of tithes by the clergy, and the exclusive right of noblemen to hunt game on their lands. Ten months later the nobility lost their titles. Instead of a society divided into various corporate groups, each with its own privileges, France would now have only citizens, all of them equal at law. Social distinctions would be based on merit rather than birth.

The second step, taken on August 26, was the promulgation of the *Declaration of the Rights of Man and Citizen*. This document revealed the main influence of the Enlightenment on the revolution. It declared that all men, not just Frenchmen, had a natural right to liberty, property, equality before the law, freedom from oppression, and religious toleration. The statement that the "law is the expression of the general will" reflected the influence of Rousseau's *The Social Contract* (1762), while the statement that every citizen has the right to participate in the formation of that law either personally or through a representative embodied the basic principle of democracy. (See *Different Voices* in this chapter.)

The third step in this revolutionary program was a complete reorganization of the Church. To solve the problem of the national debt, the National Assembly placed land owned by the Church (about 10 percent of all French territory) at the service of the nation. The Civil Constitution of the Clergy of July 1790 in effect made the Church a department of the state, with the government paying the clergy directly. To retain their positions, the clergy were required to take an oath of loyalty to the nation.

In 1791 a newly elected Legislative Assembly—replacing the National Assembly—confirmed and extended many of these changes. A constitution, put into effect in October, formalized the end of royal absolutism. The king became a constitutional monarch, retaining only the power to suspend legislation, direct foreign policy, and command the armed forces.

The new constitution formally abolished hereditary legal privileges, thus providing equality of all citizens before the law. Subsequent legislation granted Jews and Protestants full civil rights and toleration. A law eliminating primogeniture (inheritance of the entire estate by the eldest son) gave all heirs equal rights to inherited property. The establishment of marriage as a civil contract and the right to end a marriage in divorce supported the idea of the husband and wife as freely contracting individuals.

This body of legislation destroyed the Old Regime and promoted a revolutionary view of French society as a nation composed of equal citizens possessing natural rights. Contemporaries recognized the significance of these changes. The Portuguese ambassador to France, who witnessed the events of 1789 firsthand, reported back to his government, "In all the world's annals there is no mention of a revolution like this."

The French Republic, 1792–1799

20.2 How did a second more radical revolution in 1792 create a regime that instituted the Reign of Terror?

Beginning in 1792 France experienced a second revolution that was much more radical than the first. During this revolution France was transformed from a constitutional monarchy into a republic. The state claimed far greater power than it had acquired in 1789, and it used that power to bring about a radical reform of French society.

The Establishment of the Republic, 1792

During the first two years of the revolution it appeared that the building of a new French nation would take place within the framework of a constitutional monarchy. There was little sentiment among the members of the Legislative Assembly, much less among the general population, in favor of abolishing the institution of monarchy. The only committed republicans—those supporting the establishment of a republic—in the Legislative Assembly belonged to a party known as the **Jacobins**, who found support in political clubs in Paris and in other parts of the country. By the late summer of 1792 this group of radicals, drawing upon the support of militant Parisian citizens known as *sans-culottes* (literally, those without breeches, the pants worn by noblemen), succeeded in bringing about the second, more radical revolution.

King Louis himself was in part responsible for this destruction of the monarchy. The success of constitutional monarchy depended on the king's willingness to play the new role assigned to him. In October 1789 Louis had agreed, under considerable pressure, to move his residence from Versailles to Paris, where the National Assembly had also relocated. The pressure came mainly from women, who formed the large majority of 10,000 demonstrators who marched from Paris to Versailles demanding a reduction in the price of bread. The king yielded to their demands and came to Paris. As he entered the city, accompanied by soldiers, monks, and women carrying guns and pikes, he reluctantly agreed to wear the tricolor cockade (a badge) to symbolize his acceptance of the revolution. Louis, however, could not disguise his opposition to the revolution, especially the ecclesiastical legislation of 1789. His

Jacobins A French political party supporting a democratic republic that found support in political clubs throughout the country and dominated the National Convention from 1792 until 1794.

sans-culottes The militant citizens of Paris who refused to wear the pants worn by noblemen and provided support for the Jacobins during the French Revolution; literally, those without breeches.

TRICOLOR COCKADE Louis XVI wearing the red liberty bonnet with the tricolor cockade on October 20, 1792. Refusing to be intimidated by a crowd of 20,000 people outside the royal palace, he donned the cap and proclaimed his loyalty to the constitution.

Different Voices
The Rights of Man and Woman

T *he French Revolution gave rise to formal demands for the recognition and enforcement of the rights of man, but it also led to some of the earliest appeals for the equal rights of women. These two documents present the proclamation of the rights of man by the National Assembly and a parallel statement by a female writer who called for fundamental changes in the relations between men and women.*

The passage of the Declaration of the Rights of Man and Citizen *by the National Assembly on August 26, 1789, was one of the earliest and most enduring acts of the French Revolution. A document of great simplicity and power, it was hammered out during many weeks of debate. Its concern with natural rights and equality before the law reflected the ideas of the Enlightenment.*

For Olympe de Gouges, the Declaration of the Rights of Man and Citizen *did not guarantee women the same rights as men nor address existing inequalities between the sexes. In a pamphlet titled* Declaration of the Rights of Women and the Female Citizen (1791), *which is a founding document of modern feminism, de Gouges offered a set of principles that paralleled the rights claimed in the National Assembly's demand for universal human rights.*

Declaration of the Rights of Man and Citizen (1789)

1. Men are born free and remain free and equal in rights. Social distinctions may be founded only on the common good.

2. The aim of all political association is the preservation of the natural and imprescriptible rights of man. These rights are liberty, property, security and resistance to oppression.

3. The principle of all authority rests essentially in the nation. No body nor individual may exercise any authority which does not emanate expressly from the nation.

4. Liberty consists in the freedom to do whatever does not harm another; hence the exercise of the natural rights of each man has no limits except those which assure to the other members of society the enjoyment of the same rights. These limits can only be determined by law. . . .

6. Law is the expression of the general will. Every citizen has the right to participate personally or through his representative in its formation. It must be the same for all, whether it protects or punishes. All citizens, being equal in the eyes of the law, are equally eligible to all dignities and to all public positions and occupations, according to their abilities, and without distinction except that of their virtues and talents.

7. No man may be indicted, arrested, or imprisoned except in cases determined by the law and according to the forms prescribed by law. . . .

10. No one should be disturbed for his opinions, even in religion, provided that their manifestation does not trouble public order as established by law.

11. The free communication of thoughts and opinions is one of the most precious of the rights of man. Every citizen may therefore speak, write, and print freely, but shall be responsible for any abuse of this freedom in the cases set by the law. . . .

17. Property being an inviolable and sacred right, no one may be deprived of it except when public necessity, determined by law, obviously requires it, and then on the condition that the owner shall have been previously and equitably compensated.

SOURCE: From P.-J.-B. Buchez and P.-C. Roux, *Histoire parlementaire de la Révolution française* (Paris, 1834).

Olympe de Gouges, Declaration of the Rights of Women and the Female Citizen (1791)

1. Woman is born free and lives equal to man in her rights. Social distinctions can be based only on common utility.

2. The purpose of any political association is the conservation of the natural and imprescriptible rights of woman and man; these rights are liberty, property, security, and especially resistance to oppression.

3. The principle of all sovereignty rests essentially with the nation, which is nothing but the union of woman and man; no body and no individual can exercise any authority which does not come expressly from it [the nation].

4. Liberty and justice consist of restoring all that belongs to others; thus, the only limits on the exercise of the natural rights of woman are perpetual male tyranny; these limits are to be reformed by the laws of nature and reason. . . .

6. The laws must be the expression of the general will; all female and male citizens must contribute either personally or through their representatives to its formation; it must be the same for all: male and female citizens, being equal in the eyes of the law, must be equally admitted to all honors, positions, and public employment according to their capacity and without other distinctions besides those of their virtues and talents.

7. No woman is an exception: she is accused, arrested, and detained in cases determined by law. Women, like men, obey this rigorous law. . . .

10. No one is to be disquieted for his very basic opinions; woman has the right to mount the scaffold; she must equally have the right to mount the rostrum, provided that her demonstrations do not disturb the legally established public order.

11. The free communication of thoughts and opinions is one of the most precious rights of woman, since this liberty assures the recognition of children by their fathers. Any female citizen thus may say freely, I am the mother of your child, without being forced by a barbarous prejudice to hide the truth; as long as she accepts responsibility for any abuse of this liberty [by lying about the paternity of the child] in cases determined by law. . . .

(continued on next page)

(continued from previous page)

17. Property belongs to both sexes whether united or separated; for each it is an inviolable and sacred right; no one can be deprived of it, since it is a true patrimony of nature, unless public necessity, determined by law, requires it, and then only with a just compensation, settled in advance.

SOURCE: Olympe de Gouges, *Les Droits de la femme* (Paris, 1791).

For Discussion

1. What is the basis of Olympe de Gouges's demand for equal rights for women?
2. Did the two declarations differ in their views of the nation? Did they differ in their view of the proper function of law?

opposition led many people to suspect that he was encouraging the powers of Europe to invade France to restore the Old Regime.

Louis XVI had few personal resources upon which he might draw to win the confidence of his subjects. He was not as intelligent as his grandfather, Louis XV, nor did he have the skills necessary to dispel his subjects' growing distrust of him. Neither Louis nor his Austrian wife, Marie Antoinette, commanded much respect among the people. For many years the royal couple had been the object of relentless, sometimes pornographic satire. Critics lampooned the king for his rumored sexual inadequacies and the queen for a series of alleged infidelities with the king's brother and a succession of female partners. Whatever confidence Parisian citizens might have retained in the royal couple evaporated in June 1791, when the king and queen attempted to flee the country. The National Guard apprehended them at Varennes, close to the eastern French border, and forced them to return to Paris, where they were kept under guard at the palace of the Tuileries.

The development that actually precipitated the downfall of the monarchy and led to the establishment of a republic was the decision by the Legislative Assembly to go to war. After the flight to Varennes and the capture of the royal family, Frederick William II of Prussia and Emperor Leopold II of Austria, the brother of Marie Antoinette, signed an alliance and called upon the other European monarchs "to restore to the king of France complete liberty and to consolidate the bases of monarchical government." In response to this threat a small group of republicans, headed by the eloquent orator Jacques-Pierre Brissot (1754–1793), convinced the assembly that an international conspiracy against the revolution would end in an invasion of their country. Brissot and his supporters also believed that France could be lured into a foreign war, the king and queen would be revealed as traitors, and the monarchy would be destroyed. Exploiting xenophobic and revolutionary sentiment, and claiming that the strength of a citizen army would win a quick and decisive victory, Brissot and his allies won the support of the entire assembly. They also appealed to the international goals of the revolution, claiming that the French army would inspire revolution against "the tyrants of Europe" everywhere they went.

The Legislative Assembly declared war on Austria in April 1792. Instead of a glorious victory, however, the war resulted in a series of disastrous defeats at the hands of the Austrians and their Prussian allies. This military failure contributed to a mood of paranoia in France, especially in Paris. Fears arose that invading armies, in alliance with nobles, would undermine the revolution and destroy the assembly itself. In July the assembly officially proclaimed the nation to be in danger, calling for all citizens to rally against the enemies of liberty at home and abroad. Women petitioned for the right to bear arms. When the Austrians and Prussians threatened to torch the entire city of Paris and slaughter its population if anyone laid a hand on the royal family, Parisian citizens immediately demanded that the king be deposed.

On August 10 a radical republican committee overthrew the Paris commune, the city government that had been installed in 1789, and set up a new, revolutionary commune. A force of about 20,000 men, including volunteer troops from various parts of the kingdom, invaded the Tuileries, which was defended by about 900 Swiss guards. When the members of the royal bodyguard fled, members of the Paris crowds pursued them,

Le Sans Culotte intrépide

THE INTREPID *SANS-CULOTTE* In this satirical image of a *sans-culotte*, killing a nobleman conveys both the militancy of the *sans-culottes*, who were armed Parisian radicals who supported the Republic, and their distinctive dress. Male *sans-culottes* wore trousers rather than the breeches (*culottes*) that were in style among the members of the French nobility.

stripped them of their red uniforms, and hacked 600 of them to death with knives, pikes, and hatchets. The attack on the Tuileries forced the king to take refuge in the nearby Legislative Assembly. The assembly promptly suspended the monarchy and turned the royal family over to the commune, which imprisoned them in the Temple, a medieval fortress in the northeastern part of the city. The Assembly then ordered its own dissolution and called for the election of a new legislative body that would draft a new constitution.

The fall of the monarchy did nothing to allay the siege mentality of the city, especially after further Prussian victories in early September escalated fears of a Prussian invasion. The foreign invasion never materialized. On September 20, 1792 a surprisingly well-disciplined and well-trained army of French citizens, inspired by dedication to France and the revolution, repulsed the Prussian army at Valmy. This victory saved the revolution. Delegates to a new National Convention, elected by **universal male suffrage**, had already arrived in Paris to write a new constitution. On September 22 the Convention

universal male suffrage The granting of the right to vote to all adult males.

declared that the monarchy was formally abolished and that France was a republic. France had now experienced a second revolution, more radical than the first, but dedicated to the principles of liberty, equality, and fraternity, which soon became the motto of the revolution.

The Jacobins and the Revolution

By the time the Republic had been declared, the Jacobins had become the major political party in the Legislative Assembly. Soon, however, factional divisions began to develop within Jacobin ranks. The main split occurred between the followers of Brissot, known as **Girondins**, and the radicals known as Montagnards, or "**the Mountain**." The latter acquired their name because they occupied the benches on the side of the convention hall, where the floor sloped upward. The Girondins occupied the lower side of the hall, while the uncommitted deputies, known as "the Plain," occupied the middle.

Both the Mountain and the Girondins claimed to be advancing the goals of the revolution, but they differed widely on which tactics to pursue. The Mountain took the position that as long as internal and external enemies threatened the state, the government needed to centralize authority in the capital. The Mountain thought of themselves as the representatives of the common people, especially the *sans-culottes* in Paris. Many of their leaders, including Georges-Jacques Danton (1759–1794), Jean-Paul Marat (1743–1793), and Maximilien Robespierre (1758–1794), were in fact Parisians. Their mission was to make the revolution even more egalitarian and to establish a republic characterized by civic pride and patriotism, which Robespierre referred to as the **Republic of Virtue**.

The Girondins, known as such because many of their leaders came from the southwestern department of Gironde, took a more conservative position than the Mountain on these issues. Favoring the economic freedom and local control desired by merchants and manufacturers, they were reluctant to support further centralization of state power. They believed that the revolution had advanced far enough and should not become more radical. They were also afraid that the egalitarianism of the revolution, if unchecked, would lead to a leveling of French society and result in social anarchy.

The conflict between the Girondins and the Mountain became apparent in the debate over what to do with the deposed king. Louis had been suspected of conspiring with the enemies of the revolution, and the discovery of his correspondence with the Austrian government led to his trial for treason against the nation. The Girondins had originally expressed reluctance to bring him to trial, preferring to keep him in prison. Once the trial began, they joined the entire National Convention in voting to convict him, but they opposed his execution. This stance led the Mountain to accuse the Girondins of being secret collaborators with the monarchy. By a narrow vote the Convention decided to put the king to death, and on January 21, 1793, Louis was executed at the Place de la Révolution, formerly known as the Place de Louis XV. (See *Justice in History* in this chapter.)

The instrument of death was the guillotine, an efficient and merciful but nonetheless terrifying decapitation machine first pressed into service in April 1792. It took its name from Dr. Joseph-Ignace Guillotin, who had the original idea for such a device, although he did not invent it. The guillotine was inspired by the conviction that all criminals, not just those of noble blood, should be executed in a swift, painless manner. The new device was to be put to extensive use during the next 18 months, and many Girondins fell victim to it.

The split between the Mountain and the Girondins became more pronounced as the republican regime encountered increasing opposition from foreign and domestic enemies. Early in 1793 Great Britain and the Dutch Republic allied with Prussia and Austria to form the First Coalition against France; within a month Spain and the Italian kingdoms of Sardinia and Naples joined them. The armies of these allied powers defeated French forces in the Austrian Netherlands in March of that year, and once again an invasion seemed imminent. At the same time internal rebellions against the revolutionary regime took place in various outlying provinces, especially in the

Girondins The more conservative members of the Jacobin party who favored greater economic freedom and opposed further centralization of state power during the French Revolution.

The Mountain Members of the radical faction within the Jacobin party during the French Revolution who advocated the centralization of state power and instituted the Reign of Terror.

Republic of Virtue The ideal form of government proposed by Maximilien Robespierre and other Jacobins during the French Revolution. Its proponents wished to make the republic established in 1792 more egalitarian and secular and inspire civic pride and patriotism in the people.

 Read the **Document**

Maximilien Robespierre, "Speech to National Convention"

district of the Vendée in western France. Noblemen and clerics led these uprisings, but they also had popular support, especially from tenant farmers who resented the increased taxation imposed by the new revolutionary government.

In the minds of Robespierre and his colleagues, the Girondins were linked to these provincial rebels, whom they labeled as *federalists* because they opposed the centralization of the French state and thus threatened the unity of the nation. In June 1793, 29 Girondins were expelled from the Convention for supporting local officials accused of hoarding grain. This purge made it apparent that any political opponent of the Mountain, even those with solid republican credentials, could now be identified as an enemy of the revolution.

The Reign of Terror, 1793–1794

To deal with its domestic enemies, the French republican government claimed powers that far exceeded those exercised by the monarchy in the age of absolutism. The Convention passed laws that set up special courts to prosecute enemies of the regime and authorized procedures that deprived those accused of their legal rights. These laws laid the legal

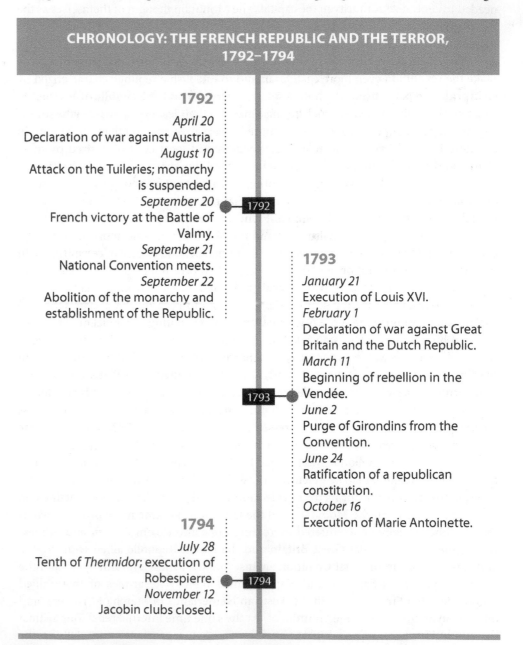

CHRONOLOGY: THE FRENCH REPUBLIC AND THE TERROR, 1792–1794

1792

April 20
Declaration of war against Austria.
August 10
Attack on the Tuileries; monarchy is suspended.
September 20
French victory at the Battle of Valmy.
September 21
National Convention meets.
September 22
Abolition of the monarchy and establishment of the Republic.

1793

January 21
Execution of Louis XVI.
February 1
Declaration of war against Great Britain and the Dutch Republic.
March 11
Beginning of rebellion in the Vendée.
June 2
Purge of Girondins from the Convention.
June 24
Ratification of a republican constitution.
October 16
Execution of Marie Antoinette.

1794

July 28
Tenth of *Thermidor*; execution of Robespierre.
November 12
Jacobin clubs closed.

foundation for the **Reign of Terror**, a campaign to rid the state of its internal enemies. A Committee of Public Safety, consisting of 12 members entrusted with the executive power of the state, superintended this process. Although technically subordinate to the Convention, the Committee of Public Safety became, in effect, a revolutionary dictatorship.

The man who emerged as the main figure on the Committee of Public Safety was Maximilien Robespierre. A brilliant student as a youth, Robespierre had taken offense when the royal carriage splashed him with mud as he was waiting to read an address to the king. A man with little sense of humor, he was passionate in his quest for justice. As a lawyer who defended indigent clients, Robespierre was elected to the Third Estate in 1789 and became a favorite of the *sans-culottes,* who called him "The Incorruptible." That he may have been, but he was also susceptible to the temptation to abuse power for partisan political purposes. Like Rousseau, whose work he admired, he was also willing to sacrifice individual liberty in the name of the General Will. He reasoned that because the General Will was indivisible, it could not accommodate dissent. Robespierre was primarily responsible for pushing the revolution to new extremes by establishing the program of state repression that began in the autumn of 1793.

The most intense prosecutions of the Terror took place between October 1793 and June 1794, but they continued until August 1794. By that time the revolutionary courts had executed 17,000 people, while 500,000 had suffered imprisonment. Another 20,000 either died in prison or were killed without any form of trial. Among the victims of the Terror were substantial numbers of clergy and nobility, but the overwhelming majority were artisans and peasants. One Parisian stableboy was guillotined for having said "f . . the Republic," while a baker from Alsace lost his head for predicting that "the Republic will go to hell with all its partisans."[1] Many of the victims came from the outlying regions of the country, especially the northeast, where foreign armies threatened the Republic, and the west, where a brutal civil war between the French army and Catholics and royalists was raging. Special surveillance committees identified these provincial enemies of the regime, and revolutionary tribunals tried them. The guillotine was by no means the only method of execution. In November and December 1793, about 1,800 rebels captured during the uprising in the Vendée were tied to other prisoners, placed in sinking boats, and drowned in the chilly waters of the Loire River.

Some of the most prominent figures of the Enlightenment fell victim to this paranoia. Among them was the Marquis de Condorcet, who believed passionately that all citizens, including women, had equal rights. Having campaigned against capital punishment, he committed suicide in a Parisian prison, just before he was to be executed. Another figure of the Enlightenment, the famous chemist Antoine Lavoisier (1743–1794), who had devoted himself to improving social and economic conditions in France, was executed at the same time. So too was the feminist Olympe de Gouges, who had petitioned for the equal rights of women. Many French revolutionaries, including Robespierre, used the political ideas of the Enlightenment to justify their actions, but the Terror struck down some of the most distinguished figures of that movement. In that sense the Terror marked the end of the Enlightenment in France.

The Committee of Public Safety then went after Danton and other so-called Indulgents who had decided that the Terror had gone too far. Danton's execution made everyone, especially moderate Jacobins, wonder who would be the next victim of a process that had spun completely out of control. In June 1794 the Terror reached a climax as 1,300 people went to their deaths. To stop the process, a group of Jacobins in the Convention organized a plot against Robespierre. Calling him a tyrant, they arrested him and more than 100 of his followers and guillotined them in late July 1794. In the provinces members of the White Terror, so named for the white Bourbon flag they displayed, executed leaders of local revolutionary tribunals. With these reprisals the most violent and radical phase of the French revolution came to an end.

The Reign of Terror had ended, but its memory would never be extinguished. Its horrors served as a constant warning against the dangers inherent in revolutionary

20.1

20.2

20.3

20.4

20.5

Reign of Terror A purging of alleged enemies of the French state between 1793 and 1794, superintended by the Committee of Public Safety, that resulted in the execution of 17,000 people.

 Read the Document

The National Convention, "Law on Suspects (1793)" and "Law of 22 Prairial Year II (1794)"

Justice in History
The Trial of Louis XVI

After the abolition of the monarchy and the proclamation of the French Republic in September 1792, the National Convention considered the fate of the deposed king. There was a broad consensus that Louis was guilty of treason against the nation and that he should answer for his crimes, but how he should do so became a subject of heated debate. The Convention was divided between the Girondins and the Mountain. Of the two, the Girondins were more inclined to follow due process, whereas the Mountain considered themselves to be acting as a revolutionary tribunal that had no obligation to adhere to existing French law. The Convention thus became a forum where Louis's accusers expressed competing notions of revolutionary justice.

The most divisive and revealing issue was whether there should be a trial at all. The Mountain originally took the position that because the people had already judged the king on August 10, when the monarchy had fallen and the king was taken prisoner, there was no need for a second judgment. They believed the death sentence should have been carried out immediately. Robespierre argued that a trial would have been counterrevolutionary, for it would have allowed the revolution itself to be brought before the court to be judged. A centrist majority, however, decided that the king had to be charged with specific offenses in a court of law and found guilty by due process before being sentenced.

A second issue, closely related to the first, was the technical legal question of whether Louis could be subject to legal action. Even in a constitutional monarchy, such as had been established in 1789, the legislative branch of the government did not possess authority over the king. The Convention based its decision to try Louis, however, on the revolutionary principle that he had committed crimes against the nation, which the revolutionaries claimed was a higher authority than the king. Louis, moreover, was no longer king but was now a citizen and, therefore, subject to the law in the same way as anyone else.

The third issue was Louis's culpability for the specific charges in the indictment. These crimes included refusing to call the Estates General, sending an army to march against the citizens of Paris, and conducting secret negotiations with France's enemies. The journalist and deputy Jean-Paul Marat added that "he robbed the citizens of their gold as a subsidy for their foes" and "caused his hirelings to hoard, to create famine, to dry up the sources of abundance that the people might die from misery and hunger." The king, who appeared personally to hear the

(continued on next page)

View the **Closer Look**   Execution of Louis XVI

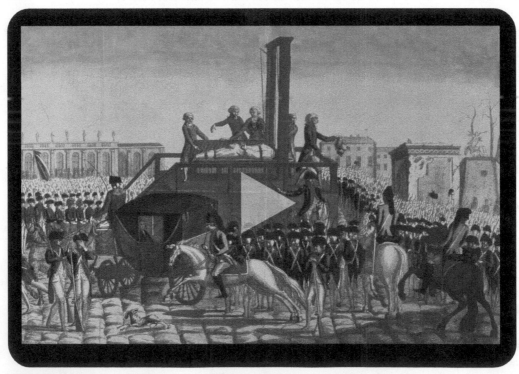

EXECUTION OF LOUIS XVI, JANUARY 21, 1793 Although the king was convicted of treason by a unanimous vote, the vote to execute him carried by a slender majority of only 27 votes.

(continued from previous page)

indictment and then respond to the charges, based his defense on the laws in force at the times he was supposed to have committed his crimes. Thus, he defended his sending of troops to Paris on the grounds that in June and July 1789 he could order troops wherever he wanted. In the same vein, he argued that he had used force solely in response to illegal intimidation. These legalisms, however, only made the members of the Convention more contemptuous of the king. His defense failed to persuade a single Convention deputy. He was convicted of treason by a vote of 693–0.

The unanimous conviction of the king did not end the factional debates over the king's fate. Knowing that there was extensive support for the king in various parts of the country, the Girondins asked that the verdict be appealed to the people. They argued that the Convention, dominated by the Mountain and supported by militants in Paris, had usurped the sovereignty of the people. A motion to submit the verdict to the people for ratification lost by a vote of 424–283.

The last vote, the closest of all, determined the king's sentence. Originally, it appeared that a majority might vote for non-capital punishment. The Marquis de Condorcet, for example, argued that although the king deserved death on the basis of the law of treason, he could not bring himself to vote for capital punishment on principle. The radical response to this argument came from Robespierre, who appealed to the "principles of nature" that justified the death penalty in such cases, "where it is vital to the safety of private citizens or of the public." Robespierre's impassioned oratory carried the day. By a vote of 361–334 the king was sentenced to "death within 24 hours" rather than the alternatives of imprisonment followed by banishment after the war or imprisonment in chains for life. The following day Louis was led to the guillotine.

All public trials, especially those for political crimes, are theatrical events, in that the various parties play specific roles and seek to convey certain messages to their audiences. The men who voted to put Louis XVI on trial wanted to create an educational spectacle in which the already deposed monarch would be stripped of any respect he might still have commanded among the people. Louis was to be tried like any other traitor, and he was to suffer the same fate, execution by the guillotine. The attempt to strip him of all privilege and status continued after his death. His corpse, with his head placed between his knees, was taken to a cemetery, placed in a wooden box, and buried in the common pit. The revolutionaries were determined to guarantee that even in death the king would have the same position as the humblest of his former subjects.

For Discussion

1. How would you describe the standard of justice that the members of the National Convention upheld in voting to execute the king? How did this standard of justice differ from the standard to which King Louis XVI appealed?

2. Evaluate the argument of Robespierre that the death penalty can be justified only in cases of public safety. Compare his argument to that of Enlightenment thinkers such as Cesare Beccaria that capital punishment was an unjust, unnecessary, and uncivilized punishment.

Taking It Further

Jordan, David P. *The King's Trial: The French Revolution vs. Louis XVI.* 1979. The most thorough account of the trial.

Walzer, Michael (ed.). *Regicide and Revolution: Speeches at the Trial of Louis XVI.* 1974. A valuable collection of speeches with an extended commentary.

movements. The guillotine, the agent of a dysfunctional and indiscriminate state terrorism, became just as closely identified with the French Revolution as its famous slogan of "Liberty, Equality, Fraternity." The contrast between those two symbols, each of them emblematic of a different stage of the revolution, helps to explain how both conservatives and liberals in the nineteenth century would be able to appeal to the experience of the revolution to support their contradictory ideologies.

The Directory, 1795–1799

A desire to end the violence of the Terror allowed moderates in the National Convention to regain control of the state apparatus that Robespierre and his allies had used to such devastating effect. They dismantled the Paris Commune and stripped the Committee of Public Safety of most of its powers. In November 1794 they closed Jacobin clubs throughout the country, which had provided support for the Terror. The moderates who now controlled the government still hoped to preserve the gains of the revolution, while returning the country to more familiar forms of authority. A new constitution of 1795 bestowed executive power on a five-man Directorate, while an assembly consisting of two houses, the Council of Elders and the Council of Five Hundred, proposed and voted on all legislation. The franchise (the right to vote) was limited to property holders, allowing only two million men out of an adult male population of seven million to vote. A system of indirect election, in which a person voted for electors who then selected representatives, guaranteed that only the wealthiest members of the country would sit in the legislative councils.

Some of the wealthier and more entrepreneurial citizens of Paris welcomed the new regime, but opposition soon arose, mainly from Jacobins and *sans-culottes*. When the government relaxed the strict price controls that had been in effect under the Jacobins, the soaring price of bread and other commodities caused widespread social discontent among the populace. The continuation of the interminable war against foreign powers only aggravated the situation. Wherever French troops went, their constant need of food and other goods resulted in serious shortages of these commodities.

By the end of 1798 conditions had grown even worse. Inflation was running out of control. The collection of taxes was intermittent at best. The paper money known as *assignats*, first issued by the government in 1791 and backed by the value of confiscated Church lands, had become almost worthless. Late in 1797 the Directory, as the new regime was called, had to cancel more than half the national debt, a step that further alienated wealthy citizens who had lent money to the government. Military setbacks in 1798 and 1799 brought the situation to a critical point. The formation of a

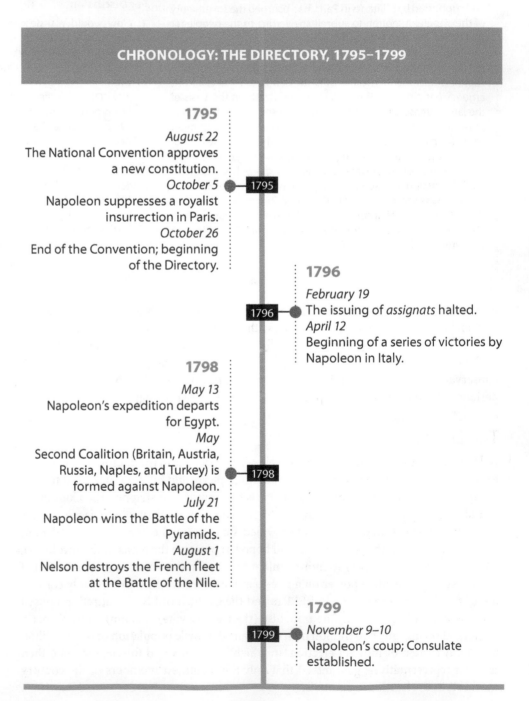

CHRONOLOGY: THE DIRECTORY, 1795–1799

1795

August 22
The National Convention approves a new constitution.
October 5
Napoleon suppresses a royalist insurrection in Paris.
October 26
End of the Convention; beginning of the Directory.

1796

February 19
The issuing of *assignats* halted.
April 12
Beginning of a series of victories by Napoleon in Italy.

1798

May 13
Napoleon's expedition departs for Egypt.
May
Second Coalition (Britain, Austria, Russia, Naples, and Turkey) is formed against Napoleon.
July 21
Napoleon wins the Battle of the Pyramids.
August 1
Nelson destroys the French fleet at the Battle of the Nile.

1799

November 9–10
Napoleon's coup; Consulate established.

Second Coalition of European powers in 1799, which included Britain, Austria, Russia, Naples, and Turkey, presented a formidable challenge to French power and ensured that the war would not end soon. These military events produced a swing to the political left and raised the specter of another Jacobin coup.

In the face of this instability, Emmanuel-Joseph Sieyès, who had been elected as one of the directors two years earlier, decided to overthrow the government. Sieyès provided a link between the early years of the revolution, when he had defended the Third Estate, and the government of the Directory. Unlike many other prominent political figures, he had managed to avoid prosecution as the revolution had become more radical. When asked what he had done during the Reign of Terror, Sieyès replied, "I survived." Now he sought to provide the country with strong government, its greatest need in a period of political, economic, and social instability. The person Sieyès selected as his partner in this enterprise, who immediately assumed leadership of the coup, was Napoleon Bonaparte (1769–1821), a 30-year-old general who in 1795 had put down a royalist rebellion in Paris with a "whiff of grapeshot."

Napoleon had already established impressive credentials as a military leader. In 1796 and 1797 he had won major victories in Italy, leading to the Treaty of Campo Formio with Austria in 1797. Those victories and his short-lived success at the Battle of the Pyramids in Egypt had made him enormously popular in Paris, where he was received as a hero when he assumed command of the armed forces in the city in 1799. (See *Encounters and Transformations* in this chapter.) His popularity, his demonstrated military leadership, and his control of a large armed force made this "man on horseback" appear to have the best chance to replace the enfeebled civilian regime of the Directory.

On November 9, 1799, Napoleon addressed the two legislative councils. He reported the discovery of another Jacobin conspiracy and called for a new constitution to give the executive branch of the government more authority. Napoleon encountered resistance from some members of the Council of Five Hundred, who demanded that he be declared an outlaw. At this stage the president of the council, Napoleon's brother Lucien, intervened and called in troops to evict the members who opposed him. The following day France had a new government, known as the Consulate.

Executive power in the new government was to be vested in three consuls. It soon became clear, however, that Napoleon would dominate this trio. In the new constitution of December 1799, which the electorate ratified by **plebiscite** (a vote to accept or reject a proposal), Napoleon was named First Consul. This appointment made him the most powerful man in France and, for all practical purposes, a military dictator. The dictatorship became more apparent in 1802, when Napoleon was named Consul for Life.

plebiscite A popular vote for or against a form of government or rule by a particular person.

Cultural Change in France During the Revolution

20.3 In what ways did the political events of the revolution change French culture?

The French Revolution was primarily a political revolution, but it also brought about profound changes in French culture. It destroyed the cultural institutions of the Old Regime and created a new revolutionary culture.

The Transformation of Cultural Institutions

Between 1791 and 1794 many of the cultural institutions of the Old Regime were either destroyed or radically transformed, and new institutions under the control of the state took their place.

ACADEMIES The Parisian scientific and artistic academies established by Louis XIV (see Chapter 16) had a monopoly over the promotion and transmission of knowledge in the sciences and the visual arts. The academies were the epitome of privilege. They controlled their own membership, determined the recipients of their prizes, and monopolized their particular branches of knowledge. They were also heavily aristocratic institutions. As many as three-quarters of their members were nobles or clergy.

During the revolution the academies were abolished as part of a general attack on corporate bodies, and various government committees replaced them. For example, the Commission on Weights and Measures, which had been part of the Academy of Science, became an independent commission. Its task was to provide uniform weights and measures for the entire kingdom. In 1795 it established the meter, calculated as one ten-millionth of the distance from the North Pole to the equator, as the standard measure of distance. Like the decimal system, which was introduced at the same time, the metric system was subsequently adopted as a universal standard in all European countries.

The Popular and Republican Society of the Arts replaced the Royal Academy of Arts. The inspiration for this new republican society, which was open to artists of all social ranks, was Jacques-Louis David (1748–1825), the greatest painter of his generation. Employed at the court of Louis XVI, David became a vocal critic of the academy at the time of the revolution. He painted some of the most memorable scenes of the revolution, including the oath taken at the tennis court by the members of the National Assembly in 1789. During the Republic David depicted heroes of the revolution, such as Jean-Paul Marat (see the illustration on page 635), and he was later appointed First Painter to Napoleon. David presided over a revival of classicism in French painting, employing Greek and Roman motifs and exhibiting a rationalism and lack of sentiment in his work.

LIBRARIES Shortly after the revolution had begun, thousands of books and manuscripts from the libraries of monasteries, royal castles, residences of the nobility, and academies came into the possession of the state. Many of these became part of the Royal Library, which was appropriately renamed the National Library. The government also intended to catalog all the books held in libraries throughout the country. This effort to create the General Bibliography of France was never completed, and while the books were being cataloged, the government decided to get rid of those that dealt with "theology, mysticism, feudalism, and royalism" by sending them to foreign countries. This decision initiated a frenzy of book sales, mainly to private individuals. Altogether about five million books were lost or sold during these years.

MUSEUMS AND MONUMENTS The day after the abolition of the monarchy the Legislative Assembly created a Commission of the Museum, whose charge was "to collect paintings, statues and other precious objects" from royal residences, churches, and houses of émigrés. The museum was to be located in the Louvre, a royal palace that also served as an art gallery. When it opened in August 1793 the Louvre included a majority of paintings with religious themes. These religious works of art remained in the collection even though they appeared to be incompatible with the republican rejection of Christianity. The revolutionaries justified this decision on the grounds that this museum was intended to be entirely historical and have no relevance to contemporary culture.

The revolutionaries did not have the same respect for the bodies of their former kings. On August 10, 1793, the first anniversary of the deposition of Louis XVI, the National Convention ordered the destruction of all the tombs of past French kings. One by one the tombs were opened and the corpses, embalmed in lead, were removed. Metals and valuables were melted down for use in the war effort. The corpses were either left to disintegrate in the atmosphere or dragged unceremoniously to the cemetery, where they were thrown into the common pit. The corpse of Louis XIV landed on top of that of Henry IV. This disrespectful treatment of the remains of France's former kings was intended to erase the memory of monarchy.

The Creation of a New Political Culture

As the state was taking over and adapting the cultural institutions of the Old Regime, revolutionaries engaged in a much bolder and original undertaking: the production of a new, revolutionary political culture. Its sole purpose was to legitimize and glorify the new regime. This culture was almost entirely political; all forms of cultural expression were subordinated to the realization of a pressing political agenda.

The main political doctrine of the revolution was popular sovereignty: the claim that the people were the highest political power in the state. The new political culture was also popular in the sense that the entire populace, not simply the literate elite, adopted it. The people who embraced the new culture most enthusiastically were the *sans-culottes*—the radical shopkeepers, artisans, and laborers of Paris. The dress of these people influenced a change in fashion among the wealthier segments of society. A simple jacket replaced the ruffled coat worn by members of the upper classes, their powdered wigs gave way to natural hair, and long trousers replaced the shorter breeches. They also donned the red liberty cap, to which a tricolor cockade was affixed. The tricolor, which combined the red and blue colors of Paris with the white symbol of the Bourbon monarchy, identified the adherents of the revolution.

Symbols of revolution could be found everywhere. The commercialization of the revolution guaranteed that the tricolor flag, portraits of revolutionary figures, and images of the Bastille appeared on household objects as constant reminders of the public's support for the revolution. An order of the government in 1792 required all men to wear the tricolor cockade. Liberty trees, first planted by peasants as protests against local landlords, became a symbol of the revolution. By May 1792 more than 60,000 trees had been planted throughout the country.

The press, no longer tightly controlled by the government and the printers' guild, became a crucial agent of revolutionary propaganda and a producer of the new culture. Pamphlets, newspapers, brochures, and posters all promoted a distinctive revolutionary language, which became one of the permanent legacies of the revolution. Political leaders used the same rhetoric in their political speeches. *Sans-culottes* sang satirical songs and ballads, many of them to tunes well known in the Old Regime. The most popular of the songs of the revolutionary period was the *Marseillaise*, first sung by soldiers preparing for battle against the Austrians, but soon adopted by the civilian population and sung at political gatherings.

Much of this new political culture stemmed from the conviction that the doctrine of popular sovereignty should be practiced in everyday life. *Sans-culottes* did this by joining the political clubs organized by different factions within the National Assembly, by addressing others as citizens, and by using the more familiar form of the pronoun *you* (*tu* rather than *vous*) in all conversations. They also participated in the revolution by taking public oaths. On the first anniversary of the fall of the Bastille, as many as 350,000 people, many of them members of the "federations" of National Guards throughout the country, gathered on the royal parade ground outside Paris to take an oath "to the Nation, to the Law, to the King." Direct democracy was not possible in a society of 27 million people, but these cultural practices allowed people to believe that they were participating actively in the political process.

The new revolutionary culture was emphatically secular. In its most extreme form, it was blatantly anti-Christian. In September 1793 the radical Jacobin and former priest Joseph Fouché inaugurated a program of **de-Christianization**. Under his leadership, radical Jacobins closed churches and removed religious symbols such as crosses from cemeteries and public venues. In an effort to establish a purely civic religion, they forbade the public practice of religion and renamed churches "temples of reason." In their public pronouncements the architects of de-Christianization avoided reference to the Christian period of French history, which covered the entire national past.

de-Christianization A program inaugurated in France in 1793 by the radical Jacobin and former priest Joseph Fouché that closed churches, eliminated religious symbols, and attempted to establish a purely civic religion.

  Read the Document

Saint-Just on Democracy, Education, and Religion (1790s)

OATH TAKING On July 14, 1790, the first anniversary of the fall of the Bastille, as many as 350,000 people gathered on a field outside Paris to take an oath of loyalty to the new French nation. The event was referred to as the Feast of the Federation, because most of the oath takers were members of the regional federations of National Guards. The oath taking, which had many characteristics of a religious gathering, was led by the king himself, and it marked the most optimistic period of the revolution.

This de-Christianization campaign became the official policy of the Paris Commune and the National Convention. The program, however, did not win widespread support, and even some Jacobins claimed that in rejecting Christianity it had undermined a belief in God and the afterlife. In 1794 Robespierre attempted to modify the excesses of de-Christianization by launching the Cult of the Supreme Being. He promoted a series of festivals acknowledging the existence of a deity and the immortality of the soul. This new cult paid lip service to traditional religious beliefs, but it still served secular purposes. The cult was designed to direct the spiritual yearnings of the French people into patriotic undertakings and promote republican virtue.

In an effort to destroy all vestiges of the Old Regime, the government also instituted a new calendar in October 1793. The dates on the calendar began with September 22, 1792, the day the Republic was established. That became the first day of the year I, while the weeks now had ten days instead of seven. The new months were given names to evoke the different seasons, such as *Brumaire* for the first month of wintry weather, *Germinal* for the season of planting, and *Thermidor* for the warmest month of the summer. Hostile British contemporaries gave their own humorous renditions of these names, translating them as Freezy, Flowery, Heaty, and so on. The new calendar was intended to make the revolution a part of people's everyday consciousness. It remained in effect until the last day of 1805. The new revolutionary culture was disseminated widely, but it was always contested. Royalists trampled on the tricolor cockade, refused to adopt the new style of dress, and pulled up the liberty trees. During the Directory many wealthy members of society donned

JACQUES-LOUIS DAVID, *THE DEATH OF MARAT* (1793) The Jacobin journalist Jean-Paul Marat was stabbed to death in his bathtub by a noblewoman, Charlotte Corday, in July 1793. Marat holds the letter from his murderer that gave her entrance to his residence. The painting depicts the slain victim in the manner of the dead Christ in Michelangelo's *Pietà*. The painting thus shows how new secular culture of the revolution incorporated many elements of the Christian culture that had prevailed before the revolution began.

fancy and opulent clothes and revived the high social life of the capital. This resistance from counterrevolutionary forces guaranteed that, when the revolution was reversed, much of the new political culture would disappear. Napoleon did little to perpetuate it in the first decade of the nineteenth century, and the restored monarchy was openly hostile to it. Like the political revolution, however, some elements of revolutionary culture, such as the tricolor and the rhetoric of the revolutionary press, could never be suppressed. Not only did these cultural innovations inspire revolutionaries for the next 100 years, but they also became part of the mainstream of Western civilization.

The Napoleonic Era, 1799–1815

20.4 Did the rule of Napoleon from 1799 to 1814 confirm or betray the achievements of the French Revolution?

The coup d'état on November 9, 1799, or the eighteenth of *Brumaire* on the revolutionary calendar, marked a turning point in the political history of France. The Consulate ushered in a period of authoritarian rule. Liberty was restricted in the interest of order; republicanism gave way to dictatorship. The French Revolution had apparently run its course. But the period between 1799 and 1815 was also a time of considerable innovation, especially in the realm of politics and diplomacy. Those innovations were primarily the work of one man, Napoleon Bonaparte, who controlled the French government for the next 15 years.

Napoleon's Rise to Power

Napoleon Bonaparte was born on the Mediterranean island of Corsica. His father, Charles-Marie de Buonaparte, was an attorney who had supported the cause of winning Corsica's independence from the Italian state of Genoa. His mother, Letizia, came from an old noble family in the northern Italian region of Lombardy. In 1770 the new French government, which had gained control of the island the previous year, accepted the Buonaparte family as nobility. In 1779 the young Napoleon, whose native language was Corsican, received an appointment to a French military school. He survived both the rigors of the course of study and the taunting of his classmates, who mocked him for his accent and his poverty. Displaying a natural gift for military science, he won a position in the artillery section of the national military academy in Paris.

The events of the French Revolution made possible Napoleon's rapid ascent to military prominence and political power. When the revolution broke out, Napoleon returned to Corsica, where he organized the National Guard and petitioned the government to grant full rights of citizenship to his people. After becoming a Jacobin, he was commissioned to attack federalist and royalist positions in the south of France. Unlike many of his fellow Jacobins, he found favor with the Directory. In 1796 Napoleon was given command of the Army of Italy, at which time he abandoned the Italian spelling of his name for Bonaparte. His decisive victories against the Austrians and his popularity in Paris attracted the attention of Sieyès and others who wished to give the country strong, charismatic leadership.

Napoleon's personality was ideally suited to the acquisition and maintenance of political power. A man of unparalleled ambition, he was driven by an extraordinarily high assessment of his abilities. After one of his military victories he wrote, "I realized I was a superior being and conceived the ambition of performing great things." To the pursuit of his destiny he harnessed a determined and stubborn will and enormous energy. Temporary setbacks never seemed to thwart his single-minded pursuit of glory. He brought enormous energy to his military and political pursuits. He wrote more than 80,000 letters during his life, many of them transmitting orders to his officers and ministers. Authoritarian by nature, he used both intimidation and paternalism to cultivate the loyalty of his subordinates. Like many authoritarian leaders, he had difficulty delegating authority, a trait that weakened his regime. Finally, in an age dominated by high-minded causes, he exhibited an instinctive distrust of ideology and the doctrinaire pronouncements of philosophes such as Rousseau. Napoleon's military training led him to take a pragmatic, disciplined approach to politics, in which he always sought the most effective means to the desired end.

Napoleon's acquisition of power was systematic and shrewd. Playing on the need for a strong leader, and using the army as his main political tool, he maneuvered himself into the position of first consul in 1799. In 1802 he became consul for life, and two years later he crowned himself emperor of the French and his wife, Josephine, empress. The title of emperor traditionally denoted the height of monarchical power.

It is ironic that Napoleon, while continuing to hunt down and execute royalists, accepted a title of royalty himself and made his position, just like the French kingship, hereditary. By becoming emperor he not only betrayed his republican principles but also gave the French monarchy more power than it had in the Old Regime. As one royalist declared in 1804, "We have done more than we hoped. We meant to give France a king, and we have given her an emperor." Napoleon's coronation also made a negative impression outside France. The great German composer Ludwig van Beethoven, having dedicated his *Third Symphony* (1803) to Napoleon for overthrowing tyranny in France, scratched the emperor's name from the dedication after he assumed his new title the following year.

  Read the Document

Madame de Rémusat on the Rise of Napoleon

EMPEROR NAPOLEON CROWNING HIS WIFE, JOSEPHINE, EMPRESS OF THE FRENCH IN THE CATHEDRAL OF NOTRE DAME, 1804 This painting by Jacques-Louis David depicts secular and religious figures gathered around Napoleon not as members of privileged orders, but as representatives of the nation. Pope Pius VII remains seated as Napoleon places the crown on Josephine's head. Napoleon had already crowned himself emperor of the French.

SOURCE: Jacques-Louis David (1748–1825), "Consecration of the Emperor Napoleon I and Coronation of Empress Josephine," 1806–07. Louvre, Paris. Bridgeman-Giraudon/Art Resource, NY.

Napoleon and the Revolution

What was the relationship between Napoleon's rule and the French Revolution? Did Napoleon consolidate the gains of the revolution or destroy them? Did he simply redirect the revolutionary commitment to liberty, equality, and fraternity into more disciplined channels of expression after 1799? Or did he reverse the political trends that had prevailed from 1789 to 1799, crushing liberty in all its forms and establishing a ruthless, authoritarian dictatorship?

Napoleon always thought of himself as the heir of the revolution rather than its undertaker. He used the radical vocabulary of the revolution to characterize his domestic programs and his military campaigns. He presented himself as the ally of the common man against entrenched aristocratic privilege. He proclaimed a love for the French people and gave his support to the doctrine of popular sovereignty. He often referred to the rulers of other European countries as tyrants and presented himself as the liberator of their subjects.

Yet Napoleon's commitment to liberty was almost entirely rhetorical. Behind the appeals to the slogans of the revolution lurked a domineering will that was stronger than that of any eighteenth-century absolute monarch. Napoleon used the language of liberty and democracy to disguise a thoroughgoing authoritarianism, just as he used the rhetoric of republicanism to legitimize his own dictatorial regime. He orchestrated and controlled elections to make it appear that his rule reflected the will of the people. When the empire was established he told his troops that they had the freedom to vote for or against the new form of government, but if they voted against it, they would be shot.

We can make a stronger case for Napoleon's egalitarianism. He demonstrated a commitment to providing equality of opportunity in the service of the state, and he supported the equality of all Frenchmen (but not Frenchwomen) before the law. This egalitarianism laid the foundation for the support he received from peasants, soldiers, and workers. He brought equality and political stability to France in exchange for political liberty. He synthesized the egalitarianism of the revolution with the authoritarianism of the Old Regime.

Napoleon was the heir of the revolution in two other ways. First, he continued the centralization and growth of state power and the rational organization of the administration that had begun in 1789. Each of the successive regimes between 1789 and 1815, even the Directory, had contributed to this pattern of state-building, and Napoleon's contribution was monumental. Second, he continued and extended France's military mission to export the revolution to its European neighbors. The two achievements are related to each other because the war effort necessitated the further growth and centralization of state power.

Napoleon and the French State

Once Napoleon had gained effective control of the French state, he sought to make it more efficient, organized, and powerful. In addition to turning the government into a de facto dictatorship, Napoleon settled the long struggle between Church and state, laid down a new law code that imposed legal uniformity on the entire country, and made the civil bureaucracy more centralized and uniform. He did all this with the intention of making the state an effective instrument of social and political control.

CONCORDAT WITH THE PAPACY Napoleon's first contribution to the development of the French state, achieved during the Consulate, was to resolve the bitter struggle between Church and state. A committed secularist, Napoleon was determined to bring the Church under the direct control of the state. This had been the main purpose of the Civil Constitution of the Clergy of 1790. Napoleon also realized, however, that the Civil Constitution had divided the clergy between those who had taken an oath to the nation and those who had refused. Clerical independence had also become a major rallying cry of royalists against the new regime, thereby threatening the stability of the country.

The death of Pope Pius VI (r. 1775–1799), an implacable foe of the revolution, gave Napoleon the opportunity to address this problem. The new pope, Pius VII (r. 1800–1823), who was more sympathetic to liberal causes, was eager to come to terms with the French government. The Concordat, which Napoleon and Pope Pius agreed to in 1801, gave something to both sides, although Napoleon gained more than he conceded. The pope agreed that all the clergy who refused to swear their loyalty to the nation would resign their posts, thus ending the bitter divisions of the past 12 years. The pope would appoint new bishops, but only with Napoleon's prior approval. The state would pay all clerical salaries, and the Church would abandon its claims to the ecclesiastical lands seized by the state at the beginning of the revolution.

These provisions represented formidable concessions to state power, and many French bishops found the terms of the Concordat too unfavorable to the Church. But the pope did manage to secure a statement that Roman Catholicism was the religion of the majority of citizens, and Napoleon agreed to scrap the secular calendar introduced in 1793, thereby restoring Sundays and holy days. Church attendance, having reached historic lows during the period of the Republic, began to rise. The Church regained respect and the freedom to function in French society, and more young recruits joined the clergy. Napoleon did not make many concessions to the Church, but they were significant enough to alienate a group of liberal philosophers and writers known as the Ideologues, who objected to what they saw as the return of "monkish superstition."

With the pope somewhat appeased, Napoleon took unilateral steps to regulate the administration of the French church. In a set of regulations known as the Organic Articles, which were added to the Concordat in 1802, the French church became a department of state, controlled by a ministry, just like any other bureaucratic department. Pronouncements from the pope required prior government approval, and the clergy were obliged to read government decrees from the pulpit. The state also gained control of Protestant congregations, which were given freedom of worship, and their ministers were also paid by the state. Jews received the protection of the state, but the government did not pay the salaries of rabbis.

THE CIVIL CODE Napoleon's most enduring achievement in the realm of state building was the promulgation of a new legal code, the Civil Code of 1804. A legal code is an authoritative and comprehensive statement of the law of a particular country. The model for modern legal codes in Europe was the *Corpus Juris Civilis* of the Roman Empire, which Justinian decreed at Constantinople between 529 and 534 C.E. That code had replaced the thousands of constitutions, customs, and judicial decisions that had been in effect during the Roman Republic and Empire. In compiling the new French code Napoleon, who had just proclaimed himself emperor of the French, imitated Justinian's legal achievement.

The Civil Code also met a long-standing set of demands to reform the confusing and irregular body of French law. Ever since the Middle Ages, France had been governed by a multiplicity of laws. In the southern provinces of the country, those closest to Italy, the law had been influenced by Roman law. In the north, the law was based on local or provincial customs. France needed a common law for all its people. Efforts to produce an authoritative written law code for all parts of the country had begun during the revolution, but Napoleon completed the project and published the code.

The Civil Code, which consisted of more than 2,000 articles, reflected the values of Napoleonic France. Articles guaranteeing the rights of private property, equality before the law, and freedom of religion enshrined key revolutionary ideas. The values promoted by the Civil Code, however, did not include the equality of the sexes. It granted men control of all family property. Women could not buy or sell property without the consent of their husbands. All male heirs were entitled to inherit equal shares of a family estate, but daughters were excluded from the settlement.

The Civil Code, which dealt only with the rights and relationships of private individuals, was the first and most important of six law codes promulgated by Napoleon. Others dealt with civil procedure (1806), commerce (1807), and criminal law (1811). Renamed the **Napoleonic Code** in 1806, the Civil Code had an impact on the law of several countries outside France. It became the basis for the codification of the laws of Switzerland, northern Italy, Poland, and the Netherlands, and it served as a model for the codes of many German territories controlled by France during the Napoleonic period. The Napoleonic Code also influenced the law of French-speaking North America, including the civil law of the state of Louisiana, which bears signs of its influence even today.

Napoleonic Code The name eventually given to the Civil Code of 1804, promulgated by Napoleon, which gave France a uniform and authoritative body of law.

ADMINISTRATIVE CENTRALIZATION Napoleon laid the foundation of modern French civil administration, which acquired the characteristics of rational organization, uniformity, and centralization. All power emanated from Paris, where Napoleon presided over a Council of State. This body consisted of his main ministers, who handled all matters of finance, domestic affairs, and war and oversaw a vast bureaucracy of salaried, trained officials. The central government also exercised direct control over the provinces. In each of the departments, the administrative divisions of France organized in 1790, an official known as a *prefect,* appointed by the central government, enforced orders coming from Paris (see **Map 20.1**). Paid the handsome annual salary of 20,000 francs, the prefects were responsible for the maintenance of public order. They enforced conscription, collected taxes, and supervised local public works, such as the construction and improvement of roads.

MAP **20.1** FRENCH DEPARTMENTS DURING THE REVOLUTION In 1790 France was divided into the 83 departments, each roughly equal in population. A preoccupation with uniformity, a product of the Enlightenment, became a major feature of French revolutionary culture. Note the departments of Vendée, a major center of counterrevolution in 1793, and Gironde, from which the Girondins, the moderate Jacobin party, took their name. In what other ways did the Enlightenment influence the French Revolution?

The men who served in the government of the French Empire belonged to one of two institutions: the civil bureaucracy and the army officer corps. The two were closely related, because the main purpose of the administrative bureaucracy was to prepare for and sustain the war effort. Both institutions were organized hierarchically, and those who held positions in them were trained and salaried. Appointment and promotion were based primarily on talent rather than birth.

The idea of "a career open to all talents," as Napoleon described it, ran counter to the tradition of noble privilege. This was one of the achievements of the revolution that Napoleon perpetuated during the empire. The new system did not amount to a **meritocracy**, in which advancement depends solely on ability and performance, because Napoleon himself made or influenced many appointments on the basis of friendship or kinship. The system did, however, allow people from the ranks of the bourgeoisie to achieve upward social mobility. To recognize their new status, Napoleon created a new order of nonhereditary noblemen, known as *notables*. Instead of inheriting status, these men acquired their titles by governmental service. Napoleon created more than 3,500 notables during his rule, thereby encouraging service to the state and strengthening loyalty to it.

meritocracy The practice of appointing people to office solely on the basis of ability and performance rather than social or economic status.

Napoleon, the Empire, and Europe

Closely related to Napoleon's efforts to build the French state was his creation of a sprawling European empire. This empire was the product of a series of military victories against the armies of Austria, Prussia, Russia, and Spain between 1797 and 1809. The instrument of these victories was the massive army that Napoleon assembled. With more than one million men under arms, it was the largest military force controlled by one man up to this time in European history.

Napoleon's victories against Austria in 1797 and 1800 resulted in territorial gains in Italy and control over the southern Netherlands, now called Belgium. A temporary peace with Britain in 1802 gave Napoleon free rein to reorganize the countries that bordered on France's eastern and southeastern boundaries. In Italy he named himself the president of the newly established Cisalpine Republic, and he transformed the cantons of Switzerland into the Helvetic Republic. Victories over Prussian forces at Jena and Auerstädt in 1806 gave him the opportunity to carve a new German kingdom of Westphalia out of Prussian territory in the Rhineland and to install his brother Jerome as its ruler. In the east Napoleon created the duchy of Warsaw out of Polish lands he seized from Prussia and Austria. In 1806 he formally dissolved the ancient Holy Roman Empire and replaced it with a loose association of 16 German states known as the Confederation of the Rhine (see **Map 20.2**).

Napoleon's final step in his effort to achieve mastery of Europe was the invasion and occupation of Spain. This campaign began as an effort to crush Portugal, an ally of Britain. In May 1808, as French armies marched through Spain en route to Lisbon, the Portuguese capital, a popular insurrection against Spanish rule occurred in Madrid. This spontaneous revolt, which led to the abdication of King Charles IV and the

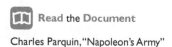

Read the Document

Charles Parquin, "Napoleon's Army"

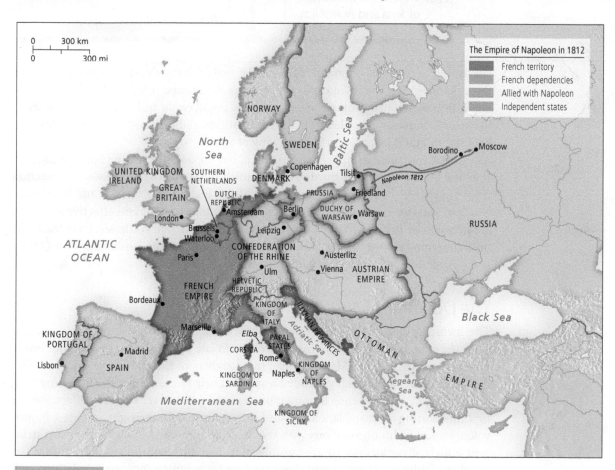

MAP **20.2** THE EMPIRE OF NAPOLEON IN 1812 At its peak the official French Empire had 44 million inhabitants. The population of dependent states in Spain, Italy, Germany, and Poland brought the population of the "Grand Empire" to 80 million people. Why was Napoleon unable to include Russia in his Grand Empire?

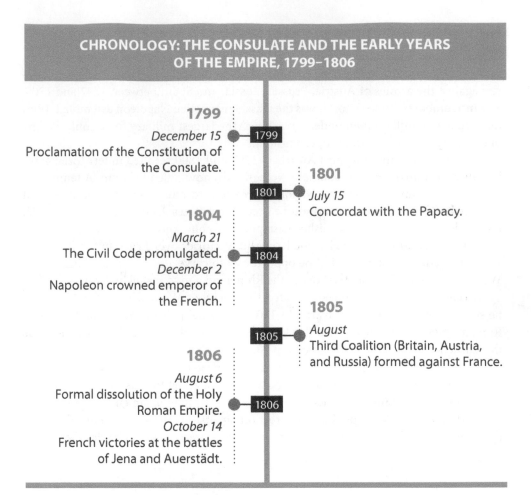

CHRONOLOGY: THE CONSULATE AND THE EARLY YEARS
OF THE EMPIRE, 1799–1806

1799
December 15
Proclamation of the Constitution of
the Consulate.

1799

1801

1801
July 15
Concordat with the Papacy.

1804
March 21
The Civil Code promulgated.
December 2
Napoleon crowned emperor of
the French.

1804

1805
August
Third Coalition (Britain, Austria,
and Russia) formed against France.

1805

1806
August 6
Formal dissolution of the Holy
Roman Empire.
October 14
French victories at the battles
of Jena and Auerstädt.

1806

succession of his son Ferdinand VII, was the first of many developments that caused the collapse of the Spanish Empire in America. In Europe it led to the absorption of Spain into the French Empire. Sensing that he could easily add one more territory to his list of conquests, Napoleon forced Ferdinand to abdicate and summoned his own brother, Joseph Bonaparte, to become king of Spain.

Joseph instituted some reforms in Spain, but the abolition of the Spanish Inquisition and the closing of two-thirds of the Spanish convents triggered a visceral reaction from the Spanish clergy and the general populace. Fighting for Church and king, small bands of local guerillas subjected French forces to intermittent and effective sabotage. An invasion by British forces under the command of Arthur Wellesley, later the Duke of Wellington (1769–1852), in what has become known as the Peninsular War (1808–1813), strengthened Spanish and Portuguese resistance.

 **Read the Document**

Sir Harry Smith on Napoleon's Army
in Spain

The Downfall of Napoleon

The turning point in Napoleon's personal fortunes and those of his empire came in 1810. After securing a divorce from Josephine in late 1809 because she had not borne him an heir, he married Marie-Louise, the daughter of the Habsburg emperor. This diplomatic marriage, which produced a son and heir to the throne the following year, should have made the French Empire more secure, but it had the opposite effect. For the first time during his rule, Napoleon faced dissent from both the right and the left, provoked in part by his negotiations with the Austrian Habsburgs. Despite the most stringent efforts at censorship, royalist and Jacobin literature poured off the presses. The number of military deserters and those evading conscription increased. Relations with the papacy reached a breaking point when Napoleon annexed the Papal States, at which point Pope Pius VII, who had negotiated the Concordat of 1801, excommunicated him.

Dissent at home had the effect of driving the megalomaniacal emperor to seek more glory and further conquests. In this frame of mind Napoleon made the ill-advised decision to invade Russia. The motives for engaging in this overly ambitious military campaign were not completely irrational. Victory over Russia promised to give France control of the Black Sea, and that in turn could ultimately have led to the control of Constantinople and the entire Middle East. More immediately, defeating Russia would have been necessary to enforce the French blockade of British goods, which Russia had refused to support.

The problem with a Russian invasion was that it stretched Napoleon's lines of communication too far and his resources too thin. Even before the invasion it was becoming increasingly difficult to feed, equip, and train the huge army he had assembled. The Grand Army that crossed from Poland into Russia in 1812 was not the efficient military force that Napoleon had commanded in the early years of the empire. Many of his best soldiers were fighting in the guerilla war in Spain. Casualties and desertions had forced Napoleon to call up new recruits who were not properly trained. Half the army, moreover, had been recruited from the population of conquered countries, making their loyalty to Napoleon uncertain.

The tactics of the Russians contributed to the failure of the invasion. Instead of engaging the Grand Army in combat, the Russian army kept retreating, pulling Napoleon further east toward Moscow. On September 7 the two armies clashed at Borodino, suffering a staggering 77,000 casualties in all. The Russian army then continued its retreat eastward. When Napoleon reached Moscow he found it deserted, and fires deliberately set by Muscovites had destroyed more than two-thirds of the city. Napoleon, facing the onset of a dreaded Russian winter and rapidly diminishing supplies, began the long retreat back to France. Skirmishes with the Russians along the way, which cost him 25,000 lives just crossing the Beresina River, conspired with the cold and hunger to destroy his army. During the entire Russian campaign his army lost a total of 380,000 men to death, imprisonment, or desertion. In the midst of this horror Napoleon, oblivious to the suffering of his troops, reported back to Paris, "The health of the emperor has never been better."

Not to be discouraged, Napoleon soon began preparing for further conquests. Once again his enemies formed a coalition against him, pledging to restore the independence of the countries that had become his satellites or dependents. Napoleon scored a few victories in the late summer of 1813, but in October allied forces inflicted a crushing defeat on him in the Battle of the Nations at Leipzig. Austrian troops administered another blow to the French in northern Italy, and the British finally drove them out of Spain. Napoleon's army was pushed back into France. A massive allied force advanced into Paris and occupied the city. After extensive political maneuvering, including a vote by the Senate to depose him, Napoleon abdicated on April 6, 1814. The allies promptly exiled him to the Mediterranean island of Elba. As he made the journey to the coast, crowds surrounding his coach shouted "Down with the tyrant!" while some villagers hanged him in effigy.

This course of events led to the restoration of the Bourbon monarchy. By the terms of the first Treaty of Paris in May 1814, the allies restored the brother of Louis XVI, the Count of Provence, to the French throne as Louis XVIII (r. 1814–1824). An implacable foe of the revolution, Louis strove to undermine its achievements. The white Bourbon flag replaced the revolutionary tricolor. Catholicism was once again recognized as the state religion. Exiled royalists returned to their high-ranking positions in the army. Nonetheless, Louis accepted a Constitutional Charter that incorporated many of the changes made between 1789 and 1791. Representative government, with a relatively limited franchise, replaced the absolutism of the Old Regime. The Constitutional Charter reaffirmed equality before the law, freedom of religion, and freedom of expression. Even more important, the powers of the state that the National Assembly and the Directory had extended and Napoleon had enhanced were maintained. The

Encounters and Transformations

The French Encounter the Egyptians, 1798–1801

Napoleon's expedition to Egypt in 1798 marked one of the few times during the revolutionary period that the French came in direct contact with non-Western peoples. The expedition resulted in the military occupation of the country for three years and set the stage for the first extensive encounters between Egyptians and Europeans since the Ottoman conquest of Egypt in the sixteenth century. At that time Egypt had become a semiautonomous province of the Ottoman Empire and had very little contact with the West. Egypt's isolation from the West meant that it had little exposure to the scientific and technological discoveries that had taken place in western Europe during the previous 300 years.

In addition to 38,000 soldiers, Napoleon brought with him 165 scholars who were organized in a Commission of Science and Arts. These men came from virtually every branch of learning: surveyors, cartographers, civil engineers, architects, botanists, physicians, chemists, and mineralogists. The commission also included artists, archaeologists, writers, and musicians. Their purpose was to give Napoleon information on the people and the resources of the country so that he could more easily subject it to French domination. A small group of these scholars set up an Institute of Egypt, whose mission was to propagate the Enlightenment and to undertake research on the history, people, and economy of the country. This involved the scholarly study of Egyptian antiquities, including the pyramids.

This work of the institute ushered in a long period in which many artifacts of Egyptian antiquity were taken from the country and transported to European museums and palaces. Members of the institute encouraged this cultural plundering, arguing that these Egyptian additions to the collections of the Louvre would embellish the glory of France. This ransacking of native Egyptian antiquities represented a form of cultural imperialism that continued unabated during the nineteenth century.

A description of Egypt, *Travels in Upper and Lower Egypt* (1802), written by a member of the institute, Dominique-Vivant Denon, reflected a different sort of French cultural imperialism. In this two-volume work, Vivant Denon described the different "races" of Egyptians whom he had encountered in the port town of Rosetta. He described the Copts, the most ancient Egyptians, as "swarthy Nubians" with flat foreheads, high cheekbones, and short broad noses and tendencies toward "ignorance, drunkenness, cunning, and finesse." He described the physical and personal characteristics of the Arabs and the Turks in more appealing terms, but they too were often reduced to the "degraded state of animals."

Expressions of French cultural superiority permeated other contemporary accounts of Napoleon's expedition. A multivolume work, *The Description of Egypt*, claimed that Napoleon wanted to procure for Egyptians "all the advantages of a perfected civilization." It praised him for bringing modern knowledge to a country that had been "plunged into darkness." These attitudes provided a justification for the subsequent economic exploitation of Egypt, first by the French and later by the British, during the nineteenth century.

JEAN-CHARLES TARDIEU, *THE FRENCH ARMY HALTS AT SYENE, UPPER EGYPT, ON FEBRUARY 2, 1799* This painting depicts a cultural encounter between French soldiers and Egyptians in the city of Syene (now Aswan) during the Egyptian campaign of 1798–1799. The soldiers are scribbling on the ruins of ancient Egypt, indicating a lack of respect for Egyptian culture.

SOURCE: Jean-Charles Tardieu (1765–1830), "Troops Halted on the Banks of the Nile, 2nd February 1812," oil on canvas. Chateau de Versailles, France/Lauros/Giraudon/The Bridgeman Art Library.

For Discussion

In what ways did Vivant Denon's work reflect the values that were cultivated during the Enlightenment?

administrative division of France into departments continued, and the Napoleonic Code remained in force. France had experienced a counterrevolution in 1814, but it did not simply turn the political clock back to 1788. Some of the political achievements of the previous 25 years were preserved.

Despite his disgrace and exile, Napoleon still commanded loyalty from his troops and large segments of the population. While in power he had constructed a legend that

JOAQUIN SOROLLA Y BASTIDA, *THE 2ND OF MAY IN MADRID* This painting depicts the unsuccessful Spanish revolt against Napoleon's military forces in Madrid on May 2, 1808. A French unit executed hundreds of the rebels the following day.

SOURCE: Art Resource XJL 186995.

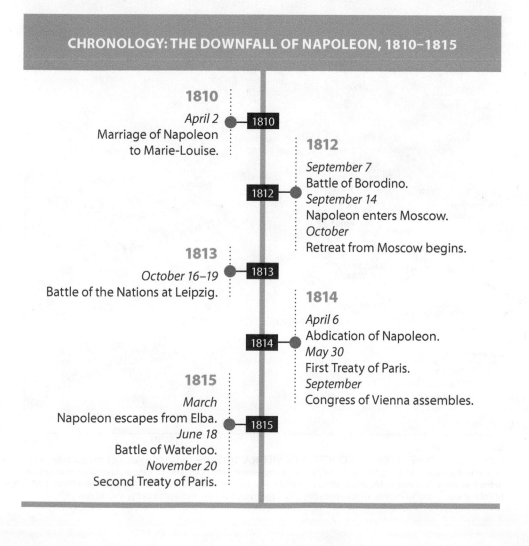

CHRONOLOGY: THE DOWNFALL OF NAPOLEON, 1810–1815

1810

April 2
Marriage of Napoleon
to Marie-Louise.

1812

September 7
Battle of Borodino.
September 14
Napoleon enters Moscow.
October
Retreat from Moscow begins.

1813

October 16–19
Battle of the Nations at Leipzig.

1814

April 6
Abdication of Napoleon.
May 30
First Treaty of Paris.
September
Congress of Vienna assembles.

1815

March
Napoleon escapes from Elba.
June 18
Battle of Waterloo.
November 20
Second Treaty of Paris.

drew on strong patriotic sentiment. Supporters throughout France continued to promote his cause in the same way that royalists had maintained that of the Bourbon monarchy since 1792. The strength of the Napoleonic legend became apparent in March 1815, when Napoleon escaped from Elba and landed in southern France. Promising to rid the country of the exiled royalists who had returned and thereby save the revolutionary cause, he won over peasants, workers, and soldiers. Regiment after regiment joined him as he marched toward Paris. By the time he arrived, Louis XVIII had gone into exile once again, and Napoleon found himself back in power.

But not for long. The allied European powers quickly began to assemble yet another coalition. Fearing that the allies would launch a massive invasion of France, Napoleon decided to strike first. He marched an army of 200,000 men into the Austrian Netherlands, where the allies responded by amassing 700,000 troops. Near the small village of Waterloo, south of Brussels, Napoleon met the British forces of the Duke of Wellington, who had turned the tide against him during the Peninsula War. Reinforced by Prussian troops, Wellington inflicted a devastating defeat on the French army, which lost 28,000 men and went into a full-scale retreat. Napoleon abdicated once again and was exiled to the remote South Atlantic island of St. Helena, from which escape was impossible. He died there in 1821.

Read the Document

Napoleon's Exile to St. Helena (1815)

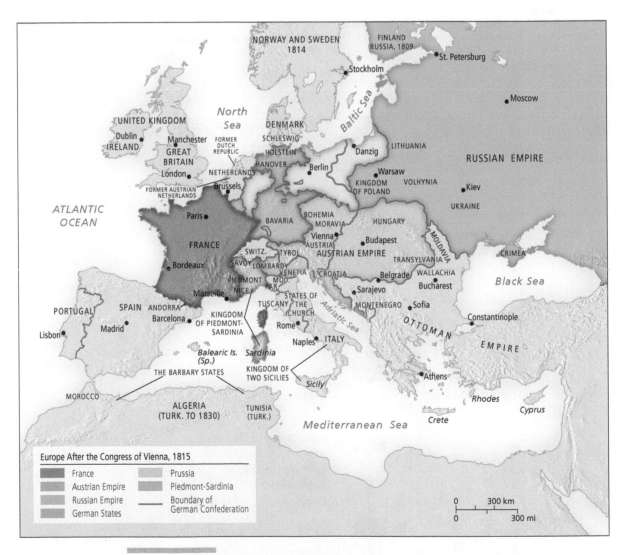

MAP **20.3** EUROPE AFTER THE CONGRESS OF VIENNA, 1815 The Congress scaled back the boundaries of France to their status in 1790, ceded territory to Austria in western and northeastern Italy, and created the Kingdom of the Netherlands, a new German Confederation, and a new Kingdom of Poland ruled by Russia. The western part of Poland was ceded to Prussia. Which states benefited the most from this redrawing of the map of Europe?

Even before the Battle of Waterloo, the major powers of Europe had gathered in Vienna to redraw the boundaries of the European states that had been created, dismembered, or transformed during the preceding 52 years (see **Map 20.3**). Under the leadership of the Austrian foreign minister, Prince Klemens von Metternich (1773–1859), this conference, known as the **Congress of Vienna**, worked out a settlement that was intended to preserve the balance of power in Europe and at the same time uphold the principle of dynastic legitimacy. By the terms of a separate Treaty of Paris (the second in two years) the boundaries of France were scaled back to what they had been in 1790, before it had begun its wars of expansion. To create a buffer state on the northern boundary of France, the Congress annexed the Austrian Netherlands to the Dutch Republic, which now became the Kingdom of the Netherlands with William I, a prince of the House of Orange, as its king. The treaty ceded territory along the Rhineland to Prussia, while Austria, now named the Austrian Empire, gained territory in Italy. In place of the defunct Holy Roman Empire, the Congress established a new German Confederation, a loose coalition of 39 separate territories with a weak legislative assembly. The duchy of Warsaw, established in 1807 and renamed the Kingdom of Poland in 1812, was partitioned between Prussia and Russia. The five major powers that had drawn this new map of Europe—Britain, Austria, Prussia, Russia, and France—agreed to meet annually to prevent any one country, especially France but also Russia, from achieving military dominance of the European Continent.

Congress of Vienna A conference of the major powers of Europe in 1814–1815 to establish a new balance of power at the end of the Napoleonic Wars.

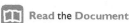 Read the Document

The German Act of Confederation 1814

The Legacy of the French Revolution

20.5 In what ways did the French Revolution change the course of European and Western history?

With the conclusion of the Congress of Vienna a tumultuous period of European and Western history finally came to an end. Not only had France experienced a revolution, but every country in Europe and America had felt its effects. Governments were toppled in countries as far apart as Poland and Peru. Added to this turbulence was the experience of incessant warfare. France was at war for more than 20 years during the Republic and the Empire, and it had involved almost all European powers in the struggle. With armies constantly in need of provisions and supplies, high taxation, galloping inflation, and food shortages inflicted economic hardship on a large portion of the European population.

The cost of all this instability and warfare in terms of human life was staggering. Within the space of one generation almost two million European soldiers were killed in action, wasted by disease, or starved or frozen to death. In France alone just under 500,000 soldiers died during the revolutionary wars of 1792–1802 and another 916,000 during the wars of the Empire. Internal political disturbances took the lives of hundreds of thousands of civilians from all ranks of society, not only in France, but throughout Europe. Unprecedented fears of internal and external subversion fed the violence at all levels. Government officials, collaborators, counterrevolutionaries, and imagined enemies of the state were all executed. This spate of violence and death—much of it in the name of liberty—occurred almost entirely at the hands of the state or its enemies.

What was achieved at this extraordinary price? How did the France of 1815 differ from the France of 1788? What on balance had changed? Historians once argued that as a result of the revolution the bourgeoisie, composed of merchants, manufacturers, and other commoners of substantial wealth, had replaced the nobility as the dominant social and political class in France. This argument can no longer be sustained. The nobility certainly lost many of their privileges in 1789, and many of them went into exile during the revolutionary period, but the position they had in French society in 1815 did not differ greatly from what it had been under the Old Regime. In both periods there was considerable blurring of the distinctions between nobility and bourgeoisie. The revolutionary period did not witness the emergence of a new class of industrial entrepreneurs either. The only group that definitely profited from the revolution in the long run was men of property, regardless of their membership in any social category or "class." Wealthy men emerged triumphant in the Directory, found favor during the Napoleonic period, and became the most important members of political society after the monarchy was restored.

It would be difficult to argue that *women* of any social rank benefited from the revolution. During the early years of the revolution, women participated actively in public life. They were involved in many demonstrations in Paris, including the storming of the Bastille and the march to Versailles. But women never achieved the position of equality with men for which the Marquis de Condorcet and Olympe de Gouges had hoped. The radical Jacobins dealt that goal a major setback when they banned all women's clubs and societies on the grounds that female participation in public life would harm the institution of the family. This action ended the extensive participation of women in political life, which had begun during the eighteenth century, especially in the salons. During the nineteenth century French women exercised influence in the private sphere of the home, but not in the public sphere of politics.

It is even more difficult to identify permanent economic changes as a result of the revolution. The elimination of the remnants of feudalism may have made France marginally more capitalist than it had been before the revolution, but agricultural and mercantile capitalism had long been entrenched in French society. Nor did the Continental System, the blockade of British goods from all European ports initiated in 1806, allow French industry to catch up with that of Great Britain. Whatever economic gains were made under the protective shield of the state were offset by the adverse economic effects of 22 years of nearly continuous warfare. In the long run the revolutionary period delayed the process of industrialization that had entered its preliminary stages in France during the 1780s and retarded the growth of the French economy for the remainder of the nineteenth century.

The permanent legacy of the French Revolution lies in the realm of politics. First, the period from 1789 to 1815 triggered an enormous growth in the competence and power of the state. This trend had begun before the revolution, but the desire of the revolutionaries to transform every aspect of human life in the service of the revolution, coupled with the necessity of utilizing all the country's resources in the war effort, gave the state more control over the everyday life of its citizens than ever before. Fifteen years of Napoleonic rule only accentuated this trend, and after 1815 many of those powers remained with the government.

A second permanent political achievement of the French Revolution was the promotion of the doctrine of popular sovereignty. The belief that the people constituted the highest political authority in the state became so entrenched during the revolution that it could never be completely suppressed, either in France or in the other countries of Europe. Napoleon recognized its power when he asked the people to approve political changes he had already made by his own authority. After the restoration of the monarchy the doctrine of popular sovereignty was promoted mainly by the press, which continued to employ the new revolutionary rhetoric to keep alive the high ideals and aspirations of the revolution. The doctrine also contributed to the formation of two nineteenth-century ideologies, liberalism and nationalism, which will be discussed in Chapter 22.

CONCLUSION

The French Revolution and Western Civilization

The French Revolution was a central event in the history of the West. It began as an internal French affair, reflecting the social and political tensions of the Old Regime, but it soon became a turning point in European and Western history. Proclamations of the natural rights of humanity gave the ideals of the revolution widespread appeal, and a period of protracted warfare succeeded in disseminating those ideals outside the boundaries of France.

Underlying the export of French revolutionary ideology was the belief that France had become the standard-bearer of Western civilization. French people believed they were *la grande nation,* the country that had reached the highest level of political and social organization. They did not believe they had acquired this exalted status by inheritance. Unlike the English revolutionaries of the seventeenth century, the French did not claim that they were the heirs of a medieval constitution. French republicans of the 1790s attributed none of their national preeminence to the monarchy, whose memory they took drastic steps to erase. They considered the secular political culture that emerged during the French Revolution to be entirely new.

The export of French revolutionary political culture during the Republic and the Empire led to widespread changes in the established order. Regimes were toppled, French puppets acquired political power, boundaries of states were redrawn, and traditional authorities were challenged. Liberal reforms were enacted, new constitutions were written, and new law codes were promulgated. The Europe of 1815 could not be mistaken for the Europe of 1789.

The ideas of the French Revolution, like those of the Enlightenment that had helped to inspire them, did not go unchallenged. From the very early years of the revolution they encountered determined opposition, both in France and abroad. As the revolution lost its appeal in France, the forces of conservatism and reaction gathered strength. At the end of the Napoleonic period, the Congress of Vienna took steps to restore the legitimate rulers of European states and to prevent revolution from recurring. It appeared that the revolution would be completely reversed, but that was not the case. The ideas born of the revolution continued to inspire demands for political reform in Europe during the nineteenth century, and those demands, just like those in the 1790s, met with fierce resistance.

MAKING CONNECTIONS

1. Did the events of 1789 constitute a revolution in the sense that they brought about a fundamental change in the system of government? In what sense did the establishment of the Republic in 1792 represent a more radical change in French politics?
2. To what extent did the ideas of the Enlightenment inspire the events of the French Revolution?
3. How did the Jacobin commitment to equality lead to the Reign of Terror?
4. Did the French Revolution end in 1799 or did Napoleon perpetuate it in any significant ways?
5. Why did Napoleon fail to realize his diplomatic and military objectives?

TAKING IT FURTHER

For suggested readings see page R-1.

On MyHistoryLab

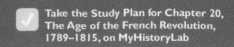

✓ Take the Study Plan for Chapter 20,
The Age of the French Revolution,
1789–1815, on MyHistoryLab

Chapter Review

The First French Revolution, 1789–1791

20.1 Why did the Old Regime collapse in 1789, and what revolutionary changes took place during the next two years?

A financial and political crisis due to the king's efforts to pay off debts from protracted periods of warfare, combined with a social crisis fueled by the high price of bread, caused a breakdown of social order. The revolution eliminated noble and clerical privileges, reorganized the Church, and instituted the idea that all men had a natural right to liberty, property, and equality before the law, freedom from oppression, and religious toleration. The king became a constitutional monarch, retaining only the power to suspend legislation, direct foreign policy, and command the armed forces.

The French Republic, 1792–1799

20.2 How did a second more radical revolution in 1792 create a regime that instituted the Reign of Terror?

Military failures abroad fueled paranoia at home, where fears that invading armies would undermine or destroy the revolution grew. The formal abolishment of the monarchy and the declaration of France as a republic dedicated to the principles of liberty, equality, and fraternity soon followed. Internal dissent within the government festered as the republican regime encountered increasing opposition from foreign and domestic enemies. The revolutionary courts executed 17,000 people, including substantial numbers of clergy and nobility, but a majority of the Terror's victims were artisans and peasants.

Cultural Change in France During the Revolution

20.3 In what ways did the political events of the revolution change French culture?

A new, revolutionary political culture was established, its sole purpose to legitimize and glorify the new government. All other forms of culture were subordinated to this new culture, with millions of books deemed to have royalist or religious themes sold off or lost, and museums like the Louvre created to house works of art that seemed incompatible with the republican rejection of Christianity.

The Napoleonic Era, 1799–1815

20.4 Did the rule of Napoleon from 1799 to 1814 confirm or betray the achievements of the French Revolution?

Napoleon combined the egalitarian values of the revolution with the authoritarianism of the Old Regime. He supported the equality of all Frenchmen, especially equality of opportunity in service of the state,

but his use of the language of liberty disguised what was essentially a dictatorship. He continued the centralization and growth of state power and administration begun during the revolution, and he extended France's military mission to spread the revolution throughout Europe.

The Legacy of the French Revolution

20.5 In what ways did the French Revolution change the course of European and Western history?

The French Revolution's legacy was mostly political. First, the revolutionaries' goal to transform every aspect of life in service of the revolution and the need to use all of the country's resources in the war effort supported the growth and power of the state. Second, the belief that the highest political authority in the state was its people is an idea that became so entrenched during the revolution that it could never be completely suppressed, either in France or in the other countries of Europe.

Chapter Time Line

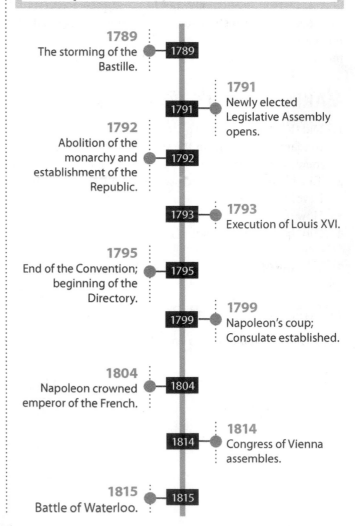

1789 The storming of the Bastille.
— 1789

1791 Newly elected Legislative Assembly opens.
— 1791

1792 Abolition of the monarchy and establishment of the Republic.
— 1792

1793 Execution of Louis XVI.
— 1793

1795 End of the Convention; beginning of the Directory.
— 1795

1799 Napoleon's coup; Consulate established.
— 1799

1804 Napoleon crowned emperor of the French.
— 1804

1814 Congress of Vienna assembles.
— 1814

1815 Battle of Waterloo.
— 1815

21 The Industrial Revolution

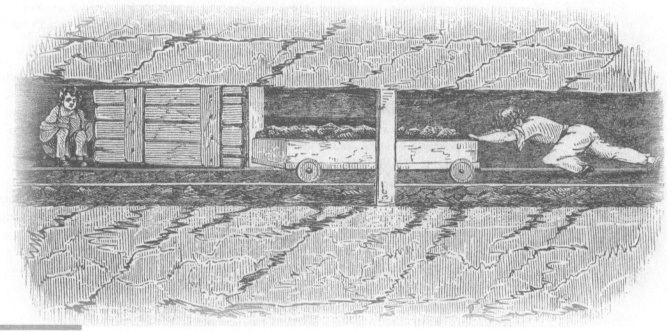

CHILD LABOR IN THE MINES A child hurrying coal through a tunnel in a mine.

I **n 1842 a 17-year-old girl, Patience Kershaw, testified before a British** parliamentary committee regarding the practice of employing children and women in the nation's mines. When the girl made her appearance, the members of the committee observed that she was "an ignorant, filthy, ragged, and deplorable-looking object, such as one of uncivilized natives of the prairies would be shocked to look upon." Patience, who had never been to school and could not read or write, told the committee that she was one of ten children, all of whom had at one time worked in the coal mines, although three of her sisters now worked in a textile mill. She went to the pit at five in the morning and came out at five at night. Her job in the mines was to hurry coal, that is, to pull carts of coal through the narrow tunnels of the mine. Each cart weighed 300 pounds, and

LEARNING OBJECTIVES

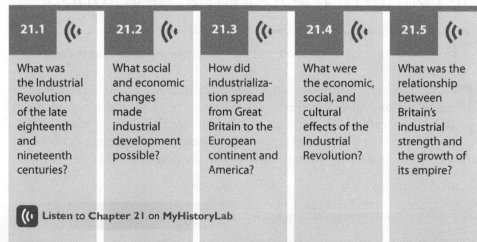

21.1	21.2	21.3	21.4	21.5
What was the Industrial Revolution of the late eighteenth and nineteenth centuries?	What social and economic changes made industrial development possible?	How did industrialization spread from Great Britain to the European continent and America?	What were the economic, social, and cultural effects of the Industrial Revolution?	What was the relationship between Britain's industrial strength and the growth of its empire?

Listen to Chapter 21 on MyHistoryLab

⊙ Watch the Video Series on MyHistoryLab

Learn about some key topics related to this chapter with the *MyHistoryLab Video Series: Key Topics in Western Civilization*

every day she hauled 11 of them one mile. The carts were attached to her head and shoulders by a chain and belt, and the pressure of the cart had worn a bald spot on her head. Patience hurried coal for 12 hours straight, not taking any time for her midday meal, which she ate as she worked. While she was working, the men and boys who dug the coal and put it in the carts would often beat her and take sexual liberties with her. Patience told the committee, "I am the only girl in the pit; there are about 20 boys and 15 men. All the men are naked. I would rather work in a mill than a coal pit."[1]

Patience Kershaw was one of the human casualties of a development that historians refer to as the Industrial Revolution. This process, which fundamentally transformed human life, involved the extensive use of machinery in the production of goods. Much of that machinery was driven by steam engines, which required coal to produce the steam. Coal mining itself became a major industry, and the men who owned and operated the mines tried to hire workers, many of them children, at the lowest possible wage. This desire to maximize profits led to the employment, physical hardship, and abuse of girls like Patience Kershaw.

The Industrial Revolution did more than create harrowing labor conditions. It resulted in a staggering increase in the volume and range of products made available to consumers, from machine-produced clothing to household utensils. It made possible unprecedented and sustained economic growth. The Industrial Revolution facilitated the rapid transportation of passengers as well as goods across large expanses of territory, mainly on the railroads that were constructed in all industrialized countries. It brought about a new awareness of the position of workers in the economic system, and it unleashed powerful political forces intended to improve the lot of these workers.

The Industrial Revolution thus played a crucial role in redefining and reshaping the West. Until the late nineteenth century industrialization took place only in Western nations. During that century "the West" gradually became identified with countries that had industrial economies. When some non-Western countries introduced mechanized industry in the twentieth century, largely by imitating Western example, the geographical boundaries of the West shifted.

This chapter will address the following question:

How did the Industrial Revolution transform Western civilization?

The Nature of the Industrial Revolution

21.1 What was the Industrial Revolution of the late eighteenth and nineteenth centuries?

The Industrial Revolution, which took place in Great Britain during the late eighteenth and early nineteenth centuries and in other European countries and America after 1815, consisted of four closely related developments: the introduction of new industrial technology, the utilization of mineral sources of energy, the concentration of labor in factories, and the development of new methods of transportation.

New Industrial Technology

The Industrial Revolution ushered in the machine age, and to this day machines are the most striking feature of modern industrial economies. In the late eighteenth century industrial machines were novelties, but their numbers increased dramatically in the early nineteenth century. For example, the power loom, a machine used for weaving cloth, was invented in Britain in 1787 but not put into widespread use until the 1820s. By 1836 there were more than 60,000 power looms in just one English county.

Machines became so common in Britain that machine-making itself became a major industry, supplying its products to other manufacturers rather than to individual consumers. Machines were introduced in the textile, iron, printing, papermaking, and engineering industries and were used in every stage of manufacture. Machines extracted minerals for use as either raw materials or sources of energy, transported those materials to the factories, saved time and labor in the actual manufacturing of commodities, and carried the finished products to market. Eventually machines were used in agriculture, facilitating both the plowing of fields and the harvesting of crops.

The most significant of the new machines were devices for producing textiles and the steam engine, which were first used in mining and the iron industry. These pieces of machinery became almost synonymous with the Industrial Revolution, and their invention in the 1760s appropriately marked its beginning.

TEXTILE MACHINERY Until the late eighteenth century, Europeans produced textiles entirely by hand. They spun yarn on spinning wheels and wove cloth on hand looms. Wool remained the main textile produced in Europe until the early eighteenth century, when a new material, cotton, became immensely popular, mainly because of its greater comfort. The demand for cotton yarn was greater than the quantities spinners could supply. To meet this demand a British inventor, James Hargreaves, in 1767 constructed a new machine, the spinning jenny, which greatly increased the amount of cotton yarn that could be spun and thus made available for weaving. The original jenny, a hand machine used in the homes of spinners, consisted of only eight spindles, but it later accommodated as many as 120.

📖 Read the Document

Richard Guest, *The Creation of the Steam Loom*

🔍 View the **Closer Look**   The Great Exhibition in London

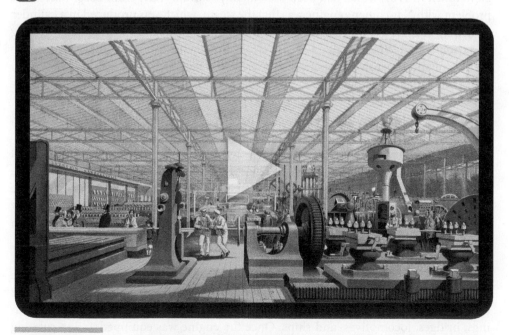

EXHIBIT OF MACHINERY AT THE CRYSTAL PALACE EXHIBITION IN LONDON IN 1851 During the Industrial Revolution the manufacture of heavy machinery itself became an industry.

The spinning of yarn on the jenny required a stronger warp, the yarn that ran lengthwise on a loom. A power-driven machine, the water frame, introduced by the barber and wigmaker Richard Arkwright in 1769, made the production of this stronger warp possible. In 1779 Samuel Crompton, using tools he had purchased with his earnings as a fiddle player at a local theater, combined the jenny and the frame in one machine, called the mule. Crompton worked on his machine only at night to keep it secret, and the strange noises coming out of his workshop made his neighbors think his house was haunted. The mule, which could spin as much as 300 times the amount of yarn produced by one spinning wheel, became the main spinning machine of the early Industrial Revolution. Both the water frame and the mule required power, and that requirement led to the centralization of the textile industry in large rural mills located near rivers so that their water wheels could drive the machinery.

The tremendous success of the mule eventually produced more yarn than the weavers could handle on their hand looms. Edmund Cartwright, an Oxford-educated clergyman, supported by monies from his heiress wife, addressed that need with the invention of the power loom in 1787. In that same year he put his new invention to use in a weaving mill he built near the town of Doncaster. The power loom, like the spinning jenny, the water frame, and the mule, met a specific need within the industry. It also gave the producer a competitive advantage by saving time, reducing the cost of labor, and increasing production. Two power looms run by a 15-year-old boy, for example, could produce more than three times what a skilled hand loom weaver could turn out in the same time using only the old hand device, the flying shuttle. The net effect of all these machines was the production of more than 200 times as much cotton cloth in 1850 as in 1780. By 1800 cotton became Britain's largest industry, producing more than 20 percent of the world's cloth; by 1850 that percentage had risen to more than 50 percent. Indeed, by midcentury, cotton accounted for 70 percent of the value of all British exports.

Read the Document

Leeds Woolen Workers, "Petition"

THE STEAM ENGINE The steam engine was even more important than the new textile machinery because it was used in almost every stage of the productive process, including the operation of textile machinery itself. James Watt, a Scottish engineer, invented the steam engine in 1763. Watt's steam engine improved the engine invented by Thomas Newcomen in 1709, which had been used mainly to drain water from deep mines. The problem with Newcomen's engine was that the steam, which was produced in a cylinder heated by coal, had to be cooled to make the piston return, and the process of heating and cooling had to be repeated for each stroke of the piston. The engine was therefore inefficient and expensive to operate. Watt created a separate chamber where the steam could be condensed without affecting the heat of the cylinder. The result was a more efficient and cost-effective machine that could provide more power than any other source. Watt's pride in his invention was matched only by his pride in his Scottish nationality. Upon receiving a patent for the new device, he boasted, "This was made by a Scot."

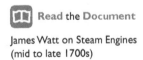

Read the Document

James Watt on Steam Engines
(mid to late 1700s)

After designing the steam engine, Watt teamed up with a Birmingham metal manufacturer, Matthew Boulton, to produce it on a large scale. Boulton provided the capital necessary to begin this process and hire the skilled laborers to assemble the machines. He also had ambitious plans for marketing the new invention throughout the world. "It would not be worth my while to make for three countries only," Boulton said, "but I find it well worth my while to make for the whole world."

The steam engine soon became the workhorse of the Industrial Revolution. Not only did it pump water from mines, but it also helped raise minerals such as iron ore from those mines. It provided the intense blast of heat that was necessary to re-smelt pig iron into cast iron, which in turn was used to make industrial machinery, buildings, bridges, locomotives, and ships. Once the engine was equipped with a rotating device, it drove factory machinery in the textile mills, and it eventually powered the railroad locomotives that carried industrial goods to market.

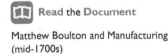

Read the Document

Matthew Boulton and Manufacturing
(mid-1700s)

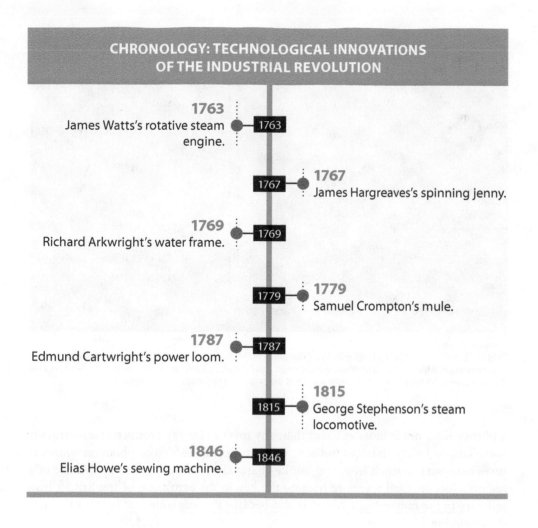

CHRONOLOGY: TECHNOLOGICAL INNOVATIONS OF THE INDUSTRIAL REVOLUTION

1763
James Watts's rotative steam engine.

1767
James Hargreaves's spinning jenny.

1769
Richard Arkwright's water frame.

1779
Samuel Crompton's mule.

1787
Edmund Cartwright's power loom.

1815
George Stephenson's steam locomotive.

1846
Elias Howe's sewing machine.

Mineral Sources of Energy

Until the late eighteenth century, either humans or beasts provided the power for most economic activity. Either people tilled the soil themselves, using a spade, or they yoked oxen to pull a plow. Either they carried materials and goods on their backs or they used horses to transport them. In either case the energy for these tasks came ultimately from organic sources, the food that was needed to feed farmers or their animals. If workers needed heat, they had to burn an organic material, wood or charcoal, to produce it. The amount of energy that these sources generated was therefore limited by the capacity of a geographical region to produce sufficient wood, charcoal, or food.

Organic sources of energy were of course renewable, in that new crops could be grown and forests replanted, but the long periods of time that these processes took, coupled with the limited volume of organic material that could be extracted from an acre of land, made it difficult to sustain economic growth. The only viable alternatives to organic sources of energy before the eighteenth century were those that tapped the forces of nature: windmills, which drained fields mainly in the Netherlands, and water wheels, which were driven by water pressure from river currents, waterfalls, or human-made channels that regulated the flow of water. The energy produced by wind and water was difficult to harness, however, and was available only in certain places. Moreover, these natural sources of energy could not produce heat.

The decisive change in harnessing energy for industrial purposes was the successful use of minerals, originally coal but in the twentieth century also oil and uranium, as the main sources of energy in the production and transportation of goods. These minerals were not inexhaustible, but the supplies could last for centuries,

PHILIPPE JACQUES DE LOUTHERBOURG, *COALBROOKDALE BY NIGHT* (1801) This painting depicts the intense heat produced by the coal bellows used to smelt iron in Coalbrookdale, an English town in the Severn Valley that was one of the key centers of industrial activity at the beginning of the nineteenth century.

and they were much more efficient than any form of energy produced from organic materials, including charcoal and peat. Coal produced the high combustion temperatures necessary to smelt iron, and unlike charcoal it was not limited by the size of a region's forests. Coal therefore became the key to the expansion of the British iron industry in the nineteenth century. It also became the sole source of heat for the new steam engine.

As the Industrial Revolution progressed, it relied increasingly on coal as its main fuel. Largely because of the demands of the mining, textile, and metal industries, coal mining became a major industry itself with an enormous labor force. By 1850 British mines employed about 5 percent of the entire national workforce. These miners were just as instrumental as textile workers in making Britain an industrial nation.

The Growth of Factories

During the Industrial Revolution, mechanized factories gradually replaced two types of workplaces in which most industrial production took place. These two predecessors of the factory were the rural industrial cottage and the large urban handicraft workshop.

Beginning in the late sixteenth century, capitalist entrepreneurs began employing families in the countryside to spin and weave cloth and make nails and cutlery. In this **domestic system** the entrepreneur provided the workers with raw materials and later paid them a fixed rate for each finished product. The workers performed their labor in their cottages, which were situated in agricultural areas. One feature of the domestic system was that all the members of the family, including children, participated in this industrial work, mainly when they were not engaged in planting or harvesting their crops.

In the early nineteenth century rural cottage industry gradually gave way to production in large factories. The great advantage of factory production over that of the rural cottage was mechanization, which became cost-efficient in a central industrial workplace. In factories, moreover, the entrepreneur could reduce the cost of labor and transportation, exercise tighter control over the quality of goods, and increase

domestic system An economic arrangement developed in the sixteenth century in which capitalist entrepreneurs employed families in rural areas to spin and weave cloth and make nails and cutlery.

productivity by concentrating workers in one location. Temporary labor shortages sometimes made the transition from rural industry to factory production imperative.

The second type of industrial workplace that the factory replaced was the large handicraft workshop. Usually located in towns and cities, rather than in the countryside, these workshops employed relatively small numbers of people with different skills who worked collectively on the manufacture of a variety of items, such as pottery and munitions. The owner of the workshop supplied the raw materials, paid the workers' wages, and gained a profit from selling the finished products.

The large handicraft workshop made possible a **division of labor**—the assignment of one stage of production to each worker or group of workers. The effect of the division of labor on productivity was evident even in the manufacture of simple items such as buttons and pins. In *The Wealth of Nations* (1776), the economist Adam Smith (1723–1790) used a pin factory in London to illustrate how the division of labor could increase per capita productivity from no more than 20 pins a day to the astonishing total of 4,800 pins in the same period of time.

Like the cottages engaged in rural industry, the large handicraft workshop eventually gave way to the mechanized factory. The main difference between the workshop and the factory was that the factory did not require a body of skilled workers. The factory worker's job was simply to tend to the machinery. The only skill factory workers needed was manual dexterity to operate the machinery. Only those workers who made industrial machinery remained craftsmen or skilled workers in the traditional sense of the word.

With the advent of mechanization, factory owners gained much tighter control over the entire production process. Indeed, they began to enforce an unprecedented discipline among their workers, who had to accommodate themselves to the boredom of repetitive work and a timetable set by the machines. Craftsmen who had been accustomed to working at their own pace now had to adjust to an entirely new and more demanding schedule. "While the engine runs," wrote one critical contemporary, "the people must work—men, women, and children yoked together with iron and steam. The animal machine—breakable in the best case, subject to a thousand sources of suffering—is chained fast to the iron machine which knows no suffering and no weariness."[2]

division of labor The assignment of one stage of production to a single worker or group of workers to increase efficiency and productive output.

 Read the Document
Adam Smith, *The Wealth of Nations*

MULE SPINNING A large mechanized spinning mill in northern England, about 1835. The workers did not require any great skill to run the machinery.

New Methods of Transportation

As industry became more extensive and increased its output, transport facilities, such as roads, bridges, canals, and eventually railroads, grew in number and quality. High industrial productivity required the efficient movement of raw materials to production sites and the transportation of finished products to markets. During the early phase of the Industrial Revolution in Britain, water transportation supplied most of these needs. A vast network of navigable rivers and human-made canals, eventually more than 4,000 miles in length, transported goods to and from areas that did not have access to the coast. For routes that had no access to water, the most common method of transportation was by horse-drawn carriages on newly built turnpikes or toll roads, many of them made of stone so that they were passable even in wet weather.

The most significant innovation in transport during the nineteenth century was the railroad. Introduced as the Industrial Revolution was gaining momentum, the railroad provided quick, cheap transportation of heavy materials such as coal and iron over long distances. Its introduction in Britain during the 1820s and throughout Europe and America during the following decades illustrated the transition from an economy based on organic sources of energy to one that relied on mineral sources of energy. Driven by coal-burning, steam-powered locomotives, the railroads freed transport from its dependence on animal power, especially the horses that were used

THE STOCKTON AND DARLINGTON RAILWAY The inaugural run of George Stephenson's locomotive on the Stockton and Darlington railway, the first in Britain, took place in 1825. The main function of the railway was to carry materials and goods to and from towns producing iron in the northern counties of England.

to pull coaches along turnpikes, barges along canals, and carts along parallel tracks in mines. Railroads rapidly became the main economic thoroughfares of the industrial economy. They linked towns and regions that earlier had not been easily accessible to each other. They also changed the travel habits of Europeans by making it possible to cover distances in one-fifth the time it took by coach.

The construction and operation of railroads became a major new industry, employing thousands of skilled and unskilled workers and providing opportunities for investment and profit. The industry created an unprecedented demand for iron and other materials used to build and equip locomotives, tracks, freight cars, passenger cars, and signals, thus giving a tremendous boost to the iron industry and the metalworking and engineering trades. By the 1840s the railroads had become the main stimulus to economic growth throughout western Europe and the United States. Transport in industrialized economies continued to experience frequent innovation. During the twentieth century, for example, new methods of transportation, including automobiles, airplanes, and high-speed rails, sustained economic growth in all industrialized countries; like the railroads, they have become major industries themselves.

View the Map

Great Britain: Railroads, ca. 1850

21.1

21.2

21.3

21.4

21.5

Conditions Favoring Industrial Growth

21.2 What social and economic changes made industrial development possible?

The Industrial Revolution occurred first in Britain because a set of social and economic developments encouraged the mechanization of industry. These conditions were the steady increase in the British population, improved agricultural productivity, the accumulation of large amounts of capital, and sufficient demand for manufactured goods.

Population Growth

Industrialization required a sufficiently large pool of labor to staff the factories and workshops of the new industries. One of the main reasons why the Industrial Revolution occurred first in Britain was that its population during the eighteenth century increased more rapidly than that of any country in continental Europe. Between 1680 and 1820 the population of England more than doubled, while that of France grew at less than one-third that rate, and the population of the Dutch Republic hardly grew at all.

One of the reasons this growth in the British population took place was that famines, which had occurred periodically throughout the early modern period, became less frequent during the eighteenth century. The last great famine in Britain took place in 1740, only a generation before industrialization began. Mortality from epidemic diseases, especially typhus, influenza, and smallpox, also decreased. Plague, which had decimated the European population periodically since the fourteenth century, struck England for the last time in the Great Plague of London in 1665. It made its last European appearance at Marseilles in 1720 but did not spread beyond the southern parts of France.

A second and even more important factor in British population growth was an increase in fertility. More people were marrying, and at a younger age, which increased the birthrate. The spread of rural industry encouraged this early-marriage pattern. Wage-earning textile workers tended to marry a little earlier than agricultural workers, probably because wage earners did not have to postpone marriage to inherit land or to become self-employed, as was the case with farm workers.

Increase in European Population, 1680–1820		
	Population Totals (millions)	
	1680	*1820*
France	21.9	30.5
Italy	12.0	18.4
Germany	12.0	18.1
Spain	8.5	14.0
England	4.9	11.5
Netherlands	1.9	2.0
Western Europe	71.9	116.5
Percentage Growth Rates, 1680–1820		
England	133%	
Spain	64	
Italy	53	
Germany	51	
France	39	
Netherlands	8	
Western Europe	73	

SOURCE: E. A. Wrigley, "The Growth of Population in Eighteenth-Century England: A Conundrum Resolved," *Past and Present* 98 (1983): 122, by permission of Oxford University Press.

This increase in population facilitated industrialization by swelling domestic demand for manufactured goods and by increasing the number of people available to work in the factories and mines. The increase in the British population, however, was not so large that it retarded industrialization. If population growth was too rapid, it could lead to declining incomes, put pressure on agriculture to feed more people than possible, and prevent the accumulation of wealth. Most important, overpopulation could discourage factory owners from introducing costly machinery. If labor was plentiful and cheap, it could cost less for workers to produce the same volume of goods by hand. Industrialization therefore required a significant but not too rapid increase in population—the exact scenario that occurred in Britain during the eighteenth century.

Agricultural Productivity

Like population growth, expanding agricultural output fostered the Industrial Revolution in Britain. Between 1700 and 1800 British agriculture experienced a revolution, resulting in a substantial increase in productivity. A major reason for this increase was the consolidation of all the land farmed by one tenant into compact fields. During the Middle Ages and most of the early modern period, each tenant on a manorial estate leased and farmed strips of land scattered throughout the estate. Decisions regarding the planting and harvesting of crops in these "open fields" were made collectively in the manorial court. Beginning in the sixteenth century, some of the wealthier tenants on these estates agreed to exchange their strips of land with their neighbors to consolidate their holdings into large compact fields, with hedges, bushes, or walls defining their boundaries. This process of **enclosure** allowed individual farmers to exercise complete control over the use of their land. In the eighteenth and nineteenth centuries the number of enclosures increased dramatically when the British Parliament, most of whose members were landowners, passed legislation authorizing them.

With control of their lands, farmers could make them more productive. The most profitable change was to introduce new crop rotations, often involving the alternation of grains such as rye or barley with root crops such as turnips or grasses

enclosure The consolidation of scattered agricultural holdings into large, compact fields which were then closed off by hedges, bushes, or walls, giving farmers complete control over the uses of their land.

such as clover. These new crops and grasses restored nutrients to the soil and therefore made it unnecessary to let fields lie fallow once every three years. Farmers also introduced a variety of new fertilizers and soil additives that made harvests more bountiful. Farmers who raised sheep took advantage of discoveries regarding scientific breeding that improved the quality of their flocks.

More productive farming meant that fewer agricultural workers were required to feed the population. This made it possible for more people to leave the farms to work in the factories and mines. The expanded labor pool of industrial workers, moreover, was large enough that factory owners did not have to pay workers high wages; otherwise, the prospect of industrializing would have lost much of its appeal. The hiring of children and women to work in the factories and mines also kept the labor pool large and the costs of labor low.

Capital Formation and Accumulation

A third development that encouraged British industrialization was the accumulation of capital. The term **capital** refers to all the assets used in production. These include both the factories and machines that produce other goods (fixed capital) and the raw materials and finished products that go to market (circulating capital). Other forms of capital are the railroads and barges that transport raw materials to the places of production and finished products to market. Mechanized industry involves the extensive and intensive use of capital to do the work formerly assigned to human beings. An industrial economy therefore requires large amounts of capital, especially fixed capital.

Capital more generally refers to the money that is necessary to purchase these physical assets. This capital can come from individuals, such as wealthy landlords, merchants, or industrialists who invest the profits they have accumulated in industrial machinery or equipment. In many cases the profits derived from industrial production are reinvested in the firm itself. Alternatively, capital can come from financial institutions in the form of loans. Very often a number of individuals make their wealth available to an industrial firm by buying shares of stock in that company's operations. This, of course, is the main way in which most capital is accumulated today. In countries that have only recently begun to industrialize in Latin America and Southeast Asia, capital often comes from public sources, such as governments, or from international institutions, such as the International Monetary Fund.

In Britain the capital needed to achieve industrialization came almost entirely from private sources. Some of it was raised by selling shares of stock to people from the middle and upper levels of society, but an even larger amount came from merchants who engaged in domestic and international trade, landowners who profited from the production of agricultural goods (including those who owned plantations in America), and the industrial entrepreneurs who owned mines, ironworks, and factories. In Britain, where all three groups were more successful than in other parts of Europe, the volume of capital made available from these sources was substantial. These people could invest directly in industrial machinery and mines or, more commonly, make their wealth available to others indirectly in the form of loans from banks where they kept their financial assets.

Banks supplied a considerable amount of the funds necessary for industrialization. In Britain the possibilities for such capital were maximized in the late eighteenth century when financial institutions offered loans at low interest rates and when the development of a national banking system made these funds readily available throughout the country, especially in the new industrial cities, such as Leeds, Sheffield, and Manchester. The number of English banks rose from a mere dozen in 1750 to more than 300 in 1800. Many bankers had close ties with industrialists, thereby facilitating the flow of capital from the financial to the industrial sector of the economy.

capital All the physical assets used in production, including fixed capital, such as machinery, and circulating capital, such as raw materials; more generally the cost of these physical assets.

supply The amounts of capital, labor, and food that are needed to produce goods for the market as well as the quantities of those goods themselves.

demand The desire of consumers to acquire goods and the need of producers to acquire raw materials and machinery.

Demand from Consumers and Producers

The conditions for industrialization discussed so far all deal with **supply**, that is, the amounts of capital, labor, food, and skill necessary to support the industrial process. The other side of the economic equation is **demand**, which is the desire of consumers to purchase industrial goods and of producers to acquire raw materials and machinery. Much of the extraordinary productivity of the Industrial Revolution arose from the demand for industrial products. Many of the technological innovations that occurred at the beginning of the revolution also originated as responses to the demand for more goods. For example, the demand for more cotton goods spurred the introduction of the spinning jenny, the water frame, and the mule. Likewise, the demand for coal for industrial and domestic use led to the development of an efficient steam engine to drain mines so that those supplies of coal could be extracted.

During the early years of British industrialization the domestic market was the main source of demand for industrial products. Demand was especially strong among the bourgeoisie. A "consumer revolution" had taken place during the eighteenth century, as bourgeois individuals and families strove to acquire goods of all sorts, especially clothing and household products, such as pottery, cutlery, furniture, and curtains. The desire of the bourgeoisie to imitate the spending habits of the aristocracy helped to fuel this consumer revolution, while commercial manipulation, including newspaper advertising, warehouse displays, product demonstrations, and the distribution of samples, helped to facilitate it. An entirely new consumer culture arose, one in which women played a leading role. Advertisements promoting the latest female fashions, housewares, and children's toys became more common than those directed at adult male consumers. One ad in a local British paper in 1777, capitalizing on reports that mice were getting into ladies' hair at night, promoted "night caps made of silver wire so strong that no mouse or even a rat can gnaw through them." Advertisements therefore created a demand for new products and increased the demand for those already on the market.

If this consumer revolution had been restricted to the middle ranks of society, it would have had only a limited effect on the Industrial Revolution. The bourgeoisie constituted at most only 20 percent of the entire population of eighteenth-century Britain, and most of the goods they craved, with the exception of the pottery produced in Josiah Wedgwood's factories (which is still made today), were luxury items rather than the types of products that could be easily mass-produced. A strong demand for manufactured products could develop only if workers were to buy consumer goods such as knitted stockings and caps, cotton shirts, earthenware, coffeepots, nails, candlesticks, watches, lace, and ribbon. The demand for these products came from small cottagers and laborers as well as the middle class. The demand for stockings for both men and women was particularly strong. In 1831 the author of a study of the impact of machinery on British society declared, "Two centuries ago, not one person in a thousand wore stockings; one century ago, not one person in five hundred wore them; now not one person in a thousand is without them."[3]

Demand for manufactured products from the lower classes was obviously limited by the amount of money that wage earners had available for nonessential goods, and real wages did not increase very much, if at all, during the eighteenth century. Nevertheless, the income of families in which the wife and children as well as the father worked for wages did increase significantly both during the heyday of rural industry and during the early years of industrialization. In many cases family members worked longer and harder just so they could afford to buy new products coming on the market. As the population increased, so too did this lower-class demand, which helped sustain an economy built around industrial production.

The Spread of Industrialization

21.3 How did industrialization spread from Great Britain to the European continent and America?

The Industrial Revolution did not occur in all European countries at the same time. As we have seen, it began in Britain in the 1760s and for more than four decades was confined exclusively to that country (see **Map 21.1**). It eventually spread to other European and North American countries, where many industrial innovations were modeled on those in Britain. Belgium, France, Germany, Switzerland, Austria, Sweden, and the United States all experienced their own Industrial Revolutions by the middle of the nineteenth century. Only in the late nineteenth century did countries outside the traditional boundaries of the West, mainly Russia and Japan, begin to industrialize. By the middle of the twentieth century, industrialization had become a truly global process, transforming the economies of a number of Asian and Latin American countries.

Great Britain and the Continent

Industrialization occurred on the European continent much later than it did in Great Britain. Only after 1815 did Belgium and France begin to industrialize on a large scale, and it was not until 1840 that Germany, Switzerland, and Austria showed significant signs of industrial growth. Other European countries, such as Italy, Spain, and Russia, did not begin serious efforts in this direction until the late nineteenth century. It took continental European states even longer to rival the economic strength of Britain. Germany, which emerged as Britain's main competitor in the late nineteenth century, did not match British industrial output until the twentieth century.

Four factors explain the slower development of industrialization on the European continent. The first relates to the political situations in those countries. Well into the nineteenth century, most continental European states had numerous internal political barriers that impeded the transportation of raw materials and goods from one part of the country to another. In Germany, for example, which was not politically united until 1871, scores of small sovereign territorial units charged tariffs whenever goods crossed their boundaries. Only in 1834 did a customs union, the *Zollverein*, eliminate some of these barriers. In Poland the removal of customs barriers did not take place until 1851. The relatively poor state of continental roads and the inaccessibility of many seaports from production sites aggravated this political situation.

In contrast, Britain achieved economic unity early in the eighteenth century. After 1707, when Scotland was united to England and freedom of internal trade was established between the two countries, the United Kingdom of Great Britain constituted the largest free-trade zone in Europe. Raw materials and finished products could therefore move from one place to another in Britain, up to a distance of more than 800 miles, without payment of any internal customs or duties. The system of inland waterways was complete by 1780, and seaports were accessible from all parts of the country.

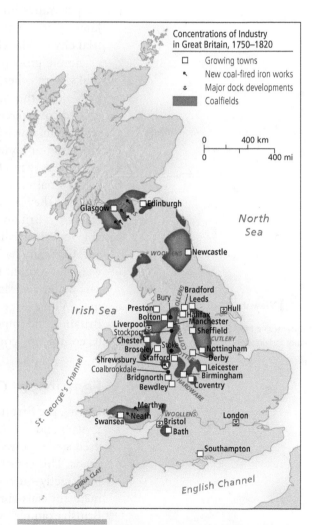

MAP **21.1** THE CONCENTRATIONS OF INDUSTRY IN GREAT BRITAIN, 1750–1820 The most heavily industrialized regions were in northern England, where the population of cities such as Manchester, Liverpool, and Sheffield grew rapidly. Why did northern England become more industrialized than the southern part of the country?

A second factor that weakened the industrial potential of many continental European countries was the imposition of protective tariffs on goods imported from other countries. The purpose of this mercantilist policy was to develop national self-sufficiency and maintain a favorable balance of trade, but it also had the negative effect of limiting economic growth. For example, in the Dutch Republic (the Kingdom of the Netherlands after 1815) a long tradition of protecting established industries prevented that country from importing the raw materials and machines needed to develop new industries. Because protectionism invited retaliation from trading partners, it also tended to shrink the size of potential overseas markets. Britain adopted a policy of free trade during the 1840s, and it pressured other European countries to adopt the same policy.

A third obstacle to European industrialization was aristocratic hostility, or at least indifference, to industrial development. British aristocrats were themselves often involved in capitalist enterprise and did not have the same suspicion of industry and trade that their counterparts in France and Spain often harbored. Many members of the British aristocracy, such as the entrepreneur "Turnip Townshend" (see Chapter 19), were agricultural capitalists who improved the productivity of their estates. Others were involved in mining. The Duke of Devonshire encouraged the exploitation of the copper mines on his estate, while the Duke of Bridgewater employed the engineer James Brindley to build a canal from the duke's coal mines in Worsley to the industrial city of Manchester in 1759. One reason for the British aristocracy's support for economic growth was that many of its members, especially the gentry, rose into its ranks from other social and economic groups. These individuals tended to be sympathetic to the values of a commercial and an industrial society. The same attitude toward commerce and industry did not exist among the nobility in France before the revolution, much less among German *Junkers*. These groups had little connection with industrial or commercial society, whose values they held in very low regard. Consequently, they rarely invested in industry.

A final reason for the slow industrialization of continental European countries was that they lacked the abundant raw materials that formed the basis of an industrial economy. Britain's large deposits of coal and iron ore, both of which were indispensable to industrialization, gave it an advantage over other European countries. France and Germany had some coal deposits, but they were more difficult to mine and they were not located near ocean ports. Continental countries also lacked access to other raw materials, especially cotton, which Britain could import from its overseas colonies. With a large empire on four continents and the world's largest merchant marine, Britain could import these raw materials less expensively and in larger quantities than its continental competitors.

View the Map

Interactive Map: European Industrialization

Features of Continental Industrialization

During the first half of the nineteenth century, especially after 1830, Belgium, France, Switzerland, Germany, and Austria introduced machinery into the industrial process, used steam power in production, concentrated labor in large factories, and built railroads. This continental European version of the Industrial Revolution was often—but incorrectly—described as an imitative process, one in which entrepreneurs or government officials simply tried to duplicate Britain's economic success by following the British example. Although continental European nations did indeed rely to some extent on British industrial technology, each European nation, responding to its own unique combination of political, economic, and social conditions, followed its own course of industrialization. Three features, however, characterized these diverse industrial paths.

First, once countries such as Belgium and Germany began to industrialize, their governments played a much more active role in encouraging and assisting in the process. In contrast to Britain, whose government allowed private industry to function with few economic controls, continental governments became active partners in the industrial process. They supplied capital for many economic ventures, especially building railroads and roads. In Prussia the state owned a number of manufacturing and mining enterprises. Many continental governments also imposed protective tariffs to prevent an influx of cheap British goods from underselling the products of their own fledgling industries. In a few cases, continental European governments even provided financial support for investors in an effort to encourage capital formation (see **Map 21.2**).

A second major feature of continental European industrialization was that banks, particularly in Germany and Belgium, played an active role in industrial development. Drawing on the resources of both small and large investors, these corporate banks became in effect industrial banks, building railroads and factories themselves in addition to making capital available for a variety of industrial ventures.

A third distinct feature of continental European industrialization was that the railroads actually contributed to the beginning of industrial development. In Britain the railroads were introduced some 60 years after industrialization had begun and thus helped sustain an ongoing process of economic development. By contrast, the railroads on the European continent provided the basic infrastructure of its new economy and became a major stimulus to the development of other industries. Railroads also gave continental European governments the ability to transport military troops quickly in time of war, which helps to explain why governments supported railroad construction with such enthusiasm. In Belgium, which was the first continental European nation to industrialize, the new government built a national railroad system during the 1830s and 1840s not only to stimulate industry, but also to unify the newly independent nation.

MAP **21.2** CUSTOMS UNIONS IN CONTINENTAL EUROPE One of the reasons for the relatively slow progress of industrialization on the European continent was the existence of internal tariff barriers. This map shows the dates when customs unions, such as the *Zollverein* of 1834 in the German Confederation, were established or the customs barriers were eliminated. By contrast, all internal customs duties within Great Britain had been eliminated more than a century earlier when England and Scotland were united in 1707. Why did continental European states find it more difficult than Britain to eliminate internal tariff barriers?

KRUPP STEELWORKS IN ESSEN, GERMANY, IN 1875 Smoke rises from the stacks of a steel mill in the Ruhr region, the center of German industry.

Q **View the Image**

Excelsior Iron Works

Industrialization in the United States

Industrialization in the United States began during the 1820s, not long after Belgium and France had begun to have their own industrial revolutions. It occurred first in the textile industry in New England, where factories using water power produced goods for largely rural markets. New England also began producing two domestic hardware products—clocks and guns—for the same market. In the 1840s New York began to produce products made from iron. Between 1850 and 1870 a second region between Pittsburgh and Cleveland became industrialized. This area specialized in heavy industry, especially steelmaking and the manufacture of large machinery, and it relied on coal for fuel. Railroads linked this industrialized region with that of the Northeast.

American industrialization included features of both the British and continental European patterns. As in Britain and France, the development of cottage industry in the United States preceded industrialization. As in most continental European countries, American railroads played a crucial role in the early years of industrialization. Most of the industrial machinery in the United States during the nineteenth century was modeled on imports from Britain. The most significant American technological innovation before 1900 was the sewing machine, which Elias Howe patented in 1846 and Isaac Singer improved in the 1850s. This new machine was then introduced in Europe, where it was used in the production of ready-to-wear garments.

The United States became known for its use of machinery in all industries and its efficient organization of factory labor. Toward the beginning of the twentieth century, American manufacturers streamlined the production process by introducing the assembly line, a division of labor in which the product passed from one operation to the next until it was fully assembled. The assembly line required the production of interchangeable parts, another American innovation, first used in the manufacture of rifles for the U.S. government.

Like Britain, the United States possessed vast natural resources, including coal. It also resembled Britain in the absence of governmental involvement in the process of industrialization. The main difference between the industrializations of the two countries was that during the nineteenth century labor in America was in relatively short supply. This placed workers in a more advantageous situation in dealing with their employers and prevented some of the horrors of early British industrialization from recurring on the other side of the Atlantic. Only with the influx of European immigrants in the late nineteenth century did the condition of American workers deteriorate and begin to resemble the early-nineteenth-century British pattern.

Industrial Regionalism

Although we have discussed the industrialization of entire states, the process usually took place within smaller geographical regions. There had always been regional specialization in agriculture, with some areas raising crops and others livestock. During the Industrial Revolution, however, entire economies acquired a distinctly regional character. Regional economies began to take shape during the days of the domestic system, when merchants employed families in certain geographical areas, such as Lancashire in England, to produce textiles. Related industries, such as those for finishing or dyeing cloth, also sprang up close to areas where spinning and weaving took place.

As industrialization spread outside Britain, this regional pattern became even more pronounced. In France the centers of the textile industry were situated near the northeastern border near Belgium and in the area surrounding Lyons in the east-central part of the country. Both of these areas had attracted rural household industry before the introduction of textile machinery. In Germany the iron industry was centered in the Ruhr region, where most of the country's coal was mined. In the city of Essen on the Ruhr River, the industrialist Alfred Krupp (1812–1887) established an enormous steelmaking complex that produced industrial machinery, railroad equipment, and guns for the Prussian army. Within the Habsburg Empire, most industry was located in parts of Bohemia (now the Czech Republic).

The development of regional economies did not mean that markets were regional. The goods produced in one region almost always served the needs of people outside that particular area. Markets for most industrial goods were national and international, and even people in small agricultural villages created a demand for manufactured goods. The French iron industry, for example, was centered in the eastern part of the country, but it catered to the needs of the wealthier segments of its own and other European populations, as did the iron industry in the Ruhr region in Germany and the textile industry in the north of England.

Regional industrial development helps to explain the striking contrast that persisted well into the twentieth century between the parts of countries that had become heavily industrialized and those that retained at least many of the appearances of a pre-industrial life. Some areas in all industrialized countries remained exclusively agricultural, while others continued a tradition of rural industry. This pattern was particularly evident in France, where mechanized industry was concentrated in a limited number of centers in the northeastern half of the country. In 1870 more than two-thirds of the French population still lived in rural areas. As economic growth and industrial development continued, however, agricultural regions eventually began to lose their traditional character. Even if industry itself did not arrive, the larger industrial economy made its mark. Agriculture itself became mechanized, while railroads and other forms of mechanized transport integrated these areas in a national economy.

The Effects of Industrialization

21.4 What were the economic, social, and cultural effects of the Industrial Revolution?

The Industrial Revolution had a profound impact on virtually every aspect of human life. The changes that it brought about were initially most evident in Britain, but over time they have occurred in every country that has industrialized, including the United States. Industrialization encouraged the growth of the population and the economy, affected the conditions in which people lived, changed family life, created new divisions within society, and transformed the traditional rural landscape.

Population and Economic Growth

The most significant of these changes was the sustained expansion of both the population and the economy. As we have seen, a significant population increase in the eighteenth century helped to make the Industrial Revolution in Britain possible. That growth had created a plentiful supply of relatively cheap labor, which in turn increased industrial output. As industry grew, population kept pace, and each provided a stimulus to the growth of the other.

Most contemporary observers in the late eighteenth century did not believe that this expansion of both the population and the economy could be sustained. The most pessimistic of these commentators was Thomas Malthus (1766–1834), an English clergyman who wrote *An Essay on the Principle of Population* in 1798. Malthus argued that population had a natural tendency to grow faster than the food supply. Thus, unless couples exercised restraint by marrying late and producing fewer children, the population would eventually outstrip the resources necessary to sustain it, resulting in poor nutrition, famine, and disease. These "positive checks" on population growth, sometimes aggravated by war, would drive population back to sustainable levels. These checks on population

Malthusian population trap The theory of Thomas Malthus (1766–1834) that the natural tendency of population to grow faster than the food supply would eventually drive the size of populations back to sustainable levels and end periods of economic expansion that usually accompany the growth of population.

growth also ended periods of economic expansion, which generally accompany increases in population. If this demographic and economic pattern had recurred, the significant expansion of the population and the economy that took place in eighteenth-century Britain would have reached its limits, just around the time that Malthus was writing.

This predicted cyclical contraction of both the population and the economy did not take place. Europe for the first time in its history managed to escape the **Malthusian population trap**. Instead of being sharply reduced after 1800, the population continued to expand at an ever-faster rate, doubling in Britain between 1800 and 1850. At the same time the economy, instead of contracting or collapsing, continued to grow and diversify.

Developments in industry explain why Europe was able to escape the Malthusian population trap. The accumulation of capital over a long period of time was so great that industry could employ large numbers of workers, even during the 1790s and 1800s, when Europe was at war. Because they had income from wages, workers were willing to marry earlier and have larger families. With lower food prices because of higher agricultural productivity, they could also afford to maintain a healthier diet and purchase more manufactured goods. Thus, the Industrial Revolution itself, coupled with the changes in agriculture that accompanied it, proved Malthus wrong.

While the increase of population in all industrialized societies is incontestable, the record of continued economic growth is not so clear. Economic growth in industrialized countries has not always been rapid or continuous. During the first six decades of industrialization in Britain, for example, economic growth was actually fairly slow, mainly because so much capital went into subsidizing the long war against France (1792–1802; 1804–1815). To claim that the Industrial Revolution resulted in sustained economic growth, we have to take a broad view, looking at an overall pattern of economic development and ignoring cyclical recessions and depressions. More important, industrialized nations have not yet experienced the type of economic contraction or collapse that Malthus predicted. For that reason, we can say that the Industrial Revolution has resulted in sustained economic growth in the West.

Standards of Living

Ever since the early years of the Industrial Revolution, a debate has raged over the effect of industrialization on the standard of living and the quality of life of the laboring population. The two main schools of thought on this issue are often referred to as the *optimists* and the *pessimists*. The optimists emphasize the positive effects of both the process of mechanization and the system of industrial capitalism that arose during the revolution. They focus on the success that industrialized nations have achieved in escaping the Malthusian population trap and in experiencing sustained economic growth. The Industrial Revolution, so they argue, has resulted in an unprecedented rise in individual income, which has made it possible for the mass of a country's population to avoid poverty for the first time in human history.

The main yardstick that the optimists use to measure the improvement in living standards is *per capita real income*, that is, income measured in terms of its actual purchasing power. Real income in Britain rose about 50 percent between 1770 and 1850 and more than doubled during the entire nineteenth century. This increase in income allowed workers to improve their diets as well as to purchase more clothing and other basic commodities. These increases, however, were only averages, concealing disparities among workers with different levels of skill. Only in the late nineteenth and twentieth centuries did industrialization raise the real income of all workers to a level that made the benefits of industrialization apparent.

The long-term increase in real income has never been substantial enough to persuade the pessimists that industrialization was on balance a positive good, at least for the working class. Pessimists have always stressed the negative effects of industrial development on the people on the lower levels of society. In their way of thinking, industrialization

📖 Read **the Document**

Andrew Ure, from *The Philosophy of Manufactures*

was an unmitigated disaster. The cause of this disaster in their eyes was not mechanization itself, but the system of **industrial capitalism**. This form of capitalism, which is characterized by the private ownership of factories and the employment of wage labor, involved a systematic effort to reduce costs and maximize profits. In the pursuit of this goal, employers tried to keep wages as low as possible and increase production by introducing labor-saving technology, thus preventing workers from improving their lot.

Pessimists usually claim a moral basis for their position. In this respect they follow in a tradition begun by the poet William Blake (1757–1827), who referred to the new factories as "satanic mills," and the socialist Friedrich Engels (1820–1895), who in *The Condition of the Working Class in England in 1844* (1845) accused the factory owners in England of mass murder and robbery.

Most of the evidence that social critics use to support the pessimist position comes from the early period of industrialization in Britain, when workers' real wages either stagnated or declined and when conditions in factories and towns were most appalling. Working-class housing was makeshift and crowded, and there were few sanitary facilities. A new word, *slum,* was coined to refer to these poverty-stricken working-class neighborhoods. Poor drainage and raw sewage gave rise to a host of new hygienic problems, especially outbreaks of typhus and cholera. Between 1831 and 1866 four epidemics of cholera killed at least 140,000 people in Britain, most of whom lived in poorer districts.

The impact of industrialization and urbanization on the environment was no less harrowing. The burning of coal and the use of industrial chemicals polluted the urban atmosphere. The famous London fogs, which were actually smogs caused by industrial pollutants, presented a serious public health problem throughout the nineteenth century and did not begin to disappear until the introduction of strict regulations on the burning of coal in the 1950s.

While life in the city was bleak and unhealthy, working conditions in the factory were monotonous and demeaning. Forced to submit to a regimen governed by the operation of the machine, workers lost their independence as well as any control whatsoever over the products of their labor. They were required to work long hours, often 14 hours a day, six days a week, with few breaks. Factory masters locked the doors during working hours and assessed fines for infractions such as opening a window when the temperature was unbearable, whistling while working, and having dirty hands while spinning yarn. Work in the mines was a little less monotonous, but it was physically more demanding and far more dangerous. (See *Different Voices* in this chapter.)

Women, Children, and Industry

During the early Industrial Revolution in Britain, the industrial workforce, especially in the textile and mining industries, included large numbers of children and women. In the woolen industry in the western part of England, for example, female and child labor together accounted for 75 percent of the workforce. Children under age 13 made up 13 percent of the cotton factory workforce, and those under age 18 made up 51 percent. This pattern of employment reflected the demands of industrialists, who valued the hand skills and dexterity that children possessed as well as the greater amenability of both children and women to the discipline of factory labor. Some of the machines that were introduced into the textile industry in the late eighteenth century were specifically designed for women and children.

Female and child labor was both plentiful and cheap. Children received only one-sixth to one-third the wages of a grown man, while women generally took home only one-third to one-half of that adult male income. Yet women and children sought these low-paying jobs. In a family dependent on wages, everyone needed to work, even when a large labor pool kept wages depressed.

The participation of women and children in the workforce was *not* new. In an agricultural economy all members of the family contributed to the work, with parents

industrial capitalism A form of capitalism characterized by the ownership of factories by private individuals and the employment of wage labor.

and children, young and old, all being assigned specific roles. Rural industry also involved the labor of all members of the family. When people began working in the factories, however, they were physically separated from the home, making it impossible for workers to combine domestic and occupational labor.

As the workplace became distinct from the household, family life underwent a fundamental change, although it did not occur immediately. During the early years of the Industrial Revolution, members of many families found employment together in the factories and mines. Factory owners also tried to perpetuate many aspects of family life in the new industrial setting, defining the entire factory community as an extended family, in which the factory owner played the paternalistic role. Gradually, however, mothers found it impossible to care for their youngest children on the job, and most of them dropped out of the full-time workforce. The restriction of child labor by the British Factory Act of 1833 reinforced this trend and led to the establishment of a fairly common situation in which the male wage earner worked outside the home while his wife stayed home with the children. As one young girl who worked in the mines testified before a parliamentary commission investigation of child labor in 1842, "Mother takes care of the children." (See *Justice in History* in this chapter.)

The Industrial Revolution did nothing to improve the status of women. Neither the pay these women received nor the jobs they performed gave them financial autonomy or social prestige. Becoming an independent wage earner meant little when women's wages were on average one-third to one-half those of men. The jobs assigned to women within industry, such as operating textile machinery, generally required the least skill. When men and women worked in the same factory, the women were invariably subordinated to the authority of male workers or foremen, thereby perpetuating the patriarchal patterns that prevailed in preindustrial society. Even their exclusion from certain occupations, such as mining by an act of Parliament in 1842, only made the sexual division of labor more rigid than in preindustrial society.

Class and Class Consciousness

As Europe became more industrialized and urbanized, and as the system of industrial capitalism became more entrenched, writers began to use a new terminology to describe the structure of society. Instead of claiming that society consisted of a finely graded hierarchy of ranks to which individuals belonged by virtue of their occupations or their legal status, they divided society into three classes on the basis of the type of property people owned and the manner in which they acquired it. At the top of this new social hierarchy was the aristocracy, consisting of those who owned land and received their income in the form of rent. The middle class or bourgeoisie, which included the new factory owners, possessed capital and derived their income from profits, whereas the working class owned nothing but their own labor and received their income from wages.

Historians and social scientists disagree over the extent to which men and women in the nineteenth century were actually conscious of their membership in these classes. Some historians claim that the growth of wage labor, the exploitation of the working class, and conflicts between capital and labor encouraged workers to think of themselves not so much as individuals who occupied a position in a social hierarchy, but as members of a large class of workers who shared the same relationship to the means of production. These historians have pointed to the growth of trade unions, political campaigns for universal male suffrage, and other forms of working-class organization and communication as evidence of this awakening of **class consciousness**.

Other historians argue that people were less conscious of their class. True, at certain times in the early nineteenth century some workers thought of themselves as members of a class whose interests conflicted with those of factory owners and financiers. It was much more common, however, for them to think of themselves primarily as practitioners of a particular craft, as members of a local community, or as part

class consciousness The awareness of people from different occupations that they belonged to a class.

Different Voices
The Social and Cultural Effects of Industrialization

C ontemporaries and historians have debated whether the condition of the working class improved or deteriorated as a result of the Industrial Revolution. These two descriptions of the working class in England in the first half of the nineteenth century present evidence to support the two sides of the debate. In his history of the cotton industry, which he greatly admired, the English journalist Richard Guest focused on the improved educational opportunities offered to workers, mainly in the Sunday schools. The German social philosopher Friedrich Engels, who collaborated with Karl Marx (1818–1883) in writing The Communist Manifesto (1848), emphasized the exploitation and brutalization of the lower classes as they were turned into a wage-earning proletariat. In his first book, The Condition of the Working Class in England in 1844, which was inspired by his service as a manager in a factory in Manchester, Engels focused on the deplorable living conditions of industrial workers.

A Journalist Celebrates the Improvement in the Life of Industrial Workers

The progress of the cotton manufacture introduced great change in the manners and habits of the people. The operative workmen being thrown together in great numbers, had their faculties sharpened and improved by constant communication. Conversation wandered over a variety of topics not before essayed; the questions of peace and war, which interested them importantly, inasmuch as they might produce a rise or fall of wages, became highly interesting, and this brought them into the vast field of politics and discussions on the character of their government and the men who composed it. They took a greater interest in the defeats and victories of their country's arms, and from being only a few degrees above their cattle in the scale of intellect, they became political citizens.

To these changes the establishment of Sunday Schools has very much contributed; they have been a great means of forwarding this wonderful alteration. Before their institution the lower orders were extremely illiterate; very few of them could read, and still fewer of them could write, and when one of them learned to read, write and cast accounts, those requirements elevated him to a superior rank. His clerkly skill exempted him from manual labour, and as shopman, book-keeper or town's officer—perchance in the higher dignity of parish clerk or schoolmaster—he rose a step above his original station in life....

The facility with which the weavers changed their masters, the constant effort to find out and obtain the largest remuneration for their labor, the excitement to ingenuity which the higher wages for fine manufacturers and skilful workmanship produced, and a conviction that they depended mainly on their own exertions produced in them that invaluable feeling, a spirit of freedom and independence, and that guarantee for good conduct and improvement of manners, a consciousness of the value of character and of their own weight and importance.

SOURCE: Richard Guest, *A Compendious History of the Cotton Manufacture* (1823).

Friedrich Engels Deplores the Living Conditions of Industrial Workers

Since capital, the direct or indirect control of the means of subsistence and production, is the weapon with which this social warfare is carried on, it is clear that all the disadvantages of such a state must fall upon the poor man. For him no one has the slightest concern. Cast into the whirlpool, he must struggle through as well as he can. If he is so happy as to find work, i.e., if the bourgeoisie does him the favour to enrich itself by means of him, wages await him which scarcely suffice to keep body and soul together; if he can get no work he may steal, if he is not afraid of the police, or starve, in which case the police will take care that he does so in a quiet and inoffensive manner....

Every great city has one or more slums, where the working class is crowded together . . . these slums are pretty equally arranged in all the great towns of England, the worst houses in the worst quarters of the towns; usually one or two-storied cottage in long rows, perhaps with cellars used as dwellings, almost always irregularly built.... The streets are generally unpaved, rough, dirty, filled with vegetable and animal refuse, without sewer or gutters, but supplied with foul, stagnant pools instead. Moreover, ventilation is impeded by the bad, confused method of building of the whole quarter, and since many human beings here live crowded into a small space, the atmosphere that prevails in these working men's quarters may readily be imagined....

Liverpool, with all its commerce, wealth and grandeur yet treats its workers with the same barbarity. A full fifth of the population, more than 45,000 human beings, live in narrow, dark, damp, badly-ventilated cellar dwellings, of which there are 7,862 in the city. Besides these cellar dwellings there are 2,270 courts, small spaces built up on all four sides and having but one entrance, a narrow, covered passageway, the whole ordinarily very dirty and inhabited exclusively by proletarians.... In Nottingham there are in all 11,000 houses, of which between 7,000 and 8,000 are built back to back with a rear party-wall so that no through ventilation is possible, while a single privy usually serves for several houses.

SOURCE: Friedrich Engels, *The Condition of the Working Class in England* (1845).

For Discussion

1. Is it possible that these two accounts of working-class life in the industrial age could both be accurate? Which account do you find more persuasive and why?
2. How do the political agendas of the two authors influence their assessments of the effects of industrialization?
3. In what ways do these descriptions of industrial working class reflect the optimistic and pessimistic interpretations of industrialization discussed in this chapter?

CAPITAL AND LABOR This cartoon, drawn by the illustrator Gustave Doré, depicts wealthy industrialists gambling with workers tied together as chips.

of a distinct ethnic minority, such as the Irish in Britain. When they demanded the right to vote, workers based their claim on their historic constitutional rights, not the interests of all wage earners. When they demonstrated in favor of the 10-hour working day, they did so to improve the conditions in which they worked, not to advance the struggle of all workers against the middle class. The work experiences of laborers were too varied to sustain a widespread awareness that they belonged to one homogeneous group. Consequently, appeals for working-class solidarity to a large extent fell on deaf ears.

It is true that on certain occasions workers took violent action against their employers. In 1812 groups of hand loom weavers in the highly industrialized Midland region of England engaged in a determined campaign to destroy the new power looms that they blamed for rising unemployment and low wages. Often disguised and operating at night, these "Luddites," who took their name from their mythical leader Ned Ludd, smashed the new textile machinery that factory owners had introduced. (Even today people who object to the introduction of new technology are referred to as Luddites.) These men, however, did not identify with other British workers, especially those tending textile machinery in the factories.

Nevertheless, occasional encounters between workers and bourgeoisie did heighten an awareness of class divisions in British society. In August 1819, 60,000 workers gathered in St. Peter's Field in Manchester to demand the right to vote and better working conditions. Frightened by the size of the demonstration and opposed to the workers' demands, the volunteer cavalrymen of the city, who belonged to the middle class, attacked the crowd, killing 11 people and injuring another 400. This violent confrontation, known as the Peterloo Massacre, did not lead to revolution or sustained class warfare, but it did contribute to the perception, shared by an increasingly large number of people, that British society was divided into large groups of people based on their economic position in society.

 Read the Document

A Luddite Pamphlet

Justice in History

The Sadler Committee on Child Labor

((• 📖 Read the Document

British Parliament, "Inquiry into Child Labor"

The widespread use of child labor in British factories and mines during the early decades of the Industrial Revolution led to efforts by social reformers and Members of Parliament to regulate the conditions under which children worked. Parliament passed legislation restricting the number of hours that all children could work in textile mills in 1819 and 1829, but neither of these laws was enforced effectively, and they did not apply to all industries. Complaints of inhumane treatment, moral degradation, and exploitation of child workers continued to surface. In 1831 Michael Sadler (1780–1835), a Tory member of the British Parliament, introduced a bill in Parliament to limit the number of hours that all children could work to 10 hours per day. Like many social reformers, Sadler was inspired by what he considered his Christian duty to protect dependent members of the community.

Sadler chaired the committee to which his bill was referred. To muster support for the bill, Sadler held hearings in which child workers themselves came before the committee to report on the conditions under which they lived and worked. The success of his bill was by no means guaranteed. Many Members of Parliament were deeply committed to the policy of *laissez-faire*, according to which the government should not intervene in the operation of the economy, treating it instead as a self-regulating machine. Sadler had to convince his colleagues that they should modify that policy in the case of children, on the grounds that the state was obliged to provide for the welfare of children when their parents were unable to do so. He also needed to make the Members of Parliament and the broader public aware of the brutality of the conditions under which the children worked.

The hearings that took place were not a trial in the strict sense of the word, but they possessed many of the features of a judicial investigation, not unlike those conducted by American grand juries in criminal cases. Sadler intended the committee's proceedings to expose, condemn, and ultimately remedy misconduct by the factory owners. Procedurally the committee members had more latitude than courts of law. Because such parliamentary committees were designed to extract

CHILD LABOR IN THE TEXTILE INDUSTRY Children walking to work in a textile mill in northern England in the nineteenth century.

information rather than to bring offenders to trial, they did not need to adhere to any established judicial guidelines. There was no cross-examination of witnesses, nor could factory owners present a defense. The witnesses in this investigation were chosen because Sadler knew they would reveal the evils of the factory system.

The testimony presented to the Sadler Committee produced abundant evidence of the exploitation and physical abuse of child workers. Some of the most harrowing testimony came from the examination of a 17-year-old boy, Joseph Hebergam, on July 1, 1832. Hebergam revealed that he had begun the work of worsted spinning at age 7, that he worked at the factory from 5 A.M. until 8 P.M., and that he had only 30 minutes for lunch at noon, leaving him to eat his other meals while standing on the job. In the factory there were three overlookers (supervisors), one of whom was responsible for greasing the machinery and another for disciplining the workers. The latter overlooker walked continually up and down the factory with whip in hand.

When asked where his brother John was working, Joseph replied that he had died three years before at age 16. Sadler then inquired into the cause of his brother's death. The boy responded, "It was attributed to this, that he died from working such long hours and that it had been brought on by the factory. They have to stop the flies [part of the textile machinery] with their knees, because they go so swift they cannot stop them with their hands; he got a bruise on the shin by a spindle-board, and it went on to that degree that it burst; the surgeon cured that, then he was better; then he went to work again; but when he had worked about two months more his spine became affected, and he died." The witness went on to explain that his own severe labor had damaged his knees and ankles so much so that he found it painful to walk. His brother and sister would help carry him to the factory, but when they arrived late, even by as little as five minutes, the overlooker beat all three of them "till we were black and blue."[4] At the request of

(continued on next page)

(continued from previous page)

the committee, Joseph then stood up to show the condition of his limbs. He reported the death of another boy who had sustained massive injuries when he was caught in the shaft of the machinery he was running. Joseph concluded his testimony by recounting how the factory owners had threatened him and his younger brothers with losing their jobs if they testified before the committee.

Although widely publicized, the hearings of the Sadler Committee fell short of realizing their original objective. The bill, which eventually was approved by Parliament as the Factory Regulations Act of 1833, prohibited the employment of children under age nine in all factories. Boys and girls were allowed to work up to nine hours a day from age nine until their thirteenth birthday, and up to 12 hours a day from age 13 until their eighteenth birthday. Nevertheless, the long-term effect of this legislation was to establish in Western industrialized countries the principle that early childhood was a period of life set aside for education rather than work.

For Discussion

1. This investigation was concerned with the achievement of social justice rather than the determination of criminal culpability. What were the advantages of using legislative committees in such an undertaking?
2. Child labor was not a new phenomenon in the early eighteenth century. Why did the Industrial Revolution draw attention to this age-old practice?

Taking It Further

Horn, Pamela. *Children's Work and Welfare, 1780–1890*. 1996. An examination of the scale and nature of child employment in Britain and changing attitudes toward the practice.

The Industrial Landscape

As industry spread throughout Europe, urban and rural areas underwent dramatic changes. The most striking of these transformations took place in the new industrial towns and cities, some of which had been little more than country towns before the factories were built. Manchester, for example, grew from a modest population of 23,000 people in 1773 to a bustling metropolis of 105,000 by 1820. Large factories with their smokestacks and warehouses, ringed by long rows of houses built to accommodate the

THE PETERLOO MASSACRE, 1819 This drawing of the Peterloo Massacre shows the mounted yeomen of Manchester, with swords drawn, attacking the demonstrators, who had gathered to hear the speeches by the reformers on the platform above.

armies of new industrial workers, gave these cities an entirely new and for the most part grim appearance.

Cities experienced the most noticeable changes in physical appearance, but the countryside also began to take on a new look, mainly as a result of the transport revolution. The tunnels, bridges, and viaducts that were constructed to accommodate the railroad and the canals that were built to improve inland water transportation made an indelible imprint on the countryside. In many ways this alteration of the landscape demonstrated the mastery over nature that human beings had achieved at the time of the Scientific Revolution. The Industrial Revolution finally fulfilled the technological promise of that earlier revolution, and one of its effects was the actual transformation of the physical world.

The advent of modern industry also brought about a change in attitudes toward the landscape. The destruction of natural beauty in the interest of economic progress stimulated an appreciation of nature that had not been widespread during the medieval and early modern periods. Before the Industrial Revolution many features of the countryside, especially mountains, were viewed as obstacles to either travel or human habitation, not as objects of aesthetic appreciation. Urbanization and industrialization changed those perceptions, triggering a nostalgic reaction that became one of the sources of the romantic movement, which we shall consider in greater detail in the next chapter.

Industry did not always blight the landscape or offend artistic sensibilities. Some of the new industrial architecture, especially the viaducts and aqueducts that traversed valleys in the mountainous regions of the country, were masterpieces of modern engineering and architecture. Sir Walter Scott (1771–1832), the Scottish romantic novelist, claimed that the cast-iron Pontcysyllte aqueduct in Wales, which carried the waters of the Caledonian Canal 127 feet above the River Dee, was the most beautiful work of art he had ever seen. The railroad also had the ability to inspire the artistic imagination, as it did in Joseph Turner's (1775–1851) romantic painting *Rain, Steam and Speed*, which captured the railroad's speed and beauty.

JOSEPH M. W. TURNER, RAIN, STEAM AND SPEED: THE GREAT WESTERN RAILWAY (1844) This was one of the first oil paintings that had the railroad locomotive as its theme.

Industry, Trade, and Empire

21.5 What was the relationship between Britain's industrial strength and the growth of its empire?

In the middle of the nineteenth century, Britain towered above all other nations in the volume of its industrial output, the extent of its international trade, and the size of its empire. In industrial production it easily outpaced all its competitors, producing two-thirds of the world's coal, about half of its cotton cloth, half of its iron, and 40 percent of its hardware. Little wonder that Britain became known as "the workshop of the world." Britain controlled about one-third of the world's trade, and London emerged as the undisputed financial center of the global economy. Britain's overseas empire, which included colonies in Canada, the Caribbean, South America, India, Southeast Asia, and Australia, eclipsed those of all other European powers and continued to grow during the second half of the century.

These three great British strengths—industry, trade, and empire—were closely linked. Britain's colonies in both Asia and the Americas served as trading depots, while the promotion of trade led directly to the acquisition of new imperial possessions. Even when Britain did not formally acquire territory, it often established exclusive trading relationships with those countries, thereby creating an informal "empire of trade." Trade and empire in turn served the purposes of industry. Many of the raw materials used in industrial production, especially cotton, came from Britain's imperial possessions. Those possessions also provided markets for Britain's mass-produced manufactured goods. Such imperial markets proved immensely valuable when France blockaded its ports during the Napoleonic wars and thereby cut into British trade with the entire European continent.

The great challenge for British industrialists during the nineteenth century was to find new markets for their industrial products. Domestic demand had been strong at the beginning of the Industrial Revolution, but by the 1840s British workers did not possess sufficient wealth to purchase the increasingly large volume of hardwares and textiles manufactured in the mills and factories. Britain had to look overseas to find markets in which to sell the bulk of its industrial products. One possibility was to market them in other European countries, such as France and Germany, where demand for manufactured goods was high. These countries, however, were in the midst of their own industrial revolutions, and their governments had often legislated high protective tariffs against British goods to encourage the growth of their own industries. British industrialists, therefore, marketed their goods in less economically developed parts of the world, including British colonies. In all these areas, moreover, British military power and diplomatic influence advanced the interests of industry, trade, and empire.

East Asia: The Opium War, 1839–1842

British conflict with China provides the best illustration of the way in which the British desire to promote trade led to the acquisition of new colonies. For three centuries the Chinese had tightly controlled their trade with European powers. By 1842, however, British merchants, supported by the British government, managed to break down these barriers and give Britain a foothold in China, allowing it to exploit the East Asian market.

The conflict arose over the importation of opium, a narcotic made from poppy seeds and produced in great quantities in India. This drug, which numbed pain but also had hallucinogenic effects and could cause profound lethargy, was in widespread use in Europe and had an even larger market in Asia. In China opium had became a national addiction by the middle of the eighteenth century. The situation became much worse when British merchants increased the volume of illegal imports from India to China in the early nineteenth century. The Chinese government prohibited the use of opium, but because it had difficulty enforcing its own edicts, it decided to put an end to the opium trade.

Chinese efforts to stop British merchants from importing opium led to an increase in tensions between China and Britain. The situation reached a climax in 1839, when the Chinese seized 20,000 chests of opium in the holds of British ships and spilled them into the China Sea. It is unknown what effect the opium had on the fish, but the incident led to a British attack on Chinese ports. In this conflict, the first Opium War (1839–1842), the British had the advantage of superior naval technology, itself a product of the Industrial Revolution. The first iron-clad, steam-driven gunboat used in combat, the *Nemesis,* destroyed Chinese batteries along the coast, and an assault by 75 British ships on Chinkiang forced the Chinese to come to terms. In a treaty signed in 1842 China ceded the island of Hong Kong to the British, reimbursed British merchants for the opium it had destroyed, and opened five Chinese ports to international trade. As part of this settlement, each of these ports was to be governed by a British consul who was not subject to Chinese law. In this way Britain expanded its empire, increased its already large share of world trade, and found new markets for British manufactured goods in East Asia.

India: Annexation and Trade

The interrelationship of industry, trade, and empire became even clearer in India, which became known as the jewel in Britain's imperial crown. As we saw in Chapter 18, Britain gained control of the Indian province of Bengal in the eighteenth century and subsequently acquired other Indian states. After the Sepoy Mutiny of 1857 the British government brought all of India under its direct control.

Political control of India during the nineteenth century served the interests of British trade in two ways. First, it gave British merchants control of the trade between India and other Asian countries. Second, Britain developed a favorable balance of trade with India, exporting more goods to that country than it imported. Taxes paid to the British government by Indians and interest payments on British loans to India increased the flow of capital from Calcutta to London. The influx of capital from India was largely responsible for the favorable balance of payments that Britain enjoyed with the rest of the world until World War I. The capital that Britain received from these sources as well as from trade with China was funneled into the British economy or invested in British economic ventures throughout the world.

Control of India also served British interests by supplying British industries with raw materials while giving them access to the foreign markets they needed to make a profit. This promotion of British industry came at the expense of the local Indian economy. The transportation of cotton grown in India to British textile mills only to be returned to India in the form of finished cloth certainly retarded, if it did not destroy, the existing Indian textile industry. Resentment of this economic exploitation of India became one of the main sources of Indian nationalism in the late nineteenth century.

Latin America: An Empire of Trade

British policy in Latin America developed differently from the way it had in China and India, but it had the same effect of opening up new markets for British goods. Great Britain was a consistent supporter of the movements for independence that erupted in South America between 1810 and 1824 (see Chapter 18). Britain supported these movements not simply because it wished to undermine Spanish and Portuguese imperialism, but also because it needed to acquire new markets for its industrial products. Britain did not need to use military force to open these areas to British trade, as it did in China. Once the countries became independent, they attracted large volumes of British exports. In 1840 the British cotton industry shipped 35 percent of its exports to Latin American countries, especially to Argentina, Brazil, Uruguay, Mexico, and Chile. British financiers also exported large amounts of capital to these Latin American countries by investing vast sums of money in their economies. Britain thus established an informal "empire of trade" in Latin America. Britain did not govern these countries, but they developed the same economic relationship with Britain as other parts of the British Empire.

British investment and trade brought the newly independent states of Latin America into the industrial world economy. These countries, however, assumed a dependent position in that economy, not unlike the position India acquired about the same time. One effect of this dependence was to transform the small, self-sufficient village economies that had developed alongside the large plantations in Central and South America. Instead of producing goods themselves and selling them within their own markets, these villages now became suppliers of raw materials for British industry. This transformation made the Latin American population more dependent upon British manufactured goods, retarded or destroyed native Latin American industry, and created huge trade deficits for Latin American countries by the middle of the nineteenth century.

Ireland: The Internal Colony

Of all the imperial possessions with which Britain engaged in trade, the position of Ireland was the most anomalous. Despite its proximity to England, Ireland had always been treated as a colony. In 1801, after the unsuccessful Irish rebellion of 1798 discussed in Chapter 18, the British government incorporated Ireland into the United Kingdom and abolished the Irish Parliament. Although a small minority of Irishmen elected their representatives to sit in the British Parliament, and although Ireland thus became a part of the British state, Britain nonetheless continued to treat the country as an imperial possession.

Throughout the nineteenth century Ireland remained almost entirely agricultural. Industrialization occurred only in the northern province of Ulster, which produced ready-to-wear undergarments for women and shirts for men. Ireland's vast agricultural estates, many of them owned by absentee British landlords, provided Britain with large imports of grain. Unable to afford the high cost of grain, which British protectionist legislation priced artificially high, and without the opportunity to find employment in industry, Irish tenants eked out an existence on the land, relying on a diet consisting almost entirely of potatoes. When a blight destroyed the potato crop in 1845, the country experienced a devastating famine that killed more than one million people and forced another million to emigrate—many of them to the United States and Canada—between 1845 and 1848. The famine occurred despite the fact that Irish lands produced enough grain to feed the entire population. As the Lord Mayor of Dublin complained in 1845, British commercial policy inflicted on the Irish "the abject misery of having their own provisions carried away to feed others, while they themselves are left contemptuously to starve."[5] Thus, even in this internal colony, the British government's policy of promoting industry at home while importing resources from its imperial possessions served British economic interests at the expense of the countries under its control.

CONCLUSION

Industrialization and the West

By 1850 the Industrial Revolution had initiated some of the most dramatic changes in human life recorded in historical documents. Not since the Neolithic Age, when people began to live in settled villages, cultivate grains, and domesticate animals, did the organization of society, the patterns of work, and the landscape undergo such profound changes. In many ways the Industrial Revolution marked the watershed between the old way of life and the new. It gave human beings unprecedented technological control over nature, made employment in the home the exception rather than the rule, and submitted industrial workers to a regimen unknown in the past. It changed family life, gave cities an entirely new appearance, and unleashed new and highly potent political forces, including the ideologies of liberalism and socialism, which we discuss in the next chapter.

Industrialization changed the very definition of the West. In the Middle Ages Christianity shaped the predominant cultural values of Western countries, while in the eighteenth century the rational, scientific culture of the Enlightenment became central to the idea of the West. Now, in the nineteenth century, industrialization—and the system of industrial capitalism it spawned—increasingly defined the West. In discussing the prospects of industrialization in the Ottoman Empire in 1856, a British diplomat wrote that "Europe is at hand, with its science, its labor, and its capital," but that the Qur'an and other elements of traditional Turkish culture "are so many obstacles to advancement in a Western sense."[6] The Industrial Revolution thus created new divisions between the West and the non-Western world.

Until the late nineteenth century, industrialization took place only in nations that had traditionally been a part of the West. Beginning in the 1890s, however, countries that lay outside the West or on its margins began to introduce industrial technology and methods. Between 1890 and 1910 Russia and Japan underwent a period of rapid industrialization, and in the second half of the twentieth century many countries in Asia, the Middle East, and Latin America followed suit. This process of industrialization and economic development is often described as one of Westernization, and it has usually led to conflicts within those countries between Western and non-Western values. Whether those countries that have industrialized should be considered Western is not clear. Industrialization outside Europe and the United States reveals once again that the composition of the West changes from time to time and that its boundaries are often difficult to define.

MAKING CONNECTIONS

1. Why did the Industrial Revolution begin in Great Britain?
2. What are the strengths and weaknesses of the optimistic view of the Industrial Revolution?
3. What was the relationship between the growth of the population and the Industrial Revolution?
4. How did the Industrial Revolution change the definition of the West?

TAKING IT FURTHER

For suggested readings see page R–1.

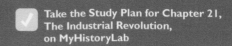
Chapter Review

The Nature of the Industrial Revolution

21.1 What was the Industrial Revolution of the late eighteenth and nineteenth centuries?

Four key developments comprised the Industrial Revolution: the introduction and implementation of new industrial technology like textile machinery and the steam engine, the use of minerals like coal as sources of energy for the production and transportation of goods, the replacement of the rural cottage system to production in large factories, and the development of new methods of transportation, like the railroad, to transport goods.

Conditions Favoring Industrial Growth

21.2 What social and economic changes made industrial development possible?

An increase in the birthrate and a decrease in the occurrence of famines allowed population growth that encouraged industrial growth. The increase in farming productivity allowed more people to leave the farms to work in the factories and mines, and the substantial growth of capital and of a consumer culture also favored industrial development.

The Spread of Industrialization

21.3 How did industrialization spread from Great Britain to the European continent and America?

Scarce resources and political and social barriers meant that industrialization occurred at a slower rate on the European continent. Once countries started to industrialize, government involvement, banks, and the already existing railroad system became key factors in the process. In America, where natural resources were abundant, the process of industrialization more closely resembled Britain's, including the absence of governmental involvement.

The Effects of Industrialization

21.4 What were the economic, social, and cultural effects of the Industrial Revolution?

The accumulation of capital meant that industry could employ workers, who in turn used their income to marry earlier and successfully maintain larger families. But unhealthy working conditions and environmental pollution were also an effect of industrialization. Unable to combine domestic and occupational labor, women left the workforce. Cities, some built up around factories, and the countryside, where canals and bridges were built to transport goods, were transformed.

Industry, Trade, and Empire

21.5 What was the relationship between Britain's industrial strength and the growth of its empire?

British military power and diplomatic influence advanced the interests of industry, trade, and empire. Colonies in both Asia and the Americas served as trading depots, while the promotion of trade led directly to the acquisition of new imperial possessions. Many of the raw materials used in industrial production came from Britain's colonies, and those same colonies were also markets for Britain's mass-produced manufactured goods.

Chapter Time Line

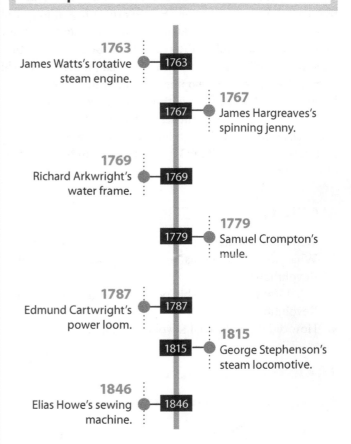

1763
James Watts's rotative steam engine.
1763

1767
1767
James Hargreaves's spinning jenny.

1769
Richard Arkwright's water frame.
1769

1779
1779
Samuel Crompton's mule.

1787
Edmund Cartwright's power loom.
1787

1815
1815
George Stephenson's steam locomotive.

1846
Elias Howe's sewing machine.
1846

22 Ideological Conflict and National Unification, 1815–1871

On March 18, 1871, the president of the French government, Adolphe Thiers, sent a small unit of troops to Paris to seize cannons that had been used against Prussian forces during their siege of the city a few months before. The cannons were in the possession of the National Guard, the citizen militia of Paris. The members of the National Guard felt that Thiers's government had abandoned them by recently concluding an armistice with the Prussians, who were still camped outside the city. They also believed that Thiers was determined to gain control of the city, which had refused to comply with the orders of the national government. When the troops reached the city, they encountered a hostile

EUGÈNE DELACROIX, *LIBERTY LEADING THE PEOPLE* (1830) The romantic representation of Liberty carrying the French tricolor during the Paris revolution of 1830 conveys the ideological inspiration and the violence of that armed uprising.

SOURCE: Eugène Delacroix (1798–1860), "July 28th, 1830; Liberty Guides the People," oil on canvas, 260 × 325 cm. Louvre, Dept. des Peintures, Paris, France. © Photograph by Erich Lessing/Art Resource, NY.

LEARNING OBJECTIVES

22.1 ((·
What were the main features of the four new ideologies of the early nineteenth century?

22.2 ((·
How did those ideologies shape the political history of Europe between 1815 and 1848?

22.3 ((·
How did liberal and conservative leaders use the ideology of nationalism to form nation-states?

22.4 ((·
How did warfare lead to political change in Russia and France between 1850 and 1871?

((· Listen to Chapter 22 on MyHistoryLab

⊙ Watch the Video Series on MyHistoryLab

Learn about some key topics related to this chapter with the *MyHistoryLab Video Series:*
Key Topics in Western Civilization

crowd of Parisians, many of whom were armed. The crowd surrounded the two generals who led the detachment, placed them up against a wall, and executed them.

This action led to a full-scale siege of Paris by government troops. In the city a committed group of radicals formed a new muhicipal government, the Paris Commune, a revival of the commune established during the French Revolution in 1792. The Commune took steps to defend the city against the government troops, and it implemented several social reforms. The Communards, as the members were known, set up a central employment bureau, established nurseries for working mothers, and recognized women's labor unions. For many decades the Commune served as a model of working-class government.

Yet the Paris Commune itself lasted only a few weeks. On May 21 the troops of the provisional government poured through the gates of the city, and during the "bloody week" that followed they took the city street by street, demolishing the barricades and executing the Communards. The Communards retaliated by executing a number of hostages, including the archbishop of Paris. They also burned down the Tuileries Palace, the hall of justice, and the city hall. During this one week at least 25,000 Communards were killed.

The short life of the Paris Commune marked the climax of a tumultuous period of European history. Between 1815 and 1871 Europe witnessed numerous movements for reform, periodic uprisings, and several revolutions. The people who participated in these momentous developments were inspired in large part by **ideologies**, theories of society and government that lay at the basis of political programs. The ideologies that developed during this period—liberalism, conservatism, socialism, and nationalism—endowed the West with a distinctive political culture. This chapter will address the following question:

ideologies Theories of society and government that form the basis of political programs.

How did these four ideologies affect the political and social history of the West from 1815 until 1871?

New Ideologies in the Early Nineteenth Century

22.1 What were the main features of the four new ideologies of the early nineteenth century?

The transformations of the West discussed in the last two chapters, the French Revolution and the Industrial Revolution, influenced the formation of the four new ideologies of the early nineteenth century.

Liberalism: The Protection of Individual Freedom

liberalism An ideology based on the conviction that individual freedom is of supreme importance and the main responsibility of government is to protect that freedom.

Liberalism is anchored in the belief that the main function of government is to promote political, social, and economic freedom. The primary objective of nineteenth-century liberals was to establish and protect individual rights, such as the freedom of the press, freedom of religion, and freedom from arbitrary arrest and imprisonment.

Liberals sought to guarantee these rights in written constitutions. Opposed to aristocratic privilege, they supported the principle of equality before the law. They also tended to be anticlerical, a position that led to frequent tension between them and the Roman Catholic Church. As defenders of individual freedom, they often campaigned to end slavery and serfdom.

The second objective of liberals was the extension of the franchise (the right to vote) to all property owners, especially the middle class. Liberals were usually opposed to giving the vote to the working class on the grounds that poor people, with little property of their own, could not be trusted to elect representatives who would protect property rights. Liberals also were opposed to giving the vote or any other form of political power to women. They believed that the proper arena for female activity was the home, where women occupied their natural domain. Liberals thus subscribed to the theory of separate spheres, which held that women were different in nature from men and that only male property holders should be allowed to participate in public affairs.

The third objective of liberals was to promote free trade with other nations and to resist government regulation of the domestic economy. This economic dimension of liberal ideology is usually referred to as **laissez-faire**, which means "let (people) do (as they choose)." Advocates of *laissez-faire* held that the government should intervene in the economy only to maintain public order and protect property rights. As merchants and manufacturers, liberals favored a policy of *laissez-faire* because it offered them the freedom to pursue their own self-interest without governmental interference and thereby realize greater profits.

One of the most influential proponents of liberal economic theory was David Ricardo (1772–1823), a British economist and stockbroker who argued that government efforts to regulate wages and prices would slow economic growth. In *Principles of Political Economy and Taxation* (1819), Ricardo argued that if wages were left to the law of supply and demand, they would fall to near subsistence levels, leading workers to limit the size of their families. Lower wages and fewer consumers would in turn keep prices low. Industrialists found Ricardo's *laissez-faire* theory appealing, but it was harder to convince workers that this "iron law of wages" would benefit them.

Liberalism found its greatest strength among the urban middle class. These people formed the group that felt most aggrieved by their exclusion from political life during the eighteenth and early nineteenth centuries and most eager to have government protect their property.

Conservatism: Preserving the Established Order

In the early nineteenth century the ideals of the Enlightenment and the radical changes ushered in by the French Revolution led to the formulation of a new ideology of **conservatism**, a set of ideas intended to prevent a recurrence of the revolutionary changes of the 1790s. The main goal of conservatives after 1815 was to preserve the monarchies and aristocracies of Europe against liberal movements.

The founder of modern conservative ideology was the Irish-born parliamentary orator Edmund Burke (1729–1797). In *Reflections on the Revolution in France* (1790), Burke insisted that rights did not derive from human nature, as Enlightenment thinkers insisted, but were privileges that had been passed down through the ages and could be preserved only by a hereditary monarchy. Burke also contended that equality, so loudly proclaimed at the time of the French Revolution, was a dangerous myth that would undermine the social order. For Burke the social order was a partnership between the living, the dead, and those who had yet to be born. By introducing revolutionary change, the French Revolution had broken that partnership.

Early nineteenth-century conservatives justified the institution of monarchy on the basis of religion as well as history. The French writer Louis de Bonald (1754–1840) argued that Christian monarchies were the final creation in the development of both religious and political society. Only monarchies of this sort could preserve public order

 Read the Document

John Stuart Mill, Excerpts from *On Liberty*

 Read the Document

David Ricardo, *On Wages*, "The Iron Law of Wages"

laissez-faire The principle that governments should not regulate or otherwise intervene in the economy unless it is necessary to protect property rights and public order.

conservatism A nineteenth-century ideology intended to prevent a recurrence of the revolutionary changes of the 1790s and the implementation of liberal policies.

and prevent society from degenerating into the savagery witnessed during the French Revolution. Like his fellow French writer, Joseph de Maistre (1754–1821), de Bonald rejected the entire concept of natural rights and reiterated the traditional doctrine of divine right, according to which kings received their power from God.

Socialism: The Demand for Equality

socialism An ideology calling for the ownership of the means of production by the community with the purpose of reducing inequalities of income, wealth, opportunity, and economic power.

Socialism, the third new ideology of the early nineteenth century, arose in reaction against the development of industrial capitalism and the liberal ideas that justified it. Socialism calls for the ownership of the means of production (such as factories, machines, and railroads) by the community, with the purpose of reducing inequalities of income, wealth, opportunity, and economic power. In small communities, such ownership can be genuinely collective. In a large country, however, the only practical way to introduce socialism is to give the ownership of property to the state, which represents the people.

The main appeal of socialism was the prospect of remedying the deplorable social and economic effects of the Industrial Revolution. As we saw in Chapter 21, the short-term effects of industrialization included wretched working conditions, low wages, a regimentation of the labor force, and a declining standard of living. Socialists did not object to the mechanization of industry as such. Like liberals, they wanted society to be as productive as possible. They did, however, object to the system of industrial capitalism that accompanied industrialization and the liberal economic theory that justified it. (See *Different Voices* in this chapter.)

The earliest socialists, known as Utopian socialists, envisioned the creation of ideal communities in which perfect social harmony and cooperation would prevail. One of these Utopian socialists, the British industrialist and philanthropist Robert Owen (1771–1858), turned his mill in New Lanark, Scotland, into a model socialist community where he housed his workers and educated their children. In 1825 he established a similar community in New Harmony, Indiana. Utopian socialism was not particularly concerned with the granting of political rights to workers, nor did it encourage class consciousness or class tensions.

View the Closer Look Socialist Utopia in New Harmony, Indiana

ROBERT OWEN'S DESIGN FOR A SOCIALIST UTOPIA IN NEW HARMONY, INDIANA The symmetry of the city's design recalls the classical notions of an ordered life.

Different Voices
Liberals and Socialists View the Middle Class

N ineteenth-century liberals, who stressed individual rights and free trade, extolled the virtues of the middle class, whom they regarded as the most progressive and productive members of society. Socialists, however, viewed the middle class or bourgeoisie as exploitative capitalists who oppressed the working class. In the first document, the liberal British economist and political philosopher James Mill (1773–1836), who supported the effort to give the middle class greater representation in the British Parliament, argues that the working class should follow the advice and example of the middle class. Karl Marx and Friedrich Engels were the leading philosophers of communism, the form of socialism that emphasized class warfare and called for a dictatorship of the proletariat. In the second document Marx and Engels condemn the middle class for their oppression and exploitation of the proletariat.

James Mill Praises the Wisdom and Leadership of the Middle Class

It is to be observed, that the class which is universally described, as both the most wise, and the most virtuous part of every community, the middle rank, are wholly included in that part of the community which is not the aristocratical. It is also not disputed, that in Great Britain the middle rank are numerous, and form a large proportion of the whole body of the people. Another proposition may be stated, with a perfect confidence of the concurrence of all those men who have attentively considered the formation of opinions in the great body of society, or, indeed, the principles of human nature in general. It is, that the opinions of that class of the people, who are below the middle rank, are formed, and their minds are directed by that intelligent and virtuous rank, who come the most immediately in contact with them, who are in the constant habit of intimate communication with them, to whom they fly for advice and assistance in all their numerous difficulties, upon whom they feel an immediate and daily dependence, in health and in sickness, in infancy and in old age; to whom their children look up as models for their imitation, whose opinions they have daily repeated, and account it their honour to adopt. There can be no doubt whatever that the middle rank, which gives their most distinguished ornaments to science, to art, and to legislation itself, to every thing which exalts and refines human nature, is that part of the community of which, if the basis of representation were now so far extended, the opinion would ultimately decide. Of the people beneath them, a vast majority would be sure to be guided by their advice and example.

SOURCE: From James Mill, *Essay on Government* (1820).

Karl Marx and Friedrich Engels Assail the Middle Class for Their Exploitation of Workers

The modern bourgeois society that has sprouted from the ruins of feudal society has not done away with class antagonisms. It has but established new classes, new conditions of oppression, new forms of struggle in place of the old ones. Our epoch, the epoch of the bourgeoisie, possesses, however, this distinct feature: it has simplified class antagonisms. Society as a whole is more and more splitting up into two great hostile camps, into two great classes directly facing each other—bourgeoisie and proletariat. . . .

The bourgeoisie, wherever it has got the upper hand, has put an end to all feudal, patriarchal, idyllic relations. It has pitilessly torn asunder the motley feudal ties that bound man to his "natural superiors," and has left remaining no other nexus between man and man than naked self-interest, than callous "cash payment." It has drowned the most heavenly ecstasies of religious fervor, of chivalrous enthusiasm, of philistine sentimentalism, in the icy water of egotistical calculation. It has resolved personal worth into exchange value, and in place of the numberless indefeasible chartered freedoms, has set up that single, unconscionable freedom—Free Trade. In one word, for exploitation, veiled by religious and political illusions, it has substituted naked, shameless, direct, brutal exploitation. . . .

The bourgeoisie has through its exploitation of the world market given a cosmopolitan character to production and consumption in every country. To the great chagrin of Reactionists, it has drawn from under the feet of industry the national ground on which it stood. All old-established national industries have been destroyed or are daily being destroyed. They are dislodged by new industries, whose introduction becomes a life and death question for all civilized nations, by industries that no longer work up indigenous raw material, but raw material drawn from the remotest zones; industries whose products are consumed, not only at home, but in every quarter of the globe. In place of the old wants, satisfied by the production of the country, we find new wants, requiring for their satisfaction the products of distant lands and climes. In place of the old local and national seclusion and self-sufficiency, we have intercourse in every direction, universal interdependence of nations. The bourgeoisie, by the rapid improvement of all instruments of production, by the immensely facilitated means of communication, draws all, even the most barbarian, nations into civilization. The cheap prices of commodities are the heavy artillery with

(continued on next page)

(continued from previous page)

which it batters down all Chinese walls, with which it forces the barbarians' intensely obstinate hatred of foreigners to capitulate. It compels all nations, on pain of extinction, to adopt the bourgeois mode of production; it compels them to introduce what it calls civilization into their midst, i.e., to become bourgeois themselves. In one word, it creates a world after its own image.

SOURCE: From Karl Marx and Friedrich Engels, *The Communist Manifesto* (1848).

For Discussion

1. How do the authors of these two documents differ in their descriptions of the relationships between the middle class and the working class?
2. What is the basis of Mill's praise for the middle class and Marx and Engels' condemnation of it?
3. How might a liberal like Mill have responded to the publication of the *Communist Manifesto*? How might a conservative have responded?

A second generation of socialists became more concerned with using the power of the state to improve their lot. The most influential of these socialists was the French democrat Louis Blanc (1811–1882), who proposed that the state guarantee workers' wages and employment in times of economic depression. He also wanted the state to support the creation of workshops where workers would sell the product of their labor directly without middlemen. The principle underlying Blanc's concept of the social order was "From each according to his abilities; to each according to his needs." Blanc's brand of socialism began a long tradition in which workers tried to improve their circumstances by influencing government. This initiative was closely related to the radical democratic goal of universal male suffrage, which became one of the main objectives of many socialists after 1840.

The German social philosopher Karl Marx (1818–1883) formulated the most radical form of nineteenth-century socialism. Marx was much more preoccupied than other socialists with the collective identity and political activities of the working class. Reading about working conditions in France during the early 1840s, he became convinced that workers in industrial society were the ultimate example of human alienation and degradation. Marx and his co-author Friedrich Engels began to think of workers as part of a capitalist system, in which they owned nothing but their labor, which they sold to capitalist producers for wages.

Marx and Engels worked these ideas into a broad account of historical change in which society moved inevitably and progressively from one stage to another. They referred to the process by which history advanced as the **dialectic**. Marx acquired the idea of the dialectic from the German philosopher Georg Wilhelm Friedrich Hegel (1770–1831), who believed that history advanced in stages as the result of the conflict between one idea and another. Marx disagreed with Hegel on the source of historical change, arguing that material or economic factors rather than ideas determined the course of history. Hence, Marx's socialist philosophy became known as **dialectical materialism**.

According to Marx and Engels, the first stage of the dialectic had taken place when the bourgeoisie, who received their income from capital, seized political power from the aristocracy, who received their income from land, during the English and French revolutions. Marx and Engels predicted that the next stage of the dialectic would be a conflict between the bourgeoisie and the working class or **proletariat**, which received its income from wages. This conflict, according to Marx and Engels, would result in the triumph of the working class. Led by a committed band of revolutionaries, the proletariat would take control of the state, establish a dictatorship so that they could implement their program without opposition, and usher in a classless society.

Marx and Engels issued this call to action in *The Communist Manifesto* (1848), which ended with the famous words, "Working men of all countries unite!" Marx's brand of socialism, **communism**, takes its name from this book. Communism is a revolutionary ideology that advocates the overthrow of "bourgeois" or capitalist institutions and the transfer of political power to the proletariat. Communism differs from other forms of socialism in its call for revolution, its emphasis on class conflict, and its

dialectic The theory that history advanced in stages as the result of the conflict between different ideas or social groups.

dialectical materialism The socialist philosophy of Karl Marx according to which history advanced as the result of material or economic forces and would lead to the creation of a classless society.

proletariat The word used by Karl Marx and Friedrich Engels to identify the class of workers who received their income from wages.

communism The revolutionary form of socialism developed by Karl Marx and Friedrich Engels that promoted the overthrow of bourgeois or capitalist institutions and the establishment of a dictatorship of the proletariat.

 Read the Document

Karl Marx and Friedrich Engels, from the *Communist Manifesto*

insistence on complete economic equality. Communism belongs to a tradition that originated among members of the extreme wing of the democratic movement at the height of the French Revolution. One of those radicals, François-Noël Babeuf (1760–1797), demanded economic and political equality, called for the common ownership of land, and spoke in terms of class warfare. Marx's achievement was to place Babeuf's radical ideas in the framework of dialectical materialism in his monumental three-volume work, *Capital* (1867–1894).

Nationalism: The Unity of the People

Nationalism, the fourth new ideology of the early nineteenth century, also took shape during and after the French Revolution. A **nation** in the nineteenth-century sense of the word refers to a large community of people who believe that they have a common homeland and share a similar culture. The ideology of **nationalism** is the belief that the people who form this nation should have their own political institutions and that the interests of the nation should be defended and promoted at all costs.

The geographical boundaries of nations, however, do not often correspond to the geographical boundaries of states, which are administrative and legal units of political organization. For example, in the early nineteenth century Germans often referred to their nation as comprising all people who spoke German. At that time there were more than a dozen German states, including Prussia, Bavaria, and Baden, and there were also many German speakers living in non-German lands, such as Bohemia. A primary goal of nationalists is to create a **nation-state**, a single political entity that governs all the members of a particular nation. The doctrine that justifies this goal is **national self-determination**, the claim that any group that considers itself a nation has the right to be ruled only by members of its own nation and to have all the members of the nation included in this state.

The ideology of nationalism had roots in the French Revolution. Most of the revolutionary steps taken in France during the 1790s were undertaken in the name of a united French people—the French *nation*. Article 3 of the *Declaration of the Rights of Man and Citizen* (1789) declared that "the principle of all authority rests essentially in the nation." The French Republic was constructed as the embodiment of the French nation. It gave an administrative unity to the French people and encouraged them to think of themselves as sharing a common cultural bond. Instead of a collection of regions, France had become *la patrie*, or the people's native land.

Nationalists emphasized the antiquity of nations, arguing that there had always been a distinct German, French, English, Swiss, or Italian people living in their respective homelands. This claim involved a certain amount of fiction, because in the past the people living in those lands possessed little cultural or linguistic unity. There was little uniformity, for example, in the languages spoken by people whom nineteenth-century nationalists identified as German, French, or Italian. Until the eighteenth century most educated Germans wrote in French, not German. Only a small percentage of Italians

KARL MARX Karl Marx, the German social philosopher who developed the revolutionary socialist doctrine of communism.

nation A large community of people who possess a sense of unity based on a belief that they have a common homeland and share a similar culture.

nationalism The belief that the people who form a nation should have their own political institutions and that the interests of the nation should be defended and promoted at all costs.

nation-state A political structure sought by nationalists in which the boundaries of the state and the nation are identical, so that all the members of a nation are governed by the same political authorities.

national self-determination The doctrine advanced by nationalists that any group that considers itself a nation has the right to be ruled only by the members of their own nation and to have all members of the nation included in that state.

687

national consciousness The awareness or belief of people that they belong to a nation.

United Kingdom The name of the British state formed by the union of England and Scotland in 1707. In 1801 Ireland became part of the United Kingdom; however, after the establishment of the Irish Free State in 1922, only the six Irish counties in the northern province of Ulster remained united to Britain.

spoke Italian (the language spoken in Tuscany), and the main language of many Italian nationalists of the nineteenth century was French. Even after nation-states were formed, a large measure of linguistic, religious, and ethnic diversity persisted within those states, making true cultural unity impossible. The nation is, therefore, something of a myth—an imagined community rather than an objective reality.

The ideal of the nation-state has proved almost impossible to realize. The boundaries of nations and states have never fully coincided. Patterns of human settlement are too fluid to prevent some members of a particular cultural group from living as a minority in a neighboring state. Some Poles, for example, have always lived in Germany, Spaniards in Portugal, and Italians in Switzerland. France at the time of the French Revolution probably came closest to realizing the ideal of a nation-state, claiming jurisdiction over most French people. Nevertheless, different cultural identities, such as those of the Basques in southwest France and the Flemish in the far northeast, both of whom spoke their own language, prevented the emergence of a powerful sense of national identity in all parts of France until the late nineteenth or early twentieth century.

In Britain the creation of a nation-state was a complicated process. **National consciousness**, which is a people's belief that they belong to a nation, developed earlier in England than in any other country in Europe. In the sixteenth century almost all English people spoke the same language, and they were also subject to the same common law. In 1536, however, the principality of Wales was united to the kingdom of England, thereby including two nations, the English and the Welsh, in the same state. In 1707 England and Scotland were united in a new state, the **United Kingdom** of Great Britain, and in 1801 Ireland was brought into the United Kingdom as well. Thus, the United Kingdom in the nineteenth century included four nations: the English, the Welsh, the Scots, and the Irish. In this multinational state, the task of building a British nation, as opposed to an English or a Scottish nation, has taken time. To this day, Britons are more accustomed to think of themselves as English, Welsh, or Scottish than as British.

Other peoples faced even more daunting obstacles in constructing nation-states. Many nations were subsumed within large empires, such as Hungarians and Croatians in the Austrian Empire and Greeks and Serbs in the Ottoman Empire. In those empires, nationalist movements often took the form of separatist revolts or wars of independence, in which a nationalist group attempted to break off and form a nation-state of its own. A very different situation prevailed in Germany and Italy, where people who shared some linguistic and cultural traditions lived under the control of many different states. In these cases, nationalist movements sought to unite the smaller states into a larger nation-state.

One of the great paradoxes of nationalism is that the acquisition of colonies overseas often strengthened nationalist sentiment at home. The military conquest of these lands became a source of pride for the people in the metropolis, and also gave them a sense of cultural superiority. The main source of British national pride was the rapid spread of British control over one-quarter of the world's surface during the eighteenth and nineteenth centuries. Nationalism could also promote the supremacy of one's own nation over others. The French revolutionaries who conquered a large part of the European continent in the early nineteenth century justified their expansion on the grounds that they were superior to the rest of the human race. In 1848 a fervent German nationalist declared his support for "the preponderance of the German race over most Slav races." The Italian national leader Giuseppe Mazzini (1805–1872) preferred to be called a patriot rather than a nationalist on the grounds that nationalists were imperialists who sought to encroach on the rights of other peoples.

Nationalism was often linked to liberalism during the early nineteenth century, when both movements supported revolutionary programs to realize the goal of national self-determination. Liberals believed that representative government and a limited expansion of the franchise would provide a firm foundation for the establishment of the nation-state. The two ideologies, however, differed in emphasis. Liberalism stressed individual freedom, whereas nationalism was more concerned with political unity. At times those different ideals came into conflict with each other. The liberal doctrine of free trade, for example, ran into conflict with the doctrine of economic nationalism, which encouraged the protection of national industries.

Nationalism was just as capable of supporting conservatism as liberalism in the early nineteenth century. Because nationalists viewed the nation as having deep roots in the distant past, some of them glorified the monarchical and hierarchical political arrangements that prevailed in the Middle Ages. In 1848 conservative Prussian landlords rallied around the cause of "God, King, and Fatherland." Later in the nineteenth century, nationalism became identified almost exclusively with conservatism when the lower middle classes began to prefer the achievement of national glory, either in warfare or in imperialistic pursuits, to the establishment of individual freedom.

Culture and Ideology

The four new ideologies of the early nineteenth century were influenced by two powerful cultural traditions: scientific rationalism and romanticism. These two traditions represented sharply divergent sides of modern Western culture.

SCIENTIFIC RATIONALISM Scientific rationalism originated in the Scientific Revolution and reached its full flowering in the Enlightenment. This tradition has provided a major source of Western identity ever since the late eighteenth century. It stresses the powers of human reason and considers science superior to all other forms of knowledge. Scientific rationalism is essentially a secular tradition, in that it does not rely on theology or Christian revelation for its legitimacy. The effort to construct a science of human nature, which was central to Enlightenment thought, belongs to this tradition, while the Industrial Revolution, which involved the application of scientific knowledge to production, was one of its products.

During the nineteenth century, scientific rationalism continued to influence Western thought and action. As scientific knowledge expanded, and as more people received a scientific education, the values of science and reason were proclaimed more boldly. Scientific knowledge and an emphasis on the importance of empirical data (that which can be tested) became essential components of much social thought. The clearest statement that science was the highest form of knowledge and would lead inevitably to human progress was the secular philosophy of **positivism**.

The French philosopher Auguste Comte (1798–1857) set forth the main elements of positivism. Like many thinkers in the Enlightenment tradition, Comte argued that human society passed through a succession of historical stages, each leading to a higher level. It had already passed through two stages, the theological and the metaphysical, and it was now in the third, the positive or scientific stage. The word *positive* in this context means that which has substance or concrete reality, as opposed to that which is abstract or speculative. Comte predicted that in the final positive stage of history the accumulation of factual or scientific knowledge would enable thinkers, whom we now call sociologists, to discover the laws of human behavior and thus make possible the improvement of society. This prediction of human progress, and Comte's celebration of the liberation of knowledge from its theological shackles, had particular appeal to liberals, especially those who harbored hostility to the Roman Catholic Church.

The values of science and the belief in its inevitable advance also influenced the social thought of Karl Marx. Friedrich Engels called Marx's ideology of communism scientific socialism, in that it too offers a vision of history determined solely by positive, in this case material or economic, developments. Marxism rejects the metaphysical, idealistic world of Hegel and the theology of all Christian religion and thus fits into the same scientific tradition to which positivism and earlier Enlightenment thought belongs.

positivism The philosophy developed by Auguste Comte in the nineteenth century according to which human society passed through a series of stages, leading to the final positive stage in which the accumulation of scientific data would enable thinkers to discover the laws of human behavior and bring about the improvement of society.

 Read the Document

Auguste Comte, "Course of Positive Philosophy"

romanticism An artistic and literary movement of the late eighteenth and nineteenth centuries that involved a protest against classicism, appealed to the passions rather than the intellect, and emphasized the beauty and power of nature.

ROMANTICISM The cultural tradition that posed the greatest challenge to scientific rationalism was **romanticism**. This tradition originated as an artistic and literary movement in the late eighteenth century, but it soon developed into a more general worldview. The artists and writers who identified themselves as romantics recognized the limits of human reason in comprehending reality. Unlike scientific rationalists, they used intuition and imagination to penetrate deeper levels of being and to comprehend the entire cosmos. Romantic art, music, and literature therefore appealed to the passions rather than the intellect.

Romantics did not think of reality as being simply material, as did the positivists. For them it was also spiritual and emotional, and their purpose as writers and artists was to communicate that nonempirical dimension of reality to their audiences. Romantics also had a different view of the relationship between human beings and nature. Instead of standing outside nature and viewing it objectively, in the manner of a scientist analyzing data derived from experiments, they considered themselves part of nature and emphasized its beauty and power.

As an art form, romanticism was a protest against classicism and, in particular, the classicism that prevailed in the late eighteenth century. As we discussed in Chapter 19, classicism reflects a worldview in which the principles of orderliness and rationality prevail. Classicism is a disciplined style that demands adherence to formal rules that govern the structure and the content of literature, art, architecture, and music. By contrast, romanticism allows the artist much greater freedom. In literature the romantic protest against classicism led to the introduction of a new poetic style involving the use of imagery, symbols, and myth. One example of this style is "Rime of the Ancient Mariner" (1798) by the English poet Samuel Taylor Coleridge (1772–1834). The poem uses the sun and moon as powerful symbols in describing a nightmarish sea voyage.

Many romantic works of literature, such as the novels of the Scottish author Sir Walter Scott (1771–1832), were set in the Middle Ages, which they saw not as a dark age of superstition but as an era that fostered spiritual and artistic pursuits. To emphasize the limits of scientific rationalism, other romantics explored the exotic, the weird, the mysterious, and even the satanic elements in human nature. Mary Shelley's introspective novel, *Frankenstein* (1818), an early example of science fiction, incorporated many of these themes. The novel, which tells the story of the creation of a large, ugly monster by the idealistic Swiss scientist Victor Frankenstein, reveals the preoccupation of romantic literature with the exotic and the mysterious. Frankenstein's rejection of the monster leads this freak of nature to kill the scientist's brother, his friend, his wife, and, ultimately, Frankenstein himself. Filled with self-loathing, this creature of modern science sets off to throw himself on his own funeral pyre.

Within the visual arts, romanticism also marked a rebellion against the classicism that had dominated eighteenth-century culture. Classicism emphasized formality and symmetry in art, and it celebrated the culture of an ideal Greek and Roman past. By contrast, romantic painters depicted landscapes that evoked a mood and an emotion rather than an objective pictorial account of the surroundings. Romantic paintings sought to evoke feeling rather than to help the viewer achieve intellectual comprehension. Some of their works conveyed the power of nature while others depicted its majesty and grandeur.

Romantic music, which also appealed to the emotions, marked a similar but more gradual departure from formal classicism. The inspirational music of Ludwig van Beethoven (1770–1827), the son of a German court musician from Bonn, marked the transition from classical to romantic forms. Beethoven's early work conformed to the conventions of classical music, but some of his later compositions, which defied traditional classical harmonies, were intended to evoke an emotional response. His famous "Ode to Joy" in his ninth and final symphony remains unequaled in its ability to rouse the passions. Another early romantic composer, Franz Schubert (1797–1828), who was born in Vienna, blended classical forms with romantic themes by incorporating

View the Closer Look

Cult of the Unattainable

CASPAR DAVID FRIEDRICH, *THE WANDERER ABOVE THE SEA OF FOG* (1818) This early nineteenth-century painting of a man observing a landscape covered by fog conveys the mystery and majesty of nature, which was a main theme of romantic art. It is unclear, however, whether the man, whose back is turned to the viewer, was awestruck by what he observed or was contemplating the difficult task of achieving human mastery over nature.

Hungarian and gypsy folk music into his compositions. The emotionally powerful operas of the German composer Richard Wagner (1813–1883), many of which were set in the mythical German past, marked the height of the romantic movement in music. That style attained its greatest popularity during the second half of the nineteenth century with the lyrical symphonies and concertos of Johannes Brahms (1833–1897) in Germany and the symphonies, ballets, and operas of Peter Tchaikovsky (1840–1893) in Russia.

Romanticism, like the rational and scientific culture it rejected, had powerful political implications, leaving its mark on the ideologies of the modern world. In the early nineteenth century, romanticism appealed to many liberals because it involved a protest against the established order and emphasized the freedom of the individual. The French romantic author Victor Hugo (1802–1885), whose epic novels *The Hunchback of Notre Dame* (1831) and *Les Misérables* (1862) depicted human suffering with great compassion, identified romanticism as "liberalism in literature." For Hugo a relationship existed between liberty in art and liberty in society. Romanticism could, however, support conservatism by idealizing the traditional social and political order of the Middle Ages and the central importance of religion in society.

Romanticism has a closer association with nationalism than with any other ideology. In the most general sense romanticism invested the idea of "the nation" with mystical qualities, thus inspiring devotion to it. Romantics also had an obsessive interest in the cultural, literary, and historical roots of national identity. The German philosopher and literary critic Johann Gottfried von Herder (1744–1803), for example, promoted the study of German language, literature, and history with the explicit purpose of giving the German people a sense of national unity.

In other parts of Europe, especially in Poland and the Balkans, romantic writers and artists gave nationalists the tools necessary to construct a common culture and history of their nations. The Polish romantic composer Frédéric Chopin (1810–1849), who emigrated to Paris in 1831, inspired Polish nationalists by drawing on native Polish dances in his works for the piano. At the same time the romantic poet Adam Mickiewicz (1798–1855), another Polish exile in Paris, wrote *The Books of the Polish Nation* (1832), exalting his country as the embodiment of freedom and predicting that by its long suffering it would eventually liberate the human race.

Ideological Encounters in Europe, 1815–1848

22.2	How did those ideologies shape the political history of Europe between 1815 and 1848?

The four new ideologies of the nineteenth century—liberalism, conservatism, socialism, and nationalism—interacted in a variety of ways, sometimes reinforcing each other and at other times leading to direct and violent political conflict. During the years between 1815 and 1831 the main ideological encounters occurred between liberalism, sometimes infused with nationalism, and conservatism. In 1815, at the time of the Congress of Vienna, it appeared that conservatism would carry the day. The determination of the major European powers to suppress any signs of revolutionary activity made the future of liberalism and nationalism appear bleak. The power of the new ideologies, however, could not be contained. Liberal and nationalist revolts took place in three distinct periods: the early 1820s, 1830, and 1848. During the latter two periods the demands of workers, sometimes expressed in socialist terms, added to the ideological mixture. In all these encounters conservatives had their say, and in most cases they emerged victorious.

Liberal and Nationalist Revolts, 1820–1825

Between 1820 and 1825 a sequence of revolts in Europe revealed the explosive potential of liberalism and nationalism and the determination of conservatives to crush those ideologies. These revolts also reflected the strength of movements for national self-determination. The three most significant revolts took place in Spain, Greece, and Russia.

THE LIBERAL REVOLTS OF 1820 IN SPAIN AND PORTUGAL The earliest clash between liberalism and conservatism occurred in Spain, where liberals ran into determined opposition from their king, Ferdinand VII (r. 1808–1833). Ferdinand had been restored to power in 1814 after his forced abdication in 1808. In 1812, during the rule of Joseph Bonaparte, the Spanish *Cortes*—the representative assembly in that kingdom—had approved a liberal constitution. This constitution provided a foundation for a limited monarchy and the protection of Spanish civil liberties. In keeping with the ideas of the French Revolution, it also declared that the Spanish nation, not the king, possessed sovereignty. The tension began when King Ferdinand declared that he would not recognize this constitution. Even worse for disheartened liberals, Ferdinand decided to reestablish the Spanish Inquisition, invited exiled Jesuits to return, and refused to summon the *Cortes*. In 1820, when the Spanish Empire in the New World had already begun to collapse (see Chapter 18), liberals in Madrid, in alliance with some military officers, seized power.

This liberal revolt proved to be a test for the **Concert of Europe**, the mechanism established at the Congress of Vienna to preserve the balance of power in Europe and prevent further revolution wherever it might arise. Klemens von Metternich, the Austrian foreign minister who had been responsible for proposing this cooperation of the major powers, urged intervention in Spain. Although the British refused because they wanted to protect their trading interests with the Spanish colonies, Austria, Prussia, and Russia agreed. These conservative powers restored Ferdinand to the throne, and again he renounced the liberal constitution of 1812. The liberals not only lost this struggle, but they also suffered bitter reprisals from the government, which tortured and executed their leaders. The situation became only marginally better in 1833, when Ferdinand died and the liberal ministers of his young daughter, Queen Isabella II (r. 1833–1868), drew up another constitution. Her reign was marked by civil war, instability, and factional strife in which liberals made few substantial gains.

Shortly after the Spanish revolt of 1820, a similar rebellion based on liberal ideas took place in Portugal. The royal family had fled to Brazil during the Napoleonic wars, leaving Portugal to be governed by a regent. A group of army officers removed the regent and installed a liberal government, which proceeded to suppress the Portuguese Inquisition, confiscate church lands, and invite King John (r. 1816–1826) to return to his native land as a constitutional monarch. After the king returned in 1822, his enthusiasm for liberal government waned. His granddaughter, Maria II (r. 1826–1853), kept the liberal cause alive, relying on support from Portugal's traditional ally, Britain, but she struggled against the forces of conservatism and had only limited success.

THE NATIONALIST REVOLT OF 1821 IN GREECE A revolt in Greece in 1821, inspired more by nationalism than liberalism, achieved greater success than did the rebellions of 1820 in Spain and Portugal. It succeeded because other members of the Concert of Europe, not just Britain, lent their support to the revolt. Greece had long been a province in the sprawling Ottoman Empire, but a nationalist movement, organized by Prince Alexander Ypsilantis (1792–1828), created a distinct Greek national identity and inspired the demand for a separate Greek state. In 1821 a series of revolts against Ottoman rule took place on the mainland of Greece and on some of the surrounding islands. These rebellions received widespread support in Europe from scholars who considered Greece the cradle of Western civilization and from religiously inspired individuals who saw this as a struggle of Christianity against Islam. Hundreds of European volunteers joined the Greek rebel forces. Thus, the insurrection became not only a liberal and national revolt, but also a broad cultural encounter between East and West. The English romantic poets George Lord Byron (1788–1824) and Percy Shelley (1792–1822) became active and passionate advocates for Greek independence, while the romantic painter Eugène Delacroix (1798–1863) depicted the horror of the Turkish massacre of the entire population of the Greek island of Chios in 1822. The link between nationalism and romanticism could not have been more explicit.

The Greek revolt placed the powers allied in the Concert of Europe in a quandary. On the one hand,

Concert of Europe The joint efforts made by Austria, Prussia, Russia, Britain, and France during the years following the Congress of Vienna to suppress liberal and nationalist movements throughout Europe.

22.1

22.2

22.3

22.4

EUGÈNE DELACROIX, *THE MASSACRE AT CHIOS* (1824) In 1821 the Greeks on the Aegean Islands rebelled against their Turkish rulers, and in April 1822 Turkish reprisals reached their peak in the massacre of the inhabitants of Chios. Romantic paintings were intended to evoke feelings, in this case horror, at the genocide perpetrated by the Turks against the Greek rebels. The painting reveals the close association of romantic art with the causes of liberalism and nationalism.

they were committed to intervene on behalf of the established order to crush any nationalist or liberal revolts, and they condemned the insurrection on those grounds when it first erupted. On the other hand, they were Western rulers who identified the Ottoman Turks with everything that was alien to Christian civilization. Moreover, Russia wanted to use this opportunity to dismember its ancient enemy, the Ottoman Empire. The European powers eventually took the side of the Greek rebels. In 1827 Britain, France, and Russia threatened the Turks with military intervention if they did not agree to an armistice and grant the Greeks their independence. When the Turks refused, the combined naval forces of those three countries destroyed the fleet of the Turks' main ally, Egypt, at Navarino off the Greek coast. This naval action turned the tide in favor of the Greeks, who in 1833 finally won their independence and placed a Bavarian prince, Otto I (r. 1833–1862), on the throne. Thus, the Greek war of independence effectively ended the Concert of Europe. Originally intended to crush nationalist and liberal revolts, the Concert in this case helped one succeed.

THE DECEMBRIST REVOLT OF 1825 IN RUSSIA The least successful of the early liberal revolts took place in Russia, where a number of army officers, influenced by liberal ideas while serving in western Europe during the Napoleonic wars, staged a rebellion against the government of Tsar Nicholas I (r. 1825–1855) on the first day of his reign. The officers, together with other members of the nobility, had been meeting for almost a decade in political clubs, such as the Society of True and Faithful Sons of the Fatherland in St. Petersburg. In these societies they articulated their goals of establishing a constitutional monarchy and emancipating the serfs.

Decembrists Russian liberals who staged a revolt against Tsar Nicholas I on the first day of his reign in December 1825.

The rebels, known as **Decembrists** for the month in which their rebellion took place, could not agree on the precise form of government they wished to institute. That disagreement, coupled with a reluctance to take action at the critical moment, led to their failure. When Tsar Alexander I died suddenly in 1825, the Decembrists hoped to persuade his brother Constantine to assume the throne and establish a representative form of government. Their hopes were dashed when Constantine refused to tamper with the succession and accepted the reign of his brother Nicholas. The reactionary Nicholas had no difficulty suppressing the revolt, executing its leaders, and leaving Russian liberals to struggle against police repression for the remainder of the nineteenth century.

Liberal and Nationalist Revolts, 1830

A second cluster of early-nineteenth-century liberal and national revolts in 1830 achieved a greater measure of success than the revolts of the early 1820s. These revolutions took place in France, the kingdom of the Netherlands, and the kingdom of Poland.

THE FRENCH REVOLUTION: THE SUCCESS OF LIBERALISM The most striking triumph of liberalism in Europe during the early nineteenth century occurred in France, where a revolution took place 15 years after the final defeat of Napoleon at Waterloo. This liberal success did not come easily. During the first few years of the restored monarchy, conservatives had their way, as they did elsewhere in Europe. Louis XVIII had approved a Charter of Liberties in 1814, but he was hardly receptive to any further liberal reforms. Between 1815 and 1828 ultraroyalists dominated French politics. These reactionaries sponsored a "white terror" (so called because they displayed the white flag of the Bourbon monarchy) against liberals and Protestants. Two men nicknamed Three Slices and Four Slices, indicating the number of pieces into which they butchered their Protestant enemies, were the main instigators of this terror.

In 1824, when the conservative Charles X (r. 1824–1830) ascended the throne and took steps to strengthen the Church and the nobility, there appeared to be little hope for liberalism. Nevertheless, liberal opposition to the monarchy gained support from

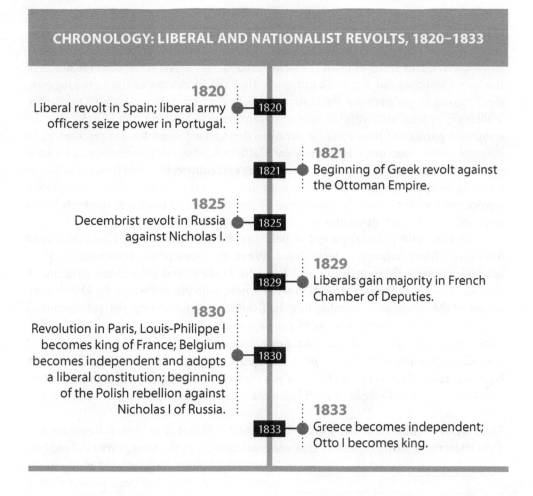

CHRONOLOGY: LIBERAL AND NATIONALIST REVOLTS, 1820–1833

1820
Liberal revolt in Spain; liberal army officers seize power in Portugal.
1820

1821
1821
Beginning of Greek revolt against the Ottoman Empire.

1825
Decembrist revolt in Russia against Nicholas I.
1825

1829
1829
Liberals gain majority in French Chamber of Deputies.

1830
Revolution in Paris, Louis-Philippe I becomes king of France; Belgium becomes independent and adopts a liberal constitution; beginning of the Polish rebellion against Nicholas I of Russia.
1830

1833
1833
Greece becomes independent; Otto I becomes king.

merchants and manufacturers, as well as from soldiers who still kept the memory of Napoleon alive. Fears that Charles would claim absolute power and a serious economic crisis in 1829 helped liberals gain a majority in the Chamber of Deputies, the French legislature.

Charles then embarked upon a perilous course. In what became known as the July Ordinances he effectively undermined the principles of the 1814 Charter of Liberties. These ordinances dissolved the new Chamber of Deputies, ordered new elections under a highly restrictive franchise, and censored the press. The public reaction to this maneuver caught the king by surprise. Thousands of students and workers, liberals and republicans alike, poured onto the streets of Paris to demonstrate. Unable to restore order, the king abdicated in favor of his grandson, but the liberals offered the crown instead to the Duke of Orléans, who was crowned as Louis-Philippe I (r. 1830–1848).

Louis-Philippe accepted a revised version of the Charter of 1814 and doubled the franchise, giving the vote to middle-class merchants and industrialists. The king catered to this bourgeois constituency by encouraging economic growth and restricting noble privilege. His reign, which is often referred to as the "bourgeois monarchy," also achieved a measure of secularization when the Chamber of Deputies declared that Roman Catholicism was no longer the state religion. In keeping with liberal ideals, however, he did nothing to encourage republicanism or radical democracy, much less socialism. Efforts to depict him as the heir to the French Revolution did not persuade the bulk of the population. When the government brought the ashes of Napoleon from St. Helena to Paris, thousands of French men and women turned out to pay homage to the former emperor. Much to his disappointment, Louis-Philippe gained little political benefit from the move. France had acquired a liberal monarchy, but it stood on a precarious foundation.

THE BELGIAN REVOLUTION: THE SUCCESS OF NATIONALISM The French Revolution of 1830 triggered the outbreak of a liberal and nationalist revolution in the neighboring country of Belgium. In 1815 the Congress of Vienna had united the Austrian Netherlands and the Dutch Republic in the new Kingdom of the Netherlands. This union of the Low Countries did not work out; soon after the formation of the new kingdom, the Belgians began pressing for their independence as a nation. With a Dutchman, William I, as king and with the seat of government in Holland, the Dutch were the dominant partner in this union, a situation that caused considerable resentment in Belgium. Moreover, most Belgians were Catholics, whereas the majority of Dutch people were Protestants. With their own history and culture, Belgians thought of themselves as a separate nation. They also were more liberal than their Dutch neighbors, advocating free trade and the promotion of industry, while resenting the high tariffs imposed by the Dutch government.

The two main political parties in Belgium, the Liberals and the Clericals, joined forces to achieve national independence. When the news of the revolution in Paris reached Brussels, fighting broke out between workers and government troops. A Belgian national congress gathered to write a new constitution; when the Dutch tried to thwart the rebellion by bombarding the Belgian city of Antwerp, Britain assembled a conference of European powers to devise a settlement. The powers agreed to recognize Belgium's independence, and they arranged for a German prince, Leopold of Saxe-Coburg, uncle of the future British Queen Victoria, to become king. The Dutch, however, refused to recognize the new government, and they renewed their military attacks on Belgium. Only in 1839 did all sides accept the new political arrangement.

THE POLISH REBELLION: THE FAILURE OF NATIONALISM The French Revolution of 1830 triggered a second uprising, this one unsuccessful, in the kingdom of Poland (see **Map 22.1**). Poland had suffered many partitions at the hands of European powers during the eighteenth century, and in 1815 the Congress of Vienna had redefined its borders once again. The congress established a separate Polish kingdom, known as Congress Poland, with Warsaw as its capital and the Russian tsar, Alexander I (r. 1815–1825), as its king. The western part of Poland, the Duchy of Poznan, went to the kingdom of Prussia, while Cracow became a free city.

With a Russian king the independence of Poland was mere fiction, but Alexander had approved a liberal Polish constitution in 1815. He grew to regret this decision, and his rule as king of Poland gradually alienated Polish liberals within the national legislature, the *Sejm*. The accession of Nicholas in 1825 aggravated those tensions. An uncompromising conservative, Nicholas accused the Polish opposition of complicity with the Russian Decembrist rebels. He brought them to the brink of rebellion when he made plans to send the Polish army, together with Russian troops, to suppress the French Revolution of 1830 and prevent the Belgians from receiving their independence.

The revolt began when army cadets in the officers' school in Warsaw attacked

MAP **22.1** EUROPEAN CENTERS OF REBELLION AND REVOLUTION, 1820–1848 All these political disturbances were inspired by ideology. Why did Britain not experience a rebellion or revolution during these years?

the residence of the Grand Duke Constantine, the governor-general of Poland, and it quickly gained the support of the entire army and the urban populace. The revolt appealed to both liberals and nationalists, and it drew inspiration from a group of romantic poets who celebrated the achievements of the Polish past. The rebels established a provisional Polish government at Warsaw, but the liberal members of the *Sejm* were unwilling to enlist the peasantry in the conflict, fearful that they would rise against Polish landlords rather than the Russians. When the powers of western Europe refused to intervene on behalf of this liberal cause, Nicholas was able to crush the rebellion, abolish the *Sejm,* and deprive the kingdom of Poland of its autonomous status. Nicholas visited a terrible revenge upon the leaders of the revolt, confiscated the lands of those who had emigrated, and shut down the University of Warsaw. His brutal repression set back the cause of liberalism and nationalism in Poland for another two generations.

22.1

22.2

22.3

View the Image

The Clemency of the Russian Monster-British Cartoon, 1832

22.4

Liberal Reform in Britain, 1815–1848

The challenges that liberals faced in Britain were somewhat different from those they confronted in most other European countries. Having maintained the status quo during the era of the French Revolution, the forces of British conservatism, which bore the ideological stamp of Edmund Burke, remained formidable. At the same time, however, Britons already enjoyed many of the rights that liberals on the European continent demanded, such as freedom of the press and protection from arbitrary imprisonment. The power of the British monarchy was more limited than in almost any other European country. The ideology of liberalism, which had deep roots in British political and social philosophy, defined the political creed of many Whigs, who formed the main opposition to the ruling Conservative or Tory party after 1815.

In this relatively favorable political climate, British liberals pursued three major goals that amounted to a program for reform rather than revolution. The first was the repeal of legislation that denied political power to Catholics and "nonconformist" Protestants who did not attend the services of the Anglican Church. Liberals were opposed on principle to religious discrimination, and many of them belonged to nonconformist congregations. The Tory prime minister, the Duke of Wellington, who had defeated Napoleon at Waterloo, eventually agreed to liberal demands. The Protestant nonconformists were emancipated in 1828 and the Catholics one year later.

The second liberal cause was the expansion of the franchise, which was realized when the Whigs, who came to power in 1830, passed the Great Reform Bill of 1832. The legislation expanded the franchise to include most of the urban middle class, created a number of new parliamentary boroughs (towns that elected representatives to sit in the House of Commons) in regions where industrial growth had led to an increase in population, and established a uniform standard for the right to vote throughout the country. In keeping with the principles of liberalism, however, the bill restricted the vote to property owners. It rejected the demands of radicals for universal male suffrage and denied all women the vote.

The third liberal cause was free trade. The target of this campaign was a series of protective tariffs on the import and export of hundreds of commodities, including raw materials used in production. The most hated protective tariff was on grain (known in Britain as corn), which kept the price of basic food commodities high to protect the interests of landlords and farmers. In 1837 a group of industrialists and radical reformers formed the Anti-Corn Law League with the purpose of bringing about the repeal of the Corn Law of 1815, which greatly restricted the importation of foreign grain into Britain. This campaign against protectionism did not succeed until 1845, when the Conservative prime minister, Sir Robert Peel, brought about repeal by securing the votes of some of his own party and combining them with those of the Whigs, all of whom favored free trade. Peel took this action only after the potato famine in Ireland, which was discussed in Chapter 21, had begun to cause widespread starvation.

 Read the Document

Karl Marx on the Question of Free Trade (1848)

Chartists A British group of workers and middle-class radicals who drafted a People's Charter in 1837 demanding universal male suffrage and other political reforms.

 **Read the Document**

Chartist Movement: The People's Petition of 1838

Unlike the liberals, socialists and radical democrats achieved little success in Britain during the first half of the nineteenth century. In 1837 workers and middle-class radicals drew up a People's Charter, demanding universal male suffrage, annual parliaments, voting by secret ballot, equal electoral districts, the elimination of property qualifications for Members of Parliament, and the payment of salaries to those same members. These **Chartists**, as they were known, gained widespread popular support when economic conditions deteriorated, but British workers showed little inclination to take to the streets. The government's reduction of indirect taxes during the 1840s, coupled with the effective use of the police force and the strict enforcement of the criminal law, also helped prevent Britain from experiencing revolution in 1848. The price of this failure was that further liberal reforms, such as the extension of the franchise to include workers, did not take place in Britain for another two decades.

The Revolutions of 1848

Unlike Britain, almost every country on the European continent experienced revolution in 1848. The revolutions took place during a period of widespread economic discontent. European countries had suffered bad harvests in 1845 and 1846 and an economic recession in 1847, leading to a decline in the standard of living for both industrial and agricultural workers. Discontent took the form of mass protests and demonstrations,

THE MEETING ON KENNINGTON-COMMON.—FROM A DAGUERREOTYPE.

THE LAST GREAT CHARTIST RALLY IN BRITAIN, APRIL 10, 1848 Government precautions, including the appointment of special constables to handle the crowd, and rain kept the number of demonstrators in London lower than anticipated. The government ordered the leader of the movement, Feargus O'Connor, to stop the planned march to Parliament.

which increased the likelihood of violent confrontation. The revolutions of 1848 were more widespread than the revolts of the 1820s and 1830, and more people participated. These revolutions also gave more attention to both nationalist and socialist issues.

THE FRENCH REVOLUTIONS OF 1848 The first of the revolutions of 1848 took place in France, where the liberal government of Louis-Philippe faced mounting criticism. Declining economic conditions led to a series of demonstrations in Paris for the right of workers to vote and receive state assistance for their trades. When troops from the Paris National Guard fired on the demonstrators and killed 40 people, the barricades once again appeared in the streets and the rebels seized government buildings. France experienced its third revolution in 60 years. To save his regime, Louis-Philippe abdicated in favor of his grandson, but the revolutionaries abolished the monarchy and declared the Second French Republic.

The Chamber of Deputies selected a provisional government that included republicans, liberals, and radical democrats. It also included two socialists, Louis Blanc and a worker who preferred to be called by the single name of Albert. The French Revolution

CHRONOLOGY: THE REVOLUTIONS OF 1848

1848

February
Revolution in Paris.
March
Insurrection in Berlin, peasant unrest in the countryside, formation of liberal governments in Prussia and other German states; revolutions in Milan and Venice; Ferdinand II issues a new constitution in Naples.
April
Elections for a new National Assembly in France.
May
Meeting of the Frankfurt Parliament; meeting of the Prussian Assembly.
June
Suppression of working-class resistance in Paris; Pan-Slav Congress in Prague; suppression of the rebellion in Prague.
October
Suppression of revolution in Vienna.
December
Election of Louis-Napoleon as president of the Second French Republic; Frankfurt Parliament issues *Declaration of the Basic Rights of the German People;* Frederick William dissolves Prussian Assembly.

1849

March
King Frederick William rejects the German crown offered by the Frankfurt Parliament.
April
Frankfurt Parliament promulgates a new constitution; Hungarian Diet proclaims Magyar independence.
May–June
Fall of the liberal ministries in German states.
August
Venetian Republic surrenders to Austrian forces; suppression of the Hungarian movement for independence.

of 1848 offered the socialists their first opportunity to realize the goal of a democratic and socialist republic. Many of the 200 clubs formed in Paris at this time, some of which were exclusively female, were either republican or socialist in their orientation. The socialist agenda included not only universal male suffrage, which the government granted immediately, but also active support for unemployed workers. Blanc secured the establishment of national workshops to give the unemployed jobs on public projects. Ordinances reduced the length of the workday to 10 hours in the city and 12 hours in rural areas.

These bold socialist initiatives did not last long. By the summer the euphoria of the revolution had dissipated and the aspirations of workers had been crushed. The elections held in April 1848 to constitute a new National Assembly and write a new constitution seated an overwhelming majority of conservative monarchists and only a small minority of republicans and socialists. Resentment of the provisional government's assistance to urban workers and anger at the levying of a surtax to pay for government programs revealed the lack of broad popular support for radical political programs. Tension between the new conservative assembly and the forces of the left mounted when the government closed the workshops and sent Parisian workers either into the army or into exile in the provinces.

These newly adopted policies led to further working-class violence in Paris in June 1848. When General Louis Cavaignac, known as "the butcher," was called in to restore order, regular army troops killed at least 1,500 insurgents and sent another 4,000 into exile in French colonies. These confrontations appeared to Karl Marx to constitute class warfare, a prelude to the proletarian revolution he predicted for the future. Louis Blanc, who was implicated in these uprisings, fled to England, where Marx himself would soon arrive and spend the rest of his life.

The revolution ended with the election of Napoleon's nephew, Louis-Napoleon Bonaparte (1808–1873), as the president of the Second French Republic in December 1848. As president, Louis-Napoleon drew support from conservatives, liberals, and moderate republicans. He also benefited from the legend that his uncle had created and the nationalist sentiment it inspired. Because the first Napoleon had become emperor, even those who preferred an empire to a republic could vote for his nephew. The younger Napoleon followed in his uncle's footsteps, dissolving the National Assembly in December 1851 and proclaiming himself emperor of the French one year later. This step brought the Second Republic to an end and established the Second Empire. The new emperor called himself Napoleon III, in deference to the uncrowned Napoleon II, the son of Napoleon I who had died in 1823.

THE REVOLUTIONS OF 1848 IN GERMANY, AUSTRIA, HUNGARY, AND BOHEMIA
Before 1848, liberalism and nationalism had achieved little success in Germany. German university students, inspired by the slogan "Honor, Freedom, Fatherland," had staged a number of large rallies during the early years of the nineteenth century, but the forces of conservatism had kept them in check. The Carlsbad Decrees of 1819, intended to suppress university radicalism, inaugurated a period of severe repression throughout Germany. The only success achieved by German liberals and nationalists prior to 1848 was the establishment of the *Zollverein,* a customs union of the various German states, in 1834. Even that project, which promoted free trade within German lands, did not attract support from all liberals.

A major opportunity for the liberal cause in Germany came in 1848 in the immediate wake of the February Revolution in France. As in France, however, radical demands from democrats and socialists for universal suffrage, including equal rights for women, competed with the more moderate liberal agenda. German radicals also demanded government assistance for artisans and workers who had suffered economic hardship as a result of industrialization. In Berlin, the capital of Prussia, these discontents led radicals to barricade the streets. The protests escalated after troops fired into the crowd, killing some 250 people. The violence spread to the countryside, where peasants demanded that landlords renounce their privileges and grant them free use of their lands. In response to these pressures, King Frederick William IV summoned an assembly, elected by universal male suffrage, to write a new Prussian constitution. Other German states also yielded to liberal pressure, establishing liberal governments known as the "March ministries."

As these events were unfolding, the contagion of revolution spread to Austria, the other major German kingdom, which formed the nucleus of the sprawling Austrian Empire. News of the revolution in Paris led to demonstrations by students and workers in Vienna. An assortment of Austrian liberal aristocrats, middle-class professionals, and discontented workers demanded an end to the long rule of the conservative minister, Klemens von Metternich. In response to the demands of these groups, Emperor Ferdinand I (r. 1835–1848) summoned a constitutional assembly and installed a moderate government. A conservative Prussian observer feared that these concessions had broken "the most secure dam against the revolutionary tide."

The main difference between the revolutions of 1848 in Austria and the other German lands was that events in Vienna awakened demands of Hungarians and Czechs for national autonomy within the empire. In Hungary the nationalist leader Lajos Kossuth (1802–1894) pushed for a program of liberal reform and national autonomy. This initiative created further tensions between the Magyars and the various national minorities within the kingdom of Hungary. Similar problems arose in Bohemia, where a revolution in Prague led to demands from the Czechs for autonomy within the Austrian Empire. In June 1848 the Czech rebels hosted a Pan-Slav Congress in Prague to advance a nationalist plan for achieving unity of all Slavic people. This idealistic proposal could not be realized, for there were many distinct Slavic nationalities, each of which had a desire to establish its autonomy. In addition, there was a large German-speaking population within Bohemia that identified with other German territories in the Confederation.

The most idealistic and ambitious undertaking of the revolution in central Europe was the meeting of the Frankfurt Parliament in May 1848. Some 800 middle-class liberals, most of whom were lawyers, officials, and university professors, came from all the German states to draft a constitution for a united Germany. The parliament produced powerful speeches in support of both liberal and nationalist ideals, and in December 1848 it promulgated a *Declaration of the Basic Rights of the German People*. This document recognized the equality of all German people before the law; freedom of speech, assembly, and religion; and the right to private property. (See *Justice in History* in this chapter.) Like so many liberal assemblies, however, the Frankfurt Parliament failed to address the needs of the workers and peasants. The delegates rejected universal male suffrage as a "dangerous experiment" and refused to provide protection for artisans who were being squeezed out of work by industrialization. For these reasons, the parliament failed to win broad popular support.

In April 1849 the Frankfurt Parliament drafted a new constitution for a united Germany, which would have a hereditary "emperor of the Germans" and two houses of parliament, one of which would be elected by universal male suffrage. Austria, however, voted against the new plan; without Austrian support, the new constitution had little hope of success. The final blow to German liberal hopes came when King Frederick William of Prussia refused the Frankfurt Parliament's offer of the German crown, which he referred to as coming from the gutter and "reeking of the stench of revolution." At that point the Frankfurt Parliament disbanded and the efforts of German liberals to unite their country and give it a new constitution came to an inglorious end.

By the middle of 1849, conservative forces had triumphed in the various German territories and the Austrian Empire. In Prussia the efforts of the newly elected assembly to restrict noble privilege triggered a reaction from the conservative nobles known as Junkers. Frederick William dismissed his liberal appointees, sent troops to Berlin, and disbanded the assembly. A similar fate befell the other German states, such as Saxony, Baden, and Hanover, all of which had installed liberal governments in the early months of the revolution. In Austria Prince Alfred Windischgrätz, who had crushed

Read the Document

Metternich on the Revolutions of 1848

Justice in History

Prostitution, Corporal Punishment, and Liberalism in Germany

In March 1822 municipal authorities in the northern German city of Bremen arrested Gesche Rudolph, a poor, uneducated 25-year-old woman, for engaging in prostitution without registering with the police. Ever since the days when troops from five different European states had occupied her neighborhood, Rudolph had been selling her sexual services as her only form of livelihood. After her arrest she was not given a formal trial, but was summarily expelled from the city and banned from ever returning. Unable to earn a living through prostitution in a village outside the city, where she resided with a brother who physically abused her, Rudolph returned to the city, where she was arrested once again for prostitution. This time she was sentenced to 50 strokes of the cane and six weeks in jail, after which she was once again expelled from the city. Returning again to Bremen, she was arrested in a drunken stupor in a whorehouse and subjected to a harsher sentence of three months' imprisonment and 150 strokes before another expulsion. This pattern of arrest, punishment, expulsion, and return occurred repeatedly during the next two decades, with the number of strokes rising to 275 and the period of imprisonment to six years. During a portion of her prison sentence she was given only bread and water for nourishment.

Rudolph's arrest in 1845 at the end of a six-year imprisonment and her subsequent expulsion and return to Bremen led to the appointment of a liberal lawyer, Georg Wilhelm Gröning, to represent her. After reviewing her case and calculating that she had been whipped a total of 893 times and imprisoned for a cumulative period of 18 years, Gröning appealed her sentence to the senate of Bremen on the grounds that her treatment was not only futile but immoral. His appeal addressed an issue that went far beyond this particular case or even the prosecution of the crime of prostitution. Gröning's action raised the controversial issue of the legitimacy and value of corporal punishment, an issue that divided liberals and conservatives, who had different notions of justice.

Until the eighteenth century the penal systems of Europe had prescribed corporal punishments, administered publicly, for most crimes. These punishments ranged from whippings and

CORPORAL PUNISHMENT IN THE NINETEENTH CENTURY A man receives the sixth of 30 lashes in 1872.

placement in the stocks for minor offenses to mutilation, hanging, and decapitation for felonies. They were justified mainly on the grounds that they provided retribution for the crime and deterred the criminal and those who witnessed the punishment from committing further crimes. These two main functions of retribution and deterrence are the same functions that capital punishment allegedly serves today. Corporal punishments were also intended to humiliate the criminal by violating the integrity of the body and subjecting the prisoner to the mockery and sometimes the maltreatment of the crowd. The torture of suspects to obtain evidence also served some of these functions, although judicial torture took place during the trial, not as part of the sentence.

The entire system of corporal punishment and torture came under attack during the eighteenth century. Prussia abolished torture in 1754, and the Prussian General Law Code of 1794 eliminated many forms of corporal punishment. This code reflected the concern of Enlightenment thinkers that all such assaults on the body were inhumane and denied the moral dignity of the individual. Because most of the people who incurred corporal punishment were poor, the system also violated the liberal principle of equality before the law.

Despite these efforts at reform, the illegal administration of corporal punishment by public and private authorities continued in Prussia and the other German states. Conservatives, who had a different notion of justice from that of liberals, defended these sentences. For them any reference to natural rights and human dignity were "axioms derived from abstract philanthropic speculation." The president of the Prussian police, Julius Baron von Minutoli, expressing the conservative position on the issue, claimed that corporal punishment was more effective than imprisonment in preventing crime, as it alone could instill terror in the criminal.

It was apparent that in the case of Gesche Rudolph, 893 strokes had not instilled terror in her or deterred her from her crime. The Senate made the young woman Gröning's ward and suspended her sentence. Gröning arranged for Rudolph to live

(continued on next page)

(continued from previous page)

in the countryside under the strict supervision of a competent countryman. This compromise solution at least broke the cycle of expulsion, return, and punishment that had failed to reform her. We do not know whether she gave up her life of prostitution.

Soon after Gesche Rudolph became Gröning's ward, the liberal critics of corporal punishment in Germany celebrated a victory. King Frederick William IV of Prussia formally abolished the practice in May 1848. Shortly thereafter the Frankfurt Parliament included freedom from physical punishment by the state in its *Declaration of the Basic Rights of the German People*. Most German states and municipalities, including Bremen, wrote this right into law in 1849. The failure of the Frankfurt Parliament, however, and the more general failure of liberalism in Germany after 1849 led to a strong conservative campaign to reinstate corporal punishment in the 1850s. They succeeded only in maintaining corporal punishment within the family, on manorial estates, and in the prisons. Liberalism had not succeeded in completely establishing its standard of justice, but it did end exposure to public shame as a punishment for crime.

For Discussion

1. Why did liberals object to corporal punishment?
2. In addition to inflicting physical pain, corporal punishment produces social shame. What is the difference between social shame and legal guilt? In what ways does shame still play a role in punishments today?

Taking It Further

Evans, Richard. *Tales from the German Underworld: Crime and Punishment in the Nineteenth Century.* 1998. Provides a full account of the prosecution of Gesche Rudolph.

the Czech rebels in June, dispersed the rebels in Vienna in October. When Hungary proclaimed its independence from the empire in April 1849, Austrian and Russian forces marched on the country and crushed the movement.

THE REVOLUTIONS OF 1848 IN ITALY The revolutions of 1848 also spread to Austrian possessions in the northern Italian territories of Lombardy and Venetia. In Milan, the main city in Lombardy, revolutionary developments followed the same pattern as those in Paris, Berlin, and Vienna. When the barricades went up, some of the Milanese insurgents used medieval pikes stolen from the opera house to fight off Austrian troops. Their success triggered rebellions in other towns in Lombardy, in Venice, and in the southern Kingdom of the Two Sicilies. In that kingdom the Spanish Bourbon king, Ferdinand II (r. 1830–1859), after suppressing a republican revolt in January, was forced to grant a liberal constitution. The spread of these revolts inspired the hope of unifying all Italian people in one nation-state.

This Italian nationalist dream had originated among some liberals and republicans during the first half of the nineteenth century. Its most articulate proponent was Giuseppe Mazzini, a revolutionary from Genoa who envisioned the establishment of a united Italian republic through direct popular action. In 1831 Mazzini founded Italy's first organized political party, Young Italy, which pledged to realize national unification, democracy, and greater social equality. Mazzini combined a passionate commitment to the ideals of liberalism, republicanism, and nationalism.

Yet in 1848 an Italian prince, not Mazzini or Young Italy, took the first steps toward Italian unification. King Charles Albert ruled Piedmont-Sardinia, the most economically advanced of the Italian states. In 1848 his army, which included volunteers from various parts of Italy, marched into Lombardy and defeated Austrian forces. Instead of moving forward against Austria, however, Charles Albert decided to consolidate his gains, hoping to annex Lombardy to his own kingdom. This decision alienated republicans in Lombardy and in other parts of Italy. The rulers of the other Italian states feared that Charles Albert's main goal was to expand the limits of his own kingdom at their expense. By August 1848 the military tide had turned. Fresh Austrian troops defeated the Italian nationalists outside Milan. The people of that city turned against Charles Albert, forcing him to return to his own capital of Turin. The Italian revolutions of 1848 had suffered a complete defeat.

THE FAILURE OF THE REVOLUTIONS OF 1848 The revolutions of 1848 in France, Germany, the Austrian Empire, and Italy resulted in victory for conservatives and defeat for liberals, nationalists, and socialists. All the liberal constitutions passed during the early phase of the revolutions were eventually repealed or withdrawn. The high hopes of national unity in Germany, Italy, and Hungary were dashed. Workers who built the barricades in the hope of achieving improvements in their working conditions gained little from their efforts.

The revolutions failed because of divisions among the different groups that began the revolutions, particularly the split between the liberals who formulated the original goals of the revolution and the lower-class participants who took to the streets. Liberals used the support of the masses to bring down the governments they opposed, but their ideological opposition to broad-based political movements and their fear of further disorder sapped their revolutionary fervor. Divisions also emerged between liberals and nationalists, whose goals of national self-determination required different strategies from those of the liberals who supported individual freedom.

National Unification in Europe and America, 1848–1871

22.3 How did liberal and conservative leaders use the ideology of nationalism to form nation-states?

Prior to 1848 the forces of nationalism, especially when combined with those of liberalism, had little to show for their efforts. Besides the Greek rebellion of 1821, which succeeded largely because of international opposition to the Turks, the only successful nationalist revolution in Europe took place in Belgium. Both of these nationalist movements were secessionist in that they involved the separation of smaller states from larger empires. Efforts in 1848 to form nations by combining smaller states and territories, as in Italy and Germany, or by uniting all Slavic people, as proposed at the Pan-Slav Congress, had failed. Between 1848 and 1871, however, movements for national unification succeeded in Italy, Germany, and the United States, each in a different way. In the vast Austrian Empire a different type of unity was achieved, but it did little to promote the cause of nationalism.

Italian Unification: Building a Fragile Nation-State

The great project of Italian nationalists, the unification of Italy, faced formidable obstacles. Austrian military control over the northern territories, which had thwarted the nationalist movement of 1848, meant that national unification would not be achieved peacefully. The dramatic economic disparities between the prosperous north and the much poorer south posed a challenge to any plan for economic integration. A long tradition of local autonomy within the kingdoms, states, and principalities made submission to a strong central government unappealing. The unique status of the papacy, which controlled its own territory and which influenced the decisions of many other states, served as another challenge. Despite these obstacles, however, the dream of a resurgence of Italian power, reviving the achievements of ancient Rome, had great emotive appeal. Hatred of foreigners who controlled Italian territory, which dated back to the fifteenth century, gave further impetus to the nationalist movement.

The main question for Italian nationalism after the failure of 1848 was who could provide effective leadership of the movement. It stood to reason that Piedmont-Sardinia, the strongest and most prosperous Italian kingdom, would be central to that undertaking. Unfortunately its king, Victor Emmanuel II (r. 1849–1861), was more known for his hunting, his carousing, and his affair with a teenage mistress than his statesmanship. Victor Emmanuel did, however, appoint a nobleman with liberal leanings, Count Camillo di Cavour (1810–1861), as his prime minister. Cavour displayed many of the characteristics of nineteenth-century liberalism. He favored a constitutional monarchy, the restriction of clerical privilege and influence, and the development of a capitalist and industrial economy. He was deeply committed to the unification of the Italian peninsula, but only under Piedmontese leadership, and preferably as a federation of states. In many ways, Cavour was the antithesis of the republican Mazzini, the central figure in Italian unification. Mazzini's idealism and romanticism led him to think of national unification as a moral force that would lead to the establishment of a democratic republic, which would then undertake an extensive program of social reform. Mazzini often wore black, claiming that he was in mourning for the unrealized cause of unification.

Mazzini's strategy for national unification involved a succession of uprisings and invasions. Cavour, however, adopted a diplomatic course of action intended to gain the military assistance of France against Austria. In 1859 French and Piedmontese forces defeated the Austrians at Magenta and Solferino and drove them out of Lombardy. One year later Napoleon III signed the Treaty of Turin with Cavour, allowing Piedmont-Sardinia to annex Tuscany, Parma, Modena, and the Romagna, while ceding to France the Italian territories of Savoy and Nice. This treaty resulted in the unification of all of northern and central Italy except Venetia in the northeast and the Papal States in the center of the peninsula (see **Map 22.2**).

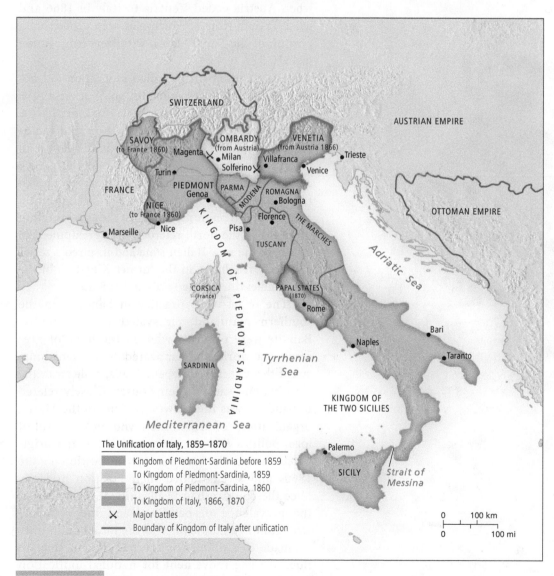

MAP **22.2** THE UNIFICATION OF ITALY, 1859–1870 The main steps to unification took place in 1860, when Piedmont-Sardinia acquired Tuscany, Parma, Modena, and the Romagna and when Garibaldi seized control of the Kingdom of the Two Sicilies in the name of King Victor Emmanuel of Piedmont-Sardinia. Who was most responsible for achieving Italian unification?

The main focus of unification efforts now turned to the Kingdom of the Two Sicilies in the south. A rebellion against the Bourbon monarch Francis II, protesting new taxes and the high price of bread, had taken place there in 1860. At that point the third figure in the story of Italian unification, the militant republican adventurer Giuseppe Garibaldi (1807–1882), intervened with decisive force. Garibaldi, who was born in Nice and spoke French rather than Italian as his main language, was determined no less than Cavour and Mazzini to drive all foreigners out of Italy and achieve its unification. Originally a supporter of Mazzini's republican goals, Garibaldi gave his support in the 1860s for Italian unification within the framework of a monarchy. A charismatic military leader, Garibaldi put together an army of volunteers, known as the Red Shirts for their colorful makeshift uniforms. In 1860 he landed in Sicily with an army of 1,000 men, took the main Sicilian city of Palermo, and established a dictatorship on behalf of King Victor Emmanuel. Garibaldi then landed on the mainland and took Naples. Shortly thereafter the people of Naples, Sicily, and most of the Papal States voted their support for union with Piedmont-Sardinia. In March 1861 the king of Sardinia assumed the title of King Victor Emmanuel of Italy (r. 1861–1878). Complete unification was achieved when Austria ceded Venetia to Italy in 1866 and when French troops, which had been protecting a portion of the Papal States, withdrew from Rome in 1870.

The achievement of Italian unification did not fully realize the lofty nationalist goals of creating a culturally unified people or a powerful central state. Economic differences between northern and southern Italy became even greater after unification than before. The overwhelming majority of the people continued to speak their local dialects or even French rather than Italian. Traditions of local political autonomy and resentment against the concentration of wealth in the north retarded the development of loyalty to the new Italian state and inspired a series of bloody rebellions in the former Kingdom of the Two Sicilies during the 1870s and 1880s.

The widespread practice of banditry in the southern mainland aggravated this instability. Bandits were peasants who, in the hope of preserving a world that appeared to be vanishing, swept through towns, opened jails, stole from the wealthy, and sacked their houses. Closely related to banditry was the growth in Sicily of the **Mafia**, organizations of armed men who took control of local politics and the economy. The Mafia originated during the struggle for unification in the 1860s and strengthened their position in Sicily once the country had been unified. Their power, the prevalence of banditry, and the enduring strength of Italian loyalty to the local community all made it difficult for the new Italian state to flourish. The movement for national unification had driven the French and the Austrians out of the peninsula, but it had failed to create a model nation-state.

GIUSEPPE GARIBALDI The uniform Garibaldi is wearing was derived from his days as a guerilla fighting in the civil war in Uruguay (1842–1846). Garibaldi also spent two years in asylum in the United States.

German Unification: Conservative Nation-Building

Like Italy, Germany experienced a successful movement for national unification after the disappointments of 1848. The German movement, like the Italian, benefited from the actions of crafty statesmen and the decisions made by other states. Unlike Italy, however, Germany achieved unification under the direction of highly conservative rather than liberal forces.

The kingdom of Prussia, with its largely German-speaking population, its wealth, and its strong army, assumed leadership of the nationalist movement. The key figure in this process was Count Otto von Bismarck (1815–1898), a lawyer and bureaucrat from an old Junker family whom King William I of Prussia appointed as his prime minister in 1862. By birth, training, and instinct, Bismarck was an inflexible conservative, determined to preserve and strengthen the Prussian nobility and monarchy and make the Prussian state strong and powerful. To achieve his goals, Bismarck did not hesitate to make alliances with any political party, including the liberals. This subordination of political means to their ends, and Bismarck's willingness to use whatever tactics were necessary, regardless of any moral considerations, made him a proponent of **Realpolitik**, the adoption of political tactics solely on the basis of their realistic chances of success.

Bismarck pursued the goal of national unification through the exercise of raw military and political power. "The great questions of the day," he said in 1862, "will not be settled by speeches and majority decisions—that was the error of 1848 and 1849—but by iron and blood." Bismarck did not share the romantic devotion of other German nationalists to the Fatherland or their desire to have a state that embodied the spirit of the German people. His determination to achieve German national unification became synonymous with his goal of strengthening the Prussian state. This commitment to the supremacy of Prussia within a united Germany explained his steadfast exclusion of the other great German power, Austria, from his plans for national unification.

Bismarck achieved German unification mainly through Prussian success in three wars (see **Map 22.3**). The first, a war against Denmark in 1864, gave Prussia and Austria joint control of the Danish duchies of Schleswig and Holstein, which had large German-speaking populations. The second war, the Austro-Prussian War of 1866, resulted in the formation of a new union of 22 German states, the North German Confederation. This new political structure replaced the German Confederation, the loose association of 39 states, including Austria, established in 1815. The North German Confederation had a central legislature, the *Reichstag*. The king of Prussia became its president and Bismarck its chancellor. Most significantly, it did not include Austria.

The third war, which completed the unification of Germany, was the Franco-Prussian War of 1870–1871. This conflict began when Napoleon III, the French emperor, challenged Prussian efforts to place a member of the Prussian royal family on the vacant Spanish throne. Bismarck welcomed this opportunity to take on the French, who controlled German-speaking territories on their eastern frontier and who had cultivated alliances with the southern German states. Bismarck played his diplomatic cards brilliantly, guaranteeing that the Russians, Austrians, and British would not support France. He then used the army that he had modernized to invade France and seize the towns of Metz and Sedan. The capture of Napoleon III during this military offensive precipitated the end of France's Second Empire and the establishment of the Third French Republic in September 1870.

As a result of its victory over France, Prussia annexed the predominantly German-speaking territories of Alsace and Lorraine. Much more important, the war led to the proclamation of the German Empire, with William I of Prussia as emperor. The empire, which included many German states, was formally a federation, just like the North German Confederation that preceded it. In practice, however, Prussia

Read the Document

A Letter from Otto von Bismarck (1866)

Realpolitik The adoption of political tactics based solely on their realistic chances of success.

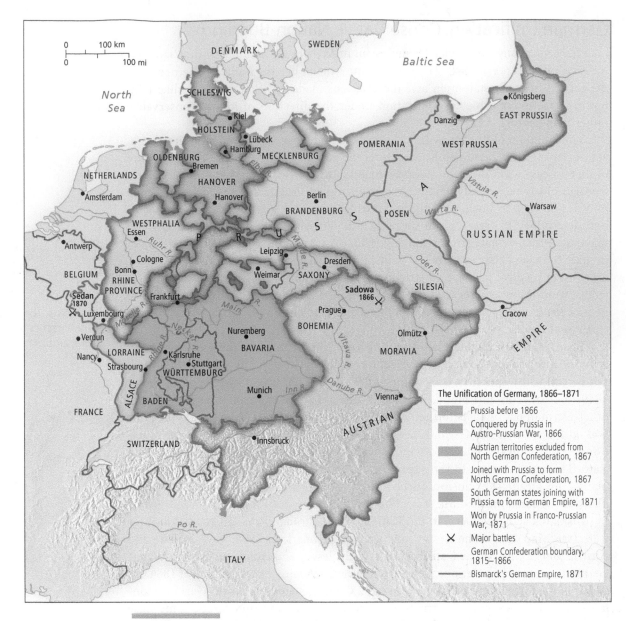

MAP **22.3** THE UNIFICATION OF GERMANY, 1866–1871 Prussia assumed leadership in uniting all German territories except Austria. Prussia was responsible for the formation of the North German Confederation in 1866 and the German Empire in 1871. Why was Austria not included in a united Germany?

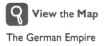

View the Map

The German Empire

dominated this political structure, and the new German imperial government, just like that of Prussia, was highly autocratic. The government won the support of the middle class by adopting policies supporting free trade, but the ideologies that the imperial government promoted were those of conservatism and nationalism, which encouraged devotion to "God, King, and Fatherland."

Unification in the United States: Creating a Nation of Nations

At the same time that Italy and Germany were achieving national unification by piecing together disparate kingdoms, provinces, and territories, the United States of America engaged in a process of territorial expansion that brought lands acquired by purchase or conquest into the union as states. This process of unification, which proceeded in a piecemeal fashion, took much longer than the unifications of Italy and Germany in the 1860s. It included the annexation of Florida in 1819 and the admission of Texas,

PROCLAMATION OF THE GERMAN EMPIRE IN THE HALL OF MIRRORS AT VERSAILLES, JANUARY 21, 1871 King William I of Prussia, standing on the dais, is being crowned emperor of Germany. At the center of the picture, dressed in a white uniform jacket, is Otto von Bismarck, the person most responsible for the unification of all German territory in one empire.

an independent republic for nine years, to the union in 1845. After establishing its independence from Mexico in 1846, California joined the union in 1850. This process of gradual unification did not end until 1912, when New Mexico and Arizona, the last territories in the contiguous 48 states, were admitted to the union.

The great test of American unity came during the 1860s, when 11 southern states, committed to the preservation of the economic system of slavery, and determined that it should be extended into new territories acquired by the federal government, seceded from the union and formed a confederation of their own. The issue of slavery had helped to polarize North and South, creating deep cultural and ideological divisions that made the goal of national unity appear remote. The constitutional issue underlying the Civil War was the preservation of the union. In a famous speech made in 1858, Abraham Lincoln, who became president in 1861, declared that "a house divided against itself cannot stand . . . this government cannot endure permanently half slave and half free." When the war ended and slavery was abolished, that union was not only preserved but strengthened. Amendments to the U.S. Constitution provided for equal protection of all citizens under the law. The South, which had its own regional economy, was integrated into the increasingly commercial and industrial North. Gradually, the people of the United States began to think of themselves as a united people, drawn from many different nations of the world. The United States became "a nation of nations."

Nationalism in Eastern Europe: Preserving Multinational Empires

The national unifications that took place in Germany and Italy formed part of a *western* European pattern in which the main units of political organization would become nation-states. Ethnic minorities would always live within the boundaries of these states, but the states would encourage the growth of national consciousness among all their citizens. In France, Britain, and Spain, all of which achieved national unification by the beginning of the nineteenth century, the state played a central role in this process. Minority populations within these large western European states have occasionally threatened to establish a separate political identity as nations. However, with the one notable exception of Ireland, the southern portion of which became independent of Britain in the twentieth century, the large states of western Europe have maintained their unity and promoted nationalist sentiment to sustain it.

In *eastern* Europe a very different pattern prevailed, especially in the Austrian and Russian Empires. Instead of becoming unified nation-states, these two empires remained large, multinational political formations, embracing many different nationalities. This pattern was most obvious in the large, sprawling Austrian Empire, which encompassed no fewer than 20 different ethnic groups, each of which thought of itself as a nation (see **Map 22.4**). The largest of these nationalities were the Germans in Austria and the Bohemians and the Magyars in Hungary, but the Czechs, Slovaks, Poles, Slovenes, Croats, Rumanians, Ukranians, and Italians (before 1866) all formed sizable minority populations. Map 22.4 illustrates this diversity. The various nationalities within the empire had little in common except loyalty to the Austrian emperor, who defended the Catholic faith and the privileges of the nobility. National unification of the empire presented a much more formidable task than those that confronted Cavour and Bismarck.

The ideology of nationalism threatened to tear apart this precariously unified empire. It awakened demands of Hungarians, Czechs, and others for national autonomy and also spawned a movement for the national unity of all Slavs. The emperor, Francis Joseph (r. 1848–1916), recognized the danger of nationalist ideology. He also feared that liberalism, which was often linked to nationalism, would at the same time

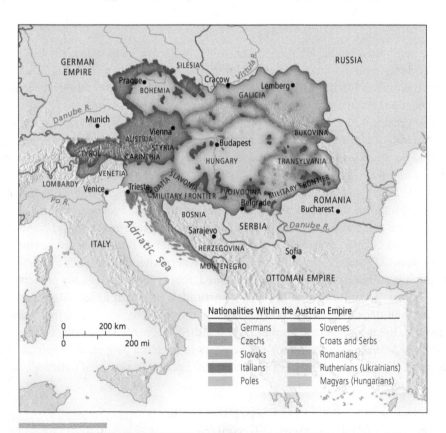

MAP **22.4** NATIONALITIES WITHIN THE AUSTRIAN EMPIRE The large number of different nationalities within the Austrian Empire made it impossible to accommodate the demands of all nationalities for their own state. In what way did the Austrian Emperor Francis Joseph differ from Bismarck in his attitude toward the ideology of nationalism?

undermine his authority, which he had reasserted with a vengeance after the failure of the revolutions of 1848. He therefore repressed these nationalist aspirations at every turn. This policy had disastrous consequences for the future history of Europe, as Slavic nationalism and separatism have remained a source of political instability in southeastern Europe until the present day.

During this volatile period Francis Joseph made only one major concession to nationalist sentiment within his sprawling empire. In 1867 he agreed to create the Dual Monarchy of Austria-Hungary, in which he would be both king of Hungary and emperor of Austria. Each monarchy would have its own parliament and bureaucracy, although matters of foreign policy and finance would be handled in Vienna. This *Ausgleich* (settlement) represented a concession to the Magyars, the dominant ethnic group in Hungary and the second largest nationality in the empire. It gave very little, however, to all the other nationalities within the two kingdoms of Austria and Hungary. The *Ausgleich* officially recognized the equality of all nationalities within the Dual Monarchy and allowed schooling to be conducted in the local language, but it permitted only Germans in Austria and Magyars in Hungary to acquire their own political identity. Instead of a unified nation-state, the emperor now presided over two multinational monarchies.

International Conflict and Domestic Politics, 1853–1871

22.4 How did warfare lead to political change in Russia and France between 1850 and 1871?

Between 1853 and 1871 two wars between European powers, one on the boundaries of the West and the other at its center, had a significant effect on domestic politics. The Crimean War of 1853–1856 led to a reluctant adoption of liberal reforms in Russia, while the Franco-Prussian War of 1870–1871 set back the cause of both liberalism and socialism in France for the remainder of the nineteenth century.

Russia and the Crimean War, 1853–1856

The Crimean War was the direct result of Russian imperial expansion. It began when Russia occupied the principalities of Moldavia and Wallachia (present-day Romania) in the Ottoman Empire to gain access to the Straits of Constantinople. Russians justified this incursion by claiming they were protecting Orthodox Christians in the Balkans from their Muslim Turkish oppressors. They also claimed that they were promoting the national unity of all Slavic people under Russian auspices. This Russian version of Pan-Slavism was, in effect, an extreme form of Russian imperialism that sought to curb the nationalist aspirations of individual Slavic minorities.

When Russia occupied Moldavia and Wallachia, the Turks responded by declaring war on Russia. Britain joined the conflict on the side of the Turks, ostensibly to preserve the balance of power in Europe, but also to prevent Russia from invading India, Britain's most important colony. The French joined the British, and both powers sent large armies to begin a siege of the port of Sebastopol on the Black Sea.

The poorly trained British forces, commanded by officers who had purchased their commissions and who had no sound knowledge of military tactics, suffered staggering losses, more of them from disease than from battle. The most senseless episode of the war occurred when a British cavalry unit, the Light Brigade, rode into a deep valley near Balaklava, only to be cut down by Russian artillery perched on the surrounding hills.

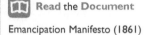 Read the Document

Emancipation Manifesto (1861)

Nevertheless, Britain, France, and Turkey, together with Piedmont-Sardinia, which entered the war in 1855, prevailed, and Russia suffered its most humiliating defeat of the nineteenth century. The defeat contributed to a crisis that led to a number of liberal reforms during the rule of Tsar Alexander II (1855–1881). Alexander, an indecisive man who had inherited the throne in the middle of the Crimean War, was hardly a liberal (he once referred to the French system of government as "vile"), but he did yield to mounting liberal pressure to emancipate 50 million serfs in 1861. Alexander also established elected local assemblies in which 40 percent of peasants had the vote, implemented a new judicial system, and instituted educational reforms.

France and the Franco-Prussian War, 1870–1871

The defeat of France in the Franco-Prussian War of 1870–1871 had a negative effect on the fortunes of both liberalism and socialism in France. When Napoleon III established the Second Empire in 1852, he tried to mask his usurpation of power by preserving the tradition of universal male suffrage and by submitting his rule to popular ratification. During the 1860s his government became known as "the Liberal Empire," a strange mixture of conservatism, liberalism, and nationalism. "The little Napoleon" gradually allowed a semblance of real parliamentary government, relaxed the censorship of the press, and encouraged industrial development. To this mixture he added a strong dose of nationalist sentiment by evoking the memory of his uncle, Napoleon I.

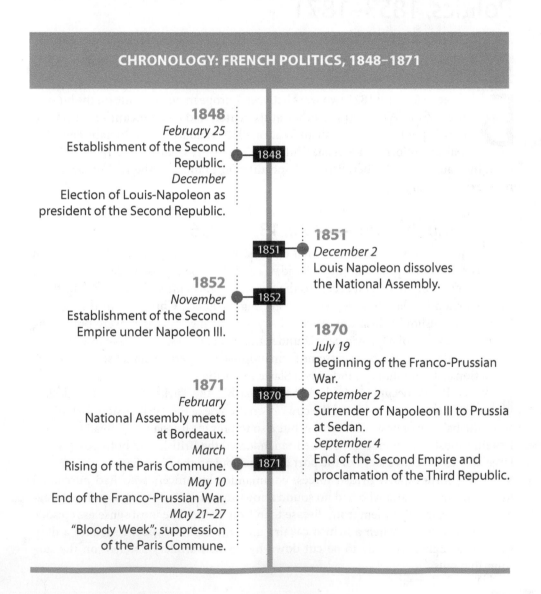

CHRONOLOGY: FRENCH POLITICS, 1848–1871

1848
February 25
Establishment of the Second Republic.
December
Election of Louis-Napoleon as president of the Second Republic.

1851
December 2
Louis Napoleon dissolves the National Assembly.

1852
November
Establishment of the Second Empire under Napoleon III.

1870
July 19
Beginning of the Franco-Prussian War.
September 2
Surrender of Napoleon III to Prussia at Sedan.
September 4
End of the Second Empire and proclamation of the Third Republic.

1871
February
National Assembly meets at Bordeaux.
March
Rising of the Paris Commune.
May 10
End of the Franco-Prussian War.
May 21–27
"Bloody Week"; suppression of the Paris Commune.

EXECUTION OF PARIS COMMUNARDS, MAY 1871 Troops of the provisional French government killed at least 25,000 Parisians during the uprising.

Military defeat, however, destroyed the regime of Napoleon III. The emperor himself was taken captive at the Battle of Sedan—a personal and national humiliation. The Second Empire collapsed. The establishment of the Third Republic in September 1870 led to a major ideological shift in French politics. The following January Adolphe Thiers (1797–1877), a veteran French statesman who hoped to establish a conservative republican regime or possibly a restoration of the monarchy, negotiated an armistice with Bismarck. This prospect gained strength when elections to a new National Assembly returned a majority of monarchists. The National Assembly then elected Thiers as president of a provisional government.

The provisional government was determined to assert its authority over the entire French nation. In particular, it wanted to curb the independence of the city of Paris. Parisians, however, were just as determined to carry on the struggle against Prussia and keep alive the French radical tradition that had flourished in the city in 1792 and again in 1848. The socialist and republican ideals of the new Paris Commune, coupled with its determination to preserve the independence of the city, culminated in the bloodshed described at the beginning of this chapter. The crushing of the Commune marked a bitter defeat for the forces of French socialism and radicalism. The Third French Republic endured, but its ideological foundation was conservative nationalism, not liberalism or socialism.

View the Map

The Paris Commune

CONCLUSION

The Ideological Transformation of the West

The ideological encounters that took place between 1815 and 1871 resulted in significant changes in the political cultures of the West. As the early nineteenth-century ideologies of liberalism, conservatism, socialism, and nationalism played out in political movements and revolutions, the people who subscribed to these ideologies often redefined their political objectives. Many British and French socialists, for example, recognizing the necessity of assistance from liberals, abandoned their call for creating a classless society and sought instead to increase wages and improve working conditions of the lower classes. The demands of socialists for greater economic equality pressured liberals to accept the need for more state intervention in the economy. The realities of conservative politics led liberal nationalists in Germany and Italy to accept newly formed nation-states that were more authoritarian than they had originally hoped to establish. Recognizing the strength of the ideologies to which they were opposed, conservative rulers such as Emperor Napoleon III and Tsar Alexander II agreed to adopt liberal reforms. Liberals, conservatives, socialists, and nationalists would continue to modify and adjust their political and ideological positions during the period of mass politics, which began in 1870 and which will be the subject of the next chapter.

The Western ideologies that underwent this process of adaptation and modification had a broad influence on world history. In the twentieth century, three of the four ideologies discussed in this chapter have inspired political change in parts of the world that lie outside the geographical and cultural boundaries of the West. Liberalism has provided the language for movements seeking to establish fundamental civil liberties in India, Japan, and several African countries. In its radical communist form, socialism inspired revolutions in Russia, a country that for many centuries had straddled the boundary between East and West, and in China. Nationalism has revealed its explosive potential in countries as diverse as Indonesia, Thailand, and the Republic of the Congo. Ever since the nineteenth century, Western ideologies have demonstrated a capacity both to shape and to adapt to a variety of political and social circumstances.

MAKING CONNECTIONS

1. Why did liberals and socialists, both of whom opposed conservatives, disagree with each other?
2. How did romanticism provide support for liberalism, nationalism, and conservatism?
3. Why did the revolutions of 1848 fail?
4. Why did the pattern of national unification succeed in western Europe and America but fail in eastern Europe?

TAKING IT FURTHER

For suggested readings see page R-1.

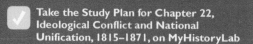
Chapter Review

New Ideologies in the Early Nineteenth Century

22.1 What were the main features of the four new ideologies of the early nineteenth century?

Establishing and protecting individual rights and freedoms, like that of the press and religion, was the primary focus of liberalism in the nineteenth century. Conservatism aimed to preserve the monarchies, aristocracies, and other hereditary rights against liberal movements, and socialism sought to reduce power and economic inequalities by allowing the community ownership of all means of production. Finally, nationalism is the belief that the unique political institutions and interests of a nation should be defended and promoted at all costs.

Ideological Encounters in Europe, 1815–1848

22.2 How did those ideologies shape the political history of Europe between 1815 and 1848?

Revolutions in European countries in the 1820s, 1830, and 1848 revealed both the potential of liberalism and nationalism and the determination of conservatives to overcome them. These revolutions achieved varying degrees of success, but in many states, especially Germany and Austria, liberal gains achieved early in the revolutions of 1848 were reversed. Ideological divisions between liberals and socialists contributed to the failure of these movements

National Unification in Europe and America, 1848–1871

22.3 How did liberal and conservative leaders use the ideology of nationalism to form nation-states?

Italian advocates of national unification appealed to a desire to revive the power of ancient Rome and to expel foreigners from their country. Bismarck achieved German unity mainly by political and military force, but the German Empire established in 1871 won conservative support from German nationalists by appealing to support for the German Fatherland. The United States cultivated a common American nationality among immigrants from other nations and by integrating the Southern states into the national economy after the Civil War. The Austrian Empire appeased Hungarian nationalist sentiment by creating the Dual Monarchy but prevented other ethnic minorities within the Austrian Empire from realizing their nationalist goals.

International Conflict and Domestic Politics, 1853–1871

22.4 How did warfare lead to political change in Russia and France between 1850 and 1871?

Russia's defeat in the Crimean War contributed to a political crisis that led Tsar Alexander II to adopt certain liberal reforms, including freeing the serfs and establishing elected assemblies in the localities. In France, conservative forces triumphed when Napoleon III was captured and defeated during the Franco-Prussian War. The collapse of his empire, which had made concessions to both nationalist and liberal groups, and the institution of a conservative republican regime defeated the forces of socialism and radicalism.

Chapter Time Line

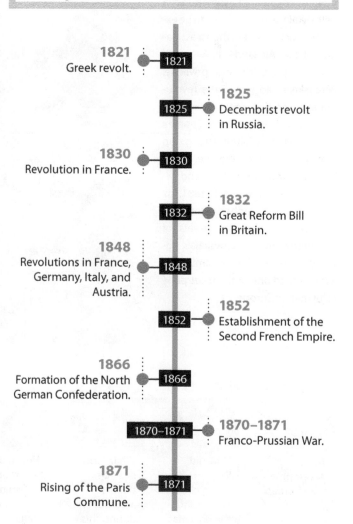

1821 Greek revolt. — 1821

1825 — **1825** Decembrist revolt in Russia.

1830 Revolution in France. — 1830

1832 — **1832** Great Reform Bill in Britain.

1848 Revolutions in France, Germany, Italy, and Austria. — 1848

1852 — **1852** Establishment of the Second French Empire.

1866 Formation of the North German Confederation. — 1866

1870–1871 — **1870–1871** Franco-Prussian War.

1871 Rising of the Paris Commune. — 1871

715

23 The Coming of Mass Politics, 1870–1914

In the spring of 1881, a harrowing scene took place in St. Petersburg, capital of the Russian Empire. A 28-year-old woman, Sofia Perovskaia, was scheduled to be executed for her part in the assassination of Tsar Alexander II. Although born into wealth and privilege, Perovskaia had joined the revolutionary socialist movement. She became a leader of the People's Will, a small revolutionary group that sought to topple the tsarist regime through sabotage and assassination. On March 1, 1881, six People's Will members stationed themselves along the streets of St. Petersburg. At Perovskaia's signal, they released their bombs and assassinated one of the most powerful men in Europe.

THE EXECUTION OF THE PEOPLE'S WILL Condemned to hang because of their role in the assassination of Tsar Alexander II, members of the revolutionary terrorist group the People's Will mount the scaffold on April 15, 1881.

LEARNING OBJECTIVES

23.1
What developments transformed Western economies and social life after 1870?

23.2
How did Western ruling classes respond to the new mass politics?

23.3
What forms did mass politics assume during this era?

23.4
How did the emergence of feminism in this period demonstrate the potential and the limits of political change?

((Listen to Chapter 23 on MyHistoryLab

◉ Watch the Video Series on MyHistoryLab

**Learn about some key topics related to this chapter with the *MyHistoryLab Video Series:*
*Key Topics in Western Civilization***

23.1

23.2

23.3

23.4

The assassins, however, were quickly arrested and sentenced to death. On the day of Perovskaia's execution, she mounted the scaffold calmly, but when the noose was placed around her neck, she grabbed hold of the platform below with her feet. It took the strength of two men to pry her feet loose so that she could hang.

The image of Sofia Perovskaia clinging to the platform with her bare feet while her executioners strained to push her to her death captures the ferocity of political struggle in Europe at the end of the nineteenth century. As we discussed in Chapter 22, ideological conflicts among liberals, conservatives, and socialists shaped the political culture of the West in the nineteenth century. These conflicts intensified and widened after 1870. The economic and social changes associated with the Industrial Revolution helped to create **mass politics**—new national political cultures characterized by the participation of men (but not yet women) outside the upper and middle classes. As industrialization spread across Europe, individuals and groups traditionally excluded from power fought for a voice in national political affairs. But, like Sofia Perovskaia's executioners, the governing classes often struggled to pry newcomers off the platform of political power—and they often succeeded. Examination of these encounters answers a key question:

mass politics A political culture characterized by the participation of non-elites.

How did the new mass politics reshape definitions of the West by the beginning of the century?

Economic Transformation

23.1 What developments transformed Western economies and social life after 1870?

Three economic developments helped shape Western actions and attitudes between 1870 and 1914: the economic depression that began in 1873, the expansion and transformation of the Industrial Revolution, and accelerated urbanization and immigration. The violent social encounters often produced by these developments helped transform the political structures and ideologies of the West.

Economic Depression and Industrial Expansion

In the 1870s, Europe's economy tilted downward—prices, interest rates, and profits all fell and remained low in many regions until the mid-1890s. Agriculture was hit hardest. By the 1890s, the price of wheat was only one-third of what it had been in the 1860s. Farmers across Europe found it difficult to make a living. Industry and commerce fared better than agriculture but declining prices for manufactured goods—often by as much as 50 percent—squeezed business profit margins.

What caused this depression? Ironically, the answer rests with the success of the Industrial Revolution. As we saw in Chapter 21, between 1760 and 1860 economic production changed dramatically, first in Britain, then in parts of western Europe. After 1860, the Industrial Revolution spread across the European continent. Railways increasingly linked Europe's diverse regions into a single economic

PRE-INDUSTRIAL CONTINUITIES This photograph of a French peasant family taking time off for a meal highlights the patchy nature of industrialization even in western Europe. Not until the 1880s and 1890s did many rural regions come within the embrace of the modern industrial economy.

network. This development opened European markets to cheap grain from the American Midwest and Ukraine—and so sent much of Europe's farming sector into economic crisis.

The spread of the Industrial Revolution is also linked to the economic depression more generally: As regions and nations industrialized, they produced more goods; yet, many industrial workers, agricultural laborers, and landowning peasants had little money to spend on industrial products. In other words, by the 1870s, a mass consumer society had not yet emerged to match the mass production created by industrialization. As production exceeded consumption, long-term agricultural and industrial depression resulted.

Industrial Change

The expansion of industrialization across Europe and the United States coincided with a new phase in the Industrial Revolution—what some historians even call the **Second Industrial Revolution**. Three factors made this industrial era different from what had come before: first, the emergence of important new industries as a result of major scientific and technical innovations; second, greater complexity in industrial organization; and third, important shifts in the marketing of industrial goods.

While textiles and coal had dominated the first Industrial Revolution, the Second Industrial Revolution rested on chemicals, steel, and electricity. The development of synthetic dyes and new techniques for refining petroleum made the chemical and oil industries into important sectors of the West's economy in the decades after 1870. Similarly, a series of new technologies and techniques enabled manufacturers to produce steel cheaply and in huge quantities, which in turn expanded production in railroads and shipbuilding.

Second Industrial Revolution A new phase in the industrialization of the processes of production and consumption, which was underway in Europe in the 1870s.

The new steel industry also transformed building construction. Combined with the inventions of the mechanical crane and stonecutter, the new steel technologies allowed builders to reach to the skies. Cityscapes changed as these new constructions thrust upward. For example, the engineering firm of Gustave Eiffel (1832–1923) built an iron and steel tower to celebrate the Paris World's Fair of 1889. Modeled on the structural supports of railway viaducts, the Eiffel Tower was ridiculed by critics as a "truly tragic street lamp" and a "half-built factory pipe," but it soon came to symbolize both Paris and the new age of industrial modernity.

The development of electric power also characterized the Second Industrial Revolution. In 1866 the English scientist Michael Faraday (1791–1867) designed the first electromagnetic generator. In 1879, the American Thomas Edison (1847–1931) invented the light bulb. These developments created a huge energy-producing industry. They also accelerated the production and distribution of other industrial goods as factories, shops, and the train and tram lines that serviced them were linked to city power grids.

Industrial organization changed as well. Businesses became larger and more complex. To control production costs in a time of declining profits, business owners developed new organizational forms, including *vertical integration*—buying the companies that supplied their raw materials and those that bought their finished products—and *horizontal integration,* linking up with companies in the same industry to fix prices, control competition, and ensure a steady profit (often called trusts or cartels). The Standard Oil Company exemplifies both trends. Formed in 1870 by John D. Rockefeller (1839–1937), Standard Oil monopolized 75 percent of the petroleum business in the United States by the 1890s, and controlled iron mines, timberland, and manufacturing and transportation businesses.

Within these new, huge, often multinational companies, organization grew more complex and impersonal. The small family firm run by the owner became rarer as layers of managers and clerical staff separated worker from owner. Even identifying "the owner" grew difficult. The need for capital to fuel these huge enterprises drove businesses to *incorporate*—to sell "shares" in the business to numerous stockholders, each of whom now shared ownership in the company.

The marketing of goods also changed. During these decades, a revolution in retailing occurred, one that culminated in a new type of business aimed at middle-class customers—the department store. In a traditional shop, the retailer (who was often also the producer) offered a small selection of products in limited quantities at fairly high prices. In contrast, in the new department stores—Bon Marché in Paris, Macy's in New York, Whiteley's in London—a vast array of products confronted the consumer. These new enterprises made their profits from a quick turnover of a large volume of low-priced products. To stimulate sales, they sought to make shopping a pleasant experience by providing well-lighted expanses filled with appealing goods sold by courteous, well-trained clerks. In-store reading rooms and restaurants pampered shoppers. Another innovation, mail-order catalogs, offered the store's delights to distant customers. Advertising became a crucial industry as business sought to persuade potential customers of new needs and desires.

On the Move: Emigration and Urbanization

Economic depression and the expansion and transformation of the Industrial Revolution accelerated patterns of urbanization and immigration. The depression hit agricultural regions particularly hard, just when population growth exerted greater pressure on land and jobs. In addition, industrial expansion undercut rural handicraft production. As a result, men and women from traditional villages sought new economic opportunities in the industrializing cities of Europe, the Americas, and Australia.

Costume original des dames au concours de vélocipèdes, à Bordeaux. (D'après le croquis de M. Sainte-Marie Prest.) 1868

THE BICYCLE REVOLUTION The bicycle exemplifies the way mass industrial production revolutionized aspects of daily life. For the first time, ordinary individuals, too poor to afford a horse or automobile, could purchase their own private means of transportation that would get them where they wanted to go in one-quarter of the time that walking required. As this engraving shows, the bicycle also contributed to the expansion of the woman's sphere.

European cities grew dramatically after 1870. In 1800, only 23 European cities had more than 100,000 inhabitants. By 1900, there were 135 cities of such a size. The European population as a whole continued to expand in this period, but the cities increased at a much faster pace. For example, in 1800 the city of Odessa in Ukraine held 6,000 inhabitants. By 1914, Odessa contained 480,000 people.

Seeking opportunities, inhabitants of industrially underdeveloped regions migrated to more economically advanced areas. Italians headed to France and Switzerland, while the Irish poured across the Irish Sea into Liverpool and Glasgow. Some immigrants headed not for the nearest city, but for a different continent. Between 1860 and 1914, more than 52 million Europeans crossed the oceans in quest of a better life. Over 70 percent of these transoceanic immigrants traveled to North America, 21 percent to South America, and the rest to Australia, New Zealand, or colonies in Asia and Africa.[1] Emigrants from eastern Europe accounted for an ever-larger share of those bound for America. In the 1880s 100,000 Poles moved to the United States. By the 1900s, however, between 130,000 and 175,000 Poles were heading to the United States *each year*.

Growing Social Unrest

Rapid economic change, combined with accelerated urbanization and immigration, heightened social tensions and destabilized political structures. The freefall in prices that characterized the depression eroded capitalist profit margins. In response, businessmen sought to reduce the number of their employees and to increase labor productivity. Workers reacted angrily. Reduced prices did mean that the living standards of *employed* workers rose, but so, too, did unemployment and underemployment. Heightened class hostilities thus characterized these decades.

In rural regions such as Spain and Ireland, the collapse in agricultural prices fostered social and economic crises. Agricultural laborers and peasants turned to violence to enforce their calls for a fairer distribution of land. The spread of industrialization into southern and eastern Europe led to unrest as handicraft producers and independent artisans fought to maintain their traditional livelihoods.

The flow of immigrants into Europe's cities raised social tensions. Cities were often unable to cope with their dramatic increases in population. Newcomers battled with established residents for jobs and apartments. The mixture of nationalities and ethnic groups often proved particularly explosive.

Read the Document

Adelheid Popp, "Finding Work: Women Factory Workers"

Defining the Nation

23.2 How did Western ruling classes respond to the new mass politics?

The economic and social changes detailed in the last section helped create mass politics. Because industrial expansion broke down local and regional cultures, loyalties, and mindsets, it cleared the way for the development of new national political identities and interests. The railroads, telegraph, and telephone shattered the barriers of distance, while new printing technologies made newspapers cheap and available to ordinary people. With access to information, they could now form opinions and participate in national and international debate as never before. The dramatic expansion of cities also created the environments in which mass political movements could grow.

Faced with the challenge of this new political culture, political leaders sought to quell social discontent and ensure the loyalty of their populations. They did so in the context of the turbulent international climate created by the national unification of Italy and Germany and the continuing decline of the Ottoman Empire (see Chapter 22). As the European balance of power shifted, governments scrambled to strengthen their states at home as well as abroad.

Nation-Making

After 1870, all but the most authoritarian European leaders recognized the importance of "nation-making," of creating a sense of national identity to overcome the conflicting regional, social, and political loyalties that divided their citizens and subjects. But while European political elites sought to make ordinary men feel a part of political life, they also tried to retain their dominant social and political position. As socialism challenged both liberal and conservative regimes, those in power had to figure out how to stay there.

FRANCHISE EXPANSION One way to stay in power was to share it, as the British example proved. In the first half of the nineteenth century, Britain's landed elite had accommodated middle-class demands for greater influence without relinquishing its own dominance. Landed aristocrats and gentlemen played leading roles in both major political parties—the Liberals and the Conservatives (also called "Tories")—but both parties encouraged industrial growth and policies that benefited the middle classes. In the last third of the century, this system expanded to include working-class men. In 1867, many urban working men won the right to vote, and in 1884 this right was extended to rural male laborers. Although Britain did not achieve universal male suffrage until after World War I, this gradual expansion of the franchise convinced many British working-class men that there was no need for revolution.

Similar patterns emerged across Europe in this era as aristocratic and middle-class politicians extended the vote to lower-class men. These political leaders regarded franchise reform as a way to avoid socialist revolution by incorporating potential revolutionaries within the system.

SOCIAL REFORM New voters, however, had to be wooed and wowed. They had to be persuaded to vote the way their leaders wished. Political parties thus turned to social welfare legislation. Both liberal and conservative politicians used social welfare reform to convince working-class voters that they had a stake in the existing political system—and thus to reduce the appeal of revolutionary socialism.

In the 1880s, for example, German Chancellor Otto von Bismarck introduced some of the most thoroughgoing social welfare measures yet seen in Europe. Bismarck, a fiercely conservative aristocrat, sought to ensure German stability and national unity. Alarmed by the popularity of the socialist German Social Democratic Party (SPD), Bismarck outlawed it in 1878, and then enacted laws to attract working-class voters. He initiated sickness benefits in 1883, coverage for industrial accidents in 1884, and old-age pensions and disability insurance in 1889.

Like their conservative opponents, liberal politicians also saw social reform as a way to stay in power and create national unity. In 1906, British trade unionists and socialists formed the Labour Party. Alarmed by this socialist threat, Britain's Liberal government enacted welfare measures, including state-funded lunches for school-children, pensions for the elderly, and sickness and unemployment benefits for some workers. A similar process occurred in Italy. Frightened by the growing appeal of revolutionary socialist parties, the Liberal Party leader Giovanni Giolitti (1842–1928) tried to improve workers' lives and convince them that real change did not require revolution. Giolitti legalized trade unions, established public health and life insurance programs, cracked down on child labor, and established a six-day workweek.

SCHOOLING THE NATION Like social welfare programs, state elementary schools served as important tools in the effort to build internally united (and therefore externally competitive) nation-states. During the late nineteenth century, most of the nations of western and central Europe established free public elementary education systems. Such schools helped foster loyalty to the nation and its leaders. In the 1880s,

MASS SCHOOLING Jean Jules Henri Geoffroy, *The Junior Class,* 1889. Geoffroy presented this painting at the World's Fair of 1889 in celebration of the 100th anniversary of the French Revolution. In France, supporters of the Republic saw the state school system as one of the French Revolution's central achievements and regarded the state school teacher as an embodiment of republican (as opposed to religious or monarchical) ideals. In keeping with these revolutionary and republican ideals, Geoffroy's classroom contains both middle-class boys (wearing white collars) and their lower-class peers.

for example, French student teachers were instructed that "their first duty is to make [their pupils] love and understand the fatherland."[2]

Schools helped forge a national identity in three ways. First, they ensured the triumph of the national language. Required to abandon their regional dialect (and sometimes brutally punished if they did not), children learned to read and write in the national language. Second, history and geography lessons taught children versions of the past that strengthened their sense of belonging to a superior people and often served a specific political agenda. For example, wall maps of France in French classrooms included the provinces of Alsace and Lorraine, even though Germany had seized these regions after the Franco-Prussian War in 1871. Finally, the schools, with their essentially captive populations, participated fully in nationalistic rituals, including singing patriotic songs such as *Deutschland Über Alles* ("Germany Over All") or *Rule Britannia,* and observing special days to commemorate military victories or national heroes.

INVENTING TRADITIONS Nationalistic ritual was not confined to the schoolroom. Making nations often meant *inventing* traditions to capture the loyalty of the mass electorate. German policymakers, for example, invented "Sedan Day." This new national holiday celebrated the victory over France in the Franco-Prussian War that helped create the new German Empire. It featured parades, flag raisings, and special services to foster a sense of German nationalism among its citizens.

Inventing a set of traditions around the monarchy and making the royal family the center of the nation were also effective nation-making tools. When the German states united in 1871, the king of Prussia, William I, became the new German emperor. William I, however, tended to identify himself more as a Prussian than a German. It was his grandson, William II (r. 1888–1918), who used personal appearances and militaristic pageantry to make the monarchy a symbolic center of the new nation. In Britain, the anniversaries of Queen Victoria's accession to the throne (the Silver Jubilee of 1887 and the Diamond Jubilee of 1897) were elaborately staged and orchestrated to make ordinary Britons feel close to the queen and therefore part of a powerful, united nation. Mass printing and production helped support this new mass politics of nationality.

GERMAN EMPEROR WILLIAM II AND HIS ENTOURAGE William preferred to wear military regalia when he appeared in public. In this way, William himself symbolized the link between the German state and Germany's military might.

723

At the Jubilees, participants could purchase illustrated commemorative pamphlets, plates etched with the queen's silhouette, teapots in the shape of Victoria's head, or even an automated musical bustle that played *God Save the Queen* whenever the wearer sat down.

Nation-Making: The Examples of France, the Russian Empire, and Ireland

By the late nineteenth and early twentieth centuries, political leaders recognized that fostering a sense of national identity among their citizens or subjects would both lessen the appeal of socialism and strengthen the nation-state in war with competitors (see **Map 23.1**). The examples of France, the Russian Empire, and Ireland, however, demonstrate the complexities of nation-making.

FRANCE: A CRISIS OF LEGITIMACY At the end of the last chapter, we saw that defeat in the Franco-Prussian War of 1870–1871 led France to return to a republican form of government, based on universal manhood suffrage. This "Third Republic" faced a crisis of legitimacy. Many Frenchmen argued that the Republic was the product of

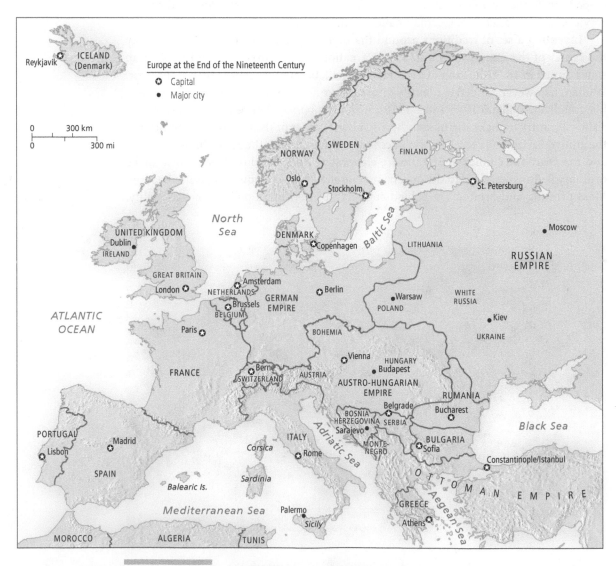

MAP **23.1** EUROPE AT THE END OF THE NINETEENTH CENTURY Compare this map with Map 20.3 ("Europe After the Congress of Vienna in 1815," page 646). How does this comparison show the impact of modern nationalism on European political geography? What changes in political borders have occurred and why?

military defeat and therefore not worth their loyalty or support. These opponents of the Third Republic included monarchists who wanted a king, Bonapartists longing for a Napoleonic empire, Catholics disturbed by republican efforts to curb the political power of the Church, and aristocrats opposed to democracy.

To understand the opposition to the Third Republic in France after 1871, it is essential to remember that "republicanism" in France meant more than "no king, no emperor." Rooted in the radical Jacobin Republic of 1792 (see Chapter 20), republicanism rested on a vision of an ideal France of male equals—small shopkeepers and independent artisans—governed by reason, not religion. Such a vision clashed with the interests and ideals of monarchists, Bonapartists, and Catholics. The clash of these rival ideologies generated chaos in French politics.

The **Dreyfus Affair** exemplified this ideological clash and revealed the lack of consensus about French political identity. (See *Justice in History* in this chapter.) In 1894, a French military court wrongly convicted Captain Alfred Dreyfus (1859–1935) of espionage. French intellectuals took up Dreyfus's case, and supporters and opponents of Dreyfus battled in the streets and the legislature. Support for Dreyfus, who was Jewish, became equated with support for the secular ideals of the Republic. The anti-Dreyfusards, in contrast, saw the affair as a symptom of everything wrong with the Republic. They believed that true French nationalism should center on the Catholic religion and respect for the military.

In some ways, the supporters of Dreyfus—and therefore of the Republic—won. Dreyfus was declared "not guilty" in 1906, and the government placed the army under civilian control and removed the Catholic Church from its privileged position. With these measures politicians aimed to separate citizenship from religious affiliation and unite the nation around the ideal of a secular Republic. In 1914, on the eve of World War I, the Third Republic was thus stronger than it had been two decades earlier.

It had not yet, however, gained the approval of all of French society. Royalist and Catholic opposition remained strong. At the same time, working-class disaffection was growing. The Radical Party, which represented the interests of small store-owners and independent craftsmen, not industrial workers, dominated political life and drew its support from rural and small-town constituencies. The Radicals opposed the high taxes necessary to establish social welfare programs and dragged their feet on social legislation such as the 10-hour workday (not passed until 1904) and old-age pensions (not established until 1910). As a result, French factory workers increasingly turned to violence.

RUSSIA: REVOLUTION AND REACTION In the sprawling and multiethnic Russian Empire, the task of nation-making was immense, but well underway by 1914. As we saw in Chapter 22, in the 1860s Tsar Alexander II instituted the "Great Reforms," which included the emancipation of 50 million serfs, the creation of a new judicial system, and the vesting of local governmental authority in elected assemblies (for which 40 percent of the peasantry was able to vote). The Reforms energized Russian provincial and press culture and enlivened local politics. As new opportunities arose for lawyers, clerks, shopkeepers, accountants, journalists, and the like, the middle classes expanded.

Many of these middle-class men and women embraced liberal political ideals and sought the reform of the tsar's autocratic regime and the expansion of political representation. Others concluded that only violent revolution would bring meaningful political change. Terrorist groups like the People's Will, as we saw at the beginning of this chapter, turned to assassination as a political weapon.

The new Russian working class also grew increasingly politicized. In the 1890s, the western regions of the Russian Empire underwent dramatic industrialization. By 1900, only Britain, Germany, and the United States produced more steel—and Russia supplied 50 percent of the industrialized world's oil. Coal mines and steel mills dotted Ukraine, and huge state-run factories dominated Moscow and St. Petersburg.

Dreyfus Affair The trials of Captain Alfred Dreyfus on treason charges dominated French political life in the decade after 1894 and revealed fundamental divisions in French society.

 Watch the Video

Russian Terrorism

Justice in History

The Dreyfus Affair: DEFINING NATIONAL IDENTITY

IN FRANCE

O n September 27, 1894, French counterespionage officers examined a disturbing document—an unsigned, undated cover letter for documents containing information on French military equipment and training. The officers concluded that the letter was intended for the German military attaché in Paris. Someone in the French officer corps was selling military secrets to the Germans.

After a brief investigation, the French investigators concluded that the traitor was Captain Alfred Dreyfus, a candidate officer on the General Staff. An unlikely traitor, Dreyfus had compiled a strong record during his military career and, by all accounts, was a staunch French patriot. Moreover, because his wife was wealthy, he had no need to sell his country for money. He was, however, an aloof arrogant man, disliked by most of his fellow officers. He was also a Jew.

Convicted of treason, Dreyfus was exiled in 1895 to Devil's Island, a former leper colony 12 miles off the coast of French Guyana in the Caribbean. Many believed he had gotten off too lightly. Public and press clamored for his execution.

The case seemed closed. But some months later, the new chief of the Intelligence Bureau, Major Marie-Georges Picquart, discovered that someone was continuing to pass military secrets to the Germans. Picquart set out to trap the man he believed to be Dreyfus's accomplice. The evidence he uncovered, however, convinced him that Dreyfus was innocent.

Picquart's efforts created a national crisis. On January 13, 1898, one of France's most famous authors, Émile Zola, alleged in a Paris newspaper that the French military was engaged in a cover-up. In an article headlined *"J'accuse!"* ("I accuse!"), Zola charged that the General Staff had deliberately convicted an innocent man. Over the next six weeks, riots broke out in French cities.

In 1899, a second military court tried Dreyfus and again found him guilty. In the subsequent riots in Paris, 100 people were wounded and 200 jailed. Ten days later, the French president pardoned Dreyfus to heal the divisions opened by the trial.

The Dreyfus Affair drew international attention, polarized French politics, and tore apart Parisian society. It sparked violent protests, duels, and trials for assault, defamation, and libel. The question "Are you for or against Dreyfus?" divided families and destroyed friendships. During the height of the controversy, for example, the painter Edgar Degas ridiculed Camille Pisarro's paintings. When reminded that he had once admired these same works, Degas said, "Yes, but that was before the Dreyfus Affair." Degas was a passionate anti-Dreyfusard, Pisarro a Dreyfus supporter.[3]

Why did the Dreyfus Affair change one painter's perception of another's work? Why was this trial not simply a case, but an *affair,* a matter of public and private debate, as well as political upheaval?

To comprehend the Dreyfus Affair, we must understand that it was less about Captain Alfred Dreyfus than about the very existence of the Third Republic, founded in 1871 in the wake of military defeat in the Franco-Prussian War and the collapse of Napoleon III's empire. The intellectuals and politicians who supported Dreyfus were defending this Republic. They sought to limit the army's involvement in France's political life and upheld a secular definition of the nation that treated Catholics no differently from Protestants, Jews, or atheists.

Dreyfus's opponents, in contrast, regarded the Third Republic as a betrayal of the true France. They wanted a hierarchical, Catholic, imperial state, steeped in military traditions. By defending the military conviction of Dreyfus, they supported the army and the authoritarian traditions that the Republic had jettisoned. The Dreyfus Affair was thus an encounter between competing versions of French national identity.

The question "What is France?" however, could not be answered without considering a second question: "Who belongs

THE DREYFUS AFFAIR GAME This board game, with portraits of the key players in the Dreyfus Affair, illustrates the dominant role of the "Affair" in late nineteenth-century French culture.

(continued on next page)

(continued from previous page)

in France?"—or more specifically, "What about Jews?" France's small Jewish community (less than 1 percent of the population) had enjoyed the rights of full citizenship since 1791—much longer than in most of Europe. Yet the Dreyfus Affair showed that even in France, the position of Jews in the nation remained uncertain. Although anti-Semitism played little role in the initial charges against Dreyfus, it quickly became a dominating feature of the affair. For many anti-Dreyfusards, Dreyfus's Jewishness explained everything. The novelist and political theorist Maurice Barrès insisted, "I have no need to be told why Dreyfus committed treason. . . . That Dreyfus is capable of treason I conclude from his race."[4] Anti-Semites such as Barrès regarded Jewishness as a kind of hereditary disease that made Jews unfit for French citizenship. To the anti-Semitic nationalist, "the Jew" was a person without a country, unconnected by racial or religious ties to the French nation—the opposite of a patriot.

In 1906, a French high court exonerated Dreyfus. Not until 1995, however, did the French military acknowledge his innocence. Dreyfus survived to serve his country with distinction in the First World War.

Like Dreyfus, the Third Republic survived the Dreyfus Affair. Outrage over the army's cover-up led republican leaders to limit the powers of the army and so lessened the chances of a military coup. Anti-Semitism, however, remained pervasive in French politics and cultural life well into the twentieth century.

For Discussion

1. What does the Dreyfus Affair reveal about definitions of national identity in late-nineteenth-century Europe?
2. Many French men and women believed that for the sake of the national interest, Dreyfus's conviction had to be upheld—whether he was actually guilty or not. In what situations, if any, should "national interest" override an individual's right to a fair trial?

Taking It Further

Begley, Louis. *Why the Dreyfus Affair Matters.* 2009. Begley, a novelist and a lawyer, uses the history of the Dreyfus Affair to reflect on contemporary political and legal issues.

Burns, Michael. *France and the Dreyfus Affair: A Documentary History.* 1999. An accessible collection of primary documents.

Industrialization created a small but significant urban working class. With a literacy rate approaching 70 percent, these workers had access to both liberal and socialist political ideas.

Such ideas, however, clashed with the absolutist convictions of the tsarist regime. Convinced that God had appointed them to rule, Alexander III (r. 1881–1894) and Nicholas II (r. 1894–1917) clung to absolutism. To catch up with the West, the tsarist regime adopted Western industrialization but had no intention of accepting Western ideas of representative government. It could not, however, completely block the flow of these ideas into the Russian Empire.

Nor could it stamp out the social upheaval created by economic change. Rapid state-imposed industrialization produced cities simmering with discontent. Factory workers labored 11 hours a day in poor conditions, but both strikes and unions were illegal. In the countryside, heavy taxation and rapid population growth increased competition for land and intensified peasant discontent.

The tsarist regime's efforts at "nation-making" proved even more divisive. Under Alexander III and even more intensely under Nicholas II, **Russification** became official state policy throughout the empire. Originally designed to limit Polish influence in the western borderlands of the empire, Russification required that the Russian language be used in schools and government institutions and that traditional local legal and social customs conform to those imposed by the central, Russian state. Russification also meant an increasing emphasis on the Russian Orthodox religion as an element of "Russianness." Orthodox believers who did not conform to official Russian Orthodox practice, as well as Roman Catholics and Lutherans, faced increasing persecution. So, too, did non-Christians, including Buddhists, Muslims, and especially Jews.

While Russification did enhance the national identity of Orthodox, Russian-speaking subjects of the tsar, it aroused hostility among even formerly loyal peoples. The Finns, for example, who had come under Russian imperial rule in 1809, had generally regarded the tsarist state as far preferable to their former Swedish overlords. The tsarist efforts to Russify Finland, which began in the 1890s, rapidly destroyed the Finns' positive view of the tsarist regime. In areas such as Poland, Lithuania, and Ukraine, too, Russification intensified nationalist resentment against Russian imperial rule.

Read the Document

"Working Conditions of Women in the Factories," M. I. Pokrovskaia

Russification Tsarist policy from the 1890s until the outbreak of World War I; Russification imposed the use of Russian language and emphasized Russian Orthodox religious and cultural practices.

THE REVOLUTION OF 1905 IN THE MOVIES On Bloody Sunday, January 22, 1905, Russian troops opened fire on more than 100,000 citizens who had gathered in St. Petersburg to present a petition to the tsar. Rather than subduing the revolt, the massacre sparked a revolution. This photograph, supposedly of the moment when the tsar's troops began to shoot the demonstrators, is one of the most familiar images of the twentieth century—yet it is *not* in fact a documentary record. Instead, it is a still taken from *The Ninth of January,* a Soviet film made in 1925.

In 1905, popular and nationalist discontent flared into revolution. That year Japan trounced the Russian Empire in a war sparked by competition for territory in Asia. This military disaster made the tsarist regime seem incompetent and provided an opening for political reformers and nationalist groups. On a day that became known as "Bloody Sunday" (January 22, 1905), 100,000 workers and their families attempted to present to the tsar a petition calling for higher wages, better working conditions, and political rights. Troops fired on the unarmed crowd. At least 70 people were killed and more than 240 wounded. The massacre strengthened the call for revolution. Across the empire, workers went on strike and demanded economic and political rights. In June, parts of the navy mutinied. Nationalist groups grabbed the opportunity to demand autonomous states.

With the empire in chaos, Tsar Nicholas II gave in to demands for the election of a national legislative assembly, the Duma. Yet the revolution continued. In December a military mutiny sparked an uprising in Moscow. As buildings burned and street battles raged, revolutionary socialists controlled parts of the city.

By the time the first Duma met in April of 1906, however, tsarist forces had regained the offensive and terrorized much of the opposition. Because most of the army remained loyal, the tsarist regime was able to quell the Moscow uprising and then move to suppress revolutionary forces across the empire. But just as importantly, the violence and radicalism displayed in Moscow horrified middle-class liberals, who now refused to cooperate with revolutionary or socialist groups. Nicholas succeeded in limiting the Duma's legislative role and, by 1907, regained many of his autocratic powers.

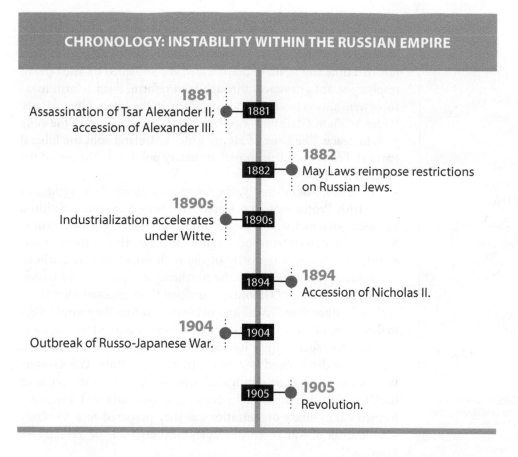

CHRONOLOGY: INSTABILITY WITHIN THE RUSSIAN EMPIRE

1881
Assassination of Tsar Alexander II; accession of Alexander III.
1881

1882
1882
May Laws reimpose restrictions on Russian Jews.

1890s
Industrialization accelerates under Witte.
1890s

1894
1894
Accession of Nicholas II.

1904
Outbreak of Russo-Japanese War.
1904

1905
1905
Revolution.

The Revolution of 1905, then, did not overthrow the tsarist regime or transform it into a limited or liberal monarchy. Yet it was not a complete failure. Trade unions, strikes, and political parties were now legal. The Duma did exist and helped connect the still-thriving provincial and urban political cultures with the central state. The revolution's most important success, however, was the loosening of censorship. The already influential local press expanded further, as did the numbers of all sorts of publications. Public opinion now became a crucial force in Russian imperial politics. Nicholas's unshaken commitment to autocracy and Russification, however, ensured that the Empire remained politically unstable.

THE IRISH IDENTITY CONFLICT Chapter 21 described Ireland as an "internal colony," officially part of the United Kingdom since 1801 but governed with British rather than Irish economic interests in mind. In this internal colony, the growth of Irish nationalism led to political instability and the threat of civil war.

The United Kingdom comprised two islands—Britain and Ireland—and four nations—the English, the Welsh, the Scottish, and the Irish. By the 1870s, a chasm yawned between the first three overwhelmingly Protestant and industrialized nations, and the largely Roman Catholic, largely peasant culture of Ireland. Economic grievances fused with a deeply rooted sense of political and religious repression among Irish Catholics and convinced many of the need for independence from Britain. Not all Irish nationalists, however, were Roman Catholic. Many Irish Protestants also embraced the ideal of an independent Ireland.

Irish nationalism took two forms. A minority of Irish nationalists was revolutionary and republican: These "Fenians" (from the Old Irish word for "warrior") sought an Irish republic with no ties to the British monarchy or the British Empire. Convinced that the only way to achieve this republic was through armed struggle, they carried out a number of terrorist attacks in Ireland and Britain from the 1860s on. The larger, more moderate group of Irish nationalists aimed not at an independent

MAP **23.2** THE UNITED KINGDOM OF GREAT BRITAIN AND IRELAND IN 1910 What were the factors weakening the Union between Great Britain and Ireland by 1910? In what ways did the emergence of the Unionist movement (in favor of retaining the Union) further destabilize the political status quo?

republic but rather at the more limited ideal of "Home Rule"—an Irish Parliament in Dublin to govern Irish domestic issues.

Faced with growing Irish nationalism, the British government resorted time and again to martial law, accompanied by attempts to resolve peasant grievances through land reform. Such reform measures were always too little, too late. Then, in the 1880s, Liberal Party leader William Gladstone embraced Irish Home Rule as the only path to peace. The issue of Home Rule for Ireland split the Liberal Party and convulsed British parliamentary politics for the rest of the nineteenth century.

Even more significantly, the prospect of Home Rule frightened many Irish Protestants who feared becoming a minority within a Catholic-governed state. "Home Rule," they said, equaled "Rome Rule." The descendants of English and Scottish settlers, Protestants constituted a minority of the Irish population as a whole, but made up the majority in the northernmost province of Ulster. These Ulstermen, or "Unionists," defined their national identity as "British" rather than "Irish" and made it clear that they would fight to defeat Home Rule and preserve the union of Ireland with Britain.

By 1914, such a fight looked inevitable. The Liberals, back in office, were determined to achieve Irish Home Rule. The Conservatives were just as determined to oppose it, even to the point of backing military rebellion. In Ireland, nationalists and Unionists formed paramilitary organizations as they prepared to fight. Only the outbreak of war in Europe postponed civil war in Ireland (see **Map 23.2**).

The New Mass Politics

23.3 What forms did mass politics assume during this era?

We have seen that by expanding the franchise, passing social welfare legislation, and inventing nationalist traditions, liberal and conservative political leaders sought to win the loyalty of the lower classes. Mass support for socialist and racist-nationalist political parties, however, challenged the power of traditional political leaders and parties.

The Politics of the Working Class

The rise of working-class socialist political parties and the emergence of more radical trade unionism reflected an escalation of class hostilities. Workers often rejected the political authority of their bosses and landlords and sought power on their own terms.

THE WORKERS' CITY The impact of agricultural crisis and industrial expansion created large working-class communities in the rapidly growing industrial cities. At the same time, technological developments such as electrified tram lines and the expansion of the railway system enabled wealthy Europeans to retreat from overcrowded, dirty, disease-ridden city centers to the new suburbs. Increasingly isolated from the middle and upper classes, industrial workers developed what sociologists call "urban villages," closely knit neighborhoods in which each family had a clear and publicly acknowledged place.

Sharply defined gender roles played an important part in ordering this world. The home became the woman's domain (although many working-class women also worked outside the home). Wives often controlled the family income and made most decisions about family life. Men built their own cultural and leisure institutions—the corner pub, the music hall, the football club, the brass band. These institutions not only provided an escape from the confines of work and home, they also secured the bonds of male working-class identity. This identity rested on a sharp distinction between "Us"—ordinary men, workers, neighbors—and "Them," bosses, owners, landlords, those with privilege and power.

WORKING-CLASS SOCIALISM AND THE REVOLUTIONARY PROBLEM The emergence of working-class socialist political parties embodied this class identity. By 1914, 20 European countries had socialist parties.

Why socialism? As we saw in Chapter 22, by 1870 Karl Marx had published his economic and political theory of revolutionary socialism. Not many workers had the time, education, or energy to study Marx's complex ideas. But Marx's basic points, presented to workers by socialist activists and organizers, resonated with many workers. Quite simply, these laborers had already identified their boss as the enemy, and Marx assured them that they were right. His insistence that class conflict was inherent within the industrial system accorded with workers' own experience of social segregation and economic exploitation. The onset of economic depression in the 1870s also appeared to confirm Marx's prediction that capitalism would produce economic crises until it finally collapsed.

The most dramatic socialist success story was in Germany. In the elections of 1912, the socialist SPD won 35 percent of the national vote and became the largest party in the German Reichstag or parliament. German socialism was, however, more than just party politics. The SPD provided German workers with an alternative community. They could send their children to socialist day care centers and bury their parents in socialist cemeteries. They could spend their leisure time in socialist bicycling clubs and chess teams. They could read socialist newspapers, sing socialist songs, save their money in socialist banks, and shop at socialist cooperatives.

By the 1890s, the rapid growth of socialist parties throughout Europe persuaded many activists that working-class revolution was just around the corner. In 1885 the SPD leader August Bebel (1840–1913) declared, "Every night I go to sleep with the thought that the last hour of bourgeois society strikes soon."[5]

Yet Bebel was wrong. Ironically, the immediate success of socialist parties ensured their long-term failure to foment a working-class revolution. To continue to attract voters, socialist parties needed to pass legislation that would appeal to workers. But minimum wage laws, pension rights, and the like improved workers' lives within a *non-socialist* system—and so made socialist revolution more remote. Why resort to violent revolution when participation in parliamentary politics was paying off? Why overthrow capitalism when workers were benefiting from it?

In Germany, the quest for an answer to these questions led to **socialist revisionism**, a set of political ideas most closely associated with Eduard Bernstein (1850–1932). Bernstein rejected the Marxist faith in inevitable violent revolution and argued instead for the gradual and peaceful evolution of socialism through parliamentary politics. He called for German socialists to form alliances with middle-class liberals and carry out social and economic reforms.

In 1899, the SPD condemned Bernstein's revisionism and reaffirmed its faith in the inevitability of capitalism's collapse and violent, working-class revolution. Bernstein had lost the battle—but he won the war. For, in practice if not in theory, the SPD acted like any other parliamentary party. It focused on improving the lot of its constituency through legislative change. As a result, the German political system grew more responsive to workers' needs—and workers grew less revolutionary.

Read the Document

"Socialism: The Gotha Program"

socialist revisionism The belief that an equal society can be built through participation in parliamentary politics rather than through violent revolution.

Socialist parties across Europe tended to follow the pattern of the SPD: They voiced the rhetoric of revolution while working for gradual change through parliamentary politics. Despite the almost hysterical fears of many middle- and upper-class Europeans, the successes of socialist political parties strengthened parliamentary politics more than they stirred up revolution.

RADICAL TRADE UNIONISM AND THE ANARCHIST THREAT Much of the support for socialist parliamentary parties came from the trade union movement. As we have seen, the onset of economic depression in the 1870s shattered middle-class confidence and shrank capitalists' profit margins. Looking to cut costs, businessmen sought to reduce the number of laborers, increase production, and decrease wages. To protect workers from this onslaught, unions grew more radical. First, while the unions of the 1850s and 1860s had tended to be small, craft-based groupings of skilled workers, the new unions aimed to organize all the male workers in an entire industry—for example, all male textile workers, rather than just the skilled weavers. And second, these new unions were also more willing to resort to strikes and violence. Unionized workers in barbershops were even encouraged to "inflict nonfatal cuts on the clients of their capitalist masters."[6]

The ideology of **syndicalism** further radicalized the union movement. Syndicalists sought to use the economic clout of the working class to topple capitalism and create a worker-controlled, egalitarian society. In the syndicalist vision, if every worker in a nation went on strike—a **general strike**—the resulting disruption of the capitalist economy would lead to working-class revolution. The French syndicalist leader Georges Sorel (1847–1922) did not actually believe that a general strike was possible, but he argued that the *idea* of the general strike served as an essential myth, an inspirational idea that would give workers the motivation and self-confidence to make a revolution.

In their rejection of parliamentary politics and their willingness to use violence to achieve their revolutionary ends, syndicalists were influenced by **anarchism**. Anarchists shunned politics and opted for direct action such as street fighting and assassination. Whereas Marxists sought working-class control of the state, anarchists aimed to destroy the state entirely. The Russian anarchist Mikhail Bakunin (1814–1876) insisted that the great obstacle to a just and egalitarian society was the state itself, not capitalism or the industrial middle class.

The combined impact of both syndicalism and anarchism created a climate of social unrest and political turmoil in much of Europe before 1914. In the 1890s anarchists carried out a terrorist campaign in Paris that began with a series of bombings and culminated in the fatal stabbing of President Sadi Carnot. Other anarchist victims included Empress Elisabeth of Austria in 1898, King Umberto I of Italy in 1900, and U.S. President William McKinley in 1901.

The Politics of Race and Nation

Just as "the masses" consisted of more than urban factory workers, so mass politics were not limited to socialism, syndicalism, and anarchism. Members of the lower middle class (or "petit-bourgeoisie"), for example, rarely joined socialist parties or trade unions: Fighting to protect their middle-class status, these clerks, shop assistants, and small store owners regarded the socialist vision of working-class rule as a nightmare. Socialism also possessed little appeal in areas just beginning to industrialize, such as much of eastern Europe, which still contained many independent artisans and peasants threatened by the modernization that socialism represented. Many within these social groups turned to political parties based on ethnic identity or racism rather than class.

Part of the appeal of **nationalist-racist politics** lay in its radical style. Possessing only a basic education, most of the newly enfranchised had little time for reading or

syndicalism Ideology of the late nineteenth and early twentieth century that sought to achieve a working-class revolution through economic action, particularly through mass labor strikes.

general strike Syndicalist tactic that called for every worker to go on strike and thus disrupt the capitalist economy and force a political revolution.

anarchism Ideology that views the state as unnecessary and repressive and rejects participation in parliamentary politics in favor of direct, usually violent action.

 Read the Document

Mikhail Bakunin, "Principles and Organization of the International Brotherhood"

nationalist-racist politics Anti-liberal politics that appeal to race-based identities and fears.

ANARCHISM AND ASSASSINATION The anarchist Luigi Lucheni assassinated Empress Elisabeth of Austria-Hungary in 1898. Lucheni targeted the empress not for anything she had done, but simply for who she was. He wrote in his diary, "How I would like to kill someone, but it must be someone important so it gets in the papers."

sustained intellectual work. They worked long hours and needed to be entertained. They needed a new style of politics—one based more on visual imagery and symbolism than on the written word. Nationalist politics fit the bill perfectly. Unlike socialists, who placed faith in education and rational persuasion, nationalist-racist politicians relied on emotional appeals. By waving flags, parading in historical costumes or military uniforms, and singing folk songs, they tapped into powerful personal and community memories to persuade voters of their common identity, based not on shared economic interests but on ethnic, religious, or linguistic ties—and a mistrust of those who did not share those ties.

NATIONALISM IN THE OTTOMAN AND AUSTRO-HUNGARIAN EMPIRES: THE POLITICS OF DIVISION Nationalist mass politics proved powerful in the multiethnic, industrially underdeveloped Ottoman and Austro-Hungarian Empires. These regions possessed a diversity of ethnic, linguistic, and religious groups. Nationalist ideology taught these groups to identify themselves as nations and to demand independent statehood.

By the 1870s, as we saw in Chapter 22, nationalism had already weakened the Ottoman Empire's rule over its European territories. Determined to hold on to his empire, the Ottoman sultan in 1875 and 1876 suppressed nationalist uprisings in Bosnia-Herzegovina and Bulgaria with ferocity. But this repression gave Russia the excuse it needed to declare war on behalf of its Slavic "little brothers" in the Balkans. As a result of this Russo-Turkish War (1877–1878), the Ottomans lost most of their remaining European territories. **Map 23.3** shows that Montenegro, Serbia, and Romania became independent states, while Austria-Hungary took Bosnia-Herzegovina. Bulgaria received autonomy, which the Bulgarians widened into full independence in 1908. A series of Balkan Wars in the early twentieth century meant even more losses for the Ottoman Empire.

Ottoman weakness appeared to make Austria-Hungary stronger. The appearance of strength, however, was deceptive. Straining under the pressures of late industrialization, Austria-Hungary's numerous ethnic and linguistic groups competed for power and privileges (see Map 22.4, page 710). In the age of mass politics, these divisions shaped political life.

Language became a key battleground in this political competition. In a multilingual empire, which language would be taught in the schools or used in official communications or guarantee career advancement? Politicians agitated for the primacy of their own native language and pushed for the power needed to ensure it. In the Hungarian half of the empire, for example, the ruling Magyar-speaking Hungarian landlords redrew constituency boundaries to give maximum influence to Magyar speakers in parliament and undercut the power of other ethnic groups. "Magyarization"

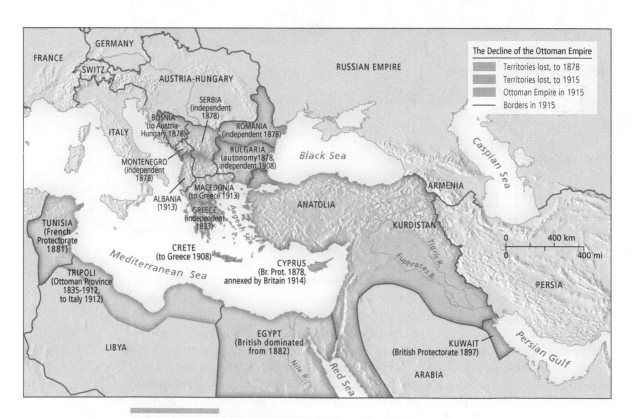

MAP **23.3** THE DISINTEGRATION OF THE OTTOMAN EMPIRE During the nineteenth century, the Ottoman regime lost territory and political control over much of its once-mighty empire to both nationalist independence movements and to rival European powers. From the 1870s on, mass nationalism accelerated Ottoman disintegration. What territories had the Ottoman regime lost by 1880? What territories were lost between 1880 and 1915? How did the disintegration of the Ottoman Empire change the balance of power in Europe?

in governmental offices and schools bred resentment among non-Hungarians. They formed their own political parties and began to dream of political independence. Similarly, in the Austrian half of the empire, the struggle between Germans and Czechs over language laws became so intense that no party could establish a majority in parliament, and in 1900 Emperor Francis Joseph (r. 1848–1916) resorted to ruling by decree.

ANTI-SEMITISM IN MASS POLITICS Anti-Semitism played a central role in the new nationalist mass politics. Across Europe, anti-Semitic parties emerged, while established conservative parties adopted anti-Semitic rhetoric to attract voters. Three developments explain this heightened anti-Semitism.

Anti-Semitism grew stronger after 1870, first, because of an increasing tendency to racialize national identity. Concepts such as "the English race" or the "racial heritage" of the French had no scientific basis, but the perception of the racial roots of nationhood was powerful. Nationalism raised the question, "Who does *not* belong to the nation?" For many Europeans and Americans, race provided the answer. As the "nation" came to be defined in racial terms, so did "Jewishness." This shift from a religious to a more racial definition of Jewishness strengthened anti-Semitism. If national identity grew from racial roots, then for many, Jews were foreign plants, outsiders who threatened national unity.

Growing immigrant Jewish populations in much of Europe and the United States in the 1880s and 1890s heightened the perception of Jews as outsiders. Mass Jewish immigration is thus the second factor that helps explain the heightened anti-Semitism after 1870. Events in the Russian Empire help explain the upsurge in Jewish immigration. We saw at the beginning of this chapter that a group of terrorists assassinated Tsar Alexander II in 1881. Tsar Alexander III believed that a Jewish conspiracy was responsible for his father's assassination and responded with the May Laws of 1882. The May Laws reimposed restrictions on Jewish economic and social life within the Russian Empire, which now included most of Poland, the heartland of European Jewry. **Pogroms**—mass attacks on Jewish homes and businesses, sometimes organized by local officials—escalated. Fleeing this persecution, Jews migrated to Paris, London, Vienna, and other European cities.

The encounter between these immigrant Jewish communities and their hosts was often hostile. Extremely poor, the immigrants spoke Yiddish rather than the language of their new home, dressed in distinctive clothing, and sometimes practiced an ardently emotional style of Judaism that resisted assimilation. As the numbers of Jews rose in Europe's cities, these clearly identifiable immigrants were blamed for unemployment, disease, crime, and any other difficulty for which desperate people sought easy explanations.

A third factor in explaining later nineteenth-century anti-Semitism is what one historian has labeled the "rise of the Jews,"[7] a development linked to Jewish emancipation and assimilation. At the start of the nineteenth century, most European Jews had few political rights and were often confined to specific economic roles and required to live in restricted territories or city districts. In the second half of the century, however, most European Jews were *emancipated*: They gained civil and political rights. Many Jews assumed new economic roles and moved into new regions; not surprisingly, as economic newcomers, they often took up positions in the newest sectors of the industrial economy. They became department store owners or newspaper editors rather than farmers or small craftsmen.

During this period, many Jews also *assimilated* into European societies: They dropped distinctive dress styles, stopped speaking Yiddish, and discarded or modernized their practice of Judaism. Because many assimilated Jews secularized the traditional Jewish emphasis on studying the Torah into an emphasis on educational and artistic excellence, they also moved into professional and cultural fields.

pogroms An organized and often officially encouraged riot or attack to persecute a particular ethnic or religious group, especially associated with eastern European attacks against Jews.

THE RESULTS OF ANTI-SEMITISM In this 1905 painting by Samuel Hirszenberg, Hasidic Jews in Russian-governed Poland bury the victim of a pogrom. Hirszenberg called his painting *The Black Banner* in reference to both "The Black Hundreds," armed thugs who belonged to the anti-Semitic "Union of the Russian People," and *The Russian Banner,* the Union's newspaper that was partially funded by the tsar.

As a result of both emancipation and assimilation, then, Jewish communities became significant in European economic, artistic, and intellectual life. In Budapest in 1900, for example, Jews formed 25 percent of the population, yet they accounted for 45 percent of the city's lawyers, more than 40 percent of its journalists, and more than 60 percent of its doctors. In Germany, Jews owned almost all the large department stores; in the German cities of Frankfurt, Berlin, and Hamburg, Jews owned all the large daily newspapers.

While most Jews remained very poor, this visible Jewish success in emerging areas of the industrial economy meant that many Europeans linked Jewishness to industrialization and modernity. For many independent shopowners, traditional artisans, and small farmers with much to lose from industrialization, Jews became the symbol of the modernity that they feared.

ZIONISM: JEWISH MASS POLITICS The heightened anti-Semitism of the late nineteenth century convinced some Jews that the Jewish communities of Europe would be safe only when they gained their own state. The ideology of Jewish nationalism became known as **Zionism** because many Jewish nationalists called for the establishment of a Jewish state in "Zion," the biblical land of Palestine.

Zionism Nationalist movement that emerged in the late nineteenth century and sought to establish a Jewish political state in Palestine (the Biblical Zion).

Zionism became a mass movement under the guidance of Theodor Herzl (1860–1904), an Austrian Jewish journalist. In his early adulthood, Herzl epitomized the assimilated Jew. He was a proud German who did not practice Judaism and refused to allow his son to be circumcised. In the 1890s, however, Herzl witnessed the rise to power of Vienna mayor Karl Lueger, whose Christian Social party attracted voters with an explicitly anti-Semitic platform. Herzl concluded that Jews would always be outsiders in Europe. In 1896, he published *The Jewish State,* a call for Jews to build a state of their own.

By 1914 some 90,000 Jews had settled in Palestine, where they hoped to build a Jewish state. Zionism, however, faced strong opposition. The idea of Palestine as the Jewish "homeland" aroused Arab nationalists, whose vision of an independent Arab state free from Ottoman control included Palestine and its population of 700,000 Arabs. Ultraorthodox Jews also condemned Zionism because they believed that only God could accomplish the Jewish return to Zion. In addition, many Jews in western European nations such as Britain feared that Zionism played into the hands of anti-Semites who argued that Jews could not be trusted to be good citizens or loyal subjects within European states.

The Women's Revolt

23.1

23.2

23.3

23.4

23.4 How did the emergence of feminism in this period demonstrate the potential and the limits of political change?

As more men from the laboring classes received the vote, middle-class women demanded that they, too, receive this key political right. The campaign for women's suffrage, however, was only part of a multifaceted international middle-class **feminist movement**. For feminists, the vote was a way to transform cultural values and expectations. Nineteenth-century feminism rejected the liberal ideology of separate spheres—the insistence that both God and biology destined middle-class men for the public sphere of paid employment and political participation, and women for the private sphere of the home. In seeking political rights, feminists sought not just to enter the public, masculine sphere, but to obliterate many of the distinctions between the public and private spheres altogether.

feminist movement International movement that emerged in the second half of the nineteenth century and demanded broader political, legal, and economic rights for women.

 Watch the Video

British Women's Suffrage

Changes in Women's Experiences and Expectations

The nineteenth-century feminist movement was almost entirely a middle-class event. One important explanation for the lack of working-class involvement rests in a revolutionary change that occurred in middle-class, but not in working-class, families. In the last third of the nineteenth century, middle-class couples began to limit the size of their families by using already well-known methods of birth control such as abstinence, withdrawal, and abortion. For example, the average British middle-class family in the 1890s had fewer than three children, versus an average of six children in 1850. This basic change meant that married middle-class women no longer spent much of their adult life pregnant or nursing and were thus free to pursue other interests, including feminist activism.

Why did working-class families not follow the same pattern? The answer is largely economic. As economic depression cut into business profits, middle-class families looked to cut expenses. Family limitation made sense: Middle-class children remained in school through much of their teenaged years and so constituted a long-term drain on family resources. Working-class children, however, left school by age 11 or 12 and so began to contribute to the family income much earlier. Because children constituted an economic asset rather than a drain, working-class families remained large. To women struggling to rear large families in poverty, the vote must have seemed largely irrelevant.

Moreover, politically active working-class women tended to agree with Karl Marx that class, not gender, was the real dividing line in society. To better their lives, they turned to labor unions and socialism. The British activist Selina Cooper (1868–1946), for example, fought hard for women's rights, but within the British Labour movement. Cooper, who was sent to work in a textile mill at age 10, viewed the widening of women's opportunities and the achievement of working-class political power as two sides of the same coin.

Changing economic and social conditions for middle-class women also help explain the emergence of the feminist movement. In 1850, the unmarried middle-class woman who had to support herself had little choice but to become a governess or a paid companion to a widow. But by the 1870s, the expansion of the Industrial Revolution and the widening of state responsibilities created new opportunities. Middle-class single women became typists, telephone and telegraph operators, sales clerks, and bank tellers. During the 1860s in England, the number of women working as commercial clerks and accountants increased tenfold.

Read the Document

Doris Viersbeck, "Life Downstairs: A Servant's Life"

MIDDLE-CLASS WOMEN MOVING INTO THE PUBLIC SPHERE Julius LeBlanc Stewart, *The Goldsmith Girls in a Peugeot Voiturette in the Bois de Boulogne in 1897,* 1901. As this turn-of-the-century painting testifies, new leisure opportunities for women challenged the middle-class ideal of the "Angel in the House."

The same period saw governments assume greater responsibility for the welfare and education of the poor. Middle-class women, who had served as volunteers and charity workers, quickly claimed both paying and elected positions in the new local and state bureaucracies. Women served on school and welfare boards, staffed government inspectorates, and managed poorhouses. In some states, they voted in local (but not national) elections and were elected to local (but not national) office. Compulsory mass education also created a voracious demand for teachers and thus a new career path for unmarried women.

Expectations also began to change for married middle-class women as they moved into a new public role as consumers. It was the woman who was the principal target of the new advertising industry, the woman whom the new department stores sought to entice with their window displays and courteous clerks, the woman who rode the new tram lines and subways to take advantage of sales.

As middle-class women's opportunities widened, they confronted legal, political, and economic disabilities. An international feminist movement emerged and fought for four goals: removing the legal impediments faced by married women, widening opportunities for female employment and higher education, erasing the double standard of sexual conduct, and obtaining national women's suffrage.

Married Women and the Law

In the nineteenth century, European legal systems strongly reinforced the liberal ideology of separate spheres for men and women. Law codes often classified women with children, criminals, and the insane. Article 231 of the Napoleonic Code, the legal system of France and the basis of the legal codes of much of Europe, declared that "the husband owes protection to his wife; the wife owes obedience to her husband." In Russia a woman could not travel without her father's or husband's permission, and the husband was also the legal guardian of all children. He alone picked their schools, determined their punishments, and approved their marriage partners. In Prussia only the husband could decide when his baby should stop breastfeeding. According to English common law, "the husband and wife are one person in law," and that person was the husband. Most property brought into a marriage, given to a woman, or earned by her while married became the property of her husband.

From the mid-nineteenth century on, women's groups fought to improve the legal rights of married women. The results were uneven. By the end of the 1880s, English married women could own their own property, control their own income, and keep their children. Two decades later, French women could claim similar rights. In contrast, the German Civil Code of 1900 granted all parental authority to the husband—even over his stepchildren. While married women could keep money they earned, all property owned by the wife before marriage or given to her after marriage became the husband's.

Read the Document

Henrik Ibsen, *A Doll's House*, Act Two

Finding a Place: Employment and Education

Feminists also worked to widen women's educational and employment opportunities. Even girls from privileged families rarely received rigorous educations before 1850. The minority who did go to school spent their time learning ladylike occupations such as fancy embroidery, flower arranging, and piano playing. Posture was more important than literature or science. Widening the world of women's education, then, became a crucial feminist aim and an area in which they achieved considerable, but limited, success.

Feminists' educational campaigns had three main emphases: improving the quality of girls' secondary education, expanding the number of girls' secondary schools, and opening universities to women. The fight to upgrade the quality of girls' secondary education was difficult. Many parents opposed an academic curriculum for girls, a position reinforced by medical professionals who argued that girls' brains could not withstand the strain of an intellectual education. Dorothea Beale (1831–1906) established one of the first academic high schools for girls in London in the 1850s, but she faced an uphill battle persuading parents to allow her to teach their daughters mathematics. In France, feminists achieved their goal of a state system of secondary schools for girls in the 1880s. They lost the battle for a university-preparatory curriculum, however, which made it difficult for girls to pass the exams necessary to enter the French university system.

Opportunities for university education for women varied. While few women entered French universities in this period, in the United States, one-third of all students in higher education were women by 1880. In Germany, however, women were not admitted as full-time university students until 1901. In Russia, full-time university study became available to women in Moscow in 1872, and by 1880 women in Russia had some of the best opportunities for higher education in Europe. But then in 1881, as we saw at the start of this chapter, a group of young assassins killed Alexander II—a group that included Sofia Perovskaia, an educated woman. The tsarist government concluded that revolutionary politics and advanced female education went hand in hand and cut off women's access to the universities.

Despite such limitations and reverses, the range of jobs open to European women did broaden. In 1900, French women won the right to practice law, and in 1903 a French woman lawyer presented a case in a European court for the first time. In 1906, the Polish-born physicist and Nobel Prize winner Marie Curie became the first woman to hold a university faculty position in France. By the early twentieth century, women doctors, although still unusual, were not unheard of. In Russia, women accounted for 10 percent of all physicians by 1914.

No More Angels

The campaigns for women's legal rights and the expansion of employment and educational opportunities helped women move into the public sphere. But the third goal of feminist activity—eradicating the double standard of sexual conduct—posed a more radical challenge to separate-sphere ideology. By arguing that the same moral standards should apply to men and women, feminists questioned whether separate spheres should exist at all.

The ideology of separate spheres glorified women's moral purity and held that the more aggressive, more animal-like natures of men naturally resulted in such pastimes as heavy drinking and sexual adventurism. The laws and the wider culture reflected these assumptions. For example, in France, a woman with an illegitimate child could not institute a paternity suit against the father: Premarital sex was a crime for the woman, but not for the man. Similarly, the English divorce legislation of 1857 declared that a woman's adultery was sufficient for a husband to sue for divorce; however, for a wife to divorce her husband, she had to prove that he had committed not just adultery, but bigamy, incest, or bestiality.

To feminists, applying different moral standards to men and women degraded men and blocked women's efforts to improve their own lives and society as a whole. As the French feminist leader Maria Deraismes explained, "To say that woman is an angel is to impose on her, in a sentimental and admiring fashion, all duties, and to reserve for oneself all rights. . . . I decline the honor of being an angel."[8]

To erase the moral distinctions between men and women, feminists fought on several fronts. One key struggle was over the regulation of prostitution. By the 1870s, many European countries, as well as the United States, had established procedures that made it safer for men to hire prostitutes, while still treating the women involved as criminals. In England, the Contagious Diseases Act, passed in 1870 to address the problem of venereal disease, declared that the police could require any woman suspected of being a prostitute to undergo a genital exam. Feminists such as Josephine Butler (1857–1942) contended that such legislation made it easier for men to indulge their sexual appetites, while punishing the impoverished women who had to sell their bodies to feed themselves and their children. For almost 20 years Butler led a campaign both to repeal the legislation that regulated prostitution and to focus public attention on the lack of employment opportunities for women.

Abuse of alcohol was another battleground for the women's movement. Feminists argued that the socially accepted practice of heavy male drinking impoverished families and caused domestic violence. The temperance or prohibitionist cause thus became a women's rights issue. Temperance organizations spread across much of the western world and, between 1916 and 1919, succeeded in pushing through prohibitionist legislation in Iceland, Finland, Norway, the United States, and many Canadian provinces. Prohibition, however, did little to transform gender relations, proved difficult to enforce, and was fairly rapidly repealed.

Other feminist moral reform campaigns achieved only limited success. The regulation of prostitution did end in England in 1886 and in the United States, France, and the Scandinavian countries by 1914, but remained in effect in Germany. By 1884 in France, a husband's adultery, like a wife's, could end a marriage; in England, however, the grounds for divorce remained differentiated by gender until 1923. In all European countries and in the United States, the sexual double standard remains embedded in much of middle- and working-class culture.

The Fight for Women's Suffrage

The slow pace and uneven progress on both the legal and moral fronts convinced many feminists that they needed the political clout of the *national* suffrage to achieve their goals. In 1867 the National Society for Women's Suffrage was founded in Britain. Over the next three decades, suffrage societies emerged in the rest of Europe. The French feminist leader Hubertine Auclert (1848–1914) described the vote as "the keystone that will give [women] all other rights." She refused to pay taxes on the grounds of "no

Different Voices
The Debate over Women's Suffrage

T *he debate over a woman's right to vote did not divide along gender lines. Many men supported women's suffrage, and many women, including Britain's Queen Victoria, regarded it as a violation of the natural order. The following excerpts present arguments in the women's suffrage debate. The best-selling British novelist Mary Ward—or, as she always presented herself, Mrs. Humphry Ward (1851–1920)—wrote the first document, a letter to the editor of an influential magazine, in 1889. Many well-known and influential women signed the letter. The second excerpt comes from a French suffragist pamphlet published in 1913.*

An Anti-Suffrage Argument: Mrs. Humphry Ward

We, the undersigned, wish to appeal to the common sense and the educated thought of the men and women of England against the proposed extension of the Parliamentary suffrage to women.

While desiring the fullest possible development of the powers, energies and education of women, we believe that their work for the State, and their responsibilities towards it, must always differ essentially from those of men, and that therefore their share in the working of the State machinery should be different from that assigned to men. . . . To men belong the struggle of debate and legislation in Parliament; the working of the army and navy; all the heavy, laborious, fundamental industries of the State, such as those of mines, metals, and railways; the lead and supervision of English commerce, the service of that merchant fleet on which our food supply depends.

At the same time we are heartily in sympathy with all the recent efforts which have been made to give women a more important part in those affairs of the community where their interests and those of men are equally concerned; where it is possible for them not only to decide but to help in carrying out, and where, therefore, judgment is weighted by a true responsibility, and can be guided by experience and the practical information which comes from it. As voters for or members of School Boards, Boards of Guardians, and other important public bodies, women have now opportunities for public usefulness which must promote the growth of character, and at the same time strengthen among them the social sense and habit. But we believe that the emancipation process has now reached the limits fixed by the physical constitution of women, and by the fundamental difference which must always exist between their main occupations and those of men. The care of the sick and the insane, the treatment of the poor; the education of children: in all these matters, and others besides, they have made good their claim to larger and more extended powers. We rejoice in it. But when it comes to questions of foreign or colonial policy, or of grave constitutional change, then we maintain that the necessary and normal experience of women does not and can never provide them with such materials for sound judgment as are open to men.

In conclusion: nothing can be further from our minds than to seek to depreciate the position or the importance of women. It is because we are keenly alive to the enormous value of their special contribution to the community, that we oppose what seems to us likely to endanger that contribution. We are convinced that the pursuit of a mere outward equality with men is for women not only vain but demoralizing. It leads to a total misconception of women's true dignity and special mission. It tends to personal struggle and rivalry, where the only effort of both the great divisions of the human family should be to contribute the characteristic labour and the best gifts of each to the common stock.

SOURCE: Mrs. Humphry Ward. "An Appeal Against Female Suffrage," *Nineteenth Century* 147 (June 1889): 781–785.

A Pro-Suffrage Argument: The French Union for Womens' Suffrage

We are going to try to prove that the vote for women is a just, possible and desirable reform. . . .

A woman has responsibility in the family; she ought to be consulted about the laws establishing her rights and duties with respect to her husband, her children, her parents.

Women work—and in ever greater numbers; a statistic of 1896 established that . . . the number of women workers was 35 percent of the total number of workers, both male and female.

If she is in business, she, like any businessman, has interests to protect. . . .

If a woman is a worker or a domestic, she ought to participate as a man does in voting on unionization laws, laws covering workers' retirement, social security, the limitation and regulation of work hours, weekly days off, labor contracts, etc.

. . . .

Finally, her special characteristics of order, economy, patience and resourcefulness will be as useful to society as the characteristics of man and will favor the establishment of laws too often overlooked until now.

The woman's vote will assure the establishment of important social laws.

All women will want:

To fight against alcoholism, from which they suffer much more than men;

To establish laws of health and welfare;

To obtain the regulation of female and child labor;

To defend young women against prostitution;

Finally, to prevent wars and to submit conflicts among nations to courts of arbitration.

SOURCE: A report presented to Besançon Municipal Council by the Franc-Comtois Group of the Union Française pour le Suffrage des Femmes. Besançon, March 1913, 6–9.

For Discussion

1. How does the argument of Mrs. Humphrey Ward reflect the liberal ideology of separate spheres for men and women?
2. What is the basic argument presented by the French Union for Women's Suffrage? Why did the suffragists argue that the women's vote would create a better world?
3. How does this argument in the pro-suffrage pamphlet reflect rather than reject separate sphere ideology?

suffragists Feminists who sought to achieve the national vote for women through rational persuasion and parliamentary politics.

suffragettes Feminist movement that emerged in Britain in the early twentieth century. Unlike the suffragists, who sought to achieve the national vote for women through rational persuasion, the suffragettes adopted the tactics of violent protest.

  Read the Document

Emmeline Pankhurst, "Freedom or Death"

taxation without representation" and was the first woman to describe herself as a "feminist," a word that entered the English language from French around 1890.

Auclert and other **suffragists** had little success. Only in Finland (1906) and Norway (1913) did women gain the national franchise in this period. The social upheaval of World War I brought women the vote in Russia (1917), Britain (1918), Germany (1918), Austria (1918), the Netherlands (1919), and the United States (1920). But women in Italy had to wait until 1945, in France until 1944, and in Greece until 1949. Swiss women did not vote until 1971.

As these dates indicate, feminists faced significant obstacles in their battle for the national franchise. (See *Different Voices* in this chapter.) In Roman Catholic countries such as France and Italy, the women's suffrage movement met two key barriers. First, the Church opposed the women's vote. Second, Catholicism empowered women in different ways. In its veneration of the Virgin Mary and other female saints, in its exaltation of family life, in the opportunity it offered for religious vocation as a nun, Catholicism provided women with many non-political avenues for emotional expression and intellectual satisfaction.

In Britain, feminists' failure to win the national franchise persuaded some activists to abandon the suffragist emphasis on working through the political system and to adopt more radical tactics. Led by the imposing mother-and-daughters team of Emmeline (1858–1928), Christabel (1880–1958), and Sylvia Pankhurst (1882–1960), the **suffragettes** formed a breakaway women's suffrage group in 1903. The suffragettes argued that male politicians would never simply give the vote to women; instead, they had to grab it by force. Adopting as their motto the slogan "Deeds, Not Words," suffragettes disrupted political meetings, chained themselves to the steps of the Houses of Parliament, shattered shop windows, burned churches, destroyed mailboxes, and even, in a direct attack on a cherished citadel of male middle-class culture, vandalized golf courses.

In opting for violence, suffragettes assaulted a central fortification of middle-class culture—the ideal of the passive, homebound woman. Their opponents reacted with fury. Police broke up suffragette rallies with sexually focused brutality: They dragged suffragettes by their hair, stomped on their crotches, punched their breasts, and tore off their blouses. Once in jail, hunger-striking suffragettes endured the horror of forced feedings. Jailers pinned the woman to her bed while the doctor thrust a tube down her throat, lacerating her larynx, and pumped in food until she gagged.

CONCLUSION

The West in an Age of Mass Politics

The clash between the suffragettes and their jailers was only one of a multitude of encounters, many of them violent, among those seeking access to political power and those seeking to limit that access, between 1870 and the start of World War I in 1914. Changing patterns of industrialization and accelerated urbanization gave rise to other sorts of encounters—between the liberal and the socialist, or between the manager seeking to cut production costs and the employee aiming to protect his wages, or between newly arrived immigrants in the city and long-established residents who spoke different languages.

Out of such encounters emerged key questions about the definition of "the West." Did democracy define the West? Should it? Was the West synonymous with white, western European men or could people with olive-colored or black skin—or women of any color—participate fully in Western culture and politics? Was "the West" defined by its rationality? In the eighteenth century, Enlightenment thinkers had looked to reason as the path to social improvement. The rise of nationalist politics, based on emotional appeal and often racist hatred, challenged this faith in reason. But at the same time, developments in industrial organization and technology, which helped expand European national incomes, pointed to the benefits of rational processes.

As we will see in the next chapter, the expansion of Western control over vast areas of Asia and Africa in this period led many Europeans and Americans to highlight economic prosperity and technological superiority as the defining characteristics of the West. Confidence, however, was accompanied by anxiety as these years also witnessed a far-reaching cultural and intellectual crisis. Closely connected to the development of mass politics and changes in social and gender relations, this crisis eroded many of the pillars of middle- and upper-class society and raised questions about Western assumptions and values.

MAKING CONNECTIONS

1. How did the economic transformation of the West after 1870 contribute to changes in middle-class women's roles—and in at least some women's expectations?
2. How did both socialism and racist-nationalist politics challenge the liberal definition of "the West"?
3. Why did anti-Semitism emerge as a powerful political force after 1870?

TAKING IT FURTHER

For suggested readings, see page R-1.

Take the Study Plan for Chapter 23, The Coming of Mass Politics, 1870–1914, on MyHistoryLab

Chapter Review

Economic Transformation

23.1 What developments transformed Western economies and social life after 1870?

An economic depression and industrial changes led to accelerated emigration and urbanization patterns that eventually contributed to social unrest. Social tensions were heightened and political structures weakened when businessmen reacted to the depression by reducing employees and attempting to increase productivity. The results were angry workers, a rise in unemployment, and violent social encounters.

Defining the Nation

23.2 How did Western ruling classes respond to the new mass politics?

Political and social elites tried to eliminate social discontent and win the loyalty of the populations in three ways: by expanding the franchise, by providing social welfare programs, and by creating a sense of national identity that could rise above conflicting loyalties. At the same time they were committed to retaining their domination of social and political positions.

The New Mass Politics

23.3 What forms did mass politics assume during this era?

On the left side of the political spectrum, the ideologies of socialism, syndicalism, and anarchism all promised radical change and a more equal society. While socialist parties used the rhetoric of revolution and proved popular among urban workers, they increasingly worked for gradual change through political and legislative routes. Nationalist-racist politics dominated rightwing mass politics and proved appealing in areas that industrialized late and that contained competing ethnic and linguistic groups.

The Women's Revolt

23.4 How did the emergence of feminism in this period demonstrate the potential and the limits of political change?

The international feminist movement fought to remove legal barriers faced by married women, increase opportunities for female employment and higher education, eliminate the double standard of sexual conduct, and obtain the right to vote for all women. In all instances, the pace was slow and success uneven, although opportunities for women did increase.

Chapter Time Line

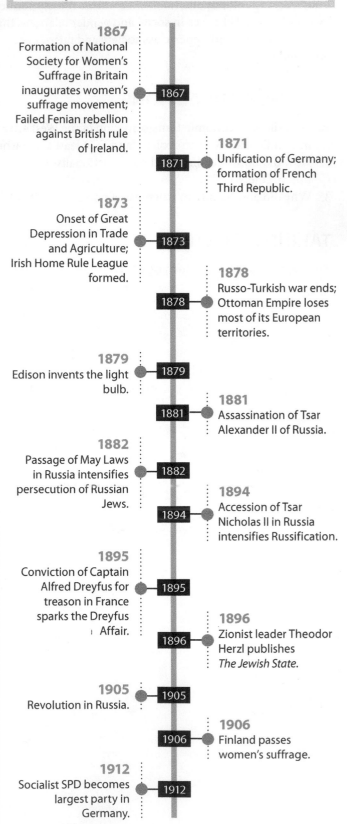

1867
Formation of National Society for Women's Suffrage in Britain inaugurates women's suffrage movement; Failed Fenian rebellion against British rule of Ireland.

1871
Unification of Germany; formation of French Third Republic.

1873
Onset of Great Depression in Trade and Agriculture; Irish Home Rule League formed.

1878
Russo-Turkish war ends; Ottoman Empire loses most of its European territories.

1879
Edison invents the light bulb.

1881
Assassination of Tsar Alexander II of Russia.

1882
Passage of May Laws in Russia intensifies persecution of Russian Jews.

1894
Accession of Tsar Nicholas II in Russia intensifies Russification.

1895
Conviction of Captain Alfred Dreyfus for treason in France sparks the Dreyfus Affair.

1896
Zionist leader Theodor Herzl publishes *The Jewish State*.

1905
Revolution in Russia.

1906
Finland passes women's suffrage.

1912
Socialist SPD becomes largest party in Germany.

24 The West and the World: Cultural Crisis and the New Imperialism, 1870–1914

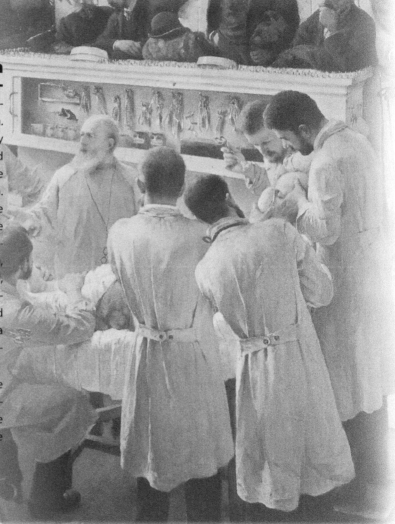

I n the summer of 1898, British troops invaded the Sudan in northeast Africa. On September 2, 40,000 Sudanese soldiers retaliated against British defenses at Omdurman.

The Sudanese soldiers possessed a reputation for military fierceness, but they attacked with swords, spears, and outdated firearms. Equipped with repeating rifles and Maxim guns (a type of early machine gun), British troops simply mowed them down. After only five hours of fighting, 11,000 Sudanese lay dead. The British lost just 40 men. According to one soldier—the future prime minister Winston Churchill—the biggest danger to the British troops was boredom: "The mere physical act [of loading, firing, and reloading] became tedious." In contrast, Churchill recalled, "all the time out on the plain on the other side bullets were shearing through flesh, smashing and splintering bone; blood spouted from terrible wounds; valiant men were struggling through a hell of whistling metal, exploding shells, and spurting dust— suffering, despairing, dying."[1]

The lopsided Battle of Omdurman was one episode in the story of new imperialism, the final phase in the Western conquest of the globe. This often violent encounter between the West and the rest of the world was closely connected to the

LEARNING OBJECTIVES

24.1 📢
How did scientific developments during this period lead to both optimism and anxiety?

24.2 📢
Why did many Europeans in this period believe they were living in a time of cultural crisis?

24.3 📢
What were the causes and consequences of the new imperialist ideology for the West and non-Western societies?

ADELBERT SELIGMANN, *GERMAN SURGEON THEODOR BILLROTH AT WORK IN VIENNA* (1890) Modern surgery in the making: The patient has been anesthetized, but the modern operating room does not yet exist, nor are the doctors wearing gloves or masks. Billroth, the director of the Second Surgical Clinic in Vienna, pioneered surgical techniques for gastrointestinal illnesses and cancer.

📢 **Listen to Chapter 24 on MyHistoryLab**

 **Watch the Video Series on MyHistoryLab**

Learn about some key topics related to this chapter with the *MyHistoryLab Video Series:*
Key Topics in Western Civilization

📖 Read the Document

Winston Churchill, *The River War:*
Chapter 15 The Battle of Omdurman

political and economic upheavals examined in Chapter 23. An understanding of new imperialism, however, also demands a close look at scientific, intellectual, and cultural developments between 1870 and 1914. As Western adventurers risked life and limb to chart Africa's rivers and exploit Asia's resources, artists and scientists explored new worlds of thought and perception that challenged the social order and even the meaning of reality itself. This chapter examines the scientific, artistic, and physical explorations that characterized these decades and asks:

> ### In what ways did these explorations redefine the West and its relationship with the rest of the world?

Scientific Transformations

24.1 How did scientific developments during this period lead to both optimism and anxiety?

S cientific advances after 1870 improved the health and hygiene of the Western world. Yet these changes also deepened the cultural anxiety of Europeans and Americans in this period as they pushed men and women into new encounters with the human body and the wider physical universe. In the crowded cities, the threat of contagious disease forced policymakers, physicians, and scientists to rethink the way the human body interacted with other bodies, human and microscopic. The work of biologists highlighted the way bodies had evolved to meet the challenges of survival, while the experiments of chemists and physicists exposed key flaws in the accepted model of the physical world.

Medicine and Microbes

In the nineteenth century, a series of developments transformed the practice of Western medicine. Before this time, physicians assumed that bad blood caused illness and so relied on practices such as leeching (attaching leeches to the skin) and bloodletting (slicing open a vein). Ignorant of the existence of bacteria and viruses, doctors attended one patient after another without bothering to wash their hands or surgical instruments. The only anesthetic available was alcohol. Patients and doctors regarded pain as inevitable, something to be endured rather than eased.

Urbanization overwhelmed such traditional medical practices. Expanding urban populations served as seedbeds for contagious diseases. Cholera outbreaks first forced doctors and public officials to pay attention to the relationship between overcrowding, polluted water, and epidemic disease. In 1848, for example, a cholera epidemic persuaded British officials to build the sewer system that still serves London today.

Neither officials nor doctors, however, understood the causes of disease until the 1860s, when the chemist Louis Pasteur (1822–1895) discovered the source of contagion to be microscopic living organisms—bacteria. Building on this discovery, Pasteur developed vaccines against anthrax, rabies, and many other diseases. (His process of purifying milk and fermented products is still known as pasteurization.) Following Pasteur, Robert Koch (1843–1910), professor of public health in Berlin, isolated the tuberculosis bacillus in 1882 and the bacteria that cause cholera in 1883. The work of Pasteur, Koch, and other scientists in tracing the transmission of disease improved Western medical practice. Between 1872 and 1900, the number of European deaths from infectious diseases dropped by 60 percent.

The use of anesthetics marked another important medical advance. In 1847 a Scottish physician first delivered a baby using chloroform to dull the mother's pain. Although condemned by theologians (who regarded pain as a necessary part of sinful human existence), the use of anesthetics spread quickly. Britain's Queen Victoria, who gave birth to nine children, expressed the feelings of many patients when she greeted the use of anesthetics in the delivery room with delight: "Oh blessed chloroform!"

These medical advances gave Europeans genuine confidence that the scientific conquest of nature would create a healthier environment. But the widespread awareness of germs also heightened anxiety. After the 1870s, Europeans were aware that they lived in a world populated by potentially deadly but invisible organisms, carried on the bodies of their servants, their employees, their neighbors, and their family members. Isolation of the bacilli that caused an illness did not immediately translate into its cure, and viral infections such as measles continued to be killers. Those who could afford to isolate themselves from danger often did so. As wealthy Europeans fled from urban centers of contagion, suburbs and seaside resorts multiplied.

The Triumph of Evolutionary Science

Developments in geology and biology also led to both confidence and anxiety. Evolutionary science provided a scientific framework in which educated Europeans could justify their own superior social and economic positions. Yet it challenged basic religious assumptions and depicted the natural world in new and unsettling ways.

Christians had long relied on the opening chapters of the Bible to understand the origins of nature and humanity, but nineteenth-century geologists challenged the biblical account. Although a literal reading of the Bible dated the Earth at 6,000 years old, geologists such as Charles Lyell (1797–1875) argued that the Earth had formed over millions of years. In *Principles of Geology*—a best-seller that went through 11 editions—Lyell refuted the orthodox Christian position that the biblical account of Noah's flood and other divine interventions explained geological change and the extinction of species. He argued that the material world must be seen as the product of natural forces still at work, still observable today.

But how did natural processes explain the tremendous variety of plant and animal species in the world? The British scientist Charles Darwin (1809–1882) answered this question in a way that proved satisfying to large numbers of educated Europeans—and horrifying to others. In the 1830s Darwin participated in a global expedition. On this trip he observed that certain species of animal and plant life, isolated on islands, had developed differently from related species on the coast. After returning to Britain, Darwin read the population theory of Thomas Malthus (see Chapter 21). Malthus argued that all species produce more offspring than can actually survive. Putting together Malthus's theory with his own observations, Darwin concluded that life is a struggle for survival, and that small biological variations can help an individual member of a species win this struggle. From this understanding came the **Darwinian theory of evolution**.

Darwin's evolutionary hypothesis rested on two ideas: *variation* and *natural selection*. Variation refers to the biological advantages that assist in the struggle for survival. A bird with a slightly longer beak, for example, might gain easier access to scarce food supplies. Over generations, the individuals with the variation displace those without. Variation, then, provides the means of natural selection, the process by which new species evolve.

Darwinian theory of evolution
Scientific theory associated with the nineteenth-century scientist Charles Darwin that highlights the role of variation and natural selection in the evolution of species.

 Read the Document

Charles Darwin, *Autobiography*

DARWIN'S DISTURBING MIRROR Simplified and often ridiculous versions of Darwin's ideas almost immediately entered popular culture. Here a monkey version of Darwin holds up a mirror to his fellow creature, who seems surprised by his reflection.

Darwin provided an explanation for evolutionary change, but two factors remained problematic. First, the process of variation that he described required many, many generations. Could it account for the multitude of variations apparent in the biological world? Second, how did variations first emerge and how are they inherited?

The answers lay embedded in the research of an Austrian monk, Gregor Mendel (1822–1884). Experimenting in his vegetable garden, Mendel developed the laws of genetic heredity. Mendel's work, however, was ignored until the end of the nineteenth century, when the Dutch botanist Hugo DeVries (1848–1935) used Mendel's data to hypothesize that evolution occurred through radical mutations in the reproductive cells of an organism, which pass on to offspring at the moment of reproduction. Mutations that offer an advantage in the struggle for existence enable the mutated offspring to survive—and to produce more mutant offspring. Thus, evolution can proceed by leaps, rather than over a very long period of time.

Long before these genetic underpinnings of evolution were understood, however, Darwin's theories proved influential. Published in 1859, *On the Origin of Species* aroused immediate interest and debate. Controversy intensified when, in 1871, Darwin published *The Descent of Man*, in which he argued that human beings, like other species, evolved over time. This denial of humanity's special place within the universe horrified many Christians. They found the Darwinian view of nature even more troubling. According to orthodox Christian theology, the beauty of nature reveals God to the believer. In the Darwinian universe, however, nature does not display God's hand at work. Instead, it is a blood-filled arena in which organisms compete for survival—"nature red in tooth and claw," as the British poet Alfred Lord Tennyson put it. In such a universe, ideas of purpose and meaning seemed to disappear.

Nevertheless, many Europeans and Americans welcomed Darwin's evolutionary theory because it seemed to confirm their faith in the virtues of competition and in the inevitability of progress. As Darwin himself wrote, because "natural selection works solely by and for the good of each being, all [physical] and mental development will tend to progress toward perfection."

Social Darwinism and Racial Hierarchies

While Darwin used his theory of evolution to explain biological change, the British writer Herbert Spencer (1820–1902) insisted that evolutionary theory should be applied to social policy as well. A champion of *laissez-faire* economics (see Chapter 22), Spencer coined the phrase "the survival of the fittest." He argued that charity or government assistance for the poor slowed the evolution of a better society by enabling the weak—the less fit—to survive.

Social Darwinists Followers of the later-nineteenth-century application of the theory of evolution to entire human societies.

Social Darwinists applied Spencer's concept of the survival of the fittest to entire races. They argued that the nonwhite races in Africa and Asia stood below white

Europeans on the evolutionary ladder. Hence, G. A. Henty, a British novelist and Social Darwinist, insisted that the "intelligence of the average negro is about equal to that of a European [male] child of ten years old."[2] Social Darwinists used such pseudoscientific arguments to justify Western imperialism. Evolutionary backwardness, they argued, doomed the nonwhite races to conquest and even extinction. These lines from a bestselling British novel sum up the Social Darwinist worldview: "Those who are weak must perish; the earth is to the strong. . . . We run to place and power over the dead bodies of those who fail and fall; ay, we win the food we eat from out the mouths of starving babes. It is the scheme of things."[3]

Social Darwinists used evolution to justify not only racial but also gender hierarchies. Arguing that the bodies of women were less evolved than those of men, they identified women as mentally and physically inferior. Such ideas spread throughout Western culture in the late nineteenth century. Leading intellectuals such as the psychiatrist Sigmund Freud, for example, argued that "the female genitalia are more primitive than those of the male," while the French social theorist Gustave Le Bon compared the average female brain to that of a gorilla.

Wrenched out of its biological framework and misapplied to social and international affairs, evolutionary theory thus justified the central assumptions of nineteenth-century society: the benefits of competition, the rightness of white rule and male dominance, and the superiority of Western civilization. Yet evolutionary science also worked to undermine Western confidence because with the idea of evolution came the possibility of *regression*: Was the traffic on the evolutionary ladder all one-way, or could species descend to a lower evolutionary level? Could humanity regress to its animal origins?

The concept of the **inheritance of acquired characteristics**, associated with the work of the French scientist Jean-Baptiste Lamarck (1744–1829), strengthened these fears of regression. More than 50 years before Darwin published his *Origin of Species,* Lamarck theorized that "acquired characteristics"—traits that an individual developed in response to experience or the environment, such as the stooped back of a miner, the poor vision of a lace maker, or the promiscuity of a prostitute—could be "acquired" by the individual's children. Because the process of genetic reproduction was not yet understood, Lamarck's theories remained influential throughout the nineteenth century. Middle-class Europeans and Americans feared that the impoverished masses in the expanding city slums were acquiring undesirable characteristics, ranging from physical deformity to sexual immorality and violent criminality. Using Lamarck's theories, they concluded that if growing numbers of poor children inherited these traits, the evolutionary ascent of the West could slow or even reverse.

 Read the Document

Herbert Spencer, "Illustrations of Universal Progress"

inheritance of acquired characteristics Now discredited scientific theory of evolutionary change, powerful in the nineteenth century.

The Revolution in Physics

A revolution in physics also began in this era. Although its most dramatic consequences—atomic weapons and nuclear energy—would not be realized for another half century, this revolution contributed to both the exhilaration and the uncertainty that characterized Western intellectual and cultural history after 1870.

At the core of the revolution in physics lay the question, "What is matter?" The triumph of the theories of Isaac Newton had ensured that, for 200 years, educated Westerners had a clear, certain answer: Matter was what close observation and measurement showed it to be (see Chapter 17). Three-dimensional material bodies, made up of the building blocks called atoms, moved against a fixed backdrop of space and time. Like a machine, nature was predictable. Using reason, observation, and common sense, then, human beings could understand, control, and improve the material world.

A series of discoveries and experiments challenged this commonsense view of the universe and offered in its place a more mysterious and unsettling vista. The discovery of the X-ray in 1895 disrupted prevailing assumptions about the solidity of matter. These assumptions crumbled further when the Polish chemist Marie Sklodowska Curie (1867–1934) found a new element, radium, which did not behave the way matter was supposed to behave: Continually emitting subatomic particles, radium did not possess a

MARIE SKLODOWSKA CURIE AND PIERRE CURIE IN THEIR LABORATORY IN 1904 Both Curies won Nobel Prizes.

constant atomic weight. Two years later, the German scientist Max Planck (1858–1947) theorized that a heated body radiates energy not in the continuous, predictable stream most scientists envisaged, but rather in irregular clumps, which he called *quanta*. Most scientists dismissed Planck's hypothesis as contrary to common sense, but soon his "quantum theory" helped shape a new model of a changeable universe.

These scientific discoveries provided the context for the work of Albert Einstein (1879–1955), the most famous scientist of the twentieth century. Bored by his job as a patent clerk, Einstein passed the time speculating on the nature of the cosmos. In 1905, he directly challenged the Newtonian model of the universe by publishing his **theory of relativity**. With this theory, Einstein offered a model of a four-dimensional rather than three-dimensional universe. To height, width, and depth, Einstein added *time*. He theorized that time and space are not fixed. They shift, relative to the position of the observer. Similarly, matter itself shifts because the mass of a material object changes with its motion. In the Einsteinian model, then, time, space, and matter intermingle in a universe of relative flux. Einstein used his own everyday experiences to explain his model. He noticed that as the streetcar in which he was traveling passed a fixed object, like a house, the object appeared to narrow. The faster the streetcar, the more the object narrowed. In other words, the dimension of width varies according to the speed and position of the viewer.

theory of relativity Albert Einstein's revolutionary model of the physical universe as four-dimensional.

Despite such efforts at everyday explanation, the revolution in physics made much of science incomprehensible to ordinary men and women. Most importantly, the new science challenged the basic assumptions that governed nineteenth-century thought by offering a vision of the universe in which what you see is *not* what you get, in which objective reality might well be the product of subjective perception.

Social Thought: The Revolt Against Positivism

Just as the revolution in physics presented a new and unsettling picture of the physical universe, so also troubling theories about the nature of human society surfaced in "social thought" (the research and publications that lay the foundations for disciplines such as sociology, psychology, and anthropology). As Chapter 22 explained, the mainstream of nineteenth-century thought was **positivist**: It placed great faith in human reason. At the end of the century, however, social thinkers revolted against positivism by emphasizing the role of nonrational forces in determining human conduct.

Gustave Le Bon (1841–1931), for example, developed his theory of crowd or collective psychology by studying how appeals to emotion, particularly in the form of symbols and myths, influenced group actions. For Le Bon, the new mass politics (see Chapter 23) was a form of such crowd behavior: Uneducated voters made choices on the basis of emotion, not logical argument. Le Bon concluded that democracy relinquished political control to the irrational masses and so would lead only to disaster.

While Le Bon focused on the crowd, the German social theorist Max Weber (1864–1920) explored the "bureaucratization" of modern life—the tendency of political and economic institutions to become more and more bureaucratic, and therefore standardized and impersonal. Weber saw the triumph of bureaucracy as generally positive, the victory of reason and science over tradition and prejudice. But he also recognized that bureaucracies could crush ideals and individuals and so threaten personal freedom.

Troubled by the vision of individuals trapped within "the iron cage of modern life," Weber in 1898 suffered a nervous breakdown. According to his wife, "an evil something out of the subterranean unconscious . . . grasped him by its claws."[4] This view of the individual as a captive of the unconscious was central to the revolt against positivism and reached its fullest development in the influential work of the Viennese scientist and physician Sigmund Freud (1856–1939). Freud's effort to treat patients suffering from nervous disorders persuaded him that the conscious mind plays a limited role in shaping an individual's actions. In *The Interpretation of Dreams* (1900), Freud argued that beneath the rational surface of each human being surge all kinds of hidden desires, including such irrational drives as the longing for death and destruction. Freud believed that he could understand human behavior (and treat mental illness) by diving below the rational surface and exploring the submerged terrain of unconscious desire. The emergence of Freudian psychology, however, convinced many educated Western individuals not that the irrational could be uncovered and controlled, but rather that the irrational was *in* control.

positivist The emphasis on the use of the scientific method to reach truth; a stress on observable fact.

Cultural Crisis: The *Fin-de-Siècle* and the Birth of Modernism

24.2 Why did many Europeans in this period believe they were living in a time of cultural crisis?

The recognition of the power of the irrational contributed to a growing cultural crisis. The French phrase *fin-de-siècle*, literally translated as "end of the century," served as a shorthand term for the mood of uneasiness that characterized much of Western society in this era. Fast-moving economic, technological,

fin-de-siècle French term for the "turn of the century"; used to refer to the cultural crisis of the late nineteenth century.

EDGAR DEGAS, *ABSINTHE* (1876–1877) Parisian café-goers often indulged in absinthe, a strong alcoholic drink flavored with anise. Degas's portrait of one such absinthe drinker is a picture of deterioration: This woman's lined face, weary posture, and isolation provide an evocative image of the *fin-de-siècle*.

SOURCE: Edgar Degas, "The Glass of Absinthe," 1876. Oil on canvas, 36 × 27 in. Musee d'Orsay, Paris. Scala/Art Resource, NY.

modernism Term applied to artistic and literary movements from the late nineteenth century through the 1950s. Modernists sought to create new aesthetic forms and values.

 Read the Document

Emile Zola, *Nana*

and social changes, coupled with new scientific theories, convinced many that old solutions no longer worked. The quest for new answers fostered the birth of **modernism**, a broad label for a series of unsettling and inspiring developments in thought, literature, and art. Many Europeans and Americans celebrated modernism as a release from restraining middle-class codes. Others, however, responded fearfully.

The *Fin-de-Siècle*

The sense that the West was in a state of decline fostered *fin-de-siècle* anxiety. A number of factors contributed to these fears of degeneration. As cities spread, so did perceptions of rising crime rates. Such perceptions went hand in hand with the reality of increasing drug and alcohol use. Diners in high society finished their sumptuous meals with strawberries soaked in ether, and respectable bourgeois men offered each other cocaine as a quick "pick-me-up" at the end of the working day. Middle-class mothers fed restless babies opium-laced syrups, while workers bought enough opium-derived laudanum on Saturday afternoon to render them unconscious until work on Monday morning. Using Lamarck's theory of the inheritance of acquired characteristics, scientists contended that criminality and drug addictions would be passed on from generation to generation, thus contributing to social decline.

Popular novels also contributed to the fear of degeneration by depicting Western culture as diseased or barbaric. In *Nana* (1880), the French novelist Émile Zola (1840–1902) used the title character, a prostitute, to embody his country. Watching as French soldiers march to defeat in the Franco-Prussian War, Nana is dying of smallpox, her face "a charnel-house, a heap of pus and blood, a shovelful of putrid flesh."[5] Works such as *Dr. Jekyll and Mr. Hyde* (1886) and *Dracula* (1897) showed that beneath the cultured exterior of a civilized man lurked a primitive, bloodthirsty beast.

The writings of the German philosopher and poet Friedrich Nietzsche (1844–1900) epitomized the mood of the *fin-de-siècle*. Nietzsche dismissed most members of modern society as little more than sheep, penned in by outdated rules and beliefs. Middle-class morality, rooted in Christianity, had sapped Western culture of its vitality. "Christianity has taken the side of everything weak," Nietzsche insisted.

Nietzsche traced the weakness of Western culture beyond Christianity, however, back to the ancient Greek emphasis on rationality. He argued that by overemphasizing rational thought, Western societies repressed powerful instinctive and emotional forces. Even the style of his publications reflected Nietzsche's impatience with reason. Rather than write carefully constructed essays that proceeded logically from one fact to another, he adopted an elusive, poetic style characterized by disconnected fragments, more accessible to intuitive understanding than to rational analysis.

Nietzsche's call to "become what you are" attracted young enthusiasts throughout Europe in the 1890s. These Nietzsche fans embraced his conviction that the confining codes of middle-class morality held back the individual from personal liberation. "God is dead," Nietzsche proclaimed, "and we have killed him." If God is dead, then "there is nobody who commands, nobody who obeys, nobody who trespasses." Such declarations alarmed other readers, who viewed Nietzsche's work as a cause rather than a critique of Western decay.

Tightening Gender Boundaries

Fear of degeneration also expressed itself in late-nineteenth-century efforts to strengthen the boundaries that separated "maleness" from "femaleness." The feminist and the homosexual joined the criminal, the drug addict, and the prostitute in the list of dangerous and degenerate beings. (See *Justice in History* in this chapter.)

In the decades after 1870, as middle-class women began to move into the public spheres of university education and paid employment, feminism emerged as a political force (see Chapter 23). Many Europeans and Americans viewed these developments with alarm. They argued that the female body and brain could not withstand the strains of public life. In the antifeminist view, a woman who pursued higher education or a career not only risked her own physical and mental breakdown, she also tended to produce physically and morally degenerate children and so threatened the evolutionary advance of Western societies.

Like feminists, homosexuals were singled out as threats to the social order in this period. Before 1869, *homosexual* was not a word: Coined by a Hungarian scientist seeking a new label for a new concept, it entered the English language in 1890. Traditionally, Europeans and Americans had viewed same-sex sexual practice as a form of immoral behavior, indulged in by morally lax—but otherwise normal—men. (Few considered the possibility of female homosexual behavior.) In the later nineteenth century, however, the emphasis shifted from *actions* to *identity*, from condemning a type of behavior to denouncing a type of person: the homosexual.

Three developments heightened the fear of homosexuality. First, the anonymity and mobility of urban life offered homosexuals space in which they could express a more confident homosexual identity. Throughout Western cities, homosexual subcultures became more numerous and more visible—and, therefore, more threatening.

Second, the rise of corporate capitalism (see Chapter 23) undercut the liberal masculine ideal. Liberal ideology depicted middle-class men as aggressive, self-reliant initiators. Now these men found themselves bound to desks and taking orders. No longer masters of their own fates, they were now bit players in the drama of corporate capitalism. Condemnation of not only homosexuality but also feminism provided a way to redefine and strengthen masculine identity.

Finally, a new science of sexuality contributed to new fears. During the final decades of the nineteenth century, scientists made important breakthroughs in the understanding of human reproduction and sexual physiology. In 1879, for example, scientists first witnessed, with the aid of the microscope, a sperm

Read the Document

Richard Freiherr von Krafft-Ebing, *Psychopathia Sexualia*

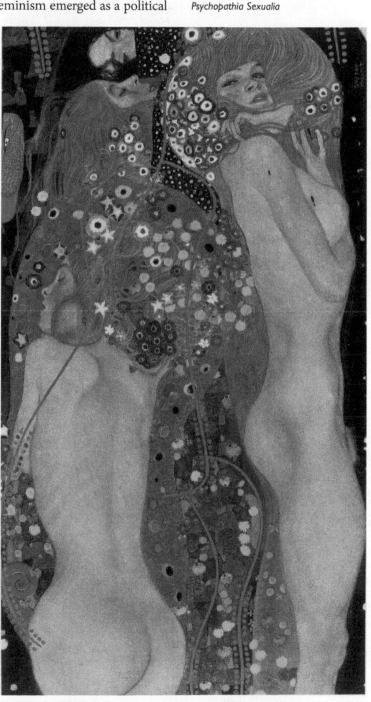

GUSTAV KLIMT, *WATER SERPENTS* (1904–1907) Klimt's paintings often featured women as alluring but engulfing elemental forces. Here he uses the mythological imagery of sea serpents to depict women as unabashedly sensual, even as creatures on the prowl—quite a contrast to the passive woman of separate-sphere ideology.

753

cell penetrating an egg. Greater understanding of sexual *physiology*, however, went hand in hand with the effort to define normal sexual *practice* and to the medical condemnation of homosexuality as pathology.

Heightened concern about gender boundaries pervaded not only the science, but also the art of the late-nineteenth-century West. In the visual arts, women often appeared as elemental forces, creatures of nature rather than civilization, who threatened to trap, emasculate, engulf, suffocate, or destroy the unwary man. The Austrian Gustav Klimt (1862–1918) frequently painted women as creatures of nature, often provocatively sexual. Such images recur even more graphically in the work of Klimt's student, Egon Schiele (1890–1918). In his short life Schiele created more than 3,000 works on paper and 300 paintings, many of these depictions of dangerous women. Works such as *Black-Haired Girl with Raised Skirt* (1911) used harsh colors and brazen postures to present an unsettling vision of female sexuality.

The Birth of Modernism

modernist movement Term applied to the artistic and literary movements from the late nineteenth century through the 1950s. Modernists sought to create new aesthetic forms and values.

Schiele's disturbing paintings exemplify the new **modernist movement**. In the final decades of the nineteenth century, modernist artists such as Schiele tossed aside the rules and embarked on a series of bold experiments. No single style characterized modernism, but modernist artists, musicians, and writers shared an impatience with the middle-class liberal worldview.

Modernists challenged liberalism, first, by rejecting the idea of art as an instrument of moral or emotional uplift. Liberals believed that the arts served a useful purpose in civilized society. Visiting art galleries was a popular activity, rather like going to the movies today. Respectable workers and middle-class men and women crowded into exhibitions where they viewed paintings that told an entertaining story and had a clear moral message. In contrast, modernists declared "art for art's sake." Modernist painters did not seek to tell a story or to preach a sermon, but rather to experiment with line, color, and composition.

Second, modernists rejected the middle-class faith in the power of human reason and observation, and instead emphasized the role of individual experience and intuition in shaping human understanding. In Paris, for example, a group of artists centered on

Justice in History
The Trial of Oscar Wilde

In March 1895 the Marquis of Queensberry left a message with the porter of a gentleman's club in London. The message, written on Queensberry's calling card, read "To Oscar Wilde, posing as a *somdomite*." What Queensberry meant to write was *sodomite*, a common term for a man who engaged in sexual relations with other men. By handing the card to the porter, Queensberry publicly accused Wilde, a famous novelist and playwright, of homosexual activity. Ten years earlier the British Parliament had declared illegal all homosexual activity, even consensual relations between adults in a private home. Queensberry's accusation, then, was serious. Oscar Wilde responded by suing Queensberry for libel—and set in motion a legal process that led to Wilde's imprisonment, and indirectly, to his early death.

Wilde made a reckless mistake when he chose to sue for libel, for in fact Queensberry had not libeled him. Wilde was a homosexual. He and Queensberry's son, Lord Alfred Douglas, were lovers. Why, then, did Wilde dare to challenge Queensberry? Perhaps he thought that the fact that he was married, with two children, shielded him against the charge. Or perhaps his professional successes gave Wilde a sense of invulnerability. With two of his plays then appearing on the London stage to favorable reviews, he stood at the pinnacle of his career in the spring of 1895.

Wilde had built that career by flouting middle-class codes of morality. He saw himself as an artist and insisted that art should be freed from social convention and moral restraint. His "High

(continued on next page)

Society" comedies about privileged elites living scandalous lives and exchanging witty epigrams were far from the morally uplifting drama expected by middle-class audiences.

Wilde also used his public persona to attack the conventional, the respectable, and the orthodox. Widely recognized for his outrageous clothing and conversation, he had consciously adopted the mannerisms of what nineteenth-century Britons called a "dandy"—a well-dressed, irreverent, artistic, leisured, and effeminate man. Before his trial, such effeminacy did not serve as a sign of, or a code for, homosexual inclinations, but it did signal to many observers a lavish—and loose—lifestyle. Oscar Wilde, then, was a man many British men and women loved to hate.

Even so, when his trial opened Wilde appeared to be in a strong position. Because Wilde had Queensberry's card with the "sodomite" charge written on it, Queensberry faced certain conviction unless he could show that Wilde had engaged in homosexual activity. Wilde knew that Queensberry would not risk shining the legal spotlight on his own son's homosexuality.

At first, Queensberry's attorney, Edward Carson, focused on Wilde's published works, trying to use Wilde's own words to showcase his immorality. It proved an ineffective strategy. On the witness stand, Wilde reveled in the attention and made Carson seem like a man of little culture and no humor.

On the second day of the libel trial, however, Carson interrogated Wilde about his associations with male prostitutes. Suddenly the issue was no longer the moral worth of Wilde's published writings, but rather his sexual life. At this point, Wilde withdrew his libel charge against Queensberry, and the court declared the marquis not guilty.

If Queensberry was innocent of libel in calling Wilde a sodomite, then by clear implication, Wilde was guilty of homosexual activity and therefore a criminal. On May 25, 1895—just three months after Queensberry had left his misspelled message with the club porter—Wilde was found guilty of seven counts of gross indecency with other men. The presiding judge, Sir Alfred Wills, characterized the trial as "the worst case I have ever tried," and described Wilde as "the centre of a circle of extensive corruption of the most hideous kind." Wills declared, "I shall under the circumstances be expected to pass the severest sentence the law allows. In my judgment it is totally inadequate for such a case." He sentenced Wilde to two years at hard labor. The physical punishment took its toll. Wilde died in 1900 at age 46.

OSCAR WILDE AND LORD ALFRED DOUGLAS Although the British government pursued its case against Wilde, it made no effort to put together a case against Douglas.

How do we account for the intensity of Wills's language and the severity of Wilde's sentence? Why did the condemnation of homosexuality grow harsher in the closing decades of the nineteenth century? One answer is that in a time of rapid change, boundaries became more important, a way to create and enforce social order. Wilde crossed those boundaries and so seemed to threaten social stability.

Secondly, by the end of the nineteenth century, the state had assumed new responsibilities. Desperate to enhance national strength in a period of heightened international competition, Western governments intervened in areas previously considered to be the domain of the private citizen. To strengthen national productivity and military viability, governments now compelled parents to send their children to school, regulated the hours adults could work, supervised the sale of food and drugs, set new standards for housing construction—and policed sexual boundaries.

The policing of sexual boundaries became easier after the well-publicized Wilde trial because it provided a homosexual personality profile, a "Wanted" poster to hang on the walls of Western culture. Wilde became the embodiment of The Homosexual, a particular and peculiar type of person, and a menace to cultural stability. The Wilde trial linked "dandyism" to this new image. Outward stylistic choices such as effeminacy, artistic sensibilities, and flamboyant clothing and conversation became, for many observers, the telltale signs of inner corruption. Thus, the Wilde case marked a turning point in the construction and the condemnation of a homosexual identity.

For Discussion

1. How does this trial illustrate the role of medical, legal, and cultural assumptions in shaping sexual identity in the late nineteenth century?
2. Did the trial of Oscar Wilde achieve justice? If so, what kind and for whom?

Taking It Further

An Ideal Husband. 1999. This film adaptation of Oscar Wilde's hilarious play exemplifies his lighthearted but devastating critique of conventional manners and morals.

The Real Trial of Oscar Wilde: The First Uncensored Transcript of The Trial of Oscar Wilde vs. John Douglas (Marquess of Queensberry), 1895. 2003. Includes an introduction by Wilde's grandson Merlin Holland.

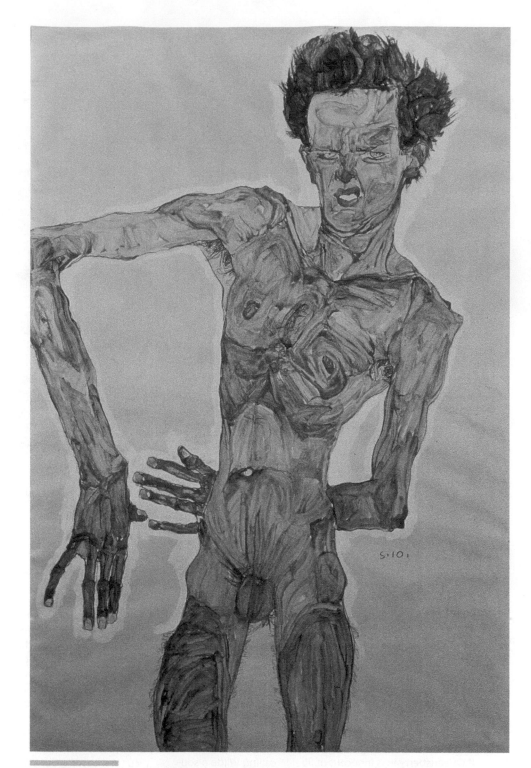

EGON SCHIELE, *NUDE SELF-PORTRAIT WITH OPEN MOUTH* (1910) Schiele's paintings exemplify the Expressionist movement with their bold use of color and their no-holds-barred exploration of human emotion and sexuality.

SOURCE: Egon Schiele (1890–1918), "Standing Nude, Facing Front (Self Portrait), 1910." Graphische Sammlung Albertina, Vienna, Austria/ The Bridgeman Art Library.

Cubists Followers of the early twentieth century modernist artistic movement that emphasized the fragmentation of human perception through visual experiments with geometric forms.

Expressionism Modernist artistic movement of the early twentieth century that used bold colors and experimental forms to express emotional realities.

the Spaniard Pablo Picasso (1881–1973) juxtaposed different perspectives and points of view on a single canvas. They called themselves **Cubists.** In one cultural historian's apt description, "Cubists cracked the mirror of art."[6] Their fragmented, jagged, energetic works no longer reflected the world "out there," but instead revealed the artist's fluid and contradictory vision. (See *Encounters and Transformations* in this chapter.)

This emphasis on art as a personal expression is also seen in the **Expressionist** movement, centered not in France as was Cubism, but in central and eastern Europe.

Expressionists such as Egon Schiele argued that art should express the artist's interior vision, not the exterior world. In nude self-portraits, Schiele depicted himself as ugly and emaciated, a graphic expression of his tormented internal universe.

Finally, modernists challenged the liberal worldview by insisting that history was irrelevant. Liberals viewed history as an important source of moral lessons and as a key to understanding the present and improving the future. Modernists, however, argued that fast-moving industrial and technological change shattered the lines connecting past, present, and future. Painters such as the Futurists in Italy (one of the many artistic movements that clustered under the modernist umbrella) reveled in the new machine age, a world cut off from anything that had gone before. In their paintings they depicted human beings as machines in motion, moving too fast to be tied down to history. The Futurists also challenged traditional ways of living, epitomized in their declaration of war on spaghetti.

New musical styles emerging in popular and high culture in these decades also demonstrated this modernist sense of discontinuity. Ragtime, for example, combined syncopation with unexpected rhythms and sudden stops, while jazz, which developed around the turn of the century in black urban neighborhoods in the United States, created a musical universe of constant spontaneous change. In Europe, symphonic musicians such as Russian composer Igor Stravinsky (1882–1971) and his Austrian counterpart Arnold Schoenberg (1874–1951) shocked their audiences with pieces that broke all the rules. In Stravinsky's ballet, *The Rite of Spring* (1913), the meter shifts 28 times in the final 34 bars of the central dance. Similarly, Schoenberg eliminated repetition from his works and used rapid tempo changes.

Audiences tended to greet modernist works with incomprehension and outrage. At the first performance of Schoenberg's *Five Orchestral Pieces* in London in 1912, one listener reported that "the audience laughed audibly all through . . . and hissed vigorously at the end." The next year in Vienna, the performance of a different Schoenberg piece had to be abandoned after the audience rioted. Similarly, reviewers routinely condemned modernist painting as sick, pornographic, or simply insane. One London critic

24.1

24.2

24.3

View the Closer Look

Futurism: Unique Form of Continuity in Space

GINO SEVERINI: *SUBURBAN TRAIN ARRIVING AT PARIS,* 1915 The interlapping geometric forms and images of tilting buildings, as well as the subject matter—a train arriving—illustrate the Futurist emphasis on change and movement, as well as their delight in the new machine age.

WILLIAM HOLMAN HUNT, *THE LIGHT OF THE WORLD* (1852) In this devotional painting, Jesus, the light of the world, stands knocking at the closed door of a lost soul. The overgrown weeds and fallen fruit symbolize sin and the lantern stands for Christ's illuminating power. The stars and crescents on the lantern represent Holman Hunt's hope for the conversion of Jews and Muslims to Christianity. The popularity of this work highlights the limited appeal of modernist art in the pre-1914 era.

SOURCE: William Holman Hunt (1827–1910), "The Light of the World," C. 1852, oil on canvas. © Manchester Art Gallery, UK/TheBridgeman Art Library.

dismissed the painter Paul Cézanne (1869–1954) as "an artist with diseased retinas."

This hostility to modernism shows that most audiences remained firmly within a cultural milieu in which paintings revealed pretty scenes, novels told a moral tale, and music offered harmonious charm. In the early twentieth century, one of the most popular pieces of art in the English-speaking world was *The Light of the World* by William Holman Hunt (1827–1910). This moralistic piece with its easy-to-understand and uplifting story, at odds with every modernist principle, triumphantly toured the British Empire from 1905 to 1907. Enthusiastic crowds jostled for tickets and hailed the painting as a religious and artistic masterpiece.

Popular Religion and Secularization

As the response to Holman Hunt's depiction of Jesus reveals, religious belief remained a powerful force in the decades after 1870. In Britain, Sunday worship continued to be a central aspect of middle-class culture, and the still-strong Sunday School movement and religious instruction in state schools ensured that working-class children were taught the fundamentals of the Christian faith. On the Continent, many Europeans connected unbelief with revolutionary anarchy after the Communards—the Parisian radicals who tried to set up a revolutionary government in 1871—executed the Archbishop of Paris. The excesses of the Paris Commune (discussed in Chapter 22) thus contributed to a religious revival. Popular Catholic religiosity often focused on the cult of the Virgin Mary: By the 1870s, the shrine at Lourdes, the site of Mary's miraculous appearance in 1858, was attracting hundreds of thousands of Catholic pilgrims.

Three additional factors contributed to the religiosity of late-nineteenth-century Europe. First, the high rate of immigration meant that many people found themselves searching for something familiar in foreign cities. They often turned to the religious cultures of the homeland. In English cities, for example, Irish immigrants looked to the local Roman Catholic Church for spiritual solace, material support, and social contacts. Second, in many regions nationalism strengthened religious belief and practice. Hence, for Polish nationalists dreaming of independence from Russian rule, Roman Catholicism was a key part of a separate national identity. Finally, as we shall see in the next section, the expansion of Western empires across the globe appeared to provide clear evidence of the ongoing triumph of Christianity.

Yet this triumphalism met growing anxiety as Christians faced new challenges. As we saw in our discussion of Darwin, developments in biology undermined the orthodox Christian view of nature as harmonious and divinely directed. Medical advances also narrowed the appeal of traditional religion. People had once accepted diseases

PILGRIMAGES IN FRANCE—DEPARTURE FROM A PROVINCIAL STATION OF "SACRED HEART" PILGRIMS FOR LOURDES.

PILGRIMAGE TO LOURDES This 1873 engraving from an American newspaper shows "Sacred Heart" pilgrims in France departing from a provincial station near Lourdes to continue their journey on foot.

such as cholera as "acts of God," but now they understood their natural causes. Scientists, in other words, seemed able to answer questions previously thought the province of theologians. Finally, the emergence of the social sciences directly challenged Christianity by dismissing the question of religious truth and asking instead, what is the function of religious belief in a society? Emile Durkheim (1858–1917), one of the founders of French sociology, dared to lump Christianity with "even the most barbarous and the most fantastic rites and the strangest myths." Durkheim insisted that no religion was more true than any other—each filled a social need.[7]

The Christian response to these challenges varied. Many Protestants embraced the scientific method as a gift from God. They argued that the study of the Bible as a historical and literary document—as a collection of divinely inspired texts produced by all-too-human writers—promised to free Christians *from* antiquated beliefs impossible to sustain in the new scientific age and *for* a more relevant, reform-oriented religious life. Protestant fundamentalists, however, insisted on retaining a belief in the literal, historical, and scientific accuracy of the Christian scriptures, a stance that led them to oppose science as the enemy of religion.

The Roman Catholic papacy also adopted a defiant pose in the face of modern challenges. In 1864, Pope Pius IX (r. 1846–1878) issued a *Syllabus of Errors,* which condemned the notion that the pope should "harmonize himself with progress, with liberalism, and with modern civilization." Six years later, a church council—the first called since the sixteenth-century Catholic Reformation—proclaimed the doctrine of **papal infallibility**. According to this doctrine, when the pope issues a decree that concerns matters of faith and morality, that decree is free from error and valid for all time and all places. The proclamation of papal infallibility rebuked those Catholic theologians who argued that Christianity had to adapt to the modern world.

The Roman Catholic Church also faced important political challenges in these decades. In countries with a large Catholic population, the Church's alliance with conservatism pushed **anticlericalism** to a dominant position on the liberal agenda. In France, for example, Catholics dominated the political parties that demanded a return

📖 Read the Document

Matthew Arnold, *Dover Beach*

📖 Read the Document

Pope Leo XIII, *Of New Things*

papal infallibility The doctrine of the Roman Catholic Church proclaimed at the First Vatican Council in 1870 that the pope could not err when making solemn declarations regarding faith or morals.

anticlericalism Opposition to the political influence of the Roman Catholic Church.

to monarchical or authoritarian rule; liberal Frenchmen who wanted the Third Republic to survive thus fought to reduce the Church's influence. More generally, the spread of socialism provided European workers with a belief system and source of communal life outside of, and opposed to, the Church.

The most significant challenge faced by religious institutions after 1870, however, emerged not from parliamentary assemblies, socialist rallies, or scientific laboratories, but rather from the department stores and sports fields. In the growing industrial cities, working- and middle-class individuals enjoyed new, secular sources of entertainment, inspiration, and desire. Energies once focused on religious devotion centered increasingly on the activities of consumption and recreation. Whereas shared religious worship had once cemented community life, the rituals of spectator sports now forged new bonds of loyalty and identity. The ever-changing array of colorful products displayed in shop windows promised fulfillment and satisfaction in the here and now, an earthly paradise rather than a heavenly reward.

The New Imperialism

24.3 What were the causes and consequences of the new imperialist ideology for the West and non-Western societies?

Many of those items on display behind the new plate-glass shop windows were the products of imperial conquest. **New imperialism** intertwined with many of the developments we have already examined in this chapter and in Chapter 23. Telegraphs ensured rapid communication from far-flung empires and mass printing technologies guaranteed that illustrated tales of imperial achievement made their way into homes and schools. Social Darwinism supplied a supposedly scientific justification for the conquest of peoples deemed biologically inferior, while swift military victories over other societies helped quell anxiety about European degeneration. For many Europeans—particularly the British, who presided over the largest empire in the world—imperialist domination served as reassuring evidence of the apparent superiority of Western civilization.

Understanding the New Imperialism

Imperialism itself was not new. In the fifteenth century, Europeans had embarked on the first phase of imperialism, with the extension of European control across coastal ports of Africa and India, and into the New World of the Americas (see Chapter 13). In the second phase, which began in the late seventeenth century, European colonial empires in Asia and the Western Hemisphere expanded as governments sought to increase their profits from international trade (see Chapter 18).

As in these earlier phases of imperialism, trade motivated much of the imperial activity after 1870 as well. The need to protect existing imperial interests also impelled further conquests. For example, the desire to protect India—the "Jewel in the Crown" of the British Empire—explains much of British imperial acquisition throughout the nineteenth century. Britain's annexation of Burma and Kashmir, its establishment of spheres of influence in the Middle East, and its interests along the coast of Africa were all linked to its empire in India.

Defense of existing empires and commercial considerations, however, do not fully explain new imperialism. After 1870 and particularly after 1880, the West's expansion became much more aggressive. In just 30 years, European control of the globe's land surface swelled from 65 to 85 percent. In addition, new players joined the expansionist game. Recently formed nation-states such as Germany and Italy jostled for colonial

new imperialism The third phase of modern European imperialism that occurred in the late nineteenth and early twentieth centuries and extended Western control over almost all of Africa and much of Asia.

territory in Africa, the United States began to extend its control over the Western Hemisphere, and Japan initiated its imperialist march into China and Korea. What factors lay behind this new imperialism?

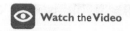
TECHNOLOGY, ECONOMICS, AND POLITICS Part of the answer lies in the economic developments examined in Chapter 23. Because of the Second Industrial Revolution, European and American economies increasingly depended on raw materials available only in regions such as Asia, Africa, and South America. Rubber insulated the electrical and telegraph wires now encircling the globe—but rubber trees did not grow in Europe or the United States. Palm oil from Africa provided the lubricant needed for industrial machinery. The slaughter of Africa's once-plentiful elephant herds provided the ivory for many of the new consumer goods now decorating middle-class parlors, such as piano keys and billiard balls. Relying on these primary resources, Western states were quick to respond to perceived threats to their economic interests. The Germans even coined a word to describe this fear of losing access to essential raw materials: *Torschlusspanik,* or "fear of the closing door."

Competition for markets also accelerated imperial acquisition. With the onset of economic depression in the 1870s (discussed in Chapter 23), industrialists faced declining demand for their products in Europe. Imperial expansion seemed to provide a solution, with annexed territories seen as captive markets. As a French newspaper editorial explained in 1891, "every gunshot opens another outlet for French industry."[8]

By the mid-1890s, however, the depression had ended in most regions—yet the pace of imperialist expansion did not slow. Instead, a global investment boom ensured continuing imperialist expansion. European capital financed railway lines, mines, and public utilities across the world. With each railroad or coal mine or dam, European interests in non-European regions expanded, and so did the pressure on European governments to assume formal political control should outside competitors or local political instability threaten those interests.

In addition to these economic factors, domestic political pressures encouraged imperialist acquisition. In the age of mass politics, political leaders needed to find issues that would appeal to new voters. Tales of dangerous explorations and decisive military victories proved popular. Imperialist conquest assured ordinary men that they were part of a superior, conquering people.

As the *Different Voices* feature in this chapter illustrates (see page 763), international competition also fostered imperialism. Newly formed nations such as Italy and Germany sought empires outside Europe as a way to gain power and prestige within Europe. The nineteenth-century German historian Heinrich von Treitschke explained, "All great nations in the fullness of their strength have desired to set their mark on barbarian lands and those who fail to participate in this great rivalry will play a pitiable role in time to come."[9] Similar concerns about status and strategic advantages motivated nations such as Britain and France to defend and expand their empires.

THE IMPERIAL IDEA New imperialism functioned as a belief system that permeated middle-class and mass culture in the decades after 1870. To educate viewers in the "imperial idea," exhibitions and fairs displayed goods and peoples from conquered regions. Images of empire appeared in boys' adventure stories, glossy ads for soap and chocolates, picture postcards, cookie tins, and cheap commemorative china plates and mugs. In the music halls and theaters, imperialist songs and dramas received popular applause.

At the center of the imperial idea stood the assumption that Western dominance over the world was a good thing. Europeans would not have sought to remake the world in the European image had they not been convinced of the superiority of that image. What led them to believe they had the right and the responsibility to take charge of other cultures and continents?

A LESSON IN THE IMPERIAL IDEA As this alphabet reader makes clear, education in imperial ideology began early.

One key factor was the perceived link between Western Christianity and "civilization." Christian missionaries served as a vanguard of Western culture throughout the nineteenth century. The celebrated Scottish explorer David Livingstone (1813–1873), who mapped out much of central and southern Africa, was a Protestant missionary (although not a very successful one—his only convert eventually renounced the Christian faith). Missionary society publications introduced their readers to exotic territories, while the societies themselves lobbied for Western territorial expansion to promote the spread of Christian missions.

Technology also seemed to justify Western imperialism. Before the eighteenth century, the technological gap between the West and other societies had not loomed large. In some cases, such as China, non-Western societies had held the technological advantage. Industrialization, however, gave the West the technological edge. Thus, the British adventurer Mary Kingsley (1862–1900) wrote, ". . . . [W]hen I come back from a spell in Africa, the thing that makes me proud of being one of the English is . . . a great railway engine. . . . [I]t is the manifestation of the superiority of my race."[10]

Finally, Social Darwinism seemed to provide scientific authority for the imperial idea. The British Lord Milner (1854–1925) explained in a speech in South Africa in 1903: "The white man must rule, because he is elevated by many, many steps above the black man; steps which it will take the latter centuries to climb, and which it is quite possible that the vast bulk of the black population may never be able to climb at all."[11]

Read the Document

Karl Pearson, "Social Darwinism and Imperialism"

Imperialists believed that empire—whether ordained by God or by biology—was a moral duty: Men and women in the West were obliged to bring the benefits of their civilization to the rest of the world. The British poet Rudyard Kipling (1865–1936) famously articulated this idea in 1899, in a poem urging American policymakers to conquer the Philippines:

> Take up the White Man's burden—
> Send forth the best ye breed—
> Go bind your sons to exile,
> To serve your captives' need;
> To wait in heavy harness
> On fluttered folk and wild—
> Your new-caught sullen peoples,
> Half devil and half child.[12]

Different Voices
Advocates of New Imperialism

N ew imperialism resulted from a variety of fears and ambitions, as these two documents illustrate. While some advocates of imperial expansion sought to convert the world's populace to Christianity, others insisted that overseas possessions strengthened a nation's ability to compete with its rivals, not only in the economic but also in the military, diplomatic, and even cultural arenas.

Jules Ferry, Speech Before French National Assembly, July 1883

Jules Ferry (1832–1893), who served two terms as premier (prime minister) of France, supported French imperial expansion. As the interruptions and objections to his speech reveal, Ferry faced opposition, particularly from socialist politicians.

M.* JULES FERRY: Gentlemen.... I believe that there is some benefit in summarizing ... the principles, the motives, and the various interests by which a policy of colonial expansion may be justified.

In the area of economics, I will allow myself to place before you ... the considerations which justify a policy of colonial expansion from the point of view of that need, felt more and more strongly by the industrial populations ... of our own rich and hard working country: the need for export markets.... Why? Because next door to us Germany is surrounded by barriers, because beyond the ocean, the United States of America has become protectionist ... because not only have these great markets ... become more difficult of access for our industrial products, but also these great states are beginning to pour products not seen heretofore onto our own markets....

Gentlemen, there is a second point ... the humanitarian and civilizing side of the question. On this point the honorable M. Camille Pellatan [an anti-imperialist opponent of Ferry's] has jeered in his own refined and clever manner; he jeers, he condemns, and he says "What is this civilization which you impose with cannonballs? What is it but another form of barbarism? Don't these populations, these inferior races, have the same rights as you? Aren't they masters of their own houses? Have they called upon you? You come to them against their will, you offer them violence, but not civilization."...

Gentlemen, I must speak from a higher and more truthful plane. It must be stated openly that, in effect, superior races have rights over inferior races. *[Movement on many benches on the far left.]*

M. JULES MAIGNE [a socialist opponent]: Oh! You dare to say this in the country which has proclaimed the rights of man!....

FERRY: I repeat that superior races have a right, because they have a duty. They have the duty to civilize inferior races. .... *[Approbation from the left. New interruptions from the extreme left and from the right.]* ...

*"M."= abbreviation for "Monsieur" ("Mister").
†These words were shouted out in the assembly by other legislators.

Gentlemen, there are certain considerations which merit the attention of all patriots. The conditions of naval warfare have been profoundly altered. ["Very true! Very true!"][†] At this time, as you know, a warship cannot carry more than 14 days' worth of coal ... and a ship which is out of coal is a derelict on the surface of the sea, abandoned to the first person who comes along. Thence the necessity of having on the oceans provision stations, shelters, ports for defense and revictualling. *[Applause at the center and left. Various interruptions.]* And it is for this that we needed Tunisia, for this that we needed Saigon and the Mekong Delta, for this that we need Madagascar ... and will never leave them! *[Applause from a great number of benches.]* Gentlemen, in Europe as it is today, in this competition of so many rivals which we see growing around us, ... in a Europe, or rather in a universe of this sort, a policy of peaceful seclusion or abstention is simply the highway to decadence! ...

France ... cannot be merely a free country ... she must also be a great country, exercising all of her rightful influence over the destiny of Europe ... she ought to propagate this influence throughout the world and carry everywhere that she can her language, her customs, her flag, her arms, and her genius. *[Applause at center and left.]*

Friedrich Fabri, *Does Germany Need Colonies?* (1879)

A pastor and theology professor, Friedrich Fabri (1824–1891) directed an interdenominational German missionary society that worked in southern Africa and the East Indies. In 1879, Fabri published Does Germany Need Colonies? *His answer was unequivocal.*

In looking for colonial possessions Germany is not prompted by the desire for expanding its power; it wants only to fulfill a national, we may even say a moral duty....

The German nation has long experience on the oceans, is skilled in industry and commerce, more capable than others in agricultural colonization, and furnished with ample manpower like no other modern highly cultured nation. Should it not also enter successfully upon this new venture? ... There is much bitterness, much poisonous partisanship in our newly united Germany; to open a promising new course of national development might have a liberating effect, and move the national spirit in a new direction.

Even more important is the consideration that a people at the height of their political power can successfully maintain their historic position only as long as they recognize and prove themselves as the bearers of a cultural mission. That is the only way which guarantees the stability and growth of national prosperity, which is the necessary basis for an enduring source of power. In past years Germany has contributed only its intellectual and literary work to this century; now we have turned to politics and become powerful. But if the goal of political power becomes an end in itself, it leads to hardness, even to barbarism, unless that

(continued on next page)

(continued from previous page)

nation is willing to undertake the inspirational, moral, and economic leadership of the times. . . . [L]ook around the globe and assess the ever-increasing colonial possessions of Great Britain, the strength which it draws from them, the skills of its administration, and the dominant position which the Anglo-Saxon stock occupies in all overseas countries. . . . It would be well if we Germans began to learn from the colonial destiny of our Anglo-Saxon cousins and emulate them in peaceful competition. When, centuries ago, the German empire stood at the head of the European states, it was the foremost commercial and maritime power. If the new Germany wants to restore and preserve its traditional powerful position in future, it will conceive of it as a cultural mission and no longer hesitate to practice its colonizing vocation.

SOURCES: Jules Ferry, Speech Before French National Assembly, 1883, in Ralph A. Austin (ed.), *Modern Imperialism: Western Overseas Expansion and Its*

Aftermath, 1776–1965 (Lexington, Mass.: D.C. Heath, 1969), 70–73. Friedrich Fabri, *Does Germany Need Colonies?* (Gotha, Germany: Perthes, 1879). Translated by Theodore von Laue. In Perry et al., *Sources of the Western Tradition*, 4th ed., Vol. 2. (New York: Houghton Mifflin, 1999), 235–237. Copyright © 1999 Wadsworth, a part of Cengage Learning, Inc. Reproduced by permission. www.cengage.com/permissions.

For Discussion

1. What are the four reasons Ferry gives for imperial expansion? Do they differ from Fabri's?

2. Which sections of these documents might any nineteenth-century imperialist of any nationality have articulated? Which sections make sense only within the specific French and German contexts?

3. The "imperial idea" played an important role in shaping Western identities at the end of the nineteenth century. How would Ferry and Fabri have defined the West? How would Ferry's parliamentary opponents?

Not all Europeans and Americans embraced the idea of the "White Man's burden," and many rejected the imperialist assumption of Western superiority. As the example of Picasso makes clear (see *Encounters and Transformations* in this chapter), some modernist artists looked to non-Western cultures for artistic inspiration. The Fauves ("wild beasts"), a Paris-based circle of artists that included Henri Matisse (1869–1954) and Paul Gauguin (1848–1903), condemned most Western art as artificial, and sought in their own brilliantly colored works to rediscover the vitality that they found in non-Western cultures.

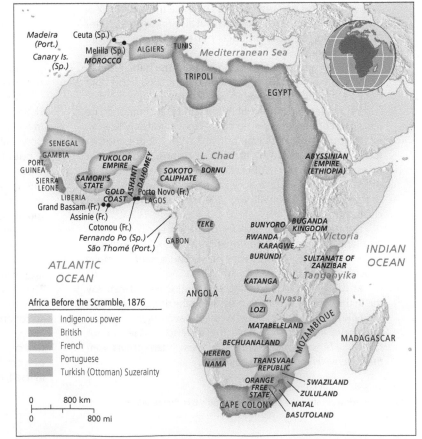

MAP 24.1 (A) AFRICA BEFORE THE SCRAMBLE, 1876 AND (B) AFRICA AFTER THE SCRAMBLE, 1914 A comparison of these two maps reveals the dramatic impact of the new imperialism on African societies. Indigenous empires such as the Sokoto Caliphate came under Western rule, as did tribal societies such as the Herero. Even states ruled by whites of European descent came under European rule, as the examples of the Transvaal and the Orange Free State in South Africa illustrate. Which African states remained independent of European control? What was the impact of Western imperialism on Ottoman power in north Africa?

Critics of empire often focused on its domestic political and economic implications. The British economist J. A. Hobson (1858–1940) charged that overseas empires benefited only wealthy capitalists while distracting public attention from the need for political and economic reform at home. Hobson argued that unregulated capitalism led almost inevitably to imperialist expansion because it generated huge surpluses in capital for a small elite, who must then find somewhere to invest these surpluses. Hobson's ideas influenced European socialists, who condemned imperialism along with capitalism.

The Scramble for Africa

New imperialism reached its zenith in Africa. As **Maps 24.1A** and **24.1B** show, in just 30 years, between 1875 and 1905, Europeans established 30 new colonies and protectorates encompassing 10 million square miles of territory and controlling 110 million Africans. By 1905, 90 percent of Africa was under European control. The conquest of the African continent was so rapid and dramatic that as early as 1884 mystified Europeans began to talk about the **Scramble for Africa**.

OVERCOMING THE OBSTACLES European efforts to establish settlements in the African interior faced three key obstacles: the climate, disease, and African resistance. The inhospitable climate meant that Africa was known as "the white man's grave." Over 75 percent of the white soldiers sent to West Africa in the early nineteenth century died there, and another 20 percent became invalids. Temperatures of more than 100 degrees Fahrenheit in some regions and constant rainfall in others made travel extremely difficult. The mosquito and the tsetse fly made it deadly. Mosquito bites brought malaria, while the tsetse fly carried trypanosomiasis, or sleeping sickness, an infectious illness that ended in a deadly paralysis. Sleeping sickness killed livestock as well as people.

Scramble for Africa The frenzied imposition of European control over most of Africa that occurred between 1870 and 1914.

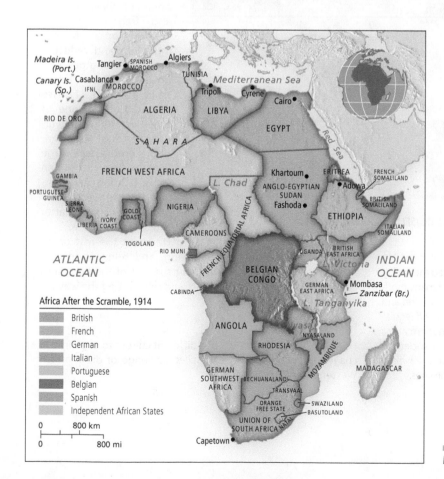

Africa After the Scramble, 1914

- British
- French
- German
- Italian
- Portuguese
- Belgian
- Spanish
- Independent African States

0   800 km

0   800 mi

MAP **24.1** (B)

Encounters and Transformations
Picasso Goes to the Museum

After months of work and more than 800 preparatory sketches, Pablo Picasso judged the painting finished at last. But when he showed *Les Demoiselles d'Avignon* to his friend and rival Matisse, the Frenchman thought the work a joke. Another friend and fellow painter, Georges Braques, found it appalling. Picasso did not exhibit the painting for several years and it remained largely unknown until 1939 when it went on display at the Museum of Modern Art in New York City. Today, *Demoiselles* is one of the most well-known modernist works of art in the Western world, "the amazing act on which all the art of our century is built."[13] It helped transform the history of Western art and even, perhaps, the history of perception itself.

With its in-your-face sexuality, *Demoiselles* retains its ability to shock. Five naked whores (*demoiselles* means "prostitutes") advertise for trade, twisting their bodies into erotic, even pornographic poses. The painting's eroticism alone, however, does not explain its impact.

The painting as we now know it resulted from a specific encounter that occurred when Picasso went to a museum in Paris. Sometime in 1906 or 1907, when he was already deeply involved in this painting, Picasso viewed African tribal masks on exhibit at the Ethnographic Museum in the Trocadero. This museum visit profoundly excited and upset the Spanish painter. His girlfriend Fernande Olivier reported, "Picasso is going crazy over Negro works and statues."[14] In Picasso's view, these "Negro works and statues" possessed the vitality and authenticity missing from Western art. Picasso and many modernists believed that Western civilization, with its urbanization and industrialism, its organizations and academies, its codes and regulations, had stifled artistic expression. They saw most modern art as weak and lifeless—the tired-out product of a worn-out society. In contrast, they argued, African art resembled the pictures drawn by children: energetic, playful, creative, colored outside the lines.

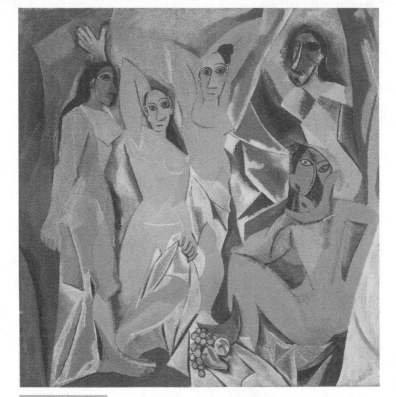

PABLO PICASSO, *LES DEMOISELLES D'AVIGNON* (1907)

This notion of African culture as childlike, of course, reflected the imperialist idea of "backward peoples." Picasso and other modernists rejected the imperialist notion of Western superiority and criticized Western empires, yet they could not escape imperialist stereotypes. Within the limits of these stereotypes, however, some modernists turned the cultural relationship of the West and Africa upside down. Picasso went to African art to learn, not to conquer.

Picasso's encounter with the African masks transformed this specific painting and modern art itself. After his Trocadero visit, Picasso reconfigured the faces of the two women on the right so that their mask-like appearances now clash awkwardly with those of the three other prostitutes. This step destroyed any unity of narrative or composition in the painting: The five figures are no longer part of a single story or share a single point of view. Picasso also fragmented each of the bodies, flattening them and reducing them to jutting geometric forms. Thus, *Demoiselles* pushed Picasso toward Cubism, one of the most influential artistic styles of the twentieth century (see page 756). As the art historian John Golding has written, "In the *Demoiselles* Picasso began to shatter the human figure. . . . He spent the rest of his artistic life dissecting, reassembling, and reinventing it."[15] After Picasso, Western artists spent the rest of the twentieth century dissecting, reassembling, and reinventing the way we see and depict our world.

For Discussion

How did Picasso use the art of a different culture to explain and challenge his own? Did *Demoiselles* challenge or did it affirm Western imperialist ideas?

In regions with endemic trypanosomiasis, such as equatorial, southern, and eastern Africa, the use of horses and oxen was impossible. Despite these difficulties, Europeans did endeavor to establish inland settlements in Africa, but were usually defeated by African resistance. In the seventeenth century, for example, the Portuguese set up forts and trading centers in modern Zimbabwe but were driven out by local African populations.

Beginning around 1830, however, a series of developments altered the relationship between Europe and Africa and made European conquest possible. First, European explorers changed the Western understanding of Africa. Between 1830 and 1870, adventurers mapped out the chief geographical features of Africa's interior and so illuminated the "Dark Continent" for Europeans. They discovered that central Africa was not the empty desert that Europeans had assumed, but rather a territory with abundant agricultural and mineral resources—and lots of people, all of them potential consumers of European goods.

The shift in the European vision of Africa—from desert to treasure house—coincided with important political changes within Africa itself. Many of these political shifts were the unintended consequences of Western efforts to abolish the slave trade. In the 1830s, Britain and other European powers, pressured by humanitarian and missionary groups, sought to wipe out the West African slave trade. They succeeded—and the slave trade shifted to central and eastern Africa. This shift caused great political instability. African slaving nations relied on frequent military raids to obtain their human merchandise. These raids—carried out by Africans against Africans—disrupted agricultural production, shattered trade networks, and undermined the authority of existing political rulers. With political systems in disarray, many African regions were vulnerable to European encroachment.

Finally, three specific inventions shifted the balance of power in the West's favor. First, steam power proved crucial in enabling Western imperialists to overcome the obstacles to traveling through Africa by allowing them to use the continent's extensive but shallow river system. While steam enabled Westerners to penetrate the African interior, the quinine prophylaxis helped them survive once they got there. Doctors had long prescribed quinine for malaria. Death and disability rates from the disease remained high, however, until some chance discoveries revealed the importance of taking quinine prophylactically—of saturating the system with quinine *before* any infection. By the 1860s, Westerners routinely ingested quinine in preparation for postings in Africa—and their death rates dropped dramatically.

African death rates, however, soared because of the third crucial invention of imperialism—the repeating, breech-loading rifles Europeans carried from the 1870s on. Before the development of these rifles, Europeans used muskets or muzzle-loading rifles. These weapons fouled easily, particularly in damp weather, and could be loaded only one ball at a time—usually while the rifleman was standing up. The musket-armed European did not gain a significant military advantage, even over spears. With the repeating rifle, however, "any European infantryman could now fire lying down, undetected, in any weather, 15 rounds of ammunition in as many seconds at targets up to half a mile away." As we saw at the beginning of this chapter, the repeating breech-loader and its descendant, the machine gun, made the European conquest of regions such as the Sudan "more like hunting than war."[16]

SLICING THE CAKE: THE CONQUEST OF AFRICA In the decades after 1870, convinced that the conquest of African territories would guarantee commercial prosperity and strengthen national power, European states moved quickly to beat out their rivals and grab a piece of the continent. As King Leopold II of Belgium (1865–1909) explained in a letter to his ambassador in London in 1876, "I do not want to miss a good chance of getting us a slice of this magnificent African cake."[17]

Leopold's slice proved enormous. He wanted the Congo, a huge region of central Africa comprising territory more than twice as large as central Europe. After a decade of quarreling, representatives of the European powers met in Berlin in 1884 and agreed to Leopold's demands. They also used this Berlin Conference to regulate the Scramble for Africa. According to the terms established in Berlin, any state claiming a territory in Africa had to establish "effective occupation" and to plan for the economic development of that region.

But as the history of the Congo Free State demonstrated, such economic development served European, not African, interests. Leopold's personal mercenary army turned the Congo into a hellhole of slavery and death. By claiming all so-called vacant land, Leopold deprived villagers of the grazing, foraging, and hunting grounds they needed to survive. He levied rubber quotas for each village, forcing villagers to harvest wild rubber for up to 25 days each month while their families starved. Brutal punishments ensured compliance: Soldiers chopped off the hands of villagers who failed to meet their quota. The Belgians also forced Africans to serve as human mules, a practice that spread sleeping sickness from the western coast into the interior. As an estimated three million people died from the combined effects of forced labor, brutal punishments, starvation, and disease, Leopold II's enormous profits from the Congo enabled him to indulge his hobby of building elaborate tourist resorts on the Riviera.

King Leopold's brand of imperialism proved so scandalous that in 1908 the Belgian government replaced Leopold's personal rule with state control over the Congo. Yet the king's exploitation of the Congo differed only in degree, not in kind, from the nature of European conquest elsewhere in Africa. Forced labor was common throughout European-controlled areas, as were brutal punishments for any Africans who dared resist. Faced with tribal revolt in Southwest Africa, the German colonial army commander in 1904 ordered the extermination of the entire Herero tribe. His soldiers drove 20,000 men, women, and children from their villages into the desert to die of thirst.

Read the Document

Carl Peters, "A Manifesto for German Colonization"

AFRICAN RESISTANCE As the Herero rebellion demonstrated, Africans frequently resisted imperial regimes, but to no avail. The only successful episode of African resistance to European conquest occurred in northern Africa, in the kingdom of Ethiopia (also called Abyssinia). By the time of the European Scramble for Africa, Ethiopia had developed not only a modern standing army, but also an advanced infrastructure and communications system. In 1896 these factors enabled the Ethiopian nation to defeat the Italian army at the Battle of Adowa.

Adowa, however, was the exception. The technological gap between the indigenous peoples and their European conquerors doomed most African resistance. Africans did have guns, the result of a booming arms trade between European rifle manufacturers and African states. Frequently, however, the arms shipped to Africa were inferior models—muskets or single-firing muzzle-loaders rather than the up-to-date and deadly efficient repeating rifles and early machine guns possessed by the European invaders. African military leaders who did obtain advanced weaponry often failed to make the strategic leap necessary to adapt their military tactics to new technologies. (As we will see in Chapter 25, European military leaders made similar mistakes in World War I.)

Asian Encounters

Unlike most of Africa, many of the diverse states of Asia had already been woven into the web of the Western economy well before 1870 as a part of the eighteenth-century mercantilist empires established by Dutch, British, Portuguese, and French trading companies (see Chapter 18). Throughout the nineteenth century, European governments strengthened their control over many of these regions, primarily to protect trade routes or to ensure access to profitable commodities such as rubber, tin, tobacco, and sugar. The Dutch, for example, expanded their East Indies empire, moving from control of the island of Java in 1815 to domination over almost the entire archipelago several decades later (see **Map 24.2**).

Four factors accelerated the pace of imperialist acquisition in Asia after 1870. First, in the age of steam, Western powers needed Pacific islands to serve as coaling stations for their commercial and naval fleets. Second, new industrial processes heightened the economic value of many of these regions. The development of a process for producing dried coconut, for example, made Samoa so valuable that Germany, Britain, and the United States competed for control over the tiny islands. Third, as in Africa, international competition accelerated imperialism. Territorial gains by one power led to anxiety and a quicker pace of expansion by its rivals.

Finally, the steady erosion of Chinese political stability—itself a result of encounters with the West—intensified this "Scramble for Asia." As Western powers competed for access to Chinese markets, Western empires expanded throughout Asia. The quest for a protected trade route to China, for example, impelled the French to extend their control over neighboring Indochina. By 1893, the Union of French Indochina included the formerly independent states of Laos, Cambodia, Annam, and Tonkin—the latter two better known by their contemporary name of Vietnam.

 **Read** the **Document**

"Letter of Phan Chu Trinh to the French Governor-General"

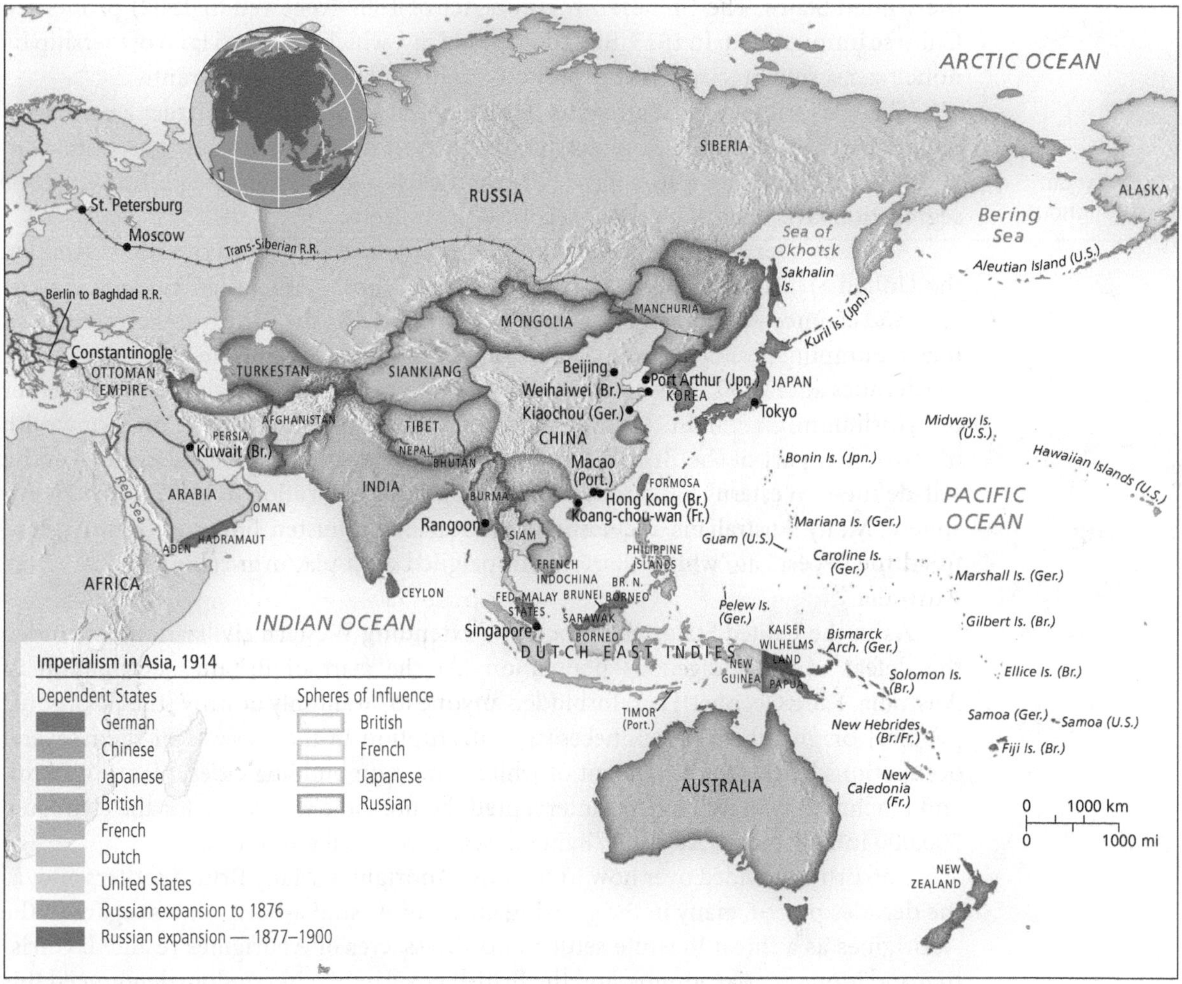

MAP **24.2** IMPERIALISM IN ASIA, 1914 The impact of the new imperialism on Asia was not as dramatic as in Africa, but the spread of Western rule is significant nonetheless. This map shows a key development: the entry of non-European powers—Japan and the United States—into the imperialist game. What it does not show is the extent of Western and Japanese influence in China. Profoundly destabilized by foreign intervention, China in 1914 was in the midst of revolution. Which states emerged as the most powerful in Asia by 1914?

EXPANDING THE WEST: THE UNITED STATES AND AUSTRALIA In the latter half of the nineteenth century, the United States and Australia established themselves as extensions of the West. As these states expanded and consolidated their territories and subdued indigenous populations, race-based versions of national identity that had justified European imperialist adventures came to be applied to all peoples of color.

For the United States, the acquisition of an empire in Asia followed consolidation of control over most of North America. After emerging victorious from a war with Mexico in 1846, the United States gained the territories of California, Nevada, Utah, Arizona, New Mexico, and southern Colorado. The completion of the transcontinental Union Pacific railroad in 1869 accelerated the pace of westward settlement. The conquest of the continent, however, depended on the defeat, and often decimation, of its indigenous peoples. A series of "Indian wars" punctuated the decades from 1860 through 1890 as the United States expanded westward.

Once its borders reached the Pacific Ocean, the United States quickly emerged as an imperialist power in Asia. In 1853, Commodore Matthew Perry used his squadron of four warships to open Japan to American commerce; during the 1860s and 1870s the United States participated with the European powers in chipping away at China's national sovereignty to ensure favorable terms of trade there. By the end of the century, the United States had annexed Hawaii and part of Samoa, and as a result of the Spanish-American War had acquired Guam, the Philippines, Cuba, and Puerto Rico.

American acquisition of empire in Asia heightened anti-Asian sentiment within the United States. The Chinese Exclusion Act of 1882 (renewed in 1902) prohibited Chinese immigration. In 1913, the Alien Land Law, which outlawed land ownership by noncitizens, sought to restrict the property rights of Japanese immigrants.

These efforts paralleled attempts in the American South to construct a version of national identity confined to whites. Southern legislators used literacy tests, poll taxes, and violent intimidation to deprive blacks of their right to vote, while **Jim Crow** or segregation laws defined blacks as second-class citizens.

Australia's territorial expansion and its emergence as a Western state resembled the United States' development in many respects. After Captain James Cook discovered and claimed Australia for the British Crown in 1770, the British government used it as a dumping ground for convicts. But with the expansion of the wool industry in the decades after 1830, the six British colonies established in Australia became a center of British immigration. In 1901, these colonies joined together in the Commonwealth of Australia, part of the British Empire but a self-governing political entity—and a self-defined "Western" nation, despite its geographical location in the Eastern Hemisphere. Many Australians, including the first prime minister, Edmund Barton, identified the "West" as "white." Barton campaigned on a platform calling for a "White Australia."

As in the United States, the process of extending Western civilization demanded the defeat of the indigenous population. At the start of Britain's occupation of Australia, King George III had forbidden anyone to "wantonly destroy [the Aboriginal peoples] or give them any unnecessary interruption in the exercise of their several occupations."[18] But the settlement of whites intent on building cities, planting farms, and fencing in land for pastures interrupted the nomadic way of life for the estimated 500,000 inhabitants of Australia, living in scattered tribal groupings.

The British divided over how to treat the Aborigines. Many British settlers and, as the decades passed, many in the growing group of Australia-born whites regarded the Aborigines as a threat to white settlements. Massacres of Aborigines resulted. Christian and humanitarian groups, and the British government in London, denounced this violence and insisted that the Aborigines should be westernized and Christianized, rather than exterminated. From the 1820s on, mission stations housed and educated Aboriginal children. Forcibly removed from their homes, these children were schooled in British ways and then at age 15 placed in employment as apprentices and domestic

Jim Crow Series of laws mandating racial segregation throughout the American South.

servants. Despite these missions, few Aborigines assimilated to the Western way of life. In the final decades of the nineteenth century, official policy shifted from assimilation to "protection." The Australian government declared Aborigines and mixed-race individuals to be legal wards of the state and required them to live on reserves. Aborigines did not receive Australian citizenship until 1967.

Many white Australians perceived not only Aborigines but also Asian immigrants as threats to their Western identity. By the 1850s, tens of thousands of Chinese had migrated to Australia. Arriving as indentured servants, they worked under brutal conditions. Many labored in the gold mines, where they received one-twelfth of the wages paid to a European. As the numbers of Chinese immigrants grew, so, too, did anti-Chinese sentiment. One newspaper editor noted, "The Chinese question never fails. At every meeting . . . visions of millions of the barbarians swooping upon the colony . . . rise in the mental horizons of every man present."[19] In 1888, the Australian government turned back ships containing Chinese immigrants. Legislation to restrict Chinese immigration soon followed.

THE CONTINUED EXPANSION OF THE RUSSIAN EMPIRE As in the United States and Australia, imperial expansion in nineteenth-century Russia took the form of territorial consolidation across a continent. **Map 24.3** shows that by 1914, the Russian Empire stretched from Warsaw in central Europe to Vladivostok on the Sea of Japan—one-seventh of the global land surface. Ethnic Russians accounted for only 45 percent of the population of this empire.

The colonization of Siberia began in the sixteenth century when Russian serfs fled eastward in search of land and freedom. The end of serfdom actually accelerated the flow to Siberia, because peasants now needed to escape the debts imposed on them by the emancipation legislation of 1861 (see Chapter 22). The tsarist policy of exiling political dissenters to Siberia added to the outflow, while the completion of the trans-Siberian railway in the 1890s made the journey easier. Between 1800 and 1914, seven million Russians settled in or were deported to Siberia.

Just as American expansion westward and the British conquest of Australia dramatically depleted Indian and Aboriginal numbers, so Russian migration into Siberia displaced that region's original population. Until 1826 Russians could trade Siberians as slaves and many died because of brutal treatment. In addition, the immigrants

MAP **24.3** THE EXPANSION OF THE RUSSIAN EMPIRE Throughout the nineteenth century, the Russian Empire expanded to the west and south. After Russia's acquisition of territories in the Caucasus and Black Sea region, more Muslims lived under tsarist rule than in the Ottoman Empire. Which states were threatened by Russian expansion?

brought with them new epidemic diseases and the booming fur trade depleted the animal herds that served as the Siberians' main food source. Disease and famine decimated the Siberian population.

Russia also expanded southward into central Asia, primarily as a preemptive response to the growth of British power in India. Fearing that the British might push northward, the Russians pushed south. By 1885, the Black Sea region, the Caucasus, and Turkestan had all fallen to Russian imperial control, and Muslims constituted a significant minority of the tsar's subjects. Over the next three decades the oil fields of the Caucasus became a crucial part of the Russian industrial economy.

The expansion of the Russian Empire eastward encroached upon Chinese territory and thus helped destabilize China. It also led to growing hostilities between Russia and Japan, as both regimes coveted Chinese Manchuria. We saw in Chapter 23 that the growing antagonism between Russia and Japan led to the Russo-Japanese War in 1904 and that defeat in this war helped provoke the Russian Revolution of 1905. Imperialism could be a risky business.

JAPANESE INDUSTRIAL AND IMPERIAL EXPANSION Japan's victory over Russia in 1905 signaled its rise to global power and its emergence as an imperialist player. In the 1630s the Japanese emperor sealed Japan from the West by closing Japanese ports to all foreigners except a small contingent of Dutch and Chinese traders confined to the city of Nagasaki. The Japanese government rebuffed all Western overtures until 1853, when, as we have seen, Commodore Perry forced Japan to open two of its ports to American ships. Over the next 15 years, Western powers pushed to expand their economic influence in Japan, and Japanese elites fought over how to respond. Anti-Western terrorism became endemic, civil war broke out, and a political revolution ensued.

Japan emerged from this turbulent time with a new government. For more than 200 years effective political control had rested in the hands not of the Japanese emperor, but rather of the "Shogun," the military governor of Japan. In 1868, however, Japan's warrior nobility tossed the Shogun from power and restored the young Emperor Mutsuhito (1867–1912) to effective rule—the Meiji Restoration.

Japan's new government determined that the only way to resist Western conquest was to adopt Western industrial and military technologies and techniques. Over the next four decades, a revolution from the top occurred, as a modern centralized state, modeled on France, replaced Japan's feudal political system and as a system of state schools, modeled on U.S. public schools, was constructed. Funds poured into building a modern navy, modeled on Britain's, and a powerful conscript-based army, modeled on Germany's. An imperial decree of 1871 even ordered that government officials abandon kimonos for western suits.

Beginning in the 1890s, Japan also adopted western-style imperialism. Wars with China in 1894 and Russia in 1904 led to the Japanese seizure of Taiwan and Korea, and expanded Japanese economic influence in Manchuria. One writer, Tokutomi Soho (1863–1957), proclaimed that Japan's imperial conquests showed that "civilization is not a monopoly of the white man."[20] Certainly imperialist violence was not a white man's monopoly: The Japanese brutally punished Koreans and Taiwanese who dared to protest against their new rulers.

SCRAMBLING IN CHINA While Japan used its encounter with the West to modernize and militarize its society, China proved less successful in withstanding Western hegemony. Throughout the nineteenth century, Chinese national sovereignty slowly eroded as European powers, the United States, and Japan jostled for access to China's markets and resources. In 1899, European states with interests in China did agree to back the American "open door" policy, which opposed the formal partitioning of China (as had just occurred in Africa). This policy, however, actually increased rather than blocked Western interference in Chinese economic and political affairs.

THE BOXER REBELLION QUELLED Although never formally controlled by Western powers, China was, by the end of the nineteenth century, a Western "sphere of influence," as the aftermath of the Boxer Rebellion of 1900 made clear. At the insistence of the Western powers, the Chinese government publicly executed the Boxer ringleaders in front of the foreign troops who had defeated the rebels.

Many Chinese resented Western encroachment, and in 1900, a secret society devoted to purging China of Western influence began attacking foreigners. Because members of the society practiced the martial arts, this event was called the Boxer Rebellion. With the covert support of the Chinese government, the rebels attacked European diplomatic headquarters in Beijing and killed more than 200 missionaries and several thousand Chinese Christians. The West responded in fury. A combined military force, drawing 16,000 soldiers from Russia, Germany, Austria-Hungary, France, Britain, Japan, and the United States, crushed the rebellion and sacked Beijing. Required to grant further trade and territorial concessions to its invaders, the Chinese central government was fatally weakened. In 1911, revolution engulfed China and propelled it into four decades of political and social tumult.

A Glimpse of Things to Come: The Boer War

In the 1840s, a British journalist in China urged the Chinese to accept what he regarded as the crucial lesson of history: "Ever since the dispersion of man, the richest stream of human blessings has, in the will of Providence, followed a western course." To many Europeans, Australians, and Americans, the rapid expansion of Western imperial control across the globe after 1870 confirmed this lesson. At the end of the nineteenth

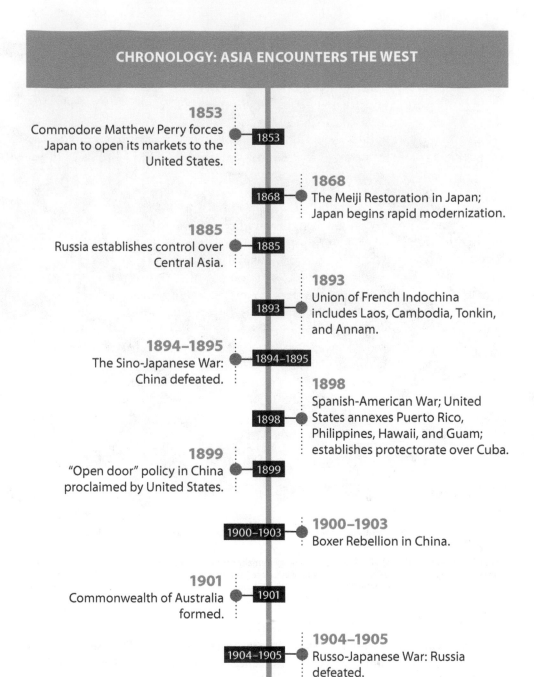

CHRONOLOGY: ASIA ENCOUNTERS THE WEST

1853
Commodore Matthew Perry forces Japan to open its markets to the United States.

1853

1868

1868
The Meiji Restoration in Japan; Japan begins rapid modernization.

1885
Russia establishes control over Central Asia.

1885

1893

1893
Union of French Indochina includes Laos, Cambodia, Tonkin, and Annam.

1894–1895
The Sino-Japanese War: China defeated.

1894–1895

1898

1898
Spanish-American War; United States annexes Puerto Rico, Philippines, Hawaii, and Guam; establishes protectorate over Cuba.

1899
"Open door" policy in China proclaimed by United States.

1899

1900–1903

1900–1903
Boxer Rebellion in China.

1901
Commonwealth of Australia formed.

1901

1904–1905

1904–1905
Russo-Japanese War: Russia defeated.

1911
Revolution in China: Overthrow of Manchu Dynasty.

1911

century, however, the British found themselves embroiled in a conflict that challenged this complacency. The Boer War of 1899–1902 shook British self-confidence and foreshadowed the total warfare and the crumbling of empires that marked the experience of the West in the twentieth century.

The Boer War was the culmination of a century of hostility among British imperialists, Dutch settlers (called Boers, the Dutch word for "farmer"), and indigenous Africans in the southern triangle of Africa. Germany's move into Southwest Africa in 1884 worsened this conflict: The British in the Cape Colony (see **Map 24.4**) feared that the Boers would work with Germany against British interests. The discovery in 1886 of diamonds and gold in the Transvaal, an independent Boer republic, intensified the conflict. British investors in the profitable diamond and gold mines resented Boer taxation and labor policies, and pressed the British government to invade the Boer republics and place them under British rule.

In 1899, these imperialists got the war they had demanded, but it turned out to be different from what they expected. The Boers proved formidable enemies, skilled riflemen who knew the land and were fighting for their homes. Mired in a guerilla war, the British command decided to smoke out the Boer fighters through a scorched-earth policy. British troops burned more than 30,000 farms to the ground and confined Boer women and children, and their black African servants, in poorly provisioned concentration camps. Diseases such as diphtheria and typhus soon took their toll. Almost 20,000 Boer women and children, and at least 14,000 blacks, died in these camps.

The British finally defeated the Boers in April 1902, but two factors limited this victory. First, the Boer states came under British control, but the Boers (or Afrikaners) outnumbered other whites in the newly created Union of South Africa. After South Africa received self-government in 1910, the Afrikaners dominated the political system and created a nation founded on racial segregation. Second, Britain emerged from the Boer War with its military and its humanitarian reputation severely tarnished. The war aroused strong opposition inside Britain and showed that popular support for imperialism would rapidly disappear if the costs proved too high.

The sort of conflict between imperialism's opponents and supporters would be repeated many times over the next several decades as nationalist challenges against

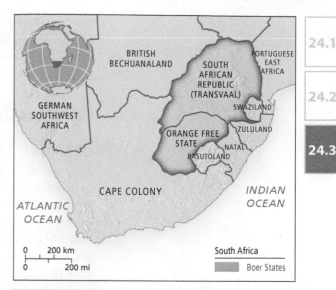

MAP **24.4** SOUTH AFRICA After the defeat of the Boer states—the Transvaal and the Orange Free State—in the Boer War in 1902, the Union of South Africa comprised the Cape Colony and the two Boer republics. Why did the British government regard South Africa as a crucial part of the British Empire?

👁 **Watch the Video**

John Cox, *The Origins of the Holocaust*

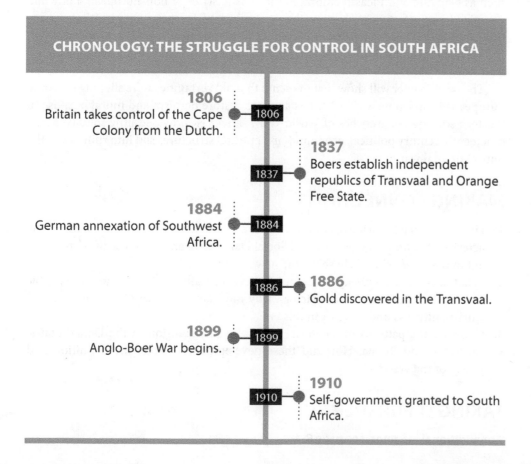

CHRONOLOGY: THE STRUGGLE FOR CONTROL IN SOUTH AFRICA

1806
Britain takes control of the Cape Colony from the Dutch.
1806

1837
1837
Boers establish independent republics of Transvaal and Orange Free State.

1884
German annexation of Southwest Africa.
1884

1886
1886
Gold discovered in the Transvaal.

1899
Anglo-Boer War begins.
1899

1910
1910
Self-government granted to South Africa.

775

imperial rule multiplied and the imperial idea grew less and less persuasive. More ominously, the sight of noncombatants confined—and dying—in concentration camps would soon become all too familiar. The Boer War thus served as a prophetic opening to the twentieth century.

CONCLUSION

Reshaping the West: Expansion and Fragmentation

Africans and Asians who saw their political and social structures topple under the imperialist onslaught would probably have agreed with the Austrian poet Hugo von Hoffmansthal (1874–1929) when he wrote in 1905 that "what other generations believed to be firm is in fact sliding." Hoffmansthal, however, was not commenting on Africa or Asia. He was describing the Western cultural and intellectual landscape that, like colonial political boundaries, underwent enormous and disturbing change in the decades after 1870. In this era, matter itself began to slide, as the Newtonian conception of the world gave way to a new, more unsettling picture of the physical universe. Changes in medical practice, the triumph of Darwin's evolutionary theory, and the revolt against positivism helped undermine established assumptions and contributed to the sense that the foundations of Western culture were shifting. So, too, did the birth of modernism and broader changes, such as middle-class women's move into the public sphere and the redefinition of sexual boundaries, push Western culture in a new direction.

In the later nineteenth century, then, a series of encounters reshaped the West. Its geographic boundaries expanded as non-European regions such as the United States emerged as significant economic and imperial powers. With Australians claiming Western identity, "the West" even spilled over into the Eastern Hemisphere. Yet fragmentation as well as expansion characterized the Western experience after 1870. At the same time that social thinkers proclaimed white cultural superiority, European artists such as Gauguin and Picasso embraced the artistic styles of non-European, nonwhite societies in an effort to push open the boundaries of Western culture. While scientific and technological achievements convinced many Europeans and Americans that the West would conquer the globe, others regarded these developments with profound uneasiness.

The next chapter will show that the sense that old certainties were slipping led some Europeans to welcome war in 1914 as a way to restore heroism and moral purpose to Western society. The trenches of World War I, however, provided little solidity. Many nineteenth-century political, economic, and cultural structures slid into ruin under the impact of total war.

MAKING CONNECTIONS

1. How did Social Darwinism contribute to the mood of cultural uneasiness that characterized the *fin-de-siècle*? How did Social Darwinism and the sense of crisis inherent in the *fin-de-siècle* help shape the new imperialism?

2. What factors strengthened religious beliefs and allegiances in late-nineteenth-century Europe? Given these factors, why did many Western Christians feel that Christianity was under attack in this era?

3. Compare the patterns of territorial and political expansion in the United States, Australia, and Russia. How did these developments change the definition and power of the West?

TAKING IT FURTHER

For additional readings, see page R-1.

On MyHistoryLab

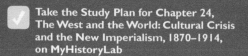

Take the Study Plan for Chapter 24,
The West and the World: Cultural Crisis
and the New Imperialism, 1870–1914,
on MyHistoryLab

Chapter Review

Scientific Transformations

24.1 How did scientific developments during this period lead to both optimism and anxiety?

Medical advances in disease prevention inspired confidence in the power of scientific discoveries to benefit humankind, but an increased awareness and fear of germs increased anxiety. Developments in evolutionary science were used to justify existing social and economic hierarchies, but also contributed to unease since they challenged basic religious assumptions and heightened fears of racial and national degeneration. New research in the social sciences highlighted the power of irrational forces in determining human conduct. Finally, the revolution in physics unseated traditional depictions of the natural world and made much of science incomprehensible to ordinary men and women.

Cultural Crisis: The *Fin-de-Siècle* and the Birth of Modernism

24.2 Why did many Europeans in this period believe they were living in a time of cultural crisis?

Perceptions of rising rates of crime and disease in the rapidly growing cities, combined with the unsettling impact of changing gender roles, contributed to the sense that the West was in a state of decline. So, too, did modernist art and literature, which challenged central middle-class ideas about the role of art in society. A growing sense of religious crisis also heightened anxieties, although popular religiosity remained vibrant.

The New Imperialism

24.3 What were the causes and consequences of the new imperialist ideology for the West and non-Western societies?

Competition for captive markets, pressure to secure global investments in these markets by formally controlling them, and the fact that Western dominance over the world appealed to voters eager to think of themselves as a superior people were factors in the rapid imperial acquisition of the time. Speedy and dramatic conquests of entire continents, like Africa and Australia, reassured many Westerners of their own racial and cultural superiority, while decimating indigenous cultures.

Chapter Time Line

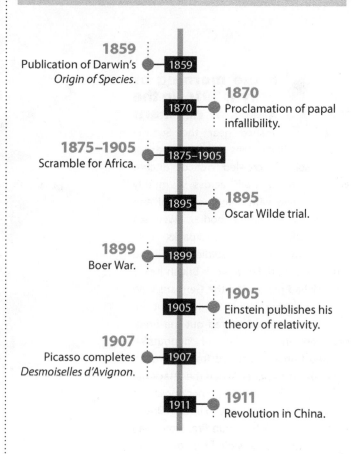

1859
Publication of Darwin's
Origin of Species.
1859

1870
1870
Proclamation of papal
infallibility.

1875–1905
Scramble for Africa.
1875–1905

1895
1895
Oscar Wilde trial.

1899
Boer War.
1899

1905
1905
Einstein publishes his
theory of relativity.

1907
Picasso completes
Desmoiselles d'Avignon.
1907

1911
1911
Revolution in China.

25 The First World War

On the morning of July 1, 1916, in the fields of northern France near the Somme River, tens of thousands of British soldiers crawled out of ditches and began to walk across a muddy expanse filled with shards of metal and decomposing human bodies. Weighed down with 60-pound backpacks, they trudged forward. The soldiers expected little opposition. For a week British heavy artillery had pummeled the Germans who lay on the other side of the mud. But the German troops had waited out the bombardment in the safety of "dugouts"—fortified bunkers scooped from the earth beneath the trenches. When the attack began, they raced to their gunnery positions and raked the evenly spaced lines of British soldiers with machine-gun fire. More than 20,000 British soldiers died that day, thousands within the first minutes of the attack. Another 40,000 were wounded. Yet the attack went on. Between July 1 and November 18, 1916, when the Battle of the Somme finally ended, almost 420,000 soldiers from Britain and the British Empire were killed or

THE BATTLE OF THE SOMME, 1916
British (left) and German troops recover casualties during a lull in the fighting.

LEARNING OBJECTIVES

25.1 	25.2	25.3	25.4
What factors led Europe into war in 1914?	When, where, and how did the Allies defeat the Central Powers?	How did total war structure the home fronts?	What were the consequences of this war for the European and the global political order?

Listen to Chapter 25 on MyHistoryLab

Watch the Video Series on MyHistoryLab

Learn about some key topics related to this chapter with the *MyHistoryLab Video Series: Key Topics in Western Civilization*

25.1

25.2

25.3

25.4

wounded. Their French allies lost 200,000 men to death or injury. German casualties are estimated at 450,000.

Such carnage became commonplace during the First World War. Between 1914 and 1918, European commanders sent more than eight million men to their deaths in a series of often futile attacks. The total number of casualties—killed, wounded, and missing—reached more than 37 million. These casualty figures were in part the products of the Industrial Revolution, as the nations of the West used their factories to churn out ever more efficient tools of killing. The need for machine guns, artillery shells, poison gas canisters, and other implements of modern warfare meant that World War I was the first **total war**, a war that demanded that combatant nations mobilize their industrial economies and their armies, and thus a war that erased the distinction between civilian and soldier. In total war, victory depended on the woman in the munitions factory as well as the man on the front lines.

This first total war redefined the West. By shattering the authoritarian empires of eastern and central Europe and integrating the United States more fully in European affairs, the war ensured that commitment to democratic values became central to one dominant twentieth-century definition of "the West." But the war also strengthened anti-democratic forces: It catapulted into power a communist regime in Russia, intensified eastern Europe's ethnic and nationalist conflicts, and undermined many of the economic structures on which Western stability and prosperity rested. This chapter explores a key question:

Read the Document

"British Soldiers on the Battle of the Somme"

total war A war that demands extensive state regulation of economic production, distribution, and consumption; and that blurs (or erases entirely) the distinction between civilian and soldier.

How did the encounter with total war transform Western cultures?

The Origins of the First World War

25.1 What factors led Europe into war in 1914?

On June 28, 1914, ethnic Serbian terrorists assassinated Archduke Franz Ferdinand (1863–1914), the heir to the throne of the Austro-Hungarian Empire. One month after the archduke's death, Austria declared war on Serbia. One week later, Europe was at war. Germany entered the war on Austria's side. These two **Central Powers** squared off against not only small Serbia, but also the colossal weight of the **Allies**, the combined forces of Russia, France, and Britain. By the time the war ended in late 1918, it had embraced states from around the globe.

Why did the murder of one man on the streets of a Balkan city lead to the deaths of millions? To understand the origins of World War I, we need to examine four interlocking factors: the destabilizing impact of eastern European nationalism, the creation of rival alliance systems, the requirements of an industrialized military, and the "will to war"—the conviction among both policymakers and ordinary people that war provided a resolution to social and cultural crisis.

Central Powers Germany and Austria-Hungary in World War I.

Allies During World War I, the states allied against the Central Powers of Germany and Austria-Hungary. During World War II, the states allied against the regimes of Nazi Germany, fascist Italy, and imperial Japan.

Nationalism in Eastern Europe: Austria-Hungary and the Problem of Serbia

In eastern Europe, where ethnic, religious, or linguistic identities rather than political citizenship defined the "nation," nationalism served as an explosive force. For the Czechs, Slovenians, Serbs, Poles, Ukrainians, and many other groups, translating national identity into political identity—creating a "nation-state"—demanded the breakup of empires and a redrawing of political boundaries.

The divisive impact of nationalism in eastern Europe explains why officials within the Austro-Hungarian Empire regarded the small state of Serbia as a major threat. A multiethnic, multilinguistic empire, Austria-Hungary's survival depended on damping down the fires of nationalism wherever they flamed up. Yet Serbian politics centered on fanning the nationalist flame. In 1903, a group of Serbian army officers had shot Serbia's despised king and queen, chopped their bodies into bits, and threw the pieces out the window. To remain in power and avoid such a grisly fate, the new king catered to the demands of radical nationalists who sought the unification of all Serbs into a Greater Serbian state. Because more than seven million Serbs lived not in Serbia, but in Austria-Hungary, the Austrian monarchy regarded this call for Serbian unification as a serious threat to the Austro-Hungarian Empire.

The hostile relations between Serbia and Austria-Hungary led directly to the outbreak of the war. In 1908 Austria annexed Bosnia, a region with a large Serbian population. The Serbian government responded by encouraging Bosnian Serb separatist and terrorist groups. One such group, the Black Hand, assassinated Archduke Franz Ferdinand in the summer of 1914. That assassination convinced Austrian officials to declare war on Serbia.

Read the Document

Borijove Jevtic, "The Murder of Archduke Franz Ferdinand at Sarajevo, 1914"

ARREST OF GAVRILO PRINCIP Princip was only 18 years old when he assassinated Archduke Franz Ferdinand and set into motion the sequence of events that led to the First World War. Because of his age, he did not receive the death penalty but instead was sentenced to 20 years in prison. He died at age 22 of tuberculosis.

International Competition and Rival Alliance Systems

To understand what transformed this Austro-Serbian conflict into a European war, we need to look at the rival alliance systems that helped escalate a regional conflict into a European and then a global war. These alliances emerged in response to heightened international competition.

The unification of Germany in 1871 upset the balance of power by creating a military and economic powerhouse in the middle of Europe. Until 1890, however, the diplomatic maneuvers of Otto von Bismarck, the new Germany's chancellor, ensured stability. Bismarck recognized that the Franco-Prussian War of 1870 (which brought about German unification) had made antagonism toward Germany central to French foreign policy. He also recognized that Germany's position in the center of Europe made it vulnerable to encirclement, should France succeed in forming an anti-German alliance with another European state. To avoid such encirclement, Bismarck maintained alliances with Russia, Austria, and Italy. The Dual Alliance between Germany and the Austro-Hungarian Empire in 1879 became the **Triple Alliance** of 1882, which joined Germany, Austria, and Italy in a defensive treaty. With the Reinsurance Treaty of 1887, Russia and Germany agreed to remain neutral if either was attacked.

But in 1888, a new emperor, Kaiser William II (r. 1888–1918), ascended the German throne. William, an ambitious and impatient young man, dismissed Bismarck in 1890 and launched Germany down a more dangerous path. The new kaiser broke with Bismarck's policies in two areas. First, William let the Reinsurance Treaty with Russia lapse, thus allowing anti-German France to join with Russia in the Franco-Russian Alliance of 1894. Germany now faced exactly the sort of encirclement by hostile powers, and the resulting threat of a two-front war, that Bismarck had sought to avoid.

Second, William favored a new "world policy" (*Weltpolitik*) for Germany that alienated Britain. Whereas Bismarck had confined Germany's interests to Europe, William and many prominent Germans wanted to see Germany claim its "place in the sun" as a global power: Germany needed a mighty overseas empire and a navy to defend it. Such policies were guaranteed to aggravate the British. As an island state dependent on its overseas empire, Britain based its defense on its naval supremacy. From the British point of view, a strong German navy challenged British national security and an expanding German empire conflicted with British imperial interests.

Hostility toward German ambitions overcame Britain's long tradition of "splendid isolation" from continental entanglements. In the first decade of the twentieth century, a series of military and economic arrangements formed ever-tighter links between Britain, Russia, and France, clearing the way for the formation of the **Triple Entente** among these three powers. An informal association rather than a formal alliance, the Triple Entente did not *require* Britain to join in a war against Germany. Many British officials, however, viewed Germany as the major threat to British interests.

In this situation, German policymakers placed heavy emphasis on the alliance with Austria-Hungary. Strengthening this crucial ally became paramount. In July 1914, then, when Austrian officials debated their response to the assassination of Franz Ferdinand, the German government urged a quick and decisive blow against Serbia. Kaiser William assured the Austrian ambassador that Germany would stand by Austria no matter what the cost.

Both German and Austrian policymakers recognized that the cost might well be war with Russia. Eager to expand its influence in the Balkan region (and so gain access to the Mediterranean Sea), the Russian imperial regime had for decades positioned itself as the champion of Slavic peoples in the Balkans and as the protector of independent Slavic states such as Serbia. Thus, if Austria attacked Serbia, Russia might well mobilize in Serbia's defense.

German officials gambled, however, that Russia was not yet strong enough to wage war on Serbia's behalf. A decade earlier, Russia's defeat in the Russo-Japanese

Triple Alliance Defensive alliance of Germany, Austria-Hungary, and Italy, signed in 1882.

Triple Entente Informal defensive agreement linking France, Great Britain, and Russia before World War I.

War (see Chapter 23) had exposed its military weakness. Yet if Russia did choose war, then, the German chancellor Theobald von Bethmann-Hollweg explained, Germany's chances of victory were "better now than in one or two years' time."[1] Bethmann-Hollweg and his advisers knew that the tsarist government, in response to its loss to Japan, had implemented a military reform and rearmament program. Russia would only grow stronger.

Mobilization Plans and the Industrialized Military

The alliance system helps explain the beginnings of World War I: Germany's alliance with Austria emboldened Austrian policymakers to attack Serbia, while the links between Serbia and Russia made it likely that this attack would pull in the Russian Empire—and Russia was allied with France. Alliances alone, however, did not transform the Austro-Serbian conflict into a European war. No alliance *required* either Russia or Britain to enter the fray. Moreover, Italy, a member of the Triple Alliance with Germany and Austria, did not join these two powers in declaring war in August 1914. In fact, when Italy entered the war in 1915, it fought *against* Germany and Austria (see **Map 25.1**).

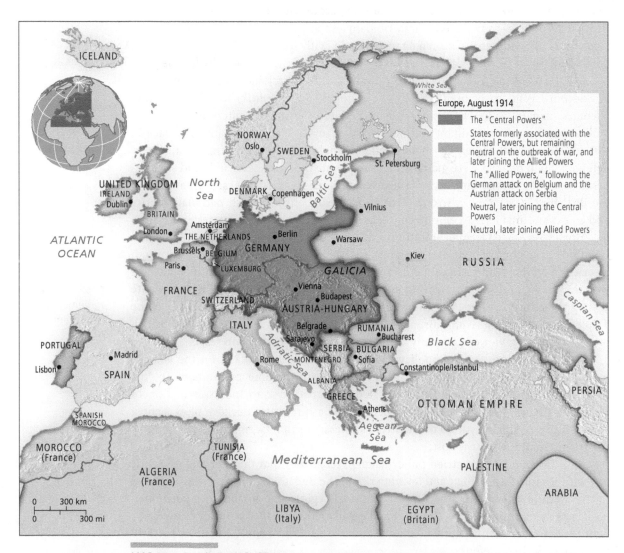

MAP **25.1** EUROPE, AUGUST 1914 In August 1914 each of the Central Powers faced the challenge of war on two fronts, but the entry of the Ottoman Empire into the war on the side of the Central Powers in November 1914 blocked Allied supply lines to Russia through the Mediterranean. What advantages did the alliance with the Ottoman Empire confer on Germany and Austria-Hungary?

To understand the origins of World War I, then, we need to look not only at the impact of rival alliance systems, but also at the widening gap between the expectations of traditional diplomacy and the requirements of an industrialized military. This growing gap ensured that when preparations for war began in the summer of 1914, control of the situation slipped out of the hands of the diplomats and their political superiors and into the grasp of the generals. The generals had planned for a European war. Once set in motion, their plans dictated events.

An important factor in these plans was the railroad, which enabled military planners to move large numbers of men quickly to precise locations. The speed with which governments could now throw armies into battle muddled the distinction between mobilization and actual war. *Mobilization* refers to the transformation of a standing army into a fighting force—calling up reserves, requisitioning supplies, enlisting volunteers or draftees, moving troops to battle stations. Traditionally, mobilization meant preparation for a possible fight, a process that took months and could be halted if the diplomats succeeded in avoiding war. But the railroads accelerated the mobilization process and thereby altered military planning. Aware that the enemy could also mobilize quickly, planners stressed the importance of preventive attacks, of striking before being struck. Once a state mobilized, the momentum toward war seemed almost irresistible.

These developments help explain the **Schlieffen Plan**, the military blueprint that structured German actions—and Allied reactions—in the summer of 1914. After the creation of the Franco-Russian Alliance in 1894, German military planners had to prepare for a two-front war. They devised the Schlieffen Plan for just that eventuality. The plan assumed that Russia's mobilization would take time: The vastness of its territory and the underdevelopment of its industrial infrastructure (including railroads) would slow its military mobilization and so guarantee that Russian troops would not pose an immediate threat to German borders. According to the Schlieffen Plan, then, the smaller Austrian army would hold off the slowly mobilizing Russians while the German army moved with lightning speed against France (see **Map 25.2**). After a quick knock-out blow against France, the Germans would concentrate on defeating Russia.

The Schlieffen Plan's need for speed thus pressured German politicians to treat a Russian declaration of mobilization as a declaration of war itself. As soon as Russia began to mobilize, German military leaders pushed their political counterparts to break off diplomatic negotiations so that the troop-laden trains could set off. Only two days elapsed between Russia's order of mobilization and the German declaration of war.

The need for speed also dictated that the attack against France would proceed via Belgium. Because German planners knew that the French expected any German attack to come through Alsace and Lorraine (the provinces that the Germans had taken from France after the Franco-Prussian War), the Schlieffen Plan called for the bulk of the German army to avoid France's fortified northeastern border (see Map 25.2) and instead swing to the west. Moving in a wide arc, the German army would flood into France through Belgium, encircle Paris, and scoop up the French forces before their generals knew what had hit them. With France out of the fight, the German troops would then board trains and speed back to the Eastern Front to join their Austrian allies.

By invading Belgium, German policymakers knew they risked bringing Britain into the war, as a longstanding international agreement appointed Britain Belgium's protector. Yet German policymakers gambled that Britain would stay out of the conflict. Again their gamble failed. Convinced that Germany threatened British economic and imperial interests, Britain's policymakers regarded the German invasion of Belgium as the pretext they needed to enter the war with mass support. Thus, just six weeks after a Serbian terrorist shot an Austrian archduke in Bosnia, British and German soldiers were killing each other in the mud of northern France.

Schlieffen Plan German military plan devised in 1905 that called for a sweeping attack on France through Belgium and the Netherlands.

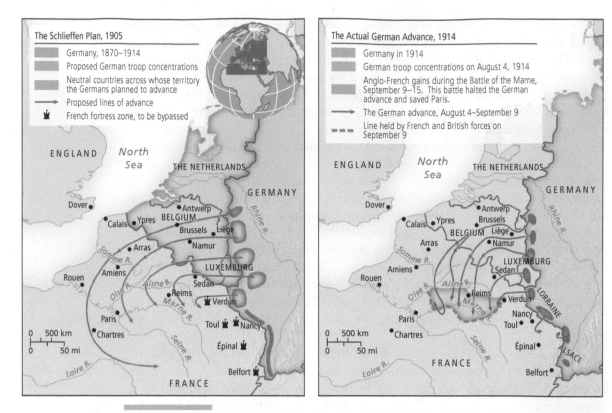

MAP 25.2 (A) THE SCHLIEFFEN PLAN, 1905 AND (B) THE ACTUAL GERMAN ADVANCE, 1914 Count Alfred von Schlieffen's original plan of 1905 called for the sleeves of the German soldiers on the right flank to brush the English Channel: The German army would sweep in a huge arching movement west. In the fall of 1914 Helmuth von Moltke modified Schlieffen's plan: Compare these two maps. Why do some military historians argue that Schlieffen's plan would have succeeded if carried out in its original form?

The Will to War

The needs of an industrialized military outweighed traditional diplomacy and pushed those soldiers into that mud. Similarly, new pressures from public opinion constrained diplomats in the summer of 1914. This public pressure, or the "will to war," constituted the fourth factor in the outbreak of World War I.

Still drawn largely from the aristocracy, diplomats sought to maintain the balance of power in a Europe unbalanced by the forces of not only nationalism and industrial change, but also mass politics. The widening of the franchise meant that public opinion now played a role in international relations. Most new voters relied on the popular press—cheap newspapers marketed to a semiliterate public—for their understanding of foreign affairs. The banner headlines, large photographs, and short, simplified stories in these newspapers transformed the dense complexities of foreign relations into a compelling drama of Good Guys versus Bad Guys. Well-schooled in national identity, ordinary Europeans by 1914 tended to view foreign affairs as a giant nationalistic competition. They wanted evidence that "we" were ahead of "them."

In the last weeks of July 1914, pro-war crowds gathered in large cities, but not all Europeans welcomed the prospect of war. In Berlin, for example, 30,000 middle-class men and women paraded through the streets on the evening of July 25, singing patriotic songs and massing around statues of German heroes, while in working-class neighborhoods antiwar demonstrations received solid support. The declaration of war, however, silenced these demonstrations. Opposition to the war muted after August 1914, even among working-class socialists. National loyalty proved stronger than class solidarity.

What made the idea of war so appealing to so many in 1914? Some Europeans saw war as a powerful cleanser that would scour society of corruption. As Chapter 24

CHRONOLOGY: THE OUTBREAK OF THE FIRST WORLD WAR, 1914

June 28
Assassination of Archduke Franz Ferdinand.
June 28

July 28
July 28
Austro-Hungarian declaration of war against Serbia.

July 30
Russian mobilization.
July 30

July 31
July 31
French, Austrian, and German mobilization.

August 1
German declaration of war on Russia.
August 1

August 3
August 3
German declaration of war on France.

August 4
German invasion of Belgium; British declaration of war against Germany.
August 4

explained, fears of racial degeneration and gender confusion marked the years before 1914. War seemed to provide an opportunity for men to reassert their virility and their superiority. It also offered them the chance to be part of something bigger than themselves—to move beyond the boundaries of their often-restricted lives and join in what was presented as a great national crusade. Carl Zuckmayer, a German playwright and novelist who volunteered to fight, later explained that men like him welcomed the war as bringing "liberation . . . from . . . the saturation, the stuffy air, the petrifaction of our world."[2]

For political leaders, war provided the opportunity to mask social conflicts and to displace domestic hostilities onto the battlefield. Violent trade unionism, socialist demands for revolutionary changes, anarchist-inspired assassinations, ethnic terrorism, and feminist protests had shaken the West in the decades before 1914. To many European elites, their society seemed on the verge of disintegration. But, as the future British prime minister Winston Churchill explained, war united societies with "a higher principle of hatred."

The war for which university students cheered, politicians schemed, and generals planned was not anything like the war that happened, however. Most people anticipated a short war. Theorists argued that the cost of waging an industrial war was so high that no state could sustain a conflict for long. The men who marched off to war in August 1914 expected that they would be home by Christmas. Instead, if they survived, which few of them did, they would spend not only that Christmas, but the next three, in the midst of unprecedented horror.

The Experience of Total War

Counting on *élan*, the French military spirit, to see them to victory, French troops swung into battle sporting bright red pants and flashy blue tunics. At their head rode the cream of the French military education system, the graduates of the Saint-Cyr military academy, who charged wearing their parade dress of white gloves and plumed hats. All that color and dash made easy targets for the German machine guns. As one military historian wrote, "Never have machine-gunners had such a heyday. The French stubble-fields became transformed into gay carpets of red and blue."[3] Those "gay carpets," colored with the blood and broken bodies of young French men, signaled that this would be a war of unexpected slaughter.

The Western Front: Stalemate in the Trenches

Implementing a modified version of the Schlieffen Plan (see Map 25.2), German troops swept through Belgium into France. By the first week of September they seemed poised to take Paris. This rapid advance, however, overstretched German supply lines, allowing French and British forces to turn back the Germans at the Marne River. In an episode that signaled the importance of the internal combustion engine—and the oil that fueled it—in modern warfare, an ingenious French commander exploited a gap in the German lines by moving troops rapidly from Paris to the front in the only vehicles available: taxicabs. (The army paid the drivers full fare for the trip.)

Taxicabs saved Paris, but the Allied forces failed to push the Germans out of France. By the middle of October, German, British, and French soldiers huddled in trenches that eventually extended more than 300 miles from the Belgian coast to the borders of Switzerland. There they stayed for the next four years.

HOLES AND DITCHES Siegfried Sassoon, a British poet and a World War I veteran, insisted that "when all is said and done, this war was a matter of holes and ditches."[4] From the strategic point of view, these holes and ditches—the trenches—were defensive fortifications, and the long stalemate on the Western Front shows that they worked well. Attacking infantry units walked forward against an enemy armed with machine guns and sheltered behind wide barbed-wire fences and a thick wall of dirt and sandbags. Despite numerous attempts between the fall of 1914 and the spring of 1918, neither side was able to break through the enemy line.

A discussion of trench strategy, however, conveys nothing of the appalling misery summed up by the term *trench warfare*. Imagine standing in a ditch about seven or eight feet deep and about three or four feet wide. The walls of the ditches are packed mud, propped up with sandbags. Wooden boards cover the floor, but the mud squelches between them. Piles of sandbags and barbed-wire barricades on the enemy's side of the ditch deepen your sense of being underground. Moreover, the trenches do not run in tidy straight lines. Instead, they zigzag at sharp angles, restricting the range of fire for enemy snipers and limiting the impact of explosives, but also ensuring that everywhere you look you see a wall of mud. Because you are in northern France, it is probably raining. Thus, you are standing not on but *in* mud—if you are lucky. In some parts of the line, soldiers stand in muddy water up to a foot deep. On the other side of your sandbag defenses stretches **no-man's-land**, the territory dividing the British and French trench systems from the German. Pocked with deep craters from heavy shelling, often a sea of mud churned up by the artillery, no-man's-land is littered with stinking corpses in various states of decomposition—all that is left of the soldiers who

no-man's-land The area between the combatants' trenches on the Western Front during World War I.

⌕ **View the Closer Look**　Trench Warfare

LIFE AND DEATH IN THE TRENCHES　The dead, the dying, and the surviving jostle one another in a French trench.

died during previous attacks. Your constant companions are lice (the term *lousy* was coined on the Western Front) and rats. For the rats, the war is an endless feast as they grow enormously fat, nibbling their way through the piles of dead.

From 1915 on, the horror of the Western Front escalated with the introduction of a new killing tool—poison gas, first deployed by the Germans in the spring of 1915. The Allies condemned the use of poison gas as inhumane, but within months the British and French, too, were firing poison gas canisters across the lines. The consequences were appalling: blinded eyes, blistered skin, seared lungs, death by asphyxiation. By

A BATTERY SHELLED BY PERCY WYNDHAM LEWIS (1919) The mechanical nature of the war on the Western Front dominated many soldiers' accounts. Seeking the chance to be heroes, men volunteered to fight and found themselves reduced to interchangeable parts in a colossal war machine. In works such as *A Battery Shelled*, British artist Percy Wyndham Lewis (1882–1957) used modernist techniques to represent the reality of mechanized war. Lewis served in a British artillery unit and, in 1917, became an "Official War Artist," charged with recording and memorializing the war through painting. In this work, a burial party digs a grave for a gunner killed by enemy shells. The three soldiers in the foreground, however, seem utterly detached, as distanced from the death as the men who fired the shells.

SOURCE: Bridgeman IWM 28827.

1916, with the gas mask a standard part of every soldier's uniform, military companies resembled hordes of insects.

And, like insects, they were easily squashed. In the summer of 1915 an average of 300 British men became casualties on the Western Front every day, not because they were wounded in an attack, but because they were picked off by snipers, felled by an exploding shell, or wasted by disease brought on by living in the mud amid putrefying corpses.

THE OFFENSIVES The offensives, the attacks launched by both sides on the Western Front, sent the numbers of dead and wounded soaring. None of the elderly commanders—the Germans Helmuth von Moltke and Erich von Falkenhayn, the French Joseph Joffre and Ferdinand Foch, and the British Douglas Haig and John French—knew what to make of trench warfare. Schooled to believe that war was about attacking, they sought vainly to move this conflict out of the ditches by throwing masses of both artillery and men against the enemy lines. But time and time again the machine gun foiled these mass attacks.

The Battle of the Somme, described in the opening of this chapter, illustrates a typical offensive on the Western Front. By the end of 1917, the death tolls on the Western Front rose to astonishing levels, yet neither side had gained much ground. Many soldiers, who enlisted not for a specific term or tour of duty but "for the duration"— until the war ended—became convinced that only the dead escaped from the trenches. (See *Different Voices* in this chapter.)

 Read the Document

Erich Maria Remarque, *All Quiet on the Western Front*

The War in Eastern Europe

The Western Front was only one of several theaters of war. The Italian and Austrian armies, for example, fought along a stationary front for two brutal years after Italy joined the war on the Allies' side. Characterized by futile offensives and essential immobility, the war in Italy mirrored the conflict on the Western Front. In eastern Europe, however, a different plot unfolded.

Different Voices

The Cultural Impact of the Western Front

Many of the upper- and middle-class officers fighting on the Western Front volunteered out of love for their country, an idealistic view of war as a heroic mission, and a longing for adventure. British recruiting posters described the war as the "Greatest Game of All." Trench warfare defied these expectations. The following poems, written by two young upper-middle-class British officers, illustrate the shift from the initial enthusiasm for the war to later disillusionment and despair. Neither man survived the war: Rupert Brooke died of blood-poisoning on his way to Gallipoli in 1915. Wilfred Owen was killed in battle in 1918, just days before the war ended.

In the sonnet series "1914," written just as the war began, Rupert Brooke not only welcomed the war but, as his first subtitle indicates, linked the outbreak of war, and the chance of heroic death, to the coming of internal or personal peace.

1914. I. Peace

Now, God be thanked Who has matched us with His hour,
And caught our youth, and wakened us from sleeping,
With hand made sure, clear eye, and sharpened power,
To turn, as swimmers into cleanness leaping,
Glad from a world grown old and cold and weary
Leave the sick hearts that honor could not move,
And half-men, and their dirty songs and dreary,
And all the little emptiness of love.

Oh! we, who have known shame, we have found release there,
Where there's no ill, no grief, but sleep is mending,
Naught broken save the body, lost but breath;
Nothing to shake the laughing heart's song peace there
But only agony, and that has ending;
And the worst friend and enemy is but Death.

1914. III. The Dead

Blow out, you bugles, over the rich Dead!
There's none of these so lonely and poor of old,
But, dying, has made us rarer gifts than gold.
These laid the world away; poured out the red
Sweet wine of youth; gave up the years to be
Of work and joy, and that unhoped serene,
That men call age; and those who would have been,
Their sons, they gave, their immortality.
Blow, bugles, blow! They brought us, for our dearth,
Holiness, lacked so long, and Love, and Pain.
Honour has come back, as a king, to earth,
And paid his subjects with a royal wage;
And Nobleness walks in our ways again;
And we have come into our heritage.

SOURCE: From "Peace" from "1914" Five Sonnets by Rupert Brooke. London: Sidgwick & Jackson, 1915.

Owen composed this piece, one of the most famous poems written during World War I, in several drafts between October 1917 and March 1918. The poem flatly describes a soldier being asphyxiated by poison gas while Owen and the rest of the company watch.

Dulce et Decorum Est by Wilfred Owen

Bent double, like old beggars under sacks,
Knock-kneed, coughing like hags,
we cursed through sludge,
Till on the haunting flares we turned our backs
And towards our distant rest began to trudge.
Men marched asleep. Many had lost their boots
But limped on, blood-shod. All went lame; all blind;
Drunk with fatigue; deaf even to the hoots
Of tired, outstripped Five-Nines that dropped behind.
Gas! Gas! Quick, boys!—An ecstasy of fumbling,
Fitting the clumsy helmets just in time;
But someone still was yelling out and stumbling
And flound'ring like a man in fire or lime . . .
Dim, through the misty panes and thick green light,
As under a green sea, I saw him drowning.
In all my dreams, before my helpless sight,
He plunges at me, guttering, choking, drowning.

If in some smothering dreams you too could pace
Behind the wagon that we flung him in,
And watch the white eyes writhing in his face,
His hanging face, like a devil's sick of sin;
If you could hear, at every jolt, the blood
Come gargling from the froth-corrupted lungs,
Obscene as cancer, bitter as the cud
Of vile, incurable sores on innocent tongues,—
My friend, you would not tell with such high zest
To children ardent for some desperate glory,
The old Lie: "Dulce et decorum est
Pro patria mori."*

SOURCE: "Dulce et Decorum Est" from Poems by Wilfred Owen, with an Introduction by Siegfried Sassoon. London: Chatto and Windus, 1920.

For Discussion

1. Why did Brooke see the war as a path to some sort of personal peace? How might his enthusiasm for war reflect the power of what Owen labeled "The old Lie"?

2. Compare the language and imagery in the two poems. How do the words themselves demonstrate a shift in the view of war?

3. Did disillusionment of soldiers on the Western Front differ from the disillusionment experienced by most soldiers, regardless of time or place? Is not the experience of combat always a rude awakening from innocence into brutal knowledge?

*"It is sweet and right to die for one's country."

A WAR OF MOVEMENT If the war on the Western Front was a war of mud and ditches, the conflict on the Eastern Front was a war of movement. For three years, massive armies surged back and forth, as the plains and mountains of eastern Europe echoed with the tumult of spectacular advances, headlong retreats, escalating ethnic conflict, and, finally, political revolution.

When the war began in August 1914, Russian troops headed in a two-pronged onslaught against Germany and against Austria (see **Map 25.3**). Although surprised by the speed of the Russian advance, German troops in East Prussia turned the Russian tide at the Battle of Tannenberg and then advanced steadily into the Russian Empire. The next year, a combined German and Austrian assault forced the Russian army to retreat more than 300 miles into its own territory. Russian military losses by the end of 1915 were astounding, with well over one million soldiers killed, another million wounded, and 900,000 taken prisoner. Russian soldiers pushed back into Austria-Hungary in June 1916, but could not sustain the attack. They advanced again in the summer of 1917, but this offensive also soon disintegrated into a retreat.

These retreats revealed that the Russian Empire's economic and political structures could not withstand the pressures of total war. Russian supply lines were so overextended that the poorly fed and inadequately clothed Russian troops found themselves without ammunition and unable to press ahead. Demoralized, they began to desert in large numbers.

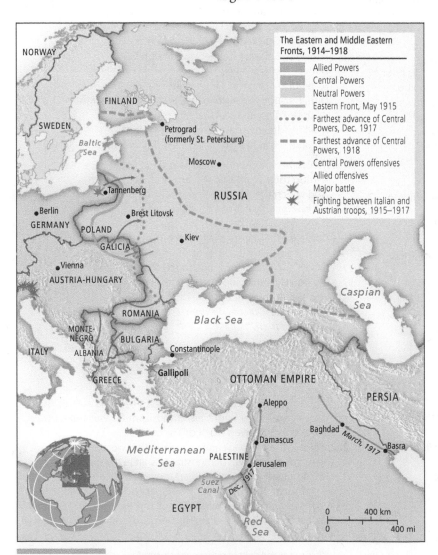

MAP **25.3** THE EASTERN AND MIDDLE EASTERN FRONTS, 1914–1918 Unlike the Western Front, the Eastern Front was far from stationary. How does this map help explain why many Germans found their country's defeat in November 1918 to be incomprehensible?

Ⓠ **View the Map**

Russian Armies on the Eastern Front in World War I

Civilians within the Russian Empire also suffered enormously. As its army retreated, the tsarist regime ordered a "scorched earth" policy: Russian soldiers bombed their own cities, dismantled factories, burned farm buildings and crops, and killed livestock. Many groups who lived in the borderlands and were judged potentially disloyal—including Poles, German-speaking Lutherans, and Jews—were deported to the east. These deportations, combined with the scorched earth policy that left millions without a means of subsistence, created a massive wave of refugees, what one historian has termed "a whole empire walking."[5]

By 1917 the Russian Empire hovered on the brink of collapse. Soldiers, workers, and peasants grew impatient with wartime deprivations and demands. Linguistic and religious minorities, particularly those who endured forcible deportation, turned increasingly to anti-Russian nationalist politics.

This disaffection and disintegration led to the Russian Revolution. As we will explore in detail later in this chapter, revolution forced the tsar to abdicate in February 1917. In October, a small group of socialist revolutionaries called the Bolsheviks seized control and moved quickly to pull Russia out of the war.

GERMANY AND THE EAST The German army thus *defeated* its enemy on the Eastern Front. From 1915 on, the German army

"A WHOLE EMPIRE WALKING" This hand-colored slide features a group of refugees in wartime Russia. By 1917, approximately seven million refugees wandered the Russian Empire, subject to months or years of hunger, cold, disease, rape, looting, and beatings.

occupied huge swathes of what had been the Russian Empire. The **Treaty of Brest-Litovsk**, signed in 1918, confirmed this occupation by ceding to Germany all of imperial Russia's western territories and one-third of its population.

Many of the regions that German soldiers occupied between 1915 and 1919 were less industrially developed and urbanized than Germany; moreover, these lands had been systematically "scorched" by the retreating Russian troops. Confronted with societies in the midst of chaos, the Germans concluded that "the East" was primitive and barbaric, in need of German civilization and order.

German rule, however, only intensified the suffering of the borderland populations. High taxation rates, forced labor, and the confiscation of scarce food and supplies resulted in famine in many occupied areas by 1917. Rather than Germanizing these peoples, German rule helped strengthen national identities. As Lithuanians, Poles, Ukrainians, and others fought for survival, they increasingly began to think of themselves in national terms.

THE FORGOTTEN FRONT: THE BALKANS In southeastern Europe, World War I was in many ways the "Third Balkan War," yet another installment in an ongoing competition for territory and power. In 1912 and again in 1913, Greece, Bulgaria, Romania, and Serbia had fought each other in the First and Second Balkan Wars. Hence, in 1915 Bulgaria allied with the Central Powers to gain back the territory it had lost in the Second Balkan War while Romania joined the Allies in 1916 to protect its hold on that territory.

For most of the war, the Central Powers controlled the Balkans. A joint Bulgarian, German, and Austro-Hungarian invasion crushed Romania. The Serbian experience was even bleaker. By November of 1915, the Serbian army had been pushed to the Albanian border. Some 200,000 Serbian soldiers fled over the snow-swept mountains of Albania to the Adriatic Sea in the disastrous "Winter March." Austrian troops occupied Serbia and placed the country under military rule. By the war's end, approximately 25 percent of Serbian citizens lay dead.

Treaty of Brest-Litovsk Treaty between Germany and Bolshevik-controlled Russia, signed in March 1918, that ceded to Germany all of Russia's western territories.

The World at War

The imperialist expansion of the later nineteenth century ensured that as soon as the war began, it jumped outside European borders. The British and French Empires supplied the Allies with invaluable military and manpower resources. Australia, New Zealand, Canada, India, South Africa, and Ireland supplied no less than 40 percent of Britain's military manpower during the war. More than 650,000 men from Indochina, Algeria, and French West Africa assisted the French war effort.

Fighting fronts multiplied around the globe as combatants struggled for imperial and European supremacy (see **Map 25.4**). Portugal joined the Allies largely because it hoped to expand its colonial possessions in Africa. Japan seized the opportunity to snatch German territories in China while using its navy to protect Allied troop and supply ships. By the end of 1914, Japanese, Australian, and New Zealander troops occupied most of Germany's island colonies in the Pacific as well.

The Middle East also became a key theater of war. Once the Ottoman Empire joined the Central Powers, Britain's Middle Eastern economic and military interests lay vulnerable. Britain was desperate to protect Allied access to the Suez Canal—a vital link to the soldiers and supplies of India, Australia, and New Zealand—and to Persian oil fields, an important source of fuel for the British navy.

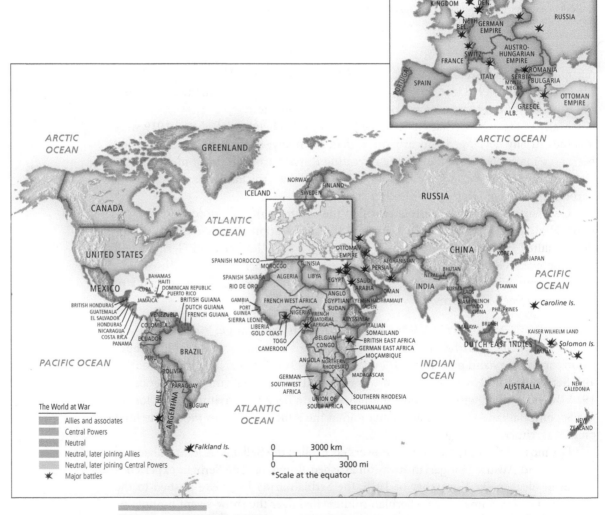

MAP **25.4** THE WORLD AT WAR Imperialist relationships and global economics ensured that a European conflict became a world war. In Africa, for example, Portuguese and South African troops fought a bush war against German and native soldiers. How does this map illustrate the emergence of Japan and the United States as global powers? Why do you think that several Latin American countries declared war on Germany in April 1917?

To defeat the Ottoman Empire in the Middle East, the British joined forces with Arab nationalists. Led by a British soldier named T. E. Lawrence (1888–1935)—better known as "Lawrence of Arabia"—and inspired by promises of postwar national independence, Arab nationalists used guerilla warfare to destroy what remained of Ottoman rule in the Middle East. By 1917 the Ottomans had lost control of almost the entire coastal region of the Arabian Peninsula bordering the Red Sea, and Lawrence and his Arab allies had captured Jerusalem.

THE WAR AT SEA AND THE ENTRY OF THE UNITED STATES While infantrymen rotted in trenches and froze in mountain passes, the German and British navies fought a critical war at sea. German submarines sought to cut Britain's imperial lifeline and starve out its civilian population by sinking ships before they could reach British ports. Almost 14,000 British sailors and civilians died in these submarine attacks. In turn, British destroyers stretched a blockade across all ocean and sea passageways to Germany and its allies.

The Allied blockade prevented food and other essential raw materials from reaching Germany, Austria-Hungary, and their associates. Food shortages sparked riots in more than 30 German cities in 1916. When the potato crop that year failed and eliminated one of the only remaining sources of nutrition, children's rations fell to *one-tenth* of their actual needs.

Desperate to win the war quickly, German policymakers in 1917 decided to escalate their submarine war against Britain. Suspecting (correctly) that supposedly neutral American passenger ships were delivering essential war materiel to Britain, the German government ordered its submarines to sink without warning any ship heading for British shores. The Germans recognized that this unrestricted submarine warfare would probably pull the United States into the war. But Germany stood on the brink of economic collapse, and German policymakers decided they had no choice. They gambled that they would defeat the Allies in a last-ditch effort before the United States' entry into the war could make much of a difference.

The United States declared war on Germany in April 1917. Outrage over American deaths at sea served as the most immediate cause of American entry into the war. Four other factors also played a role. First, Franco-British news stories about German atrocities during the invasion of Belgium persuaded many Americans that right rested on the Allied side. Second, the Russian Revolution removed an important obstacle to American cooperation with the Allies—the tsarist regime. Americans had balked at the idea of allying with the repressive government of Tsar Nicholas II, but the February Revolution, which overthrew Nicholas, offered American policymakers a more acceptable wartime partner. Third, by the time President Woodrow Wilson asked the U.S. Congress for a declaration of war, the American economy was intertwined with that of the Allies. Trade between the United States and the Allied states had grown from $825 million in 1914 to more than $3 billion in 1916, and American bankers

A WORLD AT WAR: ALGERIAN SOLDIERS Crammed into a freight car, Algerian soldiers receive drinks before heading to the Western Front. Forces from Europe's overseas empires fought on both the Western and Eastern Fronts.

had loaned more than $2 billion to the Allied governments. Finally, the German government committed a serious blunder in the spring of 1917 when it offered to assist Mexico in recovering New Mexico, Arizona, and Texas in exchange for Mexican support should war break out between Germany and the United States. The interception of a telegram sent by the German foreign minister Arthur Zimmermann exposed this offer and inflamed anti-German sentiment in the United States. The German policy of unrestricted submarine warfare, then, put flame to kindling that was already in place.

The U.S. declaration of war (followed by those of Brazil, Costa Rica, Cuba, Guatemala, Haiti, Honduras, Nicaragua, and Panama) provided an immediate psychological boost for the Allies, but several months passed before American troops arrived on the battlefield in significant numbers. By July 1918, however, the United States was sending 300,000 fresh soldiers to Europe each month. The Allies now had access to an almost unlimited supply of military materials and men. Eventually nearly two million American soldiers were sent to Europe and almost 49,000 American soldiers died in battle.

BACK IN MOTION: THE WESTERN FRONT IN 1918 Faced with the prospect of having to fight fresh American forces, German policymakers decided to gamble one more time. On March 2, 1918—before the bulk of the U.S. army had been deployed—the German army launched an overwhelming ground assault against British and French lines. The gamble almost succeeded. In just 30 minutes the German troops broke through the British front line. By April the German army stood just 50 miles from Paris.

What explains this sudden shift on the Western Front from a conflict characterized by stalemate to a war of decisive movement? As we have seen, in the first years of the war commanders remained committed to offensive techniques suited to an age of preindustrial warfare—the mass charge, the cavalry attack—even though industrial technologies such as the machine gun had transformed the power of defensive war. Certainly, Western commanders were well-acquainted with the killing potential of the machine gun. In the imperial conflicts discussed in Chapter 24, the machine gun enabled small European forces to defeat larger indigenous armies. But on the Western Front, both sides possessed the machine gun. In other words, both sides were good on defense but poor on offense.

In 1918, however, the Germans came up with new offensive strategies. Instead of a frontal assault dictated by commanders sitting well behind the lines, Germany's offensive of 1918 consisted of a series of small group attacks aiming to cut behind British and French positions rather than straight on against them. In addition, the Germans in 1918 scrapped the preliminary artillery barrage that signaled when and where an attack was about to begin. In place of the barrage they employed sudden gas and artillery bursts throughout the offensive. The rapid German advance in the spring of 1918 showed that technique had caught up with technology.

In July, however, the Allies stopped the German advance. In August they broke through the German lines and began to push the German army backward. Throughout the summer the push continued. By September the Western Front, which had stood so stationary for so long, was rolling eastward at a rapid clip.

The final German gamble failed for three reasons: First, the rapidity of the advance overstrained German manpower and supply lines. Second, the Allies learned from their enemies and adopted the same new offensive strategies. And third, the Allies figured out how to make effective use of a new offensive technology—the tank. Developed in Britain, the tank obliterated the defensive advantages of machine-gun-fortified trenches. A twentieth-century offense met a twentieth-century defense, and the war turned mobile.

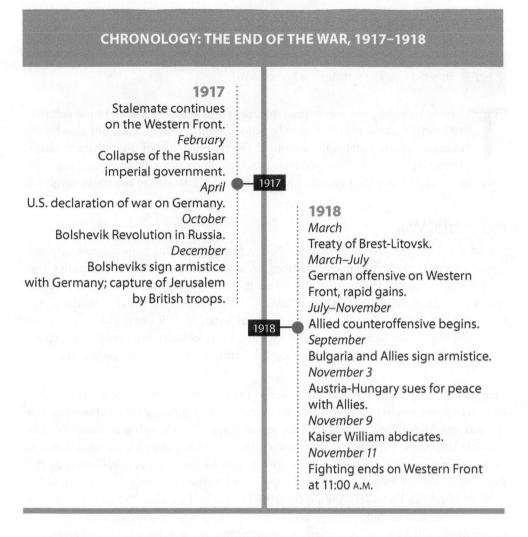

CHRONOLOGY: THE END OF THE WAR, 1917–1918

1917
Stalemate continues
on the Western Front.
February
Collapse of the Russian
imperial government.
April
U.S. declaration of war on Germany.
October
Bolshevik Revolution in Russia.
December
Bolsheviks sign armistice
with Germany; capture of Jerusalem
by British troops.

1917

1918
March
Treaty of Brest-Litovsk.
March–July
German offensive on Western
Front, rapid gains.
July–November
Allied counteroffensive begins.
September
Bulgaria and Allies sign armistice.
November 3
Austria-Hungary sues for peace
with Allies.
November 9
Kaiser William abdicates.
November 11
Fighting ends on Western Front
at 11:00 A.M.

1918

Reinforced with fresh American troops and the promise of more to come, the Allied forces surged forward against the hungry and demoralized Germans. When the Bulgarian, Ottoman, and Austrian armies collapsed in September and October, Germany stood alone. On November 11, 1918, German leaders signed an armistice and the war ended. The Treaty of Brest-Litovsk was declared void, and in 1919 German troops withdrew from the eastern lands they had occupied.

A VERY DIFFERENT BATTLE As the war drew to a close in 1918, a very different battle began. In the spring, American soldiers training at Camp Funston, Kansas, began to sicken with a severe form of influenza—the flu. When American units from the camp arrived on the Western Front, the flu virus traveled along with them and soon spread throughout the armies and then, via demobilized soldiers, nurses, and administrators, back to their home countries. By August, a flu pandemic was underway.

The influenza pandemic of 1918–1919 claimed the lives of approximately 50 million victims—far more than died in battle during the war. (Some estimates range as high as 100 million.) No other recorded epidemic killed so many people so quickly. Few people at the time, however, realized the extent of the outbreak. Horrified by what the pandemic might do to civilian morale in a time of total war, governments on both sides censored press reports. Ironically, the pandemic came to be known as the Spanish Flu, because in neutral Spain the government did not restrict press coverage.

 Read the Document

Anna Eisenmenger, "A German Soldier Returns Home"

The Home Fronts

25.1

25.2

25.3

25.4

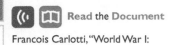

Read the Document

Francois Carlotti, "World War I:
A Frenchman's Recollections"

25.3 How did total war structure the home fronts?

The term *home front* was coined during World War I to highlight the fact that this conflict was fought not only by soldiers on the front lines, but also by civilians at home. Total war demanded the mobilization of a combatant state's productive capacity. Total war recast and in some cases revolutionized not only the economies, but also the political, social, and gender relations of the states involved.

Industrial War

World War I was the first industrial war. Poison gas and machine guns, barbed wire and shovels, canned foods and mass-produced uniforms—all poured out of factories and helped shape this war. Industrialization made it possible for governments to deploy the masses of men mobilized in this conflict. While 170,000 men fought in the Battle of Waterloo in 1815 and 300,000 soldiers in the Battle of Sedan in 1870, *one million* combatants were swept up in the Battle of the Marne in 1914. Only industrialized production could keep these huge armies supplied with weapons, ammunition, and other necessities.

THE EXPANSION OF THE STATE At first, no government realized the crucial role that industrial labor would play in this war. Both military and political leaders believed that the war would end quickly and that success depended on throwing as many men as possible into the front lines. In France, even munitions factories were shut down and their workers sent to the front. Governments practiced "business as usual"—letting the free market decide wages, prices, and supply—with disastrous results. Soaring inflation, growing black markets, public resentment over war profiteering (the practice of private businessmen making huge profits off the war), and, most crucially, shortages of essential military supplies, including ammunition, proved that a total war economy needed total regulation.

Beginning in 1915, both the Allied and Central Powers' governments gradually assumed the power to requisition supplies, dictate wages, limit profits, and forbid workers to change jobs. In Germany, the increasing regulation of the economy was called *war socialism*, a misleading term because it was big business that benefited. The German army worked in partnership with large industrial firms to ensure the supply of war materiel to the front lines, while the Auxiliary Service Law of 1916 drafted all men age 17 to 60 for war work. Measures such as these greatly expanded the size and power of the central governments in the combatant states. For example, in 1914 the British office in charge of military purchases employed 20 clerks. By 1918, it had become the Department of Munitions, a bureaucratic empire with 65,000 employees overseeing more than three million workers in government-owned and -operated munitions plants.

This expansion of governmental power corresponded with restricted individual freedom, even in traditionally liberal states such as Britain. Flying in the face of tradition, in 1916 Britain's government imposed the draft—a clear example of the requirements of the state overriding the desires of the individual. By the war's end, the British government had also restricted the hours that pubs could be open (as a way of encouraging workers to show up for work sober) and tampered with time itself by inventing Daylight Saving Time as a means of maximizing war production.

THE POLITICS OF TOTAL WAR The war's reliance on industrial production greatly empowered industrial producers—the workers. In 1915 both France and Britain abandoned political party competition and formed coalition governments that included socialist and working-class representatives. In return, French and British union leaders agreed to a ban on labor strikes and accepted the temporary "deskilling" of certain jobs—a measure that allowed unskilled laborers, particularly women, to take the place of skilled workers at lower rates of pay.

Nevertheless, the number of labor strikes rose in Britain and France in 1916 and in 1917. Faced with the potential of disintegration on the home front, British and French political leaders reacted similarly. They formed war governments committed to total victory. In Britain, David Lloyd George (1863–1945) became prime minister at the end of 1916. A Welsh artisan's son who had fought hard to reach the top of Britain's class-bound, English-dominated political system, Lloyd George was not a man to settle for a compromise peace. One year later, Georges Clemenceau (1841–1929) became prime minister of France. Nicknamed "the Tiger," Clemenceau demanded victory. When asked to detail his government's program, he replied simply, *Je fais la guerre!*" ("I make war!").

But making war, French and British officials realized, demanded public support. They cultivated this support in two ways. First, they sought to depict the war as a struggle between democracy and authoritarianism—a crusade not for national power or economic gain, but for a better world. Second, they recognized that if they failed to meet the basic needs of ordinary citizens, civilian morale would plummet. Both governments intervened regularly in the economy to ensure that workers received higher wages, better working conditions, and a fair distribution of food stocks. In state-owned munitions factories, workers for the first time received benefits such as communal kitchens and day care. Food rationing actually improved the diets of many poor families. Living standards among employed workers in France and in Britain rose during the war.

The situation in Germany differed significantly. Until the last weeks of the war German political leadership remained in the hands of the conservative elite and the military. Increasingly, Generals Hindenburg and Ludendorff—the heroes of the Battle of Tannenberg—dictated political affairs. The army and big industrial firms seized control of German economic life. Given the power to set prices and profit

BERLIN, 1917. As German civilians line up for scarce food supplies in Berlin in the winter of 1917, an elderly woman collapses, most likely from hunger.

margins, industrialists—not surprisingly—made a killing. Their incomes soared, while escalating inflation and chronic food shortages ground down ordinary workers. In 1917, industrial unrest slowed German war production, civilian discontent reached dangerous levels, and the success of the Allied blockade meant Germans were starving.

The World Turned Upside Down

By the war's end, changes in the relations among classes and between men and women caused many Europeans to feel as if their world had turned upside down. European workers grew more radical as they realized the possibilities of their own collective power and the potential of the state as an instrument of social change. The fact that by 1917 many of these workers were women also had revolutionary implications. In the work world and in society at large, gender roles, like class relations, underwent a marked shift.

THE WAR'S IMPACT ON SOCIAL RELATIONS In the trenches and on the battlefields, World War I had a leveling effect. For many young, middle-, and upper-class soldiers, the war provided their first sustained contact with both manual labor and manual laborers. In letters home, they testified to a newfound respect for both, as the horrors of the war experience broke down rigid class barriers.

On the home front, however, social relations grew more rather than less hostile. During the war years, inflation eroded the savings of middle-class men and women and left them scrambling to maintain their social and economic status. In Germany and throughout eastern Europe, food shortages and falling wages produced a revolutionary situation. By contrast, in Britain and France, a rising standard of living demonstrated to workers the benefits of an interventionist state. Yet class hostilities rose in western Europe, too. Working-class activists demanded that the state continue to regulate the economy in peacetime to improve the standard of living of ordinary workers. Having finally tasted the economic pie, workers fought for a bigger piece, while the middle class struggled to defend its shrinking slice.

THE WAR'S IMPACT ON GENDER RELATIONS By 1916, labor shortages in key military industries, combined with the need to free up as many men as possible for fighting, meant that governments on both sides actively recruited women for the paid workforce. Women were suddenly visible in the public sphere as bus drivers, elevator operators, and train conductors. In eastern Europe, the agricultural labor force came to consist almost entirely of women. In western Europe, women took on dangerous positions in munitions factories, worked just behind the front lines as ambulance drivers and nurses, and in 1917 and 1918 often led the way in walking off the job to demand better conditions.

The impact of the war on women's roles should not be exaggerated, however. Throughout the war, more women continued to work in domestic service—as cooks, maids, nannies—than in any other sector of the economy. The great majority of the women who did move into skilled industrial employment were not new to the paid workforce. Before 1914 they had worked in different, lower-paying jobs. And they certainly were not treated as men's equals. In government-run factories in Britain, women received as little as 50 percent of men's wages for the same job.

Nevertheless, for many women, the war was a liberating experience. With their husbands away, many wives made decisions on their own for the first time. Female munitions workers in Britain received wages three times higher than their prewar earnings. But middle- and upper-class women experienced the sharpest change. In the prewar years, immobility and passivity continued to mark the lives of many middle-class girls—sheltered within the family home, subject to paternal authority, waiting for a marriage proposal. The war threw women into the public space. The middle-class girl who before 1914 was forbidden to travel without a chaperone might be driving an ambulance, splashing through the mud and blood, or washing the bodies of naked working-class soldiers.

At the same time that the war smashed many of the boundaries that had restricted women, it narrowed the world of the middle-class male soldier. While women were on the move—driving buses, flying transport planes, ferrying the wounded—men were stuck in the mud, confined to narrow ditches, waiting for orders. Expecting to be heroic men of action, they found themselves instead living the sort of immobile, passive lives that had characterized the prewar middle-class woman's experience. In total war, even gender roles turned upside down.

Yet when the war ended, many of these radical changes proved to be only temporary. The wartime movement of women into skilled factory jobs and public positions such as bus drivers and train conductors was rapidly reversed. For example, by the terms of the British Restoration of Pre-War Practices Act (1919), women who had taken up skilled factory jobs received two weeks' pay and a train ticket home.

Other changes appeared more permanent. France in 1919 possessed 10 times as many female law students and three times as many female medical students as it had in 1914. British women over age 30 received the vote on a limited basis; in the United States, Germany, and most of the new states in eastern Europe, meanwhile, the achievement of female suffrage was more complete. Cultural changes also seemed to signal a gender revolution. Women smoked in public, raised their hemlines, cut their hair, and threw away their corsets.

ROLE REVERSAL The imagery in this British Red Cross poster infantilized the soldier while making the nurse into a figure of saintly power. Many men found the forced confinement and passivity of trench warfare profoundly unsettling, while many women experienced the war as a time of liberation.

Identifying the Enemy: From Propaganda to Genocide

Many of the changes in gender and class relations resulted from government efforts to regulate the economy for total war. To ensure that their citizens remained committed to the war effort, governments also sought to regulate the production and distribution of ideas. Pacifists and war objectors faced prison sentences and even execution. In France, journalists and rival politicians—even the former prime minister—who dared suggest negotiations with Germany were thrown in prison.

Wartime governments worked to create ideas that would encourage a total war mentality. Propaganda emerged as a crucial political tool. By censoring newspapers and doctoring photographs, politicians ensured that the public viewed the war positively. Poster campaigns using new techniques developed in the advertising industry aroused patriotic fervor.

Fostering a total war mentality also required stirring up hatred for those labeled as the Enemy. In words that were soon set to music and became a popular wartime song, poet and army private Ernst Lissauer (1882–1937) urged Germans to "hate [England] with a lasting hate.... Hate of seventy millions, choking down."[6] Meanwhile in Britain, anti-German feelings ran so high that the royal family changed its name from Hanover

THE HARVEST OF WAR The Turkish massacre of more than one million Armenians illustrates the destructive consequences of combining nationalist hatred with total war. This criminal horror is often seen as foreshadowing the Jewish Holocaust during World War II.

to Windsor in an effort to erase its German lineage. In the ethnic cauldron of eastern Europe, hatred of the enemy often fed hostility toward ethnic minorities, perceived as the enemy within. In Austria-Hungary, for example, more than 500 Bosnian Serbs and hundreds of Ukrainians were shot without trial because they were seen as Russian sympathizers.

The most horrific result of the tendency to look for the enemy at home occurred in the Ottoman Empire, where suspicion of the Armenian minority resulted in mass murder. The brutal "solution" to the so-called "Armenian question" began in April 1915. After arresting Armenian elites (and thus removing potential resistance leaders from Armenian communities), Turkish troops rounded up and killed Armenian men. In some cases, soldiers marched the men outside their town or village and then shot them. In other instances, they were pushed into caves and asphyxiated by fires blocking the entrances. The Ottoman government then ordered the women, children, and the elderly deported to Syria. Driven from their homes on short notice, they marched through mountain and desert terrain without food or water. Rapes and executions were commonplace. Between 1915 and 1918, more than one million Armenian men, women, and children died in this attempt at **genocide**, the murder of an entire people.

genocide The murder of an entire people.

   Read the Document

"A Turkish Officer Describes the Armenian Massacres"

War and Revolution

25.4 What were the consequences of this war for the European and the global political order?

Total war tore at the social and political fabric of European societies. As seams began to fray and gaping holes appeared, many welcomed the opportunity to tear apart the old cloth and weave something new. Some of these revolutionaries were Marxists, aiming to build a socialist Europe. Others were nationalists, determined to assert the rights of their ethnic or linguistic group, or to overthrow their colonial rulers. Yet not all revolutionaries belonged to underground or terrorist groups. The president of the United States, Woodrow Wilson, also demanded a new world order. The peace settlement, however, failed to realize these revolutionary expectations.

The Russian Revolutions

Tsarist Russia began the war already divided. In regions such as Latvia, Lithuania, Poland, and Ukraine, anti-Russian sentiment flared high, and nationalists saw the war as opening the door to independent statehood. Throughout the empire, the clash between Tsar Nicholas II's vision of Russia as a divine autocracy and the political demands of the growing middle and working classes created an explosive situation.

The war brought political chaos to the Russian Empire. Nicholas, a man with a remarkable capacity for self-delusion, insisted on going to the front and commanding his army. He left political affairs in the hands of his wife Alexandra (1872–1918) and her spiritual mentor Grigori Rasputin (1869–1916). Rasputin is one of the more intriguing characters in twentieth-century history. An illiterate, unwashed faith healer from a peasant background, he possessed a well-documented and still-unexplained ability to stop the bleeding of Alexei, the young hemophiliac heir to the throne. Many high-ranking Russians, however, argued that Rasputin was not a miracle worker but a traitor. Because Rasputin opposed the war against Germany, they perceived him as a voice of treason whispering in the German-born tsarina's ear. In 1916 Russian noblemen murdered Rasputin, in hopes of restoring authority and stability to the tsarist government.

THE FEBRUARY REVOLUTION Rasputin's removal achieved little. The French ambassador in Russia wrote in January 1917, "I am obliged to report that, at the present moment, the Russian Empire is run by lunatics."[7] Almost two million Russian soldiers had died and many more had been wounded or taken prisoner. Economic and communications networks had broken down, bread prices were rising, and people were hungry. Even members of the tsarist government began to ask not *if* revolution would occur, but *when*.

The answer came on February 24, 1917 (March 8 on the western calendar). A group of women workers in Petrograd (formerly St. Petersburg) demonstrated to protest inadequate food supplies. Over the course of the next few days, similar demonstrations flickered across the city. On February 27, they coalesced into revolutionary fire when the troops who were ordered to put down the protest joined it instead. Governmental orders lost all authority, and on March 2 Tsar Nicholas was forced to abdicate. The Russian Revolution had begun.

Who now controlled Russia? Two competing centers of power emerged: the Provisional Government and the Petrograd Soviet. On March 12, the Duma, or Russian parliament, created a Provisional Government from among its members. Like the Duma, the new Provisional Government was dominated by members of the gentry and middle classes: professionals, businessmen, intellectuals, bureaucrats. These men tended to be liberals who believed that Russia was now moving along the path toward a parliamentary democracy. They quickly enacted important reforms such as universal suffrage, the eight-hour workday, and civic equality for all citizens. The Provisional Government, however, was exactly what its name indicated: provisional. Its members believed they should not take any drastic measures. Their task was to serve as a caretaker government until an elected Constituent Assembly wrote a constitution for the new Russia.

But at the same time that the Provisional Government was struggling to bring order to the chaos of revolutionary Russia, across the empire socialists, industrial workers, and soldiers formed **soviets**, or councils, to articulate their grievances and hopes.

soviets Workers' and soldiers' councils formed in Russia during the Revolution of 1917.

THE REVOLUTIONARY SPARK On March 8, 1917, thousands of women took to the streets of Petrograd to protest the imposition of bread rationing. Their cries for "Peace and Bread" sparked the Russian Revolution.

The Petrograd Soviet, led by revolutionary socialists, soon became a powerful political rival to the less radical Provisional Government.

But neither the liberals in the Provisional Government nor the socialists in the Petrograd Soviet could control the revolution. A *popular* revolution—a revolution *of the people*—had overthrown Nicholas II, and at the core of this popular revolution stood a simple demand: "Peace, Land, Bread." Soldiers—and most Russians—wanted an immediate end to a war that had long ceased to make any sense to them. Peasants, as always, wanted land, their guarantee of survival in a chaotic world. And city dwellers wanted bread—food in sufficient quantities and at affordable prices.

The Provisional Government could not satisfy these demands. It did promise the gradual redistribution of royal and Church lands, but peasants, unconstrained by the liberal regard for law and the rights of private property, wanted land immediately. More important, by the summer of 1917 no Russian government could have provided bread without providing peace. Russia no longer had the resources both to continue its war effort and to reconstruct its economy. The urban population dwindled as food disappeared from the shops, factories ceased operation because of shortages of raw materials, and the currency lost all value. Peace appeared impossible, however. Not only did Russia have commitments to its allies, but German armies stood deep within Russian territory. A separate peace with Germany would mean huge territorial losses. Only a constitutionally elected government would have the legitimacy to take such a drastic step, most Provisional Government members believed. And so the war continued.

And so, too, did the revolution. Peasants made their own land reform by seizing the land they wanted. Soldiers declared their own peace by deserting. (Of every 1,000-man Russian troop sent to the front, fewer than 250 men made it into combat. The rest deserted.) The Provisional Government grew more unpopular. Not even the appointment of the well-liked socialist and Petrograd Soviet member Alexander Kerensky (1881–1970) as prime minister stabilized the government's position.

THE OCTOBER REVOLUTION This tumultuous situation created the opportunity for the **Bolsheviks**, one of the socialist factions in the Petrograd Soviet, to seize control. In April 1917, the Bolshevik leader, Vladimir Lenin (1870–1924), returned from almost 20 years in exile. While still in his teens, Lenin had committed himself to revolution after his older brother was executed for trying to assassinate Tsar Alexander III. Iron-willed and ruthlessly pragmatic, Lenin argued that a committed group of professional revolutionaries could force a socialist revolution on Russia. In a largely peasant society, the agent of revolutionary change could not be the urban industrial working class (as Karl Marx had theorized). The masses could not make the revolution, and so the Bolshevik or Communist Party, the revolutionary "vanguard," must make it for them.

By the fall of 1917, Bolshevik membership had grown from 10,000 to 250,000, and the party held a majority in the Petrograd Soviet. Lenin now demanded the immediate overthrow of the Provisional Government. On October 25 (November 7 on the Western calendar), Bolshevik fighters captured the Winter Palace in Petrograd, where the Provisional Government was meeting.

The *second* Russian Revolution was underway. The Bolsheviks declared a policy of land and peace—land partition with no compensation to estate owners and an immediate peace with Germany, regardless of the cost. (As we have seen, the cost was high: According to the terms of the Treaty of Brest-Litovsk, signed with Germany in 1918, Russia lost its western territories.)

Promises of peace and land did not win over everyone in Russia, however. Civil war erupted as rival socialists, liberals, and tsarist supporters resisted Bolshevik rule. These "Whites" (distinguished from "Red" Bolsheviks) received assistance from foreign troops. Fearing the spread of communist revolution, 14 countries (including the United States, Britain, France, and Japan) sent 100,000 soldiers to Russia. Non-Russian nationalists fighting for independent statehood joined in the conflict. (See *Justice in History* in this chapter.)

As the war raged, transportation systems shut down, the water supply ceased to run, and furniture became the only source of fuel. When the furniture ran out, entire families froze to death inside apartment blocks. Urban areas emptied as their inhabitants fled to the countryside. By 1921, Moscow had lost half its residents and Petrograd (formerly St. Petersburg) lost two-thirds. Yet rural conditions were also brutal, a consequence of the Bolshevik policy of "War Communism": the nationalization of all land and industry, the suppression of private trade, and a food levy that deprived peasants of almost all they produced. The peasants resisted—actively, with violence, and passively, by refusing to plant crops. Famine resulted.

The civil war killed off more combatants than had World War I, but by 1922 the Bolsheviks emerged victorious over the Whites and many of the nationalist uprisings. Poland, Finland, and the Baltic states (Estonia, Latvia, and Lithuania) retained their

Bolsheviks Minority group of Russian socialists, headed by Vladimir Lenin, who espoused an immediate transition to a socialist state. It became the Communist Party in the Soviet Union.

25.1

25.2

25.3

25.4

View the Closer Look

Bolshevik Revolution Propaganda Poster

 Read the Document

"Bolshevik Seizure of Power, 1917"

Justice in History
Revolutionary Justice: THE NONTRIAL
OF NICHOLAS AND ALEXANDRA

O n July 16, 1918, Bolshevik revolutionaries shot and killed Nicholas II, tsar of Russia; his wife, the tsarina Alexandra; his heir, 14-year-old Alexei; their four daughters—Olga (age 23), Tatiana (age 21), Maria (age 19), and Anastasia (age 17); their three servants; and their physician.

When leaders in other states heard the news of the deaths, they condemned the killings as murders. The Bolsheviks, however, termed them acts of revolutionary justice.

(continued on next page)

(continued from previous page)

After the October Revolution, the Bolsheviks imprisoned the tsar and his family in a house in Ekaterinburg, 900 miles east of Moscow in a region controlled by the Bolshevik Ural Regional Soviet. Throughout the spring of 1918, the Bolshevik government prepared to try Nicholas publicly for crimes against the Russian people.

But the trial never happened. By July, an anti-Bolshevik army was

TSAR NICHOLAS II AND FAMILY Tsar Nicholas II, the Tsarina Alexandra, and their family.

approaching Ekaterinburg. If these troops freed the imperial family, they would score a crucial victory. The Ural Soviet decided—probably with Lenin's approval—to execute the tsar and his family immediately.

Pavel Medvedev, one of the tsar's guards, recounted the events of the evening of July 16. As he watched, the royal family entered a downstairs room: "The Tsar was carrying the heir [Alexei] in his arms. . . . In my presence there were no tears, no sobs and no questions." Medvedev's commander ordered him to leave. When he returned a few minutes later, he said,

> . . . . [I] saw all the members of the Tsar's family lying on the floor with numerous wounds to their bodies. The blood was gushing. The heir was still alive—and moaning. [The commander] walked over to him and shot him two or three times at point blank range. The heir fell still.[8]

Medvedev did not relate the more gruesome details of the execution. Trying to preserve part of the family fortune, the tsar's daughters wore corsets into which they had sewn diamonds. When they were shot, the bullets, in the words of one eyewitness, "ricocheted, jumping around the room like hail."[9] Even after several pistols were emptied, one of the girls remained alive. The guards resorted to bayonets.

The Ural Regional Soviet announced the tsar's execution, but said nothing about his family. The official statement from Moscow reported that "the wife and son of Nicholas Romanov were sent to a safe place."[10]

These lies reveal the Bolsheviks' own uneasiness with the killings. Why, then, did they shoot the family? Determination to win the civil war provides part of the answer. According to Trotsky, Lenin "believed we shouldn't leave the Whites [the anti-Bolshevik forces] a live banner to rally around."[11] Any member of the royal family could have become such a banner. In addition, Trotsky argued, the killings were essential "not only to frighten, horrify, and to dishearten the enemy, but also in order to shake up our own ranks, to show them that there was no turning back, that ahead lay either complete victory or complete ruin."[12] The killing of Tsar Nicholas and his family thus formed part of the

pattern of escalating violence that characterized World War I and its revolutionary aftermath.

In the blood of these killings, however, we can also see reflected two ideas that shaped Bolshevik politics: the subordination of law to the revolutionary state and the concept of collective guilt. The Bolsheviks dismissed the liberal ideal of impartial justice as a myth. They argued that justice is never blind, that it always serves the interests of those in power. In a discussion of the tsar's killing, a Bolshevik pamphlet admitted, "Many formal aspects of bourgeois justice may have been violated." But, the pamphlet argued, such a violation of "bourgeois" standards of justice did not matter because "worker-peasant power was manifested in the process."[13] "Worker peasant power," embodied in the revolutionary state, trumped such "formal aspects of bourgeois justice" as legal rights.

While this concept of the law as subordinate to the state helps us understand the tsar's execution without trial, the concept of collective guilt provides a context for the killing of his children. The Bolshevik model of socialism assumed that *class* constituted objective reality. Aristocratic and middle-class origins served as an indelible ink, marking a person permanently as an enemy of the revolutionary state—regardless of that person's own actions or inclinations. From the Bolshevik perspective, royal origins tainted the tsar's children. When their continuing existence threatened the revolution, they were shot. Over the next four decades, the concept of collective guilt contributed to millions of deaths in the former Russian Empire.

For Discussion

1. How was the murder of the Russian royal family the by-product of total war rather than the result of any revolutionary ideals?
2. Were the Bolsheviks correct in arguing that "justice" is never blind, that legal systems reflect the interests of a society's dominant groups? Is there such a thing as impartial justice?

Taking It Further

Kozlov, Vladimir, and Vladimir Khrustalëv. *The Last Diary of Tsaritsa Alexandra.* 1997. A translation of Alexandra's diary from 1918.

Steinberg, Mark, and Vladimir Khrustalëv. *The Fall of the Romanovs.* 1999. A detailed account of the last two years of the tsar and his family, based on archives opened only after the collapse of the Soviet Union.

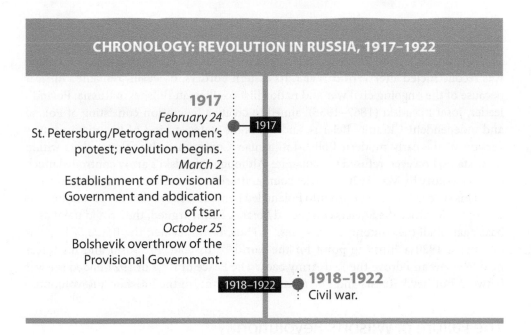

CHRONOLOGY: REVOLUTION IN RUSSIA, 1917–1922

1917
February 24
St. Petersburg/Petrograd women's
protest; revolution begins.
March 2
Establishment of Provisional
Government and abdication
of tsar.
October 25
Bolshevik overthrow of the
Provisional Government.

1918–1922
Civil war.

hard-won independence. The "Union of Soviet Socialist Republics" (USSR, or Soviet Union) replaced the Russian Empire.

THE SPREADING REVOLUTION The victory of the Russian Bolsheviks inspired socialists across Europe and around the world. In January 1919, communists in Buenos Aires, Argentina, led by Russian immigrants, controlled the city for three days until they were crushed by the Argentine army. British dockworkers struck in support of the Bolshevik Revolution, and in French cities general strikes caused chaos. In Austria, revolutionaries attempted to take control of government buildings in Vienna but were quickly defeated by the Austrian army. In Hungary, Bela Kun, a journalist who had come to admire the Bolsheviks while a prisoner of war in Russia, established a short-lived soviet regime in the spring of 1919.

Revolution also swept through defeated Germany. In October 1918, its military commanders recommended that the German government enter into peace negotiations, but the Allies refused to negotiate until the Germans democratized their political system. As a result, representatives of left-wing and centrist parties—including the SPD, the largest socialist party in Europe—joined the German government.

This "revolution from above" coincided and competed with a "revolution from below." Inspired by the Bolshevik Revolution, many German socialists condemned the SPD as too moderate; instead, they supported the more radical Spartacists (named after Spartacus, the gladiator who led a slave revolt against Rome in the first century B.C.E.). Directed by Karl Liebknecht (1871–1919) and Rosa Luxemburg (1870–1919), the Spartacists demanded an immediate communist revolution. By November 8, German communists declared the establishment of a Soviet republic in the province of Bavaria and the Red Flag—symbol of communism—flew over 11 German cities.

On November 9, the kaiser abdicated and the head of the SPD, Friedrich Ebert (1871–1925), became chancellor of Germany. From the window of the Reichstag building in Berlin, one of Ebert's colleagues in the SPD proclaimed that Germany was now a parliamentary democracy. Almost at that very moment, Karl Liebknecht stood at another window in Berlin (in the occupied royal palace) and announced that Germany was now a revolutionary communist state. With two opposing versions of revolution on offer, civil war raged until the spring of 1919, when the SPD defeated the communists.

THE REVOLUTION HALTED Even after the failure of communist revolution in Germany, however, Lenin hoped that the communist revolution would spread throughout western Europe. The Polish-Soviet War of 1919–1921 inspired and then crushed this hope of a European communist revolution.

Partitioned among Prussia, Austria, and Russia in the eighteenth century, Poland was reconstructed after World War I. Its eastern borders, however, remained unclear because of the ongoing civil war and nationalist conflicts in Bolshevik Russia. Poland's leader, Josef Pilsudski (1867–1935), aimed to create a federation consisting of Poland and independent Ukraine, Belarus, and the Baltic states, a kind of twentieth-century version of the early modern Polish-Lithuanian Commonwealth. Nationalists within these states, however, refused to cooperate. Although Pilsudski's army controlled much of this territory by May 1920, a Soviet counterattack in June forced the Poles to retreat.

This successful Soviet push into Poland led Lenin to believe that the revolution was unstoppable. Once the Soviets conquered Poland, Lenin argued, they could use it as "a base against all the contemporary states."[14] Thus, Lenin termed the Battle of Warsaw of August 1920 a "turning point for the world."[15] Instead, Pilsudski and his forces held Warsaw and drove the Red Army back. The Peace of Riga of 1921 ended the war between Bolshevik Russia and Poland and set the limits of the Bolshevik Revolution.

The Failure of Wilson's Revolution

At the beginning of 1919, representatives of the victorious Allies gathered in Paris to draw up the peace treaties. These officials aimed for more than ending the war. They wished to construct a new Europe. At the center of this high endeavor was the American college professor-turned-president Woodrow Wilson. Wilson based his version of revolutionary change on the ideal of national self-determination—a world in which "every people should be left free to determine its own polity, its own way of development, unhindered, unthreatened, unafraid, the little along with the great and powerful." Wilson foresaw a new map of Europe, with independent, ethnically homogenous, democratic nation-states replacing the old authoritarian empires.

Wilson envisioned that these new nation-states would interact differently from the empires of the past. In what he called his **Fourteen Points**, Wilson demanded a revolution in international relations. He argued that "Points" such as freedom of the seas, freedom of trade, and open diplomacy (an end to secret treaties) would break down barriers and guarantee peace and prosperity for all peoples. The cornerstone of this new world order would be an international organization, the **League of Nations**. By overseeing the implementation of the Fourteen Points and resolving disputes between states through negotiation, the League would guarantee that World War I was "the war to end all wars." Because all states—big and small, European and non-European—would have an equal voice in the League, the systems of secret diplomacy and Great Power alliances that had led to total war would disappear.

Wilson's vision, however, went unrealized. In Paris in 1919 and 1920, the Allies and their defeated enemies signed a series of treaties, the most important of which was the Treaty of Versailles with Germany. The treaty writers sought to create a new international order based on three features: a democratic Germany, national self-determination in eastern Europe, and a viable system of international arbitration headed by the League of Nations. They failed in all three.

THE TREATY OF VERSAILLES AND GERMAN DEMOCRACY At the center of the new Europe envisioned by Woodrow Wilson was to be a new democratic Germany, but the French leader, Georges Clemenceau, did not share this vision. After surviving two German invasions of his homeland, he wished to ensure that Germany could never again threaten France. Clemenceau proposed the creation of a Rhineland state in Germany's industrialized western region as a buffer zone between France and Germany and as a way to reduce Germany's economic power. The British leader David Lloyd George promised his people that he would squeeze Germany "until the pips squeak"

Fourteen Points The principles outlined by U.S. President Woodrow Wilson as the basis for a new world order after World War I.

League of Nations Association of states set up after World War I to resolve international conflicts through open and peaceful negotiation.

and publicly supported Clemenceau's hard-line approach. In private, Lloyd George feared that this approach would feed the flames of German resentment and undermine the structures of German democracy.

Lloyd George's fears proved well-grounded. The German people bitterly resented the **Versailles Treaty**, which they perceived as unjustly punitive. By the terms of the treaty, Germany lost all of its overseas colonies, 13 percent of its European territory, 10 percent of its population, and its ability to wage war. The treaty limited the German army to a defensive force of 100,000 men, with no aircraft or tanks. Clemenceau failed to create a separate Rhineland state, but the Rhineland was demilitarized, emptied of German soldiers and fortifications. In addition, the Versailles Treaty ceded the coal-fields of the Saar region to France for 15 years (see **Map 25.5**).

Most significantly, the treaty declared that German aggression had caused the war and therefore that Germany must recompense the Allies for their costs. In 1921, the Allies presented Germany with a bill for **reparations** of 132 billion marks ($31.5 billion). As Chapter 26 details, this reparations clause helped set up an economic cycle that proved devastating for both global prosperity and German democratic politics.

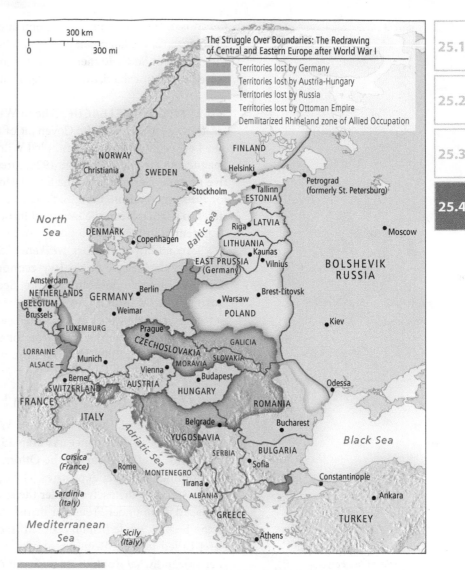

MAP **25.5** THE STRUGGLE OVER BOUNDARIES: THE REDRAWING OF CENTRAL AND EASTERN EUROPE AFTER WORLD WAR I Compare this map with Map 25.1 on page 782. How did the war redraw the political map of central and eastern Europe? Which states gained and which states lost territory? Which states were new creations?

THE FAILURE OF NATIONAL SELF-DETERMINATION The peace settlement sought to redraw eastern Europe on national lines. Map 25.5 shows that the old multinational empires of eastern and central Europe disappeared, replaced with independent nation-states. Poland again became a state, with pieces carved out of the German, Austro-Hungarian, and Russian Empires. One entirely new state—Czechoslovakia—was formed out of the rubble of the Austro-Hungarian Empire. Romania, Greece, and Italy all expanded as a result of serving on the winners' side, while Serbia became the heart of the new Yugoslavia. The defeated states shrank, some dramatically. Austria, for example, became a mere rump of what had been the mighty Habsburg Empire, and Hungary was reduced to one-third of its prewar size. All that remained of the Ottoman Empire was Turkey.

President Wilson heralded these changes as the victory of "national self-determination." But as Wilson's own secretary of state complained, "This phrase is simply loaded with dynamite. It will raise hopes which can never be realized." Wilson had called for "every people" to be left free to determine its political destiny—but who constituted "a people"?

Even after the peace settlements redrew the map, 30 million eastern Europeans remained members of minority groups. Fewer than 70 percent of Hungarians, for example, lived in Hungary—more than three million were scattered in other states. Over nine million Germans resided outside the borders of Germany. In the newly created

Versailles Treaty Treaty between Germany and the victorious Allies after World War I.

reparations Payments imposed upon Germany after World War I by the Versailles Treaty to cover the costs of the war.

View the Image

LA Times Cartoon: France Demands War Reparations from Germany

View the Map

"Shifting Borders: Eastern Europe after World War II"

Czechoslovakia, one-third of the population was neither Czech nor Slovak. The new state of Yugoslavia contained an uneasy mixture of several ethnic groups, most resentful of the dominant Serbs. Rather than satisfying nationalist ambitions, the peace settlements served to inflame them, thus creating a volatile situation for the post-World War I world.

THE LIMITS OF THE LEAGUE True to Wilson's vision of a new international order, the treaty makers included the Covenant of the League of Nations in each of the treaties. The League, however, never fulfilled Wilson's hopes of making war obsolete. When the League met for the first time in 1920, three significant world powers had no representative present: Germany and the Soviet Union were excluded, and, in a stunning defeat for President Wilson, the U.S. Senate rejected membership. The failure of these three states to participate in the League at its beginning stripped the organization of much of its potential influence.

Two additional factors weakened the League. First, it had no military power. Although the League could levy economic sanctions against states that flouted its decisions, it could do nothing more. Second, the will to make the League work was lacking. With Wilson removed from the picture, European leaders pursued their own more traditional visions of what the League should be. French politicians, for example, believed that its primary reason for existence was to enforce the provisions of the Versailles Treaty rather than to restructure international relations.

The Making of the Modern Middle East

In the Middle East, the end of World War I meant an entirely new map, but not the end of European dominance. As **Map 25.6** shows, under terms set by the new League of Nations, the Allies carved the Ottoman territory in the Middle East into separate and nominally independent states. The League, however, judged these states as "not yet able to stand by themselves under the strenuous conditions of the modern world" and so placed them under French or British control (or "Mandate"). Syria and Lebanon fell to the French, while Britain claimed Iraq (Mesopotamia), Palestine, and Transjordan (later called Jordan). Britain also continued to exercise its influence over Egypt, Iran (Persia), and what would become Saudi Arabia.

 **View the Video**

The Continuing Legacy of World War I in the Middle East

Three factors explain why this remaking of the Middle East failed to effect a lasting settlement in the region. First, the new boundaries violated wartime promises and so created a long-lasting legacy of mistrust and resentment against the West. Second, the new states imposed on the region were artificial, the creation of the Allied victors rather than a product of historical evolution or of the wishes of the inhabitants themselves. And finally, Western mandatory supervision (which in actual practice differed little from old-fashioned imperial rule) brought with it Western practices and concepts that destabilized regional social and economic structures.

The early history of Iraq exemplifies these three factors. In 1915, Sharif Husayn (Hussein) ibn Ali, head of the Hashemite dynasty that guarded the Islamic holy sites, agreed to fight the Central Powers in exchange for British support of an independent Arab state. The British argued they fulfilled this promise when they placed Husayn's son Faisal on the throne of the newly created Iraq. Husayn and his supporters, however, felt betrayed. They believed that the British had reneged on the promise of an independent Arab kingdom centering on what became Syria and including Palestine.

The artificiality of Iraq also created a revolutionary situation. In creating Iraq, the Allies glued together three provinces—Basra, Baghdad, and Mosul—that the Ottomans had never treated as a single political or economic unit. The population of this new state

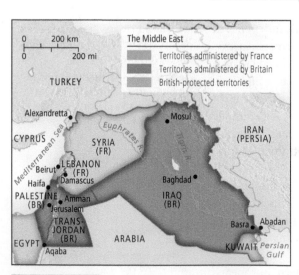

MAP **25.6** THE MIDDLE EAST AFTER WORLD WAR I In the wake of the war, the newly created League of Nations redrew the political boundaries of the Middle East under a new system of "mandates." Whose interests did this new system serve?

FAISAL AT THE HEAD OF HIS TROOPS, 1917 Sharif Husayn ibn Ali's son Faisal led Arab troops in an alliance with the British against Ottoman forces. After the war, Faisal became king of Iraq.

consisted of a volatile mixture of ethnicities (including Arab, Kurd, and Assyrian) and religions (including Shi'ite and Sunni Muslims, Christians, Jews, and Zoroastrians). These groups did not identify as "Iraqi" nor did they feel any sense of allegiance to their new ruler. They regarded Faisal as an imperialist puppet, jumping as British "advisers" pulled the strings.

Finally, the British inadvertently destabilized Iraq's social structures by introducing British legal and economic concepts that destroyed indigenous traditions. For example, by applying the concept of private land ownership to Iraqi customary relations, the British transformed the traditional tie between tribal sheikh and tribesmen into an economic arrangement between landowner and tenants—one that tended to enrich the landowner while impoverishing the tenants.

The settlement of Palestine destabilized the Middle East even further. Husayn and his supporters believed that the British government had promised them an independent Arab kingdom that would include Palestine. Yet during the war British officials also pledged support for a Jewish state in Palestine. Influenced by the anti-Semitic myth of a powerful Jewish elite wielding influence over world affairs, British policymakers believed (wrongly) that Jewish influence could determine whether the United States entered and Russia remained in the war. Desperate to ensure both, the British government in 1917 issued the **Balfour Declaration**, which announced that Britain favored the Zionist goal of a Jewish national homeland in Palestine.

After the war, Palestine passed into British hands as a League of Nations mandate. The British remained formally committed to the Balfour Declaration. Some 90 percent of the inhabitants of Palestine in 1920, however, were Arabs (both Christians and Muslims). They viewed the Balfour Declaration as an effort to take away their land and give it to Europeans. Arab protests and riots in Palestine erupted, and by 1922 the British government decided to slow the pace of Jewish immigration into the region to alleviate Arab fears. Over the next two decades the British faced continuous pressure from both Arab and Jewish nationalist forces. Like the remaking of eastern Europe, the remaking of the Middle East ushered in decades of political turmoil and violence.

 Read the Document

"The Balfour Declaration"

Balfour Declaration Declaration of 1917 that affirmed British support of a Jewish state in Palestine.

👁 **Watch the Video**

The Origins and Importance of World War I

CONCLUSION

The War and the West

The idea of "the West" changed as a result of World War I. The entry of American forces in the final year of the war signaled that, in the twentieth century, the United States would feature in any definition of "Western culture" or "Western civilization." At the same time, the spread of the war to the Middle East and Africa and the significant role played by soldiers from imperial territories such as Tunisia, India, and Australia demonstrated the global framework that complicated and constrained Western affairs.

The war's revolutionary aftermath also had consequences for formulations of "Western identity." With the triumph of the Bolshevik Revolution, two versions of modernity now presented themselves—one associated with the United States and capitalism, and the other represented by Russia and its communism. The Bolshevik Party's intellectual roots lay in Marxism, a Western ideology shaped by Western ideals of evolutionary progress and the triumph of human reason. But after the Russian Revolution, many in the West viewed communism as the "Other" against which the West identified itself.

The carnage of World War I challenged the faith of many Europeans that industrial development ensured the West's continual moral and material progress. In the final decades of the nineteenth century, European and American soldiers had used repeating rifles and machine guns to conquer huge sections of the globe in the name of Western civilization. In 1914, European and American soldiers turned their machine guns on each other. The world the war created was one of unprecedented destruction. Millions lay dead, with millions more maimed for life. Vast sections of northern France and eastern Europe became giant cemeteries filled with rotting men and rusting metal. Across central and eastern Europe, starvation continued to claim thousands of victims. In the new world shaped by relentless conflicts such as the Battle of the Somme, the pessimism and sense of despair that had invaded the arts in the decade before the war became more characteristic of the wider culture. For many Europeans, the optimism and confidence of nineteenth-century liberalism died in the trenches.

Yet, paradoxically, the war also fostered high hopes. Wilson declared that this had been the war to end all wars. The fires of revolution burned brightly and many in the West believed that, on top of the ashes of dismantled empires, they would now build a better world. The task of reconstruction, however, proved immense. Seeking stability, many Europeans and Americans did their best to return to prewar patterns. The failure of the peace settlement ensured that the "war to end all wars" set the stage for the next, more destructive total war.

MAKING CONNECTIONS

1. Compare and contrast the Eastern, Western, and Middle Eastern Fronts in World War I: How and why did the experiences of ordinary soldiers in these war zones differ? Which front was more important for shaping the postwar West?
2. What do the phrases "total war politics" and a "total war mentality" mean? How did total war politics and mentalities affect European women? The working class? National minorities?
3. How did the Wilsonian and Leninist visions of postwar Europe differ? Which was more "Western" and why? Which was more successful and why?

TAKING IT FURTHER

For suggested readings, see page R-1.

Chapter Review

The Origins of the First World War

25.1 What factors led Europe into war in 1914?

The volatile force of nationalism in Eastern Europe increased over-all tensions, while a complicated system of international alliances heavily influenced who declared war and when. Once in motion, the machine of war was difficult to stop given the widening gap between traditional diplomatic policy and the needs of an increasingly industrialized military. Public sentiment was heavily swayed toward the idea of war as a way to prove national superiority.

The Experience of Total War

25.2 When, where, and how did the Allies defeat the Central Powers?

The war was fought in the muddy trenches on the Western Front, in a series of advances and retreats in Eastern Europe, around the globe in places like the Middle East, and at sea in the form of blockades and submarine attacks. Germany proved victorious on the Eastern Front by the beginning of 1918 but the struggling Allies received needed reinforcements when the United States entered the war. A final surge against the starving and demoralized Germans led to the fall of the Central Powers and eventually Germany's withdrawal from the eastern lands its troops had occupied.

The Home Fronts

25.3 How did total war structure the home fronts?

The crucial role of industrial production in total war empowered industrial workers. Class relations shifted when workers, many of whom were women, realized the importance of their collective power. Gender relations also shifted as women moved into more public roles. To maintain morale and shape public perception of the war, states turned to censorship and propaganda. Demonization of the enemy and the need for a total war mentality fostered a climate of violence and even genocide.

War and Revolution

25.4 What were the consequences of this war for the European and the global political order?

The strain of total war led to revolution in Russia and the establishment of the world's first communist state. The punitive peace imposed on Germany weakened the new democratic German state while the re-drawing of state boundaries in central and eastern Europe heightened rather than resolved nationalist tensions. Similarly, the remapping of the Middle East betrayed wartime promises to competing national groups and failed to foster political stability or economic prosperity in the region.

Chapter Time Line

1914
June
Assassination of Archduke Francis Ferdinand of Austria-Hungary.
August
Outbreak of World War I.
October
Stalemate on the Western Front begins.

1916
Food shortages in German cities.

1917
February
Popular revolution in Russia.
April
U.S. joins the Allies.
October
Bolshevik Revolution in Russia.

1918
March
Treaty of Brest-Litovsk: Germany victorious in East.
August
Global flu pandemic underway.
November
Germany surrenders.

26 Reconstruction, Reaction, and Continuing Revolution: The 1920s and 1930s

On September 14, 1927, a convertible accelerated down a street in Nice in southern France. In its passenger seat sat Isadora Duncan, who let her long silk shawl whip in the wind. One of the most famous dancers in the Western world, Duncan had pioneered a revolutionary style of dance that replaced toe shoes and tutus with bare feet and simple tunics. Attacking classical ballet as an artificial form that deformed the female body, the American-born Duncan created dances that did not impose movement on the body, but instead flowed from the body itself. Speeding down the streets in a convertible, Duncan provides a fitting image for Western culture after World War I. She was an American, and in these decades American culture came to represent for many Europeans the limitless future. Like Duncan in her car, Americans and Europeans in the postwar era wanted to move in new directions, break traditional barriers, and push toward greater liberation. Even

OTTO DIX, *FLANDERS* (1934–1935) In this painting, the bodies of soldiers shape the Flanders landscape. Like these soldiers—and much of postwar European culture—Dix, a veteran, could not escape the war. His paintings reveal a man permanently wounded.

LEARNING OBJECTIVES

26.1 ((	26.2 ((	26.3 ((	26.4 ((	26.5 ((	26.6 ((
What was the impact of World War I on European cultural life?	What circumstances explain the collapse of democracy throughout much of interwar Europe?	How did the Nazis succeed in establishing a dictatorship in Germany?	Why did the Soviet Union seem a success and how did the democracies respond?	What changed, and what did not, in women's experiences after World War I?	How did the interaction between the West and the world outside change after World War I?

((Listen to Chapter 26 on MyHistoryLab

26.1

26.2

26.3

26.4

26.5

26.6

Watch the Video Series on MyHistoryLab

Learn about some key topics related to this chapter with the *MyHistoryLab Video Series: Key Topics in Western Civilization*

Duncan's clothing—loose tunics, free-flowing scarves, fluid shawls—symbolized a love of freedom and mobility.

Yet freedom is sometimes dangerous and movement can be violent. On that autumn day in 1927 Duncan's scarf became entangled in the wheel of the car and strangled the dancer. Gruesome as it is, this image, too, symbolizes the West in the turbulent interlude between World War I and World War II. The American president, Woodrow Wilson, hailed World War I as the "final war for human liberty." Many Europeans agreed. They thought that the war would propel their society down a new road. In much of Europe, however, the drive toward freedom ended with the triumph of ideologies that viewed human liberty as an illusion and mass murder as a tool of the state.

The strangulation of democracy in eastern and southern Europe during these decades highlights a central theme of this book: the contested definition of "the West." In the Wilsonian vision, the West promoted individual freedom through democratic politics and capitalist economics. But in the 1920s and 1930s, anti-democratic and anti-capitalist ideologies defined the West differently. Examination of the aftermath of World War I answers the question:

Why was the link between "Western" and "democratic" so fragile in this era?

Cultural Despair and Desire

26.1 What was the impact of World War I on European cultural life?

After World War I, many in the West turned from the future in despair. Others, however, dreamed of building a new world.

The Waste Land

Within a few years of the war's end, war memorials dotted cities and villages throughout France and Britain. These memorials rarely celebrated the Allies' victory. They focused instead on dead soldiers—on slaughter, not success. At Verdun, for example, the memorial was an ossuary, a gigantic receptacle for the skulls and bones of 130,000 men. In some ways, European culture after the war took the form of an ossuary, as intellectuals and artists looked at the death tolls from the war and concluded that the end product of human reason and scientific endeavor was mass destruction.

In the English-speaking world, "The Waste Land" (1922), a poem by the American expatriate T. S. Eliot (1888–1965), supplied an evocative portrait of postwar disillusion. Like a Cubist painting, this lengthy poem contains no straightforward narrative. Instead, it comprises fragments of conversation, literary allusions, disjointed quotations, and mythological references, all clashing in a modernist cry of despair:

> White bodies naked on the low damp ground
> And bones cast in a little low dry garret,
> Rattled by the rat's foot only, year to year.

26.1

26.2

26.3

26.4

26.5

26.6

Pessimism also marked theology and philosophy. In the nineteenth century, theologians and philosophers emphasized humanity's progressive evolution, but World War I raised doubts about the moral progress of human society. In his writings, the Swiss theologian Karl Barth (1886–1968) emphasized human sinfulness and argued that an immense gulf separated humanity from God. Human intellectual effort could not bridge the gap. Reaching God demanded a radical leap of faith.

Barth's German colleague Rudolf Bultmann (1884–1976) made the leap of faith even more radical. Bultmann argued that the Jesus Christ depicted in the New Testament—the foundation of Christianity—was largely fictional. In Bultmann's view, the New Testament resembled Eliot's "Waste Land" in its layered fragments originating from myth and folk tale, capable of multiple interpretations. Bultmann, a Lutheran pastor, argued that in this Christian mythology persons can find spiritual—although not scientific or historical—truth.

Bultmann's form of Christianity is often called Christian **existentialism** because Bultmann put a Christian twist on the existentialist philosophy that emerged in the interwar era. Existentialists such as Jean-Paul Sartre (1905–1980) taught that existence has no built-in meaning—no religious purpose or moral value. It just *is*. To overcome the fear, alienation, even *Nausea* (the title of one of Sartre's novels, published in 1938) of mere existence, a person must consciously choose actions that create meaning and a sense of self. As Sartre put it, each person is "condemned to be free."

existentialism Twentieth-century philosophy that emerged in the interwar era and influenced many thinkers and artists after World War II. Existentialism emphasizes individual freedom in a world devoid of meaning or coherence.

Building Something Better

In *Flanders,* painted in 1934, the war veteran Otto Dix (1891–1969) depicted a nightmare of trench soldiers, rotting like blasted trees. Stuck in the mud, Dix's soldiers provide a haunting image of interwar culture. A different vision, however, takes shape when we examine the work of Dix's contemporaries in the *Bauhaus.* Established in Berlin in 1919 as a school for architects, craftsmen, and designers, the Bauhaus epitomized postwar Western idealism rather than despair. Its members sought to eliminate the barriers between "art" (what we put on our walls or see in museums) and "craft" (what we actually use in daily life: furniture, textiles, dishes, and the like). By making daily living more effective, efficient, and beautiful, the Bauhaus's founder Walter Gropius (1883–1969) and his students hoped to become "the architects of a new civilization."[1] Like Gropius, many artists abandoned the prewar modernist ideal of "art for art's sake" and produced work steeped in political passion and the hope of radical social change.

Faith in technology characterized this optimistic side of interwar culture. Having demonstrated the destructive power of machines during World War I, human beings would now use their mechanical powers to reconfigure modern society. Architecture illustrated this mechanical faith. A house, explained the Swiss architect Le Corbusier (1887–1965), was "a machine for living in." Le Corbusier and his fellow modernist architects stripped their buildings of ornamentation and exposed the machinery—the supporting beams, the heating ducts, the elevator

ARCHITECTS OF A NEW CIVILIZATION This Bauhaus design for a "public transport interconnecting stop, electric transformer and urinal" first appeared in a French architecture journal in 1925. Many architects and city planners saw public transport systems as the means of making modern urban life not only more efficient but also more connected and cohesive.

26.1

26.2

26.3

26.4

26.5

26.6

shafts. Concrete, steel, and glass became the building materials of choice as modernist skyscrapers—glittering rectangles—transformed urban skylines and testified to the triumph of the human-made.

This enthusiasm for the mechanical also influenced interwar popular culture. The chorus line embodied the interwar obsession with mechanization, with each dancer reduced to working as a standardized component in a mass formation. Similarly, in the Charleston, a dance craze of the 1920s, the dancers' arms and legs fired like pistons, the entire body a fast-moving machine.

Along with the movies, the car and the airplane symbolized this new era of technological possibilities. The export of the assembly line from the United States to Europe cut the cost of automobile manufacturing: The rich man's toy became a middle-class necessity. The airline industry also took off in this era, with air passenger service between London and Paris beginning in 1919. In 1927, when the American Charles Lindbergh (1902–1974) completed the first solo flight across the Atlantic, he became an international hero, a symbol of human resourcefulness and technological mastery.

Scientific Possibilities

The ongoing scientific revolution also offered new possibilities. As Chapter 24 explained, from the 1890s on, a new model of the universe began to take shape. By the 1920s, Albert Einstein's concept of matter as "frozen energy" engaged scientists from all over the world. In theory, if the energy could be "thawed out," then this energy could be released. But could this theory become reality? In 1936, the British scientist Ernest Rutherford (1871–1937), head of one of the most important research laboratories in the West, dismissed the idea of unlocking the atom to release energy as "moonshine."

Four years earlier, however, a scientist working in Rutherford's laboratory had in fact found the key to unlocking the atom, although no one realized it at the time. In 1932, James Chadwick (1891–1974) discovered that atoms contain not only positively charged protons and negatively charged electrons, but also neutrons. Because neutrons possess no electrical charge, neither the protons nor electrons repel them. Thus, a bombardment of heavy neutrons could, in theory, split an atom's nucleus—a process called *nuclear fission*. The split nucleus itself would then emit neutrons, which would burst open other atoms, which in turn would emit further neutrons . . . and on and on in a nuclear chain reaction. The result: a colossal burst of energy that could be harnessed for industrial production—or for military destruction.

Such possibilities remained theoretical until 1938 when German scientists Otto Hahn (1879–1968) and Fritz Strassmann (1902–1980) broke open the uranium atom. Within a year, more than 100 articles on the implications of this discovery appeared in scientific journals. As one historian noted, "Physicists viewed the discovery of nuclear fission like the finding of a lost treasure map."[2]

Read the Document

Werner Heisenberg, "Uncertainty"

The Appeal of Authoritarianism and the Rise of Fascism

26.2 What circumstances explain the collapse of democracy throughout much of interwar Europe?

The extremes of pessimism and utopianism that characterized cultural developments in the post-World War I era were mirrored in the increasing polarization of political life. Facing the mass destruction wrought by total war, many in the West concluded that the age of liberalism, with its faith in individual reason

26.1

26.2

26.3

26.4

26.5

26.6

and the give-and-take of parliamentary democracy, had ended and that the new era demanded authoritarian, single-party politics. As we will see in the next section, many turned leftward, to the communism of the Soviet Union. But others turned in the other direction, to conservative authoritarianism, or even further, to the new politics of fascism.

The Collapse of Democracy in Eastern and Central Europe

We saw in Chapter 25 that the politicians and diplomats who drew up the peace settlements after World War I envisioned a new Europe of independent, democratic nation-states. As **Map 26.1** shows, postwar eastern Europe certainly *looked* markedly different from its prewar counterpart. Lines on the map, however, did not change key political realities. Few of these new states had any democratic traditions or history, and few of their new political leaders had mastered the consensus-building essential to stable parliamentary government.

MAP **26.1** EUROPE IN THE 1920S AND 1930S This map shows the political boundaries of European states in the interwar period. How did these boundaries clash with national identities and ambitions?

26.1

26.2

26.3

26.4

26.5

26.6

More importantly, the lines drawn on the new map actually worked to destabilize these new states. Rather than quelling nationalist hostilities, the peace settlement inflamed them. Ethnic nationalism formed the ideological basis of these new states: Poland for the Poles, Czechoslovakia for Czechs and Slovaks, Latvia for Latvians, and so forth. Yet all of these nation-states contained sizeable ethnic minorities—groups who did not regard themselves (or were not regarded by the majority) as part of the "nation" that now controlled the state. Some resorted to violence: In Poland, for example, Ukrainian nationalist groups waged a terrorist campaign throughout the 1920s and 1930s to subvert the new Polish state. Other groups turned to parliamentary politics. They formed ethnically based political parties that sought to destroy the postwar political settlement. In many of the new states, then, forming an effective government became impossible as political allegiances fractured and parties found no common ground. In Poland, where Jewish, Ukrainian, and German minorities made up one-third of the population, 18 different parties contended for control.

Economic problems exacerbated these nationalist conflicts. Much of eastern, southern, and central Europe remained a world of impoverished peasants and aristocratic landlords. In Romania, Poland, and Hungary, at least 60 percent of the population worked the land. In Bulgaria and Yugoslavia, the figure was 80 percent (versus 20 percent in industrialized Britain). With little industrial growth in these regions and few cities to absorb labor, unemployment rates rose and land hunger grew more intense. Parliaments torn apart by nationalist hostilities failed to devise effective economic development policies.

In contrast, authoritarianism offered at least the illusion of strong leadership. In every eastern European state except Czechoslovakia, democracy gave way to authoritarian government during the 1920s or 1930s.

◉ View the Map

Authoritarian Regimes in Europe in the Mid-1930s

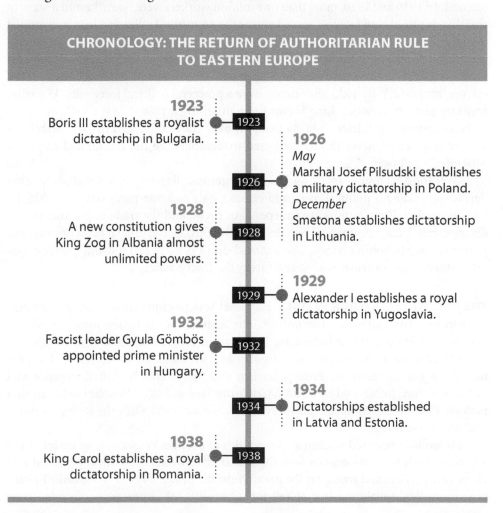

CHRONOLOGY: THE RETURN OF AUTHORITARIAN RULE TO EASTERN EUROPE

1923
Boris III establishes a royalist dictatorship in Bulgaria.

1926
May
Marshal Josef Pilsudski establishes a military dictatorship in Poland.
December
Smetona establishes dictatorship in Lithuania.

1928
A new constitution gives King Zog in Albania almost unlimited powers.

1929
Alexander I establishes a royal dictatorship in Yugoslavia.

1932
Fascist leader Gyula Gömbös appointed prime minister in Hungary.

1934
Dictatorships established in Latvia and Estonia.

1938
King Carol establishes a royal dictatorship in Romania.

26.1

26.2

26.3

26.4

26.5

26.6

fascism Twentieth-century political ideology that rejected the existing alternatives of conservatism, communism, socialism, and liberalism. Fascists stressed the authoritarian power of the state, the efficacy of violent action, the need to build a national community, and the use of new technologies of influence and control.

Read the Document

Benito Mussolini, from "The Political and Social Doctrine of Fascism"

The Fascist Alternative

At the same time, developments in Italy highlighted a new type of authoritarian politics—**fascism**. Conceived in the coupling of wartime exhilaration and postwar despair, fascism offered an alternative to existing political ideologies. Fascism was more than a set of political ideas, however. As presented by its creator, Benito Mussolini (1883–1945), fascism was an ongoing performance, a spectacular sound-and-lights show with a cast of millions.

MUSSOLINI'S RISE TO POWER Fascism originated in Italy as a product of World War I. When Italy entered the war on the side of the Allies in 1915, many Italians welcomed the war as a cleansing force, a powerful disinfectant that would purify Italian society. Mussolini, a socialist journalist, shared these views. Because the Socialist Party opposed Italy's entry into the war, Mussolini broke with the socialists, joined the army, and fought until he was wounded in 1917. When the war ended, he sought to create a new politics that would build on the camaraderie and exhilaration of combat.

In March 1919, Mussolini and about 100 men and some women gathered in Milan and declared themselves the fascist movement. Like Mussolini, many of these "fascists of the first hour" were war veterans. A number had served in the *arditi*, elite commando units that fought behind enemy lines. The arditi uniform, a black shirt, became the fascist badge of identity. The arditi slogan, *me ne frego* ("I don't give a damn"), became the blackshirts' creed, a fitting expression of their willingness to throw aside conventional standards and politics.

Just three and a half years after the first fascist meeting in Milan, Mussolini became prime minister of Italy. His rise to power occurred against a backdrop of social turmoil. In 1919 and 1920, more than one million workers were on strike and a wave of socialist-inspired land seizures spread across the countryside. Fearing that communist revolution would engulf Italy just as it had destroyed tsarist Russia, landowners and industrialists looked to Mussolini's fascists for help. Fascist squads disrupted Socialist Party meetings, broke up strikes, beat up trade unionists, and protected aristocratic estates from attack. By 1922, the fascists were a powerful political force with 35 parliamentary seats. In October, King Victor Emmanuel III (r. 1900–1946) asked Mussolini to become prime minister. Fascists from all over Italy converged in the "March on Rome," a piece of street theater designed to demonstrate the disciplined might of Mussolini's followers.

Over the next four years Mussolini used legal and illegal methods, including murder, to eliminate his political rivals and remake Italy as a one-party state. By 1926, he had succeeded. Party politics, an independent press, and the trade union movement disappeared. Victor Emmanuel remained on the throne, the official head of state, but power lay in Mussolini's hands. The restored death penalty and a strong police apparatus stood ready to crush dissent and fortify the fascist state.

THE FASCIST REVOLUTION IN ITALY But what was fascism? As a political ideology, fascism was, first, intensely *nationalistic*. The interests of the nation took precedence over any tradition, class, or individual. Fascism was also *statist* and *anti-democratic*. A centralized state, governed by a single party and led by an authoritarian leader, protected the nation's interests. Finally, fascism was *militaristic*. It exalted violence and military action. Influenced by Social Darwinism (see p. 748), Mussolini believed that nations, like species, competed for survival in a hostile world. Only the strong would—and should—survive.

Mussolini presented fascism as the politics of change. With a strong leader at the wheel, with violent action as its fuel, the fascist state would crash through social and economic barriers and transport the nation into the modern age. Yet Mussolini's supposedly radical revolution in fact reinforced traditional upper-class interests. Early fascist promises of land redistribution were never realized. In theory, fascism promised to replace capitalist competition and the profit motive with **corporatism**: Committees (or "corporations") made up of representatives of workers, employers, and the state would direct the economy for the good of the nation. In actuality, workers' rights disappeared while industrialists' profits remained untouched.

Although Mussolini had no intention of giving *genuine* political power to ordinary people, he did recognize the importance of giving them the *illusion* of power. Fascism made individuals feel a part of a mighty nation. "After-work" recreational groups connected ordinary people to the fascist state by serving as a channel for fascist propaganda and occupying their leisure hours.

The "Cult of the Duce" also fostered a sense of national community. Mussolini insisted, "I am Fascism." Choreographed public appearances gave ordinary Italians the chance to see, hear, and adore their Duce ("Leader"), and, through contact with his person, to feel a part of the new Italy. Mussolini paid careful attention to his public image. He ordered the press to ignore his birthdays and the births of his grandchildren: The Duce could not be seen to age. Instead, Mussolini appeared as a man of action. Depicted in planes, trains, and racing cars, he was always on the move, always pressing forward. (See *Different Voices* in this chapter.)

Mussolini combined up-to-date advertising and mass media technologies with age-old rituals inspired largely by the Catholic Church. Huge public rallies set in massive arenas, carefully staged with lighting and music, inspired his followers. A popular fascist slogan summed up the leadership cult: "Believe, Obey, Fight." Italians were not to think or question. They were to *believe*. What were they to believe? Another slogan provided the answer: "Mussolini is always right."

THE GREAT DEPRESSION AND THE SPREAD OF FASCISM AFTER 1929 In the 1920s, fascism possessed little appeal outside Italy. The key factor in the spread of fascism was the **Great Depression**. On October 24, 1929, the U.S. stock market collapsed. Over the next two years, the American economic crisis evolved into a global depression as banks closed, businesses collapsed, and unemployment rates rose to devastating levels.

corporatism The practice by which committees (or "corporations") made up of representatives of workers, employers, and the state direct the economy.

🔍 View the **Closer Look**

The Face of Fascism: Benito Mussolini

Great Depression Calamitous drop in prices, reduction in trade, and rise in unemployment that devastated the global economy in 1929.

26.1

26.2

26.3

26.4

26.5

26.6

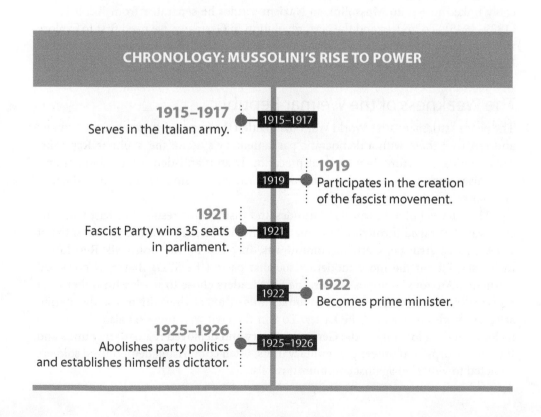

CHRONOLOGY: MUSSOLINI'S RISE TO POWER

1915–1917
Serves in the Italian army.
1915–1917

1919
1919
Participates in the creation of the fascist movement.

1921
Fascist Party wins 35 seats in parliament.
1921

1922
1922
Becomes prime minister.

1925–1926
Abolishes party politics and establishes himself as dictator.
1925–1926

26.1

26.2

26.3

26.4

26.5

26.6

The Depression spread so quickly because World War I had shifted the world's economic center from Europe to the United States. To pay for the war, European states had sold off their assets and borrowed heavily. By the end of 1918 Allied states owed the United States more than $9 billion. New York's stock market rivaled London's, and the United States moved from the position of debtor to creditor. The problem of wartime indebtedness soon became entangled with the issue of German reparations. Britain, France, and Italy could pay off their debts to the United States only if Germany paid reparations to them. American credit became the fuel that kept the European economy burning. American investors loaned money to Germany, which used the money to pay reparations to the Allies, which in turn used the money to pay back the United States. With the collapse of the U.S. stock market, however, American creditors liquidated European investments, and European economies tumbled.

The political and social disarray that accompanied the Great Depression enhanced the appeal of fascist promises of stability, order, and national strength. Over the next decade fascist movements emerged across Europe and existing authoritarian regimes adopted fascist trappings to stay in power.

Nazism and the Defeat of Democracy in Germany

26.3 How did the Nazis succeed in establishing a dictatorship in Germany?

O n the political spectrum, fascism comes under the heading of the **Radical Right**. Unlike nineteenth-century conservatism, Radical Right ideologies rejected existing social and political hierarchies, and fought not to defend but to uproot the status quo. In Germany, the Nazi Party offered a different version of Radical Right ideology. Just as the emergence of fascism was inextricably linked to Benito Mussolini, so **Nazism** cannot be separated from Adolf Hitler (1889–1945). To understand the Nazi revolution in Germany, we need first to explore the weakness of German democracy, and then Hitler's rise to power and the impact of Nazi rule on ordinary people.

The Weakness of the Weimar Republic

The peace settlement after World War I dismantled the imperial structures of Germany and replaced them with a democratic parliamentary system: the **Weimar Republic**. This political structure, however, sat precariously atop anti-democratic foundations. The kaiser was gone, but powerful anti-democratic forces remained to weaken the new Germany.

The survival of authoritarian attitudes and institutions resulted in part from the civil war that raged throughout Germany in the fall of 1918 and the first months of 1919. In this struggle, German communists, inspired by the Bolshevik Revolution in Russia, fought the more moderate socialist party (the SPD) that now governed Germany. Anxious to impose order, the SPD leaders chose to work with rather than replace the existing civil service, even though this meant allying with pro-authoritarian aristocrats who had served the kaiser. To win the civil war, the SPD also abandoned its longstanding loathing of the German military and deployed regular army units and the "Free Corps" (volunteer paramilitary units, often comprising demobilized soldiers addicted to violence) against communist rebels.

Radical Right Refers to extremist ideologies on the far right of the political spectrum, such as fascism and Nazism.

Nazism Twentieth-century political ideology associated with Adolf Hitler that adopted many fascist ideas but with a central focus on racism and particularly anti-Semitism.

Weimar Republic The democratic German state constructed after defeat in World War I and destroyed by the Nazis in 1933.

26.1

26.2

26.3

26.4

26.5

26.6

By the spring of 1919, this strange alliance of moderate socialists, traditional aristocrats, and thugs had crushed the communist uprising. The SPD had won—and yet it lost. By allying with the civil service, the army, and the Free Corps, the SPD crushed not only the communist revolution, but also its own chances of achieving significant social change. Many of the officers in the army and aristocrats in the civil service opposed democracy. Continuing in positions of power and influence, they constituted an authoritarian force at the heart of the new Germany. The approximately 400,000 men who made up the Free Corps also regarded democracy with contempt—"an attempt of the slime to govern."[3] Its slogan summed up the Free Corps attitude: "Everything would still have been all right if we had shot more people."[4] (See *Justice in History* in this chapter.)

Resentment of the Versailles Treaty strengthened these anti-democratic forces. Many Germans could not separate the birth of the Weimar Republic from the national humiliation imposed by Versailles. They blamed the moderate socialist government that signed the treaty for this humiliation. Army officers encouraged the idea that Germany could have kept on fighting had the SPD not "stabbed it in the back." This "stab-in-the-back" legend helped undermine support not only for the SPD's moderate socialism, but for democracy itself.

Hyperinflation further weakened Weimar democracy. In 1923, the German mark collapsed completely and paper money ceased to have any value. The mark, which in 1914 could be traded for the American dollar at a rate of 4:1, plummeted by October 1923 to an exchange rate of 440,000,000:1. Families who had scrimped for years found they had only enough savings to buy a loaf of bread.

This hyperinflation resulted from the Weimar government's effort to force the Allies to reconsider the reparations payments demanded by the Versailles Treaty. In 1922, the government halted payments and requested a new economic agreement. When the French retaliated by sending troops into Germany's Ruhr Valley to seize coal as a form of reparations, German miners went on strike. To pay the striking workers, the German government began printing money with abandon. The inflation rate surged upward—and then out of control.

Faced with the potentially disastrous collapse of the German economy, Allied and German representatives drew up the Dawes Plan in 1924, which renegotiated reparations. By the end of 1924, the German economy had stabilized. But hyperinflation seriously eroded support for the Weimar Republic. For many Germans, democracy meant disorder and degradation.

GEORGE GROSZ, *THE PILLARS OF SOCIETY* (1926) A World War I veteran like Otto Dix (see page 814), the Expressionist artist and communist George Grosz used his art to criticize the Weimar Republic. In this painting, a drunken military chaplain preaches while soldiers rampage behind his back. In the foreground sits a lawyer, supposedly a modern professional, but out of his head bursts a cavalry officer bent on destruction. To the lawyer's right, a publisher with a chamber pot on his head clutches the newspapers that guarantee his fortune and delude the masses. To the lawyer's left totters an SPD politician. His pudgy, drink-reddened cheeks, the steaming pile of excrement on his head, and the pamphlet he presses to his chest (headlined "Socialism Is Work") indicate Grosz's contempt for reformist socialism.

hyperinflation Catastrophic price increases and currency devaluation, such as that which occurred in Germany in 1923.

26.1

26.2

26.3

26.4

26.5

26.6

Hitler's Rise to Power

These events provide the backdrop for the emergence of Adolf Hitler and his Nazi movement as a force in German politics. Hitler, a German nationalist, was not a citizen of Germany for most of his life. Born in the Austrian half of the Austro-Hungarian Empire, Hitler came of age in Vienna, where he made a meager living as a painter while absorbing the anti-Semitic German nationalism that permeated this capital city. By the time World War I broke out, however, Hitler had settled in Germany. Delighted by the chance to fight the war in a German rather than an Austrian uniform, Hitler regarded army life as "the greatest of all experiences." He served as a German soldier until he was temporarily blinded by poison gas in 1918. Hitler then returned to Munich, home to large bands of unemployed war veterans and a breeding ground for nationalist and racist groups.

The Nazi Party began as one of these groups, with Hitler quickly emerging as its leader. *Nazi* is shorthand for National Socialist German Workers' Party, but this title, like all of Nazi ideology, was an empty promise. Nazism opposed socialism, communism, and trade unionism. Like fascism, Nazism was a nationalist, statist, anti-democratic, and militarist ideology.

In Nazism, however, racism, particularly anti-Semitism, played the central role. To Hitler, all history was the history of racial struggle; in that racial struggle, the Jews were always the principal enemy. Hitler regarded Jewishness as a biological rather than a religious identity, a toxic infection that threatened "Aryans," a linguistic term that Hitler misused to identify the "racially pure"—white northern Europeans. In Hitler's distorted vision, Jewishness and communism formed two parts of the same evil whole. He saw the Bolshevik victory in Russia as part of a wider struggle for Jewish world domination, and he promised his followers that the Aryan race would defeat the forces of "Judeo-Bolshevism" and establish a mighty empire encompassing all of eastern Europe, including the Soviet Union.

The early Nazi movement appealed to men like Hitler, individuals without power or, apparently, much chance of getting it—unemployed ex-soldiers, small shopkeepers wiped out by postwar inflation, lower middle-class clerks anxious to preserve their shaky social status, and workers who had lost their jobs. Nazism offered a simple explanation of history, a promise of future glory, and someone to blame for personal and national woes. By November 1923, party membership stood at about 55,000—a small, insignificant fringe party.

That month, however, Hitler and his supporters achieved national renown by attempting to overthrow the Weimar government. Although this "Beer Hall Putsch," as it came to be called (because it originated in a beer hall), failed miserably, it won Hitler a wide audience. His speeches during the ensuing trial for treason and *Mein Kampf* ("My Struggle"), the book he wrote while in prison, publicized his racialized view of German political history.

After Hitler emerged from prison, he concentrated on transforming the Nazis into a persuasive political force. To infiltrate German society at all levels, Nazis formed university and professional groups, labor unions, and agrarian organizations, while the Nazi paramilitary organization, the SA (*Sturmabteilung*), terrorized opponents. The party held meetings and rallies incessantly, not just during election periods, and so ensured that Germany was saturated with its message. Even so, in the elections of 1928, Nazi candidates won only 2.6 percent of the vote.

The Great Depression shifted the political playing field in Hitler's favor. As German industrial output fell by 46 percent and its number of jobless grew to more than six million, the Weimar political system began to collapse. No German political leader could put together a viable governing coalition. In all of 1932 the federal parliament met for only 13 days. With the mechanisms of parliamentary democracy faltering, political polarization accelerated. By July 1932, the Nazis were the largest party

Read the Document

Adolf Hitler, *Mein Kampf*

26.1

26.2

26.3

26.4

26.5

26.6

Justice in History
The Trial of Adolf Hitler

O n February 24, 1924, Adolf Hitler appeared in court in Munich on a charge of high treason. The trial marked a turning point in Hitler's career. It gave him a national platform and convinced him of the futility of an armed offensive against the state. From 1925 on, Hitler would work through the parliamentary system to destroy it. But the trial of Adolf Hitler was also significant in what it revealed about the power of anti-democratic forces in the new Germany. The trial made clear that many in positions of authority and responsibility in the Weimar Republic shared Hitler's contempt for the democratic state. By treating Hitler not as a traitorous thug, but rather as an honorable patriot, his prosecutors helped weaken the already fragile structures of German democracy.

Hitler's attempt to overthrow the Weimar Republic by force occurred at the height of hyperinflation. By November 8, 1923, when Hitler took up arms, the German mark was worth only one-trillionth of its prewar value. As the currency eroded, the Weimar government saw its political legitimacy seeping away as well. Hitler believed he could channel this political discontent into a national revolution. His supporters included one of the most important men in Germany, the World War I hero, General Erich von Ludendorff. Seeking to avoid the blame for Germany's defeat in 1918, Ludendorff insisted that his army could have won the war had it not been stabbed in the back by the Social Democratic politicians who now ran the government. Like many German conservatives—and like Hitler—Ludendorff viewed the Weimar Republic as illegitimate.

On November 8 Hitler

HITLER IN LANDSBERG PRISON, 1924 This photo of Hitler during his short imprisonment was made into a postcard, to be purchased by his supporters.

made his move. Standing in a Munich beer hall, he declared that the German federal government had been overthrown and that he was now the head of Germany, with Ludendorff as his commander-in-chief. Around noon the next day, Hitler, Ludendorff, and several thousands of their followers marched toward one of Munich's main squares. Armed police blocked their passage and the ensuing firefight killed 17 men. Despite the bullets whizzing through the air, Ludendorff marched through the police cordon and stood in the square awaiting arrest. Hitler ran away. Police found him two days later, cowering in a supporter's house.

The Beer Hall Putsch had failed. In jail awaiting trial, Hitler contemplated suicide. Yet later he described his defeat as "perhaps the greatest stroke of luck in my life." The defeat meant a trial and a trial meant a national audience.

During the trial Hitler admitted that he had conspired to overthrow the democratically elected Weimar government. He insisted, however, that he was not guilty of treason, that the real treason occurred in November 1918, when the Social Democratic government surrendered to the Allies: "I confess to the deed, but I do not confess to the crime of high treason. There can be no question of treason in an action which aims to undo the betrayal of this country in 1918. . . . I consider myself not a traitor but a German."

In his testimony, Hitler depicted himself as a patriot, a nationalist motivated by love of Germany and hatred of communists and socialists. "The eternal court of history" would judge him and his fellow defendants "as Germans who wanted the best for their people and their Fatherland, who were willing to fight and to die."[5]

Despite Hitler's admission of conspiring against the government, the presiding judge could persuade the three lay judges (who took the place of a jury) to render a guilty verdict only by arguing that Hitler would soon be pardoned. The reluctance of the judges to convict Hitler highlights the extraordinary sympathy shown to him and to his political ideas throughout the trial and during his imprisonment. The chief prosecutor offered a rather surprising description of an accused traitor: "Hitler is a highly gifted man, who has risen from humble beginnings to achieve a respected position in public life, the result of much hard work and dedication." In delivering the verdict, the judge emphasized Hitler's "pure patriotic motives and honorable intentions." Rather than being deported as a foreign national convicted of a serious crime (Hitler was still an Austrian citizen), he was given a slight sentence of five years, which made him eligible for parole in just six months. Prison officials treated Hitler like a visiting dignitary—they exempted him from work

(continued on next page)

(continued from previous page)

and exercise requirements, cleaned his rooms, and provided a special table decorated with a swastika banner in the dining hall. When Hitler was released in September, his parole report described him favorably as "a man of order."[6]

Hitler's gentle treatment revealed the precarious state of democratic institutions in Germany after World War I. Many high-ranking Germans in positions of power and influence (such as judges and prosecutors) loathed parliamentary democracy. The trial also revealed the willingness of conservative aristocrats to ally with Radical Right groups such as the Nazis. Not yet strong, the Nazis in 1923 were easily reined in. A decade later, however, the conservatives who thought they could ride Hitler to power found that they were no longer in control.

For Discussion

1. Imagine you are a German war veteran reading about this case in the newspaper in 1924. Why might you be attracted to the party of Adolf Hitler?
2. Hitler appealed to the "eternal court of history." What do you think he meant? How would Hitler have defined "justice"?

Taking It Further

The Hitler Trial Before the People's Court in Munich, trans. H. Francis Freniece, Lucie Karcic, and Philip Fandek (3 vols.). 1976. An English translation of the court transcripts.

Kershaw, Ian. *Hitler 1889–1936: Hubris*. 1999. A compelling (and massive) account of Hitler's early life and rise to power.

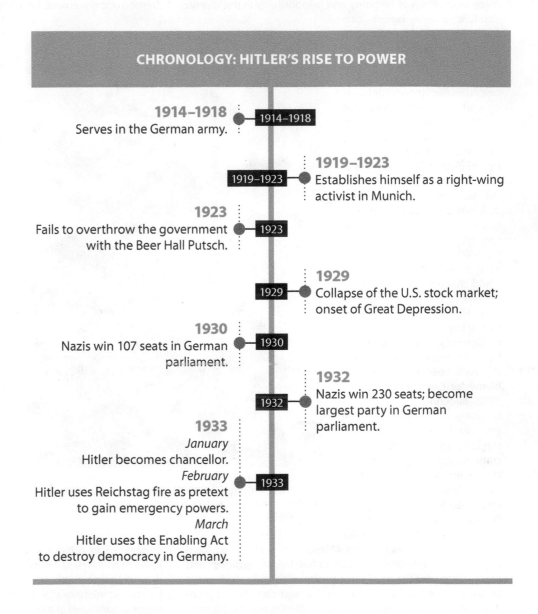

CHRONOLOGY: HITLER'S RISE TO POWER

1914–1918
Serves in the German army.

1919–1923
Establishes himself as a right-wing activist in Munich.

1923
Fails to overthrow the government with the Beer Hall Putsch.

1929
Collapse of the U.S. stock market; onset of Great Depression.

1930
Nazis win 107 seats in German parliament.

1932
Nazis win 230 seats; become largest party in German parliament.

1933
January
Hitler becomes chancellor.
February
Hitler uses Reichstag fire as pretext to gain emergency powers.
March
Hitler uses the Enabling Act to destroy democracy in Germany.

 **Read the Document**

Heinrich Hauser, "With Germany's Unemployed"

in the parliament, winning 37 percent of German votes. Support for their communist rivals also continued to grow.

In this unstable climate, Chancellor Heinrich Bruning turned to an emergency measure in the German constitution—rule by presidential decree. This practice meant that power shifted from parliament to the president, the World War I hero General

26.1

26.2

26.3

26.4

26.5

26.6

Paul von Hindenburg. Already in his 80s, Hindenburg was a weak man who was easily manipulated by a small circle of aristocratic advisers. These men, terrified of communism and convinced that the Nazis could be easily controlled, persuaded Hindenburg to offer Hitler the position of chancellor in January 1933. One of the group, Baron Franz von Papen, reassured a friend that Hitler posed "no danger at all. We have hired him for our act. In two months' time we'll have pushed Hitler so far into the corner, he'll be squeaking."[7]

It was a poor prediction. Almost as soon as Hitler took office he persuaded Hindenburg to pass an emergency decree ordering the seizure of all Communist Party presses and buildings. Then in February a fire destroyed the German parliament building. Declaring (wrongly) that the fire was part of a communist plot against the state, Hitler demanded the power to imprison without warrant or trial. Arrests of more than 25,000 of his political opponents followed—communists, socialists, and anyone who openly opposed him. At the end of March, German politicians, cowed by Nazi threats of imprisonment, passed the Enabling Act, giving Hitler the power to suspend the constitution and pass legislation without a parliamentary majority. By the summer of 1933, Hitler had destroyed German democracy and established a dictatorship.

Life (and Death) in the Nazi Dictatorship

Often presented as a model of authoritarian efficiency, the Nazi dictatorship was actually a confusing mass of overlapping bureaucracies, in which ambitious officials competed with each other for power and influence. This planned chaos ensured that none of Hitler's deputies acquired too much authority. It also enhanced the mystery of the state. The individual citizen attempting to make a complaint or resolve a problem would soon feel as if he were engaged in a battle with a multi-limbed monster.

This monster, however, had only one head: Adolf Hitler. Like Mussolini, Hitler realized the importance of personalizing his rule. In his early years of power, he was constantly on the move, using cars and planes to visit city after city, to deliver speech after speech, to touch person after person. Leaders of the Hitler Youth swore this oath: "Adolf Hitler is Germany and Germany is Adolf Hitler. He who pledges himself to Hitler pledges himself to Germany."[8]

NATIONAL RECOVERY When the Nazis seized control in 1933, depression gripped the German economy. The rules of economic orthodoxy dictated that in times of depression, a government should cut spending and maintain a balanced budget. Hoping to jump-start the stalled economy, Hitler's immediate predecessors in office had set aside these rules and begun to plan programs based on deficit spending. Hitler took these plans and ran with them. He invested heavily in public works and after 1936 poured money into rearmament. These programs created thousands of jobs. Unemployment dropped from 44 percent in 1932 to 14.1 percent in 1934 to less than 1 percent in 1938—while unemployment rates in the double digits persisted in democratic states such as Britain and France.

Germans and non-Germans alike hailed Nazi Germany as an economic success, yet under Nazi rule, real wages fell and workers' rights disappeared. Emphasis on rearmament led to shortages in food supplies and in consumer goods. Still, many Germans *believed* themselves to be much better off. The expansion of social welfare assistance (for those considered "Aryan") helps explain this perception, as does the establishment of the "Strength through Joy" program that provided workers with cheap vacations, theater and concert tickets, and weekend outings. But most important, under the Nazis, Germans were working. The abundance of jobs—despite the low wages, despite the disappearance of workers' rights, despite the food shortages—made Hitler an economic savior to many.

26.1

26.2

26.3

26.4

26.5

26.6

View the **Closer Look**   A Nazi Rally

HEIL (HAIL) *HITLER!* An enthusiastic crowd salutes Hitler at a Nazi Party rally. The women in the traditional costumes illustrate a key aspect of the Nazis' appeal: their promise to restore women to their traditional domestic roles. The men in military uniform indicate a second source of Nazi popularity: the restoration of military strength and national pride.

Many Germans also viewed him as a national savior who restored Germany's pride and power. German payments of war reparations halted in 1930 because of the global economic crisis. Hitler never resumed payment. He also ignored the treaty's military restrictions and rebuilt Germany's armed forces. By 1938, parades featuring row after row of uniformed troops signaled the revitalization of German military might. For many ordinary Germans, traumatized and shamed by the sequence of national disasters—military defeat, loss of territory, hyperinflation, political and fiscal crises, unemployment—the sight of troops goose-stepping under the German flag meant personal and national renaissance. As one Nazi song proclaimed, "And now the me is part of the great We."[9] (See *Different Voices* in this chapter.)

CAMPAIGNS OF REPRESSION AND TERROR   The creation of the "great We" depended on the demonization and repression of the "not Us," those defined as outside or opposed to the nation. Hitler used the existing German police force and his own paramilitary troops—the brownshirted SA and the blackshirted SS (*Schutzstaffel*)—to terrorize those he defined as enemies of the nation. By 1934 half of the 300,000 German Communist Party members were in prison or dead and most of the rest had fled the country. The Nazis also persecuted specific religious groups on the basis of their actual or presumed opposition to the Nazi state. Roman Catholics faced constant harassment and about half of Germany's 20,000 Jehovah's Witnesses were sent to concentration camps. Homosexuals, too, faced harsh persecution. Between 1933 and 1939, 10,000 Germans were killed by the Nazi regime.

The groups that the Nazis deemed biologically inferior suffered most severely. Beginning in 1933, the Nazi regime forced the sterilization of the mentally and physically handicapped and mixed-race children (in most cases, the offspring of German women and black African soldiers serving in the French occupation force in the Rhineland). The campaign was soon extended to the Roma (Gypsies). By 1939, 370,000 men and women had been sterilized.

The brunt of Nazi racial attacks, however, fell on Germany's Jewish community—less than 1 percent of the population. To Nazi anti-Semites, Hitler's accession to the German chancellorship was like the opening of hunting season. They beat up Jews in the streets, vandalized Jewish shops and homes, threatened German Christians who associated with Jews, and violently enforced boycotts of Jewish businesses. Anti-Jewish legislation piled up. In 1933, the Nazi government dismissed "non-Aryans" (Jews) from the civil service and the legal profession, and restricted the number of Jewish students in high schools and universities. Every organization in Germany—youth clubs, sports teams, labor unions, charitable societies—underwent "Nazification," which meant the dismissal of all Jewish members and the appointment of Nazis to leadership roles. In 1935, the "Nuremberg Laws" deprived German Jews of their citizenship and declared marriage or sexual relations between German Jews and non-Jews a serious crime. By 1938, 25 percent of Germany's Jewish population had fled the country.

26.1

26.2

26.3

26.4

26.5

26.6

The Soviet Alternative and the Democracies' Response

26.4 Why did the Soviet Union seem a success and how did the democracies respond?

The apparent successes of fascist Italy and Nazi Germany appealed to many Europeans and Americans disenchanted with democracy. During this period, the Soviet Union also seemed a success story. While the capitalist states struggled with high unemployment rates and falling industrial output, the Soviet Union appeared to be performing economic miracles. Politics in the West thus became increasingly polarized into the Radical Left and the Radical Right. Politicians and policymakers in the United States and in western Europe struggled to maintain the middle ground, to retain democratic values in the face of extremist challenges.

The Soviet Union: Revolution Reconstructed, Terror Extended

Created out of the rubble of revolution and civil war, the new Soviet Union embarked on a different path from the rest of the West in the post–World War I period. Under the dictatorial rule of the Bolshevik—now called the Communist—Party, peoples of over 100 different national groups, speakers of over 200 languages and dialects, struggled to create a new political order.

NEP AND NATIONALITIES We saw in Chapter 25 that after four years of bitter fighting, the Bolsheviks won the civil war. Once in power, Lenin imposed single-party rule, silenced debate, and used intimidation and murder to crush dissent. The rule of the tsar gave way not to democracy, but to the rule of the commissar, the Communist Party functionary. Party bureaucrats became a privileged upper class, with access to the best jobs, food, clothing, and apartments.

Even the harshest authoritarian control could not, however, make up for the immense economic damage wrought by the years of civil war. With famine in the countryside and the economy in disarray, Lenin in 1921 declared a strategic retreat from "War Communism" and the effort to abolish capitalist enterprise. Under the **New Economic Policy (NEP)**, peasants were allowed to sell their produce for profit. Although the state continued to control heavy industry, transport, and banking, NEP actually encouraged small private businesses and farms. Under this policy the Soviet

 Read the Document

Nadezhda Krupskaya, "What a Communist Ought to Be Like"

New Economic Policy (NEP) Vladimir Lenin's economic turnaround in 1921 that allowed and even encouraged small private businesses and farms in the Soviet Union.

 Read the Document

A. Dubova, "Living Someone Else's Life"

26.1

26.2

26.3

26.4

26.5

26.6

economy stabilized, small businessmen (called "Nepmen") increased in number, and many peasants prospered.

The New Economic Policy accompanied a new nationalities program. The Soviet Union included enormous numbers of non-Russians. Recognizing that many of these peoples resented the tsar's Russification policies (see p. 727), Lenin abandoned Russification. Rather than crushing non-Russian national identities, the new program sought to foster local language and cultures—and thus, Lenin hoped, win the allegiance of non-Russians to the new communist order. The Soviet Union itself was a federation of the semi-autonomous republics of Russia, Ukraine, Byelorussia (Belarus), and Transcaucasia. Ethnic Russians living in non-Russian republics were required to learn local languages, and local elites were encouraged to join the Communist Party and take on leadership positions.

FROM LENIN TO STALIN The deputy who helped Lenin create the nationalities program was himself a non-Russian from Georgia, as his last name—Dzhugashvili—indicated. But most Soviets knew him by his revolutionary name: Stalin, man of steel. Like Lenin, Joseph Stalin (1879–1953) was a professional revolutionary, an "old Bolshevik" who had labored in the underground opposition to the tsarist regime. Although an important man in the party, he was not widely expected to succeed Lenin as leader when Lenin died in 1924. As party secretary, however, Stalin controlled who belonged to this all-powerful group. By the mid-1920s, large numbers of ordinary communists owed their party privileges and their livelihoods to him. After a protracted leadership struggle, Stalin emerged in 1927 as Lenin's successor and the head of the Soviet Union.

To solidify and expand his authority, Stalin constructed a gargantuan personality cult. Innumerable posters and statues ensured that Stalin's figure remained constantly in front of Soviet citizens. Textbooks rewrote the history of the Bolshevik Revolution and linked every scientific, technological, or economic advance in the Soviet Union to him. The scores of letters personally addressed to "Comrade Stalin" testify that millions of Soviet citizens saw Stalin as their protector. (See *Different Voices* in this chapter.)

In many of the omnipresent images of Stalin, he appeared alongside Lenin, as Stalin always carefully (and deceptively) painted himself as Lenin's chosen heir. The key characteristics of Leninism—authoritarian rule and the use of terror as a tool of state—not only remained central but grew more pronounced under Stalin. We will see, however, that in important ways Stalin shifted the direction of Soviet policies.

THE "REVOLUTION FROM ABOVE": COLLECTIVIZATION Once Stalin established his control over the Soviet Union, he dismantled Lenin's New Economic Policy and launched the Soviet economy into full-scale industrialization. This economic transformation, however, rested on dead bodies, millions of dead bodies, as mass murder became even more an integral part of the Soviet regime.

To catapult the Soviet Union into the ranks of the industrialized states, Stalin called for "the revolution from above"—the abandonment of NEP and the acceleration of state control over the economy. The first stage of this revolution was **collectivization**, the replacement of private and village farms with large cooperative agricultural enterprises run by communist managers according to directives received from the central government. Regarded as more modern and efficient, collective farms were expected to produce an agricultural surplus and thereby raise the capital needed for industrialization. In addition, collectivization would realize communist ideals by eradicating the profit motive, abolishing private property, and transforming peasants into modern state employees.

To initiate collectivization, Stalin announced at the end of 1929 that the **kulaks** would be "liquidated as a class." A "kulak" was a wealthier peasant, depicted in

collectivization The replacement of private and village farms with large cooperative agricultural enterprises run by state-employed managers. Collectivization was a key part of Joseph Stalin's plans for modernizing the Soviet economy and destroying peasant opposition to communist rule.

kulak Russian term for a peasant who is relatively prosperous.

26.1

26.2

26.3

26.4

26.5

26.6

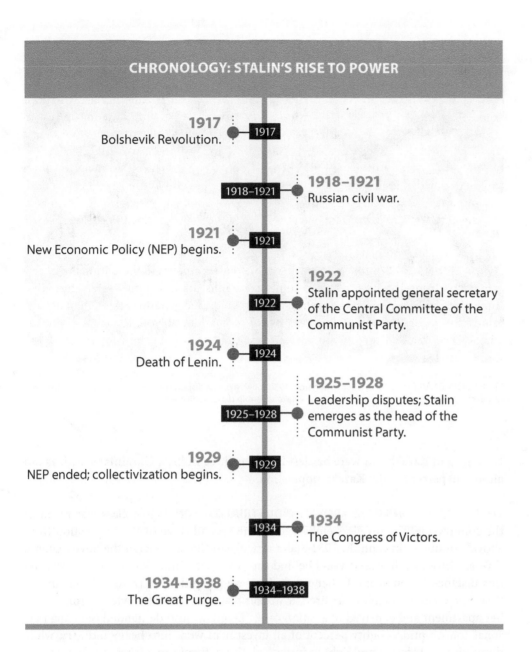

CHRONOLOGY: STALIN'S RISE TO POWER

1917
Bolshevik Revolution.
1917

1918–1921
1918–1921
Russian civil war.

1921
New Economic Policy (NEP) begins.
1921

1922
1922
Stalin appointed general secretary of the Central Committee of the Communist Party.

1924
Death of Lenin.
1924

1925–1928
1925–1928
Leadership disputes; Stalin emerges as the head of the Communist Party.

1929
NEP ended; collectivization begins.
1929

1934
1934
The Congress of Victors.

1934–1938
The Great Purge.
1934–1938

Soviet propaganda as an oppressor who grew fat off the labor of others, an enemy of the ongoing revolution. Kulaks tended to be the leaders in their localities, those who had prospered under NEP and those with the most to lose from collectivization. Over the next few years, almost two million kulaks were stripped of all their possessions, forced onto freezing freight cars, and deported to **the Gulag**, the network of forced labor camps and special settlements that stretched across Siberia and Kazakhstan.

The "liquidation" of the kulaks served as the opening onslaught in what became an undeclared war against Soviet peasants, who resisted collectivization by burning their crops, slaughtering their livestock, and fighting with shovels and hoes. They proved no match for the armed might of the Stalinist state.

Peasant resistance did, however, disrupt agricultural production. Faced with low harvest yields in 1932, Stalin responded by deploying starvation as a weapon. Brigades of communist activists moved into rural regions and confiscated all food supplies. The numbers of deaths resulting from collectivization and famine remain controversial, but the available evidence points to death figures between five and seven million.

the Gulag Term for the network of forced labor and prison camps in the Soviet Union.

 **Read the Document**

Irina Ivanovna Kniazeva, "A Life in a Peasant Village"

26.1

26.2

26.3

26.4

26.5

26.6

"THE PEOPLE'S VERMIN" This photograph from 1930 shows a public display used as publicity for the collectivization campaign. The gigantic masks depict the kulaks as vermin to be eradicated.

Ukraine and Kazakhstan were hardest hit. Over three million Ukrainians died, as did almost 40 percent of the Kazakh population.

THE "REVOLUTION FROM ABOVE": INDUSTRIALIZATION While class war raged in the countryside, city dwellers embarked on the second stage of the "revolution from above"—industrialization. In 1931 Stalin articulated the task facing the Soviet Union: "We are fifty or a hundred years behind the advanced countries. We must catch up this distance in ten years. Either we do it or we go under."[10] "Doing it" demanded, first, fierce labor discipline. If fired, a worker was automatically evicted from his or her apartment and deprived of a ration card. "Doing it" also demanded reducing personal consumption. Eighty percent of all investment went into heavy industry, while domestic construction and light industry—clothing, furniture, dishes, appliances, and the like—were ignored. Scarcity became the norm, long lines and constant shortages part of every city-dweller's existence. Soviet citizens endured an estimated 40 percent fall in their already low standard of living between 1929 and 1932.

While millions starved in the countryside and urban living standards plummeted, young communists acclaimed these years of hardship and horror as an era of heroism. They volunteered to organize collective farms, to work in brutal conditions at construction sites, to labor long hours in factories and mines. Propaganda campaigns aimed at persuading laborers to work harder kept this enthusiasm at a fever pitch. The most productive workers earned medals and material gifts. Publicity focused on gargantuan engineering achievements—the cities built atop swampland, the hydroelectric projects with their enormous dams and power plants, the Moscow subway system. Such publicity made party members feel part of a mighty endeavor. A popular song announced, "We were born to make fairy tales come true."[11]

No propaganda campaign and no amount of effort from enthusiastic communists, however, could provide the Soviet Union with the labor it needed to catch up with the West in 10 years. Forced labor was crucial. Throughout the 1930s, Gulag prison camps housed up to two million men, women, and children at any one time. Many of the huge engineering triumphs of the decade rested on the backs of these prisoners.

By the end of the 1930s, Stalin's "revolution from above" had achieved its aim. The pouring of resources into heavy industry and the wringing of every ounce of labor out of an exhausted, cold, and hungry populace succeeded in building the foundations of an industrial society, one that would pass the test of total war in the 1940s. Press censorship ensured that the mass killing and forced labor that fueled this economic transformation remained hidden.

STALIN'S CONSOLIDATION OF POWER: THE GREAT PURGE AND SOVIET SOCIETY The 17th Communist Party Congress in 1934 called itself the "Congress of Victors," as the party celebrated its industrial successes and the achievement of collectivization. But within five years, half of the 2,000 delegates had been arrested. Of the 149 elected members of the Congress's Central Committee, 98 were shot dead. These Congress delegates fell victim to the **"Great Purge."** So, too, did an estimated 700,000 of their fellow Soviet citizens, with millions more imprisoned and deported.

The most well-known victims of the Great Purge were top-ranking Communist Party officials, "old Bolsheviks" like Stalin who had fought in the revolution. By charging these powerful men with conspiring against the communist state, Stalin reduced the chances that any competitor might oust him. The purge, however, moved beyond the top ranks of the party and swallowed up low-level party members, managers in state agencies, factory directors, and engineers—and their families and friends. Many were killed without trial, others executed after a legal show, and still others deported to labor camps to be worked to death on Stalin's construction projects.

In 1937 the Purge broadened even further. Even prisoners already in the Gulag were not safe: In the Siberian city of Omsk, for example, the Gulag chief and his men shot 1,300 people in one single night. This phase of the Purge targeted members of national minorities, particularly ethnic Poles. Party officials who had faithfully implemented Lenin's nationalities program and worked to develop non-Russian languages and cultures found themselves condemned for the crime of fostering "bourgeois nationalism." An estimated 250,000 Soviet citizens were executed in 1937 and 1938 on the grounds of their nationality.

Through deportation, mass killing, and general terror, the Great Purge consolidated Stalin's hold on the Soviet Union. It eliminated all potential competitors and, strangely, it gave many people a reason to believe in their leader. Individuals who moved into the positions left vacant by the purge's victims had a material and psychological stake in believing that these victims were guilty and that the purge was justified.

The Response of the Democracies

In the 1930s, democratic states faced powerful challenges, as many in the West concluded that democracy simply did not work. Yet in western Europe and the United States, governments took important steps to ensure that democracy survived.

A THIRD WAY? THE SOCIAL DEMOCRATIC ALTERNATIVE The effort to meet the challenge of the Great Depression accelerated the development of the political model that would dominate western Europe after World War II: **social democracy**. In a social democracy, a democratically elected government accepts the responsibility of ensuring a decent standard of living for its citizens. To achieve this goal, the government assumes two functions—first, regulating an economy containing both private enterprise and

26.1

26.2

26.3

26.4

26.5

26.6

Read the Document

John Scott, Excerpt from *Behind the Urals: An American Worker in Russia's City of Steel*

Great Purge Period of mass arrests and executions particularly aimed at Communist Party members in the Soviet Union.

social democracy Political system in which a democratically elected parliamentary government endeavors to ensure a decent standard of living for its citizens through both economic regulation and the maintenance of a welfare state.

26.1
26.2
26.3
26.4
26.5
26.6

Different Voices

The Cult of the Leader

Stalinism stood on the extreme left of the political spectrum; Nazism and fascism, on the extreme right. Mussolini's fascists came to national prominence by beating up socialists, and Hitler ranked communists alongside Jews as enemies of the German nation. Yet Radical Right and Radical Left states resembled each other in many ways. Fascist Italy, Nazi Germany, and the Stalinist Soviet Union shared contempt for individual rights and a willingness to use violence as an instrument of the state. These states also all relied on the cult of personality (or the leadership cult). Searching for a way to mobilize the masses without granting them actual political power, Mussolini, Hitler, and Stalin used their own images to personify and personalize the state and to make their authoritarian rule more extensive and more acceptable. The following excerpts illustrate the cults of personality that helped shape the West in the 1930s.

I. Description of an Early Nazi Rally by Louise Solmitz, Schoolteacher

The April sun shone hot like summer and turned everything into a picture of gay expectation. There was immaculate order and discipline . . . the hours passed. . . . Expectations rose. There stood Hitler in a simple black coat and looked over the crowd. Waiting. A forest of swastika pennants swished up, the jubilation of this moment was given vent in a roaring salute. . . . How many look up to him with a touching faith! As their helper, their savior, their deliverer from unbearable distress—to him who rescues the Prussian prince, the scholar, the clergyman, the farmer, the worker, the unemployed, who leads them from the parties back into the nation.

SOURCE: "Description of an Early Nazi Rally by Louise Solmitz, Schoolteacher," copyright © 1988 by Claudia Koonz. From *Mothers in the Fatherland: Women, the Family, and Nazi Politics* by Claudia Koonz. New York: St. Martin's Press, 1987.

II. Letter from a Nazi Party member, a "Party Comrade," to Hitler, 1936

My Führer! . . . I feel compelled by unceasing love to thank our creator daily for, through his grace, giving us and the entire German people such a wonderful Führer, and in a time . . . where our beautiful dear Fatherland was threatened with the most horrible destruction through Jewish bolshevism. It does not bear thinking about what floods of tears, what blood after the scarcely healed wounds of the World War, would have flowed, if you, my beloved Führer, in all your anguish for such a great people had not found the courage, with at that time a small band of seven men, to win through as the saviour of 66 million Germans, in that through your great love of every individual, from the smallest child to the most aged, you captured all, all, women, men, and the whole of German youth. . . . It is a pleasure for me, not a compliment, not hypocrisy, to pray for you, my Führer, that the Lord God who has created you as a tool for Germany should keep you healthy, that the love of the people towards you should grow, firm and hard like the many oak trees which have been planted in love and honour to you, my Führer, even in the smallest community in Germany. . . . A Heil to the Führer for victory with all the former front-line fighters who still remain today devoted to the Führer to death. For Germany must live even if we must die.

SOURCE: Quoted in Ian Kersaw, *The Hitler Myth*, Oxford: Oxford University Press, 1987, p. 81. By permission of Oxford University Press. Copyright © 1987 by Ian Kershaw.

III. Account by Maria Demchenko, collective farm laborer, of her meeting with Stalin at an award ceremony

Comrade Stalin was standing among his assistants smiling, waving his hand to us (like this!) and looking at the *kolkhozniks* very, very closely and with a special kind of warmth. When the cheers had quieted down, he looked at me and said, 'Well, comrade Demchenko, tell us your story. . . . "

I told him everything.

I was looking at comrade Stalin—at how he was listening, and I could tell by his face that he hadn't missed a single word: now he would smile, then look thoughtful, or nod like this his head, as if to say that's right!

After the *kolkhoz* women he started talking himself. His whole speech, his every word as so engraved on my memory that I'll never forget them. . . .

SOURCE: "Account by Maria Demchenko, collective farm laborer, of her meeting with Stalin at an award ceremony," from *Stalin's Peasants: Resistance and Survival in the Russian Village After Collectivization* by Sheila Fitzpatrick. Copyright © 1994 by Oxford University Press, Inc. Published by permission of Oxford University Press.

IV. Speech by a Woman Delegate at a Workers' Conference in the Soviet Union

Thank you comrade Stalin, our leader, our father, for a happy, merry kolkhoz* life!

He, our Stalin, put the steering-wheel of the tractor in our hand. . . . He, the great Stalin, carefully listens to all of us in this meeting, loves us with a great Stalinist love (*tumultuous applause*), day and night thinks of our prosperity, of our culture, of our work. . . .

Long live our friend, our teacher, the beloved leader of the world proletariat, comrade Stalin! (*Tumultuous applause, rising to an ovation. Shouts of "Hurrah!"*)

SOURCE: "Speech by a Woman Delegate at a Worker's Conference in the Soviet Union," from *Stalin's Peasants: Resistance and Survival in the Russian Village After Collectivization* by Sheila Fitzpatrick. Copyright © 1996 by Oxford University Press, Inc. Published by permission of Oxford University Press.

For Discussion

1. Why did Radical Right and Radical Left movements include cults of personality? Do these excerpts reveal any differences between the leadership cults of these states?

2. How and why did the cult of personality take on religious dimensions? Should we view modern nationalism as a secular religion?

3. Can we take these documents at face value? In a dictatorial state, where any dissent risks punishment and even death, people often hide their true feelings and beliefs. How do we know that the individuals speaking here were not putting on an act to survive or to get ahead?

*kolkhoz = collective farm

26.1

26.2

26.3

26.4

26.5

26.6

nationalized, or state-controlled, businesses, and second, overseeing a welfare state, which guarantees citizens access to unemployment and sickness benefits, pensions, family allowances, and health services. Although social democracy did not triumph in the West until after a second total war, interwar Western societies took important steps on this third path, an alternative to the extremes of the Radical Right and the Radical Left.

One of the most striking experiments in changing the relationship between democratic governments and the economy occurred in the United States. Franklin Delano Roosevelt (1882–1945) was elected president in 1932 at the height of the Great Depression, when unemployment stood at 24 percent and federal troops in Washington, D.C. fought rioting unemployed veterans. Promising a "New Deal" of "Relief, Recovery, Reform," Roosevelt tackled the depression with an activist governmental policy that included agricultural subsidies, public works programs, and the Social Security Act of 1935, which set the foundations of the U.S. welfare program.

Yet even with this sharp upswing in government activity, unemployment in the United States remained high—10 million workers were without jobs in 1939—and the gross national product (GNP) did not recover to 1929 levels until 1941. In the view of some economists, Roosevelt failed to solve the problem of unemployment because he remained committed to the ideal of a balanced budget. In contrast, the British economist John Maynard Keynes (1883–1946) insisted that in times of depression the state should not reduce spending and endeavor to live within its budget, but instead should adopt a program of deficit spending to stimulate economic growth. Only when prosperity returned, Keynes advised, should governments increase taxes and cut expenditures to recover the deficits.

The experience of Sweden appeared to confirm **Keynesian economics**. The Swedish Social Democratic Party took office in 1932 with the intention of using the powers of the state to revive the economy. The government allowed its budget deficit to climb while it financed public works and increased welfare benefits, ranging from unemployment insurance to maternity allowances to subsidized housing. By 1937 unemployment was shrinking rapidly as the manufacturing sector boomed.

> **Keynesian economics** Economic theories associated with the British economist John Maynard Keynes that advocate using the power of the democratic state to ensure economic prosperity.

Throughout most of western Europe, however, governments proved reluctant to embrace new policies. For example, Britain's limited economic recovery in the later 1930s stemmed largely from the emergence of new private industries aimed at domestic consumption (such as radios and other small electronics). In the areas hardest hit by depression—northern British cities, home to export industries such as coal, shipbuilding, textiles, and steel—the lack of government intervention meant continuing unemployment and widespread poverty throughout the 1930s.

POPULAR FRONTS IN FRANCE AND SPAIN The limited success of democratic governments in addressing the problems of the Great Depression meant that many experienced the 1930s as a hard, hungry decade. The examples of France and Spain illustrate the political polarization occurring in Europe in the 1930s, as well as the sharp limits on governments seeking both to maintain democratic politics and to improve living conditions.

The Great Depression hit France later than most other European states, but in 1931 the French economy plummeted. Social unrest grew, and so, too, did the appeal of fascism. The fascist threat, combined with the deepening national emergency, led to the formation of the **Popular Front**, a coalition comprising radicals, socialists, and communists. In 1936, the Popular Front won the national elections and Socialist Party leader Léon Blum (1872–1950) took office as prime minister. Over the next year, Blum nationalized key industries and gave workers pay increases, paid vacations, and a 40-hour workweek.

> **Popular Front** A political coalition of liberals, socialists, and communists to defeat fascist and racist-nationalist political rivals.

Many conservative French voters saw Blum's policies of social reform as the first step on the road to Stalinism. They cried, "Better Hitler than Blum!"—in other words,

26.1

26.2

26.3

26.4

26.5

26.6

THE SPANISH CIVIL WAR The Spanish Civil War mobilized women as well as men. These soldiers, fighting in the uniform of the anarchist militia, are defending the barricades of Barcelona against rebel attack.

better the Radical Right than the Stalinist Left. The global business community pulled capital out of France, which brought on a major financial crisis and the devaluation of the French franc. Dependent on foreign loans, Blum's government tried to retreat from its social and economic reforms. Its working-class constituency responded with riots, and the Popular Front in France disintegrated.

In Spain, the Popular Front was defeated not by economic pressures, but by civil war. In 1931, a democratically elected republican government replaced the Spanish monarchy; in 1936, a Popular Front government, comprising socialists and communists, took office. Army officers, led by General Francisco Franco (1892–1975), rebelled and civil war began.

The struggle between the left-wing Republican government and the right-wing rebels quickly became an international issue. Fascist Italy and Nazi Germany supported the rebellion. The Republic of Spain appealed to the democracies for aid, but the only state that came to its assistance was the Soviet Union. Unnerved by Soviet involvement, the French, British, and American governments remained neutral, although 15,000 of their citizens joined the International Brigades to fight for Spanish democracy. All total, over 59,000 volunteers from 55 countries fought in these brigades.

The Spanish Civil War raged until March 1939, when the last remnants of the Republican forces surrendered to Franco. At least 400,000 men and women died in the war, and Franco executed another 200,000 after he took power and established an authoritarian state.

The Reconstruction of Gender

26.5   What changed, and what did not, in women's experiences after World War I?

W e saw in Chapter 25 that the demands of total war meant that women moved into economic areas previously designated as "men only." World War I seemed an important turning point in the history of Western women. But here, as in the democratization of eastern and central Europe, World War I was in many ways the turning point that failed to turn.

The New Woman

At first sight, the postwar period seemed to be an era of profound change for women. In the films, magazines, novels, and popular music of the 1920s, the "New Woman" took center stage. Living, working, and traveling on her own, sexually active, she stepped out of the confines of home and family. Women's dress and hairstyles reinforced the sense of change. Whereas nineteenth-century women's clothing had accentuated the womanly body while restricting movement, the clothing of the 1920s ignored a woman's curves and became less confining. Sporty new "bobs" replaced the long hair that had long been a sign of proper femininity.

This perception of the New Woman rested on changing political and economic expectations. By 1920 women in the United States and many European countries had received the right to vote in national elections and to hold national office. In all the industrialized countries, expansion of the health care and service sectors meant new jobs for women as nurses, social workers, secretaries, telephone operators, and clerks. Women's higher education opportunities also widened in this period.

The biggest change affecting the lives of ordinary women, however, was more intimate: the spreading practice of family limitation. We saw in Chapter 23 that by the 1870s middle-class women in Western countries were practicing birth control. In the 1920s and 1930s, an increasing number of working-class women began to do so as well. Fewer pregnancies and fewer mouths to feed improved women's health and living standards.

The Reconstruction of Traditional Roles

Despite these important changes, however, women's *roles* altered little in the two decades after World War I. Governments and ordinary citizens recoiled from wartime gender upheaval and worked to reconstruct nineteenth-century masculine and feminine ideals.

The war's lengthy casualty lists and the drop in the average family size provoked widespread fear about declining populations—and thus declining national strength. Governments, religious leaders, and commercial entrepreneurs joined together to convince women that their destiny lay in motherhood. Sales and purchases of birth control devices became illegal during the 1920s in France, Belgium, Italy, and Spain. France outlawed abortions in 1920. In Britain after 1929, a woman who had an abortion could be sentenced to life imprisonment. To encourage population growth, governments expanded welfare services. By providing family allowances, subsidized housing, school lunches, health insurance, and prenatal and well-baby care, politicians and policymakers hoped to ensure that married women stayed at home and produced large families.

Eugenics (the effort to improve the physical and intellectual capacities of the population by encouraging individuals with "desirable" traits to reproduce) played an important role in this legislation. National leaders wanted to increase not only the quantity, but the quality of the population. On the positive side, this meant improving the health of babies and mothers. More ominously, welfare policy rhetoric often focused on separating the "fit" from the "unfit," with class and race used to designate who was "fit" to produce children for the nation.

Despite the calls for women to remain at home, many women had to work in paid employment. In the work world, just as in the family, traditional roles strengthened

THE "NEW WOMAN" Almost every aspect of the "New Woman" (captured in this 1927 French magazine illustration) offended traditionalists: The bobbed hair, manly fashions, and aggressive strutting crossed the border into masculine terrain.

eugenics The effort to improve the physical and intellectual capacities of the population by encouraging individuals with "desirable" traits to reproduce and/or by discouraging those individuals designated as "undesirable" from reproducing.

835

26.1

26.2

26.3

26.4

26.5

26.6

after World War I. Most working women returned to jobs in domestic service or to factory positions labeled unskilled and therefore low-paying. Because employers still tended to bar women from management positions, assign them to the most repetitive tasks, and pay them by piecework, the wage gap between male and female laborers remained wide. The numbers of women employed in the clerical and service sectors did rise in this era, but the movement of women into these positions meant such jobs were reclassified as "women's work," a guarantee of low pay and little power.

WOMEN AND THE RADICAL RIGHT Fascism and Nazism promised to restore order to societies perceived to be on the verge of disintegration. Restoration of order meant the return of women to their proper place. According to Nazi propaganda, "the soil provides the food, the woman supplies the population, and the men make the action."[12] Hitler proclaimed, "The Nazi Revolution will be an entirely male event." Mussolini agreed: "Woman must obey. . . . In our State, she must not count."[13]

The Nazi government offered financial and cultural incentives to encourage women to stay at home and produce babies. These measures ranged from marriage loans (available only if the wife quit her job) and income tax deductions for families to the establishment of discussion, welfare, and leisure groups for housewives. The Nazis also used disincentives. One of the first actions of Hitler's government was to restrict women's employment in the civil service and to rule that female physicians could work only in their husbands' practices. By 1937, female physicians and women with PhDs had lost the right to be addressed as "Doctor" or "Professor." Women could no longer work as school principals. Coeducational schools were abolished. Birth control became illegal and penalties for abortion increased while prosecutions doubled.

In fascist Italy, Mussolini's government focused its legislation on both men and women. Unmarried men over age 30 had to pay double income tax (priests were exempt) and fatherhood became a prerequisite for men in high-ranking public office. Quotas limited the number of women employed in the civil service and in private business, while women found themselves excluded entirely from jobs defined as "virile," a list that included boat captains, diplomats, high school principals, and history teachers. A wide-ranging social welfare program that included family allowances, maternity leaves, and marriage loans sought to strengthen the traditional family. Despite these provisions, birth rates in Italy actually declined because low wages meant families could not afford more children.

WOMEN IN THE SOVIET UNION In contrast to these efforts to reinforce traditional family structures, in Russia the Bolsheviks promised to revolutionize gender roles. Lenin believed that the family was a middle-class institution doomed to "wither away." He declared that in the ideal communist society, marriage would be a mutually beneficial—and in many cases temporary—arrangement between two equally educated and equally waged partners, and housework and child care would move from the private domestic household into the public sphere of paid employment. Nevertheless, in revolutionary Soviet society, too, continuities linked the pre- and postwar experience of women.

One month after seizing power, the Bolsheviks legalized divorce and civil marriages. In 1918, a new family legal code declared women and men equal under the law and abolished the distinction between legitimate and illegitimate children. To free women from housework—described by Lenin as "barbarously unproductive, petty, nervewracking, and stultifying drudgery"[14]—the Bolsheviks promised communal child care centers, laundries, and dining rooms. In 1920, just as other states were outlawing

Read the Document

Gertrud Scholtz-Klink, "Speech to the Nazi Women's Organization"

26.1

26.2

26.3

26.4

26.5

26.6

abortion, the practice became legal in Bolshevik Russia. A Women's Bureau instructed women in their new rights, challenged the traditional patriarchy of peasant households, and encouraged Muslim women to remove their veils.

But in 1922, as we have seen, Lenin retreated from communist ideology by instituting the New Economic Policy. NEP also meant reversals in the gender revolution. By 1923, the dining halls had closed and more than half of the day care centers shut down. Throughout the 1920s, Soviet women's wages averaged 65 percent of men's. Moreover, in rural and Islamic regions, the Bolshevik attempt at gender revolution aroused strong and sometimes violent resistance. The majority of Soviet women remained in subordinate roles.

This retreat from gender revolution accelerated once Stalin took control of the Soviet Union. In 1936, the Soviet government outlawed abortion and made divorce more difficult. Like Western leaders, Stalin also tried to increase birth rates by granting pregnant women maternity stipends and improving prenatal care.

Stalin made no effort to pull women out of the workforce, however. Of the more than four million new workers entering the labor force between 1932 and 1937, 82 percent were women. Soviet women continued to have access to higher education and professional jobs—working as doctors, engineers, scientists, and high-ranking government officials—and, like men, they were deported and executed in huge numbers.

"WORKING WOMEN IN THE STRUGGLE FOR SOCIALISM AND THE STRUGGLE AGAINST RELIGION" This Soviet propaganda poster proclaims a new age of liberation for Soviet women. The light of socialism, reached through Lenin's writings (top left) and visible in clean, modernist design (top right), penetrates the darkness of superstition and patriarchal abuse (bottom left and right). The woman who dominates the poster, an architect designing the socialist future, represents the ideal Soviet woman.

The West and the World: Imperialism in the Interwar Era

((• 📖 **Read the Document**

Soviet Union "Law Code on Marriage" and "Law Code on Motherhood"

26.6 How did the interaction between the West and the world outside change after World War I?

During World War I the Allies championed national self-determination in Europe, but they had no intention of allowing the nations under their imperial rule to determine their own government. Britain and France emerged from the war with their empires greatly expanded: They divided up Germany's overseas colonies in Africa and Asia, and became the dominant powers in the Middle East. Belgium and Portugal retained their African colonies, while in Asia, some of the spoils went to Japan, Australia, and New Zealand. Popular imperialism reached its zenith after the war as well, as filmmakers and novelists found that imperial settings formed the perfect backdrop for stirring tales of individual heroism and limitless adventure.

26.1

26.2

26.3

26.4

26.5

26.6

The Irish Revolution

In this period, however, important challenges to the imperial idea emerged. The most successful occurred in Ireland. World War I radicalized the Irish nationalist movement. We saw in Chapter 23 that before 1914, the mainstream of Irish nationalism supported "Home Rule"—Irish political autonomy within the framework of the British Empire. By 1919, Home Rule was too little, too late, and popular opinion had swung behind the radical demand for an Irish Republic independent of Britain.

The British response to the Easter Rising of 1916 helped push popular Irish nationalism in a radical direction. A small group of revolutionary nationalists mounted an armed rebellion on Easter Monday in Dublin. Few Irish men or women participated and many condemned the Rising—but then the British government made the fatal error of executing the leaders of the rebellion and treating the population of Dublin with brutality. Public opinion shifted rapidly. The executed leaders became martyrs for the sacred cause of nationhood.

The British decision in 1918 to impose military conscription in Ireland aroused further anger and completed the radicalization process. The result was the Anglo-Irish War of 1919–1921, in which the Irish rebels utilized the tactics of guerilla warfare to battle against their much stronger foe.

With much of its public weary of war, the British government in 1921 offered a peace settlement based on limited independence for Ireland: The new "Irish Free State" was to retain its membership within the British Empire, and the six northern counties within the province of Ulster, dominated by Protestants of English and Scottish descent who opposed Irish independence, were to remain part of the United Kingdom.

Appalled that Irish leaders would have to continue to swear an oath of allegiance to the British monarchy and that the island would be partitioned, a minority of the Irish rejected the peace settlement—and declared war against the new Irish Free State. The Irish Civil War of 1922–1923 created lasting divisions in Irish political and cultural life. The Irish Free State finally severed its ties with the British Empire and became the Republic of Eire in 1949. Northern Ireland today retains its constitutional links to Britain (see **Map 26.2**).

Changing Power Equations: Ideology and Economics

Ireland's revolt against British imperial rule was unusual in this era because it succeeded. In other regions, European powers were able to retain imperial control. Nevertheless, during the 1920s and 1930s, mass nationalist movements grew stronger in many regions, the result of both the spread of communist ideology and the impact of the Great Depression.

Communist ideology played an important role in undermining European empires. Lenin argued that capitalist competition for markets led inevitably to imperialism and thus that anti-capitalism and anti-imperialism went hand in hand. Declaring itself the defender of oppressed nationalities everywhere, the Soviet Union provided ideological and material assistance to nationalist independence movements in Indonesia, Indochina, Burma, and, most significantly, China, where Soviet advisers helped form the Communist Party in 1921.

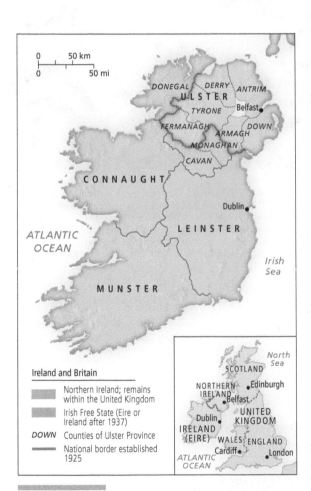

MAP 26.2 IRELAND AND BRITAIN The treaty of 1921 that ended the Anglo-Irish War partitioned the Irish island. Six northern counties (or "Ulster") remain part of the British state (officially the United Kingdom of Great Britain and Northern Ireland). The rest of Ireland became the Irish Free State, an independent state within the British Empire. In 1937, a new constitution changed the name of the Free State to Eire. Eire declared itself a republic in 1949. What was the significance of this 1949 declaration?

Economic developments proved as important as ideological arguments, however. The Great Depression brought a sharp fall in the prices of primary products across the globe. The price decline spelled disaster for many colonial regions that relied on the production of cash crops for export. More directly, the response of imperial regimes to the economic challenges of the Depression diminished their own effectiveness. Looking for ways to reduce expenditures, European governments cut funds to colonial schools, public services, and health care. Direct taxation rates rose while unemployment rates soared. In response, nationalist movements exploded.

Postwar Nationalism, Westernization, and the Islamic Challenge

Anti-Western sentiment in imperial territories also took religious form. In Africa, for example, a revival of animist religion expressed an explicit rejection of the Christian teachings brought by European and American missionaries and an implicit refusal of Western cultural and political styles.

Throughout many African regions and in much of Asia, however, Islam possessed the most potent appeal. In the growing cities, immigrants cut off from their villages and traditional religious practices found that Islam provided an alternative cultural identity to the one offered by their European rulers.

The end of World War I marked the beginning of a new era in Islamic history. The Ottoman Empire had symbolized a unified Islam: As caliph, the Ottoman sultan claimed religious authority over all Muslims, even those not under Ottoman political rule. The collapse of the Ottoman Empire and the abolition of the Ottoman caliphate in the wake of World War I created a new religious and political environment for Muslims. Many followed Western secular models. Others, however, found spiritual solace and political identity in Islamic revival movements.

NATIONALIST MODELS For many Muslims in the Middle East, **pan-Arabism** emerged as a powerful form of ethnic nationalism. Just as pan-Slavism promoted the ideal of a single Slavic state (see p. 701), so pan-Arabism insisted that all Arabs—including the minority who were not Muslim—should unite in an Arab state.

Not all Arab nationalists, however, embraced pan-Arabism. In states such as Egypt, where the national boundaries had not been imposed by Western armies or institutions, nationalism tended to coalesce around the state itself. Hence, in Egypt, the nationalist political party, *Wafd,* called for Egyptian national freedom, not for pan-Arabic unity.

For nationalists such as those in Wafd, the successful nationalist revolution in Turkey provided a source of inspiration. In the tumultuous period immediately following the end of World War I, Turkish nationalists led by Mustafa Kemal Pasha overthrew the Ottoman sultan and forced the Allies to back away from imposing a treaty that would have limited the new state of Turkey's national sovereignty.

But while Kemal had no intention of letting Western powers control Turkey, he was not anti-Western. Kemal viewed the West as modern—and he wanted to modernize Turkey. Thus, he declared Turkey a secular republic, outlawed polygamy, granted women civil and legal rights, and required all Turks to take surnames. He became known as Kemal "Ataturk" ("Father of the Turks"). A mass literacy program aimed to teach Turks how to read and write using the Latin alphabet. Schoolmasters who dared use Arabic lettering were arrested. Ataturk even condemned the traditional form of Turkish headwear, the fez, as "an emblem of ignorance, negligence, fanaticism, hatred of progress and civilization."[15] To represent Turkey's new Western orientation, Turkish men were ordered to wear Western suits and English bowler hats.

Read the Document

Ho Chi Minh, "Equality!"

Read the Document

Jomo Kenyatta, from Facing Mt. Kenya: The Tribal Life of the Gokuyu

26.1
26.2
26.3
26.4
26.5
26.6

pan-Arabism Nationalist ideology that called for the political unification of all Arabs, regardless of religious affiliation.

26.1

26.2

26.3

26.4

26.5

26.6

Ataturk was less enthusiastic about English political freedom. Despite setting up a parliament elected by universal suffrage, he used executive power to govern with an iron grip over a one-party state. He also continued the Ottoman policies of repression toward Turkey's Armenian minority.

Kemal Ataturk's secularist, Westernized model of nationalism proved alluring. During the 1920s and 1930s nationalists in the Middle East, Africa, and Asia tended to embrace Western models, even as they rejected Western (or Western-imposed) rulers. They formed parliamentary political parties, advocated Western political ideologies such as liberalism and communism, regarded the state as secular, and saw political independence as a crucial step toward industrial modernization and economic prosperity.

THE ISLAMIC CHALLENGE Beneath the surface of political life, however, different movements with different aims were coalescing. Throughout the new states of the Middle East, soaring sales of popular biographies of the Prophet Muhammad and the proliferation of Islamic leagues and clubs hinted that many ordinary people found secular nationalism as alien as the faces of their Western-imposed rulers and as meaningless as the boundaries on the new map. These sentiments did not harden into political movements until the 1940s; during the interwar decades, however, the Wahhabi religious revival in central Arabia and the Muslim Brotherhood in Egypt set a new direction for Islam's relationship to the West.

Founded by Muhammad Abd al-Wahhab (1703–1787) in the eighteenth century, **Wahhabism** sought to purify Islam by returning to a strict interpretation of the *Sharia*, or Islamic law. Wahhabism revived in the tumultuous period after World War I because its reassertion of fundamental truths and practices proved reassuring in a time of unsettling political change. Moreover, the postwar Wahhabi revival had a powerful patron: Abd al-Aziz Ibn Saud (ca. 1888–1953), the head of the Saudi dynasty whose conquests on the Arabian peninsula became the basis for the kingdom of Saudi Arabia. Wahhabism's call for Islamic purification soon embraced sharp opposition to Western culture.

A different sort of movement that had similar goals emerged in Egypt in 1928. Like the Wahhabis, the Islamic Brotherhood (or *Ikhwan*) rejected modernizing interpretations of Islam, reasserted the universal jurisdiction of Islamic law, and viewed Western societies as corrupt. For the Brotherhood, Islam governed not just religious belief, but all areas of life. Working through youth groups, educational institutes, and business enterprises, the Brotherhood spread from its Egyptian base throughout the Middle East during the 1930s.

Moral Revolution in India

During this era, an anti-Western protest movement also took shape in India under the leadership of Mohandas Gandhi (1869–1948). Gandhi had spent 20 years in South Africa fighting to improve the lot of indentured Indian laborers under British imperial rule and developing his commitment to social and political change through nonviolent protest and civil disobedience.

After he returned to India in 1916, Gandhi transformed Indian nationalism into a mass movement by appealing to traditional Indian customs and religious identities. He did not oppose modernization, but he argued that modernization did not mean Westernization. India could—and should—follow its own path. Gandhi rejected Western dress and presented himself in the role of the religious ascetic, a familiar and honored figure in Indian culture. In his insistence that the nationalist struggle be one of "moral force" rather than a physical fight, Gandhi drew on the Hindu tradition of nonviolence. He was careful, however, not to equate "Indian" with "Hindu." Gandhi strove to incorporate the minority Muslim community into the nationalist movement, and he broke with the traditional Hindu caste system by campaigning for the rights of those deemed "untouchable." (*See Encounters and Transformations* in this chapter.)

Wahhabism A religious reform and revival movement founded by Muhammad Abd al-Wahhab (1703–1787) in the eighteenth century to purify Islam by returning to a strict interpretation of the *Sharia*, or Islamic law. Revived during the 1920s in Saudi Arabia.

26.1

26.2

26.3

26.4

26.5

26.6

Encounters and Transformations

From Mohandas to Mahatma:
GANDHI'S TRANSFORMATION

In April 1893, a young, well-dressed Indian lawyer purchased a first-class train ticket from Durban to Pretoria (South Africa). The first part of the journey proceeded uneventfully, but then another traveler, a white man, entered the first-class compartment. He turned around and returned with two guards, who demanded that the Indian man sit in third class, with the other "colored" passengers. The young lawyer refused and so was thrown off the train at the next stop.

Mohandas Gandhi's experience on the train to Pretoria was not unusual. The Indian immigrant community in South Africa had long endured legal discrimination, economic exploitation, and frequent violence, while the black African community suffered far worse. But the 24-year-old Gandhi knew little about such things. Growing up as the spoiled youngest son in an upper-caste family in India, he had known privilege rather than prejudice. Even the three years he spent in London studying law did not expose him to racial discrimination. Gandhi, in fact, felt that when he left Britain he was leaving "home." He returned to India in 1891 convinced of the superiority of British law and culture. He banned Indian-style clothing from his household, insisted that his illiterate young wife learn English, and decreed that his children eat porridge and cocoa for breakfast. He saw himself as a successful British lawyer.

But others did not see him that way. When Gandhi asked a British official for a favor for his brother, he was humiliated and actually pushed out the door by a servant. "This shock changed the course of my life," Gandhi later noted.[16] Offered a job in South Africa, he went—and on that train to Pretoria encountered further humiliation. By the time Gandhi finally reached Pretoria, he had decided to fight. He became the leader of the Indian civil rights movement in South Africa.

Gandhi lived in South Africa for 21 years. During these decades, the westernized, Britain-loving lawyer became a Hindu

THE MAHATMA Gandhi drew on Hindu and Western traditions in formulating his moral protest.

holy man. Mohandas became Mahatma, the "great-souled one." This transformation occurred in part because of Gandhi's sense of betrayal as he encountered the racial discrimination embedded in British imperialism. His time in London had taught Gandhi that Britain epitomized the Western ideals of impartial justice and individual rights. But the British colonial regime he encountered in South Africa violated those ideals. Disillusioned, Gandhi turned back to his Hindu roots.

Western culture also, however, played a positive role in Gandhi's transformation. During his time in South Africa, Gandhi read widely in Christian and Western texts, including the New Testament, and books by nineteenth-century European social and cultural critics that exposed the spiritual and material failures of industrial society. Gandhi's intellectual encounter with these texts helped him formulate the idea of *Satyagraha* ("Truth-Force"). In its most specific sense, Satyagraha is a political tool. Through nonviolent mass civil disobedience, the powerless persuade the powerful to effect political change. But Satyagraha is also a spiritual act, the victory of goodness over violence and evil.

Gandhi's specific encounters with the injustice of imperial rule, first in the home of a British official in India and then on his South African train ride, forced him to embark on a different sort of spiritual and political journey, an exploration of both Western and Hindu thought. This journey transformed Gandhi from Mohandas into Mahatma and led him to Satyagraha—and the transformation of Indian nationalism into a mass movement. By 1948, this movement made it impossible for the British to govern India.

For Discussion

Encounters with Western ideas and Western people helped transform Gandhi "from Mohandas to Mahatma." How have Gandhi's ideas transformed Western culture and politics?

26.1

26.2

26.3

26.4

26.5

26.6

📖 Read the Document

Jawaharlal Nehru, from *The Autobiography of Jawaharlal Nehru*

Unable to decide whether to arrest Gandhi as a dangerous revolutionary or to negotiate with him as a representative of the Indian people, the British did both. In 1931, Gandhi and the viceroy of India (literally the "vice-king," the highest British official in India) met on equal terms for a series of eight meetings. A few months later Gandhi was in prison, along with 66,000 of his nationalist colleagues.

Successive British governments passed a series of measures granting Indians increasing degrees of self-government, but Gandhi and the Indian National Congress demanded full and immediate national independence. The resulting impasse led to escalating unrest and terrorist activity, despite Gandhi's personal commitment to nonviolence. India remained the jewel in Britain's imperial crown, but the glue holding it in place was deteriorating rapidly by the end of the 1930s.

The Power of the Primitive

When asked what he thought of "Western civilization," Gandhi replied, "I think it would be a very good idea." Just as nationalists outside of the West such as Gandhi began to challenge the equation of the West with civilization, so too did Westerners themselves. In the nineteenth century, imperialists insisted that "civilization" gave the West the right to rule the "barbarians" in the rest of the world. But by 1918, in the wake of the war, at least some Europeans asked, "Who is the barbarian now?"

Developments in psychology further eroded the boundaries between barbarian or "primitive" and modern cultures. In his postwar writings, Sigmund Freud emphasized that human nature was fundamentally aggressive, even bestial. Freud's three-part theory of personality, developed in the 1920s, argued that within each individual the *id,* the unconscious force of primitive instinct, battles against the controls of the *ego,* or conscious rationality, and the *superego,* the moral values imposed by society. Although Freud taught that the continuity of civilization depended on the repression of the id, many Freudian popularizers insisted that the individual should allow his or her primitive self to run free.

The work of Freud's onetime disciple Carl Jung (1875–1961) also stressed the links between the primitive and the modern. Jung contended that careful study of an individual's dreams will show that they share common images and forms— "archetypes"—with ancient mythologies and world religions. These archetypes point to the existence of the "collective unconscious," shared by all human beings, regardless of when or where they lived. Thus, in Jung's analysis the boundary between "civilized" and "primitive," "West" and "not West," disappeared.

In the work of other thinkers and artists, that boundary remained intact, but Western notions of cultural superiority turned upside down. The German novelist Hermann Hesse (1877–1962) condemned modern industrial society as spiritually

THE POWER OF THE PRIMITIVE When the American dancer Josephine Baker first hit the stage in Paris in 1925, her audience embraced her as the image of African savagery, even though Baker was a city kid from St. Louis. A Parisian sensation from the moment she arrived, Baker's frenetic and passionate style of dancing—and her willingness to appear on stage wearing nothing but a belt of bananas—epitomized for many Europeans the freedom they believed their urbanized culture had lost, and that the United States and Africa retained. Baker's belt of bananas, designed by her white French employer, shows that racist stereotypes shaped this idealization of the primitive. Yet Baker's blackness and her Americanness represented a positive image of liberation to many Parisians.

26.1

26.2

26.3

26.4

26.5

26.6

barren and celebrated Eastern mysticism as a source of power and wisdom. Many writers agreed that the West needed to look to outside its borders for vibrancy and vitality. The belief that Western culture was anemic, washed out, and washed up also led to a new openness to alternative intellectual and artistic traditions. As the energetic rhythms of African American jazz worked their way into white musical traditions, they transformed popular music.

Similarly, the *Négritude* movement stressed the history and intrinsic value of black African culture. Founded in Paris in 1935 by French colonial students from Africa and the West Indies, Négritude condemned European culture as weak and corrupted and called for blacks to recreate a separate cultural and political identity. The movement's leading figures, such as Leopold Senghor (1906–2001), who later became the first president of independent Senegal, opposed Western imperialism and demanded African self-rule. Drawing together Africans, Afro-Caribbeans, and black Americans, Négritude assumed the existence of a common black culture that transcended national and colonial boundaries. The movement stole the white racists' stereotype of the "happy dancing savage" and refigured it as positive: Black culture fostered the emotion, creativity, and human connections that white Western industrial society destroyed.

CONCLUSION

The Kingdom of Corpses

In 1921, the Goncourt Prize, the most prestigious award in French literature, was awarded not to a native French writer, but to a colonial: René Maran, born in the French colony of Martinique. Even more striking than Maran's receiving the prize was the content of the novel for which he was honored. In *Batouala,* Maran condemned Western culture: "Civilization, civilization, pride of the Europeans and charnel house of innocents. . . . You build your kingdom on corpses."[17]

For many in the West, Maran's description of Europe as a kingdom of corpses appeared apt in the aftermath of total war. During the 1920s and 1930s Soviet communism on the left and Nazism and fascism on the right rejected such key Western ideals as individual rights and the rule of law. These extremist ideologies seemed persuasive in the climate of despair produced not only by the war, but also by the postwar failure of democracy in eastern Europe and the collapse of the global economy after 1929. As a result, the kingdom of corpses grew: in Nazi Germany, in Spain, and most dramatically in the Soviet Union. The kingdom of corpses was, however, a particularly expansionist domain. As the 1930s ended, the West and the world stood on the brink of another total war, one in which the numbers of dead spiraled to nearly incomprehensible levels.

MAKING CONNECTIONS

1. The Soviet Union stood on the far left of the political spectrum; fascist Italy and Nazi Germany stood on the far right. Yet these ideological opponents shared many common features: What were they? How do you explain these commonalities?
2. What were the key developments in governmental policies toward women, welfare, and the family in the interwar era? How can we explain the similarities in Radical Right, democratic, and Radical Left policies?

TAKING IT FURTHER

For suggested readings, websites, and films, see page R-1.

On MyHistoryLab

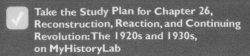

Take the Study Plan for Chapter 26, Reconstruction, Reaction, and Continuing Revolution: The 1920s and 1930s, on MyHistoryLab

Chapter Review

Cultural Despair and Desire

26.1 What was the impact of World War I on European cultural life?

The massive destruction of total war led many Europeans to embrace pessimistic assessments of human nature and human society. Others, however, argued that the war had created the possibility of radical social improvement, particularly through technological and scientific research and development.

The Appeal of Authoritarianism and the Rise of Fascism

26.2 What circumstances explain the collapse of democracy throughout much of interwar Europe?

Nationalist conflicts and economic underdevelopment weakened the new democracies of eastern Europe. As the Great Depression stalled the global economy, many voters and politicians embraced aspects of fascism, a new form of Radical Right politics that emerged in Italy after World War I. An intensely nationalistic ideology, fascism exalted the power of the state, dismissed democracy as weak, and glorified military action. It also used mass spectacles to generate enthusiasm and a sense of belonging to a mighty movement.

Nazism and the Defeat of Democracy in Germany

26.3 How did the Nazis succeed in establishing a dictatorship in Germany?

The Nazis remained a fringe party until the Great Depression weakened German democracy and polarized voters and political leaders. Once in political power, the Nazis used terror and intimidation to destroy all that remained of German democracy. The Nazi economic program lowered the standard of living for many Germans but also lowered unemployment rates. Nazi racial and political ideology demonized many groups, most particularly Germany's Jewish community.

The Soviet Alternative and the Democracies' Response

26.4 Why did the Soviet Union seem a success and how did the democracies respond?

Through violence and dictatorial rule, Stalin imposed mass modernization on the Soviet economy but the vast cost of his collectivization of Soviet agriculture and his industrial program remained largely hidden. In western Europe and the United States, governments moved toward social democratic programs and policies. In France and Spain, Popular Front governments sought to unite non-fascist parties together in democratic governments but faced defeat or overthrow.

The Reconstruction of Gender

26.5 What changed, and what did not, in women's experiences after World War I?

In many, although not all, western states, women received the national franchise after World War I and had wider employment and educational opportunities. Gender ideology, however, did not change very much. Both World War I's high cost in human life and falling birth rates after the war impelled political leaders to find ways to encourage women to remain in the home and to produce more children.

The West and the World: Imperialism in the Interwar Era

26.6 How did the interaction between the West and the world outside change after World War I?

The French and British empires grew as a result of the war, but so, too, did anti-colonialist nationalist movements. The Great Depression strained the economies of overseas territories and increased indigenous resentment against European imperial rule. The growth of anti-Western Islamic movements in the 1920s and 1930s also weakened the hold of European powers on their empires and dependencies. At the same time, many Western thinkers and artists began to see non-Western cultures as a source of the vitality and creativity that they believed to be disappearing from industrial societies.

On MyHistoryLab

Take the Study Plan for Chapter 26, Reconstruction, Reaction, and Continuing Revolution: The 1920s and 1930s, on MyHistoryLab

Chapter Time Line

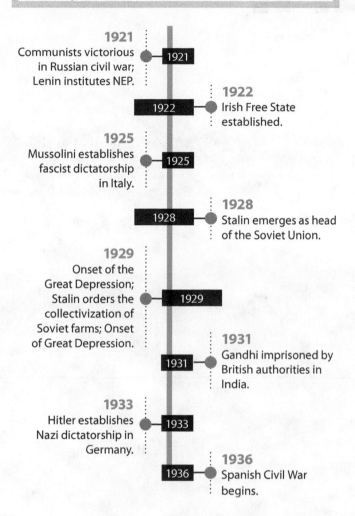

1921
Communists victorious in Russian civil war; Lenin institutes NEP.

1921

1922

1922
Irish Free State established.

1925
Mussolini establishes fascist dictatorship in Italy.

1925

1928

1928
Stalin emerges as head of the Soviet Union.

1929
Onset of the Great Depression; Stalin orders the collectivization of Soviet farms; Onset of Great Depression.

1929

1931

1931
Gandhi imprisoned by British authorities in India.

1933
Hitler establishes Nazi dictatorship in Germany.

1933

1936

1936
Spanish Civil War begins.

27 World War II

In the final weeks of World War II in Europe, many allied soldiers faced their most difficult assignment yet. Combat veterans, accustomed to scenes of slaughter, broke down and cried as they encountered a landscape of horror beyond their wildest nightmares: the Nazi concentration and death camps. As one American war correspondent put it, "We had penetrated at last to the center of the black heart, to the very crawling inside of the vicious heart."[1] The American soldiers who opened the camp in Mauthausen, Austria, never forgot their first sight of the prisoners there: "By the thousands they came streaming. . . . Hollow, pallid ghosts from graves and tombs, terrifying, rot-colored figures of misery marked by disease, deeply ingrained filth, inner decay. . . . squat skeletons in rags and crazy grins."[2]

Similarly, the sights they saw at Bergen-Belsen in Germany left an indelible mark on the British troops who liberated that camp. Bergen-Belsen had become the dumping ground for camp inmates from eastern Europe as the German army retreated in front of the advancing Soviet army. Sick and starving, these prisoners were packed, 1,200 at a time, into barracks built to accommodate a few hundred. By March 1945, drinking water and food had disappeared, excrement dripped from bunk beds and coated the floors, and dead bodies piled up everywhere. In these conditions, the only living beings to flourish were the

THE MASS GRAVES AT BERGEN-BELSEN
British soldiers liberated the Nazi concentration camp of Bergen-Belsen on April 15, 1945. For many prisoners, however, death provided their only "liberation."

LEARNING OBJECTIVES

27.1 (((•	27.2 (((•	27.3 (((•	27.4 (((•	27.5 (((•
How did military and political expectations lead to World War II?	How did Nazi Germany conquer the continent of Europe by 1941?	Why did the Allies win in 1945?	What were the context, causes, and consequences of genocide during World War II?	What did total war mean for civilians in the occupied regions and on the home front?

👁 Watch the Video Series on MyHistoryLab

**Learn about some key topics related to this chapter with the *MyHistoryLab Video Series:
Key Topics in Western Civilization***

27.1

27.2

27.3

27.4

27.5

microorganisms that caused typhus. Floundering in this sea of want, British soldiers, doctors, and nurses did what they could. Even so, 28,000 of Bergen-Belsen's 60,000 inmates died in the weeks following liberation.

In Mauthausen and Bergen-Belsen, in the piles of putrefying bodies and among the crowds of skeletal survivors, American and British soldiers encountered the results of Adolf Hitler's effort to redefine the West. In Hitler's vision, Western civilization comprised ranks of white, northern Europeans, led by Germans, marching in step to a cadence dictated by the all-powerful state. To realize this vision, Hitler turned to total war and mass murder.

This quest to reconfigure the West as a race-based German empire led Hitler to join hands with an ally outside the West: Japan. The German-Japanese alliance transformed a European war into a global conflict. Understanding World War II thus demands that we look not only at the results of Nazi racial ideology, but also at global power relations and patterns of economic dependency. The Pacific war constituted the most brutal in a long series of encounters between Japanese elites and the West. Like Hitler, Japan's governing elites longed for an empire—in their case, an Asian empire to ensure access to the resources and domination over the peoples of the Pacific region. With such access and such domination, they hoped to insulate Japan's economic and political structures from Western influence or control.

As we examine both the European and the Pacific theaters of war, we will need, then, to ask how competing definitions of "the West" helped shape this conflict. We will also confront the question of results:

How did the cataclysm known as World War II redefine the West?

The Coming of War

27.1 How did military and political expectations lead to World War II?

World War I was supposed to be the "war to end all wars." Instead, a little more than 20 years later, total war again engulfed Europe and then the world. Hitler's ambitions for a German empire in eastern Europe accounted for the immediate outbreak of war in September 1939. But a complete explanation of the origins of World War II extends beyond Hitler's aims and actions.

An Uneasy Peace

The Second World War originated in the settlement of the First. Three factors accounted for the fragility of the peace settlement. First, the Versailles Treaty created great resentment among Germans, helped weaken postwar Western economies, and enhanced Hitler's appeal. Second, the League of Nations, created to replace the alliance

THE PRELUDE TO WORLD WAR II The Japanese resumption of their war in China in 1937 added to the horrors of the 1930s. Here a photographer captured the agony of a baby separated from its parents in the railway station in Shanghai.

systems that many blamed for starting World War I, could not realize the high hopes of its planners. Lacking military power, boycotted by the United States, and at various times excluding the key states of Germany and the Soviet Union, the League proved too weak to serve as the basis of a new international order. Finally, the redrawing of the map of eastern and central Europe, intended to create cohesive nation-states, instead worsened national conflict throughout eastern and southern Europe.

The onset of the Great Depression in 1929 further destabilized the peace. Economic nationalism intensified as governments erected tariff walls to protect their own industries. Some sought to escape economic difficulties through territorial expansion. Japan, threatened by the collapse of export markets for raw silk and cotton cloth, invaded Manchuria (in eastern China) in 1931 and Italy invaded Ethiopia in 1935. The Ethiopians endured many of the horrors soon to come to the European continent, including the saturation bombing of civilians, the use of poison gas, and the establishment of concentration camps. At the end of June 1936, Ethiopia's now-exiled Emperor Haile Selassie (1892–1975) addressed the Assembly of the League of Nations and warned, "It is us today. It will be you tomorrow."[3]

One year after Italian troops invaded Ethiopia, civil war broke out in Spain. As Chapter 26 explained, the victory of General Francisco Franco's rebels seemed to signal that aggressors could act with impunity. While the Spanish Civil War raged, the Japanese resumed their advance in China. In what became known as the Rape of Nanking (Nanjing), soldiers used babies for bayonet practice, gang-raped as many as 20,000 young girls and women, and left the bodies of the dead to rot in the street.

The Expansion of Nazi Germany

Against this backdrop of military aggression and the democracies' inaction, Hitler made his first moves to establish a German empire in Europe (see **Map 27.1**). In 1933, he withdrew Germany from the League of Nations and two years later announced the creation of a German air force and the return of mass conscription—in deliberate violation of the terms of the Versailles Treaty. In 1936, Hitler allied with Mussolini in the **Rome-Berlin Axis** and again violated his treaty obligations when he sent German troops into

Rome-Berlin Axis Alliance between Benito Mussolini's Italy and Adolf Hitler's Germany formed in 1936.

the Rhineland, the industrially rich region on Germany's western border. Yet France and Britain did not respond. Two years later, in March 1938, Germany broke the Versailles Treaty once more by annexing Austria.

After the successful *Anschluss* ("joining") of Germany and Austria, Hitler demanded that the Sudetenland, the western portion of Czechoslovakia inhabited by a German-speaking majority, be joined to Germany as well. He seemed finally to have gone too far. With France and the Soviet Union pledged to protect the territorial integrity of Czechoslovakia, Europe stood on the brink of war. The urgency of the situation impelled Britain's prime minister Neville Chamberlain (1869–1940) to board an airplane for the first time in his life and fly to Munich to talk with Hitler. After negotiations that excluded the Czech government, Chamberlain and French prime minister Edouard Daladier agreed to grant Hitler the right to occupy the Sudetenland immediately. Assured by Hitler that this **Munich Agreement** satisfied all his territorial demands, Chamberlain flew home to an enthusiastic welcome. Crowds cheered when he declared "peace in our time." (See *Different Voices* in this chapter.)

"Peace in our time" lasted for six months. In March 1939, Hitler's promises were proven worthless as German troops occupied the rest of Czechoslovakia. Hitler then took out an insurance policy against fighting a two-front war by persuading Stalin to sign the **German-Soviet Non-Aggression Pact**. The pact publicly pledged the two powers not to attack each other. It also secretly divided Poland between them and promised Stalin substantial territorial gains in eastern Poland and the Baltic regions.

On September 1, 1939, German troops invaded Poland and within weeks were implementing racial policies that murdered millions of Poles. The British and French declared war against Germany on September 3. Two weeks after German troops crossed Poland's borders in the west, the Soviets pushed in from the east and imposed a regime characterized by mass deportations and death. World War II had begun.

Evaluating Appeasement

Could Hitler have been stopped before he catapulted Europe into World War II? The debate over this question has centered on British policy during the 1930s. With France weakened by economic and political crises, the United States remaining aloof from European affairs, and the communist Soviet Union regarded as a pariah state, Britain assumed the initiative in responding to Hitler's rise to power and his demands.

British policymakers—particularly Neville Chamberlain, who was prime minister in the late 1930s—pursued a policy of conciliation and negotiation in their dealings with Hitler. After World War II broke out, that policy was called **appeasement**, a word now equated with passivity and cowardice. Chamberlain, however, was not a coward and was far from passive. Convinced he had a mission to save Europe from war, he actively sought to accommodate Hitler.

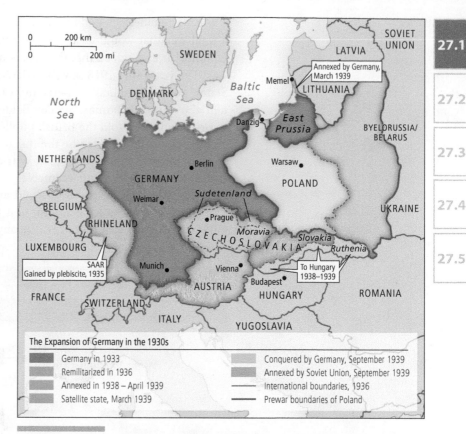

The Expansion of Germany in the 1930s

Germany in 1933	Conquered by Germany, September 1939
Remilitarized in 1936	Annexed by Soviet Union, September 1939
Annexed in 1938 – April 1939	International boundaries, 1936
Satellite state, March 1939	Prewar boundaries of Poland

MAP 27.1 THE EXPANSION OF GERMANY IN THE 1930s Beginning with the remilitarization of the Rhineland in 1936, Hitler embarked on a program of German territorial expansion. This map also indicates the expansion of the Soviet Union into Poland as a result of the secret terms of the German-Soviet Non-Aggression Pact. Which of Germany's expansionist moves could Hitler argue were based on "national self-determination"?

Munich Agreement The agreement in 1939 between the governments of Nazi Germany, Britain, and France that granted Germany sovereignty over the Sudetenland; part of the effort to appease the Nazi government and avoid a second total war in Europe.

German-Soviet Non-Aggression Pact Signed by Joseph Stalin and Adolf Hitler in 1939, the agreement publicly pledged Germany and the Soviet Union not to attack each other and secretly divided up Poland and the Baltic states between the two powers.

 View the Map

German Expansion Under the Third Reich

Read the Document

Adolf Hitler, The Obersalzberg Speech, 1939

appeasement British diplomatic and financial efforts to stabilize Germany in the 1920s and 1930s and so avoid a second world war.

For Chamberlain, and many other Europeans, the alternative to appeasement was a total war that would destroy Western civilization. They remembered the last war with horror and agreed that the next war would be even worse, for it would be an air war. The years after 1918 saw the aviation industry take off in Europe and the United States, and both military experts and ordinary people recognized the disastrous potential of airborne bombs. Stanley Baldwin (1867–1947), Chamberlain's predecessor as prime minister, told the British public, "The bomber will always get through." The civilian casualties inflicted by the Italian air force in Ethiopia and by the bombing of Spanish cities in the Spanish Civil War convinced many that Baldwin was right, and that war was, therefore, unacceptable.

Motivated by the desire to avoid another horrible war, appeasement rested on two additional pillars—the assumption that many of Germany's grievances were legitimate and the belief that only a strong Germany could neutralize the threat posed

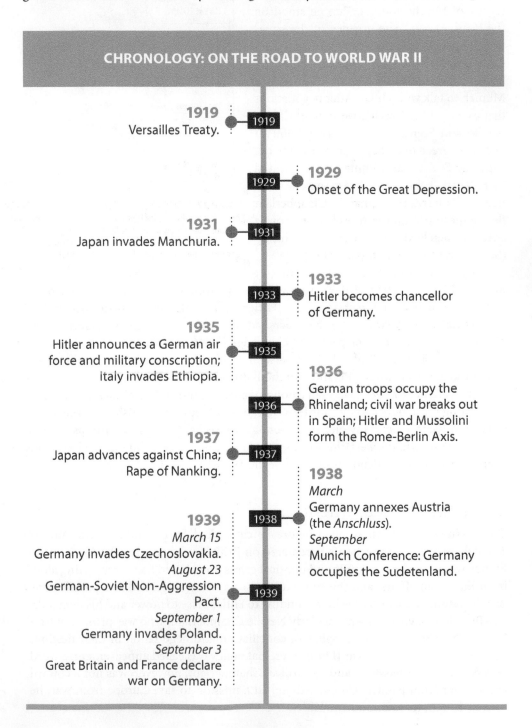

CHRONOLOGY: ON THE ROAD TO WORLD WAR II

1919 `1919`
Versailles Treaty.

`1929` **1929**
Onset of the Great Depression.

1931 `1931`
Japan invades Manchuria.

`1933` **1933**
Hitler becomes chancellor
of Germany.

1935
Hitler announces a German air `1935`
force and military conscription;
Italy invades Ethiopia.

1936
German troops occupy the
`1936` Rhineland; civil war breaks out
in Spain; Hitler and Mussolini
form the Rome-Berlin Axis.

1937 `1937`
Japan advances against China;
Rape of Nanking.

1938
March
Germany annexes Austria
1939 `1938` (the *Anschluss*).
March 15 *September*
Germany invades Czechoslovakia. Munich Conference: Germany
August 23 occupies the Sudetenland.
German-Soviet Non-Aggression
Pact. `1939`
September 1
Germany invades Poland.
September 3
Great Britain and France declare
war on Germany.

by Soviet communism. During the 1920s, many scholars and policymakers studied the diplomatic records concerning the outbreak of World War I. They concluded that the treaty makers at Versailles were wrong in blaming Germany for starting the war. Convinced that the Versailles Treaty had treated Germany unjustly, British leaders sought to renegotiate reparations, to press the French into softening their anti-German policies, and to draw Germany back into the network of international diplomatic relations. Hitler's rise to power gave added impetus to a policy already in place. British leaders argued that they could rob Hitler of much of his appeal by rectifying legitimate German grievances. Fear of communism reinforced this desire to stabilize Germany. Many politicians applauded Hitler's suppression of German communists and welcomed a remilitarized Germany as a strong barricade against the threat posed by Soviet Russia. The startling announcement of the German-Soviet Non-Aggression Pact in the summer of 1939, however, revealed this barricade to be hollow.

Europe at War, 1939–1941

27.2 How did Nazi Germany conquer the continent of Europe by 1941?

Within just two years, Hitler appeared to have achieved his goal of establishing a Nazi empire in Europe. By the autumn of 1941, almost all of continental Europe was either allied to or occupied by Nazi Germany.

A New Kind of Warfare

The four-year stalemate on the Western Front in World War I demonstrated that an entrenched defense, armed with machine guns, could easily withstand an infantry assault. Postwar German military strategists, seeking to avoid the stalemate of trench warfare, theorized that the airplane and the tank could together act as an "armored fist" strong and swift enough to break through even the most well-fortified enemy defenses. The bomber plane would provide a mobile bombardment to shatter fortifications, break communication links, and clog transport routes. Simultaneously, motorized infantry and tank formations would punch through enemy lines.

Germany's successes in the first years of World War II illustrated the effectiveness of a mobile, mechanized offensive force. Germany's only defeat during these years came in the Battle of Britain, when Germany confronted a mobile, mechanized defense. Like Germany's victories, this defeat highlights a crucial theme of this chapter: the central role of industrial production in modern war.

BLITZKRIEG During the invasion of Poland, most of the German army moved on foot or horseback, as soldiers had done for centuries. Motorized divisions, however, bludgeoned through the Polish defenses, penetrated deep into enemy territory, and secured key positions. While these units wreaked havoc on the ground, the Luftwaffe—the German air force—rained ruin from the air. Over 1,300 planes shrieked across the Polish skies and destroyed the Polish air force.

Western newspaper reporters christened Nazi Germany's offensive techniques **blitzkrieg**—lightning war. Western Europeans experienced blitzkrieg firsthand in the spring of 1940 when the German army invaded Denmark and Norway in early April and moved into western Europe in May. The Netherlands fell in four days. Belgium, supported by French and British units as in World War I, held out for two weeks.

By the end of May, the Germans had trapped the British army and several divisions of the French force in a small pocket on the northern French coast called Dunkirk. While the British Royal Air Force (RAF) held off the Luftwaffe, the British navy and a

blitzkrieg "Lightning war"; an offensive military tactic making use of airplanes, tanks, and motorized infantry to punch through enemy defenses and secure key territory. First demonstrated by the German army in World War II.

 Read the Document

Marc Bloch, *Strange Defeat*

Vichy regime Authoritarian state established in France after defeat by the German army in 1940.

View the Map

The Division of France

flotilla of fishing and recreational boats piloted by British civilians evacuated the troops. By June 4, 110,000 French and almost 240,000 British soldiers had been brought safely back to Britain. But, as the newly appointed British prime minister, Winston Churchill (1874–1965), reminded his cheering people, "Wars are not won by evacuation."

On June 14, German soldiers marched into Paris. The French Assembly voted to disband and to hand over power to the World War I war hero Marshal Philippe Pétain (1856–1951), who established an authoritarian government. On June 22 this new **Vichy regime** (named after the city Pétain chose for his capital) signed an armistice with Germany and pledged collaboration with the Nazi regime. Theoretically, Pétain's authority extended over all of France, but as **Map 27.2** illustrates, in actuality the Vichy regime was confined to the south (and to the French colonial regions). As of June 1940, Germany not only occupied western and northern France, but—with its allies and satellites—held most of the continent.

THE BATTLE OF BRITAIN After the fall of France, Hitler hoped that Britain would accept Germany's domination of the continent and agree to a negotiated peace, but his hopes went unrealized. The failure of appeasement and the subsequent military disasters had thoroughly discredited Prime Minister Neville Chamberlain. A member of Chamberlain's own party spoke for the nation, "In the name of God, go!" Chamberlain went. The British parliament suspended party politics for the duration of the war, and power passed to an all-party coalition headed by Winston Churchill, a critic of Britain's

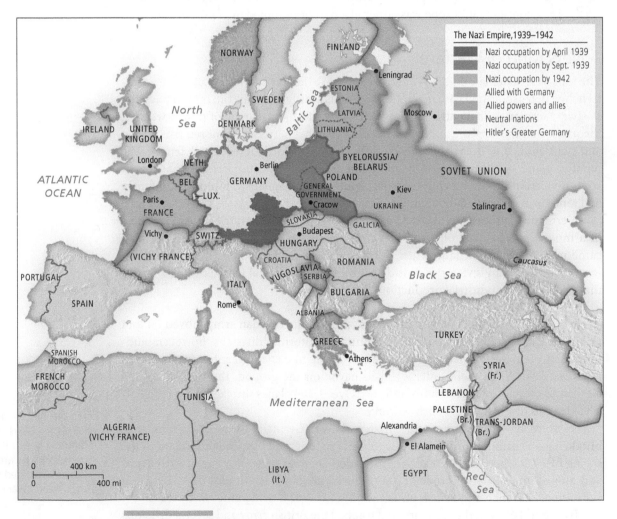

MAP **27.2** THE NAZI EMPIRE, 1939–1942 By 1942, Nazi Germany controlled most of Europe and much of North Africa and the Middle East. Which states were conquered by Germany? Which allied with Germany? Which states remained neutral?

Different Voices

Appeasement and the Munich Agreement

A fter World War I the victorious Allies redrew the map of central Europe and assigned the Sudetenland, a crescent-shaped region on the edge of what had been the Austro-Hungarian province of Bohemia, to Czechoslovakia. During the 1920s and 1930s, ethnic German Sudetenlanders experienced discrimination in education, employment, and political life, while German nationalist politicians fanned the flames of discontent and, in some cases, worked secretly with Hitler to prepare the ground for a Nazi takeover. In 1938, following his successful annexation of Austria, Hitler demanded the Sudetenland. After a series of meetings, Hitler, the British prime minister Neville Chamberlain, and the French premier Eduard Daladier announced the "Munich Agreement," which gave the Sudetenland to Germany. On his return to Britain, Chamberlain made his infamous proclamation of "peace in our time." The majority of British citizens cheered the Munich Agreement. One who did not was Winston Churchill, a member of Chamberlain's Conservative Party, but a critic of Chamberlain's appeasement policy.

In the first excerpt, Chamberlain defends appeasement in a speech before the House of Commons. In the second excerpt, Churchill attacks the Munich Agreement.

I. Neville Chamberlain in the House of Commons, 1938

War today . . . is a different thing . . . from what it used to be. . . . When war starts today, in the very first hour, before any professional soldier, sailor or airman has been touched, it will strike the workman, the clerk, the man-in-the-street or in the 'bus, and his wife and children in their homes. . . . [Y]ou cannot ask people to accept a prospect of that kind . . . unless you feel yourself, and can make them feel, that the cause for which they are going to fight is a vital cause—a cause that transcends all the human values. . . .

Since I first went to Berchtesgaden* more than 20,000 letters and telegrams have come to No. 10, Downing Street.† . . . the people who wrote did not feel that they had such a cause for which to fight. . . . That is my answer to those who say that we should have told Germany weeks ago that, if her army crossed the border of Czechoslovakia, we should be at war with her. . . .

What is the alternative to this bleak and barren policy of the inevitability of war? . . . we should seek by all means in our power to avoid war, by analysing possible causes, by trying to remove them, by discussion in a spirit of collaboration and good will. . . . even if it does mean the establishment of personal contact with dictators. . . .

I am asked how I can reconcile an appeal to the country to support the continuance of [the rearmament program]‡

---

*"Berchtesgaden": Hitler's mountain retreat where the political leaders met.
†"No. 10, Downing Street"—the address of the British prime minister's residence.
‡British governments adopted a policy of increased expenditure on armaments from 1934 on.

with . . . my belief that we might have peace for our time . . . I never meant to suggest that we should [secure peace] by disarmament, until we can induce others to disarm too. Our past experience has shown us only too clearly that weakness in armed strength means weakness in diplomacy. . . .

SOURCE: *Parliamentary Debates*. Fifth Series. Volume 339. House of Commons Official Report (London, 1938), 544–552.

II. Winston Churchill in the House of Commons, October 5, 1938

[W]e have sustained a total and unmitigated defeat. . . . The utmost my right hon. Friend the Prime Minister has been able to secure . . . has been that the German dictator, instead of snatching the victuals from the table, has been content to have them served to him course by course. . . .

After [Germany's] seizure of Austria in March . . . I ventured to appeal to the Government . . . to give a pledge that in conjunction with France and other Powers they would guarantee the security of Czechoslovakia while the Sudeten-Deutsch [Sudeten-German] question was being examined either by a League of Nations Commission or some other impartial body. . . . Between submission and immediate war there was this third alternative, which gave a hope not only of peace but of justice. It is quite true that such a policy in order to succeed demanded that Britain should declare straight out and a long time beforehand that she would, with others, join to defend Czechoslovakia against an unprovoked aggression. . . .

All is over. Silent, mournful, abandoned, broken, Czechoslovakia recedes into the darkness. . . . I think you will find that in a period of time which may be measured by years, but may be measured only by months, Czechoslovakia will be engulfed in the Nazi regime. . . .

It must now be accepted that all the countries of Central and Eastern Europe will make the best terms they can with the triumphant Nazi power. . . . Many of those countries . . . have already got politicians, Ministers, Governments, who were pro-German, but there was always an enormous popular movement in Poland, Rumania, Bulgaria, and Yugoslavia which looked to the Western democracies and loathed the idea of having this arbitrary rule of the totalitarian system thrust upon them, and hoped that a stand would be made. All that has gone by the board. . . .

The Prime Minister desires to see cordial relations between this country and Germany. There is no difficulty at all in having cordial relations between the peoples. . . . But never will you have friendship with the present German Government. You must have diplomatic and correct relations, but there can never be friendship between the British democracy and the Nazi power. . . .

(continued on next page)

(continued from previous page)

27.1

27.2

27.3

27.4

27.5

I do not grudge our loyal, brave people ... the natural, spontaneous outburst of joy and relief when they learned that the hard ordeal would no longer be required of them at the moment; but they should know the truth. They should know that there has been gross neglect and deficiency in our defences; they should know that we have sustained a defeat without a war ...

And do not suppose that this is the end. This is only the beginning of the reckoning. This is only the first sip, the first foretaste of a bitter cup which will be proffered to us year by year unless by a supreme recovery of moral health and martial vigour, we arise again and take our stand for freedom as in the olden time.

SOURCE: http://www.winstonchurchill.org/i4a/pages/index.cfm?pageid=1189. Accessed 12-12-07.

For Discussion

1. How did Chamberlain defend the Munich Agreement? What was he trying to achieve?
2. What alternatives did Churchill offer to the Munich Agreement? How realistic were these alternatives?
3. At the end of 1918, ethnic German delegates from Bohemia and Moravia rejected inclusion in Czechoslovakia and instead declared the union of German-majority regions (such as the Sudetenland) with Austria. In response, the new Czech government mobilized its army to enforce its boundaries—even though these boundaries contained over three million ethnic Germans. Does awareness of this history change your assessment of the Munich Agreement? If so, how and why?

appeasement policy since 1933. Never a humble man, Churchill wrote that when he accepted the position of prime minister, "I felt as if I were walking with Destiny, and that all my past life had been but a preparation for this hour and this trial ... I was sure I should not fail." In his first speech as prime minister, Churchill promised, "Victory—victory at all costs."

Faced with the British refusal to negotiate, Hitler ordered his General Staff to prepare for a land invasion of Britain. But placing German troops in the English Channel while the RAF still controlled the skies would be a certain military disaster. The destruction of Britain's air power had to come first. On July 10, German bomber raids on English southern coastal cities opened the Battle of Britain, a battle waged in the air and in the factories, and Germany's first significant defeat.

The British had three important advantages in the Battle of Britain. First, RAF pilots were flying in the skies above Britain—which meant that pilots who survived crashes could be rescued to fight again, whereas German survivors sat out the rest of the war as prisoners. Second, the rearmament program begun in 1934 had constructed a chain of anti-aircraft gun installations and radar stations that protected the British Isles and increased German losses. And finally, and most significantly for the future course of the war, Britain's industrial productivity outweighed Germany's. In the summer of 1940, British factories each month produced twice the number of fighter aircraft coming out of German plants. On September 17, 1940, Hitler announced that the invasion of Britain was "postponed."

The Invasion of the Soviet Union

War against Britain had never been one of Hitler's central goals, however. His dreams of the **Third Reich**, a German empire that was to last a thousand years, centered on capture of the agricultural and industrial resources of the Soviet Union. But Hitler sought far more than resources. He envisioned war with the Soviet Union as an apocalyptic clash of Good versus Evil: the superior German race against the twin evils of "Judeo-Bolshevism." The Soviet Union was, of course, the center of global "Bolshevism," or communism, while the majority of European Jews lived in Soviet-controlled eastern Polish lands or in the Soviet Union itself.

Third Reich Term for Adolf Hitler's Germany; articulates the Nazi aim of extending German rule across Europe.

A CRUCIAL POSTPONEMENT In July 1940, as the Battle of Britain began, Hitler ordered his military to plan a Soviet invasion. By December the plan was set: German troops were to invade the Soviet Union in April 1941. But they did not. Hitler postponed the invasion for two crucial months because the ambitions of an incompetent ally—Mussolini—threatened to undermine the economic base of the Nazi war machine.

Hoping to expand his Mediterranean empire, Mussolini ordered Italian troops into British imperial territories in North Africa in July 1940, followed by an invasion of Greece in October. But with a military budget one-tenth the size of Germany's, outdated tanks and aircraft, no aircraft carriers or anti-aircraft defenses, and a limited industrial base, Italy was ill-equipped to fight a total war. By the spring of 1941, the British army had pushed the Italians back into Libya while the Greeks mounted a strong resistance.

Hitler feared the consolidation of British power in Africa and was even more terrified of a British advance into eastern Europe. If Britain were able to build air bases in Greece, the Balkans would lie open to British bombing runs that could cripple the German war effort. Germany received 50 percent of its cereal and livestock from the Balkan region, 45 percent of its aluminum ore from Greece, 90 percent of its tin from Yugoslavia—and most of its oil from Romania. Without oil, there would be no *blitz* in *blitzkrieg*.

These considerations led Hitler to delay the invasion of the Soviet Union while the German army mopped up Mussolini's mess in the Balkans and North Africa. In April 1941, German armored units punched through Yugoslavian defenses and encircled the Yugoslav army. Greece came next. Meanwhile, in North Africa German troops recaptured all the territory taken by the British the previous year. As Map 27.2 shows, by the summer of 1941, Germany stood triumphant, with dramatic victories in North Africa and the Balkans. But these victories came at a high price: the postponement of the German invasion of the Soviet Union from April to June.

EARLY SUCCESS At first, that postponement seemed to matter little. On June 22, 1941, the largest invading force the world had yet seen began to cross the Soviet borders. Three million German soldiers, equipped with 2,770 modern aircraft and 3,350 tanks, went into battle. In a matter of days, most of the Soviet air force was destroyed. By October, the Germans had taken Kiev, besieged Leningrad, and stood 80 miles from Moscow. Almost 45 percent of the Soviet population was under German occupation, and the Germans controlled access to much of the Soviet Union's natural and industrial

GERMAN MASSACRE AT KERCH In one of the most famous Soviet photographs taken during the war, relatives try to identify their dead after German troops massacred all the men in the village of Kerch. Such atrocities as this strengthened the will of the Polish, Baltic, and Soviet peoples to resist their German occupiers.

resources, including more than 45 percent of its grain and 65 percent of its coal, iron, and steel. On October 10, Hitler's spokesman announced to the foreign press corps that the destruction of the Soviet Union was assured. German newspapers proclaimed, "CAMPAIGN IN THE EAST DECIDED!"[4]

Why was Germany so successful at the start of the invasion? Blitzkrieg provides part of the answer. Germany's spearhead force of tank and motorized infantry divisions shattered the Soviet defensive line and seized key targets. Stalin's stubborn refusal to believe that Hitler would violate the Non-Aggression Pact also weakened Russian defenses. Soviet intelligence sources sent in more than 80 warnings of an imminent German attack. Stalin classified these messages as "doubtful" and ordered the messengers themselves punished. Moreover, the initial German advance occurred in territories where Soviet rule had brought enormous suffering and where, therefore, the population had little reason to defend the Soviet state. Ukraine, for example, was still recovering from the Stalinist-inflicted famine of the 1930s, while eastern Poland and the Baltic states, which Stalin had gained through the German-Soviet Non-Aggression Pact, were still bleeding from the Soviet takeover in 1939.

THE FATAL WINTER Yet in the winter of 1940–1941, the German advance stalled. Leningrad resisted its besiegers, and Moscow remained beyond the Germans' reach. Three obstacles halted the German invasion. First, German atrocities strengthened local resistance against the occupiers. The troops in occupied Soviet territory treated the local populations with utter cruelty. SS and army units moved through eastern Poland, the Baltics, and Soviet lands, seizing key resources and murdering at will. The Nazi governor of Ukraine insisted, "I will pump every last thing out of this country."[5] By 1941, human-made famine devastated Ukraine and Galicia.

As partisan units worked behind the German lines, sabotaging their transportation routes, hijacking their supplies, and murdering their patrols, they found the Germans vulnerable to guerilla attack because of the second factor in halting the

REBUILDING THE INDUSTRIAL MIGHT OF THE SOVIET UNION The stalling of the German offensive in the winter of 1941–1942 gave the Soviet Union the essential advantage of time: time to rebuild their industrial strength. Thousands of factories were dismantled and shipped to safety east of the Urals. In this photo, workers begin the massive job of putting their factory back together. Before the war, they made railway cars. Now they would build tanks.

invasion: Germany's overstretched lines. Since June the German army had advanced so far so fast that it overstrained its supply and communication lines.

The weather, the third and most crucial obstacle for the Germans, worsened these logistical problems. Had the Germans invaded in April, as originally planned, they might have captured Moscow and pushed even further east well before winter set in. Instead, the crucial postponement meant that German troops were first mired in mud and then stuck in snow. An early October snowfall, which then melted, turned Russia's dirt roads to impassable mud. By the time the ground froze several weeks later, the German forces, like Napoleon's army 130 years earlier, were fighting the Russian winter. Subzero temperatures wreaked havoc with transportation lines. Horses froze to death, and machinery refused to start. Men fared just as badly. Dressed in lightweight spring uniforms, German soldiers fell victim to frostbite. By the end of the winter, the casualty list numbered more than 30 percent of the German East Army.

At the start of 1942, this army still occupied much of the Soviet Union and controlled the majority of its agricultural and industrial resources. More than three million Soviet soldiers had been killed and another three million captured. But the failure to deal the Soviets a quick death blow in 1941 gave Stalin and his high command a crucial advantage—*time*. During the German advance, Soviet laborers dismantled entire factories to transport them east, to areas out of German bombing range. Between August and October 1941, 80 percent of the Soviet war industry was in pieces. The *time* gained in the winter of 1941–1942 allowed the Soviets to put these pieces back together: They rebuilt their factories and focused the colossal productive power of the Soviet Union on the war effort. By 1943, Russia was outproducing Germany: 24,000 tanks versus 17,000; 130,000 artillery pieces versus 27,000; 35,000 combat aircraft versus 25,000. In a total war, in which victory occurs on the assembly line as well as on the front line, these statistics threatened Hitler's dreams of a German empire.

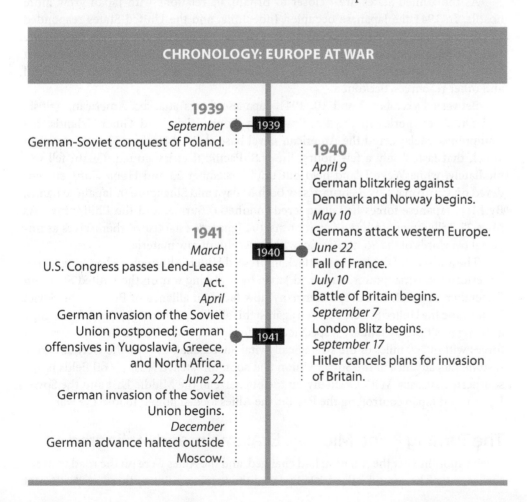

CHRONOLOGY: EUROPE AT WAR

1939
September
German-Soviet conquest of Poland.

1940
April 9
German blitzkrieg against Denmark and Norway begins.
May 10
Germans attack western Europe.
June 22
Fall of France.
July 10
Battle of Britain begins.
September 7
London Blitz begins.
September 17
Hitler cancels plans for invasion of Britain.

1941
March
U.S. Congress passes Lend-Lease Act.
April
German invasion of the Soviet Union postponed; German offensives in Yugoslavia, Greece, and North Africa.
June 22
German invasion of the Soviet Union begins.
December
German advance halted outside Moscow.

The World at War, 1941–1945

27.3   Why did the Allies win in 1945?

I n December 1941, as the German advance slowed in the Soviet Union, Japanese expansionism in the Pacific fused with the war in Europe and drew the United States into the conflict. Over the next four years, millions of soldiers, sailors, and civilians lost their lives in a gargantuan and complicated conflict waged around the world.

The Globalization of the War

Even before 1941, Europe's imperialist legacy ensured that World War II was not confined to Europe. Mussolini's desire to expand his Mediterranean empire pushed the fighting into North Africa, while Britain would never have been able to stand alone in 1940 against the German-occupied continent without access to the manpower and materials of its empire. German efforts to block British access to these resources spread the war into the Atlantic, where British merchant marines battled against German submarines to keep open the sea lanes to Britain.

Those sea lanes provided a crucial connection between Britain and the still-neutral United States, on whose resources Britain drew heavily. In March 1941, the U.S. Congress passed the **Lend-Lease Act**, which guaranteed that the United States would supply Britain with necessary military supplies, with payment postponed until after the war ended. The passage of Lend-Lease was one of the most important decisions in all of World War II. It gave first Britain and then the Soviets access to American industrial might.

As the United States drew closer to Britain, its relations with Japan grew more hostile. In 1941 the Japanese occupied Indochina, and the United States responded by placing an embargo on trade in oil with Japan. Japanese policymakers viewed the embargo as tantamount to an act of war. Japan's imperial ambitions demanded that it move decisively before its oil ran out. The South Pacific, a treasure house of mineral and other resources, beckoned.

Between December 7 and 10, 1941, Japanese forces attacked American, British, and Dutch territories in the Pacific—Hong Kong, Wake and Guam Islands, the Philippines, Malaya, and the American naval base at Pearl Harbor, Hawaii. After an attack that lasted only a few hours, the U.S. Pacific fleet lay gutted. Guam fell immediately, while Wake Island held out until December 23 and Hong Kong surrendered on Christmas Day. February saw both Malaya and Singapore in Japanese hands. By May, Japanese forces had conquered Indonesia, Burma, and the Philippines. As **Map 27.3** illustrates, in just a few months, the Japanese established themselves as imperial overlords of the South Pacific, with its wealth of raw materials.

The audacity of the Japanese attack impressed Hitler. Although he had long feared American industrial power, he joined Japan by declaring war on the United States on December 11, 1941. In Europe Germany now faced an alliance of Britain, the Soviet Union, and the United States. Yet even against this alliance, Germany appeared to occupy a strong position. By January a spectacular offensive in North Africa brought German forces within 200 miles of the strategically vital Suez Canal. In June the German army resumed its advance in the Soviet Union and soon threatened Russia's oil fields in the southern Caucasus. With Germany on the offensive in the Middle East and the Soviet Union, and Japan controlling the Pacific, the Allies looked poised to lose the war.

The Turning Point: Midway, El Alamein, and Stalingrad

Twelve months later the situation had changed, and the Allies were on the road to eventual victory. The second half of 1942 proved the turning point as three very different

Lend-Lease Act Passed in March 1941, the act gave Britain access to U.S. industrial products during World War II, with payment postponed for the duration of the war.

 **Read the Document**

Japanese Total War Research Institute, Plan for the Greater East Asia Co-Prosperity Sphere, 1942

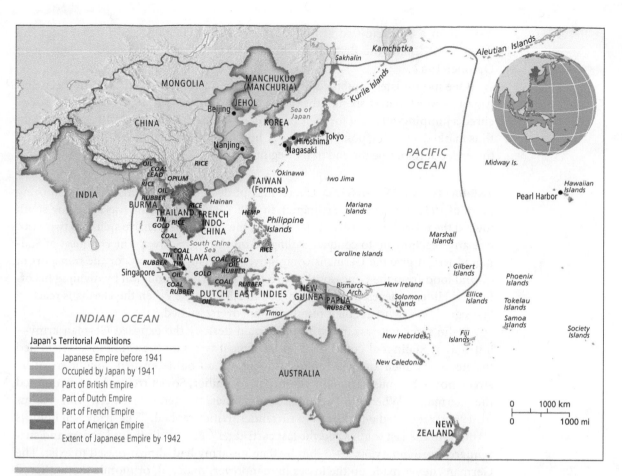

MAP **27.3** JAPAN'S TERRITORIAL AMBITIONS Lacking its own supply of natural resources, Japan embarked on imperial conquest. What mineral and agricultural resources were crucial? Which European powers lost territory to Japan?

battles transformed the course of the war. In the Pacific, victory at the Battle of Midway gave the U.S. forces a decisive advantage. In North Africa, British forces experienced their first battlefield victory at El Alamein. And in Europe, the Battle of Stalingrad dealt Germany a blow from which it never recovered.

THE BATTLE OF MIDWAY The Battle of Midway resulted from the Japanese effort to ensure its air supremacy by destroying U.S. aircraft carriers. To do so, the Japanese attacked Midway Island, a U.S. outpost, on June 4, 1942. By mid-morning the Japanese had shot down two-thirds of the American planes. But then an American dive-bomber group, which had gotten lost, suddenly found itself above the main Japanese carriers. Their decks cluttered with gas lines and bombs, these ships were caught in the act of refueling and rearming the strike force. In five minutes, the bombers destroyed three of Japan's four carriers. The fourth sank later in the day. The destruction of the Japanese carriers dealt Japan a blow from which it could not recover. The United States possessed the industrial resources to rebuild its lost ships and airplanes. Japan did not. In five explosive minutes at Midway the course of the Pacific war changed.

THE BATTLE OF EL ALAMEIN In contrast, the Battle of El Alamein marked the culmination of over two years of fighting in North Africa. As we have already seen, in the spring of 1941 German troops came to the aid of retreating Italian forces in Libya; by June 1941, they had muscled the British back into Egypt. For more than a year the two armies pushed each other back and forth across the desert. But finally the British caught the Germans by surprise at El Alamein in October 1942.

One month later combined British and American forces landed in Morocco and Algeria. Over the next six months they pushed Germany out of North Africa and secured a jumping-off point for their invasion of southern Italy in July 1943. El Alamein thus marked a turning point in the war. Churchill said of it, "It is not the beginning of the end, but it may be the end of the beginning."[6]

THE BATTLE OF STALINGRAD Churchill's apt description also fits the third turning point of 1942, the Battle of Stalingrad. In July the German army was sweeping south toward the oil-rich Caucasus. Hitler ordered the southern offensive split into two, with one arm reaching up to conquer Stalingrad on the Volga River. The conquest of Stalingrad would give the Germans control over the main waterway for the transport of oil and food from the Caucasus to the rest of the Soviet Union. But by dividing his offensive, Hitler widened his front from 500 to 2,500 miles. When the Germans reached Stalingrad on August 23, their resources were overstretched.

Stalin's generals assured him they could destroy the exposed German army—but only if Stalingrad could hold on for almost two months while they assembled the necessary men and machinery. An epic urban battle ensued, fought street by street, house by house, room by room. By November, Soviet troops had surrounded the Germans. When the German commander, General Friedrich von Paulus (d. 1953), requested permission to surrender, Hitler replied, "The army will hold its position to the last soldier and the last cartridge."[7] Paulus disobeyed orders and surrendered on January 30, 1943, but by then his army had almost ceased to exist. The Germans never made up the losses in manpower, material, or morale they suffered at Stalingrad.

The Allied Victory in Europe

Map 27.4 illustrates that the Allies moved to the offensive in 1943. The destructive fury of total war increased exponentially, as German military death statistics reveal: By July of 1944, 2.8 million German soldiers had died; in the remaining nine months of the war, another 4.8 million were killed.

THE INVASION OF ITALY Stalin had long been pleading with his Allies to relieve the pressure on Soviet troops by opening a "Second Front" in Europe. On July 10, 1943, British and American forces landed in Sicily, prepared to push up the Italian peninsula, described by Churchill as the "soft underbelly" of German-controlled Europe. The Italian offensive at first appeared a success. Within just 15 days, Mussolini had been overthrown and his successor opened peace negotiations with the Allies.

Yet the Italian invasion did not prove decisive. The German army occupied Italy, rescued Mussolini, and pushed back against the Allied offensive. Ridged with mountains and laced with rivers, the Italian peninsula formed a natural defensive fortress. In an eight-month period, Allied forces advanced only 70 miles.

THE DECISIVE FRONT The European war was thus decided not in the mountains of Italy, but in the East. Beginning in the summer of 1943, the Soviets steadily pushed back the Germans on a front that ran from Leningrad in the far north to the Crimea in the south. The battles between the Soviet Union and Nazi Germany were some of the largest military confrontations in history. An estimated 75 percent of German military losses in World War II came on the Eastern Front.

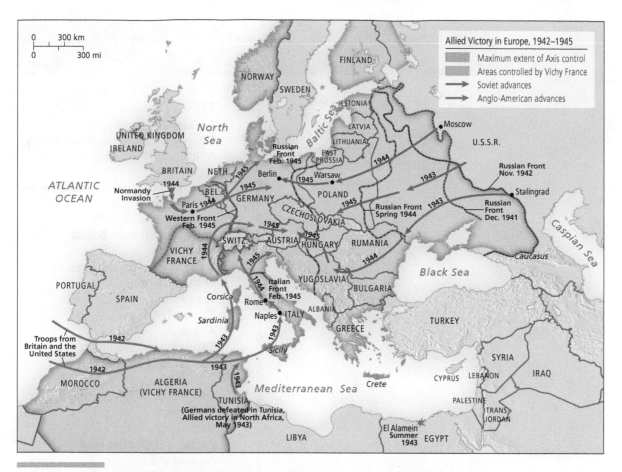

MAP **27.4** ALLIED VICTORY IN EUROPE, 1942–1945 In 1943, Allied forces moved onto the offensive. Where and when were the crucial battles? How does this map illustrate the pivotal role of the Eastern Front in deciding the outcome of the war?

The Soviet advance from 1943 on demonstrated that the Red Army had mastered and improved upon German blitzkrieg tactics. The Soviets concentrated their tanks into forces that combined motorized infantry regiments, tanks, antitank battalions, and mobile anti-aircraft artillery. They also multiplied their number of radios and field telephones to avoid the organizational chaos that had greeted the invasion of 1941.

Such mobile armored forces depended on factories churning out steel, rubber, oil, and all the various machine parts needed by a modern army. Achievements in industrial production thus constituted a key factor in the Soviet victory. While Lend-Lease supplied the Soviet Union with the basics needed to keep its army moving—aircraft and tanks, rails and locomotives, trucks and gasoline, and 15 million pairs of boots—the Soviets did not rely on imports alone. In 1943, Russia manufactured four times as many tanks as it imported, and Soviet production of tanks and antitank guns doubled Germany's.

THE FALL OF GERMANY As the Red Army closed in on Germany from the east, the British, Canadians, and Americans pushed in from the west. On June 6, 1944, the Allies carried out the largest amphibious operation in history. Five seaborne divisions (two American, two British, and one Canadian) and three airborne divisions (two American and one British) crossed the English Channel and landed on the coast of northern France. The **D-Day** landings illustrated the Allied advantage in manpower and material. Against the Allies' eight divisions, the Germans had four and against the Allies' 5,000 fighter planes, the Germans could send up 169.

Yet the strength of the German resistance—particularly on Omaha Beach, where U.S. troops sustained more than 4,000 casualties—signaled that the road to Berlin

D-Day Common term for June 6, 1944, when 150,000 Allied troops landed on the shores of northern France to open an effective second front against German-occupied Europe.

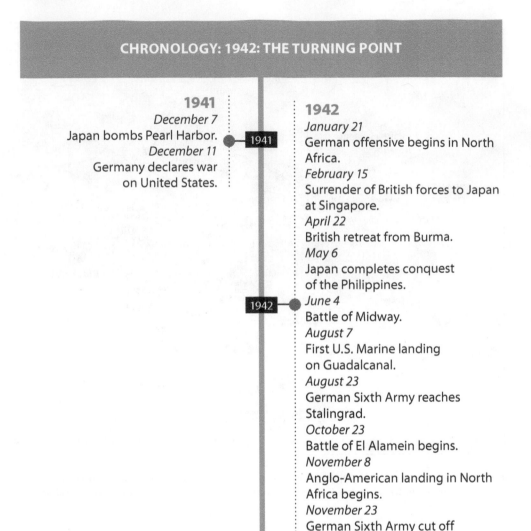

CHRONOLOGY: 1942: THE TURNING POINT

1941

December 7
Japan bombs Pearl Harbor.
December 11
Germany declares war
on United States.

1942

January 21
German offensive begins in North Africa.
February 15
Surrender of British forces to Japan at Singapore.
April 22
British retreat from Burma.
May 6
Japan completes conquest of the Philippines.
June 4
Battle of Midway.
August 7
First U.S. Marine landing on Guadalcanal.
August 23
German Sixth Army reaches Stalingrad.
October 23
Battle of El Alamein begins.
November 8
Anglo-American landing in North Africa begins.
November 23
German Sixth Army cut off at Stalingrad.

would not be easy. The Allies faced the task of uprooting the Germans from territory where they had planted themselves five years earlier. For 10 months, American, British, and other Allied troops fought a series of hard-won battles.

As these troops pushed in on Germany from the west, the Soviets accelerated their onslaught in the east. Just over two weeks after D-Day—and three years to the day since Germany had invaded the Soviet Union—the Soviet army mounted Operation Bagration, described by one historian as "the most overwhelming single military assault in history."[8] Two and a half million Soviet troops attacked along a 450-mile front that ran from the Baltics through Byelorussia (Belarus). Outmanned and outgunned, the Germans broke. One Polish civilian, who saw the Germans retreating, wrote, "They were no longer soldiers, but moving human tatters."[9] By early August, Soviet tank units were within reach of Warsaw, and Hitler's dream of a 1,000-year Reich was crumbling (see Map 27.4).

In March 1945, the Soviet army approached Berlin from the east and the British and American armies reached Germany's Rhine border. The Allies agreed to leave the conquest of Berlin to the Soviet Army. In this climactic battle of the European war, 320,000 Germans, many of them young boys, fought three million Soviet troops. Even so, it took 11 days before the city's commander surrendered on May 2. Two days earlier, Hitler took a cyanide capsule and then shot himself. On May 7, 1945, General Alfred Jodl (1890–1946) signed the unconditional surrender of German forces.

THE BATTLE FOR BERLIN On April 20, 1945, Hitler celebrated his fifty-sixth birthday and made a rare visit out of his Berlin bunker to visit with the troops defending his city. As this photograph shows, these "soldiers" were just children. Ten days later, Hitler committed suicide.

The Air War, the Atom Bomb, and the Fall of Japan

When Germany surrendered in the spring of 1945, the war in the Pacific still raged. After the Midway battle of 1942, the United States steadily, but slowly, agonizingly, pushed the Japanese back island by island. Japanese industry could not make up for the weapons and ammunition expended in these battles. In contrast, American factories were

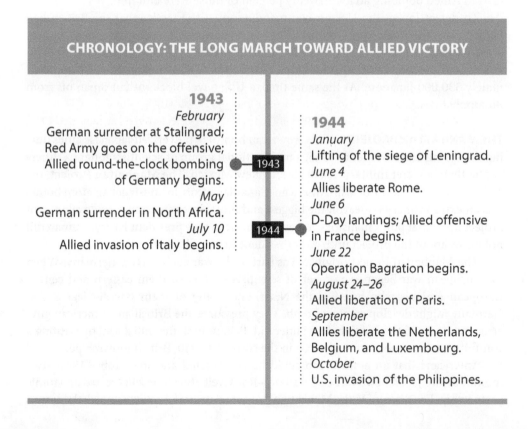

CHRONOLOGY: THE LONG MARCH TOWARD ALLIED VICTORY

1943

February
German surrender at Stalingrad;
Red Army goes on the offensive;
Allied round-the-clock bombing
of Germany begins.
May
German surrender in North Africa.
July 10
Allied invasion of Italy begins.

1943

1944

1944

January
Lifting of the siege of Leningrad.
June 4
Allies liberate Rome.
June 6
D-Day landings; Allied offensive
in France begins.
June 22
Operation Bagration begins.
August 24–26
Allied liberation of Paris.
September
Allies liberate the Netherlands,
Belgium, and Luxembourg.
October
U.S. invasion of the Philippines.

just gearing up. Whereas in 1940 American assembly lines produced only a little more than 2,000 aircraft, by 1944 they had manufactured over 96,000 bombers and fighters. American productivity per worker hour was five times that of Japan.

While U.S. troops moved closer to the Japanese mainland, British and Indian troops rebuffed a Japanese attempt to invade India and pushed the Japanese out of Burma. Australian forces, with American assistance, held the line at New Guinea and forestalled a Japanese invasion of Australia. By February 1945, then, when American marines landed on the small island of Iwo Jima, just 380 miles from Japan's home islands, the Japanese war effort was in tatters and an Allied victory ensured.

Obtaining this final victory, however, was not easy. In the month of fighting on Iwo Jima, one-third of the American landing force died or suffered injury. The April conquest of Okinawa was even more hard-won. Outnumbered two to one, the Japanese endured staggering losses—110,000 of the 120,000 soldiers on the island died. Yet they still inflicted serious damage on the attacking force, killing or wounding 50,000 Americans before the fight was over. Nobody counted how many Okinawans died in a battle they had done nothing to provoke, although estimates ranged as high as 160,000.

THE AIR WAR After the capture of Iwo Jima and Okinawa, American forces had the bases needed to bomb Japanese cities. This air war utilized tactics and technologies the Allies developed over the previous five years in the war against Germany. Their victory in the Battle of Britain in 1940 shielded the British from an invasion but not from bombing. By May 1941, German planes had bombed almost every major industrial city in Britain, killing 43,000 noncombatants. But from January 1941 on, British bombers retaliated in kind, and as the war wore on, developed new techniques of airborne destruction. In May 1942, for example, British planes destroyed Cologne with the world's first 1,000-bomber raid. One year later, the British bombing of Hamburg created the world's first **firestorm**. In this human-made catastrophe, fires (caused by incendiary bombs) combine with winds to suck the oxygen out of the air and raise temperatures to combustible levels. As one survivor of the Hamburg bombing recalled, "The smallest children lay like fried eels on the pavement."[10] More than 500,000 German civilians died in Allied bombing attacks. Twenty percent of those were children.

To defeat Japan, the U.S. air command adopted the tactics that the British had perfected in the skies over Germany. On a single March evening, American bombs and the ensuing firestorm killed 85,000 residents of Tokyo. Over the next five months, American bombers hit 66 Japanese cities, burned 180 square miles, and killed approximately 330,000 Japanese. At the same time, a U.S. naval blockade cut Japan off from its supply lines.

THE MANHATTAN PROJECT While American bombers pulverized Japanese cities during the spring and summer of 1945, a multinational group of scientists fought a different battle in a secret military installation in New Mexico. The **Manhattan Project**, the code name for the joint British-American-Canadian effort to construct an atom bomb, was an extraordinary endeavor, the biggest and most expensive weapons development project up to that point in history. Yet even American vice president Harry Truman did not know about the project until after President Roosevelt died.

The Manhattan Project originated as part of the war against Nazi Germany. When the European war began, a number of scientists—many of them eastern and central European émigrés who had fled the Nazis, and many of them Jewish—feared that Germany might develop an atom bomb. They pressured the British and American governments to build the Bomb before Hitler did. Britain took the initial lead by creating a committee to oversee atomic research in the spring of 1940. British research persuaded the Americans that an atom bomb could be constructed and in October 1941—two months *before* Japan bombed Pearl Harbor—Roosevelt and Churchill created an atomic partnership. For three years the Manhattan Project scientists labored to unlock the atom's

firestorm Catastrophe in which fires combine with winds to suck the oxygen out of the air and raise temperatures to combustible levels. First experienced during the British bombing of the German city of Hamburg in World War II.

Manhattan Project Code name given to the secret Anglo-American project that resulted in the construction of the atom bomb during World War II.

power. They succeeded on July 16, 1945, when the world's first atomic explosion—the Trinity test—detonated over the desert of New Mexico. But by the time of the Trinity test, Nazi Germany had already fallen. The threat of a Nazi atom bomb disappeared.

The Pacific War, however, raged on. The decision to use atom bombs against Japan generated immediate controversy. Many of the scientists on the Manhattan Project opposed the decision as a step across a crucial moral dividing line, as did important American military officials such as General Dwight Eisenhower (1890–1969), supreme commander of the Allied forces in Europe, and General Douglas MacArthur (1880–1964), supreme Allied commander in the Pacific. Those in favor of the decision argued that if atom bombs were not used, the Allies would have to invade Japan. U.S. Army planners warned that if casualty rates were as high as those on Okinawa, the numbers of Americans killed in the first phase of the invasion could reach 50,000. Admiral William Leahy (Truman's Chief of Staff) and others, however, argued that an invasion was not necessary, that if the Allies maintained the naval blockade and continued to attack Japanese cities with conventional bombs, Japan would surrender by the end of the year. From President Truman's perspective, however, continuing the war—with or without an invasion of Japan—meant continuing to put Allied soldiers in harm's way. The Bomb promised to end the war quickly and bring Allied servicemen home.

A LIGHT BRIGHTER THAN A THOUSAND SUNS At 8:15 A.M. on August 6, 1945, an American plane named the *Enola Gay* (after the pilot's mother) dropped an atom bomb above the city of Hiroshima (see Map 27.3). A light "brighter than a thousand suns" flashed in the sky. Temperatures at the site of the atomic explosion reached 5,400 degrees Fahrenheit. All those exposed within two miles of the center suffered primary thermal burns—their blood literally boiled and their skin peeled off in strips. Of Hiroshima's wartime population of 400,000, 140,000 died by the end of 1945, with another 60,000 dying in the next five years.

The Japanese reacted to the atomic bombing of Hiroshima with incomprehension and confusion. They did not know what had hit them. Within the high levels of the Japanese government, gradual realization of the atomic bomb's power strengthened the position of those officials who recognized that Japan must now give up. A hard-line faction of the military, however, wished to fight on.

Then, on August 8, the Soviet Union declared war on Japan. The next day American forces dropped an atom bomb on the city of Nagasaki and killed 70,000 outright (with another 70,000 dying over the next five years). On August 10, Emperor Hirohito (1901–1989) told his military leaders to surrender. Viewed in the West as an implacable warlord, Hirohito actually possessed fairly limited political power and had been pressing for peace since June. Negotiations between the Allies and the Japanese continued until August 15, when the war ended.

27.1

27.2

27.3

27.4

27.5

 Read the Document

The Franck Report

 Read the Document

John Siemes, An Eyewitness to Hiroshima

MUSHROOM CLOUD The detonation of the atomic bomb over Hiroshima on August 6, 1945, produced what would become one of the most familiar images of the post–World War II age.

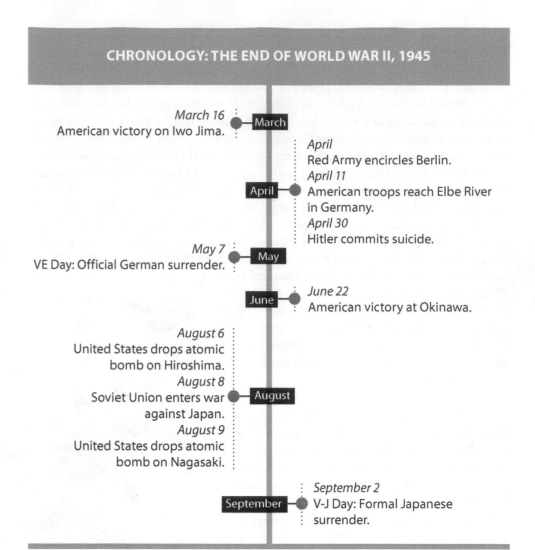

27.1

27.2

27.3

27.4

27.5

CHRONOLOGY: THE END OF WORLD WAR II, 1945

March 16
American victory on Iwo Jima.

March

April
Red Army encircles Berlin.

April 11
April
American troops reach Elbe River in Germany.

April 30
Hitler commits suicide.

May 7
VE Day: Official German surrender.

May

June 22
June
American victory at Okinawa.

August 6
United States drops atomic bomb on Hiroshima.

August 8
Soviet Union enters war against Japan.

August

August 9
United States drops atomic bomb on Nagasaki.

September 2
September
V-J Day: Formal Japanese surrender.

In Hiroshima and Nagasaki, however, another fight was underway, this time against an unseen and at first unrecognized enemy: radiation. The lingering horror of radiation sickness, which many Americans and British first dismissed as Japanese propaganda, signaled that the atom bomb was not just a bigger weapon. In the months after the war's end, both policymakers and ordinary people came to recognize that the revolutionary new force of atomic power had introduced the world to new possibilities—and new horrors.

The Wars Within the War

27.4 What were the context, causes, and consequences of genocide during World War II?

Armies and advanced weaponry tell only part of the story of World War II. Inside and alongside the military war, other wars raged.

THE EASTERN KILLING ZONE Most of the killing occurred in what the historian Timothy Snyder has termed the "bloodlands," the multilinguistic, multiethnic regions from central Poland in the west to western Russia in the east and embracing Ukraine, Belarus, and the Baltics.[11] The "bloodlands" first endured the expansion of Stalinist rule and then became a laboratory for genocide. Civilian death counts in this killing zone are staggering. By the war's end, 20 percent of Poland's prewar population was dead. So, too, were over three million Ukrainian civilians. Half of the prewar population of Belarus had either died or been displaced.

As specified in the secret clauses of the German-Soviet Non-Aggression Pact, the Soviet Union occupied eastern Poland and the Baltic states in 1939. Immediately the inhabitants of these regions endured the full ferocity of Stalinist terror. In Poland, for example, over 400,000 individuals, primarily ethnic Poles and Jews, were deported to the Gulag—pulled out of their homes, deprived of their possessions, crowded onto freezing freight cars, and trundled hundreds of miles eastward. Another 30,000 were executed as Stalinist forces moved to establish control over Polish society, including 22,000 army officers who were gunned down and buried in ditches in the Katyn forest and surrounding region.

Meanwhile, German-occupied Poland became the staging ground for the Nazi racial reordering of Europe. As **Map 27.5** shows, Germany annexed much of western Poland, which Hitler envisaged as prime territory for German "re-colonization." Between September 1939 and June 1941, a brutal deportation program forced Poles and Jews out of their homes. The remainder of German-held Poland, or the "General Government," became the dumping ground for deported Poles and Jews and a vast labor reservoir for the German war effort. Hitler intended the Slavic populations, defined in his racist hierarchy as biologically inferior, to serve as a labor pool for their German superiors. To reduce the Polish people to slaves, the Nazis attempted to destroy Polish society and culture. They seized businesses and bank accounts, replaced Polish place names with German names, closed universities and high schools, and murdered Polish intellectuals and professionals.

The German invasion of the Soviet Union (including Soviet-occupied Poland and the Baltics) intensified this race-based violence and extended the killing zone. As we saw earlier in this chapter, the advancing German army treated the local populations with horrifying brutality and deployed mass starvation as a weapon of war. Dreaming of transforming Ukraine into a vast German agricultural colony, the Nazis viewed the local populations as completely expendable.

MAP **27.5** POLAND DURING WORLD WAR II In September 1939, the Germans and Soviets invaded and divided Poland between them. The Germans split their territory in two. Western Poland became part of Greater Germany, with the Polish and Jewish residents displaced to make room for new German settlers. The rest of German-occupied Poland became the General Government, a vast forced labor and killing zone. Where were the death camps located? What factors explain this location?

The War Against the Jews

The war against the Jews, usually called the **Holocaust** or the Shoah, took place within this political context of racial reordering and within the physical context of the "bloodlands." According to Nazi racial ideology, two "races" posed an inherent threat to the Reich: the Roma (Gypsies) and Jews. War gave the Nazis the opportunity to attempt what had seemed impossible: the complete destruction of these peoples. Somewhere between 220,000 and 600,000 Romani died in the *Porajmos*—the Devouring—including almost all those living in the Baltic states and Czechoslovakia. The much larger Jewish population of Europe was, however, the special target of Hitler's hatred. The Holocaust claimed the lives of approximately six million Jews. Children were especially vulnerable. Of the Jewish children living in 1939 in the regions already or soon to be under German control, only 11 percent survived.

Holocaust Adolf Hitler's effort to murder all the Jews in Europe during World War II.

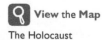

View the Map

The Holocaust

867

THE EVOLUTION OF THE "FINAL SOLUTION" In 1939, the Nazi government had no defined "Jewish policy," even as the conquest of western Poland brought almost two million Jews under German control. Amidst vague plans of exporting the Jewish population eastward or even to the African island of Madagascar, German officials in Poland focused on identifying Jews and moving them into isolated and easily controlled areas. Under this policy of "ghettoization," the German occupiers expelled Jews from their homes and confined them in ghettos sealed off from their non-Jewish neighbors. Packed into overcrowded apartments, with inadequate food and sanitation, the ghetto populations lived in a nightmare of disease, starvation, and death. In the almost two-year period between the invasion of Poland and the invasion of the Soviet Union, an estimated 30,000 Jews died, killed outright by German soldiers or dead from starvation and disease as a result of deportation and ghettoization. Yet the suffering had only begun.

The invasion of the Soviet Union provided the context in which Nazi policy shifted to outright mass murder. Alongside the regular German army marched special units of the SS called *Einsatzgruppen* ("strike forces"). With the army providing logistical support, these small motorized units (about 3,000 men in all) took on the task of murdering Jews. Most of these murders followed the same general pattern: SS soldiers—often aided by local populations—rounded up all of the Jewish men, women, and children in a town or village and marched them in batches to a field or woods. They ordered the first batch to dig a large ditch. They stripped their victims of their clothing, lined them up on the edge of the ditch, and shot them at point-blank range. They then lined up subsequent batches and shot them as well, so that by the end of a day's worth of killing, dead and dying bodies filled the ditch. A thin layer of soil thrown on top transformed the ditch into a mass grave. Estimates of the final death count of the Einsatzgruppen actions range from 1.5 to 2 million, including almost the entirety of the historic Jewish communities in the Baltics and Ukraine.

In December of 1941, with the German military offensive in the Soviet Union stalled, Hitler called for the total annihilation of European Jews, whom he blamed for Germany's military disasters. On January 20, 1942, senior German officials met in a villa in Wannsee, outside Berlin, to draw up plans for genocide, which they termed the **Final Solution**. Even the Jewish populations in neutral countries such as Sweden and Ireland showed up on the target list. The Wannsee Conference marked the beginning of a more systematic approach to murdering European Jews.

This systematic approach built on the experience in mass murder gained by the Einsatzgruppen. By trial and error, these squads discovered the most efficient ways of identifying and rounding up Jews, shooting them, and burying the bodies. But the Einsatzgruppen actions also revealed the limits of conventional methods of killing. Shooting took time, used up valuable ammunition, and required many men. Moreover, even well-trained and indoctrinated soldiers cracked under the strain of shooting unarmed women and children at close range. The Nazis needed a technological approach, one that would provide a comfortable distance between the killers and the killed. The death camp filled this need.

GENOCIDE BY ASSEMBLY LINE *Death camps* were not the same as *concentration camps*. From 1933 on, Hitler's government sentenced communists, homosexuals, Jehovah's Witnesses, Romani, and anyone else defined as an enemy of the regime to forced labor in concentration camps. After the war began, the camp system expanded dramatically throughout German-controlled Europe. Concentration camps became an essential part of the Nazi war economy. Important German businesses set up factories inside or right next to camps, to have ready access to their supplies of slave labor. Concentration camp inmates died in huge numbers from brutal physical labor, torture, and diseases linked to malnutrition, inadequate shelter, and poor sanitation. Yet death in these camps was a by-product rather than central aim. In contrast, the death camps of

Final Solution Nazi term for the effort to murder every Jew in Europe during World War II.

Read the Document

The Wannsee Protocol

Watch the Video

The Origins of the Holocaust

EINSATZGRUPPEN ACTION A soldier shoots the last remaining Jew in a Ukrainian village.

Belzec, Majdanek, Sobibor, and Treblinka had only one purpose: murder, primarily the murder of Jews.

Beginning in early 1942, Jewish ghettos throughout Poland emptied. Selected in batches, groups received orders to gather at the railway station for deportation to "work camps" farther east. Soldiers packed them into cattle cars, more than 100 people per car, all standing up for the entire journey. Deprived of food and water, with hardly any air, often for several days, many died en route. (See *Justice in History* in this chapter.)

The survivors stumbled off the trains into a vast machine of death. Forced to undress, they were then herded into a fake communal shower—actually a gas chamber. After the poison had done its work, Jewish slaves emptied the chamber and buried the bodies in mass graves or burned the bodies in crematoria, modeled after industrial bake ovens. The death camps thus used the techniques and technologies of industrial production for human destruction. Along a murderous assembly line, the human raw material moved from arrival through selection to undressing rooms to the gas chamber to the crematoria.

869

THE DEATH FACTORY OF AUSCHWITZ-BIRKENAU Auschwitz-Birkenau combined the labor camp with the death camp. Auschwitz originated in 1940 as a concentration camp for Poles and, after 1941, for Soviet POWs. It grew into an industrial complex covering several square miles, with barracks for 70,000 prisoners who slaved in its coal mines, synthetic rubber and oil factories, and several smaller military industries. Its inmate population eventually included not only Poles and Russians, but also peoples from across Europe. Given just enough food for survival (the official diet permitted a prisoner to remain alive for an average of three months), Auschwitz's inmates endured daily hard labor and the constant, indiscriminate brutality of their captors.

Once the "Final Solution" was underway, Auschwitz's cruel empire expanded to encompass a death camp: Birkenau. Jews deemed strong enough (never more than 20 percent of a typical transport) were selected for hard labor in the main camp. The rest perished in Birkenau's gas chambers, their bodies burned in one of five crematoria. The writer Elie Wiesel, deported to Auschwitz with his family when he was 15, recalled the selection process:

> 'Men to the left! Women to the right!' Eight words spoken quietly, indifferently, without emotion. Eight short, simple words. Yet that was the moment when I parted from my mother.[12]

Wiesel's mother and younger sister, and almost one million others, died in the gas chambers of Auschwitz-Birkenau.

THE ALLIES' RESPONSE Allied leaders had access to information about the Holocaust from very early on. In July 1939, before the war had begun, Polish Intelligence provided the British government with a copy of "Enigma," the German coding machine. Throughout the war, then, British code breakers translated German military radio transmissions such as this one from an Einsatzgruppen unit in the Soviet Union on August 27, 1941: "Regiment South shot 914 Jews; the special action staff with police battalion 320 shot 4,200 Jews." By June 1942, Allied leaders knew that death camps existed and in December of that year the British and American governments issued an inter-Allied declaration that described and condemned Hitler's efforts to murder European Jews.

Despite this public acknowledgment, the Allies did not act directly to stop the killings. Should the Allies then be considered bystanders in the crime of the Holocaust? Some historians contend that anti-Semitism in both British and American societies prevented their leaders from exploring ways to stop the Holocaust (such as sending in commando units, bombing the rail lines into the death camps, or even bombing the camps themselves). Other historians argue that these alternatives were not militarily feasible and that the Allies did the only thing they could do for Europe's Jews: Win the war as quickly as possible.

In the months after the war ended, Allied leaders struggled to bring Nazi leaders to trial to account for their crimes. What one participant called "the greatest trial in history" opened in November 1945. For 11 months, a four-man tribunal—American, British, French, and Soviet—sat in a courtroom in the German city of Nuremberg to judge 19 prominent German military, political, and industrial leaders. The **Nuremberg trials** introduced the category of "crimes against humanity" into international law. The participation of the Soviets, however, undercut the trials' effectiveness. The judges carefully avoided any mention of the Soviets' own war crimes of forcible deportation and mass murder.

The Resistance and Its Limits

Throughout German-occupied Europe, Jewish and non-Jewish Europeans joined the **Resistance**, the underground struggle against Nazi rule. Resistance movements hid

Read the Document

The Holocaust—Memoirs from the Commandant of Auschwitz

Nuremberg trials Post-World War II trials of members of the Nazi Party and German military; conducted by an international tribunal.

Watch the Video

Conformity and Opposition in Nazi Germany

Resistance Label given to the many different underground political and partisan movements directed against Nazi rule in German-occupied Europe during World War II.

870

Justice in History
The Trial of Adolf Eichmann

On May 23, 1960, David Ben-Gurion (1886–1973), the prime minister of Israel, made a spectacular announcement: Israeli secret service agents had kidnapped Adolf Eichmann, a wanted Nazi war criminal, and smuggled him into Israel to await trial. As the head of the Gestapo's Jewish Affairs unit, Eichmann had sorted through the complicated bureaucratic procedures to ensure that European Jews moved expeditiously along the murderous assembly line, from identification to ghettoization to deportation to death. After the war Eichmann fled to Argentina, where, as "Ricardo Klement," he lived a quiet, respectable life with his wife and children—until 1960.

From the moment of Ben-Gurion's sensational announcement, the Eichmann case occupied the attention of the world. Six hundred foreign correspondents attended the trial, one of the first to be filmed by television cameras. More than 120 witnesses, many of them Holocaust survivors, testified.

The Eichmann trial told the story of Jewish suffering during World War II to the widest possible audience. Both Ben-Gurion and the chief prosecutor, Gideon Hausner, saw the trial as "a living record of a gigantic human and national disaster" that would educate the world in the causes and consequences of the Holocaust.[13] In his emotional opening statement, Hausner

EICHMANN ON TRIAL Adolf Eichmann sits behind bulletproof glass and is guarded by Israeli soldiers.

described himself as the spokesman for "six million accusers . . . [whose] ashes were piled up in the hills of Auschwitz and in the fields of Treblinka, or washed away by the rivers of Poland."[14]

By the time the prosecution rested its case, it was clear that Eichmann had played an essential role in the murder of millions. Yet the Eichmann trial attracted an enormous amount of criticism and continues to arouse great controversy. Critics charged that to achieve *moral justice* for Holocaust victims and survivors, the Israeli court committed a *legal injustice* against Eichmann. Not only did Eichmann's kidnapping violate international law, but the trial itself was filled with irregularities, including the introduction of testimony that did not pertain to the specific crimes charged. Critics also disputed Israel's legal right to try Eichmann: The crimes had not occurred in Israeli territory, nor were Eichmann's victims Israeli citizens. (The state of Israel did not exist until 1948.)

In reply to these critics, Hausner and other supporters of the prosecution insisted that justice demanded that Eichmann be brought to trial and that the Israeli government had pursued the only course of action open to it. In the Eichmann trial, then, we confront a case in which what was legal on the one hand and what was just on the other appeared very much at odds. There is no doubt that Eichmann was guilty of horrendous crimes. There is also no doubt that the Israeli government stepped beyond established legal boundaries in trying and condemning Eichmann.

The Eichmann trial also raised important questions about the nature of the Holocaust. Was it a crime perpetrated by a few evil men, or did the evil penetrate deep into German, and European, society? The prosecution's case sought to depict Eichmann as a monster, a demonic mastermind responsible for the deaths of millions of Jews. As Hausner contended, "it was [Eichmann's] word that put gas chambers into action; he lifted the telephone, and railway trains left for the extermination centers; his signature it was that sealed the doom of tens of thousands."[15] Such a depiction provided a comforting explanation for the Holocaust—monstrous devils rather than ordinary human beings perpetrated this colossal crime.

Yet many trial observers and subsequent historians argued that such a depiction was wrong. This argument structured the most well-known critique of the prosecution—Hannah Arendt's *Eichmann in Jerusalem: A Report on the Banality of Evil,* published in 1963. Arendt (1906–1975), a Jewish philosopher who had fled Nazi Europe in 1941, argued that the trial showed Eichmann to be a plodding bureaucrat obsessed with trivial details—an ordinary man, capable of extraordinary evil.

Should ordinary men be held responsible for following evil orders? Defense attorney Robert Servatius insisted that the Holocaust was an "act of state," a crime carried out by a political regime, for which no civil servant could bear the blame. Eichmann only did as he was told. Servatius concluded his arguments by

(continued on next page)

(continued from previous page)

asking Eichmann how he viewed "this question of guilt." Eichmann replied,

> Where there is no responsibility, there can be no guilt. . . . I condemn and regret the act of extermination of the Jews which the leadership of the German state ordered. But I myself could not jump over my own shadow. I was a tool in the hands of superior powers and authorities.[16]

Eichmann's judges disagreed. In declaring Eichmann guilty of genocide, they argued,

> We reject absolutely the accused's version that he was nothing more than a "small cog" in the extermination machine. . . . He was not a puppet in the hands of others. His place was among those who pulled the strings.[17]

Eichmann died by hanging on May 31, 1962, the first execution in Israel, which had abolished capital punishment for all crimes except genocide.

For Discussion

1. What if Eichmann really was only "a tool in the hands of superior powers and authorities"? Would he still have been responsible for his actions?
2. In the Eichmann case, the letter of the law and justice appeared at odds. In what situations—if any—must we break the law to ensure that justice prevails? Who has the authority to make such a judgment?

Taking It Further

Cesarini, David. *Becoming Eichmann: Rethinking the Life, Crimes, and Trial of a "Desk Murderer."* 2004. A fascinating exploration of Eichmann's life and significance.

The Trial of Adolf Eichmann: Record of Proceedings in the District Court of Jerusalem. Vols. 1–9. 1993–1995. The basic primary source.

Jews and others on the run, disrupted transportation systems, assassinated Nazi officials, and relayed secret information to the Allies. In Poland, the Resistance developed into a secret "state within a state" that included an underground parliament, school system, printing press, and a "Home Army" of 350,000 men and women. In areas where the terrain offered shelter for guerillas (such as parts of the Soviet Union and the mountainous regions of Yugoslavia, Italy, and southern France), the Resistance formed partisan groups that attacked German army units.

The story of the Resistance is one of great heroism, yet only a minority of Europeans joined. The Germans' military strength and ruthlessness made resistance seem futile. In one of the best-known cases, Jews in the Warsaw ghetto rose up in the spring of 1943 and—armed with only one or two submachine guns and a scattering of pistols, rifles, hand grenades, and gasoline bombs—held off the Germans for more than a month. But in the end, the Germans leveled the ghetto and deported its survivors to death camps.

The German policy of exacting collective retribution also undercut mass support for anti-German efforts. In 1942, for example, British intelligence forces parachuted Czech agents into German-held Czechoslovakia. The agents assassinated the chief SS official in the region, Reinhard Heydrich (1904–1942), but they were immediately betrayed. In retaliation, the Germans massacred the entire population of the village of Lidice.

In countries allied to (rather than conquered by) the Germans, potential resisters had to convince themselves that patriotism demanded working against their own government. Thus, in France until 1943, joining the Resistance meant opposing the lawfully instituted collaborationist Vichy government. As a result, many French men and women viewed Resistance fighters as traitors, not heroes. By 1943, however, an alternative focus of national loyalty had emerged: the Free French headed by General Charles De Gaulle (1890–1970). De Gaulle had gone into exile rather than accept the armistice with Nazi Germany. After the Anglo-American landings in North Africa in November 1942, De Gaulle claimed Algeria as a power base, declared himself the head of a Free French provisional government, and called on all loyal French men and women to resist Nazi rule and Vichy collaboration.

Civil War and Nationalist Savagery

Divisions within the Resistance both limited its impact and increased the human costs of the war. In Greece, for example, the communist-dominated National Liberation Front battled a rival Resistance group that fought for the return of the Greek monarchy.

◯ **View** the **Closer Look**   Liberating the Concentration Camps

27.1

27.2

27.3

27.4

27.5

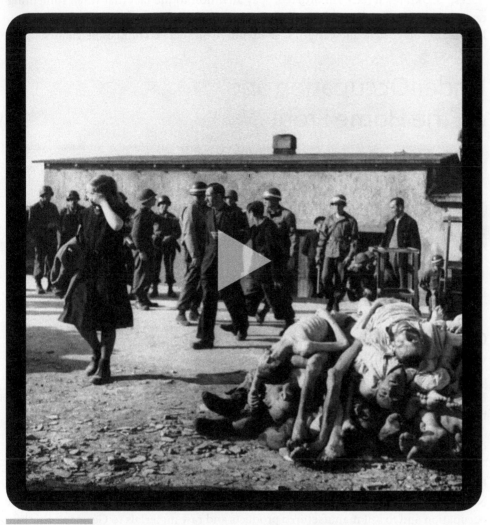

THE LIBERATION OF BUCHENWALD CONCENTRATION CAMP IN GERMANY, APRIL 25, 1945 A German woman cries as she is led, with other German citizens, past a pile of murdered prisoners at Buchenwald. The crowd in this picture is a group of people from a nearby town, brought to view the camps so they could not deny what had taken place.

There was, then, no single "Resistance," and fighting among Resistance groups often shaded into civil war.

The bloodletting in Yugoslavia exemplifies this link between the Resistance and civil war. The Nazi puppet state of Croatia, established after the German invasion of 1941, enthusiastically adopted policies of mass murder aimed at Jews, Muslims, and Serbs. The Resistance movement that emerged in Croatia and the rest of Yugoslavia split along both nationalist and political lines. The "Chetniks," Serbian guerillas who supported the return of the exiled Serb monarchy and the restoration of Serbian supremacy in Yugoslavia, not only fought Croats and Germans (and slaughtered Jews and Muslims), but also battled the communist "Partisans." Led by Josip Broz (1892–1980), alias "Tito," these Partisans won the civil war, drove the Germans out of Yugoslavia, and established a postwar communist state. Beneath the uniform surface created by communist ideology, however, the jagged edges of nationalist division in Yugoslavia remained sharp.

In the killing zones of the East—the Baltic states, Belarus, Ukraine, and eastern Poland—the retreat of German forces from 1943 on ushered in a period of vicious conflict between nationalist groups who sought to position themselves for postwar supremacy. Ukrainian guerilla groups, for example, attacked German and Polish settlements in territory that they had staked out for an independent Ukraine. At least 50,000 Poles died, with tens of thousands of others forced to flee westward. "Liquidate all Polish traces," a Ukrainian partisan ordered, "pay attention to the fact that when something remains that is Polish, then the Poles will have pretensions to our land."[18] In response, Polish units in Galicia and eastern Poland turned on their Ukrainian neighbors.

Under Occupation and on the Home Front

27.5 What did total war mean for civilians in the occupied regions and on the home front?

For the men, women, and children in the occupied zones of Europe, there was no "home front"; the war's reach extended everywhere. But even in states not under enemy occupation, the home front was not a place of safety, but a place where a different kind of war was underway. World War II obliterated the distinction between combatant and noncombatant, blurred gender roles, and provoked calls for radical social change.

Occupation Policies and Forced Labor

We have already seen in this chapter that in German-occupied Europe, Nazi racial ideals determined ordinary people's reality. The Nazis drew a sharp line between western Europeans—the Dutch, Norwegian, Danes, and Flemish, all considered of racially superior "Germanic stock"—and the Slavs of eastern Europe. The Nazis believed that "Germanic" peoples could be taught to become good Nazis and therefore spared them the extreme violence that characterized German occupation in the east.

Yet German occupation in the west, although less brutal than in the east, remained harsh. Anyone who spoke out against the Nazis faced imprisonment or death. The Nazis forced occupied countries to pay exorbitant sums to cover the costs of their own occupation and to sell manufactured products and raw materials to Germany at artificially low prices. The occupation grew even more fierce after 1943 as German military losses piled up, stocks of food and other supplies dwindled, and German demands for civilian labor increased.

For millions of men and women in both eastern and western Europe, the war meant forced labor in Germany. With the need to free up men for the front lines, the Nazis faced labor shortages in almost every economic sector. Placing the economy on an all-out war footing would have meant imposing unpopular measures such as conscripting women for industrial labor, lengthening working hours, and prohibiting holidays. The Nazis chose instead to "recruit" labor from conquered territories. By August 1944, German farmers and factory owners employed over 5.7 million foreign civilian laborers (one-third of whom were women) and almost two million POWs. These foreign workers accounted for more than half the labor in German agriculture and munitions plants and one-third of the labor force in key war industries such as mining, chemicals, and metals.

Foreign labor not only fueled the German war machine, it also maintained German civilian morale. Foreign labor cushioned Germans on the home front from the impact of total war and reassured them that they belonged to a superior race. Nazi regulations stipulated that German workers regard themselves as the masters of the foreigners working alongside them. Many German factory owners were relieved to find they now employed laborers with few political rights. The director of one aircraft manufacturing firm explained, "The great advantage of employing foreigners . . . is that we only have to give orders. There is no refusal, no need to negotiate."[19]

"THE HEROINES OF 1940" Designed in 1946, this Greek poster commemorated the contributions of women in the Greek Resistance movement.

The Women's War

World War II was in every way a women's war. The bombs falling on urban neighborhoods did not distinguish between sexes; forced labor, mass deportation, and genocide all swept up women as well as men. In occupied countries, women fought and died in the Resistance. In countries not occupied by enemy forces, women tended to bear the brunt of home front deprivation, as they were usually the ones who had to get a meal on the table and clothe their children in the face of severe rationing. Basic household goods such as frying pans, toothbrushes, bicycle tires, baby bottles, and batteries almost disappeared. Food was in short supply and clothing had to be recycled. Women became experts at "make do and mend," as British government pamphlets advised.

In total war, military victory depended on the women in the assembly lines as well as the men in the front lines, and so women were mobilized for war work. British women did not serve in combat, but they were drafted for service in civilian defense, war-related industry, or the armed forces. Women accounted for 25 percent of the civilians who worked in Britain's Air Raid Protection services as wardens, rescuers, and telephone operators. The numbers of women employed in male-dominated industries such as metals and chemicals rose dramatically.

Only the Soviet Union mobilized women more fully than Britain. Soviet women constituted 80 percent of the agricultural and 50 percent of the industrial labor force. All Soviet adult men and women under age 45 who were not engaged in essential war work were required to work 11 hours a day constructing defenses. Soviet women also served in combat. By 1944, 246,000 women were in front-line units. For all Soviet citizens, male and female, life on the home front meant endless labor, inadequate food supplies, and constant surveillance under martial law.

Until 1943, the German home front contrasted sharply with that of Britain and the Soviet Union. The Nazi policy toward female employment rested on Hitler's conviction that Germany had lost World War I in part because of the collapse of morale on the home front. In the first years of the war, then, the Nazi government did not dramatically cut consumption levels. Moreover, Hitler believed that the future of the "German race" depended on middle-class women being protected from the strains of paid labor so that they could bear healthy Aryan babies. The use of foreign labor took the place of the full-scale mobilization of women, until military necessity undercut Nazi gender ideology.

The fall of Stalingrad marked the turning point for German women. With losses on the Eastern Front averaging 150,000 men per month, the German army needed more men. Hitler's deputy Joseph Goebbels (1897–1945) ordered a total mobilization of the home front. The final, desperate year of the war saw a concentrated use of female labor in Nazi Germany.

Of all the combatant states, the United States stood out as unique with regard to the home front. More than 70 percent of American women remained outside the paid workforce. Rationing was comparatively minimal and consumption levels high. In fact, for many families, the war years brought prosperity after years of economic depression. American cities were never bombed, and thus the United States was able to maintain a clear distinction between soldier and civilian, man and woman—a distinction that was blurred in other combatant nations.

What Are We Fighting For?

To mobilize their populations for total war, governments had to convince their citizens to support the war effort. Maintaining morale and motivating civilians and soldiers to endure deprivation and danger demanded that leaders supply a persuasive answer to the question: What are we fighting for?

MYTH AND MORALE All states—democratic or authoritarian—rely on *myths*, on stories of origins and identity, to unify disparate individuals, classes, and groups. In times of total war, such myths become crucial. Combatant governments enlisted artists, entertainers, and the technologies of the mass media for mythmaking and morale-building. In Britain, for example, Henry Moore's (1898–1986) drawings of ordinary people in air raid shelters (completed under an official commission) evoked the survival of civilized values in the midst of unspeakable degradation. In Germany, strict censorship before the war had already subordinated the arts and entertainment industries to the demands of the Nazi state. The war heightened this control as censorship tightened even further, paper shortages limited the production of books and periodicals, and the threat of being drafted for the Eastern Front kept artists in line.

During the war, film came into its own as an artistic form capable of creating important myths of national unity. Laurence Olivier's version of Shakespeare's *Henry V* (1944) comforted British moviegoers with its classic story of a stirring English military victory against huge odds. In Italy, a group of filmmakers known as the Neo-Realists created a set of films that dramatized the Resistance spirit of national unity. Shot on location, with amateur actors and realistic sets, movies such as Roberto Rossellini's *Open City* (1945) depicted lower-class life with honesty and respect and called for the creation of a better society from the rubble of the old.

PLANNING FOR RECONSTRUCTION Rossellini's call for the creation of a new society was echoed throughout Europe during the war. A consensus emerged on the need for social democracy, a society in which the state intervenes in economic life to ensure both public welfare and social justice (see p. 831). As early as December 1942, a British government committee set out a radical plan for postwar society. In rather unusual language for an official document, the committee's report identified "five giants on the road to reconstruction": Want, Disease, Ignorance, Squalor, and Idleness. To slay these giants, the committee recommended that the state assume responsibility for ensuring full employment and a minimum standard of living for all through the provision of family allowances, social welfare programs, and a national health service. The Beveridge Report (named after the committee's chairman) became a best-seller in Britain and the basis for a number of postwar European social welfare plans.

Three factors explain this radical reorientation of European politics. First, and most important, as the war dragged on and the death tolls mounted, European men and women demanded that their suffering be worthwhile. They wanted to know that they were fighting not to rebuild the depressed and divided societies of the 1930s, but to construct a new Europe. In France, for example, the Resistance Charter of 1944 demanded the construction of a "more just social order" through the nationalization of key industries, the establishment of a comprehensive social security system, and the recognition of the rights of workers to participate in management.

Second, the war (and the ongoing revelations of Nazi atrocities) discredited the politics of the far right. This sort of politics, whether fascist, Nazi, or conservative-authoritarian, disappeared from legitimate political discussion. But in Europe (although less so in the United States) the liberal ideal of the free and self-interested individual competing in an unregulated economy also lay in ruins, the victim of the prewar Great Depression. The new Europe, then, had to be built along different lines.

Finally, both the Resistance and the experience of wartime mobilization taught that the power of the state could be used to improve the well-being of its citizens without trampling on the rights of the individual. In the 1930s, Hitler and Mussolini on the Radical Right, and Stalin on the Radical Left, had persuaded many that the individual was not important, that only the state mattered. But the Resistance reasserted the essential significance of the individual and the choices he or she makes. At the same time, the combatant nations' success in mobilizing their economies for total war indicated the positive possibilities of state action. If governments could regulate economies to fight wars, why could they not regulate economies for peacetime prosperity and greater social justice? In the postwar era, then, democracy reclaimed the activist state from fascism and Nazism on the one hand and Stalinism on the other.

CONCLUSION

The New West: After Auschwitz and the Atom Bomb

The wartime encounter with the Nazi vision of the West as a race-based authoritarian order was crucial. From it emerged a sharpened commitment within the West to the processes and values of democracy. But to present the Second World War as a conflict between democracy and Nazism is to oversimplify. To defeat Nazi Germany, the democracies of Britain and the United States allied with Stalin's Soviet Union, a dictatorial regime that matched Hitler's Germany in its contempt for democratic values and human rights and that surpassed it in state-sanctioned mass murder.

The Soviet Union emerged from the war as the dominant power in eastern Europe. As we will see in the next chapter, the presence of the Soviet Army obliterated any chance to establish democratic governments in this region. The tensions inherent in the Anglo-American alliance with the Soviets led directly to the Cold War, the ideological and political conflict that dominated the post-World War II world and that again forced a redefinition of the West. From 1949 until 1989, drawing the West on any map was easy: One shaded in the United States and the countries allied to it—and against the Soviet Union. At the same time, however, a new division emerged. World War II marked the beginning of the end of European imperial control over the non-European world. The postwar era would thus see growing tensions between "North" and "South"—between the industrially developed nations and the underdeveloped regions seeking to shrug off their colonial past.

Much of the impetus for imperial control over non-European regions had come from the conviction of Western supremacy. During World War II, however, Japanese victories had exposed the illusion of Western military invincibility. And after the war, the gradual realization of the full horror of the Holocaust demolished any lingering claim to Western cultural superiority. What sort of superior position could be claimed by a culture in which educated, supposedly civilized men sent children into gas chambers disguised as showers? The atomic bombings of Hiroshima and Nagasaki added more questions to the ongoing debate about the meaning of the West. With the best of intentions, some of the greatest minds in the Western world had produced weapons designed to kill and maim tens of thousands of civilians within seconds. Had Western technology outdistanced Western ethics? And what about the implications of such technologies in a democratic society? For example, would the need to control such weapons lead to measures that eroded individual freedom?

Thus, the assembly-line techniques of mass murder developed by the Nazis and, in very different ways, the sheer efficiency of the atom bomb in obliterating urban populations forced both individuals and their political leaders to confront the destructive potential of Western industrialism. For centuries, the use of the methods of scientific inquiry to uncover truth and achieve both material and moral progress had supported Westerners' self-identification and their sense of cultural superiority. But World War II demonstrated that the best of science could produce the worst of weapons, that technology and technique could combine in the death factory. The task of accepting this knowledge, and facing up to its implications, helped shape Western culture after 1945.

MAKING CONNECTIONS

1. Why do historians assert that World War II in Europe was won on the Eastern Front?
2. How did the home fronts of World War I differ from those in World War II? What explains the similarities? The differences?

TAKING IT FURTHER

For suggested readings, films, and websites, see page R-1.

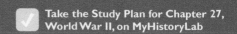
Chapter Review

The Coming of War

27.1 How did military and political expectations lead to World War II?

Supposed to be the "war to end all wars," World War I set up World War II. The peace settlements exacerbated nationalist tensions in eastern Europe and aroused German and Japanese resentment at the same time that the destruction of total war convinced many Europeans of the necessity of avoiding war at all costs. Throughout the 1930s, both Germany and Japan expanded their territorial base and military might.

Europe at War, 1939–1941

27.2 How did Nazi Germany conquer the continent of Europe by 1941?

With the techniques and technologies of blitzkrieg, German military strategists overcame the defensive stalemate that had characterized the Western Front during World War I. Although frustrated in the Battle of Britain, the Germans experienced initial success in the invasion of the Soviet Union.

The World at War, 1941–1945

27.3 Why did the Allies win in 1945?

In the defeat of Nazi Germany, the fighting on the Eastern Front proved crucial. In addition, Great Britain, the Soviet Union, and the United States outpaced Nazi Germany and its allies, including Japan, in the industrial production and scientific developments that fueled total war. Nazi atrocities also strengthened resistance throughout occupied Europe.

The Wars Within the War

27.4 What were the context, causes, and consequences of genocide during World War II?

The conquest of western Poland marked the beginnings of the Nazi regime to reorder the racial/ethnic composition of eastern Europe. With the invasion of the Soviet Union, the so-called Final Solution, which included the industrialization of mass murder in the death camps, took shape. At the same time, World War II heightened nationalist and ethnic tensions that in many areas erupted into civil war. It also provided further incentives for the Stalinist government of the Soviet Union to tighten its murderous hold on the peoples under its control.

Under Occupation and on the Home Front

27.5 What did total war mean for civilians in the occupied regions and on the home front?

Many Europeans were forced to labor for the Nazi war effort, while others opted to join the Resistance, the underground fight against the Nazi regime. Total war also meant the experience of massive bombing campaigns as well as the unprecedented economic and military mobilization of women. In western Europe, government efforts to ensure civilian morale, as well as the more general experience of wartime suffering, produced a widespread commitment to the idea and ideals of social democracy.

Chapter Time Line

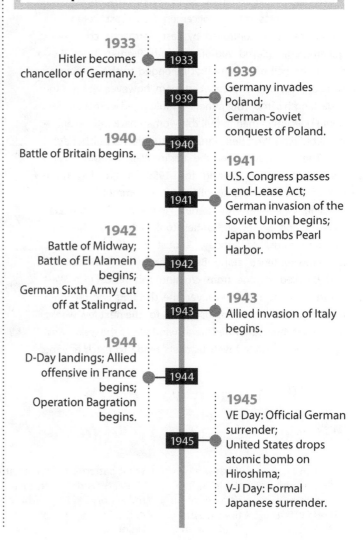

1933
Hitler becomes chancellor of Germany.
`1933`

1939
Germany invades Poland; German-Soviet conquest of Poland.
`1939`

1940
Battle of Britain begins.
`1940`

1941
U.S. Congress passes Lend-Lease Act; German invasion of the Soviet Union begins; Japan bombs Pearl Harbor.
`1941`

1942
Battle of Midway; Battle of El Alamein begins; German Sixth Army cut off at Stalingrad.
`1942`

1943
Allied invasion of Italy begins.
`1943`

1944
D-Day landings; Allied offensive in France begins; Operation Bagration begins.
`1944`

1945
VE Day: Official German surrender; United States drops atomic bomb on Hiroshima; V-J Day: Formal Japanese surrender.
`1945`

28 Redefining the West After World War II

On an apparently ordinary day in August 1961, western European television viewers witnessed an extraordinary sight. While the news cameras rolled, policemen from East Berlin—the section of Berlin controlled by East Germany's communist government—played tug-of-war with firemen from West Berlin, the half of the city that belonged to the democratic state of West Germany. Between them, however, was not the usual length of rope, but rather a middle-aged woman. As East Berlin policemen tried to pull this woman back into an apartment building, West Berlin firemen struggled to pull her out.

The construction of the Berlin Wall set this bizarre contest in motion. During the 1950s a growing number of East Germans sought to flee communist rule by crossing into (free) West Berlin. Finally in 1961, the East German and Soviet authorities took action. In the early morning hours of Sunday, August 13, they erected a barbed-wire fence along Berlin's east-west dividing line and blocked anyone from crossing this fence into West Berlin. In some cases, however, the dividing line ran right through apartment buildings and so, for the next few weeks, these apartments provided literal "windows to the west." West Berlin firemen waited with blankets ready to catch anyone

TUG-OF-WAR AT THE BERLIN WALL Caught by the television cameras, this woman sought to escape through her window into West Berlin. She succeeded.

LEARNING OBJECTIVES

28.1	28.2	28.3	28.4
Why and how did the world step from World War II to the Cold War?	What was the impact of decolonization and the Cold War on the global balance of power?	What patterns characterized the history of the Soviet Union and eastern Europe after the death of Stalin?	What patterns characterized the history of western Europe in the 1950s and 1960s?

 Listen to Chapter 28 on MyHistoryLab

⊙ Watch the Video Series on MyHistoryLab

Learn about some key topics related to this chapter with the *MyHistoryLab Video Series: Key Topics in Western Civilization*

28.1

28.2

28.3

28.4

willing to jump out of a window—and out of communist eastern Europe. These windows closed quickly. The communist authorities first bricked up windows facing West Berlin. Later they leveled entire apartment buildings. The barbed-wire fence became a concrete wall buttressed by gun towers, lit by searchlights, and patrolled by armed guards with "shoot to kill" orders.

The unidentified woman dangling out of the window, literally caught between West and East, symbolizes Europe during the 1950s and 1960s. In these decades, the Cold War between the United States and the Soviet Union helped shape European politics, culture, and society. As the woman's desperation to reach the West indicates, American influence in western Europe did not parallel Soviet domination of eastern Europe. Nevertheless, many Europeans in the West as well as the East felt that they no longer fully controlled their own societies.

The Cold War was in part an encounter of two clashing ideologies, as much a battle of ideas and values as weapons and warriors. Both sides laid claim to universal cultures—to have achieved a way of life that would benefit *all* human societies. This ideological encounter forced a redefinition of "the West." Previous chapters have described the way in which this cultural construct shifted over time. By the late nineteenth century, Christianity, although still important, played a less central role in defining "the West" than did such factors as industrial technology, the illusion of white racial superiority, and faith in capitalist economics and liberal political values. The Cold War added fears of the Soviet Union and communist ideology to the mix. These fears at times eroded the Western commitment to democracy, particularly within the developing world.

Significantly, the Cold War turned "hot" not in Europe, but in places such as Korea, Cuba, and Vietnam. This era witnessed a widening economic gap between "North" and "South"—between the industrialized nations, largely located in the Northern Hemisphere, and economically underdeveloped regions, many south of the equator, many now shrugging off colonial rule. As the Cold War moved beyond Europe's borders to the developing regions two different contests—North versus South and West versus East—intertwined.

How, then, did these contests shape the ever-evolving idea of the West?

A Dubious Peace, 1945–1949

28.1 Why and how did the world step from World War II to the Cold War?

World War II ended in the spring and summer of 1945, but the killing did not. Postwar purges, deportations, and civil wars ensured that the death totals continued to mount. As the "hot" war waned, the Cold War began between the Soviet Union and the countries it controlled on the one hand and the United States and its Western allies on the other.

Devastation, Death, and DPs

Germany's surrender in May 1945 did not bring immediate peace to Europe. Many regions in southern and eastern Europe experienced civil war, while in other areas victors turned with vengeful fury against the vanquished. In the Baltic states and Ukraine, guerilla groups opposed to Soviet annexation fought until the early 1950s. Those left alive in post-World War II Europe faced the overwhelming task of reconstruction. Intensive bombing rendered most highways, rail tracks, and waterways unusable. With laborers, seed, fertilizer, and basic equipment all in short supply, agricultural production in 1945 stood below 50 percent of prewar levels. Less visible, but just as devastating, was the destruction of the financial system. Few European currencies were worth much. In defeated Germany, cigarettes replaced marks as the unit of exchange.

Map 28.1 indicates one of the most serious problems facing postwar Europe: that of the refugees or displaced persons (DPs). The DP problem stemmed, first, from

MAP 28.1 AFTER WORLD WAR II: SHIFTING BOUNDARIES, SHIFTING POPULATIONS World War II and its aftermath resulted in the movements of millions. Political ambitions and military concerns fused with racial and ethnic hatreds and the emerging Cold War to create new state boundaries that resulted in the exchange of entire populations. One boundary line, shifted one-quarter inch on a map, meant hundreds of thousands of men, women, and children were forced out of their homes and into strange new cities or villages, in the midst of postwar economic breakdown and social upheaval. What were the significant changes in state borders after the war? Which populations were most affected by these changes?

the war itself, with millions made homeless by invasions and mass bombing. Second, Hitler's attempts at racial reordering also caused DP numbers to skyrocket, as concentration and death camp survivors now stumbled through the wreckage of war-torn Europe.

A third factor in the worsening DP problem was the peace settlement itself, which redrew the boundaries of Germany and reaffirmed the Soviet annexation of eastern Poland and the Baltic states. In a brutal resolution to what was perceived as the problem of national minorities, the Allies and eastern European governments agreed on a policy of population transfers. More than 18 million Europeans were forced out of their homes and homelands, as ancient multi-linguistic and multi-ethnic communities were destroyed, replaced by ethnically homogenous nation-states. Germans suffered particularly severely as the Soviet, Polish, Czech, Romanian, Yugoslav, and Hungarian governments all forcibly deported their German populations. Often forced on the road with no food or supplies, approximately two million Germans died in this postscript to World War II.

From Hot to Cold War

The conflict that posed the greatest threat to the dubious peace after 1945 was the **Cold War**, the struggle for global supremacy between the United States and the Soviet Union. Within just a few years of the defeat of Germany and Japan, the allies became enemies, and what Winston Churchill called the **"Iron Curtain"** dropped between eastern and western Europe.

Cold War Struggle for global supremacy between the United States and the Soviet Union, waged from the end of World War II until 1990.

Iron Curtain Metaphor for the Cold War division of Europe after World War II.

  Read the Document

Winston Churchill, "Iron Curtain Speech"

THE DELICATE FABRIC OF THE WARTIME ALLIANCE A common wartime enemy rather than shared postwar aims wove together the alliance of Britain, the Soviet Union, and the United States. To ensure Soviet (and his own) security and power, Joseph Stalin demanded that Soviet boundaries extend westward and that the Soviet "sphere of influence" include the states along the Soviet Union's western borders. He noted bluntly, "The more you've got, the safer you are."[1]

Stalin's demands for "friendly" and therefore communist-dominated governments in eastern Europe conflicted with American and British aims. The American president, Franklin D. Roosevelt, saw the establishment of democracies throughout Europe—including along the Soviet borders—as essential to international security and American prosperity. One American official explained to Congress, "If you create good governments in foreign countries, you will have better markets for ourselves."[2] The third Allied leader, Winston Churchill, the British prime minister, regarded the extension of Soviet influence westward as a threat to the European balance of power. He saw Stalin's plans for Poland as a particular problem: Britain had gone to war in September 1939 because of the Nazi invasion of Poland and over 200,000 Polish soldiers were fighting for the Allies.

Poland was very much on the agenda in November 1943 when the **Big Three**— Stalin, Churchill, and Roosevelt—met together for the first time in the Tehran Conference. Stalin insisted on the restoration of the *1940* Polish-Soviet border—the boundary line drawn by the secret clauses of the German–Soviet Non-Aggression Pact. Churchill and Roosevelt recognized that if they agreed, they would be affirming the brutal Soviet invasion of eastern Poland in 1939. Yet they also knew that Soviet soldiers were dying by the millions on the Eastern Front and they were eager to retain Stalin's full commitment to the alliance. At Tehran, then, they agreed—secretly—that Poland's postwar borders would shift hundreds of miles westward.[3]

By February 1945, when the Big Three met in the Crimean seaside town of Yalta, Stalin stood in an even stronger negotiating position. As he said, "Everyone imposes his own system as far as his armies can reach"—and in 1945, the Soviet army had a long reach, with its soldiers occupying Poland, Romania, Bulgaria, Hungary, and much of

Big Three Term applied to the British, Soviet, and U.S. leaders during World War II: until 1945, Winston Churchill, Joseph Stalin, and Franklin Roosevelt; by the summer of 1945, Clement Attlee, Joseph Stalin, and Harry Truman.

THE BIG THREE I (YALTA, FEBRUARY 1945) From 1941 until April 1945, the Big Three meant Churchill, Roosevelt, and Stalin. At the very end of the war, however, the composition of the Big Three suddenly changed, as Harry Truman replaced Roosevelt and Clement Attlee replaced Churchill.

Yalta Conference Meeting in 1945 of the leaders of the Allied states of Britain, the Soviet Union, and the United States to devise plans for postwar Europe.

Czechoslovakia. Roosevelt's desire to obtain Stalin's commitment to enter the war against Japan also strengthened Stalin's hand. The **Yalta Conference** thus produced a contradictory compromise. Stalin promised free and democratic elections in eastern Europe while Roosevelt and Churchill agreed that such freely elected democratic governments should be pro-Soviet. They did not, however, define "free" or "democratic," and made no arrangements to oversee or regulate the elections. Stalin noted privately, "A freely elected government in any of these countries would be anti-Soviet, and that we cannot allow."[4]

The Big Three also differed on the fate of Germany. Stalin hoped to wring every available resource out of Germany to pay for Soviet reconstruction. Roosevelt, however, became convinced that the economic revival of Europe depended on a prosperous Germany. Moreover, he and Churchill feared that a weak or partitioned German state would invite Soviet expansion into central Europe. At Yalta, the Big Three did not resolve the issue of Germany's future, but they agreed to divide Germany and the symbolically and strategically vital city of Berlin into occupation zones controlled by the United States, the Soviet Union, France, and Britain (see Map 28.1).

Reluctant to place too much pressure on the alliance's fraying seams, Roosevelt opted for postponing the hard decisions at Yalta. He hoped that a new international body, the United Nations (UN), would settle the controversial questions after the war. If the Soviet Union refused to participate, however, the UN, like the interwar League of Nations, would be a failure. Therefore, Roosevelt sought to avoid confrontations that might give Stalin a reason to block Soviet membership.

Roosevelt also hoped that new international economic structures would stabilize the postwar order. In 1944 leading American and European economists had gathered in New Hampshire to construct a system for postwar economic revival. Aware of the economic chaos that had followed World War I and desperate to avoid a repeat of the Great Depression of the 1930s, they drew up the **Bretton Woods Agreement**, the framework for the Western postwar economic order. To keep the global economy

Bretton Woods Agreement Agreement signed in 1944 that established the post-World War II economic framework in which the U.S. dollar served as the world's reserve currency.

running smoothly, Bretton Woods recognized the American dollar as the world's reserve currency and fixed currency exchange rates. It also established two new international economic institutions—the International Monetary Fund (IMF), to maintain the stability of member currencies, and the World Bank, to encourage global economic development.

FRAYING SEAMS, 1945–1946 The final Big Three conference in the German city of Potsdam in July 1945 did not bridge the gap between the Soviet Union and its allies. Stalin faced two unfamiliar negotiating partners. The new American president Harry Truman (1884–1972) replaced Roosevelt, who had died in April, and midway through the summit, the new British prime minister, the Labour Party leader Clement Attlee, arrived to take Churchill's place. The changes made little difference. Stalin demanded control over the territories occupied by his armies, while the British and Americans increasingly saw this demand as a threat to democratic ideals and the European balance of power.

Two additional factors heightened the hostility between the Allied leaders during the **Potsdam Conference**. First, the British foreign secretary, Ernest Bevin (1881–1951), the man who largely determined foreign policy in Attlee's government, had a history of fighting communist efforts to control British unions. A fierce anti-Stalinist as well as an ardent British nationalist, Bevin believed that a stronger Soviet Union threatened Britain's status as a Great Power. He urged the United States to stand tough against Soviet demands.

The second factor was more dramatic. During the summit Truman received a telegraph informing him of the successful Trinity test of the atomic bomb in New Mexico (see Chapter 27). This news meant that the war against Japan would soon be over—and that the Americans and British no longer needed or wanted Stalin to join the war in the Pacific. An important Western incentive for placating Stalin disappeared.

Yet the wartime alliance remained intact after Potsdam. Truman resisted the idea of a permanent American military presence in Europe and so for the next few months sought to resolve the conflicts that divided the Allied leaders. Stalin, too, was unwilling to push too far. He feared American military might and hoped to reduce military expenditures to revive the Soviet economy. Thus, in regions that he viewed as part of the Western sphere of influence, Stalin adopted a policy of passivity. He refused to assist communists seeking to overthrow the British-backed monarchy in Greece, and he ordered communist parties in western Europe to participate with noncommunists in coalition governments.

TORN IN TWO, 1946–1948 Stalin, however, adopted no such policy of passivity in eastern Europe. Throughout 1945 and 1946 communists in these states used legal and illegal methods—including intimidation, torture, and kidnapping—to expand their power base and to co-opt, silence, or expel noncommunist leaders. In Poland, for example, Stalin ordered top-ranking members of the wartime underground government secretly arrested, flown to Moscow, and thrown into prison. Those Poles who had fought in the Home Army against German rule were shipped to Soviet labor camps.

Disagreements over the fate of Germany also helped tear apart the alliance. At Yalta the Allies had agreed to share the postwar occupation, and at Potsdam, Truman and Attlee gave in to Stalin's demand for German reparations: The British, American, and French occupying governments shipped manufactured goods and machines from the more industrialized western regions of Germany to the largely agricultural Soviet zone in the east. In exchange, the Soviets agreed to provide food and raw materials from their zone to the western territories. The Soviets, however, proved more interested in plundering their zone than in establishing a workable joint economic policy. By 1946, British and American authorities recognized that Germans faced starvation. Convinced that economic recovery must be made an immediate priority, they

Potsdam Conference The meeting in July 1945 of the Allied leaders of Britain, the Soviet Union, and the United States in the German city of Potsdam.

Read the Document

Joseph Stalin, "Soviet Victory" Speech

28.1

28.2

28.3

28.4

 Read the **Document**

George F. Kennan, The Long Telegram

Truman Doctrine Named after U.S. president Harry Truman, the doctrine that in 1947 inaugurated the Cold War policy of resisting the expansion of communist control.

Marshall Plan The use of U.S. economic aid to restore stability to Europe after World War II and so undercut the appeal of communist ideology.

 Read the **Document**

George Marshall, The Marshall Plan

combined their zones into a single economic unit and stopped reparations deliveries to the Soviets. With all pretense of a united Allied policy in Germany now dropped, Truman reversed his initial plan to withdraw American troops from Germany as soon as possible. "We are staying here," declared Secretary of State James Byrnes in September 1946. And stay they did: As of 2013, American forces remain in Germany.

The announcement of the **Truman Doctrine** in 1947 exposed the widening rift between Stalin and the West. An American policy, the Truman Doctrine evolved in response to British actions. In February 1947 the British government informed Truman's administration that it could not afford to continue to assist the Greek government in its fight against communist rebels. The United States immediately assumed Britain's role in Greece. More important, Truman used this development to issue the Truman Doctrine, which committed the United States to the policy of containment: resisting communist expansion wherever in the world it occurred.

The **Marshall Plan**—and more particularly, Stalin's rejection of it—reinforced the division of Europe into two hostile camps. In 1947, U.S. Secretary of State George Marshall (1880–1959) toured Europe and grew alarmed at the devastation and despair that he observed. Fearing that hungry Europeans might turn to communism, Marshall proposed that the United States underwrite Europe's economic recovery. Marshall's proposal at first received little attention, but in Britain Foreign Secretary Ernest Bevin heard a report of it on the radio. Convinced that an ongoing American presence in Europe would serve British interests, Bevin hailed the Marshall Plan as "a lifeline to sinking men."

Bevin's French counterpart, Foreign Minister Georges Bidault (1899–1983), shared his enthusiasm, and together they helped make the Marshall Plan a reality. With representatives from 12 other European states, Bevin and Bidault devised a four-year plan for European economic reconstruction that accelerated western Europe's leap into postwar prosperity. Eventually the United States sent $13 billion to Europe, and a new international body, the Organization for European Economic Cooperation (OEEC), worked to eliminate trade barriers and stabilize currencies.

By some estimates, the wealth that the Soviet Union siphoned from eastern Europe roughly equaled the amount of Marshall aid that the United States injected into western Europe. The United States offered aid to every European state; if a state did accept aid, however, it also had to join the OEEC. Because Stalin viewed the OEEC as an instrument of American domination, he banned eastern European governments from receiving Marshall funds. When the Czechs tried to do so, Stalin engineered a communist coup in February 1948 that destroyed what remained of democracy in Czechoslovakia—and the last remnant of parliamentary democracy in eastern Europe.

THE COLD WAR BEGINS Over the next few years, eastern Europeans endured what Soviet citizens had suffered in the 1920s and 1930s: the extension of Communist Party control over the armed forces and the state bureaucracy, forced collectivization, the sacrifice of the standard of living to fuel heavy industrialization—and Stalinist terror.

Stalin's tightening grip over eastern Europe solidified American and western European suspicions of Soviet aims. Yet the spread of Stalinism in eastern Europe originated in part from Stalin's *loss* of control over a key eastern European state. In 1948, the Yugoslav communist leader, Tito, broke with Stalin. Alarmed by Tito's independence, Stalin cracked down across the rest of eastern Europe. He first purged eastern European Communist Parties of any potential "titoists"—leaders who might threaten his dominance. Between 1948 and 1953 more communists were killed by their own party members than had died at the hands of the Nazis during World War II. (See *Justice in History* in this chapter.) The terror then spread beyond communist ranks. Labor and prison camps dotted the eastern European landscape. Only Stalin's death in 1953 caused the wave of persecution to recede.

Stalin's break with Tito and the resulting spread of terror throughout eastern Europe coincided with the first "battle" of the Cold War. In June 1948, Stalin ordered

Justice in History

Show Time: THE TRIAL OF RUDOLF SLÁNSKÝ

On the night of July 31, 1951, Rudolf Slánský, general secretary of the Communist Party of Czechoslovakia (CPC), left his fiftieth birthday party and headed home, a frightened man. Outwardly, nothing was wrong. The CPC had celebrated the day in style. The communist president, Klement Gottwald, presented Slánský with the medal of the Order of Socialism, the highest honor awarded in Czechoslovakia. Congratulations poured in from all over the country. But Slánský knew he was in trouble: Stalin had not acknowledged his birthday. In the upper ranks of Czechoslovakia's Communist Party in 1951, signs of Stalin's approval or disapproval were literally matters of life or death. The Stalinist purge of eastern Europe was raging, with thousands arrested, tortured, imprisoned, or killed.

Slánský knew he was vulnerable on three counts. First, he held a rank high enough to ensure a spectacular show trial. As the Soviet Great Purge of the 1930s had demonstrated, trials and executions of leading communists cemented mass loyalty to the regime by rousing ordinary citizens to perpetual vigilance—but for a trial to be a genuine show, the defendant had to be worth showing. Any trial with Slánský, the CPC general secretary, as defendant would be the perfect show.

Second, Slánský was a Czech, and Stalin viewed his Czech colleagues with particular suspicion. Czechoslovakia was the only state in eastern Europe with a history of successful democracy. Moreover, the CPC had participated with noncommunists in a coalition government longer than any other eastern European communist party. Such differences linked the CPC to the ideology of "national communism," which taught that each state should follow its own route to communism, that the Soviet path was not the only way. After the Yugoslav communist leader Tito had dared to defy Stalin's leadership in 1948, Stalin became obsessed with rooting out "national communism" and punishing any potential "titoists."

Finally, Slánský knew that he occupied a vulnerable position because he was a Jew. Aiming to establish a Soviet presence in the Middle East after the war, Stalin had tried to persuade the new state of Israel to align with the Soviet Union by offering diplomatic recognition and arms deals. But Stalin's efforts failed. By 1950, Israel had become an ally of the United States. In response, Stalin regarded all Jews as potential "Zionists" (that is, as pro-Israel and therefore pro-Western and anti-Soviet in their allegiances).

Slánský's birthday fears turned out to be correct. Shortly before midnight on November 24, 1951, security agents arrested him at his home. A lifelong atheist, Slánský could say nothing except "Jesus Maria." He knew what was coming. Instrumental in initiating the Stalinist terror in Czechoslovakia, Slánský had approved the arrests and torture of many of his colleagues. Ironically, he had drafted the telegram asking Stalin to send Soviet advisers to assist in the Czech purge—the very same advisers who decided to target Slánský.

For the next year, Slánský endured mental and physical torture, directed by these advisers. Common torture tactics included beatings and kickings; prolonged periods in a standing position and/or without sleep, food, or water; and all-night interrogation sessions. One interrogator recalled, "Instead of getting evidence, we were told that they were villains and that we had to break them."[5]

Before the show trial began on November 20, 1952, party officials had already determined the verdict and sentences. Prosecutors, defense attorneys, judges, and the accused spoke the lines of a script written by security agents. Slánský pleaded guilty to the crimes of high treason, espionage, and sabotage. This founding member of the CPC said he had conspired to overthrow the communist government. This Resistance fighter confessed to collaborating with the Nazis. This zealous Stalinist announced that he was a titoist-Zionist working for the United States.

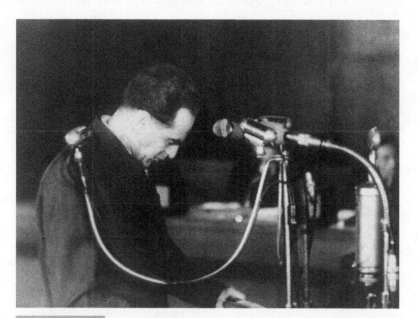

RUDOLF SLÁNSKÝ ON TRIAL Slánský, already a broken man, bows his head as he hears his death sentence on November 27, 1952.

(continued on next page)

(continued from previous page)

Why did Slánský make such a ludicrous confession? Fear of further torture was clearly one motive, but other factors also came into play. Communists such as Slánský believed that the interests of the party always came first, ahead of individual rights, ahead of abstractions such as "truth." Slánský may have believed that his confession, false though it was, served the party. As one experienced interrogator noted about a different defendant, "He'll confess; he's got a good attitude toward the party."[6] In addition, Slánský may have been promised, as were other show trial defendants, that his life would be spared and his family protected if he confessed.

Slánský hanged on December 3, 1952. His family was deported with only the barest essentials to a designated district and assigned to manual labor.

For Discussion

1. How did Cold War concerns shape Slánský's trial?
2. Slánský supervised the start of the Terror in Czechoslovakia. Did he, then, "get what he deserved"? What sort of justice was served in the trial of Rudolf Slánský?

Taking It Further

Lukes, Igor. "The Rudolf Slánský Affair: New Evidence." *Slavic Review* 58, 1 (Spring 1999): 160–187. Illuminating study of the role of Cold War intrigue in determining Slánský's fate.

Kaplan, Karel. *Report on the Murder of the General Secretary.* 1990. Kaplan emigrated from Czechoslovakia to West Germany in the late 1970s and wrote this report.

the western sectors of the city of Berlin—those areas controlled by the United States, France, and Britain—blockaded. Stalin hoped to force the Western powers to resume the delivery of reparations payments from western Germany or, at the very least, to give up control of West Berlin. Instead, the British and Americans responded with the Berlin Airlift. For almost a year, planes landed in West Berlin every three minutes, day and night, delivering 12,000 tons of daily supplies. In May 1949 Stalin recognized

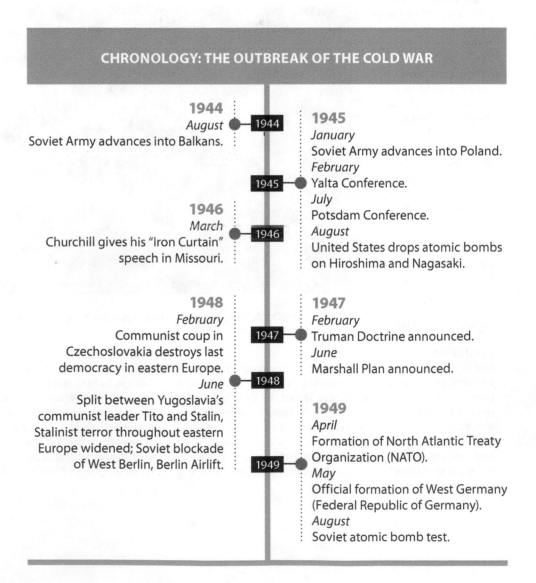

CHRONOLOGY: THE OUTBREAK OF THE COLD WAR

1944
August
Soviet Army advances into Balkans.

`1944`

1945
January
Soviet Army advances into Poland.
February
Yalta Conference.

`1945`

July
Potsdam Conference.
August
United States drops atomic bombs on Hiroshima and Nagasaki.

1946
March
Churchill gives his "Iron Curtain" speech in Missouri.

`1946`

1948
February
Communist coup in Czechoslovakia destroys last democracy in eastern Europe.

1947
February
Truman Doctrine announced.

`1947`

June
Marshall Plan announced.

June
Split between Yugoslavia's communist leader Tito and Stalin, Stalinist terror throughout eastern Europe widened; Soviet blockade of West Berlin, Berlin Airlift.

`1948`

1949
April
Formation of North Atlantic Treaty Organization (NATO).

`1949`

May
Official formation of West Germany (Federal Republic of Germany).
August
Soviet atomic bomb test.

defeat and called off the blockade. The city of Berlin, like Germany itself, remained divided for the next 40 years.

In 1949, three additional developments wove the final threads into the basic Cold War pattern. First, the British and American zones of occupied Germany, joined with the French zone, became the Western-allied state of West Germany, while the Soviet zone became communist East Germany. Second, in April 1949 nine western European nations allied with the United States and Canada in the **North Atlantic Treaty Organization (NATO)**, a military alliance specifically aimed at repelling a Soviet invasion of western Europe. And third, on August 29, 1949, the Soviet Union tested its own atomic bomb. Over the next few years, Stalin forced his eastern European satellites into an anti-Western military alliance (finalized as the **Warsaw Pact** in 1955), and the United States and the Soviet Union developed hydrogen or thermonuclear bombs, weapons with far more destructive might than their atomic predecessors. Europe stood divided into two hostile military blocs, each dominated by a superpower in possession of a nuclear arsenal.

The West and the World: Decolonization and the Cold War

28.2 What was the impact of decolonization and the Cold War on the global balance of power?

The conflict between East and West soon blended with a very different struggle, one between the peoples of the developing nations and European imperialism. The Soviet Union and the United States used economic and military aid, as well as covert action, to cajole and coerce newly independent nations into choosing sides in what became the global Cold War conflict.

The End to the Age of European Empires

In the economic hard times following World War II, European governments regarded their empires as more crucial than ever. States such as Britain and France looked to their imperial possessions to give them international power and prestige. Britain's Foreign Minister Ernest Bevin, for example, saw the British Empire as the means "to develop our own power and influence to equal that of the U.S. of A. and the U.S.S.R."[7] The war, however, strengthened colonial independence movements, with nationalists highlighting the inherent contradiction between the Allies' fight for democracy in Europe and the denial of democratic rights to the imperial subjects of European states.

When the war ended, these nationalists resisted European efforts to reimpose imperial rule, and a series of bloody colonial conflicts resulted. In Indonesia, war raged from 1945 to 1949 as the Dutch fought to keep hold of a region they viewed as vital to their economic survival. They lost the fight, and in 1949 the nationalist Ahmed Sukarno (1949–1966) led his country into independence. Similarly, nationalists in Indochina rose up against the return of French rule and began a lengthy war for independence.

The British, too, found much of their empire in revolt in the postwar period at precisely the moment when the economic and military demands of total war significantly weakened Britain's ability to control its far-flung possessions. To retain Britain's hold on its essential imperial territories, the first postwar prime minister, Clement Attlee, adopted a policy of jettisoning those regions that Britain no longer needed—or could no longer afford.

The British first jettisoned the Indian subcontinent. During World War II, the refusal of Indian nationalists to cooperate with the war effort made clear that Britain could no longer control India. After the war, therefore, Attlee's government opened

View the Map

Shifting Borders—Eastern Europe After World War II

28.1

28.2

North Atlantic Treaty Organization (NATO) Defensive anti-Soviet alliance of the United States, Canada, and the nations of western Europe established in 1949.

28.3

Warsaw Pact Military alliance of the Soviet Union and its eastern European satellite states in the Cold War era.

28.4

 Read the Document

Franz Fanon, The Wretched of the Earth

independence negotiations. Muslim nationalists led by Muhammad Ali Jinnah (1876–1948) refused to accept citizenship in a Hindu-dominated India and won from the British the creation of a separate Muslim state—Pakistan. India and Pakistan, as well as Burma (Myanmar), received independence in August 1947 (see **Map 28.2**). Just as the redrawing of boundary lines in eastern Europe resulted in mass deportations and death, so the partition of the Indian subcontinent sparked widespread devastation. More than 10 million people fled their homes and became refugees—Muslims fearing Hindu rule, Hindus fearing Muslim rule, Sikhs fearing both. Mahatma Gandhi begged for an end to the killing, but the death tolls reached 250,000—and included Gandhi himself, who was shot by an assassin just six months after India achieved independence.

In Palestine, too, British retreat led to bloodshed. After the war in Europe ended, Jewish refugees, persuaded by Hitler that a Jew could be safe only in a Jewish state, demanded that they be allowed to settle in Palestine. The British, however, sought to limit Jewish immigration to maintain regional political stability (and protect their own interests). But faced with mounting violence as well as growing international pressure to grant Jewish demands for statehood, the British announced they would leave Palestine and turned the problem over to the new United Nations. At the end of 1947, the UN announced a plan to partition Palestine into a Jewish and an Arab state. Arab leaders rejected the plan, however, and British troops left in May 1948 without transferring authority to either party. Jewish leaders proclaimed the new state of Israel, and the region erupted into war. After nine months of fighting, an uneasy peace descended, based on a partition of Palestine among Israel, Jordan, and Egypt (see Map 28.4 on page 899). Approximately 750,000 Palestinian Arabs became stateless refugees.

By withdrawing from hot spots such as India and Palestine, the British hoped to preserve what remained of the British Empire. During the 1950s, successive British governments sought to diminish the force of nationalism by diverting it down channels of constitutional reform and systems of power sharing—and stomping on nationalists who broke out of these channels. But neither compromise nor coercion stemmed the nationalist tide.

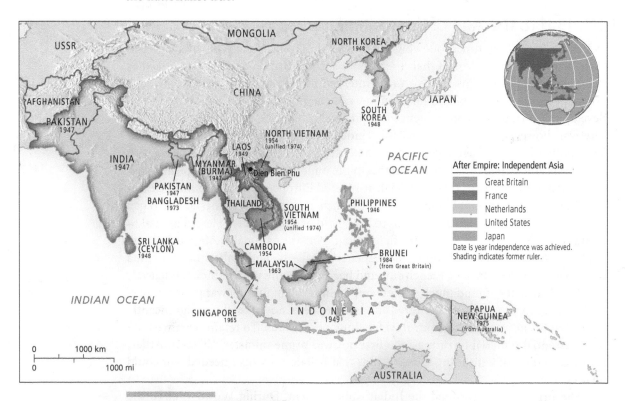

MAP **28.2** AFTER EMPIRE: ASIA Dates of national formation often give no indication of the continuing political upheaval and violence that afflicted the countries of Asia in the postwar period. Which of these newly formed states experienced prolonged warfare in the aftermath of independence?

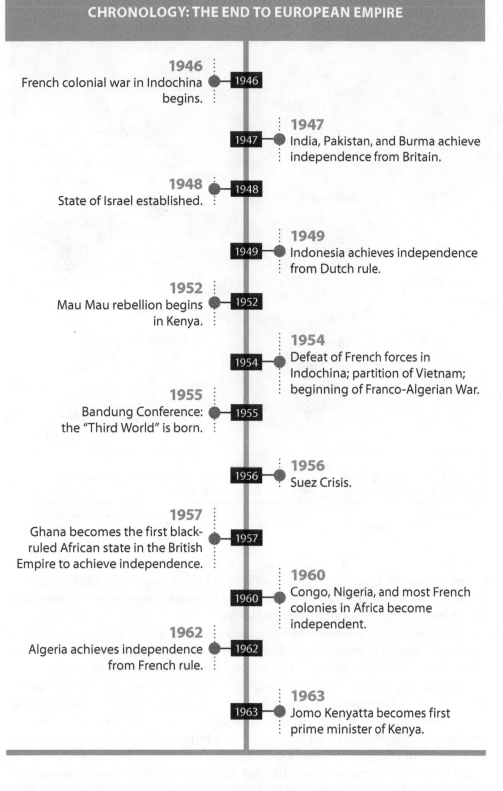

CHRONOLOGY: THE END TO EUROPEAN EMPIRE

1946
French colonial war in Indochina begins.
`1946`

1947
`1947`
India, Pakistan, and Burma achieve independence from Britain.

1948
State of Israel established.
`1948`

1949
`1949`
Indonesia achieves independence from Dutch rule.

1952
Mau Mau rebellion begins in Kenya.
`1952`

1954
`1954`
Defeat of French forces in Indochina; partition of Vietnam; beginning of Franco-Algerian War.

1955
Bandung Conference: the "Third World" is born.
`1955`

1956
`1956`
Suez Crisis.

1957
Ghana becomes the first black-ruled African state in the British Empire to achieve independence.
`1957`

1960
`1960`
Congo, Nigeria, and most French colonies in Africa become independent.

1962
Algeria achieves independence from French rule.
`1962`

1963
`1963`
Jomo Kenyatta becomes first prime minister of Kenya.

In Kenya, for example, Britain offered a gradual process of constitutional reforms leading toward eventual self-government, but these reforms were too slow and limited to satisfy Kenyan nationalists. The result, in 1952, was the "Mau Mau" rebellion, actually a combined peasant uprising, nationalist insurgence, and civil war. Britain imposed a brutal "villagization" program, intended to cut off Mau Mau supply lines. British forces imprisoned much of the population in enclosed villages, where they were deprived of adequate food and shelter, commandeered for forced labor, and often

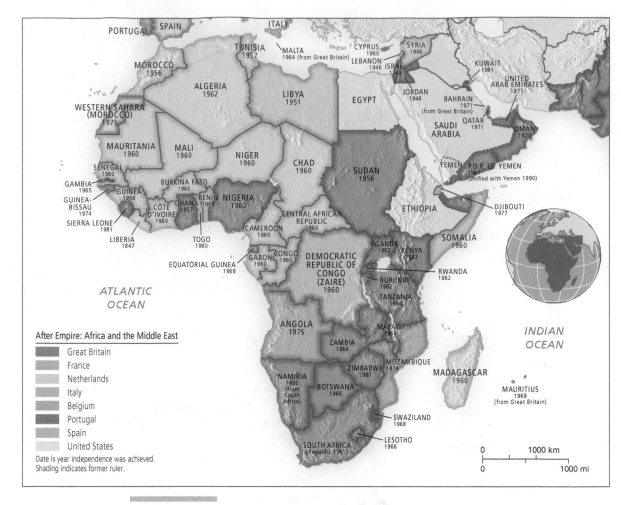

MAP **28.3** AFTER EMPIRE: AFRICA We saw in Chapter 24 that in just three decades, between 1880 and 1910, European nations divided up between them almost the entire African continent in the notorious "Scramble for Africa." African nationalists effected an even more dramatic scramble of European imperial regimes *out* of sub-Saharan Africa. Which was the first African state to become independent? How many African states became independent in the years between 1957 and 1967?

beaten and tortured. Yet all of this bloodshed did little to stop Kenyan independence. In 1963, Jomo Kenyatta (1889–1978), imprisoned for seven years because of his role in the uprising, became Kenya's first elected leader.

Many African leaders followed Kenyatta on the path from a British prison cell to a prime ministerial or presidential office (see **Map 28.3**). By the end of the 1960s, the British Empire had been reduced to an assortment of small island territories.

France, too, saw its empire disintegrate in the postwar decades despite efforts to resist nationalist movements. In Indochina, the nationalist leader Ho Chi Minh (1890–1969) adopted the U.S. Declaration of Independence for his model when he proclaimed independence in September 1945. The stirring rhetoric failed to convince the French, who fought for almost a decade to retain their hold in southeast Asia. But in 1954, the French army suffered a decisive defeat at Dien Bien Phu in Vietnam, and French rule in Indochina ended (see Map 28.2).

Humiliated by this defeat, French army officers responded ferociously to the outbreak of a nationalist revolt in Algeria that same year. Many French men and women shared the army's view that France had been pushed too far and had to stand fast. The result was the Franco-Algerian War. By the time Algeria claimed independence in 1962, approximately 200,000 Algerian nationalist fighters had been killed or imprisoned. Fifteen thousand French soldiers and auxiliary forces were dead, as were almost 23,000 Algerian and French civilians.

The Franco-Algerian War seriously divided French society, called into question the meaning of French democracy, and transformed France's political structure. Supporters of the French army in Algeria saw it as a force fighting on behalf of Western civilization against barbarism (Muslim and communist). Critics, pointing to the evidence that the French army used torture against its enemies, argued that the war threatened to corrupt French society. (See *Different Voices* in this chapter.) By 1958 France teetered on the brink of civil war, with French army officers preparing for an assault on Paris. The World War II hero Charles De Gaulle forced through a new constitution, which sharply tilted the balance of power in French domestic politics toward the president (conveniently De Gaulle himself).

The Globalization of the Cold War

The process of **decolonization** often became entangled with Cold War rivalries, and in many regions, superpower influence replaced imperial control. Despite fears of World War III and a Europe devastated by nuclear weapons, the Cold War actually turned hot only in the developing nations, at the intersection of superpower rivalries and nationalist conflicts.

THE KOREAN WAR, 1950–1953 The first such intersection occurred in Korea. Once part of the Japanese Empire, Korea, like Germany, was divided after World War II. A Soviet-linked communist regime assumed power in North Korea, and an anticommunist state propped up by the United States controlled the south (see Map 28.2, p. 890). In 1950, North Korean troops invaded South Korea in an attempt to unite the country under communist rule. This civil war, a struggle between rival groups of Korean nationalists, soon became a new theater of the Cold War. A UN-sponsored, largely American army fought alongside South Korean troops, while the Soviet Union supplied arms and Communist China provided soldiers to support North Korea.

IMPERIAL SACRIFICE This poster reminded French men and women of the sacrifice made by their army at the Battle of Dien Bien Phu in Vietnam: "They sacrificed themselves for your liberty." The memory of the army's defeat at Dien Bien Phu helped strengthen French determination to hold on to Algeria.

decolonization The retreat of Western powers from their imperial territories.

The Korean War accelerated the globalization of the Cold War. Convinced that communism was on the march, Truman's administration supported France's struggle against the nationalists in Indochina, thus drawing the United States onto the path that would lead to its war in Vietnam. The conflict in Korea also welded Japan firmly into the Western alliance. As the U.S. army turned to the Japanese for vital military supplies, more than $3.5 billion poured into and rejuvenated the Japanese economy. (American military orders for trucks guaranteed the success of a struggling new Japanese firm called Toyota.) Transformed from an occupied enemy to a staunch ally and an economic powerhouse, Japan became the dam holding back "the red tide that threatens to engulf the world."[8] Thus, in a curious way, Japan—geographically as far "East" as one can get—became a part of the "West."

The Korean War also solidified the Cold War within Europe. The escalating costs of the war led Truman's administration to demand that its European allies strengthen their own military forces and permit the rearmament of West Germany. With the trauma of German conquest so recently behind them, many Europeans were horrified

brinkmanship Style of Cold War confrontation in which each superpower endeavored to convince the other that it was willing to wage nuclear war.

by the second demand. Britain's prime minister Attlee warned, "The policy of using Satan to defeat Sin is very dangerous." But after four years of controversy, West Germany rearmed under the NATO umbrella.

CHANGING TEMPERATURES IN THE COLD WAR, 1953–1960 In 1953, both sides in the Cold War changed leaders. Stalin died in March, just a few months after a new Republican administration headed by President Dwight Eisenhower (1890–1969) took office in the United States. This change of leadership heralded a new phase in the Cold War. When Eisenhower took office, he condemned Truman's policy of *containing* communism as defeatist, a "negative, futile and immoral policy . . . which abandons countless human beings to a despotism and Godless terrorism."[9] Instead, Eisenhower committed the United States to *roll back* communism and insisted that communist aggression would be met with massive nuclear retaliation. The term **brinkmanship** entered the Cold War vocabulary when Eisenhower's Secretary of State John Foster Dulles (1888–1959) warned, "If you try to run away from [nuclear war], if you are scared to go to the brink, you are lost."[10]

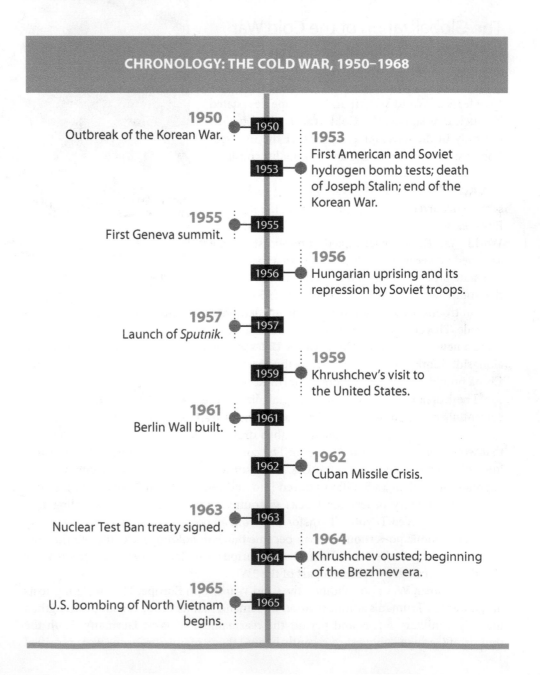

CHRONOLOGY: THE COLD WAR, 1950–1968

1950
Outbreak of the Korean War.

1953
First American and Soviet hydrogen bomb tests; death of Joseph Stalin; end of the Korean War.

1955
First Geneva summit.

1956
Hungarian uprising and its repression by Soviet troops.

1957
Launch of *Sputnik*.

1959
Khrushchev's visit to the United States.

1961
Berlin Wall built.

1962
Cuban Missile Crisis.

1963
Nuclear Test Ban treaty signed.

1964
Khrushchev ousted; beginning of the Brezhnev era.

1965
U.S. bombing of North Vietnam begins.

Different Voices

Torture and Terrorism in the French-Algerian War

The French-Algerian War shattered France's postwar political system and raised troubling questions about French identity. Much of the controversy aroused by the war centered on the revelations that French police and the French military routinely used torture to interrogate captured Algerian rebels. In the following excerpts we hear the voices of soldiers—the first, a high-ranking officer, the second, a volunteer paratrooper.

I. War Against Terrorism

Roger Trinquier (1908–1985) served in both World War II and Indochina before becoming commander of the 3rd Colonial Airborne Regiment in Algeria. In Modern Warfare: A French View of Counterinsurgency, Trinquier identified terrorism—and the fight against it—as the quintessential form of modern warfare.

The goal of modern warfare is control of the populace, and terrorism is a particularly appropriate weapon, since it aims directly at the inhabitant. . . . What characterizes modern terrorism, and makes for its basic strength, is the slaughter of generally defenseless persons. . . . The terrorist should not be considered an ordinary criminal. Actually, he fights within the framework of his organization, without personal interest, for a cause he considers noble and for a respectable ideal, the same as the soldiers in the army confronting him. On the command of his superiors, he kills without hatred individuals unknown to him, with the same indifference as the soldier on the battlefield. His victims are often women and children. . . . But during a period of history when the bombing of open cities is permitted, and when two Japanese cities were razed to hasten the end of the war in the Pacific, one cannot with good cause reproach him. The terrorist has become a soldier, like the aviator or the infantryman.

But the aviator . . . knows that anti-aircraft shells can kill or maim him. . . . It never occurs to [the infantryman] . . . to ask . . . that his enemy renounce the use of the rifle, the shell, or the bomb. . . . [The terrorist] must be made to realize that, when he is captured, he cannot be treated like an ordinary criminal. . . . No lawyer is present for such an interrogation. If the prisoner gives the information requested, the examination is quickly terminated; if not, specialists must force his secret from him. . . . The terrorist must accept this as a condition inherent in his trade and in the methods of warfare that, with full knowledge, his superiors and he himself have chosen. . . .

Interrogations in modern warfare should be conducted by specialists perfectly versed in the techniques to be employed. . . . The interrogators must always strive not to injure the physical and moral integrity of individuals. Science can easily place at the army's disposition the means for obtaining what is sought. But we must not trifle with our responsibilities. It is deceitful to permit artillery or aviation to bomb villages and slaughter women and children, while the real enemy usually escapes, and to refuse interrogation specialists the right to seize the truly guilty terrorist and spare the innocent.

If . . . our army refused to employ all the weapons of modern warfare, it could no longer fulfill its mission. We would no longer be defended. Our national independence, the civilization we hold dear, our very freedom would probably perish.

SOURCE: *Modern Warfare: A French View of Counterinsurgency* by Roger Trinquier, translated from the French by Daniel Lee; with an introduction by Bernard B. Fali; Foreword by Eliot A. Cohen (New York: Frederick Praeger, 1964), 16, 17, 20–21, 23, 115. Copyright © 1964, 2006 by Praeger Security International.

II. The Torture Room

In 1954 Pierre Leuillette enlisted in the French Army. After he finished his tour of duty in Algeria, he wrote St. Michael and the Dragon: Memoirs of a Paratrooper, *published in France in 1961.*

A volunteer paratrooper is never at the start anything but a grown-up little boy, at best an enthusiastic boy scout, dreaming of cuts and bruises, of bursts of machine-gun fire, of his parachute spread in the wind, and of the glamorous uniform, red beret, jungle-green combat suit, and commando dagger slipped into the boot. . . . He leaves everything, parents, friends, school, work, for "adventure." It's his first free act. It will be his last, too, for a long time: the enlistment is for three years. . . .

I shall speak of the torture room of the 1st Company of the 2nd R. P.C., my company. . . . Every day, the lieutenant on duty, assisted by Sergeant T., of the Signal Corps, and another sergeant, a very muscular Alsatian, spends several hours there. They have plenty to do. . . . With interrogation for a pretext, their work really amounts to torturing naked, bound prisoners, one after another, from morning to night. [Leuillette describes the various torture methods ranging from the basic slap to simulated drowning to crushing the genitals in a vise.] Our principal implement did not, however, exist in the Middle Ages. This refinement of civilization presents at first glance a quite innocuous appearance: simply an electric wire attached to a floor plug. . . . Besides being efficacious, [torture by electricity] has the added advantage of leaving no marks. . . .

Even if the great majority of those we interrogate are criminals of the most evil sort, there are also among them men only suspected—of, for example, harboring [rebels], or of collecting money for them; and there are some completely innocent, who, like most innocent people, cannot possibly prove it. . . .

(continued on next page)

(continued from previous page)

To civilians . . . I tell about what I see every day. They have always had a lofty idea of the greatness of France. They listen politely. But I sense their unbelief. They are thinking, "This isn't possible. We'd have known about it." Will they ever know about it? The German people, after the war, never stopped saying, and it was probably true, "We didn't know." . . . Have they ever realized that not knowing is also a way of being guilty?

[His tour of duty complete, Leuillette sails back to France.] On the boat my joy is so great that all night long I whistle and sing. . . . The [ship] comes into Marseilles and my excited joy suddenly dissolves. For there on the dock several hundred soldiers are waiting to leave, just as I was three years ago. I am afraid, afraid for them. . . . For I now know that they risk more than death. They risk the loss of everything that could make them men.

SOURCE: Pierre Leuillette, *St. Michael and the Dragon: Memoirs of a Paratrooper.* Trans. John Edmonds (Boston: Houghton Mifflin, 1964), 1–2, 286–288, 298–299, 334. Originally published in French as *Saint Michel et le dragon.* Copyright © 1961 by Les Editions de Minuit. Reprinted by permission of Georges Borchardt, Inc., for Les Editions de Minuit.

For Discussion

1. Why was the French-Algerian War so divisive in France? What issues did it raise about French national identity?
2. The controversy over French police and military tactics in Algeria raised a question that is much debated today: Does the fight against terrorism demand the use of torture, or is the turn to torture as much a threat to Western values as terrorism itself? Can we use the history of the French-Algerian War to answer this question? How do we "learn from history," given the uniqueness of each historical event?

📖 Read the Document

Nikita Khrushchev, "Speech to the 22nd Congress of the Communist Party"

This newly aggressive American stance was matched on the other side of the Cold War divide. After a period of uncertainty following Stalin's death in 1953, Nikita Khrushchev (1955–1964) emerged in 1955 as the new Soviet leader. Loud and boisterous, given to off-the-cuff remarks and spontaneous displays of emotion, Khrushchev contrasted sharply with the reserved Stalin. (It is hard to imagine Stalin taking off his shoe and beating it on a table, as Khrushchev did in front of the television cameras at an assembly of the United Nations.) Khrushchev played a dangerous game of nuclear bluff, by which he convinced allies and foes alike that the Soviet Union possessed a stronger nuclear force than it actually did.

Khrushchev and Eisenhower recognized, however, that nuclear weapons made total war unwinnable. Thus, the period from 1953 until 1964 witnessed thawing superpower relations followed by the icy blasts of renewed hostilities. In 1955, for example, representatives of Britain, France, the United States, and the Soviet Union met in Geneva for the first summit of the Cold War. This initial thaw ended one year later when Khrushchev sent tanks into Hungary to crush an anti-Soviet rebellion.

The Soviets' successful launch of the first human-made satellite, *Sputnik,* in 1957 was even more chilling. Khrushchev claimed—falsely—that the Soviets possessed an advanced intercontinental ballistic missile (ICBM) force and that Soviet factories were producing rockets "like sausages from a machine."[11] *Sputnik* had ominous implications, especially for western Europeans. If the Soviets could launch a satellite into space, they seemed capable of delivering a nuclear bomb to American as well as European cities. If the Soviets invaded western Europe with conventional forces, would the Americans defend Europe—and so open their own cities to nuclear retaliation? Would the United States risk Chicago to save Paris?

Yet in the late 1950s, the Cold War ice seemed to be breaking once again. In 1958 the Soviet Union announced it would suspend nuclear testing. The United States and Britain followed suit and nuclear test ban talks opened in Geneva. The next year Khrushchev spent 12 days touring the United States. (Much to his regret, security concerns kept him from visiting Disneyland.) The communist leader impressed Americans as down-to-earth, a man rather than a monster. Khrushchev ended his U.S. visit with the promise of another four-power summit in 1960.

ON THE BRINK: THE BERLIN WALL AND THE CUBAN MISSILE CRISIS These warming relations, however, turned frosty in 1960 after the Soviet Union announced it had shot

A MILITARY PARADE IN RED SQUARE, MOSCOW, NOVEMBER 7, 1963 The development of new weapons—often nuclear—became a central focus of Cold War competition between the United States and the Soviet Union. Displays such as this one, held on Revolution Day, served as a display of the Soviet Union's military might to the rest of the world.

down an American spy plane and captured its pilot. This announcement aborted the planned summit and initiated one of the most dangerous periods in the post-World War II era, one that saw the construction of the **Berlin Wall** and an escalation of the arms race. As we saw at the beginning of this chapter, the continuing outflow of East Germans to the West through Berlin led the East German communist leader Walter Ulbricht (1893–1973) and Khrushchev to erect the wall. Two weeks later, the Soviet Union resumed nuclear testing. The new American president John F. Kennedy

Berlin Wall Constructed by the East German government, a wall that physically cut the city of Berlin in two and prevented East German citizens from access to West Germany; stood from 1961 to 1989.

897

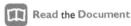
Third World Term coined in 1955 to describe nations that did not align with either the Soviet Union or the United States; commonly used to describe the industrially underdeveloped nations.

(1917–1963) increased military spending and called for an expanded civil defense program to prepare for nuclear war. Across Europe, men and women feared that their continent would become a nuclear wasteland.

Such a war was narrowly avoided in the fall of 1962 as once again the Cold War intersected with a nationalist struggle. In 1959, a nationalist revolutionary movement led by Fidel Castro (b. 1926) toppled Cuba's pro-U.S. dictator. Castro aligned Cuba with the Soviet Union. In 1962, Kennedy learned that the Soviets were building missile bases in Cuba. What he did not know was that the Soviet forces in Cuba were armed with nuclear weapons—and had the power to use these weapons if U.S. forces attacked. Some of Kennedy's advisers urged just such an attack, but instead the president used secret diplomatic channels to broker a compromise. Khrushchev removed the missiles; in exchange, Kennedy withdrew NATO's nuclear missiles from Turkey and guaranteed that the United States would not invade Cuba.

In the aftermath of the Cuban Missile Crisis, the United States and the Soviet Union backed off from brinkmanship. In 1963, the superpowers agreed to stop aboveground nuclear testing with the Nuclear Test Ban treaty and set up between them the "hotline," a direct communications link to encourage immediate personal consultation in the event of a future crisis.

The retreat from brinkmanship did not, however, slow the globalization of the Cold War. The superpowers served as magnetic poles, attracting competing nationalist and regional forces. Many newly independent nations resisted being drawn in, as the Bandung Conference of 1955 made clear. Bandung brought together "nonaligned" states who sought to establish themselves as a collective force separate from both superpowers. French journalists at the conference gave these nations a collective label— neither the first (Western, capitalist) nor the second (Eastern, communist), but rather the **Third World**. Genuine independence, however, proved difficult to retain.

COLD WAR ARENAS: VIETNAM AND THE MIDDLE EAST The transformation of the Vietnam War from a struggle against French imperial rule into a Cold War conflict illustrates the way in which the superpowers tended to replace European empires as global powerbrokers. After the defeat of French forces at Dien Bien Phu in 1954, rival Vietnamese nationalists fought to control the Indochinese peninsula. Ho Chi Minh and his communist regime in North Vietnam relied on the Soviet Union and China for support, while American military and economic aid propped up an anticommunist (but not democratic) government in South Vietnam. Under the Kennedy presidency (1961–1963), the number of military advisers in Vietnam expanded rapidly, as did American involvement in South Vietnamese politics. When Kennedy's successor, Lyndon Johnson (1908–1973), took office, he issued a clear order, "Win the war!" In 1964, the U.S. Congress granted Johnson the authority to take "all necessary measures" to do so. By 1968, more than 500,000 American soldiers were fighting in Vietnam. About 58,000 U.S. soldiers died during the war—as did well over one million Vietnamese.

Like Vietnam, the Middle East became a Cold War arena in the 1950s. Events in Egypt proved pivotal. In 1954 the revolutionary nationalist Gamal Abdel Nasser (1918–1970) overthrew the British-dominated Egyptian monarchy. The United States immediately sought to woo Nasser to the West by offering aid to build the Aswan Dam, a huge hydroelectric project on the Nile River. But when Nasser arranged a weapons deal with Czechoslovakia, outraged American policymakers denied him funds for the dam. The Egyptian leader retaliated by aligning with the Soviet Union and by nationalizing the Suez Canal.

This series of events set off what is known as the Suez Crisis, a dramatic demonstration of the waning power of European empires and of the rising dominance of the superpowers. Angered by Nasser's seizure of the canal, the British and French governments conspired with Israel to topple him from power. Israeli forces invaded Egypt, according to plan, on October 31, 1956. Posing as peacekeepers, the British and French demanded that both sides pull back from the Canal Zone. When, as they expected,

Nasser refused, British and French troops invaded. But then the plan unraveled under superpower pressure. With the Soviet Union threatening a nuclear strike against the invading forces, President Dwight Eisenhower telephoned the British prime minister, Anthony Eden, and exploded, "Is that you, Anthony? Well, this is President Eisenhower, and I can only presume you have gone out of your mind!" Eisenhower's administration blocked Britain's IMF loan application and pushed Britain to the edge of financial collapse. Eden's government had no choice but to declare a cease fire and withdraw British troops.

While the Suez Crisis highlighted superpower dominance in the Middle East, the Six-Day War of 1967 marked a clear Cold War division of the region. In six days of fighting, Israel gained possession of the Sinai Peninsula from Egypt, the West Bank from Jordan, the Golan Heights from Syria—and one million stateless Palestinian refugees (see **Map 28.4**). In the wake of the war, American foreign policy shifted to decisive support for Israel. In turn, Egypt, Syria, Iraq, Sudan, and Libya aligned with the Soviet Union.

28.1

28.2

28.3

28.4

📖 Read the Document

Gamal Abdel Nasser, Speech on the Suez Canal

🔍 View the Map

The Formation of Modern Israel

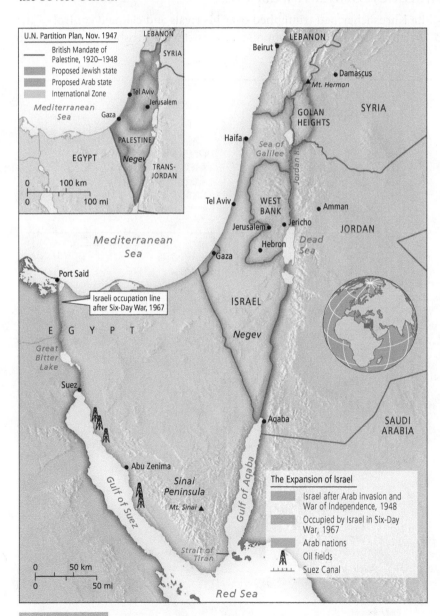

MAP **28.4** THE EXPANSION OF ISRAEL The map inset outlines the United Nations' plan to partition Palestine into Jewish and Arab states, with Jerusalem as an international zone. This plan was not implemented; instead, Israel carved out its own boundaries as a result of war with the surrounding Arab powers. What was the impact of the Six-Day War in 1967 on those boundaries?

The Soviet Union and Eastern Europe in the 1950s and 1960s

28.3 What patterns characterized the history of the Soviet Union and eastern Europe after the death of Stalin?

D ivided by the Cold War, the peoples of western and eastern Europe in the 1950s and 1960s followed separate paths (see **Map 28.5**). For the citizens of eastern Europe and the Soviet Union, Stalin's death in 1953 inaugurated a period of political reform and hope for prosperity. By the end of the 1960s, however, economic stagnation and political discontent characterized life in the Soviet bloc.

De-Stalinization Under Khrushchev

By 1955 Nikita Khrushchev had triumphed over his rivals and claimed control of the post-Stalin Soviet Union. A true communist success story, Khrushchev was born to

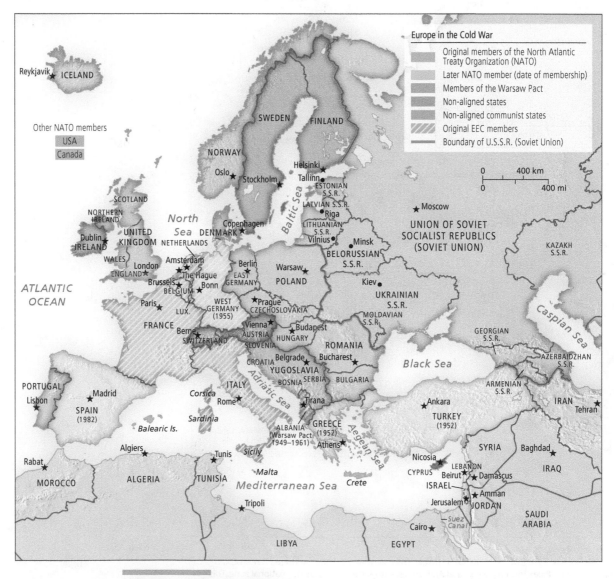

MAP **28.5** EUROPE IN THE COLD WAR As this map shows, during the Cold War the "West" was defined culturally and politically, rather than in geographic terms. Which "eastern" states belonged to the "West"? Which European states were neutral?

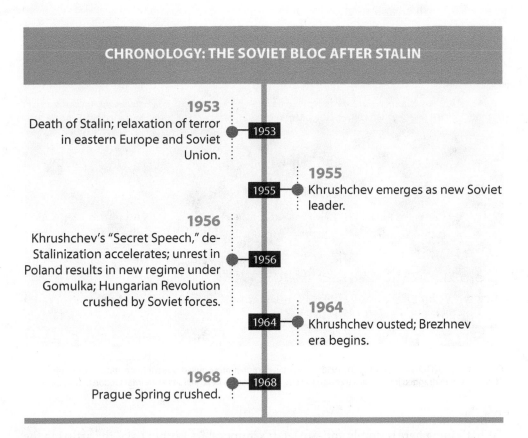

CHRONOLOGY: THE SOVIET BLOC AFTER STALIN

1953
Death of Stalin; relaxation of terror in eastern Europe and Soviet Union.

1953

1955
1955
Khrushchev emerges as new Soviet leader.

1956
Khrushchev's "Secret Speech," de-Stalinization accelerates; unrest in Poland results in new regime under Gomulka; Hungarian Revolution crushed by Soviet forces.

1956

1964
1964
Khrushchev ousted; Brezhnev era begins.

1968
1968
Prague Spring crushed.

illiterate peasants and began work as a coal miner at age 14. Recognized as a man with talent by the Communist Party, he trained as an engineer and helped build the Moscow subway system. Khrushchev owed everything to the Communist Party, and he never forgot it. Confident in the moral and material superiority of communism, Khrushchev believed that the Soviet Union would win the Cold War on the economic battlefield. But this victory would occur only if Soviet living standards substantially improved and only if the Stalinist systems of terror and rigid centralized control were dismantled. Khrushchev's accession to power thus ushered in the era of **de-Stalinization**, a time of greater openness in the Soviet bloc as governments lifted many of the controls on speech and publication. For the first time in years, dissent and debate reappeared in public life.

The most dramatic sign of de-Stalinization was the release of at least four and a half million prisoners from slave labor camps. As one Soviet citizen recalled, their return was disturbing: "In railway trains and stations, there appeared survivors of the camps, with leaden grey hair, sunken eyes, and a faded look; they choked and dragged their feet like old men."[12] These survivors often returned to find their spouses remarried, their children embarrassed by their presence, their world destroyed. Some, such as the writer Alexander Solzhenitsyn, wrote horrifying accounts of their experiences. Solzhenitsyn's books narrated the daily degradation of prison life and provided a detailed map of the network of slave labor camps that he christened "The Gulag Archipelago."

Yet in 1959, four years after the start of de-Stalinization, the Gulag still held at least one million prisoners. De-Stalinization did not end political and religious repression or artistic control. Under Khrushchev, Soviet Jews continued to suffer harassment and imprisonment while Orthodox Christians experienced an intensified anti-Christian campaign, which destroyed churches, imprisoned clergy, closed seminaries and monasteries, and in some cases removed children from Christian homes. Artists who dared challenge the standards of Socialist Realism (see Chapter 26) also suffered. An exhibition of long-hidden works by Picasso inspired many Soviet artists to experiment with abstract art; when Khrushchev saw their work on show, however, he thundered,

de-Stalinization Nikita Khrushchev's effort to decentralize political and economic control in the Soviet Union after 1956.

DE-STALINIZATION On October 31, 1956, Hungarian demonstrators pulled down a huge statue of Joseph Stalin and then dragged it two miles through the city center. Stalin's head still sits at an intersection in Budapest.

"What's hung here is simply anti-Soviet. It's immoral."[13] Within days, the artists in the show were censured, expelled, or unemployed.

De-Stalinization was also limited in its economic impact. In agriculture in particular, the Soviet Union continued to lag behind the West. Refusing to retreat from collectivization, Khrushchev instead implemented a series of poorly planned reforms, including rapid mechanization, a massive chemical fertilizer program, and the plowing of virgin lands. The fundamental productivity problem remained unsolved—and worsened in the long term because of the ecological damage inflicted on the Soviet countryside. Soil erosion increased exponentially, nitrogen runoff from fertilized fields contaminated water supplies, and soil fertility declined. The full force of these problems would not be felt until the 1980s, but as early as 1963 the Soviet Union had to import Western grain, a humiliating admission of failure for Khrushchev's regime.

Re-Stalinization and Stagnation: The Brezhnev Era

De-Stalinization unsettled many high-ranking communists who forced Khrushchev out of office in 1964. After a short period of collective leadership, Leonid Brezhnev (1906–1982) emerged as the new Soviet leader. A polite man with no interest in original ideas, Brezhnev was far more reassuring to Soviet bureaucrats than the flamboyant Khrushchev, whose boisterous embrace of ambitious schemes had proven destabilizing. Fifty-eight years old and already physically ailing when he assumed the party leadership, the increasingly decrepit Brezhnev matched his era.

Under Brezhnev the Soviet economy stagnated. Growth rates in industrial production and labor productivity slowed during the second half of the 1960s and almost disappeared in the 1970s. Improving living standards, however, masked this economic stagnation. Brezhnev continued Khrushchev's policies of free higher education and rising wages, while accelerating the expansion of consumer goods. State subsidies ensured that the cost of utilities, public transport, and rents remained far lower than in the West (although apartments were in short supply), and an extensive welfare system eased pressures on ordinary people.

By the middle of the 1960s, the Soviet Union appeared to have achieved a sort of stability. It was, however, a stability relying on repression. Judging de-Stalinization to be too risky, Brezhnev and his colleagues withdrew the limited cultural and intellectual freedoms introduced under Khrushchev. Those who expressed dissident views soon found themselves denied employment and educational opportunities, imprisoned, sent to the Gulag, or confined indefinitely in psychiatric wards.

Yet dissent did not disappear. Soviet society may have resembled a stagnant pond by the 1970s, but beneath the surface churned dangerous currents that, in the late 1980s, would engulf the entire communist system. Nationalism among the non-Russian populations served as the source of much discontent, as did resentment about political repression. Reviving a practice employed by reformers under the tsarist regime, dissidents evaded the censors by *samizdat* or "self-publishing." Novels, plays, poetry, political treatises, and historical studies were circulated privately, copied by hand, or duplicated on treasured (and often confiscated) typewriters and photocopiers and distributed more widely. Nonconformist artists, banned from official exhibitions, used private apartments to show their work.

Diversity and Dissent in Eastern Europe

Despite the uniformity imposed by Soviet-style communist systems during these decades, the nations of eastern Europe developed in different ways. De-Stalinization accelerated this diversification. In 1956, Khrushchev declared, "It is ridiculous to think that revolutions are made to order"[14] and so indicated that communist nations could follow paths diverging from the road traveled by the Soviet Union.

Read the **Document**

Henry Myers, East Berliners Rise Up Against Soviet Oppression

1956 AND AFTER But just how far from the Soviet road could those paths go? The contrasting fates of Poland and Hungary in 1956 provided the answer. In Poland, protests against Stalinist controls proved strong enough to bring back into power Wladyslaw Gomulka (1905–1982). An influential Polish communist who had been purged in the Stalinist terror in 1951, Gomulka succeeded in establishing a uniquely Polish brand of communism, one that abandoned collective farming and gave a certain amount of freedom to the Roman Catholic Church in Poland, yet remained loyal to the Warsaw Pact.

Hungary also pursued a de-Stalinizing "New Course" under the leadership of the reformist communist Imre Nagy (1896–1958). Unlike Gomulka, however, Nagy gave in to popular demands for a break with the Soviet Union. On October 31, 1956, Hungary withdrew from the Warsaw Pact—or tried to. A few days later, Khrushchev sent in the tanks. At least 4,000 Hungarians died as the Red Army crushed all resistance. Nagy was executed in 1958.

The smashing of the Hungarian revolt defined the limits of de-Stalinization in eastern Europe: The satellite states of the Soviet Union could not follow paths that led out of the Warsaw Pact. Within the confines of this structure and of the one-party state, however, the governments of eastern Europe pursued different courses. Poland held onto its small family farms, with less than one-eighth of farmland collectivized by 1960, in contrast to collectivization rates of 84 percent in Romania, and 87 percent in Czechoslovakia. In Hungary, the post-1956 government of János Kádár (1912–1989)—who had survived torture and imprisonment during the Stalinist terror of the early 1950s—instituted the New Economic Mechanism in the second half of the 1960s. This "mechanism" sharply reduced the state's control of the economy. In contrast, Romanians endured the reign of the "mini-Stalins," Gheorghe Gheorghiu-Dej (1901–1965) and Nicolae Ceauşescu (1918–1989), who imposed not only one-party but one-man control over the country through Stalinist methods of terror.

Within the diverse experiences of eastern Europeans, certain commonalities characterized the post-1956 era. Except in Romania and even more oppressive Albania, living standards improved, particularly in comparison with the hard times of the 1930s and 1940s. Educational opportunities expanded, the supply of consumer goods increased, and political repression became less overt. Even so, over-centralization, bureaucratic mismanagement, and political corruption ensured that living standards remained below those of the West. Moreover, the very consumer goods that were supposed to persuade eastern European citizens of the superiority of the communist system instead demonstrated its deficiencies. With a radio, a Hungarian teenager could tune into Radio Free Europe and hear of a livelier, more abundant society in the West. In East Germany, television watchers could view West German networks and catch a glimpse of Western prosperity.

THE PRAGUE SPRING Discontent simmered throughout the Eastern bloc during the 1960s and then, in 1968, boiled over in Czechoslovakia. During the 1960s, a reform movement emerged in the ranks of the Czechoslovakian Communist Party. It included Slovaks, who believed that the regime's centralized policies favored Czechs, and younger, university-educated managers and scientists who resented the power of uneducated party superiors. At the beginning of 1968, demands for reform fueled an intraparty revolution that brought to power the Slovakian communist Alexander Dubček (1921–1992). Dubček embarked on a program of radical reform aimed at achieving "socialism with a human face." This more humane socialism included freedom of speech, press, assembly, and travel; the removal of Communist Party controls from social and cultural life; and decentralization of the economy. Dubček's effort to reform the system from the top quickly merged with a wider popular protest movement that had arisen among intellectuals, artists, students, and workers. The result was the "**Prague Spring**"—the blossoming of political and social freedoms throughout Czechoslovakia, but especially in the capital city of Prague.

Well aware of the fate of Hungary in 1956, Dubček reassured Brezhnev that his reforms would not lead Czechoslovakia out of the Warsaw Pact. But by the summer of 1968, word of the Prague Spring had reached other eastern European countries and the Soviet Union itself. In Ukraine, nationalist protesters looked to Prague for inspiration, while in Poland, student rioters waved placards reading "Poland is awaiting its own Dubček." Frightened communist leaders throughout the Eastern bloc demanded that Brezhnev stifle the Prague Spring.

On the night of August 20–21, 80,000 Soviet, Polish, Hungarian, and East German troops crossed the Czech border, and over the next several weeks crushed the Prague Spring. That fall, Brezhnev acknowledged that Soviet domination in eastern Europe rested on force alone when he articulated what came to be known as the "Brezhnev Doctrine." Formally a commitment to support global socialism, the Brezhnev Doctrine essentially promised to use the Red Army to destroy any effort to achieve fundamental change within the Soviet bloc.

Prague Spring Short-lived popular effort in 1968 to reform Czechoslovakia's political structures; associated with the phrase "socialism with a human face."

The West: Consensus, Consumption, and Culture

28.4 What patterns characterized the history of western Europe in the 1950s and 1960s?

As in eastern Europe, in western Europe both World War II and the Cold War shaped the 1950s and 1960s. The desire to make the suffering of the war years worthwhile, and opposition to communism, fueled economic integration and strengthened political centrism. The dominant fact of the postwar years was, however, material prosperity as western European economies embarked on two decades of dramatic economic growth and consumer spending.

The Triumph of Democracy

In contrast to the interwar years, the parties in power in western Europe in the 1950s and 1960s and the voters who put them there agreed on the virtues of parliamentary democracy. The new constitutions of France, West Germany, and Italy guaranteed the protection of individual rights, and French and Italian women achieved suffrage. The democratic ideal of the universal franchise had finally been realized in most of western Europe.

Citizenship, though, meant more than the right to vote after 1945. With the triumph of *social democracy* throughout western Europe, the meaning of citizenship broadened to include the right to a decent standard of living. Through the nationalization of key industries, the establishment of public agencies to oversee and encourage investment and trade, and the manipulation of interest rates and currency supplies, governments assumed the task of ensuring full employment and material well-being for their citizens. A slogan of the German Social Democratic Party—"as much competition as possible, as much planning as necessary"—summed up an approach common to much of western Europe at this time.

Social democracy also meant the construction of comprehensive welfare states to guarantee citizens adequate incomes and medical care. By the end of the 1950s, the average western European working-class family received 63 percent of its income from wages. The substantial remaining income came from welfare benefits such as family allowances, national health services, sickness and disability insurance, and old-age pensions. In addition, state-run vaccination and inoculation programs, stricter sanitation regulation, and the development of policies to control communicable diseases all meant an improvement in the health of Europe's populations.

As we saw in Chapter 27, the victory of social democracy was rooted in the suffering of World War II, when Europeans grew determined to create a better world out of the rubble of total war. This determination remained, but wartime radicalism receded as the Cold War constricted the parameters of political debate. The mainstream political parties—Christian Democrats or Conservatives on the right, Social Democrats or Socialists on the left—agreed in refusing to allow Communist Party members to participate in governing coalitions. In France and Italy, communist parties consistently drew 20 to 30 percent of the vote, but were effectively marginalized by their exclusion from office after 1948.

With the communists isolated, and with the ideologies of the extremist Right such as fascism and Nazism discredited by the horrors of the war, western European politics became more centrist. **Christian Democracy**—which has no American or British counterpart—flourished on the European Continent. Drawing on a largely Roman Catholic base for support, Christian Democrats espoused a conservative social ideology combined with a progressive commitment to the welfare state. Christian Democrats dominated much of European politics in the 1950s and 1960s: They played significant roles in the political life of France and Belgium, governed West Germany between 1949 and 1969, and provided every prime minister except two in Italy between 1945 and 1993.

Three factors account for Christian Democracy's success. First, as anticommunists and advocates of the free market, Christian Democrats benefited from Cold War anxieties and more directly from American aid. Second, because they were based on religion (Roman Catholicism) rather than class, Christian Democratic parties appealed to middle-class and working-class voters, and particularly to women, who tended to be more religious and to vote more conservatively than men. Finally, the triumph of Christian Democracy rested on its transformation from a right-wing to a centrist political movement. In the interwar period, Christian Democracy, rooted in a religious and political tradition based on hierarchy and authoritarianism, had veered close to fascism. But during World War II, many Catholics served in the Resistance, where they absorbed progressive political ideas. The war-inspired desire to use the power

Christian Democracy Conservative and confessionally based (Roman Catholic) political parties that dominated much of western European politics after World War II.

of the state to improve the lives of ordinary people blended with traditional Catholic paternalism. After the war the Christian Democrats embraced democracy and supported the construction of comprehensive welfare states.

Prosperity in the West

These political developments unfolded against an economic backdrop of increasing prosperity. In the first half of the 1950s, Europeans moved rapidly from the austerity of the immediate postwar years to an age of affluence.

ECONOMIC INTEGRATION The greater coordination of western European economies contributed to this new prosperity. World War II provided the initial impetus for this economic integration. Fighting in conditions of unprecedented horror, Europeans looked for ways to guarantee a lasting peace. In July 1944, Resistance leaders from France, Italy, the Netherlands, and a number of other countries met in Geneva to declare their support for a federal Europe.

No such radical restructuring occurred, but Cold War concerns helped western Europeans see themselves as part of a single region with common interests. In addition, American policymakers required any state that received Marshall aid to develop transnational economic institutions. Looking back on this early stage of European economic integration, the Belgian prime minister (and ardent proponent of European union) Paul-Henri Spaak (1899–1972) wrote in the later 1960s, "Europeans, let us be modest. It is the fear of Stalin and the daring views of Marshall which led us into the right path."[15]

Efforts at European economic integration culminated with the formation of the **European Economic Community (EEC)** or Common Market in 1957. Consisting of Germany, France, Italy, and the "Benelux" states (Belgium, the Netherlands, and Luxembourg), the EEC sought to establish a free trade zone across member boundaries and to coordinate policies on wages, prices, immigration, and social security. Between 1958 and 1970, trade among its six member states increased fivefold. The rapid movement of goods, services, and even workers ensured that the economies of member states flourished. In contrast, Britain, which chose to remain outside the EEC to preserve its preferential trading relationships with its former and current colonies, struggled with growth rates below those of its continental competitors.

THE AGE OF AFFLUENCE By the mid-1950s, western Europe entered an age of consumption. After years of wartime rationing, Europeans went on a spending spree and did not stop. Climbing real wages—by 80 percent in England, for example, between 1950 and 1970—help explain why. So too does the construction of the welfare state. With full employment and comprehensive welfare services offering unprecedented financial security, Europeans shrugged off habits of thrift. Credit buying (what the British called "buying on the never-never") became commonplace and made possible even more consumption.

This spending spree transformed the interiors of European homes and their exterior environment. Housing construction boomed, and with new houses came new household goods. Items such as refrigerators and washing machines, once unaffordable luxuries, now became increasingly common in ordinary homes. In France, the stock of home appliances rose by 400 percent between 1949 and 1957. At the same time, the automobile revolutionized the rural and urban landscape. Highways, few and far between in 1950, cut across the countryside, and parking meters, unknown in Europe before 1959, dotted city streets. In 1964, the archbishop of Florence presided over a thanksgiving service in a gas station to celebrate the completion of a highway linking Milan and Naples. Out-of-town shopping centers, geared to the convenience of car owners, proliferated while city centers decayed.

European Economic Community (EEC) Originally comprising West Germany, France, Italy, Belgium, Luxembourg, and the Netherlands, the EEC was formed in 1957 to integrate its members' economic structures and so foster both economic prosperity and international peace. Also called the Common Market.

 **Read the Document**

A Common Market and European Integration

Western Culture and Thought in the Age of Consumption

Cultural developments in Western society highlight the shift from an era structured by the austerity and suffering of World War II to an age of affluence and opportunity. By the second half of the 1950s, artists began to retreat from engagement with the horrors of war and instead produced works that commented on and reveled in the cascade of consumer abundance.

FINDING MEANING IN THE AGE OF AUSCHWITZ AND THE ATOM BOMB In the years immediately after 1945, existentialism (which first emerged in the despair of the 1930s) remained a powerful cultural force. Jean-Paul Sartre's conviction that existence has no intrinsic meaning and yet that the individual retains the freedom to act and therefore make meaning, resounded in a world that had experienced both the Holocaust and the Resistance. The existentialist emphasis on individual action as the source of meaning could lead to a life of political activism. Sartre, for example, worked with the French Resistance and became a prominent participant in left-wing political causes in the 1950s and 1960s. Yet existentialist anxiety also justified political disengagement. In the Irish-French playwright Samuel Beckett's (1906–1989) *Waiting for Godot* (1952), two tramps sit in an empty universe, waiting for someone who never comes. In this absurd void, politics has no relevance or resonance.

Existentialist themes echoed throughout the visual arts in the early 1950s. The sculptures of the Swiss artist Alberto Giacometti (1901–1966) embody existentialism—fragile, insubstantial, they appear ready to crack under the strain of being. While Giacometti's sculptures exemplify existentialist terror, the works of the preeminent British painter of the 1950s, Francis Bacon (1909–1992), evoke outright nausea. Bacon's canvases are case studies in the power of the subconscious. He painted the people he saw around him, but his perceptions were of a society disfigured by slaughter. Slabs of meat, dripping in blood, figure prominently. Bacon explained, "When you go into a butcher's shop . . . you can think of the whole horror of life, of one thing living off another."[16]

The terrors of the nuclear age also shaped cultural consciousness in this period. Because figurative painting seemed utterly incapable of capturing the power and terror of the atomic age, the Bomb reinforced the hold of abstract art over the avant-garde. But abstract art itself changed. Before the war, formal geometric compositions predominated. After the war, a type of modernism, Abstract Expressionism, displayed more spontaneous styles. The Abstract Expressionist Jackson Pollock (1912–1956), for example, invented an entirely new way of painting. Placing the canvas on the ground, he moved around and in it, dripping or pouring paint. In Pollock's works (see p. 909), the canvas has no clear center, no focal point. Instead, it disintegrates, like matter itself. As Pollock explained, "New needs need new techniques. . . . The modern painter cannot express his age, the airplane, the atom bomb . . . in the old forms."[17]

ALBERTO GIACOMETTI, *MAN POINTING* (1947) Giacometti's sculptures embodied existentialist anguish. His account of this piece's creation seems to be lifted from a Samuel Beckett play or one of Jean-Paul Sartre's novels: "Wanting to create from memory [the figures] I had seen, to my terror the sculptures became smaller and smaller, they had a likeness only when they were small, yet their dimensions revolted me, and tirelessly I began again, only to end several months later at the same point."

FRANCIS BACON, *FIGURE WITH MEAT,* 1954 Bacon's disturbing images resonated with a European public still struggling with the impact of total war. *Figure with Meat* is one of a series of paintings that Bacon modeled on Diego Velazquez's *Portrait of Pope Innocent X* (1649–1650). By replacing the draperies in Velazquez's masterpiece with slabs of meat, Bacon challenged the solace and authority of traditional religion.

Most people confronted their nuclear fears not in art galleries, but rather in movie theaters and popular fiction. In the movies, various nuclear-spawned horrors, such as giant spiders, ants, and turtles, wreaked weekly havoc on the Western world. Fittingly enough, many of these films were produced in Japan. Throughout the 1950s, nuclear war and the postnuclear struggle for survival also filled the pages of popular fiction. Probably the most important "nuclear" novel, however, confined mention of atomic bombs to a single sentence. In *Lord of the Flies* (1954), British author William Golding (1911–1993) told the simple but brutal story of a group of schoolboys stranded on an island after they flee atomic attack. Their moral deterioration poses basic questions about the meaning of civilization, a question brought to the forefront of Western society by its use of advanced science and technology to obliterate civilian populations during World War II.

CULTURE AND IDEAS IN THE WORLD OF PLENTY In the later 1950s, artists began to turn away from such big questions and to focus instead on the material stuff of everyday existence. Works such as the British artist Richard Hamilton's *Just What Is It That Makes Today's Homes So Different, So Appealing?* (1956) satirized and yet celebrated the plethora of material objects pouring off assembly lines (see p. 910). Hamilton was a leading force in the Independent Group, a loose association of British artists, designers, and architects that explored the "aesthetics of plenty"—the idea that consumer affluence had smashed the barriers between fine art and popular culture. The Independent Group, along with other movements such as "New Realism" in France and "Capitalist Realism" in West Germany, helped shape what became known as **pop art**.

pop art Effort by artists in the 1950s and 1960s both to utilize and to critique the material abundance of post-World War II popular culture.

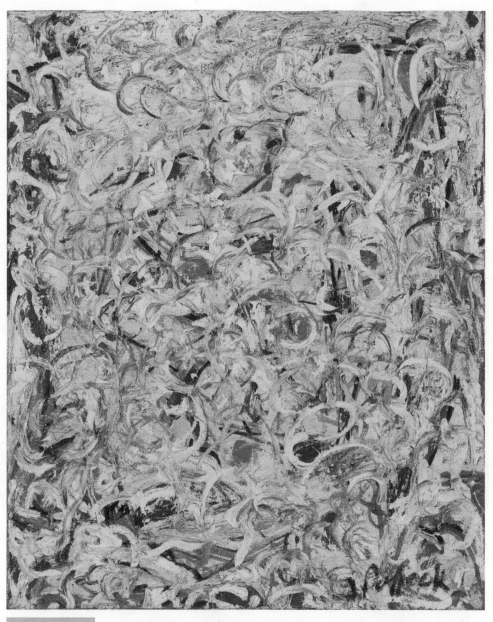

JACKSON POLLOCK, *SHIMMERING SUBSTANCE* (1946) Many of Pollock's postwar works—huge paintings that pulse with power—show an obsession with heat and light, surely no coincidence in the dawn of the nuclear age.

Pop artists dismissed the anguish of Bacon and Giacometti as the concerns of an older generation still mired in World War II. Pop art looked outward rather than inward and focused on the material rather than the spiritual. Pop artists spoke in the vocabulary of mass materialism, relied on mass production and mass marketing, and challenged accepted ideas about the role of art and the artist in Western society. When Gerhard Richter (b. 1932) placed himself in the furniture display of a West German department store and called the resulting "piece" *Living with Pop* (1963) he turned the artist, as well as art, into a commodity, something to be bought and sold just like anything else. In the age of consumption, pop advocates declared, the individual artist's intentions were unimportant, and concepts such as artistic genius were irrelevant.

Similar themes also characterized developments in social thought. Existentialism had elevated the individual as the only source of meaning in an absurd universe. In the late 1950s, however, a new social theory, **structuralism**, pushed the individual off center stage. Structuralism, which French anthropologist Claude Lévi-Strauss

structuralism Influential post-World War II social theory that explored the common structures of language and thought.

909

RICHARD HAMILTON, *JUST WHAT IS IT THAT MAKES TODAY'S HOMES SO DIFFERENT, SO APPEALING?* (1956) British artist Richard Hamilton was one of the leading figures in the pop art movement of the 1950s. The image plays with the consumerism and domesticity that marked the postwar period.

(1908–2009) first introduced to a wide audience, transformed a number of academic disciplines, including literary criticism, political theory, sociology, and history. Lévi-Strauss argued that the stories that people told, whether medieval French peasants or contemporary Londoners, shared "deep structures," repeated patterns such as pairings and oppositions that shape the way individuals perceive the world. The stories themselves—and the storytellers—were unimportant.

SCIENCE AND RELIGION IN AN AGE OF MASS CONSUMPTION At the same time that structuralists depicted the individual as stuck within a cultural and linguistic web, breakthroughs in the biological sciences suggested that perhaps the web lay *inside* the individual. In 1953, the British biologist Francis Crick (1916–2004) and his American colleague James Watson (b. 1928) discovered the structure of DNA, the basic building block of genetic material. Crick and Watson's model of the "double helix," the intertwined spirals of chemical units that, in a sense, issue the instructions for an individual's development, caught the attention of the world. As biologists and geneticists furthered their investigations into human genetic inheritance, they raised exciting yet disturbing possibilities, such as the cloning of living organisms and genetic manipulation. These possibilities added a new dimension to the perennial debate about individual freedom.

Other scientific developments assured human beings more freedom from their physical environment than ever before. Motivated by the Cold War, the space race launched humanity beyond the confines of Earth, culminating in 1969 with American astronaut Neil Armstrong's moon walk. Large-scale production of penicillin transformed ordinary medical care, as did rapid development of vaccines against many childhood killers such as measles. In 1953, the American doctor Jonas Salk announced the first successful clinical trial of a polio vaccine. Blood transfusions became more commonplace, along with the development of organ transplants, following the first successful kidney transplant in Chicago in 1950. Like washing machines and television sets, a long and healthy life suddenly appeared accessible to many people in the West.

While scientists were claiming more control over the physical environment, the organized churches continued to offer spiritual authority and sustenance. Church attendance, which had declined in most Western countries in the interwar period, rose during the 1950s. In the United States between 1942 and 1960, church membership per capita grew faster than at any time since the 1890s. No European nation shared this dramatic religious upsurge. Nevertheless, except in Scandinavia, western Europe experienced a gentle religious revival. In Britain during the 1950s, church membership, Sunday school enrollment, and the numbers of baptisms and religious marriages all increased. In West Germany, the rate of churchgoing rose among Protestants from 1952 until 1967. Throughout Catholic Europe, the vibrancy of Christian Democratic politics reflected the vital position of the Roman Catholic Church in society.

In the 1960s, however, the situation changed as Europeans abandoned the church sanctuary in favor of the department store, the sports stadium, and the sofa in front of the television set. Declining rates of church attendance, a growing number of civil rather than religious marriage ceremonies, and an increased reluctance to obey Church teaching on issues such as premarital sexual relations all pointed to the secularization of European society. By the 1970s, churchgoing rates in both Protestant and Catholic countries were in freefall.

Yet the churches did not remain stagnant during this time of change. A number of Protestant theologians argued that Christianity could maintain its relevance in

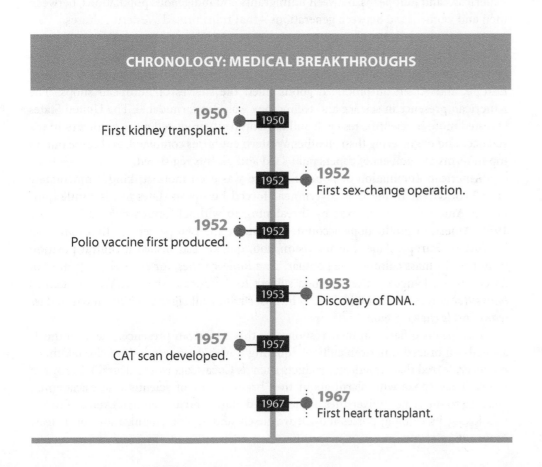

CHRONOLOGY: MEDICAL BREAKTHROUGHS

1950
First kidney transplant.
1950

1952
1952
First sex-change operation.

1952
Polio vaccine first produced.
1952

1953
1953
Discovery of DNA.

1957
CAT scan developed.
1957

1967
1967
First heart transplant.

Vatican II Popular term for the
Second Vatican Council that convened in 1963 and introduced a
series of changes within the
Roman Catholic Church.

this more secular society by adapting the biblical message to a modern context. The
British theologian (and Anglican bishop) John Robinson achieved great notoriety in
1963 when he proclaimed the "death of God." Most of those who jeered at or cheered
for Robinson's statement missed his point—that Christians had to update the language
in which they articulated their faith to make sense in the modern world.

The biggest change occurred in Roman Catholicism. In 1962 the Second Vatican
Council—widely known as **Vatican II**—convened in Rome, the first Catholic council
to meet since 1870. In calling the council, Pope John XXIII (r. 1958–1963) sought to
modernize the Church, a process that, he recognized, would demand "a change in
mentalities, ways of thinking and prejudices, all of which have a long history."[18]

John did not live to see this change in mentalities take place, but his successor
Paul VI (r. 1963–1978) presided over a quiet revolution. The Church emerged from
Vatican II less hierarchical, with local and regional councils sharing more power with
the papacy. For ordinary Catholics, the most striking changes occurred in the worship service, where a number of reforms narrowed the gap between priest and people. The
priest moved behind the altar, so that he could face the congregation; he spoke in the vernacular rather than in Latin; and all worshipers, not only the priest, received the wine at
communion.

Vatican II was less revolutionary in its approach to sexual issues and gender roles.
The council said nothing about homosexuality, reaffirmed the traditional doctrine of
clerical celibacy, and insisted that only men could be ordained as priests. The council left
open the question of birth control; three years later, however, the pope declared contraceptive use to be contrary to Catholic teaching. The issues of clerical celibacy, women's
ordination, and contraceptive use would bedevil the Church for the rest of the century.

Social Encounters in the Age of Affluence

With the prosperity of the postwar years came a series of encounters—between
Americans and Europeans, between immigrants and indigenous populations, between
men and women, and between generations—that transformed Western cultures.

AMERICANIZATION, COCA-COLONIZATION, AND THE GAULLIST PROTEST In the
postwar decades, U.S.-based corporations scattered branch offices throughout western
Europe, and American-produced goods filled the shelves of European shops. The
American presence in science and technology was also formidable. The United States
invested more in scientific research and development, produced more graduates in the
sciences and engineering than all other Western countries combined, and came out on
top in terms of numbers of papers published and patents registered.

American domination of popular culture was even more striking. Immediately
after World War II, the U.S. government forced European states to dismantle quotas on American film imports by threatening to withhold much-needed loans. By
1951, American productions accounted for more than 60 percent of films showing
in western Europe. American television, too, quickly established a central position
in European mass culture. The popular *Lone Ranger* series, for example, appeared in
24 countries. Language itself seemed subject to American takeover. Words such as
babysitter and *comics* entered directly into German, while French children coveted *les
jeans* and *le chewing-gum*.

Europeans differed in their response to this American presence. Many enthusiastically embraced American culture, equating it with openness and freedom. Others,
however, feared that American products such as Coca-Cola would degrade European
tastes. They spoke with alarm about the "brain drain" of scientists and academics
heading to the richer universities of the United States and argued that even as Europe
was losing its colonial possessions, it was itself undergoing colonization, or at least
"coca-colonization."[19]

One of the most powerful voices protesting "coca-colonization" belonged to Charles De Gaulle, France's president throughout the 1960s. De Gaulle combined anticommunism and traditional social values with a commitment to a strong state and centralized direction of the economy. Perhaps most of all, **Gaullism** championed France and Frenchness. In De Gaulle's imagination, France was "like the princess in the fairy stories or the Madonna in the frescoes, as dedicated to an exalted and exceptional destiny . . . France cannot be France without greatness."[20]

De Gaulle did not sympathize with the Soviet Union, but he believed that American "coca-colonization" posed the more immediate threat to the French way of life. Taken in 1960 to view a new highway in California, De Gaulle gazed somberly at the sight of cars weaving in and out on a traffic cloverleaf and commented, "I have the impression that all this will end very badly."[21] To reduce American influence in Europe, and thus to restore France to its rightful position of grandeur and glory, De Gaulle pursued independent foreign and military policies. He extended diplomatic recognition to communist China, made a state visit to Moscow, and withdrew French forces from NATO command (although France remained formally a part of the NATO alliance). In 1960 France exploded its own atomic bomb.

Like De Gaulle, Europeans across the political spectrum feared that their countries might become secondhand versions of the United States, yet the cultural history of this era was one of reciprocal encounters rather than one-way Americanization. Europeans consumed American products with gusto, but in the process they adapted these products to suit their own needs. In the late 1950s, for example, four young working-class men from the northern British seaport of Liverpool latched on to the new American rock-and-roll music, mixed in their own regional musical styles, and transformed popular music not only in Europe, but also in the United States. The impact of the Beatles testified to the power of European culture to remake American cultural products. Even McDonald's, when it arrived in European cities in the 1960s, made subtle changes to the composition of its fast food to appeal to the differing tastes of the new markets.

IMMIGRATION AND ETHNIC DIVERSITY Rising numbers of immigrants who brought with them new and, in many cases, non-Western cultural traditions also transformed European societies during this era. Two developments—decolonization and economic prosperity—explain the upsurge in immigration. With the collapse of European imperial control, white settlers retreated to their country of origin, and colonial "losers"— indigenous groups that had allied with the colonial powers—fled because they feared persecution and discrimination. At the same time, the soaring economies of western Europe created a voracious demand for labor that governments and businesses sought to fill by recruiting outside their state borders. By the beginning of the 1970s, approximately nine million immigrants had settled in western Europe. Half of these came from the less prosperous Mediterranean states of Portugal, Spain, Italy, and Greece, and the other half from Turkey, Yugoslavia, and countries in Asia, Africa, and the Caribbean.

These workers did the dirtiest, most dangerous, least desirable jobs. They worked the night shifts, emptied the bedpans, dug the ditches, and cleaned the toilets. They lived in substandard housing, often confined to isolated dormitories or inner-city slums, and accepted low, often illegally low, pay rates. The reason they did so is starkly presented in Table 28.1. Despite racial discrimination and economic exploitation, western Europe offered greater economic opportunities than were available in the immigrants' homelands.

The majority of the early immigrants were single men. They tended to see themselves, and were seen by their host countries, as "guestworkers," temporary laborers who would earn money and then return home to their native lands. From the 1970s on, however, families began to join these men, and a second generation of "immigrants" was born. This generation changed the face of Europe.

Gaullism The political ideology associated with twentieth-century French political leader Charles De Gaulle. Gaullism combined the advocacy of a strong, centralized state with social conservatism.

TABLE **28.1** ANNUAL PER CAPITA GROSS NATIONAL PRODUCT: MID-1960s

Pakistan	$125
Jamaica	$520
Turkey	$353
Spain	$822
Italy	$1,272
Britain	$1,977
France	$2,324

SOURCE: Leslie Page Moch, *Moving Europeans: Migration in Western Europe Since 1650* (Bloomington: Indiana University Press, 1992), 177.

The emergence of urban ethnic subcultures enlivened European cultures and economies (and diets). It also complicated domestic politics and raised challenging questions about the relationship between national and ethnic identity. Racism became more overt, first, because the white settler groups who returned "home" in the wake of decolonization often brought with them hardened racist attitudes and, second, because the presence of nonwhite minority groups, clustered in certain cities, sparked resentment in societies unused to cultural diversity.

THE SECOND SEX? A third area of encounters that shaped postwar western culture was that between men and women. In 1949, the French writer Simone de Beauvoir (1908–1986) published *The Second Sex.* In this influential critique of gender divisions in Western industrial society, de Beauvoir argued that women remained the "second sex"—that despite political and legal changes, a woman's relationship to men, rather than her own actions or achievements, still defined her. Over the next two decades, the new prosperity pushed women into higher education and the labor force and so, in the long run, worked to undermine the traditional gender roles that de Beauvoir described. In the short run, however, affluence accentuated women's identity as the second sex.

Demographic changes reflected and reinforced postwar domesticity. Marriage rates rose and the marriage age dropped in the postwar years. In the United States between 1940 and 1957, the fertility rate rose by 50 percent. Europe experienced a baby "boomlet" rather than a baby boom with birth rates rising in the late 1940s but dropping in the 1950s.

By exalting women's maternal identity, both religion and popular culture provided a potent ideology for these demographic changes. The Roman Catholic Church of the 1950s placed renewed emphasis on Mary, the paragon of motherhood. Pope Pius XII (r. 1939–1958) particularly encouraged the growth of devotion to Mary. He proclaimed in 1950 that Mary had ascended bodily into heaven (the Doctrine of the Assumption) and designated 1954 as the Year of Mary. This Marian devotion encouraged women to regard motherhood as a holy calling. Popular culture reinforced this religious message, with its glossy images of what families should look like and how they should interact. In television programs and in the articles and advertisements of women's magazines, the woman stayed at home, presiding over an expanding array of household machines that, in theory, reduced her housework burden and freed her to focus on the satisfactions of motherhood.

Cold War concerns also accentuated the Western woman's domestic role. First, anticommunist propaganda hailed domesticity as a sign of Western superiority by contrasting the favorable lot of Western women to their Soviet counterparts, who combined their domestic duties with full-time outside employment, often in jobs involving heavy manual labor, and with the tiresome task of lining up for hours each day to purchase scarce goods. Second, the nuclear age made the nuclear family seem all the more important. Feeling increasingly helpless in a superpower-dominated world on the brink of nuclear annihilation, Europeans tended to withdraw for shelter to family life.

For some women, this shelter was more like a prison. In *The Feminine Mystique* (1963), the American journalist Betty Friedan (1921–2006) identified what she called "the problem that had no name," a crisis of identity and purpose among middle-class, educated women confined in the role of housewife and mother. The research of British sociologist Hannah Gavron (1936–1965) supported Friedan's argument. In *The Captive Wife* (1966), Gavron used interviews and other sociological data to explore "the conflicts of housebound mothers." She asked, "Have all the great changes in the position of women in the last one hundred and fifty years come to nothing?" A 29-year-old wife and mother of two young sons, Gavron committed suicide the year before her work was published.

Whether a nightmare or a dream, the domestic ideal remained removed from the reality of many women's lives in the postwar era. In the poorer social classes, women by necessity continued to work outside the home, as they always had. At the same time, the new culture of consumption demanded that many women, clinging precariously to middle-class status, take on waged employment to pay for the ever-expanding list of household necessities.

A new pattern of employment emerged that reconciled renewed domesticity with the needs of expanding economies and ambitious consumers. Increasingly, single women worked until they married. Many continued to do so until the first child arrived and resumed paid employment after the last child had left home or at least started school. This work was regarded, however, as secondary to their main job—the making of a home and the rearing of children. Part-time employment, with lower wages and few or no benefits, expanded accordingly. Everywhere pay rates for men and women remained unequal.

THE PROTEST ERA The unprecedented prosperity of the West in this era permitted a dramatic expansion of higher education systems. By the later 1960s, these universities became the center of powerful protests as political demonstrations exploded in almost every Western country and in the developing nations as well. In France, a student demonstration blossomed into a full-scale social revolt. Within a few days, eight million French men and women were on strike. "Paris '68" came to symbolize the political and social discontent of many in the West, particularly the youth, during these years.

Much of this discontent focused on the **New Left** argument that ordinary people, even in democratic societies, possessed little power. Appalled by the inhumanity of Stalinism, New Leftists differed from the "old" Left in their suspicion of the state. New Left thinkers such as the German philosopher Herbert Marcuse (1898–1979) warned that expanding state power threatened the individuality and independence of the ordinary citizen. They argued that debate might seem open, but that experts and elites, not ordinary people, made the actual choices. Hence, the protesters demanded "participatory" rather than parliamentary democracy, the revitalization of citizenship through active participation in decision making.

New Left Left-wing political and cultural movement that emerged in the late 1950s and early 1960s; it sought to develop a form of socialism that rejected the overcentralization, authoritarianism, and inhumanity of Stalinism.

PARIS, 1968. *La chienlit* means masquerade or carnival, a time when rules are lifted. After protests erupted in Paris and across France in 1968, General Charles De Gaulle appeared on television. In a scatological play on words, he declaimed *"La réforme, oui. La chie-en-lit, non,"* literally translated as "Reform, yes, crap in bed, no." De Gaulle thus dismissed the protests as both a meaningless carnival and as something comparable to human excrement. The protesters picked up on De Gaulle's phrase, reverted back to the original *la chienlit*, and, under an image of De Gaulle's famous profile, proclaimed, "The carnival (and crap)—it's him!"

Discarding orthodox political solutions went hand-in-hand with overturning traditional social rules. In their demand for "liberation," the students focused as much on cultural as on economic and political issues. As behaviors labeled immoral or bohemian in the 1950s became commonplace—for example, couples living together before marriage or individuals engaging in sexual relationships with a variety of partners—commentators began to talk about a sexual revolution.

The protests of the later 1960s were also linked to the wider context of decolonization and the Cold War. Protesters identified their struggle for more open politics with colonial independence movements. Rejecting both Soviet-style communism and free-market capitalism, protesters turned for inspiration to the newly emerging nations of Latin America and Asia. Seeking to break free from the confines of the Cold War, they fiercely criticized American involvement in Vietnam, in which they believed the United States served not as "the leader of the free world," but rather as an imperialist oppressor.

CONCLUSION

New Definitions, New Divisions

When Soviet tanks rolled through the streets of Budapest in 1956, they flattened not only the Hungarian Revolution, but also any illusions about the democratic nature of Soviet-style communism. Yet the hope that the communist system could be reformed, that Marx's original concern for social justice and political equality could be reclaimed, remained—until 12 years later when the tanks rolled again in an eastern European city. The crushing of the Prague Spring destroyed any hope of a democratic eastern Europe under Soviet domination.

In contrast, democracy took firm root in western Europe during the postwar era, even in nations with anti-democratic cultural traditions such as West Germany and Italy. Yet in 1968, protesters in Paris and in cities throughout the world challenged the easy linkage of "the West" with democracy. They pointed out that the increasing scale and complexity of industrial society deprived ordinary people of opportunities for genuine participation in political decision making. And they pointed to the way that Cold War divisions superseded democratic commitments. Within the Cold War context, "the West" sometimes seemed to mean simply "anti-Soviet."

By the early 1970s, the sharp bipolarities of West versus East had begun to break down. Over the next three decades, economic crisis, combined with revolutionary changes in eastern European and Soviet affairs, would reshape the contemporary world. By the early 1990s, the Cold War was over and nationalist conflicts, often fueled by vicious ethnic and religious hatreds, once again played front and center after 20 years of being upstaged by superpower hostilities.

MAKING CONNECTIONS

1. Was the Cold War inevitable? If so, why? If not, what event constituted the "point of no return" and why?
2. How did consumerism structure Western economies, culture, and politics in the 1950s and 1960s?

TAKING IT FURTHER

For suggested readings, see page R-1.

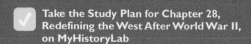
Chapter Review

A Dubious Peace, 1945–1949

28.1 Why and how did the world step from World War II to the Cold War?

A common enemy rather than shared aims cemented the alliance of the Soviet Union with the Western democracies. Differences over the political settlement of eastern and central Europe, particularly the borders of Poland and the division of Germany, strained the alliance, as did Stalin's murderous policies in the areas under Soviet control. The Truman Doctrine, the Marshall Plan, and the formation of NATO and the Warsaw Pact all marked key steps in the outbreak of the Cold War.

The West and the World: Decolonization and the Cold War

28.2 What was the impact of decolonization and the Cold War on the global balance of power?

Although European imperial powers emerged from World War II determined to hold onto their overseas territories, the economic and political costs proved too great. Already by the late 1940s, decolonization signaled a contraction of European global power. At the same time, however, Cold War rivalries increased Soviet and American intervention around the world, as events such as the Korean War, the Suez Crisis, and the Vietnam War illustrated.

The Soviet Union and Eastern Europe in the 1950s and 1960s

28.3 What patterns characterized the history of the Soviet Union and eastern Europe after the death of Stalin?

In an effort to stabilize political life and accelerate economic growth, Nikita Khrushchev initiated de-Stalinization, an effort at limited decentralization and the restoration of some civil liberties. Khrushchev's reform efforts shuddered to a halt in 1964, when he was removed from power. Economic stagnation and renewed political persecution characterized the Brezhnev years. In eastern Europe, the crushing of the Hungarian Revolution in 1956 signaled the sharp limits of de-Stalinization, a lesson reinforced in 1968 when the reform movement known as the Prague Spring in Czechoslovakia was defeated.

The West: Consensus, Consumption, and Culture

28.4 What patterns characterized the history of western Europe in the 1950s and 1960s?

The artistic shift from existentialism and Abstract Expressionism to Pop Art reflected the wider western move from austerity into affluence, as consumerism became a way of life throughout western Europe and the United States. This was also a period marked by political stability, founded on the social democratic consensus, and by efforts at European economic unification through the Common Market. Prosperity and stability attracted immigrants; by the 1970s many European societies were well on their way to becoming multi-colored, multi-cultural societies.

Chapter Time Line

1945 Potsdam Conference.

1945

1947 Truman Doctrine announced; Marshall Plan announced; India, Pakistan, and Burma achieve independence from Britain.

1947

1948 Split between Yugoslavia's communist leader Tito and Stalin, Stalinist terror throughout eastern Europe widened; Soviet blockade of West Berlin, Berlin Airlift; State of Israel established.

1948

1950 Outbreak of the Korean War.

1950

1954 Defeat of French forces in Indochina; partition of Vietnam; beginning of Franco-Algerian War.

1954

1956 Khrushchev's "Secret Speech," de-Stalinization accelerates; unrest in Poland results in new regime under Gomulka; Hungarian Revolution crushed by Soviet forces.

1956

1957 Formation of EEC (Common Market).

1957

1961 Berlin Wall built.

1961

1962 Vatican II convenes; Cuban Missile Crisis.

1962

1968 Protests in Paris; Prague Spring crushed.

1968

917

29

The West in the Contemporary Era: New Encounters and Transformations

On the evening of November 9, 1989, East German border guards at the Berlin Wall watched nervously as thousands of East Berliners crowded in front of them and demanded to be allowed into West Berlin. This demand was extraordinary: In the 28 years that the Berlin Wall had stood, some 200 people had been shot trying to cross from east to west. But the autumn of 1989 was no ordinary time. A reformist regime had emerged in the Soviet Union and proclaimed that eastern European governments could no longer rely on the Red Army to crush domestic dissent. Poland and Hungary were in the process of replacing communist governments with pluralist parliamentary systems. And in East Germany, over one million disaffected citizens had joined illegal protest demonstrations.

In response to this overwhelming public pressure, the East German government had decided to relax the requirements for obtaining an exit visa to visit West Germany. But at a press conference on the morning of November 9, the East Berlin Communist Party boss

🔍 View the **Closer Look** Collapse of the Berlin Wall

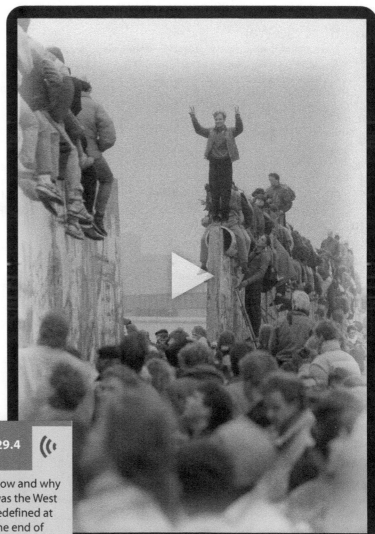

AND THE WALL CAME TUMBLING DOWN In the weeks after the opening of the Berlin Wall on November 9, Berliners from both East and West appropriated this once forbidden zone as their own space for celebration.

LEARNING OBJECTIVES

29.1 🔊	29.2 🔊	29.3 🔊	29.4 🔊
How did developments in the 1970s and 1980s de-stabilize post-World War II national and international structures?	What factors explain not only the outbreak but also the success of the revolutions of 1989–1991?	What were the consequences of the revolutions of 1989–1990 for the societies of eastern Europe?	How and why was the West redefined at the end of the twentieth century and the beginning of the twenty-first?

🔊 Listen to Chapter 29 on MyHistoryLab

Watch the Video Series on MyHistoryLab

Learn about some key topics related to this chapter with the *MyHistoryLab Video Series: Key Topics in Western Civilization*

Gunter Schabowski stated, wrongly, that anyone who wanted to head to the West could obtain an automatic exit visa at the border. As huge crowds gathered at the checkpoints that dotted the Berlin Wall, the border guards had no idea what to do. Panicked, they opened the gates. While television cameras broadcast the scene to an astonished world, tens of thousands of East Berliners walked, ran, and danced across the border that had for so long literally and symbolically divided West from East. Elated with their new freedom and energized with a sense of power and possibility, they jumped upon the Wall. An instrument of coercion and division became a platform for partying. Within a few days, and again without any official approval, ordinary Germans, equipped with hammers and chisels, began to dismantle the Wall erected almost three decades earlier.

The fall of the Berlin Wall has come to symbolize the dramatic events that closed the twentieth century: the collapse of communist regimes throughout eastern Europe, the end of the Cold War, the disintegration of the Soviet Union, and the onset of civil war in Yugoslavia and in many formerly Soviet regions. In the subsequent decades, governments and ordinary people—not only in Europe but across the globe—struggled to build new structures to suit the transformed geopolitical landscape.

What, then, were the causes and consequences of these developments? And what were their implications for Western identity—and for the future of Western civilization?

Economic Stagnation and Political Change: The 1970s and 1980s

29.1 How did developments in the 1970s and 1980s destabilize post-World War II national and international structures?

The 1970s and 1980s saw the post-World War II political settlement, in national and international terms, begin to collapse. The stark clarity—the "Them versus Us"—of the Cold War grew more opaque at the same time that economic crisis widened divisions within Western societies and eroded the social democratic political consensus.

A More Uncertain Era

In the early 1970s, the West entered a new era. **Détente**, the effort to stabilize superpower relations through negotiations and arms control, shifted the Cold War status quo while the easy affluence of the postwar period abruptly ended. At the same time, an upsurge in terrorism unsettled western European societies. With its dramatic rejection of the processes of democratic decision making, terrorism challenged some of the most basic assumptions of the postwar order in the West.

THE ERA OF DÉTENTE West German diplomacy caused the first shift in Cold War relations. In 1969 the West Berlin mayor and Social Democratic Party (SPD) leader Willy

détente During the 1970s, a period of lessened Cold War hostilities and greater reliance on negotiation and compromise.

Brandt (1913–1992) became chancellor. For the first time in its history, West Germany had a government not led by a Christian Democrat. Brandt proceeded to implement a new *Ostpolitik* or "Eastern policy"—the opening of diplomatic and economic relations between West Germany and the Soviet Union and its satellite states. Ostpolitik reached its climax when East and West Germany recognized the legitimacy of each other's existence in 1972 and both Germanys entered the United Nations in 1973.

Economic pressures led the leaders of the superpowers to embrace a much wider version of Ostpolitik: détente. By the end of the 1960s, the Soviet and the American economies were stagnating. With both states spending colossal sums on nuclear weapons, their leaders looked for a new approach to the Cold War. Thus, in November 1969 Soviet and American negotiators began the Strategic Arms Limitation Talks (SALT). Signed in 1972, the agreement froze the existing weapons balance. SALT left the superpowers with sufficient nuclear weaponry to destroy the globe several times over, but it helped slow the armaments spiral and ease Cold War tensions.

Détente also extended to U.S. relations with the other great communist power: China. In 1971 President Richard Nixon (1913–1994) announced the lifting of travel and trade restrictions with China and then visited China himself. "East versus West" had formed a basic building block of international relations throughout the 1950s and 1960s. In the era of détente, however, the shape of international politics became more fluid.

ECONOMIC CRISIS IN THE WEST The economic outlook also blurred in this era as the 1970s brought an unprecedented combination of high inflation and high unemployment rates. Commentators labeled this new reality **stagflation**—the escalating prices of an overheated economy combined with the joblessness of economic stagnation. Between 1974 and 1976 the average annual growth rate within western European nations dropped to zero.

stagflation Term coined in the 1970s to describe an economy troubled by both high inflation and high unemployment rates.

War and oil helped create this economic crisis. In October 1973, the Yom Kippur War began when Egyptian and Syrian armies attacked Israel. In retaliation for American assistance to Israel, the oil-producing Arab states in OPEC (the Organization of Petroleum Exporting Countries) imposed an embargo on sales to the United States and quintupled the price of a barrel of oil. In 1979 political revolution in Iran doubled the price again. These two "oil crises" vastly accelerated the inflationary spiral.

Two other factors also contributed to the economic crisis. First, in 1973 President Nixon acted to defend the weakening dollar by letting it "float." Market forces rather than fixed exchange rates now determined the dollar's value against other currencies. This decision gutted the Bretton Woods Agreement, which had governed international economic affairs since World War II (see Chapter 28), and introduced a less regulated, more volatile economic era. In the two decades after the collapse of Bretton Woods, 69 countries experienced serious banking crises as currency speculators destabilized national economies and the annual economic growth rates of the developing nations fell by one-third.

A second factor in the economic crisis of the 1970s was international competition as Asian, South American, and Latin American economies industrialized. Because Western societies possessed a politicized workforce that demanded relatively high wages and extensive social services, manufacturing firms began to move south and east to take advantage of the lack of labor regulation and protection in the developing world.

CONSEQUENCES OF THE CRISIS As the economic pie appeared smaller, competition for slices increased. The 1970s saw a resurgence of industrial unrest. For example, conflict with unions brought down three successive British governments in a decade. Throughout the West images of picketing workers, often fighting with police, dominated televised news broadcasts.

Racial conflict also escalated, with the nine million immigrants residing in northern and western Europe making easy targets for those individuals and groups who sought someone to blame for their economic hardships. By 1975 West Germany, France, the Netherlands, Britain, Belgium, Sweden, and Switzerland had all banned further immigration; ironically, this legislation actually increased the size of immigrant communities. Foreign workers scrambled to get into western Europe before the doors shut, and those already established hastened to bring in family members. By 1991, 25 percent of the inhabitants of France were either immigrants or the children or grandchildren of immigrants.

The resulting encounters among peoples of different religious and cultural traditions transformed European societies. In Britain, for example, Afro-Caribbean styles of dress and music radically reshaped white working-class youth culture, while the growing southeast Asian community injected new flavors into the British diet.

Yet the European tendency, dominant since the nineteenth century, to identify "nation" not with a set of ideas (what we call "civic nationalism") but rather with race or ethnicity ("ethnic nationalism"), complicated the integration of the new residents into the wider national community. Hence, British journalists in the 1980s often described an individual born in Britain to British citizenship as a "third-generation immigrant," a label that revealed the "whiteness" of popular notions of British identity.

But at least in Britain, as well as in France, immigrants could become (or already were) legal citizens. In contrast, in West Germany, Switzerland, and the Scandinavian countries, immigrants remained "foreign," with no chance of obtaining citizenship. Thus, their children grew up in a society in which they had no political rights. These "foreigners" experienced widespread discrimination in education, housing, and employment.

THE TURN TO TERRORISM As we saw in the last chapter, the 1960s witnessed a wave of student protests across much of the world. In the 1970s, frustrated with their failure to effect real change through protest and persuasion, a minority of student activists turned to terror. The Weathermen in the United States, the Red Brigades in Italy, and Baader-Meinhof in West Germany all dived underground and resorted to bombings, assassinations, and abductions in an effort to weaken the structures of Western capitalism. In Italy, a terrorist culture emerged, with approximately 2,000 acts of terrorism committed each year during the 1970s, including the Red Brigade's dramatic kidnapping, and subsequent murder, of the Christian Democratic Party leader and former prime minister Aldo Moro in 1978.

Left-wing student groups were not the only groups to embrace the politics of the bullet and the bomb in the 1970s. Nationalism also provided fertile soil for terrorism's growth. The first confirmed killing by the Basque separatist group ETA (*Euskadi Ta Askatasuna*—"Basque Homeland and Freedom") occurred in 1968, the opening move in what became a four-decades-long campaign of terror in Spain that claimed over 800 lives. In Northern Ireland, "the Troubles" began in the early 1970s. The Irish Republican Army (IRA) sought to join the province to independent Ireland; its Unionist opponents fought to maintain the union with Britain. Both regarded innocent civilians as prime targets.

Conflict in the Middle East also bled over into western Europe in the 1970s. Palestinian nationalist groups turned to hijackings and bombings in an effort to influence international diplomacy. In 1972, at the Olympic Games in Munich, West Germany, one such group murdered 11 members of the Israeli Olympic team. The "Munich massacre" not only made an absolute mockery of Olympic internationalism, it also persuaded many of the fragility of the postwar order.

The End of Political Consensus in the West

In this new and more uncertain era, the postwar political consensus crumbled. Two offshoots of the protests of the 1960s—new feminism and environmentalism—demanded a reorientation of social democratic politics, while New Conservatives rejected social democratic fundamentals.

new feminism Reemergence of the feminist movement in the 1970s.

NEW CHALLENGES AND NEW IDENTITIES: NEW FEMINISM New feminism (also called "Second Wave feminism") emerged directly out of the student protest movement of the 1960s, when female activists grew frustrated with their limited role—"We cook while the men talk of revolution."[1] Their efforts to liberate women from political and cultural limits gave birth to an international feminist movement.

Although new feminists worked for the election of female candidates and other such political goals, they refused to confine their efforts to parliamentary politics. Asserting that "the personal is political," new feminists attacked beauty pageants, critiqued the fashion industry, and demanded equal access for girls to sporting funds and facilities. They also sought to outlaw spousal rape and to legalize abortion. Abortions became legal first in northern Europe: in Britain in 1967, in Denmark in 1970. Catholic Europe followed: In Italy abortions became legally available in 1978, France followed suit in 1979.

New feminism extended its critique of gender inequalities to the economic and educational spheres. Feminists demanded equal pay for equal work and greater access for women to professional opportunities. They pressed for more generous parental leave policies, family allowances, and child care provisions. With women accounting for approximately half of the university students in many Western countries, feminists also began to alter the content of the curriculum. Challenging the biases that had regarded women's contributions as irrelevant and women's lives as insignificant, feminists brought to light the "hidden history" of women.

NEW CHALLENGES AND NEW IDENTITIES: ENVIRONMENTALISM Environmentalists added their voice to the political cacophony of the 1970s and 1980s. At the heart of environmentalism was the idea of natural limits, often conceptualized as "Spaceship Earth," the vision of the planet as a "single spaceship, without unlimited reservoirs of anything."[2] This vision led environmentalists to question the fundamental structures of industrial economies (capitalist and communist), particularly their inherent emphasis on "more, bigger, faster, now." The movement argued that quantitative measures of economic growth (such as the GNP) failed to factor in environmental destruction and social dislocation and that in many contexts, "small is beautiful."

Read the Document

Marshall Sahlins, "The Original Affluent Society"

THE NEW FEMINISM In 1971, women in Paris hit the streets to demand the legalization of abortion and free access to information about contraceptives.

The environmentalist movement's concern with ecological sustainability helped create "Green" political parties. **Green politics** drew on two other sources: new feminism and the New Left. The Greens contended that the degradation of the natural environment stemmed from the same root as discrimination against women—an obsession with physical power and an unwillingness to tear down hierarchical structures. Green politics also championed the key New Leftist goal of participatory democracy (see Chapter 28) and so articulated a basic challenge to the political status quo: "We are neither left nor right; we are in front." By the late 1980s Green Parties had sprouted in 15 western European countries. The Greens were the most successful in West Germany, where they sat in the legislature from 1983 and formed an important voting bloc.

THE NEW CONSERVATIVES Discontented by the economic crisis and social unrest of the 1970s, voters throughout the West looked for new answers. In Spain, Portugal, and Greece, they turned to socialist parties. Throughout most of western Europe and in the United States, however, **New Conservatism** dominated political society. Three leaders epitomized the New Conservatism: the Republican Ronald Reagan in the United States (1911–2004), the Christian Democrat Helmut Kohl in West Germany (b. 1930), and the Conservative Margaret Thatcher in Britain (1925–2013). New Conservatives rejected the postwar emphasis on social improvement in favor of individual achievement. They argued that rising social expenditures, funded by rising taxes, bore the blame for surging inflation and declining economic growth rates. As Kohl demanded during his 1983 campaign, "Less state, more market; fewer collective burdens, more personal performance; fewer encrusted structures, more mobility, self-initiative, and competition."

The New Conservative agenda included lifting regulations on business, privatizing nationalized or state-owned industries, and reining in the welfare state. Most dramatically, New Conservatives abandoned the central feature of the postwar social democratic consensus: the conviction that the state has the responsibility to ensure full employment. By imposing high interest rates on their economies, New Conservative leaders such as Thatcher lowered damaging double-digit inflation rates. But high interest rates hurt domestic manufacturing and led to rising unemployment numbers. In Britain, 13 percent of the workforce was unemployed by 1984. In West Germany, too, Kohl's policies of holding down taxes and government expenditures accompanied unemployment rates over 9 percent in the mid-1980s.

THE END OF DÉTENTE Like the emergence of New Conservatism, rising superpower tensions accelerated the breakdown of the post-World War II political consensus within Western societies. Those tensions had appeared to be receding in the early 1970s as the leaders of the superpowers embraced détente. In 1975 representatives of 32 European states, Canada, the United States, and the Soviet Union signed the **Helsinki Accords**, which ratified existing European borders, agreed to the joint notification of major military exercises (to reduce the chances of accidental nuclear war), and promised to safeguard human rights.

The Helsinki Accords came about because of détente—yet they helped destroy it. Eastern European and Soviet dissidents used the Helsinki human rights clauses to publicize the abuses committed by their governments and to demand justice. Dissident activities expanded throughout the Soviet bloc, as did efforts at repression. When U.S. president Jimmy Carter took office in 1976, he placed human rights at the center of his foreign policy. Carter's approach infuriated Soviet leaders. Détente finally died in December 1979, when Soviet troops invaded Afghanistan. Calling the invasion "the most serious threat to peace since the Second World War," Carter warned that if the Soviets moved toward the Middle East, he would use nuclear weapons.

The election of New Conservatives such as Thatcher in 1979 and Reagan in 1980 intensified the rejection of détente and the renewal of the Cold War. Reagan labeled

Green politics A new style of politics and set of political ideas resulting from the confluence of environmentalism, feminism, and New Left politics.

New Conservatism Political ideology that emerged at the end of the 1970s combining the free market approach of nineteenth-century liberalism with social conservatism.

Helsinki Accords Signed by representatives of 32 European states, Canada, the United States, and the Soviet Union in 1975; often regarded as the apex of détente.

NEW CONSERVATIVES AT WORK British Prime Minister Margaret Thatcher and German Chancellor Helmut Kohl address the press after a meeting in London in 1988. Although they shared many New Conservative assumptions, the two leaders did not like each other, as their body language reveals.

(( )) 📖 Read the Document

Margaret Thatcher, The Iron Lady Speech

the Soviet Union the "Evil Empire"—a reference to the popular *Star Wars* film series released in the 1970s—and revived the anticommunist attitudes and rhetoric of the 1950s. Thatcher strongly supported Reagan's decision to accelerate the arms buildup begun by Carter. Her hard-line anticommunism won her the nickname "Iron Lady" from Soviet policymakers.

Revolution in the East

29.2 What factors explain not only the outbreak but also the success of the revolutions of 1989–1991?

Between 1989 and 1991, revolution engulfed eastern Europe and the Soviet Union and set in motion a series of breathtaking changes: Soviet control over eastern Europe ended, the Cold War came to an abrupt halt, and the Soviet Union itself ceased to exist. Mikhail Gorbachev (1931–1991), appointed Soviet Communist Party secretary in 1985, played a pivotal role in these events. But Gorbachev did not control the story. Ordinary people developed their own plot lines. What the Czech dissident (and future president) Václav Havel called "the power of the powerless" proved powerful indeed.

The Crisis of Legitimacy in the East

While Western countries in the 1970s struggled with stagflation, the Soviet Union posted record-breaking production figures. But Soviet statistics ignored the quality of goods produced, the actual demand for a product, or the cost of producing it. Soviet leaders boasted that they had completed the heavy industrial expansion planned by Khrushchev in the early 1960s; microchips now counted for more than iron ore, however, and fiber optics, not steel, buttressed the new modernity. The rigid Soviet command economy could not keep up. By the 1980s, its only growth sectors were oil and vodka—and then the bottom dropped out of the oil market. After peaking in 1981, oil prices began a steady decade-long fall—and so, too, did the Soviet economy.

The Soviet Union's satellite states in eastern Europe also lurched from apparent prosperity into economic crisis during this period. During the 1970s, two factors cushioned eastern Europe from the economic crisis in the West. First, eastern governments could purchase Soviet oil at prices below market value. (In return these states had to sell their own products to the Soviets at similar discounts.) Second, loans from Western banks helped mask fundamental problems such as overcentralization and underproductivity. But in the 1980s, the Soviet Union, struggling with its own faltering economy, began charging higher oil prices at the same time that debt loads overwhelmed eastern European economies.

THE BEGINNING OF THE END: SOLIDARITY Events in Poland indicated the fragility of the communist system and initiated the process that led to the system's collapse. Faced with negative economic growth rates, the Polish government announced in July 1980 a rise in prices for meat and other essentials. Workplace strikes protesting the price increases spread throughout Poland. Then, workers at the Lenin Shipyard in Gdansk, led by a charismatic electrician named Lech Wałęsa (b. 1943), demanded the right to form a trade union independent of communist control. One month later, they did so— **Solidarity** was born. More than a trade union, Solidarity demanded the liberation of political prisoners, an end to censorship, and a rollback of governmental power. Within just a few months, more than 11 million Poles joined Solidarity.

How could Solidarity become such a powerful political and social presence so quickly? The answer rests in the concept of **civil society**: public organizations and activities separate from the state, commerce, or the family. Ranging from church and charitable groups to sports and hobby clubs, from theater companies to rock bands to radio stations, these organizations and activities help create community life—and in such communities, an individual creates his or her own sense of independent identity. In Soviet-style communism, where the state aimed to control not only public life but even private consciousness, such a self-identity, forged outside state control, threatened the entire political system. (See *Encounters and Transformations* in this chapter.)

Solidarity Trade union and political party in Poland that led an unsuccessful effort to reform the Polish communist state in 1981; survived to lead Poland's first non-communist government since World War II in 1989.

civil society Public organizations and activities separate from the state, commerce, or the family that help to create community life and a sense of identity.

THE MOMENT OF SOLIDARITY In August 1980, Lech Walesa addressed Solidarity supporters outside the Lenin Shipyard in Gdansk. Note the picture of Pope John Paul II and the other symbols of Roman Catholicism on the wall below: Throughout the communist era, the Catholic Church served as an important non-communist focus of Polish identity and loyalty.

Encounters and Transformations
Rock and the Velvet Revolution

In September 1968, less than one month after the armies of the Soviet Union and its satellite states crushed the Prague Spring (see Chapter 28), a Czech bass player named Milan Hlavsa formed a rock band. He did not see forming a rock band as a political act. The military invasion and the subsequent political crackdown appalled Hlavsa, but it never occurred to him that he could do anything to change the harsh reality of life in the communist bloc. He simply liked Western rock music (particularly the "psychedelic" music of American rocker Frank Zappa) and wanted to play in a rock band. Yet the encounter between the communist state and the anarchic energy of rock helped undermine communist rule and so contributed to the transformation of eastern Europe.

Hlavsa and his friends called their band "The Plastic People of the Universe" (PPU), after a Frank Zappa song. PPU quickly became popular in Prague, but almost as quickly the band ran into trouble. As part of the post-1968 crackdown, the Czech communist government insisted that musical groups conform to a set of official guidelines governing how, what, and where they performed. PPU refused and, in January 1970, lost its professional license. In the communist system, the state not only controlled broadcasting and recording, but even owned the distribution of musical instruments and electrical equipment. Without a license, PPU lost access to rehearsal and recording space and their instruments as well.

But the band played on by repairing cast-off instruments and constructing amplifiers from old transistor radios. Banned in 1972 from performing in Prague, PPU moved to the countryside. Banned in 1974 from playing anywhere, PPU dove underground. Fans alerted other fans when the band would be playing at some remote farm, while recordings made in houses and garages circulated illegally.

ROCKING THE BLOC In 1977, the Plastic People of the Universe play an illegal concert in Václav Havel's farmhouse.

During this period PPU became more than just a rock band. It stood at the center of what manager Ivan Jirous labeled the "Second Culture." An alternative to the official communist "First Culture," the "Second Culture" comprised musicians, fans, artists, writers, and anyone else who sought to carve out a space of individuality and integrity in a society based on conformity and lies.

On March 17, 1976, the Secret Police arrested 27 musicians, including every member of PPU. Six months later rock music went on trial. In response to international protests, the Czech government released most of the 27 rockers. But Jirous and PPU's saxophonist, Vratislav Brabenec, as well as two musicians from other bands, were found guilty of "organized disturbance of the peace" and sentenced to between 8 and 18 months in prison.

The sentence infuriated Václav Havel, a well-known playwright and an ardent Frank Zappa fan. After the trial, Havel opened his farmhouse to PPU for illegal concerts and recording sessions. More important, he decided to challenge communism openly. On January 1, 1977, Havel and other artists and intellectuals announced the formation of Charter 77 to publicize human rights abuses under communism. Over the next decade many Charter members, including Havel, spent time in prison. Yet, by calling the state to account for its crimes, Charter 77 helped weaken the communist regime. When revolution came in 1989, that regime toppled with astounding ease. PPU had split up two years before but one of the first individuals that President Václav Havel invited to the new free Czechoslovakia was an aging psychedelic rocker named Frank Zappa.

For Discussion

Imagine that the post-1968 Communist government in Czechoslovakia simply ignored the PPU. Would events have unfolded any differently? Why or why not?

In Poland, however, communist control had never entirely destroyed civil society, in part because of the key role of the Roman Catholic Church. Participation in the Church had long been a way for Poles to express not only their religious faith but also their Polishness—an identity not controlled by the communist government. The power of this Catholic identity became clear in 1979, when Pope John Paul II (r. 1978–2005) visited Poland. This visit marked the first time any pope traveled to a communist country—but John Paul II was not just any pope. Born Karol Wojtyla, he was the first non-Italian pope since 1523 and the first Polish pope ever. Twelve million people—one-third of the Polish population—greeted the pope during his visit. Many Solidarity members testified to the importance of this visit in empowering them to challenge the communist order.

Solidarity's growing popularity soon threatened communist control of Poland. In December 1981 Prime Minister Wojciech Jaruzelski declared martial law and arrested more than 10,000 Solidarity members (including Wałęsa). Like the Hungarian Revolution in 1956 and the Prague Spring of 1968, Solidarity seemed to be one more noble but defeated protest in eastern Europe.

 Read the Document

Lech Wałęsa, "Nobel Lecture"

But Solidarity refused to be defeated. It remained a political presence and a moral force in Polish society throughout the 1980s. Solidarity members met in small groups, published newspapers, and organized election boycotts. At the same time, activists throughout Hungary, Czechoslovakia, East Germany, and the Soviet Union itself drew on Solidarity for inspiration and practical lessons in resistance.

Before 1989 no other eastern European state experienced a protest movement as dramatic as Solidarity, yet throughout much of the region two important developments marked the later 1970s and the 1980s. First, economic hardship fed widespread political alienation and a deepening longing for radical change. And second, activists and ordinary people worked to create the structures of civil society.

ENVIRONMENTAL PROTEST For many eastern Europeans, environmental activism helped create at least the beginnings of civil society. For decades, the conquest of nature had been a key part of communist ideology: "We cannot wait for favors from nature; our task is to take from her."[3] Governments throughout the Soviet bloc ignored the most basic environmental precautions, dumping untreated sewage and nuclear waste into lakes and rivers and pumping poisons into the air. But because communist officials regarded the natural environment as insignificant, they tended to view environmentalist protest as unimportant, a "safe" outlet for popular frustration. Thus, by the later 1970s, many Soviet and eastern European citizens had joined environmentalist groups. Environmental activism worked like a termite infestation, nibbling away at communist structures. In Hungary, public outrage over a Czech-Hungarian collaboration to dam the Danube River resulted in the formation of environmentalist organizations that encouraged Hungarians to question not only the Danube project, but also the priorities and policies of the entire communist system.

Environmentalism also fueled nationalist protest among the non-Russian peoples within the Soviet Union. The various national and ethnic groups of the Soviet empire watched their forests disappear, their lakes dry up, and their ancient cities bulldozed as a result of decisions made in far-away Moscow by men they regarded as foreigners—as *Russians* rather than *comrades* or fellow Soviets. By the 1980s, for example, with schools in Latvia forced to issue gas masks as a routine safety precaution because of the dangers of chemical spills, many Latvians concluded that they would be better off in an independent Latvia.

 Read the Document

"Scientists Examine Russia's Economy and Environment"

Gorbachev and Radical Reform

As these discontents simmered among the peoples of the Soviet bloc, a series of deaths ushered in an era of dramatic change. In 1982, the decrepit Leonid Brezhnev died—and so, in rapid succession, did his successors, Yuri Andropov (1914–1984) and Konstantin Chernenko (1911–1985). The time had come for a generational shift. When Mikhail Gorbachev succeeded Chernenko, he was 54 years old. Compared with his elderly colleagues on the Politburo, he looked like a teenager.

Gorbachev's biography encompassed the drama of Soviet history. Born in 1931, Gorbachev experienced Stalinism at its worst. One-third of the inhabitants of his native village in Stavropol were executed, imprisoned, or died from famine or disease in the upheavals of collectivization. Both of his grandfathers were arrested during the Great Purge. His father served in the Red Army during World War II and was wounded twice. Yet Gorbachev's family continued to believe in the communist dream. In 1948 Gorbachev and his father together won the Order of Red Banner of Labor for harvesting almost six times the average crop. This achievement, and his clear ability, won Gorbachev a university education. After earning degrees in economics and law, Gorbachev rose through the ranks of the provincial and then the national Communist Party.

Although an ardent communist, Gorbachev became convinced that the Soviet system was ailing, and that the only way to restore it to health was through radical surgery. What he did not anticipate was that such surgery would, in fact, kill the patient. Gorbachev's surgical tools were *glasnost* and *perestroika*, two Russian terms without direct English equivalents.

glasnost Loosely translated as openness or honesty; Gorbachev's effort after 1985 to break with the secrecy that had characterized Soviet political life.

GLASNOST AND PERESTROIKA Glasnost, sometimes translated as "openness," "publicity," or "transparency," meant abandoning the deception and censorship that had always characterized the Soviet system for a policy based on open admission of failures and problems. According to Gorbachev, "Broad, timely, and frank information is testimony of faith in people . . . and for their capacity to work things out themselves."[4]

Soviet citizens remained wary of Gorbachev's talk of glasnost—until April 1986 and the Chernobyl nuclear power plant disaster. Operator error at the Ukrainian power plant led to the most serious nuclear accident in history. In the days following the accident, 35 plant workers died. Over the next five years the cleanup effort claimed at least 7,000 lives. The accident placed more than four million inhabitants of Ukraine and Belarus at risk from excess radiation and spread a radioactive cloud that extended all the way to Scotland. When news of the accident first reached Moscow, party officials acted as they had always done: They denied it. But after monitors in Western countries recorded the radiation spewing into the atmosphere, Gorbachev dared to release accurate information to the public. In 1986, 93 percent of the Soviet population had access to a television set and what they saw on their screens convinced them that glasnost was real. A powerful change had occurred in Soviet political culture.

Through glasnost Gorbachev aimed to overcome public alienation and apathy and so convince Soviet citizens to participate in reforming political and economic life—or

perestroika Loosely translated as "restructuring"; Gorbachev's effort to decentralize, reform, and thereby strengthen Soviet economic and political structures.

 Read the Document

Mikhail Gorbachev, "Speech to the 27th Congress of the Communist Party of the Soviet Union"

perestroika, often translated as "restructuring" or "reconstruction." Gorbachev believed he could reverse Soviet economic decline by restructuring the economy through modernization, decentralization, and the introduction of a limited market. Gorbachev knew, however, that even limited economic reforms threatened the vested interests of communist bureaucrats and that these bureaucrats would block his reforms if they could. Thus, economic perestroika would not succeed without political perestroika—restructuring the political system, opening it up to limited competition to allow new leaders and new ideas to triumph. So in 1990 Gorbachev ended the Communist Party's monopoly on parliamentary power, and the Soviet Union entered the brave new world of multiparty politics.

ENDING THE COLD WAR Restructuring Soviet economics and politics led almost inevitably to restructuring international relations—and to ending the Cold War. By the 1980s, the arms race absorbed at least 18 percent of the Soviet GNP, as the Soviets

GLASNOST Mikhail Gorbachev meets with workers in Moscow in 1985.

scrambled to keep pace with the Reagan military build-up. Gorbachev concluded that the Soviet Union could not afford the Cold War. To signal to the West his desire for a new international order, Gorbachev reduced Soviet military commitments abroad and asked to resume arms control negotiations. In December 1987, Gorbachev and Reagan signed the INF (Intermediate Nuclear Forces) Treaty, agreeing to eliminate all land-based intermediate-range nuclear missiles. In 1991, the Soviets and Americans signed the Strategic Arms Reduction Treaty (START I), in which they pledged to reduce inter-continental ballistic missiles. The nuclear arms race was over.

Gorbachev also moved to restructure Soviet policies in eastern Europe. He realized, first, that western leaders would not end the Cold War as long as the Soviet Union sought to dictate eastern European affairs, and second, that the Soviet Union could no longer afford to control its satellite states. In his first informal meetings with eastern European communist leaders in 1985, Gorbachev told these aging communist stalwarts that the Red Army would no longer enforce their will on rebellious populations. By the time Gorbachev addressed the UN General Assembly at the end of 1988 and declared that the nations of eastern Europe were free to choose their own paths, dramatic changes were underway.

Revolution in Eastern Europe

Hungary and Poland were the first states to jettison communist rule. Even before Gorbachev took power, economic crisis and public discontent had driven the Polish and Hungarian governments to embrace reform. In the early 1980s Hungary moved toward a Western-oriented, market-driven economy by joining the World Bank and the International Monetary Fund (IMF) and establishing a stock market. In 1985, independent candidates for the first time appeared on Hungarian ballots—and many won. In Poland, Jaruzelski's government also experimented with restoring some measures of a market economy and with limited political reform. Once martial law ended in 1983, censorship loosened. Newspapers published criticisms of governmental policy that would never have been permitted before 1980.

Once Gorbachev came to power, the pace of reform in these two states accelerated. In January 1989, Hungary legalized noncommunist political parties and trade unions. In February, Solidarity and Polish communist officials began "roundtable talks" aimed

CHRONOLOGY: REVOLUTION IN EASTERN EUROPE

1980
Formation of Solidarity in Poland.

— 1980

1981
Martial law declared in Poland; Solidarity made illegal.

1981 —

1983
End of martial law in Poland, political and economic reforms begin; political reforms liberalize Hungarian elections.

— 1983

1985
Independents allowed to run for election in Hungary; Gorbachev becomes Soviet leader.

1985 —

1988
Gorbachev's address to UN: eastern European nations free to choose their own paths.

— 1988

1989
January
Noncommunist parties and unions legalized in Hungary.
February
Roundtable talks between Polish government and Solidarity.
June
Free elections in Poland.
September
Solidarity forms government in Poland.
November
Fall of Berlin Wall; reformist communists overthrow Zhivkov in Bulgaria.
December
Collapse of communist government in Czechoslovakia and East Germany; execution of Ceauşescu in Romania.

1989 —

1990
March
Free elections in East Germany and Hungary.
October
Reunification of Germany.
December
Wałęsa elected president of Poland.

— 1990

1993
Division of Czechoslovakia into the Czech Republic and Slovakia.

1993 —

at restructuring Poland's political system. In June, Poland held the first free elections in the Soviet bloc. Solidarity swept the contest and formed the first noncommunist government in eastern Europe since 1948.

These remarkable events sparked revolutions throughout the Soviet bloc. In the fall of 1989, mass protests toppled communist governments in Czechoslovakia and East Germany. In November, as the introduction to this chapter detailed, East Berliners succeeded in tearing down the Berlin Wall. One month later the world watched in wonder as the dissident playwright Václav Havel (1936–2011) became Czechoslovakia's president.

IT'S OVER! CZECHS ARE FREE! This graffiti on a bus stop in Prague sums up the revolutions of 1989.

Quickly the revolutionary fire spread to Bulgaria and Romania. There, however, communism was reformed rather than overthrown. In Bulgaria, reform-minded Communist Party members ousted the government of Todor Zhivkov, who had been in power for 35 years. The Romanian revolution was similar in outcome—but much bloodier. In December 1989, Romania's dictator Nikolae Ceauşescu ordered his army to fire on a peaceful protest and hundreds died. In a matter of days, however, the soldiers turned against Ceauşescu. He and his wife went into hiding, but on Christmas Day they were caught and executed by a firing squad. A new government formed under Ion Iliescu, a communist reformer who had attended Moscow University with Gorbachev.

The final chapter of the eastern European revolutions featured a redrawing of political borders—and a corresponding shift of political identities. In October of 1990, the line dividing West and East Germany disappeared; Germany was once again a single nation-state. But three years later, the nation-state of Czechoslovakia cracked apart, as President Havel was unable to satisfy the demands of Slovakian nationalists. Out of Czechoslovakia came two new states: the Czech Republic and Slovakia.

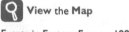 **View the Map**

Events in Eastern Europe, 1989–1990

The Disintegration of the Soviet Union

Western political leaders and ordinary people praised Gorbachev for ending the Cold War and removing the Soviet hold on eastern Europe. Gorbachev, however, regarded these changes as the international means to a domestic end—freeing the Soviet economy for prosperity and thereby saving the communist system. But prosperity eluded his grasp, and the system Gorbachev sought to save disintegrated. Economic perestroika proved a failure. By 1990, food and other essential goods were scarce, prices had risen by 20 percent since the year before, and productivity figures and incomes were falling. Dramatic increases in the number of prostitutes, abandoned babies, and the homeless population all signaled the economic and social breakdown of the Soviet Union.

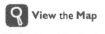

MAP **29.1** THE FORMER SOVIET UNION In December 1991, the Soviet empire disintegrated. What took its place?

As these problems escalated, Gorbachev faced growing opposition from hardline communists and from reformers who wanted a thoroughly capitalist economy. These reformers found a spokesman in Boris Yeltsin (1931–2007), a charismatic, boisterous politician who became the president of Russia (as distinct from the Soviet Union) in 1991. When the hard-liners attempted to overthrow Gorbachev in August 1991, Yeltsin led the popular resistance that blocked the coup. From that point on, Yeltsin, not Gorbachev, dominated Soviet politics.

Yet nationalism rather than the hardliners or Yeltsin's pro-capitalist movement toppled Gorbachev—and destroyed the Soviet Union. The success of eastern European nations in freeing themselves from Soviet domination encouraged separatist nationalist movements within the Soviet Union. Although Gorbachev deployed troops to quell nationalist rioting in Azerbaijan and Georgia and to counter independence movements in the Baltic states, the Soviet Union broke apart anyway. On December 25, 1991, Gorbachev resigned his office as president of a state that no longer existed (see **Map 29.1**).

View the Map

Break-Up of the Soviet Union

In the Wake of Revolution

29.3 What were the consequences of the revolutions of 1989–1990 for the societies of eastern Europe?

The collapse of communist regimes in eastern Europe and the disintegration of the Soviet Union meant exhilarating yet exhausting change. Democracy-building proved to be a colossal task in societies burdened with the communist legacies of social division, political skepticism, and economic stagnation.

Russia After the Revolution

In contrast to states such as Poland, where the dismantling of communism came as the result of popular protests, in the Soviet Union change had been initiated from above. Moreover, unlike in eastern Europe, Russians could point with pride to at least some achievements of communism: They had created an industrial society, won World War II, and become a superpower. In the 1990s, then, Russians struggled to come to terms with their unexpected—and for some, unwanted—revolution.

RUSSIA'S ECONOMIC AND SOCIAL CRISIS As the first president of post-Soviet Russia, Boris Yeltsin promised to accelerate his nation's transformation into a prosperous capitalist democracy. But he proved unable to do so. Three interlocking developments—continuing economic crisis, widening corruption and criminality, and growing socioeconomic inequality—characterized the Yeltsin era.

In January 1992, Yeltsin applied "shock therapy" to the ailing Russian economy. He lifted price controls, abolished subsidies, and privatized state industries. But the economy did not prosper. Prices climbed dramatically, and the closure of unproductive businesses worsened unemployment; at the same time, cuts in government spending severed welfare lifelines. By 1995, 80 percent of Russians were no longer earning a living wage. Food consumption fell to the same level as the early 1950s. The economic situation worsened in 1998 when Russia effectively went bankrupt. The value of the ruble collapsed, and the state defaulted on its loans. Even Russians with jobs found it difficult to make ends meet. Many resorted to barter and the black market to survive.

This economic crisis worsened as a result of widespread corruption and crime. In the 1990s Russians suddenly had the right to own private property, but they could not count on the state to protect that property. Russia's policing and judicial systems could not keep up with the new demands placed upon them. As a result, a new force appeared in Russian life—the "Russian Mafia," crime syndicates that offered "protection" at a high price and used extortion and intimidation to seize control of large sectors of the economy.

Economic crisis, combined with criminality and corruption, meant growing inequality. By 1997, *seven* individuals controlled an estimated *50 percent* of the Russian economy. Clearly a minority of powerful and influential Russians experienced the 1990s as years of extraordinary opportunity and wealth accumulation. For many other Russians, however, the ending of the Soviet regime meant freedom of the worst kind—freedom to be hungry, homeless, and afraid. In 1999, almost 40 percent of Russians fell beneath the official poverty line.

The end of the 1990s coincided with the end of the Yeltsin era. In December of 1999 the former KGB officer Vladimir Putin (b. 1952) assumed control of Russia. Well-manicured and austere, Putin provided stable and competent government—a welcome change to the roller-coaster ride of the Yeltsin years. The economy became stronger and prosperity more widespread. By 2012, the number of Russian citizens living in poverty had fallen to 13 percent. Economic stabilization, however, came at a political price: the return to authoritarianism and the denial of civil rights. Putin centralized political power and ran roughshod over such key democratic touchstones as freedom of the press and the right to a fair trial. Demonstrations demanding greater political freedom spread across Russian cities preceding elections in the spring of 2012, but as of this writing, Putin remained firmly in control of the Russian political system.

NATIONALIST CHALLENGES IN THE FORMER SOVIET UNION The breakup of the Soviet Union did not bring an end to nationalist violence in the region. Popular nationalist movements vaulted states such as Georgia, Ukraine, and the Baltic republics to independence, but many new governments then found themselves facing their own nationalist challenges. Georgia, Armenia, and Azerbaijan all experienced civil war in the 1990s as regions within these new states sought to break away and form their own independent states.

Russia, too, faced continuing violent efforts to redraw its boundaries. Russia remained an enormous multinational federation—and not all of its national minorities wanted to remain part of Russia. The sharpest challenge came from Chechnya, one of 21 autonomous republics within the larger Russian Federation. When the Soviet Union broke up, Chechens saw no reason that Chechnya should not follow the path of Georgia or Azerbaijan toward independence. The dispute simmered until 1994 when Yeltsin sent in the Russian army to force Chechnya back within Russia's embrace. In the ensuing 20-month conflict, 80,000 died and 240,000 were wounded—80 percent of these Chechen civilians. Yeltsin negotiated a truce in the summer of 1996, but four years later Putin renewed the war. In 2009, Russia declared the successful end of its "counter-terrorism operation" in Chechnya; Chechen nationalists, however, continue to mount sporadic attacks.

Central and Eastern Europe: Toward Democracy?

Like the former Soviet Union, the states of eastern Europe found the path from communist rule to democracy strewn with obstacles. By the end of the 1990s, much of the region—but not all of it—had successfully negotiated that path and achieved political and economic stability.

STRUGGLES WITHIN THE REUNITED GERMANY Almost half the population of East Germany crossed the border into West Germany in the first week after the fall of the Berlin Wall. They returned home dazzled by the consumer delights they saw in store windows and eager for a chance to grab a piece of the capitalist pie. The West German chancellor, Helmut Kohl, recognized the power of these desires and skillfully forced the pace of reunification. When the two Germanys united at the end of 1990, Kohl became the first chancellor of the new German state.

Kohl trusted that West Germany's economy was strong enough to pull its bankrupt new partner into prosperity, but he proved overly optimistic. The residents of the former East Germany soon found their factories closing and their livelihoods gone. These economic troubles leached over into the western regions of Germany. By 1997, German unemployment stood at 12.8 percent—the highest since World War II. Economic difficulties were most concentrated in the former East Germany, where over 20 percent of the population was out of work in the later 1990s.

A wide cultural gap also divided "Wessies" (West Germans) and "Ossies" (East Germans). Women of the former East Germany, for example, often found it difficult to adjust to a culture in which more conventional gender roles and conceptions of sexual morality dominated. Ossie women expected to work full time and to have access to state-provided day care, contraceptives, and abortion. In West Germany, however, the concept of the male breadwinner/head of household was enshrined in the legal code until the end of the 1970s and prominent in West German culture for a long time after.

In the 1990s, the divide between Wessie and Ossie sometimes seemed unbridgeable. In 2005, however, the election of Angela Merkel (b. 1954) as chancellor marked an important symbolic moment for united Germany. The first woman to head the German Christian Democrats (and a Protestant in a heavily Catholic party), Merkel was also an Ossie, the first East German to hold such a prominent political office in the new Germany. Under Merkel, the divide between East and West began to wane. The economy also stabilized after the trauma of reunification. By the end of 2011, Germany's unemployment rate was the lowest it had been in two decades.

WINNERS AND LOSERS AFTER 1989 East Germany, of course, was unique among the former Soviet bloc states because of its rapid unification with West Germany, but peoples throughout the region experienced hard times immediately after 1989. Western advisers and the International Monetary Fund (IMF), which controlled access to much-needed loans, insisted that the new governments follow programs of "austerity" aimed at cutting government spending and curbing inflation. The result was economic hardship far beyond what any Western electorate would have endured.

In the second half of the 1990s, however, Poland, Hungary, the Czech Republic, and the Baltic countries saw their economies stabilize and their overall standard of living rise rapidly. In 2002, the average Pole's purchasing power was 40 percent higher than in 1989. But in countries such as Slovakia, Bulgaria, Romania, and Albania, the economies continued to flounder. In Albania, conditions were so dire that some 40 percent of Albanians of working age went abroad for jobs between 1994 and 1998. An important divide opened up in eastern Europe between the "winners" and the "losers" in the struggle to adjust to post-1989 conditions. The same divide appeared in political development. By the end of the 1990s, the "winners" had successfully negotiated the transition to stable democratic politics, while elsewhere power remained concentrated in the hands of a few.

Three factors explain this new divide between "winners" and "losers" in eastern and central Europe. First, Poland and Hungary already had begun moving toward market reforms well before 1989 and so were best prepared for the transition to capitalism, while Czechoslovakia and the Baltic states could look back to pre-World War II national independence. Second, proximity to markets in and investment from western Europe played an important role. But third and most significant of all is a factor we have already discussed: the construction of civil society. The states that floundered in the post-1989 world were those in which opposition to communist rule before 1989 had not yet coalesced in a vibrant civil society. The revolutions of 1989 in Bulgaria and Romania, for example, were carried out by reformers within the communist system, not by citizens with a sense of identity apart from—and opposed to—that system.

WHO WAS GUILTY? Many eastern Europeans wanted to draw a curtain on the communist era. Others, however, argued that those who participated in and benefited from what they regarded as a criminal regime should be punished. Yet who should be put on trial? Communism had been "normal" in eastern Europe for 40 years. Almost every citizen participated in some way or another with the communist regime just to get by.

For a solution, many of the former communist states considered **lustration**, a policy that banned anyone who had collaborated with the communist state from "public office," a category that often included jobs in state-run media and in universities. In Czechoslovakia and Germany, lustration became official policy and soon proved controversial. Lustration did not distinguish between an informer whom the communist state had brutalized into collaboration and who did her best to avoid giving any usable information, and someone who had volunteered to inform and who benefited for years because of it. Concluding that lustration constituted vengeance rather than justice, lustration's opponents argued that it threatened to undermine democratic politics. Yet the disagreements over lustration occurred in public—in parliamentary debates, newspaper columns, television and radio talk shows, and political campaigns. Dissent was not driven underground or punished. In many ways, then, the controversy bore witness to the success of democracy-building in eastern and central Europe since 1989.

lustration Implemented in many former communist states in the 1990s, this policy banned former communists and communist collaborators from public office.

The Breakup of Yugoslavia

Across eastern and central Europe in the early 1990s, many had feared that hate-based nationalist politics and policies would fill the ideological vacuum left by communism's collapse. These concerns escalated as minority populations such as the Roma became targets of discrimination and violence and as neo-Nazi movements emerged. But while racism and the treatment of minority groups remained problematic (as was the case throughout the West), fears that eastern Europe might descend once again into the whirlwind of genocidal slaughter proved unfounded—except in Yugoslavia. There the revival of nationalist hostilities led to state-sanctioned mass murder and scenes of carnage not seen in Europe since the 1940s.

When the communist guerilla leader Tito seized control of the Yugoslav state after World War II, he sought to separate Yugoslavia from the divisive battles of its recent past. To construct a united nation, Tito utilized two tools—federalism and communism. A federal political structure comprising six equal republics prevented Serbia, or any other of the republics, from dominating Yugoslavia. Communism served as a unifying ideology, a cluster of ideas that transcended divisions of ethnicity, religion, and language. Tito declared ethnic identities and rivalries unacceptable, part of the bourgeois past that Yugoslavs left behind.

Yugoslavs often said, however, that their nation consisted of "six nationalities, five languages, four religions . . . and one Tito." According to this folk wisdom, Tito—not communism, not federalism—glued together this diverse state. In 1980, Tito died. Ominously, the year after his death saw the outbreak of riots between ethnic Albanians and Serbs in the Serbian province of Kosovo. Even more ominously, Tito's death coincided with the onset of economic crisis. Rising oil prices undercut the Yugoslav economy as did its debt load. By 1987, inflation was raging at 200 percent per year; two years later it had burst through into hyperinflation—200 percent *per month*.

Under pressure from this economic crisis, the federal structure Tito built began to collapse. The wealthier Yugoslav republics such as Croatia sought to loosen their ties to poorer republics such as Serbia. Then, in 1989, the revolutions that swept through the Soviet satellite states shattered the hold of communism on Yugoslavia as well. Ethnic nationalism, long simmering under the surface of Yugoslavian political life, poured into the resulting ideological void.

In Serbia, the former communist functionary Slobodan Milošević (1941–2006) transformed himself into a popular spokesman for aggressive Serbian nationalism. To enhance Serbia's power, Milošević opposed the efforts of Croatian and other leaders to dismantle the Yugoslav federation. If Yugoslavia split apart, Serbia would be nothing but a small, poor, powerless state. As long as Yugoslavia remained intact, however, Serbia could continue to siphon the economic resources of the other, wealthier republics. Milošević also encouraged Serbs living in the other Yugoslav republics to believe that their security and prosperity depended on Yugoslav unity.

War began in 1991, when Croatia declared independence and the Serb-dominated Yugoslav army mobilized against the separatists. In 1992 the war spread to Bosnia-Herzegovina after its government, too, declared independence. Civilians endured horrendous brutality as **ethnic cleansing** became widespread during this war. To create all-Serb zones within Croatia and Bosnia, Serb paramilitary units embarked on a campaign of terror designed to force Muslims and Croats to abandon their homes and villages. They burned mosques, closed schools, vandalized houses, and imprisoned women and girls in special camps where they were subjected to regular, systematic rape. The brutality proved contagious—soon, all sides were practicing ethnic cleansing. These atrocities impelled NATO into combat for the first time in its history when, in 1994, NATO planes began bombing Serb positions. The following year, an uneasy peace settled on the now-independent Bosnia and Croatia (see **Map 29.2**).

Peace eluded Serbia during this period, however. Milošević's brand of vicious nationalism demanded a constant supply of enemies and a continuous cycle of violence. In 1998, fighting between Serbs and ethnic Albanians erupted in the province of Kosovo. Ethnic cleansing, mass rape, and a huge exodus of refugees began again. After a NATO bombing campaign in Serbia, NATO and Russian troops moved into Kosovo, which declared its independence from Serbia in 2008.

ethnic cleansing A term introduced during the wars in Yugoslavia in the 1990s; the systematic use of murder, rape, and violence by one ethnic group against members of other ethnic groups in order to establish control over a territory.

📖 Read the Document

Zlata Filipovi, *Zlata's Diary: A Child's Life in Sarajevo*

MAP **29.2** THE FORMER YUGOSLAVIA What factors impelled the breakup of Yugoslavia?

Rethinking the West

29.4 How and why was the West redefined at the end of the twentieth century and the beginning of the twenty-first?

At the start of the 1990s, triumphalism characterized much of Western culture—at its simplest, expressed as "we won the Cold War." But who was "we"? For 40 years, the Cold War had provided a clear enemy and thus a clear identity: The West was anticommunist, anti-Soviet, anti-Warsaw Pact. The fall of communism, the disintegration of the Soviet Union, and the disappearance of the Warsaw Pact demanded that the West revise itself. But so, too, did other important social, political, and cultural changes that occurred in the wake of the tumultuous events of the later 1960s and the economic downturn of the 1970s.

The European Union

With the ending of the Cold War, the states of western Europe moved to take on a much more important role in global affairs. As **Map 29.3** shows, during the 1970s and 1980s the European Economic Community (EEC) widened its membership and became the European Community (EC), a political and cultural as well as economic organization. In 1979, Europeans voted in the first elections for the European Parliament, while the European Court of Justice gradually asserted the primacy of the European over national law.

Then, in 1991, the European Community (EC) became the **European Union (EU)**, defined by France's President François Mitterrand as "one currency, one culture, one social area, one environment." The establishment of the EU meant visible changes for ordinary Europeans. They saw their national passports replaced by a common EU document and border controls eliminated. The creation of a single EU currency—the euro, which replaced many national currencies in 2002—tore down one of the most significant economic barriers between European countries. At the same time, the powers of the European Parliament expanded and member states moved toward establishing common social policies such as labor rights.

As these developments were underway, Europeans confronted the unexpected challenge posed by the ending of the Cold War. Should the European Union (often called simply "Europe") now include East as well as West? Attracted by the EU's prosperity, the nations of the former Soviet bloc answered "Yes." Hesitant to join their countries to eastern Europe's shattered economies and divided societies, western European leaders drew up a list of qualifications for applicant nations. To belong to "Europe," nations had to meet financial requirements that demonstrated their economic stability and their commitment to market capitalism. Thus, the EU defined "Europe" first of all as capitalist. But a set of political requirements made clear that "Europe" also meant a commitment to democratic politics. Applicants' voting processes, treatment of minority groups, policing methods, and judicial systems were all scrutinized. Map 29.3 shows that in 2004 and again in 2007 the EU expanded to embrace much of central and eastern Europe.

Controversy greeted both the greater economic integration of the EU and its expansion. Britain, Denmark, and Sweden refused to adopt the euro, fearing that their economies would be dragged down by slower-performing EU states. Small traders and independent producers often felt overwhelmed by the EU bureaucracy, while many workers in western Europe feared having to compete for jobs with lower-paid eastern Europeans.

Nevertheless, during the 1990s and early 2000s, the EU seemed a resounding success. Although European unemployment rates often stood higher than in countries

European Union (EU) A successor organization to the EEC; the effort to integrate European political, economic, cultural, and military structures and policies.

📖 **Read the Document**

Jorg Haider, "The Freedom I Mean"

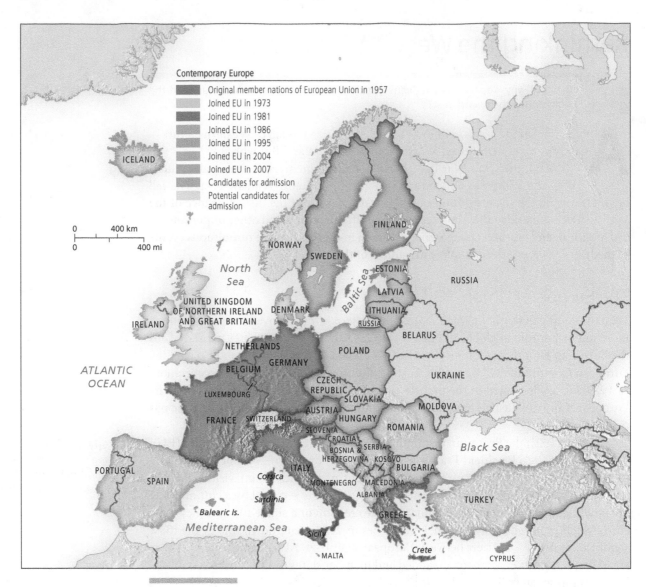

Contemporary Europe

- Original member nations of European Union in 1957
- Joined EU in 1973
- Joined EU in 1981
- Joined EU in 1986
- Joined EU in 1995
- Joined EU in 2004
- Joined EU in 2007
- Candidates for admission
- Potential candidates for admission

0   400 km

0   400 mi

MAP **29.3** CONTEMPORARY EUROPE The revolutions of 1989 and their aftermath mark a clear turning point in European history, as a comparison of this map and that of Map 28.5, "Europe in the Cold War" (p. 890), shows. What significant changes in political borders have occurred? How does the widening membership of the European Union reflect a new European order?

not aligned with the EU, the Union's economies boomed. Countries like Ireland experienced unprecedented economic expansion and prosperity. Much of this boom, however, was fueled by debt, as individuals, banks, corporations—and some EU governments—amassed huge deficits.

Then, in 2008, the globalized economy sharply declined when a real estate–related financial bubble in the United States burst. The effects soon ravaged not only the American but the global economy. In the United States, unemployment rates rose sharply, housing foreclosures escalated, and millions of people saw their retirement pensions dwindle. In western Europe, government borrowing ballooned. By 2012, the EU faced a debt crisis, with the stability of the euro imperiled by the financial instability of a number of member states, including Portugal, Italy, Spain, Ireland, and Greece. The debt crisis exposed significant weaknesses in the EU structure and, for some, called into question the entire project of European unity. As the financially sound states such as Germany demanded that their weaker partners impose politically unpopular austerity programs on electorates, older nationalist hostilities resurfaced. A German magazine, for example, featured an image of the famous Greek statue of the

Venus de Milo wrapped in a tattered Greek flag and bearing the slogan, "The Frauds of Europe," while anti-austerity demonstrators in Greece burned the German flag and labeled German EU negotiators "Nazis."

Nevertheless, European leaders remained committed to the European project. Ordinary people were more ambivalent, but even after 2008, the percentages of Europeans regarding their country's membership in the EU as "a good thing" continued to outweigh those who described belonging to the Union as "a bad thing." In the Eurobarometer poll of May 2011, only the United Kingdom and Croatia showed more people who rejected rather than affirmed EU membership.

Islam and the West

At the same time that the EU struggled to integrate Europe's diverse economies, European states contended with the challenge of integrating increasingly diverse cultures within their boundaries—and, in particular, of reconciling European identity with a growing Islamic cultural and political presence. As minarets joined church steeples in the skylines of European cities, questions about the definitions of and relationships between Islamic, European, and Western identities intensified.

MUSLIM COMMUNITIES IN EUROPE In eastern European countries such as Bulgaria, Albania, and Bosnia, Muslims belonged to the indigenous nation, the descendants of those who converted to Islam during the centuries of Ottoman rule. In western Europe, by contrast, Muslim communities were relatively recent, the result of the post-World War II immigration discussed earlier in this chapter. By 1990 Muslims—drawn from many different ethnic groups and embracing a wide variety of religious practices and cultural traditions—constituted about 4 percent of Europe's population and constituted the most rapidly growing immigrant group.

In most significant ways, the Muslim experience in Europe conformed to common immigrant patterns. The Muslim struggle to adapt to new social norms reflected the usual experience of immigrants whose countries of origins are more traditional than their host societies. Like Italian Catholic or eastern European Jewish immigrants to North American cities in the 1890s, many Muslim immigrants were particularly shocked by European gender relations and sexual freedoms. Family tensions often became acute because of the conflict between immigrant parents and children, especially daughters (again, a common immigrant pattern).

ISLAMISM AND THE WEST The emergence of **Islamism** as a powerful global force complicated the integration of Islamic communities in western Europe. An umbrella term, Islamism embraces a variety of movements that call for a return to what adherents see as a purer form of Islam. As Chapter 26 discussed, movements such as Wahhabism in Saudi Arabia and the Islamic Brotherhood in Egypt emerged in the interwar period as a reaction against corrupt Western puppet regimes and a response to unsettling economic change. Explicitly anti-Western, Islamism views Western culture as a threat to Islamic identity. In its extreme form, it accepts violence, including the murder of civilians, as an acceptable means to its ends.

A number of developments fostered support for Islamism. The ongoing Palestinian-Israeli conflict played an important role, particularly given the high level of American economic and military support for Israel. (Between 1949 and 1998, Israel received more American aid than any other country.) Because more than 90 percent of Palestinians are Muslim and because the United States is widely seen as the standard-bearer of the West, Islamists framed the conflict as a battle between the West and Islam.

The Iranian Revolution of 1979 was also critical. That year a popular revolution overthrew the western-backed authoritarian regime of Shah Mohammad Reza Pahlavi

Islamism The ideology that insists that Islam demands a rejection of Western values and that violence in this struggle against the West is justified.

and vaulted the Ayatollah Khomeini (1901–1989) into power. Khomeini rapidly reversed the westernizing and modernizing policies of the Shah and condemned the United States as the "Great Satan." Under his regime Iran became a prominent supporter of violent Islamist groups, such as Hezbollah in Lebanon. Khomeini became an international Islamist hero during the "Iranian hostage crisis" of 1979–1980, when Iranian students took over the U.S. Embassy in Tehran, kidnapped 66 Americans, and held most of them for over a year. Khomeini's decision 10 years later to issue a death sentence against the British writer Salman Rushdie for what he considered to be a blasphemous portrayal of the prophet Muhammad widened the gap between his Islamist regime and the West and, once again, made him a popular hero among Islamists. (See *Justice in History* in this chapter.)

The wars in Bosnia and Chechnya in the 1990s further intensified the Islamist conviction that Muslims were under attack. The initial passivity of western Europe and the United States during the Bosnian war—while Muslim men and boys were slaughtered and Muslim women and girls raped—convinced many Muslims that Western governments had an anti-Islamic agenda. This perception grew stronger when Western states refused to back the Chechens (who are Muslim) in what many viewed as the Chechen war of independence against Russian oppression.

Finally, Islamism fed on the alienation of some Muslims, particularly young men, in immigrant communities in western Europe. Many European Muslim families lived in urban industrial areas where manufacturing jobs had been plentiful in the 1960s and 1970s but where few work opportunities were available by the 1990s. Thus, the generation coming of age in this decade saw little point in the economic aspirations that had driven their parents and grandparents. Unemployment rates in largely Muslim areas stood at double that of the national average in many western European states, and even higher among men under age 25. Moreover, while their parents and grandparents often had maintained strong ties to their country of origin, the new generation, less bound by such ties, proved more open to transnational forms of Islamic thought and practice—such as those associated with Islamism.

THE WEST AND ISLAMIST TERRORISM This textbook has traced the way in which "the West" changed meaning, often in response to places and peoples defined as "not West." With the ending of the Cold War, the West lost its main enemy, but a replacement stood readily at hand. In 1996, the American president Bill Clinton (b. 1946) identified terrorism as "the enemy of our generation." In the post–Cold War world, Islamist terrorism replaced communism as the new foe against which the West defined itself.

Because it short-circuits the democratic process by shifting decision making from the ballot box to the bomb, terrorism directly opposes what many now regard as the bedrock of Western culture—a commitment to democracy. Both this equation of the West with democracy and this definition of terrorism as "non-Western," however, conveniently ignore the history of the West and of terrorism itself: The Fenians in mid-nineteenth-century Ireland, anarchist groups throughout Europe in the 1890s, and the surge of terrorist activity throughout western Europe in the 1970s reveal that terrorism has long been part of "Western civilization." Nevertheless, as the twenty-first century opened, many in the West regarded terrorism as an outside threat, usually bearing an Arabic face and carrying a copy of the Qur'an.

This perception rested on the emergence of Islamist groups that embraced violence as a political weapon. From the 1980s on, a number of groups carried out violent attacks throughout not only the Middle East but also Africa, parts of Asia, Europe, and the United States—and, in 2001, one of the most deadly terrorist episodes yet seen. On September 11, an Islamist group called Al Qaeda hijacked four passenger planes and smashed them into the World Trade Center in New York City and the Pentagon

Justice in History
The Sentencing of Salman Rushdie

In February 1989, the Ayatollah Khomeini, political and spiritual leader of Iran, offered an award of $2.5 million to any faithful Muslim who killed the novelist Salmon Rushdie. Rushdie, a British citizen, went into hiding, where he remained for several years. His death sentence ignited the "Satanic Verses Affair," a tumultuous international crisis caused by a resounding clash of cultural assumptions and expectations.

The crisis centered on a book. In the early autumn of 1988 Viking Penguin published Rushdie's *The Satanic Verses,* a difficult novel about the complexities and contradictions of the modern immigrant experience. Born in India and raised in an Islamic home, Rushdie wrote *The Satanic Verses* to describe "migration, metamorphosis, divided selves, love, death, London, and Bombay."[5] The novel received immediate critical acclaim, with reviewers praising it as an astonishing work of postmodernist fiction.

Many Muslims, however, regarded the book as a direct attack on the foundations of their religious faith. One scene in the novel particularly horrified devout Muslims. In this episode, the central character has a psychotic breakdown and falls into a dream: The prophet Muhammad appears as a corrupt businessman, and prostitutes in a brothel take on the names of the Prophet's wives.

The novel aroused controversy from the moment of its publication. The government of India banned it almost immediately. Within a matter of weeks, several other states followed suit. Anti-Rushdie demonstrations in India and Pakistan turned violent. Bookstores received bombing and death threats. In western Europe, hostilities between Muslims and non-Muslims intensified. Then, on February 14, 1989, an announcer on Radio Tehran read aloud the text of a *fatwa,* or decree, issued by the Ayatollah Khomeini:

I would like to inform all the intrepid Muslims of the world that the author of the book entitled *The Satanic Verses,* which has been compiled, printed and published in opposition to Islam, the Prophet and the Koran, as well as those publishers who were aware of its contents, have been

CULTURE CLASH In 2007, Britain's Queen Elizabeth awarded Salman Rushdie a knighthood for his services to literature. The award sparked protests within the Islamic world, including this one in Lahore, Pakistan, where demonstrators burned the British flag to express their outrage.

sentenced to death. I call on all zealous Muslims to execute them quickly, wherever they find them.... Whoever is killed on this path will be regarded as a martyr, God willing.

Western governments reacted quickly. The 12 states of the European Community, the United States, Sweden, Norway, Canada, Australia, and Brazil all condemned Khomeini's judgment, recalled their ambassadors from Tehran, and cancelled high-level diplomatic contacts with Iran.

Large numbers of Muslims, including many who spoke out against Rushdie's book, also condemned Khomeini's fatwa. Some Muslim scholars contended that the Ayatollah's fatwa was a scholarly opinion, not a legally binding judgment. Others argued that Rushdie could not be condemned without a trial or that Rushdie, who lived in a society without an Islamic government, was not bound by Islamic law.

But many ordinary Muslims ignored these theological and legal arguments and greeted the Ayatollah's fatwa with delight. The news of the Ayatollah's fatwa brought crowds of cheering Muslims into city streets across Europe. In Manchester and Bradford, young British Muslim men insisted they would kill Rushdie if given the chance. In Paris, demonstrators marched to cries of "We are all Khomeinists!"

Why did Khomeini's fatwa arouse such enthusiasm among Western Muslims? A partial answer is that many Muslims were frustrated with what they regarded as the unequal application of the laws of censorship. Faced with what they saw as a hate-filled, pornographic caricature of Islam, they had demanded that Western governments use existing laws censoring pornography and banning hate crimes to block the publication of Rushdie's book—and they had gotten nowhere. But the controversy was not simply a dispute about censorship. For some Muslims, Rushdie's *Satanic Verses* epitomized Western secular society with its scant regard for tradition or religious values. Dr. Kalim Siddiqui of the pro-Iranian Muslim Institute in Britain proclaimed, "Western

(continued on next page)

civilization is fundamentally an immoral civilization."[6] From this perspective, Khomeini's fatwa condemned not just one book or one author, but an entire culture.

The anti-Western stance of some Muslims was mirrored by the anti-Islam position soon occupied by some Rushdie supporters. In all of his books, Rushdie condemned British racism and exposed the falsehood of Western claims to cultural superiority. Yet in an ironic twist, many of his champions now articulated precisely the sort of Western cultural chauvinism against which Rushdie had written so passionately. Many western Europeans agreed with the conclusion drawn in this letter to a British daily newspaper: "The lesson of the Rushdie affair is that it was unwise to let Muslim communities establish themselves in our midst."[7] They equated Islam with irrationalism and barbarity, while they linked the "West" to reason and civilization. At precisely the moment when the crumbling of communism and the ending of the Cold War deprived the West of one of its defining attributes, the Satanic Verses Affair offered up a new Other against which the West could define itself.

For Discussion

On what grounds are publications censored in Western societies? Given the existence of this censorship, should Rushdie's book have been banned?

Taking It Further

Bowen, David G., ed. *The Satanic Verses: Bradford Responds.* 1996. This collection of essays and documents helps explains why many British Muslims viewed the British government's failure to censor Rushdie's book as an act of injustice.

Pipes, Daniel. *The Rushdie Affair: The Novel, the Ayatollah, and the West.* 2003. An informative overview by a controversial scholar.

(the U.S. military headquarters in Washington, D.C.); the fourth plane crashed in Pennsylvania. Almost 3,000 people died.

The attacks on "9/11" opened an even more violent phase in the history of the West and Islamism. After intelligence linked Al Qaeda to the Islamist government of Afghanistan, the United States invaded Afghanistan and, with a multinational coalition, sought to destroy Al Qaeda and uproot its Afghan supporters. In March 2003, this war took a new turn when U.S. and British forces attacked Iraq. Because the Iraqi government had played no role in the attacks on 9/11, this war divided American society and proved vastly unpopular in western Europe. It also strengthened Islamist hostility toward the West, as subsequent terrorist attacks in Europe made clear. On March 11, 2004, approximately 200 people died after four bombs exploded on commuter trains during the rush hour in Madrid. Al Qaeda linked the bombing to Spain's support of the Iraq war. One year later, on July 7, 2005, a similar spate of bombings during the morning rush hour in London killed over 50 people and injured more than 700.

The men involved in the 7/7 London attacks were not only linked to Al Qaeda, they were also British. The London bombings thus revealed the power of Islamism within the West. In the wake of 9/11 and the attacks that followed, then, the question of Western identity was more troublesome than ever, as a "Them" versus "Us" mentality that ignored the long, complex history of Islam in the West became more prevalent.

EURO-ISLAM Yet the encounter between Islam and Europe was far from wholly negative. The majority of European Muslims rejected Islamism. Many, particularly those of the second and third generations of immigrant families, endeavored to create a new identity: **Euro-Islam**. Regarding themselves as fully Muslim and fully European, these individuals insisted that no contradiction existed between Islam and what many view as the core values of the West—democratic politics, respect for individual differences, and civil liberties guaranteed by law to all, regardless of race and gender.

Euro-Islam produced significant theological and social innovations within the Islamic community. European Muslim women fought to eradicate such traditional practices as female circumcision and the forced marriage of young girls to men from their parents' or grandparents' homelands. More generally, they claimed an equal place for women within the context of both Europe and Islam. European Muslim theologians reinforced this claim. Traditional Islamic theology cut the world into two: the "house of Islam" and the "house of war." In the "house of Islam," Islamic law prevails. In the

Euro-Islam The identity and belief system being forged by European Muslims who argue that Islam does not contradict or reject European values.

"house of war," or societies where Islamic law is not followed, Muslims live in a state of constant spiritual battle. Euro-Islamic proponents such as the Swiss scholar Tariq Ramadan (b. 1962) argued that Muslims should not view Europe and the United States as the "house of war." Instead, these regions form a third "house," the "house of testimony," where Muslims freely profess and live their faith in community with non-Muslims.

Into the Postmodern Era

The end of the Cold War, the formation of the European Union, and the growth of significant Muslim communities within western Europe all demanded a reevaluation and redefinition of West. So, too, did a number of intellectual, artistic, and technological developments that together helped created the postmodern era. Although the term **postmodernism** covers an array of styles and stances, at its core postmodernism rejects Western cultural supremacy. More specifically, postmodernism challenges the idea that Western science and rationality have constructed a single, universally applicable form of "modernity."

THE MAKING OF THE POSTMODERN Postmodernism first took form in architecture, perhaps because the failures of modernist architecture were so obvious by the early 1970s. Motivated by their faith in human rationality and modern technology, modernist architects had erected buildings that they believed would enable people to live better, more beautiful lives. But the concrete high-rises they constructed failed to connect with the needs and emotions of their inhabitants, and many became derelict, crime-ridden, graffiti-scarred tenements.

THE NEW EUROPE Muslim women exchange greetings at an outdoor market in Gouda in the Netherlands.
SOURCE: Alamy BKWKJW.

Faced with this failure, a new generation—the postmodernists—insisted that modernist architecture was too elitist. The American architect Charles Jencks (b. 1939) argued that because people tend to rely on the familiar to make sense of their world, modernism was wrong to reject traditional forms. For example, most Europeans and Americans connect domestic housing with gabled roofs (ask a child to draw a picture of a house and see if he or she draws a flat roof). Was it surprising, Jencks asked, that the concrete rectangles so typical of modernist houses alienated so many people? Postmodernist *anti-elitism* thus led to *eclecticism,* to re-creating and combining forms and styles from past eras (such as gabled roofs), and to efforts to revive local and regional styles. Why should the streets of Tokyo look like the center of London or downtown Chicago? Instead, postmodernists embraced an architecture rooted in the specifics of time and place. In addition to being anti-elitist and eclectic, then, postmodernist architecture was also *anti-universalist*: It condemned modernism for its assumption that the same modern (and Western) ideals and forms fit all individuals and all societies.

The same sorts of criticism of modernism surfaced in the art world, as the politics of the late 1960s and early 1970s transformed the visual arts in three ways. First,

  Read the Document

Justin Vaisse, "Veiled Meaning"

postmodernism Umbrella term covering a variety of artistic styles and intellectual theories and practices; in general, a rejection of a single, universal, Western style of modernity.

in the wake of the protests of 1968, artists—many coming out of left-wing activist environments—rejected ideologies based on hierarchy and authority. This rejection led to an attack on the modernist idea of the "avant-garde," the concept of artistic geniuses fighting on the frontiers of aesthetic excellence. Second, the experience of political protest led many artists to try to communicate with a wider public—and, hence, to look to the past and to popular culture for forms and material that their audience would find familiar. As the art critic Edit DeAk explained, postmodernist art relied on "the shock of recognition instead of the shock of the new."[8] Finally, feminism influenced the new art. Feminists highlighted the systematic exclusion of women from gallery and museum exhibitions. They also questioned the aesthetic hierarchy that fixed the patronizing label of "craft" to traditionally female art forms such as weaving.

By the end of the 1970s, postmodernist practices in art and architecture blended with a growing body of literary and cultural theory often called *poststructuralism*. The theory of poststructuralism centered on the work of an assorted group of French thinkers whose ideas were taken up in American universities and then filtered back into European intellectual circles. These thinkers included Roland Barthes (1915–1980) and Jacques Derrida (1930–2004) in literary studies, Michel Foucault (1926–1984) in history, and Jacques Lacan (1901–1981) in psychoanalytic theory.

Like postmodernist theories in architecture and art, poststructuralism began as an exploration into the problems of communication. Barthes declared the "Death of the Author," by which he meant that the purpose of literary study is not to ask, "What does the author mean?" but instead to explore the way in which the reader creates his or her

POSTMODERNISM AT PLAY IN THE WEST Using the "shock of recognition," Marco Ventura blends six familiar images from the Western tradition in this playful painting that he entitled "Mona Lisa Contemplating the Bust of Nefertiti as God Creates Order Out of Chaos on a Starry Night on the Island of La Grande Jatte as the Infanta Margarita Looks On" (1993).

SOURCE: Marco Ventura, "Mona Lisa Contemplating the Bust of Nefertiti as God Creates Order Out of Chaos on a Starry Night on the Island of La Grande Jatte as the Infanta Margarita Looks On," 1993, oil on gessoed paper, 10"w × 821/2"h. Painting by Marco Ventura 1993.

own meanings. Building on Barthes, Derrida argued that the world we experience is structured by language—we cannot even understand or express our very selves apart from language. But because there is no inherent match between a word (what Derrida called a "signifier") and the thing or idea to which that word refers (the "signified"), communication is never straightforward. An endless variety of meanings and interpretations results, and thus, Derrida argued, we must abandon the idea of a fixed or single truth, of ultimate or universal meaning.

This effort to challenge any single "right answer" or any center of authority (sometimes called "decentering") linked the poststructuralist concern with communication to its analysis of power. Foucault and Lacan dissected hierarchies of authority (not only in the political sphere, but also in academic disciplines, for example, or in the medical world), and the way these authorities used seemingly objective bodies of knowledge to retain their hold on power.

The blending of these poststructuralist theories of communication and power with the critique of modernism already flourishing in architecture and the arts produced postmodernism. The postmodern view of culture as a global contest for power disturbed more traditional thinkers (with "modernist" now perceived as traditional), who insisted that criteria of aesthetic excellence ("Beauty") and objective standards of knowledge ("Truth") did exist, and who warned that cultural "decentering" would destroy the social cohesion and political stability of the West. (See *Different Voices* in this chapter.)

POSTMODERN CULTURES AND POSTINDUSTRIAL TECHNOLOGIES In many ways popular culture confirmed postmodern theories. In Britain, for example, the "Big Beat" songs that dominated the club scene in the late 1990s were produced by disc jockeys who lifted snatches from old records, played them at different speeds, and combined them with contrasting styles. Like postmodernist paintings, Big Beat contained chunks of the past, recycled in new ways.

Read the Document

Václav Havel, "The Need for Transcendence in the Postmodern World"

MAKING BUILDINGS DANCE Designed by the American architect Frank Gehry and his Czech collaborator Vlado Mulunić, the "Dancing Building" fills a bomb site left vacant in central Prague since World War II. Also called "Fred and Ginger" (after the famous Hollywood dancing duo Fred Astaire and Ginger Rogers), this postmodernist piece delighted and enraged the people of Prague.

postindustrial society A service-based, rather than manufacturing-based, economy characterized by an emphasis on marketing and information and by a proliferation of communications technologies.

More generally, a series of technological developments meant that popular culture was "decentered," that a multitude of popular cultures coexisted, and that the individual consumer of culture, like Barthes's reader, was free to make meaning as he or she chose. The videocassette recorder (VCR), first marketed in 1975, and its technological successors not only transported film viewing from the public to the private sphere, they also provided the film viewer with the possibility to tailor the movie to his or her own preferences—to adjust the volume or choose another soundtrack entirely, to omit or fast-forward through certain scenes, to replay others endlessly. Similarly, the proliferation of cable and satellite television stations during the 1980s and 1990s fragmented the viewing audience and made it impossible to speak of popular culture in the singular.

Postmodernist concerns with communication, with the way in which interpretations can be endlessly modified, and with the abolition of a single center of authority certainly seemed appropriate for "the Information Age" or the **postindustrial society**. Emphasis on production characterized the industrial phase of economic development. But in the postindustrial phase, *making* things became less important than *marketing* them. If the factory symbolized industrial society, then the epitome of the postindustrial era was the home computer, with its capacity to disperse information, market products, and endlessly duplicate yet constantly alter visual and verbal images—all without any central regulating authority. Governments scrambled to impose control on the proliferating technologies of the postindustrial age, but in true postmodern fashion the centers of authority broke down. Existing laws that regulated pornography, for example, proved difficult to apply to the Internet, the vast global communications web.

Similarly, developments in medical technologies raised important questions about authority and ownership. In 1978, Louise Brown was born in Britain, the world's first "test-tube baby." Over the next 20 years, assisted fertility treatment resulted in more than one million births. As the technology grew more sophisticated, so did the ethical and political questions. Societies struggled to determine the legality of practices such as commercial surrogate motherhood, in which a woman rents her womb to a couple, and postmenopausal motherhood, in which a woman past childbearing age is implanted with a fertilized egg.

Genetic research provoked even more debate about which authorities or what principles should guide scientific research. In 1997, British scientists introduced the world to Dolly the sheep, the first mammal cloned from an adult. Many scientists assumed that the cloning of human beings, long part of science fiction and horror stories, was inevitable, even if religious leaders deemed it immoral and political authorities declared it illegal. The announcement in February 2001 that scientists had decoded the human genome—that they had mapped the set of instructions in every cell in the human body—raised such questions as, Who owns this information? Who has the authority to decide how it is to be used?

POSTMODERN PATTERNS IN RELIGIOUS LIFE Postmodern patterns—the fragmentation of cultures, the collapse of centers of authority, the supremacy of image—also characterized Western religious faith and practice after the 1970s. Christianity no longer served as a common cultural bond. In a time of increasing immigration and cultural diversity, Islam was the fastest-growing religious community in western Europe. In Britain, Muslims outnumbered Methodists by two to one. By the end of the twentieth century, regular churchgoers were a small minority of the European population—well under 20 percent in most countries. Religious faith became a private matter, the mark of subcultures (often defined by an "Us versus Them" mentality), rather than a bond tying together individuals and groups into a cohesive national culture.

Different Voices
History in a Postmodern World

In the late 1980s, postmodernist ideas penetrated the study of history. While many historians—such as Joan Wallach Scott, who wrote the first excerpt that follows—embraced postmodernist theories and methodologies, others—such as Gertrude Himmelfarb, the author of the second excerpt—condemned postmodernism as relativism run amok. This debate resonated beyond the rather small world of professional historians, as the third excerpt shows. In an effort to establish uniform standards in elementary and secondary education, Margaret Thatcher sought a national curriculum for British state schools. As her account reveals, Thatcher's ideas about history clashed with those of professional historians.

I. Joan Wallach Scott: A "New" Historian's Defense

By "history," I mean not what happened, not what "truth" is "out there" . . . but what we *know* about the past, what the rules and conventions are that govern the production and acceptance of the knowledge we designate as history. My first premise is that history is . . . constructed by historians. Written history both reflects and creates relations of power. Its standards of inclusion and exclusion, measures of importance, and rules of evaluation are not objective criteria but politically produced conventions. What we know as history is, then, the fruit of past politics. . . .

The pluralization of the subject of history challenges the notion . . . that "man" can be studied through a focus on elites. Instead, attention to women, blacks, and other Others demonstrates that history consists of many irreconcilable stories. Any master narrative—the single story of the rise of American democracy or Western civilization—is shown to be not only incomplete but impossible of completion in the terms it has been written. For those master narratives have been based on the forcible exclusion of Others' stories. They are . . . stories which in their telling legitimize the actions of those who have shaped the laws, constitutions, and governments—"official stories."

The proliferation of Others' histories . . . has raised questions about difference and power: . . . . How has the exclusion of some stories from the record of the past perpetuated inequalities based on attributions of difference? What is the connection between contemporary social hierarchy and measures of importance in historical writing? Answers to these questions . . . undermine claims by orthodox historians that . . . their history is but a transcription of how things really happened in the past. . . .

. . . [H]istory is an interpretive practice, not an objective, neutral science. To maintain this does not signal the abandonment of all standards. . . . [Historians] share a commitment to accuracy and to procedures of verification and documentation. . . . [But we see] that the meanings attributed to events of the past always vary, that the knowledge we produce is contextual, relative, open to revision and debate, and never absolute.

SOURCE: Joan Wallach Scott, "History in Crisis? The Others' Side of the Story," *American Historical Review*, 1989, 94:3, 681, 682–683,689–690. Reprinted by permission of the author.

II. Gertrude Himmelfarb: An "Old" Historian Rejects the New

Historians have always quarreled about the meaning and interpretation of facts and, indeed, about the facts themselves. But they . . . have traditionally assumed some correspondence between interpretation and fact, between language and reality. They are painfully aware of the imperfection of that correspondence—a past that always eludes them, a reality that is never fully revealed to them . . . But they have also been acutely aware of the need to try to close that gap as much as possible. . . . Today, [however,] more and more historians . . . are making the past far more indeterminate, more elusive, less real than it has ever been—thus permitting themselves to be as creative, innovative, and inventive as possible in interpreting the past. These have become the new "possibles" of history: the possibilities suggested by the historian's imagination and sensibility rather than by the contemporary experience*. . . . Contemporaries may have thought that their history was shaped by kings and statesmen, politics and diplomacy, constitutions and laws. New historians know better. . . . Race/gender/class—word-processors [early personal computers] all over the country must be programmed to print that formula with a single touch of a key. . . . The assumption that race, gender, and class are, and always have been, the basic determinants of history deconstructs the past not only as historians have known it but, in many cases, as contemporaries knew it. . . . Those benighted contemporaries, the argument goes, speak with no authority, because they were deluded by the "hegemonic culture" that was itself irredeemably sexist, racist, and elitist. Thus, all the past has to be deconstructed and constructed anew.

SOURCE: Gertrude Himmelfarb, "Some Reflections on the New History," *American Historical Review*, 1989, 94:3, 665–666, 667, 668. Reprinted by permission of the author.

III. Margaret Thatcher: A Politician Weighs In

Perhaps the hardest battle I fought on the national curriculum was about history. Though not an historian myself, I had a very clear—and I had naively imagined uncontroversial—idea of what history was. History is an account of what happened in the past. Learning history, therefore, requires knowledge of events . . . [and] knowing dates. No amount of imaginative sympathy for historical characters or situations can be a substitute for the initially tedious but ultimately rewarding business of memorizing what actually happened. . . .

In July 1989 the History Working Group produced its interim report. I was appalled. It put the emphasis on interpretation and enquiry as against content and knowledge. There

*Here and throughout this essay, Himmelfarb uses the term contemporary to mean the period in the past that the historian is studying.

(continued on next page)

(continued from previous page)

was insufficient weight given to British history. There was not enough emphasis on history as chronological study. . . .

[The *final report arrived in March 1990. Thatcher was not pleased.*] The attainment targets it set out did not specifically include knowledge of historical facts, which seemed to me extraordinary [and] the coverage of some subjects—for example, twentieth-century British history—was too skewed to social, religious, cultural and aesthetic matters rather than political events. . . . By now I had become thoroughly exasperated. . . .

SOURCE: Margaret Thatcher, *The Downing Street Years*, 1993, 595–596. Copyright © 1993 by Margaret Thatcher. Reprinted by permission of HarperCollins Publishers.

For Discussion

1. What does Scott mean when she argues that "what we know as history" is actually "the fruit of past politics"? How would Thatcher have replied?

2. Himmelfarb argues that an overemphasis on race, gender, and class characterizes postmodernist interpretations of history. Why might postmodernists emphasize these three categories? Why does Himmelfarb object? Would Thatcher have sympathized with Himmelfarb's argument?

3. Imagine that you are present *in 1989* at a debate featuring Scott, Himmelfarb, and Thatcher. Each woman has been asked to define "the West." How do you think each might have responded?

CHRONOLOGY: MEDICAL CHALLENGES AND ACHIEVEMENTS

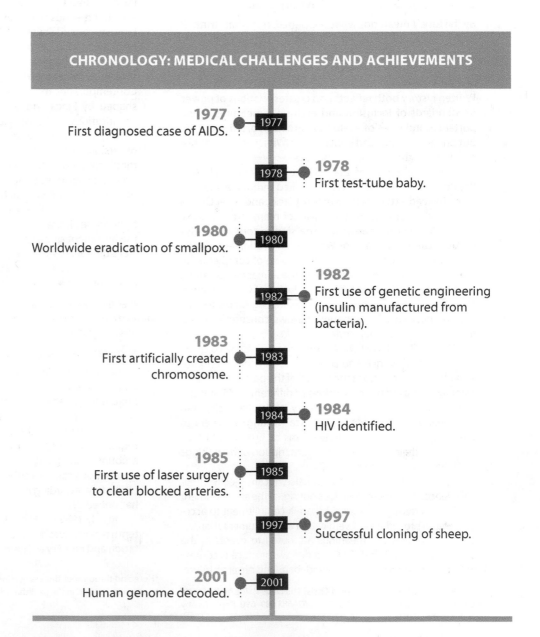

1977
First diagnosed case of AIDS.

1978
First test-tube baby.

1980
Worldwide eradication of smallpox.

1982
First use of genetic engineering (insulin manufactured from bacteria).

1983
First artificially created chromosome.

1984
HIV identified.

1985
First use of laser surgery to clear blocked arteries.

1997
Successful cloning of sheep.

2001
Human genome decoded.

But at the same time, the long-reigning Pope John Paul II experienced unprecedented popularity. The most well-traveled and populist-oriented of twentieth-century popes, John Paul II became a media star, greeted with the same sort of cheering crowds and tee-shirt vendors that accompanied famous rock bands. Much of his popularity rested on his intimate connection with Poland's Solidarity and, therefore, with an image of liberation. But the pope's support for Solidarity did not mean he supported other forms of rebellion against authority. He adopted a firmly centralized approach to church government and opposed birth control, married clergy, and the ordination of women. Confronted with the postmodernist message that authority had fragmented and that no universal truth existed, many Christians found the pope's uncompromising stand a source of great comfort.

Yet throughout the West the pope's flock moved out of his control. In the United States, millions turned out to cheer John Paul II waving from an open car (the "popemobile"), yet the percentage of American Catholics using birth control—in direct violation of papal teachings—mirrored that of the population at large. Catholic Italy boasted the second-lowest birth rate in the world (after China), with the one-child family becoming the norm. It was hard to avoid the conclusion that in much of Western Roman Catholicism, as in much of postmodern society, image ruled while authority dissipated.

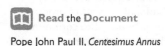

Read the Document

Pope John Paul II, *Centesimus Annus*

SEXUAL PRACTICE AND IDENTITY IN A POSTMODERN WORLD The postmodern rejection of a single "right" answer or central authoritative voice was also apparent in sexual behaviors and the debates this behavior provoked. As many in the West abandoned traditional moral codes, rates of extramarital sex and divorce soared, the age at which individuals became sexually active tumbled, and sexual imagery in films, advertising, and publishing became more explicit.

Three developments contributed to this sexual revolution. First, the declining rates of religious belief and observance meant that religious-backed codes of sexual behavior carried less weight. At the same time, the rebellions of the 1960s and early 1970s glorified resistance to traditional conventions and rules. Second, breaking those rules seemed less risky for women as oral and barrier contraceptives and—particularly in eastern Europe—abortion became widely available. Third, feminism played an important role in encouraging women to see themselves as sexual beings.

The sexual revolution also meant greater visibility for sexual identities that did not conform to the dominant heterosexual pattern. Denmark became the first European state to legalize homosexual acts in 1933, but most European countries moved toward equalizing the legal treatment of homosexuality and heterosexuality during or after the 1960s. In England, for example, homosexual acts became legal in 1967, in Scotland in 1980. Denmark moved to the forefront once again in 1989 when it became the first state to legalize registered partnerships (also called civil unions) between couples of the same sex. By 2006, 20 European countries had done so. In the Netherlands, Belgium, Spain, Portugal, Norway, Sweden, Iceland, Canada, and South Africa, gays and lesbians can legally marry on the same basis as heterosexuals.

The ongoing sexual revolution differentiated the West from much of the rest of the world, where more traditional sexual cultures remained strong. It also escalated the continuing debate within Western societies over what the "West" really means. Many Europeans and Americans, for example, saw the legalization of homosexual marriage as a logical and just extension of the concept of human rights—a central aspect of Western identity. Their opponents emphasized a different definition of the West when they argued that such a step violated the foundational Judeo-Christian values of Western culture. The growing numbers of Western citizens who were not Jewish or Christian but who adhered to religiously sanctioned sexual codes and roles—Muslim, Hindu, Sikh, and many others—intensified the debate still further.

The West in the Twenty-First Century

At the beginning of the twenty-first century, a worldwide environmental crisis raised significant questions about the ecological sustainability of Western habits of consumption. Environmental issues revealed the permeability of national borders and the limits of traditional political responses. As early as 1985, 257 multilateral treaties mandated some form of environmental protection—restrictions on trade in endangered species, wetlands preservation, forest conservation, or regulation of industrial emissions. Yet the degradation of the planet proceeded apace. By 2000, half of the world's rivers were polluted or running dry, the number of people displaced by water crises stood at 25 million (versus 21 million war-related refugees), and the potential catastrophe of global warming loomed. Faced with this potential catastrophe, representatives of 192 countries from around the world gathered in Copenhagen for a United Nations-sponsored conference on climate change in December 2009.

globalization The process by which global systems of production, distribution, and communication link together the peoples of the world.

Environmental issues such as climate change underlined the fact that global systems of production, distribution, and consumption linked the peoples of the world. Technological developments accelerated this **globalization.** Fiber-optic cables that transmitted signals 4,000 times faster than their copper predecessors made instant communication across national boundaries a reality. In this global economy, multinational corporations, with quick access to cheap Third World labor and raw materials, possessed significant economic—and political—power. So, too, did the World Bank and the IMF, the institutions that directed the flow of aid and loans throughout much of the world. The IMF, for example, insisted that governments receiving loans cut government spending on social and welfare programs and restrict the money supply to reduce inflation. Thus, economists or investors in offices far away, not elected leaders, called the shots in much of the world.

Multinational corporations, the World Bank, and the IMF embodied the characteristic Western confidence of the post-World War II era. Expert economists and agronomists taught that an infusion of Western capital and expertise would set the rest of the world on the path to economic growth. The growing gap between "North" and "South," however, called into question the reliability of Western economic models. Beginning in the 1990s, anti-globalization campaigners disrupted meetings of the World Bank, the IMF, and the "G8" (Japan, the United States, Britain, Canada, France, Germany, Italy, and Russia). These protesters sought to highlight the social costs of global capitalism and challenged the sustainability of Western models of economic growth.

CONCLUSION

Where Is the West Now?

In England, the most popular fast food is not fish and chips, long the quintessential English national supper, nor is it the Big Mac, as opponents of economic globalization might predict. Instead it is curry, the gift of the minority South Asian immigrant community. In the twenty-first century, "the West" may no longer serve as an important conceptual border marker. By many of the criteria explored in this textbook—economic, technological, political, and cultural—Tokyo would be defined as a Western city. So, too, would Melbourne—or Budapest or Shanghai. Nevertheless, the economic and social trauma that afflicted Russia and the poorer nations of the former Soviet bloc such as Romania and Bulgaria after 1989 demonstrates that the "West" retains its distinct identity, for the gap between it and the "East" remains wide. The admittedly hesitant, still incomplete spread of the Western ideal of democracy has thrown a fragile bridge across that gap. But perhaps the real divide for the twenty-first century stretches between "North" and "South"—the huge and growing difference between the global Haves and the Have-Nots. Whether any bridge can stretch across that span remains to be seen.

MAKING CONNECTIONS

1. What do historians mean when they talk about the "postwar political consensus"? When did this consensus break apart and why?
2. How does the Hungarian uprising of 1956 and the Prague Spring (see Chapter 28) compare with Solidarity? Why did Solidarity succeed when the two earlier popular risings failed?
3. How can Western technological, religious, and sexual developments since 1980 be described as "postmodern"? How have these developments shaped the relationship between the West and the rest of the world?

TAKING IT FURTHER

For suggested readings, see page R-1.

On MyHistoryLab

Take the Study Plan for Chapter 29,
The West in the Contemporary Era:
New Encounters and Transformations,
on MyHistoryLab

Chapter Review

Economic Stagnation and Political Change: The 1970s and 1980s

29.1 How did developments in the 1970s and 1980s destabilize post-World War II national and international structures?

As the superpowers attempted to stabilize relations through negotiation and arms control, rising tensions due to economic crisis escalated industrial unrest and political conflict, eroding the social democratic political consensus and leading to the crumbling of détente.

Revolution in the East

29.2 What factors explain not only the outbreak but also the success of the revolutions of 1989–1991?

Economic hardship contributed to a longing for radical change, while activists and ordinary people worked to create the structures of civil society that were crucial for the successful revolutions that tore through the Soviet bloc.

In the Wake of Revolution

29.3 What were the consequences of the revolutions of 1989–1990 for the societies of eastern Europe?

The complicated and exhausting process of building new nations divided eastern Europe into "winners," states that were able to stabilize their economies and establish democratic governments, and "losers," those with economies that continued to flounder and where power was concentrated with just a few.

Rethinking the West

29.4 How and why was the West redefined at the end of the twentieth century and the beginning of the twenty-first?

Islamist terrorism replaced communism as the new foe of the West, and intellectual, artistic, and technological developments contributed to a postmodernism rejection of Western cultural supremacy. The struggle to integrate diverse economies within the European Union, as well as increasingly diverse cultures within societies, continues to redefine the West.

Chapter Time Line

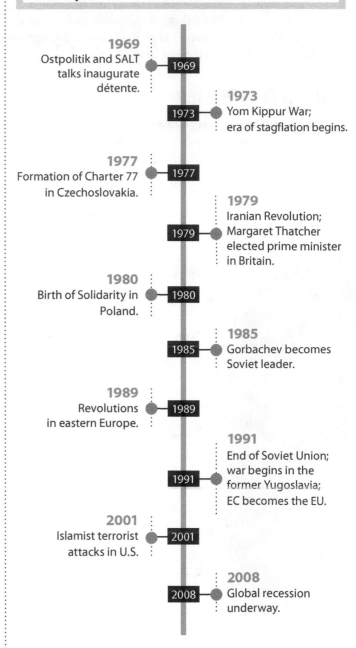

1969 Ostpolitik and SALT talks inaugurate détente.

1973 Yom Kippur War; era of stagflation begins.

1977 Formation of Charter 77 in Czechoslovakia.

1979 Iranian Revolution; Margaret Thatcher elected prime minister in Britain.

1980 Birth of Solidarity in Poland.

1985 Gorbachev becomes Soviet leader.

1989 Revolutions in eastern Europe.

1991 End of Soviet Union; war begins in the former Yugoslavia; EC becomes the EU.

2001 Islamist terrorist attacks in U.S.

2008 Global recession underway.

GLOSSARY

absolutism (p. 493) A theory and form of government in the seventeenth and eighteenth centuries in which a ruler claimed unrivaled power.

acropolis (p. 80) The defensible hilltop around which a polis grew. In classical Athens, the Acropolis was the site of the Parthenon (Temple of Athena).

agora (p. 81) An open area in the town center of a Greek polis that served as a market and a place for informal discussion.

agricultural revolution (p. 298) Refers to technological innovations that began to appear during the eleventh century, making possible a dramatic growth in population. The agricultural revolution came about through harnessing new sources of power with water and windmills, improving the pulling power of animals with better collars, using heavy plows to better exploit the soils of northern Europe, and employing a three-field crop rotation system that increased the amount and quality of food available.

alchemy (p. 531) The practice, rooted in a philosophical tradition, of attempting to turn base metals into precious ones. It also involved the identification of natural substances for medical purposes. Alchemy was influential in the development of chemistry and medicine in the sixteenth and seventeenth centuries.

aldeias (p. 412) Settlements for natives who had converted to Christianity in Brazil. In these settlements the Jesuit fathers protected the natives from enslavement.

Alexandrianism (p. 131) A style of Hellenistic poetry that demonstrated a command of meter and language and appealed more to the intellect than the emotions.

Allies (p. 779) During World War I, the states allied against the Central Powers of Germany and Austria-Hungary. During World War II, the states allied against the regimes of Nazi Germany, fascist Italy, and imperial Japan.

Anabaptism (p. 447) Meaning "to rebaptize"; refers to those Protestant radicals of the sixteenth century who rejected infant baptism and adopted adult baptism. Anabaptists treated the Bible as a blueprint for reforming not just the church but all of society, a tendency that led them to reject the authority of the state, to live in self-governing "holy communities," and in some cases to practice a primitive form of communism.

anarchism (p. 732) Ideology that views the state as unnecessary and repressive and rejects participation in parliamentary politics in favor of direct, usually violent, action.

anticlericalism (p. 759) Opposition to the political influence of the Roman Catholic Church.

Antonine Age (p. 172) Almost one hundred years of political stability in the Roman Empire, inaugurated when Nerva adopted Trajan as his son and heir.

Antonine Decree (p. 180) In 212 C.E. the emperor Aurelius Antoninus, called Caracalla, issued a decree that granted citizenship to all the free inhabitants of the Roman Empire. The decree enabled Roman law to embrace the entire population of the empire.

Apocalypse (p. 439) In the language of the Bible, the end times which would lead into Christ's Second Coming.

appeasement (p. 849) British diplomatic and financial efforts to stabilize Germany in the 1920s and 1930s and so avoid a second world war.

Arians (p. 212) Christians who believe that God the Father is superior to Jesus Christ his Son. Most of the Germanic settlers in western Europe in the fifth century were Arians.

aristocracy (p. 587) A term that originally applied to those who were considered the most fit to rule and later identified the wealthiest members of society, especially those who owned land.

asceticism (p. 214) The Christian practice of severely suppressing physical needs and daily desires in an effort to achieve a spiritual union with God. Asceticism is the practice that underlies the monastic movement.

auto-da-fé (p. 468) Meaning literally a "theater of faith," an *auto* was practiced by the Catholic Church in early modern Spain and Portugal as an extended public ritual of penance designed to cause physical pain among the sinful and promote fear of God's judgment among those who witnessed it.

auxiliary (p. 176) Soldiers in the Roman imperial army who were drawn from subject peoples. Auxiliaries received Roman citizenship after their term of service.

Babylonian Captivity of the Church (p. 352) Between 1305 and 1378, seven consecutive popes voluntarily chose to reside in Avignon, France, in order to escape anarchy in the streets of Rome. During this period the popes became subservient to the kings of France.

Babylonian Exile (p. 69) The period of Jewish history between the destruction of Solomon's temple in Jerusalem by Babylonian armies in 587 B.C.E., and 538 B.C.E, when Cyrus of Persia permitted Jews to return to Palestine and rebuild the temple.

balance of power (p. 501) An arrangement in which various countries form alliances to prevent any one state from dominating the others.

Balfour Declaration (p. 809) Declaration of 1917 that affirmed British support of a Jewish state in Palestine.

barbarians (p. 112) A term used by Greeks to describe people who did not speak Greek and who were therefore considered uncivilized.

baroque (pp. 129, 498) A dynamic style in art, architecture, and music that was intended to elicit an emotional response.

Baroque buildings were massive, imposing structures with sweeping façades. The baroque style represented a development of Greek classicism in the Hellenistic period. In the seventeenth century the baroque style was closely associated with royal absolutism.

Berlin Wall (p. 897)   Constructed by the East German government, the wall physically cut the city of Berlin in two and prevented East German citizens from access to West Germany; stood from 1961 to 1989.

Big Three (p. 883)   Term applied to the British, Soviet, and U.S. leaders during World War II: until 1945, Winston Churchill, Joseph Stalin, and Franklin Roosevelt; by the summer of 1945, Clement Attlee, Joseph Stalin, and Harry Truman.

Black Death (p. 330)   An epidemic disease, possibly Bubonic plague, that struck Europe between 1348 and the 1350s, killing at least one-third of the total population.

blitzkrieg (p. 851)   "Lightning war"; offensive military tactic making use of airplanes, tanks, and motorized infantry to punch through enemy defenses and secure key territory. First demonstrated by the German army in World War II.

boers (p. 557)   Dutch settlers, most of them farmers, who settled in the Dutch colony established at the Cape of Good Hope in southern Africa.

Bolsheviks (p. 803)   Minority group of Russian socialists, headed by Vladimir Lenin, who espoused an immediate transition to a socialist state. It became the Communist Party in the Soviet Union.

boule (p. 85)   A council of 400 male citizens established by Solon in Greece in the sixth century B.C.E. It served as an advisory body for the general assembly of all male citizens.

Bourbon reforms (p. 559)   Measures introduced by the Bourbon kings of Spain in the eighteenth century to make the Spanish Empire more manageable and profitable.

bourgeoisie (p. 594)   A social group, technically consisting of those who were untitled people living in the towns, that included prosperous merchants and financiers, members of the professions, and some skilled craftsmen known as "petty bourgeoisie." In later centuries, synonymous with "middle class."

boyars (p. 487)   Upper-level nobles who dominated Russian society until the tsars began to supplant them in the fifteenth and sixteenth centuries.

Bretton Woods Agreement (p. 884)   Agreement signed in 1944 that established the post-World War II economic framework in which the U.S. dollar served as the world's reserve currency.

brinkmanship (p. 894)   Style of Cold War confrontation in which each superpower endeavored to convince the other that it was willing to wage nuclear war.

Byzantine Empire (p. 225)   The eastern half of the Roman Empire, which lasted from the founding of Constantinople in 324 to its conquest by the Ottoman Turks in 1453.

caliphate (p. 248)   The Islamic imperial government that evolved under the leadership of Abu Bakr (r. 632–634), the successor of the prophet Muhammad. The sectarian division within Islam between the Shi'ites and Sunni derived from a disagreement over how to determine the hereditary succession from Muhammad to the caliphate, which combined governmental and some religious responsibilities.

calling (p. 443)   The Calvinist doctrine that God calls the Elect to perform his will on Earth. God's calling gave Calvinists a powerful sense of personal direction.

canon law (p. 276)   The collected laws of the Roman Catholic Church. Canon law applied to cases involving the clergy, disputes about church property, and donations to the Church. It also applied to the laity for annulling marriages, legitimating bastards, prosecuting bigamy, protecting widows and orphans, and resolving inheritance disputes.

capital (p. 661)   All the physical assets used in production, including fixed capital, such as machinery, and circulating capital, such as raw materials; more generally, the cost of these physical assets.

caravels (p. 397)   Hybrid three-masted ships developed about 1450 in the Iberian peninsula by combining the rigging of square with triangular lateen sails. These ships could be sailed in a variety of winds, carry large cargoes, be managed by a small crew, and be defended by guns mounted in the castle superstructure.

Carolingian Renaissance (p. 275)   The "rebirth" of interest in ancient Greek and Latin literature and language during the reign of the Frankish emperor Charlemagne (r. 768–814). Charlemagne promoted the intensive study of Latin to promote governmental efficiency and to propagate the Christian faith.

Catholic Reformation (p. 451)   A series of efforts during the sixteenth century to purify the Church that evolved out of late medieval spirituality and that included the creation of new religious orders, especially the Society of Jesus.

Central Powers (p. 779)   Germany and Austria-Hungary in World War I.

Chalcedonians (p. 213)   Christians who followed the doctrinal decisions and definitions of the Council of Chalcedon in 451 C.E. stating that Christ's human and divine natures were equal, but entirely distinct and united in one person "without confusion, division, separation, or change." Chalcedonian Christianity came to be associated with the Byzantine Empire and is called Greek Orthodoxy. In western Europe it is known as Roman Catholicism.

Chartists (p. 698)   A British group of workers and middle-class radicals who drafted a People's Charter in 1837 demanding universal male suffrage and other political reforms.

chinoiserie (p. 576)   A French word for an eighteenth-century decorative art that combined Chinese and European motifs.

Christian Democracy, Christian Democratic parties (p. 905) Conservative and confessionally based (Roman Catholic) political parties that dominated much of western European politics after World War II.

Christian humanists (p. 429)   During the fifteenth and sixteenth centuries these experts in Greek, Latin, and Hebrew subjected the Bible to philological study in an attempt to understand the precise meaning of the founding text of Christianity.

Church Fathers (p. 219)   Writers in late antiquity from both the Greek- and Latin-speaking worlds who sought to reconcile Christianity with classical learning.

circuit court (p. 317)   Established by King Henry II (r. 1154–1189) to make royal justice available to virtually anyone in England. Circuit court judges visited every shire in England four times a year.

civic humanism (p. 376)   A branch of humanism introduced by the Florentine chancellor Leonardo Bruni, who defended the republican institutions and values of the city. Civic humanism promoted the ethic of responsible citizenship.

civic virtue (p. 167)   The belief that the success of a republic depended on its citizens' possession of personal traits that contributed to the common good.

civilization (p. 11)   The term used by archaeologists to describe a society differentiated by levels of wealth and power, and in which religious, economic, and political control are based in cities.

civil society (p. 925)   Public organizations and activities separate from the state, commerce, or the family that help to create community life and a sense of identity.

clans or kin groups (p. 267)   The basic social and political unit of Germanic society consisting of blood relatives obliged to defend one another and take vengeance for crimes against the group and its members.

class (p. 588)   A social group with similar economic and political interests.

class consciousness (p. 670)   The awareness of people from different occupations that they belonged to a class.

classicism (p. 591)   A style in art, architecture, music, and literature that emphasizes proportion, adherence to traditional forms, and a rejection of emotion and enthusiasm.

Cluny (p. 304)   A monastery founded in Burgundy in 910 that became the center of a far-reaching movement to reform the Church that was sustained in more than 1,500 Cluniac monasteries, modeled after the original in Cluny.

Cold War (p. 883)   Struggle for global supremacy between the United States and the Soviet Union, waged from the end of World War II until 1990.

collectivization (p. 828)   The replacement of private and village farms with large cooperative agricultural enterprises run by state-employed managers. Collectivization was a key part of Joseph Stalin's plans for modernizing the Soviet economy and destroying peasant opposition to communist rule.

Columbian exchange (p. 417)   The trade of peoples, plants, animals, microbes, and ideas between the Old and New Worlds that began with Columbus.

Columbian question (p. 420)   The debate among historians and epidemiologists about whether syphilis or its ancestor disease originated in the Americas and was brought to the Old World after Columbus's voyages.

communes (p. 301)   Sworn defensive associations of merchants and workers that appeared in north-central Italy after 1070 and that became the effective government of more than a hundred cities. The communes evolved into city-states by seizing control of the surrounding countryside.

communism (p. 686)   The revolutionary form of socialism developed by Karl Marx and Friedrich Engels that promoted the overthrow of bourgeois or capitalist institutions and the establishment of a dictatorship of the proletariat.

Companions (p. 113)   Elite regiments of cavalrymen armed with heavy lances formed by Philip of Macedon in the fourth century B.C.E.

Concert of Europe (p. 693)   The joint efforts made by Austria, Prussia, Russia, Britain, and France during the years following the Congress of Vienna to suppress liberal and nationalist movements throughout Europe.

Conciliar Movement (p. 352)   A fifteenth-century movement that advocated ending the Great Schism and reforming church government by calling a general meeting or council of the bishops, who would exercise authority over the rival popes.

confessions (p. 460)   The formal sixteenth-century statements of religious doctrine: the Confession of Augsburg for Lutherans, the Helvetic Confessions for Calvinists, the Thirty-Nine Articles for Anglicans, and the decrees of the Council of Trent for Catholics.

Congress of Vienna (p. 647)   A conference of the major powers of Europe in 1814–1815 to establish a new balance of power at the end of the Napoleonic Wars.

conquistadores (p. 407)   Spanish adventurers in the Americas who explored and conquered the lands of indigenous peoples, sometimes without legal authority but usually with a legal privilege granted by the king of Spain who required that one-fifth of all things of value be turned over to the crown. The conquistadores extended Spanish sovereignty over new lands.

conservatism (p. 683)   A nineteenth-century ideology intended to prevent a recurrence of the revolutionary changes of the 1790s and the implementation of liberal policies.

corporatism (p. 819)   The practice by which committees (or "corporations") made up of representatives of workers, employers, and the state direct the economy.

Cortes (p. 494)   Legislative assemblies in the Spanish kingdoms.

cosmology (p. 134)   A theory concerning the structure and nature of the universe such as those proposed by Aristotle in the fourth century B.C.E. and Copernicus in the sixteenth century.

counties (p. 275)   Territorial units devised by the Carolingian dynasty during the eighth and ninth centuries for the administration of the empire. Each county was administered by a count who was rewarded with lands and sent to areas where he had no family ties to serve as a combined provincial governor, judge, military commander, and representative of the king.

courtly love (p. 323)   An ethic first found in the poems of the late twelfth- and thirteenth-century troubadours that portrayed the ennobling possibilities of the love between a man and a woman. Courtly love formed the basis for the modern idea of romantic love.

creoles (p. 559)   People of Spanish descent who had been born in Spanish America.

Crusades (p. 287)   Between 1095 and 1291, Latin Christians heeding the call of the pope launched eight major expeditions and many smaller ones against Muslim armies in an attempt to gain control of and hold Jerusalem.

Cubism (p. 756)   Modernist artistic movement of the early twentieth century that emphasized the fragmentation of human perception through visual experiments with geometric forms.

Cubists (p. 756)   Followers of the early twentieth century modernist artistic movement that emphasized the fragmentation of human perception through visual experiments with geometric forms.

cultural relativism (p. 421)   A mode of thought first explored during the sixteenth century to explain why the peoples of the New World did not appear in the Bible. Cultural relativism recognized that many (but not necessarily all) standards of judgment are specific to particular cultures rather than the fixed truths established by natural or divine law.

culture (p. 11)   The knowledge and adaptive behavior created by communities that helps them to mediate between themselves and the natural world through time.

cuneiform (p. 24)   A kind of writing in which wedge-shaped symbols are pressed into clay tablets to indicate words and ideas. Cuneiform writing originated in ancient Sumer.

curia (p. 307)   The administrative bureaucracy of the Roman Catholic Church.

Cynics (p. 133)   Followers of the teachings of Antisthenes (ca. 445–360 B.C.E.) who rejected pleasures, possessions, and social conventions to find peace of mind.

Darwinian theory of evolution (p. 747)   Scientific theory associated with the nineteenth-century scientist Charles Darwin that highlights the role of variation and natural selection in the evolution of species.

D-Day (p. 861)   Common term for June 6, 1944, when 150,000 Allied troops landed on the shores of northern France to open an effective second front against German-occupied Europe.

Decembrists (p. 694)   Russian liberals who staged a revolt against Tsar Nicholas I on the first day of his reign in December 1825.

de-Christianization (p. 633)   A program inaugurated in France in 1793 by the radical Jacobin and former priest Joseph Fouché that closed churches, eliminated religious symbols, and attempted to establish a purely civic religion.

decolonization (p. 893)   The retreat of Western powers from their imperial territories.

deduction, deductive reasoning (p. 533)   The logical process by which ideas and laws are derived from basic truths or principles.

Defenders (p. 581)   Irish Catholic peasants who joined the United Irishmen in the rebellion against Britain in 1798.

deism (p. 597)   The belief that God created the universe and established immutable laws of nature but did not subsequently intervene in the operation of nature or in human affairs.

deists (p. 543)   Seventeenth- and eighteenth-century thinkers who believed that God created the universe and established immutable laws of nature but did not subsequently intervene in the operation of nature or in human affairs.

Delian League (p. 94)   The alliance among many Greek cities organized by Athens in 478 B.C.E. in order to fight Persian forces in the eastern Aegean Sea. The Athenians gradually turned the Delian League into the Athenian Empire.

demand (p. 662)   The desire of consumers to acquire goods and the need of producers to acquire raw materials and machinery.

democracy (p. 84)   A form of government in which citizens devise their own governing institutions and choose their leaders; began in Athens, Greece, in the fifth century B.C.E.

de-Stalinization (p. 901)   Nikita Khrushchev's effort to decentralize political and economic control in the Soviet Union after 1956.

détente (p. 919)   During the 1970s, a period of lessened Cold War hostilities and greater reliance on negotiation and compromise.

dialectic (p. 686)   The theory that history advanced in stages as the result of the conflict between different ideas or social groups.

dialectical materialism (p. 686)   The socialist philosophy of Karl Marx according to which history advanced as the result of material or economic forces and would lead to the creation of a classless society.

Diaspora (p. 195)   Literally "dispersion of population"; usually used to refer to the dispersion of the Jewish population after the Roman destruction of the Temple in Jerusalem in 70 C.E.

diets (p. 494)   Legislative assemblies in German territories.

divination (p. 23)   The practice of discerning the future by looking for messages imprinted in nature.

divine right (p. 494)   The theory that rulers received their power directly from God.

division of labor (p. 657)   The assignment of one stage of production to a single worker or group of workers to increase efficiency and productive output.

domestic system (p. 656)   An economic arrangement developed in the sixteenth century in which capitalist entrepreneurs employed families in rural areas to spin and weave cloth and make nails and cutlery.

Dreyfus Affair (p. 725)   The trials of Captain Alfred Dreyfus on treason charges, which dominated French political life in the decade after 1894 and revealed fundamental divisions in French society.

dualistic (pp. 88, 534)   A term used to describe a philosophy or a religion in which a rigid distinction is made between body and mind, good and evil, or the material and the immaterial world.

Dutch Revolt (p. 479)   The rebellion against Spanish rule of the seven northern provinces of the Netherlands between 1579 and 1648, which resulted in the independence of the Republic of the United Provinces.

Edict of Nantes (p. 476)   Promulgated by King Henry IV in 1598, the edict allowed the Huguenots to build a quasi-independent state within the kingdom of France, giving them the right to have their own troops, church organization, and political autonomy within their walled towns, but banning them from the royal court and the city of Paris. King Louis XIV revoked the edict in 1685.

empires (pp. 19, 554)   Large political formations consisting of different kingdoms or territories outside the boundaries of the states that control them.

empiricism (p. 532)   The practice of testing scientific theories by observation and experiment.

enclosure (p. 660)   The consolidation of scattered agricultural holdings into large, compact fields which were then closed off by hedges, bushes, or walls, giving farmers complete control over the uses of their land.

encomienda (p. 409)   The basic form of economic and social organization in early Spanish America, based on a royal grant awarded to a Spaniard for military or other services that gave the grantee and his successors the right to gather tribute from the Indians in a defined area.

English Parliament (p. 318)   King Edward I (r. 1272–1307) began to call the English Parliament in order to raise sums of money for his foreign wars. The English Parliament differed from similar assemblies in Europe. It usually included representatives of the "commons," which consisted of townsmen and prosperous farmers who lacked titles of nobility, but whom the king summoned because he needed their money. As a result, a broader spectrum of the population joined Parliament than in most other medieval kingdoms.

enlightened despots (p. 611)   The term assigned to absolute monarchs who initiated a series of legal and political reforms in an effort to realize the goals of the Enlightenment.

Enlightenment (p. 595)   An international intellectual movement of the eighteenth century that emphasized the use of reason and the application of the laws of nature to human society.

Epicureans (p. 132)   Followers of the teachings of the philosopher Epicurus (341–271 B.C.E.). Epicureans tried to gain peace of mind by choosing pleasures rationally.

Estates General (p. 494)   The legislative assembly of France in the Old Regime.

ethnic cleansing (p. 936)   A term introduced during the wars in Yugoslavia in the 1990s; the systematic use of murder, rape, and violence by one ethnic group against members of other ethnic groups in order to establish control over a territory.

Eucharist (p. 313)   Also known as Holy Communion or the Lord's Supper, the Eucharistic rite of the Mass celebrates Jesus's last meal with his apostles when the priest-celebrant consecrates wafers of bread and a chalice of wine as the body and blood of Christ. In the Middle Ages the wafers of bread were distributed for the congregation to eat, but drinking from the chalice was a special privilege of the priesthood. Protestants in the sixteenth century and Catholics in the late twentieth century began to allow the laity to drink from the chalice.

eugenics (p. 835)   The effort to improve the physical and intellectual capacities of the population by encouraging individuals with "desirable" traits to reproduce and/or by discouraging those individuals designated as "undesirable" from reproducing.

Euro-Islam (p. 942)   The identity and belief system being forged by European Muslims who argue that Islam does not contradict or reject European values.

European Economic Community (EEC) (p. 906)   Originally comprising West Germany, France, Italy, Belgium, Luxembourg, and the Netherlands, the EEC was formed in 1957 to integrate its members' economic structures and so foster both economic prosperity and international peace. Also called the Common Market.

European Union (EU) (p. 937)   A successor organization to the EEC; the effort to integrate European political, economic, cultural, and military structures and policies.

excommunication (p. 306)   A decree by the pope or a bishop prohibiting a sinner from participating in the sacraments of the Church and forbidding any social contact whatsoever with the surrounding community.

existentialism (p. 814)   Twentieth-century philosophy that emerged in the interwar era and influenced many thinkers and artists after World War II. Existentialism emphasizes individual freedom in a world devoid of meaning or coherence.

Expressionism (p. 756)   Modernist artistic movement of the early twentieth century that used bold colors and experimental forms to express emotional realities.

factories (p. 415)   Trading posts established by European powers in foreign lands.

fanatic (p. 474)   Originally referring to someone possessed by a demon, during the sixteenth century a fanatic came to mean a person who expressed immoderate enthusiasm in religious matters or who pursued a supposedly divine mission, often to violent ends.

fascism (p. 818)   Twentieth-century political ideology that rejected the existing alternatives of conservatism, communism, socialism, and liberalism. Fascists stressed the authoritarian power of the state, the efficacy of violent action, the need to build a national community, and the use of new technologies of influence and control.

feminism, feminist movement (p. 737)   International movement that emerged in the second half of the nineteenth century and demanded broader political, legal, and economic rights for women.

Fertile Crescent (p. 13)   Also known as the Levantine Corridor, this 25-mile-wide arc of land stretching from the Jordan River to the Euphrates River was the place where food production and settled communities first appeared in southwest Asia (the Middle East).

feudalism (p. 281)   A term historians use to describe a social system common during the Middle Ages in which lords granted fiefs (tracts of land or some other form of income) to dependents, known as vassals, who owed their lords personal services in exchange. Feudalism refers to a society governed through personal ties of dependency rather than public political institutions.

fief (p. 281)   During the Middle Ages a fief was a grant of land or some other form of income that a lord gave to a vassal in exchange for loyalty and certain services (usually military assistance).

Final Solution (p. 868)   Nazi term for the effort to murder every Jew in Europe during World War II.

fin-de-siecle (p. 751)   French term for the "turn of the century"; used to refer to the cultural crisis of the late nineteenth century.

firestorm (p. 864)   Human-made catastrophe: incendiary bombs cause fires, which combine with winds to suck the oxygen out of the air and raise temperatures to combustible levels. First experienced during the British bombing of the German city of Hamburg in World War II.

First Triumvirate (p. 163)   The informal political alliance made by Julius Caesar, Pompey, and Crassus in 60 B.C.E. to share power in the Roman Republic. It led directly to the collapse of the Republic.

Forms (p. 103)   In the philosophical teachings of Plato, these are eternal, unchanging absolutes such as Truth, Justice, and Beauty that represent true reality, as opposed to the approximations of reality that humans encounter in everyday life.

Fourteen Points (p. 806)   The principles outlined by U.S. President Woodrow Wilson as the basis for a new world order after World War I.

freemasons (p. 609)   Members of secret societies of men and women that flourished during the Enlightenment, dedicated to the creation of a society based on reason and virtue and committed to the principles of liberty and equality.

French Wars of Religion (p. 475)   A series of political assassinations, massacres, and military engagements between French Catholics and Calvinists from 1560 to 1598.

friars (p. 312)   "Brothers" who wandered from city to city and throughout the countryside begging for alms. Unlike monks who remained in a cloister, friars tried to help ordinary laypeople with their problems by preaching and administering to the sick and poor.

Gaullism (p. 913)   The political ideology associated with twentieth-century French political leader Charles de Gaulle. Gaullism combined the advocacy of a strong, centralized state with social conservatism.

general strike (p. 732)   Syndicalist tactic that called for every worker to go on strike and thus disrupt the capitalist economy and force a political revolution.

genocide (p. 800)   The murder of an entire people.

German-Soviet Non-Aggression Pact (p. 849)   Signed by Joseph Stalin and Adolf Hitler in 1939, the agreement publicly pledged Germany and the Soviet Union not to attack each other and secretly divided up Poland and the Baltic states between the two powers.

Girondins (p. 625)   The more conservative members of the Jacobin party who favored greater economic freedom and opposed further centralization of state power during the French Revolution.

glasnost (p. 928)   Loosely translated as openness or honesty; Gorbachev's effort after 1985 to break with the secrecy that had characterized Soviet political life.

globalization (p. 950)   The process by which global systems of production, distribution, and communication link together the peoples of the world.

Gnostic (p. 197)   Religious doctrine that emphasizes the importance of *gnosis*, or hidden truth, as a way of releasing spiritual reality from the prison of the essentially unreal or evil material world.

Gothic (p. 325)   A style in architecture in western Europe from the late twelfth and thirteenth centuries, characterized by ribbed vaults and pointed arches, which drew the eyes of worshipers upward toward God. Flying buttresses, which redistributed the weight of the roof, made possible thin walls pierced by large expanses of stained glass.

grand jury (p. 318)   In medieval England after the judicial reforms of King Henry II (r. 1154–1189), grand juries were called when the circuit court judge arrived in a shire. The sheriff assembled a group of men familiar with local affairs who constituted the grand jury and who reported to the judge the major crimes that had been committed since the judge's last visit.

Great Depression (p. 819)   Calamitous drop in prices, reduction in trade, and rise in unemployment that devastated the global economy in 1929.

Great Persecution (p. 206)   An attack on Christians in the Roman Empire begun by the emperor Galerius in 303 C.E. on the grounds that their worship was endangering the empire. Several thousand Christians were executed.

Great Purge (p. 831)   Period of mass arrests and executions particularly aimed at Communist Party members in the Soviet Union.

Great Schism (p. 352)   The division of the Catholic Church (1378–1417) between rival Italian and French claimants to the papal throne.

Green movement, Green politics (p. 923)   A new style of politics and set of political ideas resulting from the confluence of environmentalism, feminism, and anti-nuclear protests of the 1970s.

guilds (p. 343)   Professional associations devoted to protecting the special interests of a particular trade or craft and to monopolizing production and trade in the goods the guild produced.

Gulag (p. 829)   Term for the network of forced labor and prison camps in the Soviet Union.

habiru (p. 55)   Peasants who existed outside the palace system of the Late Bronze Age; often seen as bandits.

haciendas (p. 409)   Large landed estates that began to be established in the seventeenth century and replaced encomiendas throughout much of Spanish America.

Hallstatt culture (p. 124)   The first Celtic civilization in central Europe; from about 750 to about 450 B.C.E., Hallstatt Celts spread throughout Europe.

Hellenistic (p. 112)   The word used to describe the civilization, based on that of Greece, that developed in the wake of the conquests of Alexander the Great.

helots (p. 84)   The brutally oppressed subject peoples of the Spartans. Tied to the land they farmed for Spartan masters, they were treated little better than beasts of burden.

Helsinki Accords (p. 923)   Signed by representatives of 32 European states, Canada, the United States, and the Soviet Union in 1975; often regarded as the apex of détente.

heresy (p. 196)   A teaching or belief not considered orthodox.

hetairai (p. 98)   Elite courtesans in ancient Greece who provided intellectual as well as sexual companionship.

hieroglyphs (p. 31)   Ancient Egyptian system of writing that represented both sounds and objects.

Holocaust (p. 867)   Adolf Hitler's effort to murder all the Jews in Europe during World War II.

Homo sapiens sapiens (p. 12)   Scientific term meaning "most intelligent people"; applied to physically and intellectually modern human beings that first appeared between 200,000 and 100,000 years ago in Africa.

hoplites (p. 82)   Greek soldiers in the Archaic Age who could afford their own weapons. Hoplite tactics made soldiers fighting as a group dependent on one another. This contributed to the internal cohesion of the polis and eventually to the rise of democracy.

Huguenots (p. 474)   The term for French Calvinists, who constituted some 10 percent of the population by 1560.

humanists (p. 374)   During the Renaissance, writers and orators who studied ancient Latin and sometimes Greek texts. Their principal interests were grammar, rhetoric, poetry, history, and ethics.

Hundred Years' War (p. 345)   A series of engagements (1337–1453) between England and France over England's attempts to assert its claims to territories in France.

hyperinflation (p. 821)   Catastrophic price increases and currency devaluation, such as that which occurred in Germany in 1923.

iconoclasm (p. 241)   The destruction of religious images in the Byzantine Empire in the eighth century.

icons (p. 240)   The Christian images of God and saints found in Byzantine art.

ideologies (p. 682)   Theories of society and government that form the basis of political programs.

Indo-European (p. 45)   Parent language of a majority of modern European languages as well as modern Armenian and Persian; sometimes used to refer to the people who spoke this language.

induction (pp. 24, 532)   The process of reasoning that formulates general hypotheses and theories on the basis of specific observation and the accumulation of data.

indulgences (p. 352)   Certificates that allowed penitents to atone for their sins and reduce their time in purgatory. Usually these were issued for going on a pilgrimage or performing a pious act; however, during the Babylonian Captivity of the Church (1305–1378) popes began to sell them, a practice Martin Luther protested in 1517 in an act that brought on the Protestant Reformation.

industrial capitalism (p. 669)   A form of capitalism characterized by the ownership of factories by private individuals and the employment of wage labor.

inheritance of acquired characteristics (p. 749)   Now discredited scientific theory of evolutionary change, which was powerful in the nineteenth century.

intendants (p. 496)   French royal officials who became the main agents of French provincial administration in the seventeenth century.

interdict (p. 307)   A papal decree prohibiting the celebration of the sacraments in an entire city or kingdom.

Investiture Controversy (p. 306)   A dispute that began in 1076 between the popes and the German emperors over the right to invest bishops with their offices. The most famous episode was the conflict between Pope Gregory VII and Emperor Henry IV. The controversy was resolved by the Concordat of Worms in 1122.

Iron Age (p. 57)   Historical period following the Bronze Age; marked by the prevalent use of iron.

Iron Curtain (p. 883)   Metaphor for the Cold War division of Europe after World War II.

Islamism (p. 939)   Ideology that insists that Islam demands a rejection of Western values and that violence in this struggle against the West is justified.

Jacobins (p. 621)   A French political party supporting a democratic republic that found support in political clubs throughout the country and dominated the National Convention from 1792 until 1794.

Jim Crow (p. 770)   Series of laws mandating racial segregation throughout the American South.

Julio-Claudian dynasty (p. 172)   Established by Octavian Augustus, this hereditary monarchy drawn from members of his extended family ruled Rome until 68 C.E.

Junkers (p. 508)   The traditional nobility of Prussia.

justification by faith (p. 432)   Refers to Martin Luther's insight that humanity is incapable of performing enough religious good works to earn eternal salvation. Salvation is an unmerited gift from God called grace. Those who receive grace are called the Elect.

Keynesian economics (p. 833)   Economic theories associated with the British economist John Maynard Keynes that advocate using the power of the democratic state to ensure economic prosperity.

knight (p. 281)   During the Middle Ages a knight was a soldier who fought on horseback. A knight was a vassal or dependent of a lord, who usually financed the knight's expenses of armor and weapons and of raising and feeding horses with a grant of land known as a fief.

Koine (p. 127)   The standard version of the Greek language spoken throughout the Hellenistic world.

kulak (p. 828)   Russian term for a peasant who was relatively prosperous.

laissez-faire (p. 683)   The principle that governments should not regulate or otherwise intervene in the economy unless it is necessary to protect property rights and public order.

late antiquity (p. 202)   The period between about 250 and 600, which bridged the classical world and the Middle Ages.

Late Bronze Age (p. 44)   The period from 1500 to 1100 B.C.E., characterized by an unprecedented degree of international trade and diplomatic exchange.

La Tène culture (p. 125)   A phase of Celtic civilization that lasted from about 450 to 200 B.C.E. La Tène culture became strong especially in the regions of the Rhine and Danube Rivers.

Latin Christendom (p. 214)   The parts of medieval Europe, including all of western Europe, united by Christianity and the use of Latin in worship and intellectual life. Latin served as an international language among the ruling elites in western Europe, even though they spoke different languages in their daily lives.

Latin War (p. 145)   A war that the Latin peoples of Italy waged against the Roman Republic between 340 and 338 B.C.E.

Law of the Twelve Tables (p. 142)   A body of written law inscribed on 12 bronze tablets and published in 451 B.C.E. This written summary of existing law was the first body of written law in Rome.

lay investiture (p. 305)   The practice of nobles, kings, or emperors installing churchmen and giving them the symbols of office.

League of Nations (p. 806)   Association of states set up after World War I to resolve international conflicts through open and peaceful negotiation.

Lend-Lease Act (p. 858)   Passed in March 1941, the act gave Britain and later the Soviet Union access to U.S. industrial products during World War II, with payment postponed for the duration of the war.

Levantine Corridor (p. 13)   Also known as the Fertile Crescent, this arc of land stretching from the Jordan River to the Euphrates River was the place where food production and settled communities first appeared in southwest Asia (the Middle East).

liberalism (p. 682)   An ideology based on the conviction that individual freedom is of supreme importance and the main responsibility of government is to protect that freedom.

"Linear B" (p. 49)   The earliest written form of Greek, used by the Mycenaeans.

linear perspective (p. 382)   In the arts, the use of geometrical principles to depict a three-dimensional space on a flat, two-dimensional surface.

liturgy (p. 263)   The forms of Christian worship, including the prayers, chants, and rituals to be said, sung, or performed throughout the year.

lord (p. 280)   During the Middle Ages, a lord was someone who offered protection to dependents, known as vassals, who took an oath of loyalty to him. Most lords demanded military services from their vassals and sometimes granted them tracts of land known as fiefs.

lustration (p. 935)   Implemented in many former communist states in the 1990s, this policy banned former communists and communist collaborators from public office.

ma'at (p. 30)   Ancient Egyptian concept of the fundamental order established by the gods.

Macedonian Renaissance (p. 242)   During the Macedonian dynasty's rule of Byzantium (867–1056), aristocratic families, the Church, and monasteries devoted their immense riches to embellishing Constantinople with new buildings, mosaics, and icons. The emperors sponsored historical, philosophical, and religious writing.

Mafia (p. 706)   Organizations of armed men who took control of local politics and the economy in late nineteenth-century Sicily.

magic (p. 470)   Learned opinion described two kinds of magic: natural magic, which involved the manipulation of occult forces believed to exist in nature, and demonic magic, which called upon evil spirits to gain access to power. This was widely accepted as a reality until the middle of the seventeenth century.

Magisterial Reformation (p. 440)   Refers to Protestant churches that received official government sanction.

Magna Carta (p. 318)   In 1215 some English barons forced King John to sign the "great charter," in which the king pledged to respect the traditional feudal privileges of the nobility, towns, and clergy. Subsequent kings swore to uphold it, thereby accepting the fundamental principle that even the king was obliged to respect the law.

Malthusian population trap (p. 668)   The theory of Thomas Malthus (1766–1834) that the natural tendency of population to grow faster than the food supply would eventually drive the size of populations back to sustainable levels and end periods of economic expansion that usually accompany the growth of population.

Manhattan Project (p. 864)   Code name given to the secret Anglo-American project that resulted in the construction of the atom bomb during World War II.

manor (p. 299)   A medieval unit of agricultural management in which a lord managed and served as the presiding judge over peasants who worked the land.

marches (p. 275)   Territorial units of the Carolingian Empire for the administration of frontier regions. Each march was ruled by a margrave who had special powers necessary to defend vulnerable borders.

Marshall Plan (p. 886)   The use of U.S. economic aid to restore stability to Europe after World War II and so undercut the appeal of communist ideology.

martyr (p. 199)   In Christian tradition, believers who chose to die rather than to renounce or deny their Christian beliefs.

mass politics (p. 717)   A political culture characterized by the participation of non-elites.

matriarchy/matriarchal (p. 48)   A social or cultural system in which family lineage is traced through the mother and/or in which women hold significant power.

mechanical philosophy (p. 534)   The seventeenth-century philosophy of nature, championed by René Descartes, holding that nature operated in a mechanical way, just like a machine made by a human being.

megalith (p. 16)   A very large stone used in prehistoric European monuments between 5000 and 1500 B.C.E.

mercantilism (p. 499)   The theory that the wealth of a state depended on its ability to import fewer commodities than it exported and thus acquire the largest possible share of the world's monetary supply. The theory encouraged state intervention in the economy and the regulation of trade.

meritocracy (p. 640)   The practice of appointing people to office solely on the basis of ability and performance rather than social or economic status.

mesmerism (p. 610)   A pseudoscience developed by Franz Anton Mesmer in the eighteenth century that treated sickness by massaging or hypnotizing the patient to produce a crisis that restored health.

mestizos (p. 573)   People of mixed white and Indian ancestry.

metropolis (p. 553)   The parent country of a colony or imperial possession; the "mother state" that controlled an empire.

Middle Kingdom (p. 32)   In ancient Near Eastern history, refers to the period of Egyptian history from 2040 to 1720 B.C.E.

Middle Passage (p. 569)   The journey taken by European ships bringing slaves from Africa to the Americas.

Mishnah (p. 195)   Completed around 220, a collection of homilies and decisions to explain Jewish law.

Modern Devotion (p. 354)   A fifteenth-century religious movement that stressed individual piety, ethical behavior, and intense religious education. The Modern Devotion was promoted by the Brothers of the Common Life, a religious order whose influence was broadly felt through its extensive network of schools.

modernism, modernist (pp. 752, 754)   Term applied to artistic and literary movements from the late nineteenth century through the 1950s. Modernists sought to create new aesthetic forms and values.

monastic movement (p. 215)   In late antiquity, Christian ascetics organized communities where men and women could pursue a life of spirituality through work, prayer, and asceticism. Called the monastic movement, this spiritual quest spread quickly throughout Christian lands.

Monophysites (p. 214)   Christians who do not accept the Council of Chalcedon (see Chalcedonians). Monophysites believe that Jesus Christ has only one nature, equally divine and human.

monotheism (p. 39)   The belief in only one god, first attributed to the ancient Hebrews. Monotheism is the foundation of Judaism, Christianity, Islam, and Zoroastrianism.

mosque (p. 246)   A place of Muslim worship.

Mountain, the (p. 625)   Members of the radical faction within the Jacobin party during the French Revolution who advocated the centralization of state power and instituted the Reign of Terror.

mulattos (p. 565)   People of mixed white and black race.

Munich Agreement (p. 849)   The agreement in 1939 between the governments of Nazi Germany, Britain, and France that granted Germany sovereignty over the Sudetenland; part of the effort to appease the Nazi government and avoid a second total war in Europe.

nabobs (p. 575)   Members of the British East India Company who made fortunes in India and returned to Britain, flaunting their wealth.

Napoleonic Code (p. 639)   The name eventually given to the Civil Code of 1804, promulgated by Napoleon, which gave France a uniform and authoritative code of law.

nation (p. 687)   A large community of people who possess a sense of unity based on a belief that they have a common homeland and share a similar culture.

national consciousness (p. 688)   The awareness or belief of people that they belong to a nation.

nationalism (p. 687)   The belief that the people who form a nation should have their own political institutions and that the interests of the nation should be defended and promoted at all costs.

nationalist-racist politics (p. 732)   Anti-liberal politics that appeal to race-based identities and fears.

national self-determination (p. 687)   The doctrine advanced by nationalists that any group that considers itself a nation has the right to be ruled only by the members of their own nation and to have all members of the nation included in that state.

nation-state (p. 687)   A political structure sought by nationalists in which the boundaries of the state and the nation are identical, so that all the members of a nation are governed by the same political authorities.

natural law (p. 144)   A law that is believed to be inherent in nature rather than established by human beings.

nawabs (p. 573)   Native provincial governors in eighteenth-century India.

Nazism (p. 820)   Twentieth-century political ideology associated with Adolf Hitler that adopted many fascist ideas but with a central focus on racism and particularly anti-Semitism.

neoclassicism (p. 591)   The revival of the classical art and architecture of ancient Greece and Rome in the eighteenth century.

Neolithic Age (p. 11)   The New Stone Age, characterized by the development of agriculture and the use of stone tools.

Neoplatonism (pp. 221, 536)   A philosophy based on the teachings of Plato and his successors that flourished in late antiquity, especially in the teachings of Plotinus. Neoplatonism influenced Christianity in late antiquity. During the Renaissance Neoplatonism was linked to the belief that the natural world was charged with occult forces that could be used in the practice of magic.

New Conservatism (p. 923)   Political ideology that emerged at the end of the 1970s combining the free market approach of nineteenth-century liberalism with social conservatism.

New Economic Policy (NEP) (p. 827)   Vladimir Lenin's economic turnaround in 1921 that allowed and even encouraged small private businesses and farms in the Soviet Union.

new feminism (p. 922)   Reemergence of the feminist movement in the 1970s.

new imperialism (p. 760)   The third phase of modern European imperialism, which occurred in the late nineteenth and early twentieth centuries and extended Western control over almost all of Africa and much of Asia.

New Kingdom (p. 35)   In ancient Near Eastern history, the period in Egyptian history from 1550 to 1150 B.C.E. During the New Kingdom, Egyptian kings first took the title of pharaoh and established an empire that reached to the Euphrates River.

New Left (p. 915)   Left-wing political and cultural movement that emerged in the late 1950s and early 1960s; sought to develop a form of socialism that rejected the overcentralization, authoritarianism, and inhumanity of Stalinism.

New Testament (p. 196)   The collection of texts that together with the Hebrew Bible, or Old Testament, comprise the Christian Bible. New Testament texts include the Epistles (letters of Paul of Tarsus to early Christians), the Gospels (stories of Jesus Christ's life, death, and resurrection), and other early Christian documents.

95 theses (p. 434)   Propositions about indulgences Martin Luther announced he was willing to defend in debate. The publication of the 95 theses in 1517 started the Protestant Reformation.

nobility (p. 588)   Members of the aristocracy who received official recognition of their hereditary status, including their titles of honor and legal privileges.

nobility of the robe (p. 588)   French noblemen whose families acquired their status by appointment to office.

no-man's-land (p. 786)   The area between the combatants' trenches on the Western Front during World War I.

North Atlantic Treaty Organization (NATO) (p. 889)   Defensive anti-Soviet alliance of the United States, Canada, and the nations of western Europe established in 1949.

northern Renaissance (p. 430)   A movement in northern Europe that built on the foundations of the Italian Renaissance, especially to subject the Bible and the sources of Christianity to critical scrutiny.

Nuremberg trials (p. 870)   Post-World War II trials of members of the Nazi Party and German military; conducted by an international tribunal.

Old Kingdom (p. 29)   In ancient Near Eastern history, the period in Egyptian history from ca. 2680–2200 B.C.E., formed by the unification of the kingdoms of Upper Egypt and Lower Egypt.

Old Regime (p. 611)   The political order of eighteenth-century France, dominated by an absolute monarch and a privileged nobility and clergy.

oligarchy (p. 84)   A government consisting of only a few people rather than the entire community.

Olympic Games (p. 81)   Greek athletic contests held in Olympia every four years between 776 B.C.E and 217 C.E.

orthodox, orthodoxy (p. 196)   In Christianity, the term indicates doctrinally correct belief.

Ottonian Renaissance (p. 284)   Under the patronage of the Saxon Emperor Otto I (936–973) and his brother Bruno,

learned monks, Greek philosophers from Byzantium, and Italian scholars gathered at the imperial court, stimulating a cultural revival in literature and the arts. The writers and artists enhanced the reputation of Otto.

pagan (p. 210)   The Christian term for polytheist worship (worshiping more than one god). In the course of late antiquity, the Christian Church suppressed paganism, the traditional religions of the Roman Empire.

palace system (p. 53)   Late Bronze Age social system that concentrated religious, economic, political, and military power in the hands of an elite, who lived apart from most people in monumental fortified compounds.

pan-Arabism (p. 839)   Nationalist ideology that called for the political unification of all Arabs, regardless of religious affiliation.

papacy (p. 209)   The bishop of the city of Rome, sometimes referred to as "Father." The papacy refers to the administrative and political institutions controlled by the Pope. The papacy began to gain strength in the sixth century in the absence of Roman imperial government in Italy.

papal infallibility (p. 759)   The doctrine of the Roman Catholic Church proclaimed at the First Vatican Council in 1870 that the pope could not err when making solemn declarations regarding faith or morals.

paradigm (p. 536)   A conceptual model or intellectual framework within which scientists conduct their research and experimentation.

parlements (p. 496)   The highest provincial courts in France, the most important of which was the Parlement of Paris.

patriarchy (p. 28)   A social or cultural system in which men occupy the positions of power; in a family system, a father-centered household.

patricians (p. 141)   In ancient Rome, patricians were aristocratic clans with the highest status and the most political influence.

patrons and clients (p. 156)   In ancient Roman society, a system in which a powerful man (the patron) would exercise influence on behalf of a social subordinate (the client) in anticipation of future support or assistance.

Pax Romana (p. 170)   Latin for "Roman Peace," this term refers to the Roman Empire established by Augustus that lasted until the early third century C.E.

Pentateuch (p. 73)   The first five books of the Hebrew Bible.

perestroika (p. 928)   Loosely translated as "restructuring"; Gorbachev's effort to decentralize, reform, and thereby strengthen Soviet economic and political structures.

personal rule (p. 515)   The period from 1629 to 1640 in England when King Charles I ruled without Parliament.

phalanx (p. 82)   The military formation favored by hoplite soldiers. Standing shoulder-to-shoulder in ranks often eight men deep, hoplites moved in unison and depended on one another for protection.

pharaoh (p. 35)   Title for the Egyptian king, used during the New Kingdom period.

philology (p. 374)   A method reintroduced by the humanists during the Italian Renaissance devoted to the comparative study of language, especially to understanding the meaning of a word in a particular historical context.

philosophes (p. 596)   The writers and thinkers of the Enlightenment, especially in France.

pilgrimages (p. 217)   Religious journeys made to holy sites in order to encounter relics.

Pillars of Islam (p. 248)   The five basic principles of Islam as taught by Muhammad.

plantation colony (p. 398)   First appearing in the Cape Verde Islands and later in the tropical parts of the Americas, these colonies were established by Europeans who used African slave labor to cultivate cash crops such as sugar, indigo, cotton, coffee, and tobacco.

plebeians (p. 141)   The general body of Roman citizens.

plebiscite (p. 631)   A popular vote for or against a form of government or rule by a particular person.

pogroms (p. 735)   An organized and often officially encouraged riot or attack to persecute a particular ethnic or religious group, especially associated with eastern European attacks against Jews.

polis (p. 80)   A self-governing Greek city-state.

polytheistic (p. 23)   The belief in many gods.

pop art (p. 908)   Effort by artists in the 1950s and 1960s both to utilize and to critique the material abundance of post-World War II popular culture.

Popular Front (p. 833)   A political coalition of liberals, socialists, and communists designed to defeat fascist and racist-nationalist political rivals.

positivism (p. 689)   The philosophy developed by August Comte in the nineteenth century according to which human society passed through a series of stages, leading to the final positive stage in which the accumulation of scientific data would enable thinkers to discover the laws of human behavior and bring about the improvement of society.

positivist (p. 751)   The emphasis on the use of the scientific method to reach truth; a stress on observable fact.

postindustrialism, postindustrial society (p. 946)   A service-based, rather than manufacturing-based, economy characterized by an emphasis on marketing and information and by a proliferation of communications technologies.

postmodernism (p. 943)   Umbrella term covering a variety of artistic styles and intellectual theories and practices; in general, a rejection of a single, universal, Western style of modernity.

Potsdam Conference (p. 885)   The meeting in July 1945 of the Allied leaders of Britain, the Soviet Union, and the United States in the German city of Potsdam.

Pragmatic Sanction of Bourges (p. 387)   An agreement in 1438 that guaranteed the virtual autonomy of the French Church from papal control, enabling the French king to interfere in religious affairs and exploit Church revenues for government purposes.

Prague Spring (p. 904)   Short-lived popular effort in 1968 to reform Czechoslovakia's political structures; associated with the phrase "socialism with a human face."

predestination (p. 442)   The doctrine promoted by John Calvin that since God, the all-knowing and all-powerful being, knew everything in advance and caused everything to happen, then the salvation of any individual was predetermined.

prerogative (p. 515)   The set of powers exercised by the English monarch alone, rather than in conjunction with Parliament.

Price Revolution (p. 464)   The period between about 1540 and 1640 in which Europe, after a long period of falling or stable prices that stretched back to the fourteenth century, experienced sustained price increases. This caused widespread social and economic turmoil.

priesthood of all believers (p. 435)   Martin Luther's doctrine that all those of pure faith were themselves priests, a doctrine that undermined the authority of the Catholic clergy over the laity.

primogeniture (p. 513)   The legal arrangement by which the eldest son inherits the entire estate upon the death of the father.

proletariat (p. 686)   The word used by Karl Marx and Friedrich Engels to identify the class of workers who received their income from wages.

prophetic movement (p. 72)   An important phase in the development of what became Judaism. In the ninth century B.C.E., Hebrew religious reformers, or prophets, demanded the transformation of religious and economic practices to reflect ideals of social justice and religious purity.

protectionism (p. 561)   The policy of shielding domestic industries from foreign competition through a policy of levying tariffs on imported goods.

Protestant Reformation (p. 427)   Period that dominated European affairs between 1517 and 1560 when the movement for religious reform begun by Martin Luther led Germany, Britain, and most of northern Europe to break away from the Catholic Church.

Radical Reformation (p. 440)   Refers to Protestant movements that failed to gain official government recognition and were at best tolerated, at worst persecuted, during the sixteenth century.

Radical Right (p. 820)   Refers to extremist ideologies on the far right of the political spectrum, such as fascism and Nazism.

rationalism (p. 533)   The theory that the mind contains rational categories independent of sensory observation; more generally that reason is the primary source of truth.

Realpolitik (p. 707)   The adoption of political tactics based solely on their realistic chances of success.

redistributive economies (p. 19)   Type of economic system characteristic of ancient Mesopotamian societies. The central political authority controls all agricultural resources and their redistribution.

regency (p. 496)   Rule by relative of a monarch during a period when the monarch was too young to rule or otherwise incapacitated.

Reign of Terror (p. 627)   A purging of alleged enemies of the French state between 1793 and 1794, superintended by the Committee of Public Safety, that resulted in the execution of 17,000 people.

relativity, theory of (p. 750)   Albert Einstein's revolutionary model of the physical universe as four-dimensional.

relics (p. 217)   In Christian belief, relics are sacred objects that have miraculous powers. They are associated with saints, biblical figures, or some object associated with them. They served as contacts between Earth and Heaven and were verified by miracles.

Religious Peace of Augsburg (p. 440)   In 1555 this peace between Lutherans and Catholics within the Holy Roman Empire established the principle of *cuius regio, eius religio,* which means "he who rules determines the religion of the land." Protestant princes in the Empire were permitted to retain all church lands seized before 1552 and to enforce Protestant worship, but Catholic princes were also allowed to enforce Catholic worship in their territories.

Renaissance (p. 365)   A term meaning "rebirth" used by historians to describe a movement that sought to imitate and understand the culture of antiquity. The Renaissance generally refers to a movement that began in Italy and then spread throughout Europe from about 1350 to 1550.

reparations (p. 807)   Payments imposed upon Germany after World War I by the Versailles Treaty to cover the costs of the war.

republic (p. 141)   A state in which political power resides in the people or their representatives rather than in a monarch.

republicanism (p. 366)   A political theory first developed by the ancient Greeks, especially the philosopher Plato, but elaborated by the ancient Romans and rediscovered during the Italian Renaissance. The fundamental principle of republicanism as developed during the Italian Renaissance was that government officials should be elected by the people or a portion of the people.

Republic of Letters (p. 596)   An international community of Enlightenment writers and thinkers in the eighteenth century.

Republic of Virtue (p. 625)   The ideal form of government proposed by Maximilien Robespierre and other Jacobins during the French Revolution. Its proponents wished to make the republic established in 1792 more egalitarian and secular and inspire civic pride and patriotism in the people.

requerimiento (p. 407)   A document read by conquistadores to the natives of the Americas before making war on them. The document briefly explained the principles of Christianity and commanded the natives to accept them immediately along with the authority of the pope and the sovereignty of the king of Spain. If the natives refused, they were warned they would be forced to accept Christian conversion and subjected to Spain anyway.

Resistance, the (p. 870)   Label given to the many different underground political and partisan movements directed against Nazi rule in German-occupied Europe during World War II.

revisionism, socialist revisionism (p. 731)   The belief that an equal society can be built through participation in parliamentary politics rather than through violent revolution.

rhetoric (p. 374)   The art of persuasive or emotive speaking and writing, which was especially valued by the Renaissance humanists.

Romanesque (p. 324)   A style in architecture that spread throughout western Europe during the eleventh and the first half of the twelfth centuries and was characterized by arched stone roofs supported by rounded arches, massive stone pillars, and thick walls.

Romanization (p. 177)   The process by which conquered peoples absorbed aspects of Roman culture, especially the Latin language, city life, and religion.

romanticism (p. 690)   An artistic and literary movement of the late eighteenth and nineteenth centuries that involved a protest against classicism, appealed to the passions rather than the intellect, and emphasized the beauty and power of nature.

Rome-Berlin Axis (p. 848)   Alliance between Benito Mussolini's Italy and Adolf Hitler's Germany formed in 1936.

Russification (p. 727)   Tsarist policy from the 1890s until the outbreak of World War I that imposed the use of Russian language and emphasized Russian Orthodox religious and cultural practices.

salons (p. 609)   Private sitting rooms or parlors of aristocratic French women where discussions of philosophy, science, literature, and politics took place in the eighteenth century.

sans-culottes (p. 621)   The militant citizens of Paris who refused to wear the pants worn by noblemen and provided support for the Jacobins during the French Revolution; literally, those without breeches.

satraps (p. 117)   Persian provincial governors who collected taxes and oversaw the bureaucracy.

Schlieffen Plan (p. 783)   German military plan devised in 1905 that called for a sweeping attack on France through Belgium and the Netherlands.

scholasticism (p. 320)   A term referring to a broad philosophical and theological movement that dominated medieval thought and university training. Scholasticism used logic learned from Aristotle to interpret the meaning of the Bible and the writings of the Church Fathers, who created Christian theology in its first centuries.

Scramble for Africa (p. 765)   The frenzied imposition of European control over most of Africa that occurred between 1870 and 1914.

scriptorium (p. 271)   The room in a monastery where monks copied books and manuscripts.

Sea Peoples (p. 55) Name given by the Egyptians to the diverse groups of migrants whose attacks helped bring the International Bronze Age to an end.

Second Industrial Revolution (p. 718) A new phase in the industrialization of the processes of production and consumption, which was underway in Europe in the 1870s.

Second Triumvirate (p. 166) In 43 B.C.E. Octavian (later called Caesar Augustus), Mark Antony, and Lepidus made an informal alliance to share power in Rome while they jockeyed for control. Octavian emerged as the sole ruler of Rome in 31 B.C.E.

secularization (p. 545) The reduction of the importance of religion in society and culture.

seigneur (p. 593) The lord of a French estate who received payments from the peasants who lived on his land.

separate spheres (p. 607) The theory that men and women should conduct their lives in different social and political environments, confining women to the domestic sphere and excluding them from the public sphere of political involvement.

sepoys (p. 574) Indian troops serving in the armed forces of the British East India Company.

Septuagint (p. 127) The Greek translation of the Hebrew Bible (Old Testament).

serfs (p. 299) During the Middle Ages serfs were agricultural laborers who worked and lived on a plot of land granted them by a lord to whom they owed a certain portion of their crops. They could not leave the land, but they had certain legal rights that were denied to slaves.

settler colony (p. 398) A colony authorized when a private person obtained a license from a king to seize an island or parcel of land and occupied it with settlers from Europe who exported their own culture to the new lands. Settler colonies first appeared among the islands of the eastern Atlantic and portions of the Americas.

simony (p. 305) The practice of buying and selling church offices.

skepticism (p. 541) A tendency to doubt what one has been taught or is expected to believe.

Social Darwinism (p. 748) The later-nineteenth-century application of the theory of evolution to entire human societies.

social democracy (p. 831) Political system in which a democratically elected parliamentary government endeavors to ensure a decent standard of living for its citizens through both economic regulation and the maintenance of a welfare state.

socialism (p. 684) An ideology calling for the ownership of the means of production by the community with the purpose of reducing inequalities of income, wealth, opportunity, and economic power.

socialist revisionism (p. 731) The belief that an equal society can be built through participation in parliamentary politics rather than through violent revolution.

Social War (p. 160) The revolt of Rome's allies against the Republic in 90 B.C.E. demanding full Roman citizenship.

Solidarity (p. 925) Trade union and political party in Poland that led an unsuccessful effort to reform the Polish communist state in 1981; survived to lead Poland's first non-communist government since World War II in 1989.

Sophists (p. 103) Professional educators who traveled throughout the ancient Greek world, teaching many subjects. Their goal was to teach people the best ways to lead better lives.

soviets (p. 801) Workers' and soldiers' councils formed in Russia during the Revolution of 1917.

Spanish Armada (p. 478) A fleet of 132 ships, which sailed from Portugal to rendezvous with the Spanish army stationed in the Netherlands and launch an invasion of England in 1588. The English defeated the Armada as it passed through the English Channel. The defeat marked a shift in the power balance from Spain to England.

Spanish Reconquest (p. 259) Refers to the numerous military campaigns by the Christian kingdoms of northern Spain to capture the Muslim-controlled cities and kingdoms of southern Spain. This long, intermittent struggle began with the capture of Toledo in 1085 and lasted until Granada fell to Christian armies in 1492.

spiritualists (p. 448) A tendency within Protestantism, especially Lutheranism, to emphasize the power of personal spiritual illumination, called the "inner Word," a living form of the Scriptures written directly on the believer's soul by the hand of God.

stagflation (p. 920) Term coined in the 1970s to describe an economy troubled by both high inflation and high unemployment rates.

standing armies (p. 494) Trained and equipped military forces that were not disbanded after the conclusion of war. Standing armies often helped maintain order and enforce governmental policy at home.

states (p. 553) Consolidated territorial areas that have their own political institutions and recognize no higher political authority.

Stoics (p. 133) Followers of the philosophy developed by Zeno of Citium (ca. 335–ca. 263 B.C.E.) that urged acceptance of fate while participating fully in everyday life.

structuralism (p. 909) Influential post-World War II social theory that explored the common structures of language and thought.

Struggle of the Orders (p. 142) The political strife between patrician and plebeian Romans beginning in the fifth century B.C.E. The plebeians gradually won political rights and influence as a result of the struggle.

suffragettes (p. 742) Feminist movement that emerged in Britain in the early twentieth century. Unlike the suffragists, who sought to achieve the national vote for women through rational persuasion, the suffragettes adopted the tactics of violent protest.

suffragists (p. 742) Feminists who sought to achieve the national vote for women through rational persuasion and parliamentary politics.

supply (p. 662)   The amounts of capital, labor, and food that are needed to produce goods for the market as well as the quantities of those goods themselves.

syncretism (p. 70)   The practice of blending foreign religious beliefs with an indigenous religious system; a common practice throughout the Roman Empire.

syndicalism (p. 732)   Ideology of the late nineteenth and early twentieth century that sought to achieve a working-class revolution through economic action, particularly through mass labor strikes.

Talmud (p. 216)   Commentaries on Jewish law. Rabbis completed the Babylonian Talmud and the Jerusalem Talmud by the end of the fifth century C.E.

tetrarchy (p. 204)   The government by four rulers established by the Roman emperor Diocletian in 293 C.E. that lasted until 312. During the tetrarchy many administrative and military reforms altered the fabric of Roman society.

Third Estate (p. 618)   The component of the Estates General in Old Regime France that technically represented all the commoners in the kingdom.

Third Reich (p. 854)   Term for Adolf Hitler's Germany; articulates the Nazi aim of extending German rule across Europe.

Third World (p. 898)   Term coined in 1955 to describe nations that did not align with either the Soviet Union or the United States; commonly used to describe the industrially underdeveloped nations.

Thomism (p. 322)   A branch of medieval philosophy associated with the work of the Dominican thinker, Thomas Aquinas (1225–1274), who wrote encyclopedic summaries of human knowledge that confirmed Christian faith.

Time of Troubles (p. 489)   The period from 1604 to 1613 when Russia fell into chaos, which ended when the national assembly elected Tsar Michael Romanov, whose descendants ruled Russia until they were deposed in 1917.

Torah (p. 73)   Most commonly, the first five books of the Hebrew Bible; also used to refer to the whole body of Jewish sacred writings and tradition.

total war (p. 779)   A war that demands extensive state regulation of economic production, distribution, and consumption; a war that blurs (or erases entirely) the distinction between civilian and soldier.

trading posts (p. 400)   Areas built by European traders along the coasts of Africa and Asia as a base for trade with the interior. Trading posts or factories were islands of European law and sovereignty, but European authority seldom extended very far beyond the fortified post.

transubstantiation (p. 313)   A doctrine promulgated at the Fourth Lateran Council in 1215 that distinguished the difference between the outward appearances and the inner substance of how the Eucharistic bread and wine changed into the body and blood of Christ.

Treaty of Brest-Litovsk (p. 791)   Treaty between Germany and Bolshevik-controlled Russia, signed in March 1918, that ceded to Germany all of Russia's western territories.

trial by jury (p. 318)   When disputes about the possession of land arose after the late twelfth century in England, sheriffs assembled a group of 12 local men who testified under oath about the claims of the plaintiffs; the circuit court judge then made his decision on the basis of their testimony. The system was later extended to criminal cases.

Triple Alliance (p. 781)   Defensive alliance of Germany, Austria-Hungary, and Italy, signed in 1882.

Triple Entente (p. 781)   Informal defensive agreement linking France, Great Britain, and Russia before World War I.

triremes (p. 91)   Greek warships with three banks of oars. Triremes manned by the poorest people of Athenian society became the backbone of the Athenian Empire.

troubadours (p. 323)   Poets from the late twelfth and thirteenth centuries who wrote love poems, meant to be sung to music, which reflected a new sensibility, called courtly love, about the ennobling possibilities of the love between a man and a woman.

Truman Doctrine (p. 886)   Named after U.S. president Harry Truman, the doctrine that in 1947 inaugurated the Cold War policy of resisting the expansion of communist control.

Twelfth-Century Renaissance (p. 321)   An intellectual revival of interest in ancient Greek philosophy and science and in Roman law in western Europe during the twelfth and early thirteenth centuries. The term also refers to a flowering of vernacular literature and the Romanesque and Gothic styles in architecture.

tyrants (p. 83)   Rulers in Greek city-states, usually members of the aristocracy, who seized power illegitimately rather than acquiring it by heredity or election. Tyrants often gained political support from the hoplites and the poor.

Unitarians (p. 449)   A religious reform movement that began in the sixteenth century and rejected the Christian doctrine of the Trinity. Unitarians (also called Arians, Socinians, and Anti-Trinitarians) taught a rationalist interpretation of the Scriptures and argued that Jesus was a divinely inspired man, not God who became a man, as other Christians believed.

United Kingdom (p. 688)   The name of the British state formed by the union of England and Scotland in 1707. In 1801 Ireland became part of the United Kingdom, but after the establishment of the Irish Free State in 1922, only the six Irish counties in the northern province of Ulster remained united to Britain.

universal law of gravitation (p. 530)   A law of nature established by Isaac Newton in 1687 holding that any two bodies attract each other with a force that is directly proportional to the product of their masses and indirectly proportional to the square of the distance between them. The law was presented in mathematical terms.

universal male suffrage (p. 624)   The granting of the right to vote to all adult males.

vassals (p. 280)   During the Middle Ages, men voluntarily submitted themselves to a lord by taking an oath of loyalty. Vassals owed the lord certain services—usually military assistance—and sometimes received in exchange a grant of land known as a fief.

Vatican II (p. 912) Popular term for the Second Vatican Council that convened in 1963 and introduced a series of changes within the Roman Catholic Church.

vernacular languages (p. 480) The native spoken languages of Europe, which became literary languages and began to replace Latin as the dominant form of learned expression during the sixteenth century.

Versailles Treaty (p. 807) Treaty between Germany and the victorious Allies after World War I.

Vichy, Vichy regime, Vichy government (p. 852) Authoritarian state established in France after its defeat by the German army in 1940.

vizier (p. 36) The chief minister of state in New Kingdom Egypt, the vizier supervised the administration of the entire kingdom.

Vulgate (p. 213) The Latin translation of the Bible produced about 410 by the monk Jerome. It was the standard Bible in western Christian churches until the sixteenth century.

Wahhabism (p. 840) A religious reform and revival movement founded by Muhammad Abd al-Wahhab (1703–1787) in the eighteenth century to purify Islam by returning to a strict interpretation of the *Sharia,* or Islamic law. Revived during the 1920s in Saudi Arabia.

Warsaw Pact (p. 889) Military alliance of the Soviet Union and its eastern European satellite states in the Cold War era.

Weimar Republic (p. 820) The democratic German state constructed after defeat in World War I and destroyed by the Nazis in 1933.

wergild (p. 267) In Germanic societies, the term referred to what an individual was worth in case he or she suffered an injury. It was the amount of compensation in gold that the wrongdoer's family had to pay to the victim's family.

witch-hunt (p. 470) Refers to the dramatic increase in the judicial prosecution of alleged witches in either church or secular courts from the middle of the sixteenth to the middle of the seventeenth centuries.

Yahwism (p. 70) The worship of Yahweh ("Jehovah"); the form of early Israelite religious belief.

Yalta Conference (p. 884) Meeting in 1945 of the leaders of the Allied states of Britain, the Soviet Union, and the United States to devise plans for postwar Europe.

ziggurat (p. 23) Monumental tiered or terraced temple characteristic of ancient Mesopotamia.

Zionism (p. 736) Nationalist movement that emerged in the late nineteenth century and sought to establish a Jewish political state in Palestine (the Biblical Zion).

Zoroastrianism (p. 88) The monotheistic religion of Persia founded by Zoroaster that became the official religion of the Persian Empire.

SUGGESTIONS FOR FURTHER READING

CHAPTER 1 THE BEGINNINGS OF CIVILIZATION, 10,000–1150 B.C.E.

Andrews, Anthony P. *First Cities*. 1995. An excellent introduction to the development of urbanism in Southwest Asia, Egypt, India, China, and the Americas.

Crawford, Harriet. *Sumer and the Sumerians*. 2004. A comprehensive study of the interplay between the physical environment, emerging political structures, and technological change. Clearly illustrated.

Dalley, Stephanie. *Mari and Karana: Two Old Babylonian Cities*. 1984. Despite the rather forbidding title, a delightful exploration of daily life in the eighteenth century B.C.E., using excavations of two small kingdoms in northwest Mesopotamia.

Fagan, Brian. *People of the Earth: An Introduction to World Prehistory*. 1998. A comprehensive textbook that introduces basic issues with a wealth of illustrations and explanatory materials.

Hornung, Erik. *History of Ancient Egypt: An Introduction*, trans. David Lorton. 1999. A concise and lucid overview of Egyptian history and life.

Kuhrt, Amélie. *The Ancient Near East, ca. 3000–330 B.C.*, 2 vols. 1995. A magisterial overview, with an excellent bibliography. The place to start for a continuous historical narrative of the region.

Redford, Donald B. *Egypt, Canaan, and Israel in Ancient Times*. 1993. A distinguished Egyptologist discusses 3,000 years of uninterrupted contact between Egypt and southwestern Asia.

Sasson, Jack M, ed. *Civilizations of the Ancient Near East*, vol. 2. 1995. Contains a number of very helpful essays, particularly on Egypt.

Schmandt-Besserat, Denise. *How Writing Came About*. 1996. A highly readable and groundbreaking argument that cuneiform writing developed from a method of counting with tokens.

Schulz, Regine, and Matthias Seidel, eds. *Egypt: The World of the Pharaohs*. 1999. A sumptuously illustrated collection of essays on all aspects of Egyptian society and life by leading experts.

Snell, Daniel C. *Life in the Ancient Near East*. 1997. A concise account of the major developments over 5,000 years.

Spindler, Konrad. *The Man in the Ice: The Discovery of a 5,000-Year-Old Body Reveals the Secrets of the Stone Age*. 1994. A leader of the international team of experts interprets the corpse of a Neolithic hunter found in the Austrian Alps.

Stiebing, William H. *Ancient Near Eastern History and Culture*. 2008. Clear and comprehensive survey of important political and cultural events.

Trigger, Bruce G. *Early Civilizations: Ancient Egypt in Context*. 1995. A leading cultural anthropologist examines Old and Middle Kingdom Egypt through comparison with the early civilizations of China, Peru, Mexico, Mesopotamia, and Africa.

Van De Mieroop, Marc. *A History of the Ancient Near East ca. 3000–323 B.C.* 2007. Authoritative and up-to-date history.

Wenke, Robert J. *Patterns in Prehistory: Humankind's First Three Million Years*, 4th ed. 1999. An often witty, highly readable account.

CHAPTER 2 THE AGE OF EMPIRES: THE INTERNATIONAL BRONZE AGE AND ITS AFTERMATH, CA. 1500–550 B.C.E.

Bryce, Trevor. *Life and Society in the Hittite World*. 2002. A lively look at Hittite customs, laws, and social structures.

Bryce, Trevor. *The Letters of the Great Kings of the Ancient Near East: The Royal Correspondence of the Late Bronze Age*. 2003. Bryce explores the Club of the Great Powers through their surviving correspondence.

Bryce, Trevor. *The Trojans and Their Neighbors*. 2005. An up-to-date examination of the historical Troy.

Cohen, Raymond, and Raymond Westbrook, eds. *Amarna Diplomacy: The Beginnings of International Relations*. 2000. An intriguing collaboration of archaeologists, linguists, and specialists in international diplomacy, this book looks at the Amarna Letters from the context of modern international relations.

Dever, William G. *What Did the Biblical Writers Know and When Did They Know It?: What Archaeology Can Tell Us About the Reality of Ancient Israel*. 2001. A clear and often entertaining account of the writing of the Hebrew Bible.

Dever, William G. *Who Were the Early Israelites and Where Did They Come From?* 2003. A clear and lively account that takes the reader step-by-step through the various historical, archaeological, and political controversies that bedevil the study of ancient Israel.

Dickinson, Oliver. *The Aegean Bronze Age*. 1994. Now the standard treatment of the complex archaeological data.

Dothan, Trude, and Moshe Dothan. *People of the Sea: The Search for the Philistines*. 1992. A survey of the archaeological material, written for non-specialists.

Finkelstein, Israel, and Neil Asher Silberman. *David and Solomon: In Search of the Bible's Sacred Kings and the Roots of the Western Tradition.* 2006. An important, if controversial, archaeological interpretation that views David and Solomon as tribal chieftains and the "United Monarchy" as a fiction, this elegantly written study also explores the impact of the biblical story on Western identity.

Fitton, J. Lesley. *Minoans: Peoples of the Past.* 2002. Accessible account of recent research and conclusions.

Fitton, J. Lesley. *The Discovery of the Greek Bronze Age.* 1996. A lucid and well-illustrated study of the archaeologists who brought the Greek Bronze Age to light in the nineteenth and early twentieth centuries.

Kuhrt, Amélie. *The Ancient Near East, ca. 3000–330 B.C.,* 2 vols. 1995. A magisterial overview, with an excellent bibliography. The place to start for a continuous historical narrative of the region.

Latacz, Joachim. *Troy and Homer: Towards a Solution of an Old Mystery.* 2004. One of the most recent efforts to solve the puzzle of the historicity of Homer's account of the Trojan War.

Markoe, Glenn. *Phoenicians.* 2000. An important treatment of Phoenician society by a noted expert.

Miller, Patrick D. *Chieftains of the Highland Clans: A History of Israel in the 12th and 11th Centuries B.C.* 2003. Uses not only archaeological and textual evidence but also anthropological methodology to explore the history of the early Israelites.

Redford, Donald B. *Egypt, Canaan and Israel in Ancient Times.* 1992. An excellent, detailed synthesis of textual and archaeological evidence that emphasizes interconnections among cultures.

Stiebing, William H. *Ancient Near Eastern History and Culture.* 2008. A comprehensive survey that also pays close attention to historiographical and archaeological controversies. The chapter on the end of the International Bronze Age is particularly well done.

van de Mieroop, Marc. *A History of the Ancient Near East ca. 3000–323 B.C.* 2007. An excellent survey, with clear maps and useful time lines.

Walker, Christopher, ed. *Astronomy Before the Telescope.* 1996. A fascinating collection of essays about astronomy in the premodern period, which makes clear Western civilization's enormous debt to the Babylonians.

CHAPTER 3   GREEK CIVILIZATION

Boardman, John. *Persia and the West: An Archaeological Investigation of the Genesis of Achaemenid Art.* 2000. A brilliantly illustrated study that stresses intercultural influences in every aspect of Persian art.

Boyce, Mary. *A History of Zoroastrianism,* vol. 2. 1975. This authoritative examination provides a masterful overview of the religion of the Persian Empire.

Burkert, Walter. *The Orientalizing Revolution: Near Eastern Influence on Greek Culture in the Early Archaic Age,* trans. Margaret Pinder and Walter Burkert. 1993. Explains how the Semitic East influenced the development of Greek society in the Archaic Age.

Cohn, Norman. *Cosmos, Chaos, and the World to Come: The Ancient Roots of Apocalyptic Faith.* 1993. Expert critical analysis of apocalyptic religions in the West, including Zoroastrianism, ancient Judaism, Christianity, and other faiths.

Finkelstein, Israel, and Neil Asher Silberman. *The Bible Unearthed: Archaeology's New Vision of Ancient Israel and the Origin of the Sacred Texts.* 2001. An important archaeological interpretation that challenges the narrative of the Hebrew Bible and offers a reconsideration of biblical history.

Gottwald, Norman K. *The Hebrew Bible: A Socio-Literary Introduction.* 1985. Combines a close reading of the Hebrew Bible with the latest archaeological and historical evidence.

Just, Roger. *Women in Athenian Law and Life.* 1989. Provides an overview of the social context of women in Athens.

Kuhrt, Amélie. *The Ancient Near East, ca. 3000–330 B.C.,* vol. 2. 1995. This rich and comprehensive bibliography is a remarkably concise and readable account of Persian history with excellent discussion of ancient textual evidence. Many important passages appear in fluent translation.

Lindberg, David C. *The Beginnings of Western Science: The European Scientific Tradition in Philosophical, Religious, and Institutional Context, 600 B.C. to A.D. 1450.* 1992. This highly readable study provides an exciting survey of the main developments in Western science.

Markoe, Glenn. *Phoenicians.* 2000. The best and most up-to-date treatment of Phoenician society by a noted expert.

Murray, Oswyn. *Early Greece.* 1983. A brilliant study of all aspects of the emergence of Greek society between the Dark Age and the end of the Persian Wars.

Osborne, Robin. *Greece in the Making, 1200–479 B.C.* 1996. An excellent narrative of the development of Greek society with special regard to the archaeological evidence.

Stewart, Andrew. *Art, Desire, and the Body in Ancient Greece.* 1997. A provocative study that examines Greek attitudes toward sexuality and art.

Walker, Christopher, ed. *Astronomy Before the Telescope.* 1996. A fascinating collection of essays about astronomy in the premodern period, which makes clear our enormous debt to the Babylonians.

Wieshöfer, Josef. *Ancient Persia from 550 B.C. to A.D. 650,* trans. Azizeh Azodi. 1996. A fresh and comprehensive overview of Persian cultural, social, and political history that relies on Persian evidence more heavily than on biased Greek and Roman sources.

CHAPTER 4   HELLENISTIC CIVILIZATION

Auatin, Michel. *The Hellenistic World from Alexander to the Roman Conquest: A Selection of Ancient Sources in Translation,* 2nd ed. 2006. A major collection of more than 325 documents from this period.

Boardman, John, Jasper Griffin, and Oswyn Murray, eds. *Greece and the Hellenistic World. The Oxford History of the Classical World.* 1988. A synthesis of all aspects of Hellenistic life, with excellent illustrations and bibliography.

Bosworth, A. B. *Alexander and the East: The Tragedy of Triumph.* 1997. A negative interpretation of Alexander as a totalitarian ruler.

Bugh, Glenn R. *The Cambridge Companion to the Hellenistic World.* 2006. A collection of essays on 15 different aspects of Hellenistic politics and culture.

Cartledge, Paul, Peter Garnsey, and Erich Gruen, eds. *Hellenistic Constructs: Essays in culture, history and historiography.* 1997. Emphasizes the cultural interaction between Greek and non-Greek societies during this period.

Cohen, Getzel M. *The Hellenistic Settlements in Europe, the Islands, and Asia Minor.* 1996. The standard reference work on the cities founded in these areas during the Hellenistic period.

Cohn, Norman. *Cosmos, Chaos, and the World to Come: The Ancient Roots of Apocalyptic Faith.* 1993. This brilliant study explains the development of ideas about the end of the world in the cultures of the ancient world.

Cunliffe, Barry. *The Ancient Celts.* 1997. This source analyzes the archaeological evidence for the Celtic Iron Age, with many illustrations and maps.

Cunliffe, Barry, ed. *The Oxford Illustrated Prehistory of Europe.* 1996. A collection of well-illustrated essays on the development of European cultures from the end of the Ice Age to the Classical period.

Fox, Robin Lane. *Alexander the Great.* 1994. Shows that the myth Alexander created is as influential today as it was in the ancient world.

Freeman, Philip. *Alexander the Great.* 2011. A highly readable study based on sound scholarship.

Green, Peter. *Alexander to Actium: The Historical Evolution of the Hellenistic Age.* 1990. A vivid interpretation of the world created by Alexander until the victory of Augustus.

Gruen, Erich S. *The Hellenistic World and the Coming of Rome.* 1984. An important study of how Rome entered the eastern Mediterranean world.

Kuhrt, Amélie, and Susan Sherwin-White, eds. *Hellenism in the East: The Interaction of Greek and Non-Greek Civilizations from Syria to Central Asia After Alexander.* 1987. These studies help us understand the complexities of the interaction of Greeks and non-Greeks in the Hellenistic world.

Momigliano, Arnaldo. *Alien Wisdom: The Limits of Hellenization.* 1975. A study of Greek attitudes toward the contemporary civilizations of the Romans, Celts, Jews, and Persians.

Onians, John. *Art and Thought in the Hellenistic Age: The Greek World View, 350–50 B.C.* 1979. Amply illustrated study of Hellenistic artistic and intellectual history.

Pollitt, J. J. *Art in the Hellenistic Age.* 1986. A brilliant interpretation of the development of Hellenistic art. Discusses the freedom of aristocratic Greek women in Egypt during this period.

Pomeroy, Sarah B. *Women in Hellenistic Egypt: From Alexander to Cleopatra.* 1984. Describes the lives of women in different strata of society.

Steele, James. *Hellenistic Architecture in Asia Minor.* 1992. Challenges the belief that Hellenistic architecture represented a degradation of the Greek classical style.

CHAPTER 5   THE ROMAN REPUBLIC

Bringmann, Klaus. *A History of the Roman Republic.* 2007. A useful survey that not only provides a detailed narrative but also challenges some of the traditional interpretations.

Cornell, T. J. *The Beginnings of Rome: Italy and Rome from the Bronze Age to the Punic Wars (ca. 1000–264 B.C.).* 1996. A synthesis of the latest evidence with many important new interpretations.

Crawford, Michael, *The Roman Republic*, 2nd ed. 1992. An overview by a leading scholar.

Flower, Harriet I., ed. *The Cambridge Companion to the Roman Republic.* 2004. Includes essays on political and military history, Roman society, republican territorial expansion, culture, and the influence of the Republic on the French and American revolutions.

Gardner, Jane F. *Women in Roman Law and Society.* 1986. Explains the legal position of women in the Roman world.

Goldsworthy, Adrian. *The Fall of Carthage: The Punic Wars, 265–146 B.C.* 2003. A sweeping history of one of the great military conflicts of the ancient world.

Gruen, Erich S. *The Last Generation of the Roman Republic.* 1995. An exhaustive study of a crucial period of the republic.

Lintott, Andrew. *The Constitution of the Roman Republic.* 2003. An authoritative and well-written treatment of the subject.

Orlin, Eric. *Temples, Religion and Politics in the Roman Republic.* 1997. A study of Roman religion focusing on the building and dedication of new temples.

Sherwin-White, A. N. *Roman Citizenship.* 1980. A comprehensive treatment of the subject.

Stein, Peter. *Roman Law in European History.* A superb overview, beginning with the Law of the Twelve Tables.

Wiseman, T. P. *Remembering the Roman Republic: Essays on Late Republican Politics and Literature.* 2009. Explores different aspects of the popular, democratic tradition of political ideology in the Roman Republic.

CHAPTER 6   ENCLOSING THE WEST: THE EARLY ROMAN EMPIRE AND ITS NEIGHBORS: 31 B.C.E.–235 C.E.

Barrett, Anthony A. *Livia: First Lady of Imperial Rome.* 2002. Biography of one of the most intriguing figures in the Roman Empire.

Beard, Mary, John North, and Simon Price. *Religions of Rome.* 1995. The first volume contains essays on polytheist religions, and the second contains translated ancient sources.

Chancey, Mark. *Greco-Roman Culture and the Galilee of Jesus.* 2005. A concise but broad-ranging survey of the title topic.

Crossan, J. D. *The Birth of Christianity.* 1998. Lively account of the Roman context of this new religious force.

Futrell, Alison. *Blood in the Arena: The Spectacle of Roman Power.* 1997. Explores the role of violent spectacle in creating and sustaining Roman rule.

Gardner, Jane F. *Women in Roman Law and Society.* 1987. Discusses issues pertaining to women in Rome.

Isaac, Benjamin. *The Creation of Racism in Classical Antiquity.* 2004. A highly readable discussion of ancient social prejudices and discriminatory stereotypes that influenced the development of modern racism.

Mattingly, David. *Imperialism, Power, and Identity: Experiencing the Roman Empire.* 2010. A critical look at the concept of "Romanization," with an emphasis on the experience of the ruled rather than the ambitions of the rulers.

Nickelsburg, George W. E. *Ancient Judaism and Christian Origins. Diversity, Continuity, and Transformation.* 2003. Innovative study of the emergence of Christianity from Judaism.

Ramage, Nancy H., and Andrew Ramage. *Roman Art,* 4th ed. 2005. An excellent, beautifully illustrated introduction to Roman art and architecture.

Romm, James. *The Edges of the Earth in Ancient Thought: Geography, Exploration, and Fiction.* 1992. An exciting introduction to the Roman understanding of real and imaginary peoples.

Scott, Sarah, and Jane Webster, eds. *Roman Imperialism and Provincial Art.* 2003. A collection of essays that explores new approaches to the cultural interconnections between the Romans and the peoples they ruled.

Talbert, Richard, ed. *The Barrington Atlas of the Classical World.* 2000. Contains excellent maps.

Webster, Graham. *The Roman Imperial Army,* 3rd ed. 1985. Discusses military organization and life in the empire.

Wells, Peter S. *The Battle That Stopped Rome.* 2003. A lively account of the Battle of Teutoburg Forest that provides a clear and comprehensive demonstration of the way archaeological evidence helps shape our understanding of the past.

Wolfram, Herwig. *The Roman Empire and Its Germanic Peoples.* 1997. Examines the interrelation of Romans and Germans over several centuries.

Woolf, G., ed. *The Cambridge Illustrated History of the Roman World.* 2003. Richly illustrated and comprehensive.

Woolf, Greg. *Becoming Roman: The Origins of Provincial Civilization in Gaul.* 1998. An acclaimed study of Romanization.

CHAPTER 7 LATE ANTIQUITY: THE AGE OF NEW BOUNDARIES, 250–600

Bowersock, G. W. *Hellenism in Late Antiquity.* 1990. Explains the important role of traditional Greek culture in shaping late antiquity.

Bowersock, G. W., Peter Brown, and Oleg Grabar, eds. *Late Antiquity: A Guide to the Postclassical World.* 1999. An indispensable handbook containing synthetic essays and shorter encyclopedia entries.

Brown, Peter. *The Cult of the Saints: Its Rise and Function in Late Antiquity.* 1981. A brilliant and highly influential study.

Brown, Peter. *The Rise of Western Christendom: Triumph and Diversity.* 1997. An influential and highly accessible survey.

Brown, Peter. *The World of Late Antiquity.* 1971. A classic treatment of the period.

Cameron, Averil. *The Later Roman Empire.* 1993. *The Mediterranean World in Late Antiquity.* 1997. Excellent textbooks with bibliography and maps.

Clark, Gillian. *Women in Late Antiquity: Pagan and Christian Life-Styles.* 1993. The starting point of modern discussion; lucid and reliable.

Harries, Jill. *Law and Empire in Late Antiquity.* 1999. Explores the presence and practice of law in Roman society.

Lee, A. D. *Information and Frontiers: Roman Foreign Relations in Late Antiquity.* 1993. An exciting and original investigation.

Maas, Michael. *The Cambridge Companion to the Age of Justinian.* 2005. A collection of 20 chapters by different experts on all aspects of the Mediterranean world in the sixth century.

Maas, Michael. *Readings in Late Antiquity: A Sourcebook.* 2000. Hundreds of ancient sources in translation illustrating all aspects of late antiquity.

Markus, Robert. *The End of Ancient Christianity.* 1995. Excellent introduction to the transformation of Christianity in late antiquity.

Pagels, Elaine. *The Origin of Satan: How Christians Demonized Jews, Pagans, and Heretics.* 1996. The award-winning historian Elaine Pagels tells the griping story of how early Christians transformed the gospel of love into the irrational hatred of others.

Rich, John, ed. *The City in Late Antiquity.* 1992. Important studies of changes in late antique urbanism.

Thompson, E. A. *The Huns,* rev. Peter Heather. 1997. The best introduction to major issues.

CHAPTER 8 MEDIEVAL EMPIRES AND BORDERLANDS: BYZANTIUM AND ISLAM

Bowersock, Glen, Peter Brown, and Oleg Grabar, eds. *Late Antiquity: A Guide to the Post-Classical World.* 1999. Interpretive essays combined with encyclopedia entries make this a starting point for discussion.

Brown, Thomas S. *Gentlemen and Officers: Imperial Administration and Aristocratic Power in Byzantine Italy, A.D. 554–800.* 1984. The basic study of Byzantine rule in Italy between Justinian and Charlemagne.

Bulliet, Richard W. *The Camel and the Wheel.* 1990. A fascinating investigation of the importance of the camel in history.

Cook, Michael. *Muhammad.* 1996. A short, incisive account of Muhammad's life that questions the traditional picture.

Cormack, Robin. *Writing in Gold: Byzantine Society and Its Icons.* 1985. An expert discussion of icons in the Byzantine world.

Donner, Fred M. *The Early Islamic Conquests*. 1981. Discusses the first phases of Islamic expansion.

Fletcher, Richard. *Moorish Spain*. 1992. Highly readable.

Franklin, Simon, and Jonathan Shepard. *The Emergence of Rus: 750–1200*. 1996. The standard text for this period.

Hawting, G. R. *The First Dynasty of Islam: the Umayyad Caliphate, AD 661–750*. 2000. The most up-to-date study of the Umayyads.

Herrin, Judith. *The Formation of Christendom*. 2001. An exceptionally learned and lucid book; Herrin sees Byzantium as crucial both for the development of Christianity and Islam.

Hourani, George. *Arab Seafaring in the Indian Ocean in Ancient and Early Medieval Times*. 1995. The standard discussion of Arab maritime activity.

King, Charles. *The Black Sea: A History*. 2004. A comprehensive history of the Black Sea region from antiquity to the present. It is especially useful for anyone interested in this borderland among cultures.

Lings, Martin. *Muhammad: His Life Based on the Earliest Sources*. 2006. This readable biography is based exclusively on the eighth- and ninth-century Arabic sources. The view of Muhammad is sympathetic, but the book strips away many of the later Muslim pieties and anti-Muslim rhetoric that has distorted the historical Muhammad.

Moorhead, John. *The Roman Empire Divided, 400–700*. 2001. A reliable and up-to-date survey of the period.

Norwich, John Julius. *A Short History of Byzantium*. 1998. The most readable short account. Norwich is a born storyteller, making the book a joy to read.

Petry, Carl F. *The Cambridge History of Egypt, vol. 1: Islamic Egypt, 640–1517*. 2008. The most comprehensive and up-to-date study of how Egypt became Muslim and one of the dominant powers in the Islamic world.

The Qu'ran (Oxford World Classics). Trans. Haleem, Muhammad Abdel. 2008. The best new translation of the founding text of Islam.

Robinson, Francis, ed. *The Cambridge Illustrated History of the Islamic World*. 1978. Many excellent and well-illustrated articles that will be useful for beginners.

Treadgold, Warren. *A History of the Byzantine State and Society*. 1998. A reliable narrative of Byzantine history.

Treadgold, Warren T. *A Concise History of Byzantium*. 2001. A reliable and insightful short survey.

CHAPTER 9 MEDIEVAL EMPIRES AND BORDERLANDS: THE LATIN WEST

Asbridge, Thomas. *The Crusades: The Authoritative History of the War for the Holy Land*. 2011. A sweeping study that captures the spiritual motivations behind the warfare. It is the only account that is thoroughly based on sources from both Christian and Muslim sides.

Bachrach, Bernard S. *Early Medieval Jewish Policy in Western Europe*. 1977. A significant revisionist view of the history of the Jews in Latin Christian Europe.

Bartlett, Robert. *The Making of Europe: Conquest, Colonization and Cultural Change: 950–1350*. 1993. The best, and often greatly stimulating, analysis of how Latin Christianity spread in post-Carolingian Europe.

Brown, Peter. *The Rise of Western Christendom: Triumph and Diversity A.D. 200–1000*. 2001. A brilliant interpretation of the development of Christianity in its social context.

Cohen, Jeremy. *Living Letters of the Law: Ideas of the Jew in Medieval Christianity*. 1999. A masterful investigation of early medieval Judaism.

Geary, Patrick J. *The Myth of Nations: The Medieval Origins of Europe*. 2003. Debunks the widespread idea that the European nations can trace their origins back to ethnic groups from the early Middle Ages. Geary convincingly undermines the nationalist ideologies of modern nationalist movements.

Geary, Patrick J. *The Peoples of Europe in the Early Middle Ages*. 2002. Discusses the emergence of the new kingdoms of Europe, stressing the incorporation of Roman elements.

Hollister, C. Warren. *Medieval Europe: A Short History*. 1997. This concise, crisply written text presents the development of Europe during the Middle Ages by charting its progression from a primitive rural society, sparsely settled and impoverished, to a powerful and distinctive civilization.

Jones, Gwyn. *A History of the Vikings*. 2001. A comprehensive, highly readable analysis.

Keen, Maurice, ed. *Medieval Warfare: A History*. 1999. Lucid specialist studies of aspects of medieval warfare.

Lawrence, C. H. *Medieval Monasticism*. 2001. A fine introduction to the phenomenon of Christian monasticism.

Maalouf, Amin. *The Crusades Through Arab Eyes*. 1984. Based on the works of Arab chroniclers, this book depicts a culture nearly destroyed both by internal conflicts and the military threat of the alien Christian culture.

Madden, Thomas F. *The New Concise History of the Crusades*. 2005. This crisp account helps explain the lasting legacy of the Crusades among Muslims today.

Mayr-Harting, Henry. *The Coming of Christianity to Anglo-Saxon England*. 1991. How a Germanic people were converted to Christianity.

McKitterick, Rosamond. *The Early Middle Ages*. 2001. The best up-to-date survey for the period 400–1000. It is composed of separate essays by leading specialists.

Moorhead, John. *The Roman Empire Divided, 400–700*. 2001. The best recent survey of the period.

Reuter, Timothy. *Germany in the Early Middle Ages, c. 800–1056*. 1991. A lucid explanation of the complexities of German history in this period.

Reynolds, Susan. *Fiefs and Vassals: The Medieval Evidence Reinterpreted*. 1994. The most important reexamination of the feudalism problem.

Riché, Pierre. *Education and Culture in the Barbarian West, Sixth Through Eighth Centuries*, translated from the third French edition by John J. Contreni. 1975. Demonstrates the rich complexity of learning during this period, once thought to be the Dark Ages of education.

Riché, Pierre. *The Carolingians: A Family Who Forged Europe*. 1993. Translated from the 1983 French edition, this book traces the rise, fall, and revival of the Carolingian dynasty, and shows how it molded the shape of a post-Roman Europe that still prevails today. This is basically a family history, but the family dominated Europe for more than two centuries.

Riley-Smith, Jonathan Simon Christopher. *The Crusades: A Short History*. 1987. Exactly what the title says.

Riley-Smith, Jonathan Simon Christopher. *The Oxford Illustrated History of the Crusades*. 2001. An utterly engaging, comprehensive study.

Stenton, Frank M. *Anglo-Saxon England*. 2001. This classic history covers the period ca. 550–1087 and traces the development of English society from the oldest Anglo-Saxon laws and kings to the extension of private lordship.

Strayer, Joseph B., ed. *Dictionary of the Middle Ages*. 1986. An indispensable reference work.

Webster, Leslie, and Michelle Brown, eds. *The Transformation of the Roman World*, A.D. *400–900*. 1997. A well-illustrated synthesis with maps and bibliography.

Wickham, Chris. *Early Medieval Italy: Central Government and Local Society, 400–1000*. 1981. Examines the economic and social transformation of Italy.

CHAPTER 10 MEDIEVAL CIVILIZATION: THE RISE OF WESTERN EUROPE

Bony, Jean. *French Gothic Architecture of the Twelfth and Thirteenth Centuries*. 1983. With many beautiful illustrations, this is a good way to begin an investigation of these magnificent buildings.

Colish, Marcia L. *Medieval Foundations of the Western Intellectual Tradition, 400–1400*. 1997. The best general study.

Gimpel, Jean. *The Medieval Machine: The Industrial Revolution of the Middle Ages*. 1976. A short, lucid account of the power and agricultural revolutions.

Keen, Maurice. *Chivalry*. 1984. Readable and balanced coverage of this sometimes misunderstood phenomenon.

Lambert, Malcolm. *Medieval Heresy: Popular Movements from the Gregorian Reform to the Reformation*, 2nd ed. 1992. The best general study of heresy.

Lawrence, C. H. *The Friars: The Impact of the Early Mendicant Movement on Western Society*. 1994. The best general study of the influence of Dominicans and Franciscans.

Moore, R. I. *The Formation of a Persecuting Society: Power and Deviance in Western Europe, 950–1250*. 1987. A brilliant analysis of how Europe became a persecuting society.

Morris, Colin. *The Papal Monarchy: The Western Church from 1050 to 1250*. 1989. A thorough study that should be the beginning point for further investigation of the many fascinating figures in the medieval Church.

Mundy, John H. *Europe in the High Middle Ages, 1150–1309*, 3rd ed. 1999. A comprehensive introduction to the period.

Panofsky, Erwin. *Gothic Architecture and Scholasticism*. 2005. A learned and thoughtful book by one of the twentieth century's most influential art historians. It is not an easy read, but it is enormously stimulating.

Peters, Edward. *Europe and the Middle Ages*. 1989. An excellent general survey.

Pieper, Joseph, Clara Winston, and Richard Winston. *Scholasticism: Personalities and Problems of Medieval Philosophy*. 2001. This concise book clearly explains the principal Christian thinkers of the Middle Ages and gives proper credit to the Jewish and Muslim influences.

Strayer, Joseph R. *On the Medieval Origins of the Modern State*. 1970. Still the best short analysis.

CHAPTER 11 THE MEDIEVAL WEST IN CRISIS

Aberth, John. *The Black Death: The Great Mortality of 1348–1350: A Brief History with Documents*. 2005. A useful source for research papers.

Carmichael, Ann G. *Plague and the Poor in Renaissance Florence*. 1986. An innovative study that both questions the traditional theory of the bubonic plague as the cause of the Black Death and examines how fear of the disease led to regulation of the poor.

Cohn, Samuel Kline. *The Black Death Transformed: Disease and Culture in Early Renaissance Europe*. 2003. A well-argued case that the Black Death was not caused by the bubonic plague.

Cohn, Samuel Kline. *Lust for Liberty: The Politics of Social Revolt in Medieval Europe, 1200–1425*. 2008. Challenging many of the common assumptions about medieval revolts, Cohn shows that most involved workers and artisans tried to gain political rights.

Cohn, Samuel Kline. *Popular Protest in Late Medieval Europe: Italy, France, and Flanders*. 2005. The volume presents more than 200 documents translated for the first time showing the wide range of protest over two centuries. A good source for research papers.

Duby, Georges. *France in the Middle Ages, 987–1460: From Hugh Capet to Joan of Arc*. 1991. Traces the emergence of the French state.

Gordon, Bruce, and Peter Marshall, eds. *The Place of the Dead: Death and Remembrance in Late Medieval and Early Modern Europe*. 2000. A collection of essays that shows how the placing of the dead in society was an important activity that engendered considerable conflict and negotiation.

Herlihy, David. *The Black Death and the Transformation of the West*. 1997. A pithy, readable analysis of the epidemiological and historical issues surrounding the Black Death.

Holmes, George. *Europe: Hierarchy and Revolt, 1320–1450*. 1975. Excellent examination of rebellions.

Huizinga, Johan. *The Autumn of the Middle Ages*, trans. Rodney J. Payton and Urlich Mammitzsch. 1996. A new translation of the classic study of France and the Low Countries during the fourteenth and fifteenth centuries. Dated and perhaps too pessimistic, Huizinga's lucid prose and broad vision still make this an engaging reading experience.

Imber, Colin. *The Ottoman Empire, 1300–1481*. 1990. The basic work that establishes a chronology for the early Ottomans.

Jordan, William C. *The Great Famine: Northern Europe in the Early Fourteenth Century*. 1996. The most comprehensive book on the famine.

Lambert, Malcolm. *Medieval Heresy: Popular Movements from the Gregorian Reform to the Reformation*. 1992. Excellent general study of the Hussite and Lollard movements.

Le Roy Ladurie, Emmanuel. *Times of Feast, Times of Famine: A History of Climate Since the Year 1000,* trans. Barbara Bray. 1971. The book that introduced the idea of the Little Ice Age and promoted the study of the influence of climate on history.

Lynch, Joseph H. *The Medieval Church: A Brief History*. 1992. A pithy, elegant survey of ecclesiastical institutions and developments.

Morgan, David O. *The Mongols*. 1986. Best introduction to Mongol history.

Nirenberg, David. *Communities of Violence: Persecution of Minorities in the Middle Ages*. 1996. An important analysis of the persecution of minorities that is deeply rooted in Spanish evidence.

Scott, Susan, and Christopher Duncan. *Biology of Plagues: Evidence from Historical Populations*. 2001. An analysis by two epidemiologists who argue that the Black Death was not the bubonic plague but probably a virus similar to Ebola.

Sumption, Jonathan. *The Hundred Years' War: Trial by Battle*. 1991. First volume goes only to 1347. When it is completed, it will be the best comprehensive study.

Swanson, R. N. *Religion and Devotion in Europe, c. 1215– c. 1515*. 1995. The best up-to-date textbook account of late medieval religious practice.

CHAPTER 12 THE ITALIAN RENAISSANCE AND BEYOND: THE POLITICS OF CULTURE

Appuhn, Karl. *A Forest on the Sea: Environmental Expertise in Renaissance Venice*. 2009. An original and path-breaking study of environmental history during the Renaissance.

Baxandall, Michael. *Painting and Experience in Fifteenth Century Italy: A Primer in the Social History of Pictorial Style*. 1988. A fascinating study of how the daily social experiences of Florentine bankers and church-goers influenced how these individuals saw Renaissance paintings and how painters responded to the viewers' experience. One of the best books on Italian painting.

Brown, Howard M. *Music in the Renaissance*. 1976. Dated but still the best general study of Renaissance music.

Brown, Patricia Fortini. *Art and Life in Renaissance Venice*. 1997. A delightful study about how art fit into the daily lives and homes of the Venetian upper classes.

Brucker, Gene. *Florence: The Golden Age, 1138–1737*. 1998. A brilliant, beautifully illustrated history by the most prominent American historian of Florence.

Burke, Peter. *The Italian Renaissance*. 1999. A concise and readable synthesis of the most recent research.

Ferraro, Joanne Marie. *Venice: History of the Floating City*. 2012. Brings the history of Venice up-to-date, especially by emphasizing issues of gender and identity.

Hale, J. R. *Renaissance Europe, 1480–1520*. 2000. A witty, engaging, and enlightening study of Europe during the formation of the early modern state system. Strong on establishing the material and social limitations of Renaissance society.

Kent, D. V. *Cosimo de' Medici and the Florentine Renaissance*. 2000. This beautiful book traces the vast influence of Cosimo's patronage of the arts.

King, Margaret L. *Women of the Renaissance*. 1991. The best general study of women in Renaissance Europe. It is especially strong on female intellectuals and women's education.

Kohl, Benjamin G., and Alison Andrews Smith, eds. *Major Problems in the History of the Italian Renaissance*. 1995. A useful collection of articles and short studies of major historical problems in the study of the Renaissance.

Martines, Lauro. *April Blood: Florence and the Plot Against the Medici*. 2004. One of the leading historians of Renaissance Italy unravels the famous Pazzi conspiracy against the Medici.

Martines, Lauro. *Power and Imagination: City-States in Renaissance Italy*. 1988. An excellent general survey that is strong on class conflicts and patronage.

Muir, Edward. *Civic Ritual in Renaissance Venice*. 1981. Shows how religion and politics intertwined in a Renaissance city.

Muir, Edward. *Mad Blood Stirring: Vendetta in Renaissance Italy*. 1998. The story of the bloodiest and longest lasting vendetta in the Renaissance.

Najemy, John M. *A History of Florence, 1200–1575*. 2006. The best and most up-to-date history of the home of the Renaissance.

Nauert, Charles G., Jr. *Humanism and the Culture of Renaissance Europe*. 1995. The best survey of humanism for students new to the subject. It is clear and comprehensive.

O'Connell, Monique. *Men of Empire: Power and Negotiation in Venice's Maritime State*. 2009. The best study of colonialism during the Italian Renaissance.

Pocock, J. G. A. *The Machiavellian Moment*. 1975. An immense scholarly discussion of the use of republican thought in Renaissance Europe, late seventeenth century England, and eighteenth-century British America.

Romano, Dennis. *The Likeness of Venice: A Life of Doge Francesco Foscari*. 2007. Foscari was the source of many romantic and tragic legends. Romano's study is perhaps the best biography of an Italian Renaissance politician.

Ross, Sarah Gwyneth. *The Birth of Feminism: Woman as Intellect in Renaissance Italy and England*. 2009. A highly original argument that the Renaissance produced a strong and lasting strain of feminist writing.

Skinner, Quentin. *Machiavelli: A Very Short Introduction.* 2000. This is the place to begin in the study of Machiavelli. Always clear and precise, this is a beautiful little book.

Stephens, John. *The Italian Renaissance: The Origins of Intellectual and Artistic Change Before the Reformation.* 1990. A stimulating analysis of how cultural change took place.

Vasari, Giorgio. *The Lives of the Artists.* 1998. Written by a sixteenth-century Florentine who was himself a prominent artist, this series of artistic biographies captures the spirit of Renaissance society.

Weinstein, Donald. *Savonarola: The Rise and Fall of a Renaissance Prophet.* 2011. An elegant history of Savonarola's dramatic career by the leading expert on him.

CHAPTER 13   THE WEST AND THE WORLD: THE SIGNIFICANCE OF GLOBAL ENCOUNTERS, 1450–1650

Chaudhuri, K. N. *Trade and Civilization in the Indian Ocean: An Economic History from the Rise of Islam to 1750.* 1985. Arguing for the long-term unity of trade routes, the book lays out the importance of Asian merchants to maritime trade networks from the South China Sea to the Mediterranean.

Clendinnen, Inga. *Aztecs: An Interpretation.* 1991. A provocative, sometimes disturbing book that directly confronts the implications of human sacrifice and cannibalism among the Aztecs and offers an explanation for it by analyzing Aztec religion.

Crosby, Alfred W., Jr. *The Columbian Exchange: Biological and Cultural Consequences of 1492.* 1973. The most significant study on the implications of the biological exchanges for the cultural history of both the Old and New Worlds. It has the benefit of being an exciting book to read.

Curtin, Philip D. *African History: From Earliest Times to Independence.* 1995. An excellent survey by one of the most distinguished comparative historians.

Elvin, Mark. *The Pattern of the Chinese Past: A Social and Economic Interpretation.* 1973. An excellent overview of Chinese history that covers Chinese responses to Western encounters.

Fernández-Armesto, Felipe. *Before Columbus: Exploration and Colonization from the Mediterranean to the Atlantic, 1229–1492.* 1987. Engagingly written and original in scope, this is the best single account of early European colonization efforts.

Fernández-Armesto, Felipe. *Columbus.* 1991. The 500th anniversary of Columbus's voyage in 1492 provoked a wide-ranging reappraisal of his motives and career. This pithy, engaging book is by far the most convincing in revising Columbus's image, but it deflated much of the Columbus myth and caused considerable controversy.

Leon-Portilla, Miguel. *Broken Spears: The Aztec Account of the Conquest of Mexico.* 2006. A revised version of the classic account of the native point of view.

Oliver, Roland. *The African Experience from Olduvai Gorge to the 21st Century.* 2000. A highly readable general survey.

Pagden, Anthony. *European Encounters with the New World: From Renaissance to Romanticism.* 1993. A fascinating examination of how Europeans interpreted their encounters with America.

Parry, J. H. *The Age of Reconnaissance.* 1982. An analysis of European shipping technology and the causes behind European explorations. It covers all the major voyages.

Parry, J. H. *The Spanish Seaborne Empire.* 1990. The standard study on the subject. It brings together an enormous range of material and presents it clearly and cogently.

Pennock, Caroline Dodds. *Bonds of Blood: Gender, Lifecycle, and Gender in Aztec Culture.* 2008. By paying attention to issues of gender, Pennock bequeaths a refreshing humanity to the gory history of human sacrifice among the Aztecs.

Phillips, William D., Jr., and Carla Rahn Phillips. *The Worlds of Christopher Columbus.* 1992. A balanced analysis of Columbus's attempts to find financing for his voyage that pays equal attention to his personal ambition, Christian zeal, and navigational skills.

Todorov, Tzvetan. *The Conquest of America: The Question of the Other.* 1999. Compelling and disturbing, this influential book completely reinterprets the clashes between the Spanish and the Aztecs.

CHAPTER 14   THE REFORMATIONS OF RELIGION

Bireley, Robert. *The Refashioning of Catholicism, 1450–1700: A Reassessment of the Counter Reformation.* 1999. A fair reappraisal of the major events by one of the most prominent historians of Catholicism in this period.

Bossy, John. *Christianity in the West, 1400–1700.* 1985. A short study not of the institutions of the Church but of Christianity itself, this book explores the Christian people, their beliefs, and their way of life. The book demonstrates considerable continuities before and after the Reformation and is especially useful in understanding the attitudes of common lay believers as opposed to the major reformers and Church officials.

Cameron, Euan. *The European Reformation.* 1995. The most comprehensive general survey, this bulky book covers all the major topics in considerable detail. It is excellent in explaining theological issues.

Gregory, Brad S. *Salvation at Stake: Christian Martyrdom in Early Modern Europe.* 2001. A comprehensive study of Protestant, Catholic, and Anabaptist martyrs during the Reformation. Gregory shows the religious foundations for why authorities were willing to kill and martyrs were willing to die for their faith.

Gregory, Brad S. *The Unintended Reformation: How a Religious Revolution Secularized Society.* 2012. Argues that the Protestant Reformation led to a loss of any sense of the common good and to the secularism, consumerism, and competitive capitalism of modern life.

Hsia, R. Po-chia. *The World of Catholic Renewal, 1540–1770.* 1998. An excellent survey of the most recent research.

Koenigsberger, H. G., George L. Mosse, and G. Q. Bowler. *Europe in the Sixteenth Century,* 2nd ed. 1989. A good beginner's survey. Strong on political events.

McGrath, Alister E. *Reformation Thought: An Introduction,* 3rd rev. ed. 1999. Indispensable introduction for anyone seeking to understand the ideas of the European Reformation. Drawing on the most up-to-date scholarship, McGrath offers a clear explanation of these ideas, set firmly in their historical contexts.

Muir, Edward. *Ritual in Early Modern Europe,* 2nd ed. 2005. A broad survey of the debates about ritual during the Reformation and the implementation of ritual reforms.

Oberman, Heiko A. *Luther: Man Between God and the Devil,* trans. Eileen Walliser-Schwarzbart. 1992. First published to great acclaim in Germany, this book argues that Luther was more the medieval monk than history has usually regarded him. Oberman claims that Luther was haunted by the Devil and saw the world as a cosmic battleground between God and Satan. A brilliant, intellectual biography that is sometimes challenging but always clear and precise.

O'Malley, John. *Trent and All That: Renaming Catholicism in the Early Modern Era.* 2000. O'Malley works out a remarkable guide to the intellectual and historical developments behind the concepts of Catholic reform and, in his useful term, Early Modern Catholicism. The result is the single best overview of scholarship on Catholicism in early modern Europe, delivered in a pithy, lucid, and entertaining style.

Ozment, Steven. *The Age of Reform, 1250–1550: An Intellectual and Religious History of Late Medieval and Reformation Europe.* 1986. Firmly places the Protestant Reformation in the context of late medieval spirituality and theology; particularly strong on pre-Reformation developments.

Reardon, Bernard M. G. *Religious Thought in the Reformation,* 2nd ed. 1995. A good beginner's survey of the intellectual dimensions of the Reformation.

Scribner, R. W. *For the Sake of the Simple Folk: Popular Propaganda for the German Reformation.* 1994. An innovative and fascinating study of the Lutheran use of visual images.

Scribner, R. W. *The German Reformation.* 1996. A short and very clear analysis of the appeal of the Reformation by the leading social historian of the period. Pays attention to what people actually did rather than just what reformers said they should do.

Shagan, Ethan H. *Popular Politics and the English Reformation.* 2002. In this innovative study Shagan shows how the Reformation involved political issues on the local level, not just theological debates.

Shagan, Ethan H. *The Rule of Moderation: Violence, Religion, and the Politics of Restraint in Early Modern England.* 2011. Demonstrates how the pursuit of the "middle way" between extremes could itself be a coercive and violent path.

Wandel, Lee Palmer. *The Eucharist in the Reformation.* 2005. Traces how different interpretations of the phrase "this is my body" divided the Reformation into various divisive camps.

Wandel, Lee Palmer. *The Reformation: Towards a New History.* 2011. Connects the encounters between Western Europeans and the Americas with the religious divisions of the Reformation. This is the most up-to-date and innovative history of the Protestant Reformation.

CHAPTER 15   THE AGE OF CONFESSIONAL DIVISION

Anderson, M. S. *The Origins of the Modern European State System, 1494–1618.* 1998. The best short study for students new to the subject of the evolution of the confessional states in Europe. This book is very good at establishing common patterns among the various states.

Burke, Peter. *Popular Culture in Early Modern Europe.* 1994. This wide-ranging book includes considerable material from eastern Europe and Scandinavia, as well as the more extensively studied western European countries. Extraordinarily influential, it practically invented the subject of popular culture by showing how much could be learned from studying festivals and games.

Davies, Norman. *God's Playground: A History of Poland.* Rev. ed., 2 vols. 1982. By far the most comprehensive study of Polish history, this is particularly strong for the sixteenth and seventeenth centuries. Davies offers a Polish-centered view of European history that is marvelously stimulating even if he sometimes overstates his case for the importance of Poland.

Dukes, Paul. *A History of Russia: Medieval, Modern, Contemporary, ca. 882–1996,* 3rd ed. 1998. A comprehensive survey that synthesizes the most recent research.

Dunn, Richard S. *The Age of Religious Wars, 1559–1715,* 2nd ed. 1980. An excellent survey for students new to the subject.

Evans, R. J. W. *Rudolf II and His World: A Study in Intellectual History, 1576–1612.* 1973. A sympathetic examination of the intellectual world Rudolf created. Evans recognizes Rudolf's mental problems but lessens their significance for understanding the period.

Holt, Mack P. *The French Wars of Religion, 1562–1629.* 1996. A lucid short synthesis of the events and complex issues raised by these wars.

Hsia, R. Po-chia. *Social Discipline in the Reformation: Central Europe, 1550–1750.* 1989. An excellent, lucid, and short overview of the attempts to discipline the people in Germany.

Huppert, George. *After the Black Death: A Social History of Early Modern Europe.* 1986. Engaging, entertaining, and elegantly written, this is the best single study of European social life during the early modern period.

Levack, Brian P. *The Witch-Hunt in Early Modern Europe,* 2nd ed. 1995. The best and most up-to-date short examination of the complex problem of the witch-hunt. This is the place to begin for students new to the subject.

Marshall, Peter. *The Magic Circle of Rudolph II: Alchemy and Astrology in Renaissance Prague.* 2006. In Marshall's book the strange intellectual world of the court of Emperor Rudolph II represents a bridge between medieval and modern views of science.

Ozment, Steven E. *Ancestors: The Loving Family in Old Europe.* 2001. This comprehensive study of family life demonstrates that families were actually far more loving than the theory of patriarchy would suggest.

Parker, Geoffrey. *The Dutch Revolt,* rev. ed. 1990. The classic study of the revolt by one of the most masterful historians of the period. This study is especially adept at pointing to the larger European context of the revolt.

Parker, Geoffrey. *The Grand Strategy of Philip II.* 1998. Rehabilitates Philip as a significant strategic thinker.

Wiesner, Merry E. *Women and Gender in Early Modern Europe.* 1993. The best short study of the subject. This is the best book for students new to the subject.

CHAPTER 16   ABSOLUTISM AND STATE BUILDING, 1618–1715

Aylmer, G. E. *Rebellion or Revolution.* 1986. A study of the nature of the political disturbances of the 1640s and 1650s.

Beik, William. *Louis XIV and Absolutism: A Brief Study with Documents.* 2000. An excellent collection of documents.

Collins, James B. *The State in Early Modern France.* 1995. The best general study of the French state.

Elliott, J. H. *Richelieu and Olivares.* 1984. A comparison of the two contemporary absolutist ministers and state builders in France and Spain.

Friedrich, Karin. *Brandenburg-Prussia, 1466–1806: The Rise of a Composite State.* 2012. Includes chapters on state-building and rural society.

Goffman, Daniel. *The Ottoman Empire and Early Modern Europe.* 2002. A broad survey that challenges many of the Western stereotypes of Ottoman politics and culture, including the belief that Ottoman government was tyrannical.

Harris, Tim. *Politics Under the Later Stuarts.* 1993. The best study of Restoration politics, including the Glorious Revolution.

Hughes, Lindsey. *Russia in the Age of Peter the Great.* 1998. A comprehensive study of politics, diplomacy, society, and culture during the reign of the "Tsar Reformer."

Israel, Jonathan. *The Dutch Republic: Its Rise, Greatness and Fall, 1477–1806.* 1996. A massive and authoritative study of the Dutch Republic during the period of its greatest global influence.

Lincoln, W. Bruce. *Sunlight at Midnight: St. Petersburg and the Rise of Modern Russia.* 2000. The best study of the building of Peter the Great's new capital city.

Parker, David. *The Making of French Absolutism.* 1983. A particularly good treatment of the early seventeenth century.

Parker, Geoffrey. *The Military Revolution.* 1988. Deals with the impact of the military revolution on the world as well as European history.

Rabb, Theodore K. *The Struggle for Stability in Early Modern Europe.* 1975. Employs visual as well as political sources to illustrate the way in which Europeans responded to the general crisis of the seventeenth century.

Schama, Simon. *The Embarrassment of Riches: An Interpretation of Dutch Culture in the Golden Age.* 1987. Contains a wealth of commentary on Dutch art and culture during its most influential period.

Underdown, David. *Revel, Riot and Rebellion: Popular Politics and Culture in England, 1603–1660.* 1985. Interprets the English civil war as a conflict of cultures.

Wilson, Peter H. *Absolutism in Central Europe.* 2000. Analyzes both the theory and the practice of absolutism in Prussia and Austria.

CHAPTER 17   THE SCIENTIFIC REVOLUTION

Biagioli, Mario. *Galileo, Courtier: The Practice of Science in the Culture of Absolutism.* 1993. Argues that Galileo's desire for patronage determined the type of research he engaged in and the scientific questions he asked.

Campbell, Mary Blaine. *Wonder and Science, Imagining Worlds in Early Modern Europe.* 1999. Explores the conceptual and celestial worlds opened by science as well as the geographical worlds found in voyages of discovery.

Cohen, H. Floris. *The Scientific Revolution: A Historiographical Inquiry.* 1995. A thorough account of all the different interpretations of the causes and significance of the Scientific Revolution.

Dear, Peter. *Discipline and Experience: The Mathematical Way in the Scientific Revolution.* 1995. Explains the importance of mathematics in the development of seventeenth-century science.

Debus, Allen G. *Man and Nature in the Renaissance.* 1978. Deals with the early history of the Scientific Revolution and develops many of its connections with the Renaissance.

Drake, Stillman, ed. *Discoveries and Opinions of Galileo.* 1957. Includes four of Galileo's most important writings, together with a detailed commentary.

Fara, Patricia. *Newton: The Making of Genius.* 2004. Studies the relationship between Newton's posthumous fame and the development of science.

Feingold, Mordechai. *The Newtonian Moment: Isaac Newton and the Making of Modern Culture.* 2004. A richly illustrated volume that contains valuable material on the reception of Newtonian ideas in the eighteenth century as well as a chapter on Newtonian women.

Finocchiario, Maurice A. *Retrying Galileo, 1633–1992.* 2007. Studies the debates to which the trial of Galileo gave rise.

Grayling, A. C. *Descartes: The Life and Times of a Genius.* 2006. A biography that places Descartes in his proper historical context and suggests that he may have served as a spy.

Harkness, Deborah. *The Jewel House: Elizabethan London and the Scientific Revolution.* 2007. Shows how a diverse group of men and women from various levels of society contributed to the Scientific Revolution.

Huff, Toby. *The Rise of Early Modern Science: Islam, China and the West,* 2003. Addresses the question why modern science arose only in the West despite the fact that non-Western science was more advanced in the Middle Ages.

Kuhn, Thomas S. *The Copernican Revolution.* 1957. The most comprehensive and authoritative study of the shift from an Earth-centered to a sun-centered model of the universe.

Needham, Joseph. *The Grand Titration: Science and Society in East and West.* 1979. Discusses the weaknesses and strengths of Chinese science.

Popkin, Richard. *The History of Scepticism from Erasmus to Spinoza.* 1979. Discusses skepticism as a cause as well as an effect of the Scientific Revolution.

Schiebinger, Londa. *The Mind Has No Sex? Women in the Origins of Modern Science.* 1989. Explores the role of women in all aspects of scientific endeavor.

Shapin, Steven. *The Scientific Revolution.* 1996. A study of the origins of the modern scientific worldview that emphasizes the social influences on the production of knowledge and the social purposes for which scientific knowledge was intended.

Shapin, Steven, and Simon Schaffer. *Leviathan and the Air Pump.* 1989. Discusses the difference between Robert Boyle and Thomas Hobbes regarding the value of experimentation.

Shea, William R., and Mariano Artigas. *Galileo in Rome: The Rise and Fall of a Troublesome Genius.* 2004. Attributes some of Galileo's troubles to his tactlessness and headstrong behavior.

Stewart, Matthew. *The Courtier and the Heretic: Leibniz, Spinoza, and the Fate of God in the Modern World.* 2006. Illuminates the conflicting philosophical ideas of Wilhelm Leibniz and Baruch Spinoza, arguing that Spinoza anticipated later philosophical and scientific developments by two and sometimes three centuries.

Thomas, Keith. *Man and the Natural World: A History of the Modern Sensibility.* 1983. A study of the shifting attitudes of human beings toward nature during the period from 1500 to 1800.

Webster, Charles. *The Great Instauration: Science, Medicine and Reform, 1626–1660.* 1975. Explores the relationship between Puritanism and the Scientific Revolution in England.

Westfall, Richard S. *Never at Rest: A Biography of Isaac Newton.* 1980. A superb biography of the most influential scientist in the history of the West.

CHAPTER 18 THE WEST AND THE WORLD: EMPIRE, TRADE, AND WAR, 1650–1815

Arana, Marie. *Bolívar: American Liberator.* 2013. An admiring biography of the leader of the independence movement in South America.

Bailyn, Bernard. *Ideological Origins of the American Revolution.* 1967. A probing analysis of the different intellectual traditions upon which the American colonists based their arguments for independence.

Blackburn, Robin. *The Making of New World Slavery: From the Baroque to the Modern, 1492–1800.* 1997. Places European slavery in a broad world perspective.

Boxer, C. R. *The Dutch Seaborne Empire, 1600–1800.* 1965. A thorough account covering the entire period of Dutch expansion.

Brown, Christopher L. *Moral Capital: Foundations of British Abolitionism.* 2006. Establishes the popular campaign as well as the work of parliamentary reformers like William Wilberforce.

Burbank, Jane, and Frederick Cooper. *Empires in World History: Power and the Politics of Difference.* 2010. Shows how empires accommodated, created, and manipulated differences among their populations to shape the global order.

Darwin, John. *After Tamerlane: The Global History of Empire Since 1405.* 2008. Focuses on the Great Asian Empires and challenges the idea that the "rise of the West" was inevitable.

Elliott, J. H. *Empires of the Atlantic World: Britain and Spain in America 1492–1830.* 2006. A superb comparative study of the two largest overseas empires in the early modern period.

Eltis, David. *The Rise of African Slavery in the Americas.* 2000. An analysis of the different dimensions of the slave trade based on a database of slave ships and passengers.

Goody, Jack. *The East in the West.* 1996. Challenges the idea that Western cultures are more rational than those of Asia.

Greene, Jack P. *Peripheries and Center: Constitutional Development in the Extended Polities of the British Empire and the United States, 1607–1788.* 1986. A study of the composition of the British Empire and its disintegration in North America.

Kamen, Henry. *Empire: How Spain Became a World Power.* 2003. Explains how Spain established the most extensive empire the world had ever known.

Langley, Lester D. *The Americas in the Age of Revolution, 1750–1850.* 1996. A broad comparative study of revolutions in the United States, Haiti, and Latin America.

Liss, Peggy K. *The Atlantic Empires: The Network of Trade and Revolutions, 1713–1826.* 1983. Places the American Revolution in a broader comparative setting and includes material on early Latin American independence movements.

Mungello, D. E. *The Great Encounter of China and the West, 1500–1800.* 1999. Studies China's acceptance and rejection of Western culture as well as the parallel Western reception of China.

Pagden, Anthony. *Lords of All the World: Ideologies of Empire in Spain, Britain and France, ca. 1500–ca. 1800.* 1996. Discusses the theoretical foundations of the Atlantic Empires.

Said, Edward. *Orientalism.* 1979. A study of the way in which Western views of the East have assumed its inferiority.

CHAPTER 19 EIGHTEENTH-CENTURY SOCIETY AND CULTURE

Alexander, John T. *Catherine the Great: Life and Legend.* 1989. A lively biography of the remarkable "enlightened despot."

Beckett, J. V. *The Aristocracy in England, 1660–1914.* 1986. A comprehensive study of this landholding and governing elite. Makes the important distinction between the aristocracy and the nobility.

Darnton, Robert. *The Forbidden Best-Sellers of Pre-Revolutionary France.* 1995. A study of the salacious, blasphemous, and subversive books that sold more copies than those of the philosophes in eighteenth-century France.

De Vries, Jan. *The Industrious Revolution: Consumer Behavior and the Household Economy, 1650 to the Present.* 2008. Studies the increase in consumer demand before the advent of the Industrial Revolution.

Dewald, Jonathan. *The European Nobility, 1500–1800.* 1996. A comprehensive study of this social class that emphasizes its adaptability.

Doyle, William. *The Old European Order, 1660–1800,* 2nd ed. 1999. The best general study of the period.

Dupré, Louis. *The Enlightenment and the Intellectual Foundations of Modern Culture.* 2004. A comprehensive survey that illustrates its complexity and dynamic character of the Enlightenment.

Houston, R. A. *Literacy in Early Modern Europe: Culture and Education.* 1991. The best survey of the subject for the entire period.

Israel, Jonathan. *Radical Enlightenment: Philosophy and the Making of Modernity 1650–1750.* 2001. Emphasizes the influence of the radical philosophical ideas of the followers of Benedict Spinoza on the Enlightenment.

Knott, Sarah, and Barbara Taylor, eds. *Women, Gender and the Enlightenment.* 2005. A valuable collection of 39 essays that reflect the influence of feminist scholarship on the study of the Enlightenment.

Lugee, Carolyn. *Le Paradis des Femmes: Women, Salons and Social Stratification in 17th-Century France.* 1976. A social study of the women of the salons.

Massie, Robert K. *Catherine the Great: Portrait of a Woman.* 2011. A beautifully crafted biography that illuminates the history of eighteenth-century Russia.

Outram, Dorinda. *The Enlightenment.* 1995. A balanced assessment of the major historiographical debates regarding the Enlightenment.

Robertson, John. *The Case for Enlightenment: Scotland and Naples, 1680–1760.* 2005. Argues that the main unifying theme of the Enlightenment throughout Europe was not its philosophical ideas but the determination to achieve "human betterment" and material improvement.

Root, Hilton. *Peasants and King in Burgundy: Agrarian Foundations of French Absolutism.* 1979. A study of peasant communal institutions and their relationship with the crown as well as the nobility.

Williams, David, ed. *The Enlightenment.* 1999. An excellent collection of political writings with a valuable introduction.

CHAPTER 20   THE AGE OF THE FRENCH REVOLUTION, 1789–1815

Andress, David. *The French Revolution and the People.* 2004. Focuses on the role played by the common people of France—the peasants, craftsmen, and those living on the margins of society—in the revolution.

Blanning, T. C. W. *The French Revolutionary Wars, 1787–1802.* 1996. An authoritative political and military narrative that assesses the impact of the wars on French politics.

Chartier, Roger. *The Cultural Origins of the French Revolution.* 1991. Explores the connections between the culture of the Enlightenment and the cultural transformations of the revolutionary period.

Cobban, Alfred. *The Social Interpretation of the French Revolution.* 1964. Challenges the Marxist interpretation of the causes and effects of the revolution.

Doyle, William. *The Oxford History of the French Revolution.* 1989. An excellent synthesis.

Ellis, Geoffrey. *Napoleon.* 1997. A study of the nature and mechanics of Napoleon's power and an analysis of his imperial policy.

Furet, François. *The French Revolution, 1770–1814.* 1992. A provocative narrative that sees Napoleon as the architect of a second, authoritarian revolution that reversed the gains of the first.

Hardman, John. *Louis XVI: The Silent King.* 2000. A reassessment of the king that mixes sympathy with criticism.

Higonnet, Patrice. *Goodness Beyond Virtue: Jacobins During the French Revolution.* 1998. Explores the contradictions of Jacobin ideology and its descent into the Terror.

Hunt, Lynn. *Politics, Culture and Class in the French Revolution.* 1984. Analyzes the formation of a revolutionary political culture.

Kennedy, Emmet. *The Culture of the French Revolution.* 1989. A comprehensive study of all cultural developments before and during the revolution.

Landes, Joan B. *Women and the Public Sphere in the Age of the French Revolution.* 1988. Explores how the new political culture of the revolution changed the position of women in society.

Lefebvre, Georges. *The Great Fear of 1789: Rural Panic in Revolutionary France.* 1973. Shows the importance of the rural unrest of July 1789 that provided the backdrop of the legislation of August 1789.

Schama, Simon. *Citizens: A Chronicle of the French Revolution.* 1989. Depicts the tragic unraveling of a vision of liberty and happiness into a scenario of hunger, anger, violence, and death.

Scurr, Ruth. *Fatal Purity: Robespierre and the French Revolution.* 2006. A judicious assessment of this controversial revolutionary figure.

CHAPTER 21   THE INDUSTRIAL REVOLUTION

Ashton, T. A. *The Industrial Revolution,* reprint edition with preface by P. Hudson. 1992. The classic statement of the optimist position, identifying the benefits of the revolution.

Berg, Maxine. *The Age of Manufactures, 1700–1820: Industry, Innovation and Work in Britain.* 1994. A study of the process and character of specific industries, especially those employing women.

Brinley, Thomas. *The Industrial Revolution and the Atlantic Economy: Selected Essays.* 1993. Essays challenging the view that Britain's Industrial Revolution was a gradual process.

Deane, Phyllis. *The First Industrial Revolution.* 1967. The best study of technological innovation in Britain.

Gutmann, Myron. *Toward the Modern Economy: Early Industry in Europe, 1500–1800.* 1988. A study of cottage industry, especially in France.

Hobsbawm, E. J. *Industry and Empire.* 1968. A general economic history of Britain from 1750 to 1970 that analyzes the position of Britain in the world economy.

Jacob, Margaret. *Scientific Culture and the Making of the Industrial West.* 1997. An exploration of the spread of scientific knowledge and its connection with industrialization.

Morris, Charles. *The Dawn of Innovation: The First American Industrial Revolution.* 2012. Empasizes industrial competition between Britain and the United States in the early nineteenth century.

Morris, R. J. *Class and Class Consciousness in the Industrial Revolution, 1780–1850.* 1979. A balanced treatment of the link between industrialization and class formation.

Pollard, Sidney. *Peaceful Conquest: The Industrialization of Europe, 1760–1970.* 1981. Links coal supplies to economic development.

Rule, John. *The Vital Century: England's Developing Economy, 1714–1815.* 1992. A general economic history establishing the importance of early eighteenth-century developments.

Stearns, Peter. *The Industrial Revolution in World History,* 2nd ed. 1998. The best study of industrialization in a global context.

Teich, Mikulas, and Roy Porter, eds. *The Industrial Revolution in National Context: Europe and the USA.* 1981. Essays illustrating similarities as well as national differences in the process of industrialization.

Wrigley, E. A. *Continuity, Chance and Change: The Character of the Industrial Revolution in Britain.* 1988. Includes the best discussion of the transition from an advanced organic economy to one based on minerals.

CHAPTER 22   IDEOLOGICAL CONFLICT AND NATIONAL UNIFICATION, 1815–1871

Anderson, Benedict. *Imagined Communities: Reflections on the Origin and Spread of Nationalism.* 1991. A discussion of the ways in which people conceptualize the nation.

Clark, Martin. *The Italian Risorgimento.* 1999. A comprehensive study of the social, economic, and religious context of Italian unification as well as its political and diplomatic dimensions.

Figes, Orlando. *The Crimean War: A History.* 2010. A fascinating narrative history of a brutal global war involving four empires.

Gellner, Ernest. *Nations and Nationalism.* 1983. An interpretive study that emphasizes the social roots of nationalism.

Hamerow, Theodore S. *Restoration, Revolution, Reaction: Economics and Politics in Germany, 1815–1871.* 1966. An investigation of the social basis of ideological encounters in Germany.

Holmes, Richard. *The Age of Wonder: How the Romantic Generation Discovered the Beauty and Terror of Nature.* 2009. Argues that science inspired the romantic imagination.

Honour, Hugh. *Romanticism.* 1979. A comprehensive study of romantic painting.

Hunczak, Tara, ed. *Russian Imperialism from Ivan the Great to the Revolution.* 1974. A collection of essays that illuminate Russian nationalism as well as imperialism over a long period of time.

Lichtheim, George. *A Short History of Socialism.* 1970. A good general treatment of the subject.

Nipperdey, Thomas. *Germany from Napoleon to Bismarck, 1800–1866.* 1996. An exploration of the creation of German nationalism as well as the failure of liberalism.

Onuf, Peter S. *Jefferson's Empire: The Language of American Nationhood.* 2000. A study of Jefferson's expansionary nationalism.

Pflanze, Otto. *Bismarck and the Development of Germany: The Period of Unification, 1815–1871.* 1963. The classic study of Bismarck and German unification.

Pinckney, David. *The French Revolution of 1830.* 1972. The best treatment of this revolution.

Seton-Watson, Hugh. *Nations and States.* 1977. A clearly written study of the nation-state.

Sperber, Jonathan. *The European Revolutions, 1848–1851.* 1994. The best study of the revolutions of 1848.

Steinberg, Jonathan. *Bismarck: A Life.* 2011. A critical portrait of the "Iron Chancellor" that exposes the deep flaws in his personality.

Tombs, Robert. *The War Against Paris, 1871.* 1981. A narrative history of the Paris Commune.

CHAPTER 23   THE COMING OF MASS POLITICS, 1870–1914

Bayly, C. A. *The Birth of the Modern World, 1780–1914: Global Connections and Comparisons.* 2004. Places the emergence of the modern West within a global perspective.

Clyman, Toby W., and Judith Vowles, eds. *Russia Through Women's Eyes: Autobiographies from Tsarist Russia.* 1999. Fascinating collection that allows us to see both women's history and Russian history in new ways.

Geraci, Robert. *Window on the East: National and Imperial Identities in Late Tsarist Russia.* 2001. Explores the effort to Russify the various peoples of "the East" in the empire.

Hoerder, Dirk. *Cultures in Contact: World Migrations in the Second Millennium.* 2002. Wide-ranging study of the causes and consequences of human migration.

Kern, Stephen. *The Culture of Time and Space, 1880–1918.* 1983. An important work that explores the cultural impact of technological change.

Lazarski, Christopher. *Power Tends to Corrupt: Lord Acton's Study of Liberty.* 2012. An examination of the role of the ideal of liberty in Western culture.

Lidtke, Vernon. *The Alternative Culture: Socialist Labor in Imperial Germany.* 1985. Looks beyond the world of parliamentary politics to assess the meaning and impact of working-class socialism.

Lindemann, Albert. *Esau's Tears: Modern Anti-Semitism and the Rise of the Jews.* 1997. A comprehensive and detailed survey that challenges many assumptions about the roots and nature of modern anti-Semitism.

Mayer, Arno. *The Persistence of the Old Regime: Europe to the Great War.* 1981. Argues that landed elites maintained a considerable amount of economic and political power throughout the nineteenth century.

Maynes, Mary Jo. *Taking the Hard Road: Life Course in French and German Workers' Autobiographies in the Era of Industrialization.* 1995. Fascinating study of the "life course" of industrial workers.

Nord, Philip. *The Republican Moment: Struggles for Democracy in Nineteenth-Century France.* 1996. Illuminates the struggle to define and redefine France.

Offen, Karen. *European Feminisms, 1700–1950: A Political History.* 1999. Comprehensive overview.

Pilbeam, Pamela. *The Middle Classes in Europe, 1789–1914: France, Germany, Italy, and Russia.* 1990. A comparative approach that helps clarify the patterns of social change.

Rappaport, Erica. *Shopping for Pleasure: Women in the Making of London's West End.* 2000. Important study of women and consumerism.

Richards, Thomas. *The Commodity Culture of Victorian England: Advertising and Spectacle, 1851–1914.* 1990. Fascinating study of the manufacturing of desire.

Slezkine, Yuri. *The Jewish Century.* 2004. A good companion volume to Lindemann's *Esau's Tears.*

Steenson, Gary P. *After Marx, Before Lenin: Marxism and Socialist Working-Class Parties in Europe, 1884–1914.* 1991. Examines both ideology and political practice within Europe's socialist parties.

Weber, Eugen. *Peasants into Frenchmen: The Modernization of Rural France, 1870–1914.* 1976. A very important work that helped shape the way historians think about "nation making."

CHAPTER 24 THE WEST AND THE WORLD: CULTURAL CRISIS AND THE NEW IMPERIALISM, 1870–1914

Adas, Michael. *Machines as the Measure of Men: Science, Technology, and Ideologies of Western Dominance.* 1989. A superb study of the way in which the ideology of empire was inextricably connected with cultural and intellectual developments within the West.

Barnes, David S. *The Great Stink of Paris and the Nineteenth-Century Struggle Against Filth and Germs.* 2005. Important study of developing attitudes toward public health.

Butler, Christopher. *Early Modernism: Literature, Music, and Painting in Europe, 1900–1916.* 1994. Wide-ranging and nicely illustrated.

Crews, Robert. *For Prophet and Tsar: Islam and Empire in Russia and Central Asia.* 2006. Important study of an often-overlooked aspect of imperialism.

Dijkstra, Bram. *Idols of Perversity: Fantasies of Feminine Evil in* Fin-de-Siècle *Culture.* 1986. This richly illustrated work shows how anxiety over the changing role of women permeated artistic production at the end of the nineteenth century.

Ellis, John. *The Social History of the Machine Gun.* 1975. Lively, nicely illustrated, and informative.

Gould, Stephen Jay. *The Mismeasure of Man.* 1996. A compelling look at the manipulation of scientific data and statistics to provide "proof" for racist and elitist assumptions.

Headrick, Daniel R. *The Tools of Empire: Technology and European Imperialism in the Nineteenth Century.* 1981. Highlights the important role played by technology in determining both the timing and success of Western imperialism.

Hochschild, Adam. *King Leopold's Ghost.* 1998. Blistering account of Leopold's imperialist rule in the Congo.

Hull, Isabel. *Absolute Destruction: Military Culture and the Practices of War in Imperial Germany.* 2005. Argues that a distinctive German military culture emerged in the late nineteenth century.

Pick, Daniel. *Faces of Degeneration: A European Disorder, c. 1848–1918.* 1993. Argues that concern over degeneration formed a central theme in European culture in the second half of the nineteenth century.

Showalter, Elaine. *Sexual Anarchy: Gender and Culture at the* Fin de Siècle. 1990. An illuminating look at the turbulence that characterized gender relations in the *fin-de-siècle.*

Sperber, Jonathan. *Popular Catholicism in Nineteenth-Century Germany.* 1984. A look at the religious dimensions of popular culture.

Vandervort, Bruce. *Wars of Imperial Conquest in Africa, 1830–1914.* 1998. Clearly presented study by a military historian.

Weeks, Theodore. *Nation and State in Late Imperial Russia: Nationalism and Russification on the Western Frontier.* 1966. Important study of Russian imperialism and nation-making.

Weiner, Jonathan. *The Beak of the Finch: The Story of Evolution in Our Time.* 1994. Prize-winning study of Darwin's theory and its impact.

Wesseling, H. L. *Divide and Rule: The Partition of Africa, 1880–1914.* 1996. A solid survey of complex developments.

CHAPTER 25 THE FIRST WORLD WAR

Barry, John M. *The Great Influenza: The Epic Story of the Deadliest Plague in History.* 2004. Riveting account of an often overlooked story.

Cooper, John Milton. *Breaking the Heart of the World: Woodrow Wilson and the Fight for the League of Nations.* 2001. Examines the failure of Wilson's new world order.

Cork, Richard. *A Bitter Truth: Avant-Garde Art and the Great War.* 1994. A beautifully illustrated work that looks at the cultural impact of the war.

Davis, Belinda. *Home Fires Burning: Food, Politics, and Everyday Life in World War I Berlin.* 2000. An important look at the German home front.

Ferguson, Niall. *The Pity of War.* 1999. Controversial reconsideration of many accepted interpretations of the origins and experience of the war.

Figes, Orlando. *A People's Tragedy: A History of the Russian Revolution.* 1997. Award-winning, gripping account of the revolutionary years.

Fitzpatrick, Sheila. *The Russian Revolution, 1917–1932.* 1994. As the title indicates, Fitzpatrick sees the revolutions of 1917 as the opening battle in a more than 10-year struggle to shape the new Russia.

Gatrell, Peter. *Russia's First World War: A Social and Economic History.* 2005. Comprehensive survey.

Healy, Maureen. *Vienna and the Fall of the Habsburg Empire: Total War and Everyday Life in World War I.* 2004. Explores the civilian conflict on the home front.

Higonnet, Margaret. *Lines of Fire: Women's Visions of World War I.* 1998. An important study of women's experiences.

Joll, James. *The Origins of the First World War.* 1984. One of the best and most carefully balanced studies of this complicated question.

Keegan, John. *The First World War.* 1999. Military history at its best.

Liulevicius, Vejas Gabriel. *War Land on the Eastern Front: Culture, National Identity, and German Occupation in World War I.* 2000. Path-breaking study of the German occupation of Russia.

Steinberg, M. D. *Voices of Revolution, 1917.* 2001. The Russian Revolution in the words of the ordinary people who made and experienced it.

Zuckerman, Larry. *The Rape of Belgium: The Untold Story of World War I.* 2004. Corrective account that takes a hard look at German atrocities.

CHAPTER 26 RECONSTRUCTION, REACTION, AND CONTINUING REVOLUTION—THE 1920s AND 1930s

Balderston, Theo, ed. *The World Economy and National Economics in the Interwar Slump.* 2003. Collections of essays exploring the impact of the Great Depression.

Berend, Ivan T. *Decades of Crisis: Central and Eastern Europe Before World War II.* 2001. Surveys the complex history of these crucial regions.

Blinkhorn, Martin. *Fascism and the Right in Europe 1919–1945.* 2000. A clear and concise historical and historiographical survey, with a selection of key primary documents.

Bookbinder, Paul. *Weimar Germany: The Republic of the Reasonable.* 1996. An innovative interpretation.

Bosworth, R. J. B. *Mussolini's Italy: Life under the Fascist Dictatorship.* 2007. Crucial study of a crucial place and time.

Brendon, Piers. *The Dark Valley: A Panorama of the 1930s.* 2000. Fast-paced but carefully researched and comprehensive overview of the histories of the United States, Germany, Italy, France, Britain, Japan, Russia, and Spain.

Brown, Kate. *A Biography of No Place: From Ethnic Borderland to Soviet Heartland.* 2004. Innovative and thought-provoking exploration of "no place," the borderlands between historic Poland and Russia.

Fitzpatrick, Sheila. *Everyday Stalinism. Ordinary Life in Extraordinary Times: Soviet Russia in the 1930s.* 1999. Explores the daily life of the ordinary urban worker in Stalinist Russia.

Fitzpatrick, Sheila. *Stalin's Peasants: Resistance and Survival in the Russian Village After Collectivization.* 1995. A superb history from the bottom up.

Getty, J. Arch, and Oleg V. Naumov. *The Road to Terror: Stalin and the Self-Destruction of the Bolsheviks, 1932–1939.* 1999. Interweaves recently discovered documents with an up-to-date interpretation of the Great Purge.

Gilbert, Bentley Brinkerhoff. *Britain 1914–1945: The Aftermath of Power.* 1996. Short, readable overview, designed for beginning students.

Jackson, Julian. *The Popular Front in France: Defending Democracy, 1934–1938.* 1988. A political and cultural history.

Kitchen, Martin. *Nazi Germany: A Critical Introduction.* 2004. Short, clearly written introduction and overview.

Mack Smith, Denis. *Mussolini: A Biography.* 1983. An engaging read and a now-classic account.

Marks, Sally. *The Ebbing of European Ascendancy: An International History of the World, 1914–1945.* 2002. Uses a global approach to examine the way in which the United States replaced Europe as the ascendant power in the world.

Pedersen, Susan. *Family, Dependence, and the Origins of the Welfare State: Britain and France, 1914–1945.* 1993. Shows how welfare policy was inextricably linked to demographic and eugenic concerns.

Seidman, Michael. *Republic of Egos: A Social History of the Spanish Civil War.* 2002. Examines the experiences of ordinary people in an extraordinary time.

Ward, Alan J. *The Easter Rising: Revolution and Irish Nationalism.* 2003. Short, nuanced, clear.

Wolpert, Stanley. *Gandhi's Passion: The Life and Legacy of Mahatma Gandhi.* 2001. An intellectual and spiritual biography by one of the foremost historians of modern India.

CHAPTER 27 WORLD WAR II

Alperovitz, Gar. *Atomic Diplomacy: Hiroshima and Potsdam. The Use of the Atomic Bomb and the American Confrontation with Soviet Power.* 1994. The first edition of this book, published in 1965, sparked an ongoing scholarly debate over whether or not U.S. fears about Soviet power influenced the decision to use the atomic bombs against Japan.

Browning, Christopher. *Ordinary Men: Reserve Police Battalion 101 and the Final Solution in Poland.* 1992. A powerful account of the participation of a group of "ordinary men" in mass murder.

Browning, Christopher. *The Origins of the Final Solution: The Evolution of Nazi Jewish Policy, September 1939–March 1942.* 2004. Highly recommended study of the origins of the Holocaust.

Calder, Angus. *The People's War: Britain, 1939–1945.* 1969. Lengthy—but worth the effort for students wishing to explore the war's impact on British society. (Those who want a shorter account can turn to Robert Mackay, *The Test of War: Inside Britain 1939–45* [1999].)

Frayn, Michael. *Copenhagen.* 1998. A remarkable play in which Frayn dramatizes a meeting (that actually did occur) between the German atomic physicist Werner Heisenberg and his Danish anti-Nazi colleague Niels Bohr. Contains both extremely clear explanations of the workings of atomic physics and a provocative exploration of the moral issues involved in the making of the atom bomb.

Friedlander, Saul. *Nazi Germany and the Jews, 1933–1939.* 1998. An important study of the evolution of Nazi anti-Semitic policy before the war.

Hilberg, Raul. *Perpetrators, Victims, Bystanders: The Jewish Catastrophe, 1933–1945.* 1992. As his title indicates, Hilberg looks at the three principal sets of participants in the Holocaust.

Iriye, Akira. *The Origins of the Second World War in Asia and the Pacific.* 1987. Part of Longman's "Origins of Modern Wars" series aimed at university students, this short and readable study highlights the major issues and events.

Keegan, John. *The Second World War.* 1989. Provides clear explanations of military technologies and techniques; packed with useful maps and vivid illustrations.

Kitchen, Martin. *Nazi Germany at War.* 1995. A short and nicely organized survey of the German home front.

Maudsley, Evan. *Thunder in the East: The Nazi-Soviet War 1941–1945.* 2005. A wide-ranging account that looks at social and political contexts as well as military strategy and technology.

Mazower, Mark. *Hitler's Empire: How the Nazis Ruled Europe.* 2008. Impressively wide-ranging account that challenges many assumptions.

Merridale, Catherine. *Ivan's War: Life and Death in the Red Army, 1939–1945.* 2007. "From-the-bottom-up" military history, this account looks at the often harrowing experiences of ordinary soldiers.

Moore, Bob, ed. *Resistance in Western Europe.* 2000. A collection of essays that explores recent research on this controversial topic.

Overy, Richard. *Russia's War: A History of the Soviet War Effort, 1941–1945.* 1997. A compelling account, written to accompany the television documentary *Russia's War.*

Paxton, Robert. *Vichy France: Old Guard and New Order, 1940–1944.* 1972. A now-classic study of the aims and evolution of France's collaborationist government.

Rees, Laurence. *WWII Behind Closed Doors: Stalin, the Nazis and the West.* 2008. Winner of the British Book Award for History and companion volume to the BBC Television series, this account uses recently revealed archival documents and interviews to explore the morally complex issues involved in the strange alliance between Stalin and Western democracy.

Rhodes, Richard. *The Making of the Atomic Bomb.* 1986. A lengthy but very readable account; very good at explaining the complicated science involved.

Snyder, Timothy. *Bloodlands: Europe Between Hitler and Stalin.* 2010. One of the most important works to be published in recent years.

Weinberg, Gerhard. *A World at Arms: A Global History of World War II.* 1994. Places the war within a global rather than simply a European context.

CHAPTER 28   REDEFINING THE WEST AFTER WORLD WAR II

Ansprenger, Franz. *The Dissolution of Colonial Empires.* 1989. A clear and comprehensive account (that unfortunately includes no maps).

Applebaum, Anne. *Iron Curtain. The Crushing of Eastern Europe, 1944–1956.* 2012. Now the definitive account of the origins of the Cold War.

Castles, Stephen, et al. *Here for Good: Western Europe's New Ethnic Minorities.* 1984. A useful exploration of the impact of postwar immigration, despite the rather rigid Marxist analysis.

Crampton, R. J. *Eastern Europe in the Twentieth Century—And After.* 1997. Detailed chapters on the 1950s and 1960s, including a substantial discussion of the Prague Spring.

De Grazia, Victoria. *Irresistible Empire: America's Advance Through Twentieth-Century Europe.* 2005. A study of the Americanization of Europe.

Elkins, Caroline. *Imperial Reckoning: The Untold Story of Britain's Gulag in Kenya.* 2005. This controversial work won the Pulitzer Prize for Nonfiction.

Fineberg, Jonathan. *Art Since 1940: Strategies of Being.* 1995. A big, bold, lavishly illustrated volume that makes the unfashionable argument that individuals matter.

Fink, Carole, et al. *1968: The World Transformed.* 1998. A collection of essays that explores both the international and the domestic political context for the turmoil of 1968.

Gaddis, John Lewis. *The Cold War: A New History.* 2005. A comprehensive overview by a prominent Cold War historian.

Gillingham, John. *European Integration, 1950–2003: Superstate or New Market Economy?* 2003. An important interpretive history of the European Union.

Gross, Jan T., ed. *The Politics of Retribution in Europe: World War II and Its Aftermath.* 2000. This series of essays makes clear that war did not end in Europe in May 1945.

Judge, Edward, and John Langdon. *A Hard and Bitter Peace: A Global History of the Cold War.* 1999. An extremely useful survey for students. Excellent maps.

Judt, Tony. *Postwar: A History of Europe Since 1945.* 2005. An important interpretive survey.

Judt, Tony, and Timothy Snyder. *Thinking the Twentieth Century.* 2012. Exciting survey of 20th-century intellectual history.

Keep, John. *Last of the Empires: A History of the Soviet Union, 1945–1991.* 1995. Looks beyond the Kremlin to explore social, cultural, and economic developments.

Madaraz, Jeannette. *Working in East Germany: Normality in a Socialist Dictatorship, 1961–1979.* 2006. Examines ordinary life in an extraordinary society.

Poiger, Uta. *Jazz, Rock, and Rebels: Cold War Politics and American Culture in a Divided Germany.* 2000. Explores the interplay among youth culture, Americanization, and political protest.

Rees, Laurence. *WWII Behind Closed Doors: Stalin, the Nazis and the West.* 2008. Winner of the British Book Award for History and companion volume to the BBC Television series, this account uses recently revealed archival documents and interviews to explore the compromises that created Cold War Europe.

Shepard, Todd. *The Invention of Decolonization: The Algerian War and the Remaking of France.* 2006. Explores not only the history but also the continuing impact of the Algerian fight for independence from France.

Steege, Paul. *Black Market Cold War: Everyday Life in Berlin, 1946–1949.* 2007. History "from the bottom up" that explores the ways Berlin became the symbolic center of the Cold War and its impact on the people of Berlin.

Taubman, William. *Khrushchev: The Man and His Era.* 2003. The first biography of Khrushchev to make use of sources made available since the end of the Cold War.

Taylor, Frederick. *The Berlin Wall: A World Divided, 1961–1989.* 2007. Uses the dramatic history of the Berlin Wall to explore the global impact of the Cold War.

Westad, Odd Arne. *The Global Cold War: Third World Interventions and the Making of Our Time.* 2007. Highly recommended study of the Cold War's globalization.

Wyman, Mark. *DPs: Europe's Displaced Persons, 1945–1951.* 1989. An important study of an often-neglected topic.

CHAPTER 29   THE WEST IN THE CONTEMPORARY ERA: NEW ENCOUNTERS AND TRANSFORMATIONS

NOTE: Many of the readings recommended for Chapter 28 supplement this chapter as well.

Ardagh, John. *Germany and the Germans: The United Germany in the Mid-1990s.* 1996. A snapshot of a society in the midst of social and economic change.

Jenkins, Philip. *God's Continent: Christianity, Islam, and Europe's Religious Crisis.* 2007. Balanced, sensible, historically informed; an important book.

Kenney, Padraic. *The Burdens of Freedom: Eastern Europe Since 1989.* 2006. In only 160 pages, Kenney offers a lucid and very helpful account of postrevolutionary developments.

Kotkin, Stephen. *Armageddon Averted: The Soviet Collapse, 1970–2000.* 2001. Clear and compelling account.

Lebovics, Herman. *Bringing the Empire Back Home: France in the Global Age.* 2004. Cultural history of the contemporary struggle to define French identity.

Lewis, Jane, ed. *Women and Social Policies in Europe: Work, Family and the State.* 1993. A series of essays exploring the position of women in western Europe. Packed with statistics and useful tables.

Lovell, Stephen. *Destination in Doubt: Russia Since 1989.* 2006. A clear and succinct account.

McNeill, John. *Something New Under the Sun: An Environmental History of the Twentieth Century.* 2000. Argues that twentieth-century human economic activity has transformed the ecology of the globe—an ongoing experiment with a potentially devastating outcome.

Ost, David. *The Defeat of Solidarity: Anger and Politics in Postcommunist Europe.* 2005. Fascinating and sometimes disturbing account of Polish developments since the victory of Solidarity over communism.

Rogel, Carole. *The Breakup of Yugoslavia and the War in Bosnia.* 1998. Designed for undergraduates, this work includes a short but detailed historical narrative, biographies of the main personalities, and a set of primary documents.

Rosenberg, Tina. *The Haunted Land: Facing Europe's Ghosts After Communism.* 1995. Winner of the Pulitzer Prize, this disturbing account focuses on the fundamental moral issues facing postcommunist political cultures.

Sandler, Irving. *Art of the Postmodern Era: From the Late 1960s to the Early 1980s.* 1996. Much more broad-ranging than the title suggests, this well-written, blessedly jargon-free work sets both contemporary art and the theories of the postmodern within the wider historical context.

Stokes, Gale. *The Walls Came Tumbling Down: The Collapse of Communism in Eastern Europe.* 1993. A superb account, firmly embedded in history.

Taylor-Gooby, Peter. *Reframing Social Citizenship.* 2008. An analysis of the impact of welfare reforms since the rise of New Conservatism.

Veldman, Meredith. *Margaret Thatcher: Shaping the New Conservatism.* 2014. Part of Westview Press's *On the World Stage: Biographies of Important Individuals in World History* series.

NOTES

CHAPTER 1

1. Robert J. Wenke, *Patterns in Prehistory: Humankind's First Three Million Years* (1999), 404.
2. Ibid.
3. Marc van de Mieroop, *A History of the Ancient Near East, ca 3000–323 B.C.E.* (2007), 23.
4. Wenke, *Patterns in Prehistory*, 404.
5. Quoted in Stephen Bertman, *Handbook to Life in Ancient Mesopotamia* (2003), 65.
6. Ibid., 179.
7. Quoted in van de Mieroop, *A History of the Ancient Near East*, 113.
8. Ibid.
9. Quoted in Bertman, *Handbook to Life in Ancient Mesopotamia*, 172–173.
10. Jean Bottero, *Mesopotamia: Writing, Reasoning, and the Gods*, translated by Zainab Bahrani and Marc van de Mieroop (1992), 33, 127, 129.
11. *Code of Hammurabi*, translated by J. N. Postgate, 55–56. Cited in Postgate, *Early Mesopotamia: Society and Economy at the Dawn of History* (1992), 160.
12. Samuel Greengus, "Legal and Social Institutions of Ancient Near Mesopotamia," in *Civilizations of the Ancient Near East*, ed. Jack M. Sasson, vol. 1 (1995), 471.
13. Ibid., 474.
14. *A Dispute of a Man with His Ba*, probably composed ca. 2180–2040 B.C.E. Quoted in W. Stiebing, *Ancient Near Eastern History and Culture* (2008), 153.
15. *The Admonitions of Ipuwer*, quoted in Stiebing, *Ancient Near Eastern History and Culture*, 164.

CHAPTER 2

1. Quoted in Carlo Zaccagnini, "The Interdependence of the Great Powers," in *Amarna Diplomacy: The Beginnings of International Relations*, eds. Raymond Cohen and Raymond Westbrook (2000), 149.
2. Quoted in Michael Roaf, *Cultural Atlas of Mesopotamia and the Ancient Near East* (2004), 136.
3. Quoted in Trevor Bryce, *Life and Society in the Hittite World* (2002), 113.
4. Quoted in William H. Stiebing, Jr., *Ancient Near Eastern History and Culture* (2008), 229.
5. Quoted in Marc van de Mieroop, *A History of the Ancient Near East ca. 3000–323 B.C.* (2007), 194.
6. Ibid., 195.
7. A. Kirk Grayson, in *Assyrian and Babylonian Chronicles* (1975).

8. Quoted in Stiebing, *Ancient Near Eastern History and Culture*, 281.
9. Micah 6: 6–8, Revised Standard Version.
10. Ezekiel 34: 15–20. Revised Standard Version.

CHAPTER 3

1. Demosthenes, *Orations*, 59.122.
2. From Euripides, *The Trojan Women*, translated by Peter Levi, in John Boardman, Jasper Griffith, and Oswyn Murray, eds., *The Oxford History of the Classical World* (1986), 169.
3. Plato, *Phaedo*, 1.118.

CHAPTER 4

1. Athenaios, 253 D; cited and translated in J. J. Pollitt, *Art in the Hellenistic Age* (1986), 271.

CHAPTER 5

1. From *Selected Works* by Cicero, translated by Michael Grant (Penguin Classics 1960, second revised edition 1971). Copyright © Michael Grant 1960, 1965, 1971. Reproduced by permission of Penguin Books Ltd.

CHAPTER 7

1. John Helgeland, *Christians in the Military: The Early Experience* (1985), 64–65.

CHAPTER 8

1. Al-Tabari, *The History of Al-Tabari*, vol. 17: *The First Civil War*, translated and annotated by G. R. Hawting (1985), 50.
2. Quoted in Jane S. Gerber, *The Jews of Spain: A History of the Sephardic Experience* (1992), 28.

CHAPTER 9

1. Willibald, *The Life of Boniface*, in Clinton Albertson, trans., *Anglo-Saxon Saints and Heroes* (1967), 308–310.
2. Quoted in Edward Peters, *Europe and the Middle Ages* (1989), 159.

CHAPTER 10

1. Cited in Emmanuel Le Roy Ladurie, *Montaillou: Promised Land of Error*, translated by Barbara Bray (1978), 130.
2. Ibid., 56.
3. Ibid., 63.

CHAPTER 11

1. Quoted in William Bowsky, "The Impact of the Black Death," in Anthony Molho (ed.), *Social and Economic Foundations of the Italian Renaissance* (1969), 92.
2. Cited in Philip Ziegler, *The Black Death* (1969), 20.
3. Giovanni Boccaccio, *The Decameron*, translated by Richard Aldington (1962), 30.
4. Ibid.
5. Quoted in Mark C. Bartusis, *The Late Byzantine Army: Arms and Society, 1204–1453* (1992), 133.
6. Trial record as quoted in Marina Warner, *Joan of Arc* (1981), 122.
7. Ibid., 127.
8. Ibid., 143.
9. *The Trial of Joan of Arc*, translated by W. S. Scott (1956), 134.
10. Ibid., 106.
11. Ibid., 135.
12. Johan Huizinga, *The Autumn of the Middle Ages,* translated by Rodney J. Payton and Ulrich Mammitzsch (1996), 156.
13. Quoted in Barbara W. Tuchman, *A Distant Mirror: The Calamitous 14th Century* (1978), 505–506. Translation has been slightly modified by the authors.
14. Cited in Bartlett, *The Making of Europe*, 238.

CHAPTER 12

1. Baldesar Castiglione, *The Book of the Courtier,* translated by Charles S. Singleton (1959), 43.
2. Giovanni Villani, *Cronica* vol. 7 (1823), 52. Translation by the authors.
3. Agostino di Colloredo, "Chroniche friulane, 1508–18," *Pagine friulane* 2 (1889), 6. Translation by the authors.
4. Francesco Petrarca, "Letter to the Shade of Cicero," in Kenneth R. Bartlett (ed.), *The Civilization of the Italian Renaissance: A Sourcebook* (1992), 31.
5. Quoted in Margaret L. King, *Women of the Renaissance* (1991), 197.
6. Laura Cereta, "Bibulus Sempronius: Defense of the Liberal Instruction of Women," in Margaret King and Alfred Rabil (eds.), *Her Immaculate Hand: Selected Works by and About the Women Humanists of Quattrocento Italy* (1983), 82.

CHAPTER 13

1. Christopher Columbus, quoted in Felipe Fernández-Armesto, *Columbus* (1991), 6.
2. Ibid., 154.
3. *The Life of the Admiral Christopher Columbus by His Son Ferdinand,* translated and annotated by Benjamin Keen (1959), 222.
4. Sir Arthur Helps, *The Spanish Conquest in America*, vol. 1 (1900), 1, 264–267.
5. *The Book of Chilam Balam of Chumayel*, edited and translated by Ralph L. Roy (1933), 83.
6. *The Conquistadores: First-Person Accounts of the Conquest of Mexico*, edited and translated by Patricia de Fuentes (1963), 159.

7. Quoted in Margaret T. Hodgen, *Early Anthropology in the Sixteenth and Seventeenth Centuries* (1964), 9.
8. Quoted in Ibid., 207. Spelling has been modernized.
9. Quoted in Ibid., 369.
10. Quoted in Ibid., 373–374. Spelling and syntax have been modernized.

CHAPTER 14

1. Quoted in Gordon Rupp, *Luther's Progress to the Diet of Worms* (1964), 29.
2. Ibid., 33.
3. Quote from an anonymous caricature reproduced in A. G. Dickens, *Reformation and Society in Sixteenth-Century Europe* (1966), Figure 46, 61.
4. Quoted in Roland H. Bainton, *Here I Stand: A Life of Martin Luther* (1950), 166, 181–185.
5. Translated and quoted in Thomas Head, "Marie Dentière: A Propagandist for the Reform," in Katharina M. Wilson (ed.), *Women Writers of the Renaissance and Reformation* (1987), 260.
6. Quoted in Peter Blickle, "The Popular Reformation," in Thomas A. Brady, Jr., Heiko A. Oberman, and James D. Tracy (eds.), *Handbook of European History 1400–1600: Late Middle Ages, Renaissance and Reformation*, vol. 2: *Visions, Programs and Outcomes* (1995), 171.
7. Quoted in Heiko A. Oberman, *Luther: Man Between God and the Devil* translated by Eileen Walliser-Schwarzbart (1989), 240.
8. Quoted in Dickens, *Reformation and Society*, 134.

CHAPTER 15

1. Quoted in R. Po-Chia Hsia, *Social Discipline in the Reformation: Central Europe, 1550–1750* (1989), 147–148.
2. Quoted in Norbert Elias, *The Civilizing Process*, vol. 1: *The History of Manners,* translated by Edmund Jephcott (1978), 119.
3. Quoted in R. J. Knecht, *The French Wars of Religion, 1559–1598,* 2nd ed. (1996), 13.
4. Michel de Montaigne, *Essays and Selected Writings,* translated and edited by Donald M. Frame (1963), 219–221.

CHAPTER 16

1. Thomas Hobbes, *Leviathan,* C. B. Macpherson (ed.) (1968), 186.
2. Marshall Poe, "The Truth about Muscovy," *Kritika* 3 (2002), 483.
3. Quoted in Lindsey Hughes, *Russia in the Age of Peter the Great* (1998), 92.

CHAPTER 17

1. René Descartes, *Le Monde*, Book VI.
2. Thomas S. Kuhn, *The Structure of Scientific Revolutions* (1970).
3. René Descartes, *Discourse on the Method and Meditations on First Philosophy,* edited by David Weissmann (1996), 21.

4. Galileo, "Letter to the Grand Duchess Christina," in Stilman Drake (ed.), *Discoveries and Opinions of Galileo* (1957), 186.
5. Quoted in W. Hazard, *The European Mind, 1680–1715* (1964), 362.
6. François Poullain, *De l'égalite des deux sexes* (1673), 85.
7. Francis Bacon, *The Works of Francis Bacon*, vol. 3, J. Spedding (ed.) (1857–1874), 524–539.
8. Henry Oldenburg, "To the Reader," in Robert Boyle (ed.), *Experiments and Considerations in Touching Colours* (1664).

CHAPTER 18

1. Olaudah Equiano, *The Interesting Narrative of the Life of Olaudah Equiano, or Gustavus Vassa the African* (1789).
2. Thomas Rymer (ed.), *Foedera* vol. 18 (1704–1735), 72.
3. Quoted in Robin Blackburn, *The Making of New World Slavery* (1997), 325.

CHAPTER 19

1. Baron d'Holbach, *Good Sense* (1753).
2. David Hume, *Essays Moral, Political, and Literary* (1742), Essay 10: "Of Superstition and Enthusiasm."
3. Cesare Beccaria, *An Essay on Crimes and Punishments* (1788), Chapter 47.
4. Voltaire, "Religion," *The Philosophical Dictionary* (1802).

CHAPTER 20

1. H. Wallon, *Histoire du tribunal révolutionnaire de Paris*, vol. 4 (1880–1882), 511.

CHAPTER 21

1. Lord Ashley's Commission on Mines, *Parliamentary Papers*, vols. 15–17 (1842), Appendix 1, Note 26.
2. Sir James Kay-Shuttleworth (1832), quoted in John Rule, *The Labouring Classes in Early Industrial England* (1986).
3. John Richardson, *The Friend: A Religious and Literary Journal*, 30 (1856), 97.
4. "Report of the Select Committee on the Factories Bill," *Parliamentary Papers*, vol. 20 (1833).
5. John O'Rourke, *The History of the Great Irish Famine of 1847* (1902).
6. David Gillard, ed., *British Documents on Foreign Affairs*, vol. 1: *The Ottoman Empire in the Balkans, 1856–1875* (1984–1985), 20.

CHAPTER 23

1. Leslie Moch, *Moving Europeans: Migration in Western Europe Since 1650* (1992), 147.
2. Quoted in Eugen Weber, *Peasants into Frenchmen: The Modernization of Rural France, 1870–1914* (1976), 332–333.
3. Norman Kleeblatt, *The Dreyfus Affair: Art, Truth, and Justice* (1987), 96.
4. Quoted in Eric Cahm, *The Dreyfus Affair in French Society and Politics* (1994), 167.

5. Quoted in Robert Gildea, *Barricades and Borders: Europe, 1800–1914* (1987), 317.
6. Eugen Weber, *France, Fin-de-Siècle* (1986), 126.
7. Albert Lindemann, *Esau's Tears: Modern Anti-Semitism and the Rise of the Jews* (1997).
8. Maria Desraismes, "La Femme et Le Droit," *Eve dans l'humanite* (1891), 16–17.

CHAPTER 24

1. Winston Churchill, *The River War: An Account of the Re-Conquest of the Sudan* (1933); quoted in Daniel Headrick, *The Tools of Empire: Technology and European Imperialism in the Nineteenth Century* (1981), 118.
2. Quoted in Anne McClintock, *Imperial Leather: Race, Gender, and Sexuality in the Colonial Contest* (1995), 50.
3. From Rider Haggard, *She* (1887).
4. Quoted in H. Stuart Hughes, *Consciousness and Society* (1958), 296.
5. Quoted in Shearer West, *Fin de Siècle* (1993), 24.
6. Stephen Kern, *The Culture of Time and Space, 1880–1918* (1983), 195.
7. From *Elementary Forms*, quoted in Hughes, *Consciousness and Society*, 284–285.
8. Quoted in William Schneider, *An Empire for the Masses: The French Popular Image of Africa, 1870–1900* (1982), 72.
9. Heinrich von Treitschke, *Politics* (1897).
10. Yves-Alain Bois, "Painting as Trauma," in Christopher Green, *Picasso's* Les Demoiselles d'Avignon (2001), 49.
11. Quoted in Catherine Hall, *Cultures of Empire: Colonizers in Britain and the Empire in the Nineteenth and Twentieth Centuries* (2000), p. 299.
12. Brassaï, *Conversations with Picasso*, translated by Jane Marie Todd (1999), 32.
13. John Golding, "*Les Demoiselles D'Avignon* and the Exhibition of 1988," in Green, *Picasso's* Les Demoiselles, 29.
14. Mary Kingsley, in *West African Studies* (1901), 329–330.
15. Rudyard Kipling, *Verse* (1920).
16. Headrick, *The Tools of Empire*, 101. Headrick is the historian who identified the crucial role of the steamship, the quinine prophylaxis, and the breech-loading, repeating rifle in the conquest of Africa.
17. Quoted in Thomas Pakenham, *The Scramble for Africa, 1876–1912* (1991), 22.
18. Quoted in F. K. Crowley (ed.), *A New History of Australia* (1974), 6.
19. Ibid., 207.
20. Quoted in W. G. Beasley, *Japanese Imperialism, 1894–1945* (1987), 31–33.

CHAPTER 25

1. Quoted in Niall Ferguson, *The Pity of War* (1999), 152.
2. Quoted in Eric Leeds, *No Man's Land: Combat and Identity in World War I* (1979), 17.
3. Allister Horne, *The Price of Glory: Verdun, 1916* (1967), 27.
4. Siegfried Sassoon, *Memoirs of an Infantry Officer* (1937), 228.
5. Peter Gatrell, *A Whole Empire Walking: Refugees in Russia During World War I* (2000).

6. Ernst Lissauer, "Hymn of Hate" (1914), in *Jugend* (1914), translated by Barbara Henderson, *New York Times*, October 15, 1914.

7. Quoted in W. Bruce Lincoln, *Red Victory: A History of the Russian Civil War* (1989), 32.

8. Quoted in Edvard Radzinsky, *The Last Tsar*, translated by Marian Schwartz (1993), 336.

9. From the written account of Yakov Yurovsky, quoted in Radzinsky, *The Last Tsar*, 355.

10. Quoted in William Henry Chamberlin, *The Russian Revolution, 1917–1921, vol. 2: From the Civil War to the Consolidation of Power* (1987), 91.

11. Quoted in Lincoln, *Red Victory*, 151.

12. Ibid., 155.

13. Quoted in Radzinsky, *The Last Tsar*, 326.

14. Richard Pipes et al. (eds.), *The Unknown Lenin* (1999), 6.

15. Ibid., Document 59.

CHAPTER 26

1. Quoted in Peter Gay, *Weimar Culture* (1970), 99.

2. Martin J. Sherwin, *A World Destroyed: Hiroshima and the Origins of the Arms Race* (1987), 17.

3. Quoted in Michael Burleigh, *The Third Reich: A New History* (2000), 36.

4. Quoted in Ibid., 52.

5. Quoted in Joachim Fest, *Hitler* (1973), 190–193.

6. Ibid., 192, 218.

7. Quoted in Claudia Koonz, *Mothers in the Fatherland* (1987), 130.

8. Quoted in Fest, *Hitler*, 445.

9. Quoted in Koonz, *Mothers in the Fatherland*, 194.

10. Quoted in Mark Mazower, *Dark Continent: Europe's Twentieth Century* (1998), 123.

11. Quoted in Sheila Fitzpatrick, *Everyday Stalinism* (1999), 68.

12. Quoted in Koonz, *Mothers in the Fatherland*, 178.

13. Ibid., 56; Victoria DeGrazia, *How Fascism Ruled Women: Italy, 1922–1945* (1992), 234.

14. Quoted in Wendy Goldman, *Women, the State, and Revolution: Soviet Family Policy and Social Life, 1917–1936* (1993), 5.

15. Quoted in Felix Gilbert, *The End of the European Era* (1991), 162.

16. Mohandas K. Gandhi, *An Autobiography: The Story of My Experiments with Truth* (1957), 120.

17. Quoted in Tyler Stovall, *Paris Noir: African Americans in the City of Light* (1996), 32.

CHAPTER 27

1. Quoted in Robert H. Abzug, *Inside the Vicious Heart: Americans and the Liberation of Nazi Concentration Camps* (1985), 19.

2. Quoted in Gordon Horwitz, *In the Shadow of Death: Living Outside the Gates of Mauthausen* (1991), 167.

3. Quoted in Piers Brendon, *The Dark Valley: A Panorama of the 1930s* (2000), 282.

4. Quoted in Richard Overy, *Russia's War* (1998), 95.

5. Quoted in Mark Mazower, *Dark Continent: Europe's Twentieth Century* (1999), 157.

6. Quoted in Peter Clarke, *Hope and Glory: Britain, 1900–1990* (1996), 204.

7. Quoted in Joachim Fest, *Hitler* (1973), 665.

8. Mark Mazower, *Hitler's Empire: How the Nazis Ruled Europe* (2008), 522.

9. Ibid., 523.

10. Quoted in Richard Rhodes, *The Making of the Atomic Bomb* (1988), 474.

11. Timothy Snyder, *Bloodlands: Europe Between Hitler and Stalin* (2010).

12. Elie Wiesel, *Night* (1960), 39.

13. Gideon Hausner, *Justice in Jerusalem* (1966), 291.

14. Ibid., 323–324.

15. From Hausner's opening statement; quoted in Moshe Pearlman, *The Capture and Trial of Adolf Eichmann* (1963), 149.

16. Ibid., 463–465.

17. Ibid., 603; Hausner, *Justice in Jerusalem*, 422.

18. Kate Brown, *Biography of No Place: From Ethnic Borderlands to Soviet Heartland* (2004), 221.

19. Quoted in Ulrich Herbert, *Hitler's Foreign Workers* (1997), 306.

CHAPTER 28

1. Stalin to Maxim Litvinov, cited in Vladislav Zubok and Constantine Pleshakov, *Inside the Kremlin's Cold War: From Stalin to Khrushchev* (Cambridge, 1996), 37–38.

2. Leo Crowley, director of the Foreign Economic Administration under Roosevelt and Truman; quoted in William Appleman Williams, *The Tragedy of American Diplomacy* (New York, 1972), 241.

3. Lawrence Rees, *World War II Behind Closed Doors: Stalin, the Nazis, and the West* (2008), 221, 236.

4. Quoted in William Hardy McNeill, *America, Britain, and Russia: Their Cooperation and Conflict 1941–1946* (New York, 1970), 700, note 2.

5. Quoted in Karel Kaplan, *Report on the Murder of the General Secretary* (1990), 159.

6. Ibid., 242.

7. Quoted in John Hargreaves, *Decolonization in Africa* (1996), 113.

8. Quotation from *Time* magazine, 1950; quoted in Martin Walker, *The Cold War and the Making of the Modern World* (1993), 66–67.

9. Quoted in Walker, *The Cold War*, 83.

10. Quoted in Stephen Ambrose, *Rise to Globalism* (1971), 225.

11. Quoted in Donald White, *The American Century* (1999), 286.

12. Quoted in John L. H. Keep, *Last of the Empires: A History of the Soviet Union, 1945–1991* (1995), 79.

13. Quoted in Michael Scammell, *From Gulag to Glasnost: Nonconformist Art in the Soviet Union*, eds. Alla Rosenfeld and Norton T. Dodge (1995), 61.

14. Quoted in Walker, *The Cold War*, 105.

15. Quoted in Robert Paxton, *Europe in the Twentieth Century* (1997), 578.
16. Quoted in Jonathan Fineberg, *Art Since 1940: Strategies of Being* (1995), 144.
17. Ibid., 89.
18. Quoted in Adrian Hastings, *Modern Catholicism: Vatican II and After* (1991), 29.
19. Reinhold Wagnleitner, *Coca-Colonization and the Cold War: The Cultural Mission of the United States in Austria After the Second World War* (1994).
20. Quoted in Felix Gilbert, *The End of the European Era, 1890 to the Present* (1991), 429.
21. Quoted in Richard Kuisel, *Seducing the French: The Dilemma of Americanization* (1993), 147.

CHAPTER 29

1. Quoted in Robert Paxton, *Europe in the Twentieth Century* (1997), 613.
2. Kenneth Boulding, "The Economics of the Coming Spaceship Earth," first published in 1966, reprinted in *Toward a Steady-State Economy*, ed. Herman Daly (1973).
3. Quoted in D. J. Peterson, *Troubled Lands: The Legacy of Soviet Environmental Destruction* (1993), 12.
4. Quoted in Archie Brown, *The Gorbachev Factor* (1996), 125.
5. Salman Rushdie, "Please, Read *Satanic Verses* Before Condemning It," *Illustrated Weekly of India* (October 1988). Reprinted in M. M. Ahsan and A. R. Kidwai, *Sacrilege Versus Civility: Muslim Perspectives on The Satanic Verses Affair* (1991), 63.
6. Quoted in Malise Ruthven, *A Satanic Affair: Salman Rushdie and the Wrath of Islam* (1991), 100.
7. *The Sunday Telegraph* (June 24, 1990), quoted in Ahsan and Kidwai, *Sacrilege Versus Civility*, 80.
8. Quoted in Irving Sandler, *Art of the Postmodern Era* (1996), 4.

PHOTO CREDITS

(tempera on panel), Angelico, Fra (Guido di Pietro) (c. 1387–1455)/ Louvre, Paris, France/Giraudon/The Bridgeman Art Library; page 323: Album/Art Resource, NY; page 324: AJancso/ Shutterstock; page 325: Dean Conger/Corbis; page 324: Interior view looking down the nave towards the east end (photo), French School (12th century)/Basilique Saint-Denis, France/Giraudon/ The Bridgeman Art Library; page 328: National Gallery, London/ Art Resource, NY; page 333: Canali PhotoBank Milan/SuperStock; page 334: Interfoto/Alamy; page 337: Mongol archer on horseback, from seals of the Emperor Ch'ien Lung and others, 15th–16th century (ink & w/c on paper), Chinese School, Ming Dynasty (1368–1644)/ Victoria & Albert Museum, London, UK/The Bridgeman Art Library; page 338: The Art Gallery Collection/Alamy; page 347: Fr 2643 f.165v Battle of Crecy from the Hundred Years War, from 'Froissart's Chronicle', 24th August 1346 (vellum) (detail of 42253), French School (15th century)/Bibliotheque Nationale, Paris, France/The Bridgeman Art Library; page 349: Classic Image/ Alamy; page 356: Sheila Terry/Science Source; page 357: Death, detail from The Table of the Seven Deadly Sins and the Four Last Things (oil on panel) (detail of 68744), Bosch, Hieronymus (c. 1450–1516)/Prado, Madrid, Spain/Giraudon/The Bridgeman Art Library; page 364: Scala/Art Resource, NY; page 369: Scala/Art Resource, NY; page 370: Erich Lessing/Art Resource, NY; page 371: Dea/M. Carrieri/De Agostini/Getty Images; page 379: Snark/Art Resource, NY; page 381: Scala/Art Resource, NY; page 382: Erich Lessing/Art Resource, NY; page 382: Scala/Art Resource, NY; page 383: Pietro Basilico/Shutterstock; page 384: Erich Lessing/Art Resource, NY; page 388: Erich Lessing/Art Resource, NY; page 394: GL Archive/Alamy; page 401: Michel Zabe/DK Images; page 404: Bridgeman-Giraudon/Art Resource, NY; page 406: Library of Congress, Prints & Photographs Division, [LC-USZ62-43536]; Cortes meets Montezuma, from 'Homenaje a Cristobal Colon' by Alfredo Chavero, 1892 (colour litho), Mexican School (19th century)/British Library, London, UK/© British Library Board. All Rights Reserved/The Bridgeman Art Library; page 409: Ritual drinking vessel (kero), with Inca-Spanish colonial decoration/ Werner Forman Archive/The Bridgeman Art Library; page 410: The Art Gallery Collection/Alamy; page 411: Snark/Art Resource, NY; page 419: The Granger Collection, NYC; page 423: bpk, Berlin/ Art Resource, page 426: bpk, Berlin/Alte Pinakothek, Bayerische Staatsgemaeldesammlungen, Munich, G/Art Resource, NY; page 430: Album/Art Resource, NY; page 433: bpk, Berlin/ Kupferstichkabinett, Staatliche Museen, Berlin, Germany/Joerg P. Anders/Art Resource, NY; page 435: akg-images; page 436: Schongauer, Martin (1435–1491) Saint Anthony Tormented by Demons. Engraving, sheet: 11 13/16 × 8 9/16 in. (30 × 21.8 cm). Rogers Fund, 1920 (20.5.2). The Metropolitan Museum of Art, New York, NY, USA. The Metropolitan Museum of Art. Image source: Art Resource, NY; page 438: Foto Marburg/Art Resource, NY; page 443: Destruction of relics and statues in churches, April 1566, engraving by Franz Hogenberg (1535–1590), Wars of Religion, France, 16th century/De Agostini Picture Library/ G. Dagli Orti/The Bridgeman Art Library; page 453: David Sutherland/DK Images; page 454: Scala/Art Resource, NY; page 455: The Death of the Virgin, 1605–06 (oil on canvas) (detail of 3678), Caravaggio, Michelangelo Merisi da (1571–1610)/Louvre, Paris, France/Giraudon/The Bridgeman Art Library; page 459: Erich Lessing/Art Resource, NY; page 462: bpk, Berlin/Alte Pinakothek, Bayerische Staatsgemaeldesammlungen, Munich, G/ Art Resource, NY; page 467: akg-images; page 468: A Woman Peeling Apples, c. 1663 (oil on canvas), Hooch, Pieter de (1629–84)/© Wallace Collection, London, UK/The Bridgeman Art Library; page 469: Erich Lessing/Art Resource, NY; page 471: The

Torture of a Witch, Anne Hendricks, in Amsterdam in 1571 (engraving) (b/w photo), French School (16th century)/Private Collection/The Bridgeman Art Library; page 477: Dea/G.Dagli Orti/De Agostini Picture Library/Getty Images; page 482: Credit: Queen Elizabeth I (1533–1603) being carried in Procession (Eliza Triumphans) c. 1601 (oil on canvas), Peake, Robert (fl. 1580–1626) (attr. to)/Private Collection/The Bridgeman Art Library; page 484: Erich Lessing/Art Resource, NY; page 487: JTB Photo Communications/Age Fotostock; page 488: Wojtek Buss/Age Fotostock; page 492: HIP/Art Resource, NY; page 496: Triple Portrait of the Head of Richelieu, 1642 (oil on canvas), Champaigne, Philippe de (1602–74)/National Gallery, London, UK/The Bridgeman Art Library; page 498: Erich Lessing/Art Resource, NY; page 501: Erich Lessing/Art Resource, NY; page 503: Erich Lessing/Art Resource, NY; page 506: bpk, Berlin/ Kunstbibliothek, Staatliche Museen, Berlin, Germany/Knud Petersen/Art Resource, NY; page 514: View of the Neva, the Harbour and the Exchange at St. Petersburg, illustration for June from 'A Year in St. Petersburg' etched by John H. Clark, coloured by M. Dubourg, pub. 1815 in London by Edward Orme (coloured engraving), Mornay (19th century) (after)/Private Collection/The Stapleton Collection/The Bridgeman Art Library; page 518: Trial of Charles I, 4th January 1649 (engraving), English School (17th century)/Private Collection/The Stapleton Collection/The Bridgeman Art Library; page 521: Mary Evans Picture Library/ Alamy; page 522: bpk, Berlin/Rijksmuseum, Amsterdam, The Netherlands/Hermann Buresch/Art Resource, NY; page 525: SuperStock/SuperStock; page 527: Library of Congress Prints and Photographs Division [LC-USZ62-44642]; page 527: Bettmann/ Corbis; page 528: Bettmann/Corbis; page 528: Scenographia: Systematis Copernicani Astrological Chart (c. 1543) devised by Nicolaus Copernicus (1473–1543), from 'The Celestial Atlas, or the Harmony of the Universe', 1660 (hand-coloured engraving), Cellarius, Andreas (c. 1596–1665)/British Library, London, UK/ © British Library Board. All Rights Reserved/The Bridgeman Art Library; page 529: Bridgeman-Giraudon/Art Resource, NY; page 531: Interfoto/Alamy; page 533: The Art Gallery Collection/ Alamy; page 539: Jean-Baptiste Colbert (1619–1683) Presenting the Members of the Royal Academy of Science to Louis XIV (1638–1715) c. 1667 (oil on canvas), Testelin, Henri (1616–95)/ Chateau de Versailles, France/Giraudon/The Bridgeman Art Library; page 542: Benedict Spinoza (1632–77) (oil on canvas), Dutch School (17th century)/Herzog August Bibliothek, Wolfenbuttel, Germany/The Bridgeman Art Library; page 544: RMN-Grand Palais/Art Resource, NY; page 547: Bettmann/Corbis; page 552: Punishment of Negroes, illustration from 'Voyage Pittoresque et Historique au Bresil', 1835 (colour litho), Debret, Jean Baptiste (1768–1848)/Biblioteca Nacional, Rio de Janeiro, Brazil/The Bridgeman Art Library; page 555: V&A Images, London/Art Resource, NY; page 557: INTERFOTO/Alamy; page 558: Erich Lessing/Art Resource, NY; page 568: Museum of London, London, Great Britain/HIP/Art Resource, NY; page 569: Anti-Smoking Pamphlet (woodcut) (b/w photo), English School (17th century)/Private Collection/The Bridgeman Art Library; page 572: Joseph Mallord William Turner, English, 1775–1851. Slave Ship (Slavers Throwing Overboard the Dead and Dying, Typhoon Coming On). 1840, Oil on canvas. 90.8 × 122.6 cm (35 3/4 × 48 1/4 in.) Museum of Fine Arts, Boston/Henry Lillie Pierce Fund. 99.22; page 576: Brighton Royal Pavilion, 19th century (w/c on paper), English School (19th century)/Private Collection/The Bridgeman Art Library; page 578: The Bostonian's Paying the Excise-man, or Tarring and Feathering, 1774 (hand-coloured engraving), Dawe, Philip (c. 1750–85)/Gilder Lehrman

Collection, New York, USA/The Bridgeman Art Library; page 580: Mary Evans Picture Library/SuperStock; page 586: RMN-Grand Palais/Art Resource, NY; page 589: National Gallery, London/Art Resource, NY; page 592: Exterior View of the East front, 1725–29 (photo), Burlington, 3rd Earl of (Richard Boyle) (1694–1753)/Chiswick House, London, UK/John Bethell/The Bridgeman Art Library; page 594: Mary, Duchess of Richmond (1740–96) 1764–67 (oil on canvas), Reynolds, Sir Joshua (1723–92)/Private Collection/The Bridgeman Art Library; page 598: Erich Lessing/Art Resource, NY; page 599: Credulity, Superstition and Fanaticism, 1762 (engraving), Hogarth, William (1697–1764)/The Israel Museum, Jerusalem, Israel/Vera & Arturo Schwarz Collection of Dada and Surrealist Art/The Bridgeman Art Library; page 602: arah Malcolm in Newgate Prison, illustration from 'Hogarth Restored: The Whole Works of the celebrated William Hogarth, re-engraved by Thomas Cook', pub. 1812 (hand-coloured engraving), Hogarth, William (1697–1764)/Private Collection/The Stapleton Collection/The Bridgeman Art Library; page 604: Madame de Chatelet-Lomont (1706–41) (oil on canvas), Tour, Maurice Quentin de la (1704–88) (after)/Private Collection/The Bridgeman Art Library; page 606: Lebrecht Music and Arts Photo Library/Alamy; page 613: Equestrian Portrait of Catherine II (1729–96) the Great of Russia (oil on canvas), Erichsen, Vigilius (1722–82)/Musee des Beaux-Arts, Chartres, France/The Bridgeman Art Library; page 616: The Taking of the Bastille, 14 July 1789 (oil on canvas), French School (18th century)/Chateau de Versailles, France/Giraudon/The Bridgeman Art Library; page 618: The Tennis Court Oath, 20th June 1789, 1791 (oil on canvas), David, Jacques Louis (1748–1825) (after)/Musee de la Ville de Paris, Musee Carnavalet, Paris, France/Giraudon/The Bridgeman Art Library; page 621: Snark/Art Resource, NY; page 624: Snark/Art Resource, NY; page 628: Execution of Louis XVI (1754–93) 21st January 1793 (coloured engraving) (see also 154902), French School (18th century)/Bibliotheque Nationale, Paris, France/Giraudon/The Bridgeman Art Library; page 634: The Celebration of the Federation, Champs de Mars, Paris, 14 July 1790 (oil on canvas), Thevenin, Charles (1764–1838)/Musee de la Ville de Paris, Musee Carnavalet, Paris, France/Giraudon/The Bridgeman Art Library; page 635: Bridgeman-Giraudon/Art Resource, NY; page 637: Art Resource, NY; page 644: Troops halted on the Banks of the Nile, 2nd February 1799, 1812 (oil on canvas), Tardieu, Jean-Charles (1765–1830)/Chateau de Versailles, France/Giraudon/The Bridgeman Art Library; page 645: The 2nd of May in Madrid, 1884 (oil on canvas), Sorolla y Bastida, Joaquin (1863–1923)/Museo Balaguer, Vilanova and Geltru, Spain/The Bridgeman Art Library; page 651: Library of Congress, Prints & Photographs Division, [LC-USZ62-51309]; page 653: Inside Machinery Hall (coloured litho)/Guildhall Library, City of London/The Bridgeman Art Library; page 656: Coalbrookdale by Night, 1801 (oil on canvas), Loutherbourg, Philip James (Jacques) de (1740–1812)/Science Museum, London, UK/The Bridgeman Art Library; page 657: Interior of a Cotton Mill (engraving) (b&w photo), English School (19th century)/Private Collection/The Bridgeman Art Library; page 658: George Stephenson's successful locomotive, English School (20th century)/Private Collection/© Look and Learn/The Bridgeman Art Library; page 665: AKG/Science Source; page 672: Henry Guttmann/Hulton Archive/Getty Images; page 673: SSPL/The Image Works; page 674: The Peterloo Massacre, 16th August 1819, pub. 1st October 1819 by Richard Carlile (coloured etching), Cruikshank, George (1792–1878)/Manchester Art Gallery, UK/The Bridgeman Art Library; page 675: National Gallery, London/Art Resource, NY; page 681: Erich Lessing/Art Resource, NY; page 684: Mary Evans Picture Library/Alamy; page 687: akg-images/Newscom; page 691:

The Wanderer above the Sea of Fog, 1818 (oil on canvas), Friedrich, Caspar David (1774–1840)/Hamburger Kunsthalle, Hamburg, Germany/The Bridgeman Art Library; page 693: Scenes from the Massacre of Chios, 1822 (oil on canvas), Delacroix, Ferdinand Victor Eugene (1798–1863)/Louvre, Paris, France/Giraudon/The Bridgeman Art Library; page 698: The Chartist Meeting on Kennington Common, April 1848 (engraving) (b/w photo), English School (19th century)/The Illustrated London News Picture Library, London, UK/The Bridgeman Art Library; page 702: Mary Evans Picture Library/The Image Works; page 706: Hulton-Deutsch Collection/Historical/Corbis; page 709: bpk, Berlin/Bismarck Museum, Friedrichsruh, Germany/Art Resource, NY; page 713: bpk, Berlin/Art Resource, NY; page 716: The Granger Collection, NYC; page 718: Roger Viollet/Getty Images; page 720: Original Costumes for the Velocipede Race in Bordeaux, 1868 (colour engraving), Durand, Godefroy (b. 1832)/Private Collection/The Bridgeman Art Library; page 722: The Children's Class, 1889 (oil on canvas), Geoffroy, Henri Jules Jean (1853–1924)/Ministere de L'Education Nationale, Paris, France/Archives Charmet/The Bridgeman Art Library; page 723: Henry Guttmann/Hulton Royals Collection/Getty Images; page 726: The Dreyfus Affair Game, with portraits of the various individuals involved, late 19th century (colour litho), French School (19th century)/Alliance Israelite Universelle, Paris, France/Archives Charmet/The Bridgeman Art Library; page 728: Sovfoto/Eastfoto; page 733: De Agostini/De Agostini Picture Library/Getty Images; page 736: Hirszenberg, Samuel (1865–1908) The Black Banner (Czarny Sztandar), 1905. Oil on canvas, 30″ × 81″. Gift of the Estate of Rose Mintz, JM 63-67a. Photo by Richard Goodbody, Inc. The Jewish Museum, New York/Art Resource, NY; page 738: RMN-Grand Palais/Art Resource, NY; page 745: Erich Lessing/Art Resource, NY; page 748: T06376 Professor Darwin, 'This is the ape of form' Love's Labour's Lost, Act V, scene II, Charles Darwin (1809–72) as an ape, 1861 (colour litho), English School (19th century)/Natural History Museum, London, UK/The Bridgeman Art Library; page 750: The Print Collector/Alamy; page 752: Scala/Art Resource, NY; page 753: Erich Lessing/Art Resource, NY; page 755: akg-images/Newscom; page 756: Standing nude, facing front (self portrait), 1910, Schiele, Egon (1890–1918)/Graphische Sammlung Albertina, Vienna, Austria/The Bridgeman Art Library; page 757: The Granger Collection, NYC; page 758: The Light of the World, c. 1852 (oil on canvas), Hunt, William Holman (1827–1910)/Manchester Art Gallery, UK/The Bridgeman Art Library; page 759: The Granger Collection, NYC; page 762: Bodleian Library; page 766: Les Demoiselles d'Avignon. Paris, June–July 1907. Oil on canvas, 8′ × 7′ 8″ (243.9 × 233.7 cm). Acquired through the Lillie P. Bliss Bequest. The Museum of Modern Art, New York, NY, U.S.A. © Estate of Pablo Picasso/Artists Rights Society (ARS), New York. © 2013 Estate of Pablo Picasso/Artists Rights Society (ARS), New York. Digital Image © The Museum of Modern Art/Licensed by SCALA/Art Resource, NY; page 773: Hulton Archive/Getty Images; page 778: akg-images/Alamy; page 780: Bettmann/Corbis; page 787: Hulton Archive/Getty Images; page 788: A Battery Shelled, 1919 (oil on canvas), Lewis, Percy Wyndham (1882–1957)/Imperial War Museum, London, UK/© The Wyndham Lewis Memorial Trust/The Bridgeman Art Library; page 791: Oesterreichisches Volkshochschularchiv/Imagno/Hulton Archive/Getty Images; page 793: Algerian troops on their way to the frontline, 1914 (b/w photo), Algeria/The Bridgeman Art Library; page 797: ullstein bild/The Granger Collection, NYC; page 799: Library of Congress, Prints & Photographs Division, WWI Posters, [LC-USZC4-10241]; page 800: Armin T Wegner/Hulton Archive/Getty Images; page 802: Sovfoto/Eastfoto;

INDEX